CONTENTS

The Comprehensive Guide to The UK Music Industry and Associated Service Companies

Published annually: **Number 37**

ISSN: 0267-3290
ISBN: 0 862 13144 8

Directories Database Manager: **Nick Tesco**
t 020 7921 8353 **f** 020 7921 8327
e nickt@musicweek.com

Editor-in-Chief: **Ajax Scott**
Executive Editor: **Martin Talbot**
Production Manager: **Desrae Procos**
Deputy Production Manager: **Mark Saunders**
Production Executive: **Nicky Hembra**

Business Development Manager: **Matthew Tyrrell**
t 020 7921 8352 **f** 020 7921 8372
e matthew@musicweek.com
Commercial Manager: **Judith Rivers**
Logo Sales Manager: **William Fahey**
Account Manager: **Scott Green**
Sales Executive: **Patrick Usmar**
Sales Executive: **Maria Edwards**

Circulation Development Manager: **David Pagendam**
t 020 7921 8320 **f** 020 7921 8404
e dpagendam@cmpinformation.com

Published by **Music Week**
CMP Information
8th Floor, Ludgate House
245 Blackfriars Road
London SE1 9UR
w www.musicweek.com
Printed by
Headley Brothers, The Invicta Press, Queens Road, Ashford, Kent TN24 8HH

Additional Copies are available by contacting:

Tower Publishing Services **t** 01858 438893

UK & Northern Ireland - **£65** Europe & Eire - **£70**
Rest of World 1 - **£80** Rest of World 2 - **£85**
Cheques should be made payable to CMP Information Ltd

SECTION INDEX

Industry Organisations

The Agents' Association (Great Britain) 54 Keyes House, Dolphin Square, London SW1V 3NA **t** 020 7834 0515 **f** 020 7821 0261 **e** association@agents-uk.com **w** agents-uk.com Administrator: Carol Richards. Pres: Bob James.

AIM (THE ASSOCIATION OF INDEPENDENT MUSIC)

Lamb House, Church Street, Chiswick, London W4 2PD **t** 020 8994 5599 **f** 020 8994 5222 **e** info@musicindie.com **w** musicindie.org Chief Executive: Alison Wenham. International and Membership Manager: Judith Govey. **British association of independent record companies and distributors with over 850 members. General enquiries to Christel Lacaze or Remi Harris.**

APRS (Assoc. of Professional Recording Services) PO Box 22, Totnes, Devon TQ9 7YZ **t** 01803 868600 **f** 01803 868444 **e** info@aprs.co.uk **w** aprs.co.uk Exec Director: Peter Filleul. Professional audio trade association in UK.

Arts Council of England 14 Great Peter St, London SW1P 3NQ **t** 020 7333 0100 or 020 7973 6784 **f** 020 7973 6590 **e** alan.james@artscouncil.org.uk **w** artscouncil.org.uk Head of Contemp Music: Alan James.

Arts Council of Ireland 70 Merrion Square, Dublin 2, Ireland **t** +353 1 618 0200 **f** +353 1 676 1302 **e** info@artscouncil.ie **w** artscouncil.ie Dir: Mary Cloake.

Association of British Jazz Musicians First Floor, 132 Southwark St, London SE1 0SW **t** 020 7928 9089 **f** 020 7401 6870 **e** info@jazzservices.org.uk **w** jazzservices.org.uk Hon Sec: Chris Hodgkins.

ASCAP (AMERICAN SOCIETY OF COMPOSERS, AUTHORS & PUBLISHERS)

8 Cork Street, London W1S 3LJ **t** 020 7439 0909 **f** 020 7434 0073 **e** initial+lastname@ascap.com **w** ascap.com Contact: Karen Hewson. Snr Vice President, Int: Roger Greenaway. Vice President, Membership: Sean Devine. Membership: Daniel Moore. The only American performing right society created and controlled by songwriters and publishers. The industry leader in the USA since 1914.

Association of Festival Organisers PO Box 296, Matlock, Derbyshire DE4 3XU **t** 01629 827014 **f** 01629 821874 **e** info@afouk.org **w** afouk.org Administrator: Frances Watt. The Association of Festival Organisers works for and with festival and event organisers and represents around 150 festivals. The AFO is a national body, recognised by the Events industry and the Arts.

AURA (The featured performers society) 1 York St, London W1U 6PA **t** 020 7487 5640 **f** 0870 8505 201 **e** info@aurauk.com **w** aurauk.com General Secretary: Peter Horrey.

Band Register (bandreg.com) PO Box 594, Richmond, Surrey TW10 6YT **t** 07973 297011 **e** peter@bandreg.com **w** bandreg.com MD: Peter Whitehead.

BARD (British Association of Record Dealers) 1st Floor, Colonnade House, 2 Westover Rd, Bournemouth, Dorset BH1 2BY **t** 01202 292063 **f** 01202 292067 **e** admin@bardltd.org **w** bardltd.org Dir Gen: Bob Lewis.

Bloc Music Industry Network Ltd Ty Cefn, Rectory Rd, Canton, Cardiff, South Glamorgan CF5 1QL **t** 029 2066 8127 **f** 029 2034 1622 **e** bloc@welshmusicfoundation.com **w** welshmusicfoundation.com/bloc Music Development Mgr: Claire Heat.

BMI (BROADCAST MUSIC INCORPORATED)

84 Harley House, Marylebone Road, London NW1 5HN **t** 020 7486 2036 **f** 020 7224 1046 **e** London@bmi.com **w** bmi.com Senior Executive, Writer-Publisher Relations, Europe: Brandon Bakshi. Executive Writer-Publisher Relations: Nick Robinson. Writer-Publisher Relations: Tabitha Capaldi. Administrative Executive/Office Manager, Writer-Publisher Relations: Helen Germanos. Executive Assistant, Writer-Publisher Relations: Amit Chokshi. BMI is the premier U.S. performing rights organisation which represents approximately 300,000 songwriters, composers and music publishers in all genres of music.

BPI (BRITISH PHONOGRAPHIC INDUSTRY)

Riverside Building, County Hall, Westminster Bridge Road, London SE1 7JA **t** 020 7803 1300 **f** 020 7803 1310 **e** general@bpi.co.uk **w** bpi.co.uk. Executive Chairman: Peter Jamieson.

The BRIT Awards Riverside Building, County Hall, Westminster Bridge Road, London SE1 7JA **t** 020 7803 1300 **f** 020 7803 1310 **e** brits@bpi.co.uk **w** brits.co.uk. Director, Events & Charity: Maggie Crowe.

BRIT Trust c/o BPI, Riverside Building, County Hall, Westminster Bridge Road, London SE1 7JA **t** 020 7803 1302 **f** 020 7803 1310 **e** brittrust@bpi.co.uk **w** brittrust.co.uk Director Events & Charity: Maggie Crowe.

BRITISH ACADEMY OF COMPOSERS & SONGWRITERS

British Music House, 26 Berners Street, London W1T 3LR **t** 020 7636 2929 **f** 020 7636 2212 **e** info@britishacademy.com **w** britishacademy.com. Membership Manager: Kizzy Donaldson.

British Country Music Association PO Box 240, Harrow, Middlesex HA3 7PH **t** 01273 559750 **f** 01273 559750 **e** theBCMA@yahoo.com **w** cmib.co.uk/bcma Chairman: Jim Marshall.

British Federation Of Audio PO Box 365, Farnham, Surrey GU10 2BD **t** 01428 714616 **f** 01428 717599 **e** chrisc@british-audio.org.uk **w** british-audio.org.uk Secretary: Chris Cowan. Trade association for British Audio Industry.

British Interactive Media Association Briarlea, Southend Rd, South Green, Billericay, Essex CM11 2PR **t** 01277 658107 **f** 0870 051 7842 **e** info@bima.co.uk **w** bima.co.uk Office Administrator: Janice Cable.

British Library Sound Archive 96 Euston Rd, London NW1 2DB **t** 020 7412 7676 **e** sound-archive@bl.uk **w** bl.uk/soundarchive National reference library of sound recordings.

BRITISH MUSIC RIGHTS LTD

BRITISH
MUSIC
RIGHTS:

British Music House, 26 Berners Street, London W1T 3LR **t** 020 7306 4446 **f** 020 7306 4449 **e** britishmusic@bmr.org **w** bmr.org Director General: Emma Pike. **Promoting the interests of British music composers, songwriters and publishers through lobbying to UK government and EU institutions, education, PR and events. Members: BAC&S, MPA & the MCPS-PRS Alliance.**

Broadcasting Commission of Ireland 2/5 Warrington Place, Dublin 2, Ireland **t** +353 1 676 0966 **f** +353 1 676 0948 **e** info@bci.ie **w** bci.ie CEO: Michael O'Keeffe.

BVA (British Video Association) 167 Great Portland St, London W1W 5PE **t** 020 7436 0041 **f** 020 7436 0043 **e** general@bva.org.uk **w** bva.org.uk Dir Gen: Lavinia Carey. Trade association for video publishers.

CATCO

CatCo

One Upper James Street, London W1F 9DE **t** 020 7534 1331 **f** 020 7535 1383 **e** info@catcouk.com **w** catcouk.com Contact: Clive Bishop, Sue Carty or Ian Worsfold. **The Record Industry's track level sound recording database – providing the 'one stop drop' for all sound recording data needs.**

Christian Copyright Licencing (Europe) Ltd PO Box 1339, Eastbourne, East Sussex BN21 4YF **t** 01323 417711 **f** 01323 417722 **e** info@ccli.co.uk **w** ccli.co.uk Sales Manager: Chris Williams. Licensing hymn and worship song reproduction.

CMA (Country Music Association) PO Box 6030, South Woodham Ferrers, Chelmsford, Essex CM3 7DW **t** 01245 324072 **f** 01245 425327 **e** BBoyce@CMAWorld.com **w** cmaworld.com Senior Manager International: Bobbi Boyce.

Commercial Radio Companies Association 77 Shaftesbury Avenue, London W1D 5DU **t** 020 7306 2603 **f** 020 7470 0062 **e** info@crca.co.uk **w** crca.co.uk Research & Communications: Alison Winter. UK commercial radio's trade body.

Community Media Association 15 Paternoster Row, Sheffield, South Yorkshire S1 2BX **t** 0114 279 5219 **f** 0114 279 8976 **e** cma@commedia.org.uk **w** commedia.org.uk Dir: Steve Buckley. Representing and supporting community media services.

Community Music Wales Unit 8, 24 Norbury Rd, Fairwater, Cardiff CF5 3AU **t** 029 2083 8060 **f** 029 2056 6573 **e** admin@communitymusicwales.org.uk **w** communitymusicwales.org.uk Music Director: Simon Dancey.

Copyright Advice and Anti-Piracy Hotline **t** 0845 603 4567

CPA (Concert Promoters Association) 6 St Mark's Rd, Henley-on-Thames, Oxfordshire RG9 1LJ **t** 01491 575060 **f** 01491 414082 **e** carolesmith.cpa@virgin.net Secretary: Carol Smith. Chairman: Stuart Littlewood.

DanceStar Awards 1 Mission Grove, London E17 7DD **t** 020 8520 9316 or +1 305 371 2450 **f** +1 305 371 2460 **e** andy.ruffell@dancestar.com **w** dancestar.com Founder CEO: Andy Ruffell MBE.

Department for Culture, Media and Sport 2-4 Cockspur St, London SW1Y 5DH **t** 020 7211 6200 **f** 020 7211 6032 **e** enquiries@culture.gov.uk **w** culture.gov.uk Contact: Public Enquiries

E Centre UK 10 Maltravers St, London WC2R 3BX **t** 020 7655 9001 **f** 020 7681 2290 **e** info@e-centre.org.uk **w** e-centre.org.uk Contact: Help Desk Bar coding and e-commerce standards.

EDiMA (European Digital Media Association) Friars House, Office 118, 157-168 Blackfriars Rd, London SE1 8EZ **t** 020 7401 2661 **f** 020 7928 5850 **e** info@edima.org **w** edima.org Dir: Wes Himes.

English Folk Dance & Song Society Cecil Sharp House, 2 Regent's Park Rd, Camden, London NW1 7AY **t** 020 7485 2206 **f** 020 7284 0534 **e** info@efdss.org **w** efdss.org Publications Manager: Felicity Greenland.

Enterprise Ireland Merrion Hall, Strand Rd, Sandymont, Dublin 4, Ireland **t** +353 1 206 6000 **f** +353 1 206 6400 **e** client.service@enterprise-ireland.com **w** enterprise-ireland.com

Federation Against Copyright Theft 7 Victory Business Centre, Worton Rd, Isleworth, Middx TW7 6DB **t** 020 8568 6646 **f** 020 8560 6364 **e** contact@fact-uk.org.uk **w** fact-uk.org.uk Dir General: Raymond Leinster.

Folk Arts Network PO BOx 296, Matlock, Derbyshire DE4 3XU **t** 01629 827014 **f** 01629 821874 **e** admin@folkartsnetwork.org.uk **w** folkartsnetwork.org.uk Administrator: Frances Watt

Industry Organisations

French Music Bureau Institut Franáais, 17 Queensberry Place, London SW7 2DT **t** 020 7073 1301 **f** 020 7073 1359 **e** french.music@ambafrance.org.uk **w** french-music.org/uk Asst. Manager: Vanessa Cordeiro.

GUILD OF INTERNATIONAL SONGWRITERS &COMPOSERS

Sovereign House, 12 Trewartha Road, Praa Sands, Penzance, Cornwall TR20 9ST **t** 01736 762826 **f** 01736 763328 **e** songmag@aol.com **w** songwriters-guild.co.uk Membership Sec: Carole A Jones. International songwriters' organisation representing songwriters, composers, lyricists, artistes, musicians, publishers etc. Music industry consultants. Publishers of Songwriting and Composing magazine.

Hospital Broadcasting Association 6 Abbots Grove, Pinglewick Hamlet, Belper, Derbyshire DE56 1BX **t** 0870 321 6000 **e** info@hbauk.com **w** hbauk.com

IFPI (Int Federation of the Phonographic Industry) IFPI Secretariat, 54-62 Regent St, London W1B 5RE **t** 020 7878 7900 **f** 020 7878 7950 **e** info@ifpi.org **w** ifpi.org Dir of Comms: Adrian Strain. CEO: John Kennedy. PR Exec. Communications: Fiona Harley. Representing the recording industry worldwide.

IMRO (Irish Music Rights Organisation) Copyright House, Pembroke Row, Lower Baggot St, Dublin 2, Ireland **t** +353 1 661 4844 **f** +353 1 676 3125 **e** info@imro.ie **w** imro.ie Chief Exec: Adrian Gaffney.

Interactive Media in Retail Group 5 Dryden St, London WC2E 9BN **t** 07000 464674 **f** 07000 394674 **e** market@imrg.org **w** imrg.org MD: Jo Tucker. Industry body for global e-retail.

International Association of Professional Creators 6 Cheyne Walk, Hornsea, East Yorks HU18 1BX **t** 01964 533982 **f** 01964 536193 **e** paul@digitaldomain.org **w** digitaldomain.org Administrator: Paul Cook.

International Music Managers Forum (IMMF) 1 York St, London W1U 6PA **t** 020 7935 2446 **f** 020 7486 6045 **e** nicka@immf.net **w** immf.net Exec Dir: Nick Ashton-Hart.

IRMA IRMA House, 1 Corrig Avenue, Dun Laoghaire, Co Dublin, Ireland **t** +353 1 280 6571 **f** +353 1 280 6579 **e** info@irma.ie **w** irma.ie Dir Gen: Dick Doyle.

ISA (INTERNATIONAL SONGWRITERS' ASSOCIATION)

PO Box 46, Limerick City, Limerick, Ireland **t** +353 61 228837 **f** +353 61 229464 **e** jliddane@songwriter.iol.ie **w** songwriter.co.uk. CEO: James D Liddane. Contacts: Anna M Sinden, Bill Miller.
International association for songwriters, founded 1967. Publishers of Songwriter magazine.

ISM (The Incorporated Society Of Musicians) 10 Stratford Place, London W1C 1AA **t** 020 7629 4413 **f** 020 7408 1538 **e** membership@ism.org **w** ism.org Chief Exec: Neil Hoyle. Professional association for performers, composers, teachers.

ITC (Independent Television Commission) (see Ofcom)

Jazz Services 1st Floor, 132 Southwark St, London SE1 0SW **t** 020 7928 9089 **f** 020 7401 6870 **e** info@jazzservices.org.uk **w** jazzservices.org.uk Director: Chris Hodgkins.
National jazz organisation funded by the Arts Council of England and a registered Charity.

Making Music (The Nat'l Fed. Of Music Societies) 7-15 Rosebery Ave, London EC1R 4SP **t** 0870 872 3300 **f** 0870 903 3785 **e** info@makingmusic.org.uk **w** makingmusic.org.uk Chief Executive: Robin Osterley.

Manchester City Music Network Second Floor, Fourways House, 57 Hilton St, Manchester M1 2EJ **t** 0161 228 6160 **f** 0161 228 3773 **e** network@manchester-music.org.uk **w** manchester-music.org.uk Project Manager: Karen Boardman. Manchester music business information and advice.

MCPS (Ireland) Pembroke Row, Lower Baggot St, Dublin 2, Ireland **t** +353 1 676 6940 **f** +353 1 661 1316 **e** victor.finn@mcps.ie **w** mcps.ie MD: Victor Finn.

MCPS (Mechanical Copyright Protection Society Ltd) Copyright House, 29-33 Berners St, London W1T 3AB **t** 020 7580 5544 **f** 020 7306 4455 **e** admissions@mcps-prs-alliance.co.uk **w** mcps.co.uk

Mercury Prize 3 Grand Union Centre, London W10 5AS **t** 020 8964 9964 **f** 020 8969 7249 **e** firstname@mercuryprize.co.uk **w** mercurymusicprize.com Dir: Kevin Milburn.

Merseyside Music Development Agency (MMDA) Level C, 70 Hope St, Liverpool L1 9EB **t** 0151 709 2202 **f** 0151 709 2005 **e** info@mmda.org.uk **w** mmda.org.uk

Millward Brown UK Olympus Avenue, Tachbrook Park, Warwick CV34 6RJ **t** 01926 826610 **f** 01926 826209 **e** bob.barnes@uk.millwardbrown.com **w** millwardbrown.com Charts Dir: Bob Barnes. Official UK record sales chart compilers.

MMF (Music Managers Forum) 1 York St, London W1U 6PA **t** 0870 8507 800 **f** 0870 8507 801 **e** office@ukmmf.net **w** ukmmf.net Gen Sec: James Sellar. Official representative body for music managers. Chairman: Keith Harris.

MMF Training 2nd Floor, Fourways House, 57 Hilton St, Manchester M1 2EJ **t** 0161 228 3993 **f** 0161 228 3773 **e** admin@mmf-training.com **w** mmf-training.com Project Manager: Stuart Worthington.

Mobile Entertainment Forum (MEF) 209 Westbourne Studios, 242 Acklam Rd, London W10 5JJ **t** 020 7524 7878 **f** 020 7524 7879 **e** info@m-e-f.org **w** m-e-f.org General Secretary: Rimma Perelmuter.

MOBO Awards 22 Stephenson Way, London NW1 2HD **t** 020 7419 1800 **f** 020 7419 1600 **e** info@mobo.com **w** mobo.com Founder: Kanya King MBE.

MPA (Music Publishers Association) 3rd Floor Strandgate, 20 York Buildings, London WC2N 6JU **t** 020 7839 7779 **f** 020 7839 7776 **e** info@mpaonline.org.uk **w** mpaonline.org.uk Office Assistant: Julia West. Chief Exec: Sarah Faulder. Trade association for UK music publishers.

MRIB Heckfield Place, 530 Fulham Rd, London SW6 5NR **t** 020 7731 3555 **f** 020 7731 8545 **e** contactus@mrib.co.uk **w** mrib.co.uk MD: Paul Basford. Entertainment content research and information consultants.

Music Industries Association Ivy Cottage Offices, Finch's Yard, Eastwick Rd, Great Bookham, Surrey KT23 4BA **t** 01372 750600 **f** 01372 750515 **e** office@mia.org.uk **w** mia.org.uk Chief Executive: Paul McManus. The Music Industries Association (MIA) is the UK trade association of suppliers and retailers of musical instruments and associated products.

Music Preserved Hillside Cottage, Hill Brow Rd, Liss, Hants GU33 7 **t** 01730 892148 **f** 01730 894264 **e** musicpreserved@dial.pipex.com **w** musicpreserved.org Chairman: Basil Tschaikov.

MPG (The Music Producers Guild Ltd) PO Box 32, Harrow HA2 7ZX **t** 020 7371 8888 **f** 020 7371 8887 **e** office@mpg.org.uk **w** mpg.org.uk Chairman: Andrew East. Representing producers, engineers, mixers and programmers.

musicaid.org Please, visit website for more deatils **e** mail@musicaid.org **w** musicaid.org Web-based music and aid organisation.

Musicians Benevolent Fund 16 Ogle St, London W1W 6JA **t** 020 7636 4481 **f** 020 7637 4307 **e** info@mbf.org.uk **w** mbf.org.uk Sec to Fund: Helen Faulkner. Charity helping professional musicians in need.

Musicians Union 60-62 Clapham Rd, London SW9 0JJ **t** 020 7582 5566 **f** 020 7582 9805 **e** london@musiciansunion.org.uk **w** musiciansunion.org.uk Gen Sec: John F Smith.

National Association of Youth Orchestras Central Hall, West Tollcross, Edinburgh, Midlothian EH3 9BP **t** 0131 221 1927 **f** 0131 229 2921 **e** admin@nayo.org.uk **w** nayo.org.uk GM: Susan White.

National Entertainment Agents Council PO Box 112, Seaford, East Sussex BN25 2DQ **t** 0870 755 7612 **f** 0870 755 7613 **e** info@neac.org.uk **w** neac.org.uk Gen Sec: Chris Bray. Trade body for licensed agents.

National Foundation for Youth Music (Youth Music) One America St, London SE1 0NE **t** 020 7902 1060 **f** 020 7902 1061 **e** info@youthmusic.org.uk **w** youthmusic.org.uk Chief Executive: Christina Coker. Head of Marketing: Julia Parlett. Head of Policy and Programmes: David Sulkin.Youth Music promotes and supports music making opportunities for children and young people up to 18 years, who principally live in areas of social and economic need through funding, information and advice.

National Student Music Awards The Old Laundry, 100 Irving Rd, Bournemouth BH6 5BL **t** 0870 040 6767 **e** info@nsma.com **w** nsma.com MD: Chris Jenkins.

NEMIS (New Music In Scotland) 2nd Floor, 93 Candleriggs, Merchant City, Glasgow G1 1NP **t** 0141 552 9224 or 07803 752 913 **f** 0141 572 0558 **e** alec@nemis.org **w** nemis.org Development Officer: Alec Downie.

Nordoff-Robbins Music Therapy Studio A2, 1927 Building, 2 Michael Rd, London SW6 2AD **t** 020 7371 8404 **f** 020 7371 8206 **e** lindamac@nrfr.co.uk **w** silverclef.com Appeals Manager: Linda McLean. Co-Chairmen: Derek Green & Jeremy Marsh.

Ofcom Riverside House, 2a Southwark Bridge Rd, London SE1 9HA **t** 020 7981 3000 **f** 020 7981 3333 **e** contact@ofcom.org.uk **w** ofcom.org.uk Regulatory body for independent radio.

The Official UK Charts Company Ltd 4th Floor, 58/59 Great Marlborough St, London W1F 7JY **t** 020 7478 8500 **f** 020 7478 8519 **e** info@theofficialcharts.com **w** theofficialcharts.com Chart Dir: Omar Maskatiya. Marketers and managers of the official UK music, and retail video, charts.

PAMRA (Performing Artists Media Rights Assoc.) 161 Borough High St, London SE1 1HR **t** 020 7940 0410 **f** 020 7407 2008 **e** office@pamra.org.uk **w** pamra.org.uk

The Patent Office Concept House, Cardiff Rd, Newport, Gwent NP10 8QQ **t** 01633 814000 or 08459 500505 **f** 01633 813600 **e** enquiries@patent.gov.uk **w** patent.gov.uk Advice on band trademarks and logos.

PLASA (Professional Lighting & Sound Association) 38 St Leonards Rd, Eastbourne, East Sussex BN21 3UT **t** 01323 410335 **f** 01323 646905 **e** info@plasa.org **w** plasa.org Executive Dir: Ruth Rossington. Serving the entertainment technology industry.

PPI (Phonographic Performance Ireland) PPI House, 1 Corrig Avenue, Dun Laoghaire, Co Dublin, Ireland **t** +353 1 280 6571 **f** +353 1 280 6579 **e** info@ppiltd.com **w** ppiltd.com CEO: Dick Doyle.

PPL (PHONOGRAPHIC PERFORMANCE LTD)

One Upper James Street, London W1F 9DE **t** 020 7534 1000 **f** 020 7534 1111 **e** See website for email addresses. **w** ppluk.com. Chairman & CEO: Fran Nevrkla. Director of Operations: Clive Bishop. Director of Customer Relationship Management: Sue Carty. Director of Licensing: Tony Clark. Director of Legal & Business Affairs: Peter Leathem. Director of Government Relations: Dominic McGonigal. Finance Director: Tania Smythe. Head of Public Relations: Jill Drew. **Collecting society licensing broadcast and public performance of sound recordings in the UK on behalf of record companies and performers.**

PRC (Performer Registration Centre) 1 Upper James St, London W1F 9DE **t** 020 7534 1234 **f** 020 7534 1383 **e** PRC.info@ppluk.com **w** performersmoney.ppluk.com

The Prince's Trust 18 Park Square East, London NW1 4LH **t** 020 7543 1234 or 0800 842 842 **f** 020 7543 1200 **e** info@princes-trust.org.uk **w** princes-trust.org.uk Chief Executive: Martina Milburn.

Production Services Association Centre Court, 1301 Stratford Rd, Hall Green, Birmingham B28 9HH **t** 0121 693 7127 **f** 0121 693 7100 **e** admin@psa.org.uk **w** psa.org.uk GM: Keith Owen.

PRS (Performing Right Society) Copyright House, 29-33 Berners St, London W1T 3AB **t** 020 7580 5544 **f** 020 7306 4455 **e** admissions@mcps-prs-alliance.co.uk **w** prs.co.uk Collecting royalties on behalf of music creators and publishers for the public performance and broadcast of their copyright musical works. Also at: Elgar House, 41 Streatham High Rd, London, SW16 1ER.

The Radio Academy 5 Market Place, London W1W 8AE **t** 020 7255 2010 **f** 020 7255 2029 **e** info@radioacademy.org **w** radioacademy.org Dir: John Bradford.

The Radio Advertising Bureau 77 Shaftesbury Avenue, London W1D 5DU **t** 020 7306 2500 **f** 020 7306 2505 **e** aimee@rab.co.uk **w** rab.co.uk Operations Dir: Michael O'Brien.

Radiocommunications Agency Wyndham House, 189 Marsh Wall, London E14 9SX **t** 020 7211 0211 **f** 020 7211 0507 **e** library@ra.gsi.gov.uk **w** radio.gov.uk

RAJAR (Radio Joint Audience Research) Gainsborough House, 81 Oxford St, London W1D 2EU **t** 020 7903 5350 **f** 020 7903 5351 **e** info@rajar.co.uk **w** rajar.co.uk MD: Sally de la Bedoyere.

Scottish Arts Council 12 Manor Place, Edinburgh EH3 7DD **t** 0845 603 6000 **f** 0131 225 9833 **e** help.desk@scottisharts.org.uk **w** scottisharts.org.uk

Scottish Music Information Centre 1 Bowmont Gardens, Glasgow G12 9LR **t** 0141 334 6393 **f** 0141 337 1161 **e** info@smic.dircon.co.uk **w** smic.org.uk Chief Exec: Andrew Logan. Documenting and promoting Scottish music incorporating sale and hire libraries.

SESAC (Society of European Songwriters & Composers) 6 Kenrick Place, London WIU 6HD **t** 020 7616 9284 **f** 020 7486 9934 **e** rights@sesac.co.uk **w** sesac.co.uk Chairman: Wayne Bickerton.

Sound Sense 7 Tavern St, Stowmarket, Suffolk IP14 1PJ **t** 01449 673990 **f** 01449 673994 **e** info@soundsense.org **w** soundsense.org Central Services Manager: Kati Wakefield.

South West Association of Promoters 143A East Reach, Taunton, Somerset TA1 3HN **t** 01823 332335 **f** 01823 332335 **e** weekenderlive@btopenworld.com **w** swapuk.co.uk Regional Secretary: Martin Brice.

Student Radio Association The Radio Academy, 5 Market Place, London W1W 8AE **t** 020 7255 2010 **f** 020 7255 2029 **e** chair@studentradio.org.uk **w** studentradio.org.uk Chair: Talia Kraines.

UK PERFORMER SERVICES

One Upper James Street, London W1F 9DE **t** 020 7534 1166 f 020 7534 1383 **e** team@royaltiesreunited.co.uk **w** royaltiesreunited.co.uk **Paying airplay royalties to recording artists and session musicians**

Variety & Light Entertainment Council 54 Keyes House, Dolphin Square, London SW1V 3NA **t** 020 7834 0515 **f** 020 7821 0261 Joint Secretary: Kenneth Earle. Entertainment contracts issue and arbitration service.

Variety Club Of Great Britain 93 Bayham St, London NW1 0AG **t** 020 7428 8100 **f** 020 7482 8123 **e** press@varietyclub.org.uk **w** varietyclub.org.uk The Chief Barker: Tony Frame. Children's charity.

VPL (VIDEO PERFORMANCE LTD)

1 Upper James Street, London W1F 9DE **t** 020 7534 1400 **f** 020 7534 1414 **e** See website for email addresses **w** vpluk.com. Chairman & CEO: Fran Nevrkla. Director of Operations: Clive Bishop. Director of Customer Relationship Management: Sue Carty. Director of Licensing: Tony Clark. Director of Legal & Business Affairs: Peter Leathem. Director of Government Relations: Dominic McGonigal. Finance Director: Tania Smythe. Head of Public Relations: Jill Drew. **Collecting society licensing broadcast and public performance of music videos on behalf of record companies and other copyright owners.**

Welsh Music Foundation Ty Cefn, Rectory Rd, Canton, Cardiff CF5 1QL **t** 029 2066 8127 **f** 029 2034 1622 **e** enquiries@welshmusicfoundation.com **w** welshmusicfoundation.com Chief Executive: Elliot Reuben.

Women In Music 7 Tavern St, Stowmarket, Suffolk IP14 1PJ **t** 01449 673990 **f** 01449 673994 **e** info@womeninmusic.org.uk **w** womeninmusic.org.uk Admin Officer: Louise Fiddaman.

The Worshipful Company Of Musicians 6th Floor, 2 London Wall Buildings, London EC2M 5PP **t** 020 7496 8980 **f** 020 7588 3633 **e** deputyclerk@wcom.org.uk **w** wcom.org.uk Dept Clerk: Margaret Alford.

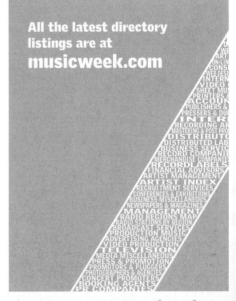

MUSICWEEK DAILY
TOP STORIES
Chili Peppers debut at one on albums
Red Hot Chili Peppers Live From Hyde Park is the highest new entry in this week's album chart after debuting at number one. [more]
Big Chill expands after festival success
Mylo, Bent, Lemon Jelly, Magnet, Big Chill moves into a permanent home in London. [more]
EMI Publishing leads pack with albums market share
albums market. [more]
Strong releases set for quarter four
Retailers can look forward to a bumper fourth quarter this year, with many of the world's biggest artists preparing studio albums for the end of the year.
outlines plans for community radio licenses
Radio stations from September 1. [more]
The news as it happens
Register for your free
Music Week Daily update at
www.musicweek.com

Retail

Retailers

23rd Precinct 23 Bath Street, Glasgow G2 1HU **t** 0141 332 4806 **f** 0141 353 3039 **e** enquiries@23rdprecinct.co.uk **w** 23rdprecinct.co.uk Directors: Billy Kiltie/David Yeats.

2Funky 62 Belgrave Gate, Leicester LE1 3GQ **t** 0116 299 0700 **f** 0116 299 0077 **e** shop@2-funky.co.uk **w** 2-funky.co.uk Manager: Vijay Mistry.

3 Beat Records 5 Slater St, Liverpool, Merseyside L1 4BW **t** 0151 709 3355 **f** 0151 709 3707 **e** info@3beat.co.uk **w** 3beat.co.uk Shop Mgr: Pezz. MD: Jonathon Barlow.

8 Ball 18 Queen St, Southwell, Notts NG25 0AA **t** 01636 813040 **f** 01636 813141 **e** info@8ball.ltd.uk **w** 8ball.ltd.uk Prop: Tim Allsopp.

A&A Music 15 Bridge St, Congleton, Cheshire CW12 1AS **t** 01260 280778 **f** 01260 298311 **e** mail@aamusic.co.uk **w** aamusic.co.uk Owner: Alan Farrar.

Aardvark Music Compton House, 9 Totnes Road, Paignton, Devon TQ2 5BY **t** 01803 664481 **f** 01803 664481 **e** cj@torrerecords.freeserve.co.uk Co-owner: Clive Jones.

AB's CDs 3A Mercury Row, Otley, West Yorkshire LS21 3HE **t** 01943 468869 **f** 01943 468869

Abergavenny Music 23 Cross St, Abergavenny, Gwent NP7 5EW **t** 01873 853394 **e** service@abergavennymusic.com **w** abergavennymusic.com Owner: James Joseph.

Acorn Records 3 Glovers Walk, Yeovil, Somerset BA20 1LH **t** 01935 425503 **f** 01935 425503 Owner: Chris Lowe.

Action Records 47 Church St, Preston, Lanc PR1 3DH **t** 01772 884772 or 01772 258809 **f** 01772 252255 **e** sales@action-records.co.uk **w** action-records.co.uk Manager: Gordon Gibson.

Adrians 36-38 High Street, Wickford, Essex SS12 9AZ **t** 01268 733 318 or 01268 733 319 **f** 01268 764 507 **e** sales@adrians.co.uk **w** adrians.co.uk Contact: Adrian Rondeau

AG Kemble Ltd 63 Leicester Rd, Wigston, Leics. LE18 1NR **t** 0116 288 1557 **f** 0116 288 3949 **e** kembles-records@btconnect.com Owners: Paul Watkins & Fiona Nicholls.

Andy Cash Music 115 High St, Harborne, Birmingham B17 9NP **t** 0121 427 8989 **f** 0121 427 9949 Owner: Andy Cash.

Asda Southbank, Great Wilson Street, Leeds, West Yorkshire LS11 5AD **t** 0113 241 8470 or 0113 243 5435 **f** 0113 241 8785 **e** aspoffo@asda.co.uk **w** asda.co.uk Entertainment Devt. Mgr.: Andy Spofforth. Music Buying Manager: Becky Oram. Chart Buyer: Denise Kilcommins.

Audiosonic 6 College St, Gloucester, Glos. GL1 2NE **t** 01452 302280 **f** 01452 302202 **w** audiosonic.uk.com Owner: Sylvia Parker.

Avalanche Records (Head Office) 2-3 Teviot Place, Edinburgh EH1 2QZ **t** 0131 226 7666 **f** 0131 226 4002 **e** avalanche.records@virgin.net **w** avalancherecords.co.uk Owner: Kevin Buckle.

Avid Records 32-33 The Triangle, Bournemouth BH2 5SE **t** 01202 295465 **f** 01202 295465 **e** paul@avidrecords-uk.com **w** avidrecords-uk.com Owner: Martin Howes.

Badlands 11 St George's Place, Cheltenham, Glos GL50 3LA **t** 01242 227724 **f** 01242 227393 **e** shop@badlands.co.uk **w** badlands.co.uk MD: Philip Jump. Head Buyer: Kane Jones.

Bailey's Records 40 Bull Ring Indoor Market, Edgbaston Street, Birmingham, West Midlands B5 4RQ **t** 0121 622 6899 **f** 0121 622 6899 **w** birminghamindoormarket.co.uk Manager: David Rock.

Banquet Records 52 Eden St, Kingston-upon-Thames KT1 1EE **t** 020 8549 5871 **e** info@banquetrecords.com **w** banquetrecords.com Owner: Dave Jarvis.

Barneys 21A Cross Keys, Market Square, St Neots PE19 2AR **t** 01480 406270 **f** 01480 406270 **e** keith.barnes2@btinternet.com Contact: Keith Barnes

Bath Compact Discs 11 Broad St, Bath BA1 5LJ **t** 01225 464766 **f** 01225 482275 **e** Bathcds@btinternet.com **w** bathcds.btinternet.co.uk Co-owner: Steve Macallister.

Beanos Ltd 7 Middle Street, Croydon, Surrey CR0 1RE **t** 020 8680 1202 **f** 020 8680 1203 **e** enquiries@beanos.co.uk **w** beanos.co.uk MD: David Lashmar.

Beatin Rhythm Records 42 Tib St, Manchester M4 1LA **t** 0161 834 7783 **e** music@beatinrhythm.com **w** beatinrhythm.com Dir: Tom Smith.

Bim Bam Records Chalfont House, Botley Rd, Horton Heath, Eastleigh SO50 7DN **t** 02380 600329 **f** 02380 600329 **e** bob@bim-bam.com **w** bim-bam.com Owner: Bob Thomas.

Black Market Records 25 D'Arblay Street, London W1F 8EJ **t** 020 7287 1932 or 020 7437 0478 **f** 020 7494 1303 **e** shop@blackmarket.co.uk MD: David Piccioni. Head Buyer: Goldie.

Blackwells Music Shop Beaver House, Hythe Bridge Street, Oxford OX1 2ET **t** 01865 333122 **f** 01865 790937 **e** vanessa.williams@blackwellsbookshops.co.uk

Boogietimes Records 3 Old Mill Parade, Victoria Road, Romford, Essex RM1 2HU **t** 01708 727029 **f** 01708 740424 **e** info@boogietimes-records.co.uk **w** boogietimes-records.co.uk Manager: Andy James.

Boots Company plc 1 Thane Road West, Nottingham NG2 3AA **t** 0115 949 4024 **f** 0115 959 2727 **w** boots.co.uk

Borders Books, Music & Video 4th Floor, 122 Charing Cross Road, London WC2 0JR **t** 020 7379 7313 **f** 020 7836 0373 **w** bordersstores.co.uk Head Buyer: Guy Raphael. Marketing Manager: Matt Taylor. Promotions Exec - Music & Video: Finn Lawrence.

Bridport Record Centre 33A South St, Bridport, Dorset DT6 3NY **t** 01308 425707 **f** 01308 458271 **e** bridrec@btinternet.com **w** bridportrecordcentre.co.uk Owners: Piers & Stephanie Garner.

Carbon Music 33-38 Kensington High St, London W8 4PF **t** 020 7373 9911 **f** 020 7938 2952 **e** info@carbonmusic.com **w** carbonmusic.com CEO: Jan Mehmet.

Cardiff Music 31-33 Castle Arcade, Cardiff CF10 1BW **t** 02920 229700 **e** service@cardiffmusic.com **w** cardiffmusic.com Manager: Paul Skyrme.

Catapult 100% Vinyl 22, Highstreet Arcade, Cardiff CF10 1BB **t** 029 2022 8990 or 029 2034 2322 **f** 029 2023 1690 **e** enquiries@catapult.co.uk **w** catapult.co.uk Prop: Lucy Squire.

Chalky's 78 High Street, Banbury, Oxon. OX16 5JG **t** 01295 271190 **f** 01295 262221 **e** richard@chalkys.com MD: Richard White.

Changes One 58 Denham Drive, Seaton Delaval, Whitley Bay, Tyne & Wear NE25 0JY **t** 0191 237 0251 **f** 0191 298 0903 **e** ian@changesone.co.uk **w** changesone.co.uk Owner: Ian Tunstall.

Citysounds Ltd 5 Kirby Street, London EC1N 8TS **t** 020 7405 5454 **f** 020 7242 1863 **e** sales@city-sounds.co.uk **w** city-sounds.co.uk Owners: Tom & Dave.

CODA Music 12 Bank Street, Edinburgh EH1 2LN **t** 0131 622 7246 **f** 0131 622 7245 **e** enquiries@codamusic.demon.co.uk **w** codamusic.co.uk Co-owner: Dougie Anderson.

Compact Discounts 258-260 Lavender Hill, Battersea, London SW11 1LJ **t** 020 7978 5560 **f** 020 7978 5931 **e** info@compactdiscounts.co.uk **w** compactdiscounts.co.uk Contact: Mark Canavan

Concepts 4A Framwellgate Bridge, Durham DH1 4SJ **t** 0191 383 0745 **f** 0191 383 0112 **e** dave-murray@lineone.net **w** concepts-durham.co.uk Owner: Dave Murray.

Connect Records 18 Badger Road, Coventry CV3 2PU **t** 024 7626 5400 **e** info@connect-records.com **w** connect-records.com Manager: Matt Green.

Coolwax Music Unit 13, The Craft Centre, Orchard Sq Shopping Centre, Sheffield S1 2FB **t** 0114 279 5878 **e** staff@coolwax.co.uk **w** coolwax.co.uk Mgr: Corey Mahoney.

Crash Records 35 The Headrow, Leeds, West Yorkshire LS1 6PU **t** 0113 243 6743 **f** 0113 234 0421 **e** info@crashrecords.co.uk **w** crashrecords.co.uk Prop: Ian De-Whytell.

Crazy Beat Records 87 Corbets Tey Road, Upminster, Essex RM14 2AH **t** 01708 228678 **f** 01708 640946 **e** sales@crazybeat.co.uk **w** crazybeat.co.uk Owner: Gary Dennis.

Crucial Music Pinery Buildings, Highmoor, Wigton, Cumbria CA7 9LW **t** 016973 45422 **f** 016973 45422 **e** simon@crucialmusicuk.co.uk **w** crucialmusicuk.co.uk MD: Simon James.

Cruisin' Records 132 Welling High St, Welling, Kent DA16 1TJ **t** 020 8304 5853 **f** 020 8304 0429 **e** john@cruisin-records.fsnet.co.uk **w** cruisinrecords.com Owner: John Setford.

Dance 2 Records 9 Woodbridge Road, Guildford, Surrey GU1 4PU **t** 01483 451002 or 01483 451006 **f** 01483 451003 **e** info@dance2.co.uk **w** dance2.co.uk MD: Hans Vind. Head Buyer: Mark Strudwick.

Deal Real 3 Marlborough Court, London W1F 7EF **t** 020 7287 7245 **f** 020 7287 7246 **e** info@dealreal.co.uk **w** dealreal.co.uk Manager: Sef Kharma.

Disc-N-Tape 17 Gloucester Road, Bishopston, Bristol BS7 8AA **t** 0117 942 2227 **f** 0117 942 2227 **e** graeme@disc-n-tape.co.uk **w** disc-n-tape.co.uk Owner: Graeme Cornish.

Discount Disc 21 Percy St, Hanley, Stoke-on-Trent, Staffs ST1 1NA **t** 01782 266888 **f** 01782 266888 **e** discountdisc@talk21.com **w** discountdisc.co.uk Manager: Ian Trigg.

Discurio Unit 3, Faraday Way, St Mary's Cray, Kent BR5 3QW **t** 01689 879101 **f** 01689 879101 **e** discurio1@aol.com **w** discurio.com Manager: Jonathan Mitchell.

Diskits 7 Outram St, Sutton-in-Ashfield, Notts NG17 4BA **t** 01623 441413 or 01623 466220 **f** 01623 441413 **e** shop@diskits.co.uk **w** diskits.co.uk Partner: Mel Vickers.

Disky.com 3 York Street, St. Helier, Jersey, Channel Islands JE2 3RQ **t** 01534 768860 **f** 01534 729525 **e** music@disky.com **w** disky.com Manager: Robert Bisson.

Disque Ltd 11 Chapel Market, Islington, London N1 9EZ **t** 020 7833 1104 **f** 020 7278 4895 **e** info@disque.co.uk **w** disque.co.uk MD: Ed Davies.

Dixons Stores Group Maylands Avenue, Hemel Hempstead, Hertfordshire HP2 7TG **t** 01442 888653 **f** 01442 353127 **e** dave.poulter@dixons.co.uk **w** dixons.co.uk Cat Mgr, DVD Software: Dave Poulter.

Dolphin Discs 56 Moore St, Dublin 1, Ireland **t** +353 1 872 9364 **f** +353 1 872 0405 **e** irishmus@iol.ie **w** irelandcd.com GM: Paul Heffernan.

Dub Vendor Records 17 Davids Rd, London SE23 3EP **t** 020 8291 6253 **f** 020 8291 1097 **e** dubvendor@dubvendor.co.uk **w** dubvendor.co.uk MD: John MacGillivray.

Earwaves Records 9/11 Paton St, Piccadilly, Manchester M1 2BA **t** 0161 236 4022 **f** 0161 237 5932 **e** info@earwavesrecords.co.uk **w** earwavesrecords.co.uk Proprietor: Alan Lacy.

Eastern Bloc Records 5-6 Central Buildings, Oldham Street, Manchester M1 1JQ **t** 0161 228 6432 **f** 0161 228 6728 **e** info@easternblocrecords.co.uk **w** easternblocrecords.co.uk Mgr: John Berry.

Easy Listening Music 224 Stratford Road, Shirley, Solihull, Birmingham, West Midlands B90 5EH **t** 0121 733 6663 or 0121 744 1524 **f** 0121 733 6663 Contact: John Corbett

The Energy 106 Store 63 High Street, Belfast, Co Antrim BT1 2JZ **t** 028 9033 3122 or 028 9032 07780 **f** 028 9033 3122 **e** cd.heaven@btclick.com Mgr: Paul Chapman.

Esprit International Limited Esprit House, 5 Railway Sidings, Meopham, Kent DA13 0YS **t** 01474 815010 or 01474 815099 **f** 01474 815030 or 01474 814414 **e** sales@eil.com **w** eil.com MD: Robert Croydon.

Essential Music 16 The Market, Greenwich, London SE10 9HZ **t** 020 8293 4982 **f** 020 8293 4982 **e** essmusco@aol.com Owner: Neil Williams.

Eukatech Records 49 Endell St, Covent Garden, London WC2H 9AJ **t** 020 7240 8060 **f** 020 7379 4939 **e** shop@eukatechrecords.com **w** eukatechrecords.com Manager: Rory Viggers.

FAB Music 55 The Broadway, Crouch End, London N8 8DT **t** 020 8347 6767 **f** 020 8348 3270 **e** fab@fabmusic.co.uk Directors: Mal Page/Kevin Payne.

Fat City Records 20 Oldham St, Manchester M1 1JN **t** 0161 237 1181 **f** 0161 236 9304 **e** shop@fatcity.co.uk **w** fatcity.co.uk Manager: Mark Torkington.

Fives 22 Broadway, Leigh-On-Sea, Essex SS9 1AW **t** 01702 711629 **f** 01702 712737 eFives@btconnect.com **w** fives-records.co.uk Mgr: Pete Taylor.

Flashback 50 Essex Rd, London N1 8LR **t** 020 7354 9356 **f** 020 7354 9358 **e** mark@flashback.co.uk **w** flashback.co.uk Owner: Mark Burgess.

Flip Records 2 Mardol, Shrewsbury SY1 1PY **t** 01743 244469 **f** 01743 260985 **e** sales@fliprecords.co.uk **w** fliprecords.co.uk Owner: Duncan Morris.

Flying Records 94 Dean Street, London W1D 3TA **t** 020 7734 0172 **f** 020 7287 0766 **e** info@flyingrecords.com **w** flyingrecords.com Manager: Anthony Cox.

Fopp Ltd Head Office, 1/2 Sciennes Gardens, Edinburgh EH9 1NR **t** 0131 668 4220 **e** info@fopp.co.uk **w** fopp.co.uk Chairman: Gordon Montgomery. MD: Peter Ellen. Director of Personnel & Finance: Angela McCourt. Product Director: Paul Turnbull.

Forest Records 7,Earley Court, High Street, Lymington, Hampshire SO41 9EP **t** 01590 676588 **f** 01590 612162 **e** forestrec@btopenworld.com Buyer: Neil Hutson.

45s Record Shop 64 Northgate Street, Gloucester GL1 1SL **t** 01452 309445 **f** 01452 309445 **e** chrismanna@onetel.net.uk Contact: Chris Manna

Gatefield Sounds 163-165 High Street, Herne Bay, Kent CT6 5AQ **t** 01227 374759 **f** 01227 374759 MD: Mike Winch.

Global Groove Records Global House, 13 Bucknall New Road, Hanley, Stoke-on-Trent, Staffs ST1 2BA **t** 01782 215554 or 01782 207234 **f** 01782 201698 **e** mail@globalgroove.co.uk **w** globalgroove.co.uk Manager: Daf.

Golden Disc Group 11 Windsor Place, Pembroke St, Dublin 2 **t** +353 1 676 8444 **f** +353 1 676 8565 **e** info@goldendiscs.ie **w** goldendiscs.ie

Good Vibrations Records 54 Howard Street, Belfast, Co Antrim BT1 6PG **t** 028 9058 2250 **f** 028 9058 2252 **w** goodvibrations.ie MD: Terri Hooley.

H & R Cloake Ltd 29 High Street, Croydon, Surrey CR0 1QB **t** 020 8686 1336 or 020 8681 3965 Contact: Richard Cloake

Hillsborough Records 35-37 Middlewood Road, Hillsborough, Sheffield S6 4GW **t** 0114 233 3449 **f** 0114 285 3110 **e** chris@hillsboroughrecords.co.uk **w** hillsboroughrecords.co.uk Owner: Chris Johnson.

Hits 10 The Arcade, Station Road, Redhill, Surrey RH1 1PA **t** 01737 773565 **f** 01737 773565 Contact: Brian Hawkins

HMV Group plc Shelley House, 2-4 York Road, Maidenhead, Berkshire SL6 1SR **t** 01628 818300 **f** 01628 818301 **e** firstname.lastname@hmvgroup.com **w** hmv.co.uk CEO: Alan Giles. Chairman: Eric Nicoli. COO: Brian McLaughlin. Group Finance Director: Neil Bright.

HMV UK Ltd

top dog for music·dvd·games

Film House, 142 Wardour Street, London W1F 8LN **t** 020 7432 2000 **f** 020 7434 1090 **e** firstname.lastname@hmv.co.uk **w** hmv.co.uk MD: Steve Knott. Product Director: Steve Gallant. Marketing Director: John Taylor. E-Commerce Director: Stuart Rowe. Operations Director: Simon Peck. Head of Music: Mark Noonan. Head of Rock & Pop: Gary Rolfe. Head of Campaigns: Grahame Davidson. Dance & Urban Manager: Steve Owen. Classical & Specialities Manager: Rudy Osorio. Head of Retail Marketing: Ged Hopkins. Head of Marketing (CRM, E-Commerce & Promotions): Gideon Lask. Head of Press & PR: Gennaro Castaldo.

HW Audio (Sound & Lighting) 180-198 St Georges Road, Bolton, Lancs BL1 2PH **t** 01204 385199 **f** 01204 364057 **e** sales@hwaudio.co.uk **w** hwaudio.co.uk Sales Dir: Richard Harfield.

Impulse Music Travel Ltd Unit 3, Campus Five, Letchworth, Herts SG6 2JF **t** 01462 677227 **f** 01462 480169 **e** firstname.lastname@imtl.co.uk **w** impulseonline.co.uk Audio Buyer: Andy Lazarewicz.

J Sainsbury 33 Holborn, London EC1N 2HT **t** 020 7695 4295 **f** 020 7695 4295 **e** julian.monaghan@sainsburys.co.uk **w** sainsbury.co.uk Music Manager: Julian Monaghan.

Jacks Records Unit 1, Aberdeen Court, 95-97 Division Street, Sheffield S1 4GE **t** 0114 276 6356 **e** sales@jacksrecords.idps.co.uk **w** jacksrecords.free-online.co.uk Owner: Ian Gadsby.

Jibbering Records 136 Alcester Rd, Moseley, Birmingham B13 8EE **t** 0121 449 4551 **e** info@jibberingrecords.com **w** jibberingrecords.com Owner: Dan Raffety.

JMF Records 86 High Street, Invergordon, Ross-shire IV18 ODL **t** 01349 853369 **f** 01349 853369 **e** james@jmf-records.co.uk Manager: James Fraser.

Jumbo Records 5-6 St Johns Centre, Leeds, West Yorkshire LS2 8LQ **t** 0113 245 5570 **f** 0113 242 5019 **e** hunter@jumborecords.fsnet.co.uk **w** jumborecords.co.uk Partners: Hunter Smith, Lornette Smith.

June Emerson Wind Music Windmill Farm, Ampleforth, York YO62 4HF **t** 01439 788324 **f** 01439 788715 **e** JuneEmerson@compuserve.com Prop: June Emerson.

Kane's Records 14 Kendrick St, Stroud, Glocs. GL5 1AA **t** 01453 766 886 **f** 01453 755 377 **e** sales@kanesrecords.com **w** kanesrecords.com Owner: Kane Jones.

Kays Music 77 Sandy Park Road, Brislington, Bristol BS4 3PQ **t** 0117 971 2353 **f** 0117 971 2353 Contact: Clive Tonkin

Ken Palk Records The Shopping Centre, Bramhall, Stockport, Cheshire SK7 1AW **t** 0161 439 8479 **f** 0161 439 0653 **e** Sales@KenPalk.co.uk **w** KenPalk.co.uk

Kingbee Records 519 Wilbraham Road, Chorlton-Cum-Hardy, Manchester M21 0UF **t** 0161 860 4762 **f** 0161 860 4762 Contact: Les Hare

Langland Records 2 Bell St, Wellington, Shropshire TF1 1LS **t** 01952 244 845 Owner: Ian Bridgewater.

The Left Legged Pineapple 24-25 Churchgate, Loughborough, Leics LE11 1UD **t** 01509 210130 or 01509 236791 **f** 01509 210106 **e** pineapple@left-legged.com **w** left-legged.com Owner: Jason White.

Lewks Music & Video 3 Wales Court, Downham Market, Norfolk PE38 9JZ **t** 01366 383762 **f** 01366 383544 **e** admin@lewks.co.uk **w** lewks.co.uk

Loco Records 5 Church Street, Chatham, Kent ME4 4BS **t** 01634 818330 **f** 01634 880321 **e** info@locomusic.co.uk **w** locomusic.co.uk Owner: Gary Turner.

Longplayer 3 Grosvenor Rd, Tunbridge Wells, Kent TN1 2AH **t** 01892 539273 **f** 01892 516770 **e** shop@longplayer.fsnet.co.uk **w** longplayer.co.uk Owner: Ali Furmidge.

Main Street Music 11 Smithfield Centre, Leek, Staffordshire ST13 5JW **t** 01538 384 315 **e** mike@demon655.freeserve.co.uk

Malcolm's Musicland Baptist Chapel, Chapel St, Chorley, Lancashire PR7 1BW **t** 01257 264 362 **f** 01257 267 636 **e** sales@cdvideo.co.uk **w** cdvideo.co.uk Prop: Malcolm Allen.

Marks & Spencer Michael House, Room A469, 47-67 Baker Street, London W1A 1DN **t** 020 7268 1121 **f** 020 7268 2607 **w** marksandspencer.com Contact: William Gill

Massive Records 30 Stephenson St, Birmingham B2 4BH **t** 0121 633 4477 **f** 0121 632 5935 **e** info@massiverecords.com **w** massiverecords.com Manager: Dan Gilbert.

MDC Classic Music Ltd 124 Camden High St, London NW1 0LU **t** 020 7485 4777 **f** 020 7482 6888 **e** info@mdcmusic.co.uk **w** mdcmusic.co.uk Dir: Alan Goulden.

Millenium Music 16-18 The Arcade, Oakhampton, Devon EX20 1EX **t** 01837 659249 **e** appleby@euphony.net Owner: Richard Appleby.

Mixmaster Records Market Square, Castlebar, Co Mayo, Ireland **t** +353 94 23732 **f** +353 94 23732 **e** mixmaster@eircom.net Owner: Pat Concannon.

Mole Jazz Ltd 311 Gray's Inn Road, London WC1X 8PX **t** 020 7278 8623 **f** 020 7278 8623 **e** jazz@molejazz.com **w** molejazz.com Mgr: Martin Allerton. Top prices paid for your unwanted jazz CDs, LPs etc.

Morning After Music Llyfnant House Shop, 22 Penrallt Street, Machynlleth, Powys SY20 8AJ **t** 01654 703767 Proprietor: Malcolm Hume.

WM Morrisons Supermarkets plc Wakefield 41 Industrial Est., Wakefield, West Yorkshire WF2 0XF **t** 01924 870000 **f** 01924 875300 Home & Leisure Dir: Andrew Pleasance.

Mr Bongo 44 Poland Street, London W1F 7LZ **t** 020 7287 5451 **f** 020 7287 1821 **e** latin@mrbongo.com **w** mrbongo.com Manager: Luis Libres.

MSM Recordstore 1st Floor, 17 Chalk Farm Road, London NW1 8AG **t** 020 7284 2527 **f** 020 7284 2504 **e** info@msmrecordstore.co.uk **w** msmrecordstore.co.uk MD: Des Carr.

The Music Box 13 Market Place, Wallingford, Oxon OX10 0AD **t** 01491 836269 **e** info@themusicbox.net Owner: Richard Strange.

Music City Ltd 122 New Cross Road, London SE14 5BA **t** 020 7277 9657 **f** 0870 7572004 **e** info@musiccity.co.uk **w** musiccity.co.uk Store Mgr: Nick Kemp.

Music Exchange 3A Crewe Road, Alsager, Stoke-on-Trent ST7 2EW **t** 01270 877 637 **f** 01270 877 637 **e** mike@demon655.freeserve.co.uk Owner: Mike Stone.

Music Room 8 North Street, Sandwick, Isle of Lewis, Outer Hebrides HS2 0AD **t** 07754 614498 **e** karen@celticmusicroom.com **w** celticmusicroom.com Contact: John Clarke

Music World The Old Armistice, 31 Hart St, Henley-On-Thames, Oxon RG9 2AR **t** 01491 572700 **e** musicworldhenley@aol.com Owner: Dave Smith.

Music Zone Direct Music Zone House, Heapriding Business Park, Ford St, Chestergate, Stockport, Cheshire SK3 0BT **t** 0161 477 5088 **f** 0161 477 5082 **e** enq@musiczone.co.uk **w** musiczone.co.uk Head of Buying: Andy Flint.

Musicbank 5 Station Way, Cheam Village, Surrey SM3 8SD **t** 020 8643 2869 **f** 020 8643 3092 Contact: Robert Bush

MVC Woolworth House, 242-246 Marylebone Rd, London NW1 6JL **t** 020 7262 1222 **f** 020 7706 5975 **e** firstname.lastname@mvc.co.uk **w** mvc.co.uk MD: Richard Izard. Head of Commercial: Jim Batchelor. Head of Mktg: Cormac Loughran.

Noise Annoys 53 Howard St, Sheffield S1 2LW **t** 0114 276 9177 **f** 0114 276 9177 **e** sales@noise-annoys.co.uk **w** noise-annoys.co.uk Mgr: Simon Baxter.

Pelicanneck Records 74-76 High St, Manchester M4 1ES **t** 0161 834 2569 **f** 0161 236 3351 **e** mailboy@boomkat.com **w** boomkat.com Owner: Shlom Sviri.

Pendulum Records 34 Market Place, Melton Mowbray, Leicestershire LE13 1XD **t** 01664 565025 **f** 01664 560310 **e** mw@pendulum-records.co.uk **w** pendulum-records.co.uk Owner: Mike Eden.

Phonica Records 51 Poland St, London W1F 7NG **t** 020 7025 6070 **e** simon@vinylfactory.co.uk **w** phonicarecords.co.uk Manager: Simon Rigg.

Piccadilly Records Unit G9, Smithfield Buildings, 53 Oldham Street, Manchester M1 1JR **t** 0161 834 8888 or 0161 834 8789 **f** 0161 839 8008 **e** mail@piccadillyrecords.com **w** piccadillyrecords.com MD: John Kerfoot.

Pied Piper Records 293 Wellingborough Rd, Northampton NN1 4EW **t** 01604 624777 **f** 01604 624777 **e** piedpiperrecords@aol.com **w** pied-piper-records.co.uk Prop: Nick Hamlyn.

Pink Panther Records 1 Chapel St, Carlisle, Cumbria CA1 1JA **t** 01228 528740 **f** 01228 592959 **e** shop@pinkpantherrecords.co.uk **w** pinkpantherrecords.co.uk Owner: Keith Jefferson.

Pinpoint Music 44a Market St, Eastleigh, Hampshire SO50 5RA **t** 023 8064 2559 **f** 023 8032 6100 **e** cdsales@pinpoint-music.co.uk **w** pinpoint-music.co.uk Manager: Drew.

Planet of Sound (Scotland) 236 High St, Ayr, South Ayrshire **t** 01292 265913 **f** 01292 265493 **e** planet-of-sound@btconnect.co.uk Manager: Ian Hollins.

Planet Phat Records 295 Caledonian Road, London N1 1EG **t** 020 7700 5450 **f** 020 7607 3334 **w** planetphat.co.uk Contact: Greg

Plastic Fantastic Records 35 Drury Lane, Covent Garden, London WC2B 5RH **t** 020 7240 8055 **f** 020 7240 7628 **e** shop@plasticfantastic.co.uk **w** plasticfantastic.co.uk Manager: Oliver MacGregor.

Popscene 97 High St, Cosham, Hants PO6 3AZ **t** 023 9242 8042 **f** 023 9279 2355 **e** enquiries@popsceneuk.com **w** popsceneuk.com Owner: Chris Lovett.

Prelude Records 25B Giles St, Norwich NR2 1JN **t** 01603 628319 **f** 01603 620170 **e** admin@preluderecords.co.uk **w** preluderecords.co.uk Partner: Andrew Cane.

Premier Record Stores 3-5 Smithfield Square, Belfast, Co Antrim BT1 1JE **t** 028 9024 0896 **f** 028 9027 8868 Contact: Ciarna McBurney

Probe Records 9 Slater St, Liverpool, Merseyside L1 4BW **t** 0151 708 8815 **f** 0151 709 7121 **e** probe-records@btconnect.com **w** probe-records.com Owner: Anne Davies.

Pure Groove Records 649 Holloway Road, London N19 5SE **t** 020 7281 4877 **f** 020 7263 5590 **e** info@puregroove.co.uk **w** puregroove.co.uk Buyers: Ziad Nashnush, Paul Christian.

Quirk's Records 29 Church Street, Ormskirk, Lancashire L39 3AG **t** 01695 570570 **f** 01695 570519 **e** quirks@email.com **w** quirks.co.uk Partner: Paul Quirk.

R&K Records 8 Clinton Arms Court, Newark, Nottinghamshire NG24 1EB **t** 01636 702653 **f** 01636 702653 Prop: Richard Young.

Range Records & Tapes 61 High St, Brownhills, West Midlands WS8 6HH **t** 01543 374299 **f** 01543 374299 **e** paul@rangerecords.com **w** rangerecords.com Prop: Paul Whitehouse.

Rap And Soul Ltd Gresham Works, Mornington Rd, London E4 7DR **t** 020 8523 9578 **f** 020 8523 9601 **e** info@rapandsoulmailorder.com **w** rapandsoulmailorder.com Director: Mike Lewis.

Rapture Records 37-38 St John's St, Colchester, Essex CO2 7AD **t** 01206 542541 **f** 01206 542546 **e** john@rapturerecords.com **w** rapturerecords.com Prop: John Parkhurst.

Ray's Jazz at Foyles 1st Floor, 113-119 Charing Cross Rd, London WC2H 0EB **t** 020 7440 3205 **e** paul@foyles.co.uk **w** foyles.com Mgr: Paul Pace.

Record Corner Pound Lane, Godalming, Surrey GU7 1BX **t** 01483 422006 **e** info@therecordcorner.co.uk **w** therecordcorner.co.uk Prop: Tom Briggs.

Record Village 8 Cole Street, Scunthorpe, North Lincs. DN15 6QZ **t** 01724 851048 **f** 01724 280582 **e** sales@recordvillage.co.uk **w** recordvillage.co.uk Prop: Dave Greaves.

Records & Cards 17, Beaufort Street, Brynmawr, Gwent NP23 4AQ **t** 01495 310 111 **f** 01495 310 555 Owner: Glenys Morgan.

Reflex 23 Nun Street, Newcastle upon Tyne NE1 5AG **t** 0191 260 3246 **f** 0191 260 3245 **e** info@reflexcd.co.uk **w** reflexcd.co.uk Owner: Alan Jourdan.

Reform Ltd Easton Buildings, Little Castle St, Exeter, Devon EX4 3PX **t** 01392 435577 **f** 01392 435577 **e** enquiries@reform-records.co.uk **w** reform-records.co.uk

Release The Groove Records 20 Denman Street, London W1V 7RJ **t** 020 7734 7712 or 020 7287 0503 **f** 020 7734 7713 **e** releasethegroove@hotmail.com **w** releasethegroove.com Managing Directors: Gary Dillon/Francesca Roucco.

Replay Records 109 High Street, Tunstall, Stoke On Trent, Staffordshire ST6 5TA **t** 01782 834660 or 01782 823456 **f** 01782 834796 **e** mack@mackstracks.freeserve.co.uk **w** replay.co.uk/replay Prop: Brian Mack.

Replay. 73 Park Street, Bristol BS1 5PF **t** 0117 904 1134 or 0117 904 1135 **f** 0117 908 3410 **e** general@replay.co.uk **w** replay.co.uk/replay Mgr: Bob Jones.

Reveal Records 37 Main Centre, Derby DE1 2PE **t** 01332 349242 **f** 01332 349141 **e** sales@revealrecords.com **w** revealrecords.com Owner: Tom Rose.

Rhythm & Rhyme Records 9 High Street, Launceston, Cornwall PL15 8ER **t** 01566 772774 **f** 01566 774678 **e** chris@rrrecords.co.uk **w** rrrecords.co.uk Owner: Chris Parsons.

Richards Records 48 St Peters St, Canterbury, Kent CT1 2BE **t** 01227 452268 **f** 01227 767785 Manager: Kerry White.

Roadkill Records 89 Oldham St, Manchester M4 1LW **t** 0161 832 4444 **e** info@roadkill-records.com **w** roadkill-records.com Mgr: Liam Stewart.

Rock Box 151 London Rd, Camberley, Surrey GU15 3JY **t** 01276 26628 **f** 01276 678776 **e** mailorder@rockbox.co.uk **w** rockbox.co.uk Owner: Alan Bush.

Rough Trade 130 Talbot Road, London W11 1JA **t** 020 7229 8541 or 020 7221 3066 **f** 020 7221 1146 **e** shop@roughtrade.com **w** roughtrade.com Contact: Nigel House

Rub A Dub 35 Howard St, Glasgow, Lanarkshire G1 4BA **t** 0141 221 9657 **f** 0141 221 9650 **e** rubadub@rad69.com **w** rad69.com Partner: Martin McKay.

Scorpion Records 110 Oxford Rd, High Wycombe, Bucks HP11 2ND **t** 01494 436619 **f** 01494 436619 Owner: Jeff Amor.

Seaford Music 24 Pevensey Rd, Eastbourne, E. Sussex BN21 3HP **t** 01323 732553 **f** 01323 417455 **e** mail@seaford-music.co.uk **w** seaford-music.co.uk

Seeds Records 7 Oxton Rd, Charing Cross, Birkenhead CH41 2QQ **t** 0151 653 4224 **f** 0151 653 3223 **e** lee@seedsrecords.co.uk **w** seedsrecords.co.uk Mgr: Lee Hessler.

Selectadisc 21 Market St, Nottingham NG1 6HX **t** 0115 947 5420 **f** 0115 941 4261 Owner: Brian Selby.

Sellanby 245 Northolt Rd, South Harrow HA2 8HR **t** 020 8864 2622 **w** sellanby.com Owners: David & Peter Smith.

Sho'nuff...Beatz Workin' 86 Main St, Bangor, Co. Down BT20 4AG **t** 028 9147 7926 **f** 028 9147 7927 **e** steve@shonuff.co.uk **w** shonuff.co.uk Owner: Steve McDowell.

Sister Ray 94 Berwick St, London W1F 0QF **t** 020 7287 8385 **f** 020 7287 1087 **e** sales@sisterray.co.uk **w** sisterray.co.uk Admin: Nick Harrison.

Slough Record Centre 241-243 Farnham Rd, Slough, Berks SL2 1DE **t** 01753 528194 or 01753 572272 **f** 01753 692110 **e** sloughrecords@btconnect.com **w** sloughrecords.co.uk Sales: Terry & Simon.

Smallfish Records 372 Old St, London EC1V 9LT **t** 020 7739 2252 **f** 020 7739 7502 **e** justusfish@smallfish.co.uk **w** smallfish.co.uk Manager: Nick Turner.

WH Smith High Street Greenbridge Road, Swindon, Wiltshire SN3 3LD **t** 01793 616161 **f** 01793 562570 **e** judith.swales@whsmith.co.uk; **w** whsmithgroup.com Entertainment Dir: Judith Swales.

Smyths Musique 12 Railway St, Newcastle, Co Down BT33 0AL **t** 028 4372 2831 **e** musique@smyths.biz **w** smyths.biz

Snv Music 8 Gammon Walk, Barnstaple, Devon EX31 1DJ **t** 01271 323382 **f** 01271 327017 **e** snv@snv2000.com **w** snv2000.com

Solo Music 22a Market Arcade, Guildhall Shopping Centre, Exeter EX4 3HW **t** 01392 496564 **f** 01392 491785 **e** admin@solomusic.freeserve.co.uk **w** solomusic.co.uk Co-Owner: Penny Keen, Maggie Garrett.

Soul Brother Records 1, Keswick Road, London SW15 2HL **t** 020 8875 1018 **f** 020 8871 0180 **e** soulbrother@btinternet.com **w** soulbrother.com Partner: Laurence Prangell.

Sound Fusion Records 209 High St, Bromley, Kent BR1 1NY **t** 020 8464 8123 **f** 020 8466 9514 **e** mail@sfrecords.co.uk **w** sfrecords.co.uk Owner: Martyn Thomas.

Soundclash 28 St Benedicts Street, Norwich, Norfolk NR2 4AQ **t** 01603 761004 **f** 01603 762248 **e** soundclash@btinternet.com **w** run.to/soundclash MD: Paul Mills.

Sounds Good 26 Clarence St, Cheltenham, Gloucs GL50 3NU **t** 01242 234604 **f** 01242 253030 **e** cds@soundsgoodonline.co.uk **w** soundsgoodonline.co.uk Partners: John & Diana Ross.

Sounds of the Universe 7 Broadwick St, London W1F 0DA **t** 020 7494 2004 **f** 020 7494 2004 **e** info@soundsoftheuniverse.com **w** souljazzrecords.co.uk Contact: Karl Shale

Spin Compact Discs 8 High Bridge, Newcastle-upon-Tyne NE1 1EN **t** 0191 261 4741 or 0191 261 4742 **f** 0191 261 4747 **e** mailorder@spinCDs.fsbusiness.co.uk **w** spincds.com Owner: Dave Dodds.

Spin It Records 13 High Rd, Willesden Green, London NW10 2TE **t** 020 8459 0761 **f** 020 8459 7464 **e** sales@spinitrecords.co.uk **w** spinitrecords.co.uk Sales Manager: Tony.

Spinadisc Records 75A Abington St, Northampton NN1 2BH **t** 01604 631144 **f** 01604 624418 **e** info@spinadisc.freeserve.co.uk **w** spinadisc.demon.co.uk Partner: Dick Raybould.

Spiral Classics 38 Baxtergate, Loughborough LE11 1TQ **t** 01509 557 846 **f** 01509 557 847 **e** sophia@spiralclassics.co.uk **w** spiralclassics.co.uk Owner: Sophia Singer.

Stand-Out 23 Fisherton Street, Salisbury, Wiltshire SP2 7SU **t** 01722 411344 **f** 01722 421505 **e** stand-out@totalise.co.uk Owner: Colin Mundy.

Stand-Out (Bournemouth) Unit 1, 169-171 Old Christchurch Road, Bournemouth, Dorset BH1 1JU **t** 01202 315954 **f** 01202 789870 **e** stand-out@totalise.co.uk Manager: Dan Kavanagh.

Stereo One 13 Old Sneddon St, Paisley, Renfrewshire PA3 2AG **t** 0141 889 4489 **f** 0141 848 1840 **e** jaz8138@aol.com **w** stereo-one.com Boss: Gordon McGinlay.

Stern's African Record Centre 293 Euston Road, London NW1 3AD **t** 020 7387 5550 or 020 7388 5533 **f** 020 7388 2756 **e** fred@sternsmusic.com **w** sternsmusic.com Mgrs: Fred Hines, Dom Raymond-Barker.

Swordfish 14 Temple Street, Birmingham B2 SBG **t** 0121 6334859 Owner: Mike Caddick.

Tempest Records 83 Bull St, City Centre, Birmingham B4 6AD **t** 0121 236 9170 **f** 0121 236 9270 **e** info@tempest-records.co.uk Manager: Mark Thornton.

Tesco Stores Ltd PO Box 44, Cirrus Building C, Shire Park, Welwyn Garden City, Herts AL7 1ZR **t** 01992 632222 **f** 01707 297690 **w** tesco.com Snr Buying Mgr, Music: Alan Hunt.

Three Shades Records 8 Lower Severn Street, Birmingham, West Midlands B1 1PT **t** 0121 687 2772 **f** 0121 687 2773 **e** martinbanks@threeshades.com **w** threeshades.com

Threshold Records 53 High St, Cobham, Surrey KT11 3DP **t** 01932 865678 **f** 01932 865678 **e** sales@threshold-cd.co.uk Mgr: Phil Pavling.

Topsounds 170 Newgate St, Bishop Auckland, Co Durham DL14 7EJ **t** 01388 609444 **f** 01388 601603 **e** topsounds@topsounds.com **w** topsounds.com

Torre Records 240 Union St, Torquay, Devon TQ2 5BY **t** 01803 291506 **f** 01803 291506 **e** cj@torrerecords.freeserve.co.uk Co-owner: Lee Jones.

Totem Records 168 Stoke Newington Church St, London N16 0JL **t** 020 7275 0234 **f** 020 7275 0111 **e** sales@totemrecords.com **w** totemrecords.com MD: Tony Fischetti.

Townsend Records 30 Queen St, Great Harwood, Lancashire BB6 7QQ **t** 01254 885995 **f** 01254 887835 **e** admin@townsend-records.co.uk **w** townsend-records.co.uk MD: Steve Bamber.

Townsend Records (2) 117 Market St, Chorley, Lancashire PR7 1SQ **t** 01257 264727 **f** 01257 264727 **e** sales@townsend-records.co.uk Manager: Adrian Crook.

Track Records 15 High Ousegate, York YO1 8RZ **t** 01904 629022 or 01904 612379 **f** 01904 610637 **e** trackrecords@btinternet.com **w** trackrecordsuk.com Owner: Keith Howe.

Tracks 14 Railway Street, Hertford SG14 1BG **t** 01992 589294 **f** 01992 587090 **e** enquiries@tracks.sonnet.co.uk **w** tracks.org.uk Buyer: Dennis Osborne.

Trading Post 23 Nelson St, Stroud, Glos **t** 01453 759116 **f** 01453 756455 **e** simon@tradingpost.freeserve.co.uk **w** the-tradingpost.co.uk

Tudor Tunes 7 Tudor Row, Lichfield WS13 6HH **t** 01543 257627 **f** 01543 257627 **e** ralph@tudortunes.fsnet.co.uk Owners: Dave & Janice Williams.

Twister Records 4 Mill St, Brierley Hill, West Midlands DY5 2RH **t** 01384 485459 **e** info@twister-records.co.uk **w** twister-records.co.uk Co-owner: Lee Skelding.

Upbeat Trevelver, Belle Vue, Bude, Cornwall EX23 8JL **t** 01288 355763 **f** 01288 355763 Owner: Keith Shepherd.

Uptown Records 3 D'Arblay Street, London W1F 8DH **t** 020 7434 3639 **f** 020 7434 3649 **e** izzy@uptownrecords.com **w** uptownrecords.com

Vinyl Addiction Record Shop 6 Inverness Street, London NW1 7HJ **t** 020 7482 1114 **f** 020 7681 6039 **e** music@vinyladdiction.ukf.net **w** vinyl-addiction.co.uk MD: Justin Rushmore.

Virgin Entertainment Group Ltd The School House, 50 Brook Green, London W6 7RR **t** 020 8752 9000 **f** 020 8752 9001 **e** firstname.lastname@virginmega.com **w** virgin.com CEO, Virgin Ent. Group: Simon Wright. Operations Director: Dennis Henderson. Head of Marketing: Andy Kendrick.

Waterside Music 1 Waterside House, The Plains, Totnes, Devon TQ9 5DW **t** 01803 867947 Prop: John Cooper.

Wax City Music 306-308 London Road, Croydon CR0 2TJ **t** 020 8665 0223 **f** 020 8665 0223 or 0709 215 9916 **e** info@waxcitymusic.com **w** waxcitymusic.com Contact: Lanre

What Records Unit 40, Abbeygate Shopping Centre, Nuneaton, Warickshire CV11 4EH **t** 02476 352904 **f** 02476 320805 **e** whatuk@aol.com **w** whatrecords.co.uk Owner: Tim Ellis.

Whitelabel Records 4,Colomberie, St Helier, Jersey, Channel Islands JE2 4QB **t** 01534 725256 **f** 01534 780956 **e** info@whitelabelrecords.co.uk **w** whitelabelrecords.co.uk Owner: Mal White.

The Woods 6 The Arcade, Bognor Regis, West Sussex PO21 1LH **t** 01243 827712 **f** 01243 842615 **e** sales@the-woods.co.uk **w** the-woods.co.uk Proprietor: Trevor Flack.

Woolworths plc Woolworth House, 242-246 Marylebone Road, London NW1 6JL **t** 020 7262 1222 **f** 020 7706 5975 **e** firstname.lastname@woolworths.co.uk **w** woolworths.co.uk CEO: Trevor Bish-Jones. Commercial Dir (Entertainment): Richard Izard. Head of Commercial (Entertainment): Jim Batchelor. Marketing Dir: Octavia Morley.

WyldPytch Records 51 Lexington St, London W1F 9HL **t** 020 7434 3472 **f** 020 7287 1403 **e** contact@wyldpytch.com **w** wyldpytch.com Owner: Digger Elias.

X-Records 44 Bridge St, Bolton, Lancs BL1 2EG **t** 01204 524018 **f** 01204 370214 **e** xrecords@xrecords.co.uk **w** xrecords.co.uk

XSF Records 39 Berwick Street, Soho, London W1F 8RU **t** 020 7287 2496 **f** 020 7437 6255 **e** info@xsfrecords.com **w** xsfrecords.com MD: J Carlos Zaghis.

Zhivago Sound And Vision 5-6 Shop Street, Galway, Ireland **t** +353 91 564198 **f** +353 91 509951 **e** info@musicireland.com **w** musicireland.com Gen Mgr: Des Hubbard.

Retail Services

Airplay The Manse, 39 Northenden Road, Sale, Cheshire M33 2DH **t** 0161 962 2002 **f** 0161 962 2112 **e** mailbox@airplay.co.uk **w** airplay.co.uk Head of Music: Paul Maunder.

Apex Retail Services Ltd 2nd Floor, Elvin House, Stadium Way, Wembley, Middx HA9 0DW **t** 020 8585 3540 **f** 020 8585 3995 **e** beth@indidist.co.uk MD: Beth Maloney.

Cardiff M Light & Sound Units 9/10, Tarran Buildings, Freeschool Court, Bridgend, Mid Glamorgan CF31 3AG **t** 01656 648170 **f** 01656 648412 **e** info@cardiffm.co.uk **w** cardiffm.co.uk MD: Philip Evans.

Chrysalis Retail Entertainment 2 Pincents Kiln, Calcot, Reading, Berkshire RG31 7SD **t** 0118 930 5599 **f** 0118 930 3360 **e** info@cre.co.uk **w** cre.co.uk PA to MD: Louise O'Sullivan.

Colorset Graphics 2-3 Black Swan Yard, Bermondsey St, London SE1 3XW **t** 020 7234 0300 **f** 020 7234 0118 **e** mail@colorsetgraphics.co.uk **w** colorsetgraphics.co.uk Dir: Frank Baptiste.

Cube Music The Factory, 2 Acre Rd, Kingston upon Thames, Surrey KT2 6EF **t** 020 8547 1543 **f** 020 8547 1544 **e** info@cube-music.com **w** cube-music.com Music & Promotions Dir: Mick Hilton.

Digital DJ Ltd 22 The Ropery, Newcastle upon Tyne NE6 1TY **t** 0191 276 2791 **f** 0191 224 0148 **e** info@digitaldjsystems.com **w** digitaldjsystems.com Dir: Paul Rogers.

Essanby Ltd Riverside Works, Amwell Lane, Ware, Herts SG12 8EB **t** 01920 870596 **f** 01920 871553 **e** shatcher@essanby.co.uk **w** essanby.co.uk MD: Steve Hatcher.

International Displays Stonehill, Stukeley Meadows Ind Estate, Huntingdon, Cambridgeshire PE29 6ED **t** 01480 414204 **f** 01480 414205 **e** info@internationaldisplays.co.uk **w** internationaldisplays.co.uk Sales & Marketing Dir.: Carl Jenkin.

Kempner Distribution Ltd 498-500 Honeypot Lane, Stanmore, MIddlesex HA7 1JZ **t** 020 8952 5262 **f** 020 8952 8061 **e** erollinson@kempner.co.uk **w** kempner.co.uk Mkting Mgr: Eddie Rollinson.

KPD London Ltd 297 Haydons Road, London SW19 8TX **t** 020 8542 9535 **f** 020 8543 9406 **e** reception@kpd.co.uk **w** kpd.co.uk MD: Ivor Heller.

Lift (UK) Triangle Business Park, Wendover Road, Stoke Mandeville, Buckinghamshire HP22 5BL **t** 01296 615151 **f** 01296 612865 **e** info@lift-uk.co.uk **w** liftsystems.com Business Manager: Gudrun Heidenbauer.

Masson Seeley & Co Ltd Howdale, Downham Market, Norfolk PE38 9AL **t** 01366 38800 **f** 01366 385222 or 01366 388025 **e** admin@masson-seeley.co.uk **w** masson-seeley.co.uk Contact: Martin Potten

Micro Video Services 24 Cobham Rd, Ferndown Industrial Estate, Wimborne, Dorset BH21 7NP **t** 01202 861696 **f** 01202 654919 **e** sales@microvideoservices.com.uk **w** microvideoservices.com Contact: Sales

MRIB Heckfield Place, 530 Fulham Road, London SW6 5NR **t** 020 7731 3555 **f** 020 7731 8545 **e** contactus@mrib.co.uk **w** mrib.co.uk MD: Paul Basford.

Musonic (UK) Unit 13, Wenta Business Centre, Colne Way, Watford, Herts WD24 7ND **t** 01923 213344 **f** 01923 213355 **e** sales@musonic.co.uk **w** musonic.co.uk Dir: Stephen Blank.

Pentonville Rubber Products Ltd 104-106 Pentonville Road, London N1 9JB **t** 020 7837 4582 **f** 020 7278 7392 **e** queries@pentonvillerubber.co.uk **w** pentonvillerubber.co.uk

Pro.Loc Europe Royal Albert House, Sheet Street, Windsor, Berks SL4 1BE **t** 01753 705030 **f** 01753 831541 **e** proloc@proloc.co.uk **w** proloc-online.com GM: Mike Vickers.

Pro.Loc UK Ltd Northgate Business Centre, 38 Northgate, Newark on Trent, Nottinghamshire NG24 1EZ **t** 01636 642827 **f** 01636 642865 **e** sales@proloc.co.uk **w** proloc-online.com Sales: Sam Jessop.

REDMUZE

REDmuze

Paulton House, 8 Shepherdess Walk, London N1 7LB **t** 020 7566 8216 **f** 020 7566 8259 **e** info@redmuze.com **w** redmuze.com. Head of Sales: Deborah Sass.

Retail Entertainment Displays Ltd (red) 27-28 Stapledon Road, Orton Southgate, Peterborough, Cambs PE2 6TD **t** 01733 239001 **f** 01733 239002 **e** info@reddisplays.com **w** reddisplays.com MD: John Findlay.

Retail Management Solutions Bloxham Mill, Barford Rd, Bloxham, Banbury OX15 4FF **t** 01295 724568 **f** 01295 722801 **e** info@rmsepos.com **w** rmsepos.com Contact: Robert Collier

Sarem & Co 43A Old Woking Road, West Byfleet, Surrey KT14 6LG **t** 01932 352535 **f** 01932 336431 **e** info@sarem-co.com **w** sarem-co.com Partner: Adrian Connelly.

Sounds Wholesale Unit 2, Park St, Burton on Trent, Staffs DE14 3SE **t** 01283 566823 **f** 01283 568631 **e** matpriest@aol.com **w** soundswholesaleltd.co.uk Dir: Matt Priest.

Mike Thorn Display & Design 30 Muswell Avenue, London N10 2EG **t** 020 8442 0279 **f** 020 8442 0496 **e** info@bear-art.com MD: Mike Thorn.

Walsh & Jenkins plc Power House, Powerscroft Road, Sidcup, Kent DA14 5EA **t** 020 8308 6300 **f** 020 8308 6340 **e** sales@walsh-jenkins.co.uk **w** walsh-jenkins.co.uk Sales Office Co-ordiantor: Jackie Read.

West 4 Tapes And Records 105 Stocks Lane, Bracklesham Bay, West Sussex PO20 8NU **t** 01243 671238 Sales Dir: Kenneth G Roe.

Wilton of London Stanhope House, 4-8 Highgate High Street, London N6 5JL **t** 020 8341 7070 **f** 020 8341 1176 Contact: The Managing Director

Direct Order Companies

ADA Mail Order PO Box 800, Belper, Derbyshire DE56 2ZA **t** 01773 850000 **f** 01773 850000 **e** info@adamailorder.co.uk **w** adamailorder.co.uk Sales Director: Michael Peat.

Alma Road Mail Order PO Box 3813, London SW18 1XE **t** 020 8870 9912 **f** 020 8871 1766 **e** mailorder@almaroad.co.uk **w** beggars.com Mail Order Manager: Jo.

Badlands Mail Order 11 St George's Place, Cheltenham, Gloucestershire GL50 3LA **t** 01242 227724 **f** 01242 227393 **e** shop@badlands.co.uk **w** badlands.co.uk MD: Philip Jump.

BMG Direct Bedford House, 69-79 Fulham High Street, London SW6 3JW **t** 020 7384 7500 **f** 020 7973 0345 Special Markets Mgr: Dom Higgins.

Bus Stop Mail Order Ltd 42-50 Steele Road, London NW10 7AS **t** 020 8453 1311 **f** 020 8961 8725 **e** info@busstop.co.uk **w** acerecords.co.uk Director: Yvette DeRoy.

Carbon Disks PO Box 28, Cromer, Norfolk NR27 9RG **t** 01263 515963 **f** 01263 515963 **e** data@carbondisks.com **w** carbondisks.com Contact: Barry Fry

Catapult 100% Vinyl 22 High Street Arcade, Cardiff CF10 2BB **t** 029 2022 8990 or 029 2034 2322 **f** 029 2023 1690 **e** enquiries@catapult.co.uk **w** catapult.co.uk MD: Lucy Squire.

CDX Music By Mail The Olde Coach House, Windsor Cresent, Radyr, South Glamorgan CF4 8AG **t** 029 2084 3604 or 029 2084 2878 **f** 029 2084 2184 **e** sales@cdx.co.uk **w** cdx.co.uk MD: Paul Karamouzis.

CeeDee Mail Ltd PO Box 14, Stowmarket, Suffolk IP14 1ED **t** 01449 770138 **f** 01449 770133 **e** CeeDeeMail@aol.com Contact: Tobias Wilcox

Celtic Music Room 8 North Street, Sandwick, Isle of Lewis HS2 0AD **t** 01851 706741 **e** info@celticmusicroom.com **w** celticmusicroom.com Contact: John Clarke

City Sounds 5 Kirby Street, London EC1N 8TS **t** 020 7404 1800 or 020 7405 5454 **f** 020 7242 1863 **e** sales@city-sounds.co.uk **w** city-sounds.co.uk Contact: Tom Henneby

The Compact Disc Club 6 The Arcade, Bognor Regis, West Sussex PO22 1LH **t** 01243 827712 **f** 01243 842615 **e** sales@the-woods.co.uk **w** the-woods.co.uk CEO: Trevor Flack.

Compact Disc Services 40-42 Brantwood Avenue, Dundee DD3 6EW **t** 01382 776595 **f** 01382 736702 **e** agcdser@aol.com **w** cd-services.com Snr Partner: Dave Shoesmith.

Cooking Vinyl Mail Order PO Box 1845, London W3 0BR **t** 020 8600 9200 **f** 020 8743 7534 **e** bob@cookingvinyl.com **w** cookingvinyl.com Direct Mktg Mgr: Bob Allan.

Copperplate Mail Order 68, Belleville Rd, London SW11 6PP **t** 020 7585 0357 **f** 020 7585 0357 **e** copperplate2000@yahoo.com **w** copperplatemailorder.com MD: Alan O'Leary.

Cyclops 33A Tolworth Park Road, Tolworth, Surrey KT6 7RL **t** 020 8339 9965 **f** 020 8399 0070 **e** postmaster@gft-cyclops.co.uk **w** gft-cyclops.co.uk MD: Malcolm Parker.

Didgeridoo PO Box 333, Brighton, East Sussex BN1 2EH **t** 01403 740289 **f** 01403 740261 **e** ukorders@didgerecords.com **w** didgerecords.com Head of Mail Order: Isabel Woods.

Direct Records Unit 12, Lodge Bank Industrial Estate, Off Crown Lane, Horwich, Bolton BL6 5HY **t** 01204 675520 **f** 01204 479006 **e** sales@directrecords.co.uk **w** directrecords.co.uk Manager: Ian Garner.

Dub Vendor Mail Order 17 Davids Rd, London SE23 3EP **t** 020 8291 8950 **f** 020 8291 1097 **e** mailorder@dubvendor.co.uk **w** dubvendor.co.uk MD: John MacGillivray.

Fair Oaks Entertainments 7 Tower Street, Ulverston, Cumbria LA12 9AN **t** 01229 581766 **f** 01229 581766 **e** fairoaksorderline@hotmail.com **w** anglefire.com/music5/roots2rockmusic Contact: JG Livingstone

Fast Forward Units 9-10 Sutherland Court, Tolpits Lane, Watford, Hertfordshire WD18 9SP **t** 01923 897080 **f** 01923 896263 **e** sales@fast-forward.co.uk MD: Ken Hill.

Freak Emporium Mail-Order PO Box 1288, Gerrards Cross, Bucks SL9 9YB **t** 01753 893008 **f** 01753 892879 **e** sales@freakemporium.com **w** freakemporium.com MD: Richard Allen.

GFT Ltd (see Cyclops)

Greensleeves Mail Order Unit 14 Metro Centre, St John's Road, Isleworth, Middlesex TW7 6NJ **t** 020 8758 2301 **f** 020 8758 0811 **e**mailorder@greensleeves.net **w** greensleeves.net Mail Order Manager: Chris O'Brien.

Hard To Find Record Vinyl House, 10 Upper Gough Street, Birmingham, West Midlands B1 1JG **t** 0121 687 7777 **f** 0121 687 7774 **e** sales@htfr.com **w** htfr.com Contact: Jason Kirby

Jim Stewart, Motown, Soul & Sixties CD Specialist 37 Main Rd, Hextable, Swanley, Kent BR8 7RA **t** 01322 613883 **f** 01322 613883 **e** jstew79431@aol.com **w** soulsearchingplus.co.uk Contact: Jim Stewart

Magpie Direct Music Ltd PO Box 20, Lewes, Sussex BN8 5ZY **t** 08700 711 611 **f** 0870 787 6143 **e** magpie@multichanneldistribution.com **w** magpiedirect.com GM: Steve Waters.

Massive Records The Dance Specialists, 95 Gloucester Green, Oxford OX1 2BU **t** 01865 250 476 **f** 01865 792 770 **e** info@massiverecords.com **w** massiverecords.com Managing Partner: Joanna Massive.

Mostly Music 28 Carlisle Close, Mobberley, Knutsford, Cheshire WA16 7HD **t** 01565 872650 **f** 01565 872650 **e** mostlymusic@btinternet.com **w** mostlymusic.co.uk Proprietor: Roger Wilkes.

Music Exchange of Manchester Mail Order Dept. X, Claverton Rd, Wythenshawe, Manchester M23 9ZA **t** 0161 946 9301 **f** 0161 946 1195 **e** mail@music-exchange.co.uk **w** music-exchange.co.uk Manager: Kevin Ackford.

Mute Bank 429 Harrow Road, London W10 4RE **t** 020 8964 0029 **f** 020 8964 3722 **e** info@mutebank.co.uk **w** mutebank.co.uk Head of Mailorder: Michael Lopatis.

Nostalgia Direct 11 St Nicholas Chambers, Newcastle-upon-Tyne NE1 1PE **t** 0191 233 1200 **f** 0191 233 1215 Contact: George Carr

Open Ear Productions Ltd. Main Street, Oughterard, Co.Galway, Ireland **t** +353 91 552816 **f** +353 91 557967 **e** info@openear.ie **w** openear.ie MD: Bruno Staehelin.

Pendulum Direct 34 Market Place, Melton Mowbray, Leicestershire LE13 1XD **t** 01664 566246 **f** 01664 560310 **e** mw@pendulum-direct.com **w** pendulum-direct.com MD: Mike Eden.

The Perennial Music Co Ltd 69 Rivington Street, London EC2A 3AY **t** 020 7613 1344 or 020 7613 3911 **f** 020 7613 3319 or 020 7613 3088 **e** oraclemusic@btinternet.com **w** forevergold.co.uk Dir: John Tracy.

Posteverything Suite 216, Bon Marche Buliding, 241 Ferndale Rd, London SW9 8BJ **t** 020 7733 2344 **f** 020 7733 5818 **e** feedback@posteverything.com **w** posteverything.com Contact: Duncan Moore

Red Lick Records Porthmadog, Gwynedd LL49 9DJ **t** 01766 512151 **f** 01766 512851 **e** sales@redlick.com **w** redlick.com MD: Ann Smith.

REDMuze Paulton House, 8 Shepherdess Walk, London N1 7LB **t** 020 7566 8216 **f** 020 7566 8259 **e** sales@redmuze.com **w** redmuze.com. Head of Sales: Deborah Sass.

Reggae Revive 27 Thamesgate, St, Edmund's Road, Dartford, Kent DA1 5ND **t** 01322 271634 **e** reggae.revive@virgin.net **w** reggaerevive.com Owner: Bob Brooks.

Rugby Songs Unlimited Whitwell, Colyford, Colyton, Devon EX24 6HS **t** 01297 553803 **e** very_funny@compuserve.com **w** rugby-songs.co.uk MD: Mike Williams.

Selections Dorchester, Dorset DT2 7YG **t** 0845 644 1560 **f** 01305 848516 **e** sales@cdselections.com **w** cdselections.com Contact: Michael Slocock

Soul Brother Records 1 Keswick Road, London SW15 2HL **t** 020 8875 1018 **f** 020 8871 0180 **e** SoulBrother@btinternet.com **w** SoulBrother.com Partner: Laurence Prangell.

Soundclash 28 St Benedicts Street, Norwich, Norfolk NR2 4AQ **t** 01603 761004 **f** 01603 762248 **e** soundclash@btinternet.com **w** run.to/soundclash MD: Paul Mills.

Soundtracks Direct 3 Prowse Place, London NW1 9PH **t** 020 7428 5500 **f** 020 7482 2385 **e** info@silvascreen.co.uk **w** soundtracksdirect.co.uk MD: Reynold D'Silva.

Spin It Records 13 High Road, London NW10 2TE **t** 020 8459 0761 **f** 020 8459 7464 **e** sales@spinitrecords.co.uk **w** spinitrecords.co.uk

Sterns Postal 293 Euston Road, London NW1 3AD **t** 020 7387 5550 **f** 020 7388 2756 **e** dave@sternsmusic.com **w** sternsmusic.com Retail Mgr: Dave Atkin.

Thirdwave Music Direct PO Box 19, Orpington, Kent BR6 9ZF **t** 01689 609481 **f** 01689 609481 **e** info@thirdwavemusic.com **w** thirdwavemusic.com MD: Matt Gall.

3 Beat Records 58 Wood Street, Liverpool, Merseyside L1 4AQ **t** 0151 709 3301 **f** 0151 707 0227 **e** info@3beat.co.uk **w** 3beat.co.uk Manager: Pezz.

Track Records 15 High Ousegate, York, South Yorkshire YO1 8RZ **t** 01904 629022 **f** 01904 610637 **e** trackrecords@btinternet.com **w** trackrecordsuk.com Mailorder Mgr: Alan Beecroft.

Tracks PO Box 117, Chorley, Lancashire PR6 0UU **t** 01257 269726 **f** 01257 231340 **e** sales@tracks.co.uk **w** tracks.co.uk Contact: Paul Wane

Universal Group Direct Ltd 76 Oxford St, London W1D 1BS **t** 020 8910 6012 **f** 020 8553 9613 **e** linda.porter@umusic.com **w** bclub.co.uk; channel.com MD: Ford Ennals.

Vinyl Tap Mail Order Music 1 Minerva Works, Crossley Lane, Kirkheaton, Huddersfield, West Yorkshire HD5 0QP **t** 01484 421446 **f** 01484 531019 **e** sales@vinyltap.demon.co.uk **w** vinyltap.co.uk Contact: Dan Browning

Vivante Music Ltd Unit 6, Fontigarry Business Pk, Reigate Road, Sidlow Nr Reigate, Surrey RG2 8QH **t** 01293 822186 **f** 01293 821965 **e** sales@vivante.co.uk **w** vivante.co.uk MD: Steven Carr.

Xsf Records 39 Berwick Street, London W1F 8RU **t** 020 7287 2496 **f** 020 7437 6255 **e** order@xsfrecords.com **w** xsfrecords.com

Online Distribution and Sales

1 Off Wax PO Box 5139, Glasgow G76 8WF **t** 0141 585 7354 **f** 0141 585 7354 **e** sales@1offwax.co.uk **w** 1offwax.co.uk Sales Director: Theresa Talbot.

101cd.com 11 Keeley Road, Croydon, Surrey CRO 1TF **t** 020 8680 5282 **f** 020 8667 9287 **e** hanifv@101cd.com **w** 101cd.com Commercial Dir: Hanif Virani.

3mv digital 3rd Floor, 7 Holyrood St, London SE1 2EL **t** 020 7378 8866 **f** 020 7378 8855 **e** info@3mv.com **w** 3mv.com CEO: Mark Hutton.

7 Digital Media 6th Floor, Palladium House, One Argyll Street, London W1F 7TA **t** 020 7494 6589 **f** 0871 733 4149 **e** info@7digitalmedia.com **w** 7digitalmedia.com Contact: Ben Drury

abovethesky.com Studio 105, 24-28 Hatton Wall, Clerkenwell, London EC1N 8JH **t** 020 7404 1005 **e** info@abovethesky.com **w** abovethesky.com Dir: A J Burt.

Action Records 47 Church St, Preston, Lancs PR1 3DH **t** 01772 884772 or 01772 258809 **f** 01772 252255 **e** sales@action-records.co.uk **w** action-records.co.uk Mgr: Gordon Gibson.

Amazon.co.uk Patriot Court, The Grove, Slough, Berkshire SL1 1QP **t** 020 8636 9200 **f** 020 8636 9400 **e** info@amazon.co.uk **w** amazon.co.uk

Atomic Sounds PO Box 2074, Lancing, East Sussex BN15 8YA **t** 01903 754341 **e** atomic1@fastnet.co.uk **w** atomicsounds.co.uk Owner: Tony Grist.

atsdigital.com Studio 105, 24-28 Hatton Wall, Clerkenwell, London EC1N 8JH **t** 020 7404 1005 **e** info@atsdigital.com **w** atsdigital.com Dir: A J Burt.

BT Rich Media (a division of BT plc) PP4E, 4th Floor, 203 High Holborn, London WC1V 7BU **t** 020 7777 7444 **f** 020 7728 7474 **e** btrminfo@bt.com **w** btrichmedia.com Dir of Music: Marco Distefano.

BUYHEAR.COM

BuyHear.com

240 High Road, Harrow Weald, Middlesex HA3 7BB **t** 020 8863 2520 **f** 020 8863 2520 **e** steve@buyhear.com **w** buyhear.com President and Musical Director: Steven Robert Glen, steve@buyhear.com. A&R Dept:Sunny Nersian, sunny@buyhear.com. Technical Director: Robert Gothan, Robert@buyhear.com www. **Buyhear.com provides and supplies successful Digital Distribution Internet Platform.**

Classical.com 3rd Floor, 82-84 Clerkenwell Rd, London EC1M 5RF **t** 020 7689 1080 **f** 020 7689 1180 **e** info@classical.com **w** classical.com Exec VP Content & Bus Dev: Roger Press.

DAW Buyers Guide Gipsy Road, London SE27 9RB **t** 020 8761 1042 **e** info@syphaonline.com **w** syphaonline.com Partner: Yasmin Hashmi.

Digital Pressure Inc. (Europe) The Peer House, 12 Lower Pembroke St, Dublin 2, Ireland **t** +353 1 662 9337 **f** +353 1 662 9339 **e** Darragh@digitalpressure.com **w** digitalpressure.com Vice President: Darragh M. Kettle.

Disky.com 3 York Street, St. Helier, Jersey JE2 3RQ **t** 01534 509687 **e** general@disky.com **w** disky.com Managing Director: Robert Bisson.

DX3 33 Glasshouse St, London W1B 5DG **t** 020 7434 5050 **f** 020 7434 5055 **e** info@dx3.net **w** dx3.net MD: Tim Newmarch. Label Relations: Ian Whitfield.

eil.com Esprit House, Railway Sidings, Meopham, Kent DA13 0YS **t** 01474 815010 **f** 01474 815030 **e** sales@eil.com **w** eil.com Marketing Manager: Simon Wright.

Elevate 3rd Floor, 7 Holyrood Street, London SE1 2EL **t** 020 7378 5818 **f** 020 7378 4761 **e** info@elevateuk.com Contact: Mark Hutton

ENTERTAINMENT UK DIRECT

Auriol Drive, Greenford Park, Greenford, Middx UB6 0DS **t** 020 8833 2888 **f** 020 8833 2967 **e** enquiriesdirect@entuk.co.uk **w** entuk.co.uk GM: Graham Lambdon. **The UK's largest direct consumer fulfilment service, offering music, VHS, DVD and multimedia. "The best Back-End in E-Business."**

ePM Online Unit 204, Saga Centre, 326 Kensal Rd, London W10 5BZ **t** 020 8964 4900 **f** 020 8962 9783 **e** melle@epm-musiconline.com **w** epm-musiconline.com Partner: Melle Boels.

Flip Records 2 Mardol, Shrewsbury SY1 1PY **t** 01743 244469 **f** 01743 260985 **e** sales@fliprecords.co.uk **w** fliprecords.co.uk Owner: Duncan Morris.

Groovetech.com 10 Latimer Industrial Estate, Latimer Road, London W10 6RQ **t** 020 8962 3350 **f** 020 8962 3355 **e** feedback@groovetech.com **w** groovetech.com US Sales Dir: Quentin Chambers.

HMV ECommerce Film House, 142 Wardour Street, London W1F 8LN **t** 020 7432 2000 **f** 020 7434 1090 **e** firstname.lastname@hmv.co.uk **w** hmv.co.uk ECommerce Dir (Europe): Stuart Rowe. HMV Internet Manager: Helen Gourley.

INTEROUTE

Walbrook Building, 195 Marsh Wall, London E14 9SG **t** 020 7025 9000 **f** 020 7025 9854 **e** isam.kelly@interoute.com **w** interoute.com Mgr, Content Dist'n: Sam Kelly. **Share! Provides secure, simple and cost effective distribution of music using the latest Internet technology.**

iTunes Europe 20 Garrick St, London WC2E 9BT **t** 020 7331 4318 **f** 020 73314513 **e** lastname.initial@euro.apple.com **w** itunes.com

Jansmusic PO Box 3136, Barnet, Herts EN5 1DY **t** 020 8447 3862 **f** 020 8447 3862 **e** jan@jansmusic.co.uk **w** jansmusic.co.uk Director: Jan Hart.

Javelin Distribution Unit 2, Water Lane, London NW1 8NZ **t** 020 7284 6500 **f** 020 7267 7235 **e** lhho@hho.co.uk **w** hho.co.uk MD: Henry Hadaway.

Lost Dog Recordings 1103 Argyle Street, Glasgow G3 8ND **t** 0141 243 2439 **e** info@lostdogrecordings.com **w** lostdogrecordings.com A&R: Jonathan Stone.

Massive Records The Dance Specialists, 95 Gloucester Green, Oxford OX1 2BU **t** 01865 250 476 **f** 01865 792 770 **e** info@massiverecords.com **w** massiverecords.com Managing Partner: Joanna Massive.

The Music Index 34 Coniston Road, Neston, Cheshire CH64 0TD **t** 0151 336 6199 **f** 0151 336 6199 **e** info@themusicindex.com **w** themusicindex.com Sales Director: Christine Randall.

Music Village PO Box 218, Haslemere, Surrey GU27 3ZR**e** info@music-village.com **w** music-village.com Sales Director: Simon Port.

Musicroom.com 11 Denmark Street, London WC2H 8TD **t** 020 7434 0066 **f** 020 7836 4810 **e** info@musicroom.com **w** musicroom.com Dir, Internet Operations: Tomas Wise.

MyCokeMusic.com bd-ntwk, The Tea Building, 56 Shoreditch High Street, London E1 6PQ **t** 020 7749 5500 **f** 020 7749 5501 **e** enquiries@mycokemusic.com **w** mycokemusic.com Group Account Dir: Sam Needham.

Napster UK 57-61 Mortimer St, London W1W 8HS **t** 020 7101 7275 **f** 020 7101 7120 **e** firstname.lastname@napster.co.uk **w** napster.co.uk Programming Dir: Jeff Smith.

Nu Urban Music Unit 3, 36 Queens Rd, Newbury, Berks RG14 7NE **t** 01635 551400 **f** 01635 550333 **e** andrew@nu-urbanmusic.co.uk **w** nu-urbanmusic.co.uk Retail Mgr: Andrew Neil.

Odyssey.fm PO Box 18888, London SW7 4FQ **t** 020 7373 1614 **f** 020 7373 1614 **e** info@outer-media.co.uk **w** odyssey.fm Dir: Gregory Mihalcheon.

On Demand Distribution (OD2) Macmillan House, 96 Kensington High Street, London W8 4SG **t** 020 7082 0850 **f** 020 7082 0847 **e** info@ondemanddistribution.com **w** ondemanddistribution.com UK Sales Dir: Paul Smith.

Oxfordmusic.net 65 George St, Oxford OX1 2BE **t** 01865 798796 **f** 01865 798792 **e** info@oxfordmusic.net **w** oxfordmusic.net MD: Andy Clyde.

peoplesound.com 20 Orange Street, London WC2H 7NN **t** 020 7766 4000 **f** 020 7766 4001 **e** enquiries@peoplesound.com **w** peoplesound.com Office Mgr: Arabella Edwards.

Pinnacle Entertainment Heather Court, 6 Maidstone Road, Sidcup DA14 5HH **t** 020 8309 3600 **f** 020 8309 3908 **e** info@pinnacle-records.co.uk **w** pinnacle-entertainment.co.uk Head Of New Media: Dominic Jones.

PlayLouder 8-10 Rhoda Street, London E2 7EF **t** 020 7729 4797 **f** 020 7739 8571 **e** site@playlouder.com **w** playlouder.com MDs: Paul Hitchman, Jim Gottlieb.

PostEverything Suite 216, Bon MarchÇ Centre, 241 Ferndale Rd, London SW9 8BJ **t** 020 7733 2344 **f** 020 7733 5818 **e** feedback@posteverything.com **w** posteverything.com Contact: Duncan Moore

Prism Leisure Corporation Unit 1, Dencora Business Centre, 1 Dundee Way, Enfield, Middlesex EN3 7SX **t** 020 8804 8100 **f** 020 8216 6645 **e** prism@prismleisure.com **w** prismleisure.com MD: Ivor Young.

Recordstore.co.uk Unit 5, Waldo Works, Waldo Road, London NW10 6AW **t** 020 8964 9020 **f** 020 8964 9090 **e** mail@recordstore.co.uk **w** recordstore.co.uk Sales Director: Simon Moxon.

Red Lick Records Porthmadog, Gwynedd LL49 9DJ **t** 01766 512151 **f** 01766 512851 **e** sales@redlick.com **w** redlick.com MD: Ann Smith.

REDMuze Paulton House, 8 Shepherdess Walk, London N1 7LB **t** 020 7566 8216 **f** 020 7566 8259 **e** sales@redmuze.com **w** redmuze.com Head of Sales: Deborah Sass.

Reggae Revive 27 Thamesgate, St, Edmund's Road, Dartford, Kent DA1 5ND **t** 01322 271634 **e** reggae.revive@virgin.net **w** reggaerevive.com Owner: Bob Brooks.

Scottish & Irish Music Store PO Box 7264, Glasgow G46 6YE **t** 0141 637 6010 **f** 0141 637 6010 **e** sales@scottish-irish.com **w** scottish-irish.com MD: Ronnie Simpson.

Secondsounds.com 54 The Lagger, Chalfont St Giles, Bucks HP8 4DJ **t** 01494 875144 **f** 08700 557774 **e** info@secondsounds.com **w** secondsounds.com Mkt Director: Kevin Rockett.

Shetland Music Distribution Griesta, Tingwall, Shetland ZE2 9QB **t** 01595 840670 **f** 01595 840671 **e** enquiries@shetlandmusicdistribution.co.uk **w** shetlandmusicdistribution.co.uk Director: Alan Longmuir.

Simbiotic Mercat House, Argyle Court, 1103 Argyle St, Glasgow G3 8ND **t** 0141 243 2439 **f** 0141 243 2449 **e** sales@simbiotic.info **w** simbiotic.info Project Manager: Colin Hardie.

Soul Brother Records 1, Keswick Road, London SW15 2HL **t** 020 8875 1018 **f** 020 8871 0180 **e** soulbrother@btinternet.com **w** soulbrother.com Partner: Laurence Prangell.

Streetsonline.co.uk Overline House, Station Way, Crawley, West Sussex RH10 1JA **t** 01293 402040 **f** 01293 402050 **e** nick.coquet@streetsonline.co.uk **w** streetsonline.co.uk Content Mgr: Nick Coquet.

thewhitelabel.com 1-3 Croft Lane, Henfield, W. Sussex BN5 9TT **t** 01273 491761 **f** 01273 491761 **e** contact@thewhitelabel.com **w** thewhitelabel.com GM: Nic Vine.

Ticketmaster UK 48 Leicester Square, London WC2H 7LR **t** 020 7344 4000 **f** 020 7915 0411 **e** sales@ticketmaster.co.uk **w** ticketmaster.co.uk National Sales Manager: Tim Chambers.

TicketWeb UK 48 Leicester Square, London WC2H 7LR **t** 020 7344 4000 **f** 020 7915 0411 or c **e** clients@ticketweb.co.uk **w** ticketweb.co.uk

TOTP Shopping Guide, beeb.com BBC Worldwide, 80 Wood Lane, London W12 0TT **t** 020 8433 1303 **f** 020 8225 7877 **e** firstname.surname@beeb.com **w** bbcshop.com Executive Producer: Greg Jarvis.

Toughshed.com First Floor, 7-13 Cotton's Garden, Shoreditch, London E2 8DN **t** 020 7613 5666 **f** 020 7739 6872 **e** orders@toughshed.com **w** toughshed.com MD: Martin Gilks.

TRIBAL2GO

TRIBAL2GO

t 020 8673 0610 **f** 020 8675 8562 **e** sales@tribal2go.co.uk **w** tribal2go.co.uk Contact: Alison Wilson , Terry Woolner , Will Keen

For efficient, cost effective services for on line sales fulfilment via your own website.

Tumi Music 8-9 New Bond Street Place, Bath BA1 1BH **t** 01225 464736 **f** 01225 444870 **e** info@tumi.co.uk **w** tumimusic.com E Commerce: Damien Doherty.

UKSounds.com PO Box 36, Nantwich, Cheshire CW5 5FQ **t** 01270 627264 **e** info@uksounds.com **w** uksounds.com MD: Russ Walton.

Universal Group Direct 76 Oxford St, London W1D 1BS **t** 020 8910 6012 **f** 020 8553 9613**e** linda.porter@umusic.com **w** bclub.co.uk; channel.com MD: Ford Ennals.

Upbeat Mail Order PO Box 63, Wallington, Surrey SM6 9YP **t** 020 8773 1223 **f** 020 8669 6752 **e** info@upbeat.co.uk **w** upbeat.co.uk MD: Liz Biddle.

Version 15 Holywell Row, London EC2A 4JB **t** 020 7684 5470 **f** 020 7684 5472 **e** info@versioncreative.com **w** versioncreative.com Dirs: Anthony Oram, Mo Chicharro.

Vinyl Tap 1 Minerva Works, Crossley Lane, Kirkheaton, Huddersfiled, West Yorkshire HD5 0QP **t** 01484 421446 **f** 01484 531019 **e** sales@vinyltap.demon.co.uk **w** vinyltap.co.uk Dir: Tony Boothroyd.

Virgin Retail School House, 50 Brook Green, Hammersmith, London W6 7RR **t** 020 8752 9000 **f** 020 8752 9001 **w** virginmega.co.uk

Vital Digital 338a Ladbroke Grove, London W10 5AH **t** 020 8324 2400 **f** 020 8324 0001 **e** firstname.lastname@vitaluk.com **w** vitaluk.com; Contact: Adrian Pope

Vitaminic 20 Orange St, London WC2H 7NN **t** 020 7766 4000 **f** 020 7766 4001 **e** info@vitaminic.co.uk **w** vitaminic.co.uk UK MD: Chris Cass.

Vivante Music Ltd Unit 6, Fontigarry Business Park, Reigate Road, Sidlow, Surrey RG2 8QH **t** 01293 822816 **f** 01293 821965 **e** sales@vivante.co.uk **w** vivante.co.uk Managing Director: Steven Carr.

WH Smith Online 1 Ashville Way, Cowley, Oxford OX4 6TS **t** 01865 771772 **f** 01865 711766 **e** support@whsmithonline.co.uk **w** whsmith.co.uk Mkting: Rowan Sadler.

YourRelease PO Box 1153, Winterbourne, Bristol BS36 1DL **t** 0870 909 0500 **f** 0870 909 0600 **e** info@yourrelease.com **w** YourRelease.com Operations Director: Pete Lockett.

Vinyl Tap 1 Minerva Works, Crossley Lane, Kirkheaton, Huddersfiled, West Yorkshire HD5 0QP **t** 01484 421446 **f** 01484 531019 **e** sales@vinyltap.demon.co.uk **w** vinyltap.co.uk Dir: Tony Boothroyd.

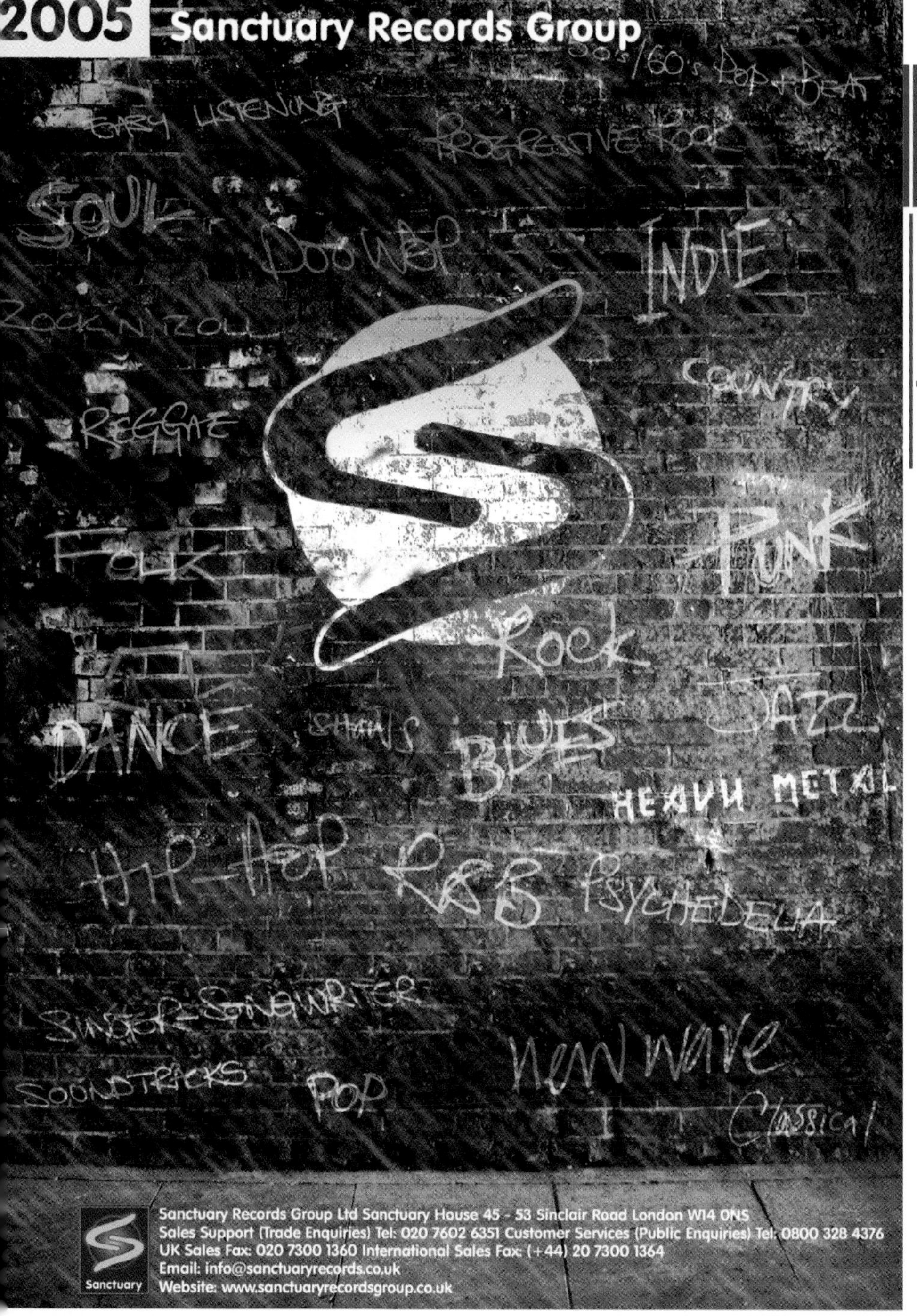
2005 Sanctuary Records Group
50's/60's Pop & Beat
Easy Listening
Progressive Rock
Soul
Doo Wop
Indie
Rock 'n' Roll
Country
Reggae
Folk
Punk
Rock
Dance
Blues
Jazz
Heavy Metal
Hip-Hop
R&B
Psychedelia
Singer-Songwriter
New Wave
Soundtracks
Pop
Classical
Sanctuary
Sanctuary Records Group Ltd Sanctuary House 45 - 53 Sinclair Road London W14 0NS
Sales Support (Trade Enquiries) Tel: 020 7602 6351 Customer Services (Public Enquiries) Tel: 0800 328 4376
UK Sales Fax: 020 7300 1360 International Sales Fax: (+44) 20 7300 1364
Email: info@sanctuaryrecords.co.uk
Website: www.sanctuaryrecordsgroup.co.uk

UK
TRADE &
INVESTMENT

Record Companies

International HQs

EMI GROUP PLC

27 Wrights Lane, London W8 5SW
t 020 7795 7000 **f** 020 7795 7001
e firstname.lastname@emimusic.com **w** emigroup.com
Chairman & CEO, EMI Music: Alain Levy. Vice Chairman, EMI Music: David Munns. General Counsel, EMI Music & EMI Group plc: Charles Ashcroft. CFO, EMI Music: Stuart Ells. Chairman & CEO, EMI Music Continental Europe: Jean-Francois Cecillon. President Classics & Jazz, EMI Music: Richard Lyttelton. SVP Global Marketing, Capitol Music: Mark Collen. SVP Global Marketing, Virgin Music: Matthieu Lauriot-Prevost.

SONY BMG INTERNATIONAL

Bedford House, 67-69 Fulham High Street, London SW6 3JW **t** 020 7384 7500.
Also at 10 Great Marlborough Street, London W1F 7LP **t** 020 7911 8200. Head of Australia, New Zealand, Canada, South Africa and UK: Tim Bowen.
Details of the new company were being confirmed at the time of going to press. For the latest information visit musicweek.com

UNIVERSAL MUSIC INTERNATIONAL

UNIVERSAL MUSIC INTERNATIONAL

8 St James's Square, London SW1Y 4JU
t 020 7747 4000 **f** 020 7747 4499
e firstname.lastname@umusic.com
w umusic.com Chairman and CEO: Jorgen Larsen. Executive VP & CFO: Boyd Muir. Executive VP, Marketing and A&R: Max Hole. General Counsel: Richard Constant. Senior VP, Commercial Affairs & Strategic Marketing: Bert Cloeckaert. Senior VP, Human Resources: Paul Howe. President, Universal Classics & Jazz: Christopher Roberts. VP, Communications: Adam White.

WARNER MUSIC INTERNATIONAL

WARNER MUSIC INTERNATIONAL

Warner Music International 28 Kensington Church St, London, W8 4EP, **t** 020 7368 2500, **f** 020 7368 2734 **e** firstname.lastname@warnermusic.com **w** wmg.com. Chairman/CEO: Paul-René Albertini. Executive VP: Gero Caccia. Executive VP Marketing: John Reid. SVP/CFO: Brian Porritt. SVP Business Affairs: John Watson. SVP Law & Corporate Affairs: Anne Mansbridge. VP Human Resources: Charlie Wolcott. SVP Business Development & Strategic Partnerships: Jay Durgan. Director Corporate Communications: Gia Rokeach. VP A&R: Ric Salmon.

Record Companies

020 Records (see Above The Sky Records / Lunastate Ltd)

1-OFF Recordings PO Box 31456, London W4 5YJ **t** 020 7384 6449 f 020 7384 6448 **e** info@1-off.co.uk **w** 1-off.co.uk MD: David Thomas. Dist: Various

10 Kilo (see Tip World)

11C RECORDINGS LTD

25 Heathmans Road, London SW6 4TJ
t 020 7371 5756 **f** 020 7371 7731 **e** office@pureuk.com **w** pureuk.com/11c. CEO: Evros Stakis. A&R: Brad Carter. Label Manager: Stewart Rowell. Dist: Various

13 Amp Recordings Ltd. 3rd Floor, 29-31 Cowper St, London EC2A 4AT **t** 020 7608 4592 **f** 020 7608 4599 **e** dean@13amp.tv **w** 13amp.tv Dirs: Dean O'Connor, John Best. Dist: Universal

14TH FLOOR RECORDS

14TH FLOOR RECORDS

The Warner Building, 28A Kensington Church St, London W8 4EP **t** 020 7368 2500 **f** 020 7368 2788 **e** firstname.lastname@warnermusic.com MD: Christian Tattersfield. GM: Peter Hall. Product Mgr: Elkie Brooks. A&R: Alex Gilbert. Asst: Chloe Stewart-Smith. Bus Affs: Rachel Evers (based at Atlantic Records UK).

21st Century Generation (see Plaza Records)

21st Century Soul 28 Tooting High Street, London SW17 0RG **t** 020 8333 5400 **f** 020 8333 5401 **e** info@21stCenturySoul.com **w** 21stCenturySoul.com MD: Tom Hayes.

2B3 Records 27 Solon Rd, London SW2 5UU **t** 020 7733 5400 or 020 7274 0782 **f** 020 7733 4449 **e** paulette@westbury.connectfree.co.uk **w** 2b3-productions.com Proprietor: Neville Thomas.

2NV Recordings 1 Canada Sq, 29th Floor Canary Wharf Tower, London E14 5DY **t** 0870 444 2506 **f** 0700 785 845 **e** info@2nvrecordings.com **w** 2nvrecordings.com Joint MDs: Chris Nathaniel, Paul Boadi. Head Of A&R: Amanda Morgan. A&R: Junior Barret. Label Co-Ordinator: Trevor Noel. Marketing Mgr: Marcus Woodland. Head Of Int'l: Mark Fokker. Dist: Pinnacle

3 Beat Breaks (see 3 Beat Music)

3 Beat Label Management 5 Slater St, Liverpool L1 4BW **t** 0151 709 2323 **f** 0151 709 3707 **e** 3blm@3beat.co.uk w 3beat.co.uk MD: Andy Jarrod. Dist: Amato

3 Beat Music 5 Slater St, Liverpool, Merseyside L1 4BW **t** 0151 709 3355 **f** 0151 709 3707 **e** mike@3beat.co.uk **w** 3beat.co.uk Label Mgr: Mike Miller. MD: Jon Barlow. General: Rob Jay. Accounts: Pezz. Shop Sales: Les. A&R: Michelle. Lbl Management: Andy Jarrod. Dist: Amato

33 Jazz Records The Hat Factory, 65-67 Bute St, Luton LU1 2EY **t** 01582 419584 **f** 01582 459401 **e** 33jazz@compuserve.com **w** 33jazz.com Director: Paul Jolly. Dist: Cadillac/Newnote

3kHz 54 Pentney Road, London SW12 0NY **t** 020 8772 0108 **f** 020 8675 1636 **e** info@3khz.com **w** 3khz.com MD: Mike Hedges.

>4 Music Morethan4 Limited, 75c Perham Road, London W14 9SP **t** 020 7610 0963 **e** info@morethan4.com **w** morethan4.com MD: Anthony Hamer-Hodges.

4AD 17-19 Alma Road, London SW18 1AA **t** 020 8870 9724 **f** 020 8874 6600 **e** fourad@almaroad.co.uk **w** 4ad.com MD: Chris Sharp. A&R: Ed Horrox. Label Assistant: Debbie Mortimer. Dist: Vital

4Real Records Myrtle Cottage, Rye Road, Hawkhurst, Kent TN18 5DW **t** 01580 754 771 **f** 01580 754 771 **e** scully4real@yahoo.co.uk **w** 4realrecords.com MD: Terry Scully. Dist: Hot Records

5.15 Records Suite 25, 9-12 Middle St, Brighton, East Sussex BN1 1AL **t** 01273 236969 **f** 01273 386291 **e** info@fivefifteenrecords.co.uk **w** fivefifteenrecords.co.uk Dirs: John Reid, Phil Barton. Dist: Sony

500 Rekords PO Box 9499, London E5 0UG **t** 020 8806 9500 or 07966 194346 **f** 020 8806 9500 **e** paul@500rekords.freeserve.co.uk MD: Paul C. Dist: Various

7Ts (see Cherry Red Records)

679 RECORDINGS

679®

Second Floor, 172a Arlington Road, London NW1 7HL **t** 020 7284 5780 **f** 020 7284 5795 **e** firstname.lastname@679recordings.com **w** 679recordings.com MD: Nick Worthington. Label Manager: Simon Rose. A&R: Dan Stacey. Label Co-ordinator: Katie Holland.

The A Label (see Numinous Music Group)

A&M (see Polydor Records)

Abaco Records 212 Piccadilly, London W1J 9HG **t** 020 7917 2854 **f** 020 7439 0262 **e** info@abaco-music.com **w** abaco-music.com A&R Manager: Vera Klefisch. Dist: Brothers/Universal

Abbey Records (SCS Music Ltd) PO Box 197, Beckley, Oxford OX3 9YJ **t** 01865 358282 **f** 0870 056 8880 **e** info@scsmusic.co.uk MD: Steve C Smith.

ABM (see Pickwick Group Ltd)

Above The Sky Records / Lunastate Ltd Studio 105, 24-28 Hatton Wall, Clerkenwell, London EC1N 8JH **t** 020 7404 1005 **e** info@abovethesky.com **w** abovethesky.com Dir: A J Burt. Dist: Alpha Magic

Absolute Records Craig Gowan, Carrbridge, Inverness-shire PH23 3AX **t** 01479 841771 **e** absolutemuse@hotmail.com **w** absoluterecords.co.uk MD: Sue Moss. Dist: Backs

Absolution Records The Old Lamp Works, Rodney Place, Merton, London SW19 2LQ **t** 020 8540 4242 **f** 020 8540 6056 **e** info@absolutemarketing.co.uk **w** absolutemarketing.co.uk MD: Simon Wills. MD: Henry Semmence. Dist: Absolute

Abstract Sounds 10 Tiverton Road, London NW10 3HL **t** 020 7286 1106 **f** 020 7289 8679 **e** abstractsounds@btclick.com **w** abstractsounds.co.uk; candlelightrecords.co.uk MD: Edward Christie. Dist: Plastic Head

Academy Records 211 Piccadilly, London W1J 9HF **t** 020 7917 2948 **e** mw@sublime-music.co.uk **w** sublime-music.co.uk Mgr: Nick Grant. Dist: Amato

Accidental Records Suite 6, 34-44 Tunstall Rd, London SW9 8DA **t** 020 7737 6464 **e** info@accidentalrecords.com **w** magicandaccident.com Label Mgr: Raphael Rundell.

Ace Eyed Records (see Blue Melon Records Ltd)

ACE RECORDS

42-50 Steele Road, London NW10 7AS t 020 8453 1311 **f** 020 8961 8725 **e** sales@acerecords.co.uk **w** acerecords.co.uk Sales & Marketing Dir: Phil Stoker.

Acid Jazz Records 146 Bethnal Green Road, London E2 6DG t 020 7613 1100 **e** info@acidjazz.co.uk **w** acidjazz.co.uk Label Manager: Danny Corr. Gen Mgr: Mark Blanch. Lbl Mgr: Danny Corr. A&R: Tristan Longworth. Dist: Recognition/Universal

ACL Records PO Box 31, Potters Bar, Hertfordshire EN6 1XR **t** 01707 644706 **f** 01707 644706 **e** WMD644706@aol.com Contact: David Thomas Dist: WMD

Acorn Records 1 Tylney View, London Rd, Hook, Hants RG27 9LJ **t** 078083 77350 **e** acornrecords@hotmail.com MD: Mark Olrog.

Acoustica Records 24 Derby St, Edgeley, Stockport, Cheshire SK3 9HF **t** 0161 476 1172 or 07950 119 151 **e** andylacallen@yahoo.co.uk **w** acoustica.tv A&R Director: Andy Callen.

Acoustics Records PO Box 350, Reading, Berkshire RG6 7DQ **t** 0118 926 8615 f 0118 935 3216 **e** mail@AcousticsRecords.co.uk **w** AcousticsRecords.co.uk MD: HA Jones. Dist: Koch

Acrobat Music & Media Limited Suite 315, MWB Business Exchange, 2 Gayton Rd, Harrow, Middx HA1 2XU **t** 020 8901 4928 **f** 020 8901 4001 **e** enquiries@acrobatmusic.net **w** acrobatmusic.net MD: John Cooper. Dist: Self distributed

Action Records 47 Church St, Preston, Lancs PR1 3DH **t** 01772 884772 or 01772 258809 **f** 01772 252255 **e** sales@action-records.co.uk **w** action-records.co.uk Mgr: Gordon Gibson.

Activa (see 4Real Records)

Activation (see ATCR: Trance Communication)

AD Music 5 Albion Rd, Bungay, Suffolk NR35 1LQ **t** 01986 894712 **f** 01986 894712 **e** admin@admusiconline.com **w** admusiconline.com Label Owner: Elaine Wright. Dist: SR Gold & Sons

Adasam Limited PO Box 8, Corby, Northants NN17 2XZ **t** 01536 202295 **f** 01536 266246 **e** adasam@adasam.co.uk **w** adasam.co.uk Label Mgr: Steve Kalidoski. Dist: Cargo

Additive EMI House, 43 Brook Green, London W6 7EF **t** 020 7605 5000 **f** 020 7605 5050 **e** firstname.lastname@emimusic.com **w** additiverecords.co.uk Director: Jason Ellis. A&R Manager: Ben Cherrill. Label Co-ordinator: Nathan Taylor.

Adelphoi 26 Litchfield St, Covent Garden, London WC2H 9TZ **t** 020 7240 7250 **f** 020 7240 7260 **e** kit@adelphoi.com **w** adelphoi.com Label Manager: Kit Wood. Dist: Ideal

Adept (see Avex Inc)

Adventure Records PO Box 261, Wallingford, Oxon OX10 0XY **t** 01491 832 183 **e** info@adventuresin-music.com **w** adventure-records.com Label Manager: Katie Conroy.

Afro Art Recordings 109 Dukes Avenue, Muswell Hill, London N10 2QD **t** 020 8374 4412 **f** 020 8374 4410 **e** simonebeedle@afroartrecords.com **w** afroartrecords.com Director: Simone Beedle.

Aftermath (see Hi-Note Music)

Ainm 5-6 Lombard Street East, Dublin 2, Ireland **t** +353 1 677 8701 **f** +363 1 677 8701 **e** fstubbs@ainm-music.com **w** ainm-music.com CEO: Frank Stubbs. Dist: IMD

Airplay Records The Sound Foundation, PO Box 4900, Earley, Berks RG10 0GA **t** 0118 934 9600 or 07973 559 203 **e** hadyn@soundfoundation.co.uk **w** soundfoundation.co.uk Label Mgr: Hadyn Wood.

AKT/Seventh (see Harmonia Mundi (UK) Ltd)

Alienor (see Harmonia Mundi (UK) Ltd)

All Action Figure Records Unit 9, Darvells Works, Common Rd, Chorleywood, Herts WD3 5LP **t** 01923 286010 f 01923 286070 **e** info@allactionfigure.co.uk **w** bigsur.co.uk MD: Steve Lowes.

All Around The World 9-13 Penny Street, Blackburn, Lancashire BB1 6HJ **t** 01254 264120 **f** 01254 693768 **e** info@aatw.com **w** aatw.com GM: Matt Cadman. MD: Cris Nuttall. Dist: Universal

All Good Vinyl (see Copasetik Recordings Ltd)

Almighty Records PO Box 12173, London N19 4SQ **t** 020 7281 3212 **f** 020 7281 8002 **e** info@almightyrecords.com **w** almightyrecords.com Label Manager: Alison Travis. Dist: BMG

Altarus Inc (UK Office) Easton Dene, Bailbrook Lane, Bath BA1 7AA **t** 01225 852323 f 01225 852523 **e** 100775.2716@compuserve.com **w** music.mcgill.ca/~schulman/sorabji.html UK Office Manager: Alistair Hinton. Dist: Kingdom

Amalie (see Loose Tie Records)

Amazing Feet (see Rotator Records)

Amazon Records Ltd Suite 3D, West Point, 36-37 Warple Way, London W3 0RG **t** 020 7727 1749 **e** face@ndirect.co.uk **w** amazonrecords.co.uk MD: Frank Sansom.

Amber PO Box 1, Chipping Ongar, Essex CM5 9HZ **t** 01277 362916 or 01277 365046 **e** recordcompany@amberartists.com **w** amberartists.com MD: Paul Tage. Dist: Vital

American Activities 29 St Michaels Rd, Leeds, West Yorks LS6 3BG **t** 0113 274 2106 f 0113 278 6291 **e** dave@bluescat.com **w** bluescat.com MD: Dave Foster. Dist: self

Amethyst (see Rainbow Quartz Records)

Amphion (see Priory Records)

Anagram (see Cherry Red Records)

Analogue Baroque (see Cherry Red Records)

Anew Music (see Crashed Music)

Angel Air Records Unicorn House, Station Road West, Stowmarket, Suffolk IP14 1ES **t** 01449 770139 **f** 01449 770133 **e** sales@angelair.co.uk **w** angelair.co.uk MD: Peter Purnell. Dist: Pinnacle

Ankst Musik Records The Old Police Station, The Square, Pentraeth, Anglesey LL75 8AZ **t** 01248 450 155 **f** 01248 450 155 **e** emyr@ankst.co.uk **w** ankst.co.uk MD: Emyr Glyn Williams. Dist: Shellshock

Anno Domini (see Talking Elephant)

Another Fine Mess (see Whoa Music)

Antara (see Line-Up PMC)

Antilles (see Island Records Group)

Apartment 22 19 Tewkesbury Road, Bristol BS2 9UL **t** 0117 955 6615 **f** 0117 955 6616 **e** caretaker@apartment22.com MD: Andy Morgan. Dist: Kudos/Pinnacle/Discovery

Ape City (see Primaudial Recordings)

APL Oddfellows Hall, London Road, Chipping Norton, Oxfordshire OX7 5AR **t** 01608 641592 **f** 01608 641969 **e** help@aitkenproductions.co.uk

Apocalypse (see Snapper Music)

Apollo Sound 32 Ellerdale Road, London NW3 6BB **t** 020 7435 5255 **f** 020 7431 0621 **e** info@apollosound.com **w** apollosound.com MD: Toby Herschmann. Dist: Kudos

Appaloosa (see Junior Boy's Own)

APR (see Harmonia Mundi (UK) Ltd)

Apropos (see Siren Music Ltd)

Arbiter (see Harmonia Mundi (UK) Ltd)

ARC Music Productions International PO Box 111, East Grinstead, West Sussex RH19 4LZ **t** 01342 328567 **f** 01342 315958 **e** info@arcmusic.co.uk **w** arcmusic.co.uk Sales & Mktg Dir: Robert Graves.

Arcana Records 198 Calder Street, Glasgow G42 7PE **t** 0141 433 9374 **e** arcanarecords@hotmail.com **w** geocities.com/arcanarecords MD: Jeff Jeffrey.

Are We Mad? (see Ariwa Sounds Ltd)

Arista (see BMG UK & Ireland Ltd)

Ariwa Sounds Ltd 34 Whitehorse Lane, London SE25 6RE **t** 020 8653 7744 **f** 020 8771 1911 **e** ariwastudios@aol.com **w** ariwa.com Label Manager: Holly Fraser. Dist: SRD

ARK 21 1 Water Lane, London NW1 8NZ **t** 020 7267 1101 **f** 020 7267 7466 **e** info@ark21.com **w** ark21.com Label Mgr: Roisin Murphy. Dist: Universal

Arpeggio Music Bell Farm House, Eton Wick, Windsor, Berkshire SL4 6LH **t** 01753 864910 or 01753 884810 MD: Beverley Campion. Dist: Universal

Arriba Records 156-158 Gray's Inn Road, London WC1X 8ED **t** 020 7713 0998 **f** 020 7713 1132 **e** info@arriba-records.com **w** arriba-records.com Dir: S-J Henry. A&R: Baby Doc & S-J. Dist: Pinnacle

Arrivederci Baby! (see Cherry Red Records)

Artfield 5 Grosvenor Sq, London W1K 4AF **t** 020 7499 9941 **f** 020 7499 9010 **e** info@artfieldmusic.com **w** artfieldmusic.com MD: BB Cooper.

Artful Records Ltd Unit 7 Grand Union Centre, West Row, Ladbroke Grove, London W10 5AS **t** 020 8968 1545 **f** 020 8964 1181 **e** info@artfulrecords.co.uk **w** artfulrecords.co.uk Contact: Danielle Chambers MD: John Lennard. Label Mgr: Steve Malins. Head of A&R & International: Ian Abraham. Dist: Fullfill/Universal

Artisan (see Snapper Music)

Artist Record Company (see ARC - Artist Record Company)

ARC - Artist Record Company 1 North Worple Way, Mortlake, London SW14 8QG **t** 020 8876 2533 **f** 020 8878 4229 **e** artistrec@aol.com **w** arcarc.co.uk Dir of Promotions: Geraldine Perry. MD: Brian Wade. Dist: Universal

Arvee (see Everest Copyrights)

Ash International (see Touch)

Ash Records Hillside Farm, Hassocky Lane, Temple Normanton, Chesterfield, Derbyshire S42 5DH **t** 01246 231762 **e** ash_music36@hotmail.com Head of A&R: Paul Townsend.

Associate (see Silverword Music Group)

Astounding Sounds, Amazing Music (see Voiceprint)

Astralwerks Kensal House, 553-579 Harrow Road, London W10 4RH **t** 020 8964 6220 **f** 020 8964 6221 **e** (through website) **w** astralwerks.com

ASV (see Sanctuary Classics)

Asylum Music PO Box 121, Hove, East Sussex BN3 4YY **t** 01273 774468 **f** 08709 223099 **e** info@AsylumGroup.com **w** AsylumGroup.com Contact: Bob James, Steve Gilmour, Scott Chester.

ATCR: Trance Communication PO Box 272, Headington, Oxford OX3 8PL **t** 01865 764568 **f** 01865 744056 **e** info@atcr.co.uk **w** atcr.org.uk Mgr: Tim Stark. Dist: Amato

Athene (see Priory Records)

ATLANTIC RECORDS UK

Electric Lighting Station, 46 Kensington Court, London W8 5DA **t** 020 7938 5500 **f** 020 7368 4900 **e** firstname.lastname@atlanticrecords.co.uk **w** atlanticrecords.co.uk MD: Max Lousada. Director of Bus Affs: Rachel Evers. Dir Proms: Damian Christian. Marketing Dir: Richard Hinkley. Dir of Press: Andy Hart. A&R Managers: Thomas Haimovici, Hugo Bedford & Joel De'ath. Creative Dir: Richard Skinner. Dist: TEN

ATMA Classique (see Harmonia Mundi (UK) Ltd)

Atomic 133 Longacre, Covent Garden, London WC2E 9DT **t** 020 7379 3010 **f** 020 7379 5583 **e** mn@atomic-london.com **w** atomic.co.uk Director: Mick Newton.

Attaboy Records Unit 4 The Pavilions, 2 East Road, S. Wimbledon, London SW19 1UW **t** 020 8545 8580 **f** 020 8545 8581 **e** mikel@simplyvinyl.com **w** simplyvinyl.com Label Mgr: Mike Loveday. Dist: THE

Attitude The Music Village, 11B Osiers Road, London SW18 1NL **t** 020 8870 0011 **f** 020 8870 2101 **e** info@attituderecords.co.uk **w** attituderecords.co.uk Director: Ian Titchner. Dist: Universal

A2 Records Tudor House, Pinstone Way, Gerrards Cross, Buckinghamshire SL9 7BJ **t** 01494 862770 **f** 01494 862770 **e** richard@a2records.com **w** a2records.com MD: Rupert Withers. Dist: Recognition/Universal

Audio Therapy 52a High Pavement, The Lace Market, Nottingham NG1 1HW **t** 0115 955 5668 **f** 0115 958 7197 **e** info@therapymusic.co.uk Dir: Sara Rowley.

Audiorec Ltd 21B Silicon Business Centre, 26-28 Wadsworth Road, Greenford, Middlesex UB6 7JZ **t** 020 8810 7779 **f** 020 8810 7773 **e** info@audiorec.co.uk **w** audiorec.co.uk Dir: Jyotindra Patel.

Audiorec Premium (see Audiorec Ltd)

Aura Records (see Mo's Music Machine)

Autograph Records 19 Longmeadow Grove, St Lawrence Court, Manchester M34 2DA **t** 0161 336 9300 **f** 0161 221 3168 **e** autograph@ntlworld.com **w** autographmusicandmedia.com Owner: Derek Brandwood.

Automatic Records Unit 5 Waldo Works, Waldo Road, London NW10 6AW **t** 020 8964 8890 **f** 020 8960 5741 **e** mail@automaticrecords.co.uk **w** automaticrecords.co.uk Label Mgr/Head of A&R: Glenn Mack. Dist: Amato

Automatic Records. The Old Vicarage, Pickering, North Yorkshire YO18 7AW **t** 01751 475502 **f** 01751 475502 **e** organised@lineone.net MD: Francis Ward.

Auvidis Astree (see Harmonia Mundi (UK) Ltd)

Auvidis Montaigne (see Harmonia Mundi (UK) Ltd)

Auvidis Taize (see Harmonia Mundi (UK) Ltd)

Auvidis Travelling (see Harmonia Mundi (UK) Ltd)

Auvidis Valois (see Harmonia Mundi (UK) Ltd)

Aux Delux (see Supreme Music)

Avalanche Records 17 West Nicolson Street, Edinburgh, Lothian EH8 9DA **t** 0131 668 2374 **f** 0131 668 3234 **e** avalanche.records@virgin.net **w** avalancherecords.co.uk MD: Kevin Buckle. Dist: Southern

Avalon Records PO Box 929, Ferndown, Dorset BH22 9YF **t** 01202 896397 **f** 01202 896397 **e** info@galahadonline.com **w** galahadonline.com Mgr: Stuart Nicholson. Dist: Voiceprint

Avant/DIW (see Harmonia Mundi (UK) Ltd)

Avex Inc The Heals Building, Unit A3, 3rd Floor, 22-24 Torrington Place, London WC1E 7HJ **t** 020 7323 6610 **f** 020 7323 6413 **e** song@avex-inc.com **w** avex.co.jp General Mgr: S.C.Song. Dist: Pinnacle

Avid Entertainment 10 Metro Centre, Dwight Road, Tolpits Lane, Watford, Herts WD18 9UF **t** 01923 281281 **f** 01923 281200 **e** info@avidgroup.co.uk **w** avidgroup.co.uk MD: Richard Lim. Mkting Mgr: Colin Davey.

Avie Records 103 Churston Drive, Morden, Surrey SM4 4JE **t** 020 8540 7357 **f** 020 8542 4854 **e** musicco@musicco.f9.co.uk MD: Melanne Mueller.

Azuli Records 25 D'Arblay Street, London W1V 8ES **t** 020 7287 1932 **f** 020 7439 2490 **e** blair@azuli.com **w** azuli.com Press & Promotions: Blair Cartwright. MD/Head of A&R: David Picconi. Dist: Vital

B-Unique Records The Matrix Studio Complex, 91 Peterborough Rd, London SW6 3BU **t** 020 7384 6464 **f** 020 7384 6466 **e** info@b-uniquerecords.com **w** b-uniquerecords.com MDs: Mark Lewis & Martin Toher. A&R Manager: Paul Harris. Product Manager: Carla Sever. Dist: TEN

Back Alley Records (see Nikt Records)

Back Door (see More Protein Ltd)

Back 2 Basics (see Back2Basics Recordings Ltd)

Back Yard Recordings 106 Gt Portland St, London W1W 6PF **t** 020 7580 0999 **f** 020 7580 8882 **e** info@black-gold-recordings.com Director: Gil Goldberg.

Backbone (see Flair Records)

Background Records (see Hi-Note Music)

Backs Recording Company St Mary's Works, St Mary's Plain, Norwich, Norfolk NR3 3AF **t** 01603 624290 or 01603 626221 **f** 01603 619999 **e** info@backs records.co.uk MD: Jonathan Appel. Dist: Backs/Shellshock

Back2Basics Recordings Ltd PO Box 41, Tipton, West Midlands DY4 7YT **t** 0121 520 1150 **f** 0121 520 1150 **e** info@back2basicsrecords.co.uk **w** back2basicsrecords.co.uk Directors: Jason Ball & Anamaria Gibbons. Dist: SRD

Bad Magic (see Wall Of Sound Recordings Ltd)

BadMeaninGood (see Whoa Music)

Baktabak Records Network House, 29-39 Stirling Rd, London W3 8DJ **t** 020 8993 5966 **f** 020 8992 0340 **e** chris@arab.co.uk **w** baktabak.com Dir: Chris Leaning.

Bamaco Vine Cottage, 255 Lower Road, Great Bookham, Leatherhead, Surrey KT23 4DX **t** 01372 450 752 **e** barrymurrayents@aol.com Contact: Barry Murray

Banana Recordings Leroy House, Unit 2L, 436 Essex Rd, London N1 3QP **t** 020 7354 7353 **f** 020 7288 2958 **e** infobanana@btconnect.com **w** bananarecordings.co.uk Dir: Richard Hermitage. Dist: Pinnacle

Bandleader Recordings Unit 3, Faraday Way, St. Mary Cray, Kent BR5 3QW **t** 01689 879090 **f** 01689 879091 **e** janice@modernpublicity.co.uk GM: Janice Whybrow. Dist: Pinnacle

Bar De Lune (see Beechwood Music Ltd)

Barely Breaking Even Records PO Box 25896, London N5 1WE **t** 020 7607 0597 **f** 020 7607 4696 **e** leeb@bbemusic.demon.co.uk **w** bbemusic.com Co Sec: Lee Bright. Dist: Beechwood Music/Flute Worldwide

Basilica Records PO Box 16671, London W8 6ZYe incoming@freakapuss.co.uk **w** freakapuss.co.uk PR Manager: Harlean Carpenter.

BBC Audio Books St James House, Lower Bristol Rd, Bath BA2 3SB **t** 01225 335 336 **f** 01225 448 005 **e** info@audiobookcollection.com **w** audiobookcollection.com MD: Paul Dempsey.

BBC Music Room A2036, Woodlands, 80 Wood Lane, London W12 0TT **t** 020 8433 1711 **f** 020 8433 1743 **e** jim.reid.01@bbc.co.uk Label Manager: Jim Reid.

Bear Family (see Rollercoaster Records)

Bearcat Records PO Box 94, Derby, Derbyshire DE22 1XA **t** 01332 332336 or 07702 564804 **f** 01332 332336 **e** chrishall@swampmusic.co.uk **w** swampmusic.co.uk Director: Chris Hall. Dist: Proper

Beat Goes On Records (BGO) 7 St. Andrews St North, Bury St Edmunds, Suffolk IP33 1TZ **t** 01284 724406 **f** 01284 762245 **e** andy@bgo-records.com **w** bgo-records.com MD: Andy Gray. Dist: Universal

Beatz (see Valve)

Beautiful Jo Records PO Box 1039, Oxford OX1 4UA **t** 01865 249 194 **f** 01865 792 765 **e** info@bejo.co.uk **w** bejo.co.uk Mgr: Tim Healey. Dist: Proper

Beautiful Records (see Media Records Ltd)

Bedrock Records Reverb House, Bennett St, London W4 2AH **t** 020 8742 7670 **f** 020 8994 8617 **e** info@bedrock.uk.net **w** bedrock.org.uk Label Manager: Nick Bates.

BEF c/o Mansfield & Co, 55 Kentish Town Rd, London NW1 8NX **t** 020 8800 1011 **f** 020 7681 3135 **e** beforeafter@heaven17.com **w** heaven17.com MD: Nick Ashton-Hart. Dist: Absolute

Beggars Banquet Records 17-19 Alma Road, London SW18 1AA **t** 020 8870 9912 **f** 020 8871 1766 **e** beggars@almaroad.co.uk **w** beggars.com Contact: Ann Wilson Dist: Vital

The Beggars Group 17-19 Alma Rd, London SW18 1AA **t** 020 8870 9912 **f** 020 8871 1766 **e** postmaster@beggars.com **w** beggars.com Chairman: Martin Mills. MD UK: John Holborow. MD International: Paul Redding. Financial Director: Nigel Bolt. Head of Promotions: Craig McNeil. Head of UK Sales & Marketing: Stewart Green. Lawyer: Rupert Skellett. Head of Group Licensing: Kathy Doherty. Head of New Media: Simon Wheeler.

Record Companies

Bell Records (see BMG UK & Ireland Ltd)

Bella Union 14 Church St, Twickenham, Middx TW1 3NJ **t** 020 8744 2777 **f** 020 8891 1895 **e** info@bellaunion.com **w** bellaunion.com Label Mgr: Fiona Glyn-Jones. Dist: Pinnacle

Berlin Records Caxton House, Caxton Ave, Blackpool, Lancashire FY2 9AP **t** 01253 591169 **f** 01253 508670 **e** berlin.studios@virgin.net **w** berlinstudios.co.uk MD: Ron Sharples.

Bespoke (see Sound Entertainment Ltd)

Better The Devil Records PO Box 45908, Kendal Avenue, London W3 0XD **t** 020 8896 8222 **f** 020 8896 8201 **e** info@btdrecords.com **w** betterthedevilrecords.com MD: Graham Stokes.

Beulah (see Priory Records)

Beyer (see Priory Records)

Beyond Beta (see Sonic360)

BGP (see Ace Records)

Bianco Music and Entertainment 4th Floor, 1 Great Cumberland Place, London W1H 7AL **t** 020 7535 3350 **f** 020 7535 3383 **e** info@biancomusic.co.uk **w** biancomusic.co.uk MD: Maddy Crass.

Biff Bang Pow Records 12 Denyer Court, Fradley, Nr Lichfield, Staffs WS13 8TQ **t** 01543 444261 **f** 01543 444261 **e** info@biffbangpow.org.uk **w** biffbangpow.org.uk MD: Paul Hooper-Keeley. Dist: F Minor

Big Bear Records PO Box 944, Birmingham, West Midlands B16 8UT **t** 0121 454 7020 **f** 0121 454 9996 **e** bigbearmusic@compuserve.com **w** bigbearmusic.com MD: Jim Simpson.

Big Beat (see Ace Records)

Big Beat (EW) (see Atlantic Records UK)

Big Cat (UK) Records PO Box 34449, London W6 0RT **t** 020 7751 0199 **f** 020 7751 0199 **e** info@bigcatrecords.com MD: Abbo.

Big Chill PO Box 7378, London N4 3RH **t** 020 7688 8081 **f** 020 7688 8082 **e** info@bigchill.net **w** bigchill.net Dirs: Pete Lawrence & Katrina Larkin. Dist: SRD

Big City (see Candid Productions Ltd)

Big Dada PO Box 4296, London SE11 4WW **t** 020 7820 3555 **f** 020 7820 3434 **e** info@bigdada.com **w** bigdada.com Lbl Mgr: Will Ashon. Dist: Vital

Big Deal Records 83 Dartmouth Park Rd, London NW5 1SL **t** 020 7681 0585 **f** 020 7681 0585 **e** Lew@Bigdealrecords.net MD: Lew Wernick.

Big Help Music Deppers Bridge Farm, Southam, Warks. CV47 2SZ **t** 01926 614640 or 07782 172 101 **e** dutch@bighelpmusic.com **w** bighelpmusic.com MD: Dutch Van Spall. Dist: Various

Big Moon Records PO Box 347, Weybridge, Surrey KT13 9WZ **t** 01932 590169 **f** 01932 889802 **e** info@tzuke.com **w** tzuke.com Label Head: Jamie Muggleton.

Big One (see Music Like Dirt)

Binliner (see Detour Records Ltd)

Biondi Records 33 Lamb Court, 69 Narrow St, London E14 8EJ **t** 020 7538 5749 **e** info@biondi.co.uk **w** biondi.co.uk Label Manager: Marc Andrewes.

Birdland (see Cargogold Productions)

Bitch Records (see Automatic Records)

Black (see Revolver Music Ltd)

Black Box Music (see Sanctuary Classics)

Black Burst Records (see Rough Trade Records)

Black Gold Recordings (see Back Yard Recordings)

Black Hole UK (see New State Entertainment)

Black Jesus (see Quiet Riot Records)

BLACKLIST ENTERTAINMENT

Fulham Palace, Bishops Avenue, London SW6 6EA **t** 020 7751 0175 **f** 020 7736 0606 **e** firstname@blacklistent.com Chairman: Clive Black. General Manager: Jayne Meegan. Dist: Vital

---

Black Magic Records 296 Earls Court Road, London SW5 9BA **t** 020 7565 0806 **f** 020 7565 0806 **e** blackmagicrecords@talk21.com **w** blackmagicrecords.com MD: Mataya Clifford. Dist: Jet Star

Black Mountain Recordings 1 Squire Court, The Marina, Swansea SA1 3XB **t** 01792 301500 **f** 01792 301500 **e** info@blackmountainmobile.co.uk **w** blackmountainmobile.co.uk MD: Michael Evans.

Black Records (see Bedrock Records)

Blackend (see Plastic Head Records Ltd)

Blackmoon Records (see BMR Entertainment Ltd)

Blakamix International Records Garvey House, 42 Margetts Rd, Bedford, Beds MK42 8DS **t** 01234 856164 or 01234 302115 **f** 01234 854344 **e** blakamix@aol.com **w** blakamix.co.uk MD: Dennis Bedeau.

Blaktrax Records (see Shaboom Records)

Blanco Y Negro 66 Golborne Rd, London W10 5PS **t** 020 8960 9888 **f** 020 8968 6715 **e** pru@roughtraderecords.com MD: Bob Harding.

Blast First (see Mute Records Ltd)

Blaster! 77 Nightingale Shott, Egham, Surrey TW20 9SU **t** 020 7272 6894 **f** 020 7687 0802 **e** martinw@netcomuk.co.uk MD: Martin Whitehead.

Bleach Records Eltime Studios, Hall Road, Maldon, Essex CM9 4NF **t** 01621 856 943 **f** 01621 855 335 **e** info@bleachrecords.co.uk Dirs: Mark Hurst, Paolo Morena. Dist: Vital

Blix Street (see Hot Records)

Blood and Fire Room 103, Ducie House, 37, Ducie Street, Manchester M1 2JW **t** 0161 228 3034 **f** 0161 228 3036 **e** info@bloodandfire.co.uk **w** bloodandfire.co.uk MD: Bob Harding. A&R Director: Steve Barrow. Asst to MD: Dom Sotgiu.

Blow Up Records Limited Unit 127, Stratford Workshops, Burford Rd, London E15 2SP **t** 020 8534 7700 **f** 020 8534 7722 **e** webmaster@blowup.co.uk **w** blowup.co.uk MD: Paul Tunkin. Dist: Vital

Blue Banana Records (see Blue Melon Records Ltd)

Blue Crystal Music Ltd Endeavour House, Cavendish Rd, Herne Bay, Kent CT6 5BE **t** 01227 749004 **f** 01227 749408 **e** info@reikimusic.co.uk **w** Bluecrystalmusic.com MD: Geoff Milner. Dist: Blue Crystal

Blue Juice Music Ltd Hobbs Barn, Wick End, Stagsden, Bedfordshire MK43 8TS **t** 01234 823452 **f** 01234 823452 **e** bluejuicemusic@aol.com MD: Rob Butterfield.

Blue Melon Records Ltd 240A High Road, Harrow Weald, Middx HA3 7BB **t** 020 8863 2520 **f** 020 8863 2520 **e** steve@bluemelon.co.uk MD: Steven Glen.

Blue Note (see EMI Music UK & Ireland)

Blue Note EMI House, 43 Brook Green, London W6 7EF **t** 020 7605 5000 **f** 020 7605 5050 **e** firstname.lastname@emimusic.com **w** emimusic.co.uk Dist: EMI

Blue Planet Records (see Blue Melon Records Ltd)

Blue Star (see East Central One Ltd)

Blue Thumb (see Universal Classics & Jazz (UK))

Blueprint (see Voiceprint)

Blueprint Recording Corporation PO Box 593, Woking, Surrey GU23 7YF **t** 01483 715336 **f** 01483 757490 **e** blueprint@lineone.net **w** blueprint-records.net MD: John Glover. A&R: Matt Glover. Admin: Julie Glover. Dist: Independent

Blues Matters Records PO Box 18, Bridgend CF33 6YW **t** 01656 743406 **e** blues.matters@ntlworld.com **w** bluesmatters.com MD: Alan Pearce.

Blunted Vinyl (see Island Records Group)

BMR Entertainment Ltd PO Box 14535, London N17 0WG **t** 020 8376 1650 **f** 020 8376 8622 **e** Pingramc2@aol.com A&R Mgr: Jef Q.

Bolshi Records Studio 11, 25 Denmark St, London WC2H 8NJ **t** 020 7240 2248 **f** 0870 420 4392 **e** sarah@bolshi.com **w** bolshi.com MD: Sarah Bolshi. Dist: SRD

Bonaire Recordings (see Blue Melon Records Ltd)

Booo! (see Direct Heat Records)

Border Community (see 3 Beat Label Management)

Border Community Recordings PO Box 38846, London W12 8YT **t** 020 8746 0407 **f** 020 8746 0407 **e** info@bordercommunity.com **w** bordercommunity.com A&R: James Holden.

Born to Dance Records PO Box 50, Brighton BN2 6YP **t** 01273 301555 **f** 01273 305266 **e** info@borntodance.com **w** borntodance.com Lbl Mgr: Natasha Brown. Dist: Pinnacle

Boss (see 3 Beat Music)

Boss Music 7 Jeffrey's Place, Camden, London NW1 9PP **t** 020 7284 2554 **f** 020 7284 2560 **e** info@bossmusic.net **w** bossmusic.net MD: Andy Ross. A&R: Adam Evans. Dist: Vital

Boss Records (see 3 Beat Label Management)

Boss Sounds (see Cherry Red Records)

Botchit & Scarper/eMotif Recordings 134-146 Curtain Road, London EC2A 3AR **t** 020 7729 8030 **f** 020 7729 8121 **e** info@botchit.com **w** botchit.com Dir: Martin Love. Dist: SRD

Boulevard (see Silverword Music Group)

Bowmans Capsule PO Box 30466, London NW6 1GJ **t** 020 7431 3129 **f** 020 7431 3129 **e** sugar@bowmanscapsule.co.uk **w** bowmanscapsule.co.uk Director: Richard Burdett. Dist: Universal

Breakbeat Kaos (see Kaos Recordings)

Breakin' Loose 32 Quadrant House, Burrell Street, London SE1 0UW **t** 020 7633 9576 or 07721 065 618 **e** sjbbreakinloose@aol.com MD: Steve Bingham.

Breathless Records Alexandra House, 6 Little Portland Street, London W1W 7JE **t** 020 7907 1733 **f** 020 7907 1734 **e** email@breathlessrecords.com **w** breathlessrecords.com Label Manager: Louis Mears. Dist: Amato/Pinnacle

Brewhouse Music Breeds Farm, 57 High Street, Wicken, Ely, Cambridgeshire CB7 5XR **t** 01353 720309 **f** 01353 723364 **e** info@brewhousemusic.co.uk **w** brewhousemusic.co.uk MD: Eric Cowell. Dist: Griffin & Co/ADA

Brickyard (see Loose Records)

Bright Star Recordings Suite 5, Emerson House, 14b Ballynahinch Road, Carryduff, Belfast BT8 8DN **t** 028 90 817111 **f** 028 90 817444 **e** brightstarrec@musicni.co.uk **w** brightstarrecordings.com MD: Johnny Davis. Label Manager: Darren Smyth. Dist: Vital

Brightside Bedford House, 69-79 Fulham High St, London SW6 3JW **t** 020 7384 7733 **f** 020 7384 7734 **e** firstname.lastname@bmg.com MD: Hugh Goldsmith. Dist: BMG

Bristol Archive (see Sugar Shack Records Ltd)

British Steel (see Cherry Red Records)

Broadley Records Broadley House, 48 Broadley Terrace, London NW1 6LG **t** 020 7258 0324 **f** 020 7724 2361 **e** admin@broadleystudios.com **w** broadleystudios.com MD: Ellis Elias.

Broken Star Recordings 10 St Marys Close, Gt Plumstead, Norwich NR13 5EY **t** 01603 712495 **f** 01603 712495 **e** recordings@brokenstar.co.uk **w** brokenstar.co.uk MD: Jon Luton.

Bronze Records Unit 1, 73 Maygrove Road, London NW6 2EG **t** 020 7209 4666 **f** 020 7209 2334 **e** info@bronzerecords.com **w** bronzerecords.com General Manager: Matthias Siefert. Dist: Absolute

Brothers Records Ltd The Music Village, 11B Osiers Road, London SW18 1NL **t** 020 8870 0011 **f** 020 8870 2101 **e** info@brothersrecords.com **w** brothersrecords.com Co-MDs: Ian Titchner & Nick Titchner.

BTM (see Gotham Records)

Bubble Gum (see Music Mercia)

Bubblin' (see Gut Recordings)

Bugged Out! Recordings 15 Holywell Row, London EC2A 4JB **t** 020 7684 5228 **f** 020 7684 5230 **e** paul@buggedout.net **w** buggedout.net Dirs: Paul Benney, John Burgess. Dist: Vital

Bulletproof (see Mohawk Records)

Burning Ice Records PO Box 48, Dorking, Surrey RH4 1YE **t** 01306 877692 **e** info@objayda.co.uk **w** objayda.co.uk Director: Tim Howe. Dist: Avid/BMG

Burning Shed c/o Windsor House, 74 Thorpe Rd, Norwich, Norfolk NR1 1QH **t** 01603 767726 **f** 01603 767746 **e** info@burningshed.com **w** burningshed.com Production: Pete Morgan. A&R: Tim Bowness.

Bushranger Records Station Lodge, 196 Rayleigh Road, Hutton, Brentwood, Essex CM13 1PN **t** 01277 222095 **e** bushrangermusic@aol.com Lbl Mgr: Kathy Lister. Dist: Nova/Pinnacle

Buttercuts Limited 5 Hasker Street, London SW3 2LE **t** 020 7225 2780 or 07957 420 492 **f** 020 7589 2278 **e** management@buttercuts.co.uk **w** Buttercuts.co.uk MD: Andrew Oury.

Butterfly Recordings (see Dragonfly Records)

Buzz Records 14 Corsiehill Road, Perth, Perthshire PH2 7BZ **t** 01738 638140 **f** 01738 638140 **e** records@thebuzzgroup.co.uk **w** thebuzzgroup.co.uk MD: Dave Arcari.

Buzz To It Records PO Box 33849, London N8 9XJ **t** 07092 047 780 **e** info@buzztoitrecords.co.uk MD: Michael Bukowski.

BXR UK (see Media Records Ltd)

Cacophonous (see Visible Noise)

Cadence Recordings (see Within Records)

Cafe de Soul 2nd Floor, 62 Belgrave Gate, Leicester LE1 3GQ **t** 0116 299 0700 **f** 0116 299 0077 **e** cafedesoul@hotmail.com **w** cafedesoul.co.uk Label Managers: Nigel Bird, Vijay Mistry. Dist: 2Funky

Cala Records 17 Shakespeare Gardens, London N2 9LJ **t** 020 8883 7306 **f** 020 8365 3388 **e** jeremy@calarecords.com **w** calarecords.com Sales & Marketing Manager: Jeremy Swerling.

Calig (see Priory Records)

Calliope (see Harmonia Mundi (UK) Ltd)

Cambridge Classics Audio House, Edison Road, St Ives, Cambridge, Cambridgeshire PE17 4LF **t** 01480 461880 **f** 01480 496100 **e** srt@btinternet.com Contact: Matthew Dilley

Camden (see BMG Commercial Division)

Camino Records Crown Studios, 16-18 Crown Rd, Twickenham, Middx TW1 3EE **t** 020 8891 4233 **f** 020 8891 2339 **e** mail@camino.co.uk **w** camino.co.uk Marketing Manager: John Wood.

Campion Records (see Disc Imports Ltd)

Candid Productions Ltd 16 Castelnau, London SW13 9RU **t** 020 8741 3608 **f** 020 8563 0013 **e** info@candidrecords.com **w** candidrecords.com MD: Alan Bates.

Candlelight Records (see Abstract Sounds)

Candy Records (see Sugar Records)

Cantankerous (see Quiet Riot Records)

Capitol (see EMI Music UK & Ireland)

Capriccio (see Delta Music plc)

Caprio (see Silverword Music Group)

Captured Music (see Above The Sky Records / Lunastate Ltd)

Cargo Records 17 Heathmans Road, London SW6 4TJ **t** 020 7731 5125 **f** 020 7731 3866 **e** phil@cargorecords.co.uk MD: Philip Hill. Dist: Cargo

Cargogold Productions 39 Clitterhouse Crescent, London NW2 1DB **t** 020 8458 1020 **f** 020 8458 1020 **e** mike@mikecarr.co.uk **w** mikecarr.co.uk MD: Mike Carr.

Caritas Records 28 Dalrymple Crescent, Edinburgh, Lothian EH9 2NX **t** 0131 667 3633 **f** 0131 667 3633 **e** caritas-records@caritas-music.co.uk **w** caritas-music.co.uk Professional Mgr: Katharine H Douglas.

Cartel Music 19c Lansdowne Road, Bournemouth, Dorset BH1 1RZ **t** 01202 296170 **f** 01202 294696 **e** info@cartelmusic.co.uk **w** cartelmusic.co.uk

Casa Nostra (see Wyze Productions)

Casa Trax (see Mo's Music Machine)

Castle Home Video (see Sanctuary Visual Entertainment)

Casual Records 65 Leonard St, London EC2A 4QS **t** 020 7613 7746 **f** 020 7613 7740 **e** info@casuallondon.com **w** casual-london.com Label Manager: Joel Davies. Dist: Vital

Catch Records (see One Step Music Ltd)

Catskills Records PO Box 3365, Brighton BN1 1WQ **t** 01273 626245 **f** 01273 626246 **e** info@catskillsrecords.com **w** catskillsrecords.com Directors: Khalid, Amr or Jonny. Dist: Vital

Catskills:Projects (see Catskills Records)

Cavalcade Records Ltd 18 Pindock Mews, London W9 2PY **t** 020 7289 7281 **f** 020 7289 2648 **e** songs@mindermusic.com **w** mindermusic.com MD: John Fogarty.

The CD Card Company 29-39 Stirling House, London W3 8DJ **t** 020 8993 5966 **f** 020 8992 0340 or 020 8992 0098 **e** cdcard@arab.co.uk **w** cdcard.com Sales Mgr: Greg Warrington. Dist: Arabesque Distribution

Cello Classics (see Naxos AudioBooks)

Celtic Collections Ltd 30-32 Sir John Rogersons Quay, Dublin 2, Ireland **t** +353 1 679 0667 **f** +353 1 679 0668 **e** info@celtic-collections.com **w** celtic-collections.com MD: Sharon Browne.

Celtic Heartbeat 30-32 Sir John Rogerson's Quay, Dublin 2, Ireland **t** +353 1 677 7330 **f** +353 1 677 7276 **e** celtic@numb.ie **w** celticheartbeat.com MD: Barbara Galvan.

Celtic Heritage Series (see Ainm)

Cent Records Melbourne House, Chamberlain Street, Wells BA5 2PJ **t** 01749 689074 **f** 01749 670315 **e** info@centrecords.com **w** centrecords.com MD: Kevin Newton.

Centaur Discs 40-42 Brantwood Avenue, Dundee DD3 6EW **t** 01382 776595 **f** 01382 736702 **e** agcdser@aol.com **w** cd-services.com MD: Dave Shoesmith.

Centric Records Regus House, George Curl Way, Southampton, Hants SO18 2RZ **t** 0870 240 4232 **f** 0870 240 4233 **e** howard.lucas@centricrecords.com W centricrecords.com Commercial Dir: Howard Lucas.

Centric Records Regus House, George Curl Way, Southampton, Hants SO18 2RZ **t** 0870 240 4232 **f** 0870 240 4233 **e** howard.lucas@centricrecords.com **w** centricrecords.com Commercial Dir: Howard Lucas.

Century Media Records 6 Water Lane, Camden, London NW1 8NZ **t** 020 7482 0161 **f** 020 7482 3165 **e** andy@centurymedia.net **w** centurymedia.net Label Mgr: Andy Turner.

Certificate18 Records Battersea Business Centre, Unit 36, 99-109 Lavender Hill, London SW11 5QL **t** 020 7924 1333 **f** 020 7924 1833 **e** info@certificate18.com **w** certificate18.com MD: Paul Arnold. Dist: SRD

Champion Records Ltd 181 High St, Harlesden, London NW10 4TE **t** 020 8961 5202 **f** 020 8961 6665 **e** mel@championrecords.co.uk **w** championrecords.co.uk Owner: Mel Medalie. Dist: Pinnacle

Chandos Records Ltd Chandos House, Commerce Way, Colchester, Essex CO2 8HQ **t** 01206 225200 **f** 01206 225201 **e** enquiries@chandos.net **w** chandos.net PA to MD: Sue Shortridge. Dist: Chandos Records

Channel 4 Recordings 124 Horseferry Rd, London SW1P 2TX **t** 020 7396 4444 **f** 020 7306 8044 **e** c4recordings@channel4.co.uk **w** channel4.com Music Manager: Liz Edmunds.

Chant du Monde (see Harmonia Mundi (UK) Ltd)

Charlie (see Snapper Music)

Charly Acquisitions Ltd. 171 Le Petit Vert, Sark, via Guernsey, Channel Islands GY9 0SB **t** 01481 832794 **f** 01481 832795 **e** info@Charly-acquisitions.com International Affairs: Jan Friedmann.

Charnel (see Harmonia Mundi (UK) Ltd)

Chateau (see Silverword Music Group)

Cheeky (see BMG UK & Ireland Ltd)

Chemikal Underground Records PO Box 3609, Glasgow G42 9TP **t** 0141 550 1919 **f** 0141 550 1918 **e** graeme@chemikal.co.uk **w** chemikal.co.uk Lbl Mgr: Andrew Savage. Dist: Vital

Cherry Red Records Unit 17, Elysium Gate West, 126-128 New Kings Road, London SW6 4LZ **t** 020 7371 5844 **f** 020 7384 1854 **e** infonet@cherryred.co.uk **w** cherryred.co.uk MD: Iain McNay. Director: Adam Velasco. Dist: Pinnacle

Chewin' Gum Records 30 Speakers Close, Tividale, Oldbury, West Midlands B69 1UX **t** 07957 692 398 **e** chewinggumrecords@aol.com Label Manager: Kev Bennison.

Chicks On Speed Records (see Labels UK)

Chillifunk Records 8 Berwick St, 3rd Floor, London W1F 0PH **t** 020 7479 7040 **f** 020 7439 0483 **e** mm@chillifunk.com **w** chillifunk.com MD: Lofty. Dist: Timewarp

Chinawhite Records (see Bianco Music and Entertainment)

Choice (see Millennium Records Ltd)

Chrome Dreams PO Box 230, New Malden, Surrey KT3 6YY **t** 020 8715 9781 **f** 020 8241 1426 **e** contactus@chromedreams.co.uk **w** chromedreams.co.uk MD: Rob Johnstone. Dist: Nova/Recognition

Chrysalis (see EMI Music UK & Ireland)

Chunk Records 139 Whitfield St, London W1T 5EN **t** 020 7380 1000 **e** info@chunkrecords.com **w** chunkrecords.com Label Mgr: Neil Stainton.

Circa (see Virgin Records)

Circulation Recordings Ltd 8 Lingfield Point, McMullen Road, Darlington, Co Durham DL1 1YU **t** 01325 365553 **f** 01325 365553 **e** Graeme.circ@ntlworld.com **w** circulationrecordings.com MD: Graeme Robinson. Dist: Shellshock/Pinnacle

Circus Records Argo House, Kilburn Park Rd., Maida Vale, London NW6 5LF **t** 020 7644 0498 **f** 020 7644 0698 **e** info@circusrecords.net **w** circusrecords.net Dir: Allison McGourty. Dist: Universal

City Rollaz inc 78 Alcester Road, Moseley, Birmingham, West Midlands B13 8BB **t** 0121 256 1311 **f** 0121 256 1318 **e** del@music.mercia.org **w** cityrollazinc.co.uk Label Manager: Del Edwards.

City Slang (see Labels UK)

Claddagh Records Dame House, Dame Street, Dublin 2, Ireland **t** +353 1 679 3664 **f** +353 1 679 3664 **e** claddagh@crl.ie **w** claddaghrecords.com Mgr: Jane Bolton. Dist: Proper

Clarinet Classics (see Naxos AudioBooks)

Classic Pictures Shepperton Int'l Film Studios, Studios Road, Shepperton, Middx TW17 0QD **t** 01932 592016 **f** 01932 592046 **e** Jo.garofalo@classicpictures.co.uk **w** classicpictures.co.uk Sales & Marketing Dir.: Jo Garofalo. Dist: Pinnacle

Claudio Records Ltd Studio 17, The Promenade, Peacehaven, E. Sussex BN10 8PU **t** 01273 580250 **f** 01273 583530 **e** Info@ClaudioRecords.com **w** ClaudioRecords.com MD: Colin Attwell. Dist: Nimbus

Clay Records (see Sanctuary Records Group)

Clean Up (see One Little Indian Records)

Cleveland City Records 52A Clifton Street, Chapel Ash, Wolverhampton, West Midlands WV3 0QT **t** 01902 838500 **f** 01902 839500 **e** info@clevelandcity.co.uk **w** clevelandcity.co.uk Contact: Mike Evans, Lee Glover

Climax Recordings Summit Studio, 3 Osborne Ave, Jesmond, Newcastle-upon-Tyne NE2 1JQ **t** 0191 212 0854 **f** 0191 281 5789 **e** james_climax@hotmail.com **w** climaxrecordings.co.uk Label Manager: James Wilson.

Clovelly Recordings Ltd 1 The Old Cannery, Hengist Road, Deal, Kent CT14 6WY **t** 01304 239356 **f** 01304 239356 **e** clovellyrecordings@hotmail.com **w** clovellyrecordings.com MD: John Perkins. Dist: BMG

Clown Records P.O Box 20432, London SE17 3WT **t** 07986 359 568 **e** office@clownrecords.co.uk **w** clownrecords.co.uk A&R: Stephen Adams.

Club du Disque Arabe (see Harmonia Mundi (UK) Ltd)

Clubscene PO Box 26723, Glasgow G1 4YY **t** 0870 922 0941 or 07785 222 205 **f** 0141 552 1184 **e** mail@clubscene.co.uk **w** clubscene.co.uk Contact: Bill Grainger

CMP (see Silva Screen Records)

Code Blue (see Atlantic Records UK)

Collecting Records LLP 21A Clifftown Road, Southend-On-Sea, Essex SS1 1AB **t** 01702 330005 **f** 01702 333309 **e** bcollent@aol.com **w** barrycollings.co.uk MD: Barry Collings.

Collective Music Ltd 2nd Floor, 80-82 Chiswick High Road, London W4 1SY **t** 020 8995 5544 **f** 020 8995 1133 **e** info@collective.mu(DO NOT PUBLISH) **w** collective.mu MD: Phil Hardy. Product Manager: Chris Tams.

Collegium Records PO Box 172, Whittlesford, Cambridge CB2 4QZ **t** 01223 832474 **f** 01223 836723 **e** info@collegium.co.uk **w** collegium.co.uk Sales & Marketing: Michael Stevens. Dist: Select Music & Video Distribution Ltd.

Comet Records 5 Cope St, Temple Bar, Dublin 2, Ireland **t** +353 1 671 8592 **f** +353 1 672 8005 **e** gforce@indigo.ie MD: Brian O'Kelly.

Commercial Recordings 12 Lisnagleer Road, Dungannon, Co Tyrone BT70 3LN **t** 028 8776 1995 **f** 028 8776 1995 **e** info@commercialrecordings.com **w** commercialrecordings.com MD: Raymond Stewart.

CommuniquÇ Records Longfield House, Bury Avenue, Ruislip, Middx HA4 7RT **t** 01895 477522 **f** 01895 477522 **e** tomdoherty@supanet.com **w** communiquerecords.com Dir: Tom Doherty. Dist: Plastic Head

Complete Control Music 2, Leckwith Place, Canton, Cardiff CF11 6QA **t** 029 2038 7620 **f** 029 2023 3022 **e** touring@communitymusicwales.org.uk **w** completecontrolmusic.com Label Manager: Jo Hunt. Dist: Shellshock

Completist (see Siren Music Ltd)

Composure Records 20 Churchward Drive, Frome, Somerset BA11 2XL **t** 07816 285809 **e** composurerecords@btinternet.com **w** composurerecords.co.uk MD: Paul Davies. Dist: Unique

CONCEPT MUSIC

Shepherds Building, Charecroft Way, London W14 0EH **t** 020 7235 4800 **f** 020 7235 4884 **e** info@conceptmusic.com **w** conceptmusic.com MD: Max Bloom.

Conception Records Ltd 40 Newman St, London W1T 1QD **t** 020 7580 4424 **f** 020 7323 1695 **e** info@conception.gb.com MD: Jean-Nicol Chelmiah. Dist: Prime

Confetti Records PO Box 11541, London N15 4DW **t** 020 8376 1876 **f** 020 8808 4413 **e** enquiries@confettirecords.co.uk **w** confettirecords.co.uk Director: John Josephs.

Congo Music Ltd 17A Craven Park Road, Harlesden, London NW10 8SE **t** 020 8961 5461 **f** 020 8961 5461 **e** congomusic@hotmail.com **w** congomusic.com A&R Director: Root Jackson.

Connoisseur Collection Ltd 2-3 Fitzroy Mews, London W1T 6DF **t** 020 7383 7773 **f** 020 7383 7724 **e** info@connoisseurcollection.co.uk **w** connoisseurcollection.co.uk Dist: Pinnacle

Connoisseur Records (see Crashed Music)

Console Sounds PO Box 7515, Glasgow G41 3ZW **t** 0141 636 6336 **f** 0141 636 6336 **e** info@consolesounds.co.uk **w** consolesounds.co.uk Dir: Stevie Middleton. Dist: Pinnacle/Unique

Constellation (see Southern Records)

Contra Music 13 Cotswold Mews, 30 Battersea Square, London SW11 3RA **t** 020 7978 7888 **f** 020 7978 7808 **e** auto@automan.co.uk **w** genenet.co.uk MD: Jerry Smith. Dist: Fullfill/Universal

Cookin' (see Good Looking Records)

Cooking Vinyl 10 Allied Way, London W3 0RQ **t** 020 8600 9200 **f** 020 8743 7448 **e** info@cookingvinyl.com **w** cookingvinyl.com MD: Martin Goldschmidt. Dist: Vital

Copasetik Recordings Ltd 9 Spedan Close, London NW3 7XF **t** 07855 551 024 **e** copasetik1@aol.com **w** copasetik.com MD/Head of A&R: Jon Sexton. Dist: Vital

Corban Recordings PO Box 2, Glasgow G44 3LB **t** 0141 637 5277 **f** 0141 637 5277 **e** alastair@corbanrecordings.com **w** corbanrecordings.co.uk Contact: Alastair McDonald

Corticol (see Harmonia Mundi (UK) Ltd)

Cowboy Records (see Amazon Records Ltd)

Cr 2 Records PO Box 718, Richmond, Surrey TW9 4XR **t** 020 8876 2216 **f** 020 8487 8831 **e** info@cr2records.co.uk **w** cr2records.co.uk MD: Mark Brown. Dist: Amato

Crai (see Sain (Recordiau) Cyf)

Cramer (see Priory Records)

Crapola Records PO Box 808, Hook, Hants RG29 1TA **t** 01256 862865 **f** 01256 862182 **e** feedback@crapola.com **w** crapolarecords.com Head of A&R: Martin Curtis.

Crashed Music 162 Church Road, East Wall, Dublin 3, Ireland **t** +353 1 888 1188 **f** +353 1 856 1122 **e** info@crashedmusic.com **w** crashedmusic.com MD: Shay Hennessy. Dist: Sony

Creamy Groove Machine Recordings (see Copasetik Recordings Ltd)

Creative World The Croft, Deanslade Farm, Claypit Lane, Lichfield WS14 0AG **t** 01543 253576 or 07885 341745 **f** 01543 253576 **e** info@creative-world-entertainment.co.uk **w** creative-world-entertainment.co.uk MD: Mervyn Spence.

Creature Music (see East Central One Ltd)

Creole (see Sanctuary Records Group)

Critical Mass (see Heat Recordings)

Crocodile Records 35 Gresse St, London W1T 1QY **t** 020 7580 0080 **f** 020 7637 0097 **e** music@crocodilemusic.com **w** crocodilemusic.com MD: Malcolm Ironton.

Crossover Urban (see Heavenly Dance)

CSA Word (Audio Books) 6A Archway Mews, London SW15 2PE **t** 020 8871 0220 **f** 020 8877 0712 **e** info@csaword.co.uk **w** csaword.co.uk MD: Clive Stanhope. Dist: Universal

Cube Soundtracks Onward House, 11 Uxbridge Street, London W8 7TQ **t** 020 7221 4275 **f** 020 7229 6893 **e** cube@bucksmusicgroup.co.uk **w** cubesoundtracks.co.uk Label Manager: Ronen Guha. Dist: Absolute

Culburnie (see Greentrax Recordings Ltd)

Cultural Foundation Dalehead, Rosedale, North Yorkshire YO18 8RL **t** 0845 458 4699 or 01751 417 147 **f** 01751 417 804 **e** info@cultfound.org **w** cultfound.org A&R: Peter Bell.

Culture Press UK 74-75 Warren Street, London W1T 5PF **t** 020 7387 3344 **f** 020 7388 2756 **e** zep@sternsmusic.com **w** sternsmusic.com / culturepress.fr Contact: Zep

Curb Records Ltd 45 Great Guildford Street, London SE1 0ES **t** 020 7401 8877 **f** 020 7928 8590 **e** firstname@curb-uk.com **w** curb.com MD: Phil Cokell. Dist: Warner/Independent Dist.

Cursery Rhymes (see Klone UK)

Cybertech Support Services Ltd 6 Cheyne Walk, Hornsea, East Yorks HU18 1BX **t** 01964 533982 **f** 01964 536193 **e** paul@csupports.co.uk **w** csupports.co.uk MD: Paul Cook.

Cycle Records 50 Stroud Green Rd, London N4 3ES **t** 01923 444440 **f** 01923 444440 **e** info@cyclerecords.co.uk **w** cyclerecords.co.uk MD: Buzz Aldrin. Dist: Discovery

Cyclops Records 33A Tolworth Park Rd, Tolworth, Surrey KT6 7RL **t** 020 8339 9965 **f** 020 8399 0070 **e** postmaster@gft-cyclops.co.uk **w** gft-cyclops.co.uk MD: Malcolm Parker. Dist: Pinnacle

CYP Limited CYP Children's Audio, The Fairway, Bush Fair, Harlow, Essex CM18 6LY **t** 01279 444707 **f** 01279 445570 **e** enquiries@cypmusic.co.uk **w** kidsmusic.co.uk MD: Mike Kitson.

D RECORDS

35 Brompton Road, London SW3 1DE **t** 020 7368 6311 **f** 020 7823 9553 **e** d@35bromptonroad.com **w** drecords.co.uk MD: Douglas Mew. Dist: Universal Music Operations

D-Mak Records 2A Downing Street, Ashton-under-Lyne, Lancashire OL7 9LR **t** 0161 292 9493 **f** 0161 344 1673 **e** d.murphy@easynet.co.uk **w** pincermetal.com MD: Dale Murphy.

D-stracted Records 4/7 Vineyard, off Sanctuary Street, Borough, London SE1 1QL **t** 020 7940 4344 **f** 020 7940 4341 **e** office@d-stracted.com **w** d-stracted.com Dir: Grant Gaze.

D.O.R. PO Box 1797, London E1 4TX **t** 020 7702 7842 **e** info@dor.co.uk **w** dor.co.uk Contact: Martin Parker Dist: D.O.R.(Infinity)

Da Doo Ron Ron Records 5 Mayfield Court, Victoria Road, Freshfield, Liverpool, Merseyside L37 7JL **t** 01704 834105 **f** 01704 834105 **e** ronellis50@hotmail.com **w** ronellis.co.uk MD: Ron Ellis.

Daisy Discs (see Hummingbird Records)

Dance Paradise UK 207 Muirfield Rd, Watford, Herts WD19 6HZ **t** 020 8421 3817 **f** 020 8387 4299 **e** dance.paradise@ntlworld.com MD: Andrei Riazanski.

Dancebeat (see Tema International)

Danceline 8 Stoney Lane, Rathcoole, Co Dublin, Ireland **t** +353 1 458 0578 or +353 1 627 1900 **f** +353 1 627 4404 **e** danceline@unison.ie **w** homepage.tinet.ie/~danceline MD: Eddie Joyce.

Dangerous Records Sandwell Manor, Totnes, Devon TQ9 7LL **t** 01803 867850 **f** 01803 867850 **e** info@dangerousrecords.co.uk **w** dangerousrecords.co.uk MD: Dennis Smith. Dist: Pinnacle

Dara (see Dolphin Music)

Dark Beat Records Holborn Gate, First Floor, 330 High Holborn, London WC1V 7QT **t** 020 7203 8366 **f** 020 7203 8409 **e** darkbeat@outlet-promotions.com **w** outlet-promotions.com MD: Glenn Wilson. Dist: After Dark

Data 103 Gaunt St, London SE1 6DP **t** 020 7740 8600 **f** 020 7403 5348 **e** jgraty@ministryofsound.com **w** datarecords.co.uk Head of A&R: Ben Cooke. Dist: Universal

The Date Tapes (see Whoa Music)

Datum (see Priory Records)

Day Release Records (see Fire Records)

db records PO Box 19318, Bath, Somerset BA1 6ZS **t** 01225 782 322 **e** info@dbrecords.co.uk **w** dbrecords.co.uk A&R: David Bates. A&R: Chris Hughes. Dist: Vital

de Wolfe Music Shropshire House, 11-20 Capper Street, London WC1E 6JA **t** 020 7631 3600 **f** 020 7631 3700 **e** info@dewolfemusic.co.uk **w** dewolfemusic.co.uk MD: Warren De Wolfe.

Dead Earnest 40-42 Brantwood Avenue, Dundee, Tayside DD3 6EW **t** 01382 776595 **f** 01382 736702 **e** deadearnest@btopenworld.com **w** deadearnest.btinternet.co.uk Owner: Andy Garibaldi.

Dead Happy Records 3B Castledown Avenue, Hastings, East Sussex TN34 3RJ **t** 01424 434778 **e** Vibezone@excite.com **w** Vibezone.co.uk Dir: David Arnold. Dist: Dead Happy / Internet

Debonair Records & Tapes Ltd Eaton House, 39 Lower Richmond Road, Putney, London SW15 1ET **t** 020 7235 9046 **f** 020 7235 7193 **e** info@eatonmusic.com **w** eatonmusic.com MD: Terry Oates.

Decca (see Universal Classics & Jazz (UK))

The Decca Music Group 347-353 Chiswick High Rd, London W4 4HS **t** 020 8747 8787 **f** 020 8994 2834 **e** firstname.lastname@umusic.com **w** deccaclassics.com President: Costa Pilavachi. Dist: Universal

Decca UK 22 St Peters Square, London W6 9NW **t** 020 8910 5000 **f** 020 8910 3130 **e** vicki.campbell@umusic.com **w** universalclassics.com Marketing Dir: Dickon Stainer. Dist: Universal

Deceptive Records Ltd PO Box 288, St Albans, Herts AL4 9YU **t** 01727 834130 **e** tony@bluff.demon.co.uk (DO NOT PUBLISH) MD: Tony Smith. Dist: Vital

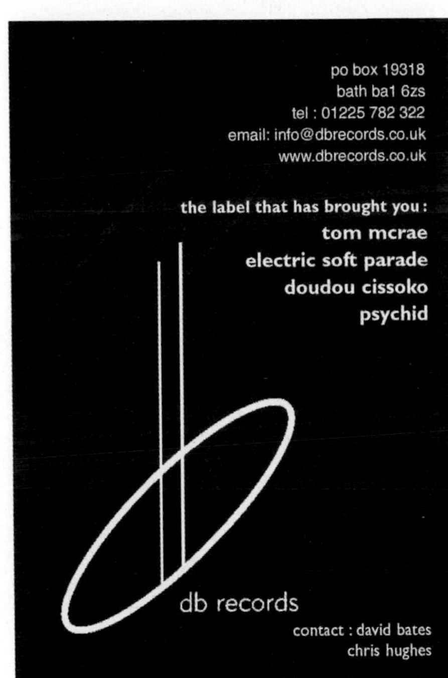

Decipher Recordings 101 Salisbury Road, Farnborough, Hants. GU14 7AE **t** 0771 289 9665 **f** 020 8995 1133 **e** decipher@decipher-recordings.com **w** decipher-recordings.com MD: Brendan Byrne. Dist: Amato

Dedicated (see Songlines Ltd)

Deep (see 3 Beat Label Management)

Deep End Records 28 Tooting High Street, London SW17 0RG **t** 020 8333 5400 **f** 020 8333 5401 **e** info@deependrecords.com **w** deependrecords.com MD: Tom Hayes.

Deep Focus (see 3 Beat Label Management)

Def Jam (see Mercury Records)

Defected Records Ltd 14/15 D'Arblay Street, London W1F 8DY **t** 020 7439 9995 **f** 020 7432 6470 **e** defected@defected.com **w** defected.com MD: Hector Dewar. A&R Dir: Simon Dunmore. Promo/Mkt Dir: Janet Bell. Press/Promo Mgr: Guy Williams. Business Affairs/Licensing: John Reed. Dist: Vital

Delerium Records Ltd PO Box 1288, Gerrards Cross, Bucks SL9 9YB **t** 01753 880873 **f** 01753 892879 **e** info@delerium.co.uk **w** freakemporium.com MD: Richard Allen. PA to MD: Corinne French. Dist: Koch

Delta Loop (see Music Mercia)

Delta Music plc 222 Cray Avenue, Orpington, Kent BR5 3PZ **t** 01689 888888 **f** 01689 888800 or 01689 888894 **e** info@deltamusic.co.uk **w** deltamusic.co.uk MD: Laurie Adams.

Deltasonic Records 102 Rose Lane, Mossley Hill, Liverpool L18 8AG **t** 0151 724 4760 **f** 0151 724 6286 **e** info@deltasonic.co.uk **w** deltasonic.co.uk Label Manager: Ann Heston. Dist: TEN

Demerara Records (see Ravensbourne Records Ltd)

Demi Monde Records Llanfair Caereinion, Powys, Wales SY21 0DS **t** 01938 810758 **f** 01938 810758 **e** demi.monde@dial.pipex.com **w** demimonde.co.uk MD: Dave Anderson. Dist: Shellshock/Backs

Demon Records Ltd 4th Floor, Holden House, 57 Rathbone Place, London W1T 1JU **t** 020 7470 8522 **f** 020 7470 6666 **e** info@demonmusicgroup.co.uk **w** vci.co.uk Sales & Mktg Dir: Danny Keene. Label Manager: Val Jennings.

DEMON MUSIC GROUP

4th Floor, Holden House, 57 Rathbone Place, London W1T 1JU **t** 020 7936 8899 **f** 020 7470 6655 **e** info@demonmusicgroup.co.uk **w** vci.co.uk GM: Neela Ebbett. Commercial Director/Licensing: Adrian Sear. Head of Marketing: Will Harris. Sales & Marketing Director: Danny Keene. Dist: Deluxe Media Services

---

Dental Records 139c Whitfield Street, London W1T 5EN **t** 020 7380 1000 **f** 020 7380 1000 **e** Neil@Nuff.co.uk Contact: Neil Stainton

DEP International 1 Andover St, Birmingham, West Midlands B5 5RG **t** 0121 633 4742 **f** 0121 643 4904 **e** enquiries@ub40.co.uk **w** ub40.co.uk Business Mgr: Lanval Storrod. Dist: Virgin

Desilu Records Ltd 6 Rookwood Park, Horsham, West Sussex RH12 1UB **t** 01403 240272 or 07788 412 867 **f** 01403 263008 **e** gbowes@desilurecords.com **w** desilurecords.com President: Graham Bowes.

Desoto (see Southern Records)

Destined Records (see Back Yard Recordings)

Destiny Music Iron Bridge House, 3 Bridge Approach, London NW1 8BD **t** 020 7734 3251 **f** 020 7439 2391 **e** nick@destinymusic.co.uk **w** carlinmusic.co.uk MD: Nick Farries.

Detour Records Ltd PO Box 18, Midhurst, West Sussex GU29 9YU **t** 01730 815422 **f** 01730 815422 **e** detour@btinternet.com **w** detour-records.co.uk Dirs: David Holmes & Tania Holmes. Dist: Various

Deutsche Grammophon (see Universal Classics & Jazz (UK))

Deux Zinoto (see Harmonia Mundi (UK) Ltd)

Deviant 12 Southam St, London W10 5PH **t** 020 8969 0666 **f** 020 8968 6128 **e** whoever@deviant.co.uk **w** deviantrecords.com MD: Rob Deacon. Dist: Vital

Different Drummer Ltd PO Box 2571, Birmingham B30 1BZ **t** 0121 603 0033 **f** 0121 603 0060 **e** info@diffdrum.co.uk **w** diffdrum.co.uk MD: Richard Whittingham. A&R/Promotion/Press: Adam Regan. Dist: Kudos/Pinnacle

Direct Heat Records PO Box 1345, Worthing, West Sussex BN14 7FB **t** 01903 202426 **f** 01903 202426 **e** dhr@happyvibes.co.uk **w** happyvibes.co.uk MD: Mike Pailthorpe. Dist: Timewarp

Dirty Blue (see 3 Beat Label Management)

Dis-funktional Recordings (see Nocturnal Recordings)

Disc Imports Ltd 1st & 2nd Floors, 7 High St, Cheadle, Cheshire SK8 1AX **t** 0161 491 6655 **f** 0161 491 6688 **e** dimus@aol.com **w** dimusic.co.uk MD: Alan Wilson. Dist: Disc Imports

Dischord (see Southern Records)

Discipline (see Vinyl Japan)

Discover (see Supreme Music)

Discovery Records PO Box 10896, Birmingham B13 0ZU **t** 0121 247 6981 or 07976 215 719 **f** 0121 247 6981 **e** rod@fruitionmusic.co.uk MD: Rod Thomson.

Discovery Records Ltd Nursteed Road, Devizes, Wiltshire SN10 3DY **t** 01380 728000 **f** 01380 722244 **e** info@discovery-records.com Commercial Director: Martin Cobb.

Disky Communications Ltd Connaught House, 112-120 High Road, Loughton, Essex IG10 4HJ **t** 020 8508 3723 **f** 020 8508 0432 **e** disky.uk@disky.nl MD: Alan Byron.

Disorient (see Mr Bongo/Disorient Recordings)

Disruptive Pattern **f** 07092 040899 **e** giles@militia.demon.co.uk Proprietor: Giles Pepperell.

Distinct'ive Records The Heals Building, Unit A3, 3rd Floor, 22-24 Torrington Place, London WC1E 7HJ **t** 020 7323 6610 **f** 020 7323 6413 **e** richard@distinctiverecords.com **w** distinctiverecords.com Head of A&R: Richard Ford.

Distinct'ive Breaks (see Distinct'ive Records)

Diverse Products (see Nu Directions)

Divine Art Record Company Ltd 8 The Beeches, East Harlsey, Northallerton, North Yorks DL6 2DJ **t** 01609 882062 or 07811 479151 **e** info@divine-art.com **w** divine-art.com MD: Stephen Sutton. Dist: DI Music/Divive Art

DMC Ltd PO Box 89, Slough, Berks SL1 8NA **t** 01628 667124 **f** 01628 605246 **e** info@dmcworld.com **w** dmcworld.com Chairman: Tony Prince. Dist: Pinnacle

DMI Arch 25, Kings Cross Freight Depot, York Way, London N1 0EZ **t** 020 7713 8130 **f** 020 7713 8247 **e** info@dmirecords.com **w** dmirecords.com Directors: Massimo Bonaddio/Dan Carey. Dist: SRD

DND Produtions Reverb House, Bennett St, London W4 2AH **t** 020 8747 0660 ext224 **f** 020 8747 0880 **e** andy.rutherford@reverbxl.com Label Manager: Andy Rutherford.

Dolphin Music Unit 4, 3-4 Great Ship Street, Dublin 8, Ireland **t** +353 1 478 3455 **f** +353 1 478 2143 **e** irishmus @iol.ie **w** irelandcd.com Export Manager: Paul Heffernan.

Dome Records Ltd 59 Glenthorne Road, Hammersmith, London W6 0LJ **t** 020 8748 4499 **f** 020 8748 6699 **e** info@domerecords.co.uk **w** domerecords.co.uk MD: Peter Robinson. Dist: Pinnacle

Domino Recording Company PO Box 47029, London SW18 1WD **t** 020 8875 1390 **f** 020 8875 1391 **e** info@dominorecordco.com **w** dominorecordco.com A&R: Flash Taylor.

Dorado Records 76 Brewer St, London W1F 9TX **t** 020 7287 1689 **f** 020 7287 1684 **e** ollie@dorado.net **w** dorado.net MD: Ollie Buckwell. Dist: Pinnacle

Dorian (see Priory Records)

Dorigen Music Unit 12, Lodge Bank Industrial Estate, Off Crown Lane, Horwich, Bolton BL6 5HY **t** 01204 675500 **f** 01204 479005 **e** simonb@uniquedist.co.uk **w** uniquedist.co.uk Label Mgr: Simon Blade. Dist: Unique

Double Dragon Music 120-124 Curtain Road, London EC2A 3SQ **t** 020 7739 6903 **f** 020 7613 2715 **e** tav@ outthere.co.uk MD: Stephen Taverner.

Dovehouse Records Crabtree Cottage, Mill Lane, Kidmore End, Oxon RG4 9HB **t** 0118 972 4356 or 0118 972 4809 **w** doverecords@btconnect.com President: Thomas Pemberton. Dist: dovehouserecords.com

Down By Law Records PO Box 20242, London NW1 7FL **t** 020 7485 1113 **e** info@proofsongs.co.uk

Dragonfly Records 67-69 Chalton St, London NW1 1HY **t** 020 7554 2100 **f** 020 7554 2154 **e** info@ dragonflyrecords.com **w** dragonflyrecords.com Label Mgr: Nick Jones. MD: Youth. Marketing & A&R Manager: Murray Rose. Dist: Arabesque

Dream Catcher Records Goodsoal Farm, Burwash Common, East Sussex TN19 7LX **t** 01435 883197 **f** 01435 883833 **e** info@dreamcatcher-records.com **w** dreamcatcher-records.com MD: Gem Howard-Kemp. Dist: Pinnacle

DreamWorks (see Polydor Records)

Dreamy Records PO Box 30427, London NW6 3FF **t** 079 6133 6121 **e** info@dreamyrecords.com **w** dreamyrecords.com MD: Tracy Lee Jackson. Dist: Prime

Drowned in Sound Recordings 72 Palatine Rd, London N16 8ST **t** 020 8969 2498 **f** 0870 164 3040 **e** thelabel@ drownedinsound.com **w**drownedinsound.com /recordings Label Mgr: Sean Adams.

Dtox Records Ltd 33 Alexander Road, Aylesbury, Bucks HP20 2NR **t** 01296 434731 **f** 01296 422530 **e** fmluk@aol.com **w** dtox.co.uk Label Manager: Joseph Stopps.

DTPM RECORDINGS

First floor, 40A Gt Eastern St, London EC2A 3EP **t** 020 7749 1199 **f** 020 7749 1188 **e** guy@blue-cube.net **w** dtpmrecordings.net Label Mgr: Guy Williams.
Send tracks for consideration to Guy Williams at above address. DJ Bookings/Tours please phone or email Simon Patterson simon@blue-cube.net.

Dulcima Records 39 Tadorne Road, Tadworth, Surrey KT20 5TF **t** 01737 812922 **f** 01737 812922 **e** dulcima@ukgateway.net **w** dulcimarecords.com MD: Johnny Douglas. Dist: Avid/Savoy Music

Dune Records 1st Floor, 73 Canning Road, Harrow, Middx HA3 7SP **t** 020 8424 2807 **f** 020 8861 5371 **e** info@dune-music.com **w** dune-music.com MD: Janine Irons. A&R: Janine Irons, Gary Crosby. Dist: New Note

Duophonic UHF PO Box 3787, London SE22 9DZ **t** 020 8299 1650 **f** 020 8693 5514 **e** duophonic@ btopenworld.com **w** duophonic.com Dir: Martin Pike. Dist: Vital

Duty Free Recordings Courtsyard Office, 68-69 Chalk Farm Rd, London NW1 8AN **t** 020 7424 0774 **f** 020 7424 9094 **e** info@dutyfreerecordings.co.uk **w** dutyfreerecordings.co.uk MD: Steffan Chandler. Dist: Vital

Dynamic (see Priory Records)

EAGLE RECORDS

EAGLE RECORDS

Eagle House, 22 Armoury Way, London SW18 1EZ **t** 020 8870 5670 **f** 020 8874 2333 **e** mail@eagle-rock.com **w** eagle-rock.com MD, Worldwide: Lindsay Brown. Artist Liaison/Repertoire Manager: Andy McIntyre. Snr. Product Manager: Ian Rowe. Snr. Intl. Marketing & Promotional Manager: Annick Barbaria. Press & Promotions: Darren Edwards. Snr Production Manager: Claire Higgins. Dist: Pinnacle

Record Companies

EAGLE ROCK ENTERTAINMENT LTD

Eagle House, 22 Armoury Way, London SW18 1EZ **t** 020 8870 5670 **f** 020 8874 2333 **e** mail@eagle-rock.com **w** eagle-rock.com Executive Chairman: Terry Shand. Deputy Chairman: Julian Paul. Chief Operating Officer: Geoff Kempin. Group Finance Director: Jonathan Blanchard. Director of Business Affairs: Martin Dacre. General Manager: Chris Cole.

Ealing Records Timperley House, 11 St.Albans Road, Skircoat Green, Halifax, W.Yorks HX3 0ND **t** 01422 367040 MD: Bill Byford.

Earache Records Ltd Suite 1-3 Westminster Building, Theatre Square, Nottingham NG1 6LG **t** 0115 950 6400 **f** 0115 950 8585 **e** mail@earache.com **w** earache.com MD: Digby Pearson.

Earthworks (see Stern's Records)

East Central One Ltd Creeting House, All Saints Rd, Creeting St Mary, Ipswich, Suffolk IP6 8PR **t** 01449 723244 **f** 01449 726067 **e** enquiries@eastcentralone.com **w** eastcentralone.com Co-Dir: Steve Fernie. Dist: Vital

Eastern Bloc Underground 5 & 6 Central Buildings, Oldham St, Manchester M1 1JT **t** 0161 228 6432 **f** 0161 228 6728 **e** info@easternblocrecords.co.uk **w** easternblocrecords.co.uk MD: John Berry.

Eastside Records Ltd Top Floor, Outset Building, 2 Grange Rd, London E17 8AH **t** 020 8509 6070 **f** 020 8509 6021 **e** info@eastside-records.co.uk **w** eastside-records.co.uk Dir: Alexis Michaelides. Dist: Essential/Millennium

Easy Street Music 333 Millbrook Road, Southampton, Hampshire SO15 0HW **t** 023 8078 0088 **f** 023 8078 0099 **e** info@easyst.co.uk **w** easyst.co.uk Dir: Jason Thomas. Dist: Vital

Easyaccess (see Silver Planet Records)

The Echo Label Ltd The Chrysalis Building, 13 Bramley Road, London W10 6SP **t** 020 7229 1616 **f** 020 7465 6296 or 020 7792 1299 **e** firstname.lastname@chrysalis.com **w** echo.co.uk MD: John Chuter. CEO Chrysalis Music Division: Jeremy Lascelles. Director of A&R: Darrin Woodford. Head of Intn'l: Dino Ostacchini.

Edel (see Blacklist Entertainment)

Edgy (see Metal Nation)

Edition (see Loose Records)

Edsel (see Demon Records Ltd)

EG Records PO Box 4397, London W1A 7RZ **t** 020 8540 9935 A&R: Chris Kettle.

Electric Music People (see 3 Beat Label Management)

Electro Caramel (see Jazz Fudge Recordings)

Electronic Projects (see Certificate18 Records)

Elefanztrunk Records 4 Vicarage St, Faversham, Kent ME13 7BD **t** 01795 538 353 **f** 01795 538 353 **e** stuart.witcher@virgin.net Partner: Stuart Witcher.

Elektra (see Atlantic Records UK)

Elemental (see One Little Indian Records)

Elusive (see Genius Records Ltd)

Emanem (see Harmonia Mundi (UK) Ltd)

Ember (see Synergy Logistics)

Emerald Music (Ireland) Ltd. 120A Coach Road, Templepatrick, Co Antrim BT39 9RT **t** 028 9443 2619 **f** 028 9446 2162 **e** info@emeraldmusic.co.uk **w** emeraldmusiconline.com MD: George Doherty. Dist: RMG

The Emergency Broadcast System PO Box 6131, London W3 8ZR **t** 020 8993 8436 **f** 020 8896 1778 **e** star_rat@hawkwind.com **w** hawkwind.com/ Contact: Eve Carr

EMI Catalogue Marketing EMI House, 43 Brook Green, London W6 7EF **t** 020 7605 5000 **f** 020 7605 5050 **e** firstname.lastname@emimusic.com **w** emimusic.co.uk Co MDs, EMI Mktg: Steve Pritchard & Peter Duckworth. Dir, Commercial Mktg: Adrienne Dunlop.

EMI Catalogue/EMI Gold/EMI Liberty EMI House, 43 Brook Green, London W6 7EF **t** 020 7605 5000 **f** 020 7605 5050 **e** firstname.lastname@emimusic.com **w** emimusic.co.uk Co MDs, EMI Marketing: Steve Pritchard & Peter Duckworth. Dir, Catalogue, EMI Liberty: Steve Davis. Hd of Range Mktg, EMI Gold: Steve Woof.

EMI CLASSICS UK

43 Brook Green, London W6 7EF **t** 020 7605 5000 **e** firstname.lastname@emimusic.com **w** emiclassics.com Managing Director, EMI Classics UK: Barry McCann. Senior Product Manager, EMI Classics UK: Gill Allis. Product Manager, EMI Classics UK: Jeff Coventry. Trade Marketing Manager, EMI Classics UK: Valérie Renaud. Head of Press & Promotion, EMI Classics UK: Louise Paul. Press Officer, EMI Classics UK: Clare Addems.

EMI CLASSICS & JAZZ

27 Wrights Lane, London W8 5SW **t** 020 795 7000 **e** firstname.lastname@emic.co.uk **w** emiclassics.com President Classics & Jazz, EMI Music: Richard Lyttelton. VP International Marketing Classics & Jazz/Virgin Classics, EMI Music: Theo Lap. VP Finance & Business Affairs Classics & Jazz, EMI Music: John King. Senior DIrector International Marketing Classics & Jazz/Virgin Classics, EMI Music: Polly Miller. Director A&R, EMI Classics: Stephen Johns. Director Business Affairs, EMI Classics: Clare Ranger.

EMI Gold (see EMI Catalogue/EMI Gold/EMI Liberty)

EMI MUSIC IRELAND

EMI House, 1 Ailesbury Road, Dublin 4, Ireland **t** +353 1 203 9900 **f** +353 1 269 6341 **e** firstname.lastname@emimusic.com **w** emimusic.co.uk MD: Willie Kavanagh. Sales & Mktg Dir: David Gogan. Head of Promotions: Gillian Waters. Fin Dir: Harry Finney. Dist: EMI

EMI MUSIC UK & IRELAND

EMI Music UK and Ireland

EMI House, 43 Brook Green, London W6 7EF **t** 020 7605 5000 **f** 020 7605 5050 **e** firstname.lastname@emimusic.com **w** emimusic.co.uk Chairman & CEO: Tony Wadsworth. President, Capitol Music UK: Keith Wozencroft. MD, EMI Records: Terry Felgate. MD, Parlophone: Miles Leonard. MD, Virgin Records: Philippe Ascoli. MD, EMI Music Ireland: Willie Kavanagh. Co-MDs, EMI Music Cat. Mktg: Peter Duckworth & Steve Pritchard. MD, Studios Group: Dave Holley. Dir Comms: Cathy Cremer. Dir HR: Michelle Emmerson. Dir Bus.Aff: Julian French. CFO: Justin Morris. Com. Dir Sales: Mike McMahon. SVP Int. Mktg: Mike Allen. DVD & New Formats Mgr: Stefan Demetriou. Dist: EMI

EMI RECORDS

EMI House, 43 Brook Green, London W6 7EF **t** 020 7605 5000 **f** 020 7605 5050 **e** firstname.lastname@emimusic.com **w** emirecords.co.uk MD: Terry Felgate. Senior A&R Mgr: George Tyekiff. Mktg & Creative Dir: John Leahy. Media Dir: Rebecca Coates. Business Affairs Dir: James Mullan.

Emmellar Recordings PO Box 1345, Ilford, Essex IG4 5FX **t** 07050 333555 **f** 07020 923292 **e** emmelleye@aol.com **w** emmellar.cwc.net MD: Phillip Hundas. Label Mgr: Paul Booth.

Emprinte Digitale (see Harmonia Mundi (UK) Ltd)

End Recordings / Plink Plonk The End, 18 West Central St, London WC1A 1JJ **t** 020 7419 9199 **f** 020 7419 9099 **e** scott@the-end.co.uk **w** the-end.co.uk Label Manager: Scott McCready.

English Garden (see Hi-Note Music)

Enriched Records 15 Spencer Mews, Lansdowne Way, London SW8 1HF **t** 07968 198 825 **e** info@enrichedrecords.com **w** enrichedrecords.com MD: Rich B. Dist: Alphamagic/Tuned

Erato (see Warner Classics)

Essence Records 10 Trevelyan Gardens, London NW10 3JY **t** 020 8930 4760 **f** 020 8451 3380 **e** info@essencerecords.co.uk **w** essencerecords.co.uk MD: Phil Cheeseman.

Estereo (see Skint Records)

Ether Music Broadway Studios, 28 Tooting High St, London SW17 0RG **t** 020 8378 6956 **f** 020 8378 6959 **e** contact@etheruk.com **w** ethermusic.net Dir: Adrian Harley. Dist: Sterns/Timewarp

Ethereal Records 68 Seabrook Rd, Hythe, Kent CT21 5QA **t** 01303 267509 **e** Robertmdrury@aol.com **w** etherealrecords.com MD: Bob Drury.

Eukabreaks (see Eukatech Records)

Eukahouse (see Eukatech Records)

Eukalounge (see Eukatech Records)

Eukatech Records 49 Endell St, Covent Garden, London WC2H 9AJ **t** 020 7240 8060 **f** 020 7379 4939 **e** hq@eukatechrecords.com **w** eukatechrecords.com Label Manager: Rory Viggers. Dist: Intergroove

Euphoric (see Almighty Records)

Eureka Music Ltd 4 Yeomans Keep, Rickmansworth Rd, Chorleywood, Herts WD3 5RU **t** 01923 284171 **e** p.summerfield@virgin.net MD: Peter Summerfield.

Evangeline Recorded Works Ltd The Old School House, Knowstone, South Molton, Devon EX36 4YW **t** 01398 341465 **f** 01398 341677 **e** evangelinemusic@aol.com **w** evangeline.co.uk Label Manager: Sarah Lock. Dist: Universal

Evasive Records Unit 18-19 Croydon House, 1 Peall Road, Croydon, Surrey CR0 3EX **t** 020 8287 8585 **f** 020 8287 0220 **e** info@evasive.co.uk **w** evasive.co.uk MD: Rob Pearson.

Eve (see Supreme Music)

Eve Nova (see Supreme Music)

Evensong Recordings Ltd PO Box 345, Harpenden, Herts AL5 2ZW **t** 01582 768020 **f** 01582 767338 **e** evensong@evensong.co.uk **w** evensong.co.uk MD: Mike Gosling.

Eventide Music PO Box 27, Baldock, Hertfordshire SG7 6UH **t** 01462 893995 **f** 01462 893995 **e** eventide.music@ntlworld.com MD: Kevin Kendle.

Everlasting Records 42 Alexandra Rd, London NW4 2SA **t** 020 8203 4197 **f** 020 8202 9805 **e** info@everlastingrecords.co.uk MD: Danny Parnes.

Everybodywantsit Music Label 1st Floor, 27 Lexington Street, London W1F 9AQ **t** 020 7287 9601 **f** 020 7287 9602 **e** info@everybodywantsit.co.uk **w** everybodywantsit.co.uk Contact: Rufus Stone

Evidente (see Harmonia Mundi (UK) Ltd)

Evolve Records The Courtyard, 42 Colwith Road, London W6 9EY **t** 020 8741 1419 **f** 020 8741 3289 **e** firstname@evolverecords.co.uk **w** evolverecords.co.uk Chairman: Oliver Smallman.

Excalibur Records (see Satellite Music Ltd)

Exceptional Records Unit 113, Buspace Studios, Conlan St, London W10 5AP **t** 020 8969 1630 **f** 020 8995 8738 **e** info@exceptionalrecords.co.uk **w** exceptionalrecords.co.uk MD: Bob Fisher. Dist: 3MV/Pinnacle

Excited Records (see Songlines Ltd)

Exotica Records 49 Belvoir Road, London SE22 0QY **t** 020 8299 2342 **f** 020 8693 9006 **e** jim@exoticarecords.co.uk **w** exoticarecords.co.uk MD: Jim Phelan. Dist: SRD

Expansion Records Skratch Music House, 81 Crabtree Lane, London SW6 6LW **t** 020 7381 8315 **f** 020 7385 6785 **e** ralph@expansion-records.co.uk **w** musiclinks.com/expansion MD: Ralph Tee.

Explicit Records 29 Oakroyd Avenue, Potters Bar, Herts EN6 2EL **t** 01707 651439 **f** 01707 651439 **e** constantine@steveconstantine.freeserve.co.uk MD: Steve Constantine.

F Communications (UK) (see PIAS Recordings Ltd)

F.I. (see Hot Lead Records)

Fabric 12 Greenhill Rents, London EC1M 6BN **t** 020 7336 8898 **f** 020 7253 3932 **e** cds@fabriclondon.com **w** fabriclondon.com Label Manager: Geoff Muncey.

Fabric Of Life (see Tidy Trax)

Fabulous (see Acrobat Music & Media Limited)

Face 2 Face (see Adasam Limited)

Fairy Cake Universe 35 Playfield Crescent, London SE22 8QR **t** 020 8299 1645 **f** 020 8299 1685 **e** aquamanda@skyfruit.com MD: Amanda Greatorex.

Faith & Hope Records 23 New Mount St, Manchester M4 4DE **t** 0161 839 4445 **f** 0161 839 1060 **e** email@faithandhope.co.uk **w** faithandhope.co.uk Contact: Neil Claxton Dist: Vital

Fall Out (see Jungle Records)

Fantastic House (see Plastic Fantastic Record Label)

Fantastic Plastic The Church, Archway Close, London N19 3TD **t** 020 7263 2267 **f** 020 7263 2268 **e** info@fantasticplastic.co.uk **w** fantasticplastic.co.uk MD: Darrin Robson. Dist: Vital

Fantasy (see Ace Records)

Far Out Productions Pant-y-blodau, Rhewl, Nr Ruthin, Denbighshire LL15 2TS **t** 01824 702579 **e** far_out@compuserve.com **w** faroutproductions.net Owner: Jeff Jones.

Far Out Recordings TBC **t** 020 8758 1233 **f** 020 8758 1244 **e** joe@faroutrecordings.com **w** faroutrecordings.com MD: Joe Davis. Dist: Mac2

Fashion Records 17 Davids Rd, London SE23 3EP **t** 020 8291 6253 **f** 020 8291 1097 **e** chrislane@dubvendor.co.uk **w** dubvendor.co.uk Studio Manager: Chris Lane.

Fast Western Group Ltd Bank Top Cottage, Meadow Lane, Millers Dale, Derbyshire SK17 8SN **t** 01298 872462 **f** 01298 872461 **e** fast.west@virgin.net MD: Ric Lee.

Fastforward Music Ltd 1 Sorrel Horse Mews, Ipswich, Suffolk IP4 1LN **t** 01473 210 555 **f** 01473 210 500 **e** sales@fastforwardmusic.co.uk Sales Director: Neil Read.

Fat Cat Records PO Box 3400, Brighton BN1 4WG **t** 01273 608300 **f** 01273 607680 **e** info@fat-cat.co.uk **w** fat-cat.co.uk Label Managers: Dave, Alex. Dist: Vital/Pias/Bubblecore

Fat City Recordings Third Floor, Habib House, 9 Stevenson Sq, Manchester M1 1DB **t** 0161 228 7884 **f** 0161 228 7266 **e** label@fatcity.co.uk **w** fatcity.co.uk Label Manager: Matt Triggs.

Fat Fox Records 24a Radley Mews, off Stratford Rd, London W8 6JP **t** 020 7376 9555 **f** 020 7937 6246 **e** felix@fatfox.co.uk **w** fatfox.co.uk Dir: Felix Bechtolsheimer. Dist: Pinnacle

Fat Records Battersea Business Centre, Unit 36, 99-109 Lavender Hill, London SW11 5QL **t** 020 7924 1333 **f** 020 7924 1833 **e** info@thefatclub.com **w** thefatclub.com MD: Paul Arnold. Dist: Intergroove

FAYMUS Productions PO Box 748, Luton, Bedfordshire LU1 5ZA **t** 01582 481222 **f** 01582 481222 **e** info@faymus.com **w** faymus.com Snr Partner: Dave Tong. A&R, Production: Mike Boreham.

Faze 2 Records (see Amazon Records Ltd)

Fellside (see Delta Music plc)

Fellside Recordings Ltd PO Box 40, Workington, Cumbria CA14 3GJ **t** 01900 61556 **e** info@fellside.com **w** fellside.com Director: Paul Adams.

Fencat Music (see East Central One Ltd)

Fenetik (see Soma Recordings Ltd)

Festivo (see Priory Records)

FF Vinyl Records 1st Floor, Warwick Hall, Off Banastre Avenue, Cardiff CF14 3NR **t** 029 2069 4450 **f** 029 2069 4338 **e** enquiries@ffvinyl.com **w** ffvinyl.com MD: Martin Bowen. Dist: Shellshock

Fierce Panda 39 Tollington Road, London N7 6PB **t** 020 7609 2789 **f** 020 7609 8034 **e** mrbongopanda@aol.com **w** fiercepanda.co.uk MD: Simon Williams. Dist: Pinnacle

Filthy Sonnix Records 12 Austral Way, Althorne, Essex CM3 6UP **t** 01621 743979 **f** 01621 743979 **e** info@filthysonnix.com **w** filthysonnix.com Manager: Dan Raynham. Manager: Mark Warner. Publishing & International Licensing Mngr: Mick Shiner. Dist: Pinnacle

Fine Style (see Fashion Records)

Finger Lickin' Records 6 Inverness St, London NW1 7HJ **t** 020 7482 1114 **f** 020 7681 6039 **e** info@fingerlickin.co.uk **w** fingerlickin.co.uk MD: Justin Rushmore. Dist: Intergroove

Fire Recordings Ltd Unit 019, Westbourne Studios, 242 Acklam Road, London W10 5JJ **t** 020 7575 3033 **f** 020 7575 3034 **e** info@openfire.co.uk **w** openfire.co.uk Label Manager: Justine Oakley.

Fire Records The Vicarage, Windmill Lane, Nottingham NG2 4QB **t** 0115 950 9590 **f** 0115 950 9590 **e** james@firerecords.com **w** firerecords.com Creative Director: James Nicholls. Dist: Pinnacle

Firebird Music Kyrle House Studios, Edde Cross Street, Ross-on-Wye, Herefordshire HR9 7BZ **t** 01989 762269 **f** on request **e** info@firebird.com **w** firebird.com CEO: Peter Martin.

Firestar Records 10 Green Acres, Glyn Ave, Barnet, Herts EN4 9PJ **t** 01709 709633 or 07740 101347 **f** 020 8275 0502 **e** mailfirestar@aol.com **w** firestarrecords.com Promotions Manager: Paul Flanaghan.

Firetraxx (see ATCR: Trance Communication)

First Bass (see Music Like Dirt)

First Night Records Ltd 3 Warren Mews, London W1T 6AN **t** 020 7383 7767 **f** 020 7383 3020 **e** info@first-night-records.com **w** first-night-records.com MD: John Craig. Dist: Pinnacle

First Time Records Sovereign House, 12 Trewartha Road, Praa Sands, Penzance, Cornwall TR20 9ST **t** 01736 762826 or 07721 449477 **f** 01736 763328 **e** panamus@aol.com **w** songwriters-guild.co.uk MD: Roderick Jones. Dist: Media UK Distribution

Flair Records 15 Tabbs Lane, Scholes, Cleckheaton, West Yorks BD19 6DY **t** 01274 851365 **f** 01274 874329 **e** nowmusic@now-music.com **w** now-music.com MD: John Wagstaff. Dist: AMD

Flamencovision 54 Windsor Road, London N3 3SS **t** 020 8346 4500 **f** 020 8346 2488 **e** info@flamencovision.com **w** flamencovision.com MD: Helen Martin. Dist: Pinnacle

Flapper (see Pavilion Records Ltd)

Flat Records 5 Doods Road, Reigate, Surrey RH2 0NT **t** 01737 210848 **f** 01737 210848 **e** flatrecords@dial.pipex.com **w** netlink.co.uk/users/sonic/flat.htm MD: Richard Coppen. Dist: Various

Flesh (see Loose)

Flo Records (see Nation Records Ltd)

Fluid Recordings UK Ltd 404 Ducie House, Ducie Street, Manchester M1 2JW **t** 0161 236 4757 **f** 0161 236 4757 **e** fluid@fluidrecordings.co.uk **w** fluidrecordings.co.uk Label Manager: Rachel Gartley. Dist: Amato

Fly Records (see Cube Soundtracks)

FM (see Revolver Music Ltd)

FM Dance (see Revolver Music Ltd)

FM Jazz (see Revolver Music Ltd)

FM-Revolver (see Revolver Music Ltd)

Focus (see Word Music)

Focus Music International Ltd 10 Dukes Court, 77 Mortlake High Street, London SW14 8HS **t** 020 8876 7111 **f** 020 8878 0331 **e** info@focus-music.com **w** focus-music.com MD: Don Reedman.

Folkprint (see Voiceprint)

Folksound Records 250 Earlsdon Avenue North, Coventry, West Midlands CV5 6GX **t** 02476 711935 **f** 02476 711191 **e** rootsrecs@btclick.com MD: Graham Bradshaw. Dist: Roots

Folktrax 16 Brunswick Square, Gloucester, Gloucestershire GL1 1UG **t** 01452 415110 **f** 01452 503643 **e** peter@folktrax.freeserve.co.uk **w** folktrax.org Mgr: Peter Kennedy.

Fontana (see Mercury Records)

Fony Records Cambridge House, Card Hill, Forest Row, E. Sussex RH18 5BA **t** 01342 822619 **f** 01342 822619 **e** mickey.modernwood@virgin.net MD: Mickey Modern. Dist: Pinnacle

Food (see Parlophone)

Forever Gold 69 Rivington Street, London EC2A 3AY **t** 020 7613 1344 or 020 7613 3911 **f** 020 7613 3319 or 020 7613 3088 **e** oraclemusic@btinternet.com **w** forevergold.co.uk Dir: John Tracy. Dist: The Perennial Music Co. Ltd

Forlane (see Harmonia Mundi (UK) Ltd)

Formula One Records 71 Alan Moss Road, Loughborough, Leicestershire LE11 5LR **t** 01509 213632 MD: Ian Barker.

Fortune and Glory Osmond House, 78 Alcester Rd, Moseley, Birmingham, West Midlands B13 8BB **t** 0121 256 1310 **f** 0121 256 1318 **e** hendricks@fortuneandglory.co.uk **w** fortuneandglory.co.uk MD: Hendricks.

four:twenty (see Hope Music Group)

Fourth & Broadway (see Island Records Group)

Fox Records Ltd 62 Lake Rise, Romford, Essex RM1 4EE **t** 01708 760544 **f** 01708 760563 **e** foxrecords@talk21.com **w** foxrecordsltd.co.uk Director: Colin Brewer. Dist: Pinnacle/AMD(Universal)

Fractal (see Harmonia Mundi (UK) Ltd)

Fragile Records Unit 3, 1 St Mary Road, London E17 9RG **t** 020 8520 4442 **f** 020 8520 2514 **e** info@fragilerecords.co.uk MD: Dave Thompson.

Frank Records (see First Time Records)

free2air recordings Fulham Palace, Bishops Avenue, London SW6 6EA **t** 020 7751 0175 **f** 020 7736 0606 **e** info@free2airrecordings.com **w** free2airrecordings.com Contact: Craig Dimech Dist: Vital

Freedom Records PO Box 283, Manchester M14 4WY **t** 0161 227 9727 or 07811 326 200 **e** info@calebstorkey.com **w** freedom.cd MD: Caleb Storkey.

The Fridge Recording Company 1 Town Hall Parade, Brixton Hill, London SW2 1RJ **t** 020 7326 5100 **f** 020 7978 9277 **e** info@fridgerecordingcompany.co.uk **w** fridgerecordingcompany.co.uk Lbl Mgr/A&R: Rich B. Dist: Tuned

Frontier Recordings 305 Canalot Studios, 222 Kensal Road, London W10 5BN **t** 020 8960 0700 **f** 020 8960 0762 **e** info@frontierrecordings.com **w** frontierrecordings.com Dir: Pete Martin. Dist: Intergroove

Fuju (see Junior Boy's Own)

Full Cycle Records Unit 23, Easton Business Centre, Felix Road, Bristol BS5 0HE **t** 0117 941 5824 **f** 0117 941 5823 **e** info@fullcycle.co.uk **w** fullcycle.co.uk Label Manager: Gerard Cantwell. Dist: Vital

Full Fat Records (see Rumour Records Ltd)

Fume Recordings 30 Kilburn Lane, Kensal Green, London W10 4AH **t** 020 8969 2909 **f** 020 8969 3825 **e** info@fume.co.uk **w** fume.co.uk MD: Seamus Morley. Dist: RSK Entertainments

FUN (see Future Underground Nation)

Functional Breaks (see Future Underground Nation)

Funky Inc 206 Golden House, 29 Great Pulteney Street, London W1R 3DD **t** 020 7434 0779 **f** 020 7434 0710 **e** funkyinc@funkyinc.com **w** funkyinc.com Contact: Brendan Donohoe Dist: Pinnacle

Furious? Records PO Box 40, Arundel, West Sussex BN18 0UQ **t** 01243 558444 **f** 01243 558455 **e** info@furiousrecords.co.uk **w** furiousrecords.co.uk Manager: Tony Patoto. Office Mgr: Clive Sherwood. Mkting/Distrib: Jonathan Brown. Dist: Fierce

Fury Records PO Box 52, Aylesham, Kent CT3 3UF **t** 01304 842 192 **f** 01304 842 325 **e** info@fury-records.com **w** fury-records.com Owner: Dell Richardson. Dist: Windsong Intl./Caroline 2

Future Earth Records 59 Fitzwilliam St, Wath Upon Dearne, Rotherham, South Yorks S63 7HG **t** 01709 872875 **e** records@future-earth.co.uk **w** future-earth.co.uk MD: David Moffitt.

Future Music (see Harmonia Mundi (UK) Ltd)

Future Underground Nation 80 Monks Rd, Exeter, Devon EX4 7BE **t** 01392 490064 **f** 01392 420580 **e** fun@fun-1.com **w** fun-1.com Label Mgr: Colin Mitchell. MD: Colin Mitchell. Dist: Amato

Futureproof Records Ltd 330 Westbourne Park Rd, London W11 1EQ **t** 020 7792 8597 **f** 020 7221 3694 **e** info@futureproofmusic.com **w** futureproofmusic.com MD: Phil Legg.

Gallic (see Silverword Music Group)

Gammer Records 39 Ivygreen Road, Chorlton, Manchester M21 9AG **t** 0161 860 4133 **e** h.gammer@virgin.net Proprietor: Gammer.

Garageband (UK) Air Studios, Lyndhurst Rd, London NW3 5NG **t** 020 7794 0660 **f** 020 7916 2784 **e** artistmanager@garageband.com **w** garageband.com UK A&R: Adam Sharp.

GAS Records 10 St John's Square, Glastonbury, Somerset BA6 9LJ **t** 01458 833040 **f** 01458 833958 **e** info@planetgong.co.uk **w** planetgong.co.uk Contact: Johnny Greene

Gaudeamus (see Sanctuary Classics)

Geffen (see Polydor Records)

Genepool Records 34 Windsor Rd, Teddington, Middlesex TW11 0SF **t** n/a **f** n/a **e** contact@genepoolrecords.com **w** genepoolrecords.com Dir: Peter Ward-Edwards. Dist: Genepool/Universal

Genius Records Ltd PO Box 22949, London N10 3ZH **t** 020 8444 0987 **e** genius@brmmusic.com **w** brmmusic.com A&R: Phillip Rose. MD: Bruce Ruffin. Dist: Avid/BMG

Genuine Recordings (see PIAS Recordings Ltd)

Georgian (see Divine Art Record Company Ltd)

Get Back (see Abstract Sounds)

Giant Pitch (see ATCR: Trance Communication)

Giant Records Woking, Surrey GU21 6NS **t** 01483 859 849 **e** mark.studio@ntlworld.com 57 Kingsway: Mark Taylor.

Giants Of Jazz (see Hasmick Promotions)

Gig Records UK (see Wayward Records)

Gimell Records PO Box 197, Beckley, Oxford, Oxfordshire 0X3 9YJ **t** 01865 358282 **f** 0870 056 8880 **e** info@gimell.com **w** gimell.com MD: Steve C Smith. Dist: Select

Glasgow Records Ltd Lovat House, Gavell Rd, Glasgow G65 9BS **t** 01236 826555 **f** 01236 825560 **e** sasha@glasgowrecords.com **w** glasgowrecords.com MD: Tessa Hartmann. Dist: AMD/Universal

Gliss (see GAS Records)

Glitterhouse Records 123c Cadogan Terrace, London E9 5HP **t** 020 8533 3577 or 07958 564 624 **e** tris@glitterhouserecords.co.uk **w** glitterhouserecords.co.uk MD: Tris Dickin.

Global Cuts/R&S Records UK PO Box 172, Hampton, Middlesex TW12 1BT **t** 020 8979 9880 or 020 8324 1980 **f** 020 8324 0016 **e** rob@globalcuts.fsnet.co.uk A&R: Rob Roar. Dist: Prime Distribution

Global Harmony Records Devonshire House, 223 Upper Richmond, London SW15 6SQ **t** 020 8780 0612 **f** 020 8789 8668 **e** steve@globalharmony.co.uk **w** globalharmony.co.uk A&R Manager: Steve Haswell. Dist: Intergroove

Global Talent Records 2nd Floor, 53 Frith St, London W1D 4SN **t** 020 7292 9600 **f** 020 7292 9611 **e** email@globaltalentgroup.com **w** globaltalentgroup.com MDs: Ashley Tabor, David Forecast.

Global Underground Kings House, Forth Banks, Newcastle upon Tyne NE1 3PA **t** 0191 232 4064 **f** 0191 232 5766 **e** firstname@globalunderground.co.uk **w** globalunderground.co.uk MD: Colin Tierney. Dist: Vital/THE

Global Warming Ltd 3rd Floor, Northburgh House, 10 Northburgh Street, London EC1V 0AT **t** 020 7549 0513 **f** 020 7549 0505 **e** globalwarming@btclick.com **w** globalwarmingrecords.com MD: John Pearson. Label Manager: Tim Soar. A&R: Trevor Holden. Dist: Pinnacle

Glossa (see Harmonia Mundi (UK) Ltd)

Going for a Song Ltd Chiltern House, 184 High Street, Berkhamsted, Hertfordshire HP4 3AP **t** 01442 877417 **f** 01442 870944 **e** sales@goingforasong.com **w** goingforasong.com Sales & Logistics C'tor: Luke White.

Gold Top Records (see Rumour Records Ltd)

Goldrush Records 9 Kinnoull Street, Perth, Scotland PH1 5EN **t** 01738 629730 **f** 01738 629730 **e** sales@goldrushrecords.co.uk **w** goldrushrecords.co.uk MD: John S. Thomson. Dist: Proper

Good Behaviour (see Fony Records)

Good Looking Records 84 Queens Road, Watford, Hertfordshire WD17 2LA **t** 01923 690700 **f** 01923 249495 **e** glo@glo.uk.com **w** glo.uk.com MD: Tony Fordham. Dist: GLD

Goom Disques (see Labels UK)

Gorgeous Music Suite D, 67 Abbey Rd, London NW8 0AE **t** 020 7724 2635 **f** 020 7724 2635 **e** production@gorgeousmusic.net **w** gorgeousmusic.net Director: David Ross. Label Mgr: Victoria Elliott. Dist: Pinnacle

Gotham Records PO Box 6003, Birmingham, West Midlands B45 0AR **t** 0121 477 9553 **f** 0121 693 2954 **e** Barry@gotham-records.com **w** gotham-records.com Proprietor: Barry Tomes.

Graduate Records PO Box 388, Holt Heath, Worcester, Worcestershire WR6 6WQ **t** 01905 620786 **f** 01905 620786 **e** davidrobertvirr@aol.com **w** graduaterecords.com MD: David Virr. Dist: Graduate

Gramavision (see Palm Pictures)

Gramophone Records Unit X, 37 Hamilton Road, Twickenham, Middx. TW2 6SN **t** 020 8894 2169 **e** Woo@radioscience.com; Reverbe@aol.com Dir: Bruce Woolley. Chairman: Matthew Seligman.

Grand Central Records Ltd Third Floor, Habib House, 9 Stevenson Square, Manchester M1 1DB **t** 0161 245 2002 **f** 0161 245 2003 **e** info@grandcentralrecords.com **w** grandcentralrecords.com Label Mgr: Iain Cooke. International: Phil Hopwood. Licensing: Rachel Wood. Dist: Vital

Grateful Dead (see Ace Records)

Great Western Records (see Rollercoaster Records)

Greensleeves Records Unit 14 Metro Centre, St John's Road, Isleworth, Middlesex TW7 6NJ **t** 020 8758 0564 **f** 020 8758 0811 **e** mail@greensleeves.net **w** greensleeves.net MD: Chris Sedgwick. Dist: Pinnacle

Greentrax Recordings Ltd Cockenzie Business Centre, Edinburgh Rd, Cockenzie, East Lothian EH32 0XL **t** 01875 814155 or 01875 815888 **f** 01875 813545 **e** greentrax@aol.com **w** greentrax.com MD: Ian D Green. Dist: Proper/Gordon Duncan

Grey Mause Records 155 Regents Park Rd, London NW1 8BB **t** 0871 900 8410 **e** info@greymause.com **w** GreyMause.com

Griffin & Co Church House, St.Mary's Gate, 96 Church St, Lancaster LA1 1TD **t** 01524 844399 **f** 01524 844335 **e** sales@griffinrecords.co.uk **w** griffinrecords.co.uk GM: Ian Murray.

GRONLAND RECORDS

9-10 Domingo Street, London EC1Y 0TA **t** 020 7553 9166 **f** 020 7553 9198 **e** thebear@groenland.com **w** gronland.co.uk MD: Rene Renner. Dist: Pinnacle

Groovefinder Records Flat 1, 19 Craneswater Park, Southsea, Portsmouth PO4 0NU **t** 07831 450 241 **e** jeff@groovefinderproductions.com **w** groovefinderproductions.com MD: Jeff Powell. Dist: Various

Groovetech Records 10 Latimer Industrial Estate, Latimer Road, London W10 6RQ **t** 020 8962 3350 **f** 020 8962 3355 **e** groovetechrecords@groovetech.com **w** groovetech.com Label Mgr: Ana Saskia Adang. Dist: Pinnacle

Groovin' Records PO Box 39, Hoylake, Cheshire CH47 2HP **t** 0151 632 6156 **e** info@groovinrecords.co.uk **w** groovinrecords.co.uk Contact: Al Willard Peterson Dist: DWM Music Company (USA)

Gross National Product (see More Protein Ltd)

Ground Groove (see Headzone Ltd)

GRP (see Universal Classics & Jazz (UK))

G2 (see Greentrax Recordings Ltd)

Guild (see Priory Records)

Gull Records (see Q Zone Ltd)

Gut (see Gut Recordings)

GUT RECORDINGS

Byron House, 112A Shirland Road, London W9 2EQ **t** 020 7266 0777 **f** 020 7266 7734 **e** general@gutrecords.com **w** gutrecords.com Chairman: Guy Holmes. MD: Steve Tandy. Creative Director: Caroline Workman. International: Fraser Ealey. A&R: Paul Martin. A&R Scout: Lucy Francis. Dist: Pinnacle

Gutta (Sweden) (see Plankton Records)

Habana Productions Ltd PO Box 370, Newquay, Cornwall TR8 5YZ **t** 01637 831011 **f** 01637 831037 **e** dimelbourne@aol.com Label Manager: Di Melbourne. MD: Rod Buckle.

Half-Inch Records PO Box 29067, London WC2H 9TD **t** 0870 2406968 **f** 0870 2406969 **e** info@half-inch.com **w** half-inch.com Label Manager: Tracie Taylor-Roberts. MD: Stephen Meade.

Hallmark (see Pickwick Group Ltd)

The Hallowe'en Society (see Adasam Limited)

Halo UK Records 88 Church Lane, London N2 0TB **t** 020 8444 0049 or 07711 062 309 **e** halomanagement@hotmail.com **w** halo-uk.net Dir: Mike Karl Maslen.

Handspun Records 45 Pembridge Road, London W11 3HG **t** 020 7727 6306 **f** 020 7792 2523 **e** handspunrecords@haveaniceday.ws **w** haveaniceday.ws Owner: Anthony Cooper.

Hannibal (see Palm Pictures)

Harbourtown Records PO Box 25, Ulverston, Cumbria LA12 7UN **t** 01229 588290 **f** 01229 588290 **e** records@hartown.demon.co.uk **w** harbourtownrecords.com MD: Gordon Jones. Dist: Proper/ADA

Hardleaders (see Kickin Music Ltd)

Harkit Records PO Box 617, Bushey Heath, Herts. WD23 1SX **t** 020 8385 7771 **f** 020 8421 8463 **e** sales@harkitrecords.com **w** harkitrecords.com MD: Michael Fishberg. Dist: Pinnacle

Harlem (see Eukatech Records)

Harmless Recordings (see Nascente World Music Label)

Harmonia Mundi (UK) Ltd 45 Vyner Street, London E2 9DQ **t** 020 8709 9509 **f** 020 8709 9501 **e** info.uk@harmoniamundi.com **w** harmoniamundi.com Press Officer: Celia Ballantyne.

Harper Collins Audio Books 77-85 Fulham Palace Road, Hammersmith, London W6 8JB **t** 020 8741 7070 or 020 8307 4618 **f** 020 8307 4517 or 020 8307 4440 **e** rosalie.george@harpercollins.co.uk **w** fireandwater.com Publishing Manager: Rosalie George.

Hasmick Promotions Unit 8, Forest Hill Trading Estate, London SE23 2LX **t** 020 8291 6777 **f** 020 8291 0081 **e** jasmine@hasmick.co.uk **w** hasmick.co.uk Contact: Carl Hazeldine Dist: Proper

Hatology (see Harmonia Mundi (UK) Ltd)

Haven Records St Mary's Works, St Mary's Plain, Norwich, Norfolk NR3 3AF **t** 01603 624290 or 01603 626221 **f** 01603 619999 **e** derek@backsrecords.co.uk **w** havenrecords.co.uk A&R: Derek Chapman/Boo Hewerdine. Dist: Backs/Shellshock

Head+Arm (see Sonic360)

Headline (see Hi-Note Music)

Headscope Headrest, Broadoak, Heathfield, East Sussex TN21 8TU **t** 01435 863994 **f** 01435 867027 **e** headscope@geesin.demon.co.uk **w** rongeesin.com Partner: Ron Geesin. Dist: Headscope Direct

Headstone Records 46 Tintagel Way, Woking, Surrey GU22 7DG **t** 01483 856 760 or 07811 387220 **e** colinfwspencer@hotmail.com MD: Colin Spencer. Dist: self

Headwrecker Records 21 Lancaster Rd, Seven Dials, Brighton BN1 5DG **t** 07810 658 764 or 07748 110 853 **e** info@headwreckerrecords.com **w** headwreckerrecords.com Dirs: Luke Bevans, Sarah Sherry. Dist: Absolute/Universal

Headzone Ltd 43 Canham Road, London W3 7SR **t** 020 8749 8860 **f** 020 8742 9462 **e** info@intergroove.co.uk **w** intergroove.co.uk MD: Andy Howarth. Dist: Intergroove

Heat Recordings 63 Hartland Rd, London NW6 6BH **t** 020 7625 5552 **f** 020 7625 5553 **e** info@heatrecordings.com **w** heatrecordings.com MD/A&R: Alex Payne. Marketing/Promotion: Rochelle McEnaney. Dist: Vital

Heavenly Recordings 47 Frith Street, London W1D 4SE **t** 020 7494 2998 **f** 020 7437 3317 **e** info@heavenlyrecordings.com **w** heavenly100.com MD: Jeff Barrett. Dist: EMI

Heavy Metal Records Ltd 152 Goldthorn Hill, Penn, Wolverhampton WV2 3JA **t** 01902 345345 **f** 01902 345155 **e** Paul.Birch@revolver-e.com **w** HeavyMetalRecords.com MD: Paul Birch. Press: Pete Black. A&R Manager: Russ Barstow. Dist: Plastic Head

Heavy Rotation Recordings PO Box 516, London HA8 7XL **t** 07905 888 865 **e** info@heavyrotation.co.uk **w** heavyrotation.co.uk Label Mgr: Simon Ross. Dist: Tuned

Hellsquad Records PO Box 44149, London SW6 2WQ **t** 020 7384 4469 or 07966 756 761 **f** 020 7384 4469 **e** tom@thedatsuns.com MD: Thomas Dalton. Dist: Pinnacle

Heraldic Jester (see Heraldic Records)

Heraldic Records Sovereign House, 12 Trewartha Road, Praa Sands, Penzance, Cornwall TR20 9ST **t** 01736 762826 **f** 01736 763328 **e** panamus@aol.com **w** songwriters-guild.co.uk MD: Roderick G Jones. Dist: Media UK

Heraldic Vintage (see Heraldic Records)

Hex Unit (see Gut Recordings)

Hi-Fi (see Everest Copyrights)

Hi-Note Music PO Box 26, Windsor, Berkshire SL4 2YX **t** 01784 432 868 **f** 01784 477 702 **e** info@hinotemusic.com **w** hinotemusic.com MD: Graham Brook.

Hidden Art Recordings (see Adasam Limited)

High Barn Records The Bardfield Centre, Great Bardfield, Braintree, Essex CM7 4SL **t** 01371 811291 **f** 01371 811404 **e** info@high-barn.com **w** high-barn.com MD: Chris Bullen.

Higher State 95-99 North Street, London SW4 0HF **t** 020 7627 5656 **f** 020 7627 5757 **e** info@higherstate.co.uk **w** higherstate.co.uk A&R Mgr: Jamie Pierce. Dist: Essential

Hip Bop (see Silva Screen Records)

Hit Mania Ltd 6, Albemarle St, London W1S 4HA **t** 020 7499 7451 **f** 020 7499 7452 **e**info@hitmania.co.uk **w** hitmania.com Office Manager: Laura Fasser.

The Hit Music Company Shepperton Film Studios, Studios Rd, Shepperton, Middx TW17 0QD **t** 01932 562 611 **e** chet@thehitmusiccompany.com W thehitmusiccompany.com MD: Chet Selwood.

HMV Classics (see EMI Classics & Jazz)

Hoax Records PO Box 23604, London E7 0YT **t** 0870 910 6666 **e** hoax@hoaxrecords.com **w** hoaxrecords.com MD: Ben Angwin.

Holier Than Thou Records Ltd 46 Rother St, Stratford on Avon, Warwickshire CV37 6LT **t** 01789 268661 **e** httrecords@aol.com **w** holierthanthourecords.com A&R Director: David Begg. Dist: Prosonic

Hombre Recordings PO Box 2051, Bristol BS99 7GJ **t** 0117 330 8778 **f** 0117 330 8778 **e** info@hombre.f2s.com **w** hombre.co.uk Label Mgr: Steve Nichols.

HomeFront Productions 47 Sydney Rd, Ealing, London W13 9EZ **t** 020 8579 4782 or 07980 822 517 **e** roland@rolandchadwick.com **w** rolandchadwick.com Director: Roland Chadwick. Dist: Red Hedgehog

Honchos Music (see NRK Sound Division Ltd)

Honeypot Records 8A Sudell Rd, Darwen, Blackburn BB3 3HD **t** 01254 771658 **f** 01254 771658 **e** natashahoneypot@hotmail.com **w** natashajones.org Label Mgr: Julie Jones.

Hook Recordings PO Box 32043, London NW1 9GE **t** +34 93 771 7241 **e** stuart@hookrecordings.com **w** hookrecordings.com Directors: Stuart Emslie/Chris Cowie. Dist: Intergroove UK

Hope Records (see Music Fusion Ltd)

Hope Music Group Loft 5, The Tobacco Factory, Raleigh Rd, Southville, Bristol BS3 1TF **t** 0117 953 5566 **f** 0117 953 7733 **e** info@hoperecordings.com **w** hoperecordings.com MD: Leon Alexander. MD: Steve Satterthwaite. Artist Manager: Matt Rickard. Label Manager: Luke Allen. Accounts: Rose Howie. Dist: Vital

Hope Recordings (see Hope Music Group)

Horatio Nelson PO Box 1123, London SW1P 1HB **t** 020 7828 6533 **f** 020 7828 1271 MD: Derek Boulton.

Hospital Records 182-184 Dartmouth Rd, Sydenham, London SE26 4QZ **t** 020 8613 0400 **f** 020 8613 0401 **e** info@hospitalrecords.com **w** hospitalrecords.com Marketing & Promotions: Tom Kelsey. Dist: SRD

Hot Dog (see Scratch Records)

Hot House Records (see Harmonia Mundi (UK) Ltd)

Hot Lead Records 2, Laurel Bank, Lowestwood, Huddersfield, Yorkshire HD7 4ER **t** 01484 846333 **f** 01484 846333 **e** HotLeadRecords@btopenworld.com **w** fimusic.co.uk MD: Ian R. Smith. Dist: Self distributed.

Hot Records PO Box 333, Brighton, East Sussex BN1 2EH **t** 01403 740260 **f** 01403 740261 **e** info@hotrecords.uk.com **w** hotrecords.uk.com GM: Andrew Bowles. Dist: Hot

Hotshot Records (see American Activities)

The House of Wax (see Global Warming Ltd)

Human Condition Records 120A West Granton Road, Edinburgh EH5 1PF **t** 0131 551 6632 **f** 0131 551 6632 **e** mail@humancondition.co.uk **w** humancondition.co.uk Dir: Jamie Watson. Dist: Shellshock

Hummingbird Records 22 Lower Leeson St, Dublin 2, Ireland **t** +353 1 662 7322 **f** +353 1 662 7323 **e** topfloor@indigo.ie **w** hummingbirdrecords.com MD: John Dunford.

Hwyl 2 The Square, Yapham, York, North Yorkshire YO42 1PJ **t** 01759 304514 **f** 01759 304514 **e** stevejparry@yahoo.co.uk **w** hwylnofio.com Director: Steve Parry. Dist: Cargo

Hydrogen Dukebox 89 Borough High Street, London SE1 1NL **t** 020 7357 9799 **e** hydrogen@dukebox.demon.co.uk **w** hydrogendukebox.com Contact: Doug Hart International & Orders: Andrew Regan. Dist: Pinnacle

Hyperion Records Ltd PO Box 25, London SE9 1AX **t** 020 8318 1234 **f** 020 8463 1230 **e** info@hyperion-records.co.uk **w** hyperion-records.co.uk Dir: Simon Perry. Dir: Simon Perry. Sales Mgr: Michael Spring. Press & Promotion: Jeanette Bevan. Dist: Select

I&B Records (Irish Music) Ltd 2A Wrentham Avenue, London NW10 3HA **t** 020 8960 9169 or 020 8960 9160 **f** 020 8968 7332 Director: Peter Browne.

I-Anka PO Box 917, London W10 5FA **t** 020 8968 6221 **f** 020 8964 2844 **e** ianka.records@mcmail.com **w** bobandy.cwc.net MD: J Punford. Dist: Jetstar

IDJ (see Incentive Music Ltd)

Iffy Biffa Records Welland House Farm, Spalding Marsh, Spalding, Lincs PE12 6HF **t** 07711 513791 **f** 01406 370478 **e** mark@iffybiffa.co.uk **w** iffybiffa.co.uk MD: Mark Bunn. Marketing & Promotion: Rob Perryman.

Ignition 54 Linhope Street, London NW1 6HL **t** 020 7298 6000 **f** 020 7258 0962 **e** mail@ignition-man.co.uk MD: Alec McKinlay. Dist: Pinnacle

IHT Records Unit 2D, Clapham North Arts Centre, 26-32 Voltaire Road, London SW4 6DH **t** 020 7720 7411 **f** 020 7720 8095 **e** rob@ihtrecords.com **w** davidgray.com Contact: Rob Holden

Ikon (see Priory Records)

Illicit Recordings 2A Southam St, London W10 5PH **t** 020 8960 3253 **f** 020 8968 5111 **e** ian@mumbo jumbo.co.uk **w** illicitrecordings.com MD: Ian Clifford. Dist: Amato

Imagemaker Sound and Vision PO Box 69, Launceston, Cornwall PL15 7YA **t** 01566 86308 **f** 01566 86308 **e** timwheater@aol.com **w** timwheater.com MD: Olive Lister.

Imaginary Music 2 Monument Cottages, Warpsgrove Lane, Chalgrove, Oxfordshire OX44 7RW **t** 01865 400286 **f** 01865 400286 **e** halls@dialin.net **w** soft.net.uk/gphall/ Contact: GP Hall

Immaterial Records PO Box 706, Ilford, Essex IG2 6ED **t** 07973 676160 **f** 020 7323 9008 **e** bij@btinternet.com Owner: Bijal Dodhia.

Immoral Recordings (see JPS Recordings)

Impact Records (see Mo's Music Machine)

Imprint (see D.O.R.)

In Jeopardy Records 3 Fleece Yard, Market Hill, Buckingham MK18 1JX **t** 01280 821170 **f** 01280 821840 **e** injeopardy@reactstudios.co.uk **w** injeopardy.co.uk Lbl Mgr: Sarah Hodgetts.

In Music Ltd 2 The Hall, Turners Green Rd, Wadhurst, East Sussex TN5 6TR **t** 01892 785005 **f** 01892 785023 **e** info@inmusicltd.co.uk **w** inmusicltd.co.uk MD: Alex Branson.

Incentive Music Ltd 103 Gaunt St, London SE1 6DP **t** 020 7740 8880 **f** 020 7740 8802 **e** incentive@incentivemusic.co.uk **w** incentivemusic.com MD: Nick Halkes. Dist: Universal

INDEPENDIENTE LTD

independiente

The Drill Hall, 3 Heathfield Terrace, Chiswick, London W4 4JE **t** 020 8747 8111 **f** 020 8747 8113 **e** firstname@independiente.co.uk **w** independiente.co.uk Chairman: Andy Macdonald. Managing Director: Mark Richardson. General Manager: Nina Frykberg. Director of Finance & Business Affairs: Neville Acaster. A&R **f** 020 8400 5399. Legal **f** 020 8995 5907. Andy's **f** 020 8400 5509. Dist: TEN

Indie 500 (see New Leaf Records)

Indigo Records (see Sanctuary Records Group)

Indipop Records P.O.Box 369, Glastonbury, Somerset BA6 8YN **t** 01749 831 674 **f** 01749 831 674 MD: Steve Coe. Dist: MACH2

Inductive Records PO Box 20503, London NW8 0WY **t** 020 7586 5427 **f** 020 7483 2164 **e** inductrec@aol.com MD: Colin Peel.

Industry (see Resist Music)

Infectious (see Atlantic Records UK)

Inferno Cool (see Inferno Records)

Inferno Records 32-36 Telford Way, London W3 7XS **t** 020 8742 9300 **f** 020 8742 9097 **e** pat@infernorecords.co.uk **w** infernorecords.co.uk Heaf of A&R: Pat Travers. Dist: Pinnacle

Infur (see Seriously Groovy Music)

INFX Records Buckinghamshire Chilterns Uni., Wellesbourne Campus, Kingshill Road, High Wycombe, Buckinghamshire HP13 5BB **t** 01494 52214 ex 4020 **f** 01494 465432 **e** fmacke01@bcuc.ac.uk **w** bcuc.ac.uk Head of Music: Frazer Mackenzie.

Ink (see Distinct'ive Records)

Inner Rhythm (see Born to Dance Records)

Inner Sanctum Recordings (see Adasam Limited)

Innerground Records 8 Roland Mews, Stepney Green, London E1 3JT **t** 020 7377 9494 **f** 020 7377 9868 **e** info@innergroundrecords.com MD: Oliver J. Brown.

INNOCENT RECORDS

Kensal House, 553-579 Harrow Road, London W10 4RH **t** 020 8962 5800 **f** 020 8962 5801 **e** firstname.lastname@virginmusic.com **w** virginrecords.co.uk Dir of A&R: Jamie Nelson. Label Mgr: Sara Freeman.

Instant Hit PO Box 34, Ventnor, Isle of Wight PO38 1YQ **t** 01983 857 079 **e** jkt@diamondisle.co.uk **w** diamondisle.co.uk MD: Jon Monks. Dist: Self

Instant Karma 2nd Floor, 9-10 Savile Row, London W1S 3PF **t** 020 7851 0900 **f** 020 7851 0901 **e** zen@instantkarma.co.uk **w** instantkarma.co.uk Chairman: Rob Dickins. Asst. to Chairman: Fiona Porter

Record Companies

Intec Records Reverb House, Bennett St, London W4 2AH **t** 020 8742 7693 **f** 020 8994 8617 **e** intec@intecrecords.com **w** intecrecords.com Label Manager: Tintin Chambers. Dist: Vital

Interactive Music Ltd 2 Carriglea, Naas Rd, Dublin 12, Ireland **t** +353 1 419 5039 **f** +353 1 429 3850 **e** info@interactive-music.com **w** interactive-music.com Dir: Suriya Moodliar. Dist: Warner

Intercom Recordings PO Box 32, Beccles NR34 9XJ **t** 01502 501414 **f** 01502 501414 **e** inter.comrecordings@virgin.net **w** intercomrecordings.com Label Manager: Jay Hurren.

Interscope (see Polydor Records)

Introducing (see Detour Records Ltd)

Intruder Records PO Box 22949, London N10 3ZH **t** 020 8444 0987 **e** intruder@brmmusic.com **w** brmmusic.com A&R: Simon Kay. MD: Bruce Ruffin. Dist: Avid/BMG

Invisible Hands Music 15 Chalk Farm Rd, London NW1 8AG **t** 020 7284 3322 **f** 020 7284 4455 **e** info@invisiblehands.co.uk **w** invisiblehands.co.uk MD: Charles Kennedy. Dist: Universal

Iodine Records (see Wayward Records)

Iona Records (see Lismor Recordings)

Ipecac (see Southern Records)

Iris Light Records 9 Station Walk, Highbridge, Somerset TA9 3HQ **t** 01278 780904 **f** 01278 780904 **e** iLIGHT@irislight.co.uk **w** irislight.co.uk MD: Adam Sykes.

IRL PO Box 30884, London W12 9AZ **t** 020 8746 7461 **f** 020 8749 7441 **e** info@independentrecordsltd.com **w** independentrecordsltd.com Dirs: David Jaymes & Tom Haxell.

Irma UK 8 Putney High Street, London SW15 1SL **t** 020 8780 0906 or 07930 381 330 **f** 020 8780 0545 **e** irmauk@btinternet.com **w** irmagroup.com Managing Director: Corrado Dierna. Licensing Manager: Elisa Molisso. Editor: Corrado Dierna.

Iron Man (see Music Mercia)

ISLAND RECORDS GROUP

Tony woods

22 St Peters Square, London W6 9NW **t** 020 8910 3333 **f** 020 8748 1998 **e** firstname.lastname@umusic.com **w** umusic.com. MD: Nick Gatfield. MD, Universal label: Paul Adam. General Manager: Jason Iley. Finance Director, David Sharpe. Legal & Business Affairs Director: Claire Sugrue. Promotions Director: Ruth Parrish. Press Director: Ted Cummings. Dist: Universal

---

Isobar Records 56 Gloucester Place, London W1U 8HW **t** 020 7486 3297 or 07956 493 692 **f** 020 7486 3297 **e** info@isobarrecords.com **w** isobarrecords.com Co-MD: Peter Morris.

It's Fabulous (see Truelove Records)

J & S Construction (see Taste Media Ltd)

Jackpot Records PO Box 2272, Rottingdean, Brighton BN2 8XD **t** 01273 304681 **f** 01273 308120 **e** steveb@a7music.com **w** a7music.com Label Manager: Steve B. Dist: Amato

Jam Central Records Unit 8, College Road Business Park, College Rd Nth, Aston Clinton, Bucks HP22 5EZ **t** 01296 633311 or 07765 258225 **f** 01296 633311 **e** admin@jamcentralrecords.co.uk **w** jamcentralrecords.co.uk MD: Stuart Robb.

Jasmine Records (see Hasmick Promotions)

JAY Productions 107 Kentish Town Rd, London NW1 8PD **t** 020 7485 9593 **f** 020 7485 2282 **e** john@jayrecords.com **w** jayrecords.com MD: John Yap. Dist: Koch Distribution

Jaygee Cassettes 5 Woodfield, Burnham on Sea, Somerset TA8 1QL **t** 01278 789352 **f** 01278 789352 **e** roger@jaygeecassettes.co.uk **w** babysooth.com Snr Partners: Roger & Patricia Wannell.

Jazz Fudge Recordings PO Box 535A, Surbiton, Surrey KT6 7WJ **t** 020 7326 0606 **f** 020 7735 6115 **e** mail@jazzfudge.co.uk **w** jazzfudge.co.uk Label Mgr: Dan Larkin. Dist: Pinnacle

Jazz Monkey (see JML Records (Jazz Monkey Limited))

Jazz Point (see Harmonia Mundi (UK) Ltd)

JBO (see Junior Boy's Own)

Jeepster Recordings Ltd PO Box 107, Winchester, Hants SO22 5ZH **t** 08451 260621 or 01962 869288 **f** 01962 850195 **e** info@jeepster.co.uk **w** jeepster.co.uk Label Manager: Kay Heath. Dist: Pinnacle

Jewish Music Heritage Recordings PO Box 232, Harrow, Middlesex HA1 2NN **t** 020 8909 2445 **f** 020 8909 1030 **e** jewishmusic@jmi.org.uk **w** jmi.org.uk MD: Geraldine Auerbach MBE.

JFM Records 11 Alexander House, Tiller Road, London E14 8PT **t** 020 7987 8596 **f** 020 7987 8596 **e** julius@amserve.com MD: Julius Pemberton Maynard. Dist: Hawk S

Jive (see BMG UK & Ireland Ltd)

JML Records (Jazz Monkey Limited) 133 Cassiobury Park Avenue, Watford, Herts WD18 7LH **t** 07941 121822 **f** 01923 227827 **e** info@jazzmonkey.co.uk **w** jazzmonkey.co.uk MD: Karalyne Chalmers. Dist: Cargo

Johnboy Records P.O Box 22877, London NW9 82S **t** 07956 811149 **f** 0870 284 7322 **e** info@johnboyrecords.com **w** johnboyrecords.com Director: Mark Uttley.

Joint Venture (see Hot Records)

JOOF Recordings Unit 5 Waldo Works, Waldo Rd, London NW10 6AW **t** 020 8964 8890 **f** 020 8960 5741 **e** mail@joof.uk.com **w** joof.uk.com A&R: John Fleming. Lbl Mgr: Russel Coultart. Dist: Amato

JPS Recordings PO Box 2643, Reading, Berks RG5 4GF **t** 0118 969 9269 or 07885 058 911 **f** 0118 969 9264 **e** johnjpsuk@aol.com MD: John Saunderson.

JSP Records PO Box 1584, London N3 3NW **t** 020 8346 8663 **f** 020 8346 8848 **e** john@jsprecords.com **w** jpsrecords.com MD: John Stedman.

Jumpin' & Pumpin' (see Passion Music)

Jungle Records Old Dairy Mews, 62 Chalk Farm Road, London NW1 8AN **t** 020 7267 0171 **f** 020 7267 0912 **e** enquiries@jungle-records.com **w** jungle-records.com Directors: Alan Hauser, Graham Combi. Dist: SRD

Junior Boy's Own The Saga Centre, 326 Kensal Rd, London W10 5BZ **t** 020 8960 4495 **f** 020 8960 3256 **e** mail@junior-records.com **w** junior-records.com A&R Dir: Paul Byrne. MD: Steven Hall. Dist: Amato

Junior Choice (see CYP Limited)

Junior Recordings (see Junior Boy's Own)

Jus Listen (see RF Records)

Just Music PO Box 19780, London SW15 1WU **t** 020 8741 6020 **f** 020 8741 8362 **e** justmusic@justmusic.co.uk **w** justmusic.co.uk Dirs: Serena & John Benedict. Dist: Pinnacle

K (see Southern Records)

K-Scope (see Snapper Music)

K-Tel Entertainment (UK) K-tel House, 12 Fairway Drive, Greenford, Middlesex UB6 8PW **t** 020 8747 7550 **f** 020 8575 2264 **e** info@k-tel-uk.com **w** k-tel.com GM: Janie Webber. Dist: K-tel

!K7 Records 1 Devonport Mews, London W12 8NG **t** 020 8762 9910 **f** 020 8762 9912 **e** katherine@k7.com **w** k7.com UK Ops Mgr: Katherine Eykelenboom. Rapster Records: rapsterrecords.com Dist: Vital

Kabuki 85 Camden St, London NW1 0HP **t** 020 7916 2142 **f** 0870 051 0158 **e** email@kabuki.co.uk **w** kabuki.co.uk Manager: Sheila Naujoks.

Kamaflage Records (see Dragonfly Records)

Kamaric (see Fury Records)

Kamera Shy (see Gotham Records)

Kamikaze (see Superglider Records)

Kaos Recordings PO Box 780, Hemel Hempstead, Herts HP1 3BD **t** 020 8871 3761 **f** 0709 200 4055 **e** ellise@sirenproductions.freeserve.co.uk Label Mgr: Ellise Theuma.

Karmagiraffe 3 Stucley Place, Camden, London NW1 8NS **t** 020 7284 4484 **f** 020 7482 6162 **e** mail@karmagiraffe.com **w** karmagiraffe.com A&R Manager: Olli Berger.

Karon Records 20 Radstone Court, Hillview Rd, Woking, Surrey GU22 7NB **t** 01483 755153 **e** ron.roker@btinternet.com MD: Ron Roker.

Keda Records The Sight And Sound Centre, Priory Way, Southall, Middlesex UB2 5EB **t** 020 8843 1546 **f** 020 8574 4243 **e** kuljit@compuserve.com **w** keda.co.uk Owner: Kuljit Bhamra.

Kent (see Ace Records)

Keswick (see Loose Records)

Kevin Mayhew (see Priory Records)

Key Recordings Evans Business Centre, Sycamore Trading Estate, Squires Gate Lane, Blackpool, Lancs FY4 3RL **t** 0870 046 6629 **f** 0870 138 9776 **e** dan@datoga.com **w** keymusicgroup.com Dir: Dan Brooks.

Keystone Records Ltd 112 Gunnersbury Ave, London W5 4HB **t** 020 8993 7441 **f** 020 8992 9993 **e** keystone@dorm.co.uk **w** keystone-records.co.uk GM: John O'Reilly.

Kickin Music Ltd Unit 8, Acklam Workshops, 10 Acklam Rd, London W10 5QZ **t** 020 8964 3300 **f** 020 8964 4400 **e** info@kickinmusic.com **w** kickinmusic.com MD: Peter Harris. Dist: SRD

KIDZ (see CYP Limited)

Kingpin (see Truelove Records)

Kingsize Records The Old Bakehouse, Hale St, Staines, Middx TW18 4UW **t** 01784 458700 **f** 01784 458333 **e** info@kingsize.co.uk **w** kingsize.co.uk Lbl Mgr: Julian Shay. Dist: Intergroove

Kingsway Music 26-28 Lottbridge Drove, Eastbourne, East Sussex BN23 6NT **t** 01323 437700 **f** 01323 411970 **e** music@kingsway.co.uk **w** kingsway.co.uk A&R Mgr: Caroline Bonnett.

Kismet Records 64 Westbourne Park Villas, London W2 5EB **t** 020 7727 5378 **f** 020 7681 1680 **e** info@kismetrecords.com **w** kismetrecords.com Director: Gilly Da Silva. Dist: Intergroove

Kitchenware Records 7 The Stables, Saint Thomas St, Newcastle upon Tyne, Tyne and Wear NE1 4LE **t** 0191 230 1970 **f** 0191 232 0262 **e** info@kware.demon.co.uk **w** kitchenwarerecords.com Administration: Nicki Turner.

Klone (see Rumour Records Ltd)

KlubDJ PO Box 5333, Daventry NN11 5FN **t** 0871 717 0450 **f** 0871 717 0460 **e** info@klubdj.co.uk **w** klubdj.co.uk General Manager: John Barnet.

Kom (see Genius Records Ltd)

Kooba Cuts 6 Westleigh Court, 28 Birdhurst Rd, South Croydon, Surrey CR2 7EA **t** 020 8667 1982 **e** simon@koobarecords.com **w** koobarecords.com Head of A&R: Simon King.

Kranky (see Southern Records)

KRL 9 Watt Road, Hillington, Glasgow G52 4RY **t** 0141 882 9060 **f** 0141 883 3686 **e** krl@krl.co.uk **w** krl.co.uk MD: Gus McDonald.

Krome Recordings Ltd (London) Sub Base Studios, 107 Holland Road, London NW10 5AT **t** 020 8961 0427 or 07958 143 966 **f** 020 8961 0427 **e** info@krome recordings.plus.com **w** kromerecordings.org MD: Andrew Radix.

Krypton Records 31 Fife St, St James, Northampton NN5 5BH **t** 01604 752800 **f** 01604 752800 **e** ray@thejets.co.uk **w** thejets.co.uk Contact: Ray Cotton Dist: Fury

KSO Records PO Box 159, Chatham, Kent ME5 7AQ **t** 07956 120 837 **e** ksorecords@hotmail.com **w** ksorecords.pwp.blueyonder.co.uk Management: Antonio Sloane, Marcus Antony. Legal Rep: Howard Livingstone.

Kudos Records Ltd 79 Fortess Rd, Kentish Town, London NW5 1AG **t** 020 7482 4555 **f** 020 7482 4551 **e** info@kudosrecords.co.uk **w** kudosrecords.co.uk Directors: Danny Ryan/Mike Hazell.

Kíla Records Charlemont House, 33 Charlemont Street, Dublin 2 **t** +353 1 476 0627 **f** +353 1 476 0627 **e** info@kilarecords.com **w** kila.ie Director: Colm O'Snodaigh.

La Cooka Ratcha (see Voiceprint)

Labels UK 429 Harrow Rd, London W10 4RE **t** 020 8960 9539 **f** 020 8968 3054 **e** Firstname.lastname@labelsmusic.com **w** cityslang.com Promotions & Market'g: Howard Corner, Liz McCudden. Dist: EMI

Lager Records 10 Barley Rise, Baldock, Hertfordshire SG7 6RT **t** 01462 636799 **f** 01462 636799 **e** dan@Lockupmusic.co.uk Dir: Steve Knight. A&R: Dan Bird. Promotion: A. Whyte. Dist: Direct

Lake (see Fellside Recordings Ltd)

Lakota Records 43 Donnybrook Manor, Donnybrook, Dublin 4, Ireland **t** +353 1 283 9071 **f** +353 1 283 9071 **e** info@lakotarecords.com **w** lakotarecords.com MD: Conor Brooks. Director: Conor O'Flaherty.

Lammas Records 34 Carlisle Avenue, St Albans, Hertfordshire AL3 5LU **t** 01727 851553 **f** 01727 851553 **e** enquiries@lammas.co.uk **w** lammas.co.uk Prop: Lance Andrews. Dist: Discovery / Griffin

LAS Records UK PO Box 14303, London SE26 4ZH **t** 07000 472572 **f** 07000 472572 **e** info@latinartsgroup.com **w** latinartsgroup.com Director: Hector Rosquete.

Laserlight (see Delta Music plc)

Late Night Tales (see Whoa Music)

Laughing Outlaw Records (UK) Clematis Cottage, Village Rd, Christleton, Chester CH3 7AS **t** 01244 335 643 or 07855 724 798 **e** laughingoutlaw@talk21.com **w** laughingoutlaw.com.au Label Mgr: Geraint Jones. Dist: Pinnacle

Laughing Stock Productions. 32 Percy St, London W1T 2DE **t** 020 7637 7943 **f** 020 7436 1666 **e** mike@laughingstock.co.uk **w** laughingstock.co.uk Dir: Mike O'Brien. Dist: Vital

Laughter Label (see Sound Entertainment Ltd)

The Leaf Label Suite 209, Bon Marche Building, 241 Ferndale Rd, London SW9 8BJ **t** 020 7733 1818 **f** 020 7733 5818 **e** leaf@posteverything.com **w** posteverything.com/leaf MD: Tony Morley. Dist: SRD

Leningrad Masters (see Priory Records)

Leopard Records 23 Thrayle House, Stockwell Road, London SW9 0XU **t** 020 7564 8476 **f** 020 7564 8476 **e** erroljoneslm@hotmail.com **w** erroljoneslm.com MD: Errol Jones. Dist: Jetstar

Lewis Recordings PO Box 12809, Hampstead, London NW3 4WT **t** 020 8523 9578 **f** 020 8523 9601 **e** info@LewisRecordings.com **w** LewisRecordings.com Director: Mike Lewis.

Lex (see Warp)

Liberty (see EMI Music UK & Ireland)

Liberty City Records 1 Tabley Close, Victoria Mansions, Macclesfield, Cheshire SK10 3SL **t** 07812 201 133 **e** darren@libertycity.biz **w** libertycity.biz Contact: Darren Eager

Lick Records (see Automatic Records)

Lifetime Records 18 St Georges Road, St Margarets, Twickenham TW1 1QR **t** 020 8892 4810 **f** 020 8744 0413 **e** gpm@pennies.demon.co.uk Dir: Graeme Perkins.

Limbo Records 23 Bath Street, Glasgow G2 1HU **t** 0141 332 4806 **f** 0141 353 3039 **e** billylimbo@aol.com **w** 23rdprecinct.co.uk MD: Billy Kiltie. Dist: Intergroove/Prime

Lindenburg (see Priory Records)

Line-Up PMC 9A Tankerville Place, Newcastle-upon-Tyne, Tyne and Wear NE2 3AT **t** 0191 281 6449 **f** 0191 212 0913 **e** info@line-up.co.uk **w** line-up.co.uk MD: Christopher Murtagh.

Linn Records Glasgow Road, Waterfoot, Eaglesham G76 0EQ **t** 0141 303 5026 **f** 0141 303 5007 **e** info@linnrecords.co.uk **w** linnrecords.com Business Manager: Caroline Dooley. Dist: ID

Lipstick (see Abaco Records)

Liquid Asset Recordings (see Tailormade Music Ltd)

Liquid Sound (see Dragonfly Records)

Lismor Recordings PO Box 7264, Glasgow, Strathclyde G46 6YE **t** 0141 637 6010 **f** 0141 637 6010 **e** lismor@lismor.com **w** lismor.com MD: Ronnie Simpson.

Lithium (see Dangerous Records)

Little Piece of Jamaica 55 Finsbury Park Road, London N4 2JY **t** 020 7359 0788 or 07973 630 729 **f** 020 7226 2168 **e** paulhuelpoj@yahoo.co.uk Dir: Paul Hue.

Livewire (see K-Tel Entertainment (UK))

Living Era (see Sanctuary Classics)

Lizard King Records 151 City Rd, London EC1V 1JH **t** 020 7253 2700 **f** 020 7253 2740 **e** chris@lizardkingrecords.com **w** lizardkingrecords.com Label Mgr: Ben Durling. Dist: Pinnacle

Loaded (see Skint Records)

Lock The Coachhouse, Mansion Farm, Liverton Hill, Sandway, Maidstone, Kent ME17 2NJ **t** 01622 858300 **f** 01622 858300 **e** info@eddielock.com **w** eddielock.co.uk A&R Mgr: Eddie Lock. Dist: Essential/Unique

Locked On Records 679 Holloway Road, London N19 5SE **t** 020 7263 4660 **f** 020 7263 9669 **e** stevehill@puregroove.co.uk **w** puregroove.co.uk MD: Tarik Nashnush.

Lockjaw Records 1 Oaklands, Cradley, Malvern, Worcestershire WR13 5LA **t** 01886 880035 **f** 01886 880135 **e** info@lockjawrecords.co.uk **w** lockjawrecords.co.uk Business Affs Mgr: Jack Turner. Dist: Pinnacle

LOE Records LOE House, 159 Broadhurst Gardens, London NW6 3AU **t** 020 7328 6100 **f** 020 7624 6384 **e** watanabe@loe.uk.net Creative Mgr: Jonny Wilson.

London Records (see Warner Bros Records)

London Independent Records PO Box 3136, Barnet, Herts EN5 1DY **t** 020 8447 3862 **f** 020 8447 3862 **e** info@london-independent.co.uk **w** london-independent.co.uk Director: Jan Hart.

LongMan Records West House, Forthaven, Shoreham-by-Sea, W. Sussex BN43 5HY **t** 01273 453422 **f** 01273 452914 **e** richard@longman-records.com **w** longman-records.com Director: Richard Durrant. Dist: Disc Imports Ltd

Loog Records (see Polydor Records)

Loose PO Box 67, Runcorn, Cheshire WA7 4NL **t** 01928 566261 **e** jaki.florek@virgin.net Contact: Jaki Florek

Loose Music Unit 205, 5-10 Eastman Road, London W3 7YG **t** 020 8749 9330 **f** 020 8749 2230 **e** info@loosemusic.com **w** loosemusic.com MD/A&R: Tom Bridgewater. Dist: Vital

Loose Records Pinery Building, Highmoor, Wigton, Cumbria CA7 9LW **t** 016973 45422 **f** 016973 45422 **e** edwards@looserecords.com **w** looserecords.com A&R: Tim Edwards. Dist: CrucialMusic.co.uk

Loose Tie Records 15 Stanhope Rd, London N6 5NE **t** 020 8340 7797 **f** 020 8340 6923 **e** paul@paulrodriguezmus.demon.co.uk MD: Paul Rodriguez. Dist: Self; Avid

Loriana Music 30A Tudor Drive, Gidea Park, Romford, Essex RM2 5LH **t** 01708 750 185 **f** 01708 750 185 **e** info@lorianamusic.com **w** lorianamusic.com MD: Jean-Louis Fargier.

Lost Dog Recordings 1103 Argyle Street, Glasgow G3 8ND **t** 0141 243 2439 **e** info@lostdogrecordings.com **w** lostdogrecordings.com Label Manager: Jonathan Stone. Dist: Vital

Lost Highway (see Mercury Records)

Lovechild Records (see Big Cat (UK) Records)

Lovers Leap (see Ariwa Sounds Ltd)

Low Quality Accident 71 Lansdowne Rd, Purley, Surrey CR8 2PD **t** 020 8645 0013 **e** flamingofleece@yahoo.com **w** geocities.com/flamingofleece MD: Alvin LeDup.

Lowriders (see 3 Beat Label Management)

Loîq (see 3 Beat Label Management)

LPMusic 14 Bellfield St, Edinburgh EH15 2BP **t** 0131 468 1716 **e** admin@lpmusic.org.uk **w** lpmusic.org.uk MD: Lee Patterson.

LPOJ (see Little Piece of Jamaica)

Lucky 7's (see Tip World)

Luggage (see Silverword Music Group)

Luminous Records P.O Box 341, Deal, Kent CT14 6AZ **t** 01304 369053 **e** luminousrecords@hotmail.com **w** luminousrecords.co.uk MD: Howard Werth.

Lunar Records 5-6 Lombard Street, East, Dublin 2, Ireland **t** +353 1 677 4229 **f** +353 1 671 0421 **e** lunar@indigo.ie Gen Mgr: Judy Cardiff. Dist: Chart

Lyrinx (see Harmonia Mundi (UK) Ltd)

Macjaz (see Corban Recordings)

Macmeanmna Gladstone Buildings, Quay Brae, Portree, Isle Of Skye IV51 9DB **t** 01478 612990 **f** 01478 613263 **e** info@gaelicmusic.com **w** gaelicmusic.com Partner: Arthur Cormack. Dist: Macmeanmna, Gordon Duncan, Highlander Music

Madacy Entertainment Group (GB) Ltd 39-41 Chase Side, Southgate, London N14 5BP **t** 020 8242 5570 **f** 020 8242 5571 **e** madacyuk@aol.com **w** madacyuk.com Operations Dir: Karen Moran.

Madfish (see Snapper Music)

Madrigal Records Guy Hall, Awre, Gloucestershire GL14 1EL **t** 01594 510512 **f** 01594 510512 **e** artists@madrigalmusic.co.uk **w** madrigalmusic.co.uk MD: Nick Ford.

Maelstrom (see New State Entertainment)

Maestro Records PO Box 2255, Mitcham, Surrey CR4 3BG **t** 020 8687 2008 **f** 020 8687 1998 **e** music@maestrorecords.com **w** maestrorecords.com MD: Tommy Sanderson. Dist: self

Magick Eye Records PO Box 3037, Wokingham, Berks RG40 4GR **t** 0118 932 8320 **f** 0118 932 8237 **e** info@magickeye.com **w** magickeye.com MD: Chris Hillman.

Magik Muzik UK (see New State Entertainment)

Main Spring Recordings PO Box 38648, London W13 9WJ **t** 020 8567 1376 **e** blair@main-spring.com **w** main-spring.com MD: Blair McDonald.

Majic Music PO Box 66, Manchester M12 4XJ **t** 0161 225 9991 **f** 0161 225 9991 **e** info@majicmusic.co.uk **w** sirenstorm.com Dir: Mike Coppock. Dist: Clubscene distribution

Mango (see Island Records Group)

Mantra (see Beggars Banquet Records)

MAP Records 27 Abercorn Place, London NW8 9DX **t** 07905 116 455 **f** 020 7624 7219 **e** anthony.pringle@virgin.net **w** mapmusic.co.uk Head of A&R: Anthony Pringle.

Marine Parade Records Loft 5, Tobacco Factory, Raleigh Road, Bristol BS3 1TF **t** 0117 953 5566 **f** 0117 953 7733 **e** luke@marineparade.co.uk **w** marineparade.net Label Manager: Luke Allen. Dist: SRD

Market Square Records Market House, Market Square, Winslow, Bucks MK18 3AF **t** 01296 715228 **f** 01296 715486 **e** peter@marketsquarerecords.co.uk **w** marketsquarerecords.co.uk MD: Peter Muir. Dist: Koch

Mastercuts (see Beechwood Music Ltd)

Matador Records Ltd PO Box 20125, London W10 5WA **t** 020 8969 5533 **f** 020 8969 6633 **e** info@matadoreurope.com **w** matadoreurope.com Gen Mgr: Mike Holdsworth. Dist: Vital

Maximum Boost Recordings 1 Andover Street, Digbeth, Birmingham B5 5RG **t** 0121 633 4742 **f** 0121 643 4904 **e** drmaximum@compuserve.com **w** maximum-boost.co.uk Contact: Carole Beirne Dist: Vinyl Distribution Ltd

Mazaruni (see Ariwa Sounds Ltd)

MC Rex 7 Northington Street, London WC1N 2JF **t** 020 7404 2647 **f** 020 7404 2647 **e** kevin.delascasas@lineone.net **w** mcsstudio.com Music Producer: Kevin de Las Casas.

MCA (see Island Records Group)

MCI (see MCI - Music Collection International)

Media Records Ltd 1 Pepys Court, 84-86 The Chase, Clapham, London SW4 0NF **t** 020 7720 7266 **f** 020 7720 7255 **e** info@mediarec.co.uk **w** mediarec.co.uk MD: Peter Pritchard.

Medium Productions 74 St Lawrence Road, Upminster, Essex RM14 2UW **t** 07939 080524 **f** 01708 640291 **e** info@mediumproductions.co.uk **w** mediumproductions.co.uk MD: Debi Zornes. Dist: Voiceprint

Mega Hit Records (UK) PO Box 56, Boston, Lincolnshire PE22 8JL **t** 07976 553624 **e** chrisdunn@megahitrecordsuk.co.uk **w** megahitrecordsuk.co.uk Contact: Chris Kamara

Megabop Records PO Box 72, Beckenham, Kent BR3 5UR **t** 020 8650 2976 **f** 0870 922 3582 **e** info@megabop.plus.com **w** Megabop.com Dir: Paul Ballance. Dist: Absolute

Melankolic 12 Pembridge Road, London W11 3HL **t** 020 7727 6320 **f** 020 7727 6319 **e** office@melankolic.co.uk MD: Marc Picken. Dist: Virgin/EMI

Mellow Monkey Records 2 Stucley Place, Camden, London NW1 8NS **t** 020 7482 6660 **f** 020 7482 6606 **e** art@mainartery.demon.co.uk MD: Jo Mirowski.

Melodic 4th Floor, 20 Dale St, Manchester M1 1EZ **t** 0161 228 3070 **f** 0161 228 3070 **e** david@melodic.co.uk **w** melodic.co.uk MD: David Cooper.

Memnon Entertainment Ltd. Habib House, 3rd Floor, 9 Stevenson Square, Piccadilly, Manchester M1 1DB **t** 0161 238 8516 **f** 0161 236 6717 **e** memnon@btconnect.com **w** memnonentertainment.com Director: Rudi Kidd. Dist: PDC

Memoir (see Delta Music plc)

Memoir Records PO Box 66, Pinner, Middlesex HA5 2SA **t** 020 8866 4865 **f** 020 8866 7804 **e** mor@memoir.demon.co.uk **w** memoir.demon.co.uk MD: Gordon Gray. Dist: Delta/BMG

Meridian Records PO Box 317, London SE9 4SF **t** 020 8857 3213 **f** 020 8857 0731 **e** mail@meridian-records.co.uk MD: John Shuttleworth. Dist: Nimbus

MERCURY RECORDS

1 Sussex Place, Hammersmith, London W6 9XS
t 020 8910 5333 **f** 020 8910 5334
e firstname.lastname@umusic.com
w mercuryrecords.com MD: Greg Castell.
Exec VP: Matt Jagger. Promotions Dir: Bruno Morelli. Marketing Dir: Richard Marshall. Commercial Dir: Stephen Cuttell. Dir of Legal & Business Affairs: Adam Barker. Creative Dir: Tom Bird. Senior National Account Manager: Brian Regan. International Dir: Sian Thomas. Dist: Universal

Mesmobeat (see Stretchy Records Ltd)

Messy Productions Ltd Studio 2, Soho Recording Studios, 22-24 Torrington Place, London WC1E 7HJ **t** 020 7813 7202 **f** 020 7419 2333 **e** info@messypro.com **w** messypro.com MD: Zak Vracelli.

Messy Records 42 City Business Centre, Lower Road, Rotherhithe, London SE16 2XB **t** 020 7740 1600 **f** 020 7740 1700 **e** tara@missioncontrol.net MD: David Samuel.

Metal Nation 2 Whitehouse Mews, The Green, Wallsend, Tyne & Wear NE28 7EPf 0191 263 8382 **e** metalnation1@hotmail.com **w** metalnationrecords.co.uk MD: Jess Cox. Dist: Cadiz/Pinnacle

Metier (see Priory Records)

Microbe 22 The Nursery, Sutton Courtenay, Oxfordshire OX14 4UA **t** 01235 845800 **f** 01235 847692 **e** john@cyard.com **w** courtyardmusic.net A&R Mgr: John Bennett. Dist: Pinnacle

Midnight Rock (see Fury Records)

Mighty Atom Records Dylan Thomas House, 32 Alexander Rd, Swansea SA1 5DT **t** 01792 476567 **f** 01792 476564 **e** info@mightyatom.co.uk **w** mightyatom.co.uk MD: Roger Hopkins. Dist: Plastic Head

Mike Lewis Entertainment Ltd (see Lewis Recordings)

Milan Music (see Atlantic Records UK)

Millennium Music Estate House, Stanmore, Bridgnorth, Shropshire WV15 5HP **t** 01746 761121 **f** 01746 711911 **e** mmpc@btclick.com **w** millenniummusicpc.com Dir A&R: Dave Coleman. Dist: Pinnacle

Millennium Records Ltd 6 Water Lane, Camden, London NW1 8NZ **t** 020 7482 0272 **f** 020 7267 4908 **e** mail@millenniumrecords.com **w** millenniumrecords.com MD: Ben Recknagel.

Mimi Entertainment 26-Hammersmith Grove, Hammersmith, London W6 7BA **t** 020 8834 1085 **f** 020 8834 1185 **e** info@mimi-music.com **w** mimi-music.com Label Manager: Nicola S.

Minimal (see 3 Beat Label Management)

Ministry Of Sound Recordings 103 Gaunt Street, London SE1 6DP **t** 020 7378 6528 **f** 020 7403 5348 **e** initial+lastname@ministryofsound.com **w** ministryofsound.com MD: Lohan Presencer. Dist: Universal

Mint (see Jungle Records)

Mint Blue Records 2nd Floor, Candleriggs, Merchant City, Glasgow G1 1NP **t** 0141 572 0234 or 01236 821890 **e** mintblue@yahoo.com **w** mintblue.com Lbl Mgr: Damian Beattie. Dist: Shellshock

Minta (see Plum Projects)

Mirabeau (see Silverword Music Group)

Miso Records (see Mutant Disc)

Miss Moneypenny's Music (see K-Tel Entertainment (UK))

Mo's Music Machine Unit 11, Forest Business Park, Argall Avenue, Leyton, London E10 7FB **t** 020 8520 7264 **f** 020 8223 0351 **e** james@mosmusic.co.uk **w** mosmusic.co.uk Production Manager: James Orfeur. Dist: Aura Surround Sound

Mo'Wax Labels Ltd 1 Codrington Mews, London W11 2EH **t** 020 8870 7511 **f** 020 8871 4178 **e** mowax@almaroad.co.uk **w** mowax.com Label Head: Toby Feltwell. Dist: Vital

Mob (see New State Entertainment)

Mobb Rule Records PO Box 26335, London N8 9ZA **t** 020 8340 8050 **e** info@mobbrule.com **w** mobbrule.com MDs: Stewart Pettey, Wayne Clements.

Mode (see Harmonia Mundi (UK) Ltd)

Mogul Records 21 Bedford Square, London WC1B 3HH **t** 020 7637 4444 **f** 020 7323 2857 **e** guy@fspg.co.uk MD: Guy Rippon. Dist: AMD

Mohawk Records Unit 3, Westmoreland House, Scrubs Lane, London NW10 6RE **t** 020 8960 4777 **f** 020 8960 7266 **e** info@alpha-magic.com **w** alpha-magic.com Label Mgr: Lee Stacy. Dist: Alphamagic

Mohock Records (see First Time Records)

Moist Records Ltd PO Box 528, Enfield, Middlesex EN3 7ZP **t** 070 107 107 24 **f** 0870 137 3787 **e** info@moistrecords.com **w** moistrecords.com MD: Rodney Lewis. Dist: Essential Direct

Moksha Recordings Ltd PO Box 102, London E15 2HH **t** 020 8555 5423 **f** 020 8519 6834 **e** recordings@moksha.demon.co.uk **w** moksha.co.uk MD: Charles Cosh.

Molecular (see Eukatech Records)

Monarch (see KRL)

Mook Records PO Box 155, Leeds, West Yorkshire LS7 2XN **t** 0113 230 4008 **f** 0113 230 4008 **e** mail@mookhouse.ndo.co.uk **w** mookhouse.ndo.co.uk Label Manager: Phil Mayne. Dist: Shellshock

Mooncrest Records (see Sanctuary Records Group)

Moonska (see Loose)

Moor Records Ltd Suite 52, Chancel House, Neasden Lane, London NW10 2TU **t** 020 8214 1430 **f** 020 8214 1431 **e** moorinfo@moor-records.com **w** moor-records.com A&R Director: Fresh de Moor.

More Protein Ltd City House, 72-80 Leather Lane, London EC1N 7TR **t** 020 7242 9730 **f** 020 7242 9731 **e** dd.mp@virgin.net Label Manager: David Davis. MD: George O'Dowd. Dist: Pinnacle

Mosquito Media PO Box 33790, 18 Chelsea Manor St, London SW3 6WF **t** 020 7286 0503 **f** 020 7286 0503 **e** mosquitomedia@aol.com **w** mosquito-media.co.uk Contact: Richard Abbott

Mother Tongue 35 Marsden St, London NW5 3HE **t** 07973 137 554 **e** Julian@takats.com MD: Julian de Takats.

Motown (see Island Records Group)

Mottete Ursina (see Priory Records)

Move (see Divine Art Record Company Ltd)

Movieplay (see Delta Music plc)

Moving Shadow Ltd PO Box 2251, London SE1 2FH **t** 020 7252 2661 **f** 0870 0512594 **e** info2004@movingshadow.com **w** movingshadow.com MD: Rob Playford. Dist: SRD

MP2 (see Multiply Records)

MPRecords 124 Sunny Bank, Spring Bank West, Hull HU3 1LE **t** 01482 343352 **f** 01482 343038 **e** rod@backtobase.demon.co.uk **w** backtobase.co.uk MD: Barbara Ray. Dist: Cargo

Mr Bongo/Disorient Recordings 2nd Floor, 24 Old Steine, Brighton BN1 1EL **t** 01273 600 546 **f** 01273 600 578 **e** info@mrbongo.com **w** mrbongo.com MD: Dave Buttle. Dist: Vital

MRR 6 Berkeley Crescent, Clifton, Bristol BS8 1HA **t** 0117 929 2393 **f** 0117 929 2696 **e** craigg.williams@virgin.net Label Manager: Craig Williams. Dist: Studio K7

Multi Vision (see Headzone Ltd)

Multiply Records 107 Mortlake High Street, London SW14 8HQ **t** 020 8878 7888 **e** info@multiply.co.uk **w** multiply.co.uk MD: Mike Hall. Dist: BMG

Multisonic (see Priory Records)

Mumbo Jumbo (see Illicit Recordings)

Mushroom (see Atlantic Records UK)

Music & Arts (see Harmonia Mundi (UK) Ltd)

Music & Elsewhere (see United World Underground)

Music City Ltd 122 New Cross Road, London SE14 5BA **t** 020 7277 9657 **f** 0870 7572004 **e** info@musiccity.co.uk **w** musiccity.co.uk Lbl Mgr: Brian Harman.

MCI - Music Collection International 4th Floor, Holden House, 57 Rathbone Place, London W1T 1JU **t** 020 7396 8899 **f** 020 7470 6655 **e** info@mcimusic.co.uk **w** vci.co.uk International Sales: Jonathan Hanscombe. Head Of Sales: Mat Newman. Sales & Mktg Dir: Danny Keene.

Music Factory Mastermix Hawthorne House, Fitzwilliam St, Parkgate, Rotherham, South Yorks S62 6EP **t** 01709 710022 **f** 01709 523141 **e** info@mastermixdj.com **w** mastermixdj.com MD: Rob Moore.

Music For Dreams (see Reverb Records Ltd)

Music For Nations 333 Latimer Road, London W10 6RA **t** 020 8964 9544 **f** 020 8964 5460 **e** mfn@music-for-nations.co.uk **w** music-for-nations.co.uk Label Manager: Sarah Haycox. Dist: Pinnacle

Music For Pleasure (MFP) (see EMI Catalogue/EMI Gold/EMI Liberty)

Music From Another Room Ltd The Penthouse, 20 Bulstrode Street, London W1U 2JW **t** 020 7224 4442 **f** 020 7224 3167 **e** patrick@julianlennon.com **w** music-from-another-room.co.uk Manager: Patrick Cousins. Dist: Pinnacle

Music Fusion Ltd Shepperton Studios, Studio Rd, Shepperton, Middx TW17 0QD **t** 01932 592016 **f** 01932 592046 **e** ben.williams@classicpictures.co.uk **w** rwcc.com Mktg Mgr: Ben Williams. Dist: Pinnacle

Music Like Dirt 9 Bloomsbury Place, East Hill, Wandsworth, London SW18 2JB **t** 020 8877 1335 **f** 020 8877 1335 **e** mld@bigworldpublishing.com **w** bigworldpublishing.com MD/A&R: Patrick Meads.

Music Masters Ltd Orchard End, Upper Oddington, Moreton-in-Marsh, Glos GL56 0XH **t** 01451 812288 **f** 01451 870702 **e** info@music-masters.co.uk **w** music-masters.co.uk MD: Nick John.

Music Mercia Osmond House, 78 Alchester Rd, Moseley, Birmingham B13 8BB **t** 0121 256 1310 **f** 0121 256 1318 **e** hendricks@music.mercia.org MD: John Hemming.

Music Of Life Records Unit 9B, Wingbury Business Village, Upper Wingbury Farm, Wingrave, Bucks HP22 4LW **t** 07770 364 268 **e** chris@musicoflife.com **w** musicoflife.com MD: Chris France. Dist: Recognition

Music With Attitude (MWA) 20 Middle Row, Ladbroke Grove, London W10 5AT **t** 020 8964 4555 **f** 020 8964 4666 **e** morgan@musicwithattitude.com **w** musicwithattitude.com MD: Morgan Khan.

MUSIQ (see 3 Beat Label Management)

Musketeer (see Start Audio & Video)

Musketeer Records 56 Castle Bank, Stafford, Staffordshire ST16 1DW **t** 01785 258746 **f** 01785 255367 **e** p.halliwell@tesco.net MD: Paul Halliwell. Dist: DA

Musoswire PO Box 100, Gainsborough DN21 3DZ **t** 01427 628826 **e** info@musoswire.com **w** musoswire.com Prop: Dan Nash.

Mutant Disc PO Box 5753, Nottingham NG2 7WN **t** 0115 941 9401 **f** 0115 958 7197 **e** mutant@deluxeaudio.com Label Mgr: Nick Gordon Brown.

Mute Records Ltd 429 Harrow Road, London W10 4RE **t** 020 8964 2001 **f** 020 8968 4977 **e** info@mutehq.co.uk **w** mute.com Chairman: Daniel Miller. Dist: Vital

MVM Records 35 Alma Rd, Reigate, Surrey RH2 0DN **t** 01737 224151 **f** 01737 241481 MD: Maryetta Midgley.

My Dad Recordings 6 Fleet St, Hyde, Cheshire SK14 2LF **t** 07967 732 616 **e** label@mydadrecordings.com **w** mydadrecordings.com MD: Paul Vella.

My Kung Fu 133 The Coal Exchange, Mount Stuart Square, Cardiff Bay, Cardiff CF10 5ED **t** 029 2019 0151 **e** carl@my-kung-fu.com **w** my-kung-fu.com Label Mgr: Carl Morris. Dist: Shellshock/Pinnacle

N2 Records (see Evolve Records)

Nachural Records PO Box 2656, Smethwick, Warley, West Midlands B66 4JF **t** 0121 505 6500 **f** 0121 505 6515 **e** info@nachural.co.uk **w** nachural.co.uk MD: Ninder Johal.

Nascente World Music Label (part of Demon Music Group), 4th Floor, Holden House, 57 Rathbone Place, London W1T 1JU **t** 020 7470 6680 **f** 020 7470 6655 **e** chris.birrell@demonmusicgroup.co.uk **w** nascente.co.uk Label Manager: Chris Birrell. Dist: DISC/THE

Nasha Records PO Box 42545, London E1 6WZ **t** 07904 145 743 **f** 020 7709 0097 **e** music@nasha.co.uk **w** nasha.co.uk Label Manager: Sobur Ahmed. Dist: Amato

Nation Records Ltd 19 All Saints Rd, Notting Hill, London W11 1HE **t** 020 7792 8167 **f** 020 7792 2854 **e** info@nationrecords.co.uk **w** nationrecords.co.uk MD: Aki Nawaz. Dist: Vital

Natural Grooves 3 Tannsfeld Rd, Sydenham, London SE26 5DQ **t** 020 8488 3677 **f** 020 8473 6539 **e** jon@naturalgrooves.co.uk **w** naturalgrooves.co.uk MD: Jonathan Sharif.

Naxos (see Naxos AudioBooks)

Naxos AudioBooks 18 High Street, Wellwyn, Herts AL6 9EQ **t** 01438 717808 **f** 01438 717809 **e** naxos_audiobooks@compuserve.com **w** naxosaudiobooks.com MD: Nicholas Soames. Dist: Select

Ncompass Records 113 Chewton Rd, Walthamstow, London E17 7DN **t** 07941 331181 **e** rich@ncompass.freeserve.co.uk A&R Director: Richard Rogers.

Nebula Music (see New State Entertainment)

Nemesis Records 1st Floor, Alexandra Buildings, 28 Queen St, Manchester M2 5LF **t** 0161 834 4500 **f** 0161 834 0014 **e** liz@nmsmanagement.co.uk MD: Nigel Martin-Smith.

Neon Records Studio One, 19 Marine Crescent, Kinning Park, Glasgow G51 1HD **t** 0141 429 6366 **f** 0141 429 6377 **e** mail@go2neon.com **w** go2neon.com Label Manager: Elaine Craig.

Nero Schwarz (see East Central One Ltd)

Nervous Records 5 Sussex Crescent, Northolt, Middlesex UB5 4DL **t** 020 8423 7373 **f** 020 8423 7773 **e** nervous@compuserve.com **w** nervous.co.uk MD: Roy Williams. Dist: Nervous

Nettwerk Productions UK Clearwater Yard, 35 Inverness St, London NW1 7HB **t** 020 7424 7500 **f** 020 7424 7501 **e** eleanor@nettwerk.com **w** nettwerk.com Dir: Gary Levermore. Dist: Pinnacle

Network (see Harmonia Mundi (UK) Ltd)

Neuropa 60 Baronald Drive, Glasgow G12 0HW **t** 0141 339 9894 **e** neuropa@talk21.com Administrator: Alexander Macpherson.

New Age Music Ltd 17 Priory Road, London NW6 4NN **t** 020 7209 2766 **f** 020 7813 2766 **e** gerrybron@easynet.co.uk **w** gerrybron.com MD: Gerry Bron.

New Christian Music (NCM Records) (see New Music Records)

New Dawn Records Box 1-2, 191 Greenhead Street, Glasgow G40 1HX **t** 0141 554 6475 **f** 0141 554 6475 **e** newdawnrecords@talk21.com **w** belles.demon.co.uk Contact: Admin Dept Dist: Shellshock

A New Day Records 75 Wren Way, Farnborough, Hampshire GU14 8TA **t** 01252 540270 or 07889 797482 **f** 01252 372001 **e** DAVIDREES1@compuserve.com **w** anewdayrecords.co.uk MD: Dave Rees. Dist: Proper

New Leaf Records 9 Church Road, Conington, Peterborough, Cambridgeshire PE7 3QJ **t** 01487 830778 **e** indie500@madasafish.com **w** indie500.co.uk Prop: Andrew Clifton. Dist: Backs

New Music Records Meredale, The Dell, Reach Lane, Heath and Reach, Leighton Buzzard, Beds LU7 0AL **t** 01525 237700 **f** 01525 237700 **e** enq@newmusicenterprises.com **w** newmusicenterprises.com Prop: Paul Davis.

New Religion 740 Alaska Buildings, Grange Road, London SE1 3BD **t** 020 7237 9985 **e** sarah@newreligionmusic.com Label Manager: Sarah Pearson.

New State Entertainment Unit 2A Queens Studios, 121 Salusbury Road, London NW6 6RG **t** 020 7372 4474 **f** 020 7372 4484 or 020 7328 4447 **e** info@newstate.co.uk **w** newstate.co.uk MD: Tom Parkinson.

New World Music Harmony House, Hillside Road East, Bungay, Suffolk NR35 1RX **t** 01986 891600 **f** 01986 891601 **e** info@newworldmusic.co.uk **w** newworldmusic.com MD: Jeff Stewart.

NGM Records North Glasgow College, 110 Flemington Street, Glasgow G21 4BX **t** 0141 558 6440 or 0141 558 9001 x 249 **f** 0141 558 9905 **e** hbrankin@north-gla.ac.uk **w** north-gla.ac.uk Senior Lecturer Music: Hugh Brankin.

Nice 'N' Ripe Records FX Promotions, Unit 30, Grenville Workshops, 502 Hornsey Rd, London N19 4EF **t** 020 7281 8363 **f** 020 7281 7663 **e** nicenripe@fxpromotions.demon.co.uk **w** fxpromotions.demon.co.uk/nicenripe MD: George Power. Dist: Various

NiceTunes 74 Pentland Close, London N9 0XN **t** 020 8351 3288 or 0781 205 2029 **f** 0870 922 3133 **e** max@nicemanproductions.com **w** nicemanproductions.com/nicetunes A&R Dir: Max Tilley.

Night & Day (see BMR Entertainment Ltd)

Nightbreed Recordings PO Box 6242, Nottingham NG1 5HY **t** 01623 401207 **f** 01623 401207 **e** trev@nightbreedmusic.co.uk **w** nightbreedmusic.co.uk Label Mgr: Trev.

Nikt Records Cadillac Ranch, Pencraig Uchaf, Cwm Bach, Whitland, Dyfed SA34 0DT **t** 01994 484294 **f** 01994 484294 **e** cadillacranch@telco4u.net Director: M Menendes. Dist: Cargo

Nimbus Records Wyastone Leys, Monmouth, Gwent NP25 3SR **t** 01600 890007 **f** 01600 891052 **e** antony@wyastone.co.uk **w** wyastone.co.uk Director: Antony Smith. MD: Adrian Farmer. Head of Press/A&R: Dominic Fyfe. Dist: Nimbus

99 North (see Higher State)

99 Degrees (see Higher State)

Ninja Tune PO Box 4296, London SE11 4WW **t** 020 7820 3535 **f** 020 7820 3434 **e** ninja@ninjatune.net **w** ninjatune.net MD: Peter Quicke. Business Affairs: Alastair Nicholson; International Marketing: Dominic Smith. Dist: Vital

NJC (see Harmonia Mundi (UK) Ltd)

NMC Recordings Ltd 18-20 Southwark Street, London SE1 1TJ **t** 020 7403 9445 **f** 020 7403 9446 **e** nmc@nmcrec.co.uk **w** nmcrec.co.uk Label Mgr: Hannah Vlcek. Executive Producer: Colin Matthews. Dist: RSK

Nocturnal Recordings PO Box 2042, Luton, Beds LU3 2EP **t** 01582 595 944 **f** 1582 612 752 **e** j.waller@nocturnalrecordings.com **w** nocturnalrecordings.com Director/A&R: Jonathan M Waller. Dist: Unique

Noise Music (see Innerground Records)

NOMADIC MUSIC

Unit 18a/b, Farm Lane Trading Estate, 101 Farm Lane, London SW6 1QJ **t** 020 7386 6800 **f** 020 7386 6801 **e** info@nomadicmusic.net **w** nomadicmusic.net Label Head: Paul Flanagan

Nonesuch (see Atlantic Records UK)

Nonesuch (see Warner Classics)

North South (see Abstract Sounds)

Nova Mute (see Mute Records Ltd)

Now And Then (see Now And Then Productions)

Now And Then Productions 208 Wigan Rd, Ashton In Makerfield, Wigan, Lancs WN4 9SX **t** 01942 513298 **e** info@nowandthen.co.uk **w** nowandthen.co.uk Label Mgr: Mark Ashton. Dist: Cargo

NoWHere Records 30 Tweedholm Ave East, Walkerburn, Peeblesshire EH43 6AR **t** 01896 870 284 or 07812 818 183 **e** michaelwild@btopenworld.com MD: Michael Wild.

NRK Sound Division Ltd 2 Princess Row, Bristol BS2 8NQ **t** 0117 9426188 **f** 0117 9424747 **e** info@nrksounddivision.com **w** nrksounddivision.com; honchosmusic.com Contact: Nick Harris Dist: Vital

Ntone (see Ninja Tune)

Nu Directions PO Box 1668, Wolverhampton, West Midlands WV3 0AE **t** 01902 423 627 **f** 01902 423 627 **e** info@nudirections.net **w** nudirections.net Label Mgr: Neil Hutchinson.

nu-republic (see 3 Beat Label Management)

NuCamp (see Wall Of Sound Recordings Ltd)

Nude Records The Zeppelin Building, 59-61 Farringdon Rd, London EC1M 3JB **t** 020 7691 8688 or 020 7691 8689 **f** 020 7691 8690 **e** saulgalpern@nuderecords.com **w** nuderecords.com MD: Saul Galpern, Ben James.

Nukleuz (see Media Records Ltd)

NuLife (see BMG UK & Ireland Ltd)

Numa Records 86 Staines Road, Wraybury, Middlesex TW19 5AA **t** 01784 483589 **f** 01784 483211 **e** tonywebb@numan.co.uk **w** numan.co.uk/ MD: Tony Webb. Dist: BMG

Numinous Music Group Figment House, Church St, Ware, Hertfordshire SG12 9EN **t** 01273 680799 **f** 01920 463883 **e** allan.james1@virgin.net **w** numinous.co.uk Dir. A&R/Marketing/Promo: Allan James. Admin/Legal Dir: John Harwood-Bee. Dist: Ideal

NYJO Records 11 Victor Road, Harrow, Middlesex HA2 6PT **t** 020 8863 2717 **f** 020 8863 8685 **e** bill.ashton@virgin.net **w** NYJO.org.uk Dir: Bill Ashton. Dist: Magnum

Nyrangongo Records 113 Cheesemans Terrace, Star Road, London W14 9XH **t** 020 7385 5447 **f** 020 7385 5447 **e** nyrangongo@yahoo.co.uk Contact: Debbie Golt

Oblong Records (see Plank Records)

Obsessive (see BMG UK & Ireland Ltd)

Ochre Records PO Box 155, Cheltenham, Glos. GL51 0YS **t** 01242 514332 **f** 01242 514332 **e** ochre@talbot.force9.co.uk **w** ochre.co.uk Prop: Talbot. Dist: Cargo

0898 Dubplate (see Direct Heat Records)

Offbeat Scotland 107 High Street, Royal Mile, Edinburgh EH1 1SW **t** 0131 556 4882 **f** 0131 558 7019 **e** iain@offbeat.co.uk **w** offbeat.co.uk MD: Iain McKinna. Dist: Highlander Music

OffDaWallMusic 4 Cliveden Close, Ferndown, Dorset BH22 9UL **t** 01202 873708 or 07776 258802 **e** info@offdawallmusic.com **w** offdawallmusic.com Co-MD: James Crompton. Co-MD: T Crompton.

Offslip Productions 3 Lion Court, Studio Way, Borehamwood WD6 5NJ **t** 07789 955 059 **e** danfeel@offslip.com **w** offslip.com Dir: Daniel Roberts.

Oh Eye Records Ltd 97 Albert St, 3F4, Edinburgh EH7 5LY **t** 0131 554 9861 **f** 0131 554 9861 **e** oheye.records@virgin.net **w** oheye.net MDs: Yvette Fugue, Pat Coll. Dist: Cargo

Okkadisc (see Harmonia Mundi (UK) Ltd)

Old Bridge Music PO Box 7, Ilkley, West Yorks LS29 9RY **t** 01943 602203 **f** 01943 435472 **e** mail@oldbridgemusic.com **w** oldbridgemusic.com Partner: Chris Newman. Dist: Proper

Olympia (see Priory Records)

On-Line-Records (see Line-Up PMC)

One Little Indian Records 34 Trinity Crescent, London SW17 7AE **t** 020 8772 7600 **f** 020 8772 7601 **e** info@indian.co.uk **w** indian.co.uk GM: Paul Johannes. Dist: Pinnacle

One Step Music Ltd Independent House, 54 Larkshall Road, London E4 6PD **t** 020 8523 9000 **f** 020 8523 8888 **e** erich@independentmusicgroup.com **w** independentmusicgroup.com CEO: Ellis Rich. Director of A&R: Andy Bailey. International Dir: Catherine Kelly. Creative Dir: Jacqui Brown.

Opal (see Pavilion Records Ltd)

Open (see Data)

Opera Rara 134-146 Curtain Rd, London EC2A 3AR **t** 020 7613 2858 **f** 020 7613 2261 **e** info@opera-rara.com **w** opera-rara.com MD: Stephen Revell. Artistic Director: Patric Schmid. Press & Promotions: Terri Robson. Dist: Select

Ophidian (see Rotator Records)

Optimum (see Silverword Music Group)

Or (see Touch)

Oracabessa Records 17 Andover St, Digbeth, Birmingham B5 5RG **t** 0121 665 6527 **f** 0121 643 8196 **e** neilhutchinson@oracabessa.com **w** oracabessa.com Lbl Mgr: Neil Hutchinson. Andy Hayes: Art Dir. Dist: Pinnacle

Orange Sync Records Quayside Business Centre, Ouseburn Buildings, Newcastle Upon Tyne NE6 1LL **t** 0191 2755000 **f** 0191 2650367 **e** orangesync@onetel.net.uk **w** web.onetel.net.uk/~orangesync MD: Ray Sharp.

Orbison Records Covetous Corner, Hudnall Common, Little Gaddesden, Herts HP4 1QW **t** 01442 842039 **f** 01442 842082 **e** mhaynes@orbison.com **w** orbison.com European Consultant: Mandy Haynes. President: Barbara Orbison.

Orbit (see Collecting Records LLP)

Orbit (see Everest Copyrights)

Ore (see Beggars Banquet Records)

Org Records Suite 212, The Old Gramophone Works, 326 Kensal Road, London W10 5BZ **t** 020 8964 3066 **e** organ@organart.demon.co.uk **w** organart.com MD: Sean Worrall. Dist: PHD

Orgy Records PO Box 8245, Sawbridgeworth, Herts CM21 9WU **t** 01279 600081 **e** info@orgyrecords.com **w** orgyrecords.com Contact: Nic Ward

Oriental Star Agency 548-550 Moseley Road, Birmingham, West Midlands B12 9AD **t** 0121 449 6437 **f** 0121 449 5404 **e** info@osa.co.uk **w** osa.co.uk Director: Mohammed Farooq.

Osceola Records PO Box 38805, London W12 7XL **t** 020 8740 8898 **e** info@osceolarecords.com **w** osceolarecords.com Proprietor: Jimmy Thomas.

Ottavo (see Priory Records)

Outafocus Recordings 146 Bethnal Green Road, London E2 6DG **t** 020 7613 1100 **f** 020 7613 1002 **e** info@outafocus.co.uk **w** outafocus.co.uk Label Manager: Danny Corr. Dist: Shellshock

Outcaste Records Limited Kensal House, 553-579 Harrow Rd, London W10 4RH **t** 020 8964 6720 **f** 020 8964 6087 **e** info@outcaste.com **w** outcaste.com MD: Shabs & Paul Franklyn.

Outdigo Records (see Shifty Disco Ltd)

Outer Recordings PO Box 18888, London SW7 4FQ **t** 020 7373 1614 **f** 020 7373 1614 **e** info@outer-media.co.uk **w** outer-recordings.co.uk MD: Greg Mihalcheon. Dist: Timewarp

Outerglobe Records 113 Cheesemans Terrace, London W14 9XH **t** 020 7385 5447 **f** 020 7385 5447 **e** golden@outerglobe.freeserve.co.uk **w** outerglobe.com MD: Debbie Golt.

Output Recordings 3rd Floor, 110 Curtain Rd, London EC2A 3AH **t** 020 7739 8560 **f** 020 7739 8561 **e** info@outputrecordings.com **w** outputrecordings.com Dist: Vital

Oval Records 326 Brixton Road, London SW9 7AA **t** 020 7622 0111 **e** charlie@ovalmusic.co.uk **w** ovalmusic.co.uk Dir: Charlie Gillett.

Ovation Recordings (see Adasam Limited)

OVC Ltd 88 Berkeley Court, Baker St, London NW1 5ND **t** 020 7402 9111 **f** 020 7723 3064 **e** Joanne.ovc@virgin.net MD: Joanne Cohen.

Oven Ready Productions PO Box 30446, London NW6 6FW **t** 07050 803 933 **f** 07050 693 471 **e** info@ovenready.net **w** ovenready.net Proprietor: Moussa Clarke.

Overground Records PO Box 1NW, Newcastle-upon-Tyne NE99 1NW **t** 0191 266 3802 **f** 0191 266 6073 **e** john@overgroundrecords.co.uk **w** overgroundrecords.co.uk MD: John Esplen. Dist: Voiceprint/Pinnacle

Overmatch Records 39 Berwick Street, London W1F 8RU **t** 020 7287 2496 **f** 020 7437 6255 **e** info@xsfrecords.com **w** xsfrecords.com Label Mgr: J Carlos Zaghis. Dist: Several

Owl Records International Limited 1 Stanaway Drive, Crumlin, Dublin 12, Ireland **t** 00 353 1 455 7750 **f** 00 353 1 455 7782 **e** owl@eircom.net **w** owlrecords.com MD: Reg Keating.

OxRecs Digital 37 Inkerman Close, Abingdon, Oxon OX14 1NH **t** 01235 550589 **e** info@oxrecs.com **w** oxrecs.com MD: Bernard Martin.

Oyster Music Limited Oakwood Manor, Oakwood Hill, Ockley, Surrey RH5 5PU **t** 01306 627277 **f** 01306 627277 **e** info@oystermusic.com **w** oystermusic.com Dirs: Chris Cooke, Adrian Fitt.

P3 Music Ltd 4 St Andrew St, Alyth, Perthshire PH11 8AT **t** 01828 633790 **f** 01828 633798 **e** records@p3music.com **w** p3music.com Dir: Alison Burns.

Pablo (see Ace Records)

Pagan (see ARK 21)

Palm Pictures 8 Kensington Park Road, Notting Hill Gate, London W11 3BU **t** 020 7229 3000 **f** 020 7229 0897 **e** firstname@palmpictures.co.uk **w** palmpictures.com MD: Andy Childs. Dist: Vital/THE

Panton (see Prestige Elite Records Ltd)

Parachute Music (see Creative World)

Parade (see Start Audio & Video)

Paradigm (see Harmonia Mundi (UK) Ltd)

Paratactile (see Harmonia Mundi (UK) Ltd)

Park Records PO Box 651, Oxford, Oxfordshire OX2 9RB **t** 01865 241717 **f** 01865 204556 **e** info@parkrecords.com **w** parkrecords.com MD: John Dagnell.

Park Lane (see The Hit Music Company)

PARLOPHONE

EMI House, 43 Brook Green, London W6 7EF **t** 020 7605 5000 **f** 020 7605 5050 **e** firstname.lastname@emimusic.com **w** parlophone.co.uk MD: Miles Leonard. Head of A&R: Dan Keeling. Mktg Dir: Mandy Plumb. Dir of Promotions: Steve Hayes. Business Affairs Dir: James Mullan. Dir of Press: Murray Chalmers.

Parlophone Rhythm Series (see Parlophone)

Partisan Recordings c/o Mute Song, 429 Harrow Road, London W19 4RE **t** 020 8964 2001 **f** 020 8968 8437 **e** mamapimp@btopenworld.com **w** emusic.com MD: Caroline Butler.

Pasadena Records Priors, Tye Green, Elsenham, Bishop's Stortford, Hertfordshire CM22 6DY **t** 01279 813240 or 01279 815593 **f** 01279 815895 **e** ProCentral@aol.com **w** pasadena.co.uk Contact: David Curtis Dist: Pinnacle

Passion Music Scratch Music House, 81 Crabtree Lane, London SW6 6LW **t** 020 7381 8315 **f** 020 7385 6785 **e** les@passionmusic.co.uk **w** passionmusic.co.uk MD: Les McCutcheon.

Past & Present Records 11 Hatherley Mews, Walthamstow, London E17 4QP **t** 020 8521 2211 **f** 020 8521 6911 **e** spencer@megaworld.co.uk **w** megaworld.co.uk Label Mgr: Spencer Kelly. Dist: Pinnacle

Past Perfect Lower Farm Barns, Bainton Rd, Bucknell, Oxon OX27 7LT **t** 01869 325052 **f** 01869 325072 **e** info@pastperfect.com **w** pastperfect.com Sales & Marketing Mgr: Jonothan Draper.

Pavilion Records Ltd Sparrows Green, Wadhurst, East Sussex TN5 6SJ **t** 01892 783591 **f** 01892 784156 **e** pearl@pavilionrecords.com **w** pavilionrecords.com MD: John Waite. Dist: Harmonia Mundi/Pinnacle

PCM (Paul Cooke Music) (see Cybertech Support Services Ltd)

Peaceville (see Snapper Music)

Peaceville Records PO Box 101, Cleckheaton, West Yorks BD19 4YF **t** 01274 878101 **f** 01274 874313 **e** hammy@peaceville.com **w** peaceville.com A&R Director: Hammy Halmshaw.

Pearl (see Pavilion Records Ltd)

Penguin Music Classics (see Decca UK)

People Music Adela Street Studio, The Saga Centre, 326 Kensal Road, London W10 5BZ **t** 020 8968 9666 **f** 020 8964 1330 **e** people@goyamusic.com **w** goyamusic.com Director: Mike Slocombe. Dist: Goya

Perceptive (see Brothers Records Ltd)

Perfect Words & Music 2 The Teak House, 37 The Avenue, Branksome Park, Poole, Dorset BH13 6LJ **t** 01202 763208 or 07810 437179 **e** philmurray.pac@talk21.com A&R: Allison Longstaff.

Perfect World Recordings PO Box 5, Sidcup, Kent DA14 6ZW **t** 020 8300 5510 **f** 020 8300 6503 **e** Kevin@perfectworldnetwork.com MD: Kevin Parkinson. Dist: Amato

Pet Sounds PO Box 158, Twickenham, Middlesex TW2 6RW **t** 07976 577 773 **f** 0871 733 3401 **e** robinhill@soundpets.freeserve.co.uk Director: Robin Hill. Dist: Pinnacle

PHAB Records High Notes, Sheerwater Avenue, Woodham, Weybridge, Surrey KT15 3DS **t** 019323 48174 **f** 019323 40921 MD: Philip HA Bailey.

Phaeton (see Claddagh Records)

Phantasm Records Unit B140-141, Riverside Business Centre, Bendon Valley, London SW18 4UQ **t** 020 8870 4484 **f** 020 8870 4483 **e** john@phantasm-uk.demon.co.uk **w** phantasm-uk.demon.co.uk MD: John Ford.

Philips (see Universal Classics & Jazz (UK))

Philips Classics (see Universal Classics & Jazz (UK))

Phonetic Recordings PO Box 172, Hampton, Middx TW12 1BT **t** 020 8255 3158 or 07989 564 293 **e** phonetic@blueyonder.co.uk Head of A&R: Rob Roar. Dist: Amato

Phonogenic 2nd Floor, Cavendish House, 69-79 Fulham High St, London SW6 3JW **t** 020 7384 7555 **f** 020 7384 7645 **e** firstname@phonogenic.net **w** phonogenic.net Dir: Paul Lisberg.

Piano (see Voiceprint)

PIAS Recordings Ltd 338A Ladbroke Grove, London W10 5AH **t** 020 8324 2500 **f** 020 8324 0010 **e** pias@piasrecordings.com **w** pias.com A&R: Carli Kapff. CEO: Nick Hartley.

Pickled Egg Records PO Box 6944, Leicester LE2 0WLe info@pickled-egg.co.uk **w** pickled-egg.co.uk Owner: Nigel Turner. Dist: Cargo

Pickwick Group Ltd 230 Centennial Park, Elstree Hill South, Elstree, Borehamwood, Herts WD6 3SN **t** 020 8236 2310 **f** 020 8236 2312 **e** info@pickwickgroup.com **w** pickwickgroup.com GM: Mark Lawton.

Pier (see Wooden Hill Recordings Ltd)

Pilgrim's Star (see Divine Art Record Company Ltd)

Pinnacle Labels (see Strange Fruit Records)

Piranha (see Star-Write Ltd)

Planet Records 11 Newmarket St, Colne, Lancashire BB8 9JB **t** 01282 866317 **f** 01282 866317 **e** pendlehawkmusic@ntlworld.com MD: Adrian Melling. Dist: Pendle Hawk

Planet1 Music PO Box 44377, London SW19 1WB **t** 01227 733 701 **f** 01227 733 701 **e** info@planet1music.com **w** planet1music.com MD: John Pepper, Sarah H.C. Dist: Self

Plank Records 9 Shaftesbury Centre, 85 Barlby Road, London W10 6BN **t** 020 8962 6244 **f** 020 8964 9551 **e** bushwacka@plank.co.uk **w** plank.co.uk Lbl Mgr: Lewis Copeland. Dist: SRD

Plankton Records PO Box 13533, London E7 0SG **t** 020 8534 8500 **e** plankton.records@virgin.net Partner: Keith Dixon.

Plantagenet (see Harmonia Mundi (UK) Ltd)

Plastic Fantastic Record Label 35 Drury Lane, Covent Garden, London WC2B 5RH **t** 020 7240 8055 **f** 020 7379 3653 **e** wes@plasticfantastic.co.uk **w** plasticfantastic.co.uk Label Manager: Wes Shearing. Dist: Amato

Plastic Head Records Ltd Avtech House, Hithercroft Rd, Wallingford, Oxon OX10 9DA **t** 01491 825029 **f** 01491 826320 **e** tom@plastichead.com **w** plastichead.com Director: Tom Doherty.

Plastica (see Plastic Fantastic Record Label)

Plastica Red (see Plastic Fantastic Record Label)

Platinum (see Prism Leisure Corporation Plc)

Platinum Collection (see Start Audio & Video)

Platipus Records Ltd Unit GM, Cooper House, 2 Michael Road, London SW6 2AD **t** 020 7731 4004 **f** 020 7731 0008 **e** platipus@platipus.com **w** platipus.com Lbl Mgr: Paul Glancy. A&R: Richard Phillips.

PLAY + LEARN (see CYP Limited)

Player Records Regents Park House, Regent St, Leeds LS2 7QJ **t** 0113 223 7665 **f** 0113 223 7514 **e** info@playerrecords.com **w** playerrecords.com Label Manager: Sarah Flay. Dist: Unique

Playtime (see CYP Limited)

Plaza Records PO Box 726, London NW11 7XQ **t** 020 8455 7965 or 020 8458 6200 **f** 020 8455 7965 or 020 8458 6200 **e** link@credo2000.com **w** etoile.co.uk/poto/poto.html MD: Roberto Danova. Dist: Independent/Universal

Pleasuredome PO Box 425, London SW6 3TXf 020 7736 9212 **e** getdown@thepleasuredome.demon.co.uk **w** pleasuredome.co.uk Chairman: Holly Johnson.

Plum Projects 8 Perseverance Place, Richmond, Surrey TW9 2PN **t** 020 8288 0531 **f** 020 8288 0531 **e** info@plumprojects.com **w** plumprojects.com Dist: Pinnacle

Point Classics (see Priory Records)

Point4 Records Unit 16 Talina Centre,, Bagleys Lane, London SW6 2BWe info@point4music.com **w** point4music.com Dirs: Paul Newton, Peter Day.

Poisoned Records (see Conception Records Ltd)

Pollytone Records PO Box 124, Ruislip, Middx HA4 9BB **t** 01895 638584 **f** 01895 624793 **e** val@pollyton.demon.co.uk **w** pollytone.com MD: Val Bird.

Polo Records (see Champion Records Ltd)

POLYDOR RECORDS

Black Lion House, 72-80 Black Lion Lane, London W6 9BE **t** 020 8910 4800 **f** 020 8910 4801 **e** firstname.lastname@umusic.com **w** polydor.co.uk. Joint MDs: David Joseph & Colin Barlow. Senior Dir, Legal & Business Affairs: James Radice. A&R Dir: Simon Gavin. Finance Dir: Geoff Harris. Dir of Press & Communications: Selina Webb. Dir of Promotions: Neil Hughes. Dir of TV & DVD: Iain Funnell. Dir of Marketing, PAL: Karen Simmonds. Dir of Marketing, PUK: Peter Loraine. Dir of International: Greg Sambrook. Head of Press: Sundraj Sreenivasan. Head of Artist Development: Orla Lee. Dist: Universal

Polyphonic Reproductions Ltd PO Box 19292, London NW10 9WP **t** 020 8459 6194 **f** 020 8451 6470 **e** sales@studio-music.co.uk MD: Stan Kitchen. Dist: BMG

Poptones (see Mercury Records)

Pork Recordings PO Box 18, Kingston Upon Hull, East Yorkshire HU1 3YU **t** 01482 441455 **f** 01482 441455 **e** pork@pork.co.uk **w** pork.co.uk MD: Dave Brennand.

Positiva EMI House, 43 Brook Green, London W6 7EF **t** 020 7605 5000 **f** 020 7605 5050 **e** firstname.lastname@emimusic.com **w** positivarecords.com Dir: Jason Ellis. A&R Mgr: Ben Cherrill. Label Co-ordinator: Nathan Taylor.

Positive Records (see Evolve Records)

Power Brothers (see Harmonia Mundi (UK) Ltd)

Power Records 29 Riversdale Road, Thames Ditton, Surrey KT7 0QN **t** 020 8398 5236 **f** 020 8398 7901 MD: Barry Evans.

Praga (see Harmonia Mundi (UK) Ltd)

The Precious Organisation The Townhouse, 1 Park Gate, Glasgow G3 6DL **t** 0141 353 2255 **f** 0141 353 3545 **e** mail@precioustoo.com MD: Elliot Davis.

Prelser (see Harmonia Mundi (UK) Ltd)

President Records Ltd Units 6 & 7, 11 Wyfold Road, Fulham, London SW6 6SE **t** 020 7385 7700 **f** 020 7385 3402 **e** hits@president-records.co.uk **w** president-records.co.uk MD: David Kassner. Dist: Independent/Universal

Prestige (see Ace Records)

Prestige Elite Records Ltd 34 Great James St, London WC1N 3HB **t** 020 7405 3786 **f** 020 7405 5245 **e** info@prestige-elite.com **w** prestige-elite.com Chairman: Keith C Thomas. Dist: NOVA/Pinnacle

Pretap Music PO Box 31890, London SE17 1XG **t** 020 7708 2098 **f** 020 7564 4406 **e** ikeleo@pretap.com **w** pretap.com A&R: Ike Leo.

Priestess Records Crouch Hill Community Centre, 83 Crouch Hill, London N8 9EG **t** 020 7263 0133 or 078146 59729 **e** katdog@chillonthehill.co.uk **w** nakedangel.co.uk MD: Kat Lee-Ryan. Dist: Changing World Distribution

Primal Rhythms (see Primate Recordings)

Primary (see Primate Recordings)

Primate Recordings 340 Athlon Road, Alperton, Middx HA0 1BX **t** 020 8601 2211 **f** 020 8601 2262 **e** primateinfo@primedistribution.co.uk **w** primedistribution.co.uk In-House Label Manager: Alistair Wells. Dist: Prime

Primaudial Recordings 35 Britannia Row, London N1 8QH **t** 020 7704 8080 **f** 020 7704 1616 **e** ski@primaudial.com **w** primaudial.com Label Manager: Tony Higgins/Ski Oakenfull.

Primevil (see Primate Recordings)

Priory Records 3 Eden Court, Eden Way, Leighton Buzzard, Beds LU7 4FY **t** 01525 377566 **f** 01525 371477 **e** sales@priory.org.uk **w** priory.org.uk MD: Neil Collier. Dist: Priory Records Ltd

Prism Leisure Corporation Plc 1 Dundee Way, Enfield, Middlesex EN3 7SX **t** 020 8804 8100 **f** 020 8216 6645 **e** music@prismleisure.com **w** prismleisure.com DVD Software Dir: Mark Pearce. Head of Licensing: Steve Brink. Exports: Simon Checketts.

Prison Records 13 Sandys Rd, Worcester WR1 3HE **t** 01905 29809 **f** 01905 613023 **e** info@prison-records.com **w** prison-records.com Co-MDs: Chris Warren, Ian Orkin.

Private Reality (see 3 Beat Label Management)

Probation Records (see FF Vinyl Records)

Profile (see Silverword Music Group)

Prolific Recordings PO Box 282, Tadworth, Surrey KT20 5WA **t** 07770 874 282 **e** andy@prolificrecordings.co.uk **w** prolificrecordings.co.uk Label Manager: Andy Lewis. Dist: Essential Direct

Prolifica Records UnitA105, Saga Centre, 326 Kensal Rd, London W10 5BZ **t** 020 8964 1917 **f** 020 8960 9971 **e** gavino@btconnect.com **w** prolifica.co.uk Label Manager: Gavino Prunas.

Proof Records (see Down By Law Records)

Proper Records Ltd Unit 1, Gateway Business Centre, Kangley Bridge Road, London SE26 5AN **t** 020 8676 5180 **f** 020 8676 5190 **e** malc@proper.uk.com **w** proper.uk.com MD: Malcolm Mills. Commercial Dir: Paul Riley. Export Manager: Roger Kent. Dist: Proper Music Distribution

Props Records Ltd 7 Croxley Road, London W9 3HH **t** 020 8960 1115 **e** info@props.co.uk **w** props.co.uk Dir: Martin Lascelles.

Prototype Recordings (see Virus Recordings)

Providence Music Ward Industries Ltd, Providence House, Brooks Road, Raunds, Northamptonshire NN9 6NS **t** 01933 624963 **f** 01933 625458 **e** Wardind1@aol.com **w** pamelaward.co.uk Mkting Dir: Paul Cherrington. Dist: Ward Industries

Provocateur Records Friendly Hall, 31 Fordwich Rd, Fordwich, Kent CT2 0BW **t** 01227 711008 **f** 01227 712021 **e** info@provocateurrecords.co.uk **w** provocateurrecords.co.uk MD: Jane Lindsey. Dist: Mac Two

PSF (see Harmonia Mundi (UK) Ltd)

Psychic Deli (see Phantasm Records)

Public Records 84A Strand On The Green, London W4 3PU **t** 020 8995 0989 **f** 020 8995 0878 **e** jcmusic@dial.pipex.com MD: John Campbell.

Pulse Records Suite 1, Regency House, Regent Road, Liverpool L5 9TB **t** 0151 298 1100 or 0151 298 2983 **f** 0151 298 2983 **e** info@pulse-records.co.uk **w** pulse-records.co.uk MDs: Rob Fennah, Alan Fennah.

Pure Delinquent 134 Replingham Rd, Southfields, London SW18 5LL **t** 07929 990 321 **f** 020 8870 0790 **e** julie@pure-delinquent.com **w** pure-delinquent.com Dir: Julie Pratt. Dist: Pinnacle

Pure Gold Records (see First Time Records)

Pure Mint Recordings The Old Post Office, 31 Penrose Street, London SE17 3DW **t** 020 7703 1239 **f** 020 7703 1239 **e** info@pure-mint.com **w** pure-mint.com MD: Anthony Hall.

Pure Silk (see Broadley Records)

PureUK Recordings (see Stirling Music Group)

PURPLE CITY LTD

P.O. Box 31, Bushey, Herts WD23 2PT **t** 01923 244673 **f** 01923 244693 **e** info@purplecitymusic.com **w** purplecitymusic.com MD: Barry Blue. Creative Dir: Lynda West. A&R Director: Jordan Jay.

Purple Records Aizlewood Mill, Nursery Street, Sheffield, South Yorkshire S3 8GG **t** 0114 233 3024 **f** 0114 234 7346 **e** ann@darkerthanblue.fsnet.co.uk **w** purplerecords.net MD: Simon Robinson. Dist: Pinnacle

Purr Records 70 The Hollow, Southdown, Bath BA2 1LZ **t** 01225 443 844 **e** info@purr.org.uk **w** purr.org.uk Contact: Dave Tinkham, Tim Orchard Dist: Shellshock

Q Music Recordings (see Suburban Soul (Music))

Qnote Records (see Cube Soundtracks)

Quannum Projects (see Ninja Tune)

Quarterstick (see Southern Records)

Quiet Riot Records 130A Plough Road, Battersea, London SW11 2AA **t** 020 7924 1948 **f** 020 7924 6069 **e** adam@grlondon.com Label Manager: Adam Records. Dist: GR London

Quixotic Records Unit 6217, 49 Greenwich High Rd, London SE10 8JL **t** 020 8691 0262 **f** 020 8691 0268 **e** info@quixoticrecords.com **w** quixoticrecords.com Label Manager: Suzanne Hunt.

Q Zone Ltd 21C Heathmans Road, Parsons Green, London SW6 4TJ **t** 020 7731 9313 **f** 020 7731 9314 **e** nicki@darah.co.uk MD: David Howells. GM: Nicki L'Amy.

R2 (see REL Records)

R2 Records PO Box 100, Moreton-in-Marsh, Gloucs GL56 0ZX **t** 01608 651802 **f** 01608 652814 **e** editor@jacobsladder.org.uk **w** jacobsladder.org.uk MD: Robb Eden.

Racing Junior (see Glitterhouse Records)

Radiate (see Virgin Records)

Radioactive (see Island Records Group)

Radiotone Records PO Box 43103, London E17 8WD **t** 07989 301910 **e** info@radiotone.co.uk **w** radiotone.co.uk Dir: Steve Cooper.

Rage (see Avex Inc)

Ragtag Music (see Fastforward Music Ltd)

Rainbow Quartz Records 74 Riverside 3, Sir Thomas Longley Road, Rochester, Kent ME2 4BH **t** +212 385 8000 **f** +212 385 7845 **e** rainbowqtz@aol.com **w** rainbowquartz.com Founder: Jim McGarry.

Rainy Day Records (see First Time Records)

Raise the Roof (see Collecting Records LLP)

Raising Grass (see Sonic360)

Ram Records Ltd PO Box 70, Hornchurch, Essex RM11 3NR **t** 01708 445851 **f** 01708 441270 **e** info@ramrecords.com **w** ramrecords.com Label Mgr: Scott Bourne. Dist: SRD

Randan 52 Osborne St, Glasgow G1 5QH **t** 0141 552 0375 **f** 0141 552 0375 **e** horse2@tinyonline.co.uk **w** horse-randan.com PA: Michelle Blair. Dist: Pinnacle

RandM Records 72 Marylebone Lane, London W1U 2PL **t** 020 7486 7458 **f** 020 8467 6997 **e** mike@randm.co.uk; roy@randm.co.uk **w** randm.co.uk MDs: Mike Andrews & Roy Eldridge.

Random House 20 Vauxhall Bridge Road, London SW1V 2SA **t** 020 7840 8400 **f** 020 7233 8791 **e** enquiries@randomhouse.co.uk **w** randomhouse.co.uk Dist: The Book Service

Rapster Records (see !K7 Records)

Rasal (see Sain (Recordiau) Cyf)

Rat Records 87 Candahar Rd, London SW11 2QA **t** 08707 501 379 **f** 08707 501 379 **e** info@ratrecords.info **w** ratrecords.info Contact: Ollywood Dist: SRD

Ravensbourne Records Ltd 34 Great James St, London WC1N 3HB **t** 020 7404 1050 **e** neil@ravensbourne.com **w** ravensbourne.com Dir: Neil March.

Raw Strings (see RF Records)

Rawkus Entertainment (see Island Records Group)

Rayman Recordings (see Adasam Limited)

RCA (see BMG UK & Ireland Ltd)

RCA International Series (see BMG Commercial Division)

RCA Red Seal (see BMG Commercial Division)

RDL Music (see Savant Records)

RDL Records 132 Chase Way, London N14 5DH **t** 020 8361 5002 or 07050 055167 **f** 0870 741 5252 **e** atlanticcrossingartists@yahoo.com **w** mkentertainments.8k.com Director: Colin Jacques. Dist: 9mm

React (see Resist Music)

Reader's Digest Association 11 West Ferry Circus, London E14 4HE **t** 020 7715 8058 **f** 020 7715 8722 or 020 7715 8181 **e** custservice@readersdigest.co.uk **w** readersdigest.co.uk Gen Mgr, Music & Vid Ops: Elaine Brooke.

Ready, Steady, Go! (see Graduate Records)

Real World Records Box Mill, Mill Lane, Box, Corsham, Wilts SN13 8PL **t** 01225 743188 **f** 01225 743787 **e** records@realworld.co.uk **w** realworldrecords.com Label Mgr: Amanda Jones. Dist: Virgin

Really Free Solutions Ichthus House, 1 Northfield Rd, Aylesbury, Bucks HP20 1PB **t** 01296 583700 **e** info@reallyfreemusic.co.uk **w** reallyfreemusic.co.uk Contact: Peter Wheeler

Really Useful Records 22 Tower St, London WC2H 9TW **t** 020 7240 0880 **f** 020 7240 8922 **e** querymaster@reallyuseful.co.uk **w** reallyuseful.com MD (Music Division): Tristram Penna.

Receiver Records (see Sanctuary Records Group)

Recharge (see Supreme Music)

The Record Label The Old Schoolhouse, 138 Lower Mortlake Road, Richmond, Surrey TW9 2JZ **t** 020 8332 7245 **f** 020 8948 6982 **e** info@recordlabel.co.uk **w** recordlabel.co.uk MD: Matt Nicholson. Dist: Pinnacle

Recoup Recordings Suite B, 2 Tunstall Rd, London SW9 8DA **t** 020 7733 5400 **f** 020 7733 4449 **e** recouprecordings@westburymusic.net **w** westburymusic.net Dist: Timewarp

Recover (see Supreme Music)

Red (see Harmonia Mundi (UK) Ltd)

Red Admiral Records The Cedars, Elvington Lane, Hawkinge., Nr. Folkestone, Kent CT18 7AD **t** 01303 893472 **f** 01303 893833 **e** Chris@kentgigs.com **w** redadmiralrecords.com MD: Chris Ashman.

Red Balloon (see 4Real Records)

Red Cat (see Scratch Records)

Red Chord (see Born to Dance Records)

Red Egyptian Records 35 Britannia Row, London N1 8QH **t** 020 7704 8080 **f** 020 7704 1616 **e** tony@headonmanagement.co.uk Label Manager: Tony Higgins.

The Red Flag Recording Company 1 Star Street, London W2 1QD **t** 020 7258 0093 **f** 020 7402 9238 **e** info@redflagrecords.com **w** redflagrecords.com Contact: Sophie Young Director: Ben Leahy.

Red Hot Records 105 Emlyn Road, London W12 9TG **t** 020 8749 3730 **e** redhotrecs@aol.com MD: Brian Leafe.

Red Lightnin' The White House, 42, The Street, North Lopham, Diss, Norfolk IP22 2LU **t** 01379 687693 **f** 01379 687559 **e** peter@redlightnin.com **w** redlightnin.com MD: Peter Shertser. Dist: Magnum/TKO/Swift/Caroline2 Ltd.

Red Records 412 Beersbridge Road, Belfast BT5 5EB **t** 08707 454640 **f** 08707 454650 **e** michael@machtwo.co.uk **w** red-records.com MD: Michael Taylor.

Red Sky Records PO Box 27, Stroud, Gloucestershire GL6 0YQ **t** 0845 644 1447 **f** 01453 836877 **e** info@redskyrecords.co.uk **w** redskyrecords.co.uk MD: Johnny Coppin. Dist: CM

Redemption 516 Queslett Road, Great Barr, Birmingham B43 7EJ **t** 0121 605 4791 **f** 0121 605 4791 **e** bhaskar@redemption.co.uk **w** redemption.co.uk MD/Head A&R: Bhaskar Dandona. Dist: Infectious

Redemption Records PO Box 5006, Reading RG10 9ZG **t** 0118 932 0687 **f** 0118 932 0807 **e** info@redemption-records.com MD: Phil Knox-Roberts.

Reel Track Records PO Box 1099, London SE5 9HT **t** 020 7326 4824 **f** 020 7535 5901 **e** gamesmaster@chartmoves.com **w** chartmoves.com A&R Manager: Dave Mombasa.

Regal Recordings EMI House, 43 Brook Green, London W6 7EF **t** 020 7605 5000 **f** 020 7605 5050 **e** firstname.lastname@emimusic.com **w** regal.co.uk Head of Label: Miles Leonard.

Regis Records Ltd Southover House, Tolpuddle, Dorset DT2 7HF **t** 01305 848983 **f** 01305 848516 **e** info@regisrecords.co.uk **w** regisrecords.co.uk GM: Robin Vaughan. Dist: Regis Records

REL Records 86 Causewayside, Edinburgh EH9 1PY **t** 0131 668 3366 **f** 0131 662 4463 **e** neil@holyroodproductions.com MD: Neil Ross.

Release (see 3 Beat Label Management)

Release Grooves (see 3 Beat Label Management)

Release Records 7 North Parade, Bath, Somerset BA2 4DD **t** 01225 428284 **f** 01225 400090 **e** aca_aba@freenet.co.uk MD: Harry Finegold.

Relentless Records Kensal House, 553-579 Harrow Road, London W10 4RH **t** 020 8964 6720 **f** 020 8964 6087 **e** firstname@mvillage.co.uk **w** relentless-records.net Co-MDs: Shabs, Paul Franklyn. A&R: Glyn Aikins. Promotions: Roland Hill. Dist: EMI

Religion Music 36 Fitzwilliam Square, Dublin 2, Ireland **t** +353 1 207 0508 **f** +353 1 207 0418 **e** info@religionmusic.com **w** religionmusic.com MD: Glenn Herlihy. Dist: Vital/Edel

Remote (see Locked On Records)

Renaissance Recordings 1st Floor, 24 Regent St, Nottingham NG1 5BQ **t** 0115 910 1111 **f** 0115 910 1071 **e** marcus@renaissanceuk.com **w** renaissanceuk.com Label Manager: Marcus James. Dist: Amato

Renegade Hardware (see TOV Music Group Ltd (Trouble on Vinyl))

Renegade Recordings (see TOV Music Group Ltd (Trouble on Vinyl))

Renk Records 189 Upton Lane, Forest Gate, London E7 9PJ **t** 020 8985 0091 **e** renkrecords@msn.com **w** renkrecords.com MD: Junior Hart. Business Affairs: Shellan Barbour. Dist: Southern

Rephlex PO Box 2676, London N11 1AZ **t** 020 8368 5903 **f** 020 8361 2811 **e** info@rephlex.com **w** rephlex.com Press/Distrib: Marcus Scott. Dist: SRD

ReprinT Records 9 The Causeway, Downend, Fareham, Hants PO16 8RN **t** 023 9257 0632 **e** water.fall@virgin.net Director: Jo Womar.

Resist Music 138B West Hill, London SW15 2UE **t** 020 8780 0305 **f** 020 8788 2889 **e** mailbox@resist-music.co.uk **w** resist-music.co.uk MD: James Horrocks. Dist: SRD

Resurgence (see Voiceprint)

Retaliate First Recordings Unit 9, Darvells Yard, Chorleywood Common, Herts. WD3 5LP **t** 01923 286010 **f** 01923 286070 **e** steve@retaliatefirst.co.uk MD: Steve Lowes. Dist: Prime

Retch Records 49 Rose Crescent, Woodvale, Southport, Merseyside PR8 3RZ **t** 01704 577835 or 07951 201407 **e** retchrecords@aol.com **w** hometown.aol.co.uk/retchrecords Owner: M Hines. Dist: Cargo/Caroline2

Retek (see Supreme Music)

Rev-Ola (see Cherry Red Records)

Reverb Records Ltd Reverb House, Bennett Street, London W4 2AH **t** 020 8747 0660 **f** 020 8747 0880 **e** records@reverbxl.com **w** reverbxl.com Label Manager: Mark Lusty.

Reverberations 27 Wallorton Gardens, London SW14 8DX **t** 020 8876 5737 **f** 020 8392 1422 **e** info@reverberations.co.uk **w** reverberations.co.uk Owner: Asad Rizvi.

Revolver Music Ltd 152 Goldthorn Hill, Penn, Wolverhampton, West Midlands WV2 3JA **t** 01902 345345 **f** 01902 345155 **e** Paul.Birch@revolver-e.com **w** revolver-records.com MD: Paul Birch. Dist: Universal

Rex (see XL Recordings)

RF Records Room B5, The Arden Centre, Sale Road, Northendon, Manchester M23 0DD **t** 0161 957 1792 or 0161 957 1795 **f** 0161 957 1742 or 0161 957 1732 **e** pellis@ccm.ac.uk **w** rfrecords.com Label Mgr: Phil Ellis.

Richmond (see Cherry Red Records)

Riddle (see Nikt Records)

Rideout Records Lillie House, 1A Conduit Street, Leicester, Leicestershire LE2 0JN **t** 0116 223 0318 **f** 0116 223 0302 **e** rideout@stayfree.co.uk **w** music.stayfree.co.uk/rideout Mkt Promo Mgr: Darren Nockles. Dist: Proper

Ridge Records 1 York Street, Aberdeen AB11 5DL **t** 01224 573100 **f** 01224 572598 **e** office@ridge-records.com **w** ridge-records.com Manager: Mike Smith. Dist: Active Media/Universal

Right Recordings (see Right Recordings Ltd)

Right Recordings Ltd 177 High Street, Harlesden, London NW10 4TE **t** 020 8961 3889 **f** 020 8961 4620 **e** info@rightrecordings.com **w** rightrecordings.com Directors: David Landau, John Kaufman. Dist: Avid/BMG

Ring-pull Records 241A East Barnet Road, East Barnet, Hertfordshire EN4 8SS **t** 020 8449 0766 **e** info@ringpullrecords.com **w** ringpullrecords.com Label Mgr: Angelique Ekart. Dist: Envy

Rinse It Out (see Labels UK)

Riot Club Records Unit 4, 27a Spring Grove Rd, Hounslow, Middx TW3 4BE **t** 020 8570 8100 **f** 020 8572 9590 **e** lee@riotclub.co.uk **w** riotclubrecords.co.uk MD: Lee Farrow.

Rise & Shine (see Wyze Productions)

Riverboat Records (see World Music Network (UK) Ltd)

Riverman Records Top Floor, George House, Brecon Road, London W6 9PY **t** 020 7381 4000 **f** 020 7381 9666 **e** info@riverman.co.uk **w** riverman.co.uk Contact: Peter Fleming Dist: Shellshock

Riviera Music & Publishing 83 Dolphin Crescent, Paignton, Devon TQ3 1JZ **t** 07071 226078 **f** 01803 665728 **e** Info@rivieramusic.net **w** rivieramusic.net MD: Kevin Jarvis.

RL-2 Bewley House, Ightham, Kent TN15 9AP **t** 01732 884606 **e** info@rl-2.com **w** rl-2.com GM: Paul Lilly. Dist: MacTwo/BMG

RMO/Chill-out Music & Film 5a Tonbridge Rd, Maidstone, Kent ME16 8RL **t** 01622 768 668 **f** 01622 768 667 Dir: Reg McLean. Dist: EMI

Road Train Recordings (see Shout Out Records)

Roadrunner Records Ealing Studios, Ealing Green, London W5 5EP **t** 020 8567 6762 **f** 020 8567 6793 **e** rrguest@roadrunnerrecords.co.uk **w** roadrunnerrecords.co.uk MD: Mark Palmer.

Rock Action Records PO Box 15107, Glasgow G1 1US **t** 0141 572 0835 **f** 0141 572 0836 **e** info@rockaction records.co.uk **w** rockactionrecords.co.uk Label Manager: Craig Hargrave. Dist: Vital

Rogue Records Ltd PO Box 337, London N4 1TW **t** 020 8340 9651 **f** 020 8348 5626 **e** rogue@frootsmag.com **w** frootsmag.com/beatnik MD: Ian Anderson. Dist: Newnote/Pinnacle

Rollercoaster Records Rock House, London Road, St Mary's, Chalford, Gloucestershire GL6 8PU **t** 0845 456 9759 or 01453 886252 **f** 0845 456 9760 **e** info@rollercoasterrecords.com **w** rollercoasterrecords.com Owner: John Beecher.

Ronco 107 Mortlake Street, London SW14 8HQ **t** 020 8392 6876 **f** 020 8392 6829 **e** ray.levy@telstar.co.uk Label Manager: Ray Levy. Dist: BMG

Roots Records 250 Earlsdon Avenue North, Coventry, W. Midlands CV5 6GX **t** 02476 711935 **f** 02476 711191 **e** rootsrecs@btclick.com MD: Graham Bradshaw. Dist: Roots

Rosette Records 12 Fairway Drive, Greenford, Middx UB6 8PW **t** 020 8575 5666 **f** 020 8575 1166 **e** info@rosetterecords.com **w** rosetterecords.com GM: Ann Clerkin.

Ross Records (Turriff) Ltd 30 Main Street, Turriff, Aberdeenshire AB53 4AB **t** 01888 568899 **f** 01888 568890 **e** gibson@rossrecords.com **w** rossrecords.com MD: Gibson Ross. Dist: Ross/Highlander/Gordon Duncan

Rotator Records Interzone House, 74-77 Magdalen Road, Oxford OX4 1RE **t** 01865 205600 **f** 01865 205700 **e** info@rotator.co.uk **w** rotator.co.uk A&R: Richard Cotton.

Rough Trade Records 66 Golborne Road, London W10 5PS **t** 020 8960 9888 **f** 020 8968 6715 **e** james@roughtraderecords.com **w** roughtraderecords.com Contact: Pru Harris Dist: Vital

Royal Palm (see Kudos Records Ltd)

RPM (see Cherry Red Records)

RPM Productions PO Box 158, Chipping Norton, Oxon OX7 6FD **t** 01993 831011 **f** 01993 831011 **e** info.rpm@ntlworld.com **w** rpmrecords.co.uk MD: Mark Stratford.

Rubber Road Records 4-10 Lamb Walk, London SE1 3TT **t** 020 7921 8353 **e** rubber_road_records@yahoo.co.uk Head of A&R: Nick Lightowlers.

Rubicon Records 59 Park View Road, London NW10 1AJ **t** 020 8450 5154 **f** 020 8452 0187 **e** rubiconrecords@btopenworld.com **w** rubiconrecords.co.uk Founder: Graham Le Fevre.

Ruff n Tumble 23 Corbyn St, London N4 3BY **t** 020 7281 1313 **e** crew@ruffntumble.co.uk **w** ruffntumble.co.uk Co-Dir: Andreas Monoyos.

RuffLife UK PO Box 38115, London W10 6XG **t** 020 8932 2860 **f** 020 7376 0779 **e** carmineperretta@ruffnation.com **w** ruffnation.com A&R: Carmine Perretta. Dist: Vital

Rulin (see Ministry Of Sound Recordings)

Rumour Records Ltd Tempo House, 15 Falcon Rd, London SW11 2PJ **t** 020 7228 6821 **f** 020 7228 6972 **e** post@rumour.demon.co.uk **w** rumourrecords.com MD: Anne Plaxton. Dist: Pinnacle

Running Man Records PO Box 32100, London N1 1GRf 020 8341 5595 **e** runningman@oysterband.co.uk **w** oysterband.co.uk Label Manager: Colin Clowtt.

Russian Season (see Harmonia Mundi (UK) Ltd)

Rykodisc 329 Latimer Road, London W10 6RA **t** 020 8960 3311 **f** 020 8960 1177 **e** info@rykodisc.co.uk **w** rykodisc.com Sales & Distribution Dir: Andy Childs. Dist: Pinnacle

S Records (see BMG UK & Ireland Ltd)

S.O.U.R. Recordings (see Tuff Street - SOSL Recordings)

S12 (see Simply Vinyl)

S:Alt Records Ltd PO Box 34140, London NW10 2WW **t** 020 8830 3355 **f** 020 8830 4466 **e** info@saltrecords.com **w** saltrecords.com Label Mgr: Sandra Ceschia.

Sacred Records 187 Freston Rd, London W10 6TH **t** 020 8969 1323 **f** 020 8969 1363 **e** info@sacred-music.com Label Manager: Adjei Amaning.

Sain (Recordiau) Cyf Canolfan Sain, Llandwrog, Caernarfon, Gwynedd LL54 5TG **t** 01286 831 111 **f** 01286 831 497 **e** sain@sain.wales.com **w** sain.wales.com Label Mgr: Dafydd Roberts.

Sakay (see Rogue Records Ltd)

Salabert (see Harmonia Mundi (UK) Ltd)

Salsoul UK (see suss'd! records - the home of Salsoul UK)

Salt Hill Recordings (see Whole 9 Yards)

SANCTUARY CLASSICS

45-53 Sinclair Road, London W14 0NS **t** 020 7300 1888 **f** 020 7300 1306 **e** info@sanctuaryclassics.com **w** sanctuaryclassics.com A&R Manager: Pollyanna Gunning. International Sales Manager: Andy West. Publicist: Karen Pitchford. Dist: Pinnacle

SANCTUARY RECORDS GROUP

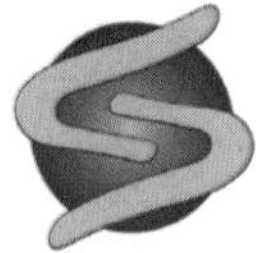

Sanctuary House, 45-53 Sinclair Road, London W14 0NS **t** 020 7602 6351 **f** 020 7603 5941 **e** info@sanctuaryrecords.co.uk **w** sanctuaryrecordsgroup.co.uk CEO: Joe Cokell. COO: Roger Semon. CFO: Ed Cook. Business Affairs Director: Paul Kernick. Senior VP A&R: John Williams. Sales Manager: Henry Yori. Intl Sales: Nick Church. VP Intl Marketing & Promotion: Julian Wall. Marketing Manager - Commercial Marketing: Lynn McPhilemy. Manager - Special Markets: John Reed. Head of Contemporary Marketing UK: Giles Green. Commercial Manager - Sanctuary Visual Entertainment: Spencer Pollard. Head of Corporate Communications: Eddy Leviten.

Sandman Records Ltd 57 Albert Road, London N22 7AA **t** 020 8881 4235 or 07961 126 990 **e** sandmandave57@hotmail.com A&R: Dave Bolton. Dist: Cargo

Sangraal (see Science Friction)

Santi Music Ltd 91 Manor Road South, Hinchley Wood, Esher, Surrey KT10 0QB **t** 020 8398 4144 or 07957 367 214 **f** 020 8398 4244 **e** steve@santimusic.com MD: Steve Weltman.

Sargasso Records PO Box 10565, London N1 8SR **t** 020 7359 7825 **f** 020 7704 2141 **e** info@sargasso.com **w** sargasso.com Dist: Impetus

Satellite Music Ltd 34 Salisbury St, London NW8 8QE **t** 020 7402 9111 **f** 020 7723 3064 **e** satellite_artists@hotmail.com MD: Eliot Cohen. Dist: Sound and Vision

Satellite. (see Soul Jazz Records)

Saucer (see Seriously Groovy Music)

Savant Records 132 Chase Way, London N14 5DH **t** 07050 055168 **f** 0870 741 5252 **e** teleryngg@msn.com **w** teleryngg.com MD: Richard Struple.

Savoy Records PO Box 271, Coulsdon, Surrey CR5 3YZ **t** 01737 554 739 **f** 01737 556 737 **e** admin@savoymusic.com **w** savoymusic.com MD: Wendy Smith.

Saydisc (see Harmonia Mundi (UK) Ltd)

Saydisc Records The Barton, Inglestone Common, Badminton, Gloucestershire GL9 1BXf 01454 299 858 **e** saydisc@aol.com **w** saydisc.com MD: Gef Lucena. Dist: Harmonia Mundi (UK)

SBS Records PO Box 37, Blackwood, Gwent NP12 2YQ **t** 01495 201116 or 07711 984651 **f** 01495 201190 **e** enquiry@sbsrecords.co.uk **w** sbsrecords.co.uk MD: Glenn Powell.

Scarlet Records Southview, 68 Siltside, Gosberton Risegate, Lincs PE11 4ET **t** 01755 841750 **f** 01755 841750 **e** info@scarletrecording.co.uk **w** scarlet recording.co.uk MD: Liz Lenten. Dist: Pinnacle

Schnitzel Records PO Box 37291, London SW11 5TX **t** 07740 700 739 **f** 07974 011 403 **e** info@schnitzel.co.uk **w** schnitzel.co.uk MD: Oliver Geywitz.

Science (see Virgin Records)

Science Friction 21 Stupton Rd, Sheffield, South Yorks S9 1BQ **t** 0114 261 1649 **f** 0114 261 1649 **e** dc@cprod.win-uk.net **w** royharper.co.uk Label Manager: Darren Crisp. Dist: Proper

Scotdisc - BGS Productions Ltd Newtown Street, Kilsyth, Glasgow, Strathclyde G65 0LY **t** 01236 821081 **f** 01236 826900 **e** info@scotdisc.co.uk **w** scotdisc.co.uk MD: Dougie Stevenson. Dist: Gordon Duncan

Scratch Records Hatch Farm Studios, Chertsey Rd, Addlestone, Surrey KT15 2EH **t** 01932 828715 **f** 01932 828717 **e** brian.adams@dial.pipex.com **w** thestoreformusic.com MD: Brian Adams. A&R (Dance/Pop): John Jules. Dist: Voiceprint/Pinnacle

Scribendum (see SilverOak Music Entertainment Ltd)

Sea Dream (see Plankton Records)

Seamless Recordings Ltd 192-194 Clapham High St, London SW4 7UD **t** 020 7498 5551 **f** 020 7498 2333 **e** amber@bargrooves.com **w** seamlessrecordings.com Label Mgr: Amber Spencer-Holmes.

Secret Records Regent House, 1 Pratt Mews, London NW1 OAD **t** 020 7267 6899 **f** 020 7267 6746 **e** partners@newman-and.co.uk MD: Colin Newman.

Sedna Records 10 Barley Mow Passage, Chiswick, London W4 4PH **t** 020 8747 4534 **e** info@sednarecords.com **w** sednarecords.com MD: Jonathan Wild. Dist: Absolute

See For Miles Records Ltd Unit 10, Littleton House, Littleton Road, Ashford, Middlesex TW15 1UU **t** 01784 247176 **f** 01784 241168 **e** sfm@highnote.co.uk **w** seeformiles.co.uk MD: Colin Miles. Dist: Koch

Seeca Records 115, Mortlake Business Centre, 20, Mortlake High St, London SW14 8JN **t** 020 8487 8622 **f** 020 8876 7467 **e** info@seeca.co.uk **w** seeca.co.uk Label Manager: Line Ebbesen.

Seedpod 11 Lindal Rd, Crofton Park, London SE4 1EJ **t** 020 8691 1564 **f** 020 8691 1564 **e** music@seedpod.biz **w** seedpod.biz Dir: Natalie Cummings.

Select Music and Video Ltd. 3 Wells Place, Redhill, Surrey RH1 3SL **t** 01737 645600 **f** 01737 644065 **e** BHolden@selectmusic.co.uk **w** naxos.com Naxos Label Mgr/Mktg Mgr: Barry Holden.

Sema (see Flat Records)

Serengeti Records 43A Old Woking Road, West Byfleet, Surrey KT14 6LG **t** 01932 351925 **f** 01932 336431 **e** info@serengeti-records.com MD: Martin Howell. Dist: Serengeti

Serious (see Renk Records)

Seriously Groovy Music 3rd Floor, 28 D'Arblay St, Soho, London W1F 8EW **t** 020 7439 1947 **f** 020 7734 7540 **e** admin@seriouslygroovy.com **w** seriouslygroovy.com Directors: Dave Holmes/Lorraine Snape. Dist: Pinnacle

Setanta Records 174 Camden Road, London NW1 9HJ **t** 020 7284 4877 **f** 020 7284 4577 **e** info@setantarecords.com **w** setantarecords.com MD: Keith Cullen. Dist: Vital

Shaboom Records PO Box 38, South Shore, Blackpool FY1 6GH **t** 01253 620039 **f** 01253 620756 **e** mail@shaboom.co.uk **w** shaboom.co.uk Co Owner: Dick Johnson. Dist: Pinnacle

Shade Factor Productions Ltd 4 Cleveland Square, London W2 6DH **t** 020 7402 6477 **f** 020 7402 7144 **e** mail@shadefactor.com **w** shadefactor.com MD: Ann Symonds.

Shadow Cryptic (see Moving Shadow Ltd)

Shamtown Records 13 St Mary's Terrace, Galway, Ireland **t** +353 91 521309 **f** +353 91 526341 **e** sawdoc@eircom.net **w** sawdoctors.com MD: Ollie Jennings. Dist: Pinnacle

Shark Records 23 Rollscourt Avenue, Herne Hill, London SE24 0EA **t** 020 7737 4580 **f** 020 7737 4580 **e** mellor@organix.fsbusiness.co.uk MD: Mr MH Mellor.

Sharpe Music 9A Irish Street, Dungannon, Co Tyrone BT70 3LN **t** 028 8772 4621 **f** 028 8775 2195 **e** info@sharpemusicireland.com **w** sharpemusicireland.com MD: Raymond Stewart.

Sheepfold 43 Broadleaf Avenue, Bishop's Stortford, Hertfordshire CM23 3JF **t** 01279 835067 or 01920 462210 **f** 01920 461187 **e** paul.burrell@virgin.net Mgr: Paul Burrell.

Shellwood Productions (see Priory Records)

Shifty Disco Ltd 65 George Street, Oxford OX1 2BE **t** 01865 798791 **f** 01865 798792 **e** info@shiftydisco.co.uk **w** shiftydisco.co.uk MD: Dave Newton. Dist: Pinnacle

Shinkansen Recordings PO Box 14274, London SE11 6ZG **t** 020 7582 2877 **f** 020 7582 3342 **e** shink@dircon.co.uk **w** shink.dircon.co.uk MD: Matt Haynes. Dist: SRD

Shock Records PO Box 301, Torquay, Devon TQ2 7TB **t** 01803 614392 **f** 01803 616271 **e** info@shockrecords.co.uk **w** shockrecords.co.uk A&R Manager: Graham Eden. Dist: Alphamagic

Shoeshine Records PO Box 15193, Glasgow G2 6LB **t** 0141 204 5654 **f** 0141 204 5654 **e** info@shoeshine.co.uk **w** shoeshine.co.uk Proprietor: Francis Macdonald. Dist: Pinnacle/Proper

Shout Out Records 51 Clarkegrove Rd, Sheffield S10 2NH **t** 0114 268 5665 **f** 0114 268 4161 **e** entsuk@aol.com MD: John Roddison.

Shrimp Platters (see Blaster!)

SI Projects (see Adelphoi)

SI Recordings (see Adelphoi)

Silent Records **t** 07957 165 391 **e** info@silentrecords.com **w** silentrecords.com MD: Julian Close.

Silva Classics (see Silva Screen Records)

Silva Screen Records 3 Prowse Place, London NW1 9PH **t** 020 7428 5500 **f** 020 7482 2385 **e** info@silvascreen.co.uk **w** silvascreen.co.uk MD: Reynold da Silva. Dist: RSK Entertainment

Silva Treasury (see Silva Screen Records)

Silver Planet Records 16 Stratford Rd, London W8 6QD **t** 020 7937 6246 **f** 020 7937 6246 **e** info@silverplanetrecordings.com **w** silverplanetrecordings.com A&R Mgr: David Conway. A&R (Easyaccess): James Holden. Dist: Intergroove

Silverscope Records (see Ncompass Records)

Silverword (see Silverword Music Group)

Simple Records First Floor, 75 Abbeville Rd SW4 9JN **t** 020 8673 1818 **f** 020 8673 6751 **e** info@simplerecords.co.uk A&R Director: Will Saul.

Simply Music (see Simply Vinyl)

Simply Recordings (see Simply Vinyl)

Simply Vinyl Unit 4, The Pavilions, 2 East Road, South Wimbledon, London SW19 1UW **t** 020 8545 8580 **f** 020 8545 8581 **e** info@simplyvinyl.com **w** simplyvinyl.com MD: Mike Loveday. Dist: THE

Single Minded Music 11 Cambridge Court, 210 Shepherd's Bush Road, London W6 7NJ **t** 0870 011 3748 **f** 0870 011 3749 **e** tony@singleminded.com **w** singleminded.com MD: Tony Byrne.

Sire (see Warner Bros Records)

Siren Music Ltd PO Box 166, Hartlepool, Cleveland TS26 9JA **t** 01429 424603 **e** daveianhill@yahoo.co.uk **w** siren-music.demon.co.uk Dir: Dave Hill. Dist: RMG

Six Degrees Records (see Collective Music Ltd)

Six Feet Deep 17 Maidavale Crescent, Styvechale, Coventry CV3 6FZ **t** 07811 469888 **e** chief@fivemileshigh.com **w** fivemileshigh.com MD: Dave Robinson.

Skindependent Leacroft, Chertion Cross, Cheriton Bishop, Exeter, Devon EX6 6JH **t** 01647 24502 **f** 01647 24502 **e** charlie35@supanet.com **w** lizardsun-music.co.uk MD: Charles Salt.

Skint Records PO Box 174, Brighton, East Sussex BN1 4BA **t** 01273 738527 **f** 01273 208766 **e** mail@skint.net **w** skint.net Dir: Damian Harris. Dist: Vital

Skyline (see New State Entertainment)

Slalom Recordings Ltd 12 Farleigh Wick, Bradford on Avon, Wiltshire BA15 2PU **t** 01225 864860 **f** 08453 339305 **e** info@slalom.co.uk **w** slalom.co.uk MD: James Reade. Dist: SRD

SLAM Productions 3 Thesiger Rd, Abingdon, Oxon OX14 2DX **t** 01235 529012 **f** 01235 529012 **e** slamprods@aol.com **w** members.aol.com/slamprods Prop: George Haslam. Dist: Cadillac

Slate Records PO Box 173, New Malden, Surrey KT3 3YR **t** 020 8949 7730 **f** 020 8949 7798 **e** john.osb1@btinternet.com Proprietor: John Osborne.

Slave Records PO Box 200, South Shore, Blackpool, Lancs FY1 6GR **t** 07714 910257 **e** sploj3@yahoo.co.uk Contact: Rob Powell

Slick Slut Recordings Brewmasters House, 91 Brick Lane, London E1 6QL **t** 020 7375 2332 **f** 020 7375 2442 **e** info@essentialdirect.co.uk **w** essentialdirect.co.uk A&R: Gary Dedman. Dist: Essential Direct

Slinky Music Ltd PO Box 3344, Bournemouth, Dorset BH1 4YB **t** 01202 652100 **f** 01202 652036 **e** info@slinky.co.uk **w** slinky.co.uk Label Manager: Dave Lea. Dist: Beechwood

Slip 'N' Slide (see Kickin Music Ltd)

Slow Graffiti 149 Albany Rd, Roath, Cardiff CF24 3NT **t** 07813 069 739 **e** buymore@slowgraffiti.com **w** slowgraffiti.com MD: Andy Davidson. Dist: Shellshock

Small Pond (see East Central One Ltd)

Smiled Records RGA Studio, 209 Goldhawk Road, London W12 8EP **t** 020 8746 7000 or 07776 188 191 **f** 020 8746 7700 **e** info@smiled.net **w** smiled.net MD: James Barton.

Snapper Music 3 The Coda Centre, 189 Munster Road, London SW6 6AW **t** 020 7610 0330 **f** 020 7386 7006 **e** sales@snappermusic.co.uk **w** snappermusic.co.uk CEO: Jon Beecher. Dist: Pinnacle

So Real Records (see East Central One Ltd)

Sobriety Records (see Shout Out Records)

Soda (see Seriously Groovy Music)

Sofa (see Seriously Groovy Music)

SOG (see 3 Beat Label Management)

Solar Music PO Box 4809, Bournemouth, Dorset BH7 6WA **t** 0776 211 3402 **f** 0870 706 4830 **e** info@solar-music.com **w** solar-music.com International Director: Stuart Wheeler.

Solarise Records PO Box 31104, London E16 4NS **t** 07980 453 628 or 07790 865 199 **e** info@solariserecords.com **w** solariserecords.com Owners: Paul/Lee.

Sole (see Console Sounds)

Solent Records 68-70 Lugley St, Newport, Isle Of Wight PO30 5ET **t** 01983 524110 **f** 0870 1640388 **e** md@solentrecords.co.uk **w** solentrecords.co.uk Owner: John Waterman. Dist: Nova/Pinnacle

Soma Recordings Ltd 2nd Floor, 342 Argyle Street, Glasgow G2 8LY **t** 0141 229 6220 **f** 0141 226 4383 **e** info@somarecords.com **w** somarecords.com MD: Dave Clarke. Dist: Vital

Sombrero (see Sonic360)

Some (see Southern Records)

Some Bizarre (see Some Bizzare)

Some Bizzare 4 Denmark Street, London WC2H 8LP **t** 020 7836 9995 **f** 020 7836 9909 **e** info@somebizarre.com **w** somebizarre.com MD: Stevo. Dist: Pinnacle

Sonar Records 82 London Rd, Coventry, West Midlands CV1 2JT **t** 024 7622 0749 **e** office@sonar-records.demon.co.uk **w** cabinstudio.co.uk MD: Jon Lord.

Songlines Ltd PO Box 20206, London NW1 7FF **t** 020 7284 3970 **f** 020 7485 0511 **e** doug@songline.demon.co.uk **w** songline.co.uk MD: Doug D'Arcy.

Sonic360 33 Riding House St, London W1W 7DZ **t** 020 7636 3939 **f** 020 7636 0033 **e** info@sonic360.com **w** sonic360.com Label Mgr: Zen Grisdale.

SonRise Records Western House, Richardson St, Swansea SA1 3JF **t** 01792 642849 **e** info@sonriserecords.co.uk **w** sonriserecords.co.uk Contact: Darren Pullin Dist: Vital

---

SONY BMG ENTERTAINMENT UK & IRELAND

Bedford House, 67-69 Fulham High Street, London SW6 3JW **t** 020 7384 7500.
Also at 10 Great Marlborough Street, London W1F 7LP **t** 020 7911 8200. Chairman/CEO: Rob Stringer.
Details of the new company were being confirmed at the time of going to press. For the latest information visit musicweek.com

---

Sorted Records PO Box 5922, Leicester LE1 6XU **t** 0116 291 1580 or 0771 128 0098 **f** 0116 291 1580 **e** sortedrecords@Hotmail.com **w** sorted-records.org.uk MD: Dave Dixey. Dist: Shellshock

SOSL Recordings (see Tuff Street - SOSL Recordings)

Soul 2 Soul Recordings 36-38 Rochester Place, London NW1 9JX **t** 020 7284 0293 **f** 020 7284 2290 **e** info@soul2soul.co.uk **w** soul2soul.co.uk MD: Jazzie B. Dist: Vital

Soul Brother (see Expansion Records)

Soul Jazz Records 7 Broadwick St, London W1F 0DA **t** 020 7734 3341 **f** 020 7494 1035 **e** info@soundsoftheuniverse.com **w** souljazzrecords.co.uk Publicity & Production: Angela Scott. Dist: Vital

Soul Note (see Harmonia Mundi (UK) Ltd)

Sound & Video Gems Ltd Quaker's Coppice, Crewe, Cheshire CW1 6EY **t** 01270 589321 **f** 01270 587438 MD: M Bates. Dist: Budget labels only

Sound Entertainment Ltd The Music Village, 11B Osiers Road, London SW18 1NL **t** 020 8874 8444 **f** 020 8874 0337 **e** info@soundentertainment.co.uk **w** soundentertainment.co.uk Dir: Bob Nolan. Dist: Disc Distribution

Sound Of Ministry (see Ministry Of Sound Recordings)

Sound Recordings 98 White Lion St, London N1 9PF **t** 020 7278 5698 **f** 020 7278 6009 **e** info@soundrecordings.net **w** soundrecordings.net Contact: Jamie Spencer Dist: Absolute

Soundclash 28 St Benedicts Street, Norwich, Norfolk NR2 4AQ **t** 01603 761004 **f** 01603 762248 **e** soundclash@btinternet.com **w** soundclash.cwc.net Manager: Spencer Took.

Soundscape Music 4 Bridgefield, Farnham, Surrey GU9 8AN **t** 01252 721096 **f** 01252 733909 **e** bobholroyd@soundscapemusic.co.uk **w** soundscapemusic.co.uk Director: Bob Holroyd.

Soundwaves Unit 4, Albert Street, Droylsden, Greater Manchester M43 7BA **t** 0161 370 6908 **f** 0161 371 8207 **e** efoulkes@aol.com Director: Bill White. Dist: BMG

Southbound (see Ace Records)

Southbound Records Ltd 9 Preston Road, Leytonstone, London E11 1NL **t** 020 8989 5005 **f** 020 8989 5006 **e** enquiries@southboundrecords.com **w** southboundrecords.com MD: Jeffrey Stothers. Dist: Ideal/Universal

Southern Cuba Records PO Box 27254, London N11 2YE **t** 020 8372 0141 **f** 020 8372 3875 **e** info@southerncubarecords.com **w** southerncubarecords.com MD: OD Hunte.

Southern Fried Records Fulham Palace, Bishops Avenue, London SW6 6EA **t** 020 7384 7373 **f** 020 7384 7392 **e** nathan@southernfriedrecords.com **w** southernfriedrecords.com A&R Manager: Nathan Thursting. Label Manager Underwater Records: Matt Stuart.

Southern Lord (see Southern Records)

Southern Records Unit 3, Cranford Way, London N8 9DG **t** 020 8348 4640 **f** 020 8348 9156 **e** info@southern.com **w** southern.net GM: Allison Schnackenberg. Dist: Shellshock/SRD

Sovereign (see Hot Lead Records)

Sovereign Lifestyle Records PO Box 356, Leighton Buzzard, Beds LU7 3WP **t** 01525 385578 **f** 01525 372743 **e** sovereignmusic@aol.com MD: Robert Lamont.

Soviet Union Records Musicdash, PO Box 1977, Manchester M26 2YB **t** 0787 0727 075 **e** sovrec@yahoo.co.uk **w** sovietunion.co.uk Director: Jon Ashley.

Space Age Recordings (see Adasam Limited)

Special Fried (see New State Entertainment)

Spin-OFF Recordings (see 1-OFF Recordings)

Spincity (see Truelove Records)

Spit and Polish Records (see Shoeshine Records)

Spitfire (see Eagle Rock Entertainment Ltd.)

Splash Records 29 Manor House, 250 Marylebone Road, London NW1 5NP **t** 020 7723 7177 **f** 020 7262 0775 **e** splashrecords.uk@btconnect.com **w** splashrecords.com Director: Chas Peate.

Splinter Recordings Terminal Studios, Lamb Walk, London SE1 3TT **t** 020 7357 8416 **f** 020 7357 8437 **e** parmesanchic@aol.com **w** sneakerpimps.com MD: Caroline Butler.

Spoilt Records PO Box 25369, London NW5 3WU **t** 020 7240 1977 **e** gillian@spoiltrecords.com **w** spoiltrecords.com Director: Gillian Pittaway. Dist: SRD

Spot On Records Unit 16, Southam Street Studios, London W10 5PH **t** 020 8964 4741 **f** 020 8960 4941 **e** info@spotonrecords.org.uk **w** spotonrecords.com Directors: Tim Stark, Katya Hilgeland. Dist: Amato

Sprawl Imprint 63 Windmill Road, Brentford, Middlesex TW8 0QQ **t** 0208 568 3145 **e** sprawl@benfo.demon.co.uk **w** dfuse.com/sprawl/ MD: Douglas Benford. Dist: SRD

Spring Recordings Dargan House, Duncairn Terrace, Bray, Co. Wicklow, Ireland **t** +353 12 861514 **f** +353 12 861514 **e** kosi@mrspring.net **w** mrspring.net MD: Mr Spring.

Springthyme Records Balmalcolm House, Balmalcolm, Cupar, Fife KY15 7TJ **t** 01337 830773 **f** 01337 831773 **e** music@springthyme.co.uk **w** springthyme.co.uk Director: Peter Shepheard. Dist: Highlander

Spundae Recordings 93b Scrubs Lane, London NW10 6QU **t** 020 8962 8255 or 07808 741 277 **f** 020 8968 3377 **e** henriette@spundae.de **w** spundae.de Label Mgr: Henriette Amiel.

Square Biz Records 65A Beresford Rd, London N5 2HR **t** 020 7354 0841 **f** 020 7503 6457 **e** sujiro.gray@btinternet.com MD: Mr J Gray. Dist: Absolute Marketing

Squeaky Records Ltd. The Squeaky Shed, 37 Baldock Road, Royston, Herts. SG8 5BJ **t** 01763 243 603 **f** 01763 245 623 **e** info@squeakyrecords.com **w** squeakyrecords.com Director: Helen Gregorios-Pippas. Dist: AMD

Squint Entertainment (see Collective Music Ltd)

Star-Write Ltd PO Box 16715, London NW4 1WN **t** 020 8203 5062 **f** 020 8202 3746 **e** starwrite@btinternet.com Dir: John Lisners.

Starfish Records Top Floor - Apartment 1, 182 Easter Road, Edinburgh EH7 5QQ **t** 0131 661 0358 or 0131 669 4657 **e** star@starfishrecords.co.uk **w** starfishrecords.co.uk Label Manager: Gavin Henderson. Dist: Cargo

Starshaped Records PO Box 28424, Edinburgh EH4 5YH **t** 0131 336 2776 or 07931 595 285 **e** info@starshaped.co.uk **w** starshaped.co.uk Label Manager: Ian White. Dist: Shellshock

Start Audio & Video 3 Warmair House, Green Lane, Northwood, Middx HA6 2QB **t** 01923 841414 **f** 01923 842223 **e** startav@compuserve.com **w** nostalgiamusic.co.uk GM: Nicholas Dicker. Dist: Koch

Start Classics (see Start Audio & Video)

State Art The Basement, 3 Eaton Place, Brighton, East Sussex BN2 1EH **t** 01273 572090 **f** 01273 572090 **e** stateart@mexone.co.uk **w** mexonerecordings.co.uk Creative Partner: Paul Mex.

State Records 6 Kendrick Place, London WIU 6HD **t** 020 7486 9878 **f** 020 7486 9934 **e** recordings@staterecords.co.uk **w** staterecords.co.uk MD: Dr Wayne Bickerton.

Stax (see Ace Records)

Sterling (see Priory Records)

Stern's Records 74-75 Warren Street, London W1T 5PF **t** 020 7387 5550 or 020 7388 5533 **f** 020 7388 2756 **e** info@sternsmusic.com **w** sternsmusic.com MD: Don Bay. Dist: Stern's

Sticky Music PO Box 176, Glasgow G11 5YJ **t** 01698 207230 **f** 0141 576 8431 **e** enquiries@stickymusic.co.uk **w** stickymusic.co.uk Partner: Charlie Irvine.

Stiff Records (see ZTT Records Ltd)

Stirling Music Group 25, Heathmans Road, London SW6 4TJ **t** 020 7371 5756 **f** 020 7371 7731 **e** office@pureuk.com **w** pureuk.com CEO: Evros Stakis. Creative Dir: Billy Royal. General Label Mgr: Stewart Rowell.

Stockholm (see Polydor Records)

Stompatime (see Fury Records)

Stoned Asia Music (see Kickin Music Ltd)

The Store For Music (see Scratch Records)

Storm Music 2nd Floor, 1 Ridgefield, Manchester M2 6EG **t** 0161 839 5111 **f** 0161 839 7898 **e** info@storm-music.com **w** storm-music.com Contact: Sam Gray Dist: Universal

Stradivarius (see Priory Records)

Strange Fruit Records 333 Latimer Road, London W10 6RA **t** 020 8964 9544 **f** 020 8964 5460 **e** sfm@strange-fruit-music.co.uk Label Mgr: Sue Armstrong. Dist: Pinnacle

Strathan Music Canisp House, Roster, Caithness KW3 6BD **t** 0870 241 2094 **f** 01593 721758 **e** mail@strathan.com **w** strathan.com Dir: Karen Brimm.

Stress Recordings (see DMC Ltd)

Stretchy Records Ltd PO Box 5520, Bishops Stortford, Herts CM23 3WH **t** 01279 865070 **f** 01279 834268 **e** simon@ozrics.com **w** ozrics.com GM: Simon Baker. MD: Tony Nunn. Dist: PHD

Strictly Rhythm (see Warner Bros Records)

Strike Back Records 271 Royal College St, Camden Town, London NW1 9LU **t** 020 7482 0115 **f** 020 7267 1169 **e** maurice@baconempire.com MD: Maurice Bacon. Dist: Pinnacle

Stringbean International Records Unit 224, 2nd Floor, 2-8 Fountayne Road, London N15 4QL **t** 020 8801 7992 **f** 020 8808 0205 **e** sales@stringbeaninternational.com **w** stringbeaninternational.com MD: Donovan Campbell.

Strong Records 33 Sunnymead Rd, London SW15 5HY **t** 020 8878 0800 **f** 020 8878 3080 **e** emily@heavyweightman.com Label Mgr: Emily Moxon. Dist: Vital

Sublime Recordings 77 Preston Drove, Brighton, East Sussex BN1 6LD **t** 01273 560605 **f** 01273 560606 **e** info@sublimemusic.co.uk **w** sublimemusic.co.uk MD: Patrick Spinks.

Substance (see Ministry Of Sound Recordings)

Suburban Soul (Music) PO Box 415, Bromley, Kent BR1 2XR **t** 020 8402 1984 or 0798 406 1954 **f** 020 8325 0708 **e** urban_music@msn.com Director: RT Brown.

Suburbia (see Eukatech Records)

Subversive Records 16 Chalk Farm Road, London NW1 8AG **t** 020 7209 2626 **f** 020 7209 0202 **e** daniel@subversiverecords.co.uk **w** subversiverecords.co.uk MD: Daniel Pope. Dist: Amato/Pinnacle

Sugar Records 8-10 Rhoda St, London E2 7EF **t** 020 7729 4797 **f** 020 7739 8571 **e** paul.hitchman@playlouder.com MDs: Paul Hitchman & Jim Gottlieb.

Sugar Shack Records Ltd PO Box 73, Fishponds, Bristol BS16 7EZ **t** 01179 855092 **f** 01179 855092 **e** info@sugarshackrecords.co.uk **w** sugarshackrecords.co.uk Dir: Mike Darby, Adrian Stiff. Dist: Shellshock

Sugar Sound 130 Shaftesbury Ave, London W1D 5EU **t** 020 7031 0971 **e** simon@thesugargroup.com **w** thesugargroup.com Label Manager: Simon Omer.

Summerhouse Records PO Box 34601, London E17 6GA **t** 020 8520 2650 **e** office@summerhouserecordsltd.co.uk **w** summerhouserecordsltd.co.uk MD: William Jones.

Sumo Records 48 Cranbury Road, Reading RG30 2XD **t** 0118 959 8282 **f** 0118 959 8282 **e** info@sumorecords.com Director: Jacqui Gresswell.

Sunday Best Studio 10, 25 Denmark St, London WC2H 8NJ **t** 020 7240 2248 **f** 0870 420 4392 **e** info@sundaybest.net **w** sundaybest.net MD: Rob Da Bank. Dist: BMG

Sundissential (see Mohawk Records)

Sunny Records Ltd 29 Fife Road, East Sheen, London SW14 7EJ **t** 020 8876 9871 **f** 020 8392 2371 **e** john.carter@amserve.net Contact: John Carter

Superglider Records First Floor, 123 Old Christchurch Rd, Bournemouth, Dorset BH1 1EP **t** 07968 345173 **e** mail@superglider.com **w** superglider.com Contact: Griff

Supersonic Records (see New State Entertainment)

Supertone 15 Carrick Court, 137 Stockwell St, Glasgow G1 7LR **t** 07904 113 034 **e** iaininm@aol.com MD: Iain MacDonald. Dist: AMD/Universal

Supertron Music 19-23 Fosse Way, London W13 0BZ **t** 020 8998 6372 or 020 8998 4372 MD: Michael Rodriguez.

Supreme Music PO Box 184, Hove, E Sussex BN3 6UY **t** 01273 556321 **f** 01273 503333 **e** info@recoverworld.com **w** recoverworld.com MD: Chris Hampshire. Dist: Amato

Supremo Recordings PO Box 8679, Dublin 7, Ireland **t** +353 1 671 7393 **f** +353 1 671 7393 **e** info@supremorecordings.com **w** supremorecordings.com MD: Philip Cartin.

Surfdog Records (see Collective Music Ltd)

Survival Records Ltd PO Box 2502, Devizes, Wilts SN10 3ZN **t** 01380 860500 **f** 01380 860596 **e** AnneMarie@survivalrecords.co.uk **w** survivalrecords.co.uk Director: David Rome. Dist: Pinnacle

Suspect Records PO Box 29287, Deptford, London SE8 3EU **t** 07764 159175 **e** info@suspectrecords.com **w** suspectrecords.com MD: Stephen Davison.

Swearbox Records (see Ravensbourne Records Ltd)

Sweet Nothing (see Cargo Records)

Swing Cafe 32 Willesden Lane, London NW6 7ST **t** 020 7625 0231 **f** 020 372 5439 **e** lauriejay@btconnect.com Head of A&R: Chas White.

Swing City (see Wyze Productions)

Switchflicker 3rd Floor, 24 Lever St, Northern Quarter, Manchester M1 1DX **t** 07803 601 885 **e** jayne@switchflicker.com **w** switchflicker.com A&R: Jayne Compton.

Swordmaker Records PO Box 55, Consett, County Durham DH8 0UX **t** 01207 509365 **f** 01207 509365 **e** enquiries@swordmaker.co.uk **w** swordmaker.co.uk A&R: Jonny Rye.

Sylvantone Records 11 Saunton Avenue, Redcar, North Yorkshire TS10 2RL **t** 01642 479898 **f** 0709 235 9333 **e** sylvantone@hotmail.com **w**country music.org.uk/tony-goodacre/index.html Prop: Tony Goodacre.

Symposium Records 110 Derwent Avenue, East Barnet, Herts EN4 8LZ **t** 020 8368 8667 **f** 020 8368 8667 **e** symposium@cwcom.net **w** symposiumrecords.co.uk

Synergy Logistics Unit 5, Pilot Trading Estate, West Wycombe Road, High Wycombe, Bucks HP12 3AB **t** 01494 450606 **f** 01494 450230 **e** synergielogistics@btconnect.com Chief Exec: Nigel Molden.

Tabitha Music Ltd 39 Cordery Road, Exeter EX2 9DJ **t** 01392 499889 **f** 01392 498068 **e** Graham@tabithamusic.fsnet.co.uk MD: Graham Sclater.

Taciturn Records PO Box 36202, London SE19 3YW **t** 020 8653 6318 **f** 020 8653 6318 **e** taciturn@chrisshields.com **w** chrisshields.com Director: Chris Shields. Dist: Nova/Pinnacle

Tahra (see Priory Records)

Tailormade Music Ltd PO Box 2311, Romford, Essex RM5 2DZ **t** 01708 734670 **f** 01708 734671 **e** info@dancelabel.com **w** dancelabel.com Dir: Dan Donnelly. Dir: Edward Short. Dist: BMG

Talking Elephant 8 Martin Dene, Bexleyheath, Kent DA6 8NA **t** 020 8301 2828 **f** 020 8301 2424 **e** talkelephant@aol.com **w** talkingelephant.com Partner: Barry Riddington. Dist: Pinnacle

Tall Pop (see Adasam Limited)

Tall Poppy Records 2 Arlington Rd, Richmond, Surrey TW10 7BY **t** 020 8948 1188 **f** 020 8948 1188 **e** man@tallpoppyrecords.com **w** tallpoppyrecords.com Directors: Lee Lindsey & Jack Guy.

Tanty Records PO Box 557, Harrow, Middlesex HA2 6ZX **t** 020 8864 4004 **f** 020 8933 1027 **e** kelvin.r@tantyrecord.com **w** tantyrecord.com Owner: Kelvin Richard. Dist: Shellshock/Pinnacle

Tara Music Company 8 Herbert Lane, Dublin 2, Ireland **t** +353 1 678 7871 **f** +353 1 678 7873 **e** info@taramusic.com **w** taramusic.com MD: John Cook.

Taste Media Ltd PO Box 31797, London SW15 2XG **t** 020 8780 3311 **f** 020 8785 9892 **e** laurie@tastemedia.com **w** tastemedia.com MD: Safta Jaffery. Creative Mgr: Mike Audley. Dir: Dennis Smith.

TeC (see Truelove Records)

Tee Hee (see Sound Entertainment Ltd)

Teldec (see Warner Classics)

Teleryngg (see Savant Records)

Telica Communications (see Supreme Music)

Telstar Music Group 107 Mortlake High Street, London SW14 8HQ **t** 020 8878 7888 **f** 020 8878 7886 **e** info@telstar.co.uk **w** telstar.co.uk Chairman: Sean O'Brien. Deputy Chairman: Neil Palmer. International CEO: Graham Williams.

Tema International 151 Nork Way, Banstead, Surrey SM7 1HR **t** 01737 219607 **f** 01737 219609 **e** music@tema-intl.demon.co.uk **w** temamusic.com Production Manager: Amanda Harris.

Temple Records Shillinghill, Temple, Midlothian EH23 4SH **t** 01875 830328 **f** 01875 830392 **e** info@templerecords.co.uk **w** templerecords.co.uk MD: Robin Morton. Dist: Gordon Duncan, Proper

Tenor Vossa Records Ltd 1 Colville Place, London W1T 2BG **t** 020 7221 0511 **f** 020 7221 0511 **e** tenor.vossa@virgin.net MD: Ari Neufeld. Dist: Pinnacle

Terminus Records (see Collective Music Ltd)

Test Recordings (see Valve)

That's Entertainment Records (see JAY Productions)

Them's Good Records (see Adasam Limited)

Theobald Dickson Productions The Coach House, Swinhope Hall, Swinhope, Market Rasen, Lincolnshire LN8 6HT **t** 01472 399011 **f** 01472 399025 **e** mail@fateocharlie.fsnet.co.uk **w** barbaradickson.net MD: Bernard Theobald.

Things To Come (see More Protein Ltd)

3rd Stone Records (see Adasam Limited)

Third World Disco (see More Protein Ltd)

Thirdwave Records PO Box 19, Orpington, Kent BR6 9ZF **t** 01689 609481 **f** 01689 609481 **e** info@thirdwavemusic.com **w** thirdwavemusic.com MD: Matt Gall. Dist: BMG/Alphamagic

13th Hour (see Mute Records Ltd)

Thirty-Seven Records 28 St. Albans Gdns, Stranmillis Rd, Belfast, Co. Antrim BT9 5DR **t** 07736 548 969 **e** sean@thirtysevenrecords.com **w** thirtysevenrecords.com Label Mgr: Sean Douglas.

Thunder (see Rollercoaster Records)

Thunderbird Records RPM Productions ltd, PO Box 158, Chipping Norton D.O., Oxfordshire OX7 6FD **t** 01993 831 011 **f** 01993 831 011 **e** thunderbird@ntlworld.com MD: Mark Stratford. Dist: Pinnacle

Tidalwave Direct Unit 83, Mill Mead Business Centre, Mill Mead Road, London N17 9QU **t** 020 8493 8848 or 020 8808 6565 **f** 020 8493 8858 **e** info@tidalwavemusic.co.uk **w** tidalwavemusic.co.uk MD: Roger Greenidge.

Tidy Trax Hawthorne House, 5-7 Fitzwilliam St, Parkgate, Rotherham, South Yorks S62 6EP **t** 01709 710 022 **f** 01709 523 141 **e** firstname.lastname@tidy.com **w** tidy.com MD: Andy Pickles. Dist: Amato(vinyl)/Pinnacle

Timbre Ltd PO Box 3698, London NW2 6ZA **t** 020 7748 3003 or 020 7748 3004 **f** 020 7691 7632 **e** info@timbre.co.uk **w** timbre.co.uk Contact: Diane M Hinds

Timbuktu Music Ltd 99C Talbot Road, London W11 2AT **t** 020 7471 3656 **f** 020 7471 3630 **e** mark.bond@vsmusic.com Gen Mgr: Mark Bond. Mktg Manager: Matt Hazelden.

Time Records U4C Studios, The Old Knows Factory, St Anne's Hill Rd, Nottingham NG3 4GP **t** 0115 847 0899 **e** mark@timerecords.biz **w** timerecords.biz Director: Mark Bagguley.

Tiny Dog Records 9 Park Rd, Wells-next-the-Sea, Norfolk NR23 1DQ **t** 01328 711115 **f** 01328 711115 **e** info@tinydog.co.uk **w** tinydog.co.uk MD: Pete Jennison.

Tip World PO Box 18157, London NW6 7FF **t** 020 8537 2675 **f** 020 8537 2671 **e** info@tipworld.co.uk **w** tipworld.co.uk Label Manager: Richard Bloor. Dist: Arabesque

Tolotta (see Southern Records)

Tongue Master Records PO Box 38621, London W13 8WG **t** 020 8723 4985 **f** 020 7371 4884 **e** info@tonguemaster.co.uk **w** tonguemaster.co.uk MD: Theodore Vlassopulos.

Too Pure 17-19 Alma Rd, London SW18 1AA **t** 020 8875 6208 **f** 020 8875 1205 **e** toopure@toopure.co.uk **w** toopure.com Label Head: Jason White. Dist: Vital

Top Notch (see Fashion Records)

Topaz (see Pavilion Records Ltd)

Topic Records 50 Stroud Green Road, London N4 3ES **t** 020 7263 1240 **f** 020 7281 5671 **e** info@topicrecords.co.uk **w** topicrecords.co.uk MD: Tony Engle. Dist: Proper

Total Control Records PO Box 1345, Ilford, Essex IG4 5FX **t** 07050 333 555 **f** 07020 923 292 **e** info@ArtistDevelopment.org A&R Director: Wendy Kickes.

Touch **t** 020 8355 9672 **f** 020 8355 9672 **e** info@touchmusic.org.uk **w** touchmusic.org.uk Directors: Jon Wozencroft/Michael Harding. Dist: Kudos

Touch And Go (see Southern Records)

TOV Music Group Ltd (Trouble on Vinyl) 120 Wandsworth Rd, London SW8 2LB **t** 020 7498 3888 **f** 020 7622 1030 **e** info@tovmusic.com **w** tovmusic.com MD: Clayton Hines. Dist: SRD

Townsend Records 30 Queen St, Gt Harwood, Lancashire BB6 7QQ **t** 01254 885995 **f** 01254 887835 **e** bruce@townsend-records.co.uk **w** townsend-records.co.uk Sales Dir: Bruce McKenzie.

Tracid Traxx (see Thirdwave Records)

Track Records PO Box 107, South Godstone, Redhill, Surrey RH9 8YS **t** 01342 892178 or 01342 892074 **f** 01342 893411 **e** ian.grant@trackrecords.co.uk **w** trackrecords.co.uk MD: Ian Grant.

Trade (see Tidy Trax)

Tradition (see Palm Pictures)

Transcopic (see Parlophone)

Transcopic Records Nettwerk, Clearwater Yard, 35 Inverness St, London NW1 7HB **t** 020 7424 7522 **e** jamie@transcopic.com **w** transcopic.com MD: Jamie Davis. Dist: Vital

Transient Records (see Automatic Records)

Transmission Recordings Ltd Bedford House, 8B Berkeley Gardens, London W8 4AP **t** 020 7243 2921 **f** 020 7243 2894 **e** notting@netcomuk.co.uk Director: Peter Chalcraft.

Traxx Music Production 6 Lillie Yard, London SW6 1UB **t** 020 7385 9000 **f** 020 7385 0700 **e** sharonrose@traxx.co.uk **w** traxx.co.uk MD: Sharon Rose.

Treasure Island Recordings Ltd Bartra Studio, Harbour Road, Dalkey, Co. Dublin, Ireland **t** +353 1 284 6336 **f** +353 1 280 0743 **e** info@treasureisland.ie **w** treasureisland.ie MD: Robert Stephenson. Dist: Gaelinn/Record Services

Tribe Recordings 30 Watermore Close, Bristol BS36 2NH **t** 07976 751 781 **e** triberecordings@hotmail.com Dir: David Cridge. Dist: SRD

Trinity Records Company 72 New Bond St, London W1S 1RR **t** 020 7499 4141 **e** info@trinitymediagroup.net **w** trinitymediagroup.net MD: Peter Murray. Dist: Brothers Distribution

---

TRIPLE A RECORDS LTD

GMC Studio, Hollingbourne, Kent ME17 1UQ
t 01622 880599 **f** 01622 880159
e records@triple-a.uk.com **w** triple-a.uk.com.
CEO: Terry Armstrong.
Part of the Triple A group of media and education companies under the parent company Triple A Multimedia Group Ltd.

Triple Earth Records (NO 3RD PARTY USE) PO Box 240, Wembley, Middlesex HA0 4FX **t** 020 8922 7216 **e** info@triple-earth.co.uk **w** triple-earth.com MD: Iain Scott. Dist: Sterns/Independent

Tripoli Trax (see Locked On Records)

Trojan Records (see Sanctuary Records Group)

Tropical Fish Music 1 Pauntley House, Pauntley Street, London N19 3TG **t** 0870 444 5462 or 07973 386 279 **f** 0870 132 3318 **e** info@tropicalfishmusic.com **w** tropicalfishmusic.com MD: Grishma Jashapara. Dist: Cargo

Tru Thoughts PO Box 2818, Brighton, East Sussex BN1 4RL **t** 01273 694617 **f** 01273 694589 **e** info@tru-thoughts.co.uk **w** tru-thoughts.co.uk Label Mgr: Paul Jonas. Dist: Pinnacle

Truck Records 15 Percy St, Oxford OX4 3AA **t** 01865 722333 **e** paul@truckrecords.com **w** truckrecords.com MD: Paul Bonham. Dist: Cargo

Truelove Records 19F Tower Workshops, Riley Rd, London SE1 3DG **t** 020 7252 2900 **f** 020 7252 2890 **e** TLM@truelove.co.uk **w** truelove.co.uk MD: John Truelove.

TrustTheDJ Records Unit 13-14, Barley Shotts Bus.Park, 246 Acklam Road, London W10 5YG **t** 020 8962 9996 **f** 020 8960 9660 **e** contact@trustthedj.com **w** trustthedj.com Label Manager: Matt Bullamore. Dist: online

Tuff Gong (see Island Records Group)

Tuff Street Recordings (see Tuff Street - SOSL Recordings)

Tuff Street - SOSL Recordings PO Box 7874, London SW20 9XD **t** 07050 605219 **f** 07050 605239 **e** sam@pan-africa.org CEO: Oscar Sam Carrol Jnr. Dist: Brothers/Universal

Tugboat Records (see Rough Trade Records)

Tumi Music Ltd 8-9 New Bond Street Place, Bath, Somerset BA1 1BH **t** 01225 464736 **f** 01225 444870 **e** mofini@tumimusic.com **w** tumimusic.com A&R Director: Mo Fini. Dist: Proper

Tune-a-Versal 78 Crown Lodge, Elystan Street, London SW3 3PR **t** 020 7581 3044 **f** 020 7589 5162 **e** grant.calton@btinternet.com **w** loramunro.com Director: Grant Calton.

23rd Precinct (see Limbo Records)

Twisted Nerve Records 6 Fleet St, Hyde, Cheshire SK14 2LF **t** 07967 732 616 **e** info@twistednerve.co.uk **w** twistednerve.co.uk Label Manager: Paul Vella. Dist: Vital

Tyrant 4a Scampston Mews, Cambridge Gardens, London W10 6HX **t** 020 8968 6815 **f** 020 8969 1728 **e** info@tyrant.co.uk **w** tyrant.co.uk Dirs: Craig Richards/Amanda Eastwood. Dist: Amato

U-Freqs 20 Athol Court, 13 Pine Grove, London N4 3GU **t** 07831 770 394 **f** 0870 1310432 **e** info@u-freqs.com **w** u-freqs.com Partner: Stevino. Dist: Intergroove

U4ria (see Flat Records)

Ugly Records (see Fume Recordings)

UGR (see Urban Gospel Records)

Ultimate Dilemma (see Atlantic Records UK)

Ultimate Groove (see Brothers Records Ltd)

Undercurrent Records Unit 4, Minerva Business Centre, 58-60 Minerva Rd, London NW10 6HJ **t** 020 8838 8330 **f** 020 8838 8331 **e** info@amatodistribution.co.uk **w** amatodistribution.co.uk Label Manager: Mario Howell. Dist: Amato

Underwater Records (see Southern Fried Records)

Union Square Music Unit 2, Grand Union Office Park, Packet Boat Lane, Cowley, Uxbridge UB8 2GH **t** 01895 458515 **f** 01895 458516 **e** info@unionsquaremusic.co.uk **w** unionsquaremusic.co.uk MD: Peter Stack.

Unique Corp 15 Shaftesbury Centre, 85 Barlby Rd, London W10 6BN **t** 020 8964 9333 **f** 020 8964 9888 **e** info@uniquecorp.co.uk **w** uniquecorp.co.uk MD: Alan Bellman.

Unisex Records (see Nascente World Music Label)

United Nations Records (see Down By Law Records)

United World Underground 6 Farm Court, Frimley, Surrey GU16 8TJ **t** 01276 27285 **e** magic@uwunderground.fsnet.co.uk **w** music-elsewhere.hypermart.net Owner: Mick Magic.

Universal Classics & Jazz (UK)

22 St Peters Square, London W6 9NW **t** 020 8910 3113 **f** 020 8910 3151 **e** firstname.lastname@umusic.com **w** universalclassics.com; deutschegrammophon.co.uk. MD: Bill Holland. Classics & Jazz Marketing Director: Dickon Stainer. Head of Classics: Mark Wilkinson. Jazz Label Mngr: Tom Lewis. Classics & Jazz Marketing Mngr: Anjali Khanduri. Press & Promotions Mngr: Linda Valentine. Promotions Exec: Becky Ram. Catalogue & Eloquence/Belart Manager: Graham Southern. Dist: Universal

Universal Egg PO Box 3, Whitland, Dyfed SA34 0YP **t** 01994 419 800 **f** 01994 419 357 **e** ue-les@lineone.net **w** wobblyweb.com Press & Promotions: Les Earthdoctor. A&R: Colin Cod. Dist: SRD

UNIVERSAL MUSIC (UK) LTD

UNIVERSAL MUSIC UK

PO Box 1420, 1 Sussex Place, London W6 9XS **t** 020 8910 5000 **f** 020 8741 4901 **e** firstname.lastname@umusic.com **w** umusic.com. CEO & Chairman: Lucian Grainge. Dir, Legal & Business Affairs: Clive Fisher. Commercial Dir: Nigel Haywood. Group Finance Dir: David Bryant. Sales Dir: Brian Rose. Snr VP International Marketing: Mark Crossingham. Distribution Dir: Russell Richards. HR Dir: Malcolm Swatton. Dir, New Media: Rob Wells. Dir of Communications: Selina Webb. Dist: Universal

Universal Music Catalogue
1 Sussex Place, London W6 9XS
t 020 8910 5000 **f** 020 8910 5039
e silvia.montello@umusic.com.
Head of Campaign and Catalogue: Silvia Montello.

Universal Music Dance 1 Sussex Place, London W6 9XS **t** 020 8910 5000 **f** 020 8910 5408 **e** firstname.lastname@umusic.com A&R: Eddie Ruffett. Marketing: Emily Balkwill. Dist: Universal

UNIVERSAL MUSIC TV

UNIVERSAL MUSIC TV

1 Sussex Place, London W6 9XS **t** 020 8910 5000 **f** 020 8910 5408 **e** firstname.lastname@umusic.com. MD: Brian Berg. General Manager: Paul Chisnall. Director of Marketing & New Media: Karen Meekings. Finance Director: Jerome Ramsey. Head of Licensing: Kevin Phelan.

Universal Records (Ireland)

9 Whitefriars, Aungier Street, Dublin 2, Ireland **t** +353 1 402 2600 **f** +353 1 475 7860 **e** firstname.lastname@umusic.com **w** universalmusic.com MD: Dave Pennefather. Chairman/CEO: Lucian Grainge. Dir of Finance: Cathy McMorrow. Dir of Sales: Freddie Blake. Mktg Mgr: Claire Meredith. Product Mgr: (Classics/Jazz) Catherine Hughes. Promotions & Mktg Executive: Anne Pennefather. Promotions & Mktg Co-ordinator: Laura Fitzgerald. Dist: Universal

Untalented Artist Inc. (see Low Quality Accident)

Untidy Trax (see Tidy Trax)

Unyque Artists PO Box 1257, London E5 0UD **t** 020 8986 1984 **e** mal@jastoy.co.uk MD: Tee.

Upbeat Classics (see Upbeat Recordings Ltd)

Upbeat Jazz (see Upbeat Recordings Ltd)

Upbeat Recordings Ltd PO Box 63, Wallington, Surrey SM6 9YP **t** 020 8773 1223 **f** 020 8669 6752 **e** admin@upbeatrecordings.co.uk - NO ATTACHMENTS **w** upbeat.co.uk MD, Exec Prod: Liz Biddle. Dist: Delta Home Ent Ltd

Upbeat Showbiz (see Upbeat Recordings Ltd)

Uptown (see Harmonia Mundi (UK) Ltd)

Urban Control Records Mayfair House, 72 New Bond St, London W1S 1RR **t** 020 8240 8787 or 07812 107 812 **f** 020 8240 8787 **e** wemakethemusic@urbancontrol.com **w** urbancontrol.com CEO: Azor. Dist: IND

Urban Dubz Recordings PO Box 12275, Birmingham B23 3AB **t** 07931 139 806 **e** info@urbandubz.com **w** urbandubz.com Prop: Jeremy Sylvester. Dist: Unique, Lasgo Chrysalis, Contact UK, Prime

Urban Gospel Records PO Box 178, Surrey SM2 6XG **t** 020 8643 6403 or 07904 255 244 **f** 020 8643 6403 **e** urbangospel@hotmail.com **w** urbangospel.com Head of A&R: P Mac. Dist: self

Urban Theory (see Beechwood Music Ltd)

Urbanite 1 Lincoln Place, 7 Hulme St, Manchester M1 5GL **t** 0161 237 9534 **f** 0161 237 9534 **e** post@urbanite.co.uk **w** urbanite.co.uk Partner: Frank Staiger.

Urbanstar Records Global House, 92 De Beauvoir Rd, London N1 4EN **t** 020 7288 2239 **f** 0870 429 2493 **e** info@urbanstarrecords.com **w** urbanstarrecords.com Dir: Nick Sellors.

Urbcom Studio 2, PO Box 13805, London NW1 9WY **t** 020 7498 0296 or 07796 975 900 **f** 020 7498 0296 **e** jerico@urbcom.net **w** urbcom.net A&R: J Van Hookens. Dist: SRD

URP (see Urban Gospel Records)

US Everest (see Everest Copyrights)

Usk Recordings 26 Caterham Road, London SE13 5AR **t** 020 7274 5610 or 020 8318 2031 **f** 020 7737 0063 **e** info@uskrecordings.com **w** uskrecordings.com Dir: Rosemary Lindsay. Dist: ID

V Ram Discs UK Nestlingdown, Chapel Hill, Pothtowan, Truro, Cornwall TR4 8AS **t** 01209 890606 Director: John Bowyer.

V2

131-133 Holland Park Avenue, London W11 4UT **t** 020 7471 3000 **e** firstname.lastname@v2music.com **f** (G) 020 7602 7198 (UK) 020 7602 4796 **w** v2music.com UK: MD: David Steele. FD: Jennifer Bentley. Director A&R: Malcolm Dunbar. Marketing Head: Richard Engler. Press: Polly Birkbeck. Promotions: Neil Ashby. Group CEO: Tony Harlow Business Affairs: Charlie Wale. CFO: Prescott Price. New Media: Beth Appleton.

VA Recordings (see Finger Lickin' Records)

Vagabond (see Silverword Music Group)

Valve Unit 24 Ropery Business Park, Anchor & Hope Lane, London SE7 7RX **t** 020 8853 4900 **f** 020 8853 4908 **e** info@valverecordings.com **w** valverecordings.com Label Manager: Josephine Serieux.

Vane Recordings P.O. Box 70, Witney, Oxon OX29 4GA **t** 01865 883671 or 07939 228435 **f** 01865 883671 **e** jerry@vane-recordings.com **w** vane-recordings.com Proprietor: Jerry Butson.

Vapour (see 3 Beat Label Management)

VC Recordings (see Virgin Records)

Veesik Records Back Charlotte Lane, Lerwick, Shetland ZE1 0JD **t** 01595 696622 **f** 01595 696622 **e** alan@veesikrecords.co.uk **w** veesikrecords.co.uk MD: Alan Longmuir. Dist: Shetland Music/Proper Music

Velvel (see Fire Records)

Venus Music & Records Ltd 13 Fernhurst Gardens, Edgware, Middx HA8 7PQ **t** 020 8952 1924 or 07956 064 019 **f** 020 8952 3496 **e** kamalmmalak@onetel.net.uk **w** venusmusicandrecords.co.uk MD: Kamal M Malak.

Vertigo (see Mercury Records)

Verve (see Universal Classics & Jazz (UK))

Vibe Entertainment (see Taste Media Ltd)

Vibezone (see Dead Happy Records)

Victo (see Harmonia Mundi (UK) Ltd)

Victoria Music Ltd Unit 215, Old Gramophone Works, 326 Kensal Road, London W10 5BZ **t** 020 7565 8193 **f** 020 8960 3834 **e** info@victoria-music.com **w** victoria-music.com Director: Charlie Hall.

Viktor Records The Saga Centre, 326 Kensal Road, London W10 5BZ **t** 020 8969 3370 **f** 020 8969 3374 **e** info@streetfeat.demon.co.uk MD: Colin Schaverien. Dist: Ideal

Village Life (see Harmonia Mundi (UK) Ltd)

Vine Gate Music 4 Vine Gate, Parsonage Lane, Farnham Common, Bucks SL2 3NX **t** 01753 643696 **f** 01753 642259 **e** vinegate@clara.net **w** salenajones.co.uk Dir: Tony Puxley. Dist: New Note

Vintage (see Collecting Records LLP)

Vinyl Japan 98 Camden Road, London NW1 9EA **t** 020 7284 0359 **f** 020 7267 5186 **e** office@vinyljapan.com **w** vinyljapan.com Label Mgr: Claire Munro. Dist: PHD

VIRGIN RECORDS

Kensal House, 553-579 Harrow Road, London W10 4RH **t** 020 8964 6000 **f** 020 8968 6533 **e** firstname.lastname@virginmusic.com **w** virginrecords.co.uk MD, Virgin: Philippe Ascoli. Mktg. Director: Mark Terry. Dir. Of Media: Steve Morton. Snr. Press Officer: John Coyne. Dist: EMI

Virus Recordings GH Cooper House, 2 Michael Rd, London SW6 2AD **t** 020 8871 3761 **f** 0709 200 4055 **e** ellise@sirenproductions.freeserve.co.uk Label Manager: Ellise Theuma.

Visceral Thrill Recordings 8 Deronda Rd, London SE24 9BG **t** 020 8674 7990 or 07775 806 288 **f** 020 8671 5548 MD: Dave Massey.

Viscous Disc (see Fluid Recordings UK Ltd)

Visible Noise 231 Portobello Road, London W11 1LT **t** 020 7792 9791 **f** 020 7792 9871 **e** julie@visiblenoise.com **w** visiblenoise.com MD: Julie Weir. Dist: Pinnacle

Vision Discs PO Box 92, Gloucester, Gloucestershire GL4 8HW **t** 01452 814321 **f** 01452 812106 **e** vic_coppersmith@hotmail.com MD: Vic Coppersmith-Heaven.

Vision Records PO Box 27442, London SW9 8WL **t** 020 7652 1168 **f** 020 7652 1168 **e** ayan@vision-records.com **w** vision-records.co.uk MD: Ayan Mohammed.

Visionquest (see Loose Tie Records)

Vital Spark Records 1 Waterloo, Breakish, Isle Of Skye IV42 8QE **t** 01471 822484 **f** 01471 822952 **e** chris@vitalsparkmusic.demon.co.uk CEO: Chris Harley.

Vixen Records (Ireland) Glenmundar House, Ballyman Rd, Bray, Co. Wicklow, Ireland **t** +353 86 257 6244 **e** picket@iol.ie Director: Deke O'Brien.

Vocaphone Records Stanley House, Stanley Road, Acton, London W3 7SY **t** 020 8735 0284 **e** vocaphone@bigupjazz.com **w** neilpyzer.com Label Manager: Cole Parker.

Voiceprint PO Box 50, Houghton-le-Spring, Tyne & Wear DH4 5YP **t** 0191 512 1103 **f** 0191 512 1104 **e** info@voiceprint.co.uk **w** voiceprint.co.uk Label Mgr: Rob Ayling.

Voltage (see New State Entertainment)

Volume Records Ltd Voysey House, Barley Mow Passage, Chiswick, London W4 4GB **t** 020 8987 2456 **f** 020 8987 2444 **e** info@volumerecords.co.uk **w** volumerecords.co.uk A&R Director: Tony Vickers.

Voluptuous Records 4th Floor, 40 Langham St, London W1W 7AS **t** 020 7323 4410 **f** 020 7323 4180 **e** carl@formidable-mgmt.com Dir: Carl Marcantonio.

VP Records UK Ltd Unit 12B, Shaftsbury Centre, 85 Barlby Rd, London W10 6BN **t** 020 8962 2760 **f** 020 8968 6791 **e** joye@vprecords.com **w** vprecords.com Mktg Mgr: Joy Ellington.

VX Records (see Planet1 Music)

Wagram Music Unit 203, Westbourne Studios, 242 Acklam Rd, London W10 5YG **t** 020 8968 8800 **f** 020 8968 8877 **e** wagrammusic@btclick.com MD: Peter Walmsley.

Wah Wah 45s Flat 12, St. Luke's Church, 38 Mayfield Rd, London N8 9LP **t** 07775 657 578 or 07812 089 629 **e** info@wahwah45s.com **w** wahwah45s.com Label Mgrs, A&R: Dom Servini & Simon Goss. Dist: Kudos

Wall Of Sound Recordings Ltd Office 2, 9 Thorpe Close, London W10 5XL **t** 020 8969 1144 **f** 020 8969 1155 **e** general@wallofsound.uk.com **w** wallofsound.net MD: Mark Jones. Dist: Vital

Walt Disney Records 3 Queen Caroline St, London W6 9PE **t** 020 8222 2281 **f** 020 8222 2283 **e** firstname.lastname@disney.com Exec Dir: Hilary Stebbings. Mktg Dir: Mike Storey. Dist: TEN

WARNER BROS RE

Waldron House, 57-63 Old Church Street, London SW3 5BS **t** 020 7761 6000 **f** 020 7761 6062 **e** firstname.lastname@warnermusic.com MD: Korda Marshall. Mktg Dir (International): Adam Hollywood. Mktg Dir (Domestic): Matt Thomas. Creative Dir: Alan Parks. Dir of Bus Affs: Gez Orakwusi. Press Director: Andy Prevezer. Promotions Director: Sarah Adams. Dist: TEN

WARNER CLASSICS

The Electric Lighting Station, 46 Kensington Court, London W8 5DA **t** 020 7938 5500 **f** 020 7368 4903 **e** firstname.lastname@warnermusic.com **w** warnerclassics.com Director: Matthew Cosgrove. Int. Mktg & Product Logistics: Stefan Bown. A&R & Catalogue Co-ordinator: Richard Maillardet. Manager, Press & Artist Relations: Lucy Bright. Press Asst: Belinda Morgan. Classics Paralegal: Emily Dowdeswell.

WARNER MUSIC (UK)

WARNER MUSIC
UNITED KINGDOM

The Warner Building, 28A Kensington Church Street, London W8 4EP **t** 020 7368 2500 **f** 020 7368 2770 **e** firstname.lastname@warnermusic.com **w** warnermusic.co.uk Chairman: Nick Phillips. Commercial Director: Alan Young. Senior VP Business Affairs WMI: John Watson. Finance Director: Keith Mullock. Director of Classics: Matthew Cosgrove. Director of WSM: Mario Warner. MD Atlantic Records UK: Max Lousada. MD Warner Bros Records: Korda Marshall. MD 679 Recordings: Nick Worthington. MD 14th Floor Records: Christian Tattersfield. HR Director: John Athanasiou. Artist Relations Director: Jason Morais. PA to Chairman: Liz Marshall.

Warner Music (Ireland) Alexandra House, Earlsfort Centre, Earlsfort Terrace, Dublin 2, Ireland **t** +353 1 676 2022 **f** +353 1 676 2602 **e** firstname.lastname@warnermusic.com **w** warnermusic.com MD: Dennis Woods. Mkting Mgr: Pat Creed. Head of A&R: Janet Kingston. Fin Dir: John Taggart.

WARNER STRATEGIC MARKETING

WARNER STRATEGIC MARKETING

The Warner Building, 28A Kensington Church Street, London W8 4EP **t** 020 7368 2500 **f** 020 7368 2773 **e** firstname.lastname@warnermusic.com Director: Mario Warner.

warner.esp (see Warner Strategic Marketing)

Warp Spectrum House, 32-34 Gordon House Road, London NW5 1LP **t** 020 7284 8350 **f** 020 7284 8360 **e** info@warprecords.com **w** warprecords.com GM: Kevin Flemming. Dist: Vital

Way Out West Records 69 Hampton Rd, Teddington, Middx TW11 0LA **t** 020 8977 6509 **f** 020 8977 6400 **e** wowrecco@aol.com **w** wowrecords.co.uk MD: Simon Davies. Dist: Proper

Wayward (see IRL)

Wayward Records PO Box 30884, London W12 9AZ **t** 020 8746 7461 **f** 020 8749 7441 **e** wayward@spiritmm.com Label Manager: Tom Haxell.

We Love You (see Wall Of Sound Recordings Ltd)

WEA London (see Warner Bros Records)

Weekend Beatnik (see Rogue Records Ltd)

Welsh Gold (see Silverword Music Group)

West Central Records (see Ravensbourne Records Ltd)

Western Union (see Dangerous Records)

Westside (see Demon Records Ltd)

What Records Ltd. PO Box 10387, Birmingham B16 8WB **t** 0121 455 6034 or 01895 824674 **f** 0121 456 5122 or 01895 822994 **e** whatrecords@blueyonder.co.uk Directors: Mick Cater/David Harper.

Whippet Records 14 Springfield Close, York, North Yorkshire YO31 1LD **t** 01904 410038 **f** 01904 410038 **e** gary@whippetpromotions.fsnet.co.uk **w** whiskypriests.co.uk MD: G Miller. Dist: Pinnacle

Whirlie Records 14 Broughton Place, Edinburgh EH1 3RX **t** 0131 557 9099 **f** 0131 557 6519 **e** info@whirlierecords.co.uk **w** whirlierecords.co.uk MD: George Brown.

White Line (see Sanctuary Classics)

Whitehouse Records (see Mo's Music Machine)

Whoa Music 2nd Floor, 40 Fordingley Rd, London W9 3HF **t** 020 8960 8338 **f** 020 8964 9495 **e** austin@whoamusic.co.uk **w** whoamusic.co.uk MD: Austin Wilde.

Whole 9 Yards PO Box 435, Walton on Thames, Surrey KT12 4XR **t** 01932 230088 **f** 01932 223796 **e** info@w9y.co.uk **w** w9y.co.uk Label Mgr: Mark Pember.

Wichita Recordings PO Box 27754, London E5 0FP **t** 020 7682 0668 or 01409 253024 **f** 01409 259415 **e** info@wichita-recordings.com **w** wichita-recordings.com Contact: Dick Green/Mark Bowen Dist: Vital

Wide-Eyed Music 24A Camden Road, London NW1 9DP **t** 020 7482 5277 **f** 020 7267 3430 **e** wem@pierconnection.co.uk Proprietor: Vid Lakhani. Dist: Pinnacle

Wienerworld Ltd Unit B2 Livingstone Court, 55-63 Peel Road, Wealdstone, Harrow, Middlesex HA3 7QT **t** 020 8427 2777 **f** 020 8427 0660 **e** wworld@wienerworld.com **w** wienerworld.com MD: Anthony Broza. A&R Dir: Lloyd Branson.

Wiiija (see 4AD)

Wild Abandon Flat 6, 27 Hereford Rd, London W2 4TQ **t** 020 7727 0335 **e** wildabandon46@aol.com **w** wildabandon.co.uk Dir: Nigel Grainge. Dist: Various

Wild Card (see Polydor Records)

Wildloops 5, Link Rd, Sale, Cheshire M33 4HW **t** 07801 454187 **e** info@wildloops.com **w** wildloops.com Label Manager: Kevin Gorman.

Winter And Winter (see Harmonia Mundi (UK) Ltd)

Wire Editions (see Harmonia Mundi (UK) Ltd)

Within Records PO Box 302, Torquay TQ2 7WA **t** 01803 605085 **f** 01803 605085 **e** within@movementinsound.com **w** movementinsound.com Dirs: Chris Clark, Stephen Gould.

Wizard (see Silverword Music Group)

Wizard Records PO Box 6779, Birmingham B13 9RZ **t** 0121 778 2218 **f** 0121 778 1856 **e** pk.sharma@ukonline.co.uk MD: Mambo Sharma.

Wolftown Recordings PO Box 1668, Wolverhampton, West Midlands WV2 3WG **t** 01902 423 627 **f** 01902 423 627 **e** info@wolftownrecordings.com **w** wolftownrecordings.com Directors: Tricksta & Late. Dist: Units/SRD

Wonderboy (see Universal Music Dance)

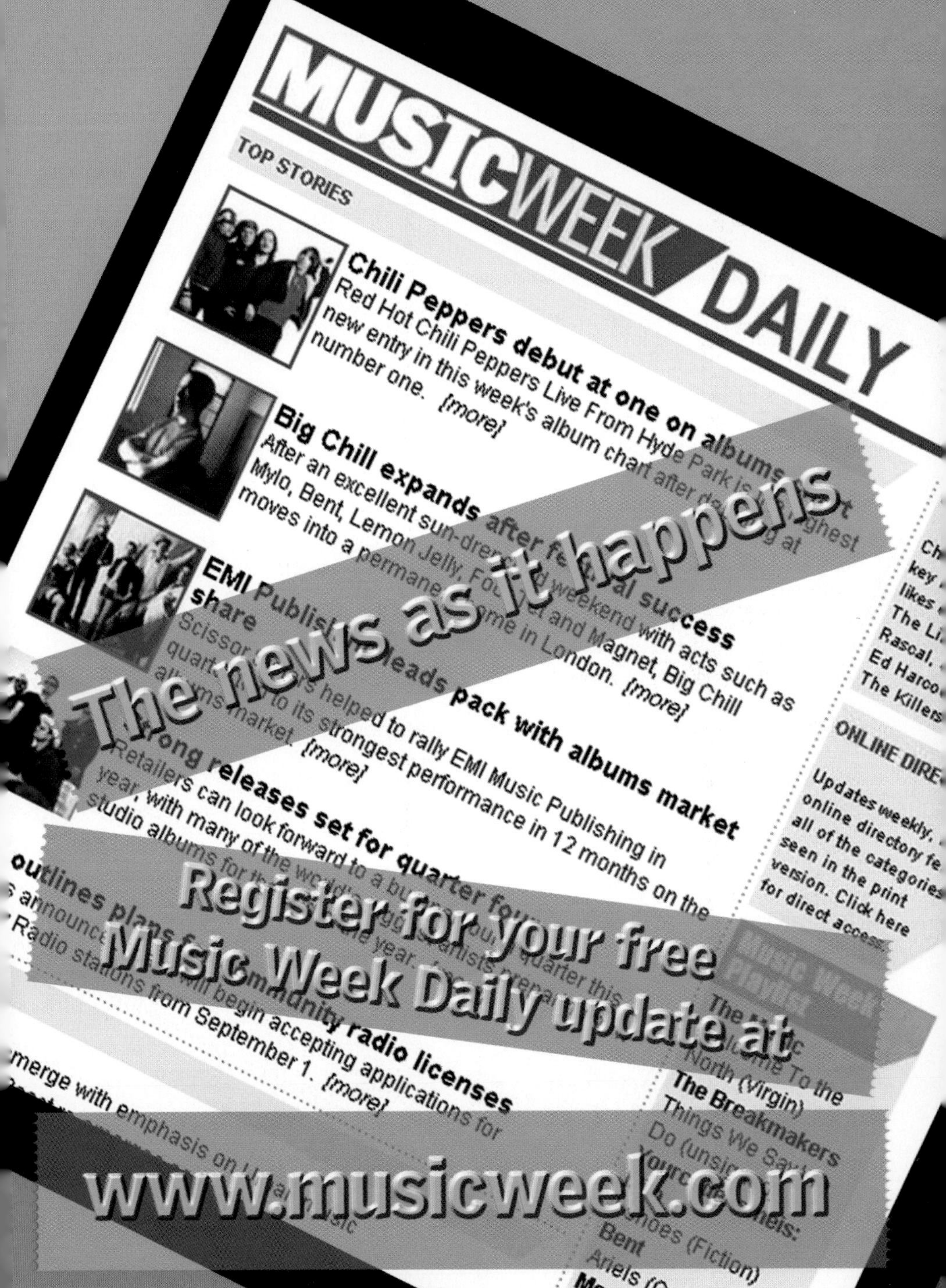

MUSIC WEEK DAILY
The news as it happens
Register for your free
Music Week Daily update at
www.musicweek.com

Wooden Hill Recordings Ltd Lister House, 117 Milton Road, Weston-super-Mare, Somerset BS23 2UX **t** 01934 644309 **f** 01934 644402 **e** cliffdane@tiscali.co.uk **w** mediaresearchpublishing.com Chairman: Cliff Dane. Dist: Proper

Word Music 9 Holdom Avenue, Bletchley, Milton Keynes, Buckinghamshire MK1 1QR **t** 01908 364218 **f** 01908 648592 **e** shelleyn@wordonline.co.uk **w** premieronline.co.uk Music Mgr: Shelley Needham. Dist: Recognition

Workers Playtime Music Co. 204 Crescent House, Goswell Rd, London EC1Y 0SL **t** 020 7490 7346 **e** bill@workersplaytime.co.uk **w** workersplaytime.co.uk MD: Bill Gilliam.

World Circuit 138 Kingsland Road, London E2 8DY **t** 020 7749 3222 **f** 020 7749 3232 **e** post@worldcircuit.co.uk **w** worldcircuit.co.uk MD: Nick Gold. Dist: New Note

World Music Network (UK) Ltd 6 Abbeville Mews, 88 Clapham Park Rd, London SW4 7BX **t** 020 7498 5252 **f** 020 7498 5353 **e** post@worldmusic.net **w** worldmusic.net MD: Phil Stanton.

Wrasse Records Wrasse House, The Drive, Tyrrells Wood, Leatherhead KT22 8QW **t** 01372 376266 **f** 01372 370281 **e** jo.ashbridge@wrasserecords.com **w** wrasserecords.com Joint MDs: Jo & Ian Ashbridge. Dist: Universal

Wren Records Unit 4, Rampart Business Pk, Greenbank Ind, Estate, Newry, Co Down BT34 2QU **t** 028 3026 2926 **f** 028 3026 2671 **e** mail@wren.ie **w** soundsirish.com MD: Canice McGarry. Dist: MVD

Wrench Records BCM Box 4049, London WC1N 3XX **f** 020 7700 3855 **e** mail@wrench.org **w** wrench.org MD: Charlie Chainsaw. Dist: Shellshock

Wrong Crowd Recording Co 1 Hulme Place, London SE1 1HX **t** 07989 010 888 **e** info@wrongcrowd.co.uk **w** wrongcrowd.co.uk Dirs: Adam McNichol & Choque Hosein. Dist: Cargo

Wundaland & Boogy Limited 65, Hazelwood Rd, Bush Hill Park, Middx. EN1 1JG **t** 020 8245 6573 **f** 020 8254 6573 **e** jemgant@yahoo.co.uk MD: Jem Gant.

Wyze Productions 2-3 Fitzroy Mews, London W1T 6DJ **t** 020 7380 0999 **f** 020 7380 1555 **e** info@wyze.com **w** wyze.com MD: Kate Ross. Dist: Various

XL Recordings 1 Codrington Mews, London W11 2EH **t** 020 8870 7511 **f** 020 8871 4178 **e** xl@xl-recordings.com **w** xl-recordings.com Contact: Jo Bagenal Dist: Vital

Xosa Music Group 130A Uxbridge Road, London W12 8AA **t** 020 7854 1400 **f** 020 7854 1500 **e** info@xosagroup.com **w** xosagroup.com MD: Dean Zepherin.

Xplosive Records 33/37 Hatherley Mews, Walthamstow, London E17 4QP **t** 020 8521 9227 **f** 020 8520 5553 **e** postmaster@xplosiverecords.co.uk **w** xplosiverecords.co.uk Partners: Terry McLeod/ Tapps Bandawe.

Xtra Mile Recordings 5-7 Vernon Yard, off Portobello Road, London W11 2DX **t** 020 7792 9400 **f** 020 7243 2262 **e** Charlie@presscounsel.com **w** xtramilerecordings.com MD: Charlie Caplowe.

Dist: Vital

Y2K (see Locked On Records)

Yellow Balloon Records Freshwater House, Outdowns, Effingham, Surrey KT24 5QR **t** 01483 281500 or 01483 281501 **f** 01483 281502 **e** yellowbal@aol.com Head of A&R: Daryl Smith.

Yolk (see High Barn Records)

York Ambisonic PO Box 66, Lancaster, Lancs LA2 6HS **t** 01524 823020 **f** 01524 824420 **e** yorkambisonic@aol.com MD: Brendan Hearne. Dist: Metrodome

Yoshiko Records Great Westwood, Old House Lane, King's Langley, Herts WD4 9AD **t** 01923 261545 **f** 01923 261546 **e** yoouchi@globalnet.co.uk **w** yoshikorecords.co.uk MD: Yoshiko Ouchi.

You Clash! Recordings PO Box 21469, Highgate, London N6 4ZG **t** 020 8340 5151 **f** 020 8340 5159 **e** james@topdrawmusic.biz Directors: Paul Masterson/James Hamilton.

Zane Records 162 Castle Hill, Reading, Berkshire RG1 7RP **t** 0118 957 4567 **f** 0118 956 1261 **e** info@zanerecords.com **w** zanerecords.com MD: Peter Thompson. Dist: Pinnacle

Zebra (see Cherry Red Records)

Zebra Traffic (see Tru Thoughts)

Zedfunk PO Box 7497, London N21 2DX **t** 07050 657 465 **e** licencing@zedfunk.com **w** zedfunk.com MD: Paul Z.

Zerga Record Co. 34 Meadowside, Cambridge Park, Twickenham TW1 2JQ **t** 020 8404 8307 **f** 020 8404 8307 **e** nicholas.dicker@zerga.co.uk **w** zerga.co.uk MD: Nicholas Dicker. Dist: RSK

Zero Tolerance (see 3 Beat Label Management)

Zeus Records Gloucester House, 68 Gloucester Rd, New Barnet, Herts EN5 1NB **t** 020 8441 7441 **f** 020 8441 7461 **e** info@zeusrecords.com **w** zeusrecords.com Directors: Ash White, Derrell King.

Zone 5 Records (see Megabop Records)

Zopf Ltd 52 King Henry's Walk, London N1 4NN **t** 020 7503 3546 **f** 020 7503 3546 **e** joanna.stephenson@penguincafe.com **w** penguincafe.com Business Affairs Mgr: Joanna Stephenson.

ZTT Records Ltd The Blue Building, 8-10 Basing St, London W11 1ET **t** 020 7221 5101 **f** 020 7221 3374 **e** info@ztt.com **w** ztt.com International & Licensing: Pete Gardiner. Dist: Pinnacle

ZYX RECORDS

11 Cambridge Court, 210 Shepherds Bush Road, London W6 7NJ **t** 020 7371 6969 **f** 020 7371 6688 or 020 7371 6677 **e** lauren.lorenzo@zyxrecords.freeserve.co.uk **w** zyx.de Gen Mgr: Lauren Lorenzo. Dist: ZYX

Video & DVD Companies

Artificial Eye Video 14 King Street, London WC2E 8HR **t** 020 7240 5353 **f** 020 7240 5242 **e** info@artificial-eye.com **w** artificial-eye.com Video/DVD Mgr: Steve Lewis.

Beckmann Visual Publishing Albion House, 133 Station Road, Hampton, Middlesex TW12 2AL **t** 020 8941 2227 or 01624 816585 **f** 020 8941 2162 or 01624 816589 **e** beckmann@enterprise.net **w** beckmanngroup.co.uk MD: David Willoughby.

Carlton Video The Waterfront, Elstree Road, Elstree, Hertfordshire WD6 3BS **t** 020 8207 6207 **f** 020 8207 5789 **e** gerry.donohoe@carltonvideo.co.uk **w** carltonvideo.co.uk MD: Gerry Donohoe.

Classic Pictures Shepperton Int'l Film Studios, Studios Road, Shepperton, Middx TW17 0QD **t** 01932 592016 **f** 01932 592046 **e** Jo.garofalo@classicpictures.co.uk **w** classicpictures.co.uk Sales & Marketing Dir.: Jo Garofalo. Dist: Pinnacle

Clear Vision 36 Queensway, Ponders End, Enfield, Middlesex EN3 4SA **t** 020 8805 1354 **f** 020 8805 9987 **e** info@clearvision.co.uk **w** silvervision.co.uk Contact: Ian Allan

Columbia Tri-Star Home Entertainment 25 Golden Square, London W1R 6LU **t** 020 7533 1200 **f** 020 7533 1172 **e** firstname_lastname@fpe.sony.com **w** cthe.co.uk

Domino Recording Company PO Box 4029, London SW15 2XR **t** 020 8875 1390 **f** 020 8875 1391 **e** info@dominorecordco.com **w** dominorecordco.com Contact: Jacqui Rice

EAGLE ROCK ENTERTAINMENT LTD.

EAGLE ROCK ENTERTAINMENT LIMITED

Eagle House, 22 Armoury Way, London SW18 1EZ **t** 020 8870 5670 **f** 020 8874 2333 **e** mail@eagle-rock.com **w** eagle-rock.com Executive Chairman: Terry Shand. Deputy Chairman: Julian Paul. Chief Operating Officer: Geoff Kempin. Group Finance Director: Jonathan Blanchard. Director of Business Affairs: Martin Dacre. General Manager: Chris Cole. Director Marketing and Sales: Lindsay Brown.

Eagle Vision

eagle vision

Eagle House, 22 Armoury Way, London SW18 1EZ **t** 020 8870 5670 **f** 020 8874 2333 **e** mail@eagle-rock.com **w** eagle-rock.com COO, Worldwide: Geoff Kempin. Dir. of Intl. Acquisitions: John Gaydon. Dir. of Intl. Sales & Marketing: Lindsay Brown. MD of Intl. Television: Peter Worsley. Dir. of Intl. TV Sales: Andrew Winter. Int'l Licensing Manager: Lesley Wilsdon. Intl. Product Manager: Nicola O'Donegan. Snr Production Manager: Claire Higgins. Business Affairs Manager: Melissa Roy.

EMI Music UK & Ireland DVD Dept. EMI House, 43 Brook Green, London W6 7EF **t** 020 7605 5332 **f** 020 7605 2526 **e** stefan.demetriou@emimusic.com DVD & New Formats Mgr: Stefan Demetriou.

Fifth Avenue Films 14 South Avenue, Hullbridge, Hockley, Essex SS5 6HA **t** 01702 232396 **f** 01702 230944 **e** fifthavenuefilms@supanet.com **w** fifthavenuefilms.co.uk Contact: Dave Harris

GUT VISION

Byron House, 112A Shirland Road, London W9 2EQ **t** 020 7266 0777 **f** 020 7266 7734 **e** general@gut-vision.com **w** gut-vision.com Chairman: Guy Holmes. Creative Director: Caroline Workman. International: Fraser Ealey. Dist: Pinnacle

K-Tel Entertainment (UK) K-tel House, 12 Fairway Drive, Greenford, Middlesex UB6 8PW **t** 020 8747 7550 **f** 020 8575 2264 **e** info@k-tel-uk.com **w** k-tel.com GM: Janie Webber. Dist: K-tel

KRL 9 Watt Road, Hillington, Glasgow G52 4RY **t** 0141 882 9060 **f** 0141 883 3686 **e** krl@krl.co.uk **w** krl.co.uk MD: Gus McDonald.

Landscape Channel Landscape Studios, Crowhurst, East Sussex TN33 9BX **t** 01424 830900 **f** 01424 830680 **e** info@cablenet.net **w** landscapetv.com

Lifetime Vision 11 St. James Square, London SW1Y 4LB **t** 020 7389 0790 **f** 020 7389 0791 **e** lifetimevision@dial.pipex.com MD: Robert Page. Dist: Universal/Carlton

MIA Video Emtertainment Ltd 4th Floor, 72-75 Marylebone High Street, London W1U 5JW **t** 020 7935 9225 **f** 020 7935 9565 **e** miavid@aol.com Gen Mgr: Vanessa Chinn.

Odyssey Video Regal Chambers, 51 Bancroft, Hitchin, Hertfordshire SG5 1LL **t** 01462 421818 **f** 01462 420393 **e** adrian_munsey@msn.com MD: Adrian Munsey. Dist: Disc

Palm Pictures 8 Kensington Park Road, Notting Hill Gate, London W11 3BU **t** 020 7229 3000 **f** 020 7229 0897 **e** firstname@palmpictures.co.uk **w** palmpictures.com MD: Andy Childs. Dist: Vital/THE

Picture Music International 30 Gloucester Place, London W1H 4AJ **t** 020 7467 2000 **f** 020 7224 5927 Director of Sales: Dawn Stevenson. Dist: EMI

Prism Leisure Corp PLC 1 Dundee Way, Enfield, Middlesex EN3 7SX **t** 020 8804 8100 **f** 020 8805 8001 **e** mpearce@prismleisure.com **w** prismleisure.com DVD Software Dir: Mark Pearce. Head Of DVD Sales: Nigel Walmsley (nwalmsley@prismleisure.com).

Sanctuary Visual Entertainment Sanctuary House, 45-53 Sinclair Rd, London W14 0NS **t** 020 7602 6351 **f** 020 7603 5941 **e** info@sanctuaryrecords.co.uk **w** sanctuarygroup.com Commercial Mgr: Spencer Pollard. Visual Rights Mgr: Andy McIntosh. Director of Sales: Maro Korkou.

Scotdisc - BGS Productions Ltd Newtown Street, Kilsyth, Glasgow, Strathclyde G65 0LY **t** 01236 821081 **f** 01236 826900 **e** info@scotdisc.co.uk **w** scotdisc.co.uk MD: Dougie Stevenson. Dist: Gordon Duncan

Silver Road Studios 2 Silver Road, London W12 7SG **t** 020 8746 2000 **f** 020 8746 0180 **e** enquiries@silver-road-studios.co.uk **w** silver-road-studios.co.uk Facilities Manager: Samantha Leese.

Start Audio & Video 3 Warmair House, Green Lane, Northwood, Middx HA6 2QB **t** 01923 841414 **f** 01923 842223 **e** startav@compuserve.com **w** nostalgiamusic.co.uk GM: Nicholas Dicker. Dist: Koch

Universal Pictures Visual Programming Oxford House, 76 Oxford Street, London W1D 1BS **t** 020 7307 7651 **f** 020 7307 7669 **e** gilly.grafton@unistudios.com **w** universalstudios.com Pres: Hugh Rees-Parnall.

Universal Pictures Video Ltd 1 Sussex Place, London W6 9XS **t** 01733 232 800 **f** 01733 230 618 **e** orders@choicesdirect.co.uk **w** choicesdirect.co.uk Manager: Lynette Young. Dist: Universal

Urban Edge Entertainment Ltd Unit B2 Livingstone Court, 55-63 Peel Road, Wealdstone, Harrow, Middlesex HA3 7QT **t** 020 8427 2777 **f** 020 8427 0660 **e** urbanedge@wienerworld.com **w** wienerworld.com MD: Anthony Broza.

The Valentine Music Group 7 Garrick Street, London WC2E 9AR **t** 020 7240 1628 **f** 020 7497 9242 **e** valentine@bandleader.co.uk **w** valentinemusic.co.uk Chairman/CEO: John Nice.

Video Collection International 76 Dean Street, London W1D 3SQ **t** 020 7396 8888 **f** 020 7396 8996 or 020 7396 8997 **e** info@vci.co.uk **w** vciplc.co.uk Contact: Amanda Morgan

The Video Pool 99A Linden Gardens, London W2 4EX **t** 020 7221 3803 or 020 7229 1723 **f** 020 7221 3280 **e** roz@videopool.com **w** videopool.com MD: Roz Bea.

Vision Video Ltd 1 Sussex Place, Hammersmith, London W6 9XS **t** 020 8910 5000 **f** 020 8910 5404 **e** firstname.lastname@unistudios.com A&R Manager: Tim Payne.

Visionary Communications 329 Clifton Drive South, Lytham St Annes, Lancashire FY8 1LP **t** 01253 712453 **f** 01253 712362 **e** nicky@visionary.co.uk **w** outlaw23.com Dir: Nicky O'Toole. Dist: PHD

Vital DVD 338a Ladbroke Grove, London W10 5AH **t** 020 8324 2400 **f** 020 8324 0001 **e** firstname.lastname@vitaluk.com **w** vitaluk.com; Contact: James Akerman

Warner Home Video Warner House, 98 Theobald's Road, London WC1X 8WB **t** 020 7984 6400 **f** 020 7984 5001 **e** neil.mcewan@warnerbros.com **w** warnerbros.com MD: Neil McEwan. Sales Dir: Roger Why.

Warner Vision International The Electric Lighting Station, 46 Kensington Court, London W8 5DA **t** 020 7938 5500 **f** 020 7368 4931 **e** julia.fiske@warnermusic.com President: Ray Still.

Wienerworld Ltd Unit B2 Livingstone Court, 55-63 Peel Road, Wealdstone, Harrow, Middlesex HA3 7QT **t** 020 8427 2777 **f** 020 8427 0660 **e** wworld@wienerworld.com **w** wienerworld.com MD: Anthony Broza. A&R Dir: Lloyd Branson.

John Williams Productions Burnfield Road, Giffnock, Glasgow, Strathclyde G46 7TH **t** 0141 637 2244 **f** 0141 637 2231 **e** jwp.sbl@virgin.net Production Manager: Karen McKay. Dist: Sports Business & Leisure

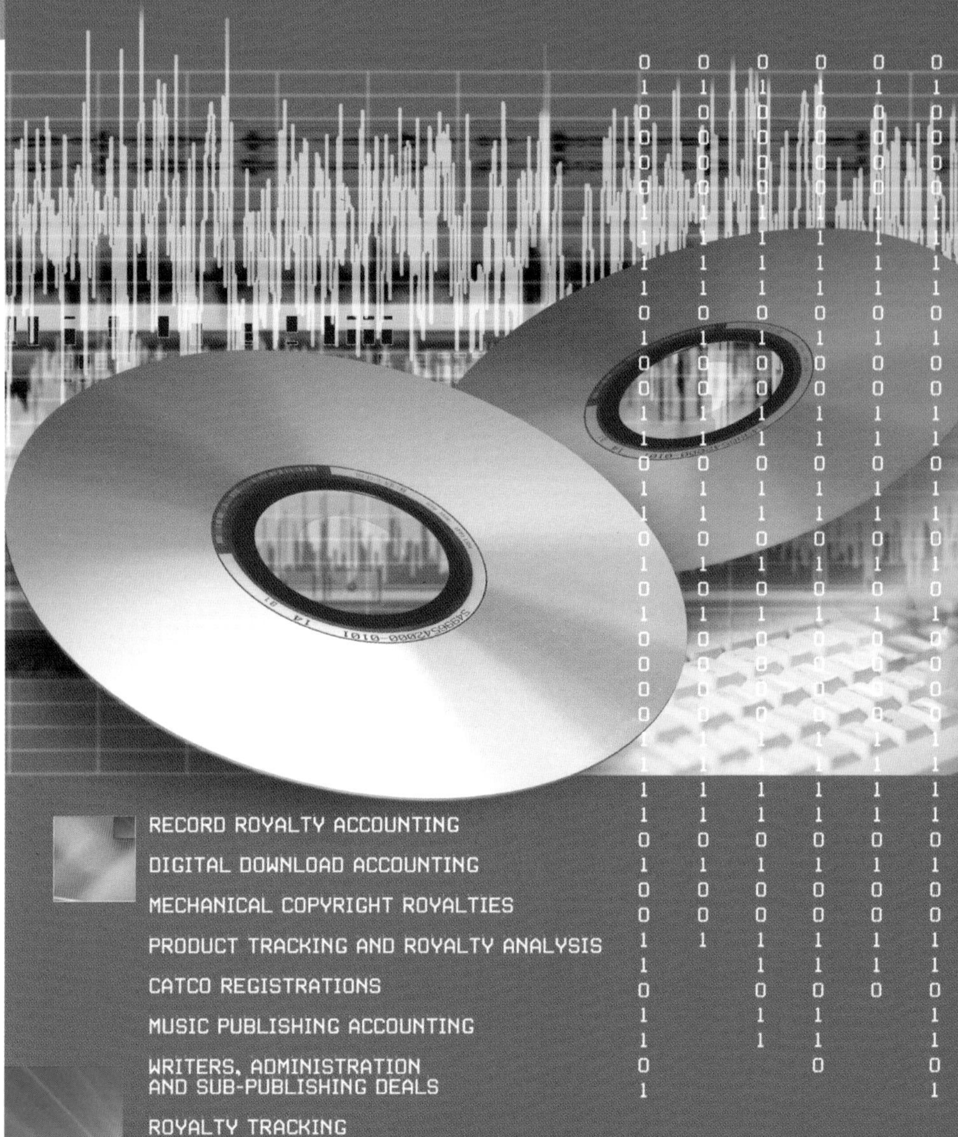
info@musicalc.com
ROYALTY ACCOUNTING SOFTWARE
musicalc
RECORD ROYALTY ACCOUNTING
DIGITAL DOWNLOAD ACCOUNTING
MECHANICAL COPYRIGHT ROYALTIES
PRODUCT TRACKING AND ROYALTY ANALYSIS
CATCO REGISTRATIONS
MUSIC PUBLISHING ACCOUNTING
WRITERS, ADMINISTRATION AND SUB-PUBLISHING DEALS
ROYALTY TRACKING
NET PUBLISHER SHARE ANALYSIS
COMMON WORKS REGISTRATIONS
COUNT ON US
+44 (0) 208 541 5135

Publishers & Affiliats

23rd Precinct Music (see Notting Hill Music (UK) Ltd)

2NV Publishing 1 Canada Sq, 29th Floor Canary Wharf Tower, London E14 5DY **t** 0870 444 2506 **f** 07000 785 845 **e** info@2nvpublishing.com **w** 2nvpublishing.com MD: Daniel Morgan. Creative Mgr: Darren Bullen. Hd Of Copyright: Jackie Jones. A&R Mgr: Nicola Stringer.

3rd Stone (see Heavy Truth Music Publishing Ltd)

4 Liberty Music (see Notting Hill Music (UK) Ltd)

4 Tunes Music PO Box 36534, London W4 3XE **t** 020 8994 2739 **f** 020 8472 0399 **e** andy@4-tunes.com **w** 4-tunes.com MD: Andy Murray.

5HQ (see Paul Rodriguez Music Ltd)

7pm Music (see A7 Music)

A Train Management (see Bucks Music Group)

A&C Black (Publishers) 37 Soho Square, London W1D 3QZ **t** 020 7758 0200 **f** 020 7758 0222 or 020 7758 0333 **e** educationalsales@acblack.com Educational Music Ed: Sheena Hodge.

Abaco Media & Publishing Ltd 212 Piccadilly, London W1J 9HG **t** 020 7917 2854 **f** 020 7439 0262 **e** info@abaco-music.com **w** abaco-music.com Dir: John Fisher.

Abacus (see Carlin Music Corporation)

Abigail London (see Warner Chappell Music Ltd)

Abood Music (see Jamdown Music Ltd)

ABRSM Publishing (see Oxford University Press)

Accolade Music 250 Earlsdon Avenue North, Coventry, West Midlands CV5 6GX **t** 02476 711935 **f** 02476 711191 **e** rootsrecs@btclick.com MD: Graham Bradshaw.

Acorn Publishing 1, Tylney View, London Road, Hook, Hants RG27 9LJ **t** 07808 377 350 **e** publishingacorn@hotmail.com MD: Mark Olrog.

Acrobat Music Publishing Suite 315, MWB Business Exchange, 2 Gayton Rd, Harrow, Middx HA1 2XU **t** 020 8901 4928 **f** 020 8901 4001 **e** enquiries@acrobatmusic.net w acrobatmusic.net MD: John Cooper.

Active (see Mute Song)

Acton Green (see EMI Music Publishing)

Acuff-Rose Music Ltd 3 Sandridge Park, Porters Wood, St Albans AL3 6PH **t** 01727 896544 **f** 01727 896545 **e** tpeters@acuffroseltd.com Gen Mgr: Tony Peters.

Ad-Chorel Music 86 Causewayside, Edinburgh EH9 1PY **t** 0131 668 3366 **f** 0131 662 4463 **e** neil@ad-chorelmusic.com MD: Neil Ross.

Addington State (see The Valentine Music Group)

ADN Creation Music Library (see Panama Music Library)

Adventures in Music Publishing PO Box 261, Wallingford, Oxon OX10 0XY **t** 01491 832 183 **e** info@adventuresin-music.com **w** adventure-records.com MD: Paul Conroy.

AE Copyrights (see Air-Edel Associates)

Ainm Music 5-6 Lombard Street East, Dublin 2, Ireland **t** +353 1 677 8701 **f** +353 1 677 8701 **e** fstubbs@ainm-music.com **w** ainm-music.com MD: Frank Stubbs.

Air (London) (see Chrysalis Music Ltd)

Air Music and Media Group Limited Chiltern House, 184 High Sreet, Berkhamsted, Hertfordshire HP4 3AP **t** 01442 877018 **f** 01442 877015 **e** info@airmusicandmedia.com **w** airmusicandmedia.com Contact: Michael Infante

Air Traffic Control Music Publishing 29 Harley St, London W1G 9QR **t** 0870 20 200 20 or 07973 270 963 **e** mark@airtrafficcontrolhq.com Dir: Mark Barker.

Air-Edel Associates 18 Rodmarton St, London W1U 8BJ **t** 020 7486 6466 **f** 020 7224 0344 **e** susan@air-edel.co.uk **w** air-edel.co.uk Publishing Manager: Susan Arnison.

Airdog Music (see Notting Hill Music (UK) Ltd)

AJ (see Kassner Associated Publishers Ltd)

Alan Price (see Carlin Music Corporation)

Alarcon Music Ltd The Old Truman Brewery, 91 Brick Lane, London E1 6QL **t** 020 7377 9373 **f** 020 7377 6523 **e** byron@bko-alarcon.co.uk Director: Byron Orme.

Alaw 4 Tyfila Road, Pontypridd, RCT CF37 2DA **t** 01443 402178 **f** 01443 402178 **e** sales@alawmusic.com **w** alawmusic.com Director: Brian Raby. Director: Meinir Heulyn.

J Albert & Son (UK) Ltd Unit 29, Cygnus Business Centre, Dalmeyer Road, London NW10 2XA **t** 020 8830 0330 **f** 020 8830 0220 **e** info@alberts.co.uk **w** albertmusic.co.uk Head Of A&R: James Cassidy.

Albion (see Complete Music)

Alexscar (see Menace Music Ltd)

Alfred Lengnick & Co (see Complete Music)

Alfred Publishing Co (UK) Ltd Burnt Mill, Elizabeth Way, Harlow, Essex CM20 2HX **t** 01279 828960 **f** 01279 828961 **e** music@alfredpublishing.demon.co.uk **w** alfreduk.com Mktng Mgr: Andrew Higgins.

All Action Figure Music Unit 9 Darvells Works, Common Rd, Chorleywood, Herts WD3 5LP **t** 01923 286010 **f** 01923 286070 **e** songs@allactionfigure.co.uk MD: Steve Lowes.

All Around The World Music Munro House, High Close, Rawdon, nr Leeds, West Yorkshire LS19 6HF **t** 01132 503338 **f** 01132 507343 **e** stewart@artandmusic.co.uk MD: Stewart Coxhead.

All Boys Music Ltd 222-224 Borough High Street, London SE1 1JX **t** 020 7403 0007 **f** 020 7403 8202 **e** helen@pwl-studios.com Mgr: Helen Dann.

All Good Music Group (see Copasetik Music)

All Media Music (see Paul Rodriguez Music Ltd)

All Zakatek Music 3 Purley Hill, Purley, Surrey CR8 1AP **t** 020 8660 0861 **f** 020 8660 0861 **e** allzakatekmusic@aol.com MD: Lenny Zakatek.

Alola Music (see Westbury Music Ltd)

Alon Music (see Charly Publishing Ltd)

Alpadon Music Shenandoah, Manor Park, Chislehurst, Kent BR7 5QD **t** 020 8295 0310 **e** donpercival@freenet.co.uk MD: Don Percival.

Amazing Feet Publishing Interzone House, 74-77 Magdalen Road, Oxford OX4 1RE **t** 01865 205600 **f** 01865 205700 **e** amazing@rotator.co.uk **w** rotator.co.uk/amazingfeet MD: Richard Cotton.

Amazon Music Ltd (see Peermusic (UK))

Ambassador Music (see Hornall Brothers Music Ltd)

Amco Music Publishing 2 Gawsworth Road, Macclesfield, Cheshire SK11 8UE **t** 01625 420163 **f** 01625 420168 **e** amco@cottagegroup.co.uk **w** cottagegroup.co.uk MD: Roger Boden.

Amigos De Musica (see Menace Music Ltd)

Amokshasong (see Tairona Songs Ltd)

Amos Barr Music (see Bucks Music Group)

Amphonic Music Ltd. Kerchesters, Waterhouse Lane, Kingswood, Surrey KT20 6HT **t** 01737 832837 **f** 01737 833812 **e** info@amphonic.co.uk **w** amphonic.co.uk MD: Ian Dale.

Anew Music (see Crashed Music)

Anglia Music Company 39 Tadorne Rd, Tadworth, Surrey KT20 5TF **t** 01737 812922 **f** 01737 812922 **e** angliamusic@ukgateway.net Dir/Co Sec: Norma Camby.

Anglia TV (see Carlin Music Corporation)

Anglo Plugging Music Fulham Palace, Bishops Avenue, London SW6 6EA **t** 020 7384 7373 **f** 020 7384 7374 **e** sue@asongs.co.uk Director: Sue Crawshaw.

Angus Publications 14 Graham Terrace, Belgravia, London SW1W 8JH **t** 07850 845280 **f** 020 7730 3368 **e** bill.puppetmartin@virgin.net **w** billmartinsongwriter.com Chairman: Bill Martin.

Anna (see Miriamusic)

Another Planet Music PO Box 158, Chipping Norton, Oxfordshire OX7 6FD **t** 01993 831 011 **f** 01993 831 011 **e** mark.rpm@ntlworld.com MD: Mark Stratford.

Anxious Music (see Universal Music Publishing Ltd)

Appleseed Music (see Bucks Music Group)

AppleTreeSongs Ltd PO Box 381, Great Missenden, Buckinghamshire HP16 9BE **t** 01494 890086 **f** 0870 054 8130 **e** nigelrush@appletreesongs.com Dir: Nigel Rush.

Applied Music (see Bucks Music Group)

Appropriate Music Ltd 65 Hazelwood Rd, Bush Hill Park, Middlesex EN1 1JG **t** 020 8245 6573 **f** 020 8245 6573 **e** jemgant@yahoo.co.uk Directors: Jem Gant/James Stewart.

Arcadia Production Music (UK) Greenlands, Payhembury, Devon EX14 3HY **t** 01404 841601 **f** 01404 841687 **e** admin@arcadiamusic.tv **w** arcadiamusic.tv Prop: John Brett.

Ardmore & Beechwood (see EMI Music Publishing)

Arena Music Hatch Farm Studios, Chertsey Rd, Addlestone, Surrey KT15 2EH **t** 01932 828715 **f** 01932 828717 **e** brian.adams@dial.pipex.com MD: Brian Adams.

Arhelger (see New Music Enterprises)

Ariel Music Malvern House, Sibford Ferris, Banbury, Oxon 0X15 5RG **t** 01295 780679 **f** 01295 788630 **e** jane@arielmusic.co.uk **w** arielmusic.co.uk Managing Partner: Jane Woolfenden.

Aristocrat Music Ltd Bournemouth Business Centre, 1052-54 Christchurch Rd, Bournemouth, Dorset BH7 6DS **t** 01202 436184 **f** 01202 423297 **e** AristocratMusic@aol.com MD: Terry King.

Arketek Music 53 Edge St, Nutgrove, St Helens, Merseyside WA9 5JX **t** 0151 430 6290 **e** info@arketek.com **w** arketek.com MD: Alan Ferreira.

ARL (see TMR Publishing)

Arloco Music (see Bucks Music Group)

Arnakata Music Ltd (see Astwood Music Ltd)

Arnisongs Unit A, The Courtyard, 42 Colwith Rd, London W6 9EY **t** 020 8846 3737 **f** 020 8846 3738 **e** info@jmanagement.co.uk MD: John Arnison.

Arpeggio Music Bell Farm House, Eton Wick, Windsor, Berkshire SL4 6LH **t** 01753 864910 **f** 01753 884810 MD: Beverley Campion.

Art Music (see Paul Rodriguez Music Ltd)

Artemis Music Pinewood Studios, Iver Heath, Bucks SL0 0NH **t** 01753 650766 **f** 01753 654774 **e** info@artemismusic.com **w** artemismusic.com MD: Mike Sheppard. Director of Publishing: James Sleigh.

Artfield 5 Grosvenor Square, London W1K 4AF **t** 020 7499 9941 **f** 020 7499 9010 **e** info@artfieldmusic.com; bbcooper@artfieldmusic.com **w** artfieldmusic.com MD: BB Cooper.

Arthur's Mother (see The Valentine Music Group)

Arts Music Publishing 185 Upton Lane, Forest Gate, London E7 9PJ **t** 020 8985 0091 **e** renkrecords@msn.com MD: Junior Hart.

Artwork (see Bucks Music Group)

Ascherberg, Hopwood & Crew (see Warner Chappell Music Ltd)

A7 Music PO Box 2272, Brighton BN2 8XD **t** 01273 304681 **f** 01273 308120 **e** info@a7music.com **w** a7music.com Director: Seven Webster. Director: Anthony DeRothschild.

Ash Music (GB) Hillside Farm, Hassocky Lane, Temple Normanton, Chesterfield, Derbyshire S42 5DH **t** 01246 231762 **e** ash_music36@hotmail.com Head of A&R: Paul Townsend.

Ashley Mark Publishing Company 1-2 Vance Court, Trans Britannia Enterprise Pk, Blaydon on Tyne, Tyne & Wear NE21 5NH **t** 0191 414 9000 **f** 0191 414 9001 **e** mail@ashleymark.co.uk **w** ashleymark.co.uk MD: Simon Turnbull. Proprietor: Maurice J Summerfield.

Asongs Publishing (see Anglo Plugging Music)

Assoc. Board of the Royal Schools of Music (Pub'g) 24 Portland Place, London W1B 1LU **t** 020 7636 5400 **f** 020 7637 0234 **e** publishing@abrsm.ac.uk **w** abrsmpublishing.co.uk Director of Publishing: Leslie East.

Associated (see Music Sales Ltd)

Associated Music International Ltd 34 Salisbury Street, London NW8 8QE **t** 020 7402 9111 **f** 020 7723 3064 **e** eliot@amimedia.co.uk **w** amimedia.co.uk MD: Eliot Cohen.

Asterisk Music Rock House, London Rd, St Marys, Stroud, Gloucestershire GL6 8PU **t** 01453 886252 or 0845 456 9759 **f** 01453 885361 **e** asterisk@rollercoasterrecords.com MD: John Beecher.

Astwood Music Ltd Latimer Studios, West Kington, Wilts SN14 7JQ **t** 01249 783 599 **f** 0870 169 8433 **e** DolanMAP@aol.com CEO: Mike Dolan.

Asylum Songs PO Box 121, Hove, East Sussex BN3 4YY **t** 01273 774468 **f** 08709 223099 **e** info@AsylumGroup.com **w** AsylumGroup.com Contact Bob James, Steve Gilmour, Scott Chester.

Atham (see Asterisk Music)

Atlantic Seven Productions/Music Library Ltd 52 Lancaster Road, London N4 4PR **t** 020 7263 4435 **f** 020 7436 9233 or 020 8374 9774 **e** musiclibrary@atlanticseven.com MD: Patrick Shart.

Atmosphere Music (see BMG Zomba Production Music)

Attic Music PO Box 38805, London W12 7XL **t** 020 8740 8898 **e** atticmusic@btinternet.com **w** atticmusic.co.uk Proprietor: Jimmy Thomas.

Audio Visual Media Music Library (see Panama Music Library)

Audio-Visual Media Music Library (see Panama Music Library)

Authentic Media 9 Holdom Avenue, Bletchley, Milton Keynes, Buckinghamshire MK1 1QR **t** 01908 364210 or 01908 644348 **e** grahamword@aol.com **w** authenticmedia.co.uk MD: Graham Williams.

Automatic Songs Ltd 5 Waldo Works, Waldo Rd, London NW10 6AW **t** 020 8964 8890 **f** 020 8960 5741 **e** mail@automaticrecords.co.uk **w** automaticrecords.co.uk MD: Russell Coultart.

Autonomy Music Publishing (see Bucks Music Group)

Avatar Music (see Notting Hill Music (UK) Ltd)

Aves (see London Publishing House)

Aviation Music Ltd (see Maxwood Music)

Aviva (see Music Sales Ltd)

B Feldman & Co (see EMI Music Publishing)

B&C Music Publishing (see Maxwood Music)

B-Unique Music Matrix Studio Complex, 91 Peterborough Rd, London SW6 3BU **t** 020 7384 6464 **f** 020 7384 6466 **e** info@b-uniquerecords.com **w** b-uniquerecords.com Co-MDs: Mark Lewis, Martin Toher.

The Bacon Empire Publishing 271 Royal College Street, Camden Town, London NW1 9LU **t** 020 7482 0115 **f** 020 7267 1169 **e** maurice@baconempire.com MD: Maurice Bacon.

Bad B Music (see Cheeky Music)

Bados Music (see Paul Rodriguez Music Ltd)

Baerenreiter Ltd Burnt Mill, Elizabeth Way, Harlow, Essex CM20 2HX **t** 01279 828930 **f** 01279 828931 **e** baerenreiter@dial.pipex.com **w** baerenreiter.com MD: Christopher Jackson.

Bamaco Vine Cottage, 255 Lower Road, Great Bookham, Leatherhead, Surrey KT23 4DX **t** 01372 450 752 **e** barrymurrayents@aol.com Contact: Barry Murray

Bandleader Music Co. 7 Garrick St, London WC2E 9AR **t** 020 7240 1628 **f** 020 7497 9242 **e** valentine@bandleader.co.uk **w** valentinemusic.co.uk MD: John Nice.

Bandleader Publications (see Kirklees Music)

Banks Music Publications The Old Forge, Sand Hutton, York, N. Yorkshire YO41 1LB **t** 01904 468472 **f** 01904 468679 **e** banksramsay@boltblue.com **w** banksmusicpublications.cwc.net Proprietor: Margaret Silver.

Barbera Music 102 Dean St, London W1D 3TQ **t** 020 7758 1494 **e** hgadsdon@barberamusic.co.uk MD: Hugh Gadsdon.

Bardell Smith (see EMI Music Publishing)

Bardic Edition 6 Fairfax Crescent, Aylesbury, Buckinghamshire HP20 2ES **t** 0870 950 3493 **f** 0870 950 3494 **e** info@bardic-music.com w bardic-music.com Proprietor: Barry Peter Ould.

Bardis Music Co.Ltd CPG House, Glenageary Office Park, Glenageary, Co Dublin, Ireland **t** +353 1 285 8711 **f** +353 1 285 8928 **e** info@bardis.ie w bardis.ie MD: Peter Bardon.

Barking Green Music 19 Ashford Carbonell, Ludlow, Shropshire SY8 4DB **t** 01584 831 474 **e** peterstretton@aol.com Contact: Peter J. Stretton

Barn Dance Publications Ltd 62 Beechwood Road, South Croydon, Surrey CR2 0AA **t** 020 8657 2813 **f** 020 8651 6080 **e** info@barndancepublications.co.uk **w** barndancepublications.co.uk MD: Derek Jones.

Barn Publishing (Slade) Ltd 1 Pratt Mews, London NW1 0AD **t** 020 7267 6899 **f** 020 7267 6746 **e** partners@newman-and.co.uk Pub: Colin Newman.

Basement Music Ltd. 20 Cyprus Gardens, London N3 1SP **t** 020 8922 4908 **f** 020 8922 4908 **e** basementmusic@btinternet.com Business Manager: John Cefai.

Batoni (see Notting Hill Music (UK) Ltd)

BBC (see BMG Music Publishing Ltd)

BBC Music Publishing A2033 Woodlands, 80 Wood Lane, London W12 OTT **t** 020 8433 1723 **f** 020 8433 1741 **e** victoria.watkins@bbc.co.uk Catalogue Manager: Victoria Watkins.

BDI Music Onward House, 11 Uxbridge St, London W8 7TQ **t** 020 7243 4101 **f** 020 7243 4131 **e** sarah@bdimusic.com **w** bdimusic.com Publisher: Sarah Liversedge.

Beacon Music (see Paul Rodriguez Music Ltd)

Beamlink (see Paul Rodriguez Music Ltd)

Bearsongs PO Box 944, Birmingham, West Midlands B16 8UT **t** 0121 454 7020 **f** 0121 454 9996 **e** bigbearmusic@compuserve.com **w** bigbearmusic.com MD: Jim Simpson.

Beat Music (see Paul Rodriguez Music Ltd)

Beat That Music Ltd (see Independent Music Group Ltd)

Beat That Music Ltd (see Independent Music Group)

Beatguru The Townhouse, 150 Goldhawk Rd, London W12 8HH **t** 020 8743 1111 or 07951 406 938 **e** andrian@beatguru.com **w** beatguru.com Dirs: Magnus Fiennes, Andrian Adams.

Beautiful (see Kassner Associated Publishers Ltd)

Bed & Breakfast Publishing (see Sublime Music)

Beechwood Music Publishing Ltd Littleton House, Littleton Rd, Ashford, Middx TW15 1UU **t** 01784 423214 **f** 01784 251245 **e** melissa@beechwoodmusic.co.uk **w** beechwoodmusic.co.uk MD: Tim Millington. Publishing Manager: Melissa Kennaway.

Beez (see Paul Rodriguez Music Ltd)

Beggars Banquet (see 4AD Music)

Beijing Publishing 105 Emlyn Road, London W12 9TG **t** 020 8749 3730 **e** brianleafe@aol.com Owner: Brian Leafe.

Belsize Music Ltd 29 Manor House, 250 Marylebone Road, London NW1 5NP **t** 020 7723 7177 **f** 020 7262 0775 e belsizemusic@btconnect.com Dir: Chas Peate.

Belwin Mills (see EMI Music Publishing)

Berkley (see Bucks Music Group)

Best Sounds (see Paul Rodriguez Music Ltd)

Bicameral (see Menace Music Ltd)

Big City Triumph Music 3 St Andrews Street, Lincoln, Lincolnshire LN5 7NE **t** 01522 539883 **f** 01522 528964 **e** steve.hawkins@easynet.co.uk **w** icegroup.co.uk MD: Steve Hawkins.

Big Life Music 67-69 Chalton Street, London NW1 1HY **t** 020 7554 2100 **f** 020 7554 2154 **e** biglife@biglife.co.uk **w** biglife.co.uk MD: Tim Parry.

Big Note Music Limited Comforts Place, Tandridge Lane, Lingfield, Surrey RH7 6LW **t** 01342 893046 **f** 01342 893562 **e** ahillesq@aol.com Contact: Deborah Beaton

Big One (see Big World Publishing)

Big One (see Big World Publishing)

Big Shot Music Ltd PO Box 14535, London N17 0WG **t** 020 8376 1650 **f** 020 8376 8622 **e** Pingramc2@aol.com Contact: P Ingram

Big Spliff (see Paul Rodriguez Music Ltd)

Big World Publishing 9 Bloomsbury Place, East Hill, Wandsworth, London SW18 2JB **t** 020 8877 1335 **f** 020 8877 1335 **e** songs@bigworldpublishing.com **w** bigworldpublishing.com MD: Patrick Meads.

Bigtime Music Publishing 86 Marlborough Road, Oxford OX1 4LS **t** 01865 249 194 **f** 01865 792 765 **e** info@bejo.co.uk **w** bejo.co.uk Administrator: Tim Healey.

Billym (see Menace Music Ltd)

Billymac (see Paul Rodriguez Music Ltd)

Biswas Music 21 Bedford Square, London WC1B 3HH **t** 020 7637 4444 **f** 020 7323 2857 **e** guy@fspg.co.uk, MD: Guy Rippon.

Black & Blue Music Ltd. PO Box 1200, London SW6 2GH **t** 020 7384 3200 **f** 020 7384 2999 **e** info@neorecords.com **w** neorecords.com MD: Darren Hamer.

Black Heat Music 13a Filey Avenue, London N16 6JL **t** 020 8806 4193 **e** tmorgan@ntlworld.com Director: Tony Morgan.

Blaster! Music 77 Nightingale Shott, Egham, Surrey TW20 9SUf **t** 01784 741 592 **e** martinw@netcomuk.co.uk MD: Martin Whitehead.

Blow Up Songs Unit 127, Stratford Workshops, Burford Rd, London E15 2SP **t** 020 8534 7700 **f** 020 8534 7722 **e** webmaster@blowup.co.uk **w** blowup.co.uk MD: Paul Tunkin.

Blue Banana Music (see Blue Melon Publishing)

Blue Cat (see Asterisk Music)

Blue Dot Music (see PXM Publishing)

Blue Melon Publishing 240A High Road, Harrow Weald, Middx HA3 7BB **t** 020 8863 2520 **f** 020 8863 2520 **e** steve@bluemelon.co.uk **w** bluemelon.co.uk MD: Steven Glen.

Blue Mountain Music Ltd 8 Kensington Park Rd, London W11 3BU **t** 020 7229 3000 **f** 020 7221 8899 **e** bluemountain@islandlife.co.uk **w** bluemountainmusic.tv MD: Alistair Norbury.

Blue Planet Music (see Blue Melon Publishing)

Blue Ribbon Music Ltd (see Hornall Brothers Music)

Blujay Music 55 Loudoun Rd, St Johns Wood, London NW8 0DL **t** 020 7604 3633 **f** 020 7604 3639 **e** info@blujay.co.uk Dirs: Steve Tannett, Carly Martin.

BMG MUSIC PUBLISHING LTD

MUSIC PUBLISHING
UNITED KINGDOM

Bedford House, 69-79 Fulham High St, London SW6 3JW **t** 020 7384 7600 **e** firstname.lastname@bmg.com **f** 020 7384 8164 **w** bmgmusicsearch.com Group Managing Director: Paul Curran. **t** 020 7384 7731. General Manager: Ian Ramage. **t** 020 7384 7706 Head of Global Marketing: Steve Levy. **t** 020 7384 7622. Director of Business and Commercial Affairs: Jackie Alway. **t** 020 7384 7806. Finance Director: Will Downs. **t** 020 7384 7737

BMG Music Publishing International Bedford House, 69-79 Fulham High Street, London SW6 3JW **t** 020 7384 7600 **f** 020 7384 8162 **e** (firstname).(lastname)@bmg.co.uk Exec. VP International: Andrew Jenkins. (BMG Music Publishing International - a unit of BMG Entertainment). Creative Mgr: Aram Walstra.

BMG ZOMBA PRODUCTION MUSIC

10-11 St Martin's Court, London WC2N 4AJ **t** 020 7497 4800 **f** 020 7497 4801 **e** musicresearch@bmgzomba.com **w** bmgzomba.com Music Researchers: Julia Dean, Andrew Stannard, Pascale Khalaf, Edward De Vroome.

BMGM Unit 207, Ducie House, Ducie Street, Manchester M1 2JW **t** 0161 236 5324 or 0161 237 3403 **f** 0161 236 4268 **e** caroline.elleray@bmg.co.uk Contact: Caroline Elleray

BMP - Broken Music Publishing Riverbank House, 1 Putney Bridge Approach, London SW6 3JD **t** 020 7371 0022 **f** 020 7371 0099 **e** ripe@compuserve.com Directors: Sharon Brooks / Jurgen Dramm.

Bob Ltd (see Notting Hill Music (UK) Ltd)

BobbySox (see Castle Hill Music)

Bobnal Music Inc (see Bucks Music Group)

Bocu Music Ltd 1 Wyndham Yard, Wyndham Place, London W1H 1AR **t** 020 7402 7433 **f** 020 7402 2833 Director: Carole Broughton.

Bolland & Bolland (see Menace Music Ltd)

Bollywood (see Notting Hill Music (UK) Ltd)

Boneless (see Menace Music Ltd)

Bonney (see Kassner Associated Publishers Ltd)

Bonskeid Music 4 Netherbank View, Edinburgh, Lothian EH16 6YY **t** 0131 666 1024 **f** 0131 666 1024 **e** info@castlesound.co.uk **w** bonskeidmusic.co.uk Dir: Freeland Barbour.

Boosey & Hawkes Music Publishers Ltd 295 Regent St, London W1B 2JH **t** 020 7291 7222 **f** 020 7436 5675 **e** booseymedia@boosey.com **w** boosey.com Music Consultant: Natasha Baldwin.

BOP Music (see The Valentine Music Group)

Boulevard Music Publishing (see Kevin King Music Publishing)

Bourne Music 2nd Floor, 207/209 Regent Street, London W1B 4ND **t** 020 7734 3454 **f** 020 7734 3385 **e** bournemusic@supanet.com Office Manager: John Woodward.

Bramsdene (see Music Sales Ltd)

Brass Wind Publications 4 St Mary's Road, Manton, Oakham, Rutland LE15 8SU **t** 01572 737409 **f** 01572 737409 **e** info@brasswindpublications.co.uk **w** brasswindpublications.co.uk

Breakin' Loose 32 Quadrant House, Burrell St, Southwark, London SE1 0UW **t** 020 7633 9576 or 07721 065 618 **e** sjbbreakinloose@aol.com MD: Steve Bingham.

Breakloose (see Bucks Music Group)

Breezy Tunes (see Jonsongs Music)

Breitkopf & Hartel Broome Cottage, The Street, Suffield, Norwich NR11 7EQ **t** 01263 768732 **f** 01263 768733 **e** sales@breitkopf.com **w** breitkopf.com Sales Rep: Robin Winter.

Brenda Brooker Enterprises 9 Cork St, Mayfair, London W1S 3LL **t** 020 7544 2893 **e** BrookerB@aol.com MD: Brenda Brooker.

Brentwood Benson Music (see Bucks Music Group)

Briar Music 5-6 Lombard Street, Dublin 2, Ireland **t** +353 1 677 4229 or +353 1 677 9762 **f** +353 1 671 0421 **e** lunar@indigo.ie MD: Brian Molloy.

Bright Music Ltd 21c Heathmans Road, Parsons Green, London SW6 4TJ **t** 020 7751 9935 **f** 020 7731 9314 **e** brightmusic@aol.com **w** brightmusic.co.uk MD: Martin Wyatt.

Brightly Music 231 Lower Clapton Road, London E5 8EG **t** 020 8533 7994 or 07973 616342 **f** 020 8986 4035 **e** abrightly@yahoo.com **w** brightly.freeserve.co.uk MD: Anthony Brightly.

Briter Music (see Asterisk Music)

Brm Music Publishing Ltd. PO Box 22949, London N10 3ZH **t** 0208 444 0987 **e** info@brmmusic.com **w** brmmusic.com MD: Bruce Ruffin. Head of Copyright: Michelle Francis.

Broadbent & Dunn 66 Nursery Lane, Dover, Kent CT16 3EX **t** 01304 825 604 **f** 0870 135 3567 **e** bd.music@broadbent-dunn.com **w** broadbent-dunn.com Company Secretary: William Dunn.

Broadley Music (Int) Ltd Broadley House, 48 Broadley Terrace, London NW1 6LG **t** 020 7258 0324 **f** 020 7724 2361 **e** admin@broadleystudios.com **w** broadleystudios.com MD: Ellis Elias.

Broadley Music Library (see Broadley Music (Int) Ltd)

Broadley Studios Ltd (see Broadley Music (Int) Ltd)

Brookside (see Asterisk Music)

Brothers Records Ltd The Music Village, 11B Osiers Road, London SW18 1NL **t** 020 8870 0011 **f** 020 8870 2101 **e** info@the-brothers.co.uk **w** brothersdistribution.co.uk Dirs: Ian Titchener, Nick Titchener.

Broughton Park Music Kennedy House, 31 Stamford Street, Altrincham, Cheshire WA14 1ES **t** 0161 941 4560 **f** 0161 941 4199 **e** harveylisberg@aol.com MD: Harvey Lisberg.

Bruco (see Menace Music Ltd)

Bryter Music Marlinspike Hall, Walpole Halesworth, Suffolk IP19 9AR **t** 01986 784 664 **f** 01986 784 664 **e** cally@antar.cc **w** brytermusic.com Proprietor: Cally.

Bs In Trees (see Menace Music Ltd)

Bill Buckley Music Saunders, Wood & Co, The White House, 140A Tatchbrook Street, London SW1V 2NE **t** 020 7821 0455 **f** 020 7821 6196 **e** nigel@s-wood.dircon.co.uk Partner: Nigel J Wood.

Bucks Music Group Onward House, 11 Uxbridge Street, London W8 7TQ **t** 020 7221 4275 **f** 020 7229 6893 **e** info@bucksmusicgroup.co.uk **w** bucksmusicgroup.com MD: Simon Platz.

Buffalo Songs 120 Ashurst Rd, North Finchley, London N12 9AB **t** 07887 983 452 **f** 020 8342 8213 **e** jonathan@buffalosongs.com **w** buffalosongs.com Creative Director: Jonathan Morley.

Bug Music Ltd Long Island House, Unit GB, 1-4 Warple Way, London W3 0RG **t** 020 8735 1868 **f** 020 8743 1551 **e** info@bugmusic.co.uk **w** bugmusic.com MD/VP International: Mark Anders.

Bugle Publishing Second Floor, 81 Rivington St, London EC2A 3AY **t** 020 7012 1416 **f** 020 7012 1419 **e** tcgleg@aol.com **w** milescopeland.com

Bulk Music Ltd 9 Watt Road, Hillington Park, Glasgow, Strathclyde G52 4RY **t** 0141 882 9986 **f** 0141 883 3686 **e** krl@krl.co.uk **w** krl.co.uk MD: Gus McDonald.

Bull-Sheet Music 18 The Bramblings, London E4 6LU **t** 020 8529 5807 **f** 020 8529 5807 **e** irene.bull@btinternet.com **w** bull-sheetmusic.co.uk; bandmemberswanted.co.uk MD: Irene Bull.

Bullish Music Inc (see Bucks Music Group)

Burlington (see Warner Chappell Music Ltd)

Burning Petals Music 5 Clover Ground, Shepton Mallet BA4 4AS **t** 0870 749 1117 **e** enquiries@burning-petals.com **w** burning-petals.com MD: Richard Jay.

Burnt Puppy (see Bucks Music Group)

Burnt Toast Music Publishing 12 Denyer Court, Fradley, Nr Lichfield, Staffs WS13 8TQ **t** 01543 444261 **f** 01543 444261 **e** phooper-keeley@softhome.net MD: Paul Hooper-Keeley.

Burton Way (see Universal Music Publishing Ltd)

Bushranger Music Station Lodge, 196 Rayleigh Road, Hutton, Brentwood, Essex CM13 1PN **t** 01277 222095 **e** bushrangermusic@aol.com MD: Kathy Lister.

C.O.R.S. Ltd (see MCS Plc)

Cactus (see SGO Music Publishing Ltd)

Cactus (see Creole Music Ltd)

Cala Music Publishing 17 Shakespeare Gardens, London N2 9LJ **t** 020 8883 7306 **f** 020 8365 3388 **e** paul@calarecords.com **w** calarecords.com Sales & Marketing Manager: Paul Sarcich.

Caleche (see Castle Hill Music)

California Phase (see Menace Music Ltd)

Campbell Connelly & Co (see Music Sales Ltd)

Candid Music 16 Castelnau, London SW13 9RU **t** 020 8741 3608 **f** 020 8563 0013 **e** info@candidrecords.com **w** candidrecords.com MD: Alan Bates.

Candle Music Ltd 44 Southern Row, London W10 5AN **t** 020 8960 0111 or 07860 912 192 **f** 020 8968 7008 **e** email@candle.org.uk **w** candle.org.uk MD: Tony Satchell. Exec Producer: Charlie Spencer.

Candor Music (see TMR Publishing)

Cara Music The Studio, R.O. 63 Station Road, Winchmore Hill, London N21 3NB **t** 020 8364 3121 **f** 020 8364 3090 **e** caramusicltd@dial.pipex.com Dir: Michael McDonagh.

Cardinal (see Carlin Music Corporation)

Cargo Music Publishing 39 Clitterhouse Crescent, Cricklewood, London NW2 1DB **t** 020 8458 1020 **f** 020 8458 1020 **e** mike@mikecarr.co.uk **w** mikecarr.co.uk MD: Mike Carr.

Caribbean Music (see Paul Rodriguez Music Ltd)

Caribbean Music Library (see Panama Music Library)

Caribbean Music Library Sovereign House, 12 Trewartha Road, Praa Sands, Penzance, Cornwall TR20 9ST **t** 01736 762826 or 07721 449477 **f** 01736 763328 **e** panamus@aol.com **w** panamamusic.co.uk Dir: Roderick Jones.

Caritas Music Publishing (see Eschenbach Editions)

Carlin Music Corporation Iron Bridge House, 3 Bridge Approach, London NW1 8BD **t** 020 7734 3251 **f** 020 7439 2391 **e** simonabbott@carlinmusic.com **w** carlinmusic.com Creative Manager: Simon Abbott. Head Of A&R: Simon Abbott.

Carnaby Music 78 Portland Road, London W11 4LQ **t** 020 7727 2063 **f** 020 7229 4188 **e** negfan@aol.com Dir: Charles Negus-Fancey.

Carte Blanche (see Fay Gibbs Music Services)

Castle Hill Music 2 Laurel Bank, Lowestwood, Huddersfield, West Yorkshire HD7 4ER **t** 01484 846333 **f** 01484 846333 **e** Hotleadrec@LineOne.net **w** fimusic.co.uk MD: Ian R Smith.

Cat's Eye Music (see Multiplay Music Ltd)

Catchphrases Library (see Karonsongs)

Cathedral Music King Charles Cottage, Racton, Chichester, West Sussex PO18 9DT **t** 01243 379968 **f** 01243 379859 **e** cathedral_music@compuserve.com Proprietor: Richard Barnes.

Catskills Music Publishing Ltd. PO Box 3365, Brighton BN1 1WQ **t** 01273 626245 **f** 01273 626246 **e** info@catskillsrecords.com **w** catskillsrecords.com Directors: Khalid, Amr or Jonny.

Cauliflower (see Bucks Music Group)

Cavendish Music (see Boosey & Hawkes Music Publishers Ltd)

Cecil Lennox (see Kassner Associated Publishers Ltd)

Cee Cee (see Asterisk Music)

Celtic Songs Unit 4, Great Ship Street, Dublin 8, Ireland **t** +353 1 478 3455 **f** +353 1 478 2143 **e** irishmus@iol.ie w irelandcd.com GM: Paul O'Reilly.

CF Kahnt (see Peters Edition)

Chain Music 24 Cornwall Rd, Cheam, Surrey SM2 6DT **t** 020 8643 3353 **f** 020 8643 9423 **e** gchurchill@c-h-a-ltd.demon.co.uk Chairman: Carole Howells.

Chain Of Love (see Sea Dream Music)

Chalumeau (see Paul Rodriguez Music Ltd)

Champion Music (see Cheeky Music)

Chandos Music Ltd Chandos House, Commerce Way, Colchester, Essex CO2 8HQ **t** 01206 225200 **f** 01206 225201 **e** shogger@chandos.net w chandos.net Music/Copyright Admin: Stephen Hogger.

Chapala Productions Rectory House, Church Lane, Warfield, Berkshire RG12 6EE **t** 01344 890001 **f** 01344 885323 Contact: Alan Bown

Chappell (see Warner Chappell Music Ltd)

Chappell Morris (see Warner Chappell Music Ltd)

Charisma Music Publishing (see EMI Music Publishing)

Charjan Music (see Paul Rodriguez Music Ltd)

Charlena (see Menace Music Ltd)

Charly Publishing Ltd Suite 379, 37 Store Street, London WC1E 7BS **t** 07050 136143 **f** 07050 136144 Contact: Jan Friedmann

Chart Music Company Ltd Island Cottage, Rod Eyot, Wargrave Road, Henley-on-Thames, Oxfordshire RG9 3JD **t** 01491 412946 **f** 01491 574361 **e** islandmusicuk@compuserve.com Dir: JW Farmer.

Chartel (see Bucks Music Group)

Chatwise Music (see Bucks Music Group)

Cheeky Music 181 High Street, Harlesden, London NW10 4TE **t** 020 8961 5202 **f** 020 8965 3948 **e** eddie@championrecords.co.uk **w** championrecords.co.uk Business Affairs: Eddie Seago.

Chelsea Music Publishing Co 124 Great Portland St, London W1W 6PP **t** 020 7580 0044 **f** 020 7580 0045 **e** eddie@chelseamusicpublishing.com **w** chelseamusicpublishing.com MD: Eddie Levy.

Cherry Red (see Complete Music)

Chester Music 8-9 Frith Street, London W1D 3JB **t** 020 7434 0066 **f** 020 7287 6329 **e** promotion@musicsales.co.uk **w** chesternovello.com MD: James Rushton.

Chestnut Music Smoke Tree House, Tilford Road, Farnham, Surrey GU10 2EN **t** 01252 794253 **f** 01252 792642 **e** keynote@dial.pipex.com MD: Tim Wheatley.

Chick-A-Boom Music (see Asterisk Music)

Chipglow (see Asterisk Music)

Chisholm Songs 36 Follingham Court, Drysdale Place, London N1 6LZ **t** 020 7684 8594 **f** 020 7684 8740 **e** deschisholm@hotmail.com Proprietor: Desmond Chisholm.

Christabel Music 32 High Ash Drive, Alwoodley, Leeds, West Yorkshire LS17 8RA **t** 0113 268 5528 **f** 0113 266 5954 MD: Jeff Christie.

Christel Music Ltd Fleet House, 173 Haydons Rd, Wimbledon, London SW19 8TB **t** 01255 421560 **e** songs@christelmusic.com **w** christelmusic.com MD: Dennis R. Sinnott.

Christian Music Ministries (see Sovereign Music UK)

Chrome Dreams PO Box 230, New Malden, Surrey KT3 6YY **t** 020 8715 9781 **f** 020 8241 1426 **e** mail@chromedreams.co.uk **w** chromedreams.co.uk GM: Andy Walker.

Chrys-A-Lee (see Chrysalis Music Ltd)

CHRYSALIS MUSIC LTD

The Chrysalis Building, 13 Bramley Road, London W10 6SP **t** 020 7221 2213 **f** 020 7465 6178 **e** firstname.lastname@chrysalis.com **w** chrysalis.com MD: Alison Donald. CEO, Chrysalis Music Division: Jeremy Lascelles. Chief Operating Officer, Chrysalis Music Division: Neil Fenton. Dir of A&R, Europe: Paul Kinder. Dir of Legal & Business Affairs: Simon Harvey. Senior Licensing Manager: Suzi Scott. Head of Copyright: Andy Godfrey. Royalty Manager: Janet Andersen. A&R Scout: Phil Catchpole.

Chuckle Music 6 Northend Gardens, Kingswood, Bristol BS15 1UA **t** 0117 783 7586 or 0789 994 8199 **e** ply501@netscapeonline.co.uk MD: Peter Michaels.

CIC UK (see Universal Music Publishing Ltd)

Cicada (see Paul Rodriguez Music Ltd)

Cinephonie Co (see Music Sales Ltd)

Cinque Port Music (see The Valentine Music Group)

Citybeat (see 4AD Music)

Class 52 Music Ltd (see Paternoster Music)

Classic Editions (see Wilson Editions)

CLM 7 Whiteford Road, Mannamead, Plymouth, Devon PL3 5LU **t** 01752 510710 **f** 01752 224281 **e** ronhancock@lineone.net Partner: Rob Hancock.

Clouseau (see SGO Music Publishing Ltd)

Clown Songs P.O Box 20432, London SE17 3WT **t** 07986 359 568 **e** office@clownmediagroup.co.uk **w** clownmediagroup.co.uk A&R: Stephen Adams.

Coda (see Bucks Music Group)

Cold Harbour Recording Company Ltd 1 York St, London W1U 6PA **t** 01449 720988 **e** enquiries@eastcentralone.com **w** eastcentralone.com MD: Steve Fernie.

Collegium Music Publications PO Box 172, Whittlesford, Cambridge CB2 4QZ **t** 01223 832474 **f** 01223 836723 **e** info@collegium.co.uk **w** collegium.co.uk Contact: Joanna Holland

Barry Collings Entertainments 21A Clifftown Road, Southend-On-Sea, Essex SS1 1AB **t** 01702 330005 **f** 01702 333309 **e** bcollent@aol.com **w** barrycollings.co.uk Proprietor: Barry Collings.

Collingwood O'Hare (see Bucks Music Group)

Columbia Publishing Wales Ltd Glen More, 6 Cwrt y Camden, Brecon, Powys LD3 7RR **t** 01874 625270 **f** 01874 625270 **e** dng@columbiawales.fsnet.co.uk **w** columbiapublishing.co.uk MD: Dafydd Gittins.

Come Again Music (see Broadley Music (Int) Ltd)

Cometmarket (see Notting Hill Music (UK) Ltd)

Comma Music (see Paul Rodriguez Music Ltd)

COMPLETE MUSIC

3rd Floor, Bishops Park House, 25-29 Fulham High Street, London SW6 3JH **t** 020 7731 8595 **f** 020 7371 5665 **e** info@complete-music.co.uk **w** complete-music.co.uk MD: Martin Costello. General Manager: Jonathan Kyte.

Concord (see The Essex Music Group)

Concord Music Hire Library (see Maecenas Music)

The Concord Partnership 5 Bushey Close, Old Barn Lane, Kenley, Surrey CR8 5AU **t** 020 8660 4766 or 020 8660 3914 **f** 020 8668 5273 **e** concordptnrship@aol.com Partner: Malcolm Binney.

Confetti Publishing PO Box 11541, London N15 4DW **t** 020 8376 1876 **f** 020 8808 4413 **e** publishing@confettirecords.co.uk **w** confettirecords.co.uk Director: Maria James.

Congo Music Ltd 17A Craven Park Road, Harlesden, London NW10 8SE **t** 020 8961 5461 **f** 020 8961 5461 **e** congomusic@hotmail.com **w** congomusic.com A&R Director: Root Jackson.

Connect 2 Music (see Zomba Music Publishers)

Connoisseur Music (see Crashed Music)

Consentrated Music (see Bucks Music Group)

Console Sounds PO Box 7515, Glasgow G41 3ZW **t** 0141 636 6336 **f** 0141 636 6336 **e** info@solemusic.co.uk **w** consolesounds.co.uk Dir: Stevie Middleton.

Constant In Opal Music (see Panama Music Library)

Constant In Opal Music Publishing Sovereign House, 12 Trewartha Road, Praa Sands, Penzance, Cornawall TR20 9ST **t** 01736 762826 **f** 01736 763328 **e** panamus@aol.com **w** songwriters-guild.co.uk MD: Roderick Jones.

The Contemporary Music Centre 19 Fishamble Street, Temple Bar, Dublin 8, Ireland **t** +353 1 673 1922 **f** +353 1 648 9100 **e** info@cmc.ie w cmc.ie Director: Eve O'Kelly.

Cooking Vinyl Ltd 10 Allied Way, London W3 0RQ **t** 020 8600 9200 **f** 020 8743 7448 **e** info@cookingvinyl.com **w** cookingvinyl.com MD: Martin Goldschmidt.

Copasetik Music 9 Spedan Close, Branch Hill, London NW3 7XF **t** 07855 551 024 **e** copasetik1@aol.com **w** copasetik.com MD/Head of A&R: Jon Sexton.

Copeberg (see Bugle Publishing)

Copperplate Music (see Bardic Edition)

Cordella Music Ltd 35 Britannia Gardens, Hedge End, Hants SO30 2RN **t** 08450 616616 or 07831 456348 **f** 01489 780909 **e** barry@cordellamusic.co.uk **w** cordellamusic.co.uk MD: Barry Upton.

Corelia Music Library (see Panama Music Library)

Corner Stone (see The Valentine Music Group)

Cornerways Music Ty'r Craig, Longleat Avenue, Craigside, Llandudno LL30 3AE **t** 01492 549759 **f** 01492 541482 **e** gordonlorenz@compuserve.com Contact: Gordon Lorenz

Cot Valley Music (see Scamp Music)

Courtyard Music 22 The Nursery, Sutton Courtenay, Oxfordshire OX14 4UA **t** 01235 845800 **f** 01235 847692 **e** andy@cyard.com **w** courtyardmusic.net A&R Mgr: Andy Ross.

CPP (see International Music Publications (IMP))

Cramer Music 23 Garrick Street, London WC2E 9RY **t** 020 7240 1612 **f** 020 7240 2639 **e** enquiries@cramermusic.co.uk MD: Peter Maxwell.

Cranford Summer School Of Music (see The Concord Partnership)

Crashed Music 162 Church Road, East Wall, Dublin 3, Ireland **t** +353 1 856 1011 **f** +353 1 856 1122 **e** shay@crashedmusic.com **w** crashedmusic.com MD: Shay Hennessy.

Creative Minds (see Bucks Music Group)

Creative Minds Units 13-14, Barley Shotts Business Park, 246 Acklam Rd, London W10 5YG **t** 020 8962 5499 **f** 020 8962 5498 **e** nick@bedrock.uk.net **w** creativemindspublishing.com Creative Director: Nick Bates.

Creative World Entertainment Ltd The Croft, Deanslade Farm, Claypit Lane, Lichfield, Staffordshire WS14 0AG **t** 01543 253576 or 07885 341745 **f** 01543 255185 **e** info@creative-world-entertainment.co.uk **w** creative-world-entertainment.co.uk MD: Mervyn Spence.

Creole Music Ltd The Chilterns, France Hill Drive, Camberley, Surrey GU15 3QA **t** 01276 686077 **f** 01276 686055 **e** creole@clara.net MD: Bruce White.

Crimson Flame (see Sea Dream Music)

Cromwell Music (see The Essex Music Group)

Cross Music (see Music Sales Ltd)

Crossbar Music (see The Valentine Music Group)

Crumbs Music South Lodge, Watlington Rd, Shirburn, Oxon OX49 5DQ **t** 01491 613 555 **f** 01491 613 591 **e** crumbsmusic@btopenworld.com MD: Ray Williams.

Crystal City (see Sea Dream Music)

CSA Word 6a Archway Mews,, 241a Putney Bridge Rd, London SW15 2PE **t** 020 8871 0220 **f** 020 8877 0712 **e** clive@csaword.co.uk **w** csatelltapes.demon.co.uk Audio Manager: Victoria Williams.

CTV Music The Television Centre, St Helier, Jersey, Channel Islands JE1 3ZD **t** 01534 816816 **f** 01534 816778 **e** broadcast@channeltv.co.uk **w** channeltv.co.uk Dir Sales/Mktg: Gordon de Ste. Croix.

Cultural Foundation Dalehead, Rosedale, North Yorks YO18 8RL **t** 01751 417147 or 0845 4584699 01751 417804 **e** info@cultfound.org **w** cultfound.org Dir: Peter Bell.

David Cunningham Music 17 Kirkland Lane, Penkhull, Stoke on Trent, Staffordshire ST4 5DJ **t** 01782 410237 or 07754 170541 **f** 01782 410237 **e** davidcunninghammusic@yahoo.co.uk Contact: David Cunningham

Curious (see Bucks Music Group)

Curious? UK (see Bucks Music Group)

Cutting Edge Music Ltd 3rd Floor, 36 King St, London WC2E 8JS **t** 020 7759 8550 **f** 020 7759 8560 **e** philipm@cutting-edge.uk.com **w** cutting-edge.uk.com MD: Philip Moross. GM: John Boughtwood. Asst: Susan Tilly.

Cutting Records Music (see Dejamus Ltd)

Cwmni Cyhoeddi Gwynn (see Cyhoeddiadau Sain)

Cwmni Cyhoeddi Gwynn Cyf 28 Heol-y-Dwr, Penygroes, Caernarfon, Gwynedd LL54 6LR **t** 01286 881797 **f** 01286 882634 **e** info@gwynn.co.uk **w** gwynn.co.uk Administrator: Wendy Jones.

Cybertech88 6 Cheyne Walk, Hornsea, East Yorkshire HU18 1BX **t** 01964 536193 **e** info@csupports.co.uk **w** csupports.co.uk MD: Paul Cooke.

Cyclo Music (see Bucks Music Group)

Cyhoeddiadau Sain Canolfan Sain, Llandwrog, Caernarfon, Gwynedd LL54 5TG **t** 01286 831111 **f** 01286 831497 **e** rhian@sain.wales.com **w** sain.wales.com Contact: Rhian Eleri

---

D MUSIC

35 Brompton Road, London SW3 1DE **t** 020 7368 6311 **f** 020 7823 9553 **e** d@35bromptonroad.com **w** drecords.co.uk MD: Douglas Mew. Sub-Publisher: Notting Hill Music

---

CYP Music Limited CYP Children's Audio, The Fairway, Bush Fair, Harlow, Essex CM18 6LY **t** 01279 444707 **f** 01279 445570 **e** sales@cypmusic.co.uk **w** kidsmusic.co.uk Sales Manager: Gary Wilmot.

Cznin Music (see Menace Music Ltd)

D-Jon Music (see Menace Music Ltd)

D.O.R Encryption PO Box 1797, London E1 4TX **t** 020 7702 7842 **e** Encryption@dor.co.uk MD: Martin Parker.

Dacara Music (see Menace Music Ltd)

Daisynook (see Notting Hill Music (UK) Ltd)

Dalmation Songs Ltd PO Box 49155, London SW20 0YL **t** 020 8946 7242 **e** w.stonebridge@btopenworld.com Directors: Bill Stonebridge, Marc Fox.

Damani Songs (see Darah Music)

Danny Thompson Music (see SGO Music Publishing Ltd)

Darah Music 21C Heathmans Rd, Parsons Green, London SW6 4TJ **t** 020 7731 9313 **f** 020 7731 9314 **e** admin@darah.co.uk MD: David Howells. GM: Nicki L'Amy.

Toby Darling Ltd 37/39 Southgate St, Winchester, Hampshire SO23 9EH **t** 01962 844480 **f** 01962 854400 **e** info@tobydarling.com **w** tobydarling.com MD: Toby Darling.

Dartsongs (see Asterisk Music)

Dash Music (see Music Sales Ltd)

Datsmaboy Music (see Menace Music Ltd)

David Paramor Publishing (see Kassner Associated Publishers Ltd)

DCI Video (see International Music Publications (IMP))

De Haske Music (UK) Ltd Fleming Road, Earlstrees, Corby, Northamptonshire NN17 4SN **t** 01536 260981 or 0800 616415 **f** 01536 401075 or 0800 616415 **e** music@dehaske.co.uk Sales & Marketing Mgr: Mark Coull.

Decentric Music 12 Tideway Yard, 125 Mortlake High Street, London SW14 8SN **t** 020 8977 4616 **f** 020 8977 4616 **e** decentricjb@talk21.com Director: James Bedbrook.

Deceptive Music PO Box 288, St Albans, Hertfordshire AL4 9YU **t** 01727 834130 **e** tony@bluff.demon.co.uk MD: Tony Smith.

Deconstruction Songs (see BMG Music Publishing Ltd)

DeeKay Songs (see Asylum Songs)

Deekers (see Eaton Music Ltd)

Deep Blue Music (see Bucks Music Group)

Deep Blue Publishing (see Sovereign Music UK)

Dejamus Ltd Suite 11, Accurist House, 44 Baker Street, London W1U 7AZ **t** 020 7486 5838 **f** 020 7487 2634 **e** info@dejamus.co.uk MD: Stephen James. Copyright Mgr: Linda Watts.

Delfont Music (see Warner Chappell Music Ltd)

Delicious Publishing Suite GB, 39-40 Warple Way, Acton, London W3 0RG **t** 020 8749 7272 **f** 020 8749 7474 **e** info@deliciousdigital.com **w** deliciousdigital.com MD: Ollie Raphael.

Demi Monde Publishing Llanfair Caereinion, Powys, Wales SY21 0DS **t** 01938 810758 **f** 01938 810758 **e** demi.monde@dial.pipex.com **w** demimonde.co.uk MD: Dave Anderson.

Denker Music (see Kassner Associated Publishers Ltd)

Design Music (see Carlin Music Corporation)

Desilu Publishing Ltd 6 Rookwood Park, Horsham, West Sussex RH12 IUB **t** 01403 240272 or 07788 412867 **f** 01403 263008 **e** gbowes@desilurecords.com MD: Graham Bowes.

Destiny Music (see Carlin Music Corporation)

Deutscher Verlag Fur Musik, Leipzig (see Breitkopf & Hartel)

Dharma Music 2nd Floor, 9-10 Savile Row, London W1S 3PF **t** 020 7851 0900 **f** 020 7851 0901 **e** zen@instantkarma.co.uk Chairman: Rob Dickins.

Dick Music (see Tabitha Music Ltd)

Digger Music 21 Bedford Square, London WC1B 3HH **t** 020 7637 4444 f 020 7323 2857 **e** tills@globalnet.co.uk CEO: Tilly Rutherford.

Dinosaur Music Publishing 5 Heyburn Crescent, Westport Gardens, Stoke On Trent, Staffordshire ST6 4DL **t** 08707 418651 **f** 08707 418652 **e** alan@dinosaurmusic.co.uk **w** dinosaurmusic.co.uk MD: Alan Dutton. Head of A&R: Alan Avon.

Diverse Music Ltd Creeting House, All Saints Road, Creeting St Mary, Ipswich, Suffolk IP6 8PR **t** 01449 720 988 **f** 01449 726 067 **e** diversemusicltd@compuserve.com MD: Diana Graham.

Dizzy Heights (see Edel Publishing)

DL Songs (see Kassner Associated Publishers Ltd)

DMX Music Forest Lodge, Westerham Road, Keston, Kent BR2 6HE **t** 01689 882200 **f** 01689 882288 **e** custserv@dmxmusic.co.uk **w** dmxmusic.co.uk Music Dir: Mick Bennett.

Do It Yourself Music (see Bucks Music Group)

Doctor Snuggles Music (see Roedean Music Ltd)

Dog Music (see Crashed Music)

Dome Music Publishing 59 Glenthorne Rd, London W6 0LJ **t** 020 8748 4499 **f** 020 8748 6699 **e** info@domerecords.co.uk MD: Peter Robinson.

Domino Music (see Tabitha Music Ltd)

Donna (see EMI Music Publishing)

Dorsey Brothers Music (see Music Sales Ltd)

Douglas Music (see Anglia Music Company)

Douglas Sahm Music (see Menace Music Ltd)

Dr Watson Music (see Sherlock Holmes Music)

Dread Music (see Bucks Music Group)

Dreaded Sunny Day Music 5 St John's Lane, London EC1M 4BH **t** 020 7549 2807 **e** info@dreadedsunnyday.com **w** dreadedsunnyday.com MD: Mark Jackson.

Dreambase Music PO Box 13383, London NW3 5ZR **t** 020 7794 2540 **f** 020 7794 7393 **e** hitman@popstar.com A&R: Tony Strong.

Drumblade Music (see Bardic Edition)

Dub Plate Music (see Greensleeves Publishing Ltd)

Dune Music 1st Floor, 73 Canning Road, Harrow, Middx HA3 7SP **t** 020 8424 2807 **f** 020 8861 5371 **e** info@dune-music.com **w** dune-music.com MD: Janine Irons.

Durham Music (see Bucks Music Group)

Eagle (see Bucks Music Group)

Earache Songs UK Ltd Suite 1-3 Westminster Building, Theatre Square, Nottingham NG1 6LG **t** 0115 950 6400 **f** 0115 950 8585 **e** mail@earache.com **w** earache.com MD: Digby Pearson.

Earlham Press (see De Haske Music (UK) Ltd)

Earthsongs (see Bucks Music Group)

Eaton Music Ltd Eaton House, 39 Lower Richmond Road, Putney, London SW15 1ET **t** 020 8788 4557 **f** 020 8780 9711 **e** info@eatonmusic.com **w** eatonmusic.com MD: Terry Oates.

Eclectic Dance Music (see Westbury Music Ltd)

Eddie Trevett Music (see Carlin Music Corporation)

Edel Publishing 12 Oval Road, London NW1 7DH **t** 020 7482 9700 **f** 020 7482 4846 **e** phil_hope@edel.com w edel.com MD: Phil Hope.

Edition (see Loose Music (UK))

Edition Kunzelmann (see Obelisk Music)

Edition Schwann (see Peters Edition)

Editions Penguin Cafe 52 King Henry's Walk, London N1 4NN **t** 020 7503 3546 **f** 020 7503 3546 **e** joanna.stephenson@penguincafe.com **w** penguincafe.com Business Affairs Manager: Joanna Stephenson. Dir: Arthur Jeffes.

Edwin Ashdown (see Music Sales Ltd)

EG Music Ltd PO Box 4397, London W1A 7RZ **t** 020 8540 9935 MD: Sam Alder.

Egleg Music (see Asterisk Music)

Publishers

ELA MUSIC

Argentum, 2 Queen Caroline Street, London W6 9DX **t** 020 8323 8013 **f** 020 8323 8080 **e** ela@ela.co.uk **w** ela.co.uk Contact: John Giacobbi.

Eldorado Music Publishing (see Future Earth Music Publishing)

Eleven East Music (see Bucks Music Group)

Eleven East Music Inc. (see Bucks Music Group)

William Elkin Music Services Station Road Industrial Estate, Salhouse, Norwich, Norfolk NR13 6NS **t** 01603 721302 **f** 01603 721801 **e** sales@elkinmusic.co.uk **w** elkinmusic.co.uk Partner: Richard Elkin.

Embassy Music (see Music Sales Ltd)

Emerson Edition Ltd Windmill Farm, Ampleforth, North Yorkshire YO62 4HF **t** 01439 788324 **f** 01439 788715 **e** JuneEmerson@compuserve.com MD: June Emerson.

EMI Film & Theatre Music (see EMI Music Publishing)

EMI MUSIC PUBLISHING

127 Charing Cross Road, London WC2H 0QY **t** 020 7434 2131 **f** 020 7434 3531 **e** firstinitial+lastname@emimusicpub.com **w** emimusicpub.co.uk Chairman/CEO: Peter Reichardt. Senior VP/Head of Business Developement: William Booth. Exec VP, Head of UK & Europe A&R: Guy Moot. Senior VP A&R: Mike Smith. Dir of Legal & Business Aff: Chris Mileson. Senior VP, Film TV & Media: Jonathan Channon. Dir KPM Music: Peter Cox.

EMI Music (see Kingsway Music)

EMI Music Publishing Continental Europe Publishing House, 127 Charing Cross Road, London WC2H 0QY **t** 020 7434 2131 **f** 020 7287 5254 **e** firstinitial+lastname@emimusicpub.com **w** emimusicpub.co.uk Chief Operating Officer Continental European: Terry Foster-Key. Dir of Fin & Admin Continental European Operations: Kevin Pallent.

Emmelle Music PO Box 1345, Essex IG4 5FX **t** 07050 333 555 **f** 07020 923 292 **e** emmelleye@aol.com **w** emmellar.cwc.net Joint MD: Penelope Hersk.

Emusic Pty Ltd (see SGO Music Publishing Ltd)

Endomorph Music Publishing 29 St Michael's Rd, Leeds, West Yorkshire LS6 3BG **t** 0113 274 2106 **f** 0113 278 6291 **e** dave@bluescat.com **w** bluescat.com MD: Dave Foster.

English West Coast Music The Old Bakehouse, 150 High Street, Honiton, Devon EX14 8JX **t** 01404 42234 **f** 07767 869029 **e** Studio@ewcm.co.uk **w** ewcm.co.uk Studio Manager: Sean Brown.

Ensign Music (see Famous Music Publishing)

ERA Music (see Express Music (UK) Ltd)

Ernst Eulenburg (see Schott & Company Ltd)

Ernvik Musik (Sweden) (see Sea Dream Music)

Eschenbach Editions 28 Dalrymple Crescent, Edinburgh EH9 2NX **t** 0131 667 3633 **f** 0131 667 3633 **e** eschenbach@caritas-music.co.uk **w** caritas-music.co.uk MD: James Douglas. MD: James Douglas.

Esoterica Music Ltd 20 Station Road, Eckington Road, Sheffield, South Yorkshire S21 4FX **t** 01246 432507 or 07785 232176 **f** 01246 432507 **e** richardcory@lineone.net MD: Richard Cory.

Esquire Music Company 185A Newmarket Road, Norwich, Norfolk NR4 6AP **t** 01603 451139 MD: Peter Newbrook.

The Essex Music Group Suite 207, Plaza 535, Kings Road, London SW10 0SZ **t** 020 7823 3773 **f** 020 7351 3615 **e** sx@essexmusic.demon.co.uk MD: Frank D Richmond.

Euterpe Music (see Paul Rodriguez Music Ltd)

EV-Web (see Bucks Music Group)

Eventide Music (see Panama Music Library)

Evergreen Music (see Music Sales Ltd)

Evita Music (see Universal Music Publishing Ltd)

Evocative Music (see G2 Music)

Evolve Music Ltd The Courtyard, 42 Colwith Road, London W6 9EY **t** 020 8741 1419 **f** 020 8741 3289 **e** firstname@evolverecords.co.uk Co-MD: Oliver Smallman. Creative Manager: Richard Belcher.

Ewan McColl Music (see Bucks Music Group)

Express Music (UK) Ltd Matlock, Brady Road, Lyminge, Kent CT18 8HA **t** 01303 863185 **f** 01303 863185 **e** siggyjackson@onetel.net.uk MD: Siggy Jackson.

Extra Slick Music (see Menace Music Ltd)

Faber Music 3 Queen Square, London WC1N 3AU **t** 020 7833 7900 **f** 020 7833 7939 **e** information@fabermusic.com w fabermusic.com

Fabulous Music (see The Essex Music Group)

Fairwood Music Ltd 72 Marylebone Lane, London W1U 2PL **t** 020 7487 5044 **f** 020 7935 2270 **e** paul.brown@fairwoodmusic.com GM: Paul Brown.

Faith & Hope Publishing 23 New Mount St, Manchester M4 4DE **t** 0161 839 4445 **f** 0161 839 1060 **e** email@faithandhope.co.uk **w** faithandhope.co.uk Contact: Neil Claxton

Fall River Music (see Bucks Music Group)

Famous Music Publishing Bedford House, 69-79 Fulham High St, London SW6 3JW **t** 020 7736 7543 **f** 020 7471 4812 **e** luke.famousmusic@bigfoot.com **w** syncsite.com A&R Director: Luke McGrellis.

Far Out Music (see Westbury Music Ltd)

Fashion Music 17 Davids Road, London SE23 3EP **t** 020 8291 6253 **f** 020 8291 1097 **e** chrislane@dubvendor.co.uk Producer: Chris Lane.

Fast Western Ltd. Bank Top Cottage, Meadow Lane, Millers Dale, Derbyshire SK17 8SN **t** 01298 872462 **f** 01298 872461 **e** fast.west@virgin.net MD: Ric Lee.

Fastforward Music Publishing Ltd 1 Sorrel Horse Mews, Ipswich, Suffolk IP4 1LN **t** 01473 210555 **f** 01473 210500 **e** sales@fastforwardmusic.co.uk Sales Dir: Neil Read.

Fat Fox Music 24a Radley Mews, off Stratford Rd, London W8 6JP **t** 020 7376 9555 **f** 020 7937 6246 **e** nick@fatfox.co.uk **w** fatfox.co.uk Director: Nick Wilde.

Favored Nations Music (see Shanna Music Ltd)

Fenette Music (see De Haske Music (UK) Ltd)

FI Music 2 Laurel Bank, Lowestwood, Huddersfield, West Yorkshire HD7 4ER **t** 01484 846 333 **f** 01484 846 333 **e** HotLeadRecords@btopenworld.com **w** fimusic.co.uk Co-Director: Ian R Smith.

John Fiddy Music Unit 3, Moorgate Business Centre, South Green, Dereham NR19 1PT **t** 01362 697922 **f** 01362 697923 **e** info@johnfiddymusic.co.uk **w** johnfiddymusic.co.uk Prop: John Fiddy.

Filthy Music 12 Austral Way, Althorne, Essex CM3 6UP **t** 01621 743979 **f** 01621 743979 **e** info@filthysonnix.com **w** filthysonnix.com Publishing & Int'l Lic.: Mick Shiner.

Fintage Music 36-38 Westbourne Grove, Newton Rd, London W2 5SH **t** 020 7313 9977 **f** 020 7221 0033 **e** entertainment.assets@fintagehouse.com **w** fintagehouse.com Contact: George Helyer, Suzanne Plesman

Fireworks Music 8 Berwick Street, Soho, London W1F 0PH **t** 020 7292 0011 **f** 020 7292 0016 **e** fwx@fireworksmusic.co.uk **w** fireworksmusic.co.uk Manager: Lizzie Prior.

First Time Music (Publishing) UK Sovereign House, 12 Trewartha Road, Praa Sands, Penzance, Cornwall TR20 9ST **t** 01736 762826 or 07721 449477 **f** 01736 763328 **e** panamus@aol.com **w** songwriters-guild.co.uk MD: Roderick Jones.

Flicknife (see Complete Music)

Flip Flop Music (see Asterisk Music)

The Flying Music Company Ltd FM House, 110 Clarendon Road, London W11 2HR **t** 020 7221 7799 **f** 020 7221 5016 **e** info@flyingmusic.co.uk **w** flyingmusic.com Directors: Paul Walden/Derek Nicol.

Focus Music (Publishing) Ltd 4 Pilgrims Lane, London NW3 1SL **t** 020 7435 8266 **f** 020 7435 1505 **e** info@focusmusic.com **w** focusmusic.com MD: Paul Greedus.

Focus Music Library (see Focus Music (Publishing) Ltd)

Folktrax & Soundpost Publications 16 Brunswick Square, Gloucester GL1 1UG **t** 01452 415110 **f** 01452 503643 **e** peter@folktrax.freeserve.co.uk **w** folktrax.org Dir: Peter Kennedy.

FON Music (see Universal Music Publishing Ltd)

FourFives Music 21d Heathman's Rd, London SW6 4TJ **t:** 020 7731 6555 **f:** 020 7371 5005 **e:** mp@fourfives-music.com **w:** fourfives-music.com MD: Neil Duckworth.

Forsyth Brothers Ltd 126 Deansgate, Manchester M3 2GR **t** 0161 834 3281 **f** 0161 834 0630 **e** info@forsyths.co.uk **w** forsyths.co.uk Publishing: Gene Colter.

Fortissimo Music 78 Portland Road, London W11 4LQ **t** 020 7727 2063 **f** 020 7229 4188 **e** negfan@aol.com

Fortunes Fading Music Unit 1, Pepys Court, 84-86 The Chase, London SW4 0NF **t** 020 7720 7266 **f** 020 7720 7255 **e** ffading@btinternet.com MD: Peter Pritchard.

Four Seasons Music Ltd Killarney House, Killarney Road, Bray, Co. Wicklow, Ireland **t** +353 1 286 9944 **f** +353 1 286 9945 **e** coulter@indigo.ie **w** philcoulter.com PA to MD: Moira Winget.

4AD Music 17-19 Alma Road, London SW18 1AA **t** 020 8871 2121 **f** 020 8871 2745 **e** postmaster@almaroad.co.uk MD: Andy Heath.

Fox Publishing (see EMI Music Publishing)

Francis Day & Hunter (see EMI Music Publishing)

Frank Chacksfield Music (see Music Sales Ltd)

Freddy Bienstock Music (see Carlin Music Corporation)

Freedom Songs Ltd PO Box 272, London N20 0BY **t** 020 8368 0340 **f** 020 8361 3370 **e** freedom@jt-management.demon.co.uk MD: John Taylor.

Friendly Overtures Walkers Cottage, Aston Lane, Henley-on-Thames, Oxon. RG9 3EJ **t** 01491 574457 **f** 01491 574457 **e** jmbatory@ukonline.co.uk Creative Dir: Michael Batory.

Frontline Music (see Shanna Music Ltd)

Frontline Music Publishing Ltd (see Purple City Ltd)

Frooty Music (see No Known Cure Publishing)

Full Cycle Music (see Bucks Music Group)

Full Flavour Music (see Dome Music Publishing)

Fundamental Music Ltd The Old Lampworks, Rodney Place, London SW19 2LQ **t** 020 8542 4222 **f** 020 8542 9934 **e** info@fundamental.co.uk MD: Tim Prior.

Fundit (see Fundamental Music Ltd)

Fungus (see Paul Rodriguez Music Ltd)

Funtastik Music 43 Seaforth Gardens, Stoneleigh, Surrey KT19 0LR **t** 020 8393 1970 **f** 020 8393 2428 **e** info@funtastikmusic.com **w** funtastikmusic.com Contact: John Burns

Future Earth Music Publishing 59 Fitzwilliam Street, Wath Upon Dearne, Rotherham, South Yorks S63 7HG **t** 01709 872875 **e** david@future-earth.co.uk **w** future-earth.co.uk MD: David Moffitt.

Future Stars Publishing Company (see Bucks Music Group)

Futureproof Music 330 Westbourne Park Rd, London W11 1EQ **t** 020 7792 8597 **f** 020 7221 3694 **e** info@futureproofmusic.com **w** futureproofmusic.com MD: Phil Legg.

FX Media Publishing (see Notting Hill Music (UK) Ltd)

G Whitty Music (see Bucks Music Group)

G&M Brand Publications PO Box 367, Aylesbury, Buckinghamshire HP22 4LJ **t** 01296 682220 **f** 01296 681989 **e** orders@rsmith.co.uk MD: Michael Brand.

G2 Music 33 Bournehall Ave, Bushey, Herts WD23 3AU **t** 020 8952 4355 **f** 020 8952 4548 **e** hitsongs@g2-music.com **w** g2-music.com CEO: Helen Gammons.

Gabsongs (see Arnisongs)

Gabsongs (see Arnisongs)

Gael Linn Music (see Crashed Music)

Garron Music Newtown Street, Kilsyth, Glasgow, Strathclyde G65 0LY **t** 01236 821081 **f** 01236 826900 **e** info@scotdisc.co.uk **w** scotdisc.co.uk MD: Bill Garden.

Publishers

Gazell Publishing International P O Box 370, Newquay, Cornwall TR8 5YZ **t** 01637 831011 **f** 01637 831037 **e** dimelbourne@aol.com Manager: Di Melbourne.

GDR Music Publishing Ltd 8 Lingfield Point, McMullen Road, Darlington, Co Durham DL1 1YU **t** 01325 365553 **f** 01325 365553 **e** Graeme.circ@ntlworld.com MD: Graeme Robinson.

Gerig, Cologne (see Breitkopf & Hartel)

Getaway Music (see Complete Music)

Ghost Music Ltd. (see Freedom Songs Ltd)

Fay Gibbs Music Services Warwick Lodge, 37 Telford Avenue, London SW2 4XL **t** 020 8671 9699 **f** 020 8674 8558 **e** faygibbs@fgmusicservice.demon.co.uk **w** fgmusicservice.co.uk MD: Fay Gibbs.

Gill Music 40 Highfield Park Road, Bredbury, Stockport, Cheshire SK6 2PG **t** 0161 494 2098 **e** a1.entertainment@btdigitaltv.com **w** a1entertainmentshowbiz.com Contact: Mrs Gill Cragen

Glad Music (see Music Sales Ltd)

Glendale Music (see Music Sales Ltd)

Glissando Music (see Edel Publishing)

Global Journey Ltd Unit 3 Boston Court, Salford Quays, Manchester M50 2GN **t** 0870 264 7484 **f** 0870 264 6444 **e** psamuels@global-journey.com **w** global-journey.com Head of A&R: Peter Samuels.

Global Talent Publishing 2nd Floor, 53 Frith St, London W1D 4SN **t** 020 7292 9600 **f** 020 7292 9611 **e** email@globaltalentgroup.com **w** globaltalentgroup.com GM: Miller Williams.

GMW (see Bucks Music Group)

Go Ahead Music Ltd Kerchesters, Waterhouse Lane, Kingswood, Tadworth, Surrey KT20 6HT **t** 01737 832 837 **f** 01737 833 812 **e** info@amphonic.co.uk MD: Ian Dale.

Golden Apple Productions (see Music Sales Ltd)

Golden Cornflake Music (see Menace Music Ltd)

Good Groove Songs Ltd Unit 217 Buspace Studios, Conlan Street, London W10 5AP **t** 020 7565 0050 **f** 020 7565 0049 **e** gary@goodgroove.co.uk Contact: Gary Davies

Goodmusic Publishing PO Box 100, Tewkesbury, Gloucestershire GL20 7YQ **t** 01684 773883 **f** 01684 773884 **e** sales@goodmusic-uk.com **w** goodmusic-uk.com

Graduate Music PO Box 388, Holt Heath, Worcester WR6 6WQ **t** 01905 620786 **f** 01905 620786 **e** davidrobertvirr@aol.com w graduaterecords.com MD: David Virr.

Grainger Society Edition (see Bardic Edition)

Grand Central Music Publishing Ltd Habib House, 3rd Floor, 9 Stevenson Square, Manchester M1 2DB **t** 0161 245 2002 **f** 0161 245 2003 **e** info@grandcentralrecords.com **w** grandcentralrecords.com CEO: Phil Hopwood.

Grapedime Music 28 Hurst Crescent, Barrowby, Grantham, Lincolnshire NG32 1TE **t** 01476 560241 **f** 01476 560241 **e** grapedime@pjbray.globalnet.co.uk A&R Manager: Phil Bray.

Grapevine Music Ltd 1 York St, London W1U 6PA **t** 01449 720988 **e** enquiries@eastcentralone.com **w** eastcentralone.com MD: Steve Fernie.

Grass Roots Music Publishing 29 Love Lane, Rayleigh, Essex SS6 7DL **t** 01268 747 077 MD: Gerald Mahlowe.

Greensleeves Publishing Ltd Unit 14, Metro Centre, St John's Rd, Isleworth, Middlesex TW7 6NJ **t** 020 8758 0564 **f** 020 8758 0811 **e** clare@greensleeves.net **w** greensleeves.net MD: Chris Sedgwick.

Gregsongs (see 4 Tunes Music)

GRG Music (see PXM Publishing)

Grin Music Hurston Mill, Pulborough, West Sussex RH20 2EW **t** 01903 741502 **f** 01903 741502 Copyright Mgr: Patrick Davis.

Gull Songs (see Darah Music)

Gut Music Byron House, 112A Shirland Road, London W9 2EQ **t** 020 7266 0777 **f** 020 7266 7734 **e** info@gut-intermedia.com **w** gutrecords.com Chairman: Guy Holmes. MD: Caroline Lewis. A&R: James O'Driscoll, Simon De Winter, Nick Burgess, Oliver Newman.

Gwynn Publishing (see Cwmni Cyhoeddi Gwynn Cyf)

Gypsy's Kiss Music Publishing 4 Vicarage Street, Faversham, Keny ME13 7BD **t** 01795 538 353 **f** 01795 538 353 **e** stuart.witcher@virgin.net Partner: Stuart Witcher. Partners: S. & J.D. Witcher.

H&B Webman & Co (see Chelsea Music Publishing Co)

Habana Music Publishing (see Gazell Publishing International)

Hal Carter Organisation 101 Hazelwood Lane, London N13 5HQ **t** 020 8886 2801 **f** 020 8882 7380 **e** info@halcarterorg.com w halcarterorg.com Managing Exec: Abbie Carter.

Halcyon Music 233 Regents Park Road, Finchley, London N3 3LF **t** 07000 783633 **f** 07000 783634 MD: Alan Williams.

Hallin Music Ltd 2 Trinity Rd, Marlow, Bucks SL7 3AW **t** 01628 483 629 **e** b.hallin@virgin.net MD: Brian Hallin.

Halo Publishing 88 Church Lane, London N2 0TB **t** 020 8444 0049 or 07711 062 309 **e** halomanagement@hotmail.com w halo-uk.net Dir: Mike Karl Maslen.

Hamburger Publishing PO Box 37291, London SW11 5TX **t** 07740 700 739 **f** 07974 011 403 **e** hamburger@schnitzel.co.uk MD: Oliver Geywitz.

Hammer Musik (see Bucks Music Group)

Hammerhead Music Suite 237, 78 Marylebone High St, London W1U 5AP **t** 07973 129068 **f** 07971 402973 **e** hammer@vizzavi.pt Director A&R: Bob Miller. CEO: Mike Hanon.

Harbrook Music (see Thames Music)

Hardmonic Music Unit 29, Cygnus Business Center, Dalmeyer Road, London NW10 2XA **t** 020 8830 0077 **f** 020 8830 0220 **e** info@hardmonic.com **w** hardmonic.com Mgr: Sandra Ceschia.

Haripa Music Publishing Ltd Unit 8, Acklam Workshops, 10 Acklam Rd, London W10 5QZ **t** 020 8964 3300 **f** 020 8964 4400 **e** info@kickinmusic.com **w** haripa.com Head Of Repetoire: Matt Ward.

Harmony Music (see Bucks Music Group)

Harrison Music (see Music Sales Ltd)

Harvard Music (see Bucks Music Group)

Hatton & Rose Publishers 46 Northcourt Avenue, Reading, Berkshire RG2 7HQ **t** 0118 987 4938 **f** 0118 987 4938 Contact: Graham Hatton

Havard Music (see Bucks Music Group)

Haynestorm (see Menace Music Ltd)

Hazell Dean Music (see Chelsea Music Publishing Co)

HBF Music (see Menace Music Ltd)

Heartbeat Music (see SGO Music Publishing Ltd)

Heartsongs (see Bucks Music Group)

Heaven Music PO Box 92, Gloucester GL4 8HW **t** 01452 814321 **f** 01452 812106 **e** vic_coppersmith@hotmail.com MD: Vic Coppersmith-Heaven.

Heavenly Music (see Paul Rodriguez Music Ltd)

Heavenly Songs 47 Frith Street, London W1D 4SE **t 020 7494 2998** f 020 7437 3317 e info@heavenlyrecordings.com w heavenly100.com MDs: Jeff Barrett, Martin Kelly.

Heavy Harmony Music (see Menace Music Ltd)

Heavy Metal Music (see Revolver Music Publishing)

Heavy Truth Music Publishing Ltd PO Box 8, Corby, Northamptonshire NN17 2XZ **t** 01536 202295 **f** 01536 266246 **e** skalidoski@heavytruth.com **w** heavytruth.com Label Mgr: Steve Kalidoski.

Hedgecock Music (see Menace Music Ltd)

Heinrichshofen (see Peters Edition)

Hello Cutie/Heru Xuti Publishing Cadillac Ranch, Pencraig Uchaf, Cwm Bach, Whitland, Carms. SA34 0DT **t** 01994 484466 **f** 01994 484294 **e** cadillacranch@telco4u.net Dir: Helios Steelgrave.

Hened Music (see Menace Music Ltd)

Henry Hadaway Organisation Satril House, 3 Blackburn Road, London NW6 1RZ **t** 020 7328 8283 **f** 020 7328 9037 **e** licensing@hho.co.uk **w** hho.co.uk MD: Henry Hadaway.

Heraldic Production Music (see Panama Music Library)

High-Fye Music (see Music Sales Ltd)

Hilltop Publishing Ltd. PO Box 429, Aylesbury, Bucks. HP18 9XY **t** 01844 238692 **f** 01844 238692 **e** info@hilltoppublishing.co.uk w brillsongs.com Director: Catherine Croydon.

Hit & Run (see EMI Music Publishing)

Hoax Music Publishing PO Box 23604, London E7 0YT **t** 0870 910 6666 **e** hoax@hoaxmusic.com **w** hoaxmusic.com MD: Ben Angwin.

Honeyhill Music (see Bucks Music Group)

Hooj Choons (see Mute Song)

Hornall Brothers Music Ltd 1 Northfields Prospect, Putney Bridge Road, London SW18 1PE **t** 020 8877 3366 **f** 020 8874 3131 **e** stuart@hobro.co.uk **w** hobro.co.uk MD: Stuart Hornall.

Hot Melt Music (see Universal Music Publishing Ltd)

Hournew Music (see Music Sales Ltd)

Howard Beach Music (see Bucks Music Group)

Howard Beach Music Inc. (see Bucks Music Group)

Howlin' Music Ltd 114 Lower Park Road, Loughton, Essex IG10 4NE **t** 020 8508 4564 or 07831 430080 **e** djone@howardmarks.freeserve.co.uk Prop/A&R: Howard Marks.

Hub Music (see Universal Music Publishing Ltd)

Hubris Music (see BDI Music)

Hucks Productions (see Bucks Music Group)

Hummingbird Productions (see Bucks Music Group)

Hummingbird Publishing 22 Lwr Leeson St, Dublin 2, Ireland **t** +353 1 662 7322 **f** +353 1 662 7323 **e** topfloor@indigo.ie **w** hummingbirdrecords.com MD: John Dunford.

Humph Music (see Paul Rodriguez Music Ltd)

Hunka Lisa Marie Music (see SGO Music Publishing Ltd)

Huntley Music (see Bucks Music Group)

Hyde Park Music 110 Westbourne Terrace Mews, London W2 6QG **t** 020 7402 8419 **f** 020 7723 6104 **e** tony@tonyhiller.com Chairman: Tony Hiller.

Hydrogen Duke Box Music Publishing (see Reverb Music Ltd)

I.L.C Music Ltd The Old Props Building, Pinewood Studios, Pinewood Rd, Iver Heath, Bucks SL0 0NH **t** 01753 785 631 **f** 01753 785 632 **e** Nigelwood@ilcgroup.co.uk Directors: Nigel Wood & Ellis Elias.

Ilona Sekacz Music (see Bucks Music Group)

Imma Play Jason Music (see Notting Hill Music (UK) Ltd)

Immortal Music Ltd (see Independent Music Group)

In The Frame Music 42 Winsford Gardens, Westcliff On Sea, Essex SS0 0DP **t** 01702 390353 **f** 01702 390355 **e** willbirch@aol.com Prop: Will Birch.

Inair Musikverlag (see BMP - Broken Music Publishing)

Inception Music Publishing Unit 1 Meadow St, Heol-y-Gors, Townhill, Swansea SA1 6RZ **t** 01792 581500 **f** 01792 581500 **e** inceptionmusic@btopenworld.com MD: Paul Scott.

Incredible Music (see Notting Hill Music (UK) Ltd)

Independent Music Group Ltd Independent House, 54 Larkshall Road, London E4 6PD **t** 020 8523 9000 **f** 020 8523 8888 **e** erich@independentmusicgroup.com **w** independentmusicgroup.com CEO: Ellis Rich. A&R Director: Andy Bailey. International Director: Catherine Kelly. Creative Director: Jacqui Brown.

Indian Hill Music (see Menace Music Ltd)

Indipop Music P.O. Box 369, Glastonbury, Somerset BA6 8YN **t** 01749 831 674 **f** 01749 831 674 MD: Steve Coe.

Industrial Music (see Bucks Music Group)

Infectious Music (see 4AD Music)

Infernal Music (see Notting Hill Music (UK) Ltd)

Inky Blackness Music Ltd PO Box 32089, Camden Town, London NW1 0NX **t** 07958 520580 **e** inky@inkyblackness.co.uk **w** inkyblackness.co.uk MD: Ian Tregoning.

Instant (see JHT Music)

International Music Network (see Independent Music Group)

International Music Network Ltd (see Independent Music Group Ltd)

International Music Publications (IMP) Griffin House, 161 Hammersmith Road, London W6 8BS **t** 020 8222 9200 **f** 020 8222 9260 **e** imp.info@warnerchappell.com w wbpdealers.com Sales Manager: Chris Statham.

International Songwriters' Music PO Box 46, Limerick City, Ireland **t** +353 61 228837 or 020 7486 5353 **f** +353 61 229464 or 020 7486 2094 **e** jliddane@songwriter.iol.ie w songwriter.co.uk MD: James D Liddane.

Intersate (see Paul Rodriguez Music Ltd)

Intuition Music Ltd 1 Devonport Mews, London W12 8NG **t** 020 7565 4750 **f** 020 7565 4751 **e** Berni@intuitionmusic.com Creative Director: Bernie Griffiths.

Iona Music (see Isa Music)

IQ Music Commercial House, 52 Perrymount Road, Haywards Heath, West Sussex RH16 3DT **t** 01444 452807 **f** 01444 451739 **e** kathie@iqmusic.co.uk Dir: Kathie Iqbal.

IRMA UK 8 Putney High Street, London SW15 1SL **t** 020 8780 0906 or 07930 381 330 **f** 020 8780 0545 **e** irmauk@btinternet.com w irmagroup.com Managing Director: Corrado Dierna.

IRS Music/IRS Songs (see Bugle Publishing)

Isa Music PO Box 7264, Glasgow, Strathclyde G46 6YE **t** 0141 637 6010 **f** 0141 637 6010 **e** isamusic@lismor.com MD: Ronnie Simpson.

Isobar Music 56 Gloucester Place, London W1U 8HW **t** 020 7486 3297 or 07956 493 692 **f** 020 7486 3297 **e** info@isobarrecords.com Co-MD: Peter Morris.

Ivy Music (see Music Sales Ltd)

Ixion (see Eaton Music Ltd)

J Curwen & Sons (see Music Sales Ltd)

J&H Publishing (see Dejamus Ltd)

J&M Music Publishing (see Paul Rodriguez Music Ltd)

Jack Good Music (see Carlin Music Corporation)

Jacobs Ladder Music Ltd 25 Bell Lane, Syresham, Northants NN13 5HP **t** 07813 894309 **e** allen.jacobs@virgin.net MD: Allen Jacobs.

Jacquinabox Music Ltd (see Independent Music Group)

Jamdown Music Ltd Stanley House Studios, 39 Stanley Gardens, London W3 7SY **t** 020 8735 0280 **f** 07970 574924 **e** othman@jamdown-music.com **w** jamdown-music.com MD: Othman Mukhlis.

Jap Songs (see Proof Songs)

Jarb Publishing (see Charly Publishing Ltd)

Javelin Music Ltd Satril House, 3 Blackburn Road, London NW6 1RZ **t** 020 7328 8283 **f** 020 7328 9037 **e** licensing@hho.co.uk **w** hho.co.uk MD: Henry Hadaway.

Jay Nick Enterprises (see Menace Music Ltd)

Jaykay Music (see Bucks Music Group)

Jazid Music (see Paul Rodriguez Music Ltd)

Jazz Art (see Bucks Music Group)

Jazz Art Music (see Bucks Music Group)

JB Max Music 142 New Cavendish St, London W1W 6YF **t** 020 7323 2420 **f** 020 7580 7776 **e** jbmax.co.uk Dirs: Adrian Bullock, Paul Moore.

Jelly Street Music Ltd Chester Terrace, 358 Chester Road, Manchester M16 9EZ **t** 0161 872 6006 **f** 0161 872 6468 **e** kevkinsella@aol.com **w** jellystrecords.co.uk MD: Kevin Kinsella Snr.

Jenjo Music Publishing 68 Wharton Avenue, Sheffield, South Yorkshire S26 3SA **t** 0114 287 9882 **f** 0114 287 9882 Contact: Mike Ward

Jetstar Publishers (see Carlin Music Corporation)

Jewel Music Co (see Warner Chappell Music Ltd)

Jewel Music Publishing Ltd (see Hornall Brothers Music)

JHT Music The Music Village, 11B Osiers Road, London SW18 1NL **t** 020 8870 0011 **f** 020 8870 2101 **e** nick@the-brothers.co.uk Dir: Nick Titchener.

Jiving Brothers (see G&M Brand Publications)

JKMC Publishing (see Dejamus Ltd)

Jobete Music (UK) Ltd (see EMI Music Publishing)

Joe Gibb (see Westbury Music Ltd)

Johi Music (see Dejamus Ltd)

John Rubie (see Paul Rodriguez Music Ltd)

John Stedman Music Publishing PO Box 1584, London N3 3NW **t** 020 8346 8663 **f** 020 8346 8848 **e** john@jsprecords.com **w** jsprecords.com Contact: John Stedman

Johnsongs (see Universal Music Publishing Ltd)

Jonalco Music (see Halcyon Music)

Jonjo Music (see Bocu Music Ltd)

Jonsongs Music 3 Farrers Place, Croydon, Surrey CR0 5HB **t** 020 8654 5829 **f** 020 8656 3313 **e** johnsongsuk@yahoo.co.uk GM: Patricia Bancroft.

Josef Weinberger 12-14 Mortimer St, London W1T 3JJ **t** 020 7580 2827 **f** 020 7436 9616 **e** general.info@jwmail.co.uk **w** josef-weinberger.co.uk Promotion: Lewis Mitchell.

Joustwise Ltd Myrtle Cottage, Rye Road, Hawkhurst, Kent TN18 5DW **t** 01580 754 771 **f** 01580 754 771 **e** scully4real@yahoo.co.uk **w** 4realrecords.com MD: Terry Scully.

JSE Music Publishing (see Independent Music Group)

JSE Music Publishing Ltd (see Independent Music Group Ltd)

Ju-Ju Bee Music (see Dejamus Ltd)

David Julius Publishing 11 Alexander House, Tiller Road, London E14 8PT **t** 020 7987 8596 **f** 020 7987 8596 **e** julius@amserve.com MD: David Maynard.

June Songs (see Chelsea Music Publishing Co)

Jupiter 2000 (see Crumbs Music)

Just Publishing PO Box 19780, London SW15 1WU **t** 020 8741 6020 **f** 020 8741 8362 **e** justmusic@justmusic.co.uk **w** justmusic.co.uk Director: John & Serena Benedict.

Justice Music (see Bucks Music Group)

K7 (see Bucks Music Group)

Kalmann Music (see Carlin Music Corporation)

Alfred A Kalmus Ltd. (Music Publishers) 48 Gt Marlborough St, London W1F 7BB **t** 020 7437 5203 **f** 020 7437 6115 **e** andrew.knowles@uemusic.co.uk Sales Promotion Manager: Andrew Knowles.

Kamara Music Publishing PO Box 56, Boston, Lincolnshire PE22 8JL **t** 07976 553624 **e** chrisdunn@kamaramusic.fsnet.co.uk **w** megahitrecordsuk.co.uk MD: Chris Dunn.

Karon Music (see Karonsongs)

Karonsongs 20 Radstone Court, Hillview Rd, Woking, Surrey GU22 7NB **t** 01483 755153 **e** ron.roker@btinternet.com MD: Ron Roker.

Kassner Associated Publishers Ltd Units 6 & 7, 11 Wyfold Rd, Fulham, London SW6 6SE **t** 020 7385 7700 **f** 020 7385 3402 **e** songs@kassner-music.co.uk **w** president-records.co.uk MD: David Kassner.

Katsback (see Menace Music Ltd)

Kaplan Kaye Music 95 Gloucester Rd, Hampton, Middlesex TW12 2UW **t** 020 8783 0039 **f** 020 8979 6487 **e** kaplan222@aol.com Contact: Kaplan Kaye

Kayenne Music (see The Valentine Music Group)

Keep Calm Music The Music Village, 11B Osiers Road, London SW18 1NL **t** 020 8870 0011 **f** 020 8870 2101 **e** info@keepcalm.co.uk **w** keepcalm.co.uk Dirs: Colin Peter, Carl Ward.

Kenny Lynch Music (see Carlin Music Corporation)

Kensington Music (see The Essex Music Group)

Kensongs (see Paul Rodriguez Music Ltd)

Kerroy Music Publishing 2 Queensmead, St John's Wood Park, London NW8 6RE **t** 020 7722 9828 **f** 020 7722 9886 **e** kerroy@btinternet.com CEO: Iain Kerr.

Keswick (see Loose Music (UK))

Kevin King Music Publishing 16 Limetrees, Llangattock, Crickhowell, Powys NP8 1LB **t** 01873 810142 **f** 01873 811557 **e** kevinkinggb@aol.com **w** silverword.co.uk MD: Kevin King.

Key Music (see Bucks Music Group)

Kickin Music (see Haripa Music Publishing Ltd)

Kickstart Music 12 Port House, Square Rigger Row, Plantation Wharf, London SW11 3TY **t** 020 7223 3300 **f** 020 7223 8777 **e** info@kickstart.uk.net Director: Frank Clark.

Kila Music Publishing Charlemont House, 33 Charlemont Street, Dublin 2 **t** +353 1 476 0627 **f** +353 1 476 0627 **e** info@kilarecords.com **w** kila.ie Director: Colm O'Snodaigh.

Killer Trax (see BMG Zomba Production Music)

King Jam Music (see Paul Rodriguez Music Ltd)

King Of Spades (see Paul Rodriguez Music Ltd)

Kingsway Music Lottbridge Drove, Eastbourne, East Sussex BN23 6NT **t** 01323 437700 **f** 01323 411970 **e** music@kingsway.co.uk **w** kingsway.co.uk Label Mgr: Stephen Doherty.

Kirklees Music 609 Bradford Road, Bailiff Bridge, Brighouse, W Yorkshire HD6 4DN **t** 01484 722855 **f** 01484 723591 **e** sales@kirkleesmusic.co.uk **w** kirkleesmusic.co.uk Partner: Graham Horsfield.

Kirschner-Warner Bros Music (see Warner Chappell Music Ltd)

Kite Music Ltd Binny Estate, Ecclesmachan, Edinburgh EH52 6NL **t** 01506 858885 **f** 01506 858155 or 01506 858931 **e** kitemusic@aol.com MD: Billy Russell.

Knox Music (see Carlin Music Corporation)

Koala Publishing (see Music Exchange (Manchester) Ltd)

Kobalt Music Group 33 Glasshouse Street, London W1B 5DG **t** 020 7434 5151 **f** 020 7434 5155 **e** info@kobaltmusic.com **w** kobaltmusic.com Creative Dir: Sas Metcalfe.

Kojam Music (see Kobalt Music Group)

Koka Media (see BMG Zomba Production Music)

KPM Music (see EMI Music Publishing)

KPM Music 127 Charing Cross Road, London WC2H 0EA **t** 020 7412 9111 **f** 020 7413 0061 **e** kpm@kpm.co.uk **w** kpm.co.uk Creative Mgr: Elaine Van Der Schoot.

Kudos Film and TV (see BDI Music)

Kunzelmann (see Peters Edition)

Lady's Gold Mercedes (see Bucks Music Group)

Lakes Music Wakefield Place, Sandgate, Kendal, Cumbria LA9 6HT **t** 01539 724433 **f** 01539 724499 **e** info@ensign.uk.com Director: Neil Clark.

Lakeview Music Pub Co (see The Essex Music Group)

Lantern Music 34 Batchelor St, London N1 0EG **t** 020 7278 4288 **f** 020 7837 2894 **e** rgoldmff@aol.com Contact: Rob Gold

Lark Music (see Carlin Music Corporation)

Latin Arts Group PO Box 14303, London SE26 4ZH **t** 07000 472 572 **f** 07000 472 572 **e** info@latinartsgroup.com **w** latinartsgroup.com Director: Hector Rosquete.

Latino Buggerveil Music (see Notting Hill Music (UK) Ltd)

Laurel Music (see EMI Music Publishing)

Laurie Johnson Music (see Bucks Music Group)

Laws Of Motion Publishing (see Westbury Music Ltd)

Leaf Songs Reverb House, Bennett Street, London W4 2AH **t** 020 8747 0660 **f** 020 8747 0880 **e** liam@leafsongs.com **w** leafsongs.com MD: Liam Teeling.

Dick Leahy Music Ltd 1 Star Street, London W2 1QD **t** 020 7258 0093 **f** 020 7402 9238 **e** info@playwrite.uk.com Office Manager: Nicky McDermott.

Legend Music Highridge, Bath Road, Farmborough, Nr. Bath BA2 0BG **t** 07161 470023 **e** davidrees55@aol.com MD: David Rees.

Leonard, Gould & Butler (see Music Exchange (Manchester) Ltd)

Leosong Copyright Service Ltd (see MCS Plc)

Les Etoiles de la Musique (see Menace Music Ltd)

Leslie Veale Music (see Scamp Music)

The Licensing Team Ltd 23 Capel Rd, Watford WD19 4FE **t** 01923 234 021 **f** 01923 249 251 **e** Lucy@TheLicensingTeam.com **w** thelicensingteam.com Director: Lucy Winch. Director: Celine Palavioux.

Lindsay Music 23 Hitchin St, Biggleswade, Beds SG18 8AX **t** 01767 316521 **f** 01767 317221 **e** office@lindsaymusic.co.uk **w** lindsaymusic.co.uk Partner: Carole Lindsay-Douglas.

Linvoy Music (see Carlin Music Corporation)

Lionrich Music (see Menace Music Ltd)

Little Diva (see Menace Music Ltd)

Little Dragon Music (see Bucks Music Group)

Little Rox Music (see Celtic Songs)

Little Venice (see Bucks Music Group)

Little Victory Music (see Menace Music Ltd)

Littlechap (see Jeff Wayne Music Group)

Livingsting Music (see Greensleeves Publishing Ltd)

Publishers

LOE Music LOE House, 159 Broadhurst Gardens, London NW6 3AU **t** 020 7328 6100 **f** 020 7624 6384 **e** watanabe@loe.uk.net MD: Hiroshi Kato.

Logo Songs (see Hornall Brothers Music Ltd)

Lomond Music 32 Bankton Park, Kingskettle, Fife KY15 7PY **t** 01337 830974 **f** 01337 830653 **e** bruce.fraser@zetnet.co.uk **w** lomondmusic.com Partners: Bruce/Pat Fraser.

London Publishing House 22 Denmark Street, London WC2H 8NG **t** 020 7240 5349 **f** 020 7379 5205 **e** music@mautoglade.fsbusiness.co.uk MD: Frank Coachworth.

Longstop Productions (see Bucks Music Group)

Loose Music (UK) Pinery Building, Highmoor, Wigton, Cumbria CA7 9LW **t** 016973 45422 **f** 016973 45422 **e** edwards@looserecords.com **w** looserecords.com A&R: Tim Edwards.

Lorna Music (see EMI Music Publishing)

Louise Music (see Menace Music Ltd)

Love Music (see Crashed Music)

Love-Ly-N-Divine (see Menace Music Ltd)

Ludix Music (see Carlin Music Corporation)

Ludwig Van Music Ltd PO Box 30884, London W12 9XA **t** 020 8746 7461 **f** 020 8749 7441 **e** info@spiritmm.com Director: David Jaymes.

Lupus Music 1 Star Street, London W2 1QD **t** 020 7706 7304 **f** 020 7706 8197 **e** morrison@powernet.co.uk MD: Cora Barnes.

Lynton Muir Music Ltd 1 Oakwood Parade, London N14 4HY **t** 020 8950 8732 **f** 020 8950 6648 **e** paul.lynton@btopenworld.com MD: Paul Lynton.

Lynwood Music 2 Church St, West Hagley, West Midlands DY9 0NA **t** 01562 886625 **f** 01562 886625 **e** downlyn@globalnet.co.uk **w** users.globalnet.co.uk/~downlyn/index.html Mgr: Rosemary Cooper.

M2 Music (see Bucks Music Group)

Machola Music (see Darah Music)

Madena (see Eaton Music Ltd)

Madrigal Music Guy Hall, Awre, Glocs GL14 1EL **t** 01594 510512 **f** 01594 510512 **e** artists@madrigalmusic.co.uk w madrigalmusic.co.uk MD: Nick Ford.

Maecenas Contemporary Composers Ltd (see Maecenas Music)

Maecenas Music 5 Bushey Close, Old Barn Lane, Kenley, Surrey CR8 5AU **t** 020 8660 4766 or 020 8660 3914 **f** 020 8668 5273 **e** maecenasmusicltd@aol.com **w** maecenasmusic.co.uk Trade Mgr: Bill Burnett.

Magic Frog Music (see Focus Music (Publishing) Ltd)

Magick Eye Publishing PO Box 3037, Wokingham, Berkshire RG40 4GR **t** 0118 932 8320 **f** 0118 932 8237 **e** info@magickeye.com **w** magickeye.com MD: Chris Hillman.

Magneil Publishing (see Bugle Publishing)

Magnet Music (see Warner Chappell Music Ltd)

Main Spring Music PO Box 38648, London W13 9WJ **t** 020 8567 1376 **e** blair@main-spring.com **w** main-spring.com MD: Blair McDonald.

Main Street (see Greensleeves Publishing Ltd)

Malahat (see Menace Music Ltd)

MAM Music (see Chrysalis Music Ltd)

Man in the Street Publishing The Old Chapel, Hardwick, Aylesbury, Bucks HP22 4DZ **t** 01296 640839 **e** maninthestreet@beeb.net **w** man_in_the_street.com Proprietor: Derik Timms. Accounts: Julia Beer.

Mann Music Ltd (see Paternoster Music)

Mansem Music (see Wilson Editions)

Market Square Music Market House, Market Square, Winslow, Bucks MK18 3AF **t** 01296 715228 **f** 01296 715486 **e** msmpub@pmpr.co.uk Adminstrator: Patrick Rob.

Marlyn Music (see Carlin Music Corporation)

Marmalade Music (see Warner Chappell Music Ltd)

Marquis Music (see Bocu Music Ltd)

George Martin Music Ltd Air Studios, Lyndhurst Rd, London NW3 5NG **t** 020 7794 0660 **f** 020 7916 2784 **e** info@georgemartinmusic.com **w** georgemartinmusic.com A&R: Adam Sharp.

Marzique Music (see Menace Music Ltd)

Match Production Music (see BMG Zomba Production Music)

Mattapan Music (see Bucks Music Group)

Matthews Music (see SGO Music Publishing Ltd)

Mautoglade Music (see Hornall Brothers Music Ltd)

Max-Hill Music (see Notting Hill Music (UK) Ltd)

Maximum Music (see Paul Rodriguez Music Ltd)

Maxwood Music Regent House, 1 Pratt Mews, London NW1 0AD **t** 020 7267 6899 **f** 020 7267 6746 **e** partners@newman-and.co.uk MD: Colin Newman.

Mayhew Music (see Kassner Associated Publishers Ltd)

Mcasso Music Publishing 32-34 Great Marlborough St, London W1F 7JB **t** 020 7734 3664 **f** 020 7439 2375 **e** music@mcasso.com w mcasso.com Professional Manager: Lisa McCaffery.

McGuinness Whelan 30-32 Sir John Rogersons Quay, Dublin 2, Ireland **t** +353 1 677 7330 **f** +353 1 677 7276 **e** jenn@numb.ie MD: Paul McGuinness.

MCI Music Publishing Ltd 4th Floor, Holden House, 57 Rathbone Place, London W1T 1JU **t** 020 7396 8899 **f** 020 7470 6659 **e** info@mcimusic.co.uk Creative Manager: James Bedbrook.

Mediant Music (see Kassner Associated Publishers Ltd)

Melankolic Songs 12 Pembridge Road, London W11 3HL **t** 020 7243 9879 **f** 020 7727 6319 **e** steve@melankolic.co.uk **w** melankolic.co.uk Consultant: Steve Lindsey.

Melody First Music (see Panama Music Library)

MCS MUSIC LTD **(A Division of Music Copyright, Solutions plc)**

MCS Music Ltd

32 Lexington Street, London W1F 0LQ **t** 020 7255 8777 **f** 020 7255 8778 **e** info@mcsmusic.com **w** mcsmusic.com Creative Director: Guy Fletcher. CEO: Brian Scholfield. Copyright Manager: Pete McGlinchey. Royalty Manager: Chris Oake. Registration Manager: Ellie Pitt. General Manager Andy Spacey. Financial Controller: Frank McAweaney.

Melody Lauren Music Unit B2 Livingstone Court, 55-63 Peel Road, Wealdstone, Harrow, Middlesex HA3 7QT **t** 020 8427 2777 **f** 020 8427 0660 **e** wworld@wienerworld.com **w** wienerworld.com MD: Anthony Broza.

Memnon Music Habib House, 3rd Floor, 9 Stevenson Square, Piccadilly, Manchester M1 1DB **t** 0161 238 8516 **f** 0161 236 6717 **e** memnon@btconnect.com **w** memnonentertainment.com Director: Rudi Kidd.

Memory Lane Music Ltd Independent House, 54 Larkshall Rd, London E4 6PD **t** 020 8523 9000 **f** 020 8523 8888 **e** erich@independentmusicgroup.com **w** independentmusicgroup.com CEO: Ellis Rich.

Menace Music Ltd 2 Park Road, Radlett, Hertfordshire WD7 8EQ **t** 01923 853789 **f** 01923 853318 **e** menacemusicmanagement@btopenworld.com MD: Dennis Collopy.

Menace USA (see Menace Music Ltd)

Menlo Music (see International Songwriters' Music)

Mercury Music (see EMI Music Publishing)

Meriden Music (Classical) The Studio Barn, Silverwood House, Woolaston, Nr Lydney, Gloucestershire GL15 6PJ **t** 01594 529026 **f** 01594 529027 **e** gdw.meriden@btclick.com Contact: The Secretary

Meringue Productions Ltd 37 Church St, Twickenham, Middlesex TW1 3NR **t** 020 8744 2277 **f** 020 8744 9333 **e** meringue@meringue.co.uk **w** meringue.co.uk Dir: Lynn Earnshaw.

Messer Music (see Bucks Music Group)

Metric Music (see Bugle Publishing)

Metro Music Library (see Amphonic Music Ltd.)

Metrophonic Tithebarns, Tithebarns Lane, Send, Surrey GU23 7LE **t** 01483 225 226 **f** 01483 479 606 **e** info@metrophonic.com **w** metrophonic.com MD: Brian Rawling. Copyright: Dean Migchelbrink.

Michael Batory Music (see Friendly Overtures)

Middle Eight Music (see Cramer Music)

Miggins Music (UK) 33 Mandarin Place, Grove, Oxon OX12 0QH **t** 01235 771577 **f** 01235 767171 **e** migginsmusic3@yahoo.com Creative Director: Des Leyton.

Mighty Iron Music (see Asterisk Music)

Mike Music Ltd Freshwater House, Outdowns, Effingham, Surrey KT24 5QR **t** 01483 281500 or 01483 281501 **f** 01483 281502 **e** yellowbal@aol.com MD: Mike Smith.

Mikosa Music 9-10 Regent Square, London WC1H 8HZ **t** 020 7837 9648 **f** 020 7837 9648 **e** mikosapanin@hotmail.com MD: Mike Osapanin.

Millennium Songs 6 Water Lane, Camden, London NW1 8NZ **t** 020 7482 0272 **f** 020 7267 4908 **e** mail@millenniumrecords.com MD: Ben Recknagel.

Milstein Music (see Dejamus Ltd)

Minerva Vision Music (see Paul Rodriguez Music Ltd)

Mio Fratello (see Dejamus Ltd)

Miracle Music (see Carlin Music Corporation)

Miriamusic 1 Glanleam Road, Stanmore, Middlesex HA7 4NW **t** 020 8954 2025 MD: Zack Laurence.

Mistletoe Melodies (see Bocu Music Ltd)

Misty River Music (see Bucks Music Group)

MINDER MUSIC LTD

18 Pindock Mews, London W9 2PY **t** 020 7289 7281 **f** 020 7289 2648 **e** songs@mindermusic.com **w** mindermusic.com. Dirs: John Fogarty, Beth Clough. Administration: Jenny Clough. Business Affairs: Roger Nickson. A&R: S Boy. Security: Jack Russell.

Mix Music PO Box 89, Slough, Berkshire SL1 6DQ **t** 01628 667124 **f** 01628 605246 **e** simon@dmcworld.com **w** dmcworld.com Business Affairs Mgr: Simon Gurney.

Mizmo International (see Notting Hill Music (UK) Ltd)

Model Music (see Kassner Associated Publishers Ltd)

Moggie Music Ltd 101 Hazelwood Lane, London N13 5HQ **t** 020 8886 2801 **f** 020 8882 7380 **e** artistes@halcarterorg.com **w** halcarterorg.com Owner: Hal Carter.

Moist Music PO Box 528, Enfield, Middx EN3 7ZP **t** 070 107 107 24 **f** 0870 137 3787 **e** moistmusic@moistrecords.com w moistrecords.com MD: Rodney Lewis.

Moncur Street Music Ltd PO Box 16114, London SW3 4WG **t** 020 7349 9909 **f** 020 7376 8532 **e** mail@moncurstreet.com **w** moncurstreet.com MD: Jonathan Simon.

Monument Music (see Diverse Music Ltd)

MoonRock Music PO Box 883, Liverpool L69 4RH **t** 0151 922 5657 **f** 0151 922 5657 **e** bstratt@mersinet.co.uk **w** mersinet.co.uk Publishing Manager: Billy Stratton.

Moonsung Music PO Box 369, Glastonbury, Somerset BA6 8YN **t** 01749 831 674 **f** 01749 831 674 Contact: Sheila Chandra

Morgan Music Co Ltd (see Maxwood Music)

Bryan Morrison Music 1 Star Street, London W2 1QD **t** 020 7706 7304 **f** 020 7706 8197 **e** morrison@powernet.co.uk MD: Bryan Morrison.

Morrison Budd Music 1 Star Street, London W2 1QD **t** 020 7706 7304 **f** 020 7706 8197 **e** morrison@powernet.co.uk MD: Carol Smith.

Morrison Evans Music (see Bryan Morrison Music)

Morrison Leahy Music 1 Star Street, London W2 1QD **t** 020 7258 0093 **f** 020 7402 9238 **e** nicky@playwrite.uk.com Contact: Nicky McDermott

Moss Music 7 Dennis Rd, Corfe Mullen, Wimborne, Dorset BH21 3NF **t** 01202 695965 **f** 01202 695965 **e** petermossmusic@onetel.net.uk MD: Peter Moss.

Mostyn Music 8 Milvil Court, Milvil Rd, Lee on the Solent, Hampshire PO13 9LY **t** 023 9255 0566 **f** 023 9255 0566 **e** Maureen@mostynmusic.com **w** mostynmusic.com Partner: Maureen Cresswell.

Mother Music 30-32 Sir John Rogersons Quay, Dublin 2, Ireland **t** 00 353 1 677 7330 **f** 00 353 1 677 7276 **e** jenn@numb.ie MD: Paul McGuinness.

Mother Tongue 35 Marsden St, London NW5 3HE **t** 07973 137 554 **e** Julian@takats.com MD: Julian de Takats.

Moving Shadow Music PO Box 2551, London SE1 2FH **t** 020 7252 2661 **f** 0870 051 2594 **e** info2004@movingshadow.com **w** movingshadow.com MD: Rob Playford.

MP Belaieff (see Peters Edition)

Mr & Mrs Music (see Dejamus Ltd)

Mr & Mrs Music Suite 11, Accurist House, 44 Baker Street, London WIU 7AZ **t** 020 7224 2280 **f** 020 7224 2290 **e** lesburgess45@aol.com MD: Les Burgess.

Mr Sunshine (see Menace Music Ltd)

MRM Ltd Cedar House, Vine Lane, Hillingdon, Middx UB10 0BX **t** 01895 251515 **f** 01895 251616 **e** mail@mrmltd.co.uk MD: Mark Rowles.

MSM (see Music Exchange (Manchester) Ltd)

Muirhead Music/IPA Anchor House, 2nd Floor, 15-19 Britten St, London SW3 3TY **t** 020 7351 5167 or 07785 226 542 **f** 0870 136 3878 **e** info@muirheadmanagement.co.uk **w** muirheadmanagement.co.uk CEO: Dennis Muirhead.

Mule UK Music PO Box 77, Leeds LS13 2WZ **t** 08709 905 078 **f** 0113 256 1315 **e** katherine@full360ltd.com MD: Katherine Canoville.

Multiplay Music Ltd 19 Eagle Way, Harrold, Bedford MK43 7EW **t** 01234 720785 or 07971 885375 **f** 01234 720664 **e** kevin@multiplaymusic.com **w** multiplaymusic.com MD: Kevin White.

Mumbo Jumbo Music 2A-6A Southam St, London W10 5PH **t** 020 8960 3253 **f** 020 8968 5111 **e** info@mumbojumbo.co.uk **w** mumbojumbo.co.uk MD: Ian Clifford.

Mummer Music 38 Grovelands Road, London N13 4RH **t** 020 8350 0613 **f** 020 8350 0613 **e** jim@jcook21.freeserve.co.uk Dir: Jim Cook.

Munka (see Paul Rodriguez Music Ltd)

Munnycroft (see Darah Music)

Murfin Music International 1 Post Office Lane, Kempsey, Worcester WR5 3NS **t** 01905 820659 **f** 01905 820015 **e** muff.murfin@virgin.net MD: Muff Murfin.

Music 1 Ltd. (see Independent Music Group Ltd)

Music Box Publications (see Paul Rodriguez Music Ltd)

Music By Design 49 Greek Street, Soho, London W1D 4EG **t** 020 7434 3244 **f** 020 7434 1064 **e** enquiries@musicbydesign.co.uk **w** musicbydesign.co.uk Producer: Angela Allen.

Music Exchange (Manchester) Ltd Claverton Road, Wythenshawe, Greater Manchester M23 9ZA **t** 0161 946 1234 **f** 0161 946 1195 **e** sales@music-exchange.co.uk w musicx.co.uk (Trade Only) Sales Director: Gerald Burns.

Music For Films (see Lantern Music)

Music Funtime (see G&M Brand Publications)

Music House (International) 2nd Floor, 143 Charing Cross Road, London WC2H 0EH **t** 020 7434 9678 **f** 020 7434 1470 **w** playmusichouse.com Gen Mgr: Simon James.

Music Like Dirt 9 Bloomsbury Place, East Hill, Wandsworth, London SW18 2JB **t** 020 8877 1335 **f** 020 8877 1335 **e** mld@bigworldpublishing.com **w** bigworldpublishing.com MD: Patrick Meads.

Music Music (see Paul Rodriguez Music Ltd)

Music Partner (see Peters Edition)

Music Sales Ltd 8-9 Frith Street, London W1V 5TZ **t** 020 7434 0066 **f** 020 7734 8416 **e** music@musicsales.co.uk **w** musicsales.com GM: Chris Butler.

Music To Picture (see The Valentine Music Group)

Musica Oscura (see Paul Rodriguez Music Ltd)

Musica Rara (see Breitkopf & Hartel)

Musicalities Limited Snows Ride Farm, Snows Ride, Windlesham, Surrey GU20 6LA **t** 01276 474181 **f** 01276 452227 **e** ivan@musicalities.co.uk **w** musicalities.co.uk MD: Ivan Chandler.

Musicare (see Paternoster Music)

Musicare Ltd 60 Huntstown Wood, Clonsilla, Dublin 15, Ireland **t** +353 1 820 6483 **f** +353 1 820 6294 **e** musicare@eircom.net Dir: Brian Barker.

Musicland (see Peters Edition)

Musik'Image Music Library (see Panama Music Library)

Musisca Publishing 34 Strand, Topsham, Exeter, Devon EX3 0AY **t** 01392 877737 **f** 01453 751911 **e** musisca@printed-music.com **w** printed-music.com/musisca Prop: Philippe Oboussier.

MusiWorks Services Ltd The Old Boiler House, Brewery Courtyard, High St, Marlow, Bucks SL7 2FF **t** 01628 488808 **f** 01628 890777 **e** mark@musiworks.com w musiworks.com Director: Mark Mumford.

Mute Song 429 Harrow Road, London W10 4RE **t** 020 8964 2001 **f** 020 8968 4977 **e** info@mutehq.co.uk **w** mute.com MD: Daniel Miller.

My Ears! My Ears! (see Mute Song)

Myers Music (see Kassner Associated Publishers Ltd)

Myra Music (see Bucks Music Group)

N2 Music Ltd (see Evolve Music Ltd)

N2K Publishing Ltd The Studios, 8 Hornton Place, Kensington, London W8 4LZ **t** 020 7937 0272 **f** 020 7368 6573 **e** marketing@n2kltd.com **w** n2k.ltd.uk Director: Marcus Shelton.

Native Songs Unit 32 Ransome's Dock, 35-37 Parkgate Rd, London SW11 4NP **t** 020 7801 1919 **f** 020 7738 1819 **e** info@nativemanagement.com **w** nativemanagement.com Contact: Anna Carpenter

Ncompass Publishing 113 Chewton Rd, Walthamstow, London E17 7DN **t** 07941 331181 **e** rich@ncompass.freeserve.co.uk MD: Richard Rogers.

Nectar Music PO Box 263, Cobham, Surrey KT11 2YZ **f** 01932 865637 **e** admin@nectarmusic.co.uk

Neon Music Studio One, 19 Marine Crescent, Kinning Park, Glasgow G51 1HD **t** 0141 423 9811 **f** 0141 423 9811 **e** mail@go2neon.com **w** go2neon.com Director: Stephanie Pordage.

Nervous Publishing 5 Sussex Crescent, Northolt, Middlesex UB5 4DL **t** 020 8423 7373 **f** 020 8423 7773 **e** nervous@compuserve.com **w** nervous.co.uk MD: Roy Williams.

Nettwerk Songs Publishing (U.K.) Ltd. Clearwater Yard, 35 Inverness Street, London NW1 7HB **t** 020 7424 7500 **f** 020 7424 7501 **e** mark@nettwerk.com **w** nettwerksongspublishing.com MD: Mark Jowett.

New Claims Music (see Graduate Music)

New Ikon Music (see The Essex Music Group)

New Music Enterprises Meredale, Reach Lane, Heath And Reach, Leighton Buzzard, Bedfordshire LU7 0AL **t** 01525 237700 **f** 01525 237700 **e** Pauldavis@newmusic28.freeserve.co.uk Prop: Paul Davis.

New Music West (see The Concord Partnership)

New State Publishing Ltd Unit 2A, Queens Studios, 121 Salusbury Rd, London NW6 6RG **t** 020 7372 4474 **f** 020 7328 4447 or 020 7372 4484 **e** info@newstate.co.uk **w** newstate.co.uk MD: Tom Parkinson.

New Town Sound Ltd (see Maxwood Music)

Newquay Music (see Bucks Music Group)

Next Century (see Bucks Music Group)

Nice 'n' Ripe Music (see Westbury Music Ltd)

Nicklewhistle Music (see Menace Music Ltd)

Niles Productions 34 Beaumont Rd, London W4 5AP **t** 020 8248 2157 **e** r.niles@richardniles.com **w** richardniles.com Dir: Richard Niles.

19 Music Unit 33, Ransomes Dock, 35-37 Parkgate Road, London SW11 4NP **t** 020 7801 1919 **f** 020 7801 1920 MD: Simon Fuller.

NKS Publishing (see Westbury Music Ltd)

No Future Music (see Complete Music)

No Known Cure Publishing 45 Kings Road, Dover Court, Harwich, Essex CO12 4DS **t** 07760 427306 **e** tomsong1@hotmail.com MD: TF McCarthy.

Noeland Productions (see Bucks Music Group)

NOMADIC MUSIC PUBLISHING

Unit 18a/b, Farm Lane Trading Estate, 101 Farm Lane, London SW6 1QJ **t** 020 7386 6800 **f** 020 7386 6801 **e** info@nomadicmusic.net **w** nomadicmusic.net Head of Publishing: Paul Flanagan.

Northern Light Music Ltd Noyna Lodge, Manor Road, Colne, Lancashire BB8 7AS **t** 01282 611547 or 0797 072 8210 **f** 01282 718901 **e** ajjh@freenetname.co.uk Director: Andrew Hall.

NorthStar Music Publishing Ltd PO Box 868, Cambridge CB1 6SJ **t** 01787 278256 **f** 01787 279069 **e** info@northstarmusic.co.uk **w** northstarmusic.co.uk MD: Grahame Maclean.

Not S'bad Music (see Crashed Music)

Notting Dale Songs (see Notting Hill Music (UK) Ltd)

NOTTING HILL MUSIC (UK) LTD

NOTTING HILL music

Bedford House, 8B Berkeley Gardens, London W8 4AP **t** 020 7243 2921 **f** 020 7243 2894 **e** info@nottinghillmusic.com **w** nottinghillmusic.com MD: David Loader. Chair: Andy McQueen. Int Dir: Peter Chalcraft. Professional Manager: Leo Whiteley. Royalty Manager: Liz Davey. Head of Administration: Charles Garside.

Novello & Co Ltd 8-9 Frith Street, London W1D 3JB **t** 020 7434 0066 **f** 020 7287 6329 **e** promotion@musicsales.co.uk MD: James Rushton.

Nowhere Publishing 30 Tweedholm Ave East, Walkerburn, Peeblesshire EH43 6AR **t** 01896 870284 **e** michaelwild@btopenworld.com MD: Michael Wild.

Numinous Music Figment House, Church Street, Ware, Hertfordshire SG12 9EN **t** 01920 484040 **f** 01920 463883 **e** allan.james1@virgin.net w numinous.co.uk Dir, A&R/Marketing/Promo: Allan James.

Nusong Unit 105 Canalot Studio, 222 Kensal Road, London W10 5BN **t** 020 8964 4778 **f** 020 8960 1344 **e** abbi@north-nusong.com **w** north-nusong.com MD: John MacLennan.

Nuthouse Music (see Notting Hill Music (UK) Ltd)

Obelisk Music 32 Ellerdale Road, London NW3 6BB **t** 020 7435 5255 **f** 020 7431 0621 MD: Mr H Herschmann.

Oblivion Music (see Accolade Music)

Ocean Music (see Express Music (UK) Ltd)

Off The Peg Songs (see In The Frame Music)

Old Bridge Music PO Box 7, Ilkley, West Yorks LS29 9RY **t** 01943 602203 **f** 01943 435472 **e** mail@oldbridgemusic.com **w** oldbridgemusic.com Partner: Chris Newman.

Old School Songs (see SGO Music Publishing Ltd)

Old Strains (see Paul Rodriguez Music Ltd)

Olrac Songs (see Asterisk Music)

One Note Music (see Asterisk Music)

Onion Music 57b Riding House St, London W1W 7EF **t** 020 7436 5434 **f** 020 7436 5431 **e** barry@7hz.co.uk **w** 7hz.co.uk/onionmusic.htm MD: Barry Campbell.

Online Music Unit 18, Croydon House, 1 Peall Road, Croydon, Surrey CR0 3EX **t** 020 8287 8585 **f** 020 8287 0220 **e** publishing@onlinestudios.co.uk **w** onlinestudios.co.uk MD: Rob Pearson.

Onward Music (see Bucks Music Group)

Opal Music Studio 1, 223A Portobello Rd, London W11 1LU **t** 020 7221 7239 **f** 020 7792 1886 **e** opal-chant@dial.pipex.com Dir: Anthea Norman-Taylor.

Openchoice (see Roedean Music Ltd)

Optimum Publishing Unit 3, 1 St Mary Road, London E17 9RG **t** 020 8520 1188 **f** 020 8520 2514 **e** info@optimumpublishing.co.uk MD: Debra Thompson.

Orange Songs Ltd 1st Floor, 28 Denmark Street, London WC2H 8NJ **t** 020 7240 7696 **f** 020 7379 3398 **e** cliff.cooper@omec.com MD: Cliff Cooper.

Orestes Music Publishing 112 Gunnersbury Avenue, London W5 4HB **t 020 8993 7441** e orestes@dorm.co.uk w orestesmusic.com GM: John O'Reilly.

Orgy Music Publishing PO Box 8245, Sawbridgeworth, Herts CM21 9WU **t** 01279 600081 **e** info@orgyrecords.com **w** orgyrecords.com Contact: Martin Hayter

Ossian (see Music Exchange (Manchester) Ltd)

Our Music (see Associated Music International Ltd)

Oval Music Ltd 326 Brixton Road, London SW9 7AA **t** 020 7622 0111 **e** charlie@ovalmusic.co.uk Dir: Charlie Gillett.

Oxford Film Co. (see Paul Rodriguez Music Ltd)

Oxford University Press Music Department, Great Clarendon St, Oxford, Oxfordshire OX2 6DP **t** 01865 353349 **f** 01865 353749 **e** music.enquiry.uk@oup.com w oup.com/uk/music Music Sales & Mktng: Suzy Gooch.

Oyster Songs Ltd Oakwood Manor, Oakwood Hill, Ockley, Surrey RH5 5PU **t** 01306 627277 **f** 01306 627277 **e** info@oystermusic.com Dirs: Adrian Fitt, Chris Cooke. MD: Adrian Fitt. Finance Director: Warren Hillier.

P3 Music 4 St Andrew St, Alyth, Perthshire PH11 8AT **t** 01828 633790 **f** 01828 633798 **e** publishing@p3music.com **w** p3music.com MD: James Taylor.

Page One Music (see Kassner Associated Publishers Ltd)

Palace Music (see Warner Chappell Music Ltd)

Palan Music Publishing Ltd Greenland Place, 115-123 Bayham Street, London NW1 0AG **t** 020 7446 7439 **f** 020 7446 7421 **e** chrisg@palan.com **w** palan.com A&R/Aquisitions Mgr: Chris Gray.

Pan Musik (see Kassner Associated Publishers Ltd)

Panache Music Ltd (see Maxwood Music)

PANAMA MUSIC LIBRARY

PANAMA MUSIC LIBRARY

Sovereign House, 12 Trewartha Road, Praa Sands, Penzance, Cornwall TR20 9ST **t** 01736 762826 or 07721 449477 **f** 01736 763328 **e** panamus@aol.com **w** panamamusic.co.uk MD: Roderick Jones. Copyright & Royalties: Carole Jones. Prod Dir: Colin Eade. Business Affairs: Anne Eade. **Suppliers of recorded mood music libraries to television, radio, audio-visual, advertising and film industries worldwide. Commissions and original music.**

Panganai Music 296 Earls Court Rd, London SW5 9BA **t** 020 7565 0806 **f** 020 7565 0806 **e** blackmagicrecords@talk21.com **w** blackmagicrecords.com MD: Mataya Clifford.

Paper Publishing (see Westbury Music Ltd)

Par Entertainment (see Charly Publishing Ltd)

Paradise Line Music (see Blue Melon Publishing)

Parliament Music Ltd PO Box 6328, London N2 0UN **t** 020 8444 9841 **f** 020 8442 1973 **e** info@parliament-management.com Director: David Woolfson.

Partisan Songs c/o Mute Song, 429 Harrow Road, London W10 4RE **t** 020 8964 2001 **f** 020 8968 8437 **e** mamapimp@btopenworld.com MD: Caroline Butler.

Pasadena Music (see Paul Rodriguez Music Ltd)

Patch Music (see SGO Music Publishing Ltd)

Paternoster Music 16 Thorpewood Avenue, London SE26 4BX **t** 020 8699 1245 **f** 020 8291 5584 **e** peterfilleul@compuserve.com MD: Peter Filleul/Sian Wynne.

Patricia Music (see Warner Chappell Music Ltd)

Paul Ballance Music PO Box 72, Beckenham, Kent BR3 5UR **t** 020 8650 2976 **f** 0870 922 3582 **e** info@megabop.plus.com **w** megabop.com MD: Paul Ballance.

Paul Rodriguez Music Ltd 15 Stanhope Rd, London N6 5NE **t** 020 8340 7797 **f** 020 8340 6923 **e** paul@paulrodriguezmus.demon.co.uk MD: Paul Rodriguez. Senior Executive: David Nash. Copyright Manager: Amy Coats.

PCM (Paul Cook Music) (see Cybertech88)

Pearl Music (see Asterisk Music)

PEERMUSIC (UK)

Peer House, 8-14 Verulam Street, London WC1X 8LZ **t** 020 7404 7200 **f** 020 7404 7004 **e** peermusic@peermusic.com **w** peermusic.com MD: Nigel Elderton. Financial Director: Duncan Toone. Business Affairs Manager: Allan Dann. Creative Manager: Richard Holley. Synch/Copyright Mgr: Samantha Stevens.

Penkiln Burn (see Bryter Music)

Penny St Music (see Bucks Music Group)

Perfect Songs The Blue Building, 8-10 Basing St, London W11 1DG **t** 020 7221 5101 **f** 020 7221 3374 **e** firstname@spz.com A&R: Paul Barton. MD: Emma Kamen. A&R: Adrian Jolly. Business Affairs: Stanley Banks.

Perfect Space Music Publishing Ichthus House, 1 Northfield Rd, Aylesbury, Bucks HP20 1PB **t** 01296 583700 **e** info@reallyfreemusic.co.uk **w** reallyfreemusic.co.uk Contact: Peter Wheeler

Performance Music (see Kassner Associated Publishers Ltd)

Perpetuity Music 21A Maury Rd, London N16 7BP **t** 020 7394 4493 **e** mowhock@aol.com **w** fucdk.com MD: Michael Gordon.

Pete Allen Music (see Paul Rodriguez Music Ltd)

Peter Maurice (see EMI Music Publishing)

Peterman & Co (see Carlin Music Corporation)

Peters Edition Hinrichsen House, 10-12 Baches Street, London N1 6DN **t** 020 7553 4000 or 020 7553 4020 (Hire) **f** 020 7490 4921 **e** sales@editionpeters.com **w** editionpeters.com Marketing Manager: Linda Hawken.

PHAB Music High Notes, Sheerwater Avenue, Woodham, Surrey KT15 3DS **t** 019323 48174 **f** 019323 40921 MD: Philip HA Bailey.

Phillday (see Menace Music Ltd)

Phoenix Music Bryn Golau, Saron, Denbighshire LL16 4TH **t** 01745 550317 **f** 01745 550560 **e** post@phoenix-music.com **w** phoenix-music.com Proprietor: Kath Banks.

Phonetic Music (see Rondor Music (London) Ltd)

PI34 Music (see Notting Hill Music (UK) Ltd)

Pinera Music (see Menace Music Ltd)

Pink Floyd Music Publishers Ltd (see Plangent Visions Music Ltd)

Pisces Publishing Limited 20 Middle Row, Ladbroke Grove, London W10 5AT **t** 020 8964 4555 **f** 020 8964 4666 **e** morgan@musicwithattitude.com **w** musicwithattitude.com MD: Morgan Khan.

Plan C Music Ltd Covetous Corner, Hudnall Common, Little Gaddesden, Herts HP4 1QW **t** 01442 842851 **f** 01442 842082 **e** christian@plancmusic.com **w** plancmusic.com MD: Christian Ulf-Hansen.

Plangent Visions Music Ltd 27 Noel Street, London W1F 8GZ **t** 020 7734 6892 **f** 020 7439 4613 **e** info@noelstreet.com MD: Peter Barnes.

Plantation Music Pub (see Independent Music Group Ltd)

Platinum Status (see Notting Hill Music (UK) Ltd)

Platypus Music Unit 3 Home Farm, Welford, Newbury, Berks RG20 8HR **t** 01488 657200 **f** 01488 657222 MD: John Brand.

Playwrite Music Limited The Penthouse, 1 Star Street W2 1QD **t** 020 7258 0093 **f** 020 7402 9238 **e** info@playwrite.uk.com Manager: Nicky McDermott.

Plaza Music (see Express Music (UK) Ltd)

Plus 8 Music Benelux (see Independent Music Group Ltd)

Plus 8 Music Europe (see Independent Music Group Ltd)

Plus Music Publishing 36 Follingham Court, Drysdale Place, London N1 6LZ **t** 020 7684 8594 **f** 020 7684 8740 Proprietor: Desmond Chisholm.

Pluto Music Hulgrave Hall, Tiverton, Tarporley, Cheshire CW6 9UQ **t** 01829 732427 **f** 01829 733802 **e** info@plutomusic.com **w** plutomusic.com MD: Keith Hopwood.

Pod Publishing 11 Lindal Rd, Crofton Park, London SE4 1EJ **t** 020 8691 1564 **f** 020 8691 1564 **e** music@podpublishing.biz Dir: Natalie Cummings.

Point4 Music Unit 16 Talina Centre, Bagleys Lane, Fulham, London SW6 2BW **e** info@point4music.com **w** point4music.com Dirs: Peter Day, Paul Newton.

Pollination Music 30 Kilburn Lane, Kensal Green, London W10 4AH **t** 020 8969 2909 **f** 020 8969 3825 **e** info@pollinationmusic.co.uk **w** pollinationmusic.co.uk A&R Dir: Seamus Morley.

Pollytone Music PO Box 124, Ruislip, Middx HA4 9BB **t** 01895 638584 **f** 01895 624793 **e** val@pollyton.demon.co.uk **w** pollytone.com MD: Val Bird.

Pop Anarchy Music 98 Camden Road, London NW1 9EA **t** 020 7284 0359 **f** 020 7267 5186 **e** office@vinyljapan.com **w** vinyljapan.com Contact: Claire Munro

Pop Muzik Haslemere, 40 Broomfield Road, Henfield, W. Sussex BN5 9UA **t** 01273 491416 **f** 01273 491417 **e** robin@robinscott.org **w** robinscott.org Director: Robin Scott.

Porpete Music (see Menace Music Ltd)

Portland Productions (see Cramer Music)

Possie Music (see Independent Music Group Ltd)

Powdermill Music Aka Ray Pillow Music (see Independent Music Group Ltd)

Power Music 29 Riversdale Road, Thames Ditton, Surrey KT7 0QN **t** 020 8398 5236 **f** 020 8398 7901 MD: Barry Evans.

Power Music Company (see Music Sales Ltd)

Preshus Child Music (see Independent Music Group Ltd)

Prestige Music (see Bocu Music Ltd)

Prime Music Publishing Ltd 340 Athlon Road, Alperton, Middx HA0 1BX **t** 020 8601 2200 **f** 020 8601 2262 **e** music@primedistribution.co.uk **w** primedistribution.co.uk MD: John Warwick.

Primitive Music Publishing 16 Stanley Hill Ave, Amersham, Bucks HP7 9BD **t** 01494 581272 **f** 01494 580852 **e** contact@primitive-music.co.uk **w** primitive-music.co.uk Dir: Simon Hill.

Primo Music 39 Bettespol Meadows, Redbourn, Herts AL3 7EN **t** 01582 626 015 or 07740 645 628 **e** tony@primomusic.co.uk MD: Tony Peters.

Producer's Workshop Music (see Carlin Music Corporation)

Promo Sonar International (SARL) Sovereign House, 12 Trewartha Road, Praa Sands, Penzance, Cornwall TR20 9ST **t** 01736 762826 **f** 01736 763328 **e** panamus@aol.com **w** panamamusic.com Dir: Roderick Jones.

Proof Songs PO Box 20242, London NW1 7FL **t** 020 7485 1113 **e** info@proofsongs.co.uk

Proper Music Publishing Ltd Unit 1, Gateway Business Centre, Kangley Bridge Road, London SE26 5AN **t** 020 8676 5152 **f** 020 8676 5190 **e** malc@proper.uk.com MD: Malcolm Mills.

PS Songs (see Bucks Music Group)

PSI Music Library (see Panama Music Library)

Psychedelic Research Lab Songs (see Independent Music Group Ltd)

Published By Patrick

PUBLISHED BY PATRICK

18 Pindock Mews, London W9 2PY **t** 020 7289 7281 **f** 020 7289 2648 **e** songs@mindermusic.com **w** mindermusic.com MD: John Fogarty. Administration: Jenny Clough. Business Affairs: Roger Nickson. A&R: Patrick Fogarty. Security: Jack Russell.

Puppet Music (see Paul Rodriguez Music Ltd)

Pure Groove Music 679 Holloway Road, London N19 5SE **t** 020 7263 4660 **f** 020 7263 5590 **e** mickshiner@puregroove.co.uk **w** puregroove.co.uk Head of A&R: Mick Shiner.

Pure Silk Music The Old Props Building, Pinewood Studios, Pinewood Rd, Iver Heath, Bucks SL0 0NH **t** 01753 785 631 **f** 01753 785 632 **e** Elliselias@ilcgroup.com MD: Ellis Elias.

Purple City Ltd PO Box 31, Bushey, Herts WD23 2PT **t** 01923 244673 **f** 01923 244693 **e** info@purplecitymusic.com **w** purplecitymusic.com MD: Barry Blue.

Purple Patch Music (see Editions Penguin Cafe)

Pushcart Music (see Independent Music Group Ltd)

PXM Publishing 45 Mount Ash Rd, Upper Sydenham, London SE26 6LY **t** 020 8699 5835 or 020 8291 1193 **f** 020 8699 5835 **e** pxm.publishing@virgin.net **w** pxmpublishing.com Director/Admin: Carolyne Rodgers.

Quaife Music Publishing 9 Carroll Hill, Loughton, Essex IG10 1NL **t** 020 8508 3639 **f** 0870 4016885 **e** Qmusic@carrollhill.freeserve.co.uk MD: Alan Quaife.

Quick Step Music (see Lomond Music)

R&E Music (see Independent Music Group Ltd)

R&E Music Ltd (see Independent Music Group)

Radical UK Music (see Sovereign Music UK)

Raeworks (see Independent Music Group Ltd)

RAK Publishing Ltd 42-48 Charlbert St, London NW8 7BU **t** 020 7586 2012 **f** 020 7722 5823 **e** rakpublishing@yahoo.com General Manager: Nathalie Hayes.

Rakeway Music (see Kirklees Music)

Ralphie Dee Music (see Independent Music Group Ltd)

RandM Music 72 Marylebone Lane, London W1U 2PL **t** 020 7486 7458 **f** 020 8467 6997 **e** roy@randm.co.uk MDs: Roy Eldridge, Mike Andrews.

Randscape Music (see Menace Music Ltd)

Rapido Music (see Bucks Music Group)

RBT Publications PO Box 640, Bromley BR1 4XZ **t** 07985 439 453 **f** 020 8290 4589 **e** rbtprodctions1@aol.com **w** rbtprodctions.co.uk Mgr: Mr MacPepple.

Reach Music International (see Bucks Music Group)

React Music Publishing 138b West Hill, London SW15 2UE **t** 020 8780 0305 **f** 020 8788 2889 **e** mailbox@react-music.co.uk **w** resist-music.co.uk MD: James Horrocks.

Real Magic Publishing (see Bucks Music Group)

Real World Music Ltd Box Mill, Mill Lane, Box, Corsham, Wiltshire SN13 8PL **t** 01225 743188 **f** 01225 744369 **e** publishing@realworld.co.uk **w** http://realworld.co.uk/publishing Publishing Manager: Rob Bozas.

Really Free Music (see Sea Dream Music)

The Really Useful Group 22 Tower St, London WC2H 9TW **t** 020 7240 0880 **f** 020 7240 8977 **e** robinsond@reallyuseful.co.uk **w** reallyuseful.com Music Publishing Manager: David Robinson.

Really Wicked Publishing 8 Martin Dene, Bexleyheath, Kent DA6 8NA **t** 020 8301 2828 **f** 020 8301 2424 **e** mholmes822@aol.com **w** htdrecords.com A&R Director: Barry Riddington.

Rebecca Music Ltd Terwick Place, Rogate, Petersfield, Hampshire GU31 5BY **t** 01730 821644 **f** 01730 821597 **e** donna@lesreed.com **w** lesreed.com Dir: Donna Reed.

Recent Future Music (see Universal Music Publishing Ltd)

Red Cherry Music (see SGO Music Publishing Ltd)

Red House Music (see Bucks Music Group)

Red Shadow Wisteria House, 56 Cole Park Rd, St Margarets, Twickenham, Middx TW1 1HS **t** 020 8891 3333 **f** 020 8891 3222 **e** julian@redshadow.co.uk Director: Julian Spear. Promotion Manager: Justin Coombes.

Red Songs (see Bucks Music Group)

Redemption Publishing 516 Queslett Road, Great Barr, Birmingham B43 7EJ **t** 0121 605 4791 **f** 0121 605 4791 **e** bhaskar@redemption.co.uk **w** redemption.co.uk MD: Bhaskar Dandona.

Redwood Music (see Carlin Music Corporation)

Reggae Giant Music (see Castle Hill Music)

Regina Music (see Music Exchange (Manchester) Ltd)

Reinforced Music (see Westbury Music Ltd)

Reliable Source Music 6 Kenrick Place, London WIU 6HD **t** 020 7486 9878 **f** 020 7486 9934 **e** library@reliable-source.co.uk **w** reliable-source.co.uk MD: Dr Wayne Bickerton. Account Exec: Alistair Wybrew.

Religion Music 36 Fitzwilliam Square, Dublin 2, Ireland **t** +353 1 207 0508 **f** +353 1 207 0418 **e** info@religionmusic.com **w** religionmusic.com MD: Glenn Herlihy.

Remission Music (see Sovereign Music UK)

Repetoire (see Bucks Music Group)

Restoration Music Ltd (see Sovereign Music UK)

Reverb 2 Music Ltd (see Reverb Music Ltd)

Reverb 3 Music Ltd (see Reverb Music Ltd)

Reverb Music Ltd Reverb House, Bennett Street, London W4 2AH **t** 020 8747 0660 **f** 020 8747 0880 **e** publishing@reverbxl.com **w** reverbxl.com Head of A&R: Paul Harris.

Revolver Music Publishing 152 Goldthorn Hill, Penn, Wolverhampton, West Midlands WV2 3JA **t** 01902 345345 **f** 01902 345155 **e** Paul.Birch@revolver-e.com **w** revolvermusic.com MD: Paul Birch.

Revue Music (see Creole Music Ltd)

Reyshell Music (see Menace Music Ltd)

Rhiannon Music (see SGO Music Publishing Ltd)

Richmond Music (see Paul Rodriguez Music Ltd)

Rickim Music Publishing Company Thatched Rest, Queen Hoo Lane, Tewin, Herts AL6 0LT **t** 01438 798395 **f** 01438 798395 **e** joyce@bigmgroup.freeserve.co.uk **w** martywilde.com MD: Joyce Wilde.

Riderwood Music (see Carlin Music Corporation)

Right Key Music (see Independent Music Group Ltd)

Right Music 177 High Street, Harlesden, London NW10 4TE **t** 020 8961 3889 **f** 020 8961 4620 **e** info@rightrecordings.com **w** rightrecordings.com Directors: David Landau, John Kaufman.

Rights Worldwide Ltd (see Faber Music)

Rinsin Music (see Bucks Music Group)

Rita (Publishing) Ltd 12 Pound Court, The Marld, Ashtead, Surrey KT21 1RN **t** 01372 276293 **f** 01372 276328 **e** thebestmusicis@ritapublishing.com **w** ritapublishing.com MD: Ralph Norton.

Riverboat (UK) Music 6 Abbeville Mews, 88 Clapham Park Road, London SW4 7BX **t** 020 7498 5252 **f** 020 7498 5353 **e** phil@worldmusic.net **w** worldmusic.net MD: Phil Stanton.

Riverhorse Songs (see MCS Music Ltd)

Rivers Music (see Independent Music Group Ltd)

RL2 Music Bewley House, Ightham, Kent TN15 9AP **t** 01732 884606 **e** info@rl-2.com **w** rl-2.com Gen Mgr: Paul Lilly.

Roba Music (see Independent Music Group Ltd)

Robbins Music Corp (see EMI Music Publishing)

Robert Forberg (see Peters Edition)

Robert Lienau (see Peters Edition)

Roberton Publications (see Goodmusic Publishing)

Robroy West Music (see Independent Music Group Ltd)

Rock Music Company Ltd (see Plangent Visions Music Ltd)

Rocksong Music (see Revolver Music Publishing)

Roedean Music Ltd 16-17 Grafton House, 2-3 Golden Sq, London W1F 9HR **t** 020 7437 1958 **f** 020 7437 3852 **e** tonyhall@btconnect.com MD: Tony Hall.

Rokstone Music Ltd (see Darah Music)

Roky Erickson (see Menace Music Ltd)

Roland Robinson Music (see Menace Music Ltd)

Rolf Baierle Music Limited (see Independent Music Group Ltd)

Rollercoaster Music (see Asterisk Music)

Rondercrest (see Loose Music (UK))

Rondor Music (London) Ltd The Yacht Club, Chelsea Harbour, London SW10 0XA **t** 020 7349 4750 **f** 020 7376 3670 **e** firstname.surname@umusic.com MD: Richard Thomas. Head Of Creative: Marc Sher. Head Of A&R: James Dewar. PA/Office Manager: Sydelle Davey. Admin/A&R Assistant: Dan Hawkins.

Ronster Music (see Independent Music Group Ltd)

Rose Rouge International Ltd Aws House, Trinity Square, St Peter Port, Guernsey, Channel Islands GY1 1LX **t** 01481 728283 **f** 01481 714118 **e** awsgroup@cwgsy.net Director: Steve Free.

Rosehill Music Publishing Co Ltd PO Box 48, Aylesbury, Buckinghamshire HP17 8DW **t** 01844 290798 **f** 01844 290757 **e** sales@rosehillmusic.com **w** rosehillmusic.com MD: Peter Wilson.

Rosette Music (see The Valentine Music Group)

The Rosewood Music Company PO Box 6754, Dublin 13, Ireland **t** +353 1 843 9713 **f** +353 1 843 9713 **e** rosewood@iol.ie **w** rosewoodmusic.ie Professional Mgr: Greg Rogers.

Rough Trade Publishing 81 Wallingford Rd, Goring, Reading, Berks RG8 0HL **t 01491 873612** f 01491 872744 e info@rough-trade.com w rough-trade.com MD: Matt Wilkinson.

The Royal School Of Church Music (RSCM) Cleveland Lodge, Westhumble, Dorking, Surrey RH5 6BW **t** 01306 872811 **f** 01306 887240 **e** musicdirect@rscm.com **w** rscm.com Mgr, Press/Music Direct: Tim Ruffer.

RT Music (see Asterisk Music)

Rubber Road Music 4-10 Lamb Walk, London SE1 3TT **t** 020 7579 4404 **f** 020 7579 4171 **e** info@rubberroadmusic.com **w** rubberroadmusic.com Creative Manager: Nick Lightowlers.

Ruben Blades (see Dejamus Ltd)

Rumour Music Publishing Tempo House, 15 Falcon Rd, London SW11 2PJ **t** 020 7228 6821 **f** 020 7228 6972 **e** post@rumour.demon.co.uk **w** rumour.demon.co.uk MD: Anne Plaxton.

Rustomatic Music (see Menace Music Ltd)

Rybar Music (see Paul Rodriguez Music Ltd)

Rydim Music (see Blue Mountain Music Ltd)

Rykomusic Ltd 329 Latimer Road, London W10 6RA **t** 020 8960 3311 **f** 020 8960 1177 **e** info@rykodisc.co.uk **w** rykomusic.com GM: Paul Lambden.

S'Od Music (see Bucks Music Group)

SA Rodger & SD Jones Publishing (see Westbury Music Ltd)

Sabre Music (see Eaton Music Ltd)

Safe (see Bucks Music Group)

St James Music 34 Great James Street, London WC1N 3HB **t** 020 7405 3786 **f** 020 7405 5245 **e** info@prestige-elite.com MD: Keith Thomas.

Salsoul Music Publish (see Independent Music Group Ltd)

Salvo West Ltd t/a Union Square (see Bucks Music Group)

Sanctuary Music Publishing Ltd Sanctuary House, 45-53 Sinclair Road, London W14 0NS **t** 020 7300 1866 **f** 020 7300 1881 **e** firstname.lastname@sanctuarygroup.com **w** sanctuarygroup.com Director of A&R: Jamie Arlon. Director of Commercial Business: Maria Forte.

Sands Music (see Independent Music Group Ltd)

Sanga Music (see Bucks Music Group)

Santi Music Ltd 91 Manor Road South, Hinchley Wood, Esher, Surrey KT10 0QB **t** 020 8398 4144 or 07957 367 214 **f** 020 8398 4244 **e** steve@santimusic.com MD: Steve Weltman.

Sarah Music Cherry Tree Lodge, Copmanthorpe, York, North Yorks YO23 3SH **t** 01904 703764 **f** 01904 702312 **e** malspence@thedandys.demon.co.uk **w** thedandys.demon.co.uk MD: Mal Spence.

Satellite Music (see Associated Music International Ltd)

Scamp Music Sovereign House, 12 Trewartha Road, Praa Sands, Penzance, Cornwall TR20 9ST **t** 01736 762826 or 07721 449477 **f** 01736 763328 **e** panamus@aol.com **w** songwriters-guild.co.uk MD: Roderick Jones.

Scaramanga Music (see Menace Music Ltd)

Scarf Music Publishing (see Sea Dream Music)

Schaeffers-Kassner Music (see Kassner Associated Publishers Ltd)

Schauer & May (see Boosey & Hawkes Music Publishers Ltd)

Schott & Company Ltd 48 Great Marlborough Street, London W1F 7BB **t** 020 7437 1246 **f** 020 7437 0263 **e** info@schott-music.com **w** schott-music.com Promotions Asst.: Rachael Oakley.

SCO Music 29 Oakroyd Avenue, Potters Bar, Hertfordshire EN6 2EL **t** 01707 651439 **f** 01707 651439 **e** constantine@steveconstantine.freeserve.co.uk MD: Steve Constantine.

Screen Gems-EMI Music (see EMI Music Publishing)

Screen Music Services (see MCS Music Ltd)

Screwbox (see Menace Music Ltd)

Sea Dream Music Sandcastle Productions, PO Box 13533, London E7 0SG **t** 020 8534 8500 **e** sea.dream@virgin.net Snr Partner: Simon Law.

Second Skin Music (see Reverb Music Ltd)

See For Miles Music Ltd Unit 10, Littleton House, Littleton Road, Ashford, Middlesex TW15 1UU **t** 01784 247176 **f** 01784 241168 **e** es95@dial.pipex.com **w** seeformiles.co.uk Dir: Colin Miles.

Seeca Music Publishing 115, Mortlake Business Centre, 20, Mortlake High Street, London SW14 8JN **t** 020 8487 8622 **f** 020 8876 7467 **e** info@seeca.co.uk **w** seeca.co.uk A&R: Louise Martins.

Semprini Music (see Carlin Music Corporation)

Sepia (see Bucks Music Group)

Seriously Groovy Music 3rd Floor, 28 D'Arblay Street, Soho, London W1F 8EW **t** 020 7439 1947 **f** 020 7734 7540 **e** admin@seriouslygroovy.com **w** seriouslygroovy.com Dir: Dave Holmes.

Seriously Wonderful Music (see Bucks Music Group)

Seven B Music (see Charly Publishing Ltd)

Seventh House Music (see Bucks Music Group)

Sexy Music Ltd PO Box 421, Aylesbury, Bucks HP17 8BS **t** 01844 290528 **f** 01844 290528 **e** unie@redd-angel.com MD: Unie Moller. Business Affairs: Shayne Trackman. A&R: Ronny Anderson. Legal: Andrew Brabyn.

SGO Music Publishing Ltd PO Box 34994, London SW6 6WF **t** 01264 811154 **f** 01264 811172 **e** sgomusic@sgomusic.com **w** sgomusic.com MD: Stuart Ongley.

Shade Factor Productions Limited 4 Cleveland Square, London W2 6DH **t** 020 7402 6477 **f** 020 7402 7144 **e** mail@shadefactor.com **w** shadefactor.com MD: Ann Symonds.

Shadows Music (see Carlin Music Corporation)

Shaftesbury (see Chrysalis Music Ltd)

Shak Music (see SGO Music Publishing Ltd)

Shake Up Music Ickenham Manor, Ickenham, Uxbridge, Middlesex UB10 8QT **t** 01895 672994 **f** 01895 633264 **e** mail@shakeupmusic.co.uk Director: Joanna Tizard.

Shalit Global Music 7 Moor Street, Soho, London W1D 5NB **t** 020 7851 9155 **f** 020 7851 9156 **e** info@shalitglobal.com MD: Jonathan Shalit.

Shanna Music Ltd (see Purple City Ltd)

Shapiro Bernstein & Company (see Music Sales Ltd)

Shaun Davey Music (see Bucks Music Group)

Shay Songs (see Crashed Music)

Shed Publishing (see Scamp Music)

Sheila Music (see Creole Music Ltd)

Shepsongs Inc (& Luxo (see Independent Music Group Ltd)

Sherlock Holmes Music 28 Foundry Street, Brighton BN1 4AT **t** 01273 607492 **f** 01273 607520 **e** mail@sherlockholmesmusic.co.uk **w** sherlockholmesmusic.co.uk MD: Vernon Rossiter.

Shipston Music (see Independent Music Group Ltd)

Shogun Music (see Eaton Music Ltd)

Shrub Music (see Menace Music Ltd)

Signia Music 20 Stamford Brook Avenue, London W6 0YD **t** 020 8846 9469 **f** 020 8741 5152 **e** info@signia.com **w** signiamusic.com MD: Dee Harrington.

Silence Music (see Independent Music Group Ltd)

Silhouette Music (see New Music Enterprises)

Silk Music (see Independent Music Group Ltd)

Silktone Songs Inc (see Independent Music Group Ltd)

Silva Screen Music Publishers 3 Prowse Place, London NW1 9PH **t** 020 7428 5500 **f** 020 7482 2385 **e** info@silvascreen.co.uk **w** silvascreen.co.uk MD: Reynold D'Silva.

Silver Cradle Music (see Independent Music Group Ltd)

Silverscope Music (see Ncompass Publishing)

Alan Simmons Music PO Box 7, Scissett, Huddersfield, West Yorkshire HD8 9YZ **t** 01924 848888 **f** 01924 849999 **e** mail@alansimmonsmusic.com **w** alansimmonsmusic.com MD: Alan Simmons.

Simon Rights Music (see Eaton Music Ltd)

Single Minded Music 11 Cambridge Court, 210 Shepherd's Bush Road, London W6 7NJ **t** 0870 011 3748 **f** 0870 011 3749 **e** tony@singleminded.com **w** singleminded.com MD: Tony Byrne.

Singletree Music (see Independent Music Group Ltd)

Sixteen Stars Music (see Independent Music Group Ltd)

Size: Music PO Box 798, London EN1 1ZP **t** 020 8350 1221 **e** simon@size-music.com **w** size-music.com Contact: Simon Nicholls

SJ Music 23 Leys Road, Cambridge CB4 2AP **t** 01223 314771 **w** printed-music.com/sjmusic Principle: Judith Rattenbury.

Skidmore Music (see Music Sales Ltd)

Skratch Music Publishing Skratch Music House, 81 Crabtree Lane, London SW6 6LW **t** 020 7381 8315 **f** 020 7385 6785 **e** les@skratchmusic.co.uk **w** passionmusic.co.uk Head of Publishing: Les McCutcheon.

Sky Blue Recordings 164D Albion Road, London N16 9JS **t** 020 7503 2258 or 0781 372 4854 **f** 020 7503 2258 **e** alyson@skybluerecordings.com **w** skybluerecordings.com MD: Alyson Gilliland.

Slam Dunk Music (see Independent Music Group Ltd)

Slamina Music (see Carlin Music Corporation)

Sleeping Giant Music International (see St James Music)

SLI Music (see Asterisk Music)

SLNB 143 Westmead Road, Sutton, Surrey SM1 4JP **t** 020 8395 3045 **f** 020 8395 3046 **e** smac143@tesco.net **w** slnb.co.uk MD: Steve McIntosh.

Smackin' Music (see Universal Music Publishing Ltd)

Smirk (see Bucks Music Group)

SMK Publishing (see Independent Music Group Ltd)

SMV Schacht Musikvalage (see Bucks Music Group)

Snappersongs (see Asterisk Music)

So Good Music (see Independent Music Group Ltd)

Solar Publishing PO Box 4809, Bournemouth, Dorset BH7 6WA **t** 0797 317 5036 **f** 0870 706 4830 **e** info@solar-music.com **w** solar-music.com A&R Director: Nic Carrington.

Solent Songs 68-70 Lugley St, Newport, Isle Of Wight PO30 5ET **t** 01983 524110 **f** 0870 1640388 **e** songs@solentrecords.co.uk **w** solentrecords.co.uk Owner: John Waterman.

Solida-Soulville Music (see Urban Music Entertainment Network (U-Men))

Songlines Ltd PO Box 20206, London NW1 7FF **t** 020 7284 3970 **f** 020 7485 0511 **e** doug@songlines.demon.co.uk **w** songlines.co.uk MD: Doug D'Arcy.

Songs For Real (see Bucks Music Group)

Songs In The Key Of Knife Red Corner Door, 17 Barons Court Road, London W14 9DP **t** 020 7386 8760 **f** 020 7381 8014 **e** info@hospitalrecords.com **w** hospitalrecords.com MD: Tony Colman.

Songstream Music Nestlingdown, Chapel Hill, Porthtowan, Truro, Cornwall TR4 8AS **t** 01209 890606 MD: Roger Bourne.

Songwriter Music (see International Songwriters' Music)

Songwriters' Showcase (see First Time Music (Publishing) UK)

Sonic Arts Network Jerwood Space, 171 Union Street, London SE1 0LN **t** 020 7928 7337 **e** phil@sonicartsnetwork.org **w** sonicartsnetwork.org Chief Exec: Phil Hallett.

Sonic Sheet (see Menace Music Ltd)

sonic360music 33 Riding House Street, London W1W 7DZ **t** 020 7636 3939 **f** 020 7636 0033 **e** info@sonic360.com **w** sonic360.com Publishing Mgr: Zen Grisdale.

SONY/ATV MUSIC PUBLISHING

Sony / ATV Music Publishing (UK) Limited

13 Great Marlborough Street, London W1F 7LP **t** 020 7911 8200 **f** 020 7911 8600 **e** firstname_lastname@uk.sonymusic.com MD: Charlie Pinder. Deputy MD: Rakesh Sanghvi. Director of Synch/Marketing: Rachel Iyer. Head of A&R: Steve Sasse.

The Sorabji Archive Easton Dene, Bailbrook Lane, Bath BA1 7AA **t** 01225 852323 **f** 01225 852523 **e** 100775.2716@compuserve.com **w** music.mcgill.ca/~schulman/sorabji.html Curator/Director: Alistair Hinton.

Soul II Soul Mad Music Ltd 36-38 Rochester Place, London NW1 9JX **t** 020 7284 0393 **f** 020 7284 2290 **e** info@soul2soul.co.uk MD: Jazzie B.

Souls Kitchens Music 7 The Stables, Saint Thomas St, Newcastle upon Tyne, Tyne and Wear NE1 4LE **t** 0191 230 1970 **f** 0191 232 0262 **e** info@kware.demon.co.uk **w** kitchenwarerecords.com Administration: Nicki Turner.

Soulstreet Music Publishing Inc (see Independent Music Group Ltd)

Sound Of Jupiter Music (see Carlin Music Corporation)

Sound Songs 98 White Lion St, London N1 9PF **t** 020 7278 5698 **f** 020 7278 6009 **e** paula@soundsongs.net **w** soundsongs.net Professional Mgr: Paula Greenwood.

Sound Stage Production Music (see Amphonic Music Ltd.)

Sounds Like A Hit Ltd 48 Shelvers Way, Tadworth, Surrey KT20 5QF **t** 01737 218899 **f** 01737 355443 **e** steve@soundslikeahit.com **w** soundslikeahit.com Dir: Steve Crosby.

Soundslike Music (see Bucks Music Group)

Sovereign Music UK PO Box 356, Leighton Buzzard, Beds LU7 3WP **t** 01525 385578 **f** 01525 372743 **e** sovereignmusic@aol.com MD: Robert Lamont.

Sovereign Lifestyle Music (see Sovereign Music UK)

SP2 Music (USA & Canada) (see Perfect Songs)

Spadesongs (see Asterisk Music)

Spectrum Music 7 Brunswick Close, Thames Ditton, Surrey KT7 0EU **t** 020 8398 1450 **f** 020 8398 1450 **e** smd.music@virgin.net Dir: Al Dickinson.

Spielman Music (see Independent Music Group Ltd)

Split Music 13 Sandys Road, Worcester WR1 3HE **t** 01905 29809 **f** 01905 613023 **e** split.music@virgin.net **w** splitmusic.com MD: Chris Warren.

Spoon Music (see Bucks Music Group)

Spring River Music (see Independent Music Group Ltd)

Springthyme Music Balmalcolm House, Balmalcolm, Cupar, Fife KY15 7TJ **t** 01337 830773 **f** 01337 831773 **e** music@springthyme.co.uk **w** springthyme.co.uk MD: Peter Shepheard.

Sprint Music Ltd High Jarmany Farm, Jarmany Hill, Barton St David, Somerton,Somerset TA11 6DA **t** 01458 851010 **f** 01458 851029 **e** info@sprintmusic.co.uk **w** sprintmusic.co.uk Consultant: John Ratcliff.

Squaw Peak Music (see Independent Music Group Ltd)

Squirrel (see Briar Music)

St Annes Music Ltd Kennedy House, 31 Stamford Street, Altrincham, Cheshire WA14 1ES **t** 0161 941 5151 **f** 0161 928 9491 **e** kse@kennedystreet.com Dir: Danny Betesh.

Stagecoach Music (see Barry Collings Entertainments)

Standard Music (see Bucks Music Group)

Standard Music Library (see Bucks Music Group)

Stanley House Music (see Jamdown Music Ltd)

Stanza Music 11 Victor Road, Harrow, Middlesex HA2 6PT **t** 020 8863 2717 **f** 020 8863 8685 **e** bill.ashton@virgin.net **w** nyjo.org.uk Dir: Bill Ashton.

Star Street Music Ltd PO Box 375, Chorleywood, Herts WD3 5ZZ **t** 01923 440608 **e** StarstreetUK@aol.com **w** Starstreetmusic.com MD: Nick Battle.

Star-Write Music PO Box 16715, London NW4 1WN **t 020 8203 5062** f 020 8202 3746 e starwrite@btinternet.com Dir: John Lisners.

State Music (see Reliable Source Music)

Stave & Nickelodeon (see Blue Melon Publishing)

Steam Power Music (see The Really Useful Group)

Steelchest Music (see Menace Music Ltd)

Steelworks Songs 218 Canalot Studios, 222 Kensal Road, London W10 5BN **t 020 8960 4443** f 020 8960 9889 e freedom@frdm.co.uk MD: Martyn Barter.

Step by Step Music (see Independent Music Group Ltd)

Steve Dan Mills Music (see Independent Music Group Ltd)

Steve Glen Music (see Blue Melon Publishing)

Steve Marriott Licensing Ltd. Unit 9B, Wingbury Business Village, Upper Wingbury Farm, Wingrave, Bucks HP22 4LW **t** 07770 364 268 **e** chris@stevemarriott.co.uk **w** stevemarriott.co.uk MD: Chris France.

Steve Warner Music (see Independent Music Group Ltd)

Stevensong Music (see Ash Music (GB))

Stickysongs Great Oaks Granary, Kennel Lane, Windlesham, Surrey GU20 6AA **t** 01276 479255 **f** 01276 479255 **e** stickysong@aol.com MD: Peter Gosling.

Still Working Music Covetous Corner, Hudnall Common, Little Gaddesden, Herts HP4 1QW **t** 01442 842039 **f** 01442 842082 **e** mhaynes@orbison.com **w** orbison.com European Consultant: Mandy Haynes. President: Barbara Orbison.

Stinkhorn Music (see Asterisk Music)

Stomp Off Music (see Paul Rodriguez Music Ltd)

Stop Drop & Roll Music Ltd Colbury Manor, Jacobs Gutter Lane, Eling, Southampton SO40 9FY **t** 0845 658 5006 **f** 0845 658 5009 **e** frontdesk@stopdroproll.com **w** stopdroproll.com Publishing Executive: Howard Lucas.

Stormking Music (see Bucks Music Group)

Strada 2 Publishing 25 Heathmans Road, London SW6 4TJ **t** 020 7371 5756 **f** 020 7371 7731 **e** office@pureuk.com **w** pureuk.com Creative Dir: Billy Royal. President: Evros Stakis.

Strange Art Music (see Miggins Music (UK))

Strathmere Music (see Independent Music Group Ltd)

Stratsong (see Carlin Music Corporation)

Strictly Confidential UK 338A Ladbroke Grove, London W10 5AH **t** 020 8365 3367 **f** 020 8374 5967 **e** mike@strictly-confidential.co.uk MD: Pierre Mossiat.

Strongsongs Publishing 107 Mortlake High St, London SW14 8HQ **t** 020 8392 6839 **f** 020 8878 7886 **e** anna.jolley@strongsongs.com MD: Anna Jolley.

Structure Music PO Box 26273, London W3 6FN **t** 0870 207 7720 **f** 0870 208 8820 **e** sound@structure.co.uk **w** structure.co.uk Contact: Olly Groves MD: Olly Groves. Bus Aff Dir: Stephen Copeland.

Studio G Cedar Tree House, Main St, Farthingstone, Northants N12 8EZ **t** 01327 360820 **f** 01327 360821 **e** library@studiog.co.uk **w** studiog.co.uk MD: John Gale.

Studio Music Company PO Box 19292, London NW10 9WP **t** 020 8830 0110 **f** 020 8451 6470 **e** sales@studio-music.co.uk **w** studio-music.co.uk Ptnr: Stan Kitchen.

Sub Rosa 13 Cotswold Mews, 30 Battersea Square, London SW11 3RA **t** 020 7978 7888 **f** 020 7978 7808 **e** auto@automan.co.uk MD: Jerry Smith.

Sublime Music 211 Piccadilly, London W1J 9HF **t** 020 7917 2948 **e** mw@sublime-music.co.uk **w** sublime-music.co.uk MD: Nick Grant.

Sublime Music Publishing 77 Preston Drove, Brighton, East Sussex BN1 6LD **t** 01273 560605 **f** 01273 560606 **e** info@sublimemusic.co.uk **w** sublimemusic.co.uk MD: Patrick Spinks.

Suburban Base Music 1 Star Street, London W2 1QD **t** 020 7706 7304 **f** 020 7706 8197 **e** morrison@powernet.co.uk Creative Manager: Carol Smith.

Suburban Base Music (see Bryan Morrison Music)

Success Music (see Kassner Associated Publishers Ltd)

Sugar Bottom Publishing (see Independent Music Group Ltd)

Sugar Music 8-10 Rhoda Street, London E2 7EF **t** 020 7729 4797 **f** 020 7739 8571 **e** paul.hitchman@playlouder.com Contact: Paul Hitchman

Sugar Songs UK (see Chelsea Music Publishing Co)

Sugarcane Music 32 Blackmore Avenue, Southall, Middlesex UB1 3ES **t** 020 8574 2130 **f** 020 8574 2130 MD: Astrid Pringsheim.

Sugarfree Music (see Bucks Music Group)

Sugarmusic (see Universal Music Publishing Ltd)

Sugarstar Music Ltd Park View House, 64 Murray St, York YO24 4JA **t** 08456 448424 **f** 0709 222 8681 **e** info@sugarstar.com **w** sugarstar.com MD: Mark J. Fordyce.

Suggsongs (see Menace Music Ltd)

Sun Star Songs (BMI) (see Independent Music Group Ltd)

Sun-Pacific Music (London) Ltd PO Box 5, Hastings, E. Sussex TN34 1HR **t** 01424 721196 **f** 01424 717704 **e** aquarius.lib@clara.net MD: Gilbert Gibson.

Sunflower Music (see John Fiddy Music)

Supreme Songs Ltd (see Independent Music Group)

Survival Music PO Box 2502, Devizes, Wilts SN10 3ZN **t** 01380 860500 **f** 01380 860596 **e** annemarie@survivalrecords.co.uk **w** survivalrecords.co.uk Dir: Anne-Marie Heighway. Dir: David Rome

Survivor Records (see Kingsway Music)

Susan May Music (see Paul Rodriguez Music Ltd)

Sutjujo Music (see Independent Music Group Ltd)

Suzuki (see International Music Publications (IMP))

Sweet 'n' Sour Songs 2-3 Fitzroy Mews, London W1T 6DF **t** 020 7383 7767 **f** 020 7383 3020 MD: John Craig.

Sweet Glenn Music Inc (see Independent Music Group Ltd)

Sweet Karol Music Inc (see Independent Music Group Ltd)

Swiggeroux Music (see SGO Music Publishing Ltd)

Swivel Publishing (see Independent Music Group Ltd)

Sylvantone Music 11 Saunton Avenue, Redcar, North Yorkshire TS10 2RL **t** 01642 479898 **f** 0709 235 9333 **e** sylvantone@hotmail.com **w** countrymusic.org.uk./tony-goodacre/index.html Prop: Tony Goodacre.

T H Music (see Chelsea Music Publishing Co)

Tabitha Music Ltd 39 Cordery Road, Exeter, Devon EX2 9DJ **t** 01392 499889 **f** 01392 498068 **e** graham@tabithamusic.fsnet.co.uk **w** eyespyonline.net MD: Graham Sclater.

Tabraylah (see Menace Music Ltd)

Tafari Music (see Greensleeves Publishing Ltd)

Tairona Songs Ltd PO Box 102, London E15 2HH **t** 020 8555 5423 **f** 020 8519 6834 **e** tairona@moksha.demon.co.uk **w** moksha.co.uk MD: Charles Cosh. General & Royalty Administration: Gwyneth Stenton.

Take It Quick Music (see Bucks Music Group)

Takes On Music (see Eaton Music Ltd)

Tales from Forever Publishing (see Independent Music Group Ltd)

Tancott Music (see Independent Music Group Ltd)

Tanspan Music (see Asterisk Music)

Tapadero Music (see Independent Music Group Ltd)

Tapestry Music (see Bucks Music Group)

Tapier Music (see Charly Publishing Ltd)

Tarantula Productions (see Bucks Music Group)

Taste Music Ltd 263 Putney Bridge Road, London SW15 2PU **t** 020 8780 3311 **f** 020 8785 9892 **e** mike@tastemedia.com **w** tastemusic.com Creative Manager: Mike Audley.

Tayborn Publishing (see Music Exchange (Manchester) Ltd)

TBM International (see Independent Music Group Ltd)

TCB Music (see Independent Music Group Ltd)

TCR Music (see Westbury Music Ltd)

Teleny Music (see Miriamusic)

Television Music Ltd Yorkshire Television, TV Centre, Leeds, West Yorkshire LS3 1JS **t** 0113 243 8283 **f** 0113 222 7166 **e** sue.clark@granadamedia.com Contact: Sue Clark

Tema International 151 Nork Way, Banstead, Surrey SM7 1HR **t** 01737 219607 **f** 01737 219609 **e** music@tema-intl.demon.co.uk **w** temadance.com Production Manager: Amanda Harris.

Temple Records & Publishing Shillinghill, Temple, Midlothian EH23 4SH **t** 01875 830328 **f** 01875 830392 **e** robin@templerecords.co.uk **w** templerecords.co.uk Prop: Robin Morton.

Termidor Music (see Editions Penguin Cafe)

Texas Red Songs (see Independent Music Group Ltd)

TGM Hammer (see Bucks Music Group)

Thames Music 445 Russell Court, Woburn Place, London WC1H 0NJ **t** 020 7837 6240 **f** 020 7833 4043 MD: C W Adams.

Thank You Music (see Kingsway Music)

The First Composers Company (see Carlin Music Corporation)

The Music Factor (see Paul Rodriguez Music Ltd)

The Music Trunk Publishing Co. Ltd (see Broughton Park Music)

The Royalty Network (see Notting Hill Music (UK) Ltd)

The Sparta Florida Music Group (see Music Sales Ltd)

Third World (see Paul Rodriguez Music Ltd)

Thirdwave Music PO Box 19, Orpington, Kent BR6 9ZF **t** 01689 609481 **f** 01689 609481 **e** info@thirdwavemusic.com **w** thirdwavemusic.com MD: Matt Gall.

Thomas & Taylor Music Works (see Independent Music Group Ltd)

Thompson Station Music (see Independent Music Group Ltd)

Three 4 Music (see Bucks Music Group)

Three Two Music (see Crashed Music)

Throat Music (see Warner Chappell Music Ltd)

Thrust Magnum Inc (see Bucks Music Group)

Thumpin' Publishing (see Independent Music Group Ltd)

Tia Music Publishing (see SGO Music Publishing Ltd)

Tidy Trax Hawthorne House, Fitzwilliam St, Parkgate, Rotherham, South Yorks S62 6EP **t** 01709 710022 **f** 01709 523141 **e** firstname.lastname@tidy.com **w** tidy.com MD: Andy Pickles. International Director: Debra Foster. Creative Director: Amadeus Mozart.

Tiger Trax Limited (see Independent Music Group Ltd)

Timbuk One Music (see Independent Music Group Ltd)

Timbuktu Music (see V2 Music Ltd.)MD: Mark Bond.

Timewarp (see Paul Rodriguez Music Ltd)

Tin Whistle Music (see Bucks Music Group)

Tinrib (see Paul Rodriguez Music Ltd)

Tiparm Music Publishers Inc (see Bucks Music Group)

Tiparm Music Publishing (see Bucks Music Group)

TKO Music Group Ltd PO Box 130, Hove, E. Sussex BN3 6QU **t** 01273 550088 **f** 01273 540969 **e** management@tkogroup.com **w** tkogroup.com Creative Manager: Warren Heal.

TM Music (see Carlin Music Corporation)

TMC Publishing (see Triad Publishing)

TMR Publishing PO Box 3775, London SE18 3QR **t** 020 8316 4690 **f** 020 8316 4690 **e** marc@wufog.freeserve.co.uk **w** Braindead-Studios.com MD: Marc Bell.

TNR Music 5B Oakleigh Mews, Whetstone, London N20 9HQ **t** 020 8343 9971 **f** 020 8445 9258 **e** tnrproductions@yahoo.co.uk **w** thenextroom.com MD: Chris Warren.

Todo Music (see Paul Rodriguez Music Ltd)

Tomake Music (see Independent Music Group Ltd)

Tomeja Music (see Independent Music Group Ltd)

Tomi Girl Music (see Independent Music Group Ltd)

Tomi Music Co (see Westbury Music Ltd)

Tonecolor Music (see Express Music (UK) Ltd)

Tony Carlisle Music (see Independent Music Group Ltd)

Tony Randolph (see Paul Rodriguez Music Ltd)

Too Pure Music (see 4AD Music)

Torgrimson Music (see Independent Music Group Ltd)

Tosca Music (see Bucks Music Group)

Townhill Music Ty Cefn, Rectory Road, Canton, Cardiff CF5 1QL **t** 029 2022 7993 **f** 029 2034 1622 **e** huwwilliams@townhillmusic.com Director: Huw Williams.

Trace Elements (see Menace Music Ltd)

Track Music PO Box 107, South Godstone, Redhill, Surrey RH9 8YS **t** 01342 892178 or 01342 892074 **f** 01342 893411 **e** ian.grant@trackrecords.co.uk **w** trackrecords.co.uk MD: Ian Grant.

Trackboyz (see Notting Hill Music (UK) Ltd)

Trackdown Music Ickenham Manor, Ickenham, Uxbridge, Middx UB10 8QT **t** 01895 672994 **f** 01895 633264 **e** mail@trackdownmusic.co.uk Dir: Joanna Tizard.

Trax On Wax Music Publishers Glenmundar House, Ballyman Road, Bray, Co. Wicklow, Ireland **t** +353 86 257 6244 **f** +353 1 216 4395 **e** picket@iol.ie Dir: Deke O'Brien.

Treasure Island Publishing Bartra Studio, Harbour Road, Dalkey, Co Dublin, Ireland **t** +353 1 284 6336 **f** +353 1 284 6336 **e** info@treasureisland.ie **w** treasureisland.ie MD: Robert Stephenson.

Tree Music (see Sony/ATV Music Publishing)

Trevor Fung (see Independent Music Group Ltd)

Treyball Music (see Notting Hill Music (UK) Ltd)

Triad Publishing PO Box 150, Chesterfield S40 0YT **t** 0870 746 8478 **e** traid@themanagementcompany.biz **w** themanagementcompany.biz MD: Tony Hedley.

Trinity Publishing Company 72 New Bond Street, London W1S 1RR **t** 020 7499 4141 **e** info@trinitymediagroup.net **w** trinitymediagroup.net MD: Peter Murray.

Triple A Publishing Ltd GMC Studio, Hollingbourne, Kent ME17 1UQ **t** 01622 880599 **f** 01622 880159 **e** publishing@triple-a.uk.com **w** triple-a.uk.com CEO: Terry Armstrong.

Tristan Music Ltd (see Hornall Brothers Music)

TRO Essex Music (see The Essex Music Group)

Truck Publishing 15 Percy Street, Oxford OX4 3AA **t** 01865 722333 **e** paul@truckrecords.com **w** truckrecords.com MD: Paul Bonham.

True Playaz Music Publishing (see Bucks Music Group)

Truelove Music 19F Tower Workshops, Riley Road, London SE1 3DG **t** 020 7252 2900 **f** 020 7252 2890 **e** truelove@truelove.co.uk **w** truelove.co.uk Business Affairs: Brian Roach.

Tsunami Sounds The Gables, Avenue Road, Cranleigh, Surrey GU6 7LE **t** 01483 271200 **f** 01483 271200 **e** info@tsunami.co.uk **w** tsunami.co.uk Director: Ken Easter.

Tuesday Music (see PXM Publishing)

Tuesday Productions (see Bucks Music Group)

Tumi Music (Editorial) Ltd 8-9 New Bond St. Place, Bath, Somerset BA1 1BH **t** 01225 464736 **f** 01225 444870 **e** info@tumimusic.com **w** tumimusic.com MD: Mo Fini.

Tune Kel Publishing (see Charly Publishing Ltd)

TVS Music (see Bucks Music Group)

Twangy Music (see Music Sales Ltd)

Two Guys Who Are Publishers (see Independent Music Group Ltd)

Two Song (see Menace Music Ltd)

Tyler Music (see The Essex Music Group)

Ubiquitunes (see Bucks Music Group)

UGR Publishing PO Box 45821, London E11 3YZ **t** 020 8503 0684 **f** 020 8503 0684 **e** urbangospel@hotmail.com Head of A&R: P. Mac.

Ultimate Dilemma Music (see Westbury Music Ltd)

Ultimate Musical Publishing Co (see The Bacon Empire Publishing)

Ultramodern Music (see Bucks Music Group)

Under The Counter Music (see Westbury Music Ltd)

Unforgettable Songs (see Perfect Songs)

Unique Corp. 15 Shaftesbury Centre, 85 Barlby Road, London W10 6BN **t** 020 8964 9333 or 07768 065661 **f** 020 8964 9888 **e** info@uniquecorp.co.uk **w** uniquecorp.co.uk MD: Alan Bellman.

Unique Publishing (see Bucks Music Group)

Unit 11 Publishing Ltd (see Independent Music Group Ltd)

United Music GBMH (see Independent Music Group Ltd)

United Music Publishers Ltd 42 Rivington Street, London EC2A 3BN **t** 020 7729 4700 **f** 020 7739 6549 **e** info@ump.co.uk **w** ump.co.uk MD: Shirley Ranger.

UNIVERSAL MUSIC PUBLISHING GROUP

UNIVERSAL MUSIC PUBLISHING GROUP

136-144 New Kings Road, London SW6 4LZ **t** 020 8752 2600 **f** 020 8752 2601 **e** firstname.lastname@umusic.com. MD & Exec VP Europe: Paul Connolly. Deputy Managing Director: Mike McCormack. European Finance Dir: Simon Baker. VP, International: Kim Frankiewicz. Head of Legal & Business Affairs: Sarah Levin. Head of UK Finance: Rob Morris. Head of Film & TV: Barbara Zamoyska. UK Licensing Manager: Ross Pelling. Creative Services Manager: Karina Masters. A&R: Willi Morrison, Claire Blackburn, Jamie Campbell, Andy Thompson, Frank Tope, Darryl Watts, Ruth Rothwell, Dougie Bruce. UK Admin: UK Copyright Mgr: David Livermore. UK Royalty Mgr: Simon Lindquist. Universal Music Publishing International: SVP Intl Bus & Legal Affairs: Crispin Evans.

United Songwriters Music (see International Songwriters' Music)

Universal Edition (see Alfred A Kalmus Ltd. (Music Publishers))

Universal Edition (London) 38 Eldon Way, Paddock Wood, Kent TN12 6BE **t** 01892 833422 **f** 01892 836038 **w** uemusic.co.uk Sales/Mktng Mgr: Andrew Knowles.

Upright Music 204 Crescent House, Goswell Road, London EC1Y 0SL **t** 020 7490 7346 **e** bill@workersplaytime.co.uk **w** workersplaytime.co.uk MD: Bill Gilliam.

Upright Songs (see Independent Music Group Ltd)

Urban Music Entertainment Network (U-Men) PO Box 7874, London SW20 9XD **t** 07050 605219 **f** 07050 605239 **e** sam@pan-africa.org CEO: Oscar Sam-Carrol Jnr.

Urbanstar Music Global House, 92 De Beauvoir Rd, London N1 4EN **t** 020 7288 2239 **f** 0870 429 2493 **e** info@urbanstarrecords.com **w** urbanstarrecords.com Dirs: Steve Wren, Nick Sellors.

Utopia Publishing Utopia Village, 7 Chalcot Road, London NW1 8LH **t** 020 7586 3434 **f** 020 7586 3438 **e** utopiarec@aol.com MD: Phil Wainman.

V2 Music Publishing Ltd 131 Holland Park Avenue, London W11 4UT **t** 020 7471 3000 **f** 020 7471 3110 **e** Mike.Sefton@V2Music.com MD: Mike Sefton.

The Valentine Music Group 7 Garrick Street, London WC2E 9AR **t** 020 7240 1628 **f** 020 7497 9242 **e** valentine@bandleader.co.uk **w** valentinemusic.co.uk MD: John Nice.

Valley Music (see Universal Music Publishing Ltd)

Valley Music Ltd. 1 Greys Road, Henley-on-Thames, Oxfordshire RG9 1SB **t** 01491 845840 **f** 01491 412855 **e** mark@valleymusicuk.com **w** valleymusicuk.com MD: Kyle Hunter.

Valliant Publishing (see Charly Publishing Ltd)

Value Added Tunes (see Independent Music Group)

Van Steene Music Publishing 23 Anthony Road, Borehamwood, Herts WD6 4NF **t** 020 8905 2878 **f** 020 8905 2879 **e** guyvansteene@macunlimited.net MD: Guy Van Steene.

Vanderbeek & Imrie Ltd 15 Marvig, Lochs, Isle Of Lewis, Scotland HS2 9QP **t** 01851 880216 **f** 01851 880216 **e** mapamundi@aol.com MD: M Imrie.

Vanessa Music Co 35 Tower Way, Dunkeswell, Devon EX14 4XH **t** 01404 891598 MD: Don Todd MBE.

Vanwarmer Music (see Independent Music Group Ltd)

Vaughan Williams Memorial Library (Sound Archive) Cecil Sharp House, 2 Regent's Park Road, Camden, London NW1 7AY **t** 020 7485 2206 **f** 020 7284 0534 **e** info@efdss.org **w** efdss.org Publications Manager: Felicity Greenland.

Vector Music (see Independent Music Group Ltd)

Veltone Music (see Independent Music Group Ltd)

Venus Music 13 Fernhurst Gardens, Edgware, Middx HA8 7PQ **t** 020 8952 1924 or 07956 064 019 **f** 020 8952 3496 **e** kamalmmalak@onetel.net.uk **w** venusmusicandrecords.co.uk MD: Kamal M Malak.

Verdi Publishing Estate House, Stanmore, Bridgnorth, Shropshire WV15 5HP **t** 01746 761121 **f** 01746 711911 **e** mmpc@btclick.com **w** milleniummusicpc.com Dir A&R: Dave Coleman.

Verge Music (see Asterisk Music)

Veronica Music (see Music Sales Ltd)

Verulam Music (see Bocu Music Ltd)

Vicki Music (see Carlin Music Corporation)

Victor Hugo Salsa PO Box 14303, London SE26 4ZH **t** 07000 472572 **f** 07000 472572 **e** victorhugo@victorhugosalsa.com **w** victorhugosalsa.com Manager: Hector Rosquete.

Victoria Kay Music (see Independent Music Group Ltd)

Vidor Publications (see Independent Music Group Ltd)

Ville de Beest (see Asterisk Music)

Vince Barranco Music (see Independent Music Group Ltd)

Vinteuil (see Rondor Music (London) Ltd)

Virgin Music (see EMI Music Publishing)

Visual Music Publishing West House, Forthaven, Shoreham-by-Sea, W. Sussex BN43 5HY **t** 01273 453422 **f** 01273 452914 **e** richard@longman-records.com **w** richard-durrant.com Director: Richard Durrant.

Vital Records (see Vital Spark Music)

Vital Spark Music 1 Waterloo, Breakish, Isle Of Skye IV42 8QE **t** 01471 822484 **f** 01471 822952 **e** chris@vitalsparkmusic.demon.co.uk CEO: Chris Harley.

Vitamin V Music 1 Sekforde Street, London EC1R OBE **t** 020 7075 6080 **f** 020 7075 6081 **e** firstname@vitaminv.tv Dir: Les Mear.

VLS Music Inc (see Independent Music Group Ltd)

Voiceprint Publishing PO Box 50, Houghton-le-Spring, Tyne and Wear DH4 5YP **t** 0191 512 1103 **f** 0191 512 1104 **e** info@voiceprint.co.uk **w** voiceprint.co.uk MD: Rob Ayling.

W Bessel, London (see Breitkopf & Hartel)

W.A.M. Music Ltd. (see Broadley Music (Int) Ltd)

Waif Productions 1 North Worple Way, London SW14 8QG **t** 020 8876 2533 **f** 020 8878 4229 **e** artistrec@aol.com **w** arcarc.co.uk General Manager: Marie Hourihan.

Walden Creek Music (see Independent Music Group Ltd)

Walk on the Wild Side 8 Deronda Road, London SE24 9BG **t** 020 8674 7990 or 07775 806288 **f** 020 8671 5548 MD: Dave Massey.

Warner Chappell Hire Library (see The Concord Partnership)

WARNER/CHAPPELL MUSIC LTD

The Warner Building, 28 Kensington Church Street, London W8 4EP **t** 020 7938 0000 **f** 020 7368 2777 **e** firstname.surname@warnerchappell.com **w** warnerchappell.com Please note that Royalties and Copyright Administration operate from Griffin House, 161 Hammersmith Road, London W6 8BS. **t** 020 8563 5800 **f** 020 8563 5801. MD: Richard Manners. Fin Dir: Mike Lavin. Exec Dir, Legal & Business Affairs: Jane Dyball. Snr Mgr Legal & Business Affairs: Honey Onile-Ere. Snr A&R Manager: David Donald. A&R Manager: Kehinde Olarinmoye. Jnr A&R Manager: Jane Rees. Snr Mgr Film & TV: Gary Downing. Standard Repertoire Mgr: Caroline Underwood. Mgr, UK & Int'l Services: Lesley Hatch. Vice President, Global Administration: John Reston. Head Of Copyright & Royalties: Steve Clark.

Warner Chappell Music International (see Warner/Chappell Music Ltd)

Wall Of Sound Music Office 2, 9 Thorpe Close, London W10 5XL **t** 020 8969 1144 **f** 020 8969 1155 **e** general@wallofsound.uk.com **w** wallofsound.net MD: Mark Jones.

Walter Neal Music (see Asterisk Music)

Wardo Music (see Bucks Music Group)

Wardour Music (see Express Music (UK) Ltd)

Warlock Music (see Rykomusic Ltd)

Water House Music (see Greensleeves Publishing Ltd)

Water Music Productions 6 Erskine Road, London NW3 3AJ **t** 020 7722 3478 **f** 020 7722 6605 **e** splash@watermusic.co.uk Producer: Tessa Lawlor.

Jeff Wayne Music Group Oliver House, 8-9 Ivor Place, London NW1 6BY **t** 020 7724 2471 **f** 020 7724 6245 **e** info@jeffwaynemusic.com **w** jeffwaynemusic.com Group Dir: Jane Jones.

Websongs The Troupe Studio, 106 Thetford Road, New Malden, Surrey KT3 5DZ **t** 020 8949 0928 **f** 020 8605 0238 **e** kip@websongs.co.uk **w** websongs.co.uk MD: Kip Trevor.

Bruce Welch Music 64 Stirling Court, Marshall Street, London W1F 9BD **t** 020 7434 1839 **f** 020 7434 1839 **e** BWML@globalnet.co.uk MD: Bruce Welch.

Welsh Media Music Gorwelion, Llanfynydd, Carmarthen, Dyfed SA32 7TG **t** 01558 668525 **f** 01558 668750 **e** dpierce@welshmediamusic.f9.co.uk MD: Dave Pierce.

Westbury Music Ltd Suite B, 2 Tunstall Road, London SW9 8DA **t** 020 7733 5400 **f** 020 7733 4449 **e** info@westburymusic.net **w** westburymusic.net MD: Caroline Robertson.

Westminster Music (see The Essex Music Group)

WGS Music (see Bardic Edition)

Whacker Music (see Independent Music Group Ltd)

Whispering Wings Music (see Independent Music Group Ltd)

Whitman (see Eaton Music Ltd)

Whole Earth Music (see Independent Music Group Ltd)

Wienerworld (see Melody Lauren Music)

Wiiija Music (see 4AD Music)

Wild Bouquet Music (see Independent Music Group Ltd)

Wildwood Music (see The Essex Music Group)

Wilhelm Music (see New Music Enterprises)

Wilson Editions 1st & 2nd Floors, 7 High Street, Cheadle, Cheshire SK8 1AX **t** 0161 491 6655 **f** 0161 491 6688 **e** dimus@aol.com **w** dimusic.co.uk MD: Alan Wilson.

Windfall (see Bucks Music Group)

Window Music (see Independent Music Group Ltd)

WINDSWEPT MUSIC (LONDON) LTD

Hope House, 40 St Peter's Road, London W6 9BD **t** 020 8237 8400 **f** 020 8741 0825 **e** firstname@windswept.co.uk **w** windsweptpacific.com Executive Director: Peter McCamley. Finance Director: Paul Flynn. Creative Co-ordinator: Emma Burgess. Copyright & Licensing Manager: Indi Chawla.

Wintrup Songs 31 Buckingham Street, Brighton, East Sussex BN1 3LT **t** 01273 880439 **e** mcgowan.allan@virgin.net Contact: Allan McGowan

Wipe Out Music Ltd PO Box 1NW, Newcastle-Upon-Tyne NE99 1NW **t** 0191 266 3802 **f** 0191 266 6073 **e** johnesplen@btconnect.com Manager: John Esplen.

WOMAD Music Ltd Box Mill, Mill Lane, Box, Wiltshire SN13 8PL **t** 01225 743188 **f** 01225 744369 **e** publishing@realworld.co.uk **w** realworld.co.uk/publishing Publisher: Annie Reed.

Wooden (see Bucks Music Group)

Woody Guthrie Publications (see Bucks Music Group)

World Music Press (see Lindsay Music)

WW Music (see Paul Rodriguez Music Ltd)

WW Norton (see Peters Edition)

Wyse Music (see Bucks Music Group)

Wyze Music (see Bucks Music Group)

Yancey Music (see Asterisk Music)

Yard Dog Music (see Independent Music Group Ltd)

Year Zero Music (see Bucks Music Group)

Yesterday's Music (see Multiplay Music Ltd)

Yok Music (see Bucks Music Group)

Yorke Edition Grove Cottage, Southgate, Fakenham, Norfolk NR21 9PA **t** 01328 823501 **f** 01328 823502 **e** info@yorkedition.co.uk **w** yorkedition.co.uk Prop: Rodney Slatford.

Yoshiko Publishing Estate Office, Great Westwood, Old House Lane, King's Langley, Hertfordshire WD4 9AD **t** 01923 261545 **f** 01923 261546 **e** yoouchi@globalnet.co.uk MD: Yoshiko Ouchi.

Young Beau Music (see Independent Music Group Ltd)

Young Man Moving (see Independent Music Group Ltd)

Your Music 39 Leyton Road, Harpenden, Hertfordshire AL5 2JB **t** 01582 715098 MD: David Blaylock.

Zagora Editions (see Independent Music Group Ltd)

Zamalama Music (see Independent Music Group Ltd)

Zane Music 162 Castle Hill, Reading, Berkshire RG1 7RP **t** 0118 957 4567 **f** 0118 956 1261 **e** info@zaneproductions.demon.co.uk MD: Peter Thompson.

Zok Music (see Bucks Music Group)

Zomba Music Publishers Bedford House, 69-79 Fulham High Street, London SW6 3JW **t** 020 7384 7500 **f** 020 7371 9298 **e** firstname.lastname@zomba.com **w** zomba.co.uk GM: Tim Smith. A&R Managers: Angel Thompson, Michael Morley. A&R Asst: Ollie Hodge.

Zonic Music (see Creole Music Ltd)

Zoo-Bee Music (see SGO Music Publishing Ltd)

Zorch Music 5 Sussex Crescent, Northolt, Middlesex UB5 4DL **t** 020 8423 7373 **f** 020 8423 7773 **e** nervous@compuserve.com **w** nervous.co.uk MD: Roy Williams.

Sheet Music Suppliers

A&C Black Howard Road, Eaton Socon, Cambridgeshire PE19 8EZ **t** 01480 212666 **f** 01480 405014 **e** custser@acblack.com Educational Support Mgr: Hilary While.

Alker & Askem Arrangements and Transcriptions The Coach House, 29 Market Square, Bicester, Oxon OX26 6AG **t** 01869 250647 **f** 01869 321552 **e** aaa@groovecompany.co.uk **w** aaarrangements.co.uk MD: Martin Alker.

Boosey & Hawkes Music Publishers Ltd 295 Regent Street, London W1B 8JH **t** 020 7580 2060 **f** 020 7291 7199 **e** marketing.uk@boosey.com **w** boosey.com Contact: David Allenby

Cramer Music 23 Garrick Street, London WC2E 9RY **t** 020 7240 1612 **f** 020 7240 2639 MD: Peter Maxwell.

William Elkin Music Services Station Road Industrial Estate, Salhouse, Norwich, Norfolk NR13 6NS **t** 01603 721302 **f** 01603 721801 **e** sales@elkinmusic.co.uk **w** elkinmusic.co.uk Partner: Richard Elkin.

Faber Music Burnt Mill, Elizabeth Way, Harlow, Essex CM20 2HX **t** 01279 828989 or 01279 828900 **f** 01279 828990 or 01279 828901 **e** sales@fabermusic.com **w** fabermusic.com Sales & Mktg Dir: Phillip Littlemore.

International Music Publications (IMP) Griffin House, 161 Hammersmith Road, London W6 8BS **t** 020 8222 9222 **f** 020 8222 9260 **e** imp.info@warnerchappell.com **w** wbpdealers.com Marketing & Creative Mgr: Matt Crossey.

Jazzwise 2B Gleneagle Mews, Ambleside Avenue, London SW16 6AE **t** 020 8769 7725 **f** 020 8677 7128 **e** admin@jazzwise.com **w** jazzwise.com MD: Charles Alexander.

Alfred A Kalmus/Universal Edition (London) 48 Gt Marlborough Street, London W1F 7BB **t** 020 7437 5203 **f** 020 7437 6115 **e** andrew.knowles@uemusic.co.uk Sales Promo Mgr: Andrew Knowles.

London Orchestrations (c/o Jazzwise)

Lookmusic 21 Presley Way, Crownhill, Milton Keynes, Buckinghamshire MK8 0ES **t** 0870 333 0091 **f** 01908 263301 **e** sales@lookmusic.com **w** lookmusic.com Head of IT: Philip Evans.

MakeMusic! Inc (see MusiWorks Services Ltd -, under Publishers)

Music Exchange (Manchester) Ltd. Claverton Road, Wythenshawe, Manchester M23 9ZA **t** 0161 946 1234 **f** 0161 946 1195 **e** sales@music-exchange.co.uk **w** musicx.co.uk (Trade Only) Sales Director: Gerald Burns.

Music Sales Ltd 8/9 Frith Street, London W1V 5TZ **t** 020 7434 0066 **f** 020 7734 8416 **e** music@musicsales.co.uk **w** musicsales.com GM: Chris Butler.

Stainer & Bell PO Box 110, Victoria House, 23 Gruneisen Road, London N3 1DZ **t** 020 8343 3303 **f** 020 8343 3024 **e** post@stainer.co.uk **w** stainer.co.uk Joint MD: Carol Wakefield.

Studio Music Company (Sheet Music Distributors) PO Box 19292, London NW10 9WP **t** 020 8830 0110 **f** 020 8451 6470 **e** sales@studio-music.co.uk Partner: Stan Kitchen.

United Music Publishers 42 Rivington Street, London EC2A 3BN **t** 020 7729 4700 **f** 020 7739 6549 **e** info@ump.co.uk **w** ump.co.uk Marketing Mgr: James Perkins.

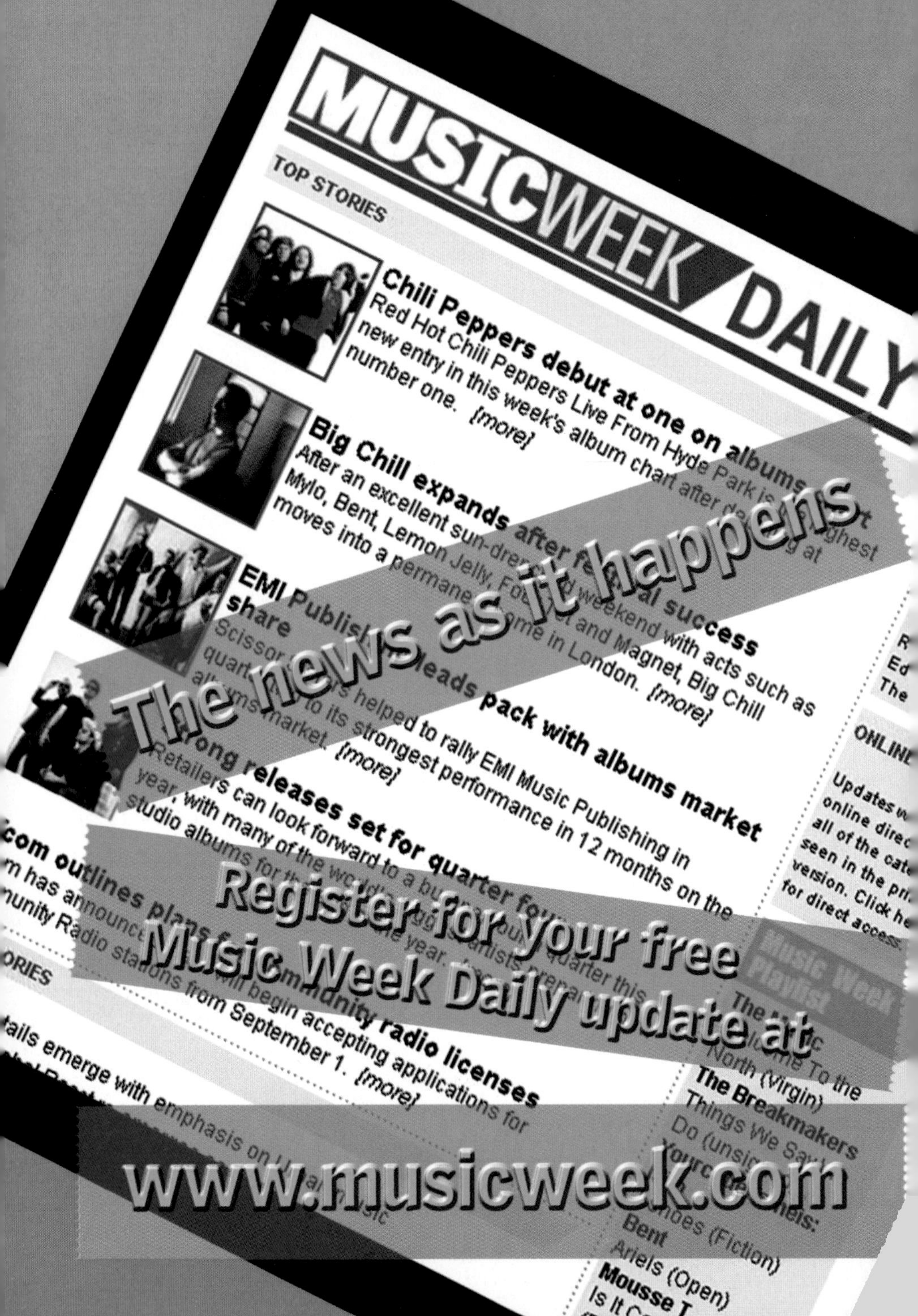

MUSICWEEK DAILY
TOP STORIES
Chili Peppers debut at one on albums chart
Red Hot Chili Peppers Live From Hyde Park is the highest new entry in this week's album chart after debuting at number one. [more]
Big Chill expands after festival success
After an excellent sun-drenched weekend with acts such as Mylo, Bent, Lemon Jelly, Four Tet and Magnet, Big Chill moves into a permanent home in London. [more]
EMI Publishing leads pack with albums market share
Scissor Sisters helped to rally EMI Music Publishing in quarter two to its strongest performance in 12 months on the albums market. [more]
Strong releases set for quarter four
Retailers can look forward to a bumper fourth quarter this year, with many of the world's biggest artists preparing studio albums for the end of the year. [more]
Ofcom outlines plans for community radio licenses
Ofcom has announced it will begin accepting applications for Community Radio stations from September 1. [more]
The news as it happens
Register for your free Music Week Daily update at
www.musicweek.com

DOUBLE TAKE!

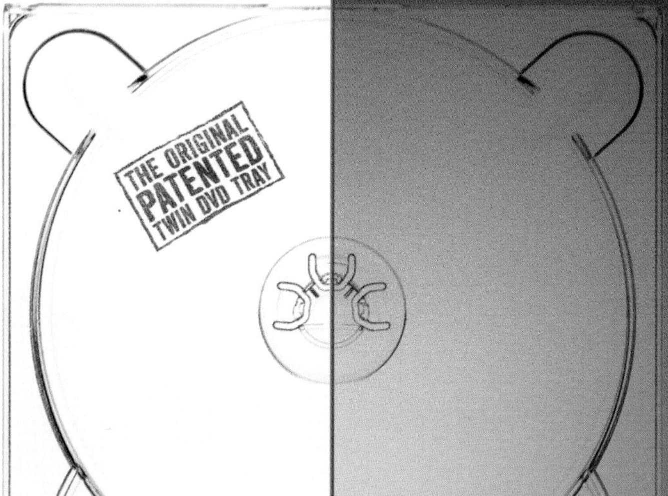

From now on, quality no longer comes at a price. By choosing the **Twin DVD Tray**, with its fully automated production process, you can save time, reduce costs and make the most of your materials.
This **Pozzoli**-designed innovation allows special packaging to become the new standard.
Now - for the first time ever - all your DVD releases can come beautifully presented in a packaging solution that's irresistible but doesn't cost the earth to produce.

Pozzoli S.p.A.
Via G. Di Vittorio 11 - 20065 Inzago (Milano), Italy
Tel. (39) 02 954341 - Fax (39) 02 95434240
www.pozzolispa.com
E-mail: mail@pozzolispa.com

Pozzoli Ltd
100 New Kings Road - London, SW6 4LX, UK
Tel. (44) 020 7384.3283 - Fax (44) 020 7384.3067
E-mail: pozzoliltd@aol.com

Pozzoli Deutschland GmbH
Zeilweg 44 - D-60439 Frankfurt am Main
Tel (49) 069 58604032 - Fax (49) 069 58604033
E-mail: pozzoligmbh@t-online.de

Design, Pressing & Distribution

Pressers and Duplicators

*	APRS members (PAD group)
CD	Compact Disc
CDi	Compact Disc Interactive
CDRom	Compact Disc Read Only Memory
DAT	Digital Audio Tape
DCC	Digital Compact Disc
DVD	Digital Versatile Disc
LD	LaserDisc
MC	Music Cassette
MD	MiniDisc
V	Vinyl
VC	Video Cassette
VCD	Video Compact Disc

10th Planet 40 Newman St, London W1T 1QJ **t** 020 7637 9500 **f** 020 7637 9599 **e** studio@10thplanet.net **w** 10thplanet.net Directors: Ben Woolley/Jon Voda. [CD CDRom]

4MC Ltd Film House, 142 Wardour Street, London W1F 8DD **t** 020 7878 0000 **f** 020 7878 7870 **e** info@4mc.co.uk **w** 4mc.co.uk Head of Sales & Mktg: Sally Hart-Ives. [DAT VC CDRom]

A2Z Music Services c/o Key Production, 8 Jeffrey's Place, London NW1 9PP **t** 020 7284 8800 **f** 020 7284 8811 **e** mail@keyproduction.co.uk **w** keyproduction.co.uk Sales & Marketing: Melodie Greenwell. [V CD MC DAT VC DCC MD CDRom]

***Accurate Disc Duplication** Queniborough Industrial Estate, Melton Road, Queniborough, Leicestershire LE7 8FP **t** 0870 774 1112 **f** 0870 774 1113 **e** info@accuratedisc.com **w** accuratedisc.com [CD MC DAT CDRom]

ACS Media Ltd 37 Bartholomew St, Newbury, Berkshire RG14 5LL **t** 01635 552237 or 01635 580448 **f** 01635 34179 **e** sales@acsmedia.co.uk **w** acsmedia.co.uk MD: Wilber Craik. [V CD MC DAT VC DCC MD CDRom]

ADS (Audio Duplication Services) 54, Woodview Estate, Castlebridge, Wexford, Ireland. **t** +353 53 59370 **f** +353 53 59371 **e** sales@duplication.ie **w** duplication.ie Sales Manager: Tom Byrne. [V CD MC]

AGR Manufacturing Ltd Suite 5, Melville House, High Street, Great Dunmow, Essex CM6 1AF **t** 01371 859 393 **f** 01371 859 375 **e** info@agrm.co.uk **w** agrm.co.uk Production Director: Ed Jones. [V CD MC CDRom]

Alfasound Duplication Old School House, 1 Green Lane, Ashton On Mersey, Sale, Cheshire M33 5PN **t** 0161 905 1361 **f** 0161 282 1360 **e** garry.adl@btinternet.com MD: Garry Bowen. **[CD MC DAT MD CDRom]**

All That Duplication 59 Sutherland Place, London W2 5BY **t** 020 7229 1779 **e** info@allthat.co.uk **w** allthat.co.uk Mgr: Darren Tai.

AND Press (Manufacturing Agents) Westfield Cottage, Scragged Oak Rd, Maidstone, Kent ME14 3HA **t** 01622 632 634 **f** 01622 632 634 **e** info@andpress.co.uk **w** andpress.co.uk MD: Andy Rutherford. [V CD]

Armco Units 1 & 2, Forest Ind Park, Forest Road, Hainault, Essex IG6 3HL **t** 020 8500 1981 **f** 020 8501 1319 **e** armco@globalnet.co.uk **w** armco.co.uk MD: Jan Fonseca. [CD MC CDRom]

Assured Manufacturing Ltd 34 Great Queen St, Covent Garden, London WC2B 5AA **t** 0870 745 3375 **f** 0870 745 3376 **e** info@assuredmanufacturing.co.uk **w** assuredmanufacturing.co.uk Production Manager: Kat Smith. Artwork Manager: Spencer King. [V CD MC CDRom]

]Audio Services Ltd (ASL)

6 Orsman Road, London N1 5QJ **t** 020 7739 9672 **f** 020 7739 4070 or 020 7729 5948 **e** asl@audio-services.co.uk **w** audio-services.co.uk Dir: Mel Gale. **[V CD MC DAT VC DCC MD CDRom]**

Audiolab West Street Studios, 3 West Street, Buckingham, Bucks MK18 1HL **t** 01280 822814 **f** 01280 822814 **e** office@alab.co.uk **w** copysound.co.uk Duplication Manager: Nigel Neill. [CD DAT CDi CDRom]

AWL Compact Disc Company 356 Scraptoft Lane, Leicester LE5 1PB **t** 0116 241 3979 **f** 0116 243 3760 Dir: Andrew Lipinski. [V CD MC]

Bluecrest International Ltd 272 Field End Rd, Eastcote, Ruislip, Middx HA4 9NA **t** 020 8582 0230 **f** 020 8582 0232 **e** info@bluecrest.com **w** bluecrest.com [CD CDRom]

C2 Productions Ltd Cromer House, Caxton Way, Stevenage, Herts SG1 2DF **t** 01438 317333 **f** 01438 317555 **e** info@c2productions.co.uk **w** c2productions.co.uk Director: Carlos Buhagiar. [CD MC VC CDRom]

Canon Video (UK) Ltd 15 Main Drive, East Lane Business Park, Wembley, Middlesex HA9 7FF **t** 020 8385 4455 **f** 020 8385 0722 **e** email@canon-video.co.uk **w** canonvideo.co.uk Sales Dir: Mike Seaman. [CD VC]

CD and Cassette Duplication Ltd. 77 Barlow Road, Stannington, Sheffield, South Yorkshire S6 5HR **t** 0114 233 0033 **f** 0114 233 0033 MD: Ian Stead. [CD MC DAT]

CD Central Ltd 3 Grange Yard, London SE1 3AG **t** 020 7231 4805 **f** 020 7237 0633 **e** sales@riverproaudio.co.uk **w** cdcentral.ltd.co.uk Contact: Joel Monger

CD Industries Units 7-10, Sovereign Park, Coronation Road, London NW10 7QP **t** 020 8961 8898 **f** 020 8961 8688 Production: Ms ME Tan. [CD MC VC CDRom]

CDA Disc Ltd Abbey House, 450 Bath Rd, Longford, Heathrow UB7 0EB **t** 020 8757 8966 **f** 020 8757 8972 **e** sales@cdadisc.com **w** cdadisc.com Sales Manager: Ian Mackay. Large independent manufacturer of all CD formats,DVD & CD-R. [CD CDRom]

CLEAR SOUND AND VISION LTD

Clarendon House, 117 George Lane, London E18 1AN **t** 020 8989 8777 **f** 020 8989 9777 **e** info@c-s-v.co.uk **w** c-s-v.co.uk MD: Clive Robins. Sales Manager: Danny Sperling. **[V CD MC VC MD CDRom]**

Chameleon Developments Ltd 71 Rampton Drift, Longstanton, Cambridge CB4 5EW **t** 0845 456 2144 **f** 01223 528449 **e** chameleon-d@btconnect.com **w** chameleon-developments.com MD: Tash Cox. [CD MC]

Cine Wessex Westway House, St Thomas Street, Winchester, Hampshire SO23 9HJ **t** 01962 865454 **f** 01962 842017 **e** info@cinewessex.co.uk **w** cinewessex.co.uk Duplication Manager: Ema Branton. [VC]

Cinram Europe 3, Shortlands, Hammersmith, London W6 8RX **t** 020 8735 9494 **f** 020 8735 9499 **e** uk.sales@cinram.com **w** cinram.com UK Sales Director: Jonathan Beddows. [CD MC VC CDRom]

COPS

The Studio, Kent House Station Approach, Barnmead Road, Beckenham, Kent BR3 1JD **t** 020 8778 8556 **f** 020 8676 9716 **e** info@cops.co.uk **w** cops.co.uk Managing Director: Jeremy Dahdi. [V CD MC CDRom]

The Cottage Group 2 Gawsworth Road, Macclesfield, Cheshire SK11 8UE **t** 01625 420163 **f** 01625 420168 **e** info@cottagegroup.co.uk **w** cottagegroup.co.uk MD: Roger Boden. [CD MC DAT VC MD CDRom]

Cutgroove Ltd (Vinyl Pressing Agency) 101 Bashley Rd, Park Royal, London NW10 6TE **t** 020 8838 8270 **f** 020 8838 2012 **e** nikki@cutgroove.com **w** inter-groove.co.uk Manager: Nikki Howarth. [V CD]

CVB Duplication 179A Bilton Road, Perivale, Middlesex UB6 7HQ **t** 020 8991 2610 **f** 020 8997 0180 **e** sales@cvbduplication.co.uk **w** cvbduplication.co.uk Sales & Marketing: Phil Stringer. [CD MC DAT VC DCC MD CDRom]

Damont Audio 20 Blyth Road, Hayes, Middlesex UB3 1BY **t** 020 8573 5122 **f** 020 8561 0979 or 020 8813 6692 **e** sales@damontaudio.com **w** damontaudio.com Commercial Dir: Chris Seymour. [V CD MC]

Diamond Black The Old Truman Brewery, 91 Brick Lane, London E1 6QL **t** 020 7053 2179 **f** 020 7053 2179 **e** diamondblackpressings@hotmail.com Sales Manager: Kat Smith. [CD CDRom]

DELUXE GLOBAL MEDIA SERVICES BLACKBURN LTD

Philips Road, Blackburn, Lancs BB1 5RZ **t** 01254 505300 **f** 01254 505421 **w** deluxemedia.com Audio Sales: Angela Kaye. CD ROM Sales: Merrick Iszatt. [CD MC VC CDi CDRom]

Deluxe Global Media Services Ltd - Southwater Southwater Business Park, Worthing Road, Southwater, West Sussex RH13 9YT **t** 0800 6008909 **f** 01403 739601 **w** deluxemedia.com Dir of European Sales & Business Dev for Optical Replication: Sue Mackie.
VP Audio Sales: Martin Bignall. Asst Audio Sales Mngr: Andrew Isbister. VP Multimedia Sales: Roger Twynham.
SVP DVD Sales & Marketing: Paul Chesney.
DVD Sales Mngr: Dean Pearce.
VP, OEM Sales & Logistics: David Williamson.
DFS Sales Manager: Simon Papworth.
[CD MC VC CDi CDRom]

DOCDATA UK LTD

DOCdata UK

Halesfield 14, Telford, Shropshire TF7 4QR **t** 01952 680131 **f** 01952 583501 **e** uksales@docdata.co.uk **w** docdata.co.uk Sales Director: Martine Tatman. [CD MC DVD]

Downsoft Ltd Downsway House, Epsom Road, Ashtead, Surrey KT21 1LD **t** 01372 272422 **f** 01372 276122 **e** work@downsway.worldonline.co.uk **w** downsoft.co.uk Mgr: Martin Dare. [MC DAT]

Elevate 3rd Floor, 7 Holyrood Street, London SE1 2EL **t** 020 7378 4760 **f** 020 7378 4761 **e** info@elevateuk.com **w** elevateuk.com Contact: Kirstie Hadlow [V CD MC VC CDRom]

EMS Audio Ltd Director, 12 Balloo Avenue, Bangor, Co. Down BT19 7QT **t** 028 9127 4411 **f** 028 9127 4412 **e** ems@musicshop.to **w** musicshop.to William Thompson: EMS. [CD MC]

EURODISC MANUFACTURING LTD

1st Floor, Howard House, The Runway, South Ruislip, Middx HA4 6SE **t** 020 8839 0060 **f** 020 8845 6679 **e** info@euro-disc.co.uk **w** euro-disc.co.uk **[V CD DVD VCD]**

Fairview Music Cavewood Grange Farm, Common Lane, North Cave, Brough, East Yorks HU15 2PE **t** 01430 425546 **f** 01430 425547 **e** sales@fairviewstudios.co.uk **w** fairviewstudios.co.uk Graphics Manager: Dave Beauchamp. [CD MC DAT VC DCC MD CDRom]

Filterbond Ltd 19 Sadlers Way, Hertford, Hertfordshire SG14 2DZ **t** 01992 500101 **f** 01992 500101 **e** jbsrecords.filterbondltd@virgin.net MD: John B Schefel. 1/4 inch tape. [MC DAT]

FocusMove.com Units 13-15 The Maltings, Station Rd, Newport, Essex CB11 3RN **t** 01799 543 605 **f** 01799 542 542 **e** sales@focusmove.com **w** cd-rmedia.co.uk Garry Le Count: Garry Le Count. [CD CDRom]

GZ Digital Media UK PO Box 37860, London SE23 3WT **t** 020 8291 3175 **e** bibby.paul@gzcd.cz **w** gzcd.com Sales Dir: Paul Bibby. [V CD]

Heathmans 7 Heathmans Road, London SW6 4TJ **t** 020 7371 0978 **f** 020 7371 9360 **e** susana@heathmans.co.uk **w** heathmans.co.uk MD: Ronnie Garrity. [V CD MC DAT MD CDRom]

Hiltongrove Multimedia Hiltongrove Business Centre, Hatherley Mews, London E17 4QP **t** 020 8521 2424 **f** 020 8521 4343 **e** info@hiltongrove.com **w** hiltongrove.com MD: Guy Davis. [CD MC DAT CDRom]

***ICC Duplication** Unit 27, Hawthorn Road Industrial Est, Eastbourne, East Sussex BN23 6QA **t** 01323 647880 **f** 01323 643095 **e** info@iccduplication.co.uk **w** iccduplication.co.uk Operations Dir: Andy Thorpe. [CD MC VC MD CDRom]

Icon Marketing Ltd Park House, 27 South Avenue, Thorpe St Andrew, Norwich NR7 0EZ **t** 01603 708050 **f** 01603 708005 **e** Icon@dircon.co.uk **w** icon-marketing.co.uk Production Manager: Sarah Neve. [V CD MC MD CDRom]

Ideal Mastering Ltd Ground Floor Shop, 696 Holloway Rd, London N19 3NL **t** 020 7263 3346 **f** 020 7263 3396 **e** mark@elcc-ideal.co.uk **w** idealmastering.co.uk Dir: Mark Saunders. Quarter inch. [CD MC DAT MD CDRom]

Impress Music Ltd

Unit 5C, Northfield Industrial Estate, Beresford Avenue, Wembley, Middx HA0 1NW **t** 020 8795 0101 **f** 020 8795 0303 **e** info@impressmusic-uk.com **w** impressmusic-uk.com Chairman: Alastair Bloom. Sales: Ros Hyman. **[V CD DVD MC MD DAT VC VCD CDi CDRom]**

***Isis Duplicating Co** Unit 11 Shaftesbury Ind Centre, The Runnings, Cheltenham, Gloucestershire GL51 9NH **t** 01242 571818 **f** 01242 571315 **e** enquiries@isis-duplicating.com **w** isis-duplicating.com Sales Mgr: Glyn Ellis Evans. [CD MC CDRom]

***ITD Cassettes Ltd** 31 Angelvale, Buckingham Industrial Park, Buckingham, Bucks MK18 1TH **t** 01280 821177 **f** 01280 821188 **e** ITDcassets@aol.com **w** ITDcassettes.com MD: Mike McLoughlin. [CD MC CDRom]

James Yorke Ltd Unit M, 40-44 The Bramery, Alstone Lane, Cheltenham, Gloucestershire GL51 8HE **t** 01242 584222 or 07900 806197 **f** 01242 222445 **e** alanb@jamesyorke.co.uk **w** jamesyorke.co.uk National Sales Exec: Alan Buckley. MD: Ken Leeks. [CD MC]

JTS 73 Digby Road, London E9 6HX **t** 020 8985 3000 **f** 020 8986 7688 **e** sales@jts-uk.com **w** jts-uk.com Studio Mgr: Keith Jeffrey. [V CD]

KDG UK Ltd Unit 5 Triangle Business Park, Pentrebach, Merthyr Tydfil, Mid Galmorgan SF48 4TQ **t** 01685 354700 **f** 01685 354701 **e** sales@kdguk.com **w** kdg-mt.com Sales Mgr: Ian Browning. Customer Services Manager: June Purnell.

KEY PRODUCTION

8 Jeffreys Place, London NW1 9PP **t** 020 7284 8800 **f** 020 7284 8844 **e** mail@keyproduction.co.uk **w** keyproduction.co.uk Sales & Marketing: Melodie Greenwell. **[CD DVD CD-ROM Vinyl MC VHS]**

Keynote Audio Services Smoke Tree House, Tilford Rd, Farnham, Surrey GU10 2EN **t** 01252 794253 **f** 01252 792642 **e** admin@keynoteaudio.co.uk **w** keynoteaudio.co.uk MD: Tim Wheatley. [V CD MC DAT MD CDRom]

KMS 79 Fortess Road, Kentish Town, London NW5 1AG **t** 020 7482 4555 **f** 020 7482 4551 **e** kms@kudos-records.co.uk Director: Danny Ryan. [CD MC VC]

Lemon Media Ltd Kings Castle Business Park, The Drove, Bridgwater, Somerset TA6 4AG **t** 01278 434 241 **f** 01278 434 243 **e** dudley@lemonmedia.co.uk Head of Music Sales: Dudley Perrin. [V CD MC DAT VC MD CDi CDRom]

Liquid Mastering Unit 6Q, Atlas Business Centre, Oxgate Lane, London NW2 7HU **t** 020 8452 2255 **f** 020 8422 4242 **e** sales@liquidmastering.co.uk **w** liquidmastering.co.uk Director: Bob Kane. [CD VC]

Logicom Sound And Vision Portland House, 1 Portland Drive, Willen, Milton Keynes, Buckinghamshire MK15 9JW **t** 01908 663848 **f** 01908 666654 **e** grayham.amos@luk.net **w** luk.net Bus Dev Mgr: Grayham Amos. [CD MC DAT VC MD CDRom]

THE LYNIC GROUP

thelynicgroup
evolutioneveryday

645 Ajax Avenue, Slough, Berkshire SL1 4BG **t** 01753 786200 **f** 01753 786201 **e** sales@lynic.com w lynic.com CEO: Jag Gill. Sales Dir: Simon Notton. Business Development Mgr: Trevor Southam. The Lynic Group is the UK's leading independent replicator of CD, DVD and 8cm Discs with in-house Glass Mastering and automated packaging. [CD VC CDi CDRom]

MacTrak Duplicating 3/2 Inveresk Industrial Estate, Musselburgh, Edinburgh EH21 7UL **t** 0131 665 5377 **f** 0131 653 6905 **e** mactrak@ednet.co.uk **w** mactrak.co.uk Prop: MD MacGregor. [CD MC CDRom]

Magic Wand Manufacturing Littleton House, Littleton Road, Ashford, Middlesex TW15 1UU **t** 01784 253 534 **f** 01784 251 267 **e** info@magicwand.co.uk **w** magicwand.co.uk MD: Rob McCartney. [V CD MC VC CDRom]

MAP Music Ltd 46 Grafton Road, London NW5 3DU **t** 020 7916 0545 or 020 7916 0544 **f** 020 7284 4232 **e** info@mapmusic.net **w** mapmusic.net MD: Chris Townsend. Marketing Manager: Trevor Agard. [CD]

Meltones Media 3 King Edward Drive, Chessington, Surrey KT9 1DW **t** 020 8391 9406 **f** 020 8391 8924 **e** tony@meltones.com **w** meltones-media.co.uk Sales/Mkt Dir: Tony Fernandez. Suppliers: CD-R and CDs. CD/CD-Rom Replication. [CD]

Metro Broadcast Ltd 5-7 Great Chapel St, London W1F 8FF **t** 020 7434 7700 **f** 020 7434 7701 **e** info@metrobroadcast.com **w** metrobroadcast.com Business Development Dir: Paul Beale. [VC CDRom]

Modo Productions Ltd Ground Floor Studio, 11 Codrington Mews, London W11 2EH **t** 020 7243 9855 **f** 020 7243 9856 **e** mail@modo.co.uk Dir: Henry Lavelle. [V CD MC]

MPO Ireland Ltd Blanchardstown Industrial Est, Snugborough Road, Blanchardstown, Dublin 15, Ireland **t** +353 1 822 1363 **f** +353 1 806 6064 **e** swalsh@mpo.ie **w** mpo.fr Sales Director: Sharon Walsh. [V CD MC LD CDRom]

MPO UK Ltd Unit 3-4, Nucleus Central Way, Park Royal, London NW10 7XT **t** 020 8963 6888 or 07714 676 925 **f** 020 8963 8693 **e** matt@mpo.co.uk **w** MPO.co.uk Audio Sales Executive: Matt Shoults. [V CD MC VC CDRom]

Multi Media Replication Ltd Unit 4 Balksbury Estate, Upper Clatford, Andover, Hampshire SP11 7LW **t** 01264 336 330 **f** 01264 336 694 **e** info@replication.com **w** replication.com MD: Philip Hall. [CD]

Music City Ltd 122 New Cross Road, London SE14 5BA **t** 020 7277 9657 **f** 0870 7572004 **e** info@musiccity.co.uk **w** musiccity.co.uk Mgr: James Woodward. CD Burning and graphics. [CD DAT]

Music Media Manufacturers Ltd Unit F11D, 1st Floor, Parkhall Road Trading Estate, 40 Martell Road, London SE21 8EN **t** 020 8265 6364 **f** 020 8265 6423 **e** mail@musicmedia-uk.com **w** musicmedia-uk.com GM: Mike Spenser. [V CD MC DAT VC CDRom]

Music With Attitude (MWA) 20 Middle Row, Ladbroke Grove, London W10 5AT **t** 020 8964 4555 **f** 020 8964 4666 **e** morgan@musicwithattitude.com **w** musicwithattitude.com MD: Morgan Khan. [V CD MC]

Musicbase Music Pressing 2 Plato Place, 72-74 St Dionis Road, London SW6 4TU **t** 020 7384 2626 **f** 020 7384 2622 **e** Kelly@musicbase.uk.com Dir: Kelly Canueto. [V CD MC CDRom]

Noisebox Digital Media Ltd Windsor House, 74 Thorpe Rd, Norwich NR1 1BA **t** 01603 767726 **f** 01603 767746 **e** info@noisebox.co.uk **w** noisebox.co.uk MD: Pete Morgan. [CD MC VC CDRom]

Offside Management Unit A, 16-24 Brewery Road, London N7 9NH **t** 020 7700 2662 **f** 020 7700 2882 **e** info@bsimerch.com **w** bsimerch.com Sales Director: Richard Cassar. [CD MC CDRom]

Open Ear Productions Ltd. Kinarva, Co. Galway, Ireland **t** +353 91 635810 **f** +353 87 58575588 **e** info@openear.ie **w** openear.ie MD: Bruno Staehelin. [CD]

Optical Technique Pinewood, Chineham Business Park, Crockford Lane, Basingstoke, Hampshire RG24 8AL **t** 01256 698016 **f** 01256 698216 **e** ho@optical-technique.com **w** opticaltechnique.com Contact: Shaun Lugg [CD MC MD CDRom]

***Orlake Records (Vinyl Specialists)** Sterling Industrial Estate, Rainham Road South, Dagenham, Essex RM10 8HP **t** 020 8592 0242 **f** 020 8595 8182 **e** info@orlakerecords.com Production Controller: Paula Pearl. [V]

PR Records Hamilton House, Endeavour Way, London SW19 8UH **t** 01423 541020 **f** 01423 540970 **e** pr@celtic-music.co.uk Cust Liason: Ruth Bulmer. [V CD MC DAT MD CDRom]

Professional Magnetics Ltd Cassette House, 329 Hunslet Road, Leeds, West Yorkshire LS10 1NJ **t** 0113 270 6066 **f** 0113 271 8106 **e** promags@aol.com **w** promags.freeserve.co.uk Dir: Hilary Rhodes. [CD MC DAT VC DCC MD CDRom]

Reflex Media Services Ltd Unit 5, Cirrus, Glebe Road, Huntingdon, Cambridgeshire PE29 7DL **t** 01480 412222 **f** 01480 411441 **e** roger@reflex-media.co.uk Dir: Roger Masterson. Sales: John Garrad. [CD MC CDRom]

Repeat Performance RPM Unit 6, Grand Union Centre, West Row, London W10 5AS **t** 020 8960 7222 **f** 020 8968 1378 **e** info@rpmuk.com **w** rpmuk.com MD: Robin Springall. [CD MC DAT DCC CDRom]

Replica North Works, Hookstone Park, Harrogate, North Yorkshire HG2 7DB **t** 01423 888979 or 01423 541020 **f** 01423 540970 **e** replica@northworks.co.uk Dir: David Bulmer. [V MC CDRom]

RMS Studios 43-45 Clifton Road, London SE25 6PX **t** 020 8653 4965 **f** 020 8653 4965 **e** studiosrms@aol.com **w** rms-studios.co.uk Duplicating Mgr: Alan Jones. [CD MC DAT MD]

***RTS Onestop** Unit M2, Albany Road, Prescot, Merseyside L34 2UP **t** 0151 430 9001 **f** 0151 430 7441 **e** rts.onestop@virgin.net MD: John Fairclough. [V CD MC DAT VC MD CDRom]

***SDC GB Ltd** Fairview Business Cent., 29-31 Clayton Rd, Hayes, Middx UB3 1AN **t** 020 8581 9200 **f** 020 8581 9249 **e** sales@sdcuk.com **w** sdc-group.com Sales Mgr: Colin Rye. Sales Audio: Lisa Dickson, Daragh McDonogh. [CD MC DAT VC CDi CDRom]

SKM Europe SKM House, Springfield Rd, Hayes, Middx UB4 0TY **t** 020 8573 0909 **f** 020 8573 9990 **e** anita@skmeurope.co.uk **w** skmeurope.co.uk Sales Dir: Steve Castle. Magnetic media. [MC]

SONOPRESS (UK)

Wednesbury One, Black Country New Road, Wednesbury, West Midlands WS10 7NY
t 0121 502 7800 **f** 0121 502 7811
e sales@sonopress.co.uk **w** sonopress.co.uk
Sales Dir - Music: Anthony Daly. MD: John Shervey.
[V CD MC DAT CDRom]

Sound & Video Services (UK) Shentonfield Road, Sharston Industrial Estate, Manchester M22 4RW **t** 0161 491 6660 **f** 0161 491 6669 **e** sales@svsmedia.com **w** svsmedia.com MD: Mike Glasspole. [CD MC DAT MD]

Sound Discs Ltd. 5 Barley Shotts Business Park, 246 Acklam Road, (off St Ervans Rd), London W10 5YG **t** 020 8968 7080 or 07721 624 868 **f** 020 8968 7475 **e** sound.discs@virgin.net **w** sound-discs.co.uk Production Director: Peter Bullick. [V CD MC DAT MD CDRom]

SOUND PERFORMANCE

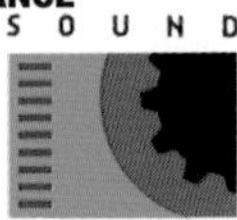

Unit 3, Greenwich Quay, Clarence Road, London, SE8 3EY
t 020 8691 2121 **f** 020 8691 3144
e sales@soundperformance.co.uk
w soundperformance.co.uk Contact: Sales
[CD, CD-Rom, Vinyl, DVD, Cassette, & Video manufacturing and all associated packaging]
Dedicated customer service, excellent quality and competitive rates.

Sound Recording Technology Audio House, Edison Road, St Ives, Cambridge PE27 3LF **t** 01480 461880 **f** 01480 496100 **e** srt@btinternet.com **w** soundrecordingtechnology.co.uk Dirs: Sarah Pownall, Karen Kenney. [CD MC DAT DCC MD CDRom]

SOUNDS GOOD LTD

- cd manufacturing
- dvd manufacturing
- audio/video cassette duplication

www.sounds-good.co.uk

12 Chiltern Enterprise Centre, Station Road, Theale, Berks RG7 4AA **t** 0118 930 1700 **f** 0118 930 1709 **e** sales-info@sounds-good.co.uk **w** sounds-good.co.uk Dir: Martin Maynard.
CD & DVD Pressing and express Duplication services. Also Cassette Duplication, DVD Authoring, CD Mastering, plus Design, Print & Packaging. [CD MC DVD VC CDRom]

Sponge Multimedia Ltd Sponge Studios, Cross Chancellor Street, Leeds, West Yorkshire LS6 2TG **t** 0113 234 0004 **f** 0113 242 4296 **e** damian@spongestudios.demon.co.uk **w** spongestudios.demon.co.uk Director: Damian McLean-Brown. [V CD MC VC DCC CDRom]

Spool Multi Media (UK) Unit 30, Deeside Industrial Park, Deeside, Flintshire CH5 2NU **t** 01244 280602 **f** 01244 288581 **e** admin@smmuk.co.uk **w** smmuk.co.uk MD: Roy Varley. [CD MC DAT CDRom]

Tapemaster (Europe) Ltd King George's Place, 764 Eastern Avenue, Newbury Park, Ilford, Essex IG2 7HU **t** 020 8518 4202 **f** 020 8518 4203 **e** tapemaster@msn.com **w** tapemaster.co.uk MD: Laji Lalli. [CD MC VC CDRom]

TC Video Wembley Commercial Centre, East Lane, Wembley, Middx HA9 7UU **t** 020 8904 6271 **f** 020 8904 0172 **e** info@tcvideo.co.uk **w** tcvideo.co.uk Marketing Manager: Lissandra Xavier. [CD VC CDRom]

TECHNICOLOR Llantarnam Park, Cwmbran, Gwent NP44 3AB **t** 01633 465259 **f** 01633 867799 **e** technicolor.europe@thomson.net **w** technicolor.com Dir, Optical Disc: Emil Dudek. [CD VC CDRom]

Telecine Ltd Video House, 48 Charlotte St, London W1T 2NS **t** 020 7208 2200 **f** 020 7208 2252 **e** shortform@telecine.co.uk **w** telecine.co.uk Head of Shortform: Claire Booth. [VC]

Thames Valley Video 660 Ajax Avenue, Slough, Berkshire SL1 4BG **t** 01753 553131 **f** 01753 554505 **e** tvv@netcomuk.co.uk MD: Nigel Morris. [VC]

Touchstone Productions TPL House, Beccles Business Park, Copland Way, Suffolk NR34 7TL **t** 01502 716056 **f** 01502 717124 **w** tpl.com Dir: Marc Barnes. [DAT VC]

Transition Mastering Studios Kemble House, Kemble Rd, London SE23 2DJ **t** 020 8699 7888 **f** 020 8699 9441 **e** info@transition-studios.co.uk **w** transition-studios.co.uk Manager: Jason Goz. [V CD]

Trend Studios A2 Canal Bank, Park West Industrial Park, Dublin 12, Ireland **t** +353 1 6160 600 **f** +353 1 6160 601 **e** muswk@trendstudios.com **w** trendstudios.com Tech Dir: Paul Waldron. [CD MC DAT CDi CDRom]

TRIBAL MANUFACTURING

11 Hillgate Place, Balham Hill, London SW12 9ER **t** 020 8673 0610 **f** 020 8675 8562 **e** sales@tribal.co.uk **w** tribal.co.uk Directors: Alison Wilson, Terry Woolner. **[V CD CDRom DVD point of sale, special packaging, repro and print]**

TSF Limited 3B Athena Avenue, Elgin Industrial Estate, Swindon, Wiltshire SN2 8HF **t** 01793 421300 **f** 01793 428724 **e** sales@tsfltd.co.uk **w** tsfltd.co.uk MD: Iain Morrison. [CD CDRom]

Vanderquest 7 Latimer Road, Teddington, Middlesex TW11 8QA **t** 020 8977 1743 **f** 020 8943 2818 **e** nick@vanderquest.co.uk MD: Nick Maingay. [VC]

***VDC Group** VDC House, South Way, Wembley, Middlesex HA9 0HB **t** 020 8903 3345 **f** 020 8900 1427 **e** enquiries@vdcgroup.com **w** vdcgroup.com Sales Executive: Aaron Williamson. [CD VC CDRom]

Vinyl Factory Productions (One Stop Service) The Basement Studios, 45 Fouberts Place, London W1F 7QH **t** 020 8526 8070 **e** paula@vinlyfactory.co.uk **w** vinylfactory.co.uk Contact: Paula Pearl.

Vinyl Pressing 308 High Street, London E15 1AJ **t** 020 8519 4260 **f** 020 8519 5187 MD: Terence Murphy. [V CD MC CDi]

Warner Music Manufacturing Europe 77 Oxford Street, London W1D 2ES **t** 020 7659 2530 **f** 020 7659 2100 **e** sam.menezes@warnermusic.com **w** wmme.co.uk UK Sales & Marketing Mgr: Sam Menezes. [CD CDRom]

Warren Recordings 59 Hendale Avenue, London NW4 4LP **t** 020 8203 0306 **f** 020 8203 0306 **e** stanley@warrenworld.fsnet.co.uk Dir: Stanley Warren. [V CD MC DAT VC]

Wyastone Estate Limited Wyastone Leys, Monmouth NP25 3SR **t** 01600 890 007 **f** 01600 891 052 **e** sales@wyastone.co.uk **w** wyastone.co.uk Business Dir: Antony Smith. [CD]

Mastering & Post Production

10th Planet 40 Newman St, London W1T 1QJ **t** 020 7637 9500 **f** 020 7637 9599 **e** studio@10thplanet.net **w** 10thplanet.net Director: Jonathan Moore. [CD CDRom]

360 Mastering Ltd 18A Farm Lane Trading Centre, 101 Farm Lane, London SW6 1QJ **t** 020 7385 6161 **f** 020 7386 0473 **e** studio@360mastering.co.uk **w** 360mastering.co.uk MD: Dick Beetham. Other format: SACD. [V CD MC DAT MD]

400 Company B3, The Workshops, 2A, Askew Crescent, London W12 9DP **t** 020 8746 1400 **f** 020 8746 0847 **e** info@the400.co.uk **w** the400.co.uk Marketing Mgr: Christian Riou.

AGR Manufacturing Suite 5, Melville House, High Street, Great Dunmow, Essex CM6 1AF **t** 01371 859 393 **f** 01371 859 375 **e** info@agrm.co.uk **w** agrm.co.uk Production Director: Ed Jones. [V CD MC DAT VC DCC MD CDRom]

Alchemy SoHo 29th Floor, Centre Point, 103 New Oxford Street, London WC1A 1DD **t** 020 7420 8000 **f** 020 7420 8001 **e** info@alchemysoho.com **w** alchemysoho.com Vinyl & CD Bookings: Emily Byrne. Voice studio bookings: Patricia Slade-Baker. CD, Dat & Cassette duplication: Phil Kinrade. [V CD MC DAT MD CDRom]

All That Music 59 Sutherland Place, London W2 5BY **t** 020 7229 1779 **e** info@allthat.co.uk **w** allthat.co.uk MGR: Darren Tai.

Assured Manufacturing Ltd 34 Great Queen St, Covent Garden, London WC2B 5AA **t** 0870 745 3375 **f** 0870 745 3376 **e** info@assuredmanufacturing.co.uk **w** assuredmanufacturing.co.uk Production Manager: Kat Smith. [V CD MC CDRom]

ADS (Audio Duplication Services) 54, Woodview Estate, Castlebridge, Wexford, Ireland. **t** +353 53 59370 **f** +353 53 59371 **e** sales@duplication.ie **w** duplication.ie Director: Tom Byrne. Technical Manager: Colin Turner. [V CD MC DAT CDRom]

Audio Edit Productions (AEP) Littleton House, Littleton Road, Ashford, Middlesex TW15 1UU **t** 01784 421996 **f** 01784 247542 **e** clive@audioedit.co.uk **w** audioedit.co.uk MD: Phil Kerby. [CD MC DAT MD CDRom]

Audio Services Ltd (ASL) 6 Orsman Rd, London N1 5QJ **t** 020 7739 9672 **f** 020 7739 4070 or 020 7729 5948 **e** asl@audio-services.co.uk **w** audio-services.co.uk Dir: Mel Gale. [V CD MC DAT VC DCC MD CDRom]

B&H Sound Services Ltd The Old School Studio, Crowland Road, Eye, Peterborough PE6 7TN **t** 01733 223535 **f** 01733 223545 **e** sound@bhsound.co.uk **w** bhsound.co.uk Recording Manager: Nicola Seager.

Boomtown (ProTools) Studio Valetta Road, London W3 7TG **t** 020 8723 9548 or 07961 405 140 **e** info@boomtownstudio.co.uk **w** boomtownstudio.co.uk Contact: Simon Wilkinson

The Classical Recording Company Ltd. 16-17 Wolsey Mews, Kentish Town, London NW5 2DX **t** 020 7482 2303 **f** 020 7482 2302 **e** info@classicalrecording.com **w** classicalrecording.com Senior Producer: Simon Weir. [V CD MC VC]

Close To The Edge 2 The Embankment, Twickenham, Middlesex TW1 3DU **t** 01225 311661 **f** 01225 482013 **e** info@positivebiz.com **w** positivebiz.com Mgr: Carole Davies. Mastering Engineer: Jon Astley. [CD MC DAT]

CopyMaster International Ltd 8 Arundel Road, Uxbridge Trading Estate, Uxbridge, Middlesex UB8 2RR **t** 01895 814813 **f** 01895 814999 **e** info@copymaster.co.uk **w** copymaster.co.uk Sales Mgr: Rachelle Peterson. [CDRom]

Cottage Media Mastering 2 Gawsworth Road, Macclesfield, Cheshire SK11 8UE **t** 01625 420163 **f** 01625 420168 **e** cmm@cottagegroup.co.uk **w** cottagegroup.co.uk MD: Roger Boden. [CD MC DAT VC MD CDRom]

Cut and Groove Prospect Farm, Main Rd, Bosham, Chichester, W. Sussex PO18 8PN **t** 01243 572381 **f** 01243 575861 **e** info@cutandgroove.com **w** cutandgroove.com Dirs: Duncan Davis, Adam Twine. [V CD]

Deluxe Global Media Services Ltd - Southwater Southwater Business Park, Worthing Road, Southwater, West Sussex RH13 9YT **t** 01403 739600 **f** 01403 739601 **e** sales@disctronics.co.uk **w** disctronics.co.uk; bydeluxe.com Gen Mgr, European Sales: Sue Mackie. [CD MC CDi CDRom]

Diamond Black Pressings 91 Brick Lane, London E1 6QL **t** 020 7053 2179 **f** 010 7053 2179 **e** diamond-blackpressings@hotmail.com Sales Manager: Katrina Smith.

Diverse Media PO Box 3, South Croydon, Surrey CR2 0YW **t** 0870 765 4343 **f** 0870 765 4344 **e** sales@diversemedia.com **w** audiomastering.co.uk; audiorestoration.co.uk MD: A Jacobs. [CD]

Edit Videos 2A Conway Street, London W1T 6BA **t** 020 7637 2288 **f** 020 7637 2299 **e** mail@editvideo.co.uk **w** editvideo.co.uk MD/Editor: Henry Stein. [VC]

***The Exchange** 42 Bruges Place, Randolph Street, London NW1 0TX **t** 020 7485 0530 **f** 020 7482 4588 **e** studio@exchangemastering.co.uk MD: Graeme Durham. [V CD MC DAT MD]

Figment DVD 341-345 Old St, London EC1V 9LL **t** 020 7729 1969 **f** 020 7739 1969 **e** mail@figment-media.com **w** figment-media.com MD: Andrew Huffer.

***Finesplice Ltd** 1 Summerhouse Lane, Harmondsworth, West Drayton, Middlesex UB7 0AT **t** 020 8564 7839 **f** 020 8759 9629 **e** info@finesplice.co.uk **w** finesplice.co.uk MD: Ben Turner. [CD DAT MD CDRom]

Firebird Suite 11 Osram Road, East Lane Business Park, Wembley, Middx HA9 7NG **t** 020 8904 4422 **f** 020 8904 3777 **e** info@thefirebirdsuite.com **w** thefirebirdsuite.com

Flare DVD Ingestre Court, Ingestre Place, London W1F 0JL **t** 020 7343 6565 **f** 020 7343 6555 **e** katy@flare-dvd.com **w** flare-dvd.com Manager: Katy Deegan.

Floating Earth Unit 14, 21 Wadsworth Rd, Perivale, Middx UB6 7JD **t** 020 8997 4000 **f** 020 8998 5767 **e** record@floatingearth.com **w** floatingearth.com Director: Steve Long. [CD DAT]

Flying Ace Productions Walders, Oldbury Lane, Ightham, Sevenoaks TN15 9DD **t** 01732 887056 or 07778 165931 **f** 01732 887056 **e** reiddick@netmatters.co.uk Dir: Will Reid Dick. [CD MC DAT MD CDRom]

Freehand Limited Dunsfold Park, Cranleigh, Surrey GU6 8TB **t** 01483 200111 **f** 01483 200101 **e** phil.kerby@freehand.co.uk **w** freehand.co.uk Contact: Phil Kerby

Glasseye Rose Cottage, The Aberdeen Centre, 22-24 Highbury Grove, London N5 2EA **t** 020 7354 8808 **f** 020 7354 8808 **e** info@glasseyeltd.com **w** glasseyeltd.com Director: Alastair Mills. [CD CDRom]

Hear No Evil 6 Lillie Yard, London SW6 1UB **t** 020 7385 8244 **f** 020 7385 0700 **e** info@hearnoevil.net **w** hearnoevil.net Dir: Steve Parr. [CD MC DAT]

Heathmans Mastering Ltd 7 Heathmans Road, London SW6 4TJ **t** 020 7371 0978 **f** 020 7371 9360 **e** susana@heathmans.co.uk **w** heathmans.co.uk MD: Ronnie Garrity. Exabyte, 1630. [V CD MC DAT MD]

Hiltongrove Multimedia Hiltongrove Business Centre, Hatherley Mews, London E17 4QP **t** 020 8521 2424 **f** 020 8521 4343 **e** info@hiltongrove.com **w** hiltongrove.com MD: Guy Davis. [CD MC DAT CDRom]

Ideal Mastering Ground Floor Shop, 696 Holloway Rd, London N19 3NL **t** 020 7263 3346 **f** 020 7263 3396 **e** mark@elcc-ideal.co.uk **w** idealmastering.co.uk Director: Mark Saunders. [V CD DAT]

International Broadcast Facilities 12 Neal's Yard, London WC2H 9DP **t** 020 7497 1515 **f** 020 7379 8562 **e** ibf.admin@ibf.co.uk **w** ibf.co.uk Facilities Dir: David Lale. [DAT VC]

Intimate Recording Studios The Smokehouse, 120 Pennington St, London E1 9BB **t** 020 7702 0789 **f** 020 7813 2766 **e** p.madden1@ntlworld.com **w** intimatestudios.com Contact: Paul Madden, Gerry Bron [V CD MC]

JRP Music Services Empire House, Hereford Rd, Southsea, Hants PO5 2DH **t** 023 9229 7839 **e** James.Perrett@soc.soton.ac.uk **w** jrpmusic.fsnet.co.uk Senior Engineer: James Perrett. [V CD]

JTS 73 Digby Road, London E9 6HX **t** 020 8985 3000 **f** 020 8986 7688 **e** sales@jts-uk.com **w** jts-uk.com Studio Mgr: Keith Jeffrey. [V CD]

Keynote Audio Services Ltd. Smoke Tree House, Tilford Rd, Farnham, Surrey GU10 2EN **t** 01252 794253 **f** 01252 792642 **e** admin@keynoteaudio.co.uk **w** keynoteaudio.co.uk MD: Tim Wheatley. [V CD MC DAT MD CDRom]

La Rocka Studios Post Mark House, Cross Lane, Hornsey, London N8 7SA **t** 020 8348 2822 **e** info@larockastudios.co.uk **w** larockastudios.co.uk Director: Pete Chapman. [CD]

***Lansdowne Studios** Lansdowne House, Lansdowne Road, London W11 3LP **t** 020 7727 0041 **f** 020 7792 8904 **e** bookings@cts-lansdowne.co.uk **w** cts-lansdowne.co.uk Bookings Mgr: Sharon Rose. [CD MC DAT MD]

Liquid Mastering Unit 6Q, Atlas Business Centre, Oxgate Lane, London NW2 7HU **t** 020 8452 2255 **f** 020 8422 4242 **e** sales@liquidmastering.co.uk **w** liquidmastering.co.uk Director: Bob Kane. [V CD VC]

Locomotion 1-8 Bateman's Building, Soho Square, London W1D 3EN **t** 020 7304 4403 **f** 020 7304 4400 **e** info@locomotion.co.uk **w** locomotion.co.uk [VC]

Loud Mastering & Loud Independent 2-3 Windsor Place, Whitehall, Taunton, Somerset TA1 1PG **t** 01823 353123 **f** 01823 353055 **e** info@loudmastering.com **w** loudmastering.com Proprietor: John Dent. Bookings Mgr: Jason Mitchell. [V CD]

The Lynic Group 645 Ajax Avenue, Slough, Berks SL1 4BG **t** 01753 786 200 **f** 01753 786 201 **e** sales@lynic.com **w** lynic.com VP Business Development: Trevor Southam. CEO: Jag Gill. VP Sales: Simon Notton. VP Operations: Louise Holder. [CD CDi CDRom]

The Machine Room 54-58 Wardour Street, London W1D 4JQ **t** 020 7734 3433 **f** 020 7287 3773 **e** paul.willey@themachineroom.co.uk **w** themachineroom.co.uk Contact: Paul Willey [VC]

Mad Hat Studios The Upper Hattons Media Centre, The Upper Hattons, Pendeford Hall Lane, Coven, Nr Wolverhampton WV9 5BD **t** 01902 840440 **f** 01902 840448 **e** studio@madhat.co.uk **w** madhat.co.uk Dir: Claire Swan.

Masterpiece Media Unit 14 The Talina Centre, Bagleys Lane, London SW6 2BW **t** 020 7731 5758 Audio or **020 7371 0700 Video f** 020 7384 1750 **e** info@masterpiecelondon.com **w** masterpiecelondon.com Studio Manager: Toni Wagner. [CD MC DAT VC DCC MD CDRom]

Mediadisc Unit 4C, Farm Lane Trading Centre, 101 Farm Lane, Fulham, London SW6 1QJ **t** 020 7385 2299 **f** 020 7385 4888 **e** studio@mediadisc.co.uk **w** mediadisc.co.uk MD: Simon Payne.

Metropolis DVD The Power House, 70 Chiswick High Road, London W4 1SY **t** 020 8742 1111 **f** 020 8742 2626 **e** reception@metropolis-group.co.uk **w** metropolis-group.co.uk Producer: Alex Sanders.

Metropolis Mastering The Power House, 70 Chiswick High Road, London W4 1SY **t** 020 8742 1111 **f** 020 8742 2626 **e** reception@metropolis-group.co.uk **w** metropolis-group.co.uk Mastering Bookings: Beta Ratel/Michelle Conroy. [V CD MC DAT MD CDRom]

***Molinare** 34 Fouberts Place, London W1F 7PX **t** 020 7478 7000 **f** 020 7478 7299 **e** bookings@molinare.co.uk **w** molinare.co.uk DigiBeta, Beta SP, U-matic, Mini DV. [CD MC DAT VC CDRom]

***M2 Facilities Group (TV Post Production only)** The Forum, 74-80 Camden Street, London NW1 0EG **t** 020 7387 5001 **f** 020 7343 6777 **e** info@m2tv.com **w** m2tv.com Mgr: Simon Partington.

Optimum Mastering Unit 5.4, Central Trading Estate, Bath Rd, Bristol BS4 3EH **t** 0117 971 6901 **f** 0117 971 0700 **e** info@optimum-mastering.com **w** optimum-mastering.com Engineers: Shawn Joseph, Matt Colton. [V CD]

The Pavement 4a Burbage House, 83 Curtain Road, London EC2A 3BS **t** 020 7749 4300 **f** 020 7749 4301 **e** info@the-pavement.com **w** the-pavement.com Sales: Guy Goodger.

The Picture House (Edit Suites) Ltd The Strand, 156 Holywood Rd, Belfast, Co Antrim BT4 1NY **t** 028 9065 1111 **f** 028 9067 3771 **e** stephen@thepicturehouse.tv **w** thepicturehouse.tv Studio Manager: Stephen Petticrew. [VC]

***Porky's Mastering** 55-59 Shaftesbury Avenue, London W1D 6LD **t** 020 7494 3131 **f** 020 7494 1669 **e** george@porkysprimecuts.com **w** porkysprimecuts.com Studio Mgr: George Peckham. [V CD DAT MD CDRom]

P3 Post 40-42 Lexington Street, London W1F 0LN **t** 020 7287 3006 **f** 020 7439 3110 **e** edit@p3post.co.uk **w** p3post.co.uk Facilities Director: Martin Price. [CD MC DAT VC DCC MD CDRom]

Red Facilities 61 Timberbush, Leith, Edinburgh EH6 6QH **t** 0131 555 2288 **f** 0131 555 0088 **e** doit@redfacilities.com **w** redfacilities.com Partner: Max Howarth.

Red Light Mastering 27 Lexington St, London W1F 9AQ **t** 020 7287 7373 or 07796 958 115 **e** craig@red-light.co.uk **w** red-light.co.uk Contact: Craig Dormer [CD MC DAT VC MD CDRom]

Redwood Studios 20 Great Chapel St, London W1F 8FW **t** 020 7287 3799 **f** 020 7287 3751 **e** andrestudios@yahoo.co.uk **w** redwoodstudios.co.uk MD/Prod: Andre Jacquemin. [CD MC DAT]

Reflex Media Services Ltd Unit 5, Cirrus, Glebe Road, Huntingdon PE29 7DL **t** 01480 412222 **f** 01480 411441 **e** roger@reflex-media.co.uk Dir: Roger Masterson. Sales: John Garrad. [CD MC CDRom]

Repeat Performance RPM 6 Grand Union Centre, West Row, London W10 5AS **t** 020 8960 7222 **f** 020 8968 1378 **e** info@rpmuk.com **w** rpmuk.com MD: Robin Springall. [CD MC DAT DCC MD CDRom]

Revolution Digital 33 St James's Square, London SW1Y 4JS **t** 020 7661 9303 **f** 020 7661 9413 **e** laura@rdigital.co.uk **w** rdigital.co.uk MD: Laura Gate-Eastley.

Reynolds Mastering 55 Albert Street, Colchester, Essex CO1 1RX **t** 01206 562655 **f** 01206 761936 **e** reynolds.mastering@virgin.net MD: Peter Reynolds. Umatic, shellac, acetate. [V CD MC DAT MD]

RTSOnestop Ltd Unit M2, Albany Road, Prescot, Merseyside L34 2UP **t** 0151 430 9001 **f** 0151 430 7441 **e** rts.onestop@virgin.net MD: John Fairclough. [CD MC DAT DCC MD CDRom]

Sanctuary Archiving 3a Oakwood Trading Park, Standard Rd, London NW10 6EX **t** 020 8963 0362 **f** 020 8963 9137 **e** tim.hunt@sanctuarygroup.com **w** sanctuarystudios.co.uk Head Engineer - Archiving: Tim Hunt.

Sanctuary Post 53 Frith St, London W1D 4SN **t** 020 7734 4480 **f** 020 7439 7394 **e** jason.elliott@sanctuary-group.com **w** sanctuarystudios.co.uk Sales & Marketing Mgr: Jason Elliott. [VC]

Sanctuary Town House Mastering Sanctuary Town House, 140 Goldhawk Road, London W12 8HH **t** 020 8932 3200 **f** 020 8932 3209 **e** mastering@sanctuarystudios.co.uk **w** sanctuarystudios.co.uk Mastering Mgr: Sophie Nathan. [V CD MC DAT DCC MD CDRom]

Saunders & Gordon 30 Gresse Street, London W1T 1QR **t** 020 7580 7316 **f** 020 7637 5085 **e** info@sgss.co.uk **w** sgss.co.uk Facilities Dir: Tim Lofts. [V CD MC DAT VC DCC MD CDRom]

Sonic Arts 85 Barlby Road, London W10 6BN **t** 020 8962 3000 **f** 020 8962 6200 **e** avi@sonic-arts.com **w** sonic-arts.com [V CD MC DAT MD CDRom]

Sound Discs CD Mastering & Manufacturing Ltd 5 Barley Shotts Business Park, 246 Acklam Road, London W10 5YG **t** 020 8968 7080 or 07721 624 868 **f** 020 8968 7475 **e** info@sound-discs.co.uk **w** sound-discs.co.uk Production Director: Peter Bullick. [CD MC DAT VC MD CDRom]

Sound Generation Unit 3, Clarence Road, Greenwich, London SE8 3EY **t** 020 8691 2121 **f** 020 8691 3144 **e** at@soundperformance.co.uk **w** soundperformance.co.uk Studio Mgr: Andrew Thompson. [CD MC]

***SOUNDS GOOD LTD**

○ cd manufacturing
○ dvd manufacturing
○ audio/video cassette duplication
www.sounds-good.co.uk

12 Chiltern Enterprise Centre, Station Road, Theale, Reading, Berks RG7 4AA **t** 0118 930 1700 **f** 0118 930 1709 **e** sales-info@sounds-good.co.uk **w** sounds-good.co.uk Dir: Martin Maynard. **Expert Mastering in SADiE studio with flat, time-aligned ATC monitoring. Professional DVD Authoring & MPEG Compression. "Director" & "Flash" Multimedia Programming [CD MC DVD VC CD Rom]**

Sound Mastering 48-50 Steele Road, London NW10 7AS **t** 020 8961 1741 **f** 020 8838 2824 **e** info@soundmastering.com **w** soundmastering.com MD: Duncan Cowell. [V CD MC DAT]

Sound Performance Unit 3, Clarence Road, Greenwich, London SE8 3EY **t** 020 8691 2121 **f** 020 8691 3144 **e** sales@soundperformance.co.uk **w** soundperformance.co.uk Contact: Sales [V CD MC VC CDRom]

***Sound Recording Technology** Audio House, Edison Road, St Ives, Cambridge, Cambridgeshire PE27 3LF **t** 01480 461880 **f** 01480 496100 **e** srt@btinternet.com **w** soundrecordingtechnology.co.uk Dirs: Sarah Pownall, Karen Kenney. [CD MC DAT DCC MD CDRom]

Design, Pressing & Distribution

The Soundmasters International Ltd The New Boathouse, 136-142 Bramley Road, London W10 6SR **t** 020 7565 3020 **f** 020 7565 3021 **e** jane@soundmasters.co.uk **w** soundmasters.co.uk Post Prodn Coordinator: Jane Long. [V CD MC DAT]

***Sounds Good Ltd** 12 Chiltern Enterprise Centre, Station Rd, Theale, Reading, Berks RG7 4AA **t** 0118 930 1700 **f** 0118 930 1709 **e** sales-info@sounds-good.co.uk **w** sounds-good.co.uk Dir: Martin Maynard. [CD MC DAT VC CDRom]

Stream Digital Media Ltd 61 Charlotte St, London W1P 1LA **t** 020 7208 1567 **f** 020 7208 1555 **e** info@streamdm.co.uk w streamdm.co.uk Head of Stream: Paul Kind. [VC]

SUPER AUDIO MASTERING

Monks Withecombe, Chagford, Devon TQ13 8JY **t** 01647 432858 or 07721 613145 **f** 01647 432308 **e** info@superaudiomastering.com **w** superaudiomastering.com MD: Simon Heyworth. **Stereo & Surround Mastering-All Formats-All Sample Rates including DSD. Authoring for SACD. Wonderful Devon Location** [CD CDi CDRom DVD]

SVC 142 Wardour Street, London W1F 8ZU **t** 020 7734 1600 **f** 020 7437 1854 **e** post@svc.co.uk **w** svc.co.uk Facilities Mgr: Jon Murray. 1/4 inch. [CD MC DAT VC CDRom]

Tangerine Dreams Riverside Studios, Crisp Road, Hammersmith, London W6 9RL **t** 0800 085 6732 or 01189 89 2306 **f** 020 8237 1220 **e** prodvd@tangerine-dreams.co.uk **w** tangerinedreams.co.uk [CD CDRom]

The Tape Gallery 28 Lexington Street, London W1F 0LF **t** 020 7439 3325 **f** 020 7734 9417 **e** info@tape-gallery.co.uk **w** tape-gallery.co.uk Studio Mgrs: David Croft & Tara Simpson.

Town House Post Production (see Sanctuary Town House)

Transfermation Ltd 63 Lant Street, London SE1 1QN **t** 020 7417 7021 **f** 020 7378 0516 **e** trace@transfermation.com **w** transfermation.com Co-ordinator: Tracey Roper. Umatic. [V CD MC DAT MD]

Transition Mastering Kemble House, Kemble Road, London SE23 2DJ **t** 020 8699 7888 **f** 020 8699 9441 **e** info@transition-studios.co.uk **w** transition-studios.com Mastering Eng: Jason Goz. 1/4 inch tape. [V CD MC DAT]

Trend A2 Canal Bank, Park West Industrial Park, Dublin 12, Ireland **t** +353 1 6060 600 **f** +353 1 6160 601 **e** muswk@trendstudios.com **w** trendstudios.com Tech Dir: Paul Waldron. [CD MC DAT MD]

VDC Group VDC House, South Way, Wembley, Middx HA9 0HB **t** 020 8903 3345 **f** 020 8900 1427 **e** enquiries@vdcgroup.com **w** vdcgroup.com Sales Executive: Aaron Williamson. [CD VC CDRom]

***Videosonics** 13 Hawley Crescent, London NW1 8NP **t** 020 7209 0209 **f** 020 7419 4460 **e** info@videosonics.com **w** videosonics.com Studio Mgr: Peter Hoskins.

VisArt The Studios, 8 Hornton Place, Kensington, London W8 4LZ **t** 020 7937 8485 **f** 020 7937 4326 **e** info@visart.co.uk **w** visart.co.uk Technical Director: Steve Bell.

Voyager Media Ltd 341 Brook Street, Broughty Ferry, Dundee DD5 2DSe voyager@sol.co.uk **w** voyager-media.co.uk Account Mgr: Brad Sutherland. [CD DAT]

Waterfall Studios 2 Silver Road, London W12 7SG **t** 020 8746 2000 **f** 020 8746 0180 **e** info@waterfall-studios.com **w** waterfall-studios.com Facilities Mgr: Samantha Leese. [VC]

***Whitfield Street Studios** 31-37 Whitfield Street, London W1T 2SF **t** 020 7636 3434 **f** 020 7580 2219 **e** gay.marshall@whitfield-street.com **w** whitfield-street.com Mastering Bkngs Mgr: Gay Marshall. [V CD MC DAT MD CDRom]

Wolf Studios 83 Brixton Water Lane, London SW2 1PH **t** 020 7733 8088 **f** 020 7326 4016 **e** bret@wolfen.netkonect.co.uk **w** wolfstudios.co.uk Manager: Dominique Brethes. MP3.

[CD MC DAT MD CDRom]

Printers and Packaging

ACS Media Ltd (Printers) 37 Bartholomew St, Newbury, Berks RG14 5LL **t** 01635 552237 or 01635 580448 **f** 01635 34179 **e** sales@acsmedia.co.uk Contact: Wilber Craik

After Dark Media Grosvenor House, Belgrave Lane, Plymouth PL4 7DA **t** 01752 294130 **f** 01752 257320 **e** nigel@afterdarkmedia.net **w** afterdarkmedia.net Manager: Nigel Muntz.

AGI Amaray Amaray House, Arkwright Road, Corby NN17 5AE **t** 01536 274800 **f** 01536 274902 **e** amaraysales@uk.agimedia.com **w** amaray.com; agimedia.com Customer Services Manager: William Millen.

AGI Media Berghem Mews, Blythe Road, London W14 0HN **t** 020 7605 1940 **f** 020 7605 1941 **e** sales@uk.agimedia.com **w** agimedia.com Marketing Exec.: Dominique O'Connor.

AGI Media Birmingham 98-138 Barford Street, Birmingham, West Midlands B5 6AP **t** 0121 607 7300 **f** 0121 607 7400 **e** birmingham@uk.agimedia.com **w** agimedia.com Sales Mgr: Christian Richards.

AGR Manufacturing Suite 5, Melville House, High Street, Great Dunmow, Essex CM6 1AF **t** 01371 859 393 **f** 01371 859 375 **e** info@agrm.co.uk **w** agrm.co.uk Production Director: Ed Jones.

Artomatic 65 Stirling Road, London W3 8DJ **t** 020 8896 6666 **f** 020 8896 6611 **e** mark@artomatic.co.uk **w** artomatic.co.uk Contact: Mark Joseph ISDN: 0181 896 6622.

Assured Manufacturing Ltd 34 Great Queen St, Covent Garden, London WC2B 5AA **t** 0870 745 3375 **f** 0870 745 3376 **e** info@assuredmanufacturing.co.uk **w** assuredmanufacturing.co.uk Artwork Manager: Spencer King.

Audioprint Wolseley Court, Wolseley Road Ind Estate, Kempston, Bedford, Bedfordshire MK42 7AY **t** 01234 857566 **f** 01234 841700 **e** audio.print@virgin.net **w** audioprint.co.uk Dir/General Manager: Peter Hull.

Bernard Kaymar Trout Street, Preston, Lancashire PR1 4AL **t** 01772 562211 **f** 01772 257813 **e** sales@bernard-kaymar.co.uk **w** bernardkaymar.co.uk MD: Mrs J Stead.

Capital Repro Suite G, Tech West House, Warple Way, London W3 0UE **t** 020 8743 0111 **f** 020 8743 0112 **e** ian@caprep.co.uk **w** caprep.co.uk Sales Director: Ian Part.

CMCS Group Plc Unit 1, Kennet Rd, Dartford, Kent DA1 4QN **t** 020 8308 5000 **f** 020 8308 5005 **e** sales@cmcs.co.uk **w** cmcs.co.uk Sales Manager: Ian Thomas.

CML CD & Multimedia Packaging Units 1&2, Crathie Road, Western Road, Kilmarnock, Ayrshire KA3 1NG **t 01563 574481 f** 01563 533537 **e** cml@btconnect.com **w** cmlpackaging.com Prod Dir: Edward McGill.

Compac Print Unit 6, The Greenbridge Centre, Greenbridge Road, Swindon, Wiltshire SN3 3JQ **t** 01793 421242 **f** 01793 421252 **e** adam.teskey@cmcs.co.uk Contact: Adam Teskey

Cops The Studio, Kent House Station Approach, Barnmead Road, Beckenham, Kent BR3 1JD **t** 020 8778 8556 **f** 020 8676 9716 **e** musicmanufacture@cops.co.uk **w** cops.co.uk/cops/ MD: Elie Dahdi.

CopyMaster International Ltd (Packaging) 8 Arundel Road, Uxbridge, Middx UB8 2RR **t** 01895 814 813 **f** 01895 814 999 **e** info@copymaster.co.uk **w** copymaster.co.uk Sales Mgr: Rachelle Peterson.

COLORS

Colors

42-44 Hanway Street, London W1T 1UT **t** 020 7637 1842 **f** 020 7637 5568 **e** studio@colors.co.uk **w** colors.co.uk Dir: Chris Green

---

Crown Impex Ltd 27 Glebe Hyrst, Sanderstead, South Croydon CR2 9JG **t 020 8651 6136 f** 020 8651 4904 **e** crown-impex@supanet.com Sales Mgr: R Vanner.

CRS (Cassette & Record Services) Ltd Woburn Road Ind. Estate, Wolseley Road, Kempston, Bedford MK42 7RA **t 01234 853777 f** 01234 857456 or 01234 841233 (ISDN) **e** sales@crsprint.co.uk **w** crsprint.co.uk Sales Director: Richard Coates.

CVB Duplication 179A Bilton Road, Perivale, Middlesex UB6 7HQ **t** 020 8991 2610 **f** 020 8997 0180 **e** sales@cvbduplication.co.uk **w** cvbduplication.co.uk Customer Service Manager: Adrian Tubman.

The Davis Group (Mailers and Cases) 48 Watersfield Way, Edgware, Middlesex HA8 6RZ **t** 020 8951 4264 **f** 020 8951 4342 **e** rdavis7054@aol.com Contact: Robbie Davis

Delga Group Seaplane House, Riverside Est., Sir Thomas Longley Rd,, Medway City Estate, Rochester, Kent ME1 4BH **t** 01322 550723 **e** info@delga.co.uk **w** delga.co.uk Sales Director: John Bridgeman.

Diamond Black The Old Truman Brewery, 91 Brick Lane, London E1 6QL **t** 020 7053 2179 **f** 020 7053 2179 **e** diamondblackpressings@hotmail.com Sales Manager: Kat Smith.

Gemini Print & Display Europa House, Denmark Street, Maidenhead, Berkshire SL6 7BN **t** 01628 410068 **f** 01628 412128 **e** kevingemini@netscapeonline.co.uk Contact: Kevin Hill

GM Printing Ltd Buttermere House, Clyde Road, Wallington, Surrey SM6 8PZ **t** 0800 216620 **f** 020 8286 4646 **e** info@gmprinting.co.uk **w** gmprinting.co.uk Contact: Steven Lo Presti

Go Digital Print Ltd 21 Wates Way, Mitcham, Surrey CR4 4HR **t** 020 8648 7060 **f** 020 8241 0989 **e** godigital@stjames.org.uk **w** godigitalprint.co.uk Production Manager: Steve Hill.

Ingersoll Printers Second Way, Wembley, Middlesex HA9 0YJ **t** 020 8903 1355 **f** 020 8795 1381 **e** tcarney@ingersoll-printers.co.uk **w** ingersoll-printers.co.uk Marketing Dir: Terry Carney.

Jigsaw (London) Ltd 64 Great Eastern Street, London EC2A 3QR **t** 020 7613 5550 **f** 020 7613 1818 **e** info@jigsawlondon.co.uk **w** jigsawlondon.co.uk Director: David Pampel. ISDN: 020 7729 8190.

Jourdans Kestral Way, Sowton Industrial Estate, Exeter, Devon EX2 7LA **t** 01392 445524 **f** 01392 445526 **e** rhino@jourdans.co.uk Mktg Dir: David Gargrave.

Key Production 8 Jeffreys Place, London NW1 9PP **t** 020 7284 8800 or 01454 886 487 **f** 020 7284 8811 or 01454 886 489 **e** mail@keyproduction.co.uk Customer Services Manager: Katy Rose.

Keyprint (Printers) Research House, Fraser Road, Greenford, Middlesex UB6 7AQ **t** 020 8566 7246 or 01992 553193 **f** 020 8566 7247 **e** sales@keyprinters.co.uk **w** keyprinters.co.uk Managing Director: Mike Keyworth. Contacts: Mike Keyworth, David Shrimpton.

Lexon Group Park Road, Risca, Gwent NP11 6YJ **t** 01633 613444 **f** 01633 601333 **e** print@lexongroup.com **w** lexongroup.com Contact: Sales Dept

Leyprint Leyland Lane, Leyland, Preston, Lancashire PR25 1UT **t** 01772 425000 **f** 01772 425001 **e** edward@leyprint.co.uk **w** leyprint.co.uk Sales & Mktg Dir: Edward Mould.

London Fancy Box Co Ltd Poulton Close, Dover, Kent CT17 0XB **t** 01304 242001 **f** 01304 240229 **e** castle@londonfancybox.co.uk **w** londonfancybox.co.uk Contact: Drew Dixon

The Lynic Group 645 Ajax Avenue, Slough, Berks SL1 4BG **t** 01753 786 200 **f** 01753 786 201 **e** sales@lynic.com **w** lynic.com VP Business Development: Trevor Southam. CEO: Jag Gill. VP Sales: Simon Notton. VP Operations: Louise Holder.

Magic Wand Printing & Packaging Littleton House, Littleton Road, Ashford, Middx. TW15 1UU **t** 01784 253 534 **f** 01784 251 267 **e** info@magicwand.co.uk **w** magicwand.co.uk MD: Rob McCartney.

Meltones Media 3 King Edward Drive, Chessington, Surrey KT9 1DW **t** 020 8391 9406 **f** 020 8391 8924 **e** sales@meltones.com **w** meltones-media.co.uk MD: Tony Fernandez.

Modo Production Ltd Ground Floor, 11 Codrington Mews, London W11 2EH **t** 020 7243 9855 **f** 020 7243 9856 **e** mail@modo.co.uk **w** modo.co.uk MD: Henry Lavelle.

MPO UK Ltd Units 3-4, Nucleus Central Way, Park Royal, London NW10 7XT **t** 020 8963 6888 **f** 020 8963 6841 **e** Sales@MPO.co.uk **w** MPO.co.uk Sales & Marketing Dir: John Barker.

MPT Colour Graphics Unit 9 Thame Park Bus.Cen., Wenman Road, Thame, Oxfordshire OX9 3XA **t** 01844 216888 **f** 01844 218999 **e** info@mptcolour.co.uk **w** mptcolour.co.uk GM: Gary Pople.

Nuleaf Graphics Ltd 37-42 Compton St., London EC1V OAP **t** 020 7250 3558 **f** 020 7251 6981 **e** peter@nuleaf-group.co.uk Contact: Keith Morgan/Peter Moran

Panmer Plastics (UK) Ltd. Unit 4-5, Delta Centre, Mount Pleasant, Wembley, Middx. HA0 1UX **t** 020 8903 7733 **f** 020 8903 3036 **e** info@panmer.com **w** panmer.com MD: Nimesh Shah.

Paul Linard Print 57-63 Brownfields, Welwyn Garden City, Hertfordshire AL7 1AN **t** 01707 333716 **f** 01707 334211 **e** Pat@linards.co.uk **w** linards.co.uk MD: Patrick Leighton.

Pollard Boxes Ltd 193 Gloucester Crescent, South Wigston, Leicestershire LE18 4YH **t** 0116 277 2999 **f** 0116 277 3888 **e** sales@pollardboxes.co.uk Director: Peter Conner.

Pozzoli Ltd 100 New Kings Road, London SW6 4LX **t** 020 7384 3283 **f** 020 7384 3067 **e** pozzoliltd@aol.com **w** pozzolispa.com Sales Dir: Luigi Pozzoli.

RAD Printing Ltd Unit 10, Block F, Northfleet Industrial Estate, Kent DA11 9SW **t** 01322 380775 **f** 01322 380647 **e** info@radprint.com **w** radprint.com Production Manager: Emilie Bish.

Reflex Media Services Ltd Unit 5, Cirrus, Glebe Road, Huntingdon PE29 7DL **t** 01480 412222 **f** 01480 411441 **e** roger@reflex-media.co.uk Dir: Roger Masterson. Sales: John Garrad.

Repeat Performance RPM 6 Grand Union Centre, West Row, London W10 5AS **t** 020 8960 7222 **f** 020 8968 1378 **e** info@rpmuk.com **w** rpmuk.com MD: Robin Springall.

Rowleys:London One Port Hill, Hertford, Herts SG14 1PJ **t** 01992 587350 or 01992 551931 **f** 01992 586059 **e** info@rowleyslondon.co.uk **w** rowleyslondon.co.uk MD: Anne Rowley.

rtsOnestop Ltd Unit M1 & M2, Albany Road, Prescot, Merseyside L34 2UP **t** 0151 430 9001 **f** 0151 430 7441 **e** rts.onestop@virgin.net **w** rtsOnestop.co.uk MD: John Fairclough.

Sarem & Co 43A Old Woking Road, West Byfleet, Surrey KT14 6LG **t** 01932 352535 **f** 01932 336431 **e** info@sarem-co.com **w** sarem-co.com Partner: Adrian Connelly. Partner: Martin Howell.

Senol Printing 6 Sandiford Road, Kimpton Road Estate, Sutton, Surrey SM3 9RD **t** 020 8641 3890 **f** 020 8641 3486 **e** info@senolprinting.co.uk **w** senol-printing.co.uk Contact: Jacqui Gunn

The Shalford Press Ltd 9 Crittall Drive, Springwood Industrial Estate, Braintree, Essex CM7 2RT **t** 01376 321125 or 01376 550856 (ISDN) **f** 01376 324535 **e** print@shalford.co.uk Sales Mgr: Pauline Braithwaite.

Shellway Press 42-44 Telford Way, Westway Estate, London W3 7XS **t** 020 8749 8191 **f** 020 8749 8721 **e** stuart@shellway.co.uk MD: Stuart Shelbourn.

ST IVES PRINT & DISPLAY (BLACKBURN) LTD

St Ives
Print & Display

Greenbank Technology Park, Challenge Way, Blackburn, Lancashire BB1 5QB **t** 01254 278800 **f** 01254 278811 **e** salesbl@stivespd.co.uk **w** stivespd.co.uk Sales Director: Allan Brown. General Manager: Mark Ord. **Manufacturers of all forms of print and packaging for CD and DVD products and general commercial print.**

ST IVES PRINT & DISPLAY (CRAYFORD) LTD

St Ives
Print & Display

Optima Park, Thames Road, Crayford, Kent DA1 4QX **t** 01322 621 560 **f** 01322 625 060 **e** sales@stivespd.co.uk **w** stivespd.co.uk Sales Director: Mark Vincent. **Manufacturers of all forms of printed packaging for CD's, Cassettes, Vinyl and Multimedia Games, Booklets, Boxes, Brochures, etc.**

St James Litho 21 Wates Way, Mitcham, Surrey CR4 4HR **t 020 8640 9438 f** 020 8241 0989 **e** production@stjames.org.uk **w** stjames.org.uk Production Manager: Vince Lowe.

The Standard Press Ltd Standard House, 7/9 Burnham St, Kingston Upon Thames, Surrey KT2 6QR **t 020 8549 1990 f** 020 8549 6500 or 020 8547 3358(ISDN) **e** sales@standardpress.co.uk **w** standard-press.co.uk Production Manager: Paul Williams.

Total Spectrum Ltd 11 Intec 2, Wade Rd, Basingstoke, Hants RG24 8NE **t 01256 814114 f** 01256 814115 **e** sales@totalspectrum.co.uk **w** totalspectrum.co.uk Contact: Sales

TSF Limited 3B Athena Avenue, Elgin Industrial Estate, Swindon, Wiltshire SN2 8HF **t 01793 421300 f** 01793 428724 **e** sales@tsfltd.co.uk **w** tsfltd.co.uk Managing Director: Iain Morrison.

VDC Group VDC House, South Way, Wembley, Middx HA9 0HB **t 020 8903 3345 f** 020 8900 1427 **e** enquiries@vdcgroup.com **w** vdcgroup.com Sales Executive: Aaron Williamson.

Art & Creative Studios

ABBEY ROAD INTERACTIVE

Abbey Road Studios, 3 Abbey Road, London NW8 9AY **t** 020 7266 7282 **f** 020 7266 7321 **e** interactive@abbeyroad.com **w** abbeyroadinteractive.com. Studio Manager: Trish McGregor. [DVD, SACD, ECD, WEB]

After Dark Media Grosvenor House, Belgrave Lane, Mutley, Plymouth PL4 7DA **t** 01752 294130 **f** 01752 257320 **e** nigel@afterdarkmedia.net **w** afterdarkmedia.net Manager: Nigel Muntz.

Airside 24 Cross St, London N1 2BG **t** 020 7354 9912 **f** 020 7354 5529 **e** info@airside.co.uk **w** airside.co.uk Studio Manager: Anne Brassier.

Alias Multimedia Unit 204, 134-146 Curtain Road, Shoreditch, London EC2A 3AR **t** 020 7684 6235 or 07968 773972 **f** 020 7684 8162 **e** info@alias-multimedia.com **w** alias-multimedia.com MD: Joel Harrison.

Amp Associates 103 Gaunt St, London SE1 6DP **t** 020 7740 8767 **f** 020 7740 8761 **e** info@ampuk.com **w** ampuk.com Head of Studio: Alison Warfield.

Antar Marlinspike Hall, Walpole Halesworth, Suffolk IP19 9AR **t** 01986 784 664 **f** 01986 784 664 **e** cally@antar.cc **w** antar.cc MD: Cally.

Art Goes Boom Weir Bank, Bray-on-Thames, Maidenhead, Berkshire SL6 2ED **t** 01628 762651 **f** 01628 762650 **e** jayne@artgoesboom.co.uk **w** artgoesboom.co.uk Contact: Jayne Holt

ArtScience Limited 3rd floor, 172 Westminster Bridge Road, London SE1 7RW **t** 020 7902 2780 **f** 020 7691 9755 **e** info@artscience.net **w** artscience.net Director: Douglas Coates, Liz Milward.

Barnes Music Engraving Ltd 21 Claremont, Hastings, Blackboys TN34 1HA **t** 01424 203344 **f** 01424 203355 **e** enquiries@barnes.co.uk Manager: Julia Bovee.

Big Active Ltd (Art Direction & Design) Unit D4, Metropolitan Wharf, Wapping Wall, London E1W 3SS **t** 020 7702 9365 **f** 020 7702 9366 **e** contact@bigactive.com **w** bigactive.com Creative Dir: Gerard Saint.

Big Screen Films York House, Empire Way, Wembley HA9 OPA **t** 020 8903 0046 **f** 020 8795 4106 **e** info@bigscreenfilms.com **w** bigscreenfilms.com Creative Director: Neil Gibbons.

Bijoux Graphics 10 L Peabody Bldgs, Clerkenwell Close, London EC1R 0AY **t** 020 7608 1316 **e** davies@bijouxgraphics.co.uk **w** bijouxgraphics.co.uk Director: David Davies.

Blue Source Ltd The Saga Centre, 326 Kensal Road, London W10 5BZ **t** 020 7460 6033 or 07778 777 922 **f** 020 7460 6021 or 020 7598 8252 **e** seb.m@bluesource.com **w** bluesource.com MD: Sebastian Marling.

Brian Burrows Ind Illustration & Graphic Design Enterprise House, 133 Blyth Road, Hayes, Middlesex UB3 1DD **t** 020 8573 8761 **f** 020 8561 9114 **e** bburrows@btinternet.com MD: Brian Burrows.

The Clinic 32-38 Saffron Hill, London EC1N 8FH **t** 020 7421 9333 **f** 020 7421 9334 **e** firstname.lastname@clinic.co.uk **w** clinic.co.uk Studio Manager: Guy Hatton.

Colors 42-44 Hanway Street, London W1T 1UT **t** 020 7637 1842 **f** 020 7637 5568 **e** studio@colors.co.uk **w** colors.co.uk Dir: Chris Green.

Coloset Graphics 2-3 Black Swan Yard, Bermondsey St, London SE1 3XW **t** 020 7234 0300 **f** 020 7234 0118 **e** info@colorsergraphics.co.uk **w** colorsergraphics.co.uk Dir: Frank Baptiste.

Crush Design & Art Direction 6 Gloucester St, Brighton BN1 4EW **t** 01273 606058 **e** info@crushed.co.uk **w** crushed.co.uk Dir: Carl.

D-Face Unit 104, 326 Kensal Rd, London W10 5BZ **t** 020 8969 5123 or 07817 806 011 **f** 020 8969 5123 **e** design@d-face.co.uk **w** d-face.co.uk Creative Director: Donna Pickup.

D-Fuse 13-14 Gt.Sutton St, London EC1V 0BX **t** 020 7253 3462 **e** info@dfuse.com **w** dfuse.com Dir: Michael Faulkner.

Darkwaveart 29 Granville St, Loughborough, Leics. LE11 3BL **t 01509 822 827 f** 01509 560 221 **e** matt@darkwaveart.co.uk **w** darkwaveart.co.uk Designer: Matt Vickerstaff.

Delga Group Seaplane House, Riverside Est., Sir Thomas Longley Rd, Medway City Estate, Rochester, Kent ME2 4BH **t** 01322 550723 **f** 01322 558020 **e** info@delga.co.uk **w** delga.co.uk Sales Director: John Bridgeman.

Demons Dressed as Designers t 0709 204 7845 **f** 0709 222 9581 **e** rina.cheung@public-art.net **w** public-art.net Design Manager: Rina Cheung.

The Design And Advertising Business 10A Berners Place, London W1T 3AE **t** 020 7580 5566 **f** 020 7580 9933 **e** designbiz@easynet.co.uk **w** dabiz.co.uk Account Director: Richard Fearn.

The Design Dell 13a Newnham St, Ely, Cambridgeshire CB7 4PG **t** 01353 659911 **f** 01353 650011 **e** dan@design-dell.com **w** design-dell.com Creative Director: Dan Donovan.

THE DESIGN CORP

design4music.com

3rd Floor, 68A Neal Street, Covent Garden, London WC2H 9PA **t** 020 7836 0007 or 020 7734 5676 **e** us@design4music.com **w** design4music.com MD: Nigel Pearce.

A full creative service for the music industry

Designers Republic Work Station, Unit 415, Paternoster Row, Sheffield, South Yorkshire S1 2BX **t** 0114 275 4982 **e** disinfo@thedesignersrepublic.com **w** thedesignersrepublic.com Creative Dir: Ian Anderson.

DS Emotion Ltd Chantry House, Victoria Road, Leeds, West Yorkshire LS5 3JB **t** 0113 225 7100 **f** 0113 225 7200 **e** studio@dsemotion.com **w** dsemotion.com

Eject Limited 5 Green Dragon Court, Borough Market, London SE1 9AW **t 020 7407 3003 f** 020 7407 3012 **e** studio@eject.it **w** eject.it Dir: Lee Murrell.

Eldamar Ltd 157 Oxford Rd, Cowley, Oxford OX4 2ES **t** 01865 77 99 44 **e** ideas@eldamar.co.uk **w** eldmar.co.uk Creative Director: Ayd Instone. Sales Director: Suzanne Bourner.

expdesign.co.uk Top Floor, 23 Charlotte Rd, London EC2A 3PB **t** 020 7729 8255 **f** 020 7729 8258 **e** creative@expdesign.co.uk **w** expdesign.co.uk Creative Director: Mark Bailey.

Eyetoeye Digital The Seed Warehouse, Maidenhead Yard, The Wash, Hertford SG14 1PX **t** 01992 558881 **f** 01992 558465 **e** info@eyetoeye.com **w** eyetoeye.com Creative Director: Andrew W. Ellis.

Farrow Design Ltd 23-24 Great James Street, London WC1N 3ES **t** 020 7404 4225 or 020 7831 4976 ISDN **f** 020 7404 4223 **e** studio@farrowdesign.com **w** farrowdesign.com Contact: Mark Farrow

Feline Design Old Employment Exchange, East Grove, off Rectory Rd, Rushden, Northants NN10 0AR **t** 01933 355095 or 07801 731177 **f** 01933 413279 **e** felineab@aol.com **w** purr-fectprint.com Graphic Designer: Andrea Billett.

Firebird.com Ltd Kyrle House Studios, Edde Cross Street, Ross-on-Wye, Herefordshire HR9 7BZ **t** 01989 762269 **e** info@firebird.com **w** firebird.com CEO: Peter Martin.

Fisher Graphics 209E St John's Hill, Wandsworth, London SW11 1TH **t** 020 7228 4740 **f** 020 7228 4762 **e** nick@fishergraphics.demon.co.uk MD: Nick Fisher.

Fluid Graphic Design Ltd Studio 1/222, The Custard Factory, Gibb Street, Birmingham, West Midlands B9 4AA **t** 0121 693 6913 **f** 0121 693 6911 **e** drop@fluidesign.co.uk **w** fluidesign.co.uk Director: James Glover. Account Manager: Victoria Betts.

Form 47 Tabernacle St, London EC2A 4AA **t** 020 7014 1430 **f** 020 7014 1431 or 020 7014 1432 ISDN **e** studio@form.uk.com **w** form.uk.com Partners: Paula Benson, Paul West.

Framous Limited Unit 12/13 Impress House, Mansell Rd, Acton, London W3 7QH **t** 020 8735 0047 **f** 020 8735 0048 **e** lucy@framous.ltd.uk **w** framous.ltd.uk Office Mgr: Lucy Walker.

Glasseye Rose Cottage, The Aberdeen Centre, 22-24 Highbury Grove, London N5 2EA **t** 020 7354 8808 **f** 020 7354 8808 **e** info@glasseyeltd.com **w** glasseyeltd.com Dir: Alastair Mills.

Graphic Design Consultancies Zeall, 5a Station Rd, Twickenham, Middx TW1 4LL **t** 020 8607 9401 **e** david@zeall.com MD: David McGeachie.

Green Ink 28 Hanbury Street, Spitalfields, London E1 6QR **t 020 7247 7248 f** 020 7247 7293 **e** design@green-ink.co.uk **w** green-ink.co.uk MD: Bruce Gill.

Harry Monk Productions Top Floor, 24-28 Hatton Wall, Farringdon, London EC1N 8JH **t** 020 7691 0088 **f** 020 7691 0081 **e** production@harrymonk.net **w** harrymonk.net Account Manager: Guy Blaskey.

Hiltongrove Hiltongrove Business Centre, Hatherley Mews, London E17 4QP **t** 020 8520 5933 or 020 8521 2424 **f** 020 8521 4343 **e** freddy@hiltongrove.com **w** hiltongrove.com Creative Director: Freddy Apeayja.

Tom Hingston Studio 76 Brewer Street, London W1R 3PH **t** 020 7287 6044 **f** 020 7287 6048 **e** info@hingston.net Contact: Tom Hingston

Hive Associates Ltd Bewlay House, 2 Swallow Place, London W1B 2AE **t** 020 7664 0480 **f** 020 7664 0481 **e** consult@hiveassociates.co.uk **w** hiveassociates.co.uk Account Director: Alex Moss.

icoico.com 2nd floor, 93 Candleriggs, Merchant City, Glasgow G1 1NP **t** 0141 572 0234 **f** 0141 572 0558 **e** info@icoico.co.uk **w** icoico.co.uk MD: Lee McLean.

Ideas Redding House, Redding, Falkirk FK2 9TR **t** 01324 716827 or 01324 718299 ISDN **f** 01324 717189 **e** creativity@ideas.co.uk **w** ideas.co.uk Creative Director: Don Jack.

Ignite Marketing (UK) 26a Stoke Newington Church St, London N16 0LU **t** 020 7502 2971 **f** 020 7241 3857 **e** paul@ignitemarketing.co.uk **w** ignitemarketing.co.uk MD: Paul West.

Impac Associates Ltd Grafton House, 2-3 Golden Square, London W1F 9HR **t** 020 7734 1134 **f** 020 7734 1135 **e** impac.tom@virgin.net Contact: Tom Heron

Intro 42 St John St, London EC1M 4DL **t** 020 7324 3244 **f** 020 7324 3245 **e** intro@intro-uk.com **w** introwebsite.com New Business Mgr: Jo Marsh.

Jeff Cummins Design 125, High Oak Rd, Ware, Herts SG12 7PA **t** 01920 411434 or 07751 549098 **f** 01920 411434 **e** info@jeffcummins.com **w** jeffcummins.com Art Director: Jeff Cummins.

Jigsaw (London) Ltd 64 Great Eastern Street, London EC2A 3QR **t** 020 7613 5550 **f** 020 7613 1818 **e** info@jigsawlondon.co.uk **w** jigsawlondon.co.uk Director: David Pampel. ISDN: 020 7729 8190.

JP3 78 Church Path, London W4 5BJ **t** 020 8747 2562 **f** 020 8747 2565 **e** mail@jp3.co.uk **w** jp3.co.uk MD: Paul McGarvey.

Chris Kay (UK) Ltd 158 Station Road, Witham, Essex CM8 3YS **t 01376 500566 f** 01376 500578 **e** sales@chriskay.com **w** chriskay.com Contact: Eddie Clark

Kleber Design Ltd Third Floor, 95A Rivington St, London EC2A 3AY **t** 020 7729 2819 **f** 020 7729 6162 **e** yes@kleber.net **w** kleber.net MD: Chris McGrail.

Kut & Payste Studios Suite 110, Hiltongrove Business Centre, Hatherley Mews, London E17 4QP **t** 020 8520 5933 **f** 020 8520 9401 **e** info@kutandpayste.com **w** kutandpayste.com Contact: Paul Akwaeoh

L&K Graphics Rock House, Wheatsheaf Corner, Shiney Row, Tyne & Wear DH4 4QX **t** 0191 385 6591 **f** 0191 385 6616 **e** keith@lkgraphics.freeserve.co.uk Senior Designer: Keith Morrell.

Lab Design The Studios, 8 Hornton Place, London W8 4LZ **t 020 7938 5329 f** 020 7937 4717 **e** info@labology.com **w** labology.com Creative Director: Kevin Points.

David Larkham Ink PO Box 257, Leatherhead, Surrey KT23 4XZ **t** 01372 458002 or 07860 461 568 **e** david.larkham@btconnect.com MD: David Larkham.

Laughing Gravy Design Ltd 3 Lionel St, Birmingham, West Midlands B3 1AG **t** 0121 605 4454 or 0121 605 5666 **f** 0121 605 5444 **e** gravy@dial.pipex.com **w** lgdgroup.co.uk Partner: Phil Jolly.

Lewis Creative Consultants 4 Quayside Mills, Leith, Edinburgh EH6 6EX **t** 0131 554 1286 **e** postman@lewis.co.uk **w** lewis.co.uk Dir: Alan Hepburn.

P Linard Marketing & Advertising 57-63 Brownfields, Welwyn Garden City, Hertfordshire AL7 1AN **t** 01707 333716 or 01707 375167 **f** 01707 334211 **e** neil@linards.co.uk **w** linards.co.uk Contact: Neil Smith

M+H Communications Ltd 36 Lexington Street, London W1F 0LJ **t** 020 7412 2000 **f** 020 7412 2020 **e** info@MandH.co.uk **w** MandH.co.uk Account Director: Mike McCraith. MD: Adrian Allen.

Mainartery Design 2 Stucley Place, London NW1 8NS **t** 020 7482 6660 **f** 020 7482 6606 **e** art@mainartery.co.uk **w** mainartery.co.uk Creative Dir: Jo Mirowski. Creative Director: Pete Hayward.

Me Company 14 Apollo Studios, Charlton Kings Rd, London NW5 2SA **t** 020 7482 4262 **f** 020 7284 0402 **e** meco@mecompany.com **w** mecompany.com Art Dir: Paul White.

Mental Block Unit 2, Archway Mews, Putney Bridge Rd, London SW15 2PE **t** 020 8877 0085 **e** laurence@mentalblock.co.uk **w** mentalblock.co.uk MD: Laurence Smith. Dirs: Laurence Smith, Johnathan Elliott.

Modo Production Ltd Ground Floor, 11 Codrington Mews, London W11 2EH **t** 020 7243 9855 **f** 020 7243 9856 **e** henry@modo.co.uk **w** modo.co.uk Creative Manager: Henry Lavelle.

Motive Unknown 7 St Marys Place, Ealing, London W5 5HA **t** 020 8579 9092 **e** darren@motiveunknown.com **w** motiveunknown.com MD: Darren Hemmings.

New Visual Media 30 Neal St, London WC2H 9PS **t** 020 7240 6767 **f** 020 7240 6768 **e** info@n-v-m.com **w** n-v-m.com Dir of Projects: Christian Renwick.

Nu Urban Design Unit 3, 36 Queens Rd, Newbury, Berks RG14 7NE **t** 01635 551400 **f** 01635 550333 **e** kevin@nu-urbanmusic.co.uk **w** nu-urbanmusic.co.uk Head of Design: Kevin Broome.

The Nuclear Family 149 Defoe House, London EC2Y 8ND **t** 020 7628 7853 or 07979 848 754 **e** mail@thenuclearfamily.co.uk **w** thenuclearfamily.co.uk Creative Dir: Red James.

OR Multimedia Ltd Marathon House, 1-9 Evelyn Street, London SE8 5RQ **t** 020 7394 1072 **f** 020 7237 3458 **e** info@or-media.com **w** or-media.com ISDN: 020 7237 3508.

Peacock Design 34 Percy St, London W1T 2DG **t** 020 7580 8868 **f** 020 7323 9780 **e** mailus@peacockdesign.com **w** peacockdesign.com MD: Keith Peacock.

Phantom Industries Studio 11, 25 Denmark St, London WC2H 8NJ **t** 020 7379 3695 **e** info@phantom-industries.com **w** phantom-industries.com Dir: Steve Rowland.

Playground Creative Services 21 Wates Way, Mitcham, Surrey CR4 4HR **t** 020 8685 9453 **f** 020 8241 0989 **e** playground@stjames.org.uk **w** playgroundcreative.com Art Director: Tim Bridle.

Plus Two Studio 153 Hagley Rd, Oldswinford, Stourbridge, West Midlands DY8 2JB **t** 01384 393311 **f** 01384 393232 **e** studio@plustwo.co.uk **w** plustwostudio.com Art Dir: Andrew Higginbotham.

Protege Design and Marketing East Dene, 5 Cromer Road, Southend on Sea, Essex SS1 2DU **t** 01702 300 176 **f** 01702 304 028 **e** info@protegedesign.co.uk **w** protegedesign.co.uk MD: Nic Cleeve.

Public Art Creative Consultants Limited , Harrow, London **t** 07092 047 845 **f** 07092 229 581 **e** info@public-art.net **w** public-art.net Design Manager: Rina Cheung.

Purple Frog Studios Ltd The Byre, Manor Farm, Aston Sandford, Aylesbury, Bucks HP17 8LP **t** 01844 295170 **f** 01844 292981 **e** sales@purplefrog.co.uk **w** purplefrog.co.uk Creative Dir: Marcus Marsh.

Qd 93 Great Titchfield, London W1P 7FP **t** 020 7462 1700 **f** 020 7636 0652 **e** info@qotd.co.uk **w** qotd.co.uk Contact: Dave Wharin ISDN: 020 7323 2061/2.

Quite Great Design Suite 1C, Langford Arch, London Rd, Sawston, Cambridge CB2 4EG **t** 01223 830111 **f** 01223 830140 **e** design@quitegreat.co.uk MD: Mark Lovell.

Raw-Paw Graphics 13-14 Great Sutton Street, London EC1 0BX **t** 020 7253 3462 **f** 020 7253 3463 **e** mike@dfuse.com **w** raw-paw.net MD: Michael Faulkner.

Real World Design Mill Lane, Box, Corsham, Wiltshire SN13 8PN **t** 01225 743188 **f** 01225 744369 **e** york.tillyer@realworld.co.uk **w** realworld.co.uk Interactive Director: York Tillyer.

Really Free Solutions Ichthus House, 1 Northfield Rd, Aylesbury, Bucks HP20 1PB **t** 01296 583700 **e** info@reallyfreesolutions.co.uk **w** reallyfreesolutions.co.uk Contact: Peter Wheeler

Red James , London EC2 **t** 020 7628 7853 **e** red@redjam.com **w** redjam.com Dir: Red James.

The Reptile House 1 Neal's Yard, Covent Garden, London WC2H 9DP **t** 020 7379 8351 **f** 020 7379 3326 **e** matt@the-reptile-house.co.uk **w** the-reptile-house.co.uk Creative Director: Matt Hughes.

Root Associates Ground Floor, 4 Ravey St, London EC2A 4QP **t** 020 7739 2277 **f** 020 7613 0342 **e** martin@rootdesign.co.uk **w** rootdesign.co.uk Creative Director: Martin Root.

Ryan Art 48A Southern Row, London W10 5AN **t** 020 8968 0966 **f** 020 8968 6418 **e** info@ryanart.com **w** ryanart.com Contact: Niamh McGovern

Seed Software The Seed Warehouse, Maidenhead Yard, The Wash, Herts SG14 1PX **t** 01992 558 881 **f** 01992 558 465 **e** info@seedsoftware.co.uk **w** seedsoftware.co.uk MD: Andrew W Ellis.

Sirenstorm Media/Majic Design PO Box 66, Manchester M12 4XJ **t** 0161 225 9991 **f** 0161 225 9991 **e** info@sirenstorm.com **w** sirenstorm.com Dir: Tony Spalding.

Sounds Good Ltd 12 Chiltern Enterprise Centre, Station Rd, Theale, Reading, Berkshire RG7 4AA **t** 0118 930 1700 **f** 0118 930 1709 **e** sales-info@sounds-good.co.uk **w** sounds-good.co.uk Dir: Martin Maynard.

STAR AWARDS DESIGN GROUP

39 Felsham Road, Putney, London SW15 1AZ **t** 0870 950 5716 **f** 020 8704 5748 **e** sales@starawardsdesign.com w starawardsdesign.com Contact: Brian Hyams, Gail Rowbotham and Kevin Coller. UK leading manufacturers of 24 carat gold discs. Sole approved supplier of BVA video/DVD awards and makers of awards to the Entertainment Industry.

Storm Media 134 Godstone Rd, Caterham, Surrey CR3 6RB **t** 01883 372639 **f** 01883 372639 **e** enquiries@stormmedia.uk.com **w** stormmedia.uk.com MD: Stephen Bailey-Johnston.

Studio Lobster & Design The Foundry, Forth Banks, Newcastle upon Tyne, Tyne & Wear NE1 3PA **t** 0191 261 2101 **f** 0191 230 0707 **e** shorty@studiolobster.com **w** studiolobster.com MD: Richard Short.

StudioMix 3rd Floor, Mayfair House, 11 Lurke St, Bedford MK40 3HZ **t** 01234 272347 **f** 01234 272327 **e** design@studiomix.co.uk **w** studiomix.co.uk Senior Designer: Mick Lowe. ISDN: 020 7251 4673.

Stylorouge 57/60 Charlotte Road, London EC2A 3QT **t** 020 7729 1005 **f** 020 7739 7124 **e** rob@stylorouge.co.uk **w** stylorouge.co.uk Dir: Rob O'Connor.

Superdead Graphics 42 Neale Rd, Chorlton, Manchester M21 9DQ **t** 07855 888 961 **e** mail@superdead.com **w** superdead.com Designer: Ed Syder.

thelongdrop Studio 12, Atlas Works, Foundry Lane, Earls Colne, Essex CO6 2TE **t** 01787 224464 **f** 01787 220434 **e** mwd@thelongdrop.com **w** thelongdrop.com/mwd Creative Dir: Andy Carne.

Mike Thorn Display & Design 30 Muswell Avenue, London N10 2EG **t** 020 8442 0279 **f** 020 8442 0496 **e** info@bear-art.com MD: Mike Thorn.

TM Ltd 33 Nutbrook Street, Peckham, London SE15 4JU **t** 020 7564 2700 **e** info@tm-ltd.co.uk

Toffeeapple Creative Media 199 Piccadilly, London **t** 020 7287 4442 **f** 020 7287 5557 **e** alex@toffeeapple-creative.com **w** toffeeapplecreative.com Account Dir: Alex Eicke.

Tourist 1 Willow St, Shoreditch, London EC2A 4BH **t** 020 7739 3011 **f** 020 7739 3033 **e** info@weare-tourist.com **w** wearetourist.com Directors: Rob Chenery, Keith White.

TWO:design Studio 20, The Arches, Hartland Rd, Camden, London NW1 8HR **t** 020 7267 1118 **f** 020 7482 0221 or 020 7424 9147(ISDN) **e** studio@twode-sign.net **w** twodesign.net Art Dir: Graham Peake.

Undertow Design No7, 9-10 College Terrace, London E3 5EP **t** 020 8983 4718 or 07966170109 **f** 020 8983 4718 **e** info@undertow-design.co.uk **w** undertow-design.co.uk Art Director: Steve Wilkins.

UnLimited Creative Fl 3 Grampian House, Meridian Gate, London E14 9YT **t** 0870 744 2643 **f** 070 9231 4982 **e** creative@unlimitedmedia.co.uk **w** unlimited-media.co.uk Dirs: Chris Cooke, Alan Ogilvie.

Version 15 Holywell Row, London EC2A 4JB **t** 020 7684 5470 **f** 020 7684 5472 **e** info@versioncreative.com **w** versioncreative.com Dirs: Anthony Oram, Mo Chicharro.

VisArt The Studios, 8 Hornton Place, London W8 4LZ **t** 020 7937 8485 **f** 020 7937 4326 **e** info@visart.co.uk **w** visart.co.uk Technical Director: Steve Bell.

Vivid Communications Littleton House, Littleton Road, Ashford, Middlesex TW15 1UU **t** 01784 252916 **f** 01784 254811 or 01784 421946(ISDN) **e** info@vivid-communications.co.uk **w** vividcommunications.co.uk MD: Jools.

Vivid Design Consultants 138 Cherry Orchard Rd, Croydon, Surrey CRO 6BB **t** 020 8649 8825 **f** 020 8667 1682 **e** paul@vividdesignconsultants.com **w** vividdesignconsultants.com Owner: Paul Jukes.

Wherefore Art? 8 Primrose Mews, Sharpleshall Street, London NW1 8YW **t** 020 7586 8866 **f** 020 7586 8800 or 020 7586 8008 (ISDN) **e** info@where-foreart.com **w** whereforeart.com Creative Director: David Costa.

Wierd & Wonderful Art & Graphic Design 177 High St, Harlesden, London NW10 4TE **t** 020 8961 3889 **f** 020 8961 4620 **e** johnkaufman@totalise.co.uk Business Affairs: John Kaufman. Artist: "Legs" Larry Smith.

Wolf Graphics 49 Belvoir Rd, London SE22 0QY **t** **020 8299 2342** **f** 020 8693 9006 **e** jim@exoti-carecords.co.uk **w** exoticarecords.co.uk MD: Jim Phelan.

ZiP Design Ltd Unit 2A Queens Studios, 121 Salusbury Road, London NW6 6RG **t** **020 7372 4474** **f** 020 7372 4484 or 020 7328 4447 **e** info@zipdesign.co.uk **w** zipdesign.co.uk Art Director: Peter Chadwick.

Web Design & Online Services

7 Digital Media 6th Floor, Palladium House, One Argyll Street, London W1F 7TA **t** 020 7494 6589 **f** 0871 733 4149 **e** info@7digitalmedia.com **w** 7digital-media.com Contact: Ben Drury

Absolute Multimedia Design 47 Park End, Bromley, London BR1 4AN **t** 020 8325 1644 **e** design@willdob-son.co.uk **w** willdobson.co.uk MD: Will Dobson.

Accent Integrated Media 51 Kingsway Place, Sans Walk, London EC1R 0LU **t** 020 7251 4411 **f** 020 7251 3311 **e** enquiries@accent.co.uk **w** accent.co.uk Contact: The MD

Airside 24 Cross St, London N1 2BG **t** 020 7354 9912 **f** 020 7354 5529 **e** info@airside.co.uk **w** airside.co.uk Studio Manager: Anne Brassier.

Airtight Productions Unit 16, Albany Rd Trading Estate, Albany Rd, Chorlton M21 0AZ **t** 0161 881 5157 **e** info@airtightproductions.co.uk **w** airtightproduc-tions.co.uk Director: Anthony Davey.

Amp Associates 103 Gaunt St, London SE1 6DP **t** 020 7740 8767 **f** 020 7740 8761 **e** info@ampuk.com **w** ampuk.com Head of Studio: Alison Warfield.

AMP Online Marketing 8-10 Rhoda St, London E2 7EF **t** 020 7739 0100 **f** 020 7739 8571 **e** info@ampunited.com **w** ampunited.com Director: Jim Gottlieb.

Anglo Plugging Fulham Palace, Bishops Avenue, London SW6 6EA **t** 020 7800 4488 **f** 020 7371 9490 **e** dylan@angloplugging.co.uk **w** angloplugging.co.uk Contact: Dylan White

AOL 80 Hammersmith Road, London W14 8UD **t** 020 7348 8000 **f** 020 7348 8002 **w** aol.com

Applied Interactive Ltd Cranfield Innovation Centre, University Way, Cranfield, Bedfordshire MK43 0BT **t** 01234 756049 or **01234 756050** **f** 01234 756138 **e** sales@applied-interactive.co.uk **w** applied-interactive.co.uk Technical Dir: Dave Fairhurst.

Artism 1 Angel Court, London EC2R 7HJ **t** 020 7886 9940 **f** 020 7886 9941 **e** david@artism.com **w** artism.com Ops Mgr: David Otzen.

ArtScience Ltd 172 Westminster Bridge Rd, London SE1 7RW **t** 020 7902 2780 **f** 020 7691 9755 **e** info@artscience.net **w** artscience.net Director: Douglas Coates, Liz Milward.

Avantnoise Limited 5th Floor Crown House, Linton Road, Barking, Essex IG11 8HJ **t** 020 8591 1125 **f** 020 8591 0110 **e** info@avantnoise.com **w** avantnoise.com MD: Adrian Turner.

Beatwax Communications 91 Berwick St, Soho, London W1F 0NE **t** 020 7734 1965 **f** 020 7292 8333 **e** jamie.danan@beatwax.com **w** beatwax.com Online Manager: Jamie Danan.

Big Picture Interactive Ltd 9 Parade, Leamington Spa, Warwickshire CV32 4DG **t** 01926 422002 **f** 01926 450945 **e** enquiries@thebigpic.co.uk **w** thebigpic.co.uk PA: Sarah Pannell.

Bite It Ltd 563 Bury Road, Rochdale, Gtr. Manchester OL11 4DQ **t** 01706 525220 or 0800 975 7112 **f** 01706 639818 **e** declan@biteit.net **w** biteit.net MD: Declan Cosgrove.

Bloc Media Ltd 3rd Floor, 18 Charlotte Road, London EC1A 3PB **t** 020 7739 1718 **f** 020 7739 1115 **e** contact@blocmedia.com **w** blocmedia.com Director: Liz Vaughan. Creative Director: Rick Palmer.

Blue Marble Warwick House, Kensington Village, Avonmore Road, London W14 8HQ **t** 020 7751 1663 **f** 020 7348 3859 **e** peter.hollins@bluemarble.co.uk **w** bluemarble.co.uk MD: Peter Hollins.

Blue Source Ltd. Saga Centre, 326 Kensal Road, London W10 5BZ **t** 020 7460 6020 **f** 020 7598 9252 **e** info@bluesource.com **w** bluesource.com Company Director: Seb Marling.

Broadchart Limited Shelana House, 31-32 Eastcastle St, London W1W 8DW **t** 020 7341 0999 **f** 020 7341 0888 **e** info@broadchart.com **w** broadchart.com CEO: Andy Hill.

C-Burn Systems Ltd 33 Sekforde St, London EC1R 0HH **t** 020 7250 1133 **f** 020 7253 8553 **e** info@c-burn.com **w** c-burn.com Sales & Marketing: Neil Phillips.

Cake New Media 10 Stephen Mews, London W1T 1AG **t** 020 7307 3100 **f** 020 7307 3101 **e** newbiz@cakemedia.com **w** cakenewmedia.com Dir: Jez Jowett.

Classical.com Limited 8 Bloomsbury Square, London WC1A 2LP **t 020 7916 2000** **f** 020 7916 2030 **e** info@classical.com **w** classical.com Director: Tim Lloyd.

Clear Sound & Vision Ltd Clarendon House, 117 George Lane, London E18 1AN **t** 020 8989 8777 **f** 020 8989 9777 **e** info@c-s-v.co.uk **w** c-s-v.co.uk MD: Clive Robins. Sales Manager: Danny Sperling.

Clever Cherry Victoria Works, Birmingham B1 3PE **t** 0121 236 1060 **e** info@clevercherry.com **w** clevercherry.com MD: Ian Allen.

The Clinic 32-38 Saffron Hill, London EC1N 8FH **t** 020 7421 9333 **f** 020 7421 9334 **e** firstname.lastname@clinic.co.uk **w** clinic.co.uk Creative Director: David Dragan.

Complete Websites 159A High Road, Romford, Essex RM6 6NL **t** 08707 440717 **f** 08701 340920 **e** info@completewebsites.co.uk **w** completewebsites.co.uk

Compuserve UK 80 Hammersmith Road, London W14 8UD **t** 020 7348 8000 **f** 020 7348 8002 **w** compuserve.com

Connolly Associates 6 Brookfields, Crickhowell, Powys NP8 1DJ **t** 01873 811633 **f** 01873 811992 **e** steve@connolly-associates.co.uk **w** connolly-associates.co.uk Owner: Steve Connolly.

Consolidated Independent 8-10 Rhoda St, London E2 7EF **t** 020 7729 8493 **e** info@cissme.com **w** consolidatedindependent.com Director: Paul Sanders.

Counterpoint Systems Ltd 74-80 Camden Street, London NW1 0EG **t** 020 7543 7500 **f** 020 7543 7600 **e** info@counterp.com **w** counterp.com CEO: Amos Biegun.

Cybertech Support Services Ltd 6 Cheyne Walk, Hornsea, East Yorks HU18 1BX **t** 01964 536193 **f** 01964 533925 **e** info@csupports.co.uk **w** csupports.co.uk Music Industry Consultant: Paul Cooke.

D-Fuse 13-14 Gt.Sutton St, London EC1V 0BX **t** 020 7253 3462 **e** info@dfuse.com **w** dfuse.com Director: Michael Faulkner.

Demon Imaging Unit 110, Bon Marche Centre, 241-251 Ferndale Road, London SW9 8BJ **t** 020 7738 6492 **f** 020 7274 8504 **e** info@demonimaging.com **w** demonimaging.com Dir: Jamie Baker.

Design Esti 23 New Mount St, Manchester M4 4DE **t** 0161 953 4102 **f** 0161 953 4091 **e** Mail@DesignEsti.com **w** designesti.com Marketing Director: Steven Oakes.

Digital Press Kit 11 St. Bede's Terrace, Christchurch, Sunderland SR3 8HS **t** 0191 565 2429 **e** info@martinjames.demon.co.uk **w** digitalpresskit.co.uk MD: Martin James.

digitalfist Devonshire House, Devon St, Liverpool L3 8HA **t** 0151 207 8600 **f** 0151 207 8601 **e** digitalfist@digitalfist.co.uk **w** digitalfist.com Account Manager: Andrew Law.

Direct Choice TV Communications 42 Edith Grove, London SW10 0NJ **t** 020 7352 6688 or 020 7352 6633 **f** 020 7352 6677 **e** jthomas@directchoicetv.com **w** directchoicetv.com Business Dev'**t** Mgr: Johanna Thomas.

Diverse Interactive 6 Gorleston Street, London W14 8XS **t** 020 7603 4567 **f** 020 7603 2148 **e** firstname@diverse.co.uk **w** diverse.co.uk Interactive Prod Mgr: Nicola Wells.

djindex.com 32 Wells House Road, London NW10 6EE **t** 020 8961 2577 **f** 020 8961 2576 **e** info@djindex.com **w** djindex.com Dir: Roy Marsh.

DMCC - Online Marketing and Search Engines 34 Hereford Road, London W2 5AJ **t** 07092 047 348 **f** 07092 047 348 **e** SearchFindUse@DMCC.net **w** dmcc.net Projects Director: Fiona Austin.

Domainssale.co.uk 17-20 Moorhurst Road, St Leonards on Sea, East Sussex TN38 9NA **t** 01424 853200 **f** 01424 756007 **e** teepee@globalnet.co.uk **w** domainssale.co.uk Partner: Tony Pankhurst.

DS Emotion Ltd Chantry House, Victoria Rd, Leeds LS5 3JB **t 0113 225 7100 f** 0113 225 7200 **e** studio@dsemotion.com **w** dsemotion.com

d2 design 50 Malting House, Oak Lane, London E14 8BS **t** 020 7987 6378 **f** 020 7987 6378 **e** info@d2design.co.uk **w** d2design.co.uk MD: Steven Cook.

DVDeye Tossa House, Main Road, Smalley, Derby DE7 6EF **t** 01332 881779 **f** 01332 780008 **e** johnb@dvd-eye.net **w** webconnectedDVD.com MD: John Barker.

eJay Empire Interactive Europe Ltd, The Spires, 677 High Rd, North Finchley, London N12 0DA **t** 020 8492 1049 **f** 020 8343 7447 **e** eJayinfo@empire.co.uk **w** eJay.com Brand Manager: Cate Swift.

Eject Limited 5 Green Dragon Court, Borough Market, London SE1 9AW **t** 020 7407 3003 **f** 020 7407 3012 **e** studio@eject.it **w** eject.it Dir: Lee Murrell.

Emporium Internet 49 Windmill Road, London W4 1RN **t** 020 8742 2001 **e** charlie@emporium.org **w** emporium.org MD: Charlie Carne. Low-priced domain name registration, web-hosting, email marketing solutions, ISP.

The Epic Group plc 52 Old Steine, Brighton, East Sussex BN1 1NH **t** 01273 728686 **f** 01273 821567 **e** marketing@epic.co.uk **w** epic.co.uk Events Mgr: Marnie Harnden.

eTank 17 Braganza Street, London SE17 3RD **t** 020 7582 1409 or 07905 118 299 **f** 020 7582 1409 **e** contact@medix.to **w** etank.to Music Director: Jakob Illeborg. Research, web based.

Eyetoeye Digital The Seed Warehouse, Maidenhead Yard, The Wash, Hertford SG14 1PX **t** 01992 558 881 **f** 01992 558 465 **e** drew@eyetoeye.com **w** eyetoeye.com Creative Director: Andrew W. Ellis.

Fastchanges 15 Barlby Gardens, London W10 5LW **t** 07956 218 159 **f** 07092 279 089 **e** webdesign@fastchanges.com **w** fastchanges.com Design Director: Jude Samuel.

Fastrax Allan House, 10 John Prince's Street, London W1G 0JW **t** 020 7468 6888 **f** 202 7468 6889 **e** info@fastrax.co.uk **w** fastrax.co.uk Fastrax Manager: Ross Priestley.

Firebrand 3 Wish Road, Eastbourne, East Sussex BN21 4NX **t** 01323 430700 **f** 01323 430223 **e** enq@firebrand.co.uk **w** firebrand.co.uk Creative Director: Michael Dale.

Fourmiles Media Services 7 Masefield Grove, Bletchley, Milton Keynes MK3 5AS **t** 0709 222 3643 **f** 0705 069 8195 **e** sales@fourmiles.com **w** fourmiles.com MD: David Wright.

Freeway Internet 30 Victoria Street, Brighton, East Sussex BN1 3FQ **t** 01273 263737 **e** david@freewayinternet.co.uk **w** freewayinternet.co.uk MD: David Pinless.

Glasseye Rose Cottage, The Aberdeen Centre, 22-24 Highbury Grove, London N5 2EA **t** 020 7354 8808 **f** 020 7354 8808 **e** info@glasseyeltd.com **w** glasseyeltd.com Director: Alastair Mills.

Global Communications Group 12 The Pines Business Park, Broad Street, Guildford, Surrey GU3 3BH **t** 01483 456000 **f** 01483 456001 **e** info@globalgroup.co.uk **w** globalgroup.co.uk Sales Mgr: Jan Karumaratme.

Good Technology 332B Ladbroke Grove, London W10 5AH **t** 020 7565 0022 **f** 020 7565 0020 **e** info@goodtechnology.com **w** goodtechnology.com MD: Richard Davies.

Graphico New Media Ltd Goldwell House, Old Bath Road, Newbury, Berkshire RG14 1JH **t** 01635 522810 **f** 01635 580621 **e** info@graphico.co.uk **w** graphico.co.uk Sales & Marketing Dir: Graham Darracott.

Griots.net t 07961 589 616 **f** 07050 695 366 **e** info@griots.net **w** griots.net GM: Marva Jackson Lord. Web promotions for artists.

Harry Monk Productions 24-28 Hatton Wall, London EC1N 8JH **t** 020 7691 0088 **f** 020 7691 0081 **e** production@harrymonk.net **w** harrymonk.net Account Manager: Guy Blaskey.

Hiltongrove Multimedia Hiltongrove Business Centre, Hatherley Mews, London E17 4QP **t** 020 8521 2424 **f** 020 8521 4343 **e** info@hiltongrove.com **w** hiltongrove.com MD: Guy Davis.

Ignite Marketing 26A Stoke Newington Church St, London N16 0LU **t** 020 7502 2971 **f** 020 7241 3857 **e** paul@ignitemarketing.co.uk **w** ignitemarketing.co.uk MD: Paul West.

Infogrames United Kingdom Landmark House, Hammersmith Bridge Road, London W6 9DP **t** 020 8222 9700 **e** mwoodley@uk.infogrames.com **w** infogrames.com UK Marketing Director: Matthew Woodley.

Informer Interactive Research Ltd 52 Shaftesbury Avenue, London W1V 7DE **t** 020 7734 2331 **f** 020 7734 4350 **e** danm@informer-interactive.com **w** informer.com Mktng Dir: Alan Price.

Inner Ear Argyle House, 16 Argyle Court, 1103 Argyle St, Glasgow G3 8ND **t** 0141 226 8808 **f** 0141 226 8818 **e** info@innerear.co.uk **w** innerear.co.uk Sales & Marketing Dir: Tom Lousada.

Interface New Media 20A Brownlow Mews, London WC1N 2LA **t** 020 7416 0702 **f** 020 7416 0700 **e** info@interface-newmedia.com **w** interface-newmedia.com Dir: Neil Jones.

Intro 42 St John St, London EC1M 4DL **t** 020 7324 3244 **f** 020 7324 3245 **e** intro@intro-uk.com **w** introwebsite.com Creative Director: Adrian Shaughnessy. Design & Production for web & print.

iomart Fleming Pavilion, Todd Campus, West of Scotland Science Park, Glasgow, Scotland G20 0XA **t** 0141 931 7000 **f** 0141 931 7001 **e** forrest@iomart.com **w** iomart.com Sales: Forrest Duncan. ADSL systems.

Kleber Design Ltd Third Floor, 95A Rivington St, London EC2A 3AY **t** 020 7729 2819 **f** 020 7729 6162 **e** yes@kleber.net **w** kleber.net MD: Chris McGrail. Full service design company.

KLegal, solicitors 1-2 Dorset Rise, London EC4Y 8AE **t** 020 7694 2500 **f** 020 7694 2501 **e** Philip.Daniels@KPMG.co.uk **w** klegal.com e-commmerce lawyer: Philip Daniels. E-commerce/digital media lawyer

Kusala Ltd Sheffield Science Park, Arundel Street, Sheffield S1 2NS **t** 0114 221 1858 **f** 0845 334 4846 **e** info@kusala.com **w** kusala.com MD: Richard Wakefield.

Larkspur Elesy House, 24-30 Great Titchfield Street, London W1W 8BF **t** 020 7580 0990 **f** 020 7580 0660 **e** info@larkspur.co.uk **w** larkspur.co.uk MD: Victoria Collis.

Lateral Net Ltd Charlotte House, 47-49 Charlotte Road, London EC2A 3QT **t** 020 7613 4449 **f** 020 7613 4645 **e** studio@lateral.net **w** lateral.net Client Services Dir: David Hart.

Lewis Multimedia 4 Quayside Mills, Leith, Edinburgh EH6 6EX **t** 0131 554 1286 **f** 0131 555 2600 **e** ideas@lewismultimedia.co.uk **w** lewismultmedia.co.uk Interactive Media Mgr: Alan Hepburn.

Liquid Audio Europe Plc PO Box 25094, London SW4 9GW **t** 020 8772 0774 **e** info@liquidaudio.com **w** liquidaudio.com Head of Business Devt: Gary Crock.

LoFly Web Technology Unit 2A Queens Studios, 121 Salusbury Road, London NW6 6RG **t** 020 7372 4474 **f** 020 7328 4447 **e** info@lofly.co.uk **w** lofly.co.uk New Media Programmers: Peter Gill, Tom Parkinson.

Luna Internet Ltd 8 Triumph Way, Woburn Road Industrial Estate, Kempston, Bedford MK42 7QB **t** 0845 345 0175 **f** 01234 299 009 **e** info@luna.co.uk **w** luna.co.uk Sales & Mktg Dir: Spencer Ecclestone.

M3M Media Group 563 Bury Road, Rochdale, Greater Manchester OL11 4DQ **t** 0800 975 6004 or 01706 525 760 **f** 01706 639 818 **e** info@m3mmedia.com **w** m3mmedia.com MD: Declan Cosgrove.

Macromedia Europe Ltd Century Court, Millennium Way, Bracknell, Berkshire RG12 2XN **t** 01344 458600 **f** 01344 458666 **e** fcoughlan@macromedia.com **w** macromedia.com MD: Fiona Coughlan.

Magex Limited 4th Floor Walbrook House, 23 Walbrook, London EC4N 8BN **t** 020 7070 4000 **f** 020 7070 4999 **e** ask@magex.com **w** magex.com President: Alexander Grous.

Magic Wand Littleton House, Littleton Road, Ashford, Middlesex TW15 1UU **t** 01784 253 534 **f** 01784 421 946 **e** info@magicwand.co.uk **w** magicwand.co.uk Dir: Rob McCartney.

Mando Group 30-32 Faraday Road, Wavertree Tech Park, Liverpool L13 1EH **t** 0151 281 4040 **f** 0151 281 0060 **e** liverpool@mandogroup.com **w** mandogroup.com

Martello Media Limited 4 Islington Avenue, Sandycove, Co Dublin, Ireland **t** 00 353 1 284 4668 **f** 00 353 1 280 3195 **e** info@martellomm.ie **w** martellomm.ie Mkting Mgr: Edel Peppard.

MatinÇe Sound & Vision Ltd 132-134 Oxford Road, Reading, Berkshire RG1 7NL **t** 0118 957 5876 **f** 0118 959 4936 **e** info@matinee.co.uk **w** matinee.co.uk Marketing Co-ordinator: Miranda Harley.

Mekon Ltd Mekon House, 31-35 St Nicollas Way, Sutton, Surrey SM1 1JN **t** 020 8722 8400 **f** 020 8722 8500 **e** info@mekon.com **w** mekon.com Sales Dir: Julian Murfitt.

Mental Block Unit 2, Archway Mews, Putney Bridge Rd, London SW15 2PE **t** 020 8877 0085 **e** laurence@mentalblock.co.uk **w** mentalblock.co.uk MD: Laurence Smith.

Microsoft - MSN Microsoft House, 10 Great Pulteney Street, London W1R 3TG **t** 0870 60 10 100 **w** mircrosoft.com/uk/info

Midas Multimedia The Media Village, Grampion Television, Queens Cross, Aberdeen AB15 4XJ **t** 01224 627327 **f** 01224 627427 **e** info@midas-multimedia.com **w** midas-multimedia.com Partner: Scott Brown.

Mode International Ltd. 19 Bolsover Street, London W1P 7HJ **t** 020 7665 9600 **f** 020 7665 9630 **e** info@mode.net **w** mode.net CEO: Ian Foley.

Moonfish Ltd 6th Floor, 121 Princess Street, Manchester M1 7AD **t** 08700 704321 **f** 0161 236 3598 **e** fish.market@moonfish.com **w** moonfish.com New Business Dir: Stuart Johnson.

Motive Unknown 7 St Marys Place, Ealing, London W5 5HA **t** 020 8579 9092 **e** darren@motiveunknown.com **w** motiveunknown.com Managing Director: Darren Hemmings.

Music & Media Software 24 Annandale Rd, London SE10 0DA **t** 020 8858 6241 **e** info@backbeatsolutions.com **w** backbeatsolutions.com Contact: Chris Chambers

Music On-Line PO Box 221, Manchester M60 1NN **t** 0161 228 3217 **f** 0161 228 3217 **e** mailbox@musicon-line.com **w** musicon-line.com MD: Ian Sibbald.

Musix Ltd Lower Gatley, Steeple Morden, Herts SG8 0NR **t** 01763 853303 **f** 01763 853573 **e** musix@epix.to Chief Executive: Rino Coladangelo.

Netbod Promotions 22 Morrish Road, London SW2 4EH **t** 020 8674 9493 **e** zenbeat@hotmail.com; wendy@ninjatune.net New Media Marketing: Wendy K.

Newtronic Ltd 165 Malpas Road, London SE4 1BQ **t** 020 8691 1087 **e** sales@newtronic.com **w** newtronic.com MD: Martin Griese.

ntl: 90 Long Acre, London WC2E 9RA **t** 020 7909 2100 **f** 020 7909 2101 **e**(firstname).(surname)@ntl.com **w** ntl.co.uk Contact: Mark James

The Nuclear Family 149 Defoe House, London EC2Y 8ND **t** 020 7628 7853 or 07979 848 754 **e** mail@thenuclearfamily.co.uk **w** thenuclearfamily.co.uk Creative Dir: Red James.

OUTSIDE LINE

outside line

OUTSIDE organisation

OUTSIDE management

Butler House, 177-178 Tottenham Court Road, London W1T 7NY **t** 020 7636 5511 **f** 020 7636 1155 **e** ant@outsideline.co.uk **w** outsideline.co.uk Dir: Anthony Cauchi. **A digital media specialist with departments covering creative online and mobile marketing, online street teams, site management and web & dvd production.**

onedotzero Unit 212C, Curtain House, 134-146 Curtain Road, London EC2A 3AR **t** 020 7729 0072 **f** 020 7729 0057 **e** info@onedotzero.com **w** onedotzero.com Director: Shane Walter.

OR Multimedia Ltd Marathon House, 1-9 Evelyn Street, London SE8 5RQ **t** 020 7394 1072 **f** 020 7237 3458 **e** info@or-media.com **w** or-media.com Dir: Peter Gough.

Oxfordmusic.net ltd 65 George St, Oxford OX1 2BE **t** 01865 798796 **f** 01865 798792 **e** info@oxfordmusic.net **w** oxfordmusic.net MD: Andy Clyde.

PBI Media 19 Thomas More Street, London E1 9YW **t** 020 7423 4686 **f** 020 7423 4501 **e** icanhelp@pbimedia.com **w** pbimedialtd.com

Perfect World Programs Ltd 1 Decima Studios, Decima Street, London SE1 4QR **t** 0207 407 8992 **e** enq@perfect-world.co.uk **w** perfect-world.co.uk MD: Denise Proctor.

Permission 60 Maltings Place, London SW6 2BX **t 0845 665 3221 e** contact@getpermission.co.uk **w** getpermission.co.uk MD: Matt McNeill.

Phoenix Video Ltd Global House, Denham, North Orbital Road, Uxbridge, Middlesex UB9 5HL **t** 01895 837000 **f** 01895 833085 **e** info@phoenix-video.co.uk **w** phoenix-video.co.uk MD: Terry Young. Full broadcast company.

Poptel Internet Services 21-25 Bruges Place, Randolph Street, London NW1 0TF **t** 0845 052 2000 **f** 020 7284 6901 **e** info@poptel.net **w** poptel.net Contact: The Sales Dept

Prezence 35 Denby Buildings, Regent Grove, Leamington Spa, Warcs CV32 4NY **t** 01926 422004 **f** 01926 422005 **e** info@prezence.co.uk **w** prezence.co.uk MD: Tim Bishop.

Pro-Motion 33 Kendal Rd, Hove, East Sussex BN3 5HZ **t** 01273 327175 **e** info@martinjames.demon.co.uk Executive Producer: Martin James.

Probe Media 2nd Floor, The Hogarth Centre, Hogarth Lane, London W4 2QN **t** 020 8742 3636 **f** 020 8995 1350 **e** john@probemedia.co.uk **w** probemedia.co.uk Account Director: John Dicks.

Radiopromotions.co.uk PO Box 20, Banbury, Oxfordshire OX17 3YT **t** 0129 581 4995 **e** info@radiopromotions.co.uk **w** radiopromotions.co.uk MD: Steve Betts.

RD2 Media Ltd 3 Hurst Rd, Sidcup, Kent DA15 9BA **t** 020 8308 4444 **f** 020 8308 4450 **e** post@rd2media.com **w** rd2media.com Creative Director: Gary Haslam.

Real Time The Unit, 2 Manor Gardens, London N7 6ER **t** 020 7561 6700 **f** 020 7561 6701 **e** hq@realtimeinfo.co.uk **w** realtimeinfo.co.uk Director: Simon Edwards.

Real World Multimedia Box Mill, Millside, Mill Lane, Box, Wiltshire SN13 8PL **t** 01225 743188 **f** 01225 744369 **e** york.tillyer@realworld.co.uk **w** realworld.co.uk Creative Dir: York Tillyer.

RealNetworks Europe Ltd. Abbey Barn, Abbey Green, Chertsey, Surrey KT16 8RF **t** 01932 58 1000 **f** 01932 58 1010 **e** gfraser@real.com **w** real.com Sales Director: George Fraser.

Recognition Media Ltd (D-Rom) Unit 28, 49 Effra Road, London SW2 1BZ **t** 020 7738 7644 **f** 020 7924 0402 **e** ukoffice@recognitionmedia.net **w** recognitionmedia.net Contact: Mark Pearce

REDMuze Paulton House, 8 Shepherdess Walk, London N1 7LB **t** 020 7566 8216 **f** 020 7566 8259 **e** sales@redmuze.com **w** redmuze.com Head of Sales: Deborah Sass.

Rednet Ltd 6 Cliveden Office Village, Lancaster Road, High Wycombe, Buckinghamshire HP12 3YZ **t** 01494 513 333 **f** 01494 443 374 **e** contactus@red.net **w** red.net Mktg Mgr: Zoe Marrett.

Ricall Limited Suites 1-4, 97 Mortimer St, London W1W 7SU **t** 020 7927 8305 **f** 020 7927 8306 **e** mail@ricall.com **w** ricall.com MD: Richard Corbett. Online research and licensing.

Rootsmusic.com 22 Oregon Avenue, Manor Park, London E12 5TD **t** 020 8553 1435 **f** 020 8553 1435 **e** info@rootsmusic.co.uk **w** rootsmusic.co.uk MD: Ayo Bamidele.

Sandbag Ltd 59/61 Milford Rd, Reading RG1 8LG **t** 0118 9505812 **f** 0118 9505813 mungo@sandbag.uk.com **w** sandbag.uk.com Contact: Christiaan Munro

Seed Software The Seed Warehouse, Maidenhead Yard, The Wash, Herts SG14 1PX **t** 01992 558 881 **f** 01992 558 465 **e** info@seedsoftware.co.uk **w** seedsoftware.co.uk MD: Andrew W Ellis. ISDN: 020 7235 8327.

Sign-Up.to (E-Marketing) 60 Maltings Place, London SW6 2BX **t 0845 644 4184 e** contact@sign-up.to **w** sign-up.to MD: Matt McNeill.

Simbiotic Mercat House, Argyle Court, 1103 Argyle St, Glasgow G3 8ND **t** 0141 243 2439 **e** sales@simbiotic.info **w** simbiotic.info Project Manager: Colin Hardie.

Single Minded Productions 11 Cambridge Court, 210 Shepherd's Bush Road, London W6 7NJ **t** 0870 011 3748 **f** 0870 011 3749 **e** tony@singleminded.com **w** singleminded.com MD: Tony Byrne.

Small Japanese Soldier 4th Floor, 53-55 Beak St, London W1F 9SH **t** 020 7734 9956 **f** 020 7734 9957 **e** Jungle@smallJapanesesoldier.com **w** smalljapanesesoldier.com MD: Andy Hunns.

Smartcreds Ltd 2nd Floor, Griffin House, 161 Hammersmith Road, London W6 8BS **t** 020 8846 2300 **f** 020 8846 2400 **e** smartservice@smartcreds.co.uk **w** smartcreds.co.uk Brand Mgr: Paul Basham.

Solaris Media 20 Damien St, London E1 2HX **t** 020 7791 1555 **f** 020 7791 1545 **e** info@solarismedia.co.uk **w** solarismedia.co.uk MD: Rob Davis.

Songplayer Plc Wilsons House, Wilsons Park, Newton Heath, Manchester M40 8WN **t** 0161 205 8885 **f** 0161 205 8887 **w** songtones.com CEO: John Doyle.

Sony Psygnosis Ltd Napier Court, Wavertree Technology Park, Liverpool, Merseyside L13 1HD **t** 0151 282 3000 **f** 0151 282 3001 **e** (firstname)_(surname)@scee.net **w** playstation.com

Soundengineer.co.uk 49 Liddington Road, London E15 3PL **t 020 8536 0649 f** 07092 022897 **e** ian@soundengineer.co.uk **w** soundengineer.co.uk Sound Engineer: Ian Hasell.

Spot On Design Ltd 3A Tremadoc Road, Clapham, London SW4 7NF **t** 020 7498 0951 **f** 020 7498 0962 **e** al@spotondesign.co.uk **w** spotondesign.co.uk Creative Director: Al Hunter.

Starcom Motive Partnership 24-27 Great Pultney Street, London W1F 9NJ **t** 020 7453 4444 **f** 020 7437 2401 **e** john.owen@uk.starcomworldwide.com **w** starcomworldwide.com Head of Digital Services: John Owen.

state51 8-10 Rhoda Street, London E2 7EF **t** 020 7729 4343 **f** 020 7729 8494 **e** intouch@state51.co.uk **w** state51.co.uk Director: Paul Sanders. Host & run sites.

Stream UK Centa House, 61 Birkenhead Street, London WC1H 8BB **t** 020 7843 4339 **f** 020 7278 3466 **e** joe@streamuk.com **w** streamuk.com Dir: Joe Bray.

Stylorouge 57/60 Charlotte Rd, London EC2A 3QT **t** 020 7729 1005 **f** 020 7739 7124 **e** rob@stylorouge.co.uk **w** stylorouge.co.uk Dir: Rob O'Connor.

Tele-Cine 48 Charlotte Street, London W1T 2NS **t** 020 7208 2200 **f** 020 7208 2251 **e** alex.reid@telecine.co.uk **w** telecine.co.uk Sales: Alex Reid.

Telepathy Interactive Media Hardy House, High Street, Box, Wiltshire SN13 8NF **t** 01225 744225 **f** 01225 744554 **e** info@telepathy.co.uk **w** telepathy.co.uk Dir: Nigel Milk.

Ten-Two 35 Gweal Wartha, Helston, Cornwall TR13 0SN **t** 01326 569524 **e** office@ten-two.co.uk **w** ten-two.co.uk MD: Jon Wills.

TheFireFactory.com 13 William Rd, Westbridgeford, Nottingham NG3 **t** 07870 553 717 **e** info@thefirefactory.com **w** thefirefactory.com Producer: Jake Shaw.

Toffeeapple Creative Media 199 Piccadilly, London **t** 020 7287 4442 **f** 020 7287 5557 **e** alex@toffeeapplecreative.com **w** toffeeapplecreative.com Account Dir: Alex Eicke.

Tornado Virtue PLC Tornado House, Pound Lane, Marlow, Bucks SL7 2AF **t** 01628 498600 **f** 01628 498610 **e** info@tornadovirtue.com **w** tornadovirtue.com Business Development Dir: Nick English.

Total Connectivity Providers 12 New Road, Southampton, Hampshire SO14 0AA **t** 023 8057 1300 **e** sss@tcp.net.uk **w** tcp.co.uk GM: Mr S Shahi.

Totally Brilliant Media Ltd at Sphere Studios, 2 Shuttleworth Road, London SW11 3EU **t** 020 7326 9494 **f** 020 7326 9495 **e** andyh@totallybrilliant.com **w** totallybrilliant.com MD: Andy Hilton.

Turnround Multi-Media 16 Berkeley Mews, 29 High Street, Cheltenham, Gloucestershire GL50 1DY **t** 01242 224360 **f** 01242 226566 **e** studio@turnround.co.uk **w** turnround.co.uk MD: Ross Lammas.

TWO:design London Studio 20, The Arches, Hartland Rd, Camden, London NW1 8HR **t** 020 7267 1118 **f** 020 7482 0221 **e** studio@twodesign.net **w** twodesign.net Creative Director: Graham Peake.

UK Multimedia Special Interest Group The Old Office Block, Elmtree Road, Teddington, Surrey TW11 8ST **t** 020 8977 7670 **f** 020 8943 3377 **e** Neil_Sandford@compuserve.com **w** mmsig.org.uk Coordinator: Neil Sandford.

UnLimited Creative Fl 3, Grampian House, Meridian Gate, London E14 9YT **t** 0870 744 2643 **f** 070 9231 4982 **e** chris@unlimitedmedia.co.uk **w** unlimitedmedia.co.uk MD: Chris Cooke.

Via Net.Works UK Ltd 830 Birchwood Boulevard, Birchwood, Warrington, Cheshire WA3 7QZ **t** 0845 330 4959 **f** 01925 484 468 **e** support@vianetworks.co.uk **w** vianetworks.co.uk Mgr, Tech Support: Steven Wiggins.

Virgin Interactive Entertainment 74A Charlotte Street, London W1T 4QN **t** 020 7551 4236 **f** 020 7551 4267 **e** clifford_harry@hotmail.com **w** vie.co.uk Tech Support Rep.: Clifford Harry.

Virgin Net Norfolk House, 31 St James Square, London SW1Y 4JR **t** 020 7664 6000 **f** 020 7664 6006 **e** media@london.virgin.net **w** virgin.net

Virtual Festivals.com 4 Rowan Court, 56 High St, Wimbledon SW19 5EE **t** 020 8605 2691 **f** 020 8605 2255 **e** steve@virtualfestivals.com **w** virtualfestivals.com Managing Ed: Steve Jenner.

Visualeyes Imaging Services 24 West Street, Covent Garden, London WC2H 9NA **t** 020 7836 3004 **f** 020 7240 0050 **e** imaging@visualeyes.ltd.uk **w** visualeyes.ltd.uk Sales & Marketing Manager: Tracy Berry.

Vitaminic Ltd 20 Orange St, London WC2H 7NN **t** 020 7766 4000 **f** 020 7766 4001 **e** info@vitaminic.co.uk **w** vitaminic.co.uk MD: Chris Cass.

WayOutWebs.co.uk PO Box 1345, Ilford, Essex IG4 5FX **t** 07050 333 555 **f** 07020 923 292 **e** info@ArtistDevelopment.Org **w** wayoutwebs.co.uk Business Devt Director: Paul Booth.

Web Sheriff Argentum, 2 Queen Caroline St, London W6 9DX **t** 020 8323 8013 **f** 020 8323 8080 **e** websheriff@websheriff.com **w** websheriff.com MD: John Giacobbi.

Wheel Beaumont House, Kensington Village, Avonmore Road, London W14 8TS **t** 020 7348 1000 **f** 020 7348 1111 **e** jillian.cross@wheel.co.uk **w** wheel.co.uk Business Dev't Mgr: Jillian Cross.

Xebec McGraw-Hill Wellington House, Bath Road, Woodchester, Stroud, Gloucestershire GL5 5EY **t** 01453 835482 **f** 01453 832241 **e** info@xebec.co.uk **w** xebec-online.com Sales Admin: Diana May.

XO Communications 6th Floor, 141 Wardour Street, London W1F 0UT **t** 20 7025 9900 **f** 20 7025 9950 **e** enquiries@uk.xo.com **w** uk.xo.com Contact: Sales Dept

YourRelease PO Box 1153, Winterbourne, Bristol BS36 1DL **t** 0870 909 0500 **f** 0870 909 0600 **e** info@YourRelease.com **w** YourRelease.com Operations Director: Peter Lockett.

ZDNet UK Ltd International House, 1 St Katharine's Way, London E1W 1XQ **t** 020 7903 6800 **f** 020 7903 6000 **e** firstname.lastname@zdnet.co.uk **w** zdnet.co.uk Ops Dir: Jill Hourston.

Zen Internet Ltd Moss Bridge Road, Rochdale, Lancashire OL16 5EA **t** 0870 6000 971 **f** 0870 6000 972 **e** sales@zen.co.uk **w** zen.co.uk Markeing Exec: Rod Fielding.

Zomba Production Music 10-11 St Martin's Court, London WC2N 4AJ **t** 020 7497 4800 **f** 020 7497 4801 **e** promotions@zpm.co.uk **w** zpm.co.uk MD: Stephen Cole.

Zynet Rockeagle House, Pynes Hill, Exeter, Devon EX2 5AZ **t** 01392 209500 **f** 01392 421762 **e** sales@zynet.net **w** zynet.net Business Mgr: Steve Bennett.

Merchandise Companies

ABC Shirts Unit 16, Greenwich Centre Business Park, 53 Norman Road, London SE10 9QF **t** 020 8853 1103 **f** 020 8293 1746 **e** sales@abcshirts.com **w** abcshirts.com Contact: Jane Cheese

Action Jacket Company PO Box 1180, Stourbridge, West Midlands DY9 0LX **t** 01562 887096 **f** 01562 882010 **e** info@actionjacket.co.uk Prop: Brian Smith.

Active Merchandising (T Shirts) 58, Overn Avenue, Buckingham MK18 1LT **t** 01280 814510 **f** 01280 814519 **e** leonprice@lineone.net MD: Leon Price.

Adrenalin Merchandising Unit 5, Church House, Church Street, London E15 3JA **t** 020 8503 0634 **f** 020 8221 2528 **e** scott@adrenalin-merch.demon.co.uk **w** adrenalin-merch.demon.co.uk Contact: Scott Cooper

Airborne Packaging Pegasus House, Beatrice Rd, Leicester LE3 9FH **t 0116 253 6136 f** 0116 251 4485 **e** sales@airbornebags.co.uk **w** airbornebags.co.uk Sales Manager: Chris Milton.

Alchemy Carta Ltd The Alembic, Hazel Drive, Narborough Road South, Leicester LE3 2JE **t** 0116 282 4824 **f** 0116 282 5202 **e** info@alchemygroup.co.uk **w** alcemygroup.co.uk Sales Dir: Sandra Philipson.

Alex Co 94 Guildford Road, Croydon, Surrey CR0 2HJ **t** 020 8683 0546 **f** 020 8689 4749 **e** alexco@btinternet.com MD: Stuart Alexander.

Alister Reid Ties 9 Applegate House, Applegate, Brentwood, Essex CM14 5PL **t** 01277 375329 **f** 01277 375331 **e** colin@arties.fsbusiness.co.uk Sales Manager: Colin Stoddart.

The Alternative Display Company 874 Pershore Road, Selly Park, Birmingham, West Midlands B29 7LS **t** 0121 414 0436 **f** 0121 440 7837 **w** alternativedisplay.co.uk MD: Pauline Carr.

Backstreet International Merchandise Ltd. Unit A, 1st Floor, 16-24 Brewery Road, London N7 9NH **t** 020 7700 2662 **f** 020 7700 2882 **e** sales@bsimerch.com **w** backstreetmerch.com Senior Sales Dir: Roy Jenkins.

Baskind Promotions Ltd 54 Otley Rd, Headingley, Leeds, West Yorkshire LS6 2AL **t** 0113 389 4100 **f** 0113 389 4101 or 0113 278 8307 ISDN **e** simon@baskind.com **w** baskind.com MD: Simon Baskind.

The Bizz 14 Finlay Street, London SW6 6HD **t** 020 7384 1528 **f** 020 7371 5651 **e** mail@the-bizz.demon.co.uk Dir: Anne Loates.

Blowfish U.V. 29 Granville St, Loughborough, Leics. LE11 3BL **t** 07900 262 052 **f** 01509 560 221 **e** anna@blowfishuv.co.uk **w** blowfishuv.co.uk MD: Anna Sandiford.

Blue Grape Tech West House, 4 Warple Way, London W3 0UE **t** 020 8740 5398 **f** 020 8749 5897 **e** wclarke@bluegrape.co.uk **w** bluegrape.gb.com Contact: Wayne Clarke

Bravado International Group 12 Deer Park Road, Windledon, London SW19 3FB **t** 020 8545 8100 **f** 020 8542 1807 **e** firstname.lastname@bravado.ws A&R Manager: Benny Lindstrom.

Caterprint Ltd Unit 3, Chaseside Works,, Chelmsford Rd, Southgate, London N14 4JN **t** 020 8886 1600 **f** 020 8886 1636 **e** info@caterprint.co.uk **w** caterprint.co.uk Contact: Leonard

Chester Hopkins International PO Box 536, Headington, Oxford OX3 7LR **t** 01865 766 766 or 020 8441 1555 **f** 01865 769 736 **e** office@chesterhopkins.co.uk **w** chesterhopkins.co.uk MDs: Adrian Hopkins, Jo Chester.

Chris Kay (UK) Ltd 158 Station Road, Witham, Essex CM8 3YS **t** 01376 500566 **f** 01376 500578 **e** sales@chriskay.com **w** chriskay.com MD: Eddie Clark.

De-lux Merchandise Co Zetland House, 5/25 Scrutton St, London EC2A 4HJ **t** 020 7613 3550 **f** 020 7613 3555 **e** info@de-lux.net **w** de-lux.net MD: Jeremy Joseph.

EMC Advertising Gifts Derwent House, 1064 High Road, Whetstone, London N20 0YY **t** 020 8492 2200 **f** 020 8445 9347 **e** sales@emcadgifts.co.uk **w** emcadgifts.co.uk Sales Dir: John Kay.

Fair Oaks Entertainments 7 Towers Street, Ulverston, Cumbria LA12 9AN **t** 01229 581766 **f** 01229 581766 **e** fairoaksonline@audiohighway.net **w** ahwy.net/fairoaksonline/files/mainpage.doc Contact: JG Livingstone

---

FEZBOROUGH LIMITED

Manor Farm Studio, Cleveley, Oxfordshire OX7 4DY **t** 01608 677100 or 07889 787600 **f** 01608 677101 **e** kellogs@fezbro.com Promotional Merchandise Director: John Kalinowski.

Fifth Column T Shirt Design & Print 276 Kentish Town Road, London NW5 2AA **t** 020 7485 8599 **f** 020 7267 3718 **e** info@fifthcolumn.co.uk **w** fifthcolumn.co.uk MD: Rodney Adams.

Finally Fan-Fair PO Box 153, Stanmore, Middx HA7 2HF **t** 01923 896 975 **f** 01923 896 985 **e** hrano@fan-fair.freeserve.co.uk MD: Mike Hrano.

Flag Standards Compass House, Waldron, East Sussex TN21 0RE **t** 01435 810080 **f** 01435 810082 **e** sales@flagstandards.co.uk **w** flagstandards.co.uk Owner: Tim Eustace.

Framous Unit 12/13 Impress House, Mansell Road, Acton, London W3 7QH **t** 020 8735 0047 **f** 020 8735 0048 **e** info@framous.ltd.uk **w** framous.ltd.uk Office Administrator: Lucy Walker.

GB Posters 1 Russell Street, Kelham Island, Sheffield S3 8RW **t** 0114 276 7454 **f** 0114 272 9599 **e**enquiries@gbposters.com **w** gbposters.co.uk Licensing Director: Robert G Edwards.

GMerch 2 Glenthorne Mews, London W6 0LJ **t** 020 8741 7100 **f** 020 8741 1170 **e** Paula.Campbell@gmerch.com **w** gmerch.com MD: Mark Stredwick.

The Gold Disc.com Moose Towers, 2 Beattie Ave, Newcastle-under-Lyme, Staffs ST5 9LS **t** 01782 634 149 **e** sales@thegolddisc.com **w** thegolddisc.com MD: Dave Breese.

Green Island Promotions Ltd Unit 31, 56 Gloucester Rd, Kensington, London SW7 4UB **t** 0870 789 3377 **f** 0870 789 3414 **e** greenisland@btinternet.com Dir: Steve Lucas.

IDD Enterprises Ltd The Old Boat House, 66 London Rd, Sheffield, South Yorkshire S2 4HL **t** 0114 273 9848 **f** 0114 278 7855 **e** ian@iddltd.co.uk **w** iddltd.co.uk Sales Director: Ian Bell.

Independent Posters PO Box 7259, Brentwood, Essex CM14 5ZA **t** 01277 372000 **f** 01277 375333 **e** info@independentposters.co.uk Publishing Manager: Kim Miller.

Inkorporate 10A Lower Mall, Hammersmith, London W6 9DJ **t** 020 8748 3311 **f** 020 8563 7999 **e** sales@inkorporate.co.uk **w** inkorporate.co.uk Sales Director: Melvyn de Villiers.

JTL Printed And Embroided Leisurewear Unit 12, Worcester Road Industrial Est, Chipping Norton, Oxfordshire OX7 5XW **t** 0845 2250725 **f** 01608 645529 **e** sales@jtlembroidery.co.uk Sales Director: Mike Yallop.

Klobber Ltd 443 Streatham High Road, London SW16 3PH **t** 020 8679 9289 **f** 020 679 9775 **e** info@fruitpiemusic.com **w** fruitpiemusic.com Director: Kumar Kamalagharan.

Lasgo Chrysalis Ltd Unit 2, Chapmans Park, 378 High Road Willesden, London NW10 2DY **t** 020 8459 8800 **f** 020 8451 5555 **e** merchandise@lasgo.co.uk **w** lasgo.co.uk Dance Sales & Purchasing: Jeff Ward.

LOGO Promotional Merchandise Ltd 10 Crescent Terrace, Ilkley, West Yorkshire LS29 8DL **t** 01943 817 238 **f** 01943 605 259 **e** alan@logomerchandising.co.uk **w** logomerchandising.co.uk Director: Alan Strachan.

Masons Music Dept. 260, Drury Lane, Ponswood Industrial Est, St Leonards On Sea, East Sussex TN38 9BA **t** 01424 427562 **f** 01424 434362 **e** sales@masonsmusic.co.uk **w** masonsmusic.co.uk Sales Admin: Alastair Sutton.

Metro Merchandising Ltd The Warehouse, 60 Queen Street, Desborough, Northamptonshire NN14 2RE **t** 01536 763100 **f** 01536 763200 **e** mailbox@metro-ltd.co.uk **w** metro-ltd.co.uk MD: Martin Stowe.

Mick Wright Merchandising 185 Weedon Road, Northampton NN5 5DA **t** 07000 226397 or 07802 500054 **f** 08701 372735 **e** tshirts@mickwright.com **w** mickwright.com CEO: Mick Wright.

Montfleury Kardelton House, Arthur Rd, Windsor, Berks SL4 1SE **t** 01753 778989 **f** 01753 778988 **e** info@montfleury.com **w** montfleury.com Dir: Shami Kalra.

Olympus Designs Unit 3, Balthane, Ballasalla, Isle of Man IM9 2AJ **t** 01624 825396 **f** 01624 825423 **e** olympus@advsys.co.uk MD: Chris Beards.

Pagan 1A Kirk Lane, Ruddington, Nottinghamshire NG11 6NN **t** 0115 984 4224 **f** 0115 984 3227 **e** PAGAN.BYH@btinternet.com Contact: Garry Sharpe-Young

PKA Promotions 6 South Folds Road, Oakley Hay Industrial Estate, Corby, Northamptonshire NN18 9EU **t** 01536 461122 **f** 01536 744668 **e** PKaPromotions@aol.com MD: Mr D Dias.

Promotional Condom Co PO Box 111, Croydon, Surrey CR9 6WS **t** 0033 29751 2950 **f** 0033 29739 3306 **e** promotionalcondoms@btopenworld.com Dir: Andrew Kennedy.

Propaganda Symal House, 423 Edgware Road, London NW9 0HU **t** 020 8200 1000 **f** 020 8200 4929 **e** sales@propa.net **w** propa.net Sales Manager: Jason Stevens.

Pyramid Posters The Works, Park Road, Blaby, Leicester LE8 4EF **t** 0116 264 2642 **f** 0116 264 2640 **e** mordy.benaiah@pyramidposters.com **w** pyramidposters.com Licensing Director: Mordy Benaiah.

Razamataz 4 Derby Street, Colne, Lancashire BB8 9AA **t** 01282 861099 **f** 01282 861327 **e** sales@razamataz.com **w** razamataz.com Contact: Simon Hartley, Rachel Redfearn

Rock-It! Promotions Old Employment Exchange, East Grove, (off Rectory Rd), Rushden, Northants NN10 0AR **t** 0800 980 4660 **f** 01933 413279 **e** rock-it@easynet.co.uk **w** promoclothing.com Sales Manager: Andy Campen.

Rowleys:London One Port Hill, Hertford, Herts SG14 1PJ **t** 01992 587350 or 01992 551931 **f** 01992 586059 **e** info@rowleyslondon.co.uk **w** rowleyslondon.co.uk MD: Annie Rowley.

RTG Branded Apparel The Old Dispensary, 36 The Millfields, Plymouth, Devon PL1 3JB **t** 01752 253888 **f** 01752 255663 **e** sales@rtg.co.uk **w** rtg.co.uk Sales Dir: Andy Moulding.

Sandbag Ltd 59/61 Milford Rd, Reading RG1 8LG **t** 0118 9505812 **f** 0118 9505813 **e** mungo@sandbag.uk.com **w** sandbag.uk.com Contact: Christiaan Munro

Shirty Shirts 144 Algernon Road, London SE13 7AW **t** 020 8690 7658 **f** 020 7692 9258 **e** justin@shirtyshirts.screaming.net Ops Dir: Justin Simpson.

Stop Press Screen Printing 38 Torquay Gardens, Redbridge, Ilford, Essex IG4 5PT **t** 020 8551 9005 **f** 020 8551 9005 **e** g4gql@aol.com.uk Contact: Alan Shipman

Sweet Concepts Symal House, 423 Edgware Road, London NW9 0HU **t** 020 8200 5000 **f** 020 8200 4929 **e** sales@sweetconcepts.com **w** sweetconcepts.com MD: Stephen Taylor.

T.O.T. Shirts 14B Banksia Rd, Eley Estate, Edmonton, London N18 3BH **t** 020 8807 8083 **f** 020 8345 6095 **e** sales@t-o-t-shirts.co.uk w t-o-t-shirts.co.uk Snr Account Dir: Paul Whiskin.

Tabak Marketing Ltd Network House, 29-39 Stirling Road, London W3 8DJ **t** 020 8993 5966 **f** 020 8992 0340 or 020 8893 1396 **e** tabak@arab.co.uk Mgr: Chris Leaning.

Target Transfers Ltd Anglia Way, Chapel Hill, Braintree, Essex CM7 3RG **t** 01376 326351 **f** 01376 345876 **e** info@targettransfers.com **w** targettransfers.com Managing Director: Robin Bull.

TDC Neckwear 34 Chandlers Rd, St Albans, Hertfordshire AL4 9RS **t** 01727 840548 **f** 01727 840552 **e** djt@tieman.co.uk **w** tieman.co.uk MD: David Taylor.

Mike Thorn Display & Design 30 Muswell Avenue, London N10 2EG **t** 020 8442 0279 **f** 020 8442 0496 **e** info@bear-art.com Contact: Mike Thorn

Tie Rack Corporate Neckwear Capital Interchange Way, Brentford, Middlesex TW8 0EX **t** 020 8230 2345 **f** 020 8230 2350 **e** corp.sales@tie-rack.co.uk **w** tierackcorporate.com MD: Peter Hirsch.

The Tradewinds Merchandising Company Ltd Cranford Way, London N8 9DG **t** 0208 341 9700 **f** 0208 341 6295 **e** sales@tradewinds.eu.com **w** tradewinds.eu.com Sales Manager: Les Deacon.

West Country Marketing & Advertising Kyre Park, Kyre, Tenbury Wells, Worcestershire WR15 8RP **t** 01885 410247 **f** 01885 410398 **e** info@wcma.co.uk **w** wcma.co.uk Sales Director: Simon Adam.

Wyrd Sects 1A Kirk Lane, Ruddington, Nottinghamshire NG11 6NN **t** 0115 984 4224 or 0800 3281382 **f** 0115 984 3227 **e** PAGAN.BYH@btinternet.com Contact: Garry Sharpe-Young

Zephyr Flags And Banners Midland Road, Thrapston, Northamptonshire NN14 4LX **t** 01832 734484 **f** 01832 733064 **e** sskey@zephyrflags.com **w** zephyrflags.com Sales Mgr: Simon Skey.

Distributors

4am Distribution 1 Campaspe Park, Fordbridge Road, Sunbury On Thames, Middx TW16 6AX **t** 01932 769760 **f** 01932 780481 **e** sales@4amdistribution.co.uk w 4amdistribution.co.uk Dir: Dan Pepperrell. [R]

ABSOLUTE MARKETING & DISTRIBUTION LTD.

The Old Lamp Works, Rodney Place, Wimbledon, London SW19 2LQ **t** 020 8540 4242 **f** 020 8540 6056 **e** info@absolutemarketing.co.uk w absolutemarketing.co.uk MD: Henry Semmence. GM: Simon Wills. [R]

ADA Distribution PO Box 800, Belper, Derbyshire DE56 2ZA **t** 01773 850000 **f** 01773 850000 **e** info@adamailorder.co.uk **w** adamailorder.co.uk Sales Director: Michael Peat. [R V]

African Caribbean Asian Entertainment Stars Building, 10 Silverhill Close, Nottingham NG8 6QL **t** 0115 951 9864 **f** 0115 951 9874 **e** acts@african-caribbean-ents.com **w** african-caribbean-ents.com Contact: Mr Sackey [R]

Alternative Music Distribution Unit 29 Cygnus Business Centre, Dalmeyer Rd, London NW10 2XA **t** 020 8830 4401 **f** 020 8830 4466 **e** Info@altmusic-dist.com **w** altmusic-dist.com Sales Dir: Matt Stoddart. [R V]

AMATO DISTRIBUTION

amato distribution

4, Minerva Business Centre, 58-60, Minerva Road, London NW10 6HJ **t** 020 8838 8330 **f** 020 8838 8331 **e** info@amatodistribution.co.uk **w** amatodistribution.co.uk MD: Mario Howell.
Label Enquiries - 020 8838 8335.
UK Sales Enquiries - 020 8838 8333.
International Sales Enquiries - 020 8838 8834. [R]

Apex Entertainment Group Ltd 2nd Floor, Elvin House, Stadium Way, Wembley, Middx HA9 0DW **t** 020 8585 3540 **f** 020 8585 3995 **e** info@indidist.co.uk **w** indidist.co.uk MD: Nigel Reveler. Chairman: Harry Maloney. [R]

Arabesque Distribution Network House, 29-39 Stirling Road, London W3 8DJ **t** 020 8992 7732 or 020 8992 0098 **f** 020 8992 0340 or 020 8993 1396 **e** sales@arab.co.uk **w** arab.co.uk MD: Brian Horn. [R V G]

ARC Music Distribution UK Ltd PO Box 111, East Grinstead, West Sussex RH19 4FZ **t** 01342 312161 **f** 01342 325209 or 01342 315958 **e** info@arcmusic.co.uk **w** arcmusic.co.uk Executive Director: Phil Collinson. [R]

Avanti Records Unit 11, Airlinks Ind Estate, Spitfire Way, Heston, Middlesex TW5 9NR **t** 020 8848 9800 **f** 020 8756 1883 **e** sales@avanti-records.com Hd of Sales: Charlie Paulinski. [R V]

Avid Entertainment 10 Metro Centre, Dwight Rd, Tolpits Lane, Watford, Herts WD18 9UF **t** 01923 281281 **f** 01923 281200 **e** info@avidgroup.co.uk **w** avidgroup.co.uk MD: Richard Lim. [R V]

Backs Distribution St Mary's Works, St Mary's Plain, Norwich, Norfolk NR3 3AF **t** 01603 624290 or 01603 626221 **f** 01603 619999 **e** info@backsrecords.co.uk Distribution Manager: Derek Chapman. [R]

Baked Goods Distribution Ducie House, 37 Ducie Street, Manchester M1 2JW **t** 0161 236 3233 **f** 0161 236 3351 **e** simon@baked-goods.com **w** baked-goods.com Sales Director: Simon Tonkinson. [R]

BDS (Bertelsmann Distribution Services) 24 Crystal Drive, Sandwell Business Park, Warley, West Midlands B66 1QG **t** 0121 543 4000 **f** 0121 543 4399 **e** paul.dudley@bs-uk.com **w** bs-uk.com Head of Business: Paul Dudley. [R V G]

Blue Crystal Endeavour House, Cavendish Rd, Herne Bay, Kent CT6 5BE **t** 01227 749004 **f** 01227 749408 **e** info@reikimusic.co.uk **w** Bluecrystalmusic.com MD: Geoff Milner. [R]

Brothers Distribution Music Village, 11B Osiers Road, London SW18 1NL **t** 020 8870 0011 **f** 020 8870 2101 **e** info@the-brothers.co.uk **w** brothersdistribution.com MD: Nick Titchener. [R]

Cadiz Music Ltd 2 Greenwich Quay, Clarence Rd, London SE8 3EY **t** 020 8692 4691 or 020 8692 3555 **f** 020 8469 3300 **e** richard@cadizmusic.co.uk MD: Richard England. [V]

Candid Productions Ltd 16 Castelnau, London SW13 9RU **t** 020 8741 3608 **f** 020 8563 0013 **e** info@candidrecords.com **w** candidrecords.com MD: Alan Bates. [R]

Cargo Records (UK) Ltd 17 Heathmans Road, Parsons Green, London SW6 4TJ **t** 020 7731 5125 **f** 020 7731 3866 **e** info@cargouk.demon.co.uk **w** cargorecords.co.uk MD: Philip Hill. [R]

Caroline 2 Ltd 342 Athlon Road, Alperton, Middlesex HA10 1BX **t** 020 8601 2200 **f** 020 8601 2262 **e** sales@caroline2.com **w** caroline2.com Sales Director: Dave Gadsby. MD: Oliver Comberti. [R V]

Chandos Records Chandos House, Commerce Way, Colchester, Essex CO2 8HQ **t** 01206 225200 **f** 01206 225201 **e** enquiries@chandos.net **w** chandos.net Sales Mgr: Ginny Cooper. [R]

Changing World Distribution Willow Croft, Wagg Drove, Huish Episcopi, Near Langport, Somerset TA10 9ER **t** 01458 253838 **f** 01458 250317 **e** enquiries@changing-world.com **w** changing-world.com Owner: David Hatfield. Manager: Milton Cecil. [R]

Chart Records 5-6 Lombard Street East, Westland Row, Dublin 2, Ireland **t** 00 353 1 671 3426 or 00 353 1 677 9914 **f** 00 353 1 671 0237 **e** sales@chart.ie MD: Noel Cusack. [R]

Chrome Dreams PO Box 230, New Malden, Surrey KT3 6YY **t** 020 8715 9781 **f** 020 8241 1426 **e** mail@chromedreams.co.uk **w** chromedreams.co.uk GM: Andy Walker. [R]

Cisco Europe 144 Princes Avenue, London W3 8LT **t** 020 8992 7351 **f** 020 8400 4931 **e** info@ciscoeu-rope.co.uk MD: Mimi Kobayashi. [R]

Claddagh Records Dame House, Dame Street, Dublin 2, Ireland **t** +353 1 677 8943 **f** +353 1 679 3664 **e** wholesale@crl.ie **w** claddaghrecords.com Co Mgr: Jane Bolton. [R V]

Classical International Ltd 3rd Floor, 82-84 Clerkenwell Road, London EC1M 5RF **t** 020 7689 1080 **f** 020 7689 1180 **e** info@classical.com **w** classi-cal.com VP Content & Business: Roger Press.

CM Distribution North Works, Hook Stone Park, Harrogate, North Yorkshire HG2 7DB **t** 01423 888979 **f** 01423 540970 **e** info@northworks.co.uk MD: DR Bulmer. [R]

Columbia Tri-Star Home Video 25 Golden Square, London W1F 9LU **t** 020 7533 1111 **f** 020 7533 1015 **e** firstname_lastname@spe.sony.com **w** spe.sony.com [V]

The Complete Record Company Ltd 22 Prescott Place, London SW4 6BT **t** 020 7498 9666 **f** 020 7498 1828 **e** info@complete-record.co.uk MD: Jeremy Elliott. [R]

Confetti Distribution PO Box 11541, London N15 4DW **t** 020 8376 1876 **f** 020 8808 4413 **e** distribution @confettirecords.co.uk **w** confettirecords.co.uk MD: John Josephs. [R]

Contact (UK) Research House, Fraser Road, Greenford, Middlesex UB6 7AQ **t** 020 8997 5662 **f** 020 8997 5664 **e** contactukltd@btinternet.com **w** contactmusic.co.uk Dir: Michael Lo Bianco. [R]

Copperplate Distribution 68 Belleville Rd, London SW11 6PP **t** 020 7585 0357 **f** 020 7585 0357 **e** copperplate2000@yahoo.com **w** copperplatedistribution.com CEO: Alan O'Leary. [R]

Culture Press UK 74-75 Warren Street, London W1T 5PF **t** 020 7387 5550 **f** 020 7387 2756 **e** zep@sternsmusic.com **w** sternsmusic.com Contact: Zep [R]

CYP Children's Audio The Fairway, Bush Fair, Harlow, Essex CM18 6LY **t** 01279 444707 **f** 01279 445570 **e** sales@cypmusic.co.uk **w** kidsmusic.co.uk Sales Manager: Gary Wilmot. Children's audio specialists.

DA Tape & Records 56 Castle Bank, Stafford ST16 1DW **t** 01785 258746 **f** 01785 255367 **e** p.halliwell@tesco.net MD: Paul Halliwell. [R V]

David Bloom Music Sales Ltd 5 O'Feld Terrace, Ferry Rd, Felixstowe, Suffolk IP11 9NA **t** 01394 283712 **f** 01394 283712 **e** david@dbloom.co.uk **w** dbloom.co.uk Dir: David Bloom.

Delta Music PLC 222 Cray Avenue, Orpington, Kent BR5 3PZ **t** 01689 888888 **f** 01689 888800 **e** info@deltamusic.co.uk **w** deltamusic.co.uk MD: Laurie Adams. [R]

Devil Fish Distribution Unit G/H Cooper House, 2 Michael Rd, London SW6 2AD **t** 020 7384 1524 **f** 020 7384 1524 **e** info@devil-fish.com **w** devil-fish.com MD: Mark Macdonald. [R]

Digital Import Software Co The Old Coach House, Windsor Crescent, Radyr, South Glamorgan CF15 8AE **t** 029 2084 3334 **f** 029 2084 2184 **e** digitaldisc@ision.co.uk Prop: Paul Kay. [R]

Direct Dance Distribution Ltd Unit F34, Third Floor, Park Hall Rd Trading Estate, 40 Martell Rd, London SE21 8EN **t** 020 8670 9433 **f** 020 8670 8452 **e** info@directdance.co.uk **w** directdance.co.uk MD: Steve Bradley. [R]

Disc Imports Ltd 1st/2nd Floors, 7 High St, Cheadle, Cheshire SK8 1AX **t** 0161 491 6655 **f** 0161 491 6688 **e** dimus@aol.com **w** dimusic.co.uk MD: Alan Wilson. [R]

Discovery Records Ltd Nursteed Road, Devizes, Wiltshire SN10 3DY **t** 01380 728000 **f** 01380 722244 **e** info@discovery-records.com **w** discovery-records.com MD: Mike Cox. [R]

Gordon Duncan Distributions 20 Newtown Street, Kilsyth, Glasgow, Lanarkshire G65 0LY **t** 01236 827550 **f** 01236 827560 **e** gordon-duncan@sol.co.uk Contact: Jack Scott, Senga Gregor [R V]

Dynamic Entertainment Unit 22 Acton Park Estate, The Vale, London W3 7QE **t** 020 8746 9500 **f** 020 8746 9501 **e** info@dynamicentertainment.co.uk MD: Beverley King. [R V]

Elap UK Ltd 42 Keswick Close, Tilehurst, Reading, Berks RG30 4SD **t** 01189 452999 **f** 01189 451313 **e** chris.wickens@elap.com **w** elap.com GM: Chris Wickens. [R]

EMI Distribution Hermes Close, Tachbrook Park, Leamington Spa, Warwickshire CV34 6RP **t** 01926 466300 **f** 01926 466392 **e** john.williams@emimusic.com Ops Dir: John Williams. [R V]

EMI Records (Ireland) 1 Ailesbury Road, Dublin 4, Ireland **t** 00 353 1 269 3344 **f** 00 353 1 269 6341 **e** firstname.lastname@emimusic.com **w** emirecords.ie MD: Willie Kavanagh. **[R V]**

ENTERTAINMENT UK LTD

243 Blyth Road, Hayes, Middlesex UB3 1DN **t** 020 8848 7511 **f** 020 8754 6601 **e** enquiries@entuk.com **w** entuk.com MD: Lloyd Wigglesworth. Commercial Dir: Ian Foster. The UK's largest distributor of CDs, VHS and DVD. **[R V G]**

Entertainment UK Direct Auriol Drive, Greenford Park, Greenford, Middx UB6 0DS **t** 020 8833 2888 **f** 020 8833 2967 **e** enquiriesdirect@entuk.co.uk **w** entuk.co.uk GM: Graham Lambdon.

ESSENTIAL DIRECT LTD

Brewmaster House, 91 Brick Lane, London E1 6QL **t** 020 7375 2332 **f** 020 7375 2442 **e** info@essentialdirect.co.uk **w** essentialdirect.co.uk A&R/Dir: Gary Dedman. **[RV]**

Essential Exports Brewmaster House, 91 Brick Lane, London E1 6QL **t** 020 7375 2332 **f** 020 7375 2442 **e** info@essentialdirect.co.uk **w** essentialdirect.co.uk A&R/Dir: Gary Dedman. [R]

Excel Marketing Services Ltd Prism Leisure Building, Knowl Piece, Wilbury Way, Hitchin, Herts SG4 0TY **t** 01462 423231 **f** 01462 423222 **e** excelms@aol.com MD: Vinoth Kumar. [R V G]

EXO Ltd Unit 23 Cannon Wharf, 35 Evelyn Street, London SE8 5RT **t** 020 7394 7234 **f** 020 7394 7239 **e** davidwest@exoltd.fsnet.co.uk MD: David West. [R]

F Minor Ltd Unit 8, Commercial Mews North, 45A, Commercial Road, Eastbourne, East Sussex BN21 3XF **t** 01323 736598 **f** 01323 738763 **e** sales@fminor.com **w** fminor.com MD: Paul Callaghan. [R]

Fat Cat International Ltd 20 Liddell Road Estate, Maygrove Road, London NW6 2EW **t** 020 7624 4335 **f** 020 7624 4866 **e** info@fatcatint.co.uk **w** fatcatint.co.uk MD: Trevor Reidy. [R]

Fat Shadow Records Ltd Unit 23, Cygnus Business Centre, Dalmeyer Road, London NW10 2XA **t** 020 8830 2233 **f** 020 8830 2244 **e** mikekirk@fatshad.co.uk **w** fatshadowrecords.com MD: Michael Kirkman. [R V]

Fierce! Distribution PO Box 40, Arundel, West Sussex BN18 0UQ **t** 01243 558444 **f** 01243 558455 **e** info@fiercedistribution.com **w** fiercedistribution.com Director: Jonathan Brown. Director: Tony Patoto. Marketing Manager: Vanessa Carreras. [R]

Flute Worldwide Ltd 1 Campaspe Park, Fordbridge Road, Sunbury-On-Thames, Middlesex TW16 6AX **t** 01932 769760 **f** 01932 780481 **e** info@fluteworld-wide.co.uk **w** fluteworldwide.co.uk MD: Duncan Peel.

Fopp Ltd Unit 1, Eldonwall Trading Estate, Brislington, Bristol BS4 3QE **t** 0117 972 7130 **f** 0117 941 8724 **e** info@fopp.co.uk; firstname.lastname@fopp.co.uk **w** fopp.co.uk GM: Ryan Latham. Purchasing Mgr: Andy Singh. [R V G]

Fullfill Distribution Ltd Studio 54, 222 Kensal Road, London W10 5BN **t** 020 8968 1231 **f** 020 8964 1181 **e** info@fullfill.co.uk **w** fullfill.co.uk Office Manager: Danni Chambers. [R]

Global Dance Distribution Ltd The Substation, The Saga Centre, 326 Kensal Road, London W10 5BZ **t** 020 8969 9333 **f** 020 8960 7010 **e** anyone@global-dance.co.uk **w** globaldance.co.uk General Manager: Al Robertson. [R]

GOLDS

Uplands Business Park, Blackhorse Lane, Walthamstow, London E17 5QJ **t** 020 8501 9600 **f** 020 8527 3232 **w** sgolds.co.uk **e** sales@sgolds.co.uk Telesales (UK): 020 8527 1035. Fax (UK) 020 8527 3605. Sales (Export): +44 (0) 8282 7031. Fax (Export): +44 (0) 8527 3605.
Wholesaling Entertaiment Software for 50 years - 1955-2005. DVD, VHS, CD, Games, Books & Accessories [R V G]

Goya Music Distribution Ltd The Saga Centre, 326 Kensal Road, London W10 5BZ **t** 020 8968 9666 **f** 020 8969 9558 **e** info@goyamusic.com **w** goyamusic.com Directors: Mike Slocombe/Spencer Weekes. [R]

GR London Ltd 130A Plough Road, Battersea, London SW11 2AA **t** 020 7924 1948 or 020 7924 2254 **f** 020 7924 6069 or 020 7924 4271 **e** info@grlondon.com **w** grlondon.com Director: John Wright. [R]

Griffin & Co. Ltd Church House, 96 Church St, St Mary's Gate, Lancaster LA1 1TD **t** 01524 844399 **f** 01524 844335 **e** sales@griffinrecords.co.uk **w** griffin-records.co.uk GM: Ian Murray. [R]

Handleman UK Ltd 27 Leacroft Rd, Birchwood, Warrington, Cheshire WA3 6PJ **t** 0870 4445844 **f** 0870 4445944 **e** robsalter@handleman.co.uk **w** handleman.co.uk Head of Purchasing: John Misra. MD: Rob Salter. [R V]

Harmonia Mundi (UK) Ltd 45 Vyner Street, London E2 9DQ **t** 020 8709 9509 **f** 020 8709 9501 **e** info.uk@harmoniamundi.com **w** harmoniamundi.com MD: Serge Rousset. [R]

Hermanex Ltd Connaught House, 112-120 High Rd, Loughton, Essex IG10 4HJ **t** 020 8508 3723 **f** 020 8508 0432 **e** uk@hermanex.nl Director: Dave Harmer. [R V G]

Hot Records PO Box 333, Brighton, Sussex BN1 2EH **t** 01403 740260 **f** 01403 740261 **e** info@hotrecords.uk.com **w** hotrecords.uk.com GM: Andrew Bowles. [R]

Hot Shot Records 29 St Michaels Road, Leeds, West Yorkshire LS6 3BG **t** 0113 274 2106 **f** 0113 278 6291 **e** sales@bluescat.com **w** bluescat.com MD: Dave Foster. [R]

I&B Records (Irish Music) Ltd 2A Wrentham Avenue, London NW10 3HA **t** 020 8960 9160 or 020 8960 9169 **f** 020 8968 7332 Dir: Peter Browne. [R V]

Ibex Distribution Ltd. Suite 1, First Floor, 23 Percy St, Hanley, Stoke-on-Trent, Staffs ST1 1NA **t** 01782 281777 **f** 01782 208461 **e** becky@ibexdistribution.co.uk **w** ibexdistribution.co.uk Sales Manager: Becky Hall. [R]

Impetus Distribution Ltd 10 High Street, Skigersta, Ness, Isle of Lewis, Outer Hebrides HS2 0TS **t** 01851 810 808 **f** 01851 810 809 MD: Paul Acott-Stephens. [R]

IMS, Interactive Management Services Unit 4C, The Odyssey Centre, Corporation Rd, Birkenhead, Merseyside CH41 1LB **t** 0845 644 1580 **f** 0845 644 1580 **e** daveims@compuserve.com **w** heritagevideo.co.uk MD: David MacWilliam. [R V]

Independent Distribution Ltd 2nd Floor, Elvin House, Stadium Way, Wembley, Middx HA9 0DW **t** 020 8585 3540 **f** 020 8585 3995 **e** info@indidist.co.uk **w** indidist.co.uk MD: Nigel Reveler. [R V]

InterGroove Ltd 101 Bashley Rd, Park Royal, London NW10 6TE **t** 020 8838 2000 **f** 020 8838 2003 **e** info@intergroove.co.uk **w** intergroove.co.uk MD: Andy Howarth. [R]

Jazz Music Glenview, Moylegrove, Cardigan, Dyfed SA43 3BW **t** 01239 881278 **f** 01239 881296 **e** jazz.music@btinternet.com Sales Mgr: Jutta Greaves. [R V]

Jet Star Phonographics 155 Acton Lane, Park Royal, London NW10 7NJ **t** 020 8961 5818 **f** 020 8965 7008 **e** distribution@jetstar.co.uk **w** jetstar.co.uk MD: Carl Palmer. [R V]

KRD 81-82 Stour St, Birmingham B18 7AJ **t** 0121 248 2548 **f** 0121 248 2549 **e** krd1@supanet.com MD: Pat Ward. [R]

Kudos Records Ltd 77 Fortess Road, Kentish Town, London NW5 1AG **t** 020 7482 4555 **f** 020 7482 4551 **e** info@kudosrecords.co.uk **w** kudosrecords.co.uk MD: Danny Ryan. [R]

K°la Records & Distribution Charlemont House, 33 Charlemont Street, Dublin 2 **t** +353 1 476 0627 **f** +353 1 476 0627 **e** info@kilarecords.com **w** kila.ie Director: Colm O'Snodaigh. [R]

LASGO CHRYSALIS LTD

Lasgo Chrysalis

Unit 2, Chapmans Park Ind. Est., 378-388 High Road, Willesden, London NW10 2DY **t** 020 8459 8800 **f** 020 8451 5555 **e** info@lasgo.co.uk **w** lasgo.co.uk Sales Mgr: Paul Burrows. **The UK's Leading Wholesaler of CDs, DVDs, Books, Vinyl, Deals & Overstocks to the traditional & non-traditional sectors.** [CD DVD B VIN V]

Lightning Export First Floor, 141 High St, Southgate, London N14 6BX **t** 020 8920 1250 **f** 020 8920 1252 **e** Export.Information@the.co.uk **w** the.co.uk GM: Bill Brightley. [R V G]

Load Media Burghfield Bridge, Green Lane, Burghfield, Reading RG30 3XN **t** 01189 599944 **f** 01189 587416 **e** info@load-media.co.uk **w** load-media.co.uk A&R & Production: Brillo. [R]

Love Da Records 20/F New Victory House, 93-103 Wing Lok St, Hong Kong **t** +852 2264 1025 **f** +852 2264 1211 **e** tommy@love-da-records.com **w** love-da-records.com Director: Tommy Chan. [R]

Media UK Distribution Sovereign House, 12 Trewartha Road, Praa Sands, Penzance, Cornwall TR20 9ST **t** 01736 762826 or 07721 449477 **f** 01736 763328 **e** panamus@aol.com **w** songwriters-guild.co.uk MD: Roderick Jones. [R V]

Megaworld Ltd 11 Hatherley Mews, Walthamstow, London E17 4QP **t** 020 8521 2211 **f** 020 8521 6911 **e** sales@megaworld.co.uk **w** megaworld.co.uk Dir: Nigel King. [R]

Metrodome Distribution 110 Park Street, London W1K 6NX **t 020 7408 2121 f** 020 7409 1935 **e** video@metrodomegroup.com **w** metrodome group.com Head Of Marketing: Jane Lawson. [V]

Metronome Distribution Singleton Court, Wonastow Road, Monmouth NP25 5JA **t** 01600 775 395 **f** 01600 775 396 **e** info@metronome.co.uk **w** metronomedistribution.co.uk Label Manager: Colin Chambers. [R]

MIA Video Entertainment Ltd MIA Video, 4th Floor, 72-75 Marylebone High Street, London W1U 5JW **t** 020 7935 9225 **f** 020 7935 9565 **e** miavid@aol.com Prod Mgr: Vanessa Chinn. [V]

Midland Records Chase Road, Brownhills, West Midlands WS8 6JT **t** 01543 378222 or 01543 378225 **f** 01543 360988 Dir: Ms Wendy Creffield. [R V]

Aura Surround Sound Ltd. t/a Mo's Music Machine Unit 11, Forest Business Park, Argall Avenue, Leyton, London E10 7FB **t** 020 8520 7264 **f** 020 8223 0351 **e** gary@mosmusic.co.uk **w** mosmusic.co.uk Head of Sales: Gary Kay. [R V]

Movementinsound PO Box 302, Torquay TQ2 7WA **t** 01803 605085 **f** 01803 605085 **e** info@movementinsound.com **w** movementinsound.com Dirs: Chris Clark, Stephen Gould. [R]

Multiple Sounds Distribution Units 1 - 2 Bay Close, Port of Heysham Ind Estate, Heysham, Lancs LA3 2XS **t** 01524 851177 **f** 01524 851188 **e** info@multiple-sounds.com **w** multiplesounds.com MD: Mike Hargreaves. [R]

Music Box Leisure Ltd Unit 9, Enterprise Court, Lancashire Enterprise Bus Park, Centurion Way, Leyland PR26 6TZ **t** 01772 455000 **f** 01772 331199 **e** enquiries@musicboxleisure.com Sales Director: Jan Beer. MD: Trevor Allan. Head Buyer: James Allan. [R V]

Music Express Ltd Sheepscar House, Sheepscar Street South, Leeds, West Yorkshire LS7 1AD **t** 0113 234 4112 **f** 0113 234 4113 **e** office@music-express.co.uk Director: Christopher Lane. [R V G]

Music Sales (Northern Ireland) 224B Shore Road, Lower Greenisland, Carrickfergus, Co Antrim BT38 8TX **t** 028 9086 5422 **f** 028 9086 2902 **e** music-sales@dnet.co.uk **w** musicsalesni.co.uk Dir: Eddie Graham. [R V]

MVD Distribution Unit 4, Rampart Business Park, Greenbank Industrial Estate, Newry, Co Down BT34 2QU **t** 028 3026 2926 **f** 028 3026 2671 **e** mail@wren.ie **w** soundsirish.com MD: Canice McGarry. [R V G]

Nervous Records 5 Sussex Crescent, Northolt, Middlesex UB5 4DL **t** 020 8423 7373 **f** 020 8423 7773 **e** Nervous@compuserve.com **w** nervous.co.uk MD: Roy Williams. [R]

New Note Distribution Ltd Electron House, Cray Avenue, Orpington, Kent BR5 3RJ **t** 01689 877884 **f** 01689 877891 **e** mail@newnote.com **w** newnote.com Joint MD (Distrib/Admin): Graham Griffiths. [R]

North West Music 10 Magnet Road, East Lane Business Park, Wembley, Middlesex HA9 7RG **t** 020 8904 7700 **f** 020 8904 1999 **e** northwestmusic@northwestmusic.co.uk MD: Aniff Allybokus. [R]

Northern Record Supplies Ltd Star Works, Wham St, Heywood, Lancs OL10 4QU **t** 01706 367412 or 01706 620842 **f** 01706 620842 **e** nrs99@ukonline.co.uk **w** northernrecords.co.uk MD: Simon Jones. [R V]

NOVA SALES AND DISTRIBUTION (UK) LTD

Isabel House, 46 Victoria Road, Surbiton, Surrey KT6 4JL **t** 020 8390 3322 or 020 8390 6639 **f** 020 8390 3338 **e** info@novadist.co.uk **w** novadist.co.uk MD: Wilf Mann. [R V]

Nu Urban Music Unit 3, 36 Queens Rd, Newbury, Berkshire RG14 7NE **t** 01635 551400 **f** 01635 550333 **e** tobie@nu-urbanmusic.co.uk **w** nu-urbanmusic.co.uk A&R Manager: Tobie Scapes. [R]

One Nation Exports Units G11/G10, Belgravia Workshops, 159-163 Marlborough Road, London N19 4NP **t** 020 7263 3100 **f** 020 7263 3002 **e** barry@onenation.co.uk MD: Barry Milligan. [R]

The Orchard 25 Floral St, Covent Garden, London WC2E 9DS **t** 020 7031 8278 or 0788 438 1970 **e** jason@theorchard.com **w** theorchard.com MD: Jason Ojalvo. [R]

Pendle Hawk Music Distribution 2nd Floor, 11 Newmarket Street, Colne, Lancashire BB8 9BJ **t** 01282 866317 **f** 01282 866317 **e** pendlehawkmusic@ntl.world.com MD: Adrian Melling. [R]

Pickwick Group Ltd 230 Centennial Park, Elstree Hill South, Elstree, Borehamwood, Herts WD6 3SN **t** 020 8236 2310 **f** 020 8236 2312 **e** info@pickwickgroup.com **w** pickwickgroup.com GM: Mark Lawton. [R V]

PINNACLE RECORDS

Heather Court, 6 Maidstone Road, Sidcup, Kent, DA14 5HH **t** 020 8309 3600 or **f** 020 8309 3600 Cust Service **t** 020 8309 3925 Tele-Ordering

t 020 8309 3926 **f** 0208 309 3894 or orders@pinnacle-records.co.uk **e** firstname.lastname@pinnacle-records.co.uk **w** www.pinnacle-entertainment.co.uk Chairman: Sean Sullivan. MD: Tony Powell. GM: Susan Rush. Commercial Dir: Chris Maskery.Ops Dir: Alan King. **Also representing 3MV, New Note, Shellshock, Kudos, Nova, Weatherbox, Cadiz & Dynamic Music & Media.** [R V G]

PLASTIC HEAD MUSIC DISTRIBUTION LTD

Avtech House, Hithercroft Rd, Wallingford, Oxfordshire OX10 9DA **t** 01491 825029 **f** 01491 826320 admin **e** info@plastichead.com **w** plastichead.com Dir: Steve Beatty. [R V]

Play Right Distribution Crabtree Cottage, Mill Lane, Kidmore End, Oxon RG4 9HB **t** 0118 972 4356 **f** 0118 972 4809 **e** ppmusicint@aol.com **w** dovehouserecords.com Head of Sales: Lara Pavey. [R]

David Powell Distribution 182 Park Avenue, Riverside Business Park, London NW10 7XH **t** 020 8963 1717 **f** 020 8961 3910 **e** sales@dpdist.com MD: David Powell. [R]

Prime Distribution 340-341 Athlon Road, Alperton, Middlx HA0 1BX **t** 020 8601 2200 **f** 020 8997 2292 **e** music@primedistribution.co.uk **w** primedistribution.co.uk MD: John Warwick. [R]

Priory Records Ltd 3 Eden Court, Eden Way, Leighton Buzzard, Bedfordshire LU7 4FY **t** 01525 377566 **f** 01525 371477 **e** sales@priory.org.uk **w** priory.org.uk MD: Neil Collier. [R]

Prism Leisure Corp plc Unit 1, 1 Dundee Way, Enfield, Middlesex EN3 7SX **t** 020 8804 8100 **f** 020 8216 6645 **e** music@prismleisure.com **w** prismleisure.com DVD Softward Director: Mark Pearce. Head of Licensing: Steve Brink. Exports: Simon Checketts. [R V G]

Proper Music Distribution Ltd Unit 1, Gateway Business Centre, Kangley Bridge Road, London SE26 5AN **t** 0870 444 0800 **f** 0870 444 0801 **e** info@proper.uk.com **w** proper.uk.com MD: Malcolm Mills. Operations Dir: Steve Kersley. Finance Dir: John Glockler. Export Manager: Roger Kent. [R V]

Proper Music Imports Ltd The Powerhouse, Cricket Lane, Beckenham, Kent BR3 1LW **t** 020 8676 5115 **f** 020 8676 5169 **e** gaz@proper.uk.com Imports: Gary Harries. [R]

Quadrant Video 37A High Street, Carshalton, Surrey SM5 3BB **t** 020 8669 1114 **f** 020 8669 8831 **e** admin@quadrantvideo.co.uk **w** quadrantvideo.co.uk MD: Chris Jolly. **[V]**

Record Services 30-32 Sir John Rogerson Quay, Dublin 2, Ireland **t** +353 1 671 4011 **f** +353 1 671 4554 **e** rsirl@indigo.ie **w** recordservices.biz MD: Brian Wynne. [R V]

Red Lightnin' The White House, The Street, North Lopham, Diss, Norfolk IP22 2LU **t** 01379 687693 **f** 01379 687559 **e** peter@redlightnin.com **w** redlightnin.com MD: Pete Shertser. [R]

Redemption Export 516 Queslett Rd, Birmingham B43 7EJ **t** 0121 605 4791 **f** 0121 605 4791 **e** bhaskar@redemption.co.uk **w** redemption.co.uk MD: Bhaskar Dandona. [R]

Regis Records Ltd Southover House, Tolpuddle, Dorset DT2 7HF **t** 01305 848983 **f** 01305 848516 **e** info@regisrecords.co.uk **w** regisrecords.co.uk GM: Robin Vaughan. [R]

Revolver Music 152 Goldthorn Hill, Penn, Wolverhampton, West Midlands WV2 3JA **t** 01902 345345 **f** 01902 345155 **e** Paul.Birch@revolver-**e**.com **w** Revolver-Records.com MD: Paul Birch. [R]

RM Associates 46 Great Marlborough Street, London W1V 1DB **t** 020 7439 2637 **f** 020 7439 2316 **e** rma@rmassociates.co.uk MD: Reiner Moritz. [R]

RMG Chart Entertainment Ltd. 2, Carriglea, Naas Rd, Dublin 12 **t** +353 1 419 5000 **f** +353 1 419 5016 **e** info@rmgchart.ie **w** rmgchart.ie MD: Peter Kenny. [R]

Rolica Music Distribution 7 Towers Street, Ulverston, Cumbria LA12 9AN **t** 01229 581766 **f** 01229 581766 **e** fairoaksorderline@hotmail.com **w** hmpge.com /roots2rockmusic Prop: John Graeme Livingstone. [R]

Rolled Gold International Ltd Unit 4 Perth Trading Estate, Perth Ave, Slough, Berks SL1 4XX **t** 01753 691317 **f** 01753 692728 **e** rgilimited@aol.com **w** rolled-gold.net Dir: Keith Staton. [R]

Roots Records 250 Earlsdon Avenue North, Coventry, West Midlands CV5 6GX **t** 02476 711935 **f** 02476 7 1191 **e** rootsrecs@btclick.com MD: Graham Bradshaw. [R]

Rose Records 1B Ellington Street, Islington, London N7 8PP **t 020 7609 8288 f** 020 7607 7851 **e** rose.records@lineone.net MD: John Butcher. [R V]

Ross Record Distribution 29 Main Street, Turriff, Aberdeenshire AB53 4AB **t** 01888 568899 **f** 01888 568890 **e** info@rossrecords.com **w** rossrecords.com MD: Gibson Ross. [R V]

RSK ENTERTAINMENT

Unit 3, Home Farm, Welford, Newbury, Berks RG20 8HR **t** 01488 608900 **f** 01488 608901 **e** info@rskentertainment.co.uk **w** rskentertainment.co.uk Joint MDs: Rashmi Patani, Simon Carver. Label Management: Gerry Kelly, Matt Groom. **Independent Minds with Major Company Muscle, offering label management, full national accounts representation plus own field sales force, with fulfilment via Arvato** [R V]

Sain (Recordiau) Cyf Canolfan Sain, Llandwrog, Caernarfon, Gwynedd LL54 5TG **t** 01286 831111 **f** 01286 831497 **e** music@sain.wales.com **w** sain.wales.com MD: Mr D Iwan. [R V]

Sarem & Co 43A Old Woking Road, West Byfleet, Surrey KT14 6LG **t** 01932 352535 **f** 01932 336431 **e** info@sarem-co.com **w** sarem-co.com Partner: Adrian Connelly. Partner: Martin Howell. [R]

Savoy Strict Tempo Distributors PO Box 271, Coulsdon, Surrey CR5 3TR **t** 01737 554 739 **f** 01737 556 737 **e** admin@savoymusic.com **w** savoymusic.com Dir: Wendy Smith. [R]

SBI Global Ltd Oak Lodge, Leighams Road, Bicknacre, Chelmsford, Essex CM3 4HF **t** 01245 328683 **f** 020 7504 8242 **e** sales@sbiglobal.com **w** sbiglobal.com GM: Keith Page. [R]

Securicor Omega Express Sutton Park House, 15 Carshalton Road, Sutton, Surrey SM1 4LD **t** 020 8770 7000 **f** 020 8722 2974 **e** marketing@soe.securicor.co.uk **w** securicor.com/euroexpress Director of Sales: Jonathan Simpson. [R V G]

See For Miles Records Ltd 10 Littleton House, Littleton Road, Ashford, Middlesex TW15 1UU **t** 01784 247176 **f** 01784 241168 **e** sfm@highnote.co.uk **w** seeformiles.co.uk Sales & Marketing Manager: Steve Waters. [R]

Select Music & Video Distribution 3 Wells Place, Redhill, Surrey RH1 3SL **t** 01737 645600 **f** 01737 644065 **e** cds@selectmusic.co.uk **w** selectmusic.co.uk MD: Anthony Anderson. [R V]

Shellshock Distribution 23A Collingwood Road, London N15 4LD **t** 020 8800 8110 **f** 020 8800 8140 **e** info@shellshock.co.uk **w** shellshock.co.uk MD: Garreth Ryan. [R V]

Shetland Music Distribution Ltd Griesta, Tingwall, Shetland ZE2 9QB **t** 01595 840670 **f** 01595 840671 **e** enquiries@shetlandmusicdistribution.co.uk **w** shetlandmusicdistribution.co.uk Director: Ronnie Jamieson. Director: Alan Longmuir. [R]

Silver Sounds CD Ltd Unit 7, Peerglow Estate, Queensway, Ponders End, Enfield, Middlesex EN3 4SB **t** 020 8364 7711 **f** 020 8805 1135 **e** info@silversounds.co.uk **w** silversounds.co.uk MD: Murray Allan. [R V]

Silverwood Distribution 16 Limetrees, Llangattock, Crickhowell, Powys NP8 1LB **t** 01873 810142 **f** 01873 811557 **e** silvergb@aol.com **w** smgdistribution.com Managing Director: Kevin Holland King. [R]

SMG Distribution 16 Limetrees, Llangattock, Crickhowell, Powys NP8 1LB **t** 01873 810142 **f** 01873 811557 **e** smgdistribution@aol.com **w** silverword.co.uk MD: Kevin Holland King. [R]

Snapper Music plc Unit 4, The Coda Centre, 189 Munster Road, London SW6 6AW **t** 020 7610 0330 **f** 020 7386 7006 **e** sales@snappermusic.co.uk **w** snappermusic.com Head of Sales: Tony Harris. [R]

Soul Trader Unit 43, Imex-Spaces Business Centre, Ingate Place, London SW8 3NS **t** 020 7498 0732 **f** 020 7498 0737 **e** soultrader@btconnect.com MD: Marc Lessner. [R]

Sound & Video Gems Ltd Quakers Coppice, Crewe, Cheshire CW1 6EY **t** 01270 589321 **f** 01270 587438 MD: Michael Bates. [R V]

Sound And Media Ltd Unit 4, Coomber Way, Croydon, Surrey CR0 4TQ **t** 020 8684 4286 **f** 020 8684 4173 **e** info@soundandmedia.co.uk **w** soundandmedia.co.uk Ops Dir: Rob Worsfold. [R V]

Sound Entertainment Ltd The Music Village, 11B Osiers Road, London SW18 1NL **t** 020 8874 8444 **f** 020 8874 0337 **e** info@soundentertainment.co.uk Dir: Bob Nolan. [R]

Soundsrite Music Ltd Unit 4, Albert St, Droylsden, Manchester M43 7BA **t** 0161 370 6908 **f** 0161 371 8207 **e** soundsrite2me@aol.com MD: Bill White. [R]

SRD (Southern Record Distribution) 70 Lawrence Road, London N15 4EG **t** 020 8802 3000 or 020 8802 4444 **f** 020 8802 2222 **e** info@southern.com **w** southern.com MD: John Knight. [R]

ST Holdings Ltd Unit 2 Old Forge Road, Ferndown Industrial Estate, Wimborne, Dorset BH21 7RR **t** 01202 890889 **f** 01202 890886 **e** info@stholdings.co.uk **w** stholdings.co.uk Contact: Chris Parkinson [R]

Stern's Distribution 74-75 Warren Street, London W1T 5PF **t** 020 7388 5533 or 020 7387 5550 **f** 020 7388 2756 **e** sales@sternsmusic.com **w** sternsmusic.com UK Sales Mgr: Ian Thomas. [R]

Streets Ahead Record Distribution PO Box 208, Bangor, Co Down, N.Ireland BT20 3WB **t** 028 9147 4116 **f** 028 9147 4116 **e** streets.ahead@business.ntl.com MD: Paul Wyness. [R V G]

Stringbean International Records Ltd Unit 224, 2nd floor, 2-8 Fountayne Road, Tottenham, London N15 4QL **t** 020 8801 7992 **f** 020 8808 0205 **e** sales@stringbeaninternational.com **w** stringbeaninternational.com MD: Donovan Campbell. [R]

SVS Tape Distributors Shentonfield Road, Sharston Industrial Estate, Manchester M22 4RW **t** 0161 491 6660 **f** 0161 491 6669 **e** sales@svsmedia.com **w** svsmedia.com MD: Mr MJ Glasspole. [V]

Swift Record Distributors 3 Wilton Rd, Bexhill on Sea, East Sussex TN40 1HY **t** 01424 220028 **f** 01424 213440 **e** swiftrd@btinternet.com **w** swiftrd.btinternet.co.uk GM: Robin L Gosden. [R]

Synergie Logistics Unit 5, Pilot Trading Estate, West Wycombe Road, High Wycombe, Buckinghamshire HP12 3AB **t** 01494 450606 **f** 01494 450230 **e** synergielogistics@btconnect.com CEO: Nigel Molden. **[R V]**

Talking Books Ltd 11 Wigmore Street, London W1U 1PE **t** 020 7491 4117 **f** 020 7629 1966 **e** support@talkingbooks.co.uk **w** talkingbooks.co.uk Dir: Stanley Simmonds. [R]

Technicolor Distribution Services Ltd Unit 8, Northfield Industrial Estate, Beresford Avenue, Wembley, Middlesex HA0 1NW **t** 020 8900 1122 **f** 020 8900 1658 **e** sales@technicolor.com **w** technicolor.com Director: Tony Brown. [R V G]

TEN (THE ENTERTAINMENT NETWORK)

Rabans Lane, Aylesbury, Bucks HP19 7TS
t 01296 426151 f 01296 481009
e firstname_lastname@ten-distribution.com
w ten-net.com MD: Shaun Plunkett.
Finance Director: Colin Chapple. Distribution Enquiries: enquiries@ten-distribution.com [R V G]

THE (TOTAL HOME ENTERTAINMENT)

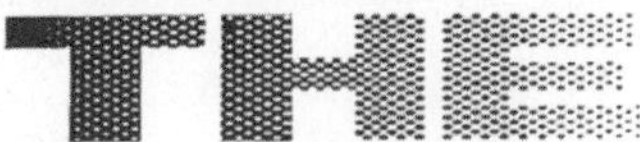

Head Office / Export, Rosevale Business Park, Newcastle-under-Lyme, Staffordshire ST5 7QT **t** 01782 566 566 **f** 01782 565 400 **e** firstname.lastname@the.co.uk **w** the.co.uk Commercial Dir: David Hollander. Audio GM: Andy Adamson. Exclusive Lbls Mgr: Mike Fay. Export Sales Mgr: Matt Glover. Buying Office: Suite 3.1, Shepherds West, Rockley Road, London, W14 ODA. **t** 020 8600 3502. **f** 020 8600 3518. **[R V G]**

Thames Distributors Ltd Unit 12, Millfarm Business Park, Millfield Rd, Hounslow, Middlesex TW4 5PY **t 020 8898 2227 f** 020 8898 2228 **e** gibbon_roger@hotmail.com **w** thamesworldmusic.com Director: Roger Gibbon. [R V]

TIMEWARP DISTRIBUTION

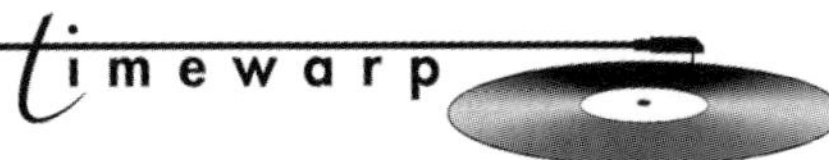

GFM House, Cox Lane, Chessington, Surrey KT9 1SD **t** 020 8397 4466 **f** 020 8397 1950 **e** info@timewarpdis.com **w** timewarpdis.com MD: Bill Shannon. [R]

Tuned Distribution Unit 26 Acklam Workshops, 10 Acklam Road, London W10 5QZ **t** 020 8964 1355 **f** 020 8969 1342 **e** info@tuned-distribution.co.uk **w** tuned-distribution.co.uk MD: Lee Muspratt. [R]

UgGR Distributions PO Box 178, Surrey SM2 6XG **t** 020 8643 6403 or 07904 255 244 **f** 020 8643 6403 **e** ugrrecords@hotmail.com **w** ugrrecords.com Hd of Marketing & Sales: P. Mac. [R]

Unique Distribution Unit 12, Lodge Bank Industrial Estate, Off Crown Lane, Horwich, Bolton BL6 5HY **t** 01204 675500 **f** 01204 479005 **e** contact@uniquedist.co.uk **w** uniquedist.co.uk Dir: James Waddicker. [R]

Universal Music Operations Chippenham Drive, Kingston, Milton Keynes, Bucks MK10 0AT **t** 020 8910 5000 or 08705 310310 **(orders) f** 01908 452600 or 08705 410410(orders) **e** information.centre@umusic.com **w** distribution.umusic.co.uk Commercial/Logistics Mgr: Clive Smith. [R V]

Vinyl UK 59-61 Milford Road, Reading, Berkshire RG1 8LG **t** 0118 960 5700 **f** 0118 960 6800 **e** info@vinyl.nu Owner: Lance Phipps. [R]

Vision Video PO Box 1420, Sussex Place, London W6 9XS **t** 020 8910 5000 **f** 020 8910 5404 **e** firstname.lastname@unistudios.com A&R Manager: Tim Payne. [V]

VITAL DISTRIBUTION

VITAL:

338A Ladbroke Grove, London W10 5AH **t** 020 8324 2400 **f** 020 8324 0001 **e** firstname.lastname@vitaluk.com **w** vitaluk.com; cwnn.org MD: Peter Thompson. Product Dir: Ian Dutt. Sales Dir: Richard Sefton. Vital Digital: Adrian Pope. Vital DVD: James Akerman. Head of International: Adrian Hughes. [R V]

Vital Ireland 30-32 Sir John Rogerson Quay, Dublin 2 **t** +353 1 679 0631 **f** +353 1 671 4554 **e** Sales@vitaliresland.com General Manager: Jay Ahern. [R V]

Vivante Music Ltd Unit 6,, Fontigarry Business Park, Reigate Road, Sidlow, Surrey RG2 8QH **t** 01293 822186 **f** 01293 821965 **e** sales@vivante.co.uk **w** vivante.co.uk MD: Steven Carr. [R]

Windsong International Heather Court, 6 Maidstone Rd, Sidcup, Kent DA14 5HH **t** 020 8309 3867 **f** 020 8309 3905 **e** enquiries@windsong.co.uk **w** windsong.co.uk Hd Of Int'l Sales: David Gadsby. [R V]

Word (UK) Music 9 Holdom Avenue, Bletchley, Milton Keynes, Buckinghamshire MK1 1QR **t** 01908 364210 **f** 01908 364141 **e** info@wordonline.co.uk **w** premiere-online.co.uk MD: Graham Williams. [R V]

WRD Worldwide Music Ltd 282 Camden Road, London NW1 9AB **t** 020 7267 6762 **f** 020 7482 4029 **e** info@wrdmusic.com **w** wrdmusic.com MD: Steve Johanson. [R V]

Wwwatt CD Gregory House, Harlaxton Road, Grantham, Lincolnshire NG31 7JX **t** 01476 577734 **f** 01476 579309 **e** malcolm@wwwatt.co.uk **w** wwwatt.com Ops Mgr: Malcolm Mclean. [R]

Zander Exports 34 Sapcote Trading Centre, 374 High Road, Willesden, London NW10 2DJ **t** 020 8451 5955 **f** 020 8451 4940 or 020 8459 5408 **e** zander@btinternet.com **w** zanderman.co.uk Dir: John Yorke. [R]

Zeit Distribution Ltd PO Box 50, Houghton-le-Spring, Tyne & Wear DH4 5YP **t** 0191 512 1103 **f** 0191 512 1104 **e** info@voiceprint.co.uk **w** voiceprint.co.uk MD: Rob Ayling. [R]

Zenith Sales & Marketing Ltd 70 Wellsway, Bath BA2 4SB **t** 01225 329806 **f** 01225 329650 **e** info@zenithltd.fsbusiness.co.uk **w** zenithlimited.com MD: Andy Richmond. [R V]

ZYX Records

11 Cambridge Court, 210 Shepherds Bush Road, London W6 7NJ **t** 020 7371 6969 **f** 020 7371 6688 or 020 7371 6677 **e** lauren.lorenzo@zyxrecords.freeserve.co.uk **w** zyx.de GM: Lauren Lorenzo. Dist: ZYX

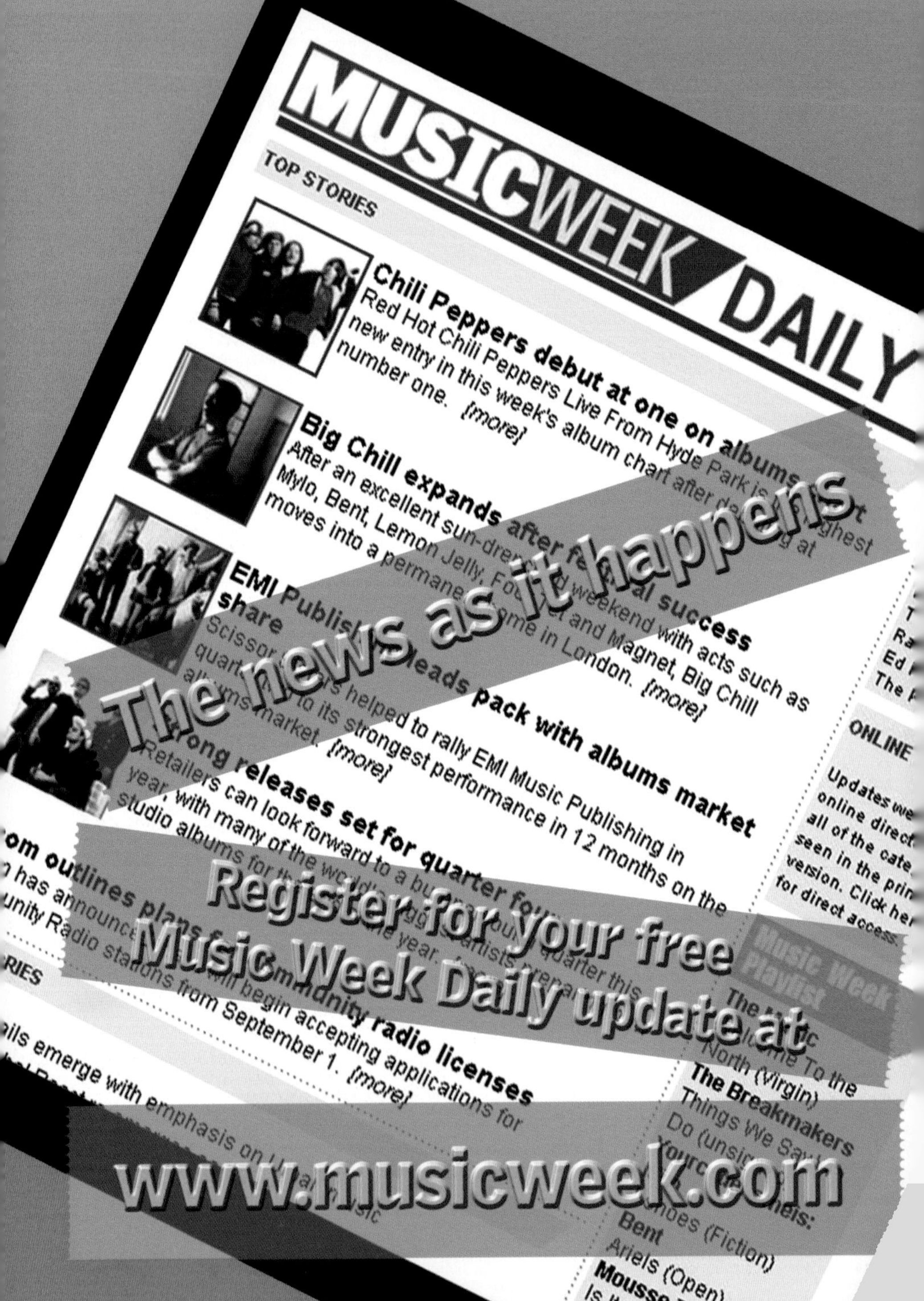
MUSIC WEEK DAILY
TOP STORIES
The news as it happens
Register for your free
Music Week Daily update at
www.musicweek.com

Distributed Labels

!K7: Vital Distribution
1-OFF Recordings: Prime Distribution
10 Kilo: InterGroove Ltd
2 Sinners: ST Holdings Ltd
2000 Black: Goya Music Distribution Ltd
211b: Pinnacle Records
3 Head: Shellshock Distribution
3D Vision: Shellshock Distribution
4 Alarm: Shellshock Distribution
441 Records: The Woods
482 Music: The Woods
541: Timewarp Distribution
6 Mile: Shellshock Distribution
7 Bridges: Timewarp Distribution
818 Music: Shellshock Distribution
A: Proper Music Distribution Ltd
A One: Gordon Duncan Distributions
A Touch of Music: Jazz Music
A&M: Universal Music Operations
AAA: BDS (Bertelsmann Distribution Services)
Aarde: Proper Music Distribution Ltd
Abacabe: Hot Shot Records
Abaco: Pinnacle Records
abCDs: New Note Distribution Ltd, Pinnacle Records
ABL: Nova Sales and Distribution (UK) Ltd
Abokadisc: Proper Music Distribution Ltd
Above Rock: Shellshock Distribution
Absolute: BDS (Bertelsmann Distribution Services), Essential Direct Ltd
Absolutely Kosher: Shellshock Distribution
Abstract Sounds: Plastic Head Music Distribution Ltd
Abuse Your Friends: Pinnacle Records, Shellshock Distribution
Acaysha: ADA Distribution
Accident Prone: Shellshock Distribution
Accidental: Baked Goods Distribution
Accolade: EMI Distribution, Roots Records
Accurate: Proper Music Distribution Ltd
Ace: Jazz Music, New Note Distribution Ltd, Pinnacle Records
Ace Eyed Records: Independent Distribution Ltd
Acetone: Cargo Records (UK) Ltd
Acid Jazz: Shellshock Distribution
Acid Stings: Plastic Head Music Distribution Ltd
Acme: F Minor Ltd
Acolwon: ZYX
Acoustics: RSK Entertainment
Acruacree: Pinnacle Records
Act: New Note Distribution Ltd, Pinnacle Records
Action: Shellshock Distribution
Active Suspension: Baked Goods Distribution
AD Music: Golds
ADA: ADA Distribution
Addis: SRD (Southern Record Distribution)
Additive: Vital Distribution
Adeline: Plastic Head Music Distribution Ltd
Adept: Pinnacle Records
ADN Creation Music Library: Media UK Distribution
Adrenaline: Plastic Head Music Distribution Ltd
ADSR: Pinnacle Records
Adult Swim: Shellshock Distribution
Advanced Bio Systems: SRD (Southern Record Distribution)
Aegean: Pinnacle Records
Aerospace: Jazz Music
AFM Records: Plastic Head Music Distribution Ltd
African Love: Jet Star Phonographics
African Music: Stern's Distribution
After Dark: BDS (Bertelsmann Distribution Services)
Afternoon Focus: Cargo Records (UK) Ltd
Age Of Panik: BDS (Bertelsmann Distribution Services)
Aggro: Proper Music Distribution Ltd
Agram: Hot Shot Records
Ahum: New Note Distribution Ltd
AIM: Proper Music Distribution Ltd
Ainm: I&B Records (Irish Music) Ltd
AIP: Shellshock Distribution
Air Mail: Harmonia Mundi (UK) Ltd
Air Movement: Universal Music Operations
Air Raid: Pinnacle Records
Airtight: Vital Distribution
Airwave Records: RSK Entertainment
AK: ADA Distribution
Akarma: Cargo Records (UK) Ltd, F Minor Ltd
Akashic: Cargo Records (UK) Ltd
AKT/Seventh: Harmonia Mundi (UK) Ltd
Al Segno: New Note Distribution Ltd
Al Sur: Discovery Records Ltd
Al's: Vital Distribution
Alam Madina: Proper Music Distribution Ltd
Alba: Pinnacle Records
Alchemy: New Note Distribution Ltd, Pinnacle Records
Aleph: RSK Entertainment
Alia Vox: Select Music & Video Distribution
Alien Trax: Amato Distribution, Pinnacle Records
Alient Recordings: SRD (Southern Record Distribution)
Alive: Pinnacle Records, Shellshock Distribution
All Around The World: Universal Music Operations
All City: Cargo Records (UK) Ltd
All Good Vinyl: Vital Distribution
All Natural: Cargo Records (UK) Ltd
All Saints: Vital Distribution
All Score Media: Shellshock Distribution
All Star Collection: Pinnacle Records
All That Records: New Note Distribution Ltd
All Tore Up: Shellshock Distribution
Alladin: Avid Entertainment
Allez-Hop: Cargo Records (UK) Ltd
Alliance: EMI Distribution
Alligator: Proper Music Distribution Ltd
Alltone: New Note Distribution Ltd
Alma Latina: Discovery Records Ltd
Almafame: Absolute Marketing & Distribution Ltd., Pinnacle Records
Almighty: BDS (Bertelsmann Distribution Services)
Almo Sounds: Pinnacle Records
Alola: Amato Distribution
Alopecia: Pinnacle Records, Shellshock Distribution
Alpaca Park: Pinnacle Records
Alpha: Pinnacle Records
Alpha & Omega: SRD (Southern Record Distribution)
Alpha Park: Pinnacle Records
Alphabet Records: Plastic Head Music Distribution Ltd
Alphabet.: SRD (Southern Record Distribution)
Alphaphone: Pinnacle Records
Alter Ego: Vital Distribution
Altered Vibes: Cargo Records (UK) Ltd
Alternative Tentacles: Plastic Head Music Distribution Ltd
AM:PM: Universal Music Operations
Amate: Jet Star Phonographics
Amazing Feet: Nova Sales and Distribution (UK) Ltd, Pinnacle Records
Ambassador: Jazz Music
Amber: Proper Music Distribution Ltd
Amberley: Cargo Records (UK) Ltd
Ambient: EMI Distribution
Ambition: RSK Entertainment
Ambush: Pinnacle Records, Shellshock Distribution
American Recordings: BDS (Bertelsmann Distribution Services)
American Clave: New Note Distribution Ltd, Proper Music Distribution Ltd
American Music: The Woods
American Pop Project: Cargo Records (UK) Ltd
American Primitive: Cargo Records (UK) Ltd
Amiata: Universal Music Operations
Amos Recordings: SRD (Southern Record Distribution)
Amphetamine Reptile USA: Plastic Head Music Distribution Ltd
Amputate: Shellshock Distribution
Anagram: Pinnacle Records
Anansi: Pinnacle Records
And Sound: Shellshock Distribution
Andmoresound: Cargo Records (UK) Ltd
Andromeda: Shellshock Distribution
Angel Air: Proper Music Distribution Ltd
Angella: Jet Star Phonographics
Angelwings: Shellshock Distribution
AniManga: New Note Distribution Ltd, Pinnacle Records
Ankst Musik: Shellshock Distribution
Another Planet: Pinnacle Records, Plastic Head Music Distribution Ltd
Ant Zen: Shellshock Distribution
Antigua Sun: Universal Music Operations
Antilles: Universal Music Operations
Antiphon: Vital Distribution
Antipop: Pinnacle Records, Shellshock Distribution
Antones: Proper Music Distribution Ltd
Anty: Vital Distribution
Anuna Teo: Proper Music Distribution Ltd
AnXious: TEN (The Entertainment Network)
Anything Goze: Nova Sales and Distribution (UK) Ltd
Anyway: Cargo Records (UK) Ltd
Apartment: Cargo Records (UK) Ltd
Apartment B: Baked Goods Distribution
Apartment 22: Kudos Records Ltd
Apati: The Woods
Ape City: Soul Trader
Aphrodite: Pinnacle Records
Apocalyptic Vision: Shellshock Distribution
Apollo: Pinnacle Records
Apollo Sound: Backs Distribution
Appaloosa: Amato Distribution
Appollo Sounds: Shellshock Distribution
April: Pinnacle Records, Shellshock Distribution
Aqua: Pinnacle Records
Aquarius: Pinnacle Records
Arabesque: Arabesque Distribution
ARC Music: ARC Music Distribution UK Ltd
Arcade: Discovery Records Ltd
Arcadia: Vital Distribution
Architex: Pinnacle Records
Archive International: Shellshock Distribution
Arctic: Pinnacle Records
Ardo: Gordon Duncan Distributions
Area Code 221: Shellshock Distribution
Arena Rock: Cargo Records (UK) Ltd, Shellshock

Distribution
Arf Arf: F Minor Ltd, Shellshock Distribution
Arg: BDS (Bertelsmann Distribution Services)
Arhoolie: Proper Music Distribution Ltd
Aries: Shellshock Distribution
Arion: Discovery Records Ltd
Arista: BDS (Bertelsmann Distribution Services)
Arka Sound: SRD (Southern Record Distribution)
Arkadia Jazz: Synergie Logistics
ARK 21: Universal Music Operations
Armed: Cargo Records (UK) Ltd
Aromasound: Vital Distribution
Arrow: Jet Star Phonographics
ARS Produktion: Vivante Music Ltd
Art & Soul: Pinnacle Records
Art Monk Construction: SRD (Southern Record Distribution)
Art-Tek: Baked Goods Distribution
Artbus: Pinnacle Records
Artefact: Cargo Records (UK) Ltd
Artelier: New Note Distribution Ltd, Pinnacle Records
Artful Records: BDS (Bertelsmann Distribution Services)
Arthaus Musik (DVD): Select Music & Video Distribution
Arthur Mix: Vital Distribution
Artificial: Universal Music Operations
Artisan: Pinnacle Records
Artist Record Company: Universal Music Operations
Artlos: Pinnacle Records
ARTS Music: The Complete Record Company Ltd
Artus: Pinnacle Records
ASC Records: New Note Distribution Ltd
Ascendant Grooves: Vital Distribution
Ascension: F Minor Ltd
ASHA: ADA Distribution
Ashe: Shellshock Distribution
Asian Man: Plastic Head Music Distribution Ltd
Aspect: ST Holdings Ltd
Asphodel: Pinnacle Records
ASPIC: Harmonia Mundi (UK) Ltd
Astor Place: New Note Distribution Ltd, Pinnacle Records
Astral: Gordon Duncan Distributions, Vital Distribution
Astralwerks: Pinnacle Records
Astree: Harmonia Mundi (UK) Ltd
ASV: Select Music & Video Distribution
Asylum: TEN (The Entertainment Network)
Ata Tak: Shellshock Distribution
Atavistic: SRD (Southern Record Distribution)
ATCR: Trance Communication: Amato Distribution
Athanor: Shellshock Distribution
Athletico: Vital Distribution
Atlantic Records: TEN (The Entertainment Network)
Atlantic Jaxx: Vital Distribution
Atlas: Universal Music Operations
ATMA Classique: Metronome Distribution
Atoll: Stern's Distribution
Atoll Music: Silver Sounds CD Ltd
Atomic: BDS (Bertelsmann Distribution Services), Shellshock Distribution
Atomic Theory: Proper Music Distribution Ltd
Attic: Gordon Duncan Distributions
Attitude: Brothers Distribution
A2: Universal Music Operations
Au Go Go: Cargo Records (UK) Ltd
Audio Archive: F Minor Ltd
Audio Couture: SRD (Southern Record Distribution)
Audio Illusion: Shellshock Distribution
Audioglobe: Plastic Head Music Distribution Ltd
Audiopharm: Timewarp Distribution
Audiophile: Delta Music PLC, Jazz Music, The Woods
Audioquest: Vivante Music Ltd
Audioview: Cargo Records (UK) Ltd, Shellshock Distribution
Augogo: Cargo Records (UK) Ltd
August: Vital Distribution
Aum Fidelity: Cargo Records (UK) Ltd
Auracle Recordings: BDS (Bertelsmann Distribution Services), Essential Direct Ltd
Ausfahrt: Shellshock Distribution
Authentic Media: Nova Sales and Distribution (UK) Ltd
Automatic: Amato Distribution
Autonomy: EMI Distribution
Autpilot: Excel Marketing Services Ltd
Auvidis Astree: Harmonia Mundi (UK) Ltd
Auvidis Ethnic: Harmonia Mundi (UK) Ltd
Auvidis Silex: Harmonia Mundi (UK) Ltd
Auvidis Tempo: Harmonia Mundi (UK) Ltd
Auvidis Textes: Harmonia Mundi (UK) Ltd
Avalon Records: Pinnacle Records
Avant: Harmonia Mundi (UK) Ltd
Avant Garde: Amato Distribution
Avantgarde: Shellshock Distribution
Avid: Avid Entertainment
Axe Killer: Cargo Records (UK) Ltd
Axiomatic: Vital Distribution
Axis: Pinnacle Records, Shellshock Distribution
Azuli: TEN (The Entertainment Network)
Azure: Jazz Music
B.T.M.: Shellshock Distribution
Ba Da Bing: Cargo Records (UK) Ltd
Ba-Da-Bing: Shellshock Distribution
Babel: Harmonia Mundi (UK) Ltd
Babi-Yaga: Cargo Records (UK) Ltd
Babushka Records: Amato Distribution
Bacchus Archives: F Minor Ltd
Back Bone: Vital Distribution
Back Door: Pinnacle Records
Back 2 Basics: SRD (Southern Record Distribution)
Back 2 Front: BDS (Bertelsmann Distribution Services), Essential Direct Ltd
Backbone: BDS (Bertelsmann Distribution Services), Essential Direct Ltd
Backburner: Shellshock Distribution
Background Records: F Minor Ltd
Backshift: ADA Distribution
Backstreet: Cargo Records (UK) Ltd
Backyard Brew: Vital Distribution
Backyard Movement: SRD (Southern Record Distribution)
Bacteria: Pinnacle Records
Bad Acid Records: Plastic Head Music Distribution Ltd
Bad Afro: Cargo Records (UK) Ltd, Shellshock Distribution
Bad Boy: Cargo Records (UK) Ltd
Bad Dog: Cargo Records (UK) Ltd
Bad Habit: Load Media
Bad Habits: BDS (Bertelsmann Distribution Services)
Bad Jazz: Cargo Records (UK) Ltd
Bad Magic: Vital Distribution
Bad Parents: Cargo Records (UK) Ltd
Bad Taste: Cargo Records (UK) Ltd, RSK Entertainment
Badman: Shellshock Distribution
Bag: BDS (Bertelsmann Distribution Services)
Baktabak: Arabesque Distribution
Ball Product: Vital Distribution
Balloonia: Shellshock Distribution
Baltic: SRD (Southern Record Distribution)
Banana: Pinnacle Records
Banana Juice: Nervous Records
Bananajuice: Nervous Records
Bandleader: BDS (Bertelsmann Distribution Services), Nova Sales and Distribution (UK) Ltd, Pinnacle Records
Bandstand: Hot Shot Records
Bankylous: Jet Star Phonographics
Baphomet: Shellshock Distribution
Bar De Lune: 4am Distribution
Baraka: Cargo Records (UK) Ltd
Barbarity: Stern's Distribution
Barber's Itch: Cargo Records (UK) Ltd
Barclay France: Discovery Records Ltd
Barely Breaking Even: 4am Distribution, Pinnacle Records
Barend Video: Plastic Head Music Distribution Ltd
Barracuda: Amato Distribution
Barraka: Shellshock Distribution
Bartrax: Jazz Music
Basedaddy: Shellshock Distribution
Basic Unit: Shellshock Distribution
Bassline Generation: Shellshock Distribution
Basswerk: Pinnacle Records, Shellshock Distribution
Basta: F Minor Ltd, Proper Music Distribution Ltd
Bay City Recordings: Pinnacle Records
BBC Audio Collection: Technicolor Distribution Services Ltd
BBC CLASSIC COLLECTION: New Note Distribution Ltd
BBC Jazz Legends: New Note Distribution Ltd
BBC Legends/Britten: New Note Distribution Ltd
BBC Proms: New Note Distribution Ltd
BBC Video: Technicolor Distribution Services Ltd
BCR International: Jet Star Phonographics
Bear Family: Swift Record Distributors
Bear Necessities: SRD (Southern Record Distribution)
Bearcat: Proper Music Distribution Ltd
Beard Of Stars: F Minor Ltd
Bearos: Cargo Records (UK) Ltd
Beat Freak: ST Holdings Ltd
Beat Goes On: Universal Music Operations
Beat Rocket: F Minor Ltd
Beat Service: Pinnacle Records, Shellshock Distribution
Beatific: Pinnacle Records
Beatnik: Pinnacle Records
Beatservice: Pinnacle Records
Beau Monde: Kudos Records Ltd, Vital Distribution
Beau Range: Cargo Records (UK) Ltd
Beau Rivage: Shellshock Distribution
Beautiful: Vital Distribution
Beautiful Jo: Pendle Hawk Music Distribution, Proper Music Distribution Ltd
Beautiful Noise: Pinnacle Records
Beautiful Place: Vital Distribution
Bedlam: Shellshock Distribution
Bedrock: Vital Distribution
Beebees: Nervous Records
Beechwood: 4am Distribution, BDS (Bertelsmann Distribution Services)
Beehive: ADA Distribution
Beemade: Shellshock Distribution

Beeswax: SRD (Southern Record Distribution)
Beggars Banquet: Vital Distribution
Bella Union: Pinnacle Records
Bella Voce: BDS (Bertelsmann Distribution Services)
Bellaphon: Pinnacle Records, Plastic Head Music Distribution Ltd
Bellboy: InterGroove Ltd
Below Zero/Timewarp: Shellshock Distribution
Beltane: ADA Distribution, Gordon Duncan Distributions
Benbecula: Baked Goods Distribution
Bentley Welcomes Careful Drivers: Cargo Records (UK) Ltd
Berlin Classics: The Complete Record Company Ltd
Bespoke: Sound Entertainment Ltd
Best Of Jazz: Discovery Records Ltd
Best Test: Pinnacle Records
Beta: SRD (Southern Record Distribution)
Better: Vital Distribution
Beyongolia: Vital Distribution
BFD: Shellshock Distribution
BGO: Pinnacle Records
BGP: Pinnacle Records
BGS Records: Metronome Distribution
Biddulph: Harmonia Mundi (UK) Ltd
Big & Complex World: Pinnacle Records
Big Balls: Cargo Records (UK) Ltd
Big Banana: BDS (Bertelsmann Distribution Services)
Big Bang: BDS (Bertelsmann Distribution Services)
Big Barber: Cargo Records (UK) Ltd
Big Boss: Hot Shot Records
Big Brother: Pinnacle Records
Big Chill: Kudos Records Ltd, SRD (Southern Record Distribution)
Big City: Candid Productions Ltd, Proper Music Distribution Ltd
Big Dada: Vital Distribution
Big Deal: Cargo Records (UK) Ltd
Big Drum: Jet Star Phonographics
Big Life: Vital Distribution
Big Musik: The Woods
Big Noise: Shellshock Distribution
Big Ship: Jet Star Phonographics
Big Star: Universal Music Operations
Big Sur: Timewarp Distribution
Big Top: Shellshock Distribution
Big Yard: Jet Star Phonographics
Bilda: ADA Distribution
Biograph: Jazz Music
Bird's Eye: Jet Star Phonographics
Birdland: New Note Distribution Ltd, Pinnacle Records
Birdman: Cargo Records (UK) Ltd
Birdsnest: Cargo Records (UK) Ltd
BIS: Select Music & Video Distribution
Bistro: Pinnacle Records
Bitch Vinyl: Pinnacle Records
Bittersweet: Vital Distribution
Bitzcore: Cargo Records (UK) Ltd
Bitzcore Records GMBH: Plastic Head Music Distribution Ltd
BKO: Absolute Marketing & Distribution Ltd.
Black: Jet Star Phonographics
Black & Blue: Discovery Records Ltd
Black & Tan: Hot Shot Records
Black Arc: Vital Distribution
Black Box Music: Select Music & Video Distribution
Black Canvas: Shellshock Distribution
Black Flag: Cargo Records (UK) Ltd
Black Gold Recordings: Shellshock Distribution, Vital Distribution
Black Hoodz: SRD (Southern Record Distribution)
Black Jack: BDS (Bertelsmann Distribution Services), Essential Direct Ltd
Black Jam: Vital Distribution
Black Jesus: GR London Ltd
Black Label: Jet Star Phonographics
Black Magic: Hot Shot Records, Jet Star Phonographics
Black Market International: Vital Distribution
Black No Sugar: ST Holdings Ltd
Black Roots: SRD (Southern Record Distribution)
Black Saint: Harmonia Mundi (UK) Ltd
Black Scorpio: Jet Star Phonographics
Black Solidarity: SRD (Southern Record Distribution)
Black Sunshine: Vital Distribution
Black Swan: Jazz Music, The Woods
Black Top: Proper Music Distribution Ltd
Black Up: BDS (Bertelsmann Distribution Services), Essential Direct Ltd
Black Vinyl: 4am Distribution, Global Dance Distribution Ltd
Black Widow: F Minor Ltd, Plastic Head Music Distribution Ltd
Blackberry: Cargo Records (UK) Ltd
Blackbox: Pinnacle Records
Blackend: Plastic Head Music Distribution Ltd
Blacker Dread: Jet Star Phonographics
Blackfish: Plastic Head Music Distribution Ltd
Blackhood: SRD (Southern Record Distribution)
Blackjack: Shellshock Distribution
Blacklabel: Jet Star Phonographics
Blackout: Vital Distribution
Blackplastic: Pinnacle Records
Blacktop: Hot Shot Records
Blakamix: SRD (Southern Record Distribution)
Blanco Y Negro: TEN (The Entertainment Network)
Blapps!: Vital Distribution
Blast: Pinnacle Records
Blast First: Vital Distribution
Blaster: Vital Distribution
Blatant: BDS (Bertelsmann Distribution Services)
Bleeding Hearts: Pinnacle Records
Blind Pig: Proper Music Distribution Ltd
Blindside: Pinnacle Records
Bliss: Pinnacle Records, Shellshock Distribution
Blissfulmusic: Metronome Distribution
Blix Street: Hot Records
Blokshok: Pinnacle Records
Blood: SRD (Southern Record Distribution)
Blood And Fire: Universal Music Operations, Vital Distribution
Blood Lust: Vital Distribution
Bloodshot: Proper Music Distribution Ltd
Bloodstained Dusk: Shellshock Distribution
Blow The Fuse: New Note Distribution Ltd, Pinnacle Records
Blow Up: SRD (Southern Record Distribution)
BLS: Jet Star Phonographics
Blue: Universal Music Operations
Blue August: Backs Distribution, Pinnacle Records, Shellshock Distribution
Blue Banana Records: Independent Distribution Ltd
Blue Chicago: Proper Music Distribution Ltd
Blue Dog: Pinnacle Records
Blue Gorilla: Universal Music Operations
Blue Harlem: Hot Shot Records
Blue Horizon: Hot Shot Records
Blue House: Jet Star Phonographics
Blue Jackel: New Note Distribution Ltd, Pinnacle Records
Blue Melon: Independent Distribution Ltd
Blue Moon: Discovery Records Ltd
Blue Music: New Note Distribution Ltd
Blue Nite: Delta Music PLC
Blue Note: EMI Distribution
Blue Planet Records: Independent Distribution Ltd
Blue Plate: Proper Music Distribution Ltd
Blue Ray: Hot Shot Records
Blue Rhythm: Nova Sales and Distribution (UK) Ltd
Blue Room: Pinnacle Records
Blue Rose: Pinnacle Records, Shellshock Distribution
Blue Sanct: Cargo Records (UK) Ltd
Blue Silver: Stern's Distribution
Blue Sting: Hot Shot Records
Blue Suit: Hot Shot Records
Blue Sun: Hot Shot Records
Blue Thumb: BDS (Bertelsmann Distribution Services)
Bluebell: Jazz Music, Pinnacle Records
Blueblood: Hot Shot Records
Bluefire: Shellshock Distribution
Blueloon: Hot Shot Records
Blueprint: Pinnacle Records
Blues Alliance: New Note Distribution Ltd, Pinnacle Records
Blues Archives: Discovery Records Ltd
Blues Beacon: New Note Distribution Ltd, Pinnacle Records
Blues Collection: Discovery Records Ltd
Blues Document: Hot Shot Records
Blues Factory: BDS (Bertelsmann Distribution Services)
Blues Works: Hot Shot Records
Bluesanct: Cargo Records (UK) Ltd
Bluesanct Music: Shellshock Distribution
Bluesrock: Hot Shot Records
Bluesting: Hot Shot Records
Bluestone: Cargo Records (UK) Ltd
Bluetonium: ZYX
Bluetrak: Hot Shot Records
Blunt: Pinnacle Records, Shellshock Distribution
Blunted Vinyl: Vital Distribution
Blut: Pinnacle Records, Shellshock Distribution
Bluurg: Shellshock Distribution
BMG Europe: Discovery Records Ltd
BNA: BDS (Bertelsmann Distribution Services)
B9: Pinnacle Records
BOA: ADA Distribution
Bob Egan: Shellshock Distribution
Bobsled: Cargo Records (UK) Ltd
Body & Soul: New Note Distribution Ltd
Boiler House!: Vital Distribution
Boka: Proper Music Distribution Ltd
Bolshi: Vital Distribution
Bomb Basic: Cargo Records (UK) Ltd
Bomb Hiphop: Cargo Records (UK) Ltd
Bomp: F Minor Ltd, Shellshock Distribution, Vital Distribution
Bomp!: Backs Distribution
Bon: Cargo Records (UK) Ltd
Bonaire Recordings: BDS (Bertelsmann Distribution Services), Essential Direct Ltd, Independent Distribution Ltd
Bond Girl: Pinnacle Records, Shellshock Distribution
Boneheddz: Shellshock Distribution
Boneshaker Records: ADA Distribution

Design, Pressing & Distribution

Bong Load: Cargo Records (UK) Ltd
Bongload: Cargo Records (UK) Ltd
Boo: KRD
Boogie Back: Vital Distribution
Boogie Man: Shellshock Distribution
Boogie Wonderland: SRD (Southern Record Distribution)
Book: Jazz Music
Boom: Pinnacle Records
Boom Shacka Lacka: Pinnacle Records
Boomba Records: Plastic Head Music Distribution Ltd
Boomtang: BDS (Bertelsmann Distribution Services)
Boot: Amato Distribution
Bootleg Net: Pinnacle Records
Booze: Nervous Records
Boplicity: Jazz Music
Borderline: F Minor Ltd
Borealis: Pendle Hawk Music Distribution
Bosca Beats: SRD (Southern Record Distribution)
Bosh: BDS (Bertelsmann Distribution Services)
Boss: SRD (Southern Record Distribution)
Boston Skyline: Metronome Distribution
Botchit & Scarper: SRD (Southern Record Distribution)
The Bottom Line: Pinnacle Records
Bottrop-Boy: Baked Goods Distribution
Bounce!!: BDS (Bertelsmann Distribution Services)
Bovinyl: Vital Distribution
Bowstone: Jazz Music
Boys: BDS (Bertelsmann Distribution Services)
Boys of the Lough: Gordon Duncan Distributions
BPitch Control: Baked Goods Distribution
Brambus: Pendle Hawk Music Distribution
Branded: Pinnacle Records
Break Butt: Pinnacle Records
Break Records 2000: BDS (Bertelsmann Distribution Services)
Break/Flow: Shellshock Distribution
Breakbeat Culture: SRD (Southern Record Distribution)
Breakdown: Pinnacle Records
Breaker Breaks: ST Holdings Ltd
Breakin: Kudos Records Ltd
Breakin': Pinnacle Records
Breathe: BDS (Bertelsmann Distribution Services)
Breeze: BDS (Bertelsmann Distribution Services)
Brick Wall: ADA Distribution, Jet Star Phonographics
Bridge: RSK Entertainment
Bright Choice: RMG Chart Entertainment Ltd.
Bright Star Recordings: Vital Distribution
Brinkman: Cargo Records (UK) Ltd
Broadstar: Vital Distribution
Brobdingnangian: Shellshock Distribution
Broken Rekids: Cargo Records (UK) Ltd
Broken.: Pinnacle Records
Bronze: SRD (Southern Record Distribution)
Brothers: Brothers Distribution, Universal Music Operations
Brown Sugar: F Minor Ltd, Timewarp Distribution
BSI: Shellshock Distribution
Bubble Core: SRD (Southern Record Distribution)
Bubblin': Vital Distribution
Bucketfull of Brains: Shellshock Distribution
Bud: Universal Music Operations
Buda: Discovery Records Ltd
Budapest Music Centre (BMC): Metronome Distribution
Buena Vista Home Video: Technicolor Distribution Services Ltd
Bulb: Shellshock Distribution
Bullion: Pinnacle Records
Bulls Eye Blues Munich: Hot Shot Records
Bulls Eye Rounder: Hot Shot Records
Bullseye: Proper Music Distribution Ltd
Bullseye Blues: Proper Music Distribution Ltd
Bumpercar: Shellshock Distribution
Bungalow: Cargo Records (UK) Ltd
Bunker: Shellshock Distribution
Burial Mix: SRD (Southern Record Distribution)
Burning Airliner: Excel Marketing Services Ltd, Pinnacle Records
Burning Rome: Vital Distribution
Burning Sounds: Universal Music Operations
Burnt Hair: Cargo Records (UK) Ltd
Bush: BDS (Bertelsmann Distribution Services), KRD
Bushranger: Pinnacle Records
Business: Jet Star Phonographics
But!: Pinnacle Records
Butcher's Wig: Pinnacle Records
Button: The Complete Record Company Ltd
Buzz: Shellshock Distribution
BXR UK: Amato Distribution
BYG Actuel: F Minor Ltd
BYO Records: Plastic Head Music Distribution Ltd
C&N: Universal Music Operations
Cabal: SRD (Southern Record Distribution)
Caber: Proper Music Distribution Ltd
Cacophonous: Vital Distribution
Cactus Island: Baked Goods Distribution
Cadillac: Jazz Music
Caipirinha: Pinnacle Records
Calligraph: Jazz Music, New Note Distribution Ltd
Calliope: Harmonia Mundi (UK) Ltd
Cam Original Soundtracks: Hot Records
Cambrian: Sain (Recordiau) Cyf
Camden: BDS (Bertelsmann Distribution Services)
Camel: Pinnacle Records
Cameo: BDS (Bertelsmann Distribution Services), Disc Imports Ltd
Camera Obscura: Cargo Records (UK) Ltd, Shellshock Distribution
Camino: Pinnacle Records
Camp Fabulous: BDS (Bertelsmann Distribution Services), Pinnacle Records
Campion Records: Disc Imports Ltd
Can: Jet Star Phonographics
Can Can: Vital Distribution
Candid: Candid Productions Ltd, Jazz Music, Proper Music Distribution Ltd
Candle: Hot Records
Candlelight Records: Plastic Head Music Distribution Ltd
Candy Ass: Vital Distribution
Caney: Discovery Records Ltd
Cantankerous: GR London Ltd
Canzona: New Note Distribution Ltd, Pinnacle Records
Capitol: EMI Distribution
Capitol Jazz: EMI Distribution
Capri Records: The Woods
Capriccio: BDS (Bertelsmann Distribution Services), Delta Music PLC
Capricorn: Universal Music Operations
Capstack: Cargo Records (UK) Ltd
Captain Oi!: Plastic Head Music Distribution Ltd
Captain Trip: F Minor Ltd, Shellshock Distribution
Cara: The Complete Record Company Ltd
Caramba: Independent Distribution Ltd
Cardas: Vivante Music Ltd
Cardina: TEN (The Entertainment Network)
Cargogold: New Note Distribution Ltd
Caribbean: Jet Star Phonographics
Caribbean Music Library: Media UK Distribution
Cariwak: Jet Star Phonographics
Carlton Video: Technicolor Distribution Services Ltd
Carmo: New Note Distribution Ltd
Caroline: Vital Distribution
Carrack UK: Absolute Marketing & Distribution Ltd.
Carrera: Pinnacle Records
Carrot Top: Shellshock Distribution
Cartel: 4am Distribution
Carzy Love: Nervous Records
Casa Nostra: Amato Distribution
Casa Trax: Pinnacle Records
Cascade: Hot Shot Records
Case Invaders: SRD (Southern Record Distribution)
Casino: Pinnacle Records
Castle Home Video: Pinnacle Records
Castle Music: Pinnacle Records
Casualty: Vital Distribution
Catalyst: BDS (Bertelsmann Distribution Services)
Catamount: Shellshock Distribution
Catcall: Vital Distribution
Catch 23: Shellshock Distribution
Catfish: Pinnacle Records
Catskills: Vital Distribution
Cause4Concern: Load Media
The CD Card Company: Arabesque Distribution
Cedille: Metronome Distribution
Cee 22: Vital Distribution
Celebrity: Candid Productions Ltd
Celtic Music: CM Distribution
Celtic Pride: Delta Music PLC
Celtophile: Proper Music Distribution Ltd
Centaur: F Minor Ltd, Pinnacle Records
Central Hill: BDS (Bertelsmann Distribution Services)
Central Station: BDS (Bertelsmann Distribution Services), Essential Direct Ltd
Centric: Pinnacle Records
Century Media: RSK Entertainment
Ceraton: Shellshock Distribution
Certificate18: SRD (Southern Record Distribution)
Chain Reaction: SRD (Southern Record Distribution)
Challenge: Jazz Music, Proper Music Distribution Ltd
Champ: Shellshock Distribution
Champagne Lake: Pinnacle Records
Champagne/Rockathon: Shellshock Distribution
Champion: BDS (Bertelsmann Distribution Services)
Chandos: Chandos Records
Changing World: Changing World Distribution, Shellshock Distribution
Channel 5: Shellshock Distribution
Channel Classics: RSK Entertainment
Channel 4: Universal Music Operations
Channel One: SRD (Southern Record Distribution)
Chant du Monde: Harmonia Mundi (UK) Ltd
Chapter 22: Vital Distribution
Charm: Jet Star Phonographics
Charnel: Harmonia Mundi (UK) Ltd
Chart: I&B Records (Irish Music) Ltd
Chase: BDS (Bertelsmann Distribution Services)
Chatback: Universal Music Operations
Chaucer: Nova Sales and Distribution (UK) Ltd

Che: Cargo Records (UK) Ltd
Checkered Past: Proper Music Distribution Ltd
Checkpoint: Vital Distribution
Cheeky: BDS (Bertelsmann Distribution Services)
Cheeky Junior: BDS (Bertelsmann Distribution Services)
Cheese International: Vital Distribution
Chemikal Underground: Vital Distribution
Cherokee: Nervous Records
Cherry Red: Pinnacle Records
Chesky: Discovery Records Ltd, Vivante Music Ltd
Chess: BDS (Bertelsmann Distribution Services)
Chiarascuro: Jazz Music
Chili Funk: Absolute Marketing & Distribution Ltd.
Chilli Funk: Vital Distribution
Chillifunk: Timewarp Distribution
China: TEN (The Entertainment Network), Pinnacle Records
Chocolate Boy: Aura Surround Sound Ltd. t/a Mo's Music Machine
Choice: Candid Productions Ltd
Choo Choo: InterGroove Ltd, Unique Distribution
Chouchen: ADA Distribution
Chris Barber Collection: New Note Distribution Ltd
Christel Deesk: Vital Distribution
Chrome Dreams: Nova Sales and Distribution (UK) Ltd
Chrome Dreams Media: Nova Sales and Distribution (UK) Ltd
Chronicles: Universal Music Operations
Chrysalis: EMI Distribution
Chug & Bump: KRD
Chute: Cargo Records (UK) Ltd
Ciano: Pinnacle Records
CIC: Claddagh Records
Cinebox: Silver Sounds CD Ltd
Cinedelic: F Minor Ltd
Circa: EMI Distribution
Circle: F Minor Ltd, Jazz Music, The Woods
Circulation: Pinnacle Records, Shellshock Distribution
Citadel: Hot Records, Proper Music Distribution Ltd
Citrus: Pinnacle Records
City Centre Offices: Baked Goods Distribution
City Rollaz: Vinyl UK
City Slang: Vital Distribution
Citywax: BDS (Bertelsmann Distribution Services), Essential Direct Ltd
Claddagh: Proper Music Distribution Ltd
Claire: Cargo Records (UK) Ltd
Clarinet Classics: Select Music & Video Distribution
Clarion: Swift Record Distributors
Clarity: Synergie Logistics, Vivante Music Ltd
Clarke & BL: Jet Star Phonographics
Classic FM: BDS (Bertelsmann Distribution Services)
Classic Records: F Minor Ltd
Classic Rock: Nova Sales and Distribution (UK) Ltd
Classics: Discovery Records Ltd, Jazz Music
Classified: Vital Distribution
Claudio: Metronome Distribution
Claytwins: Cargo Records (UK) Ltd
Clean Up: Pinnacle Records
Clear: Vital Distribution
Clearspot: Pinnacle Records
Clementine: Shellshock Distribution
Cleopatra: Cargo Records (UK) Ltd
Cleveland City: TEN (The Entertainment Network)
Clifford: Jazz Music
Climax: BDS (Bertelsmann Distribution Services)
Clinkscale: Gordon Duncan Distributions
Clive Mulcahy: Hot Shot Records
Clo lar Chonnachta: Copperplate Distribution
Cloak And Dagger: Vital Distribution
Cloud Nine: New Note Distribution Ltd
Clover U.S.: Shellshock Distribution
Club Spangle: Pinnacle Records, Shellshock Distribution
Club Tools: Vital Distribution
Club Tracks: SRD (Southern Record Distribution)
Clubscene: Universal Music Operations
Clubstar: Timewarp Distribution
Clued: SRD (Southern Record Distribution)
CMC: BDS (Bertelsmann Distribution Services)
CML: Gordon Duncan Distributions
CNN: Vital Distribution
Coalition: Plastic Head Music Distribution Ltd
Coast: SRD (Southern Record Distribution)
Cocaine: SRD (Southern Record Distribution)
Codename: Shellshock Distribution
Codex: Pinnacle Records
Cog Sinister: Pinnacle Records
Cold Blue: RSK Entertainment
Cold Meat Industry: Shellshock Distribution, Vital Distribution
Cold Spring: Shellshock Distribution, Vital Distribution
Colin Campbell: Gordon Duncan Distributions
Colin Fat: Jet Star Phonographics
Collection: Delta Music PLC
Collective Fruit: Shellshock Distribution
Collector: Synergie Logistics
Collector's Choice: Silver Sounds CD Ltd
Collector's Classics: BDS (Bertelsmann Distribution Services), Jazz Music
Collector's Edition: Pinnacle Records
Collectors Choice: RSK Entertainment
Collegium: Select Music & Video Distribution
Collins Classics: Pinnacle Records
Collision: Vital Distribution
Colombe d'Or: BDS (Bertelsmann Distribution Services)
Colony: Baked Goods Distribution
Colosseum: Pinnacle Records
Colour Blind: BDS (Bertelsmann Distribution Services), Essential Direct Ltd
Columbia: TEN (The Entertainment Network)
Columbia Tristar Home Video: TEN (The Entertainment Network)
Comet: F Minor Ltd, Music Express Ltd
Communion: Cargo Records (UK) Ltd
Communique Records: Plastic Head Music Distribution Ltd
Community: Cargo Records (UK) Ltd, Plastic Head Music Distribution Ltd
The Compact Organization: Pinnacle Records
Compiler: Shellshock Distribution
Complete Control Music: Shellshock Distribution
Complex: Universal Music Operations
Compose: SRD (Southern Record Distribution)
Compost: SRD (Southern Record Distribution)
Compressed Knowledge: Shellshock Distribution
Concept: Absolute Marketing & Distribution Ltd.
Concord: New Note Distribution Ltd, Pinnacle Records
Concord Concerto: New Note Distribution Ltd, Pinnacle Records
Concord Crossover: New Note Distribution Ltd
Concord Jazz: New Note Distribution Ltd, Pinnacle Records
Concord Picante: New Note Distribution Ltd, Pinnacle Records
Concord Vista: New Note Distribution Ltd, Pinnacle Records
Concrete: Vital Distribution
Concrete Productions: BDS (Bertelsmann Distribution Services)
Congo: Pinnacle Records
Connector: Shellshock Distribution
Connoisseur Collection: Pinnacle Records
Conqueror: Universal Music Operations
Conquistador: Pinnacle Records, Shellshock Distribution
Conscious Sounds: SRD (Southern Record Distribution)
Conspiracy: Shellshock Distribution
Constellation: Cargo Records (UK) Ltd
Contemporary: Jazz Music, New Note Distribution Ltd
Continental Song City: Proper Music Distribution Ltd
Control: Vital Distribution
Cooker: BDS (Bertelsmann Distribution Services)
Cooking Vinyl: Vital Distribution
Cool D:Vision: Timewarp Distribution
Cool Guy: Cargo Records (UK) Ltd
Cooler: Cargo Records (UK) Ltd
Cooltempo: EMI Distribution
Coop: Pinnacle Records, Shellshock Distribution
Cop International: Cargo Records (UK) Ltd
Copasetik: Vital Distribution
Copro Records: Plastic Head Music Distribution Ltd
Coral: Jet Star Phonographics
Corban: Gordon Duncan Distributions
Corduroy: F Minor Ltd
Core-Tex Records: Plastic Head Music Distribution Ltd
Cornerstone Records: The Woods
Corntreeper: Jet Star Phonographics
Corporate Image: Vital Distribution
Corpus Christi: SRD (Southern Record Distribution)
Corpus Hermeticum: Cargo Records (UK) Ltd
The Corries: Ross Record Distribution
Corrupt: Shellshock Distribution
Corrupt Conglomerate: Shellshock Distribution
Cortical: Harmonia Mundi (UK) Ltd
Corvus Corax: Shellshock Distribution
Couchblip: Baked Goods Distribution
Council of Nine: Shellshock Distribution
Counterpoint: 4am Distribution
Country Branch: ADA Distribution
Country Routes: Hot Shot Records, Jazz Music
County: Proper Music Distribution Ltd
Coup de Main: Shellshock Distribution
Cousin: Jet Star Phonographics
Cousins: Jet Star Phonographics
COW: ADA Distribution
Cowards: Cargo Records (UK) Ltd
Cowboy Records: Absolute Marketing & Distribution Ltd.
Cowsong: Proper Music Distribution Ltd
CPO: Select Music & Video Distribution
Crackle: Plastic Head Music Distribution Ltd
Crai: Proper Music Distribution Ltd, Sain (Recordiau) Cyf
Cramboy: New Note Distribution Ltd
Crammed Discs: New Note Distribution Ltd
Cramworld: New Note Distribution Ltd, Pinnacle Records

Design, Pressing & Distribution

Crazy Love: Nervous Records
Crazy Rhythm: Nervous Records
CRD: Regis Records Ltd
Cream: New Note Distribution Ltd
Cream Records: New Note Distribution Ltd
Creative Entertainment: Pinnacle Records
Creative Man: Cargo Records (UK) Ltd
Creative Wax: Vital Distribution
Creeping Bent: SRD (Southern Record Distribution)
Creole: Universal Music Operations
Crepuscule: Discovery Records Ltd
Crippled Dick: SRD (Southern Record Distribution)
Crisis: Nova Sales and Distribution (UK) Ltd
Criss Cross Jazz: Proper Music Distribution Ltd
Critical Mass: Amato Distribution
CRO: The Complete Record Company Ltd
Crocodile Bites: SRD (Southern Record Distribution)
Crosby's: Jet Star Phonographics
Cross: Baked Goods Distribution
Cross Section: ST Holdings Ltd
Crosscut: Proper Music Distribution Ltd
Crossfade: Shellshock Distribution
Crossroads: Jet Star Phonographics
Crosstown: BDS (Bertelsmann Distribution Services), Essential Direct Ltd
Crosstrax: Amato Distribution
Crowd Control: Shellshock Distribution
CRS: Jet Star Phonographics
Cruise: Jet Star Phonographics
Cruise International: BDS (Bertelsmann Distribution Services), Essential Direct Ltd
Crunch Melody: Vital Distribution
Crunk: ST Holdings Ltd
Crypt: Pinnacle Records, Shellshock Distribution
CSA Telltapes: Universal Music Operations
CTM: Shellshock Distribution
Cube Metier: The Woods
Cube Roots: ADA Distribution
Cubop: New Note Distribution Ltd, Pinnacle Records
CUIG Music: ADA Distribution
Culburnie: Gordon Duncan Distributions, Proper Music Distribution Ltd
Cuneiform: Shellshock Distribution
Cup Of Tea: Vital Distribution
Curb: Independent Distribution Ltd
Curlique: Timewarp Distribution
Curve: Pinnacle Records
Cyanide: Load Media, Vital Distribution
Cyber: Shellshock Distribution
Cyberchotik: SRD (Southern Record Distribution)
Cyclops: Pinnacle Records
Da Lick: SRD (Southern Record Distribution)
Da Music: RSK Entertainment
Da Poison: EMI Distribution
DAD International: Cargo Records (UK) Ltd
Daddy: Amato Distribution
Dagored: F Minor Ltd, RSK Entertainment
Dallas Blues Society: Hot Shot Records
Damaged Goods: Pinnacle Records
Dambuster: CM Distribution
Damnation: Vital Distribution
Damo's Network: Shellshock Distribution
Dance Mix: Vital Distribution
Dance Naked: BDS (Bertelsmann Distribution Services), Essential Direct Ltd
Dance Network: ZYX
Dance Planet: SRD (Southern Record Distribution)
Dance Pool: TEN (The Entertainment Network)
Dance Reaction: BDS (Bertelsmann Distribution Services)
Dance Street: ZYX
Dance 2: Essential Direct Ltd
Dancecop: Discovery Records Ltd
Dangerous: Proper Music Distribution Ltd
Dangerzone: Hot Shot Records
Danse Macabre: Shellshock Distribution
Danza Y Movimento: Shellshock Distribution
Dara: Independent Distribution Ltd, Universal Music Operations
Dare Dare: Cargo Records (UK) Ltd
Daring: Jazz Music, Proper Music Distribution Ltd
Dark Beat: BDS (Bertelsmann Distribution Services)
Dark Beloved: Cargo Records (UK) Ltd
Dark Beloved Cloud: Shellshock Distribution
Dark Dungeon: Vital Distribution
Dark House: Pinnacle Records
Dark Matter: Vital Distribution
Dark Sea: Pinnacle Records
Dark Skies: Shellshock Distribution
Dark Trinity: Vital Distribution
Dark Vinyl: Shellshock Distribution
Darla: Cargo Records (UK) Ltd, Shellshock Distribution
Data: Amato Distribution
Dave Cooper: Jazz Music
DBM: SRD (Southern Record Distribution)
DBX: Pinnacle Records
DC Recordings: Vital Distribution
DCC: Vivante Music Ltd
DDD: ADA Distribution
De Beek: Shellshock Distribution
De La Haye: SRD (Southern Record Distribution)
De Soto: SRD (Southern Record Distribution)
De Underground: SRD (Southern Record Distribution)
Dead Dead Good: Pinnacle Records
Dead Reckoning: Proper Music Distribution Ltd
Deadly Systems: Pinnacle Records, Shellshock Distribution
Deansville: CM Distribution
Death Becomes Me: SRD (Southern Record Distribution)
Death Row: Universal Music Operations
Deathlike Silence: Shellshock Distribution
Debonair: Pinnacle Records
Debt: Vital Distribution
Debutante: Universal Music Operations
Decca: Universal Music Operations, Vivante Music Ltd
Deceptive: Vital Distribution
Decipher: Amato Distribution
Decision: BDS (Bertelsmann Distribution Services)
Deck 8: Shellshock Distribution
Deconstruction: BDS (Bertelsmann Distribution Services)
Decoy: Vital Distribution
Dedicated: Vital Distribution
Dee Jay: SRD (Southern Record Distribution)
Deeay: Gordon Duncan Distributions
Deep Beats: Pinnacle Records
Deep Elm: Shellshock Distribution
Deep Elm Records: Plastic Head Music Distribution Ltd
Deep End: BDS (Bertelsmann Distribution Services), Essential Direct Ltd
Deep Root: SRD (Southern Record Distribution)
Deep South: Shellshock Distribution
Def Jam: Universal Music Operations
Def Soul: Universal Music Operations
Def Wish: Shellshock Distribution
Defected: TEN (The Entertainment Network), Unique Distribution
Defender: BDS (Bertelsmann Distribution Services), Essential Direct Ltd
Defiant: Pinnacle Records
DeFocus: ST Holdings Ltd
Defunked: ST Holdings Ltd
Del-Fi: Cargo Records (UK) Ltd
Delabel: Cargo Records (UK) Ltd
Delancey Street: Vital Distribution
Delerium: RSK Entertainment
Delicious Vinyl: Pinnacle Records, Shellshock Distribution
Delikatessan: Baked Goods Distribution
Delinquent: Cargo Records (UK) Ltd
Delirious: Pinnacle Records
Delmark: Proper Music Distribution Ltd
Delmonico: Shellshock Distribution
Delos: Metronome Distribution
Delta: Delta Music PLC
Dementia: Shellshock Distribution
Demerara: Nova Sales and Distribution (UK) Ltd
Demi Monde: Backs Distribution, Shellshock Distribution
Demon: BDS (Bertelsmann Distribution Services)
Demonic: ST Holdings Ltd
Dental: Universal Music Operations
DEP International: EMI Distribution
Department H: 4am Distribution
Depth: Pinnacle Records
Depth Of Field: Proper Music Distribution Ltd
Deram: Universal Music Operations
Derivative: Cargo Records (UK) Ltd
Derock: Cargo Records (UK) Ltd
Desco: Cargo Records (UK) Ltd
Desoto: Shellshock Distribution
Dessous: Shellshock Distribution
Destiny: BDS (Bertelsmann Distribution Services)
Detour: F Minor Ltd, Plastic Head Music Distribution Ltd
Detox: Vital Distribution
Deutsche Grammophon: Universal Music Operations
Deux Z/Nato: Harmonia Mundi (UK) Ltd
Deux-Elles: RSK Entertainment
Deva: Vital Distribution
Deviant: Vital Distribution
Deviation: Vital Distribution
Device Electronic Entertainment: Baked Goods Distribution
Devil in the Woods: Shellshock Distribution
Devil May Care: Amato Distribution
Devious: Jet Star Phonographics
Devon: Pinnacle Records
Dexter's Cigar: Cargo Records (UK) Ltd
DHR: Vital Distribution
Diablo: BDS (Bertelsmann Distribution Services)
Diablo Fuel: Pinnacle Records
Diagonal: Nova Sales and Distribution (UK) Ltd
Diamond: Plastic Head Music Distribution Ltd
Diamond Classics: Pinnacle Records
Diamond Range: Jet Star Phonographics
Diamond Recordings: Pinnacle Records
Dice: Synergie Logistics
Die Young Stay Pretty: Shellshock Distribution
Diesel: Jet Star Phonographics
Different Drummer: Kudos Records Ltd, Pinnacle Records
Different Recordings: Vital Distribution
Diffusion: Universal Music Operations
Dig The Fuzz: Cargo Records (UK) Ltd, F Minor Ltd

Digelius Music: ADA Distribution
Diggler: F Minor Ltd
Digi Dub: Pinnacle Records
Digital B: Jet Star Phonographics
Digital Food: Shellshock Distribution
Digital Hardcore: Vital Distribution
Digital Underground: Shellshock Distribution
Dill: Cargo Records (UK) Ltd
Dimension: Jet Star Phonographics
Din: SRD (Southern Record Distribution), Shellshock Distribution
Dionysus: Cargo Records (UK) Ltd, F Minor Ltd
Direct Disco: Unique Distribution
Direct Drive: Shellshock Distribution
Direct Heat: Arabesque Distribution
Dirt: Pinnacle Records
Dirter: Pinnacle Records, Shellshock Distribution
Disaster/Alive: Shellshock Distribution
Dischord: SRD (Southern Record Distribution)
Discipline: Pinnacle Records
Discipline Global Mobile: Pinnacle Records
Discipline Records: Plastic Head Music Distribution Ltd
Disco Peligros: Brothers Distribution
Disco 2000: BDS (Bertelsmann Distribution Services), Essential Direct Ltd
Disco Volante: TEN (The Entertainment Network)
Discocaine Production#: Amato Distribution
Discography: Pinnacle Records
Discordant: Pinnacle Records
Discotex: Jet Star Phonographics
Discribe: Jet Star Phonographics
Dishy: SRD (Southern Record Distribution)
Diskono: Baked Goods Distribution, Cargo Records (UK) Ltd
Disorient: Vital Distribution
Displeased Records: Plastic Head Music Distribution Ltd
Disque Arabe: Harmonia Mundi (UK) Ltd
Disques Solid: Vital Distribution
Disreplicant: Shellshock Distribution
Distance: Pinnacle Records
Distinct'ive Breaks: Pinnacle Records
Distortions: F Minor Ltd
Diverse: F Minor Ltd, Pinnacle Records
Diversity.: SRD (Southern Record Distribution)
Divine Art: CM Distribution
Dixiefrog: Proper Music Distribution Ltd
DJ Beat: Shellshock Distribution
Django: Jet Star Phonographics
DJC: ADA Distribution
Djenne: Stern's Distribution
DJT: Vital Distribution
DMC: Pinnacle Records
DMP: Vivante Music Ltd
DNA Records: New Note Distribution Ltd
DNM: Timewarp Distribution
Document: Hot Shot Records, Jazz Music
Dodge: Pinnacle Records, Shellshock Distribution
Dodgem Discs: New Note Distribution Ltd
Dog Eat Cat: BDS (Bertelsmann Distribution Services)
Doghouse: ADA Distribution, Plastic Head Music Distribution Ltd
Dolores Records: Plastic Head Music Distribution Ltd
Dolphin: I&B Records (Irish Music) Ltd
Dome: TEN (The Entertainment Network)
Dominance: Shellshock Distribution
Domination: ST Holdings Ltd
Domino: Vital Distribution
Domo: Pinnacle Records
Don Q: SRD (Southern Record Distribution)
Done: SRD (Southern Record Distribution)
Donside: Gordon Duncan Distributions
Doolittle: Proper Music Distribution Ltd
Doop: Pinnacle Records
Doorstep Vinyl: Cargo Records (UK) Ltd
Dope: Shellshock Distribution
Dope On Plastic: Vital Distribution
Dope Wax: Universal Music Operations
Dopesmoker: Cargo Records (UK) Ltd
Doppelganger: BDS (Bertelsmann Distribution Services)
Dorado: Pinnacle Records
Dorian: Metronome Distribution, Pinnacle Records
Dorigen: Unique Distribution
Dos Or Die: Shellshock Distribution
Dossier: Shellshock Distribution
Dot: Pinnacle Records
Double Gold: BDS (Bertelsmann Distribution Services)
Double Scoop: New Note Distribution Ltd
Double Zero: Shellshock Distribution
Douglas Music: Pinnacle Records
Down Boy: BDS (Bertelsmann Distribution Services)
Downbeat: Cargo Records (UK) Ltd
Downsall Plastics: Pinnacle Records
Downsound: Jet Star Phonographics
Downtown Soulville: Shellshock Distribution
Downwards: Plastic Head Music Distribution Ltd
Doyen: BDS (Bertelsmann Distribution Services)
Draft: Shellshock Distribution
Drag City: Cargo Records (UK) Ltd
Dragon Flight: Shellshock Distribution
Dragonfly: ADA Distribution, Vital Distribution
Dreadbeat: Proper Music Distribution Ltd
Dream Catcher: Pinnacle Records
Dream Circle: Cargo Records (UK) Ltd
Dreamscape: Flute Worldwide Ltd
DreamWorks: Universal Music Operations
Dreamy: Prime Distribution
Dress Circle: Silver Sounds CD Ltd
Dressed To Kill: Avanti Records, BDS (Bertelsmann Distribution Services)
Dreyfus: New Note Distribution Ltd, Pinnacle Records
DRG: New Note Distribution Ltd, Pinnacle Records, RSK Entertainment
DRG Records: New Note Distribution Ltd
Drive Thru: Plastic Head Music Distribution Ltd
Drive-In: Cargo Records (UK) Ltd
Droffig: Pinnacle Records
Drop Beat: Cargo Records (UK) Ltd, Shellshock Distribution
Drop Music: InterGroove Ltd
Drought: SRD (Southern Record Distribution)
Drug Squad: Vital Distribution
Drugracer: Cargo Records (UK) Ltd
Drumcode: Prime Distribution
Drunkabilly: Nervous Records
Drunken Fish: Cargo Records (UK) Ltd
DSS69: Plastic Head Music Distribution Ltd
D3: RSK Entertainment
Dtox: Universal Music Operations
DTR: Metronome Distribution
DTS: Vivante Music Ltd
Duality: Universal Music Operations
Dub Mission: SRD (Southern Record Distribution)
Dub Organiser: SRD (Southern Record Distribution)
Dubhead: SRD (Southern Record Distribution)
Dublin One: SRD (Southern Record Distribution)
Dubmission: SRD (Southern Record Distribution)
Dubology: SRD (Southern Record Distribution)
Dubwise: Shellshock Distribution
Duckdown: RSK Entertainment
Duellists: ADA Distribution
Dulcima: Savoy Strict Tempo Distributors
Dune: New Note Distribution Ltd, Pinnacle Records
Dunkeld: Gordon Duncan Distributions, Proper Music Distribution Ltd
Duophonic UHF: Vital Distribution
Dusk til Dawn: Shellshock Distribution
Dust: F Minor Ltd, SRD (Southern Record Distribution)
Duty Free: Vital Distribution
DV8: Universal Music Operations
Dwell: Plastic Head Music Distribution Ltd
Dyad: New Note Distribution Ltd
Dynamic: Jet Star Phonographics
Dynamics: Shellshock Distribution
Dynosupreme: SRD (Southern Record Distribution)
Dysfunctional: Cargo Records (UK) Ltd
E Music: Shellshock Distribution
Eagle: BDS (Bertelsmann Distribution Services)
Earache: Vital Distribution
Earful: Timewarp Distribution
Earth: Pinnacle Records, Shellshock Distribution
Earth Connection: SRD (Southern Record Distribution)
Earth Music: Cargo Records (UK) Ltd
Earthnoise: Vital Distribution
Earthsounds: Vital Distribution
Earthworks: Stern's Distribution
Earworm: Cargo Records (UK) Ltd
East Coast: SRD (Southern Record Distribution)
East Coast Empire: Plastic Head Music Distribution Ltd
East Edge: Vital Distribution
East Side Digital: SRD (Southern Record Distribution)
East Side: Load Media
East West: TEN (The Entertainment Network)
Eastern Developments: Baked Goods Distribution
Eastern Pressure: Shellshock Distribution
Eastside: BDS (Bertelsmann Distribution Services)
Eastworld: Plastic Head Music Distribution Ltd
Easy DB: Vital Distribution
Easy Jam: Universal Music Operations
Easy Star: SRD (Southern Record Distribution)
Easy!Tiger: Pinnacle Records
Easydisc: Proper Music Distribution Ltd
Eat Raw: Cargo Records (UK) Ltd
Ebony: SRD (Southern Record Distribution)
EBS: BDS (Bertelsmann Distribution Services)
Ecco.Chamber: Timewarp Distribution
Echo: Pinnacle Records
Echo Beach: Pinnacle Records, Shellshock Distribution
Echo Drop: Vital Distribution
ECI: Independent Distribution Ltd
Eclectic: Pinnacle Records
Eclipse: Gordon Duncan Distributions
ECM: New Note Distribution Ltd, Pinnacle Records
ECM Books: New Note Distribution Ltd
ECM New Series: New Note Distribution Ltd
ECM Works: New Note Distribution Ltd
Ecstatic: SRD (Southern Record Distribution)
Ecstatic Peace: Cargo Records (UK) Ltd
Edel: Vital Distribution
Eden: Gordon Duncan Distributions

Eden Productions: The Woods
Edgar Music: Pinnacle Records, Shellshock Distribution
Edgy: Proper Music Distribution Ltd
Edinburgh Tattoo: Gordon Duncan Distributions
Edsel: BDS (Bertelsmann Distribution Services)
Edward Davenport: Shellshock Distribution
Eerie Materials: Cargo Records (UK) Ltd
EFA: SRD (Southern Record Distribution)
Effortless: Shellshock Distribution
Ego: Vital Distribution
Eidechse: BDS (Bertelsmann Distribution Services), Essential Direct Ltd
18th Street Lounge: Cargo Records (UK) Ltd
Eighth Day: Amato Distribution
El Bandoneon: Discovery Records Ltd
Elastic: Cargo Records (UK) Ltd
Electric Lounge: Timewarp Distribution
Electric Melt: Amato Distribution
Electro Bunker Cologne: SRD (Southern Record Distribution)
Electro-Fi: Hot Shot Records
Electron Industries: Vital Distribution
Eledethorn: Pinnacle Records
Elefant: SRD (Southern Record Distribution)
Eleganz: Shellshock Distribution
Elegy: Plastic Head Music Distribution Ltd
Elektra: TEN (The Entertainment Network)
Elektrik Orgasm: Pinnacle Records
Elemental: Pinnacle Records
Elements Of Sound: BDS (Bertelsmann Distribution Services), Essential Direct Ltd
Elephant 6: Shellshock Distribution
Elevator Music: Plastic Head Music Distribution Ltd
Elf Cut: Pinnacle Records
Elite: Cargo Records (UK) Ltd
Elkarlanean: ADA Distribution
Elleffe: Universal Music Operations
Elliesis Arts: Stern's Distribution
Elypsia: Vital Distribution
Emanem: Harmonia Mundi (UK) Ltd
Emarcy: Universal Music Operations
Ember: Pinnacle Records
Emerald Hour: Proper Music Distribution Ltd
Emergency Broadcast System Ltd: Plastic Head Music Distribution Ltd
EMI: EMI Distribution
EMI Brazil: Stern's Distribution
EMI Classics UK: EMI Distribution
EMI Gold: EMI Distribution
EMI South Africa: Stern's Distribution
Emission: Load Media
Emissions: Vital Distribution
Emocion: New Note Distribution Ltd
Emoticon: Baked Goods Distribution
Emotif: SRD (Southern Record Distribution)
Emperor Jones: Cargo Records (UK) Ltd
Emperor Norton: Shellshock Distribution
Empreinte DIG: Harmonia Mundi (UK) Ltd
Empress: RSK Entertainment
Empty: Cargo Records (UK) Ltd, Shellshock Distribution
En Seine: Amato Distribution
The End: Shellshock Distribution
Endearing: Shellshock Distribution
Endorphin: Cargo Records (UK) Ltd
Energetic: SRD (Southern Record Distribution)
Engine: Vital Distribution
English Muffin: Baked Goods Distribution
Enja: New Note Distribution Ltd, Pinnacle Records
Enraptured: Cargo Records (UK) Ltd
Enriched: Pinnacle Records, Shellshock Distribution
Entertainment In Video: TEN (The Entertainment Network)
Entracte: Hot Records
Entropica: Changing World Distribution, Shellshock Distribution
Entropy Productions: Vital Distribution
Enviken: Nervous Records
Environ: Vital Distribution
Epic: TEN (The Entertainment Network)
Epidemic: Universal Music Operations
Epigram: Cargo Records (UK) Ltd
Episode: Universal Music Operations
Epitaph: Pinnacle Records
EPM: Discovery Records Ltd
Erato: TEN (The Entertainment Network)
Ermitage: Metronome Distribution
Ernie Smith: Jet Star Phonographics
Eruption: Pinnacle Records
ESC Records: New Note Distribution Ltd
Escapade: Cargo Records (UK) Ltd
Escape: Cargo Records (UK) Ltd, RSK Entertainment
Escape Music: Cargo Records (UK) Ltd
Eschaton: Shellshock Distribution
Eskimo Recordings: Timewarp Distribution
ESL: Cargo Records (UK) Ltd
Esoteric: Load Media
ESP Disk: F Minor Ltd
Espionage: Shellshock Distribution
Essay: Cargo Records (UK) Ltd
Essential: Pinnacle Records
Essential Music: African Caribbean Asian Entertainment
Estrus: Cargo Records (UK) Ltd
Eternal: TEN (The Entertainment Network)
Ethbo: Kudos Records Ltd
Etherean Music: Blue Crystal
Ethnic Flight: BDS (Bertelsmann Distribution Services), Essential Direct Ltd
Ethnic-Flamenco Vivo: Harmonia Mundi (UK) Ltd
Euphonious: Vital Distribution
Euphonius: Shellshock Distribution
Euphoria: F Minor Ltd
Euphoric: BDS (Bertelsmann Distribution Services)
Eureka: BDS (Bertelsmann Distribution Services)
Euro Ralph: Cargo Records (UK) Ltd
Europress: Pinnacle Records
Evans World Of Music: Harmonia Mundi (UK) Ltd
Eve: Amato Distribution
Eve Nova: Amato Distribution
Event: Cargo Records (UK) Ltd
Eventide Music: Media UK Distribution
Evil: SRD (Southern Record Distribution)
Evil Horde: Shellshock Distribution
Evil Teen: Shellshock Distribution
Evocative: Pinnacle Records
Evolution Gold: BDS (Bertelsmann Distribution Services)
Excession: Vital Distribution
Exil: Proper Music Distribution Ltd
Exoteric: BDS (Bertelsmann Distribution Services), Essential Direct Ltd
Exotica: SRD (Southern Record Distribution)
Expanding: Baked Goods Distribution
Experience: Jet Star Phonographics
Explicit: Load Media
Exploding Plastic: BDS (Bertelsmann Distribution Services), Essential Direct Ltd
Explosive: BDS (Bertelsmann Distribution Services)
Expression: Pinnacle Records
Extatique: Vital Distribution
Exterminator: Jet Star Phonographics
Extreme: Vital Distribution
Eye Q: Vital Distribution
F Communications (UK): Vital Distribution
F D M: Nova Sales and Distribution (UK) Ltd
F O D: Nova Sales and Distribution (UK) Ltd
F.O.A.D.: Shellshock Distribution
F.R.: Shellshock Distribution
Fabric: KRD
Fabric Of Life: Amato Distribution
Factory Too: Pinnacle Records
Falasha: SRD (Southern Record Distribution)
Falcone: Pinnacle Records, Shellshock Distribution
Fanboy/Garralda: Shellshock Distribution
Fantastic Plastic: Vital Distribution
Fantasy: Pinnacle Records
Fantasy Jazz: New Note Distribution Ltd
Far Out: KRD, New Note Distribution Ltd, Pinnacle Records
Farside: Timewarp Distribution
Fast Music: Plastic Head Music Distribution Ltd
Fast Western: Independent Distribution Ltd
Fat Records: InterGroove Ltd
Fat 'n' Round: Pinnacle Records
Fat Beats: Pinnacle Records
Fat Cat: SRD (Southern Record Distribution)
Fat City: 4am Distribution
Fat Eyes: Jet Star Phonographics
Fat Man: SRD (Southern Record Distribution)
Fat Wreck: Plastic Head Music Distribution Ltd
Fatal Generation: Shellshock Distribution
Fatlip: Vital Distribution
Fauve: Vital Distribution
Faze 2 Records: Absolute Marketing & Distribution Ltd.
Fear Of Music: SRD (Southern Record Distribution)
Federation: Universal Music Operations
Fedora: Proper Music Distribution Ltd
Feedback: BDS (Bertelsmann Distribution Services)
Fellside: Gordon Duncan Distributions, Proper Music Distribution Ltd
Fen Cat: Universal Music Operations
Fenetik: Kudos Records Ltd
Ferocious: Vital Distribution
Ferric Mordant: Pinnacle Records, Shellshock Distribution
Ferris Wheel: Prime Distribution
Festival: Cargo Records (UK) Ltd
Fflach TRADD: ADA Distribution
Ffrench Production: Jet Star Phonographics
ffrr: TEN (The Entertainment Network)
Fiasco: Kudos Records Ltd, Pinnacle Records
Fidelity Lo: Shellshock Distribution
Fie!: Vital Distribution
Fierce: SRD (Southern Record Distribution)
Fierce Panda: Pinnacle Records, Vital Distribution
1500: Cargo Records (UK) Ltd
Fifth Freedom: Vital Distribution
Fifty First Recordings: Pinnacle Records
Film Four: Technicolor Distribution Services Ltd
Film 2000: TEN (The Entertainment Network)
Filter: Pinnacle Records
Filth: Pinnacle Records
Filthy Sonnix: Pinnacle Records
Fine Art: Vital Distribution

Fine Balance: SRD (Southern Record Distribution)
Fine Hairy Rope Records: ADA Distribution
Fingal: Gordon Duncan Distributions
Finger: Cargo Records (UK) Ltd
Finger Lickin': InterGroove Ltd, Universal Music Operations
Finlandia: TEN (The Entertainment Network)
Finnish Folk Music Institute: ADA Distribution
Finnish Swedish Folk Music Institute: ADA Distribution
Fire Inc: Cargo Records (UK) Ltd
Fire Island: Universal Music Operations
Fire Recordings: Pinnacle Records
Fireball: Excel Marketing Services Ltd, Proper Music Distribution Ltd
Firm Music: Pinnacle Records
First Edition: Jet Star Phonographics
First Impressions: Vivante Music Ltd
First Love: Cargo Records (UK) Ltd
First Night: Pinnacle Records
First Time: Media UK Distribution
The First Time: Shellshock Distribution
Fisheye: Cargo Records (UK) Ltd
Fishtail: Hot Shot Records
555 Recordings: Cargo Records (UK) Ltd
500: BDS (Bertelsmann Distribution Services), Essential Direct Ltd
504: Proper Music Distribution Ltd
Five O Four: Jazz Music
Five Trees: Absolute Marketing & Distribution Ltd., Pinnacle Records
5HQ: SRD (Southern Record Distribution)
FJ Entertainment: Jet Star Phonographics
Flair: Absolute Marketing & Distribution Ltd., BDS (Bertelsmann Distribution Services)
Flamingo West: The Woods
Flammable: Load Media
Flapper: Pinnacle Records
Flapping Jet: Cargo Records (UK) Ltd
Flarenasch: Discovery Records Ltd
Flashlight: Synergie Logistics
Flat Earth: Cargo Records (UK) Ltd, Shellshock Distribution
Flat Rock: Proper Music Distribution Ltd
Flatline: Shellshock Distribution
Flaw: Vital Distribution
Fledg'ling: Proper Music Distribution Ltd
Flex: Jet Star Phonographics
Flexipop: Shellshock Distribution
Flintwood: Jet Star Phonographics
Flipside: Global Dance Distribution Ltd, Pinnacle Records
Fliptop Records: Plastic Head Music Distribution Ltd
Flittchen: Pinnacle Records, Shellshock Distribution
Flo Records: SRD (Southern Record Distribution)
Florida: ADA Distribution
Flotsam & Jetsam: SRD (Southern Record Distribution)
Fluffy: Pinnacle Records
Fluffy Bunny: Pinnacle Records
Fluid: Amato Distribution
Fluid Ounce: Cargo Records (UK) Ltd
Flute: BDS (Bertelsmann Distribution Services)
Flux: Vital Distribution
Fly Casual: Cargo Records (UK) Ltd
Flyboy: Shellshock Distribution
Flydaddy: Pinnacle Records, Shellshock Distribution
Flying Fish: Proper Music Distribution Ltd
Flying Rhino: SRD (Southern Record Distribution)
Flying Thorn: Proper Music Distribution Ltd
Flyright: Hot Shot Records, Jazz Music
FM: Revolver Music
Fog Area: Pinnacle Records, Shellshock Distribution
Folk Corporation: Pinnacle Records
Folk Era: Rolica Music Distribution
Folksound: ADA Distribution, CM Distribution, Roots Records
F1: TEN (The Entertainment Network)
Fono Astur: ADA Distribution
Fontana: Universal Music Operations
Food: EMI Distribution
Food For Thought: Pinnacle Records
Foot Stomping Records: ADA Distribution
For All The Right Reasons: Pinnacle Records
For Real: Amato Distribution
Force Inc: SRD (Southern Record Distribution)
Forever Forward: BDS (Bertelsmann Distribution Services)
Form & Function: Shellshock Distribution
Formacentric DisK: Cargo Records (UK) Ltd
Formaldehyde: Shellshock Distribution
Format Supremacy: Cargo Records (UK) Ltd
Formation: SRD (Southern Record Distribution)
Forsaken: Plastic Head Music Distribution Ltd
Fortress: ST Holdings Ltd
Fortuna Pop: Pinnacle Records, Shellshock Distribution
Fortunate: Pinnacle Records, Shellshock Distribution
49th Parallel: Vital Distribution
Forum: Regis Records Ltd
Forward: Jet Star Phonographics
Fotofone: Jet Star Phonographics
Foundation Sound Works: Vital Distribution
Foundling: Shellshock Distribution
Foundry Band: Gordon Duncan Distributions
Four D: Amato Distribution
4 Liberty: Pinnacle Records
4 Men With Beards: F Minor Ltd
four:twenty: InterGroove Ltd
4AD: Vital Distribution
Fourbeat: Pinnacle Records
4M: Pinnacle Records
(4most): Pinnacle Records
Fourth & Broadway: Universal Music Operations
Fragments: SRD (Southern Record Distribution)
Frances Court: Jazz Music
Frank Records: Media UK Distribution
Frankman: Shellshock Distribution
Frantic: Vital Distribution
Freak: Load Media, Pinnacle Records
FreakStreet: Pinnacle Records
Free: F Minor Ltd, Pinnacle Records
Free Booze: Pinnacle Records
Free Range: Kudos Records Ltd
Free Reed: ADA Distribution, CM Distribution
Free World: SRD (Southern Record Distribution)
Freebass: Amato Distribution
Freeform: Pinnacle Records
Freek: Cargo Records (UK) Ltd
Freeland: Shellshock Distribution
Fremeaux: Discovery Records Ltd
French Kiss: Shellshock Distribution
Frequent Soundz: Timewarp Distribution
Fresh: Pinnacle Records
Fresh Ear: Pinnacle Records
Fresh Kutt: SRD (Southern Record Distribution)
Fresh Sound: Discovery Records Ltd
Freskanova: Pinnacle Records
Fret: New Note Distribution Ltd, Pendle Hawk Music Distribution
Frog: Jazz Music
Fromage Rouge: Vital Distribution
Frontiers: Cargo Records (UK) Ltd
Fruit Tree: F Minor Ltd
Fruitbeard: Kudos Records Ltd
Fruition: Pinnacle Records
Fuel: Pinnacle Records
Fueled By Ramen: Plastic Head Music Distribution Ltd
Fuju: Amato Distribution
Fuk: Amato Distribution
Full Blown: BDS (Bertelsmann Distribution Services)
Full Circle: Vital Distribution
Full Moon: Plastic Head Music Distribution Ltd
Fullwatts: Shellshock Distribution
FUN: Pinnacle Records
Funakasaurus: Vital Distribution
Function: Load Media
Function 8: Cargo Records (UK) Ltd
Fundamental: Pinnacle Records, Shellshock Distribution
Funfundvierzig: Shellshock Distribution
Funksta: Shellshock Distribution
Funky Beats: Universal Music Operations
Funkyard: Shellshock Distribution
Furious?: Vital Distribution
Fury: Caroline 2 Ltd
Fuse: Pendle Hawk Music Distribution, Proper Music Distribution Ltd
Fused & Bruised: SRD (Southern Record Distribution)
Fusion: BDS (Bertelsmann Distribution Services)
Future Legend: Pinnacle Records
Future Primitive: Cargo Records (UK) Ltd
Future Sound & Vision: BDS (Bertelsmann Distribution Services)
Future Tense: Vital Distribution
Future Underground Nation: Amato Distribution
Future Vinyl: Shellshock Distribution
Futurus: Pinnacle Records
Fuze: Load Media, SRD (Southern Record Distribution)
G-Spot: BDS (Bertelsmann Distribution Services), Essential Direct Ltd
G.M.I.: Shellshock Distribution
GAHO Music: ADA Distribution
Gail Davies: Proper Music Distribution Ltd
Gailo: Stern's Distribution
Gala: BDS (Bertelsmann Distribution Services)
Galaktic Sound Lab: Proper Music Distribution Ltd
Galaxia: Cargo Records (UK) Ltd
Galaxy: ZYX
Gale: Metronome Distribution
Game: BDS (Bertelsmann Distribution Services)
Game Two: Shellshock Distribution
Gamp: Pinnacle Records
Gannet: Jazz Music
Garage Nation: Pinnacle Records
Garden: Pinnacle Records, Shellshock Distribution
GAS: Pinnacle Records
Gas Works: Shellshock Distribution
Gaz's: Shellshock Distribution
Gazmo: Universal Music Operations
GDI: Nova Sales and Distribution (UK) Ltd
Gear Fab: F Minor Ltd
Gear Head: F Minor Ltd
Gecko: Pinnacle Records, Shellshock Distribution
Gee Street: Pinnacle Records
Geffen: BDS (Bertelsmann Distribution Services)
Geist: Vital Distribution
Generations: Vital Distribution

Generic: Pinnacle Records, Shellshock Distribution
Genetic Stress: SRD (Southern Record Distribution)
Genius: Avid Entertainment
Gentilly: The Woods
Germstore: Baked Goods Distribution
Gern Blansten: SRD (Southern Record Distribution)
Get Back: Cargo Records (UK) Ltd, F Minor Ltd
Get Hip: F Minor Ltd
Get Real Productions: Proper Music Distribution Ltd
GHB: Jazz Music
GHB Jazz Foundation: The Woods
Ghetto Safari: Cargo Records (UK) Ltd
Ghostmeat: Shellshock Distribution
Giant: BDS (Bertelsmann Distribution Services)
Giant Claw: Cargo Records (UK) Ltd
Giant Electric Pea: Pinnacle Records
Giants Of Jazz: BDS (Bertelsmann Distribution Services), Delta Music PLC, Jazz Music, Swift Record Distributors
Gift Of Life: Cargo Records (UK) Ltd
Giga: BDS (Bertelsmann Distribution Services)
Giglo: SRD (Southern Record Distribution)
Gigolo: SRD (Southern Record Distribution)
Ginga: EMI Distribution
Ginger: Cargo Records (UK) Ltd
Girl: Vital Distribution
Girl Dependence: Pinnacle Records
Glade: ADA Distribution
Glamma: Jet Star Phonographics
Glasgow: Absolute Marketing & Distribution Ltd., Universal Music Operations
The Glass Gramophone Co: Swift Record Distributors
Glencoe: Gordon Duncan Distributions
Glenda Leigh Lewis: Jet Star Phonographics
Gliss: Pinnacle Records
Glitterhouse: Avid Entertainment
Global Harmony: Amato Distribution
Global Head: Shellshock Distribution
Global Headz: Vital Distribution
Global Labels: Vital Distribution
Global Mobile: Pinnacle Records
Global Nite Life: Pinnacle Records
Global Talent: Pinnacle Records
Global TV: BDS (Bertelsmann Distribution Services)
Global Underground: Vital Distribution
Global Warming: Cargo Records (UK) Ltd
Globestyle: New Note Distribution Ltd, Pinnacle Records, Stern's Distribution
Gloomy Prophecies: Shellshock Distribution
Glossa: Harmonia Mundi (UK) Ltd
GM Recordings: Metronome Distribution
GMM: Cargo Records (UK) Ltd, Plastic Head Music Distribution Ltd
GNP: Pinnacle Records
GNP Crescendo: ZYX
GO: ADA Distribution
Go Clubland: New Note Distribution Ltd
Go For It: InterGroove Ltd
Go Jazz: New Note Distribution Ltd, Vital Distribution
Go Kart: Pinnacle Records, Plastic Head Music Distribution Ltd
Go!Discs: Universal Music Operations
Go-Go Girl: SRD (Southern Record Distribution)
Go.Beat: Universal Music Operations
Goatboy: Shellshock Distribution
God Bless: Cargo Records (UK) Ltd
God's Pop: Pinnacle Records
Godz Greed: Shellshock Distribution
Gogo Girl: SRD (Southern Record Distribution)
Going For A Song: Synergie Logistics
Golden Triangle: Pinnacle Records
Goldmine: Vital Distribution
Goldrush: Proper Music Distribution Ltd
Golf: Plastic Head Music Distribution Ltd
Gone Clear: Jet Star Phonographics
Gonzo Circus: Pinnacle Records, Shellshock Distribution
Goo!: Pinnacle Records
Good As: Amato Distribution
Good Ink: Shellshock Distribution
Good Life: Cargo Records (UK) Ltd
Good Looking: SRD (Southern Record Distribution)
Good Sounds: TEN (The Entertainment Network)
Good Time Jazz: Jazz Music
Good Vibe: Cargo Records (UK) Ltd
Goodlife: Cargo Records (UK) Ltd
Goodlooking: Load Media
Goodtime Jazz: New Note Distribution Ltd
Goofin: Nervous Records, Synergie Logistics
Gorgeous Music: Pinnacle Records
Gosh: Pinnacle Records
Gotham: BDS (Bertelsmann Distribution Services)
GPR: Vital Distribution
Gracethril: Jet Star Phonographics
Grade: Cargo Records (UK) Ltd
Grainne: BDS (Bertelsmann Distribution Services)
Gramavision: Vital Distribution
Gran Kru: SRD (Southern Record Distribution)
Grand: Proper Music Distribution Ltd
Grand Central: Vital Distribution
Grand Larceny: SRD (Southern Record Distribution)
Grand Royal: EMI Distribution, Vital Distribution
Grand Theft Autumn: Shellshock Distribution
The Grapevine Label: I&B Records (Irish Music) Ltd, Independent Distribution Ltd, THE (Total Home Entertainment), Universal Music Operations
Grasmere: BDS (Bertelsmann Distribution Services), Delta Music PLC, Gordon Duncan Distributions
Grateful Dead: Pinnacle Records
Gratuitous Beaver: Shellshock Distribution
Grave News Ltd: Plastic Head Music Distribution Ltd
Gravitate: Cargo Records (UK) Ltd
Gravitation: Pinnacle Records
Gravity: Shellshock Distribution
Graylan: Universal Music Operations
Great British Techno: BDS (Bertelsmann Distribution Services)
Great Movie Themes: BDS (Bertelsmann Distribution Services)
Green Dolphin: Shellshock Distribution
Green Light: Vital Distribution
Green Linnet: Claddagh Records, Proper Music Distribution Ltd
Green Tea: SRD (Southern Record Distribution)
Green Vinyl: Pinnacle Records
Greenage: ADA Distribution
Greentrax: Gordon Duncan Distributions, Proper Music Distribution Ltd
Grilled Cheese: Cargo Records (UK) Ltd
Grilli: Universal Music Operations
Grimm Records: Plastic Head Music Distribution Ltd
Gringo: Pinnacle Records
Grinnigogs: ADA Distribution
Groove: SRD (Southern Record Distribution)
Groove Attack: Pinnacle Records
Groove Kissing: Vital Distribution
Groovenote: Vivante Music Ltd
Grooves Magazine: Baked Goods Distribution
Gross National Product: Pinnacle Records
Ground: Vital Distribution
Ground Control: Cargo Records (UK) Ltd
Grover: Plastic Head Music Distribution Ltd
GRP: BDS (Bertelsmann Distribution Services)
GS: ADA Distribution
G2: Proper Music Distribution Ltd
Guess What: Jet Star Phonographics
Guidance: Cargo Records (UK) Ltd
Guided Missile: Pinnacle Records
Guild: Pinnacle Records
Gun: Plastic Head Music Distribution Ltd
Gush: Shellshock Distribution
Gussie P: Jet Star Phonographics
Gut: Pinnacle Records
Gutbucket: Shellshock Distribution
Gwynfryn: Sain (Recordiau) Cyf
Gypsy: ADA Distribution
Gyration: Pinnacle Records, Shellshock Distribution
Habit: Load Media
Hades: Vital Distribution
Hadshot Haheizar: Shellshock Distribution
Hairball 8: Cargo Records (UK) Ltd
Halcyon: Jazz Music
Halesouth: Pinnacle Records
Half Moon: BDS (Bertelsmann Distribution Services)
Half-A-Cow: Cargo Records (UK) Ltd
Hall Of Sermon: Plastic Head Music Distribution Ltd
Hallmark Music & Entertainment: Technicolor Distribution Services Ltd
The Hallowe'en Society: Cargo Records (UK) Ltd
Halo: Nova Sales and Distribution (UK) Ltd, Pinnacle Records
Hammerheart: Shellshock Distribution
Hana: Universal Music Operations
Hands On: Pinnacle Records
Hangdog: Cargo Records (UK) Ltd
Hangman's Daughter: Pinnacle Records
Hannibal: Vital Distribution
Hansome: Vital Distribution
Hanssler: Select Music & Video Distribution
Happy Accident: Pinnacle Records
Happy Days: BDS (Bertelsmann Distribution Services)
Happy Gang: Gordon Duncan Distributions
Happy Go Lucky: Cargo Records (UK) Ltd
Happy Trax: Universal Music Operations
Harbinger: Pinnacle Records
Harbourtown: Proper Music Distribution Ltd
Harbourtown Records: ADA Distribution
Hard Hands: SRD (Southern Record Distribution)
Hard Times: Vital Distribution
Hardleaders: SRD (Southern Record Distribution)
Hardward Records: Plastic Head Music Distribution Ltd
Harkit: Pinnacle Records
Harlequin: Hot Shot Records, Jazz Music, Stern's Distribution
Harmless Recordings: New Note Distribution Ltd
Harmonia Mundi: Harmonia Mundi (UK) Ltd
Harp: Gordon Duncan Distributions
Harper Collins: Pinnacle Records, Sound Entertainment Ltd
Harthouse: Vital Distribution

Harvest: SRD (Southern Record Distribution)
Harzfein: Pinnacle Records
Hash: SRD (Southern Record Distribution)
Haska Music: ADA Distribution
Hat Hut: Harmonia Mundi (UK) Ltd
Hat Now: Harmonia Mundi (UK) Ltd
Hate: BDS (Bertelsmann Distribution Services), Essential Direct Ltd
Hatology: Harmonia Mundi (UK) Ltd
Hausmusic: Cargo Records (UK) Ltd
Hausmusik: Baked Goods Distribution
Havana: SRD (Southern Record Distribution)
Havek Olam: Shellshock Distribution
Haven: Backs Distribution, Shellshock Distribution
Hawkeye: SRD (Southern Record Distribution)
Hazelwood: Shellshock Distribution
Head Hunter: Cargo Records (UK) Ltd
Head Not Found: Shellshock Distribution
Header: Vital Distribution
Headhunter: Cargo Records (UK) Ltd
Headspace: Vital Distribution
Headware: Shellshock Distribution
Heard: Vital Distribution
Hearpen: Vital Distribution
Heart Beat: Jet Star Phonographics
Heartbeat: Proper Music Distribution Ltd
Heat Recordings: Vital Distribution
Heaven: Universal Music Operations
Heaven Hotel: Cargo Records (UK) Ltd
Heavenly: BDS (Bertelsmann Distribution Services), Pinnacle Records, Vital Distribution
Heavy Truth: Vital Distribution
Heavyweight: Universal Music Operations
Hebe: ADA Distribution
Hectic: Shellshock Distribution, Universal Music Operations
Hed Kandi: 4am Distribution
Hefty: Baked Goods Distribution, Cargo Records (UK) Ltd, Shellshock Distribution
Heiro Imperium: Cargo Records (UK) Ltd
Helicon Mountain: Nova Sales and Distribution (UK) Ltd
Helix: SRD (Southern Record Distribution)
Hell Yeah: Cargo Records (UK) Ltd
Hellcat: Pinnacle Records
Helter Skelter: Pinnacle Records, Plastic Head Music Distribution Ltd
Hemiola: Vital Distribution
Hendricks: BDS (Bertelsmann Distribution Services)
Henry Street: Proper Music Distribution Ltd
HEP: Jazz Music, New Note Distribution Ltd, Pinnacle Records
Hep Records: New Note Distribution Ltd
Herald: The Complete Record Company Ltd
Heraldic Records: Media UK Distribution
Heraldic Jester: Media UK Distribution
Heraldic Vintage: Media UK Distribution
Heritage: Hot Shot Records, Jazz Music
Hertz: Shellshock Distribution
Hey Presto: Music Express Ltd
Hi: BDS (Bertelsmann Distribution Services)
Hi Fashion: SRD (Southern Record Distribution)
Hi-Ball: Shellshock Distribution
Hi-Life: Universal Music Operations
Hibiscus: Cargo Records (UK) Ltd
Hidden Agenda: Cargo Records (UK) Ltd, Shellshock Distribution
Hidden Valley Music: ADA Distribution
Hideaway Blues Band: Hot Shot Records
High Action: Hot Shot Records
High Barn: Nova Sales and Distribution (UK) Ltd
High Gain Records: Plastic Head Music Distribution Ltd
High Impedance: Shellshock Distribution
High Noon: SRD (Southern Record Distribution)
High Note: Proper Music Distribution Ltd
High Octane: Cargo Records (UK) Ltd
High On Hope: Pinnacle Records
High Society: Shellshock Distribution
High Society International: Plastic Head Music Distribution Ltd
High-Life: ADA Distribution
Higher Ground: TEN (The Entertainment Network)
Higher Limits: BDS (Bertelsmann Distribution Services)
Higher Octave: EMI Distribution
Higher Plane: Hot Shot Records
Higher State: Essential Direct Ltd
Highlander: Ross Record Distribution
HighTone: Proper Music Distribution Ltd
Hightone/HMG: Proper Music Distribution Ltd
Hillside Music: RSK Entertainment
Hindsight: BDS (Bertelsmann Distribution Services), Jazz Music
Hip-No: BDS (Bertelsmann Distribution Services)
Hipster: Shellshock Distribution
HIT LABEL: Technicolor Distribution Services Ltd, Universal Music Operations
The Hit Label: Pinnacle Records
Hitback: Pinnacle Records
Hitbound: SRD (Southern Record Distribution)
Hitchcock Media: Metronome Distribution
Hitop Records: Timewarp Distribution
HMV Classics: EMI Distribution
Hobby Industries: Shellshock Distribution
Hobgoblin Records: ADA Distribution
Hocus Pocus: Universal Music Operations
Hodder Headline: Pinnacle Records
Hoe Down City: SRD (Southern Record Distribution)
Hole In The Floor: Pinnacle Records
Holistic: Pinnacle Records
Hollenfeuer: Shellshock Distribution
Hollow Planet: Pinnacle Records, Shellshock Distribution
Hollywood: Vital Distribution
Holy Moly: Amato Distribution
Holy Records: Plastic Head Music Distribution Ltd
Hom-Mega: Pinnacle Records
Hombre: SRD (Southern Record Distribution)
Hombre Mapache Brand: SRD (Southern Record Distribution)
Home Alone: BDS (Bertelsmann Distribution Services), Essential Direct Ltd
Home Entertainment: Cargo Records (UK) Ltd
Home Roots Music: ADA Distribution
Homelife: Kudos Records Ltd
Homemade Records: New Note Distribution Ltd
Homer: Pinnacle Records
Homework: Pinnacle Records
Homewreckerfoundation: Shellshock Distribution
Honalulu United: Pinnacle Records, Shellshock Distribution
Honey Bear: Cargo Records (UK) Ltd
Honibokum: Vital Distribution
Honolulu United: Pinnacle Records, Shellshock Distribution
HOOD: ADA Distribution
Hooj Choons: Vital Distribution
Hook: InterGroove Ltd
Hooley: Gordon Duncan Distributions
Hooligan: Universal Music Operations
Hope Records: Pinnacle Records
Hope Recordings: Vital Distribution
Hopeless: Cargo Records (UK) Ltd
Horseback: Pinnacle Records
Horseplay: Hot Shot Records
Hospital: SRD (Southern Record Distribution)
Hostile: Load Media
Hot: Hot Records, Vital Distribution
Hot Air: Baked Goods Distribution, Cargo Records (UK) Ltd
Hot Classics: Cargo Records (UK) Ltd
Hot House Records: Harmonia Mundi (UK) Ltd
Hot Vinyl: Jet Star Phonographics
Hot Wire: Shellshock Distribution
Hotel Lotte: Shellshock Distribution
Hotel Lotte/Kompakt: Shellshock Distribution
Hottis: Jet Star Phonographics
House Nation: ZYX
House Of God: Cargo Records (UK) Ltd
Household Names: Plastic Head Music Distribution Ltd
Houston Party: Shellshock Distribution
Howling Duck: Pinnacle Records
HPT Independent: BDS (Bertelsmann Distribution Services), Essential Direct Ltd
HRL: BDS (Bertelsmann Distribution Services)
HTD: Pinnacle Records
H2OH Recordings: Universal Music Operations
Hubbcap: Universal Music Operations
Hubris: ADA Distribution
Human: Roots Records
Human Condition: Shellshock Distribution
Hummingbird: Universal Music Operations
Hut: EMI Distribution
Hux: Pinnacle Records
Hwyl: Cargo Records (UK) Ltd
Hydrahead: Shellshock Distribution
Hydration: Universal Music Operations
Hydrogen Dukebox: Pinnacle Records
Hydroponic: SRD (Southern Record Distribution)
Hymen: Shellshock Distribution
Hyper: Pinnacle Records, Shellshock Distribution
Hyperion: Select Music & Video Distribution
Hyperspace: Cargo Records (UK) Ltd
Hypertension: Proper Music Distribution Ltd
Hypnotic: Vital Distribution
Hypnotize: Nova Sales and Distribution (UK) Ltd
I Scream Records: Plastic Head Music Distribution Ltd
I&B: I&B Records (Irish Music) Ltd
Iajrc: Jazz Music
Iboga: Shellshock Distribution
Ice Rink: Vital Distribution
ID Identity: SRD (Southern Record Distribution)
Idiot Savant: Cargo Records (UK) Ltd
IE Music: Universal Music Operations
Ignition: Vital Distribution
Igus: Discovery Records Ltd
Ikef: F Minor Ltd
Ill Recordings: Vital Distribution
Illegal: Jet Star Phonographics
Illusion: BDS (Bertelsmann Distribution Services)
Imaginary Music: Harmonia Mundi (UK) Ltd
Imago: Proper Music Distribution Ltd
Imani: Jet Star Phonographics
Immaterial: Vital Distribution
IMP: Discovery Records Ltd
Impact Records: Plastic Head Music Distribution Ltd
Imperial Dub: Pinnacle Records
Important: Vital Distribution
Impulse: BDS (Bertelsmann Distribution Services)
In & Out: Vital Distribution

In Extremo: Shellshock Distribution
In The Red: Cargo Records (UK) Ltd
In-Tec: Pinnacle Records, SRD (Southern Record Distribution)
Inakustic: Proper Music Distribution Ltd
Inbetweens: Shellshock Distribution
Incoming!: Pinnacle Records
INCredible: TEN (The Entertainment Network)
Independent: Shellshock Distribution
Independent Dealers: Shellshock Distribution, Vital Distribution
Independiente: TEN (The Entertainment Network)
India Navigation: Discovery Records Ltd
Indie 500: Backs Distribution, Pinnacle Records, Shellshock Distribution
Indigo Records: Jazz Music, New Note Distribution Ltd, Proper Music Distribution Ltd
Indochina: Pinnacle Records
Industrial Strength: Vital Distribution
Industry Standard: Amato Distribution
Inertia: SRD (Southern Record Distribution)
Infernal: Pinnacle Records
Inferno: Vital Distribution
Inferno Cool: Vital Distribution
Infiltration: Pinnacle Records, Shellshock Distribution
Infinity: Pinnacle Records
Influential: Pinnacle Records, Shellshock Distribution
Infonet: Vital Distribution
Infracom: SRD (Southern Record Distribution), Timewarp Distribution
Infrared: Pinnacle Records
Infur: Pinnacle Records
Infusion: Vital Distribution
Innerspace: Shellshock Distribution
Innerstate: Shellshock Distribution
Innocent: EMI Distribution
Inside Out: TEN (The Entertainment Network)
Instant Karma: TEN (The Entertainment Network)
Instant Mayhem: Vital Distribution
Instinct: Cargo Records (UK) Ltd
Instinctive: TEN (The Entertainment Network)
Insurrection: Cargo Records (UK) Ltd, Shellshock Distribution
Intasound: Load Media
Integral: SRD (Southern Record Distribution)
Integrity: SRD (Southern Record Distribution)
Inter City: Vital Distribution
Intercom: SRD (Southern Record Distribution)
Intermusic: Nervous Records
International Deejay Gigolos: SRD (Southern Record Distribution)
International Playboy Gigolos: SRD (Southern Record Distribution)
Internazionale: Pinnacle Records
Interra: BDS (Bertelsmann Distribution Services)
Interscope: BDS (Bertelsmann Distribution Services)
Intersound: I&B Records (Irish Music) Ltd, Jazz Music
Intrinsic: Pinnacle Records
Intruder: BDS (Bertelsmann Distribution Services), Essential Direct Ltd
Intuition: New Note Distribution Ltd, Pinnacle Records
Invicta Hi-Fi: Vital Distribution
Invisible: Pinnacle Records
Invisible Hands Records: Pinnacle Records
Invisible Records: Plastic Head Music Distribution Ltd
Involve: Baked Goods Distribution
Ion: Cargo Records (UK) Ltd
Irdial: Baked Goods Distribution
Irish: BDS (Bertelsmann Distribution Services)
Irma: BDS (Bertelsmann Distribution Services), Essential Direct Ltd, Nova Sales and Distribution (UK) Ltd
Irma On Canvas: Timewarp Distribution
Iron Man: Cargo Records (UK) Ltd
Irregular: Proper Music Distribution Ltd
Island: Universal Music Operations
Island Black Music: Universal Music Operations
Island Jamaica: Universal Music Operations, Vital Distribution
Island Masters: Universal Music Operations
Isobar Records: Pinnacle Records
Isolation: Shellshock Distribution
Israelimetal Classics: Shellshock Distribution
It Records: Vital Distribution
It's Fabulous: SRD (Southern Record Distribution)
It's Music: Pinnacle Records
Itchy Teeth: Cargo Records (UK) Ltd
ITN Corporation: Plastic Head Music Distribution Ltd
IVL Videos: Excel Marketing Services Ltd
Ivory: SRD (Southern Record Distribution)
IVP: Gordon Duncan Distributions
Ivy: Vital Distribution
Ixor Stix: Shellshock Distribution
J&M Recordings: Jazz Music
Jab: Gordon Duncan Distributions
Jagjaguwar: Cargo Records (UK) Ltd, Shellshock Distribution
JAGZ: The Woods
Jah Warrior: SRD (Southern Record Distribution)
Jah Works: SRD (Southern Record Distribution)
Jahmani: Jet Star Phonographics
Jal Premium: SRD (Southern Record Distribution)
Jam Jah: Absolute Marketing & Distribution Ltd.
Jamaica: Jet Star Phonographics
Jamal: Pinnacle Records
Jamazima: Jet Star Phonographics
Jamdown: Plastic Head Music Distribution Ltd
Jamixal: Jet Star Phonographics
Jammys: Jet Star Phonographics
Jamnic: Absolute Marketing & Distribution Ltd.
Japo: New Note Distribution Ltd
Jardis: The Woods
Jas: SRD (Southern Record Distribution)
Jasmine Records: Proper Music Distribution Ltd
Jasper: Pinnacle Records
Javelin: THE (Total Home Entertainment)
Jawbone: Shellshock Distribution
Jazz & Blues: BDS (Bertelsmann Distribution Services), Delta Music PLC
Jazz Academy: New Note Distribution Ltd
Jazz Alliance: New Note Distribution Ltd, Pinnacle Records
Jazz Archives: Discovery Records Ltd, Jazz Music
Jazz Arena: The Woods
Jazz Base: The Woods
Jazz Cat: New Note Distribution Ltd
Jazz Classics: Proper Music Distribution Ltd
Jazz Compass: The Woods
Jazz FM: 4am Distribution, Flute Worldwide Ltd
Jazz Fudge: Pinnacle Records
Jazz Hour: Jazz Music
Jazz House: New Note Distribution Ltd, Synergie Logistics
Jazz Monkey: Cargo Records (UK) Ltd
Jazz Oracle: Jazz Music
Jazz Perspective: Hot Shot Records, Jazz Music
Jazz Unlimited: Jazz Music, Proper Music Distribution Ltd
Jazzanova: SRD (Southern Record Distribution)
Jazzband: Hot Shot Records, Jazz Music
Jazzheads: The Woods
Jazzizit: New Note Distribution Ltd
Jazzizzit: Pinnacle Records
Jazzman: Timewarp Distribution
Jazzology: Jazz Music, The Woods
JB Records: The Woods
JBO: Pinnacle Records
JC Records: ADA Distribution
JDJ: Pinnacle Records
Jealous: Pinnacle Records
Jeepster: Pinnacle Records
Jeity Music: Pinnacle Records
Jel: Shellshock Distribution
Jelly Street: BDS (Bertelsmann Distribution Services)
Jesper: Pinnacle Records
Jet: Proper Music Distribution Ltd
Jetstar: Jet Star Phonographics
Jika: New Note Distribution Ltd
Jimmi Kidd: Pinnacle Records
Jive: Pinnacle Records
Jive House: Pinnacle Records
JMC: Jet Star Phonographics
JMS: New Note Distribution Ltd
JMY/Moon/IAI/Red: Harmonia Mundi (UK) Ltd
Jockey Slut: Vital Distribution
Joe Frasier: Jet Star Phonographics
Joe G's: Jet Star Phonographics
Joe Gibbs: SRD (Southern Record Distribution)
Johann's Face: Cargo Records (UK) Ltd
Johanna: Proper Music Distribution Ltd
John Holt: Jet Star Phonographics
John John: Jet Star Phonographics
Johnny Ferreira: Hot Shot Records
Johnny Kane: Shellshock Distribution
Joke Productions: SRD (Southern Record Distribution)
Joker: SRD (Southern Record Distribution)
Jonson Family: Cargo Records (UK) Ltd
Joss House: Kudos Records Ltd
Journeys By DJ: Pinnacle Records
Jowonio Productions: Baked Goods Distribution
Joy: Jazz Music
JR Productions: Jet Star Phonographics
JR Records: Jazz Music
JRB: Metronome Distribution, Shellshock Distribution
JSP: Jazz Music, Proper Music Distribution Ltd
JTC Music Group: The Woods
Juice: SRD (Southern Record Distribution), Timewarp Distribution
Juice Box: SRD (Southern Record Distribution)
Juicy Cuts: Universal Music Operations
Jukebox Jazz: Jazz Music
Jump Up: Cargo Records (UK) Ltd
Jump Wax: Shellshock Distribution, Vital Distribution
Jumpin' & Pumpin': TEN (The Entertainment Network)
Jungle: SRD (Southern Record Distribution)
Jungle Growers: Pinnacle Records
Jungle Sky: Cargo Records (UK) Ltd
Junior: Amato Distribution
Junior Productions: Jet Star Phonographics
Junior Recordings: Amato Distribution
Junk: Cargo Records (UK) Ltd
Just A Memory: Pinnacle Records
Just Another Bootleg: SRD (Southern Record Distribution)
Just Another Label: SRD (Southern Record

Distribution)
Just Frienz: Jet Star Phonographics
Justin Time: New Note Distribution Ltd, Pinnacle Records
Justine: Vital Distribution
JVC: Proper Music Distribution Ltd, Vivante Music Ltd
JW Productions: Jet Star Phonographics
JZ & Arkh - MCMLXV Productions: Baked Goods Distribution
K&K: Jet Star Phonographics
K'Boro: Pinnacle Records
K-Power: Shellshock Distribution
Kamaric: Caroline 2 Ltd
Kamera Shy: THE (Total Home Entertainment)
Kamtschatka: Shellshock Distribution
Karaoke Kalk: SRD (Southern Record Distribution)
Karma: Shellshock Distribution
Karmagiraffe: SRD (Southern Record Distribution)
Karonte: Discovery Records Ltd
Kartoonz: SRD (Southern Record Distribution)
Kat: Cargo Records (UK) Ltd
Katt Pie: CM Distribution
Kay Video: Jazz Music
Kayak: Cargo Records (UK) Ltd
Kbox: Synergie Logistics
KC: Hot Shot Records
Keith Hinchliffe: ADA Distribution
Kelero: ADA Distribution
Keltia: Discovery Records Ltd
Kemet: Jet Star Phonographics
Ken Colyer Trust: Jazz Music
Kenneth: Jazz Music
Kent: Pinnacle Records
Kent Duchaine: Hot Shot Records
Kettle: Gordon Duncan Distributions
Key: Proper Music Distribution Ltd
Keynote: Load Media
K422: Vital Distribution
KG Records: ADA Distribution
Kick On: Pinnacle Records
Kickin: SRD (Southern Record Distribution)
Kicking Mule: Pinnacle Records
Kid Rhino: Pinnacle Records
Kiff SM: Vital Distribution
Kila: Proper Music Distribution Ltd
Kill Rock Stars: Cargo Records (UK) Ltd
Kim Will Kill Me: Shellshock Distribution
Kin: Baked Goods Distribution
Kindercore: Cargo Records (UK) Ltd, Shellshock Distribution
Kindness: Vital Distribution
Kinetix: Flute Worldwide Ltd, Pinnacle Records
King: BDS (Bertelsmann Distribution Services)
King Biscuit Flower: Pinnacle Records
King Edwards: Jet Star Phonographics
King Mob: TEN (The Entertainment Network)
King Pin: SRD (Southern Record Distribution)
King Super Analogue: Vivante Music Ltd
King Syndrome Sounds: Soul Trader
Kingpin: Amato Distribution
Kings Cross: Harmonia Mundi (UK) Ltd
Kings Of Kings: Jet Star Phonographics
Kingsize: SRD (Southern Record Distribution)
Kiss Kidee: Jet Star Phonographics
Kissing Spell: F Minor Ltd
Kitchenware: Vital Distribution
Kitty Kitty Corporation: SRD (Southern Record Distribution)
Kitty Yo: Cargo Records (UK) Ltd, SRD (Southern Record Distribution)
KK Traxx: Cargo Records (UK) Ltd
Klangbad: Shellshock Distribution
Kleptomania: Cargo Records (UK) Ltd
Klone: Nova Sales and Distribution (UK) Ltd, Pinnacle Records
Knite Force: Universal Music Operations
Knitebreed: Universal Music Operations
Knitting Factory: New Note Distribution Ltd, Pinnacle Records, Shellshock Distribution
Knock On Wood: Discovery Records Ltd
Knock Out: Cargo Records (UK) Ltd
Knowsavage: Shellshock Distribution
Knoy: Cargo Records (UK) Ltd
Ko Productions: Silver Sounds CD Ltd
Koala: Pinnacle Records, Shellshock Distribution
Kollaps: Cargo Records (UK) Ltd
Kompakt: SRD (Southern Record Distribution), Shellshock Distribution
Konkurrent: SRD (Southern Record Distribution)
Konter: Pinnacle Records, Shellshock Distribution
Kontraband: Shellshock Distribution
Kooky: Cargo Records (UK) Ltd
Kool Cuts: Independent Distribution Ltd
Kool-Pop: Shellshock Distribution
Koolworld: Vital Distribution
Kopf: Shellshock Distribution
Koyote: Pinnacle Records
Krave: Shellshock Distribution
Krazy Kat: Hot Shot Records, Jazz Music
Krembo: Shellshock Distribution
KRL: Gordon Duncan Distributions, Ross Record Distribution, Vital Distribution
Krunch: SRD (Southern Record Distribution)
Krunchie: Pinnacle Records
Krush Grooves: SRD (Southern Record Distribution)
K7: Vital Distribution
Kudos: Kudos Records Ltd, Pinnacle Records
Kufe: Jet Star Phonographics
Kuff: EMI Distribution
Kuku: Pinnacle Records
Kultbox: Cargo Records (UK) Ltd
Kung Fu: Pinnacle Records
Kurbel: SRD (Southern Record Distribution)
Kus: SRD (Southern Record Distribution)
KWR: BDS (Bertelsmann Distribution Services), Essential Direct Ltd
L'Age d'Or: Shellshock Distribution
L'Attitude: Vital Distribution
La La: The Woods
La La Land: Vital Distribution
La Lichere: Discovery Records Ltd
Lab Recordings: Pinnacle Records, Shellshock Distribution
Label Bleu: New Note Distribution Ltd, Pinnacle Records
Label X: Hot Records
Labyrinth: Vital Distribution
Lacerated: Baked Goods Distribution
Lacerba: TEN (The Entertainment Network)
Ladomat: Shellshock Distribution
LaFace: BDS (Bertelsmann Distribution Services)
Lager: Proper Music Distribution Ltd
Lagoon: Jet Star Phonographics
Lake: Delta Music PLC
Lakota: Vital Distribution
Lammas Music: New Note Distribution Ltd
Lance Rock: Cargo Records (UK) Ltd
Land Speed: Cargo Records (UK) Ltd
Language: Vital Distribution
Lapwing: CM Distribution
Large Club: Amato Distribution
Laserlight: BDS (Bertelsmann Distribution Services), Delta Music PLC
Laserlight Celtic: BDS (Bertelsmann Distribution Services)
Last Call: Proper Music Distribution Ltd
Last Days: Hot Shot Records
Latent Talent: Proper Music Distribution Ltd
Laughing Stock: Vital Distribution
Lava.: SRD (Southern Record Distribution)
Law & Auder: Shellshock Distribution
LD: Vital Distribution
Le Chant Du Monde: Harmonia Mundi (UK) Ltd
Le Club Du Disque Arabe: Harmonia Mundi (UK) Ltd
Le Coq Musique: Shellshock Distribution
Le Grand Magistery: Shellshock Distribution
Le Village Vert: Pinnacle Records
LEA: Timewarp Distribution
Leader: CM Distribution
Leadmill: Vital Distribution
Left Hand: Pinnacle Records
Leo: Pendle Hawk Music Distribution
Leopard: Jet Star Phonographics
Les Productions Mille-Pattes: ADA Distribution
Liberation: Cargo Records (UK) Ltd
Liberation & Ecstasy: Shellshock Distribution
Liberation Records: Plastic Head Music Distribution Ltd
Lidocaine: Pinnacle Records
Lifelike: Baked Goods Distribution
Liftin' Spirit: SRD (Southern Record Distribution)
Light In The Attic: Timewarp Distribution
Light Town: Cargo Records (UK) Ltd
Lightning Rock: SRD (Southern Record Distribution)
Limbo: Pinnacle Records
Lime Street: Pinnacle Records, Shellshock Distribution
Limetree: New Note Distribution Ltd
Linn Records: Universal Music Operations
Lino Vinyl: Vital Distribution
Lion & Roots: SRD (Southern Record Distribution)
Lipstick: Pinnacle Records
Liquefaction: Cargo Records (UK) Ltd
Liquid: SRD (Southern Record Distribution)
Liquid Space: Shellshock Distribution
Lismor: Ross Record Distribution
Lissy's: Cargo Records (UK) Ltd
Listenable Records: Plastic Head Music Distribution Ltd
Litte Arthur: Jazz Music
Little Boy Lost: Universal Music Operations
Little Brother: Vital Distribution
Little Fish: Pinnacle Records
Little Johnny England: ADA Distribution
Little Teddy: Pinnacle Records, Shellshock Distribution
Little Tykes: BDS (Bertelsmann Distribution Services), Essential Direct Ltd
Live: SRD (Southern Record Distribution)
Live & Learn: Jet Star Phonographics
Live & Love: Jet Star Phonographics
Livid Meercat: Vital Distribution
Living Beat: Universal Music Operations
Living Tradition: Gordon Duncan Distributions
Lizard: Proper Music Distribution Ltd
LKJ: Jet Star Phonographics
Lo Fi Hi: Baked Goods Distribution
Lo Fidelity: Shellshock Distribution
Lo Recordings: SRD (Southern Record Distribution)
Load: Pinnacle Records
Loaded: Prime Distribution
Lobster Records: Plastic Head Music

Distribution Ltd
Lochshore: Proper Music Distribution Ltd
Lock Records: Essential Direct Ltd, Unique Distribution
Locked On: Vital Distribution
Lockjaw: Pinnacle Records
Locust: F Minor Ltd
Logic Records: BDS (Bertelsmann Distribution Services)
Logistic: Cargo Records (UK) Ltd
Londisc: Jet Star Phonographics
London Records: TEN (The Entertainment Network)
London Dub Plates: BDS (Bertelsmann Distribution Services), Essential Direct Ltd
London Ragtime Orchestra: Jazz Music
London Somet'ing: SRD (Southern Record Distribution)
Long Distance: Discovery Records Ltd
Long Hair: F Minor Ltd
Long Lost Brother: Vital Distribution
Loofy Records: ADA Distribution
Looking Good: Load Media
Lookout: Pinnacle Records, Shellshock Distribution
Looney Tunes: Plastic Head Music Distribution Ltd
Loose Tie: Avid Entertainment, BDS (Bertelsmann Distribution Services)
Lost & Found: Plastic Head Music Distribution Ltd
Lost Dog Recordings: Vital Distribution
Lost House: Pinnacle Records
Lost Moment: Shellshock Distribution
Lost Vegas: Pinnacle Records, Shellshock Distribution
Loud: BDS (Bertelsmann Distribution Services)
Loud & Slow: Amato Distribution
Lough: Claddagh Records
Lounge: Cargo Records (UK) Ltd
Love: Jet Star Phonographics
Love Train: SRD (Southern Record Distribution)
Low Pressings: InterGroove Ltd
Lowlands: Pinnacle Records, Shellshock Distribution
Lowlife: Vital Distribution
Lowri Records: RSK Entertainment
Lowsley Sound: Shellshock Distribution
Lowspeak: Pinnacle Records
Lplates: Load Media
LS Diezel: Vital Distribution
LSD: Cargo Records (UK) Ltd
LSO Live: Harmonia Mundi (UK) Ltd
Luaka Bop: Stern's Distribution
Lucertola Media: SRD (Southern Record Distribution)
Lumberjack: Vital Distribution
Lunar: Shellshock Distribution, Vital Distribution
Lunatec: Pinnacle Records, Shellshock Distribution
Lunch: Shellshock Distribution
Lusafrica: Discovery Records Ltd, New Note Distribution Ltd
Luscious Peach: Pinnacle Records
Luv N Haight: New Note Distribution Ltd
Lux Nigra: Baked Goods Distribution
Luxury Lounge: Shellshock Distribution
Lypsoland: Jet Star Phonographics
M People: BDS (Bertelsmann Distribution Services)
M&F: Jet Star Phonographics
M-Net: Synergie Logistics
M-Pire: Shellshock Distribution
Mac Developments: RSK Entertainment
Macca: SRD (Southern Record Distribution)
Macdada: Jet Star Phonographics
Macmeanmna: Gordon Duncan Distributions
Macmillan: Pinnacle Records
Mad: Pinnacle Records
Mad Cat: Vital Distribution
Mad Dog: Unique Distribution
Mad Entropic: Pinnacle Records
Mad 4 It: Amato Distribution
Mad Mob: Cargo Records (UK) Ltd
Mad Promotions: Cargo Records (UK) Ltd
Made in Mexico: Shellshock Distribution
Made To Measure: New Note Distribution Ltd, Pinnacle Records
Madfish: Pinnacle Records
Madhouse: Nervous Records
Maelstrom: Vital Distribution
Mag Wheel: Cargo Records (UK) Ltd
Magic: F Minor Ltd, Jazz Music
Magic Carpet: F Minor Ltd
Magic Marker: Shellshock Distribution
Magic Talent: BDS (Bertelsmann Distribution Services)
Magick Eye: SRD (Southern Record Distribution)
Magnet Records: ADA Distribution
Magnetic: Proper Music Distribution Ltd
Magneto Recordings: Cargo Records (UK) Ltd
Magnum: Synergie Logistics
Magnum Force: Synergie Logistics
Magnum Opus: Synergie Logistics
Magpie: Hot Shot Records, Jazz Music
Main Squeeze: Goya Music Distribution Ltd
Main Street: Jet Star Phonographics
Mainframe: Universal Music Operations
Mainstreet: Jet Star Phonographics
Majestic Reggae: Proper Music Distribution Ltd
Major League Productions: RSK Entertainment
Mako Music: Pinnacle Records
Malandro: Metronome Distribution
Malarky: Vital Distribution
Malawi: Universal Music Operations
Mama: Pinnacle Records
Mammoth: Cargo Records (UK) Ltd, Shellshock Distribution
Man's Ruin: Cargo Records (UK) Ltd
Manchester: Pinnacle Records
Mandala: Harmonia Mundi (UK) Ltd
Manga: TEN (The Entertainment Network)
Mangled: Kudos Records Ltd
Mango: Universal Music Operations
Manifest: Shellshock Distribution
Manifesto: Universal Music Operations
Manifesto Records Inc: Plastic Head Music Distribution Ltd
Manifold: Shellshock Distribution
Manikin: F Minor Ltd
Manteca: New Note Distribution Ltd
Mantra: Vital Distribution
Mapleshade: Vivante Music Ltd
Marble Arch: BDS (Bertelsmann Distribution Services)
Marble Bar: EMI Distribution, Vital Distribution
March: Shellshock Distribution
Marco Polo: Select Music & Video Distribution
Maree Records: Copperplate Distribution
Marginal Talent: Pinnacle Records, Shellshock Distribution
Marine Parade: SRD (Southern Record Distribution)
Mariposa: CM Distribution
Market Square: Caroline 2 Ltd, Pendle Hawk Music Distribution, RSK Entertainment, Windsong International
Marlboro Music: BDS (Bertelsmann Distribution Services)
Marquis: Metronome Distribution
Martians Go Home: Cargo Records (UK) Ltd
Mascot: Plastic Head Music Distribution Ltd
Mask: Vital Distribution
Mass Of Black: Vital Distribution
Massacre Records: Plastic Head Music Distribution Ltd
Massive: Pinnacle Records
Massive Music: Pinnacle Records
Massman: Cargo Records (UK) Ltd
Master Detective: Pinnacle Records
Master Mix: New Note Distribution Ltd
Mastercuts: 4am Distribution, BDS (Bertelsmann Distribution Services), Flute Worldwide Ltd
MasterTone Multimedia: Pinnacle Records
Matador: Vital Distribution
Matchbox: Hot Shot Records, Jazz Music
Materiali Sonori: Cargo Records (UK) Ltd
Matinee: Shellshock Distribution
Matrix: Amato Distribution
Matsuri Productions: SRD (Southern Record Distribution)
Mau Mau: BDS (Bertelsmann Distribution Services)
Maverick: TEN (The Entertainment Network)
Mawson & Wareham: CM Distribution
Max Picou: Cargo Records (UK) Ltd
Mayhem: Pinnacle Records
Mayker: Gordon Duncan Distributions
Mazaruni: SRD (Southern Record Distribution)
Mazzo: Proper Music Distribution Ltd
MC: Proper Music Distribution Ltd
MC Projects: Pinnacle Records
MC Records: RSK Entertainment
MCA: Universal Music Operations
MCC: Shellshock Distribution
MCG - Medien: Nervous Records
MCG-Medien: Nervous Records
MCI: New Note Distribution Ltd
McQueen: Vital Distribution
MDG: Chandos Records
MDMA: Shellshock Distribution
Me & My: Proper Music Distribution Ltd
Me & My Blues: Proper Music Distribution Ltd
Mean: Vital Distribution
Mean Time: Shellshock Distribution
Meantime: New Note Distribution Ltd, Pinnacle Records
Mecca: Pinnacle Records
Mecca Holding Co.: Shellshock Distribution
Med Fly: SRD (Southern Record Distribution)
Medcom: Universal Music Operations
Media: BDS (Bertelsmann Distribution Services)
Medium: Pinnacle Records, Shellshock Distribution
Medium Cool: Vital Distribution
Medusa: TEN (The Entertainment Network)
Mega: Universal Music Operations
Megahertz: Shellshock Distribution
Megaworld: Universal Music Operations
Mei Mei: Pinnacle Records, Shellshock Distribution
Melange: Baked Goods Distribution
Melankolic: EMI Distribution
Melljazz: The Woods
Mellowvibe: Jet Star Phonographics
Melodie: Discovery Records Ltd, Stern's Distribution
Melodious Fonk: Global Dance Distribution Ltd
Melt: Pinnacle Records

Memoir: BDS (Bertelsmann Distribution Services), Delta Music PLC
Memory Man: Cargo Records (UK) Ltd
Memphis Industries: Kudos Records Ltd
Menace: Pinnacle Records, Shellshock Distribution
Menlo Park: Cargo Records (UK) Ltd
Mentiras: Amato Distribution
Mephisto: Amato Distribution
Merciful Release: Vital Distribution
Merciless Records: Plastic Head Music Distribution Ltd
Mercury: Universal Music Operations
Mercyground: Shellshock Distribution
Merge: Amato Distribution
Merrymakers: Jazz Music
Mesmer: Pinnacle Records
Mess Media: Baked Goods Distribution
Metal Blade: Pinnacle Records
Metalimbo: New Note Distribution Ltd
Metamorphic: Vital Distribution
Metech Recordings: Plastic Head Music Distribution Ltd
Metro: New Note Distribution Ltd
Metro Independent: BDS (Bertelsmann Distribution Services), Essential Direct Ltd
Metrodome: Technicolor Distribution Services Ltd
Metronome: The Complete Record Company Ltd, Metronome Distribution
Metropole: Flute Worldwide Ltd
Metropolis: Shellshock Distribution, Universal Music Operations
Metropolis (Germany): Shellshock Distribution
Mextrax: Shellshock Distribution
MFS: Shellshock Distribution
Mic Mac: Vital Distribution
Michael Burks: Hot Shot Records
Microbe: Pinnacle Records
Middle Class Pig: Plastic Head Music Distribution Ltd
Middle Earth: SRD (Southern Record Distribution)
Midnight Creeper: Hot Shot Records
Midnight Rock: Caroline 2 Ltd
Midnite Jazz: Regis Records Ltd
Miguel: Cargo Records (UK) Ltd
Milan: BDS (Bertelsmann Distribution Services)
Miles Music: New Note Distribution Ltd
Milestone: New Note Distribution Ltd
Milestones: ADA Distribution, Jazz Music
Militant Funk: Pinnacle Records, Shellshock Distribution
Milk: SRD (Southern Record Distribution)
Mill: Gordon Duncan Distributions
Millennium: SRD (Southern Record Distribution)
Millennium Classics: BDS (Bertelsmann Distribution Services)
Millionaire's Bookshelf: Pinnacle Records
Milltown: Universal Music Operations
Milo: Pinnacle Records
Mind Expansion: Cargo Records (UK) Ltd
Mind The Gap: SRD (Southern Record Distribution)
Minimal: Pinnacle Records
Minimal Communication: Cargo Records (UK) Ltd
Ministry Of Sound: TEN (The Entertainment Network)
Minor Music: Vital Distribution
Mint: SRD (Southern Record Distribution), Shellshock Distribution
Mint Blue Records: Shellshock Distribution
Minta: Pinnacle Records
Minus: Cargo Records (UK) Ltd
Mir: Cargo Records (UK) Ltd
Miracle: Pinnacle Records, Shellshock Distribution
Miramar: New Note Distribution Ltd
Misanthropy: Vital Distribution
Miss Moneypennys: 4am Distribution
Missile: Prime Distribution, SRD (Southern Record Distribution)
Mission Control: Cargo Records (UK) Ltd
Mission Hall: Cargo Records (UK) Ltd
Mixmag Live!: Vital Distribution
Mixman: Pinnacle Records
Mixology: BDS (Bertelsmann Distribution Services)
MJJ: TEN (The Entertainment Network)
MK Ultra: Cargo Records (UK) Ltd
MMP: New Note Distribution Ltd
Mo Wax: Vital Distribution
Mo's Music Machine: Aura Surround Sound Ltd. t/a Mo's Music Machine
Mob: Vital Distribution
Mobile Fidelity: Vivante Music Ltd
Mobstar: Shellshock Distribution
Mock Rock: Pinnacle Records
Mode: Harmonia Mundi (UK) Ltd
Modern Invasion Music & T Shir: Plastic Head Music Distribution Ltd
Modern Love: Baked Goods Distribution
Mog: Cargo Records (UK) Ltd
Mogul: Absolute Marketing & Distribution Ltd.
Mohock Records: Media UK Distribution
Moidart: BDS (Bertelsmann Distribution Services), Gordon Duncan Distributions
Moist: Essential Direct Ltd
Moksha: ST Holdings Ltd, Shellshock Distribution
Mokum: Universal Music Operations
Mole In The Ground: Cargo Records (UK) Ltd
Moll: SRD (Southern Record Distribution), Shellshock Distribution
Moll Seleta: SRD (Southern Record Distribution)
Monarch: Gordon Duncan Distributions, Proper Music Distribution Ltd
Mondo Music: Shellshock Distribution
Money: Jet Star Phonographics
Mongo: Cargo Records (UK) Ltd
Monitor: Shellshock Distribution
Mono: Pinnacle Records
Monoplize: Universal Music Operations
Mons: Pinnacle Records
Montaigne: Harmonia Mundi (UK) Ltd
Montana: Essential Direct Ltd
Montpellier: Jazz Music
Mood Food: Cargo Records (UK) Ltd
Moof: Shellshock Distribution
Mook: Shellshock Distribution
Moon Ska Europe: Plastic Head Music Distribution Ltd
Moon Wave: Jet Star Phonographics
Moonbeam: Gordon Duncan Distributions
Mooncrest Records: Proper Music Distribution Ltd
Moonshine: Cargo Records (UK) Ltd
Moonska: Plastic Head Music Distribution Ltd
Moonstorm: Shellshock Distribution
Moonwave: SRD (Southern Record Distribution)
Morbid: Vital Distribution
Mordgrimm: Shellshock Distribution
More Music: Shellshock Distribution
More Protein: Pinnacle Records
More Rockers: Vital Distribution
Morning: BDS (Bertelsmann Distribution Services)
Morpheus: Vital Distribution
Mosaic: Vivante Music Ltd
Mosaic Movies: TEN (The Entertainment Network)
Moshi-Moshi: Cargo Records (UK) Ltd
Mosquito: SRD (Southern Record Distribution)
Moteer: Baked Goods Distribution
Motel: F Minor Ltd
Motel Kings: Hot Shot Records
Mother Stoat: Pinnacle Records, Shellshock Distribution
Mother.: Universal Music Operations
Motion: Cargo Records (UK) Ltd
Motor: Cargo Records (UK) Ltd
Motor Music: Universal Music Operations
Motorama: Pinnacle Records
Motorcoat: Shellshock Distribution
Motorway: Cargo Records (UK) Ltd
Motown: Universal Music Operations
Mount Ararat: Jet Star Phonographics, Shellshock Distribution
Mouse: Universal Music Operations
Mouthpiece: Proper Music Distribution Ltd
Mouthy Productions: Shellshock Distribution
Movement (Movement London Ltd.): SRD (Southern Record Distribution)
Movieplay Gold: Delta Music PLC
Movin' House: Essential Direct Ltd
Moving Shadow: SRD (Southern Record Distribution)
MPS: Universal Music Operations
Mr: Pendle Hawk Music Distribution
Mr Bongo: Vital Distribution
Mr Punch: Pinnacle Records
MRR&B: Hot Shot Records
Mrs Ackroyd: Proper Music Distribution Ltd
MSB: Brothers Distribution
MTM Music: RSK Entertainment
Mud: Cargo Records (UK) Ltd, Shellshock Distribution
Muddy Waters: Jazz Music
Muff Ugga: Hot Shot Records
Muffin: Shellshock Distribution
Multicultural Media: Proper Music Distribution Ltd
Multimedia: Cargo Records (UK) Ltd
Multiplex: Pinnacle Records
Multiply: TEN (The Entertainment Network)
Multiply White: Vital Distribution
Mumbo Jumbo: Hot Shot Records
Munich: Proper Music Distribution Ltd
Munster: Cargo Records (UK) Ltd, F Minor Ltd
Murena Records: Kudos Records Ltd
Murgatroid: Pinnacle Records, Shellshock Distribution
Musea: Nova Sales and Distribution (UK) Ltd
Mushi Mushi: Shellshock Distribution
Mushroom: Pinnacle Records
Music: BDS (Bertelsmann Distribution Services)
Music & Arts: Harmonia Mundi (UK) Ltd
Music And Words: Discovery Records Ltd
Music Avenue: Universal Music Operations
Music Base: Universal Music Operations
The Music Cartel: Shellshock Distribution
Music Choice: New Note Distribution Ltd
Music City: Jet Star Phonographics
Music Collection International: New Note Distribution Ltd
A Music Company: Pinnacle Records
Music For Freaks: Pinnacle Records
Music For Nations: Pinnacle Records
Music For Pleasure (MFP): EMI Distribution
Music From Another Room: Pinnacle Records
Music Fusion: Pinnacle Records

Music Is Everything: 4am Distribution
Music Lab: Jet Star Phonographics
Music Man: BDS (Bertelsmann Distribution Services)
Music Maniac: Cargo Records (UK) Ltd
Music Mecca: Jazz Music
Music Mountain: Jet Star Phonographics
Music Of Life: Nova Sales and Distribution (UK) Ltd
Music Of The World: BDS (Bertelsmann Distribution Services)
Music Unites: Pinnacle Records
Musica Latina: BDS (Bertelsmann Distribution Services), Delta Music PLC
Musica Omnia: Metronome Distribution
Musical Directions: Vital Distribution
Musical Tragedies: Shellshock Distribution
Musicbase: Pinnacle Records
Musicsysytem: Baked Goods Distribution
Musidisc: Universal Music Operations
Musik'Image Music Library: Media UK Distribution
Mustradem: ADA Distribution
Mutant Sound System: Cargo Records (UK) Ltd
Mutt Records: RSK Entertainment
Muzik Release: BDS (Bertelsmann Distribution Services), Essential Direct Ltd
Muzique Tropique: Vital Distribution
MVG: Cargo Records (UK) Ltd
MVP: Pinnacle Records
My Own Planet: Pinnacle Records, Shellshock Distribution
My Pal God: Shellshock Distribution
Mystic: Pinnacle Records
Mystic Man: Jet Star Phonographics
Mystic Productions: Plastic Head Music Distribution Ltd
Mysty Lane: F Minor Ltd
N-Coded: New Note Distribution Ltd
Nail: Vital Distribution
Naim Audio: RSK Entertainment
Naive: Cargo Records (UK) Ltd
Naked: BDS (Bertelsmann Distribution Services), Essential Direct Ltd
Nana: Shellshock Distribution
Napalm: Vital Distribution
Napalm Records: Plastic Head Music Distribution Ltd
Narada: EMI Distribution
Narcotix Lounge: SRD (Southern Record Distribution)
Nascente: New Note Distribution Ltd, Pinnacle Records, Stern's Distribution
Natasha Imports: Jazz Music
Nation: Vital Distribution
Natural History Museum: Pinnacle Records
Navras: New Note Distribution Ltd, Pinnacle Records
Navras Records: New Note Distribution Ltd
Naxos: Select Music & Video Distribution
Naxos Audiobooks: Select Music & Video Distribution
Naxos Historical: Select Music & Video Distribution
Naxos Jazz: Select Music & Video Distribution
Naxos Nostalgia: Select Music & Video Distribution
Naxos World: Select Music & Video Distribution
NC: Jet Star Phonographics
Neat: Pinnacle Records
Nebula Music: Amato Distribution
Necropolis: Plastic Head Music Distribution Ltd
Necropolis - Trade: Plastic Head Music Distribution Ltd
Necropolis Records: Plastic Head Music Distribution Ltd
Necrosis: Vital Distribution
Nectah: Vital Distribution
Nectar: Pinnacle Records
Needlework: SRD (Southern Record Distribution)
Needs: Timewarp Distribution
Negative Progression: Cargo Records (UK) Ltd
Negus Nagast: SRD (Southern Record Distribution)
Neo Ouija: Baked Goods Distribution
Neoteric: BDS (Bertelsmann Distribution Services)
Nepenta: Pinnacle Records
Nervous: Nervous Records
Nettwerk: Pinnacle Records
Network: Harmonia Mundi (UK) Ltd, Sound And Media Ltd
The Network: BDS (Bertelsmann Distribution Services)
Neurosonics: Shellshock Distribution
Neurot: Plastic Head Music Distribution Ltd
New Albion: Harmonia Mundi (UK) Ltd
New Beats: Pinnacle Records
New Beginnings: Blue Crystal
New Blue: Hot Shot Records
New Classical: Metronome Distribution
New Dawn: Sound And Media Ltd
A New Day: Proper Music Distribution Ltd
New Earth: ARC Music Distribution UK Ltd, Blue Crystal
New Electronica: BDS (Bertelsmann Distribution Services)
New Emissions: Vital Distribution
New Identity: SRD (Southern Record Distribution)
New Millenium: Pinnacle Records
New Moon: Hot Shot Records
New Note: New Note Distribution Ltd, Pinnacle Records
New Red Archives: Plastic Head Music Distribution Ltd
New World Music: Blue Crystal, Harmonia Mundi (UK) Ltd
Newsound 2000: North West Music
Next Century: SRD (Southern Record Distribution)
Next Music: Stern's Distribution
Next Plateau: Pinnacle Records
Next Step: SRD (Southern Record Distribution)
Nexus: Vital Distribution
Ngovart: Stern's Distribution
Nice: Vital Distribution
Niche: Amato Distribution
Nickel & Dime: Cargo Records (UK) Ltd
Nif Nuff: The Woods
Night & Day: Discovery Records Ltd
Nightbreed: Plastic Head Music Distribution Ltd
Nightingale: RSK Entertainment
Nightvision: Vital Distribution
Nil By Mouth: Pinnacle Records, Shellshock Distribution
9 AM: BDS (Bertelsmann Distribution Services), Essential Direct Ltd
Ninebar: SRD (Southern Record Distribution)
99 North: Essential Direct Ltd
Ninety Six: Backs Distribution, Shellshock Distribution
99 Degrees: Essential Direct Ltd
Ninja Toolz: Vital Distribution
Ninja Tune: Vital Distribution
Ninth World: Shellshock Distribution
Nitedance: BDS (Bertelsmann Distribution Services), Essential Direct Ltd
Nitro: Pinnacle Records
NMC: RSK Entertainment
NMG/Pavement Music: Plastic Head Music Distribution Ltd
No Bones: Pinnacle Records
No Choice: Jet Star Phonographics
No Fashion: Cargo Records (UK) Ltd
No Idea: Plastic Head Music Distribution Ltd
No Interference: Pinnacle Records
No Label: Cargo Records (UK) Ltd
No Master's Cooperative: Proper Music Distribution Ltd
No More Heroes: Plastic Head Music Distribution Ltd
No U Turn: SRD (Southern Record Distribution)
Nocturnal: Cargo Records (UK) Ltd, Shellshock Distribution
Nocturnal Art Manufacturing: Plastic Head Music Distribution Ltd
Nocturnal Art Productions: Plastic Head Music Distribution Ltd
Nocturne: Discovery Records Ltd
Noid Recordings: Kudos Records Ltd
Nois O Lution: Shellshock Distribution
Noise Factory: Vital Distribution
Noise Museum: Shellshock Distribution, Vital Distribution
The Nominal Recording Company: Vital Distribution
Nonesuch: TEN (The Entertainment Network)
Nons: Pinnacle Records
Noodles: SRD (Southern Record Distribution)
Normal: Proper Music Distribution Ltd
North East West: Jet Star Phonographics
North Pole Sound Lab: Pinnacle Records
North South: Pinnacle Records
North Star Music: Blue Crystal
Northern Heights: Cargo Records (UK) Ltd
Northern Sky: Proper Music Distribution Ltd
Northwest 10: Vital Distribution
Northwestside: BDS (Bertelsmann Distribution Services)
Norton: F Minor Ltd
Nostalgia: ZYX
Not Lame: Cargo Records (UK) Ltd
Note Music: The Woods
Nova Mute: Vital Distribution
Nova Tekk: Pinnacle Records
Nova Zembla: Cargo Records (UK) Ltd
Now: Absolute Marketing & Distribution Ltd., Pinnacle Records
Now And Then: Cargo Records (UK) Ltd
NOW Music: Pinnacle Records
NRK: Vital Distribution
NRK Sound Division: Vital Distribution
NSK: Shellshock Distribution
NSM Records: Plastic Head Music Distribution Ltd
Ntone: Vital Distribution
Nu Directions: Load Media, Pinnacle Records
Nu Image: TEN (The Entertainment Network)
Nu Recordings: SRD (Southern Record Distribution)
Nu Vision: Shellshock Distribution
Nuba: Discovery Records Ltd
Nubian: Vital Distribution
NuCamp: Vital Distribution
Nuclear Blast: Pinnacle Records
Nucool: New Note Distribution Ltd
Nuenergy: SRD (Southern Record Distribution)
Nukleuz: Amato Distribution
Num Num: Shellshock Distribution

Nuova Era: Metronome Distribution
Nuphonic: Vital Distribution
NV Records: Hot Shot Records
NVQ: Jet Star Phonographics
NYC: New Note Distribution Ltd, Pinnacle Records
NYC Records: New Note Distribution Ltd
NYJO: New Note Distribution Ltd
Obliqsound: Timewarp Distribution
Oblong Records: InterGroove Ltd
Obscene: Load Media
Observer: SRD (Southern Record Distribution)
Obzaki: BDS (Bertelsmann Distribution Services), Essential Direct Ltd
Oceandeep: Universal Music Operations
Ocho: New Note Distribution Ltd
Ochre: Cargo Records (UK) Ltd
OCK Records: ADA Distribution
Ocora: Harmonia Mundi (UK) Ltd
Octagon: Amato Distribution
Octopus: Pinnacle Records
Odeon: SRD (Southern Record Distribution)
Odyssey: TEN (The Entertainment Network)
Off Beat: Gordon Duncan Distributions, Pinnacle Records
Off The Wall: SRD (Southern Record Distribution)
Off Yer Face: Shellshock Distribution
Offspring: ADA Distribution
Offtime: Cargo Records (UK) Ltd
Offyerface: Backs Distribution
Oggum: Cargo Records (UK) Ltd
Ogun: Jazz Music
Oh Boy: Proper Music Distribution Ltd
Ohn.Cet: Pinnacle Records
Olarin Musiikki: ADA Distribution
Old and New Tradition: ADA Distribution
Old Bean: Jazz Music
Old Bridge: Claddagh Records, Pendle Hawk Music Distribution, Proper Music Distribution Ltd
Old Eagle: Shellshock Distribution, Vital Distribution
Old Hat: Proper Music Distribution Ltd, Shellshock Distribution
Old Prospector: Shellshock Distribution
Old Tramp: Hot Shot Records
Oldie Blues: Proper Music Distribution Ltd
Om: Pinnacle Records
On Delancey Street: Vital Distribution
On Line: Pinnacle Records
On The Air: BDS (Bertelsmann Distribution Services)
On-U Sound: SRD (Southern Record Distribution)
Ondine: The Complete Record Company Ltd
One Big Cowboy: Pinnacle Records
One Fifteen: BDS (Bertelsmann Distribution Services)
One Foot: Plastic Head Music Distribution Ltd
100 Guitar Mania: Cargo Records (UK) Ltd
One Little Indian: Pinnacle Records
One Louder: Pinnacle Records
One Step: Pinnacle Records
One Stop: RSK Entertainment
One To One: BDS (Bertelsmann Distribution Services), Essential Direct Ltd
One Way: F Minor Ltd
1+2: Cargo Records (UK) Ltd
Ongaku: Metronome Distribution
Onwards: Jet Star Phonographics
Ooh: Amato Distribution
Opaque: Pinnacle Records
Opaz: Pinnacle Records
Open: Vital Distribution
Opera House: Jet Star Phonographics
Opera Rara: Select Music & Video Distribution
Optimus: Shellshock Distribution
Opus III: Select Music & Video Distribution
Opus Kura: Metronome Distribution
Opus 3: Harmonia Mundi (UK) Ltd, Jazz Music, Proper Music Distribution Ltd, Vivante Music Ltd
Orange Egg: Pinnacle Records
Orange Shark: Shellshock Distribution
Orange Street: Excel Marketing Services Ltd, Proper Music Distribution Ltd
Orange Tree: BDS (Bertelsmann Distribution Services), Essential Direct Ltd
Orbit: Vital Distribution
Orbiter: Pinnacle Records
Ore: Vital Distribution
Oreade: Blue Crystal
Orfeo: Chandos Records
Org: Plastic Head Music Distribution Ltd
Organic: Vital Distribution
Organic Music: The Woods
Organon: Shellshock Distribution
Orgasm: Cargo Records (UK) Ltd
Orgone: Discovery Records Ltd, Shellshock Distribution
Orient: SRD (Southern Record Distribution)
Origin Music: Pinnacle Records
Original Blues Classics: Jazz Music
Original Jazz Classics: Jazz Music, New Note Distribution Ltd, Pinnacle Records
Origo Sound: Shellshock Distribution
Orkus: Shellshock Distribution
Ornament (CMA Music Production): Hot Shot Records
Orphange: Cargo Records (UK) Ltd
Orpheus: Amato Distribution
Oscar: BDS (Bertelsmann Distribution Services)
Osiris: Pinnacle Records
Osk: BDS (Bertelsmann Distribution Services), Essential Direct Ltd
Oska: Cargo Records (UK) Ltd
Osmose: Plastic Head Music Distribution Ltd
Osmosys: ADA Distribution, Proper Music Distribution Ltd, RSK Entertainment
Ossian: Claddagh Records, Proper Music Distribution Ltd
Other: Pinnacle Records
Other People's Music: Cargo Records (UK) Ltd
Otherworld: Vital Distribution
Our Choice: Shellshock Distribution
Our Time: Baked Goods Distribution
Out Of Time: Proper Music Distribution Ltd
Outafocus Recordings: Shellshock Distribution
Outcaste: Pinnacle Records
Outdigo Records: Vital Distribution
Outer Music: Pinnacle Records
Outlaw: BDS (Bertelsmann Distribution Services), Essential Direct Ltd
Outlet Records Ltd: I&B Records (Irish Music) Ltd, Proper Music Distribution Ltd
Outlet: Gordon Duncan Distributions
Outpost: BDS (Bertelsmann Distribution Services)
Output: SRD (Southern Record Distribution)
Outsider: Load Media
Oval: Universal Music Operations
Overground: Pinnacle Records
Overmatch: Prime Distribution
Ovni: Pinnacle Records, Shellshock Distribution
Own: Pinnacle Records, Shellshock Distribution
Owned & Operated: Shellshock Distribution
Oxa: ZYX
Oxingale: Metronome Distribution
Oxygen Music Works: Pinnacle Records
Ozit: Cargo Records (UK) Ltd
P.U.P Metal Mind Productions: Plastic Head Music Distribution Ltd
Pablo: Jazz Music, New Note Distribution Ltd
Pacific Jazz: EMI Distribution
Pagan: Universal Music Operations, Vital Distribution
Pagoda: Universal Music Operations
Palm Pictures: TEN (The Entertainment Network)
Pan: Vital Distribution
Panama Music (Library): Media UK Distribution
Pandaemonium: Shellshock Distribution
Pandemonium: Pinnacle Records, Shellshock Distribution
Panic: Cargo Records (UK) Ltd
Panorama: Pinnacle Records
Panther International: Amato Distribution
Paper: Vital Distribution
PAR: Jazz Music
Parachute Music: Pinnacle Records
Parade Amoureuse: Cargo Records (UK) Ltd
Paradox: Vital Distribution
Parasol: Cargo Records (UK) Ltd, Shellshock Distribution
Parasound: Shellshock Distribution
Park: Pinnacle Records
Parlophone: EMI Distribution
Parlophone Rhythm Series: EMI Distribution
Parnassus: Pinnacle Records, Regis Records Ltd
Parousia: BDS (Bertelsmann Distribution Services), Pinnacle Records
Parrot: Jazz Music
Part: Nervous Records
Partisan: Pinnacle Records
Pasadena Roof Orchestra: New Note Distribution Ltd
Passenger: Pinnacle Records
Passion 4 Music: Brothers Distribution
Passion Jazz: TEN (The Entertainment Network)
Past & Present: F Minor Ltd
Past Perfect: Swift Record Distributors
Paste Music: Shellshock Distribution
Pathfinder: Shellshock Distribution
Pati Pami: Avid Entertainment
Pavement Music: Plastic Head Music Distribution Ltd
Pavilion: Pinnacle Records
PCP: Vital Distribution
Peabody: Shellshock Distribution
Peace Feast: Kudos Records Ltd, Vital Distribution
Peace Frog: Vital Distribution
Peacemaker: Jet Star Phonographics
Peaceman: Pinnacle Records
Peaceville: Pinnacle Records
Peach: Pinnacle Records
Peak: New Note Distribution Ltd
Michael Peavy Music: Hot Shot Records
Pebble Beach: Nova Sales and Distribution (UK) Ltd
Pee Wee: Pinnacle Records
Peek A Boo: Cargo Records (UK) Ltd
Peerless: Hot Shot Records
PEK: Jazz Music
Pelican: Vital Distribution
Penalty Recordings: Pinnacle Records
Pendulum: Hot Records
Peng: Timewarp Distribution
Penguin: Pinnacle Records
Pennant Records: Silver Sounds CD Ltd
Penny Black: Pinnacle Records, ST Holdings Ltd
Penthouse: Jet Star Phonographics
People: Goya Music Distribution Ltd
People Of Rhythm: Cargo Records (UK) Ltd

Pepper: Pinnacle Records
Perceptive: Brothers Distribution, Universal Music Operations
Percheron Musique: ADA Distribution
Perfect Toy: Timewarp Distribution
Perishable: Cargo Records (UK) Ltd, Shellshock Distribution
Persevere Records: RSK Entertainment
Perspective: Universal Music Operations
Pessimiser: Cargo Records (UK) Ltd
Pet Sounds: Pinnacle Records
Petra: Shellshock Distribution
Phantasm: Vital Distribution
Phantom: Hot Records
Phantom Audio: Load Media
Pharm: Pinnacle Records
Pharma: SRD (Southern Record Distribution)
Phase 4: Cargo Records (UK) Ltd
Pheroes Entertainment: BDS (Bertelsmann Distribution Services), Essential Direct Ltd
Philips: Universal Music Operations
Philips Classics: Universal Music Operations
Philly Blunt: SRD (Southern Record Distribution)
Philo: Proper Music Distribution Ltd
Phoenix: Shellshock Distribution, Universal Music Operations
Phonetic Recordings: Prime Distribution
Phonographe: Metronome Distribution
Phonography: Vital Distribution
Phonokol: Pinnacle Records, Shellshock Distribution
Phonokol/Hom-Mega: Shellshock Distribution
Phontastic: Jazz Music
Phuzz: Amato Distribution
Piano: Pinnacle Records
Piao!: SRD (Southern Record Distribution)
Picasso: Shellshock Distribution
Pick Your Own: Proper Music Distribution Ltd
Pickled Egg: Cargo Records (UK) Ltd
Pickninny: Cargo Records (UK) Ltd
Pickout: Jet Star Phonographics
Pied Piper: Amato Distribution
Pier: Proper Music Distribution Ltd
Pig's Whiskers: Proper Music Distribution Ltd
Piknmix: SRD (Southern Record Distribution)
Pimp: SRD (Southern Record Distribution)
Pin Up: Vital Distribution
Pinhead: Pinnacle Records
Pinkerton: Vital Distribution
Pioneer Sounds: Shellshock Distribution
Piperman: Jet Star Phonographics
Piranha: New Note Distribution Ltd, Stern's Distribution
Pivotal: ST Holdings Ltd
Placid Casual: Pinnacle Records, Sain (Recordiau) Cyf
The Plague: Shellshock Distribution
Plain: F Minor Ltd
Planet: Pendle Hawk Music Distribution
Planet Dog: Pinnacle Records, Vital Distribution
Planet Nice: Pinnacle Records
Planet Of Drums: SRD (Southern Record Distribution)
Planet 3: Pinnacle Records
Planet U: Vital Distribution
Planet/MDMA: Shellshock Distribution
Planetary Consciousness: InterGroove Ltd
Plantagenet: Harmonia Mundi (UK) Ltd
Plastic: Pinnacle Records
Plastic Fantastic: Amato Distribution
Plastic Hip: Shellshock Distribution
Plastic Park: Shellshock Distribution
Plastic Raygun: Shellshock Distribution
Plastica: InterGroove Ltd
Plastica Red: InterGroove Ltd
Plastique: Pinnacle Records, Shellshock Distribution
Platipus: Vital Distribution
Play: Avid Entertainment, Shellshock Distribution
Play It Again Sam: Vital Distribution
Playasound: Harmonia Mundi (UK) Ltd
Playback: Pinnacle Records
Playtime: Pinnacle Records
Plaza: Independent Distribution Ltd, Universal Music Operations
Pleasure: Pinnacle Records
Pleasuredome: Vital Distribution
PLR: Pinnacle Records
Plum Projects: Pinnacle Records
Plusquam: Shellshock Distribution
PMM: Vital Distribution
A PMS Plan: Soul Trader
Poets Club: Shellshock Distribution
POF: Shellshock Distribution
Pohjola: Proper Music Distribution Ltd
Point Entertaiinment: Cargo Records (UK) Ltd, Independent Distribution Ltd
Point Music: Universal Music Operations
Pointblank: EMI Distribution
Pointy: Pinnacle Records, Shellshock Distribution
Poker Flat: Shellshock Distribution
Polestar: Cargo Records (UK) Ltd
Polydor: Universal Music Operations
Polyester: Amato Distribution
Polygram (Norway): Rolica Music Distribution
PolyGram Brazil: Stern's Distribution
Polyrhythmic: Shellshock Distribution
Polytox: Shellshock Distribution
Pomme: Discovery Records Ltd
Pony: Vital Distribution
Pony Canyon: Cargo Records (UK) Ltd
Pop Factory: Cargo Records (UK) Ltd
Pop God: Vital Distribution
Pop Llama: Vital Distribution
Popmafia: Cargo Records (UK) Ltd
Poppy: Pinnacle Records
Populuxe: Pinnacle Records
Pork: Kudos Records Ltd, Pinnacle Records
Pork Pie: Plastic Head Music Distribution Ltd
Porno Bass: Shellshock Distribution
Position Chrome: SRD (Southern Record Distribution)
Positiva: EMI Distribution
Possessed: Nova Sales and Distribution (UK) Ltd
Postar: Cargo Records (UK) Ltd
Postcard: Vital Distribution
Potlatch: Harmonia Mundi (UK) Ltd
Pottheadz: Shellshock Distribution
Pow!: Pinnacle Records
Power Bros: Harmonia Mundi (UK) Ltd
Power of Voice: Shellshock Distribution
Power Tool: Shellshock Distribution
Powerage: Plastic Head Music Distribution Ltd
Powerhouse: New Note Distribution Ltd
Powertool: Pinnacle Records
Praga: Harmonia Mundi (UK) Ltd
Prague Jazz: The Woods
Prank: Cargo Records (UK) Ltd
Prawn Song: Vital Distribution
Praxis: Shellshock Distribution
Preamble: Hot Records
Precious Organisation: Universal Music Operations
Precision: SRD (Southern Record Distribution)
Preiser: Harmonia Mundi (UK) Ltd
Premier Soundtracks: EMI Distribution
Preponderance: SRD (Southern Record Distribution)
President: Delta Music PLC, Independent Distribution Ltd, Jazz Music
Prestige: Jazz Music, New Note Distribution Ltd, Nova Sales and Distribution (UK) Ltd, THE (Total Home Entertainment)
Prestige Elite: Pinnacle Records
Pricepoint: Proper Music Distribution Ltd
Prima: Proper Music Distribution Ltd
Primary: Prime Distribution
Primate Recordings: Prime Distribution
Primavera: Pinnacle Records
Prime: Vital Distribution
Primedeep: Cargo Records (UK) Ltd
Primevil: Prime Distribution
Primrose: Discovery Records Ltd
Prince Buster: Jet Star Phonographics
Priority: EMI Distribution
Prism: I&B Records (Irish Music) Ltd
Prism Leisure: Prism Leisure Corp plc
Prism Leisure Classics: Prism Leisure Corp plc
Pro Logic: BDS (Bertelsmann Distribution Services)
Pro-Activ: BDS (Bertelsmann Distribution Services)
Pro-Jex: Pinnacle Records
Profile: Pinnacle Records
Progression: SRD (Southern Record Distribution)
Progressive: Jazz Music, The Woods
Progressive Form: Baked Goods Distribution
Prohibited: Shellshock Distribution
Prohibition: Pinnacle Records
Project: SRD (Southern Record Distribution)
Project 51: Load Media
Project Blowed: Cargo Records (UK) Ltd
Projector: Shellshock Distribution
Prolekult: Vital Distribution
Promo: SRD (Southern Record Distribution)
Promo Sonor International Music Library: Media UK Distribution
Prone: Shellshock Distribution
Pronoia: Nova Sales and Distribution (UK) Ltd
Proper: Proper Music Distribution Ltd
Proper Talent: Vital Distribution
Prophecy: Shellshock Distribution
Proprius: Jazz Music
Props: Universal Music Operations
Protected: Pinnacle Records
Prototype: Harmonia Mundi (UK) Ltd
Protractor: Vital Distribution
Proud: Cargo Records (UK) Ltd
Provogue: Pinnacle Records
Prox: Shellshock Distribution
Pseudonym: F Minor Ltd
PSF: Harmonia Mundi (UK) Ltd, Shellshock Distribution
Psi Fi: F Minor Ltd
PSI Music Library: Media UK Distribution
PSI Piano Bar Library: Media UK Distribution
PSM Recordings: Shellshock Distribution
Psychic: Vital Distribution
Psychomat: SRD (Southern Record Distribution)
Psychonavigation: Baked Goods Distribution
Ptolemaic Terrascope: Shellshock Distribution
Ptool/Pandemonium: Shellshock Distribution
Public Domain: Backs Distribution
Puff Daddy: BDS (Bertelsmann Distribution Services)
Puffin Audio: Pinnacle Records
Pugwash: ADA Distribution, Proper Music Distribution Ltd
Pulp Flavor: Shellshock Distribution

Pulsar: Synergie Logistics
Pulse: BDS (Bertelsmann Distribution Services)
Pulse-8: Pinnacle Records
Pulver: Timewarp Distribution
Pulverised: Vital Distribution
Pump: Pinnacle Records
Punch: SRD (Southern Record Distribution)
Punisher: Universal Music Operations
Punt Rock: SRD (Southern Record Distribution)
Pure: Amato Distribution
Pure Gold Records: Media UK Distribution
Pure Plastic: Cargo Records (UK) Ltd
Pure Silk: Absolute Marketing & Distribution Ltd., Pinnacle Records
Purple: Pinnacle Records
Purple Flower/Orkus: Shellshock Distribution
Purpose Maker: Cargo Records (UK) Ltd
Push: SRD (Southern Record Distribution)
Pussyfoot: SRD (Southern Record Distribution)
Putamayo: Universal Music Operations
Putumayo World Music: New Note Distribution Ltd, Universal Music Operations
PVC: Vital Distribution
PWL: TEN (The Entertainment Network)
Pylon: Baked Goods Distribution
Pyssy: Soul Trader
QDK Media: Proper Music Distribution Ltd
Quaint: Proper Music Distribution Ltd
Quality Control: Amato Distribution
Quality Umlaut: SRD (Southern Record Distribution)
Quality Words: Pinnacle Records
Quango: Universal Music Operations
Quark: Vital Distribution
Quartz: Jet Star Phonographics, One Nation Exports
Queen: BDS (Bertelsmann Distribution Services), Essential Direct Ltd
Queen Bee Brand: Hot Shot Records
Quench: BDS (Bertelsmann Distribution Services), Essential Direct Ltd
Quiet Riot: GR London Ltd
Quinlan Road: Claddagh Records, Proper Music Distribution Ltd
R&D: Vital Distribution
R&S: Pinnacle Records
R2 Records: 4am Distribution
Raceway: Pinnacle Records
Radarscope: Pinnacle Records
Radial: Vital Distribution
Radiate: Pinnacle Records
Radical: Plastic Head Music Distribution Ltd
Radical Ambient: Cargo Records (UK) Ltd
Radikal Fear: Vital Distribution
Radio Blast: Cargo Records (UK) Ltd
Radio France: Harmonia Mundi (UK) Ltd
Radioactive: BDS (Bertelsmann Distribution Services)
Radiotone: Cargo Records (UK) Ltd
Radius: SRD (Southern Record Distribution)
RAFR: Cargo Records (UK) Ltd
Raft: Shellshock Distribution
Rafting Dog: Proper Music Distribution Ltd
Rage: Nervous Records, Pinnacle Records
Rage of Achilles: Shellshock Distribution
Raging Bull: BDS (Bertelsmann Distribution Services)
Raid: Pinnacle Records
Railway Records: New Note Distribution Ltd
Rainbow Quartz: Pinnacle Records
Rainlight: Proper Music Distribution Ltd
Rainy Day Records: Media UK Distribution
Ram: SRD (Southern Record Distribution)
Ram Records: ST Holdings Ltd
randan: Pinnacle Records
Random: Load Media
Random House: Pinnacle Records
Randy's: Pinnacle Records
Rap Nation: Shellshock Distribution
Rapido: Cargo Records (UK) Ltd
Raputation: Pinnacle Records
Rare: SRD (Southern Record Distribution)
RAS: Proper Music Distribution Ltd
Rashaan: BDS (Bertelsmann Distribution Services), Essential Direct Ltd
Ratio: ST Holdings Ltd
Raucous: Nervous Records, Shellshock Distribution
Raven: Cargo Records (UK) Ltd, Proper Music Distribution Ltd, Shellshock Distribution
Raw Elements: SRD (Southern Record Distribution)
Raw Power: Pinnacle Records
Raw Talent: Jet Star Phonographics
Rawkus Entertainment: Pinnacle Records
Rayman Recordings: Cargo Records (UK) Ltd
RB Music: Jet Star Phonographics
RBN Recordings: Plastic Head Music Distribution Ltd
RCA: BDS (Bertelsmann Distribution Services)
RCA Classics: BDS (Bertelsmann Distribution Services)
RCA International Series: BDS (Bertelsmann Distribution Services)
RCA Victor: BDS (Bertelsmann Distribution Services)
RCA Victor Gold Seal: BDS (Bertelsmann Distribution Services)
RCR: Pinnacle Records
Re-Light/Iris Light: Shellshock Distribution
Reach Out International: Pinnacle Records
React: Vital Distribution
Reactor: Vital Distribution
Readers Digest: Talking Books Ltd
Ready Made: Shellshock Distribution
Real Authentic Sound: Proper Music Distribution Ltd
Real Life: RSK Entertainment
Real Music: Universal Music Operations
Real World: EMI Distribution
Really Useful: Universal Music Operations
Realsound: Metronome Distribution
Realty: Jazz Music
Rebel: Proper Music Distribution Ltd, Shellshock Distribution
Rebelscum: Shellshock Distribution
Rebound: Pinnacle Records
Rec 90: Absolute Marketing & Distribution Ltd.
Recall 2CD: Pinnacle Records
Receiver Records: Proper Music Distribution Ltd
Reception: Vital Distribution
Reckless: Shellshock Distribution
Rec90: Cargo Records (UK) Ltd
Recognition: Universal Music Operations
Recon: Pinnacle Records
Record Cellar: Shellshock Distribution
Record Factory: Jet Star Phonographics
The Record Label: Pinnacle Records
Recordhead: Pinnacle Records, Shellshock Distribution
Recordings Of Substance: Pinnacle Records
Recreation: 4am Distribution
Recycle Or Die: Vital Distribution
Red 'n Raw: Unique Distribution
Red Balloon: RSK Entertainment
Red Bullet: F Minor Ltd
Red Dot: Pinnacle Records
Red Egyptian Jazz: Timewarp Distribution
Red House: RSK Entertainment
Red Light: Vital Distribution
Red Lightnin': Caroline 2 Ltd, Hot Shot Records, Swift Record Distributors, Synergie Logistics
Red Pajamas: Proper Music Distribution Ltd
Red Parrot: Amato Distribution
Red Rose: Brothers Distribution, Vivante Music Ltd
Red Sky: CM Distribution
Red Square: BDS (Bertelsmann Distribution Services), Essential Direct Ltd
Red Steel: Pinnacle Records, RSK Entertainment
Red Stream: Shellshock Distribution
Red Sun: Shellshock Distribution
Red Telephone Box: Vital Distribution
Red Weed: SRD (Southern Record Distribution)
Redcliffe: Pinnacle Records
Redeye: Shellshock Distribution
Redhouse: Absolute Marketing & Distribution Ltd.
Redial: Universal Music Operations
Redwing: Proper Music Distribution Ltd
Reekie: Gordon Duncan Distributions
Reel Music: Vital Distribution
Reference: Jazz Music, Vivante Music Ltd
Refined: The Woods
Reflections: Plastic Head Music Distribution Ltd
Regal: Vital Distribution
Regency Sound: Proper Music Distribution Ltd
Reggae On Top: SRD (Southern Record Distribution)
Reggae Retro: SRD (Southern Record Distribution)
Regis: Regis Records Ltd
Rehab: SRD (Southern Record Distribution)
Rehab Music: Load Media
Rejected: Cargo Records (UK) Ltd, Plastic Head Music Distribution Ltd
REL: Gordon Duncan Distributions, Proper Music Distribution Ltd
Relapse: Pinnacle Records
Relapse Records: Plastic Head Music Distribution Ltd
Related Recordings: Pinnacle Records
Relativity: Cargo Records (UK) Ltd, TEN (The Entertainment Network)
Relaxation Co: Stern's Distribution
Relay: Shellshock Distribution
Release: Cargo Records (UK) Ltd
Relentless: TEN (The Entertainment Network)
Rembrandt: ADA Distribution
Remedy: Pinnacle Records
Renaissance: TEN (The Entertainment Network)
Renaissance Music: Amato Distribution
Renascent: Vital Distribution
Renegade Hardware: SRD (Southern Record Distribution)
Renegade Recordings: SRD (Southern Record Distribution)
Renella Records: The Woods
Repap: Vital Distribution
Repeat: Shellshock Distribution
Repellent: Vital Distribution
Repertoire: RSK Entertainment
Rephlex: SRD (Southern Record Distribution), Vital Distribution
Replay Music: Cargo Records (UK) Ltd
Replicant: Universal Music Operations
Reprise: TEN (The Entertainment Network)
ReR: Vital Distribution
Rer Megacorp: Shellshock Distribution

Reservoir: Pinnacle Records
Resolve: Vital Distribution
Resource: Pinnacle Records
Response: Pinnacle Records
Restless: Vital Distribution
Resurgence: Pinnacle Records
Resurrection Records: Plastic Head Music Distribution Ltd
Retch: Cargo Records (UK) Ltd
Retrieval: Proper Music Distribution Ltd
Retro Afric: Stern's Distribution
Retrograde: Hot Records
Retrowrek: Proper Music Distribution Ltd
Return To Sender: Proper Music Distribution Ltd
Return To The Source: Changing World Distribution, Shellshock Distribution
Rev-Ola: Pinnacle Records
Reveal: Pinnacle Records, Shellshock Distribution
Revelation: Plastic Head Music Distribution Ltd
Revenant: Cargo Records (UK) Ltd
Reverb: Pinnacle Records
Revolution: BDS (Bertelsmann Distribution Services)
RGF: Proper Music Distribution Ltd
RH Records: Pinnacle Records
Rhiannon Records: Pendle Hawk Music Distribution, Proper Music Distribution Ltd
Rhino: TEN (The Entertainment Network), Universal Music Operations
Rhythm & Freakquencies: Vital Distribution
Rhythm Division: BDS (Bertelsmann Distribution Services), Essential Direct Ltd
Rhythm King: BDS (Bertelsmann Distribution Services)
Rhythm Robbers: Amato Distribution
Rhythm Syndicate: Amato Distribution
Rhythm Vicar: Plastic Head Music Distribution Ltd
Rialto: Proper Music Distribution Ltd
Ricky-Tick: Timewarp Distribution
Riddim: SRD (Southern Record Distribution)
Rideout: Proper Music Distribution Ltd
Ridge: Gordon Duncan Distributions, Independent Distribution Ltd, Proper Music Distribution Ltd
Right: Pinnacle Records
Right Now: Pinnacle Records
Right Recordings: Pinnacle Records
Righteous: BDS (Bertelsmann Distribution Services), Vital Distribution
Righteous Babe: RSK Entertainment
Rinse Out: SRD (Southern Record Distribution)
Ripe Recordings: Pinnacle Records
Ripe 'n' Ready: Jet Star Phonographics
Rise Above: Pinnacle Records
Rising Sun Productions: Plastic Head Music Distribution Ltd
Rising Tide: BDS (Bertelsmann Distribution Services)
Ritornell: SRD (Southern Record Distribution)
Ritz: Gordon Duncan Distributions, I&B Records (Irish Music) Ltd, Independent Distribution Ltd, Universal Music Operations
River Horse: TEN (The Entertainment Network)
River Music: ADA Distribution
Riverboat Records: New Note Distribution Ltd
Riverrun: Metronome Distribution
Riverside: Jazz Music, New Note Distribution Ltd, Nova Sales and Distribution (UK) Ltd
Riverwalk Jazz: The Woods
Riviera: BDS (Bertelsmann Distribution Services)
RMD: Nervous Records
Road Cone: Cargo Records (UK) Ltd, Shellshock Distribution
Road Goes On Forever: Proper Music Distribution Ltd
Road Trip: Hot Records
Roadrunner: Universal Music Operations
Robert Parker Jazz Classics: New Note Distribution Ltd, Pinnacle Records
Robert Parker: Metronome Distribution
Robert Parker's Jazz Classics: New Note Distribution Ltd
Robinwood Productions: The Woods
Robot: Pinnacle Records
Robs: Pinnacle Records
Roc & Presta Recordings: Universal Music Operations
Roch: Proper Music Distribution Ltd
Rock Action: Vital Distribution
Rock Docs: Plastic Head Music Distribution Ltd
Rock Hard: Cargo Records (UK) Ltd
Rockadillo: ADA Distribution, Proper Music Distribution Ltd
Rockathon: Shellshock Distribution
Rockers: Jet Star Phonographics
Rocket: Universal Music Operations
Rocket Girl: Cargo Records (UK) Ltd
Rocket Racer: Cargo Records (UK) Ltd
Rockhouse: Nervous Records, RSK Entertainment
Rockingham: Shellshock Distribution
Rockstar: Nervous Records
Rockville: Gordon Duncan Distributions
Rocky One: SRD (Southern Record Distribution)
Roesch: Hot Shot Records
Rogue: Proper Music Distribution Ltd
Roir: Shellshock Distribution
Rollercoaster: Swift Record Distributors
Rollin'Rock: Nervous Records
Rolling Acres: Vital Distribution
Rolling Thunder: RSK Entertainment
Roly Records: ADA Distribution
Ronin: Soul Trader
Ronnie Scott's Jazz House: Synergie Logistics
rooArt: Cargo Records (UK) Ltd
Rooster: Proper Music Distribution Ltd
Rooster Blues: Shellshock Distribution
Ros Dubh: Gordon Duncan Distributions
Rosewood Union: Shellshock Distribution
Ross: CM Distribution, Gordon Duncan Distributions, Ross Record Distribution
Rotation: SRD (Southern Record Distribution)
Rotator: Pinnacle Records
Rough Guides: New Note Distribution Ltd
Rough Trade: Pinnacle Records
Roulette: EMI Distribution
Round: SRD (Southern Record Distribution)
Round Tower: Avid Entertainment, BDS (Bertelsmann Distribution Services)
Rounder: Proper Music Distribution Ltd
Roundtrip: Jet Star Phonographics
Rowdy: BDS (Bertelsmann Distribution Services)
Royal Jazz: Jazz Music
Royal Mint: Vital Distribution
Royal Music: Shellshock Distribution
Royal Palm: Kudos Records Ltd, Pinnacle Records
RP Media: Nova Sales and Distribution (UK) Ltd
RPM: Pinnacle Records
RRE: Vital Distribution
RSR: Universal Music Operations
RST: Hot Shot Records, Jazz Music
RST (Austria): Hot Shot Records
Rubber: Cargo Records (UK) Ltd
Ruf: Proper Music Distribution Ltd
Ruf Beat: SRD (Southern Record Distribution)
Ruff Beat: SRD (Southern Record Distribution)
Ruff Cut: Jet Star Phonographics
Ruffhouse: TEN (The Entertainment Network)
Rugger Bugger: Pinnacle Records, Shellshock Distribution
Rulin: TEN (The Entertainment Network)
Rum: Baked Goods Distribution
Rumble: Cargo Records (UK) Ltd, Nervous Records
Rumblestrip: Pinnacle Records, Shellshock Distribution
Rumour: Pinnacle Records
Runegrammofon: New Note Distribution Ltd
Runn: Jet Star Phonographics
Runnetherlands: Jet Star Phonographics
Runningz: SRD (Southern Record Distribution)
Runt: Cargo Records (UK) Ltd
Rupie: Jet Star Phonographics
Ruptured Ambitions: Shellshock Distribution
Russian Season: Harmonia Mundi (UK) Ltd
Rutland: Pinnacle Records, Shellshock Distribution
RXD Records: Silver Sounds CD Ltd
Ryko Latin: Vital Distribution
Rykodisc: Stern's Distribution, Vital Distribution
S Records: Amato Distribution
S.L.: Shellshock Distribution
Sabotage: SRD (Southern Record Distribution)
Sackville: Jazz Music
Sacred: Vital Distribution
Sad Eyes: Shellshock Distribution
Safe House: Plastic Head Music Distribution Ltd
Saigon: SRD (Southern Record Distribution)
Sain: Sain (Recordiau) Cyf
Sakay: Proper Music Distribution Ltd
Saludos Amigos: Delta Music PLC
Samsara: Shellshock Distribution
Sanctuary: Pinnacle Records
Sandman: Cargo Records (UK) Ltd
Sandy: Pinnacle Records
Sano: Pinnacle Records
Santorin: Shellshock Distribution
Sapphire: Vital Distribution
Sargasso: SRD (Southern Record Distribution)
Sarge: Jet Star Phonographics
Sarpa: Shellshock Distribution
SAS: Shellshock Distribution
Saskris: Avid Entertainment
Satellite: BDS (Bertelsmann Distribution Services)
Satellite City: Pinnacle Records
Satellite.: Vital Distribution
Satis: Jet Star Phonographics
Satisfaction: SRD (Southern Record Distribution)
Sativae: SRD (Southern Record Distribution)
Satori: Vital Distribution
Satril: Pinnacle Records
Sattva: Blue Crystal
Satyricon: Vital Distribution
Savage Bee: Cargo Records (UK) Ltd
Savant: Proper Music Distribution Ltd
Saxon: Jet Star Phonographics
Saydisc: Proper Music Distribution Ltd
SBK: EMI Distribution
Scandinavia: SRD (Southern Record Distribution)
Scared Hitless: Vital Distribution
Scared Of Girls: Vital Distribution
Scarlet: Pinnacle Records
Scat: Pinnacle Records, Shellshock Distribution
Scenario: Pinnacle Records
Scenescoff: F Minor Ltd
Schema: Jet Star Phonographics, Timewarp Distribution
Schism: Pinnacle Records, Shellshock Distribution

Schizophonic: Vital Distribution
Science: EMI Distribution
Science Fiction: Load Media
Science Friction: Pinnacle Records
Scooch Pooch: F Minor Ltd, Pinnacle Records
Scorcher: SRD (Southern Record Distribution)
Scorchio: Amato Distribution
Scorpio: BDS (Bertelsmann Distribution Services)
Scotdisc: Gordon Duncan Distributions, Ross Record Distribution
Scottish Harp: Gordon Duncan Distributions
Scratch: Cargo Records (UK) Ltd, Shellshock Distribution
Scratchy: Pinnacle Records
Screwgun: New Note Distribution Ltd, Pinnacle Records
SCSI Av: Baked Goods Distribution
Sea Breeze Jazz: The Woods
Seal: Jet Star Phonographics
Second Battle: F Minor Ltd
Second Skin: Pinnacle Records
2nd Movement: SRD (Southern Record Distribution)
Secret: Pinnacle Records, Shellshock Distribution
Secret Agent: SRD (Southern Record Distribution)
Secret Operations: Load Media
Secret Service: Pinnacle Records
Secret Sevens: Shellshock Distribution
Secretly Canadian: Cargo Records (UK) Ltd
See For Miles: RSK Entertainment
See Thru: Nova Sales and Distribution (UK) Ltd
Seed: Baked Goods Distribution
Seil: Gordon Duncan Distributions
Seismic: SRD (Southern Record Distribution)
Select: BDS (Bertelsmann Distribution Services)
Selection Club: Cargo Records (UK) Ltd
Selector: Vital Distribution
Self-Indulgent Music: Cargo Records (UK) Ltd
Self-Possessed: Shellshock Distribution
Sellwell: Shellshock Distribution
Sense UK: Amato Distribution
Senton: Baked Goods Distribution
Sequel: Pinnacle Records
Sequential: BDS (Bertelsmann Distribution Services), Essential Direct Ltd
Series 500: Vital Distribution
Serious: Vital Distribution
Serious Ent.: Shellshock Distribution
Sessions: Cargo Records (UK) Ltd
Setanta: Vital Distribution
720 Degrees: Vital Distribution
Severn: Hot Shot Records
SFRI: F Minor Ltd
Shadbury And Duxbury: Nova Sales and Distribution (UK) Ltd
Shadow: Cargo Records (UK) Ltd
Shadow Law: Load Media
Shady Acorns: Pinnacle Records
Shagadelic: F Minor Ltd
Shagpile: Cargo Records (UK) Ltd
Shake The Record Label: Cargo Records (UK) Ltd
Shamtown: Pinnacle Records
Shanachie: Independent Distribution Ltd, Jet Star Phonographics
Shang: Jet Star Phonographics
Shaping The Invisible: Proper Music Distribution Ltd
Shark: Pinnacle Records
Sharma Productions: Jet Star Phonographics
Sharp: Vital Distribution
Sharp End: Independent Distribution Ltd, Universal Music Operations
Sharp Nine: The Woods
Sharpe: BDS (Bertelsmann Distribution Services), Delta Music PLC, Gordon Duncan Distributions, I&B Records (Irish Music) Ltd
She Wolf: Pendle Hawk Music Distribution
Shedcentral: ST Holdings Ltd
Shelflife: Essential Direct Ltd
Shell: Nova Sales and Distribution (UK) Ltd
Shellshock: Cargo Records (UK) Ltd
Shellwood: Priory Records Ltd
Shielburn: Gordon Duncan Distributions
Shield: Vital Distribution
Shift: ZYX
Shifty Disco: Pinnacle Records
Shimmy Disc: Pinnacle Records, Shellshock Distribution
Shine: Pinnacle Records
Shining Path: Vital Distribution
Shinkansen: SRD (Southern Record Distribution)
Shiva Nova: Nova Sales and Distribution (UK) Ltd
Shiva Space Techonolo: Shellshock Distribution
Shiver: SRD (Southern Record Distribution)
Shock: Amato Distribution, Essential Direct Ltd
Shocking Vibes: Jet Star Phonographics
Shoebox: Pinnacle Records, Shellshock Distribution
Shoeshine: Pinnacle Records, Proper Music Distribution Ltd, Shellshock Distribution
Shongolo: BDS (Bertelsmann Distribution Services), Essential Direct Ltd
Shore: Jet Star Phonographics
Short Fuse: Shellshock Distribution
Shot: BDS (Bertelsmann Distribution Services), Essential Direct Ltd
Shout: Load Media
Shrimper: Cargo Records (UK) Ltd
Shut Up And Dance: Vital Distribution
SI Projects: Cargo Records (UK) Ltd
Siam: New Note Distribution Ltd
Side One Dummy: Plastic Head Music Distribution Ltd
Siesta: Pinnacle Records, Shellshock Distribution
Sign Language: Shellshock Distribution
Significant Music: Pinnacle Records
Silent: Shellshock Distribution
Siltbreeze: Shellshock Distribution, Vital Distribution
Silva Classics: BDS (Bertelsmann Distribution Services)
Silva CMP: RSK Entertainment
Silva Productions: RSK Entertainment
Silva Screen: RSK Entertainment
Silver Planet: InterGroove Ltd
Silverdoor: Shellshock Distribution
Silvertone: Pinnacle Records
Simax: Chandos Records
Simba: Pinnacle Records, Shellshock Distribution
Simon & Schuster: Pinnacle Records
Simple Solution: Shellshock Distribution
Simpleton: Pinnacle Records
Simply Vinyl: F Minor Ltd
Sincere Sounds: Vital Distribution
Sing Sing: Vital Distribution
Sing, Eunuchs!: Cargo Records (UK) Ltd
Sioux: Pinnacle Records
Sir Peter: Jet Star Phonographics
Sire: TEN (The Entertainment Network)
Siren Music: Zeit Distribution Ltd
Sirkus: Vital Distribution
Sirocco Jazz: New Note Distribution Ltd, Pinnacle Records
Six & Seven: Jet Star Phonographics
60 Degrees North: Pinnacle Records
Size 8: Pinnacle Records, Shellshock Distribution
SJP: Pinnacle Records
Skam: SRD (Southern Record Distribution)
Skerries: Gordon Duncan Distributions
Skiff-A-Billy: Nervous Records
Skint: Pinnacle Records
Skint Under 5s: Pinnacle Records
Skratch Music: TEN (The Entertainment Network)
Sky Ranch: Discovery Records Ltd
Skycap: Cargo Records (UK) Ltd, Shellshock Distribution
Skyline: Vital Distribution
Skyranch: Discovery Records Ltd
Skyride: Pinnacle Records
Skyway: Pinnacle Records
SL: Shellshock Distribution
Slalom: SRD (Southern Record Distribution)
SLAM: Jazz Music, Pendle Hawk Music Distribution
Slam City: Jet Star Phonographics
Slamm: Vital Distribution
Slammin' Vinyl: 4am Distribution
Slap A Ham: Cargo Records (UK) Ltd
Slappa: Pinnacle Records
Slash: Universal Music Operations
Sleepin' Corporation: Cargo Records (UK) Ltd
Sleepytown: Gordon Duncan Distributions, Ross Record Distribution
Sliced: Vital Distribution
Slick Sluts: BDS (Bertelsmann Distribution Services), Essential Direct Ltd
Slider Music: The Woods
Slinky: 4am Distribution, Shellshock Distribution
Slip 'N' Slide: Vital Distribution
Slip Discs: Proper Music Distribution Ltd
Slip'd By: BDS (Bertelsmann Distribution Services), Essential Direct Ltd
Slow Graffiti: Shellshock Distribution
Slow River: Vital Distribution
Slowdime: Shellshock Distribution
Slumberland: Cargo Records (UK) Ltd
Slut Trax: Vital Distribution
Sm:)e: Pinnacle Records
Small Stone: Cargo Records (UK) Ltd
Small Wonder: Pinnacle Records
Smalltown Supersound: Cargo Records (UK) Ltd
Smallworld: Proper Music Distribution Ltd
Smekkleysa: Shellshock Distribution
Smells Like: Cargo Records (UK) Ltd
SMG: Shellshock Distribution
Smiddymade: Gordon Duncan Distributions
Smitten: SRD (Southern Record Distribution)
Smoke: Pinnacle Records
Smokers Inc: SRD (Southern Record Distribution)
Smokin' Drum: Shellshock Distribution
Smugg: Shellshock Distribution, Vital Distribution
Snapper: Pinnacle Records
Snatch: Backs Distribution, Shellshock Distribution
SND / Premium Leisure: Baked Goods Distribution
Snowblind: SRD (Southern Record Distribution)
Soap Dodja: Pinnacle Records
Social Studies: Load Media
Sockett: SRD (Southern Record Distribution)
Sofa: Baked Goods Distribution
SoleSides: Universal Music Operations
Solid: Vital Distribution
Solistic: Discovery Records Ltd
Solistitium Records: Plastic Head Music Distribution Ltd

Solistium: Vital Distribution
Solo Art: Jazz Music, The Woods
Some: Shellshock Distribution
Some Bizarre: Pinnacle Records
Something Else: Pinnacle Records
Son: Kudos Records Ltd
Son Of Soundclash: Vital Distribution
Sona Rupa: New Note Distribution Ltd
Sonar Kollektiv: Timewarp Distribution
Sonic Art Union: Pinnacle Records
Sonic Boom: Shellshock Distribution
Sonic Images: Cargo Records (UK) Ltd
Sonic Rendezvous: Plastic Head Music Distribution Ltd
Sonic Wave: Pinnacle Records
Sonifolk: ADA Distribution
Sonig: Shellshock Distribution
Sonix: ST Holdings Ltd
Sonntag: Shellshock Distribution
Sons of Sound: The Woods
Sony Brazil: Stern's Distribution
Sony Classical: TEN (The Entertainment Network)
Sony Computer Entertainment (SCE): TEN (The Entertainment Network)
Sony Jazz: TEN (The Entertainment Network)
Sony Music TV: TEN (The Entertainment Network)
Sony Music Video (SMV): TEN (The Entertainment Network)
Sony S2: TEN (The Entertainment Network)
Sony South Africa: Stern's Distribution
Sony S3: TEN (The Entertainment Network)
Sophisticat: New Note Distribution Ltd
Sophisticuts: Pinnacle Records
Sore Thumb Records: Proper Music Distribution Ltd
Sorted: Shellshock Distribution
SOS: Plastic Head Music Distribution Ltd
Soul Beat: SRD (Southern Record Distribution)
Soul Brother: New Note Distribution Ltd, Pinnacle Records
Soul Dump: Shellshock Distribution
Soul Fire: F Minor Ltd
Soul Note: Harmonia Mundi (UK) Ltd
Soul On Wax: Vital Distribution
Soul Static Sound: SRD (Southern Record Distribution)
Soul Supply: Vital Distribution
Soulciety: Pinnacle Records
Soulja: Essential Direct Ltd
Sound Box: Jet Star Phonographics
Sound Chamber: Pinnacle Records, Shellshock Distribution
Sound Clash: SRD (Southern Record Distribution)
Sound Consortium: Global Dance Distribution Ltd
Sound Corporation: Amato Distribution
Sound Design: Vital Distribution
Sound Dimension: BDS (Bertelsmann Distribution Services), Flute Worldwide Ltd
Sound Hills: Harmonia Mundi (UK) Ltd
Sound Information: Vital Distribution
Sound Of Ministry: TEN (The Entertainment Network)
Sound Proof: BDS (Bertelsmann Distribution Services)
Sound Riot: Plastic Head Music Distribution Ltd
Soundalive: Metronome Distribution
Soundbites: Universal Music Operations
Soundboy: Vital Distribution
Soundclash: SRD (Southern Record Distribution)
Soundclash.: Backs Distribution
Soundfx: Pinnacle Records
Soundings: Talking Books Ltd
Soundjam: Universal Music Operations
Soundproof: Shellshock Distribution
Sounds Of The World: BDS (Bertelsmann Distribution Services)
Soundsational: Cargo Records (UK) Ltd
Soundscape: SRD (Southern Record Distribution)
Soundslike: Baked Goods Distribution
Soundwaves: Delta Music PLC
Soundway: Timewarp Distribution
Source: EMI Distribution
Soussol: Timewarp Distribution
South China Sea: Shellshock Distribution
South Circular: Pinnacle Records
South Of Sanity: Vital Distribution
South West: F Minor Ltd
Southbound: Universal Music Operations
Southern Cross: Hot Records
Southern Lord: Shellshock Distribution
Southland: Jazz Music
Southland Records: The Woods
Southpaw Recordings: Vital Distribution
Southside Production: SRD (Southern Record Distribution)
Sow & Reap: Jet Star Phonographics
Spa:rk: Baked Goods Distribution
Space Age Recordings: Cargo Records (UK) Ltd
Space Cadet: Shellshock Distribution
Spaceagebachelorpad: Shellshock Distribution
Spalax: Cargo Records (UK) Ltd, F Minor Ltd
Spanking Herman: Cargo Records (UK) Ltd
Spawn: Load Media
Speakers Corner Vinyl: Vivante Music Ltd
Special Emissions: Vital Distribution
Special Fried: Amato Distribution
Species: Shellshock Distribution
Spectrum: Universal Music Operations
Spectrum.: Kudos Records Ltd
Speedowax: Cargo Records (UK) Ltd
Speedway Sounds: Shellshock Distribution
Spezial Material: Baked Goods Distribution
Spinart: Cargo Records (UK) Ltd, Plastic Head Music Distribution Ltd
Spindle: Jet Star Phonographics
Spindrift: Nervous Records
Spinefarm: Pinnacle Records, Plastic Head Music Distribution Ltd
Spinning Wheel: Cargo Records (UK) Ltd
Spira: SRD (Southern Record Distribution)
Spiral: F Minor Ltd
Spiral Grooves: Amato Distribution
Spiral Trax: Pinnacle Records, Shellshock Distribution
Spirit: ADA Distribution, Amato Distribution, Vital Distribution
Spirit Of Orr: Pinnacle Records, Shellshock Distribution
Spirit Zone: Pinnacle Records
Spit and Polish Records: Pinnacle Records, Proper Music Distribution Ltd
Spitfire: Pinnacle Records
Spoilt For Choice: Pinnacle Records
Spoilt Records: SRD (Southern Record Distribution)
Spoon: Vital Distribution
Spot On: Amato Distribution
Spotlite: Jazz Music, New Note Distribution Ltd, Pinnacle Records
Sprawl: SRD (Southern Record Distribution)
Spresso: Shellshock Distribution
Springthyme: Gordon Duncan Distributions, Proper Music Distribution Ltd
Sprint: Jet Star Phonographics
SPV: RSK Entertainment
Spyda: Pinnacle Records
Spymania: Vital Distribution
Square: Pinnacle Records
Square Biz: Universal Music Operations
Squeaky: Absolute Marketing & Distribution Ltd.
Squealer: Cargo Records (UK) Ltd
Squire: Excel Marketing Services Ltd
SSR: SRD (Southern Record Distribution)
SST Records: Plastic Head Music Distribution Ltd
Staalplaat: Vital Distribution
Stable: Gordon Duncan Distributions
Stadium: BDS (Bertelsmann Distribution Services), Essential Direct Ltd
Standard: Cargo Records (UK) Ltd
Standback: Cargo Records (UK) Ltd
Star City: Shellshock Distribution
Starburst: Pinnacle Records
Stars in the Dark: Shellshock Distribution
Starshaped: Shellshock Distribution
Start: RSK Entertainment
Stash: Jazz Music
Static Caravan: Cargo Records (UK) Ltd
Static Sound: SRD (Southern Record Distribution)
Status: Jazz Music
Stayfree: Vital Distribution
Steady On: New Note Distribution Ltd
Steel Fish: Amato Distribution
Step 1 Music: Plastic Head Music Distribution Ltd
Step One: Cargo Records (UK) Ltd
Steppin' Out: Pinnacle Records
Stereo Deluxe: Timewarp Distribution
Sterling Circle: The Woods
Sterndale: BDS (Bertelsmann Distribution Services), Metronome Distribution
Sterns: Stern's Distribution
Stewardess: SRD (Southern Record Distribution)
Stickman: Cargo Records (UK) Ltd
Sticky Label: Pinnacle Records
Stiff Weapon: Nova Sales and Distribution (UK) Ltd
StiKKi TiMeS MuSiC: Harmonia Mundi (UK) Ltd
Stillwater: Rolica Music Distribution
Stim: Pinnacle Records
Stimulant: Amato Distribution
Stingray: Jet Star Phonographics
Stir 15: Shellshock Distribution
Stockwell Park: Vital Distribution
Stomp: Universal Music Operations
Stomp Off: Jazz Music, The Woods
Stompatime: Caroline 2 Ltd
Stomper Time: Nervous Records
Stone Island: BDS (Bertelsmann Distribution Services), Essential Direct Ltd
Stone Love: Jet Star Phonographics
Stone's Throw: Cargo Records (UK) Ltd
Stoned Heights: Vital Distribution
Stonedrive: BDS (Bertelsmann Distribution Services), Essential Direct Ltd
Stonelove: Jet Star Phonographics
Stoner Shit: SRD (Southern Record Distribution)
Stoptime Recordings: ADA Distribution
Storyville: Jazz Music, Proper Music Distribution Ltd
Straker's: Jet Star Phonographics
Strange & Beautiful Music: New Note Distribution Ltd
Strange Fruit: Pinnacle Records
Strategy: BDS (Bertelsmann Distribution Services), Essential Direct Ltd

Strawberry Sundae: SRD (Southern Record Distribution)
Streamline: EMI Distribution
Street Beat: Cargo Records (UK) Ltd
Street Corner: Amato Distribution
Street Vibes: Jet Star Phonographics
Streetsounds: Flute Worldwide Ltd
Stress Recordings: Pinnacle Records
Stretch: New Note Distribution Ltd, Pinnacle Records
Stretchy: Pinnacle Records, Snapper Music plc
Strictly Country: Proper Music Distribution Ltd
Strictly Rhythm: TEN (The Entertainment Network)
Stringbean: Jet Star Phonographics
Striving For Togetherness: Cargo Records (UK) Ltd
Stronghouse: Amato Distribution
Strongjazz: Amato Distribution
Strut: Vital Distribution
Strut Music: 4am Distribution
Stubborn: Nova Sales and Distribution (UK) Ltd
The Studio of Scott Grooves: Global Dance Distribution Ltd
Studio 1: SRD (Southern Record Distribution)
Stupid Cat: Pinnacle Records, Shellshock Distribution
STW: Pinnacle Records
Sub Dub: Hot Records
Sub Pop: Cargo Records (UK) Ltd, Shellshock Distribution
Sub Tub Players: Timewarp Distribution
Sub/version: Shellshock Distribution
Subkrauts: Pinnacle Records
Subliminal: F Minor Ltd
Subliminal Sounds: Shellshock Distribution
Substance: TEN (The Entertainment Network)
Subterfuge: Shellshock Distribution
Subtitles: ST Holdings Ltd
Suburban Home: Plastic Head Music Distribution Ltd
Subvert: Vital Distribution
Subvoice: Pinnacle Records
Suckapunch: Plastic Head Music Distribution Ltd
Suction: Shellshock Distribution
Sudden Def: Load Media, Pinnacle Records, Shellshock Distribution
Sugar Free: Cargo Records (UK) Ltd
Sugar Hill: Proper Music Distribution Ltd
Sugarcube: Pinnacle Records
SugarDaddy: Absolute Marketing & Distribution Ltd., Pinnacle Records
Suicidal: Shellshock Distribution
Suicide Squeeze: Shellshock Distribution
Sulphuric: Nova Sales and Distribution (UK) Ltd
Sum: BDS (Bertelsmann Distribution Services)
Summershine: Cargo Records (UK) Ltd
Summit: Metronome Distribution, Sound And Media Ltd
Sunbird: Shellshock Distribution
Sundazed: Cargo Records (UK) Ltd, F Minor Ltd
Sundown: Synergie Logistics
Sunflower: Amato Distribution
Sunjay: Synergie Logistics
Sunshine Enterprises: Timewarp Distribution
Sunshot (Japan): SRD (Southern Record Distribution)
Sunspot: F Minor Ltd
Super Classe: Shellshock Distribution
Super Discount: Vital Distribution
Super 8: Shellshock Distribution
Super Electro: Cargo Records (UK) Ltd
Super Power: Jet Star Phonographics
Superior Quality: Vital Distribution
Supernal: Shellshock Distribution, Vital Distribution
Supertone: Absolute Marketing & Distribution Ltd., Universal Music Operations
Supple Pipe: Vital Distribution
Supraphon: RSK Entertainment
Supreme Underground: Pinnacle Records
Supremo: Pinnacle Records, Shellshock Distribution
Sure Shot: Proper Music Distribution Ltd
Surehand: Plastic Head Music Distribution Ltd
Surface: Cargo Records (UK) Ltd
Surgury: Vital Distribution
SurroundedBy: Vivante Music Ltd
Survival: Pinnacle Records
SUS: SRD (Southern Record Distribution)
Susan Lawly: Cargo Records (UK) Ltd
Suspect Device: Shellshock Distribution
Swaggie: Jazz Music
Swank: SRD (Southern Record Distribution)
Swansong: TEN (The Entertainment Network)
Swarf Finger: Cargo Records (UK) Ltd
Swashbuckle: Nova Sales and Distribution (UK) Ltd
Sweat: Aura Surround Sound Ltd. t/a Mo's Music Machine, Pinnacle Records, Universal Music Operations
Sweet: Pinnacle Records, Shellshock Distribution
Sweet Nothing: Cargo Records (UK) Ltd
Swim: Cargo Records (UK) Ltd
Swirl: Timewarp Distribution
Switch: SRD (Southern Record Distribution), ST Holdings Ltd
Switchflicker: Baked Goods Distribution
Swordmaker Records (SMK): Independent Distribution Ltd, Universal Music Operations
SWS: Jet Star Phonographics
Sygnet: ADA Distribution
Sylem: Pinnacle Records, Shellshock Distribution
Symbol Records: The Woods
Sympathy For The Record Industry: Cargo Records (UK) Ltd
Syncom: SRD (Southern Record Distribution)
Syrous: ST Holdings Ltd
TAA: New Note Distribution Ltd
Taang Records: Plastic Head Music Distribution Ltd
Table Of Elements: Cargo Records (UK) Ltd
Tabu: Universal Music Operations
Tacet: Vivante Music Ltd
Tacklebox: Cargo Records (UK) Ltd
Tailormade: Pinnacle Records
Takoma: Pinnacle Records
Talkin Loud: Universal Music Operations
Tall Guy: Hot Shot Records
Tall Pop: Cargo Records (UK) Ltd
Tamoki Wambesi: SRD (Southern Record Distribution)
Tangerine: Shellshock Distribution
Tango Mi Amor: BDS (Bertelsmann Distribution Services)
Tank: Amato Distribution
Tantara Productions Inc: The Woods
Tanty: Pinnacle Records, Shellshock Distribution
Tapestry: The Woods
Tara: Claddagh Records, Proper Music Distribution Ltd
Taratn Tapes: Gordon Duncan Distributions
Target: Vital Distribution
Tartan Tapes: Proper Music Distribution Ltd
Tatra Productions Ltd: Plastic Head Music Distribution Ltd
Tax: Jazz Music
TB/Peacefrog: Vital Distribution
TCB: New Note Distribution Ltd, Pinnacle Records
TCR: SRD (Southern Record Distribution)
TDK: Nova Sales and Distribution (UK) Ltd
TDV: Vital Distribution
Tea Leaf Records: Plastic Head Music Distribution Ltd
Tealeaf: Cargo Records (UK) Ltd
TeC: SRD (Southern Record Distribution)
Technical Itch: SRD (Southern Record Distribution)
Ted Smith: Shellshock Distribution
Tee Hee: Sound Entertainment Ltd
Teem: SRD (Southern Record Distribution)
Teen-C: Shellshock Distribution
Teenage Shutdown: Pinnacle Records, Shellshock Distribution
Teenbeat: Shellshock Distribution, Vital Distribution
Telarc: New Note Distribution Ltd
Teldec: TEN (The Entertainment Network)
Telebender: Proper Music Distribution Ltd
Telica: Amato Distribution
Telica Communications: Amato Distribution
Telstar: BDS (Bertelsmann Distribution Services)
Tema: Northern Record Supplies Ltd, Savoy Strict Tempo Distributors
Tempa: Essential Direct Ltd
Temple: Gordon Duncan Distributions
Tempo Toons: SRD (Southern Record Distribution)
Temptation: Universal Music Operations
Ten Lovers: Unique Distribution
10 To 4: Pinnacle Records
Ten To Ten: The Woods
Ten Years After: Nova Sales and Distribution (UK) Ltd
Tenacious: Pinnacle Records
Tenor Vossa: Pinnacle Records
Tenth Planet: F Minor Ltd
Terra Nova: Proper Music Distribution Ltd
Terrascape: BDS (Bertelsmann Distribution Services)
Tess: Vital Distribution
Testament: The Complete Record Company Ltd, Proper Music Distribution Ltd
Textone: Nervous Records
Thang: Plastic Head Music Distribution Ltd
Thats Entertainment: RSK Entertainment
Thee Blak Label: Vital Distribution
Them's Good Records: Plastic Head Music Distribution Ltd
Themsgood Records: Plastic Head Music Distribution Ltd
Theologian Records: Plastic Head Music Distribution Ltd
Theory: Cargo Records (UK) Ltd
Thermal: Shellshock Distribution
Thick: Cargo Records (UK) Ltd, Shellshock Distribution
Things To Come: Pinnacle Records
Think Progressive: SRD (Southern Record Distribution)
Third Eye: SRD (Southern Record Distribution)
3rd Stone Records: Cargo Records (UK) Ltd
Thirdwave: Amato Distribution
Thirsty Ear: Vital Distribution
Thirteen Recording: Cargo Records (UK) Ltd
13th Moon: Nova Sales and Distribution (UK) Ltd, Pinnacle Records
30 Hertz: Vital Distribution
30Hz: Vital Distribution

33 Jazz: New Note Distribution Ltd
32 Records: Hot Records
This Is...: Flute Worldwide Ltd
This Way Up: Universal Music Operations
Thoofa: Cargo Records (UK) Ltd
Three Cord Trick: Nervous Records
Three Sevens: Shellshock Distribution
Threeman: Pinnacle Records
304: SRD (Southern Record Distribution)
Threshold: Pinnacle Records
Thrill Jockey: Vital Distribution
Thriving Underground: Pinnacle Records
Thumpin' Vinyl: SRD (Southern Record Distribution)
Thunderbird: Proper Music Distribution Ltd
Thunderbolt: Synergie Logistics
Tidy Trax: Amato Distribution
Tigerstyle: Shellshock Distribution
Timba: Shellshock Distribution
Timebomb: Cargo Records (UK) Ltd
Timeless: Jazz Music, Load Media, New Note Distribution Ltd, Pinnacle Records
Timeless Historical: New Note Distribution Ltd
Timeless Traditional: New Note Distribution Ltd
Timewave: Vital Distribution
Tin Can: BDS (Bertelsmann Distribution Services)
Tinseltones: Cargo Records (UK) Ltd
Tiny Dog: Cargo Records (UK) Ltd
Tiny Superhero: Cargo Records (UK) Ltd, Shellshock Distribution
TIP.World: Arabesque Distribution
Tiptoe: New Note Distribution Ltd, Pinnacle Records
Titan Sounds: ST Holdings Ltd
Tivoli: Pinnacle Records
TKM: New Note Distribution Ltd
TKO Magnum: Pinnacle Records
TKO Records: Plastic Head Music Distribution Ltd
Tolerance: Vital Distribution
Tolerance Records: Plastic Head Music Distribution Ltd
Tolotta: Shellshock Distribution
Tomato: Vital Distribution
Tombstone: Nervous Records
Tomcat Music: ADA Distribution
Tommy Boy: Pinnacle Records
Tone Casualties: Cargo Records (UK) Ltd
Tone Cool: Proper Music Distribution Ltd
Tone King: Hot Shot Records
Tone-Cool: Proper Music Distribution Ltd
Tongue And Groove: Vital Distribution
Tonka: BDS (Bertelsmann Distribution Services), Essential Direct Ltd
Too Pure: Vital Distribution
Tooth & Nail: Plastic Head Music Distribution Ltd
Top Banana: Vital Distribution
Top Deck: SRD (Southern Record Distribution)
Topaz: Pinnacle Records
Topaz Jazz: Pinnacle Records
Topic: Jazz Music, Proper Music Distribution Ltd
Torment: BDS (Bertelsmann Distribution Services)
Torn: Cargo Records (UK) Ltd
Torrance: Gordon Duncan Distributions
Tortured: InterGroove Ltd
Total: BDS (Bertelsmann Distribution Services)
Total Energy: F Minor Ltd
Total Music: 4am Distribution
Touch: Kudos Records Ltd, Pinnacle Records
Touch And Go: Cargo Records (UK) Ltd
Town Crier: The Woods
Townhill: Shellshock Distribution
Track: Pinnacle Records
Trade: 4am Distribution
Trade 2: Vital Distribution
Tradition: Vital Distribution
Tradition & Moderne: Proper Music Distribution Ltd
Traditional Crossroads: Stern's Distribution
Train Wreck: Proper Music Distribution Ltd
Traktor: SRD (Southern Record Distribution)
Trance: SRD (Southern Record Distribution)
Transatlantic: Pinnacle Records
Transcopic: Vital Distribution
Transglobal: Vital Distribution
Transiberian: Shellshock Distribution
Transmat: Vital Distribution
Transmission: F Minor Ltd
Transparent: Absolute Marketing & Distribution Ltd.
Trauma: BDS (Bertelsmann Distribution Services)
Travellin' Man: Jazz Music
Trax: Pinnacle Records
Tree Roots: Jet Star Phonographics
Trelik: Pinnacle Records
Tribal Drift: Shellshock Distribution
Tribal UK: Vital Distribution
Tribe: SRD (Southern Record Distribution)
Tribesman: Jet Star Phonographics
Trick: BDS (Bertelsmann Distribution Services), Essential Direct Ltd
Trickster: Shellshock Distribution
Trident: Universal Music Operations
Triefeelin: Jet Star Phonographics
Trifekta: Cargo Records (UK) Ltd
Trinidad & Tobago: Jet Star Phonographics
Trinity: Cargo Records (UK) Ltd, Shellshock Distribution
Trinity Records: Plastic Head Music Distribution Ltd
Trinity/Matrix Cube: Shellshock Distribution
Trinity/Sad Eyes: Shellshock Distribution
Trio: EMI Distribution, The Woods
Trip: The Woods
Triple Crown: Plastic Head Music Distribution Ltd
Triple Earth: Stern's Distribution, Universal Music Operations
Triple X: Plastic Head Music Distribution Ltd
Triple XXX: SRD (Southern Record Distribution)
Tripoli Trax: Vital Distribution
Tripsichord: Nova Sales and Distribution (UK) Ltd
Trisol: Shellshock Distribution
TRL: Absolute Marketing & Distribution Ltd.
Trocadero: Pinnacle Records, Shellshock Distribution
Trojan Records: Proper Music Distribution Ltd
Tropical: Discovery Records Ltd
Trouble Man: F Minor Ltd
Trouble On Vinyl: SRD (Southern Record Distribution)
Troubleman Utd: Cargo Records (UK) Ltd
TRS: Jet Star Phonographics
Tru 2 Da Game: Universal Music Operations
Truck: Shellshock Distribution
Truckadelic: Cargo Records (UK) Ltd
Truckstop: Cargo Records (UK) Ltd
True Playaz: SRD (Southern Record Distribution)
Truelove Electronic Communications: SRD (Southern Record Distribution)
Trunk: SRD (Southern Record Distribution)
Trybute: SRD (Southern Record Distribution)
Tryfan: Sain (Recordiau) Cyf
TSM Records: New Note Distribution Ltd
Tu Pierdes: Proper Music Distribution Ltd
Tuff City: Cargo Records (UK) Ltd
Tuff Gong: Universal Music Operations
Tugboat Records: Vital Distribution
Tumbao: Discovery Records Ltd
Tumi: Universal Music Operations
Tummy Touch: Pinnacle Records
Turmoil: Pinnacle Records, Shellshock Distribution
Turnbuckle: Cargo Records (UK) Ltd, Shellshock Distribution
Turning Point: F Minor Ltd
TVD Entertainment: BDS (Bertelsmann Distribution Services)
TVT: Cargo Records (UK) Ltd, F Minor Ltd
Twah!: Pinnacle Records
Tweak: Cargo Records (UK) Ltd
Tweed: Vital Distribution
23rd Precinct: Pinnacle Records
2012: Vital Distribution
Twin Arrows: Universal Music Operations
Twin Tone: Vital Distribution
Twist: F Minor Ltd, SRD (Southern Record Distribution)
Twist And Shout: Pinnacle Records
Twisted Nerve: Vital Distribution
Twisted UK: BDS (Bertelsmann Distribution Services), Vital Distribution
Twisted Village: Cargo Records (UK) Ltd
2 Bob Sounds: Pinnacle Records, Shellshock Distribution
2/4 Spoke: Pinnacle Records
2 Kool: Pinnacle Records
2.13.61: Pinnacle Records
Two To Tango: Universal Music Operations
242: Vital Distribution
Tycoon: Pinnacle Records
Tzadik: Cargo Records (UK) Ltd
U Star Records: Kudos Records Ltd
U-Star: Pinnacle Records
U.S.T.A.: Shellshock Distribution
UBC: Pinnacle Records
Ubik: Shellshock Distribution
Ubiquity: New Note Distribution Ltd, Timewarp Distribution
Ufcro: Cargo Records (UK) Ltd
UFO: F Minor Ltd, Pinnacle Records
UG: InterGroove Ltd
Ugly Bug: SRD (Southern Record Distribution)
Uglyman: Shellshock Distribution
UK Reggae Performers: Jet Star Phonographics
UK Roses: Jet Star Phonographics
Ulftone: Proper Music Distribution Ltd
Ultimate: Pinnacle Records
Ultimate Dilemma: Pinnacle Records
Ultimate Groove: Universal Music Operations
Ultra: Cargo Records (UK) Ltd
Ultra Violet: SRD (Southern Record Distribution)
Ultrapop: Pinnacle Records
Un-Disputed: Pinnacle Records
Unaware Collection: Universal Music Operations
Uncle Sam's Vinyl: BDS (Bertelsmann Distribution Services), Essential Direct Ltd
Unda-Vybe: Vital Distribution
Under One Sun: Proper Music Distribution Ltd
Under The Counter: Vital Distribution
Undercover: Cargo Records (UK) Ltd
Underground Classics: SRD (Southern Record

Distribution)
Underground Sounds: Shellshock Distribution
Underground Vibe: Pinnacle Records
Undervybe: BDS (Bertelsmann Distribution Services), Essential Direct Ltd
Underware: Vital Distribution
Unexplored Beats: Pinnacle Records
Unforscene: Pinnacle Records
Unicorn Records: Plastic Head Music Distribution Ltd
Unidisc: ZYX
Union Jack: Amato Distribution
Union Square: New Note Distribution Ltd
Unique: Pinnacle Records, Shellshock Distribution
Unique Gravity: Proper Music Distribution Ltd
Unique 2 Rhythm: Amato Distribution
Unisound Records International: Plastic Head Music Distribution Ltd
Unit 5: Brothers Distribution
United: Pinnacle Records
United DJs Of America: Pinnacle Records
United Recordings: Timewarp Distribution
Unity: Pinnacle Records
Universe: F Minor Ltd
Universal: BDS (Bertelsmann Distribution Services)
Universal Language: Vital Distribution
Universal Sound: Vital Distribution
Universal TV: Universal Music Operations
Unknown: ST Holdings Ltd, Vital Distribution
Unknown Territory: Vital Distribution
Unreleased Project: Amato Distribution
Unsigned Talent: Jet Star Phonographics
Untertainment: TEN (The Entertainment Network)
Untidy Trax: Pinnacle Records
Up & Running: Nervous Records
Up Beat: Jazz Music
Upbeat: BDS (Bertelsmann Distribution Services), Delta Music PLC
UPE: ADA Distribution
Upfront: SRD (Southern Record Distribution)
Upland: Shellshock Distribution
Upper Class: Shellshock Distribution
Uppercut: Vital Distribution
Uprising: Load Media
Uprock: Shellshock Distribution
Upstart: Proper Music Distribution Ltd
Uptempo: Jet Star Phonographics
Urban: Universal Music Operations
Urban Beat Collection: BDS (Bertelsmann Distribution Services), Essential Direct Ltd
Urban Collective: Vital Distribution
Urban Dance: Universal Music Operations
Urban Dubz: Universal Music Operations
Urban Groove: Vital Distribution
Urban House: Universal Music Operations
Urban Theory: 4am Distribution
Urgent: BDS (Bertelsmann Distribution Services)
Urningsou: Jet Star Phonographics
USG: Cargo Records (UK) Ltd
USR: Universal Music Operations
(Utmost): Pinnacle Records
Uwe: Nova Sales and Distribution (UK) Ltd
Uxbridge Street: Amato Distribution
V Recordings: SRD (Southern Record Distribution)
VA Recordings: InterGroove Ltd
Vaclav: Vital Distribution
Vagrant: Cargo Records (UK) Ltd, F Minor Ltd
Vagrant Records: Plastic Head Music Distribution Ltd
Vague: Cargo Records (UK) Ltd
Vampirella: Nervous Records, Plastic Head Music Distribution Ltd
Vampisoul: Timewarp Distribution
Van Der Linden: Hot Shot Records
Vandeleur: Universal Music Operations
Vanguard: The Complete Record Company Ltd, F Minor Ltd, New Note Distribution Ltd, Pinnacle Records
Vapours: Pinnacle Records
Varese Saraband: Pinnacle Records
Varrick: Proper Music Distribution Ltd
Vasco: Cargo Records (UK) Ltd
VC Recordings: EMI Distribution
Vee Jay: Discovery Records Ltd
Veesik: Proper Music Distribution Ltd
Velvel: Pinnacle Records
Velvet: ZYX
Vendome: Pinnacle Records, Shellshock Distribution
Venture: EMI Distribution
VeraBra: Pinnacle Records
Verbatim: Synergie Logistics
Verge: New Note Distribution Ltd
Verglas: Pinnacle Records
Vermiform: Cargo Records (UK) Ltd
Vernon Yard: EMI Distribution, Vital Distribution
Vertigo: Universal Music Operations
Verve: Universal Music Operations
Verve Forecast: Universal Music Operations
VESK: Cargo Records (UK) Ltd
Vespertine: Cargo Records (UK) Ltd
Vesuvius: SRD (Southern Record Distribution)
VHF: Cargo Records (UK) Ltd
Via: Pinnacle Records
Via Satellite: Cargo Records (UK) Ltd
Vibrations From The: Backs Distribution, Shellshock Distribution
Viceroy: BDS (Bertelsmann Distribution Services)
Vicious Vinyl: Unique Distribution
Victory Records: Plastic Head Music Distribution Ltd
Vigilante: Nova Sales and Distribution (UK) Ltd
Vigilantes Of Love: Cargo Records (UK) Ltd
Viking: Discovery Records Ltd
Villa Villakula: Shellshock Distribution
Vine Gate Music: New Note Distribution Ltd
Vinegate Music: Proper Music Distribution Ltd
Vintage Jazz Band: Jazz Music
Vintage Jazz Classics: Jazz Music
Vintage Music Company: BDS (Bertelsmann Distribution Services)
Vinyl Communications: Cargo Records (UK) Ltd
Vinyl Japan: Plastic Head Music Distribution Ltd
Vinyl Junkie: Vital Distribution
Vinyl Syndicate: ST Holdings Ltd
Viper: Pinnacle Records
Vipers Nest: Proper Music Distribution Ltd
Virgin: EMI Distribution
Virgin America: EMI Distribution
Virgin Classics: EMI Distribution
Virgin/EMI TV: EMI Distribution
Visible Noise: Vital Distribution
Vision: Shellshock Distribution
Visionary: Pinnacle Records
Visions Inc: Goya Music Distribution Ltd
Vital Cog: Cargo Records (UK) Ltd
Viva Voce: Copperplate Distribution
Vod: Shellshock Distribution
Voiceprint: Pinnacle Records
Voices Of Wonder: Shellshock Distribution
Voltage: Amato Distribution
Voltone: Shellshock Distribution
Voodoo: Proper Music Distribution Ltd, Vital Distribution
Voodoo Records: Kudos Records Ltd
Vortex: BDS (Bertelsmann Distribution Services), Essential Direct Ltd
Vox Pop: ADA Distribution
Vox Pop 45s: Timewarp Distribution
Voxx: Shellshock Distribution
Voyager: Discovery Records Ltd
Voyageur: Pinnacle Records
VP: Jet Star Phonographics
V2: Pinnacle Records
Waako: Universal Music Operations
Wabana: Pinnacle Records, Shellshock Distribution
Wackies: Jet Star Phonographics
Wafer Thin: Shellshock Distribution
Wag: Absolute Marketing & Distribution Ltd.
Wagram: Plastic Head Music Distribution Ltd
Wah Wah: Cargo Records (UK) Ltd, F Minor Ltd, Kudos Records Ltd
Wah'tup: Proper Music Distribution Ltd
Wall Of Sound: Vital Distribution
Walt Disney: Vital Distribution
Waltrop: Shellshock Distribution
Walzwerk: Cargo Records (UK) Ltd
Walzwerk Records: Plastic Head Music Distribution Ltd
Wambesi: Pinnacle Records
Waqt Recordings: Amato Distribution
War Music AB: Plastic Head Music Distribution Ltd
Warner Bros: TEN (The Entertainment Network)
Warner Home Video (WHV): TEN (The Entertainment Network)
Warner Vision (WVI): TEN (The Entertainment Network)
warner.esp: TEN (The Entertainment Network)
Water: F Minor Ltd
Watercolour: Gordon Duncan Distributions
Waterlily: Proper Music Distribution Ltd, Vivante Music Ltd
Watermelon: Proper Music Distribution Ltd
Watt: New Note Distribution Ltd, Pinnacle Records
Waulk Elektrik: Proper Music Distribution Ltd
Wave Records: New Note Distribution Ltd
Wax: BDS (Bertelsmann Distribution Services)
Wax Trax: Cargo Records (UK) Ltd
Way Out West: Proper Music Distribution Ltd
Wayward: BDS (Bertelsmann Distribution Services), Essential Direct Ltd
We Love You: Vital Distribution
WEA London: TEN (The Entertainment Network)
Weekend Beatnik: Proper Music Distribution Ltd
Weird Neighbourhood: Pinnacle Records, Shellshock Distribution
Well Charged: BDS (Bertelsmann Distribution Services), Essential Direct Ltd
Well-G Records: ADA Distribution
Welsh Teldisc: Sain (Recordiau) Cyf
The Wenlock Label: Cargo Records (UK) Ltd
Wergo: Harmonia Mundi (UK) Ltd
West Ten: SRD (Southern Record Distribution)
West 2 Recordings: Vital Distribution
Westbound: Pinnacle Records
Western: BDS (Bertelsmann Distribution Services), Essential Direct Ltd
Westmoor: BDS (Bertelsmann Distribution Services)

Westpoint: SRD (Southern Record Distribution)
What Else?: Cargo Records (UK) Ltd
What Records: Independent Distribution Ltd
Whatever: Pinnacle Records
Whatsoever: BDS (Bertelsmann Distribution Services)
When!: Pinnacle Records
Where It's At: Shellshock Distribution
Where It's At Is Where You Are: Pinnacle Records, Shellshock Distribution
Whipcord: Pinnacle Records, Shellshock Distribution
Whippa Snappa: Plastic Head Music Distribution Ltd
Whippet: Pinnacle Records
Whirl-y-Gig: Changing World Distribution
Whirlie: Gordon Duncan Distributions
Whirly Music: Shellshock Distribution
Whirlybird: Cargo Records (UK) Ltd
White: TEN (The Entertainment Network)
White Dragon: Cargo Records (UK) Ltd
White Jazz: Cargo Records (UK) Ltd
White Lines: Vital Distribution
White Water: TEN (The Entertainment Network)
The Whole Nine Yards: SRD (Southern Record Distribution)
Whoop!: InterGroove Ltd
WHV/BBC Superbudget: Technicolor Distribution Services Ltd
Why Not: Candid Productions Ltd
Wicked Music: Shellshock Distribution
Wicked Worlds: Vital Distribution
Wide: Shellshock Distribution
Widespread: Shellshock Distribution
Wigwam: Pinnacle Records
Wiiija: Vital Distribution
Wikkid: Nova Sales and Distribution (UK) Ltd
Wild Bunch: EMI Distribution
Wild Card: Universal Music Operations
Wild England: BDS (Bertelsmann Distribution Services), Essential Direct Ltd
Wildcat: Hot Shot Records
Wildgoose: ADA Distribution
Wildloops: InterGroove Ltd
Wildwood Acoustic: Pendle Hawk Music Distribution
Windsong: Pinnacle Records
Wingspan: Shellshock Distribution
Winter & Winter: Harmonia Mundi (UK) Ltd
Wire: Shellshock Distribution
The Wire Editions: Harmonia Mundi (UK) Ltd
Wirl Music: Jet Star Phonographics
Witness: Pinnacle Records
WMD: Discovery Records Ltd
WMF: Shellshock Distribution
WMO: Vital Distribution
Wolf: Hot Shot Records, RSK Entertainment
Wolfrilla: F Minor Ltd
WOMAD Select: Proper Music Distribution Ltd
Won't Stop: Pinnacle Records
Wonderboy: Universal Music Operations
Woo Me: SRD (Southern Record Distribution)
Wooded Hill Recordings: Pinnacle Records
Wooden Hill: Proper Music Distribution Ltd
Woodland: Timewarp Distribution
Woof!: Pinnacle Records
Wooligan: Jet Star Phonographics
Word Sound: SRD (Southern Record Distribution)
Words Of Warning: SRD (Southern Record Distribution)
Wordsound: SRD (Southern Record Distribution)
Worker's Playtime: Pinnacle Records
Working Party Music: ADA Distribution
World: Gordon Duncan Distributions, Plastic Head Music Distribution Ltd, Proper Music Distribution Ltd
World Circuit: New Note Distribution Ltd, Proper Music Distribution Ltd, Stern's Distribution
World Dance: Flute Worldwide Ltd
World Domination: Cargo Records (UK) Ltd
World In Sound: F Minor Ltd
World Music Network: New Note Distribution Ltd
World Service: Shellshock Distribution, Vital Distribution
World Village: Harmonia Mundi (UK) Ltd
World's Best: Shellshock Distribution
Worm Interface: Pinnacle Records
Woronzow: Shellshock Distribution
Wotre Music: Discovery Records Ltd
Wounded Bird: F Minor Ltd
Wreckage: Plastic Head Music Distribution Ltd
Wrenched: Cargo Records (UK) Ltd
Wrong Again Records: Plastic Head Music Distribution Ltd
Wu Tang: Shellshock Distribution
Wu-Tang: Vital Distribution
Wurlitzer Jukebox: Cargo Records (UK) Ltd
X-Clusive: Vital Distribution
X-Core: Shellshock Distribution
X-Tradition Records: ADA Distribution
Xacca Sounds: Nova Sales and Distribution (UK) Ltd
Xart: Shellshock Distribution
Xenophile: Proper Music Distribution Ltd
XL Recordings: Vital Distribution
Xplicit Vinyl: Vital Distribution
Xterminator: Jet Star Phonographics
Xtra Large Productions: Jet Star Phonographics
Xtravaganza: TEN (The Entertainment Network)
Xtreme: TEN (The Entertainment Network)
Y: Vital Distribution
Yard Beat: Jet Star Phonographics
Yard Face: Jet Star Phonographics
Yard High: New Note Distribution Ltd
Yard Music: SRD (Southern Record Distribution)
Yassaba: Pinnacle Records, Shellshock Distribution
Yazoo: Proper Music Distribution Ltd
Ye Gods: Pinnacle Records, Shellshock Distribution
Yeaah: Absolute Marketing & Distribution Ltd.
Yep!: Shellshock Distribution
Yo Mama: Shellshock Distribution
York Ambisonic: Metronome Distribution
Yoshiko: Vital Distribution
Young God: Cargo Records (UK) Ltd
Your Mum: BDS (Bertelsmann Distribution Services), Essential Direct Ltd
Yoyo: Shellshock Distribution
YR 3000: Plastic Head Music Distribution Ltd
Yunx Recordings: Baked Goods Distribution
Yush: Pinnacle Records
Yush Recordings: Kudos Records Ltd
Zane: Pinnacle Records
Zarnak: Pinnacle Records
Zarozinia: Shellshock Distribution
Zebra: Pinnacle Records
Zen Garden: ADA Distribution
Zeno: Shellshock Distribution
Zephyr: New Note Distribution Ltd, Pinnacle Records
Zero Hour: Pinnacle Records
Zero House: Pinnacle Records
Zerox: Vital Distribution
Zest: ST Holdings Ltd
Zev: Vital Distribution
Zhark: Pinnacle Records, Shellshock Distribution
Zimbob: Stern's Distribution
Zip: Shellshock Distribution
Ziriguiboom: New Note Distribution Ltd
Zok: BDS (Bertelsmann Distribution Services)
Zomart: BDS (Bertelsmann Distribution Services)
Zone Recordings: Pinnacle Records
Zoom Club: Plastic Head Music Distribution Ltd
Zoomshot: Shellshock Distribution
ZTT: Pinnacle Records
ZYX: ZYX
ZZZ: Cargo Records (UK) Ltd

Accountants

A & Co (Part of BKL LLP) 7 Ivebury Court, 325 Latimer Road, London W10 6RA **t** 020 8960 6644 **f** 020 8960 8437 **e** lesley.alexander@bergkaprowlewis.co.uk **w** bergkaprowlewis.co.uk Partner: Lesley E Alexander.

Addis & Co Emery House, 192 Heaton Moor Road, Stockport, Cheshire SK4 4DU **t** 0161 432 3307 **f** 0161 432 3376 **e** enquiries@a-addis.co.uk **w** a-addis.co.uk Partner: Anthony Addis.

Baker Tilly 2 Bloomsbury Street, London WC1B 3ST **t** 020 7413 5100 **f** 020 7413 5101 **e** media@bakertilly.co.uk **w** bakertilly.co.uk Head of Music Group: Tim Berg.

BEVIS & CO

4 South St, Epsom, Surrey KT18 7PF **t** 01372 840280 **f** 01372 840282 **e** cjbevis@compuserve.com **w** bevisandco.co.uk Partner: Chris Bevis Commercially experienced accountants with extensive music industry knowledge, royalty audits and catalogue valuations carried out, statutory audits, management accounts service.

BDO Stoy Hayward 8 Baker St, London W1U 3LL **t** 020 7486 5888 **f** 020 7487 3686 **e** mike.haan@bdo.co.uk **w** bdo.co.uk Partner: Michael Haan.

Bettersounds Consultancy Suite F Regency House, 6/7 Elwick Road, Ashford, Kent TN25 4NT **t** 01233 643325 **f** 01233 645570 **e** Bettersounds@btconnect.com Contact: Bernard Symonds.

BKR Haines Watts Sterling House, 177-181 Farnham Road, Slough, Berkshire SL1 4XP **t** 01753 530333 **f** 01753 576606 **e** slough@hwca.com **w** hwca.com Partner: Michael Davidson.

Blackstone Franks & Co 26-34 Old Street, London EC1V 9QR **t** 020 7250 3300 **f** 020 7250 1402 **e** RMaas@blackstones.co.uk Partner: Robert Maas.

Alan Boddy & Co Chartered Accountants Damer House, Meadoway, Wickford, Essex SS12 9HA **t** 01268 571466 **f** 01268 570638 **e** alan@albodd.freeserve.co.uk **w** alanboddy.co.uk Principal: Alan Boddy FCA.

Booth Anderson Chester & Co 1 Peterborough Road, Harrow, Middx HA1 2AX **t** 020 8422 8218 **f** 020 8423 1783 **e** ralph@boothanderson.com **w** boothanderson.com Snr Partner: Ralph Crane.

Bowker Orford 15-19 Cavendish Place, London W1G 0DD **t** 020 7636 6391 **f** 020 7580 3909 **e** mail@bowkerorford.com Partner: Michael Orford.

Bradney & Co South House, 21-37 South Street, Dorking, Surrey RH4 2JZ **t** 01306 743939 **f** 01306 740253 **e** mail@bradney.co.uk **w** bradney.co.uk MD: John Bradney.

Brebner, Allen & Trapp The Quadrangle, 180 Wardour Street, London W1F 8LB **t** 020 7734 2244 **f** 020 7287 5315 **e** partners@brebner.co.uk **w** brebner.co.uk Partner: Jose Goumal.

Brett Adams-Chartered Accountants 25 Manchester Square, London W1U 3PY **t** 020 7486 8985 **f** 020 7486 8991 **e** Info@brettadams.co.uk Music Partner: Steven Davidson.

Bright Grahame Murray Chartered Accountants 124-130 Seymour Place, London W1H 1BG **t** 020 7402 5201 **f** 020 7402 6659 **e** post@bgm.co.uk **w** bgm.co.uk Auditor: Shailesh Gor/Kevin Levine.

Brighten Jeffrey James 421a Finchley Road, Hampstead, London NW3 6HJ **t** 020 7794 7373 **f** 020 7431 5566 **e** info@brightenjeffreyjames.co.uk **w** brightenjeffreyjames.com Partner: Roger Brighten.

Brown McLeod 51 Clarkegrove Road, Sheffield, South Yorks S10 2NH **t** 0114 268 4747 **f** 0114 268 4161 **e** Jroddison@aol.com MD: John Roddison.

BSJ Finance Ltd Chartered Mgmt Accountants 60 Fernleigh Road, London N21 3AH **t** 020 8882 5622 **f** 020 8886 0930 **e** info@bsjfinance.co.uk Senior Partner: Beverley Jones.

Bullocks Ltd 142 New Cavendish Street, London W1W 6YF **t** 020 7323 2417 **f** 020 7580 7776 **e** abullock@bullocks.co.uk **w** bullocks.co.uk MD: Adrian Bullock.

Carnmores Royalties Consultants Ltd Suite 212-213, Blackfriars House, 157-168 Blackfriars Road, London SE1 8EZ **t** 020 7261 1660 **f** 020 7261 1659 **e** carnmores@aol.com **w** carnmores.com MD: Richard Jackson-Bass.

Conroy & Company 27 Beaumont Avenue, St. Albans, Herts AL1 4TL **t** 01727 858 589 **e** conroyandcompany@btconnect.com Snr Partner: A Conroy FCA, FSCA.

Coombes Wales Quinnell 100 Baker Street, London W1U 6WG **t** 020 7486 9798 **f** 020 7486 0092 **e** advice@cwq.co.uk Partner: Ian Coombes.

Cousins Brett 20 Bulstrode Street, London W1U 2JW **t** 020 7486 5791 **f** 020 7224 7226 **e** johncousins@cousinsbrett.com Partner: John Cousins.

Dales Evans & Co Ltd Chartered Accountants 4th Floor, 88/90 Baker Street, London W1U 6TQ **t** 020 7298 1899 **f** 020 7298 1871 **e** PaulMakin@dalesevans.co.uk Dir: Paul Makin.

W John Daniel FCCA The Beam House, 14 Winkfield Road, Windsor, Berkshire SL4 4BG **t** 01753 852924 **f** 01753 852924 **e** johndaniel@btconnect.com Snr Partner: John Daniel.

dBM Ltd 8 The Glasshouse, 49A Goldhawk Road, London W12 8QP **t** 020 8222 6628 **f** 020 8222 6629 **e** david@dbmltd.co.uk MD: David Hitchcock.

De La Haye Royalty Services 76 High Street, Stony Stratford, Bucks MK11 1AH **t** 01908 568800 **f** 01908 568890 **e** royalties@delahaye.co.uk **w** delahaye.co.uk MD: Roger La Haye.

Deloitte & Touche 180 Strand, London WC2R 1BL **t** 020 7007 6023 **f** 020 7303 4786 **e** cbradbrook@deloitte.co.uk **w** deloitte.co.uk Tax Partner, Music/ Media: Charles Bradbrook.

DPC Media Holed Stone Barn, Stisted Cottage Fm, Hollies Road, Bradwell, Braintree, Essex CM77 8DZ **t** 01376 551426 **f** 01376 551787 **e** info@dpcmedia.demon.co.uk Business Mgr: Dave Clark.

Business Services

EMTACS-Entertainers & Musicians Tax & Accountancy 69 Loughborough Road, West Bridgford, Nottingham NG2 7LA **t** 0115 981 5001 **f** 0115 981 5005 **e** emtacs@aol.com **w** emtacs.com Partner: Geoff Challinger.

Entertainment Accounting International 26a Winders Road, Battersea, London SW11 3HB **t** 020 7978 4488 **f** 020 7978 4492 **e** contact@eai.uk.com Proprietor: Mike Donovan.

Entertainment Audit Services Northumberland House, 11 The Pavement, Popes Lane, Ealing, London W5 4NG **t** 020 8832 7393 **f** 020 8832 7394 **e** easltd@btinternet.com Contact: Tony Hughes

Ernst & Young 1 More London Place, London SE1 2AF **t** 020 7951 2000 **f** 020 7951 9336 **e** aflitcroft@uk.ey.com **w** ey.com Partner: Alan Flitcroft.

HW Fisher & Company Acre House, 11-15 William Road, London NW1 3ER **t** 020 7388 7000 **f** 020 7380 4900 **e** info@hwfisher.co.uk **w** hwfisher.co.uk Partner: Martin Taylor.

Freedman Frankl & Taylor Reedham House, 31 King Street West, Manchester M3 2PJ **t** 0161 834 2574 **f** 0161 831 7608 **e** mail@fft.co.uk **w** fft.co.uk

FSPG 21 Bedford Square, London WC1B 3HH **t** 020 7637 4444 **f** 020 7323 2857 **e** jon@fspg.co.uk Partner: Jon Glasner.

GELFAND RENNERT FELDMAN & BROWN

Langham House, 1b Portland Place, London W1B 1GR **t** 020 7636 1776 **f** 020 7636 6331 **e** info@grfb-uk.com Contact: Stephen Marks, Robert Perez. **Accountants to the Entertainment Industry specialising in : Business Management • Royalty Examination • Tour Accounting • Taxation.**

Guy Rippon Organisation 21 Bedford Square, London WC1B 3HH **t** 020 7637 4444 **f** 020 7323 2857 **e** guy@fspg.co.uk Principal: Guy Rippon.

HARDWICK & MORRIS

Hardwick & Morris
Chartered Accountants

4 New Burlington Street, London W1S 2JG **t** 020 7287 9940 **f** 08707 065 204 **e** stephanie@hardwickandmorris.co.uk **w** hardwickandmorris.co.uk. Partner: Stephanie Hardwick.

Harold Everett Wreford, Chartered Accountants 32 Wigmore Street, London W1U 2RP **t** 020 7535 5900 **f** 020 7535 5901 **e** mail@hew.co.uk Partner, Entertainment: Jeffrey Sloneem.

HARRIS & TROTTER

65 New Cavendish Street, London W1G 7LS **t** 020 7467 6300 **f** 020 7467 6363 **e** mail@harrisandtrotter.co.uk Contact: Ronnie Harris, Russell Selwyn, Jason Boas.

George Hay & Co 83 Cambridge Street, London SW1V 4PS **t** 020 7630 0582 **f** 020 7630 1502 **e** george.hay@virgin.net Contact: The Snr Partner

Horwath Clark Whitehill 25 New Street Square, London EC4A 3LN **t** 020 7353 1577 **f** 020 7583 1720 **e** norkettt@horwathcw.co.uk **w** horwathcw.com Partner: Tim Norkett.

Immediate Business Management 61 Birch Green, Hertford, Herts SG14 2LR **t** 01992 550573 **f** 01992 550573 **e** immediate@onetel.net.uk Partner: Derek Jones.

J.E.R 4 Crescent Stables, 139 Upper Richmond Road, London SW15 2TN **t** 020 8704 5407 **f** 020 8785 1969 **e** julieeyre@btinternet.com Royalty Auditor: Julie Eyre.

Jeffrey James Chartered Accountants 421a Finchley Road, Hampstead, London NW3 6HJ **t** 020 7794 7373 **f** 020 7431 5566 **e** info@jeffreyjames.co.uk Partner: Jeffrey Kaye.

Johnsons Chartered Accountants Lancashire House, 217 Uxbridge Road, London W13 9AA **t** 020 8567 3451 **f** 020 8840 6823 **e** mail@johnsonsca.com **w** johnsonsca.com Partner: Shaukat Murad.

Jon Child & Co 202 Ducie House, Ducie St, Manchester M1 2JW **t** 0161 228 1314 **f** 0161 228 3134 **e** jonchild@msn.com Partner: Jon Child.

JW Management & Finance 380 Longbanks, Harlow, Essex CM18 7PG **t** 01279 304526 **f** 01279 304526 **e** jpweston@ntlworld.com **w** westonenterprises.co.uk Manager/Consultant: John Weston ACCA.

K.M.Malak & Co Ltd 1st Floor Rear Office, 11 The Quadrant, Edgware, Middx HA8 7LU **t** 020 8952 9500 **f** 020 8952 3496 **e** kamalmmalak@onetel.net.uk Principal: Kamal M Malak.

OJ Kilkenny & Company 6 Lansdowne Mews, London W11 3BH **t** 020 7792 9494 **f** 020 7792 1722 **e** mail@ojkilkenny.co.uk Contact: Patrick Savage

KPMG LLP Aquis Court, 31 Fishpool St, St Albans AL3 4RF **t** 01727 733063 **f** 01727 733001 **e** charles.lestrangemeakin@kpmg.co.uk **w** kpmg.com Dir: Charles Le Strange Meakin.

Leigh Philip & Partners 1-6 Clay Street, London W1U 6DA **t** 020 7486 4889 **f** 020 7486 4885 **e** mail@lpplondon.co.uk Snr Partner: Leigh Genis.

Lewis-Simler 4 Prince Albert Road, London NW1 7SN **t** 020 7482 4424 **f** 020 7482 4623 **e** advice@eles.co.uk Partner: GJ Simler.

Lloyd Piggott Blackfriars House, Parsonage, Manchester M3 2JA **t** 0161 833 0346 **f** 0161 832 0045 **e** info@lloydpiggott.co.uk **w** lloydpiggott.co.uk Tax Associate: Paula Abbott.

Lubbock Fine Russell Bedford House, City Forum, 250 City Road, London EC1V 2QQ **t** 020 7490 7766 **f** 020 7490 5102 **e** post@lubbockfine.co.uk **w** lubbockfine.co.uk Partner: Jeff Gitter.

Macnair Mason John Stow House, 18 Bevis Marks, London EC3A 7ED **t** 020 7469 0550 **f** 020 7469 0660 **e** mm@macmas.co.uk **w** macmas.co.uk Partner: Anton Luck.

Mansfield & Co, Chartered Accountants 55 Kentish Town Road, Camden Town, London NW1 8NX **t** 020 7482 2022 **f** 020 7482 2025 **e** mco@mansfields.co.uk **w** mansfields.co.uk Snr Partner: David FL Mansfield.

MARTIN GREENE RAVDEN

Martin Greene Ravden is the trading name of Martin Greene Ravden LLP
55 Loudoun Road, St John's Wood, London NW8 0DL **t** 020 7625 4545 **f** 020 7625 5265 **e** mgr@mgr.co.uk **w** mgr.co.uk Contact: David Ravden, Steve Daniel, Ed Grossman. **A division of Media Management Group.**

Morris & Shah 31 Paddington Street, London W1U 4HD **t** 020 7486 9554 **f** 020 7486 9557 **e** MorrisandShah@aol.com Partners: Jonathan Morris, Kewal Shah.

Music Business Associates Ltd 1st Floor, 4 South Street, Epsom, Surrey KT18 7PF **t** 01372 840280 **f** 01372 840282 **e** info@musicbusinessassociates.com **w** musicbusinessassociates.com Contact: Lisa, David or Michael

Music Business Services 1 Freshfields Drive, Lancing, West Sussex BN15 9LN **t** 01903 530005 **f** 01903 530005 **e** ray@rowlesmusic.co.uk **w** rowlesmusic.co.uk Contact: Ray Rowles

Music Royalties Ltd 18 Cavendish Close, Hayes, Middlesex UB4 8AJ **t** 020 8569 3936 **e** david@musicroyalties.co.uk Dir: David Rayment.

MWM Chartered Accountants & Business Advisers 6 Berkeley Cresecent, Clifton, Bristol BS8 1HA **t** 0117 929 2393 **f** 0117 929 2696 **e** office@mwmuk.com Dir: Craig Williams.

Neill & Co 25 Hill Road, Theydon Bois, Epping, Essex CM16 7LX **t** 01992 812211 **f** 01992 812299 **e** info@neill.co.uk **w** neill.co.uk Principal: Keith Neill.

Newman & Co Regent House, 1 Pratt Mews, London NW1 0AD **t** 020 7267 6899 **f** 020 7267 6746 **e** partners@newman-and.co.uk **w** newman-and.co.uk Snr Partner: Colin Newman.

Nieman Walters Niman Rosewood Suite, Teresa Gavin House, Woodford Ave, Woodford Green, Essex IG8 8FH **t** 020 8550 3131 **f** 020 8550 6020 **e** info@nwnaccounts.com **w** nwnaccounts.com Partner: Edmund Niman.

Note for Note 15 Marroway, Weston Turville, Aylesbury, Bucks HP22 5TQ **t** 01296 614966 **f** 01296 614651 **e** immbus@aol.com Proprietor: Chris Turner.

NYMAN LIBSON PAUL

Regina House, 124 Finchley Road, London NW3 5JS **t** 020 7433 2400 **f** 020 7433 2401 **e** mail@nlpca.co.uk **w** nlpca.co.uk Partner: Amin Saleh.

Pannell Kerr Forster Associates New Garden House, 78 Hatton Garden, London EC1N 8JA **t** 020 7831 7393 **f** 020 7405 6736 **e** info.london@uk.pkf.com **w** pkf.co.uk

Pearson & Co 113 Smug Oak Business Centre, Lye Lane, Bricket Wood, St Albans, Hertfordshire AL2 3UG **t** 01923 894404 **f** 01923 894990 **e** richard@stantonpearson.co.uk Partner: Richard Pearson.

PORTMAN MUSIC SERVICES LTD

38 Osnaburgh Street, London NW1 3ND **t** 01962 732033 or 07971 455 920 **f** 01962 732032 **e** maria@portmanmusicservices.com Royalty & Copyright Mgr: Maria Comiskey.

Positive Accounting Solutions 29 Langley Park, London NW7 2AA **t** 020 8906 2343 **f** 020 8906 2343 **e** simon@positiveaccounting.co.uk MD: Simon Durban.

Prager and Fenton Midway House, 27-29 Cursitor Street, London EC4A 1LT **t** 020 7831 4200 **f** 020 7831 5080 **e** mgoldberg@pragerfenton.co.uk **w** pragerfenton.com Partners: Martin Goldberg, Mark Boomla and Austin Jacobs.

PricewaterhouseCoopers 1 Embankment Place, London WC2N 6RH **t** 020 7583 5000 **f** 020 7822 4652 **e** firstname.lastname@uk.pwcglobal.com **w** pwcglobal.co.uk Head of UK E&M: Murray Legg.

RCO - ROYALTY COMPLIANCE ORGANISATION

4 Crescent Stables, 139 Upper Richmond Road, London SW15 2TN **t** 020 8789 6444 **f** 020 8785 1960 **e** ask@TheRcO.co.uk **w** rcoonline.com Partners: Mike Skeet, Gill Sharp. Dedicated royalty auditors and valuation experts with offices in London, Los Angeles and New York.

Reeds Copperfields Mount Pleasant, Crowborough, East Sussex TN6 2NF **t** 01892 668676 **f** 01892 668678 Principle: Chris Reed.

RSM Robson Rhodes LLP 186 City Road, London EC1V 2NU **t** 020 7251 1644 **f** 020 7250 0801 **e** enquiries@rsmi.co.uk **w** rsmi.co.uk Contact: Dir of Communications

Ryan & Co 4F, Shirland Mews, London W9 3DY **t** 020 8960 0961 **f** 020 8960 0963 **e** ryan@ryanandco.com **w** ryanandco.com Chartered Accountant: Cliff Ryan.

SAFFERY CHAMPNESS

Saffery Champness

CHARTERED ACCOUNTANTS

Lion House, Red Lion Street, London WC1R 4GB **t** 020 7841 4000 **f** 020 7841 4100 **e** nick.kelsey@saffery.com **w** saffery.com. Partners: Nick Kelsey, Nick Gaskell.

SEDLEY RICHARD LAURENCE VOULTERS

SEDLEY RICHARD LAURENCE VOULTERS

Kendal House, 1 Conduit Street, London W1S 2XA **t** 020 7287 9595 **f** 020 7287 9696 **e** general@srlv.co.uk **w** srlv.co.uk Snr Partner: Richard Rosenberg.

Shulman & Company 4 St George's House, 15 Hanover Square, London W1S 1HS **t** 020 7486 6363 **f** 020 7408 1388 **e** 888@shulman.co.uk **w** shulman.co.uk Principal: Neville Shulman.

Sloane & Co 36-38 Westbourne Grove, Newton Road, London W2 5SH **t** 020 7221 3292 **f** 020 7229 4810 **e** mail@sloane.co.uk **w** sloane.co.uk Contact: David Sloane

Ivan Sopher & Company 5 Elstree Gate, Elstree Way, Borehamwood, Hertfs WD6 1JD **t** 020 8207 0602 **f** 020 8207 6758 **e** accountants@ivansopher.co.uk **w** ivansopher.co.uk Proprietor: Ivan Sopher.

Synergy Business Management 143 Syon Lane, Osterley, Middlesex TW7 5PZ **t** 020 8568 0609 **f** 020 8568 6968 **e** synergy143@aol.com Partner: Eddie Bull.

Tenon Media 66 Chiltern Street, London W1U 4JT **t** 020 7535 1400 **f** 020 7535 1401 **e** julian.hedley@tenongroup.com **w** tenongroup.com MD: Julian Hedley.

CR Thomas & Co The 1929 Building, Merton Abbey Mills, Wimbledon, London SW19 2RD **t** 020 8542 4262 **f** 020 8545 0662 **e** ah@thomas-harris.com Snr Partner: Chris Thomas.

Anthony Tiscoe & Company Brentmead House, Britannia Road, London N12 9RU **t** 020 8343 8749 or 07976 661217 **f** 020 8446 6864 **e** tony@tiscoe.fsnet.co.uk Chartered Accountant: Anthony Tiscoe.

Warley & Warley Chartered Accountants 76 Cambridge Road, Kingston-Upon-Thames, Surrey KT1 3NA **t** 020 8549 5137 **f** 020 8546 3022 **e** info@warleyandwarley.co.uk **w** warleyandwarley.co.uk Partner: Andrew Wordingham.

Westbury Schotness 145-157 St John Street, London EC1V 4PY **t** 020 7253 7272 **f** 020 7253 0814 **e** Keithg@westbury.co.uk **w** westbury.co.uk Partner: Keith Graham.

William Evans & Partners 20 Harcourt Street, London W1H 4HG **t** 020 7563 8390 **f** 020 7569 8700 **e** wep@williamevans.co.uk Senior Partner: Stephen Evans.

Willott Kingston Smith 2nd Floor, Quadrant House, (Air Street Entrance), 80-82 Regent Street, London W1B 5RP **t** 020 7304 4646 **f** 020 7304 4647 **e** ghowells@kingstonsmith.co.uk **w** kingstonsmith.co.uk Partner: Geraint Howells.

Wingrave Yeats Ltd (Chartered Accountants) 65 Duke Street, London W1M 6AJ **t** 020 7495 2244 **f** 020 7499 9442 **e** wyl@wingrave.co.uk **w** wingrave.co.uk Dir: Philip Hedges.

Winters 29 Ludgate Hill, London EC4M 7JE **t** 020 7919 9100 **f** 020 7919 9019 **e** info@winters.co.uk **w** winters.co.uk Partner: Roy Bristow.

Wyndhams 177 High Street, Harlesden, London NW10 4TE **t** 020 8961 3889 **f** 020 8961 4620 **e** wyndhams@btopenworld.com Partner: David Landau.

C.C. Young & Co 48 Poland Street, London W1F 7ND **t** 020 7494 5680 **f** 020 7494 5690 **e** ccy@ccyoung.co.uk Dir: Colin Young.

Legal

Iain Adam 2 Whitmore Gardens, London NW10 5HH **t** 020 8969 5243 **f** 020 8960 2128 **e** On application. Contact: Iain Adam

Addleshaw Goddard 150 Aldersgate Street, London EC1A 4EJ **t** 020 7606 8855 **f** 020 7606 4390 **e** paddy.graftongreen@addleshawgoddard.com **w** addleshawgoddard.com Partner: Paddy Grafton Green.

ADR Chambers - Mediators 2 Heron Gate, Taunton, Somerset TA1 2LR **t** 0845 083 3000 **f** 0845 083 3001 **e** ward@clerksroom.com **w** adrchambers.co.uk Mediator: Dennis Muirhead.

Alastair Nicholas Music and Entertainment Law 89A Leathwaite Road, London SW11 6RN **t** 020 7924 1904 **f** 020 7738 1764 **e** awnicholas@btinternet.com Partner: Alastair Nicholas.

Angel & Co 1 Green Street, Mayfair, London W1K 6RG **t** 020 7495 0555 **f** 020 7495 7550 **e** legalangel@btconnect.com Contact: Nigel Angel

Barry & Co 4 Bay Terrace, Pevensey, East Sussex BN24 6EE **t** 01323 766370 Prop: Mr Barry.

Baxter McKay Suite 208 Panther House, 38 Mount Pleasant, London WC1X 0AN **t** 020 7833 9191 **f** 020 7833 9494 **e** gb@baxtermckay.com Partner: Gill Baxter.

Benedicts Grant llp Just House, Beavor Lane, London W6 9UL **t** 020 8741 6020 **f** 020 8741 8362 **e** john@benedictsgrant.biz Partners: John Benedict, Tony Grant.

SJ Berwin & Co 222 Grays Inn Road, London WC1X 8XF **t** 020 7533 2222 **f** 020 7533 2000 **e** info@sjberwin.com **w** sjberwin.com Solicitor: Nora Mullally.

Sally Bevan 14 Birchlands Ave, London SW12 8ND **t** 020 8675 5747 **f** 020 8675 9101 **e** sally@sallybevan.co.uk Principal: Sally Bevan.

Brabners Chaffe Street 1 Dale St, Liverpool L2 2ET **t** 0151 600 3000 **f** 0151 600 3009 **e** francis.mcentegart@brabnerscs.com **w** brabnerschaffestreet.com Solicitor, Media: Francis McEntegart.

Bray and Krais Solicitors Suite 10, Fulham Business Exchange, The Boulevard, London SW6 2TL **t** 020 7384 3050 **f** 020 7384 3051 **e** bandk@brayandkrais.com Senior Partner: Richard Bray.

Briffa Business Design Centre, Upper Street, Islington, London N1 0QH **t** 020 7288 6003 **f** 020 7288 6004 **e** margaret@briffa.com **w** briffa.com Snr Partner: Margaret Briffa.

BrookStreet Des Roches 1 Des Roches Square, Witan Way, Witney, Oxfordshire OX28 4LF **t** 01993 771616 **f** 01993 779030 **e** charlie@bsdr.com Partner: Charlie Seaward.

Burley & Company 10 Gray's Inn Square, Gray's Inn, London WC1R 5JD **t** 020 7404 4002 **f** 020 7405 2429 Contact: Christopher Burley

John Byrne & Co Sheraton House, Castle Park, Cambridge CB3 0AX **t** 01223 370063 **f** 01223 370065 **e** JB@johnbyrne.co.uk Principal: John Byrne.

CALVERT SOLICITORS

77 Weston Street, London Bridge, London SE1 3RS **t** 020 7234 0707 **f** 020 7234 0909 **e** mail@calvertsolicitors.co.uk Contact: Nigel Calvert.

Cambridge Civil Mediation Sheraton House, Castle Park, Cambridge CB3 0AX **t** 01223 370063 **f** 01223 370065 **e** jb@johnbyrne.co.uk Mediator: John Byrne.

Charles Law at WPF Glasner Gerber Shapiro 133 Praed Street, London W2 1RN **t** 020 7723 1656 **f** 020 7724 6936 **e** cl@wpflaw.com **w** wpflaw.com Partner: Charles Law.

Charles Russell Solicitors 8-10 New Fetter Lane, London EC4A 1RS **t** 020 7203 5116 **f** 020 7203 5002 **e** timb@cr-law.co.uk **w** charlesrussell.co.uk Partner: Tim Bamford.

CLINTONS

Clintons ©

55 Drury Lane, London WC2B 5RZ **t** 020 7379 6080 **f** 020 7240 9310 **e** amyers@clintons.co.uk **w** clintons.co.uk Partner: Andrew Myers. Contacts: David Landsman, Peter Button, Andrew Myers.

Cobbetts 39 Newhall Street, Birmingham B3 3DY **t** 0121 236 4477 **f** 0121 236 0774 **e** frances.anderson@cobbetts.co.uk **w** cobbetts.co.uk Partner: Frances Anderson.

Collins Long Solicitors 24 Pepper Street, London SE1 0EB **t** 020 7401 9800 **f** 020 7401 9850 **e** info@collinslong.com **w** collinslong.com Partners: James Collins & Simon Long.

COLLYER-BRISTOW

COLLYER ~ BRISTOW
solicitors

4 Bedford Row, London WC1R 4DF **t** 020 7242 7363 **f** 020 7405 0555 **e** cblaw@collyerbristow.com **w** collyerbristow.com Partner: Howard Ricklow. Music Consultant: Nick Kanaar.

Simon Conroy Solicitors Second Floor, 43-45 St John Street, London EC1M 4AN **t** 020 7490 1276 **f** 020 7490 1298 **e** mail@simonconroy.com **w** simonconroy.com Contact: Simon Conroy

Consigliari Ltd 18 Hackford Walk, Hackford Road, London SW9 0QT **t** 020 7587 3799 **f** 020 7587 3818 **e** info@consigliari.com Contact: Mark Melton

Jim Cook 38 Grovelands Road, London N13 4RH **t** 020 8350 0613 **f** 020 8350 0613 **e** jim@jcook21.freeserve.co.uk Solicitor: Jim Cook.

Davenport Lyons 30 Old Burlington Street, London W1S 3NL **t** 020 7468 2600 **f** 020 7437 8216 **e** jware@davenportlyons.com **w** davenportlyons.com Partner: James Ware.

DAVID WINEMAN SOLICITORS

Craven House, 121 Kingsway, London WC2B 6NX t 020 7400 7800 f 020 7400 7890 e irving.david@davidwineman.co.uk w davidwineman.co.uk Contact: Irving David Please see our full page advertisement.

DEAN MARSH & CO

Business Services

1892 Building, 54 Kingsway Place, Sans Walk, Clerkenwell, London EC1R 0LU **t** 020 7553 4400 **f** 020 7553 4414 **e** info@deanmarsh.com **w** deanmarsh.com Principal: Dean Marsh.

Dechert 2 Sergeants' Inn, London EC4Y 1LT **t** 020 7583 5353 **f** 020 7353 3683 **e** marketing@dechertEU.com **w** dechert.com Chief Exec: Sir Peter Duffell.

DLA (Solicitors) 3 Noble Street, London EC2V 7EE **t** 020 7796 6182 or 020 7796 6312 **f** 020 7796 6113 or 020 7600 1727 **e** ian.penman@dla.com **w** dla.net **Associate, Media etc.:** Ian Penman.

ENGEL MONJACK

16-18 Berners Street, London W1T 3LN **t** 020 7291 3838 **f** 020 7291 3839 **e** info@engelmonjack.com **w** engelmonjack.com. Contacts: Jonathan Monjack/Lawrence Engel.

Edmonds Bowen 4 Old Park Lane, London W1K 1QW **t** 020 7629 8000 **f** 020 7221 9334 **e** info@edmondsbowen.co.uk **w** edmondsbowen.co.uk Consultant: Nick Pedgrift.

Effective Legal Services 16 Stratford Road, London W8 6QD **t** 020 7937 6246 or 07808 741 277 **f** 020 7937 6246 **e** henriette@effectivemusicservices.com Solicitor: Henriette Amiel.

Ent-Law Solicitors 3 Grange Farm Business Park, Shedfield, Southampton, Hampshire SO32 2HD **t** 01329 834100 **f** 01329 834448 **e** paul@ent-law.co.uk Contact: Paul Lambeth LLB

Entertainment Advice Ltd. 31 Penrose Street, London SE17 3DW **t** 020 7708 8822 **f** 020 7703 1239 **e** info@entertainmentadvice.co.uk **w** entertainmentadvice.co.uk Consultants: Len Bendel, Anthony Hall.

ENTERTAINMENT LAW ASSOCIATES

Argentum, 2 Queen Caroline Street, London W6 9DX **t** 020 8323 8013 **f** 020 8323 8080 **e** ela@ela.co.uk **w** ela.co.uk Contact: John Giacobbi.

Field Fisher Waterhouse 35 Vine Street, London EC3N 2AA **t** 020 7861 4000 **f** 020 7488 0084 **e** info@ffwlaw.com **w** ffwlaw.com

Finers Stephens Innocent 179 Great Portland Street, London W1N 6LS **t** 020 7353 4000 **f** 020 7580 7069 **e** marketing@fsilaw.co.uk **w** fsilaw.com Marketing Assistant: Katie Mackenzie.

FORBES ANDERSON

16-18 Berners Street, London W1T 3LN **t** 020 7291 3500 **f** 020 7291 3511 **e** aforbes@forbesanderson.com Partner: Andrew Forbes.

Fox Williams City Gate House, 39-45 Finsbury Square, London EC2A 1UU **t** 020 7628 2000 **f** 020 7628 2100 **e** mail@foxwilliams.com **w** foxwilliams.com Snr Partner: Ronnie Fox.

P Ganz & Co 88 Calvert Road, Greenwich, London SE10 0DF **t** 020 8293 9103 **f** 020 8355 9328 **e** penny.ganz@ganzlegal.com Solicitor: Penny Ganz.

Goldkorn Mathias Gentle 6 Coptic Street, London WC1A 1NW **t** 020 7631 1811 **e** davidgentle@gmglegal.com Partner: David Gentle.

Gray & Co Habib House, 3rd Floor, 9 Stevenson Square, Manchester M1 1DB **t** 0161 237 3360 **f** 0161 236 6717 **e** grayco@grayand.co.uk **w** grayand.co.uk Partner: Rudi Kidd.

GSC Solicitors 31-32 Ely Place, London EC1N 6TD **t** 020 7822 2222 **f** 020 7822 2211 **e** info@gscsolicitors.com **w** gscsolicitors.com Managing Partner: Saleem Sheikh.

Hamlins Roxburghe House, 273-287 Regent Street, London W1B 2AD **t** 020 7355 6000 **f** 020 7518 9100 **e** ent-law@hamlins.co.uk **w** hamlins.co.uk Managing Partner: Laurence Gilmore.

HammondSuddardsEdge 7 Devonshire Square, Cutlers Gardens, London EC2M 4YH **t** 020 7655 1000 **f** 020 7655 1001 **e** enquiries@hammondse.com **w** hammondsuddardsedge.com Partner: Hubert Best.

Harbottle and Lewis Hanover House, 14 Hanover Square, London WIS 1HP **t** 020 7667 5000 **f** 020 7667 5100 **e** info@harbottle.com **w** harbottle.co.uk Partners, Hds of Music Gp: Antony Bebawi, James Sully.

Harrison Curtis Solicitors 8 Jockey's Fields, London WC1R 4BF **t** 020 7611 1720 **f** 020 7611 1721 **e** mail@harrisoncurtis.co.uk **w** harrisoncurtis.co.uk Partner: Lawrence Harrison.

Harrisons Entertainment Law Ltd Suites 5&6 46 Manchester Street, London W1U 7LS **t** 020 7486 2586 **f** 020 7486 2786 **e** info@annharrison.co.uk Principal: Ann Harrison.

Hart-Jackson & Hall 3A Ridley Place, Newcastle upon Tyne, Tyne and Wear NE1 8JQ **t** 0191 232 1987 **f** 0191 232 0429 Partner: Mr PA Hall.

Helen Searle - Legal & Business Adviser Shortbridge Mill Barn, Piltdown, East Sussex TN22 3XA **t** 01825 769356 **f** 01825 769357 **e** helen@helensearle.com Partner: Helen Searle.

Henry Hepworth 5 John Street, London WC1N 2HH **t** 020 7242 7999 **f** 020 7539 7201 **e** leisure@h2o-law.com **w** h2o-law.com

Howard Livingstone, Solicitor 37 Trinity Road, E.Finchley, London N2 8JJ **t** 020 8365 2962 **f** 020 8365 2484 **e** aooa76@dsl.pipex.com **w** fsvo.com/musiclawyer Music Lawyer: Howard Livingstone.

Howletts 60 Grays Inn Road, London WC1X 8LA **t** 020 7404 5612 **f** 020 7831 0635 **e** howletts@zoom.co.uk Partner: David Semmens.

HOWELL-JONES PARTNERSHIP

HOWELL - JONES
PARTNERSHIP
Solicitors

Flint House, 52 High Street, Leatherhead, Surrey KT22 8AJ **t** 01372 860650 **f** 01372 860659 **e** leatherhead@hjplaw.co.uk **w** hjplaw.co.uk Snr Partner: Peter Scott.
25 years advising the music industry.

John Ireland & Co 57 Elgin Crescent, London W11 2JU **t** 020 7792 1666 **e** johnny.ireland@virgin.net MD: John Ireland.

Jane Clemetson 24 Pepper Street, London SE1 0EB **t** 020 7633 0152 **f** 020 7633 9621 **e** jclemetson@btconnect.com Contact: Jane Clemetson

JAYES & PAGE

JAYES & PAGE

Universal House, 251 Tottenham Court Road, London W1T 7JY **t** 020 7291 9111 **f** 020 7291 9119 **e** enquiries@jayesandpage.com **w** jayesandpage.com Partners: Anthony Jayes, Bob Page.
Specialist music and media solicitors experienced in undertaking non-contentious and contentious work for corporate and individual clients.

Jens Hills & Co Northburgh House, 10 Northburgh Street, London EC1V 0AT **t** 020 7490 8160 **f** 020 7490 8140 **e** info@jenshills.com Principal: Jens Hills. DX 53317 Clerkenwell. Music and entertainment lawyers.

KIRKPATRICK & LOCKHART NICHOLSON GRAHAM LLP

Kirkpatrick & Lockhart
Nicholson Graham LLP

110 Cannon Street, London EC4N 6AR **t** 020 7648 9000 **f** 020 7648 9001 **e** ndavies@klng.com **w** klng.com Partner: Nigel Davies.

MC Kirton & Co 83 St Albans Avenue, London W4 5JS **t** 020 8987 8880 **f** 020 8932 7908 **e** michael@mckirton.com Snr Partner: Michael Kirton.

KLegal Solicitors 1-2 Dorset Rise, London EC4Y 8AE **t** 020 7694 2500 **f** 020 7694 2501 **e** philip.daniels@kpmg.co.uk **w** klegal.co.uk Music Industry Solicitor: Philip Daniels.

Peter Last 75 Holland Road, Kensington, London W14 8HL **t** 020 7603 4245 **f** 020 7348 0113 **e** prlast@aol.com Lawyer: Peter Last (LL.B, LL.M).

Lea & Company Solicitors Bank Chambers, Market Place, Stockport, Cheshire SK1 1UN **t** 0161 480 6691 **f** 0161 480 0904 **e** mail@lealaw.com **w** lealaw.com Partner: Stephen Lea.

Lee & Thompson Greengarden House, 15-22 St Christopher's Place, London W1U 1NL **t** 020 7935 4665 **f** 020 7563 4949 **e** mail@leeandthompson.com **w** leeandthompson.com Snr Partner: Andrew Thompson.

Lewis, Davis, Shapiro & Lewit see **Smiths**

Lipkin Gorman 61 Grosvenor Street, Mayfair, London W1K 3JE **t** 020 7493 4010 **f** 020 7409 1734 Partner: Charles Gorman.

Lovells Atlantic House, Holborn Viaduct, London EC1A 2FGlo **t** 020 7296 2000 **f** 020 7296 2001 **e** lindy.golding@lovells.com **w** lovells.com Partner: Lindy Golding.

Leonard Lowy & Co 500 Chiswick High Road, London W4 5RG **t** 020 8956 2785 **f** 020 8956 2786 **e** lowy@leonardlowy.co.uk **w** leonardlowy.co.uk Principal: Leonard Lowy.

Maclay, Murray & Spens 151 St Vincent Street, Glasgow G2 5NJ **t** 0141 248 5011 **f** 0141 248 5819 **e** murray.buchanan@mms.co.uk **w** mms.co.uk Consultant: Murray J. Buchanan.

Maclay, Murray & Spens, London 10 Foster Lane, London EC2V 6HR **t** 020 7606 6130 **f** 020 7600 0992 **e** murray.buchanan@mms.co.uk **w** mms.co.uk Consultant: Murray J. Buchanan.

Magrath & Co 52-54 Maddox Street, London W1S 1PA **t** 020 7495 3003 **f** 020 7409 1745 **e** alexis.grower@magrath.co.uk **w** magrath.co.uk Consultant: Alexis Grower.

Manches Aldwych House, 81 Aldwych, London WC2B 4RP **t** 020 7404 4433 **f** 020 7430 1133 **e** manches@manches.co.uk **w** manches.co.uk

Marriott Harrison 12 Great James St, London WC1N 3DR **t** 020 7209 2000 or 020 7209 2093 **f** 020 7209 2001 **e** tony.morris@marriottharrison.co.uk **w** marriottharrison.com Partner and Head of Media: Tony Morris.

McClure Naismith 292 St Vincent Street, Glasgow, Lanarkshire G2 5TQ **t** 0141 204 2700 **f** 0141 248 3998 **e** glasgow@mcclurenaismith.com **w** mcclurenaismith.com Associate: Euan Duncan. also at 49 Queen Street, Edinburgh EH2 3NH **t**0131 220 1002 **f**0131 220 1003 6 Laurence Pountney Hill, London EC4R 0BL **t**020 7623 9155 **f**020 7623 9154.

McDermott Will & Emery 7 Bishopsgate, London EC2N 3AQ **t** 020 7577 6900 **f** 020 7577 6950 **e** wreilly@europe.mwe.com **w** mwe.com/london Practice Dir: William Reilly.

Metcalfes Solicitors 46-48 Queen Square, Bristol BS1 4LY **t** 0117 929 0451 **f** 0117 929 9551 **e** mburgess@metcalfes.co.uk **w** metcalfes.co.uk Entertainment Lawyer: Martino Burgess.

Mishcon de Reya Summit House, 12, Red Lion Square, London WC1R 4QD **t** 020 7440 7000 **f** 020 7404 5982 **e** feedback@mishcon.co.uk **w** mishcon.co.uk Partner: Martin Dacre.

Robin Morton, Solicitor 22 Herbert Street, Glasgow G20 6NB **t** 0141 337 1199 **f** 0141 357 0655 **e** robinmorto@aol.com

Multiplay Music Consultants 19 Eagle Way, Harrold, Beds MK43 7EW **t** 01234 720785 **f** 01234 720664 **e** info@multiplaymusic.com **w** multiplaymusic.com MD: Kevin White.

Nicolaou Solicitors The Barn Studios, Burnt Farm Ride, Goffs Oak, Herts EN7 5JA **t** 01707 877707 or 07785 933377 **f** 01707 877708 **e** niclaw@tiscali.co.uk Solicitor: Constantina Nicolaou.

Nigel Dewar Gibb & Co Solicitors 43 St John Street, London EC1M 4AN **t** 020 7608 1091 **f** 020 7608 1092 **e** ndg@e-legaluk.co.uk **w** e-legaluk.co.uk Principal: Nigel Dewar Gibb.

NORTHROP MCNAUGHTAN DELLER

solicitors

The Chapel, 26a Munster Road, London SW6 4EN **t** 020 7731 8707 **f** 020 7731 6358 **e** nmd@nmdsolicitors.com Partners: Tim Northrop, Christy McNaughtan, Martin Deller.

Olswang 90 Long Acre, London WC2E 9TT **t** 020 7208 8888 **f** 020 7208 8800 **e** olsmail@olswang.com **w** olswang.com Partner: John Enser.

Pinsent Curtis Biddle 1 Gresham Street, London EC2V 7BU **t** 020 7606 9301 **f** 020 7606 3305 **e** martin.lane@pinsents.com **w** pinsents.com Managing Ptnr: Martin Lane.

ROHAN & CO SOLICITORS

ROHAN & Co

SOLICITORS

Aviation House, 1-7 Sussex Road, Haywards Heath, West Sussex RH16 4DZ **t** 01444 450901 **f** 01444 440437 **e** partners@rohansolicitors.co.uk **w** rohansolicitors.co.uk Contact: Rupert Rohan, Edward Glauser

---

Ross & Craig 12A Upper Berkeley Street, London W1H 7QE **t** 020 7262 3077 **f** 020 7724 6427 **e** david.leadercramer@rosscraig.com **w** rosscraig.com MD: David Leadercramer.

James Rubinstein & Co 149 Cholmley Gardens, Mill Lane, London NW6 1AB **t** 020 7431 5500 **f** 020 7431 5600 **e** help@jamesrubinstein.co.uk **w** jamesrubinstein.co.uk Senior Partner: James Rubinstein.

P Russell & Co, Solicitors Suite 48, London House, 271 King Street, London W6 9LZ **t** 020 8233 2943 **f** 020 8233 2944 **e** info@prcsolicitors.com Partner: Paul Russell.

Russells Regency House, 1-4 Warwick Street, London W1R 6LJ **t** 020 7439 8692 **f** 020 7494 3582 **e** media@russells.co.uk Contact: Mr R Page

Sample Clearance Services Ltd PO Box 3367, Brighton, East Sussex BN1 1WX **t** 01273 326999 **f** 01273 328999 **e** saranne@sampleclearance.com **w** sampleclearance.com MD: Saranne Reid.

Schillings Royalty House, 72-74 Dean Street, London W1D 3TL **t** 020 7453 2500 **f** 020 7453 2600 **e** legal@schillings.co.uk **w** schillings.co.uk Office Mgr: Shelley Vincent.

SEARCH (a division of Jeff Wayne Music Group) Jeff Wayne Music Group Ltd. Oliver House, 8-9 Ivor Place, London NW1 6BY **t** 020 7724 2471 **f** 020 7724 6245 **e** info@jeffwaynemusic.com **w** samplesearch.co.uk Group Dir: Jane Jones.

SEDDONS

5

Portman Square, London W1H 6NT **t** 020 7725 8000 **f** 020 7935 5049 **e**davidk@seddons.co.uk **w** seddons.co.uk Partner: David Kent.

Sheridans 14 Red Lion Square, London WC1R 4QL **t** 020 7404 0444 **f** 020 7831 1982 **e** entertainment@sheridans.co.uk Partner: Stephen Luckman.

The Simkins Partnership 45-51 Whitfield Street, London W1T 4HB **t** 020 7907 3000 **f** 020 7907 3111 **e** info@simkins.com **w** simkins.com Head of Music Group: Julian Turton.

Simons Muirhead & Burton 50 Broadwick Street, London W1F 7AG **t** 020 7734 4499 **f** 020 7734 3263 **e** info@smab.co.uk **w** smab.co.uk Partner: Simon Goldberg.

Smiths 2 Calvert's Buildings, 52 Borough High Street, London SE1 1XN **t** 020 7357 9100 **f** 020 7357 9004 **e** smiths@smiths-law.com **w** smiths-law.com Partner: Andrew Lewis.

Spraggon Stennett Brabyn Matrix Complex, 91 Peterborough Road, London SW6 3BU **t** 020 7348 7630 **f** 020 7348 7631 **e** legal@ssb.co.uk **w** ssb.co.uk Office Manager: Chris Weller.

Statham Gill Davies 52 Welbeck Street, London W1G 9XP **t** 020 7317 3210 **f** 020 7487 5925 **e** john.statham@stathamgilldavies.com Solicitor/Partner: John Statham.

Steeles Law LLP 11 Guilford St, London WC1N 1DT **t** 020 7421 1720 **f** 020 7421 1749 **e** music@steeleslaw.co.uk **w** steeleslaw.co.uk Consultant: Patrick Rackow.

Tarlo Lyons Watchmaker Court, 33 St John's Lane, London EC1M 4DB **t** 020 7405 2000 **f** 020 7814 9421 **e** info@tarlolyons.com **w** tarlolyons.com Partners: Stanley Munson, D Michael Rose.

Taylor Wessing Carmelite 50 Victoria Embankment, London EC4Y 0DX **t** 020 7300 7000 **f** 020 7300 7100 **e** london@taylorwessing.com **w** taylorwessing.com Partner: Paul Mitchell.

Teacher Stern Selby 37-41 Bedford Row, London WC1R 4JH **t** 020 7242 3191 **f** 020 7405 2964 **e** g.shear@tsslaw.co.uk **w** tsslaw.co.uk Snr Partner: Graham Shear.

Theodore Goddard 150 Aldersgate Street, London EC1A 4EJ **t** 020 7606 8855 **f** 020 7606 4390 **e** info@theodoregoddard.co.uk **w** theogoddard.com Partner: Paddy Grafton Green.

Tods Murray WS 66 Queen St, Edinburgh, Lothian EH2 4NE **t** 0131 226 4771 **f** 0131 300 2202 **e** t2m@todsmurray.com **w** t2mlaw.com Entertainment Law Partner: Richard M Findlay.

Tods Murray WS (Glasgow) 33 Bothwell Street, Glasgow G2 6NL **t** 0141 275 4771 **f** 0141 275 4781 **e** t2m@todsmurray.com **w** t2mlaw.com Partner: Richard Findlay.

Turner Parkinson Hollins Chambers 64a Bridge Street, Manchester M3 3BA **t** 0161 833 1212 **f** 0161 834 9098 **e** tp@tp.co.uk **w** tp.co.uk Partner: Andy Booth.

WEB SHERIFF

Argentum, 2 Queen Caroline Street, London W6 9DX **t** 020 8323 8013 **f** 020 8323 8080 **e** websheriff@websheriff.com **w** websheriff.com Contact: John Giacobbi. **Protecting Your Rights On The Internet.**

ZIMMERS SOLICITORS RECHTSANWÄLTE

ZIMMERs

32 Corringham Road, London NW11 7BU **t** 0870 770 0171 or 020 8457 8850 **f** 0870 770 0172 **e** hanna.weber@zimmerslaw.com European Registered Lawyer: Hanna Weber.

Insurance

Albemarle Insurance Brokers 10B Printing House Yard, Shoreditch, London E2 7PR **t** 020 7613 5919 **f** 020 7613 5839 **e** ruth@albemarleinsurance.com **w** albemarleinsurance.com MD: Ruth Sandler.

NW Brown Insurance Brokers Richmond House, 16-20 Regent St, Cambridge CB2 1DB **t** 01223 720310 **f** 01223 353705 **e** richard.rampley@nwbrown.co.uk **w** nwbrown.co.uk Account Exec: Richard Rampley.

FMW Insurance Brokers Farr House, Chelmsford, Essex CM1 1NR **t** 01245 348500 **f** 01245 356553 **e** d.macmahon@fmw.co.uk **w** fmw.co.uk Dir: Dominic MacMahon.

HCF Partnership Star House, 6 Garland Road, Stanmore, Middlesex HA7 1NR **t** 020 8731 5151 **f** 020 8951 3081 **e** enquiries@hcfltd.co.uk **w** hcf.co.uk Partner: Steven Gordon.

La Playa The Stables, Manor Farm, Milton Road, Impington, Cambridge CB4 9NF **t** 01223 522411 **f** 01223 237942 **e** media@laplaya.co.uk **w** laplaya.co.uk MD: Mark Boon.

Musicguard (Pavilion Insurance Management Ltd) Pavilion House, Mercia Business Village, Westwood Business Park, Coventry CV4 8HX **t** 02476 851000 **f** 02476 851080 **e** sales@musicguard.co.uk **w** musicguard.co.uk Sales Dir: Sarah Gow.

Robertson Taylor Insurance Brokers 5 Plato Place, 72-74 St Dionis Road, London SW6 4TU **t** 020 7510 1234 **f** 020 7510 1134 **e** enquiries@rtib.net **w** robertson-taylor.co.uk Dir: John Silcock.

Stafford Knight Entertainment Insurance Brokers 55 Aldgate High Street, London EC3N 1AL **t** 020 7481 6262 **f** 020 7481 7638 **e** tony.crawford@towergate.co.uk Divisional Dir: Tony Crawford.

FinancialAdvisors

Aaron Knight Saili & Associates 27 Lynwood Avenue, Langley, Berkshire SL3 7BJ **t** 01753 676300 **f** 01753 676301 **e** aksaili@btinternet.com Principal: Arun Saili.

Albemarle Insurance 7 Hodgkinson Farm, Boot Lane, Heaton, Bolton BL1 5ST **t** 01204 840444 **f** 01204 841411 Contact: Ruth Sandler

Chelver Media Finance First Floor, Kendal House, 1 Conduit Street, London W1S 2XA **t** 020 7287 7087 **f** 020 7287 9696 **e** steve@ccdb.cc **w** ccdb.cc Contact: Steve Cherry

Collins Financial Consultants Allum Gate House, Theobald Street, Borehamwood, Hertfordshire WD6 4RS **t** 020 8823 0316 **f** 020 8823 0305 **e** CFC@sjpp.co.uk Director: Paul Collins.

Craig Ryle Financial 62 Lake Rise, Romford, Essex RM1 4EE **t** 01708 760544 **f** 01708 760563 **e** mail@craigryle.fsnet.co.uk Director: Linda Ryle.

Credit Suisse Five Cabot Square, London E14 4QR **t** 020 7888 8560 **f** 020 7888 8591 **e** david.thompson.2@credit-suisse.ch **w** cspb.co.uk Fund Mgr: David Thompson.

Ents. & Musicians Tax and Accounts Services 69 Loughborough Road, West Bridgford, Nottingham NG2 7LA **t** 0115 9815001 **f** 0115 9815005 **e** info@emtacs.com **w** emtacs.com Mgr: Geoff Challinger.

Kingston Smith Financial Services 105 St Peter's Street, St Albans, Herts AL1 3EJ **t** 01727 896000 **f** 01727 896001 **e** ksfs@kingstonsmith.co.uk **w** kingstonsmith.co.uk Dir: Derek Prentice.

LGI Consulting - Professional Mortgage Advice 2nd Floor, 41a Church St, Weybridge, Surrey KT13 8DG **t** 01932 856699 **f** 01932 856685 **e** info@lgiconsulting.co.uk **w** lgiconsulting.co.uk Contact: Giuseppe Iannelli

MBA Corporate Solutions Flat 2, 35 Lexham Gardens, London W8 5JR **t** 07713 404 101 **e** gcalton@mbacorporatesolutions.com Dir: Grant Calton.

Merrill Lynch International Private Bank 33 Chester Street, London SW1X 7XD **t** 020 7867 6260 **f** 020 7867 6028 **e** derek_browne@ml.com Relationship Manager: Derek Browne.

Music Media IFA Bright Cook House, 139 Upper Richmond Road, London SW15 2TX **t** 020 8780 0988 **f** 020 8780 1594 **e** post@musicmedia.co.uk **w** musicmedia.co.uk Planning Dir: Malcolm Lyons.

Thomas Financial Planning Independent Financial Advisers 439 Clock Face Road, St Helens, Merseyside WA9 4QL **t** 01744 812376 **e** drphil@blueyonder.co.uk Principal: Dr Phil Thomas.

Wilkinson Turner King 10A London Road, Alderley Edge, Cheshire SK9 7JS **t** 01625 599944 **f** 01625 581442 **e** enquiries@wtkltd.com **w** wtkltd.com Dir: Andrew Wilkinson.

Artist Management

1-AM Management 1b Hollywood Lofts, 154 Commercial Street, London E1 6NU **t** 07966 213 266 **e** openconsulting@virgin.net MD: Angus Carmichael.

10 Management 10 Barley Mow Passage, Chiswick, London W4 4PH **t** 020 8747 4533 **e** info@10management.com **w** 10management.com MD: Jonathan Wild.

19 Management 33 Ransomes Dock, 35-37 Parkgate Road, London SW11 4NP **t** 020 7801 1919 **f** 020 7801 1920 **e** reception@19.co.uk **w** 19.co.uk Contact: Simon Fuller

21st Artist 1 Blythe Road, London W14 0HG **t** 020 7348 4800 **f** 020 7348 4801 **w** eltonjohn.com Creative Dir: Derek Mackillop.

360 Degree Management Appledram, Trumpsgreen Road, Virginia Water, Surrey GU25 4JA **t** 07957 467 796 **e** chelsey@360degree-management.com CEO: Chelsey Baker.

365 Artists 91 Peterborough Rd, London SW6 3BU **t** 020 7384 6500 **f** 020 7384 6504 **e** info@365artists.com **w** 365artists.com Dirs: Adam Clough. Co-MDs: Rebecca Duncan & Adam Clough.

3cord Management 54 Portobello Road, London W11 3DL **t** 020 7229 9218 **e** simon@3cord.net Manager: Simon Hicks.

3rd Stone PO Box 8, Corby, Northamptonshire NN17 2XZ **t** 01536 202295 **f** 01536 266246 **e** steve@adasam.co.uk **w** adasam.co.uk Label Mgr: Steve Kalidoski.

>4 Management Morethan4 Limited, 75c Perham Road, London W14 9SP **t** 020 7610 0963 **e** info@morethan4.com **w** morethan4.com MD: Anthony Hamer-Hodges.

4 Tunes PO Box 36534, London W4 3XE **t** 020 8749 3210 **f** 020 8742 0399 **e** andy@4-tunes.com **w** 4-tunes.com MD: Andy Murray.

7Hz Management 57b Riding House Street, London W1W 7EF **t** 020 7436 5434 **f** 020 7436 5431 **e** barry@7hz.co.uk Director: Barry Campbell.

7pm Management PO Box 2272, Rottingdean, Brighton BN2 8XD **t** 01273 304681 **f** 01273 308120 **e** info@a7music.com **w** a7music.com Director: Seven Webster.

A Crosse The World Management PO Box 23066, London W11 3FR **t** 07956 311810 **e** the@morrighan.com **w** morrighan.com Contact: Jon X

A.M.P./TBA Level 2, 65 Newman Street, London W1T 3EG **t** 020 7224 1992 **f** 020 7224 0111 **e** mail@harveygoldsmith.com MD: Harvey Goldsmith CBE.

A1 Entertainment 40 Highfield Park Road, Bredbury, Stockport, Cheshire SK6 2PG **t** 0161 494 2098 **e** a1.entertainment@btdigitaltv.com **w** a1entertainmentshowbiz.com MD: Gill Cragen.

Abbi Frutin Management Canalot Studios, 222 Kensal Road, London W10 5BN **t** 07941 868 383 **e** abbi55555@hotmail.com MD: Abbi Frutin.

ACA Music Management 7 North Parade, Bath, Somerset BA2 4DD **t** 01225 428284 **f** 01225 400090 **e** aca_aba@freenet.co.uk MD: Harry Finegold.

Acker's International Jazz Agency 53 Cambridge Mansions, Cambridge Road, London SW11 4RX **t** 020 7978 5885 **e** pamela@ackersmusicagency.co.uk **w** ackersmusicagency.co.uk Proprietor: Pamela F Sutton.

ACT Music PO Box 164, Kendal, Cumbria LA9 4WX **t** 01539 728 872 **f** 01539 727 233 **e** val@cbsman.sagehost.co.uk MD: Val Driver.

Active Music Management Suite 401, 29 Margaret Street, London W1N 7LB **t** 087 0120 7668 **f** 087 0120 9880 **e** activemm@btopenworld.com **w** activemm.net MD: Mark Winters.

Adventures in Music Management PO Box 261, Wallingford, Oxon OX10 0XY **t** 01491 832 183 **e** info@adventuresin-music.com **w** adventure-records.com MD: Paul Conroy.

AIR (Artistes International Representation Ltd) Air House, Spennymoor, Co Durham DL16 7SE **t** 01388 814632 **f** 01388 812445 **e** info@airagency.com **w** airagency.com Director: Colin Pearson.

Aire International (Air,) 2a Ferry Road, London SW13 9RX **t** 020 8834 7373 **f** 020 8834 7474 **e** info@airmtm.com **w** airmtm.com Dir: Marc Connor.

Albert Samuel Management 42 City Business Centre, Lower Road, London SE16 2XB **t** 020 7740 1600 **f** 020 7740 1700 **e** asm@mission-control.co.uk **w** asmanagement.co.uk Director: Albert & David Samuel. Manager: Amy Styles.

Vern Allen Entertainments & Management Agency P.O Box 135, Exeter, Devon EX2 9WA **t** 01392 273305 **f** 01392 426421 **e** vern@vernallen.co.uk **w** vernallen.co.uk Dir: Vernon Winteridge.

Altered States The Zeppelin Building, 59-61 Farringdon Road, London EC1M 3JB **t** 020 7691 8688 or 020 7691 8689 **f** 020 7691 8690 **e** vanessa@alteredstates.net **w** alteredstates.net MD: Saul Galpern, Vanessa Sanders.

Amber PO Box 1, Chipping Ongar, Essex CM5 9HZ **t** 01277 362916 or 01277 365046 **e** management@amberartists.com **w** amberartists.com MD: Paul Tage.

Ambush Management 32 Ransome's Dock, 35-37 Parkgate Road, London SW11 4NP **t** 020 7801 1919 **f** 020 7738 1819 **e** alambush.native@19.co.uk **w** ambushgroup.co.uk MD: Alister Jamieson.

Nita Anderson Entertainments 165 Wolverhampton Road, Sedgley, Dudley, West Midlands DY3 1QR **t** 01902 882211 **f** 01902 883356 **e** nitaandersonagency@hotmail.com **w** nitaanderson.co.uk Contact: Juanita Anderson

Andrew Miller Promotions Int. 35 Ashcombe Street, Fulham, London SW6 3AW **t** 020 7471 4775 **f** 020 7371 5545 **e** AMPILtd@aol.co.uk **w** ampi.co.uk Dir: Faye Miller.

Anger Management PO Box 6105, Birmingham, West Midlands B43 6NZ **t** 0121 357 3338 **f** 0121 580 2642 **e** anger.1965@virgin.net Manager: Carl Bedward.

Antar Marlinspike Hall, Walpole Halesworth, Suffolk IP19 9AR **t** 01986 784 664 **f** 01986 784 666 **e** cally@antar.cc Proprietor: Cally.

ARB Music Management F5 157 Wells Rd, Bristol BS4 2BU **t** 0117 977 9917 or 07768 905238 **f** 0117 977 9917 **e** anthony.braine@arbmusic.co.uk Mgr: Anthony Braine.

Archetype Management 91 Clarendon Road, London W11 4JG **t** 020 7221 5543 **f** 020 7691 7002 **e** jon@archetype.cc **w** archetype.cc MD: Jon Terry.

Ardent Music PO Box 20078, London NW2 3FA **t** 020 7435 7706 **f** 020 7435 7712 **e** info@ardentmusic.co.uk MD: Ian Blackaby.

Arketek Management 53 Edge St, Nutgrove, St Helens, Merseyside WA9 5JX **t** 0151 430 6290 **e** info@arketek.com **w** arketek.com MD: Alan Ferreira.

Armstrong Academy Artist Management GMC Studio, Hollingbourne, Kent ME17 1UQ **t** 01622 880599 **f** 01622 880020 **e** management@triple-a.uk.com **w** triple-a.uk.com MD: Scott Armstrong.

The Art & Music Corporation Munro House, High Close, Rawdon, Leeds, West Yorkshire LS19 6HF **t** 0113 250 3338 **f** 0113 250 7343 **e** stewart@artandmusic.demon.co.uk **w** acoustic-alchemy.net MD: Stewart Coxhead.

Artist Management Group 8 King Street, Covent Garden, London WC2E 8HN **t** 020 7240 5052 **f** 020 7240 4956 **e** info@qdosentertainment.plc.uk Director: Phil Dale.

ArtistManager.com 32 St Michaels Road, Worthing BN11 4RY **t** 01903 522712 **f** 01903 210068 **e** enquiries@artistmanager.com **w** artistmanager.com MD: Nicola Cairncross.

Artists & Media Devlin House, 36 St George Street, Mayfair, London W1R 9FA **t** 07951 406 938 **e** andrian@msn.com MD: Andrian Adams. Assistant Mgr: Nick Roxton, PA to MD: Sarah Golden.

Askonas Holt (classical artists only) Lonsdale Chambers, 27 Chancery Lane, London WC2A 1PF **t** 020 7400 1700 **f** 020 7400 1799 **e** info@askonasholt.co.uk **w** askonasholt.co.uk Joint Chief Executive: Robert Rattray.

David Aspden Management The Coach House, Capel Leyse, South Holmwood, Dorking, Surrey RH5 4LJ **t** 01306 712120 **f** 01306 713241 **e** d.aspden@virgin.net MD: David Aspden.

Asylum Artists PO Box 121, Hove, East Sussex BN3 4YY **t** 01273 774468 **f** 08709 223099 **e** info@AsylumGroup.com **w** AsylumGroup.com Contact: Bob James, Steve Gilmour, Scott Chester.

Atlantis Management PO Box 1419, Croydon CR9 7XG **t** 07974 755217 **e** richardbelcher1@btopenworld.com **w** atlantismanagement.co.uk Dir: Richard Belcher.

Atomic Management Elme House, 133 Long Acre, Covent Garden, London WC2H 9DT **t** 020 7379 3010 **f** 020 7240 8272 **e** info@atomic-london.com Contact: Mick Newton

Atrium Music Burlington House, 33 South Drive, Victoria Park, Liverpool L15 8JJ **t** 0151 722 0241 or 07786 537 866 **f** 0151 424 6816 **e** atrium@blueyonder.co.uk **w** atrium-music.co.uk MD: Paula McCool.

Automatic Management 13 Cotswold Mews, 30 Battersea Square, London SW11 3RA **t** 020 7978 7888 **f** 020 7978 7808 **e** auto@automan.co.uk MD: Jerry Smith.

Autonomy Music Unit 212 The Gramophone Works, 326 Kensal Rd, London W10 5BZ **t** 020 8969 9111 **f** 020 8969 9955 **e** info@autonomy-music.co.uk **w** autonomy-music.co.uk MD: Grant Bishop.

Axis Management 42 Ferry Road, Barnes, London SW13 9PW **t** 020 7751 0199 **f** 020 7751 0199 **e** jeremy.pearce@axismanagement.net MD: Jeremy Pearce.

azoffmusic management 22 Gordon Ave, St Margarets, Twickenham, Middx TW1 1NQ **t** 020 8744 2404 **f** 020 8744 2406 **e** sarahfj22@aol.com UK Representative: Sarah Ferguson-Jones.

B&H Management PO Box 475, Amersham, Bucks HP8 4ZN **t** 01494 737414 **f** 01494 737415 **e** simon@bandhmanagement.demon.co.uk MD: Simon Harrison.

BA Management PO Box 34351, London NW6 7ZW **t** 020 7372 6648 **f** 020 7372 6673 **e** enquiries@bjornagain.com **w** bjornagain.com Dir: Rod Leissle.

Back Yard Management 106 Great Portland Street, London W1W 6PF **t** 020 7580 0999 **f** 020 7580 8882 **e** info@back-yard.co.uk Manager: Phil Catchpole.

Badger Management 4 Ormonde Gardens, Belfast BT6 9FL **t** 028 9079 1666 **e** steve@badger-management.com Contact: Stephen Orr

Banchory Management PO Box 25074, Glasgow G3 8TT **t** 0141 204 2269 **f** 0141 226 3181 **e** info@banchory.net **w** banchory.net Manager: Neil Robertson, Katrina House.

Bandana Management 100 Golborne Road, London W10 5PS **t** 020 8969 0606 **f** 020 8969 0505 **e** info@banman.co.uk **w** banman.co.uk MD: Brian Lane.

Joe Bangay Enterprises River House, Riverwoods, Marlow, Buckinghamshire SL7 1QY **t** 01628 486193 **f** 01628 890239 **e** william.b@btclick.com **w** joe-bangay.com Managing Director: Joe Bangay.

Paul Barrett (Rock 'N' Roll Enterprises) 21 Grove Terrace, Penarth, South Glamorgan CF64 2NG **t** 029 2070 4279 **f** 029 2070 9989 **e** barrettrocknroll@amserve.com MD: Paul Barrett.

Barrington Pheloung Management Andrew's, off Rand Road, High Roding, Great Dunmow CM6 1NQ **t** 01371 874 022 **f** 01371 874 110 **e** info@pheloung.co.uk Contact: Jona Cox

Bastard Management 22 Charmouth House, Dorset Road, London SW8 1EU **t** 020 7582 5532 **e** bastardmgt@hotmail.com MD: Alex Holland.

The Bechhofer Agency 51 Barnton Park View, Edinburgh EH4 6HH **t** 0131 339 4083 **f** 0131 339 9261 **e** agency@bechhofer.demon.co.uk **w** bechhoferagency.com Contact: Frank Bechhofer

Bedlam Management PO Box 34449, London W6 0RT **t** 07855 528 672 **e** giselle.allier@bedlammanagement.com MD: Steven Abbott.

Beetroot Management 3/4 Portland Mews, D'Arblay Street, London W1F 8JF **t** 020 7437 7889 **f** 020 7734 9230 **e** info@beetrootmusic.com **w** beetrootmusic.com Assistant Manager: Annabel Burn.

Bermuda Management Matrix Complex, 91 Peterborough Road, London SW6 3BU **t** 020 7371 5444 **f** 020 7371 5454 **e** paul@crownmusic.co.uk MD: Paul Samuels.

Best Kept Secret Queens Wharf, Queen Caroline Street, London W6 9RJ **t** 020 8600 2664 **e** info@bestkeptsecret.uk.com **w** bestkeptsecret.uk.com GM: Nick Matthews.

Big Blue Music Windy Ridge, 39-41 Buck Lane, London NW9 0AP **t** 020 8205 2990 **f** 020 8205 2990 **e** info@bigbluemusic.biz **w** bigbluemusic.biz Manager: Steve Ancliffe.

Big Brother Management PO Box 1288, Gerrards Cross, Buckinghamshire SL9 9YB **t** 01753 880873 **f** 01753 892879 **e** richard.allen@delerium.co.uk Manager: Richard Allen.

Big Dipper Productions 3rd Floor, 29-31 Cowper Street, London EC2A 4AT **t** 020 7608 4591 **f** 020 7608 4599 **e** john@bestest.co.uk Dirs: John Best, Dean O'Connor.

Big Help Music Deppers Bridge Farm, Southam, Warwicks CV47 2SZ **t** 01926 614640 or 07782 172 101 **e** dutch@bighelpmusic.com **w** bighelpmusic.com MD: Dutch Van Spall.

Big Life Management 67-69 Chalton Street, London NW1 1HY **t** 020 7554 2100 **f** 020 7554 2154 **e** biglife@biglife.co.uk **w** biglife.co.uk MD: Jazz Summers.

Big M Productions Thatched Rest, Queen Hoo Lane, Tewin, Herts AL6 0LT **t** 01438 798395 **f** 01438 798395 **e** joyce@bigmgroup.freeserve.co.uk **w** martywilde.com MD: Joyce Wilde.

Big Out 27 Smithwood Close, Wimbledon, London SW19 6JL **t** 020 8780 0085 or 07703 165146 **f** 020 8785 4004 **e** BigOutLtd@aol.com **w** enrap-ture.com MD: Louise Porter.

Bizarre Management 29 Halifax Road, Enfield, Middlesex EN2 0PP **t** 020 8351 0872 **f** 020 8351 0872 **e** matthias@siefert.freeserve.co.uk MD: Matthias Siefert.

BKO Productions The Old Truman Brewery, 91 Brick Lane, London E1 6QL **t** 020 7377 9373 **f** 020 7377 6523 **e** byron@bko-alarcon.co.uk Director: Byron K. Orme.

Black and White Indians PO Box 706, Ilford, Essex IG2 6ED **t** 07973 676160 **f** 020 7323 9008 **e** bij@btinternet.com Owner: Bijal Dodhia.

Black Magic Management 296 Earls Court Road, London SW5 9BA **t** 020 7565 0806 **f** 020 7565 0806 **e** blackmagicrecords@talk21.com **w** blackmagicrecords.com MD: Mataya Clifford.

Terry Blamey Management PO Box 13196, London SW6 4WF **t** 020 7371 7627 **f** 020 7731 7578 **e** info@TerryBlamey.com Assistant Manager: Alli MacGregor.

Blind Faith Management 1 Allevard, Blackrock Road, Cork, Ireland **t** +353 21 4321 508 **f** +353 21 4321 508 **e** blindfaith@iol.ie **w** junofalls.com MD: Gerald O'Leary.

Blue Sky Entertainment 60 Kingly St, London W1B 5DS **t** 020 7453 4327 **f** 020 7453 4185 **e** info@blue-sky.uk.com Managers: Gordon Biggins.

Blue Stack Music 52 Abbott Avenue, London SW20 8SQ **t** 020 8540 3350 **f** 020 8540 3350 **e** bluestack@hotmail.com **w** countrymusic.org.uk/heartfield Prop: Angela Williams.

Blueprint Management PO Box 593, Woking, Surrey GU23 7YF **t** 01483 715336 **f** 01483 757490 **e** blueprint@lineone.net Dirs: John Glover/Matt Glover.

Blujay Management 55 Loudoun Road, St Johns Wood, London NW8 0DL **t** 020 7604 3633 **f** 020 7604 3639 **e** info@blujay.co.uk Mgrs: Steve Tannett, Carly Martin.

Roger Boden Management 2 Gawsworth Road, Macclesfield, Cheshire SK11 8UE **t** 01625 420163 **f** 01625 420168 **e** rbm@cottagegroup.co.uk **w** cottagegroup.co.uk MD: Roger Boden.

Bodo Music Co Ashley Road, Hale, Altrincham, Cheshire WA15 9SF **t** 07939 521 465 **f** 0161 928 8136 MD: FL Marshall.

Bold Management Ground Floor, 39 Mowbray Road, London NW6 7QS **t** 020 8830 2655 **f** 020 8964 8882 **e** jayne@boldmanagement.com MD: Jayne Griffiths.

Bond Management 500 Chiswick High Road, London W4 5RG **t** 020 8956 2785 **f** 020 8956 2786 **e** bondmgt@dial.pipex.com Dirs: Jon Barlow, Leonard Lowe.

Boom Management Cranhurst Lodge, 37-39 Surbiton Hill Road, Surbiton, Surrey KT6 4TS **t** 020 8786 2121 **f** 020 8786 2123 **e** info@boommanagement.com **w** boommanagement.com Director: Ian Titchener.

The Bootleg Beatles 10 Barley Mow Passage, London W4 4PH **t** 020 8994 8397 **f** 020 8742 7684 **e** bbeatles@atlas.co.uk **w** bootlegbeatles.com Company Manager: Raj Patel.

Boss Music 7 Jeffrey's Place, Camden, London NW1 9PP **t** 020 7284 2554 **f** 020 7284 2560 **e** info@bossmusic.net **w** bossmusic.net MD: Andy Ross.

Derek Boulton Management 76 Carlisle Mansions, Carlisle Place, London SW1P 1HZ **t** 020 7828 6533 **f** 020 7828 1271 MD: Derek Boulton.

BPR Productions 36 Como Street, Romford, Essex RM7 7DR **t** 01708 725330 **f** 01708 725322 **e** bprmusic@compuserve.com **w** bprmusic.com MD: Brian Theobald.

Tony Bramwell 9 Brooking Barn, Ashprington, Totnes, Devon TQ9 7UL **t** 07762 583489 Director: Tony Bramwell.

Braw Management 31 Hartington Place, Edinburgh EH10 4LF **t** 0131 221 0011 **f** 0131 221 1313 **e** brawmusic@yahoo.com Manager: Kenny MacDonald.

Brenda Brooker Enterprises 9 Cork Street, Mayfair, London W1S 3LL **t** 020 7544 2893 **e** BrookerB@aol.com MD: Brenda Brooker.

Brilliant 19 32 Ransomes Dock, 35-37 Parkgate Road, London SW11 4NP **t** 020 7801 1919 **f** 020 7738 1819 **e** reception@19.co.uk MD: Nick Godwyn.

Broken Star Management 10 St Marys Close, Gt Plumstead, Norwich NR13 5EY **t** 01603 712495 **f** 01603 712495 **e** management@brokenstar.co.uk **w** brokenstar.co.uk Manager: Jon Luton.

Gerry Bron Management 17 Priory Road, London NW6 4NN **t** 020 7209 2766 **f** 020 7813 2766 **e** gerrybron@easynet.co.uk **w** gerrybron.com MD: Gerry Bron.

Brotherhood Of Man Management Westfield, 75 Burkes Road, Beaconsfield, Buckinghamshire HP9 1PP **t** 01494 673073 **f** 01494 680920 **e** agency@brotherhoodofman.co.uk **w** brotherhoodofman.co.uk

Brown McLeod 51 Clarkegrove Road, Sheffield, South Yorks S10 2NH **t** 0114 268 5665 **f** 0114 268 4161 **e** entsuk@aol.com MD: John Roddison.

BTM PO Box 6003, Birmingham, West Midlands B45 0AR **t** 0121 477 9553 **f** 0121 693 2954 **e** BT@barrytomes.com **w** gotham-records.com Proprietor: Barry Tomes.

Bulldozer Management 8 Roland Mews, Stepney Green, London E1 3JT **t** 020 7377 9494 **f** 020 7377 9868 **e** oliver@bulldozermedia.com **w** bulldozermedia.com MD: Oliver J. Brown.

Mel Bush Organization Tanglewood, Arrowsmith Road, Wimborne, Dorset BH21 3BG **t** 01202 691891 **f** 01202 691896 **e** mbobmth@aol.com **w** davidessex.com & bond-music.com MD: Mel Bush.

But! Management Walsingham Cottage, 7 Sussex Square, Brighton, E. Sussex BN2 1FJ **t** 01273 680799 **e** allan.james1@virgin.net MD: Allan James.

Buzz Artist Management 14 Corsiehill Road, Perth PH2 7BZ **t** 01738 638140 **f** 01738 638140 **e** management@thebuzzgroup.co.uk **w** thebuzzgroup.co.uk MD: Dave Arcari.

CA Management Air Studios, Lyndhurst Road, London NW3 5NG **t** 020 7794 0660 **f** 020 7916 2784 **e** adam@camanagement.co.uk MD: Adam Sharp.

Caleche Studios 175 Roundhay Road, Leeds LS8 5AN **t** 0113 249 4941 **f** 0113 249 4941 **e** calechestudios@ntlworld.com MD: Leslie Coleman.

Cambrian Entertainments International 24 Titan Court, Laporte Way, Luton LU4 8EF **t** 0870 200 5000 **f** 01582 488877 **e** mailbox@cambrian.tv **w** cambrian.tv Director: Robin Breese-Davies.

Carol & Associates 57 Meadowbank, Bushy Park Road, Dublin 6, Ireland **t** +353 1 490 9339 or +353 1 660 5588 **f** +353 1 492 1100 **e** carolh@indigo.ie MD: Carol Hanna.

Hal Carter Organisation 101 Hazelwood Lane, Palmers Green, London N13 5HQ **t** 020 8886 2801 **f** 020 8882 7380 **e** artistes@halcarterorg.com **w** halcarterorg.co.uk Managing Director: Hal Carter.

CBL 1 Glenthorne Mews, 115A Glenthorne Road, London W6 0LJ **t** 020 8748 5036 **f** 020 8748 3356 **e** mail@clivebanks.com **w** clivebanks.com Management Assistant: Caroline Stewart.

CEC Management 65-69 White Lion Street, London N1 9PP **t** 020 7837 2517 **f** 020 7727 8915 **e** cec@cecmanagement.com MD: Peter Felstead.

Cent Management PO Box 2642, Wells BA5 2WX **t** 01749 677711 **f** 01749 670315 **e** info@centmanagement.com **w** centgroup.biz Manager: Shellie Newstead.

Chantelle Music 3A Ashfield Parade, London N14 5EH **t** 020 8886 6236 **e** info@chantellemusic.co.uk **w** chantellemusic.co.uk MD: Riss Chantelle.

Charabanc Music Management 18 Sparkle Street, Manchester M1 2NA **t** 0161 273 5554 **f** 0161 273 5554 **e** charabanc@btconnect.com **w** charabanc.net Manager: Richard Lynch.

Charmenko 46 Spenser Road, London SE24 0NR **t** 020 7274 6618 **e** nick@charmenko.net **w** charmenko.net MD: Nick Hobbs.

Choir Connexion & London Community Gospel Choir Brookdale House, 75 Brookdale Road, Walthamstow, London E17 6QH **t** 020 8509 7288 **f** 020 8509 7299 **e** choirconnexion@btconnect.com **w** lcgc.org.uk Principle: Bazil Meade.

Chris Griffin Management 69 Shakespeare Road, London W7 1LU **t** 07973 883 159 **f** 020 8357 9047 **e** chris@crgriffin.demon.co.uk Contact: Chris Griffin

Chunk Management 97a Scrubs Lane, London NW10 6QU **t** 020 8960 1331 **f** 020 8968 3377 **e** info@chunkmanagement.com **w** chunkmanagement.com MD: Mike Nelson.

Chute P.O. Box 211, Dundee DD1 9PH **t** 07941 286 555 **e** jan.burnett10@ntlworld.com Manager: Jan D Burnett.

Clarion/Seven Muses (Classical Artist Management) 47 Whitehall Park, London N19 3TW **t** 020 7272 4413 or 020 7272 5125 **f** 020 7281 9687 **e** admin@c7m.co.uk **w** c7m.co.uk Partners: Caroline Oakes, Nicholas Curry.

Clever Cherry Victoria Works, Birmingham, West Midlands B1 3PQ **t** 0121 236 1060 **e** info@clevercherry.com **w** clevercherry.com MD: Ian Allen.

Clown Management P.O Box 20432, London SE17 3WT **t** 07986 359 568 **e** office@clownmediagroup.co.uk **w** clownmediagroup.co.uk A&R: Stephen Adams.

CMO Management International Studio 2.6, Rockley Road, London W14 0DA **t** 020 7316 6969 **f** 020 7316 6970 **e** info@cmomanagement.co.uk **w** cmomanagement.co.uk MD: Chris Morrison.

Coalition Management Devonshire House, 12 Barley Mow Passage, London W4 4PH **t** 020 8987 0123 **f** 020 8987 0345 **e** management@coalitiongroup.co.uk Contact: Tim Vigon/ Tony Perrin

Coda Management UK 8 Grosvenor Heights, 2 Wyndham Road, Lower Parkstone, Poole, Dorset BH14 8SR **t** 01202 741816 **f** 01202 741816 **e** bazatcoda@onetel.net.uk MD: Barry Davies.

Raymond Coffer Management PO Box 595, Bushey, Herts WD23 1PZ **t** 020 8420 4430 **f** 020 8950 7617 **e** raymond.coffer@btopenworld.com Contact: Raymond Coffer

Coldplay Management Clearwater Yard, 35 Inverness Street, London NW1 7HB **t** 020 7424 7513 **f** 020 7424 7551 **e** ewilkinson@dcmhq.com; htickett@dcmhq.com Manager: Estelle Wilkinson. Asst. Manager: Holly Tickett.

Collaboration 33 Montpellier Street, Brighton, East Sussex BN1 3DL **t** 01273 730744 **f** 01273 775134 **e** nikki@collaborationuk.com **w** collaborationuk.com MD: Nikki Neave.

Conception Artist Management 40 Newman Street, London W1T 1QD **t** 020 7580 4424 **f** 020 7323 1695 **e** info@conception.gb.com MD: Jean-Nicol Chelmiah.

Congo Music 17A Craven Park Road, Harlsden, London NW10 8SE **t** 020 8961 5461 **f** 020 8961 5461 **e** congomusic@hotmail.com **w** congomusic.com A&R Director: Root Jackson.

Connected Artists P.O.Box 46758, London SW17 9YE **t** 020 8682 2460 **f** 020 8682 2460 **e** paul@connectedartists.com MD: Paul McDonald.

Consigliari 18 Hackford Walk, Hackford Road, London SW9 0QT **t** 020 7587 3799 **f** 020 7587 3818 **e** info@consigliari.com Contact: Mark Melton/Sarah Blain

Console Sounds PO Box 7515, Glasgow G41 3ZW **t** 0141 636 6336 **f** 0141 636 6336 **e** info@consolesounds.co.uk **w** consolesounds.co.uk Dir: Stevie Middleton.

Cool Badge Management Office 604, Oxford House, 49A Oxford Road, London N4 3EY **t** 020 7272 3870 **f** 020 7272 3871 **e** Russell@CoolBadge.com **w** coolbadge.com MD: Russell Yates.

Martin Coull Management 65A Dundas Street, Edinburgh EH3 6RS **t** 0131 557 5330 or 07803 137509 **f** 0131 557 1050 **e** marticoull@aol.com Proprietor: Martin Coull.

Courtyard Management 21 The Nursery, Sutton Courtenay, Oxon OX14 4UA **t** 01235 845800 **f** 01235 847692 **e** kate@cyard.com Partner: Chris Hufford.

Craig Huxley Management 13 Christchurch Road, London N8 9QL **t** 020 8374 9133 **f** 020 8292 1205 **e** craighuxleymusic@blueyonder.co.uk Proprietor: Craig Huxley.

Crashed Music 162 Church Road, East Wall, Dublin 3, Ireland **t** +353 1 888 1188 **f** +353 1 856 1122 **e** info@crashedmusic.com **w** crashedmusic.com MD: Shay Hennessy.

Crazel Town Unit 20 Monpelier Court, Station Road, Bristol BS6 5EE **t** 0117 942 6677 **f** 0117 942 6677 **e** matt@crazeltown.com **w** crazeltown.com Manager: Matt Booth.

Creation Management 2 Berkley Grove, Primrose Hill, London NW1 8XY **t** 020 7483 2541 **f** 020 7722 8412 **e** info@creationmngt.com MD: Stephen King.

Creative Music Management Unit 53, Simla House, Weston St, London SE1 3RN **t** 020 7378 1642 **f** 020 7378 1642 **e** general@creativepruk.com CEO: Dave Norton.

Creative World Entertainment The Croft, Deanslade Farm, Claypit Lane, Lichfield, Staffordshire WS14 0AG **t** 01543 253576 or 07885 341745 **f** 01543 255184 **e** info@creative-world-entertainment.co.uk **w** creative-world-entertainment.co.uk MD: Mervyn Spence.

Crisis Management The Old Granary, Ammerham, Somerset TA20 4LB **t** 01460 30846 **e** ronnie@crisis-management.org Dirs: Ronnie Gleeson, Meredith Cork.

Cromwell Management 4-5 High Street, Huntingdon, Cambridgeshire PE29 3TE **t** 01480 435600 **f** 01480 356250 **e** tricvic@lineone.net **w** jazzmanagement.ic24.net Managing Partner: Vic Gibbons.

Crown Music Management Services Matrix Complex, 91 Peterborough Road, London SW6 3BU **t** 020 7371 5444 **f** 020 7371 5454 **e** mark@crownmusic.co.uk MD: Mark Hargreaves.

Cruisin' Music Charlton Farm Studios, Hemington, Bath BA3 5XS **t** 01373 834161 **f** 01373 834164 **e** sil@cruisin.co.uk **w** cruisin.co.uk MD: Sil Willcox. ISDN: 01323 834159.

Cultural Foundation Hollin Bush, Dalehead, Rosedale, North Yorkshire YO18 8RL **t** 01751 417147 or 0845 4584699 **f** 01751 417804 **e** info@cultfound.org **w** cultfound.org MD: Peter Bell.

David Curtis Management Priors Hall, Tye Green, Elsenham, Bishop Stortford, Hertfordshire CM22 6DY **t** 01279 813240 **f** 01279 815895 **e** procentral@aol.com **w** pasadena.co.uk Director: David Curtis.

D2mm (Direct2 Music Management) 3, 6 Belsize Crescent, Belsize Park, London NW3 5QU **t** 020 7431 1609 or 07939 028 466 **f** 020 7431 1609 **e** david@d2mm.com **w** d2mm.com Director: David Otzen.

Daddy Management 15 Holywell Row, London EC2A 4JB **t** 020 7684 5219 **f** 020 7684 5230 **e** paul@daddymanagement.net MD: Paul Benney.

Dara Management Unit 4, Great Ship Street, Dublin 8, Ireland **t** +353 1 478 3455 **f** +353 1 478 2143 **e** irishmus@ioe.ie **w** irelandcd.com MD: Joe O'Reilly.

Dark Blues Management Puddephats, Markyate, Herts AL3 8AZ **t** 01582 842226 **f** 01582 840010 **e** info@darkblues.co.uk **w** darkblues.co.uk Office Mgr: Fiona Hewetson.

David Jaymes Associates (see Spirit Music & Media)

Lena Davis John Bishop Associates Cotton's Farmhouse, Whiston Road, Cogenhoe, Northamptonshire NN7 1NL **t** 01604 891487 **f** 01604 890405 Contact: Lena Davis

Davix Management Suite D, 67 Abbey Road, St John's Wood, London NW8 0AE **t** 020 7724 2635 **f** 020 7724 2635 **e** davix@gorgeousmusic.net **w** gorgeousmusic.net Artist Manager: Victoria Elliott.

Daytime Entertainments The Roundhouse, 91 Saffron Hill, Farringdon, London EC1N 8QP **t** 07973 479 191 **e** diane@daytime-ent.com MD: Diane Young.

DCM International Suite 3, 294-296 Nether Street, Finchley, London N3 1RJ **t** 020 8343 0848 **f** 020 8343 0747 **e** dancecm@aol.com **w** dancecrazy.co.uk MD: Kelly Isaacs.

Dellphonic Management 112 Bathurst Gardens, London NW10 5HX **t** 020 8969 2657 **f** 020 8969 2657 **e** dickodell@hotmail.com **w** dellphonic.com Artist Mgr: Dick O'Dell.

Deluxe Management PO Box 5753, Nottingham NG2 7WN **t** 0115 941 9401 **f** 0115 958 7197 **e** management@deluxeaudio.com MD: Nick Gordon Brown.

Deluxxe Management PO Box 373, Teddington, Middx TW11 8ZQ **t** 020 8755 3630 or 07771 861 054 **f** 020 8404 7771 **e** info@deluxxe.co.uk **w** deluxxe.co.uk MD: Diane Wagg.

Wally Dent Entertainments 121A Woodlands Avenue, West Byfleet, Surrey KT14 6AS **t** 01932 347885 or 01932 351444 **f** 01932 336229 **e** wallydent@hotmail.com MD: Wally Dent.

Tony Denton Promotions 19 South Molton Lane, London W1Y 1AQ **t** 020 7629 4666 **f** 020 7629 4777 **e** mail@tdpromo.com **w** tdpromo.com Director: Tony Denton.

Deuce Management 178b Venner Road, Sydenham, London SE26 5JQ **t** 020 8325 7337 or 0780 326 0255 **e** rob.saunders13@ntlworld.com **w** sungover.com MD: Rob Saunders.

Deutsch-Englische Freundschaft 51 Lonsdale Road, Queens Park, London NW6 6RA **t** 020 7328 2922 **f** 020 7328 2322 **e** info@d-e-f.com Mgr: Eric Harle.

Devolution Management 25 Pinehurst Court, Colville Gardens, London W11 2BH **t** 020 7229 5021 **f** 020 7229 5021 **e** info@devolution.freeserve.co.uk MD: Geremy O'Mahony.

DGM Management PO Box 1533, Salisbury, Wiltshire SP5 5ER **t** 01722 780187 **f** 01722 781042 **e** dgm@dgmhq.com **w** disciplineglobalmobile.com MD: David Singleton.

Diamond Sounds Music Management The Fox and Punchbowl, Burfield Rd, Old Windsor, Berks SL4 2RD **t** 01753 855420 **f** 01753 855420 **e** samueldsm@aol.com **w** wildthymeproductions.com Director: Julie Samuel.

Theobald Dickson Productions The Coach House, Swinhope Hall, Swinhope, Market Rasen, Lincolnshire LN8 6HT **t** 01472 399011 **f** 01472 399025 **e** tdproductions@lineone.net **w** barbaradickson.net MD: Bernard Theobald.

Direct Heat Management PO Box 1345, Worthing, West Sussex BN12 7FB **t** 01903 202426 **f** 01903 202426 **e** dhm@happyvibes.co.uk **w** happyvibes.co.uk MD: Mike Pailthorpe.

Divine Management 1 Cowcross Street, London EC1M 6DR **t** 020 7490 7271 **f** 020 7490 7273 **e** info@divinemanagement.co.uk Manager: Natalie de Pace.

DJT Management PO Box 229, Sheffield, South Yorkshire S1 1LY **t** 0114 250 9775 **f** 0114 258 3164 **e** dtaylor@djtmanagement.freeserve.co.uk Director: David Taylor.

DNA Artist Management Unit 3, St Mary Road, London E17 9RG **t** 020 8520 1188 **f** 020 8520 2514 **e** dna_management@hotmail.com MD: Debra Thompson.

Domain Music Unit 9, TGEC, Town Hall Approach Road, London N15 4RX **t** 020 8375 3608 **f** 020 8375 3487 **e** info@domainmusic.co.uk **w** domainmusic.co.uk Dir: Michael Lowe.

David Dorrell Management 2nd Floor, Lyme Wharf, 191 Royal College St, London NW1 0SG **t** 0870 420 5088 **f** 0870 420 5188 **e** shane@dorrellmanagement.com Contact: Shane Egan

Steve Draper Entertainments 2 The Coppice, Beardwood Manor, Blackburn, Lancashire BB2 7BQ **t** 01254 679005 **f** 01254 679005 **e** steve@stevedraperents.fsbusiness.co.uk **w** stevedraper.co.uk Owner: Steve Draper.

Dreaded Sunny Day Music 5 St. John's Lane, London EC1M 4BH **t** 020 7549 2807 **e** info@dreadedsunnyday.com **w** dreadedsunnyday.com MD: Mark Jackson.

Dreamscape Management 18A Green Court, Green Lane, Edgware, Middx HA8 7PP **t** 07930 732239 **f** 01727 826308 **e** dreamscape25@hotmail.com MD: Adam C Lamb.

Dreem Teem Millmead Business Centre 86, Millmead Ind Estate, Millmead Road, London N17 9QU **t** 020 8801 8800 **f** 020 8801 4800 **e** viveka@urbanhousemusic.com **w** urbanhousemusic.com Mgr: Viveka Nilsson. Bookings: Terri Lynch.

The Dune Music Company 1st Floor, 73 Canning Road, Harrow, Middx HA3 7SP **t** 020 8424 2807 **f** 020 8861 5371 **e** info@dune-music.com **w** dune-music.com MD: Janine Irons.

Duroc Media Riverside House, 10-12 Victoria Road, Uxbridge, Middx UB8 2TW **t** 01895 810831 **f** 01895 231499 **e** info@durocmedia.com **w** durocmedia.com MD: Simon Porter.

Duty Free Artist Management 3rd Floor, 67 Farringdon Road, London EC1M 3JB **t** 020 7831 9931 **f** 020 7831 9331 **e** info@dutyfreerecordings.co.uk **w** dutyfreerecords.com Booking Agent: Sacha Hearn.

DWL (Dave Woolf) 53 Goodge Street, London W1T 1TG **t** 020 7436 5529 **f** 020 7637 8776 **e** dave@dwl.uk.net MD: Dave Woolf.

Barry Dye Entertainments PO Box 888, Ipswich, Suffolk IP1 6BU **t** 01473 744287 **f** 01473 745442 **e** barrydye@aol.com **w** barrydyents.co.uk Proprietor: Barry Dye.

Dyfel Management 19 Fontwell Drive, Bickley, Bromley, Kent BR2 8AB **t** 020 8467 9605 **f** 020 8249 1972 **e** jean@dyfel.co.uk **w** dyfel.co.uk MD: J Dyne.

Dynamik Music PO Box 32146, London N4 3AX **t** 020 7272 0090 **f** 020 7171 0101 **e** giles@dynamik-music.com **w** dynamik-music.com MD: Giles Goodman.

Earth Music 50 Hadley Road, Barnet, Herts EN5 5QR **t** 020 8441 3247 **f** 020 8441 0163 **e** ricky@audiojelly.com **w** audiojelly.com Manager: Ricky Simmonds.

Easy Street Artist Management 333 Millbrook Road, Southampton, Hampshire SO15 0HW **t** 023 8078 0088 **f** 023 8078 0099 **e** jay@easyst.co.uk **w** easyst.co.uk Dir: Jason Thomas.

ECI Management PO Box 589, London SE6 4PU **t** 020 8690 6515 **f** 020 8690 6515 **e** macjaja@aol.com Director: R Mac.

Eclipse-PJM PO Box 3059, South Croydon, Surrey CR2 8TL **t** 020 8657 2627 or 07798 651691 **f** 020 8657 2627 **e** eclipsepjm@btinternet.com MD: Paul Johnson.

Effective Management 16 Stratford Rd, London W8 6QD **t** 020 7937 6246 or 07808 741 277 **f** 020 7937 6246 **e** henriette@effectivemusicservices.com Contact: Henriette Amiel

EG Management PO Box 4397, London W1A 7RZ **t** 020 8540 9935 A&R: Chris Kettle.

ELA Management (See Wild West Management)

Eleven Clements Yard , Iliffe St, London SE17 3LJ **t** 020 7820 1262 **f** 020 7820 1846 **e** eleven@dsl.pipex.com Contact: Dave Bedford, Ruth Starns.

Elite Beats Management 23 Burleigh House, St. Charles Square, London W10 6HB **t** 020 8964 4313 **f** 07092 361057 **e** simon@elitebeats.com **w** elitebeats.com Manager: Simon Sutcliffe.

Elite Squad Management Valtony, Loxwood Road, Plaistow, W Sussex RH14 0NY **t** 01403 871200 **f** 01403 871334 **e** tony@elitesquad.freeserve.co.uk MD: Tony Nunn.

Emkay Entertainments Nobel House, Regent Centre, Blackness Road, Linlithgow, Lothian EH49 7HU **t** 01506 845555 **f** 01506 845566 **e** admin@emkayentertainments.com **w** emkayentertainments.com Proprietor: Mike Kean.

Emperor Management 2 Brayburne Ave, London SW4 6AA **t** 020 7720 0826 **f** 020 7720 1869 **e** john.empson@btopenworld.com MD: John Empson.

Empire Artist Management The Blue Building, 42-46 St Lukes Mews, Notting Hill, London W11 1DG **t** 020 7221 1133 **f** 020 7221 1144 **e** marie@empire-management.co.uk Dir: Neale Easterby, Richard Ramsey.

ENC Productions The Clockhouse, 2nd Floor, 220 Latimer Road, London W10 6QY **t** 020 8962 8888 **f** 020 8964 0620 **e** lizzie.enc@virgin.net MD: Lizzie Francis.

ePM Unit 204, The Saga Centre, 326 Kensal Road, London W10 5BZ **t** 020 8964 4900 **f** 020 8962 9783 **e** oliver@electronicpm.co.uk **w** electronicpm.co.uk Partner: Oilver Way.

Escape Music Management 45 Endymion Road, London SW2 2BU **t** 0871 474 2956 **f** 0870 458 0272 **e** mail@escapeman.com **w** escapeman.com MD: Robert Davies.

Essential Entertainments 9 Church Street, Brighton, East Sussex BN1 1US **t** 01273 888787 **f** 01273 888780 **e** info@essentialents.com Contact: Ish Ali

Eurock First Floor, 5 Cope Street, Temple Bar, Dublin 2, Ireland **t** +353 1 672 8001 **f** +353 1 672 8005 **e** gforce@indigo.ie MD: Brian O'Kelly.

European Arts & Media 11-12 Warrington Place, Dublin 2, Ireland **t** +353 1 664 4700 **f** +353 1 664 4747 **e** info@euroartsmedia.com **w** euroartsmedia.com Dir: Nigel Tebay.

Evolution Management 13 Haldane Close, London N10 2PB **t** 020 8883 4486 **e** evomgt@aol.com MD: John Brice.

Excession: The Agency 242 Acklam Road, London W10 5JJ **t** 020 7524 7676 **f** 020 7524 7677 **e** bookings@excession.co.uk **w** excession.co.uk MD: Tara Morgan.

Expression Management 3D Park Mews, 213 Kilburn Lane, London W10 4BQ **t** 020 8960 5801 **f** 020 8960 0784 **e** info@manzanera.com **w** manzanera.com Director: Phil Manzanera.

Extreme Music Production 4-7 Forewoods Common, Holt, Wilts BA14 6PJ **t** 01225 782984 or 07909 995011 **e** george@xtrememusic.co.uk **w** xtrememusic.co.uk MD: George Allen.

F&G Management Unit A105, 326 Kensal Road, London W10 5BZ **t** 020 8964 1917 **f** 020 8960 9971 **e** gavino@btclick.com **w** fgmusica.com MD: Gavino Prunas.

Faithless Live PO Box 17336, London NW5 4WP **t** 020 7428 0495 **f** 020 7267 3889 **e** aubrey@faithless.co.uk **w** faithless.co.uk MD: Aubrey Nunn.

Fanatic Management PO Box 153, Stanmore, Middx HA7 2HF **t** 01923 896 975 **f** 01923 896 985 **e** hrano@fan-fair.freeserve.co.uk MD: Mike Hrano.

FBI Routenburn House, Routenburn Road, Largs, Strathclyde KA30 8SQ **t** 01475 673392 or 0795 729 2054 **f** 01475 674075 **e** wbrown8152@aol.com Owner: Willie Brown.

Feedback Communications The Court, Long Sutton, Hook, Hampshire RG29 1TA **t** 01256 862865 **f** 01256 862182 **e** feedback@crapola.com **w** crapola.com Management: Keir Jens-Smith.

Malcolm Feld Agency Malina House, Sandforth Road, Liverpool, Merseyside L12 1JY **t** 0151 259 6565 **f** 0151 259 5006 **e** malcolm@malcolmfeld.co.uk **w** malcolmfeld.co.uk Agent/Manager/Promoter: Malcolm Feld.

Fifth Element Artist Management 258 Belsize Road, London NW6 4BT **t** 020 7372 2128 **f** 020 7624 3629 **e** info@fifthelement.biz **w** fifthelement.biz Directors: Cath Hockley/Chris Hewlett.

Fintage House 36-38 Westbourne Grove, Newton Road, London W2 5SH **t** 020 7313 9977 **f** 020 7221 0033 **e** entertainment.assets@fintagehouse.com **w** fintagehouse.com Contact: George Helyer, Suzanne Plesman

Firebrand Management 12 Rickett Street, London SW6 1RU **t** 020 7381 2375 or 07885 282165 **e** vernfire@aol.com MD: Mark Vernon.

First Column Management 34 West Street, Brighton, East Sussex BN1 2RE **t** 01273 724710 **f** 01273 736004 **e** fcm@firstcolumn.co.uk Director: Phil Nelson.

First Move Management 137 Shooters Hill Road, Blackheath, London SE3 8UQ **t** 020 8305 2077 or 07717 475 433 **f** 020 8305 2077 **e** firstmoves@aol.com **w** firstmove.biz Creative Director: Janis MacIlwaine.

First Time Management Sovereign House, 12 Trewartha Road, Praa Sands, Penzance, Cornwall TR20 9ST **t** 01736 762826 or 07721 449477 **f** 01736 763328 **e** panamus@aol.com **w** songwriters-guild.co.uk MD: Roderick Jones.

FiveMilesHigh 17 Maidavale Crescent, Styvechale, Coventry CV3 6FZ **t** 07811 469888 **e** dave@fivemileshigh.com MD: Dave Robinson.

Flamecracker Management PO Box 394, Hemel Hempstead HP3 9WL **t** 01442 403445 **f** 01442 403445 **e** kdavis@aol.com **w** frantik.org Manager: Karen Davis.

Flamencovision 54 Windsor Road, Finchley, London N3 3SS **t** 020 8346 4500 **f** 020 8346 2488 **e** hvmartin@dircon.co.uk **w** flamencovision.com MD: Helen Martin.

Flamingo Record Management Thornhurst Place, Rowplatt Lane, Felbridge, East Grinstead RH19 2PA **t** 01342 317943 **f** 01342 317943 **e** ed@badgerflamingoanimation.co.uk **w** badgerflamingoanimation.co.uk MD: Ed Palmieri.

Flick Productions PO Box 888, Penzance, Cornwall TR20 8ZP **t** 01736 788798 **f** 01736 787898 **e** Flickprouk@aol.com **w** flickpro.co.uk MD: Mark Shaw.

Float Your Boat Productions 5 Ralphs Retreat, Hazlemere, High Wycombe, Bucks HP15 7DU **t** 07958 415784 **e** melinda@zore.co.uk Manager: Melinda Lawler.

The Flying Music Co FM House, 110 Clarendon Road, London W11 2HR **t** 020 7221 7799 **f** 020 7221 5016 **e** info@flyingmusic.co.uk **w** flyingmusic.com Contact: Derek Nicol, Paul Walden

Fools Paradise 15 Hartland Rd, London NW6 6BG **t** 07973 297 124 **e** julian@fools-paradise.co.uk Manager: Julian Nugent.

Formidable Management 4th Floor, 40 Langham Street, London W1W 7AS **t** 020 7323 4410 or 07939 140 774 **e** carl@formidable-mgmt.com **w** formidable-mgmt.com Dir: Carl Marcantonio.

FourFives Productions 21d Heathman's Road, London SW6 4TJ **t** 020 7731 6555 **f** 020 7371 5005 **e** mp@fourfives-music.com **w** fourfives-music.com Dir: Andrew Greasley.

Fox Records (Management) 62 Lake Rise, Romford, Essex RM1 4EE **t** 01708 760544 **f** 01708 760563 **e** foxrecords@talk21.com **w** foxrecordsltd.co.uk Director: Colin Brewer.

Frannyman Music PO Box 3418, Sheffield S11 7WJ **t** 0114 2685441 **f** 0114 2685441 **e** info@frannyman.com **w** frannyman.com Owner: Barney Vernon.

Freedom Management 218 Canalot Studios, 222 Kensal Road, London W10 5BN **t** 020 8960 4443 **f** 020 8960 9889 **e** freedom@frdm.co.uk MD: Martyn Barter.

Freshwater Hughes Management PO Box 54, Northaw, Herts EN6 4PY **t** 01707 661431 or 020 8245 0679 **f** 01707 664141 **e** fresh@btconnect.com or hughesee@tiscali.co.uk Contact: Jackie Hughes, Brian Freshwater

Friars Management 33 Alexander Road, Aylesbury, Buckinghamshire HP20 2NR **t** 01296 434731 **f** 01296 422530 **e** fmluk@aol.com **w** fmlmusic.com MD: David Stopps.

Fruit Ground Floor, 37 Lonsdale Road, London NW6 6RA **t** 020 7328 0848 **f** 020 7328 8078 **e** fruitmanagement@btconnect.com Partner: Caroline Killoury.

Fruition Management PO Box 10896, Birmingham B13 0ZU **t** 0121 247 6981 or 07976 215 719 **f** 0121 247 6981 **e** rod@fruitionmusic.co.uk MD: Rod Thomson.

Fruity Red Inc. Second Floor, The Swiss Center, 10 Wardour Street, London W1D 6QF **t** 020 7864 1300 **f** 020 7437 1029 **e** info@fruityred.com **w** fruityred.com Dir: Helen Douglas.

The Full 36ixty PO Box 77, Leeds LS13 2WZ **t** 08709 905 078 **f** 0113 256 1315 **e** katherine@full360ltd.com **w** full360ltd.com MD: Katherine Canoville.

Fundamental Management Falkland House, Falkland Road, London N8 0QY **t** 020 8376 1876 **f** 020 8808 4413 **e** fundamentaluk@yahoo.co.uk Mgr: Maria James.

funky star 4 Moray Place, Glasgow G41 2AQ **t** 0141 424 4703 or 07977 224258 **f** 0141 424 4703 **e** info@funkystar.org.uk **w** funkystar.org.uk Director: alan mccuskerthompson.

Furtive Mass Transit Systems LLP First floor, 7-13 Cotton's Gardens, Shoreditch, London E2 8DN **t** 020 7613 5666 **f** 020 7739 6872 **e** mail@furtive-mts.com **w** furtive-mts.com Contact: Tank

Future Management PO Box 183, Chelmsford, Essex CM2 9XN **t** 01245 601910 **f** 01245 601048 **e** Futuremgt@aol.com **w** futuremanagement.co.uk MD: Joe Ferrari.

G Entertaining 16 Coney Green, Abbotts Barton, Winchester, Hants SO23 7JB **t** 0845 601 6285 **e** enquiries@g-entertaining.co.uk **w** g-entertaining.co.uk MD: Peter Nouwens.

Gailforce Management 55 Fulham High Street, London SW6 3JJ **t** 020 7384 8989 **f** 020 7384 8988 **e** gail@gailforcemanagement.co.uk MD: Gail Colson.

Galaxi Artiste Management 11 Spruce Park, Crediton, Devon EX17 3HQ **t** 07968 163866 **e** ross@galaxi.tv **w** galaxi.tv MD: Ross Hemsworth.

Brian Gannon Management PO Box 106, Rochdale, Lancashire OL15 0AZ **t** 01706 374411 **f** 01706 377303 **e** brian@briangannon.co.uk **w** briangannon.co.uk Owner: Brian Gannon.

Ganz Management 88 Calvert Road, Greenwich, London SE10 0DF **t** 020 8333 9447 **f** 020 8355 9328 **e** sam.towers@ganzmanagement.com Manager: Sam Towers.

Patrick Garvey Management Top Floor, 59 Lansdowne Place, Hove, East Sussex BN3 1FL **t** 01273 206623 **f** 01273 208484 **e** patrick@patrickgarvey.com **w** patrickgarvey.com Director: Andrea McDermott.

Geronimo! Management 15 Canada Copse, Milford, Surrey GU8 5AL **t** 07960 187529 **e** barneyjeavons@supanet.com Owner: Barney Jeavons.

Global Talent Management 2nd Floor, 53 Frith Street, London W1D 4SN **t** 020 7292 9600 **f** 020 7292 9611 **e** email@globaltalentgroup.com **w** globaltalentgroup.com MD: David Forecast, Ashley Tabor.

Gola Entertainment 7 Crofton Terrace, Dun Laoghaire, Co. Dublin, Ireland **t** +353 1 202 0909 **f** +353 1 280 1229 **e** gola@iol.ie **w** moyabrennan.com Managers: Tim Jarvis & Leon Brennan.

Goldpush 38 Langham Street, London W1N 5RH **t** 020 7323 9522 **f** 020 7323 9526 **e** razgold@goldpush.com MD: Raz Gold.

Got A Loser Job At The Diner Management 71 Lansdowne Rd, Purley, Surrey CR8 2PD **t** 020 8645 0013 **e** flamingofleece@yahoo.com **w** geocities.com/flamingofleece GM: Alvin LeDup.

GR Management 974 Pollokshaws Road, Shawlands, Glasgow, Strathclyde G41 2HA **t** 0141 632 1111 **f** 0141 649 0042 **e** g.r@dial.pipex.com MDs: Rab Andrew/Gerry McElhone.

Graham Peacock Management P.O.Box 84, Hove, West Sussex BN3 6YP **t** 01273 777409 **f** 01273 777809 **e** gpmanage@aol.com MD: Graham Peacock.

Grand Union Management 93b Scrubs Lane, London NW10 6QU **t** 020 8968 7798 **f** 020 8968 3377 **e** davidbianchi@granduniongroup.com **w** granduniongroup.com Managers: David Bianchi, Nick Ember.

Grant & Foresight 192D Brooklands Road, Weybridge, Surrey KT13 0RJ **t** 01932 855337 **f** 01932 851245 or 020 8232 8160 **e** davidmanagement@aol.com MD: David Morgan.

Grapedime Music 28 Hurst Crescent, Barrowby, Grantham, Lincolnshire NG32 1TE **t** 01476 560241 **f** 01476 560241 **e** grapedime@pjbray.globalnet.co.uk A&R Manager: Phil Bray.

Stan Green Management PO Box 4, Dartmouth, Devon TQ6 0YD **t** 01803 770046 **f** 01803 770075 **e** sgm@clara.co.uk **w** keithfloyd.co.uk MD: Stan Green.

Grinning Rat Music Management 19a High Street, Midsomer Norton, Bath BA3 2DR **t** 01761 419333 **e** info@grinningrat.co.uk **w** helenaonline.com MD: Ian Softley.

Groovefinder Productions Flat 1, 19 Craneswater Park, Southsea, Portsmouth PO4 0NU **t** 07831 450 241 **e** jeff@groovefinderproductions.com MD: Jeff Powell.

Peter Haines Management Montfort, The Avenue, Kingston, Lewes, East Sussex BN7 3LL **t** 01273 475846 **e** peter@uktourist.freeserve.co.uk Manager: Peter Haines.

Harmony Entertainment 23 Ruscombe Way, Feltham, Middx TW14 9NY **t** 020 8751 6060 or 07774 856 679 **f** 020 8751 6060 MD: Mike Dixon.

Keith Harris Music PO Box 2290, Maidenhead, Berkshire SL6 6WA **t** 01628 674422 **f** 01628 631379 **e** keith@keithharris.plus.com MD: Keith Harris.

Les Hart (Southampton Entertainments) 6 Crookhorn Lane, Purbrook, Waterlooville, Hants PO7 5QE **t** 023 9225 8373 or 023 8045 6149 **f** 023 9225 8369 **e** rod@leshart.co.uk **w** leshart.co.uk Proprietor: Rod Watts.

Pete Hawkins Management 3 Vincent Close, Bromley, Kent BR2 9ED **t** 020 8402 9199 **e** pvhawkins@ntlworld.com MD: Pete Hawkins.

The Headline Agency 39 Churchfields, Milltown, Dublin 14, Ireland **t** +353 1 260 2560 **f** +353 1 261 1879 **e** info@musicheadline.com **w** musicheadline.com MD: Madeleine Seiler.

Headstone Management 46 Tintagel Way, Woking, Surrey GU22 7DG **t** 01483 856 760 **e** colinfwspencer@hotmail.com MD: Colin Spencer.

Dennis Heaney Promotions Whitehall, Ashgrove Road, Newry, Co Down BT34 1QN **t** 028 3026 8658 **f** 028 3026 6673 **e** dennis_heaney@hotmail.com **w** susanmccann.com Director: Dennis Heaney.

Heavenly Management 47 Frith Street, London W1D 4SE **t** 020 7494 2998 **f** 020 7437 3317 **e** lou@heavenlymanagement.com Dir: Martin Kelly.

Heavyweight Management 33 Sunnymead Road, London SW15 5HY **t** 020 8878 0800 **f** 020 8878 3080 **e** heavyweight@dial.pipex.com **w** heavyweightman.com MD: Simon Goffe/Emily Moxon.

Hedgehog 9 Tavistock Court, Tavistock Square, London WC1H 9HE **t** 020 7387 3220 **f** 020 7383 2832 **e** carol_hodge@hotmail.com Manager: Carol Hodge. Partner: Susan Wincott.

Henderson Management 51 Promenade North, Cleveleys, Blackpool, Lancashire FY5 1LN **t** 01253 863386 **f** 01253 867799 **e** agents@henderson-management.co.uk **w** henderson-management.co.uk MD: John Henderson.

Herotech Management 24-25 Nutford Place, London W1H 5YN **t** 020 7725 7064 **f** 020 7725 7066 **e** dylan@herotech.co.uk

Hip-Hop Cow Management 27 Church Drive, North Harrow, Middx HA2 7NR **t** 020 8866 2454 **f** 020 8429 4383 **e** hiphopcow@aol.com **w** hiphopcow.com Managing Director: Andrew East.

Hope Management Loft 5, The Tobacco Factory, Raleigh Road, Southville, Bristol BS3 1TF **t** 0117 953 5566 **f** 0117 953 7733 **e** info@hoperecordings.com **w** hoperecordings.com MD: Steve Satterthwaite. Co-MD & Remixes: Leon Alexander. Artist Mgr: Matt Rickard.

HotHouse Music Greenland Place, 115-123 Bayham Street, London NW1 0AG **t** 020 7446 7446 **f** 020 7446 7448 **e** info@hot-house-music.com **w** hot-house-music.com MDs: Becky Bentham, Karen Elliott.

Hug Management Contact: Indie Music Management

Hutt Russell Organisation PO Box 64, Cirencester, Gloucestershire GL7 5YD **t** 01285 644622 **f** 01285 642291 **e** shows@huttrussell.co.uk **w** huttrussell.co.uk Director: Steven Hutt.

Hyperactive Music Management PO Box 255, Brentford TW8 OBU **f** 020 8580 4912 **e** teresa@hyperactivemgt.com Contact: Teresa Sutterby

The ICE Group 3 St Andrews Street, Lincoln, Lincolnshire LN5 7NE **t** 01522 539883 **f** 01522 528964 **e** steve.hawkins@easynet.co.uk **w** icegroup.co.uk MD: Steve Hawkins.

Idle Eyes Management 11 Mountain Road, Caerphilly CF83 1HG **t** 07796 947 799 **e** Jon@IdleEyes.co.uk **w** idleeyes.co.uk Dir: Jonathan Rees.

IE Music 111 Frithville Gardens, London W12 7JG **t** 020 8600 3400 **f** 020 8600 3401 **e** info@iemusic.co.uk **w** iemusic.co.uk MDs: David Enthoven, Tim Clark.

Ignite Marketing (UK) 26a Stoke Newington Church Street, London N16 0LU **t** 020 7502 2971 **f** 020 7241 3857 **e** paul@ignitemarketing.co.uk **w** ignitemarketing.co.uk MD: Paul West.

Ignition Management 54 Linhope Street, London NW1 6HL **t** 020 7298 6000 **f** 020 7258 0962 **e** mail@ignition-man.co.uk

IMD PO Box 1200, London SW6 2GH **t** 020 7371 0995 **f** 020 7384 2999 **e** rachel@imd-info.com **w** imd-info.com Co Director: Rachel Birchwood- Gordon.

Immoral Management PO Box 2643, Reading, Berks RG5 4GF **t** 0118 969 9269 **f** 0118 969 9264 **e** johnjpsuk@aol.com MD: John Saunderson.

Impact Ventures 38b Brixton Water Lane, London SW2 1QE **t** 020 7274 8509 **f** 020 7274 3543 **e** info@impactventures.co.uk **w** impactventures.co.uk MD: Rachael Bee.

Imprint Bookings & Management - DJ Agency Unit 13, Barley Shotts Business Park, 246 Acklam Road, London W10 5YG **t** 020 8964 1331 **f** 020 8960 9660 **e** gareth@imprintdjs.com **w** imprintdjs.com Contact: Gareth Rees

Impro Management 35 Britannia Row, London N1 8QH **t** 020 7704 8080 **f** 020 7704 1616 **e** guy@impromanagement.com Director: Guy Trezise.

In Phase Management 55A Ditton Road, Surbiton, Surrey KT6 6RF **t** 020 8390 4583 **f** 020 8288 1597 **e** mail@inphasemanagement.com **w** inphasemanagement.com Mgr: Fay Woolven.

In2music Flat 3, 1 Prince of Wales Road, London NW5 3LW **t** 020 7428 2604 **f** 020 7424 0183 **e** jessicain2music@aol.com Contact: Jessica Peel

Independent Sound Management (ISM) 1st Floor, 39 Margaret Street, London W1G OJQ **t** 020 7493 9200 **f** 020 7493 9111 **e** nian@independentsound.net GM: Nian Brindle.

Indie Music Management 51-55 Highfield Street, Liverpool L3 6AA **t** 0151 236 5551 **e** info@indiemusicmanagement.com **w** indiemusicmanagement.com MD: Mark Cowley.

Inductive Management PO Box 20503, London NW8 0WY **t** 020 7586 5427 **f** 020 7483 2164 **e** Inductrec@aol.com Director: Colin Peel.

INS-YNC 74 Harberton Road, London N19 3JP **t** 020 7263 5299 **f** 020 7263 5299 **e** charlie@ins-ync.co.uk **w** ins-ync.co.uk MD: Charlie Inskip.

Insanity Artist Management 8 Duncannon Street, London WC2N 4JF **t** 08456 446625 **f** 08456 446627 **e** info@insanitygroup.com **w** insanitygroup.com Manager: Andy Varley.

Instinct Management 10 Nightingale Lane, London SW12 8TB **t** 020 8675 9233 **e** geoff@instinct-mgt.demon.co.uk Dir: Geoff Smith.

Intelligent Music Management 42A Malden Road, London NW5 3HG **t** 020 7284 1955 **f** 020 7424 9876 **e** verity.german@glatmanent.com MD: Daniel Glatman.

Interactive Marketing Unit One, 25a Blue Anchor Lane, London SE16 3UL **t** 020 7231 1393 **f** 020 7232 1373 **e** info@interactivem.co.uk **w** interactivem.co.uk MD: Jo Cerrone.

Interactive Music Management 2 Carriglea, Naas Road, Dublin 12, Ireland **t** +353 1 419 5039 **f** +353 1 419 5409 **e** info@interactive-music.com MD: Oliver Walsh.

Interceptor Enterprises PO Box 46572, London N1 9YL **t** 020 7278 8001 **f** 020 7713 6298 **e** info@interceptor.co.uk Manager: Charlie Charlton.

International Artistes 2nd Floor - TV House, Mount Street, Manchester M2 5FA **t** 0161 833 9838 **f** 0161 832 7480 **e** intartltd@aol.com **w** i-a-l.com Director: Stuart Littlewood.

Interzone Management Interzone House, 74-77 Magdalen Road, Oxford OX4 1RE **t** 01865 205600 **f** 01865 205700 **e** interzone@rotator.co.uk **w** rotator.co.uk MD: Richard Cotton.

Intuition Music 1 Devonport Mews, London W12 8NG **t** 020 7565 4750 **f** 020 7565 4751 **e** berni@intuitionmusic.com **w** MewsMedia.com MD: Bernie Griffiths.

INXS Music Management (London) PO Box 39464, London N10 1WP **t** 07779 340 154 **f** 020 8883 4086 **e** info@inxs.com **w** inxs.com MD: Nathan Hull.

J Management Unit A, The Courtyard, 42 Colwith Road, London W6 9EY **t** 020 8846 3737 **f** 020 8846 3738 **e** John@jmanagement.co.uk MD: John Arnison.

Jack 'N' Jill Artiste Management F3, 60 West End Lane, London NW6 2NE **t** 07050 056 175 or 07860 232 527 **f** 020 7372 3088 **e** JNJ@mgmt.fsbusiness.co.uk Dir: Joycelyn Phillips.

Jackie Davidson Management The Business Village, 3 Broomhill Rd, London SW18 4JQ **t** 020 8870 8744 **f** 020 8874 1578 **e** jackie@jdmanagement.co.uk **w** jdmanagement.co.uk MD: Jackie Davidson.

Jamdown Stanley House Studios, 39 Stanley Gardens, London W3 7SY **t** 020 8735 0280 **f** 020 8930 1073 **e** othman@jamdown-music.com **w** jamdown-music.com MD: Othman Mukhlis.

James Grant Management Syon Lodge, London Road, Isleworth, Middlesex TW7 5BH **t** 020 8232 4100 **f** 020 8232 4101 or 020 8232 4102 **e** enquiries@jamesgrant.co.uk **w** jamesgrant.co.uk Joint MD: Paul Worsley.

JBM Management 317 Portway, Woodhouse Park, Manchester M22 0DL **t** 0161 610 1856 **f** 0161 610 1856 **e** JBMManagement@aol.com MD: Jason Brierley.

JBS Management UK Apartment 11, Dean Meadow, Newton-le-Willows, Lancs WA12 9PX **t** 01925 291159 **f** 01925 291159 **e** xag84@jaybs.freeserve.co.uk Contact: John Sheffield

JC Music 84A Strand On The Green, London W4 3PU **t** 020 8995 0989 **f** 020 8995 0878 **e** jcmusic@dial.pipex.com MD: John Campbell.

Jive Entertainments PO Box 5865, Corby, Northamptonshire NN17 5ZT **t** 01536 406406 **f** 01536 400082 **e** hojive@aol.com MD: Dave Bartram.

John Taylor Management PO Box 272, London N20 0BY **t** 020 8368 0340 **f** 020 8361 3370 **e** john@jt-management.demon.co.uk MD: John Taylor.

John Waller Management & Marketing The Old Truman Brewery, 91 Brick Lane, London E1 6QL **t** 020 7247 1057 **f** 020 7377 0732 **e** john.waller@dial.pipex.com MD: John Waller.

Johnboy Productions P.O.Box 22877, London NW9 82J **t** 07956 811149 **f** 0870 284 7322 **e** johnboyproductions@hotmail.com Manager: Mark Uttley.

Jonny Paul Management 2 Downsbury Studios, 40 Steeles Rd, London NW3 4SA **t** 020 7586 3005 **f** 020 7586 3005 **e** jonny@paul66.fsworld.co.uk MD: Jonny Paul.

JPR Management Suite 25, 9-12 Middle Street, Brighton, East Sussex BN1 1AL **t** 01273 236969 **f** 01273 386291 **e** info@jprmanagement.co.uk **w** jprmanagement.co.uk Contact: John Reid

JPS Management PO Box 2643, Reading, Berks RG5 4GF **t** 0118 969 9269 or 07885 058 911 **f** 0118 969 9264 **e** johnjpsuk@aol.com MD: John Saunderson.

Jukes Productions PO Box 13995, London W9 2FL **t** 020 7286 9532 **f** 020 7286 4739 **e** jukes@easynet.co.uk **w** jukesproductions.co.uk MD: Geoff Jukes. PA to MD: Amanda Hon.

Just Another Management Co PO Box 19780, London SW15 1WU **t** 020 8741 6020 **f** 020 8741 8362 **e** justmusic@justmusic.co.uk Director: Serena Benedict.

JW Management 380 Longbanks, Harlow, Essex CM18 7PG **t** 01279 304526 **f** 01279 304526 **e** jpweston@ntlworld.com **w** westonenterprises.co.uk Manager/Consultant: John Weston ACCA.

Kabuki 85 Camden Street, London NW1 0HP **t** 020 7916 2142 **f** 0870 051 0158 **e** email@kabuki.co.uk **w** kabuki.co.uk Manager: Sheila Naujoks.

KAL Management 95 Gloucester Road, Hampton, Middlesex TW12 2UW **t** 020 8783 0039 **f** 020 8979 6487 **e** kaplan222@aol.com **w** kaplan-kaye.co.uk Dir: Kaplan Kaye.

Kamara Artist Management (UK) 81 Carlton Road, Boston, Lincolnshire PE21 8LH **t** 07952 289504 **f** 01205 270088 **e** chriskamara@megahitrecordsuk.co.uk **w** megahitrecordsuk.co.uk MD: Chris Kamara.

Karma Management Brough Cottage, Brotton, Saltburn-by-the-Sea TS12 2QR **t** 07796 364276 **e** info@karmaeg.com **w** karmaeg.com Dir: Kevin Parry.

Keep Hit Real Management 12 Molasses Row, Plantation Wharf, York Road, London SW11 3UX **t** 020 7228 2772 **f** 020 7228 2889 **e** glynnsmith55@hotmail.com Dirs: Glynn Smith, Alan Comer.

Keep It Live! Glebe Cottage, Station Road, Kildale, Whitby, North Yorkshire YO21 2RH **t** 01642 724470 **f** 01642 725143 **e** keepit.live@virgin.net **w** keepitlive.co.uk Director: Colin McCosh.

Kev Bennison Management 30 Speakers Close, Tividale, Oldbury, West Midlands B69 1UX **t** 07957 692398 **e** kev.bennison@talk21.com Manager: Kev Bennison.

Key Management 20 Lower Stephens Street, Dublin 2, Ireland **t** +353 1 478 0191 **f** +353 1 475 1324 **e** info@thecube.ie A&R Director: Mark French.

Key Music Management Evans Business Centre, Sycamore Trading Estate, Squires Gate Lane, Blackpool, Lancs FY4 3RL **t** 0870 046 6629 **f** 0870 138 9776 **e** keymusicmgmt@aol.com **w** keymusicgroup.com Artist Mgrs: Dan Brooks, Richard Jones.

Kickstart Management 12 Port House, Square Rigger Row, Plantation Wharf, London SW11 3TY **t** 020 7223 3300 **f** 020 7223 8777 **e** info@kickstart.uk.net Director: Ken Middleton.

Kim Glover Management PO Box 468, Maidstone, Kent ME14 1HQ **t** 01622 759444 **f** 01622 754749 **e** kimglovermgmt@aol.com MD: Kim Glover.

Simon King Management (SKM) 6 Westleigh Court, 28 Birdhurst Rd, South Croydon, Surrey CR2 7EA **t** 020 8667 1982 **e** simon@koobarecords.com **w** kingmanagement.co.uk MD: Simon King.

Kitchenware Management 7 The Stables, Saint Thomas Street, Newcastle upon Tyne, Tyne and Wear NE1 4LE **t** 0191 230 1970 **f** 0191 232 0262 **e** info@kware.demon.co.uk **w** kitchenwarerecords.com Administration: Nicki Turner.

KlubDJ PO Box 5333, Daventry, Northamptonshire NN11 5FN **t** 07092 171780 **f** 07092 171790 **e** info@klubdj.co.uk **w** klubdj.co.uk Contact: John Barnet

Knifedge 57b Riding House St, London W1W 7EF **t** 020 7436 5434 **f** 020 7436 5431 **e** info@knifedge.net **w** knifedge.net Director: Jonathan Brigden.

Krack Music Management East Yorkshire **t** 01405 861124 or 07764 936377 **e** alan@krack.prestel.co.uk MD: Alan Lacey.

KSO Records PO Box 159, Chathan, Kent ME5 7AQ **t** 07956 120837 **e** ksorecords@hotmail.com **w** ksorecords.pwp.blueyonder.co.uk MD: Antonio Sloane.

Kudos Management Crown Studios, 16-18 Crown Road, Twickenham, Middx TW1 3EE **t** 020 8891 4233 **f** 020 8891 2339 **e** kudos@camino.co.uk MD: Billy Budis.

Wolfgang Kuhle Artist Management PO Box 425, London SW6 3TX **t** 020 7371 0397 **f** 020 7736 9212 **e** getdown@thepleasuredome.demon.co.uk Contact: Wolfgang Kuhle

L25 Entertainment 17 Parkhill Road, London NW3 2YH **t** 07973 624 443 **f** 020 7209 4064 **e** darren.michaelson@L25entertainment.co.uk MD: Darren Michaelson.

Lamb Management PO Box 54, Hyde, Cheshire SK16 5FJ **t** 07973 724499 or 07789 502877 **f** 0870 164 1848 **e** john@easylamb.com **w** easylamb.com Managers: John Leah, Andrew Melchior.

Lateral Artist Management PO Box 29391, London W2 1GE **t** 020 8257 9470 **f** 020 8257 9470 **e** enquiries-information@lateral-am.co.uk **w** lateral-am.co.uk Dir: David Smith.

Latin Arts Services Po Box 14303, London SE26 4ZH **t** 07000 472 572 or 020 8291 9236 **f** 07000 472 572 **e** latinarts@latinartsgroup.com **w** latinartsgroup.com Director: Hector Rosquete.

Lazarus Music & Media (LM2) Suite 14 Harrow Lodge, St Johns Wood Road, London NW8 8HR **t** 020 7286 7470 **f** 020 7286 7470 **e** brad.lazarus@LM2.co.uk Director: Brad Lazarus. Director: Niki Sanderson.

Leafman Reverb House, Bennett Street, London W4 2AH **t** 020 8747 0660 **f** 020 8747 0880 **e** liam@leafsongs.com MD: Liam Teeling.

Leap 33 Green Walk, London NW4 2AL **t** 020 8202 4120 **f** 020 8202 4120 **e** leap@gideonbenaim.com MD: Gideon Benaim.

Lee & Co 3 Taylor Avenue, Silsden, Keighley, West Yorks BO20 0DY **t** 01535 653 139 or 07969 697 660 **e** erika@letstalkmusic.com Contact: Erika Lee

Let It Rock Management PO Box 3, Newport NP20 3YB **t** 07973 715875 **f** 01633 677672 **e** alan.jones@amserve.com Principal: Alan Jones.

Level 22 Management 6 Hyldavale Ave, Gatley, Cheshire SK8 4DE **t** 0161 428 3150 **f** 0161 428 3150 **e** level22uk@yahoo.co.uk Director: Randolph Mike.

LH Management Studio 205, Westbourne Studios, 242 Acklam Road, London W10 5JJ **t** 020 8968 0637 **e** info@lhmanagement.com MD: Lisa Horan.

The Liaison and Promotion Company 124 Great Portland Street, London W1W 6PP **t** 020 7636 2345 **f** 020 7580 0045 **e** garydavison@fmware.com Director: Gary Davison.

Liberation Management The Shack at Walnut Cottage, Walden Road, Hadstock, Cambs CB1 6NX **t** 01223 890 186 **e** jamiesuptonogood@aol.com Contact: Jamie Spencer

Liberty City Music 1 Tabley Close, Victoria Mansions, Macclesfield, Cheshire SK10 3SL **t** 07812 201 133 **e** darren@libertycity.biz **w** LibertyCity.Biz Contact: Darren Eager

Line-Up PMC 9A Tankerville Place, Newcastle-upon-Tyne, Tyne and Wear NE2 3AT **t** 0191 281 6449 **f** 0191 212 0913 **e** info@line-up.co.uk **w** line-up.co.uk Owner: Christopher Murtagh.

Liquid Management 1st Floor, 139 Sutherland Ave, London W9 1ES **t** 020 7286 6463 **f** 0709 238 9779 **e** info@Liquidmanagement.net Contact: David Manders

Harvey Lisberg Associates Kennedy House, 31 Stamford Street, Altrincham, Cheshire WA14 1ES **t** 0161 941 4560 **f** 0161 941 4199 **e** harveylisberg@aol.com MD: Harvey Lisberg.

Little Giant Music 35 Park Mansions, 141 Knightsbridge, London SW1X 7QT **t** 020 7287 7444 or 07779 616 552 **e** Liza@littlegiantmusic.com **w** littlegiantmusic.com Dir: Liza Kumjian-Smith.

Little Piece of Jamaica (LPOJ) 55 Finsbury Park Road, Highbury, London N4 2JY **t** 020 7359 0788 or 07973 630 729 **f** 020 7226 2168 **e** paulhuelpoj@yahoo.co.uk Dir: Paul Hue.

LJE 32 Willesden Lane, London NW6 7ST **t** 020 7625 0231 **f** 020 7372 6503 **e** lauriejay@btconnect.com MD: Laurie Jay.

LOE Entertainment LOE House, 159 Broadhurst Gardens, London NW6 3AU **t** 020 7328 6100 **f** 020 7624 6384 **e** watanabe@loe.uk.net Creative Director: Hideto Watanabe.

Rupert Loewenstein 2 King Street, St. James's, London SW1Y 6QU **t** 020 7839 6454 **f** 020 7930 4032 **e** clare@rll.co.uk Dir: Clare Turner.

Loose PO Box 67, Runcorn, Cheshire WA7 4NL **t** 01928 566261 **e** jaki.florek@virgin.net Manager: Jaki Florek.

Louis Walsh Management 24 Courtney House, Appian Way, Dublin 6, Ireland **t** +353 1 668 0309 or +353 1 668 0982 **f** +353 1 668 0721 or +353 1 2815162-ISDN **e** louiewalsh@eircom.net MD: Louis Walsh.

Machine Management 1st Floor, 93 Leonard Street, London EC2A 4RD **t** 020 7739 0622 **f** 020 7394 2133 **e** iw@machinemanagement.co.uk MD: Iain Watt.

Mad As Toast 3 Broomlands Street, Paisley PA1 2LS **t** 0141 887 8888 **f** 0141 887 8888 **e** info@madastoast.com **w** madastoast.com Dirs: John Richardson, George Watson.

Mad Management 7 The Chase, Rayleigh, Essex SS6 8QL **t** 01268 771113 **f** 01268 774192 **e** madmanagementltd@aol.com MD: Alex Rose.

Madison Management 6 Cinnamon Gardens, Guildford, Surrey GU2 9YZ **t** 07810 540 990 **e** info@madisonmanagement.co.uk **w** madisonmanagement.co.uk Artist Manager: Paul Harvey.

Madrigal Music Guy Hall, Awre, Glocs GL14 1EL **t** 01594 510512 **f** 01594 510512 **e** artists@madrigalmusic.co.uk **w** madrigalmusic.co.uk MD/Head of A&R: Nick Ford.

Magic Kingdom Management 942b Brighton Road, Purley, Surrey CR8 2LP **t** 07931 748590 **f** 020 8645 0316 **e** paul@magicking.freeserve.co.uk MD: Paul Mitchell.

Mako Music 27 Waverton Road, London SW18 3BZ **t** 020 8870 6790 **e** dombrownlow@tiscali.co.uk **w** makomusic.com MD: Dominic Brownlow.

The Management Company PO Box 150, Chesterfield S40 0YT **t** 0870 746 8478 **e** mail@themanagementcompany.biz **w** themanagementcompany.biz MD: Tony Hedley.

Manners McDade Artist Management 4th Floor, 18 Broadwick Street, London W1F 8HS **t** 020 7277 8194 **f** 020 7277 7630 **e** info@mannersmcdade.co.uk **w** mannersmcdade.co.uk MD: Catherine Manners.

Manygate Classical Management Trees, Ockham Road South, East Horsley, Surrey KT24 6QE **t** 01483 281300 **f** 01483 281811 **e** manygate@easynet.co.uk Administrator: John Boydem.

Marko Polo (UK) The Barn, Fordwater Lane, Chichester, West Sussex PO19 4PT **t** 01243 789786 **f** 01243 789787 **e** markoPolo@compuserve.com **w** markopolo.co.uk Director: Mark Ringwood.

Marshall Arts Management Leeder House, 6 Erskine Road, London NW3 3AJ **t** 020 7586 3831 **f** 020 7586 1422 **e** info@marshall-arts.co.uk **w** marshall-arts.co.uk MD: Barrie Marshall.

Marsupial Management 63 Sailmakers Court, William Morris Way, Fulham, London SW6 2UX **t** 020 7751 0020 **f** 020 7384 9797 **e** info@marsupialmanagement.com MD: John Brand. Management Assistant: Sophie Rahat.

Richard Martin Management 18 Ambrose Place, Worthing, West Sussex BN11 1PZ **t** 01903 823456 **f** 01903 823847 **e** ric@ricmartinagency.com **w** hot-chocolate.co.uk Manager: Richard Martin.

Martin Wyatt 21c Heathmans Road, Parsons Green, London SW6 4TJ **t** 020 7751 9935 **f** 020 7731 9314 **e** brightmusic@aol.com MD: Martin Wyatt.

Nigel Martin-Smith Management 1st Floor, Alexandra Buildings, 28 Queen Street, Manchester M2 5LF **t** 0161 834 4500 **f** 0161 834 0014 **e** liz@nmsmanagement.co.uk MD: Nigel Martin-Smith.

MartynLevett.com PO Box 1345, Essex IG4 5FX **t** 07050 333 555 **f** 07020 923 292 **e** info@MartynLevett.com **w** MartynLevett.com Joint MD: Paul Booth.

Massive Management The Seahouse, Pett Level Road, Pett Level, East Sussex TN35 4EH **t** 01424 812 945 **f** 01424 812 420 **e** tom@massiveman.demon.co.uk **w** qedtheband.com MDs: Tom Watkins, Darron Coppin.

Matrix Management 91 Peterborough Road, London SW6 3BW **t** 020 7384 6400 **f** 020 7384 6401 **e** flip@matrix-studios.co.uk Manager: Flip Dewar.

Maximum Music 9 Heathmans Road, Parsons Green, London SW6 4TJ **t** 020 7731 1112 **f** 020 7731 1113 **e** info@maximummusic.co.uk MD: Nicky Graham, Deni Lew.

MBL 1 Cowcross Street, London EC1M 6DR **t** 020 7253 7755 **f** 020 7251 8096 MD: Robert Linney.

Michael McDonagh Management The Studio, R.O. 63 Station Road, Winchmore Hill, London N21 3NB **t** 020 8364 3121 **f** 020 8364 3090 **e** caramusicltd@dial.pipex.com Director: Michael McDonagh.

McLeod Holden Enterprises Priory House, 1133 Hessle High Road, Hull, East Yorkshire HU4 6SB **t** 01482 565444 **f** 01482 353635 **e** info@mcleod-holden.com **w** mcleod-holden.com Chairman: Peter McLeod.

MCM Third Floor, 40 Langham Street, London W1N 5RG **t** 020 7580 4088 **f** 020 7580 4098 **e** mcmemail@aol.com Contact: Meredith Cork

MDMA 1A, 1 Adelaide Mansions, Hove, Sussex BN3 2FD **t** 01273 321602 **e** ricmdma@aol.com Manager: Rick French.

Me Me Me Management 105 Canalot Studios, 222 Kensal Road, London W10 5BN **t** 020 8960 8060 **f** 020 8960 1344 **e** sam@me-me-me.co.uk **w** me-me-me.co.uk MD: Sam Tromans.

Media Records Units 1-2 Pepys Court, 84-86 The Chase, Clapham Common, London SW4 0NF **t** 020 7720 7266 **f** 020 7720 7255 **e** info@mediarec.co.uk **w** mediarec.co.uk MD: Peter Pritchard.

Medium Productions 74 St Lawrence Road, Upminster, Essex RM14 2UW **t** 07939 080524 **f** 01708 640291 **e** info@mediumproductions.co.uk **w** mediumproductions.co.uk Director: Debi Zornes.

Memnon Entertainment (UK) Habib House, 3rd Floor, 9 Stevenson Square, Piccadilly, Manchester M1 1DB **t** 0161 238 8516 **f** 0161 236 6717 **e** memnon@btconnect.com **w** memnonentertainment.com Dir: Rudi Kidd.

Menace Management. 2 Park Road, Radlett, Hertfordshire WD7 8EQ **t** 01923 853789 or 01923 854789 **f** 01923 853318 MD: Dennis Collopy.

Mental Music Management PO Box 20750, London E3 2YU **t** 020 8980 4819 or 07900 631 883 **f** 020 8980 4819 **e** mentalmusicman@hotmail.com Mgr: Gary Heath.

Metamorphosis Management Matrix Complex, 91 Peterborough Road, London SW6 3BU **t** 020 7371 5095 **f** 020 7371 5454 **e** mark@crownmusic.co.uk Manager: Mark Hargreaves.

Method Management Matrix Complex, 91 Peterborough Road, London SW6 3BU **t** 020 7371 5065 **f** 020 7371 5454 **e** chloe@crownmusic.co.uk Manager: Chloe Griffiths.

Metro Artist Management Latimer Studios, West Kington, Wilts SN14 7JQ **t** 01249 783 599 **f** 0870 169 8433 **e** dolanmap@aol.com CEO: Mike Dolan.

Midi Management The Old Barn, Jenkins Lane, Great Hallingbury, Essex CM22 7QL **t** 01279 759067 **f** 01279 504145 **e** midi-management@btconnect.com Manager/Director: Mike Champion.

Midnight To Six Management 4th Floor, 33 Newman Street, London W1T 1PY **t** 020 7462 0026 **f** 020 7462 0012 **e** harper@midnighttosix.com Directors: Dave Harper, Tony Crean.

Mighty Music Management 2 Stucley Place, Camden, London NW1 8NS **t** 020 7482 6660 **f** 020 7482 6606 **e** art@mainartery.co.uk Director: Jo Mirowski.

John Miles Organisation Cadbury Camp Lane, Clapton In Gordano, Bristol BS20 7SB **t** 01275 854675 or 01275 856770 **f** 01275 810186 **e** john@johnmiles.org.uk MD: John Miles.

Mimi Music 26-28 Hammersmith Grove, Hammersmith, London W6 7BA **t** 020 8834 1085 **f** 020 8834 1185 **e** info@mimi-music.com **w** mimi-music.com MD: Dee Sharma.

MM Management 17-20 Moorhurst Road, St Leonards on sea, East Sussex TN38 9NA **t** 01424 853200 **f** 01424 756007 **e** teepee@globalnet.co.uk MD: Tony Pankhurst.

Mobb Rule PO Box 26335, London N8 9ZA **t** 020 8340 8050 **e** info@mobbrule.com **w** mobbrule.com MDs: Stewart Pettey, Wayne Clements.

Mockingbird Music PO Box 52, Marlow, Bucks SL7 2YB **t** 01491 579214 **f** 01491 579214 **e** mockingbirdmusic@aol.com Artiste Management: Leon B Fisk.

Modernwood Management Cambridge House, Card Hill, Forest Row, East Sussex RH18 5BA **t** 01342 822619 or 020 8947 2224 **f** 01342 822619 **e** mickey.modernwood@virgin.net Senior Partner: Mickey Modern.

Modest! Management Studios 2-3, Matrix Complex, 91 Peterborough Road, London SW6 3BU **t** 020 7384 6410 **f** 020 7384 6411 **e** initial+lastname@modestmanagement.com Partners: Richard Griffiths, Harry Magee. Co-MDs: Richard Griffiths, Harry Magee.

Moksha Management PO Box 102, London E15 2HH **t** 020 8555 5423 **f** 020 8519 6834 **e** info@moksha.demon.co.uk **w** moksha.co.uk MD: Charles Cosh.

Mondo Management Unit 2D, Clapham North Arts Centre, 26-32 Voltaire Road, London SW4 6DH **t** 020 7720 7411 **f** 020 7720 8095 **e** rob@ihtrecords.com **w** davidgray.com Contact: Rob Holden

Money Talks Management Cadillac Ranch, Pencraig Uchaf, Cwm Bach, Whitland, Dyfed SA34 0DT **t** 01994 484466 **f** 01994 484294 **e** cadillacranch@telco4u.net Manager: C Augustino.

Moneypenny Management The Stables, Westwood House, Main Street, North Dalton, Driffield, East Yorks YO25 9XA **t** 01377 217815 or 07977 455882 **f** 01377 217754 **e** nigel@adastey.demon.co.uk **w** adastra-music.co.uk/moneypenny MD: Nigel Morton.

Monster Music Management 28 Glen View Crescent, Heysham, Lancashire LA3 2QW **t** 01524 852037 **f** 01524 852037 **e** croftmc@aol.com Contact: Mike Croft

David Morgan Management 192D Brooklands Road, Weybridge, Surrey KT13 0RJ **t** 01932 855337 **f** 01932 851245 or 020 8232 8160 **e** davidmanagement@aol.com MD: David Morgan.

Mother Tongue 35 Marsden Street, London NW5 3HE **t** 07973 137 554 **e** julian@mothertongue.tv MD: Julian de Takats.

Motive Music Management 13 Bexhill Road, London SW14 7NF **t** 07779 257 577 or 07808 939 919 **e** info@motivemusic.co.uk Contact: Paul Flanagan, Nathan Leeks

MPC Entertainment MPC House, 15-16 Maple Mews, London NW6 5UZ **t** 020 7624 1184 **f** 020 7624 4220 **e** mpc@mpce.com **w** mpce.com Chief Executive: Michael Cohen.

MSM Music Consultants PO Box 10036, Halesowen B62 8WD **t** 07785 506637 **e** trevorlonguk@aol.com MD: Trevor Long.

MuchMoreMusic Management Unit 29, Cygnus Business Centre, Dalmeyer Road, London NW10 2XA **t** 020 8830 0330 **f** 020 8830 0220 **e** info@muchmoremusic.net **w** muchmoremusic.net MD: Sandra Ceschia.

Muirhead Management Anchor House, 2nd Floor, 15-19 Britten Street, London SW3 3TY **t** 020 7351 5167 or 07785 226 542 **f** 0870 136 3878 **e** info@muirheadmanagement.co.uk **w** muirheadmanagement.co.uk CEO: Dennis Muirhead.

Mumbo Jumbo Management 2a-6a Southam Street, London W10 5PH **t** 020 8960 3253 **f** 020 8968 5111 **e** ian@mumbojumbo.co.uk **w** mumbojumbo.co.uk Managing Director: Ian Clifford.

The Music & Media Partnership First Floor, 72-74 Notting Hill Gate, London W11 3HT **t** 020 7727 9111 **f** 020 7727 9911 **e** info@tmmp.co.uk MD: Rick Blaskey.

Music Company (London) 103 Churston Drive, Morden, Surrey SM4 4JE **t** 020 8540 7357 **f** 020 8542 4854 **e** musicco@musicco.f9.co.uk MD: Melanne Mueller.

The Music Partnership 41 Aldebert Terrace, London SW8 1BH **t** 020 7787 0361 **f** 020 7735 7595 **e** office@musicpartnership.co.uk **w** musicpartnership.co.uk Artist Manager: Louise Badger.

MWM Music Management 6 Berkeley Crescent, Clifton, Bristol BS8 1HA **t** 0117 929 2393 **f** 0117 929 2696 **e** office@mwmuk.com Dir: Craig Williams.

Mylestone Unit 6, Ferrier St, London SW18 1SW **t** 020 8875 0990 or 07779 026 555 **f** 020 8875 0080 **e** myles@mylestoneltd.com MD: Myles Keller.

Name Music Innovation Labs, Watford Road, Harrow, Middx HA1 3TP **t** 020 8357 7305 **f** 020 8357 7326 **e** sam@name-uk.net MD: Sam Shemtob.

Native Management Unit 32, Ransome's Dock, 35-37 Parkgate Road, London SW11 4NP **t** 020 7801 1919 **f** 020 7738 1819 **e** info@nativemanagement.com **w** nativemanagement.com MD: Peter Evans.

NBM 43d Ferme Park Road, London N4 4EB **t** 020 8342 9220 **f** 020 8340 4721 **e** nbengali@lineone.net **w** naive.fr Artist Manager: Neville Bengali.

NEM Productions (UK) Priory House, 55 Lawe Road, South Shields, Tyne and Wear NE33 2AL **t** 0191 427 6207 **f** 0191 427 6323 **e** dave@nemproductions.com **w** nemproductions.com Contact: Dave Smith

Nettwerk Management UK Clearwater Yard, 35 Inverness St, London NW1 7HB **t** 020 7424 7500 **f** 020 7424 7501 **e** eleanor@nettwerk.com **w** nettwerk.com Contact: Sam Slattery

No Half Measures Studio 19, St. George's Studios, 93-97 St. George's Road, Glasgow G3 6JA **t** 0141 331 9888 **f** 0141 331 9889 **e** info@nohalfmeasures.com **w** nohalfmeasures.com MD: Dougie Souness.

No Quarter Management 171 Tolcarne Drive, London HA5 2DN **t** 07816 870 666 **e** info@noquartermanagement.com **w** noquartermanagement.com Director: Christian Miller. Director: Nathan Horrocks.

North Unit 105 Canalot Studio, 222 Kensal Road, London W10 5BN **t** 020 8964 4778 **f** 020 8960 1344 **e** abbi@north-nusong.com **w** north-nusong.com Artist Manager: John MacLennan.

North & South PO Box 1099, London SE5 9HT **t** 020 7326 4824 **f** 020 7535 5901 **e** gamesmaster@chartmoves.com MD: Dave Klein.

Northern Lights Mangement 120 Ashurst Road, London N12 9AB **t** 07887 983 452 **f** 020 8342 8213 **e** jonny.lights@virgin.net Manager: Jonathan Morley.

Northern Music Company Cheapside Chambers, 43 Cheapside, Bradford, West Yorks BD1 4HP **t** 01274 306361 **f** 01274 730097 **e** info@northernmusic.co.uk **w** northernmusic.co.uk MD: Andy Farrow.

Northstar Artist Management PO Box 458, Rotherham S66 1YN **t** 01709 709633 or 07740 101347 **e** Paul.flanaghan1@btinternet.com **w** northstar-management.com Artist Manager: Paul Flanaghan.

Norwich Artistes Bryden, 115 Holt Road, Norwich, Norfolk NR6 6UA **t** 01603 407101 **f** 01603 405314 **e** brian@norwichartistes.co.uk **w** norwichartistes.co.uk MD: Brian Russell.

NOW Music 15 Tabbs Lane, Scholes, Cleckheaton, West Yorks BD19 6DY **t** 01274 851365 **f** 01274 874329 **e** nowmusic@now-music.com **w** now-music.com MD: John Wagstaff.

NoWHere Management 30 Tweedholm Ave East, Walkerburn, Peeblesshire EH43 6AR **t** 01896 870284 or 07812 818 183 **e** michaelwild@btopenworld.com Owner: Michael Wild.

NSE Entertainments Minster Cottage, Sincox Lane, Broomers Corner, Shipley, near Horsham, West Sussex RH13 8PS **t** 01403 741321 **e** ian@entertainment-nse.co.uk **w** entertainment-nse.co.uk Owner: Ian Long.

NSMA The Old Laundry, 100 Irving Road, Bournemouth BH6 5BL **t** 0870 040 6767 **e** info@nsma.com **w** nsma.com Dir: Chris Jenkins.

Numinous Management Figment House, Church Street, Ware, Hertfordshire SG12 9EN **t** 01920 484040 **f** 01920 463883 **e** allan.james1@virgin.net **w** numinous.co.uk Dir, A&R/Management: Allan James.

Nutty Tart Management Call for address. **t** 07951 062 566 **e** nuttytartmanagement@hotmail.com MD: Mandy Freedman.

NVA Management 1 Canada Square, 29th Floor Canary Wharf Tower, London E14 5DY **t** 0870 444 2506 **f** 07000 785 845 **e** info@newvisionarts.com **w** newvisionarts.com MD: Chris Nathaniel.

NVB Entertainments 80 Holywell Road, Studham, Dunstable, Bedfordshire LU6 2PD **t** 01582 873623 **f** 01582 873618 **e** henri12787@aol.com MD: Mr H Harrison.

NYJO - National Youth Jazz Orchestra 11 Victor Road, Harrow, Middlesex HA2 6PT **t** 020 8863 2717 **f** 020 8863 8685 **e** bill.ashton@virgin.net **w** NYJO.org.uk Chairman: Bill Ashton.

Dee O'Reilly Management 112 Gunnersbury Avenue, London W5 4HB **t** 020 8993 7441 **f** 020 8992 9993 **e** info@dorm.co.uk **w** thedormgroup.com General Manager: John O'Reilly.

O-Mix 18 Avonmore Road, London W14 8RR **t** 020 7622 4176 **f** 020 7622 4176 **e** info@o-mix.co.uk **w** o-mix.co.uk Dir: Alex Kerr-Wilson.

Offside Management Unit A, 1st Floor, 16-24 Brewery Road, London N7 9NH **t** 020 7700 2662 **f** 020 7700 2882 **e** info@bsimerch.com **w** bsimerch.com MD: Andy Allen.

OMC Management Oxford Music Central, 2nd Floor, 65 George Street, Oxford OX1 2BQ **t** 01865 798 791 **f** 01865 798 792 **e** omcmanagement@oxfordmusic.net Mgr: Dave Newton.

Omoya Entertainment 26-28 Hammersmith Grove, London W6 7BA **t** 020 8834 1085 **f** 020 8834 1100 **e** info@omoya.com **w** omoya.com Contact: Kenneth Omoya

On 10 Music Entertainment Studio 204, Westbourne Studios, 242 Acklam Rd, London W10 5JJ **t** 020 7524 7610 or 07900 055 810 **f** 020 7524 7611 **e** info@on10music.com **w** on10music.com MD: Justin Hsu.

One Fifteen 1 Prince Of Orange Lane, Greenwich, London SE10 8JQ **t** 020 8293 0999 **f** 020 8293 9525 **e** info@onefifteen.com **w** onefifteen.com MD: Paul Loasby.

One Management 43 St Albans Avenue, London W4 5JS **t** 020 8994 4422 **f** 020 8994 1930 **e** onemgmt@dircon.co.uk MD: Karin Clayton.

Onside Management 19a Ware Road, Hertford, Herts SG13 7EB **t** 01992 535126 **f** 01992 535127 **e** mail@onside.co.uk Director: Nick Boyles.

Opal-Chant Studio 1, 223A Portobello Road, London W11 1LU **t** 020 7221 7239 **f** 020 7792 1886 **e** opal-chant@dial.pipex.com Dir: Jane Geerts. Dir: Anthea Norman-Taylor.

Open Top Music 20 Market Place, Kingston upon Thames, Surrey KT1 1JP **t** 020 8255 8818 **e** mail@opentopmusic.com **w** opentopmusic.com Dir: Nick Turner.

Opium (Arts) 49 Portland Road, London W11 4LJ **t** 020 7229 5080 **f** 020 7229 4841 **e** opium@aol.com MD: Richard Chadwick.

OPL Management 4 The Limes, North End Way, London NW3 7HG **t** 020 8209 0025 **e** oplmanagement@aol.com Director: Miss Sabina Van de Wattyne.

Orgasmatron 4 Bourlet Close, London W1W 7BJ **t** 020 7580 4170 **f** 020 7900 6244 **e** info@orgasmatron.co.uk **w** guychambers.com Contact: Dylan Chambers, Louise Jeremy

Ornadel Management Clearwater Yard, 35 Inverness St, London NW1 7HB **t** 020 7424 7500 **f** 020 7424 7501 **e** guy@ornadel.com **w** ornadel.com MD: Guy Ornadel.

Out There Management Strongroom, 120-124 Curtain Road, London EC2A 3SQ **t** 020 7739 6903 **f** 020 7613 2715 **e** outthere@outthere.co.uk Manager: Stephen Taverner.

Outerglobe (Global Fusion) 113 Cheesemans Terrace, London W14 9XH **t** 020 7385 5447 **f** 020 7385 5447 **e** golden@outerglobe.freeserve.co.uk **w** outerglobe.com MD: Debbie Golt.

OUTSIDE MANAGEMENT

OUTSIDE management

outside line

Butler House, 177-178 Tottenham Court Road, London W1T 7NY **t** 020 7436 3633 **f** 020 7436 3632 **e** info@outside-org.co.uk **w** outside-org.co.uk Director: Alan Edwards

P&P Music International Crabtree Cottage, Mill Lane, Kidmore End, Oxon RG4 9HB **t** 0118 972 4356 **f** 0118 972 4809 **e** ppmusicint@aol.com **w** dovehouserecords.com President: Thomas Pemberton.

P3 Music Management. 4 St Andrew Street, Alyth, Perthshire PH11 8AT **t** 01828 633790 **e** office@p3music.com **w** p3music.com Dirs: James Taylor & Alison Burns.

Parallel Lines 16-24 Underwood Street, London N1 7JQ **t** 020 7253 2700 or 07958 549264 **f** 020 7253 2740 **e** siona@parallellinesmusic.co.uk Contact: Siona Ryan

Park Promotions PO Box 651, Oxford 0X2 9AZ **t** 01865 241717 **f** 01865 204556 **e** info@parkrecords.com **w** parkrecords.com MD: John Dagnell.

Parliament Management PO Box 6328, London N2 0UN **t** 020 8444 9841 **f** 020 8442 1973 **e** info@parliament-management.com A&R: Damian Baetens.

Part Rock Management 1 Conduit Street, London W1S 2XA **t** 020 8207 1418 **e** stewartyoung@mindspring.com MD: Stewart Young.

The Party Palace Balcony Floor, The Meridian Centre, Elm Lane, Havant, Hants PO9 1UN **t** 023 9247 7222 **f** 023 9247 7223 **e** info@thepartypalace.co.uk **w** thepartypalace.co.uk Dir: Del Mitchell.

Pat Kane 9 Crown Road South, Glasgow G12 9DJ **t** 07718 588497 **e** patkane@theplayethic.com **w** patkane.com Singer/Writer: Pat Kane.

Paul Crockford Management (PCM) Latimer House, 272 Latimer Rd, London W10 6QY **t** 020 8962 8272 **f** 020 8962 8243 **e** pcm.assistant@virgin.net MD: Paul Crockford. Assistant: Danielle Lazarus.

Pegasus Management 8 Ashington Court, Westwood Hill, Sydenham, London SE26 6BN **t** 020 8778 9918 **f** 020 8355 7708 **e** PegasusMgnt@hotmail.com Dir: James Doheny.

Justin Perry Management PO Box 20242, London NW1 7FL **t** 020 7485 1113 **e** info@proofsongs.co.uk

PEZ Management 15 Sutherland House, 137-139 Queenstown Road, London SW8 3RJ **t** 020 7978 1503 **f** 020 7978 1502 **e** perryfmorgan@hotmail.com Management: Perry Morgan.

PFB Management 9 Bowmans Lea, London SE23 3TL **t** 020 8291 3175 **f** 020 8699 6409 **e** paul@pfb-management.co.uk MD: Paul Bibby.

Pilot Management 222 Canalot Studios, 222 Kensal Road, London W10 5BN **t** 020 7565 2227 **f** 020 7565 2228 **e** dayo@pilotcreativeagency.com Manager: Amanda Fairhurst.

PJ Music 156A High Street, London Colney, Hertfordshire AL2 1QF **t** 01727 827017 or 07860 902361 **f** 01727 827017 **e** pjmusic@ukonline.co.uk **w** schmusicmusic.com Dir: Paul J Bowrey.

Plan C Management Covetous Corner, Hudnall Common, Little Gaddesden, Herts HP4 1QW **t** 01442 842851 **f** 01442 842082 **e** christian@plancmusic.com **w** plancmusic.com Manager: Christian Ulf-Hansen.

Platinum Management 42 Cheriton Close, Queens Walk, Ealing, London W5 1TR **t** 020 8997 8851 **f** 020 8997 8851 **e** carolyn@platinum.fsnet.co.uk MD: Carolyn Norman.

Plus Artist Management 36 Follingham Court, Drysdale Place, London N1 6LZ **t** 020 7684 8594 **f** 020 7684 8740 **e** deschisholm@hotmail.com Contact: Desmond Chisholm

PopWorks 1 Lopen Road, Silver Street, London N18 1PN **t** 020 8807 6268 **f** 020 8351 1497 **e** popworks1@yahoo.com MD: Linda Duff.

Porcupine Management 33-45 Parr Street, Liverpool, Merseyside L1 4JN **t** 0151 707 1050 **f** 0151 709 4090 **e** oxygenmusic@btinternet.com Partners: Pete Byrne & Peasy.

Positive Management 41 West Ella Road, London NW10 9PT **t** 020 8961 6257 or 07889 155 533 **f** 020 8963 1974 **e** Meira@positive-mgmt.co.uk **w** positive-mgmt.co.uk MD: Meira Shore.

Power Artist Management 29 Riversdale Road, Thames Ditton, Surrey KT7 0QN **t** 020 8398 5236 **f** 020 8398 7901 MD: Barry Evans.

PPM Artist Management 73 Leonard Street, London EC2A 4QS **t** 020 7739 7552 **e** music@ppmlondon.com **w** ppmlondon.com MD: Polo Piatti.

The Precious Organisation The Townhouse, 1 Park Gate, Glasgow G3 6DL **t** 0141 353 2255 **f** 0141 353 3545 **e** elliot@precioustoo.com MD: Elliot Davis.

Prestige Management 8600 Wilbur Avenue, Northridge, California, 91324 USA **t** 020 8248 0200 **f** 020 8248 0201 **e** info@prestigeuk.com; prestige@gte.net MD: Richard Rashman.

Principle Management 30-32 Sir John Rogersons Quay, Dublin 2, Ireland **t** +353 1 677 7330 **f** +353 1 677 7276 **e** jenn@numb.ie **w** u2.com MD: Steve Matthews.

PRo Management Room 56, London Fruit & Wool Exchange, Brushfield Street, London E1 6EX **t** 020 7375 3282 **f** 020 7375 3314 **e** amy@theprogroup.co.uk Director: Amy Thomson.

Pro-Rock Management Caxton House, Caxton Avenue, Blackpool, Lancashire FY2 9AP **t** 01253 508670 **f** 01253 508670 **e** promidibfp@aol.com **w** members.aol.com/promidibfp MD: Ron Sharples.

Prodmix DJ Management & Production 61 Railway Arch, Cambridge Grove, London W6 0LD **t** 020 8742 6600 **f** 020 8742 6677 **e** info@prodmix.com **w** prodmix.com Director: Karen Goldie-Sauve.

The Psycho Management Company 111 Clarence Road, London SW19 8QB **t** 020 8540 8122 **f** 020 8715 2827 **e** agents@psycho.co.uk **w** psycho.co.uk Dir: J Mabley.

Public Symphony 22 Gravesend Road, London W12 OSZ **t** 07973 295113 **e** Dobs@adagemusic.co.uk **w** adagemusic.co.uk Manager: Dobs Vye.

Pure Delinquent 134 Replingham Road, Southfields, London SW18 5LL **t** 07929 990 321 **f** 020 8870 0790 **e** julie@pure-delinquent.com **w** pure-delinquent.com Dir: Julie Pratt.

Pure Music Management 77 Beak Street, No. 306, London W1F 9DB **t** 07766 180 330 **f** 020 7439 3330 **e** puremusicmgmt@yahoo.com Contact: Michael Cox

PVA 2 High Street, Westbury On Trym, Bristol BS9 3DU **t** 0117 950 4504 **f** 0117 941 9021 **e** enquiries@pva.ltd.uk **w** pva.ltd.uk Dir: Pat Vincent.

PVA Management Hallow Park, Worcester WR2 6PG **t** 01905 640663 **f** 01905 641842 **e** pva@pva.co.uk **w** pva.co.uk PA: Cary Taylor.

Qaraj' 1 King's House, 396, King's Road, London SW10 0LL **t** 020 7352 2239 **f** 020 7349 0249 **e** info@qaraj.com **w** qaraj.com MD: Michele Baldini.

Quest Management 34 Trinity Crescent, London SW17 7AE **t** 020 8772 7888 **f** 020 8722 7999 **e** info@quest-management.com Managers: Scott Rodger/Stuart Green.

Quintessential Music PO Box 546, Bromley, Kent BR2 0RS **t** 020 8402 1984 or 07956 389 840 **f** 020 8325 0708 **e** urban_music@msn.com Senior Partner: Quincey.

R2 Management PO Box 100, Moreton-in-Marsh, Gloucestershire GL56 0ZX **t** 01608 651802 **f** 01608 652814 **e** editor@jacobsladder.org.uk **w** jacobsladder.org.uk MD: Robb Eden.

Radius Music PO Box 46770, London SW17 9YH **t** 020 8672 7030 **f** 020 8672 7030 **e** info@radiusmusic.co.uk **w** radiusmusic.co.uk Manager: Mark Wood.

Razzamatazz Management Crofters, East Park Lane, Newchapel, Surrey RH7 6HS **t** 01342 835359 **f** 01342 835433 **e** mcgrogan@tinyworld.co.uk Dir: Jill Shirley.

RDPR Music Management The Heritage, Horsley, Stroud, Glocs GL6 0PY **t** 01453 832876 **e** rachel@dunlop4917.freeserve.co.uk Proprietor: Rachel Dunlop.

Reckless 122A Highbury Road, Kings Heath, Birmingham, West Midlands B14 7QP **t** 0121 443 2186 **e** boblamb@recklessltd.freeserve.co.uk MD: Bob Lamb.

Red Onion Productions Suite 100, Hilton Grove Business Centre, 25 Hatherley Mews, London E17 4QP **t** 020 8520 3975 **f** 020 8521 6646 **e** info@redonion.uk.com **w** redonion.uk.com MD: Dee Curtis.

Redd Management The Courtyard, Unit A, 42 Colwith Road, Hammersmith, London W6 9EY **t** 020 8846 3737 **f** 020 8846 3738 **e** mail@reddmanagement.com Artist: David Moores.

Represents Artist Management Unit 10 Southam Street Studios, Southam Street, London W10 5PH **t** 020 8969 5151 **f** 020 8969 4141 **e** ben@represents.co.uk **w** represents.co.uk MD: Ben King.

Retaliate First Management Unit 9, Darvells Works, Common Road, Chorleywood, Herts WD3 5LP **t** 01923 286010 **f** 01923 286070 **e** mgmt@retaliatefirst.co.uk **w** ianbrown-online.co.uk MD: Steve Lowes.

Rheoli Ankst Management 104a Cowbridge Road East, Canton, Cardiff CF11 9DX **t** 02920 394200 **f** 02920 372703 **e** rhiannonankst1@aol.com Contact: Alun Llwyd

Richard Evans Management 15 Chesham Street, Belgravia, London SW1X 8ND **t** 020 7235 3929 **e** r.evans@pipemedia.co.uk MD: Richard Evans.

Richard Ogden Management PO Box 43729, West Kensington, London W14 8DT **t** 020 7751 1300 **f** 020 7602 8998 **e** mail@richardogdenmanagement.com **w** richardogdenmanagement.com MD: Richard Ogden. Co-MD: Matthew Szumpf.

Richman Management 66A Highgate High Street, London N6 5HX **t** 020 8374 2258 MD: Richard Shipman.

Right Management 177 High Street, Harlesden, London NW10 4TE **t** 020 8961 3889 **f** 020 8961 4620 **e** info@rightrecordings.com **w** rightrecordings.com Directors: David Landau, John Kaufman.

Riot Club Management Unit 4, 27A Spring Grove Road, Hounslow, Middx TW3 4BE **t** 020 8572 8809 **f** 020 8572 9590 **e** riot@riotclub.co.uk **w** riotclub.co.uk MD: Lee Farrow.

Riot Management 47 Hay's Mews, London W1J 5QE **t** 020 7499 3993 **f** 020 7499 0219 **e** info@riot-management.com Contact: Matt Page, Ewan Grant

Riverman Management Top Floor, George House, Brecon Road, London W6 8PY **t** 020 7381 4000 **f** 020 7381 9666 **e** info@riverman.co.uk **w** riverman.co.uk Dir: David McLean.

Riviera Music Management 83 Dolphin Crescent, Paignton, Devon TQ3 1JZ **t** 07071 226078 **f** 01803 665728 **e** Info@rivieramusic.net **w** rivieramusic.net MD: Kevin Jarvis.

RLM (Richard Law Management) 58 Marylands Road, Maida Vale, London W9 2DR **t** 020 7286 1706 **f** 020 7266 1293 **e** richard@rlmanagement.co.uk Manager: Richard Law.

Ro-lo Productions 35 Dillotford Avenue, Coventry, W. Midlands CV3 5DR **t** 02476 410388 or 07711 817475 **f** 02476 416615 **e** roger.lomas@virgin.net MD: Roger Lomas.

Robert Miller Management Suite 237, 78 Marylebone High Street, London W1U 5AP **t** 020 8908 1262 or 07973 129068 **f** 07971 402973 **e** millermusic@hotmail.com MD: Robert Miller.

Robert Owens/Musical Directions 352A Kilburn Lane, London W9 3EF **t** 020 8962 0515 **f** 020 8960 5271 **e** jackyaschroer@aol.com Manager: Jacky Schroer.

Robin Morton Consultancy 22 Herbert Street, Glasgow G20 6NB **t** 0141 337 1199 or 07870 590 909 **f** 0141 357 0655 **e** robinmorto@aol.com Mgr: Robin Morton.

Rose Rouge International AWS House, Trinity Square, St Peter Port, Guernsey, Channel Islands GY1 1LX **t** 01481 728283 **f** 01481 714118 **e** awsgroup@cwgsy.net Director: Steve Free.

Rough Trade Management 66 Golborne Road, London W10 5PS **t** 020 8960 9888 **f** 020 8968 6715 **e** kelly.kiley@roughtraderecords.com **w** roughtraderecords.com Artist Co-ordinator: Kelly Kiley.

Route One Management 24 Derby Street, Edgeley, Stockport, Cheshire SK3 9HF **t** 0161 476 1172 or 07950 119 151 **e** andylacallen@yahoo.co.uk **w** spinning-fields.com Director: Andy Callen.

RPM Management Pierce House, London Apollo Complex, Queen Caroline Street, London W6 9QU **t** 020 8741 5557 **f** 020 8741 5888 **e** marlene-rpm@pierce-entertainment.com **w** pierce-entertainment.com MD: Marlene Gaynor.

RRR Management 96 Wentworth Road, Birmingham B17 9SY **t** 0121 426 6820 **f** 0121 426 5700 **e** enquiries@rrrmanagement.com **w** rrrmanagement.com Director: Ruby Ryan.

Ruby Talent Appt 8, Goldcrest, 1 Lexington Street, London W1F 9TA **t** 020 7439 4554 **f** 020 7439 1649 **e** tara@ruby-talent.co.uk MD: Tara Joseph.

Runrig Management 1 York Street, Aberdeen AB11 5DL **t** 01224 573100 **f** 01224 572598 **e** office@runrig.co.uk **w** runrig.co.uk Manager: Mike Smith.

Billy Russell Management Binny Estate, Ecclesmachan, Edinburgh EH52 6NL **t** 01506 858885 **f** 01506 858155 **e** kitemusic@aol.com **w** kitemusic.com MD: Billy Russell.

Sacred Management 187 Freston Road, London W10 6TH **t** 020 8969 1323 **f** 020 8969 1363 **e** info@sacred-music.com Manager: Adjei Amaning.

Safe Management St Ann's House, Guildford Road, Lightwater, Surrey GU18 5RA **t** 01276 476676 **f** 01276 451109 **e** first name@safemanagement.co.uk Manager: Chris Herbert.

Safehouse Management Reverb House, Bennett Street, London W4 2AH **t** 020 8994 8889 **f** 020 8994 8617 **e** info@safehousemanagement.com **w** safehousemanagement.com Manager: Ian Hindmarsh.

Saffa Music Arena House, 12-15 Plough and Harrow Road, Edgbaston, Birmingham B16 8UR **t** 0121 694 5135 **f** 0121 248 6007 **e** info@safa.co.uk **w** rubyturner.com MD: Geoff Pearce.

Safi Sounds Management & Promotion Po Box 572, Huddersfield HD3 4ZD **t** 01484 340975 **e** info@safisounds.co.uk **w** safisounds.co.uk Mgr: Sarah Hutton.

Charles Salt Management Leacroft, Cheriton Cross, Cheriton Bishop, Exeter, Devon EX6 6JH **t** 01647 24502 **f** 01647 24052 **e** charlie35@supanet.com **w** lizardsun-music.co.uk MD: Charles Salt.

Sanctuary Artist Management Sanctuary House, 45-53 Sinclair Road, London W14 0NS **t** 020 7602 6351 **f** 020 7603 5941 **e** info@sanctuarygroup.com **w** sanctuarygroup.com

Saphron Management c/o 36 Belgrave Road, London E17 8QE **t** 020 8521 7764 or 07973 415 167 **e** saphron@msn.com Artist Manager: Annette Bennett MMF.

Satellite Artists Studio House, 34 Salisbury Street, London NW8 8QE **t** 020 7402 9111 **f** 020 7723 3064 **e** satellite_artists@hotmail.com MD: Eliot Cohen. GM: Peter Sullivan. Dir: Ray Dorset.

Scarlet Management Southview, 68 Siltside, Gosberton Risegate, Lincs PE11 4ET **t** 01755 841750 **f** 01755 841750 **e** info@scarletrecording.co.uk **w** scarletrecording.co.uk MD: Liz Lenten.

Schoolhouse Management 42 York Place, Edinburgh EH1 3HU **t** 0131 557 4242 **e** bruce@schoolhousemanagement.co.uk **w** schoolhousemanagement.co.uk MD: Bruce Findlay.

Scruffy Bird The Nest, 205 Victoria St, London SW1E 5NE **t** 020 7931 7990 **f** 020 7900 1557 **e** duncan@scruffybird.com **w** scruffybird.com Head of Management: Duncan Ellis.

Dave Seamer Entertainments 46 Magdalen Road, Oxford, Oxfordshire OX4 1RB **t** 01865 240054 **f** 01865 240054 **e** dave@daveseamer.co.uk **w** daveseamer.co.uk MD: Dave Seamer.

Seaview Music 28 Mawson Road, Cambridge CB1 2EA **t** 01223 508431 **f** 01223 508449 **e** seaview@dial.pipex.com **w** seaviewmusic.co.uk Mgr: Alison Page.

Alan Seifert Management 1 Winterton House, 24 Park Walk, London SW10 0AQ **t** 020 7795 0321 or 07958 241 733 **f** 020 7795 0321 **e** alanseifert@lineone.net MD: Alan Seifert.

Sentics 18 Coronation Court, London W10 6AL **t** 020 8968 4337 **f** 020 7598 9465 **e** raf.sentics@virgin.net Dir: Raf Edmonds.

Sentinel Management 60 Sellons Avenue, London NW10 4HH **t** 020 8961 6992 or 07932 737 547 **e** sentinel7@hotmail.com Dirs: RJ, Sandra Scott.

Serious Artist Management PO Box 13143, London N6 5BG **t** 020 8731 7300 **f** 020 8458 0045 **e** sam@seriousworld.com **w** seriousworld.com Contact: Sam O'Riordan

Session Connection 110-112 Disraeli Road, London SW15 2DX **t** 020 8871 1212 or 020 8672 7055 **f** 020 8682 1772 **e** sessionconnection@mac.com **w** thesessionconnection.com MD: Tina Hamilton.

Seven Music Promotions PO Box 2042, Luton, Beds LU3 2EP **t** 01582 595944 **f** 01582 612752 **e** j.waller@nocturnalrecordings.com Dir/A&R: Jonathan M Waller. A&R: Hamish Maclean.

Jon Sexton Management (JSM) 9 Spedan Close, Branch Hill, London NW3 7XF **t** 07855 551 024 **e** copasetik1@aol.com **w** copasetik.com MD: Jon Sexton.

SGO Music Management PO Box 34994, London SW6 6WF **t** 020 7385 9377 **f** 020 7385 0372 **e** sgomusic@sgomusic.com **w** sgomusic.com MD: Stuart Ongley. Managing Director: Stuart Ongley.

ShaftRoxy Management PO Box 39464, London N10 1WP **t** 07779 340 154 **f** 020 8883 4086 **e** nathan@shaftroxy.com **w** shaftroxy.com MD: Nathan Hull.

Shalit Global Entertainment & Management 7 Moor St, Soho, London W1D 5NB **t** 020 7851 9155 **f** 020 7851 9156 **e** info@shalitglobal.com MD: Jonathan Shalit.

Shavian Enterprises 14 Devonshire Place, London W1G 6HX **t** 020 7935 6906 **f** 020 7224 6256 **e** info@sandieshaw.com **w** sandieshaw.com Director: Louise Voss.

Show Business Entertainment The Bungalow, Chatsworth Avenue, Long Eaton, Nottinghamshire NG10 2FL **t** 0115 973 5445 **f** 0115 946 1831 **e** kimholmes@showbusinessagency.freeserve.co.uk MD: Kim Holmes.

Shurwood Management Tote Hill Cottage, Stedham, Midhurst, West Sussex GU29 0PY **t** 01730 817400 **f** 01730 815846 **e** shurley@shurwood.fsnet.co.uk GM: Shurley Selwood.

Silentway Management Unit 61B, Pall Mall Deposits, 124-128 Barlby Road, London W10 6BL **t** 020 8969 2498 **f** 020 8969 2506 **e** silentwayuk@aol.com **w** simplyred.com Manager: Ian Grenfell.

Silentway Management. (Manchester) Lock Keeper's Cottage, Century Street, Manchester M3 4QL **t** 0161 832 2111 **f** 0161 832 2333 **e** silentwayuk@aol.com **w** simplyred.com

Silverbird Amersham Common House, 133 White Lion Road, Amersham Common, Bucks HP7 9JY **t** 01494 766754 **f** 01494 766745 **e** donatella@silvrbird.demon.co.uk **w** leosayer.com Mgr: Donatella Piccinetti.

Simon Lawlor Management On request **t** 01224 647 220 or 07792 517 508 **e** simonlawlormanagement@btinternet.com **w** simonlawlor.co.uk MD: Simon Lawlor.

Sincere Management Flat B, 6 Bravington Road, London W9 3AH **t** 020 8960 4438 **f** 020 8968 8458 **e** office@sinman.co.uk Contact: Peter Jenner & Mushi Jenner

Siren Productions 5 Cavalry Gardens, London SW15 2QQ **t** 020 8871 3761 **f** 0709 200 4055 **e** ellise@sirenproductions.freeserve.co.uk Dance Music Label Const.: Ellise Theuma.

Size: Music PO Box 798, London EN1 1ZP **t** 020 8350 1221 **e** simon@size-music.com **w** size-music.com Contact: Simon Nicholls

Skeleton Key Management 102 Rose Lane, Mossley Hill, Liverpool L18 8AG **t** 0151 724 4760 **f** 0151 764 6286 **e** info@deltasonic.co.uk Managers: Alan Wills, Simon Moran.

Slap Back Management 27 Sherbourne Drive, Cox Green, Maidenhead, Berkshire SL6 3EP **t** 01628 675999 **f** 01628 676985 Prop: Keith Rowe.

Slice DJ & Artist Management 2a Exmoor Street, London W10 6BD **t** 020 8964 7623 **f** 020 8964 0101 **e** slice@slice.co.uk **w** slice.co.uk Director: Simone Young.

Slowburn Productions 18 Eastwick Lodge, 4 Village Road, Enfield, Middx EN1 2DH **t** 020 8360 4670 **e** Harry@slowburnproductions.co.uk MD: Harry Benjamin.

SMA Talent The Cottage, Church Street, Fressingfield, Suffolk IP21 5PA **t** 01379 586734 **f** 01379 586131 **e** carolynne@smatalent.com MD: Carolynne Wyper.

Small World 18a Farm Lane Trading Centre, 101 Farm Lane, London SW6 1QJ **t** 020 7385 3233 **f** 020 7386 0473 **e** tina@smallworldmanagement.com Manager: Tina Matthews.

SMI/Everyday Productions 33 Mandarin Place, Grove, Oxon OX12 0QH **t** 01235 771577 or 01235 767171 **e** smi_everyday_productions@yahoo.com Contact: VP A&R

Doug Smith Associates PO Box 1151, London W3 8HA **t** 020 8993 8436 **f** 020 8896 1778 **e** mail@dougsmithassociates.com **w** dougsmithassociates.com Partners: Doug Smith, Eve Carr.

Social Misfit Entertainment Suite 17 Hunter House, Woodfarrs, London SE5 8HA **t** 020 7924 0565 **e** socialmisfits@hotmail.com **w** social-misfit.com MD: Patrick Waweru.

Solar Management 13 Rosemont Road, London NW3 6NG **t** 020 7794 5588 **f** 020 7794 3388 **e** info@solarmanagement.co.uk **w** solarmanagement.co.uk MD: Carol Crabtree.

Solid Senders 93 Ronald Park Avenue, Westcliff On Sea, Essex SS0 9QP **t** 01702 341983 **e** irene@solidsenders.freeserve.co.uk **w** wilkojohnson.co.uk Manager/Agent: Irene Knight.

Some Bizarre 4 Denmark Street, London WC2H 8LP **t** 020 7836 9995 **f** 020 7836 9909 **e** info@somebizarre.com **w** somebizarre.com A&R Manager: Andy Pettitt.

Son Management 72 Marylebone Lane, London W1U 2PL **t** 020 7486 7458 **f** 020 8467 6997 **e** sam@randm.co.uk Mgr: Sam Eldridge.

Sound Image Unit 2B, Banquay Trading Estate, Slutchers Lane, Warrington, Cheshire WA1 1PJ **t** 01925 445742 **f** 01925 445742 **e** info@frogstudios.co.uk **w** frogstudios.co.uk MD: Steve Millington.

Sound Pets PO Box 158, Twickenham, Middlesex TW2 6RW **t** 07976 577 773 **f** 0871 733 3401 **e** robinhill@soundpets.freeserve.co.uk Director: Robin Hill.

Sounds Like A Hit 48 Shelvers Way, Tadworth, Surrey KT20 5QF **t** 01737 218899 **f** 01737 355443 **e** steve@soundslikeahit.com **w** soundslikeahit.com Director: Steve Crosby.

Spaced Out Music 11 Smithfield Centre, Leek, Staffs. ST13 5JW **t** 01782 772 989 or 01538 384 315 **e** mike@demon655.freeserve.co.uk **w** the-demon.com MD: Mike Stone.

Mal Spence Management Cherry Tree Lodge, Copmanthorpe, York, North Yorks YO23 3SH **t** 01904 703764 **f** 01904 702312 **e** malspence@aol.com **w** sugarstar.com MD: Mal Spence.

Sphinx Management 2 Unity Place, West Gate, Rotherham, South Yorkshire S60 1AR **t** 01709 820379 or 01709 820370 **f** 01709 369990 **e** tributebands@btconnect.com **w** tribute-entertainment.co.uk Dir: Anthony French.

Spirit Music & Media PO Box 30884, London W12 9AZ **t** 020 8746 7461 **f** 020 8749 7441 **e** info@spiritmm.com **w** spiritmm.com MD: Tom Haxell.

Splinter Management Terminal Studios, 4-10 Lamb Walk, London SE1 3TT **t** 020 7357 8416 **f** 020 7357 8437 **e** parmesanchic@aol.com **w** sneakerpimps.com MD: Caroline Butler.

Split Music 13 Sandys Rd, Worcester WR1 3HE **t** 01905 29809 **f** 01905 613023 **e** split.music@virgin.net **w** splitmusic.com MD: Chris Warren.

Sprint Music High Jarmany Farm, Jarmany Hill, Barton St David, Somerton,Somerset TA11 6DA **t** 01458 851010 **f** 01458 851029 **e** info@sprintmusic.co.uk **w** sprintmusic.co.uk Consultant: John Ratcliff.

Star Quality Management 50 Anne's Court, 3 Palgrave Gardens, London NW1 6EN **t** 0114 268 5665 **f** 0144 268 4161 **e** bmc@brownmcleod.co.uk MD: John Roddison.

Star-Write Management PO Box 16715, London NW4 1WN **t** 020 8203 5062 **f** 020 8202 3746 **e** starwrite@btinternet.com Dir: John Lisners.

Starone 2 Trinity Road, Marlow, Bucks SL7 3AW **t** 01628 483 629 **e** b.hallin@virgin.net MD: Brian Hallin.

Stereophonic Management PO Box 3787, London SE22 9DZ **t** 020 8299 1650 **f** 020 8693 5514 **e** duophonic@btopenworld.com Contact: Martin Pike

Steve Allen Entertainments 60 Broadway, Peterborough, Cambs PE1 1SU **t** 01733 569589 **f** 01733 561854 **e** steve@sallenent.co.uk **w** sallenent.co.uk Director: Steve Allen.

Steve Harrison Management 10-12 Hightown, Sandbach, Cheshire CW11 1AE **t** 01270 750448 **f** 01270 750449 **e** info@shmanagement.co.uk **w** shmanagement.co.uk Director: Steve Harrison. Promotions: Sue Reinhardt. PA: Jane Faulkner. Accounts: Jude Harrison.

Stirling Music 25 Heathmans Road, London SW6 4TJ **t** 020 7371 5756 **f** 020 7371 7731 **e** office@pureuk.com **w** pureuk.com Creative Dir: Billy Royal. President: Evros Stakis.

WG Stonebridge Artist Management PO Box 49155, London SW20 0YL **t** 020 8946 7242 **f** 020 7371 7722 **e** w.stonebridge@btopenworld.com Contact: Bill Stonebridge

Storm Management 134 Godstone Road, Caterham, Surrey CR3 6RB **t** 01883 372639 **f** 01883 372639 **e** enquiries@stormmanagement.uk.com **w** stormmanagement.uk.com MD: Stephen Bailey-Johnston.

Streetfeat Management Unit 105, The Saga Centre, 326 Kensal Rd, London W10 5BZ **t** 020 8969 3370 **f** 020 8960 9971 **e** info@streetfeat.demon.co.uk MD: Colin Schaverien. Directors: Colin Schaverien, Simon Napier-Bell. Artist Liason: Vicki Bannister.

Stress Management Unit 6217, 49 Greenwich High Road, London SE10 9JL **t** 020 8691 0262 **f** 020 8691 0268 **e** stressmgt01@aol.com **w** quixoticrecords.com Manager: Suzanne Hunt.

Strike Back Management 271 Royal College Street, Camden Town, London NW1 9LU **t** 020 7482 0115 **f** 020 7267 1169 **e** maurice@baconempire.com MD: Maurice Bacon.

Strongroom Management 120-124 Curtain Road, London EC2A 3SQ **t** 020 7426 5130 **f** 020 7426 5102 **e** coral@strongroom.com **w** strongroom.com/management Dir: Coral Worman.

Sublime Music 77 Preston Drove, Brighton, East Sussex BN1 6LD **t** 01273 560605 **f** 01273 560606 **e** info@sublimemusic.co.uk **w** sublimemusic.co.uk MD: Patrick Spinks.

Subversive Music Management PO Box 32160, London N4 2XY **t** 020 8800 1011 **f** 020 7681 3135 **e** nashton@subversive-music.com **w** subversive-music.com MD: Nick Ashton-Hart.

Sugar Shack Management PO Box 73, Fish Ponds, Bristol BS16 7EZ **t** 01179 855092 **f** 01179 855092 **e** mike@sugarshackrecords.co.uk **w** sugarshackrecords.co.uk Dir: Mike Darby.

Sunhand 63 Grosvenor Street, London W1X 9DA **t** 020 7493 7831 **f** 020 7491 3028 **e** info@tonygordon.com Manager: Tony Gordon.

SuperVision Management Zeppelin Building, 59-61 Farringdon Road, London EC1M 3JB **t** 020 7916 2146 **f** 020 7691 4666 **e** info@supervisionmgt.com Dirs: Paul Craig & James Sandom.

Swamp Music PO Box 94, Derby, Derbyshire DE22 1XA **t** 01332 332336 **f** 01332 332336 **e** chrishall@swampmusic.co.uk **w** swampmusic.co.uk MD: Chris Hall.

Sylvantone Promotions 11 Saunton Avenue, Redcar, North Yorkshire TS10 2RL **t** 01642 479898 **f** 0709 235 9333 **e** sylvantone@hotmail.com **w** countrymusic.org.uk/tony-goodacre/index.html Prop: Tony Goodacre.

T2 Management Dolphin Court, 42 Carleton Road, London N7 0ER **t** 020 7607 6654 or 07971 575810 **e** hilltaryn@hotmail.com Dir: Taryn Hill.

Talent Call Independent House, 54 Larkshall Road, Chingford E4 6PD **t** 020 8523 9000 **f** 020 8523 8888 **e** abailey@independentmusicgroup.com **w** independentmusicgroup.com Dir: Andy Bailey.

TARGO Ents Corp PO Box 1977, Salisbury SP3 5ZW **t** 01722 716716 or 07971 405874 **f** 01722 716413 **e** targo.entscorps@virgin.net Manager: Mathew Priest.

Teleryngg UK 132 Chase Way, London N14 5DH **t** 07050 055167 **f** 0870 741 5252 **e** teleryngg@msn.com **w** teleryngg.com MD: Richard Struple.

Tender Prey Management Studio 4, Ivebury Court, 325 Latimer Road, London W10 6RA **t** 020 8964 5417 **f** 020 8964 5418 **e** restrictedarea@tenderprey.com Mgr: Rayner Jesson.

Terra Firma Management The Courtyard, Unit A, 42 Colwith Road, Hammersmith, London W6 9EY **t** 020 8846 3737 **f** 020 8846 3738 **e** laura@terraartists.com MD: Marc Marot.

TFF Management Lovat House, Gavell Road, Kilsyth, Glasgow G65 9BS **t** 01236 826555 **f** 01236 825560 **e** tessa@tffpr.com MD: Tessa Hartmann.

TForce Open Studios, County Hall, Belevedere Road, London SE1 7PB **t** 020 7902 8411 **f** 020 7902 8460 **e** enquiry@tforce.com **w** tforce.com MD: Tim Byrne.

Thunderbird Management PO Box 44149, London SW6 2WQ **t** 020 7384 4469 or 07966 756 761 **f** 020 7384 4469 **e** tom@thedatsuns.com Contact: Thomas Dalton

Tim Prior - Artist & Rights Management The Old Lampworks, Rodney Place, London SW19 2LQ **t** 020 8542 4222 **f** 020 8540 6056 **e** info@arm-eu.com MD: Tim Prior.

TJM PO Box 46024, London W9 1WW **t** 020 7286 2230 or 07801 702 279 **f** 020 7286 5359 **e** tara@tjm.uk.com Dir: Tara Joseph.

TK1 Management PO Box 38475, London SE16 7XT **t** 020 7740 3119 **f** 020 7740 3119 **e** info@tk1management.com **w** tk1management.com Dirs: Trina Torpey & Kathryn Nash.

Toni Medcalf Management 31 Grove Road, Barnes, London SW13 0HH **t** 020 8876 2421 or 07767 832260 **f** 020 8876 6621 **e** TTMManagement@aol.com Artist Manager: Toni Medcalf.

Tony Hall Group of Companies 16-17 Grafton House, 2-3 Golden Sq, London W1F 9HR **t** 020 7437 1958 **f** 020 7437 3852 **e** tonyhall@btconnect.com MD: Tony Hall.

Top Banana Management Monomark House, 27 Old Gloucester St, London WC1N 3XX **t** 020 7419 5026 or 07961 056 369 **e** info@topbananaman.com **w** topbananaman.com Contact: Garry Kemp, Nino Pires

Top Draw Music Management PO Box 21469, Highgate, London N6 4ZG **t** 020 8340 5151 **f** 020 8340 5159 **e** info@topdrawmusic.biz **w** topdrawmusic.biz Dir: James Hamilton.

Topaz Entertainment 42 Alexandra Road, London NW4 2SA **t** 020 8203 4197 **f** 020 8202 9805 **e** info@topazentertainment.com MD: Danny Parnes.

Total Concept Management (TCM) PO Box 128, Dewsbury, West Yorkshire WF12 9XS **t** 01924 438295 **f** 01924 525378 **e** tcm@totalconceptmanagement.com **w** totalconceptmanagement.com

Total Management Flat 2, 7 Milnthorpe Road, Meads Village, Eastbourne, East Sussex BN20 7NS **t** 01323 645879 **f** 01323 728608 **e** chris@totalmgt.biz **w** catherinetran.com MD: Chris McGeever.

Touched Productions 4 Varley House, County Street, London SE1 6AL **t** 020 7403 5451 **f** 020 7403 5446 **e** toucheduk@aol.com **w** touched.co.uk Dir: Armorel Weston.

Traffik Productions Po Box 23615, Edinburgh EH1 3ZP **t** 0131 524 9591 **f** 0131 524 9581 **e** stuart@traffik.uk.com Manager: Stuart Duncan.

Traxxevents 3/2, 1 Kennoway Drive, Glasgow G11 7UA **t** 0141 341 0691 **f** 0141 341 0691 **e** info@traxxevents.com **w** traxxevents.com Dir: Mark MacKechnie.

TRC Management 23 New Mount Street, Manchester M4 4DE **t** 0161 953 4081 or 07831 803 435 **f** 0161 953 4091 **e** mail@trcmanagement.com MD: Phil Chadwick.

Trinifold Management Third Floor, 12 Oval Road, London NW1 7DH **t** 020 7419 4300 **f** 020 7419 4325 **e** trinuk@globalnet.co.uk MD: Robert Rosenberg.

TSD Records 14 Coneycroft, Dunnington, York, North Yorkshire YO19 5RL **t** 01904 489337 **e** tsdrecords@btinternet.com MD: Trevor Dawton.

Tsunami Sounds The Gables, Avenue Road, Cranleigh, Surrey GU6 7LE **t** 01483 271200 **f** 01483 271200 **e** info@tsunami.co.uk **w** tsunami.co.uk Director: Ken Easter.

TwoPointNine 7-9 Wadsworth Rd, Perivale, Middx UB6 7JD **t** 020 8566 8633 **e** info@2point9.com **w** 2point9.com Dirs: Billy Grant, Rob Stuart.

Mel Tyler Management 6 Liberty Hall Road, Addlestone, Surrey KT15 1SS **t** 01932 840 616 or 07702 272100 **f** 01932 840 616 **e** meltyler@talk21.com MD: Mel Tyler.

The Umbrella Group Call for address. **t** 07802 535 696 **f** 020 7603 9930 **e** Tommy@Umbrella-Group.com **w** umbrella-group.com MD: Tommy Manzi.

Unique Corp 15 Shaftesbury Centre, 85 Barlby Road, London W10 6BN **t** 020 8964 9333 **f** 020 8964 9888 **e** info@uniquecorp.co.uk **w** uniquecorp.co.uk MD: Alan Bellman.

Up All Night Music 20 Denmark St, London WC2H 8NA **t** 020 7419 4696 **e** info@upallnightmusic.com **w** upallnightmusic.com MD: Phil Taylor.

Upbeat Classical Management PO Box 479, Uxbridge, Middx UB8 2ZH **t** 01895 259441 **f** 01895 259341 **e** info@upbeatclassical.co.uk **w** upbeatclassical.co.uk Director: Maureen Phililps.

Upside Management 14 Clarence Mews, Balham, London SW12 9SR **t** 020 8673 8549 **f** 020 8673 8498 **e** simon@upsideuk.com Co MDs: Simon Jones & Denise Beighton.

Urban Control Mayfair House, 72 New Bond Street, London W1S 1RR **t** 020 8240 8787 or 07812 107 812 **f** 020 8240 8787 **e** wemakethemusic@urbancontrol.com **w** urbancontrol.com CEO: Azor.

Vagabond Management 8th Floor, 245 Blackfriars Road, London SE1 9UR **t** 020 7921 8353 **e** rubber_road_records@yahoo.co.uk MD: Dexter Charles.

Valley Music. 1 Greys Road, Henley-on-Thames, Oxfordshire RG9 1SB **t** 01491 845840 **f** 01491 412855 **e** mark@valleymusicuk.com **w** valleymusicuk.com Manager: Mark Woodward.

Value Added Talent Management (VAT) 1 Purley Place, London N1 1QA **t** 020 7704 9720 **f** 020 7226 6135 **e** vat@vathq.co.uk **w** vathq.co.uk MD: Dan Silver.

Denis Vaughan Management PO Box 28286, London N21 3WT **t** 020 7486 5353 **f** 020 8224 0466 **e** dvaughanmusic@dial.pipex.com Dir: Denis Vaughan.

Vex Management 21c Tressillian Road, London SE4 1YG **t** 020 8469 0800 **f** 020 8469 0800 **e** paul@vexmgmt.demon.co.uk **w** vexmanagement.com MD: Paul Ablett.

Vibe UK PO Box 173, New Malden, Surrey KT3 3YR **t** 020 8949 7730 **f** 020 8949 7798 **e** johnosb1@aol.com **w** vibeuk.com Director: John Osborne.

Vine Gate Music 4 Vine Gate, Parsonage Lane, Farnham Common, Bucks SL2 3NX **t** 01753 643696 **f** 01753 642259 **e** vinegate@clara.net **w** salenajones.co.uk Partner: Tony Puxley.

Voicebox PO Box 82, Altrincham, Cheshire WA15 0QD **t** 0161 928 3222 **f** 0161 928 7849 **e** vb@thevoicebox.co.uk **w** thevoicebox.co.uk MD: Vicki Hope-Robinson.

VRUK Management Top Floor, Voysey House, Barley Mow Passage, Chiswick, London W4 4GB **t** 020 8987 2456 **f** 020 8987 2444 **e** vruk@volumerecords.co.uk MD: Tony Vickers.

War Zones and Associates 33 Kersley Road, London N16 0NT **t** 020 7249 2894 **f** 020 7254 3729 **e** wz33@aol.com Contact: Richard Hermitage

Watercress Management The Old Vicerage, Pickering, North Yorkshire YO18 7AW **t** 01751 475502 **f** 01751 475502 **e** organised@ukonline.co.uk Dir: Ian McDaid.

What Management 3 Belfry Villas, Belfry Ave, Harefield, Uxbridge, Middlesex UB9 6HY **t** 01895 824674 **f** 01895 822994 **e** whatmanagement@blueyonder.co.uk Contact: Mick Cater/David Harper

White Tiger Management 55 Fawcett Close, London SW16 2QJ **t** 020 8677 5199 or 020 8677 5399 **f** 020 8769 5795 **e** whitetigermanagement@hotmail.com MDs: Paul & Corinne White.

Alan Whitehead Management 79 The Ryde, Hatfield, Hertfordshire AL9 5DN **t** 01707 267883 **f** 01707 267247 **e** alan_whitehead_uk@yahoo.com MD: Alan Whitehead.

Whitehouse Management PO Box 43829, London NW6 1WN **t** 020 7209 2586 **f** 020 7209 7187 **e** mail@whitehousemanagement.com MD: Sue Whitehouse.

Whitenoise Management 8 Southam Street, London W10 5PH **t** 020 8964 1002 **f** 020 8964 0021 **e** info@whitenoisemanagement.com MD: Chris Butler.

Wicked Wolf Management 4 Meadow Walk, Wallington, Surrey SM6 7EJ **t** 020 8669 1407 **e** seamus@wickedwolf.co.uk **w** dnadoll.com MD: Seamus Murphy.

WILD WEST MANAGEMENT

Argentum, 2 Queen Caroline Street, London W6 9DX **t** 020 8323 8013 **f** 020 8323 8080 **e** ela@ela.co.uk **w** ela.co.uk Contact: John Giacobbi.
A Division of ELA - Artist Celebrity & Personal Management.

Wildlife Entertainment Unit F, 21 Heathmans Road, London SW6 4TJ **t** 020 7371 7008 **f** 020 7371 7708 **e** info@wildlife-entertainment.com Managing Directors: Ian McAndrew, Colin Lester.

John Williams PO Box 423, Chislehurst, Kent BR7 5TU **t** 020 8295 3639 **f** 020 8295 3641 **e** jrwilliams@lineone.net Contact: John Williams

Allan Wilson Enterprises Queens House, Chapel Green Road, Hindley, Wigan, Lancashire WN2 3LL **t** 01942 258565 or 01942 255158 **f** 01942 255158 **e** allan@allanwilson.co.uk Owner: Allan Wilson.

Wise Buddah Talent 74 Great Titchfield Street, London W1W 7QP **t** 020 7307 1600 **f** 020 7307 1608 **e** nicole.c@wisebuddah.com **w** wisebuddah.com Mgr: Nicole Constantinou.

Wizard Management PO BOX 6779, Birmingham B13 9RZ **t** 0121 778 2218 **f** 0121 778 1856 **e** pk.sharma@ukonline.co.uk MD: Mambo Sharma.

Alan Wood Agency 346 Gleadless Road, Sheffield, South Yorkshire S2 3AJ **t** 0114 258 0338 **f** 0114 258 0638 **e** celia@alanwoodagency.co.uk **w** alanwoodagency.co.uk Contact: Alan Wood

Working Class Music Management 22 Upper Brook St, Mayfair, London W1K 7PZ **t** 020 7491 1060 **f** 020 7491 9996 **e** workingclassmusic@btinternet.com **w** workingclassmanagement.com Contact: Matt Crossey, Lisa Barker

World Famous Group Stamford Gate House, Chelsea Village, Fulham Rd, London SW6 1HS **t** 020 7385 6838 **f** 020 7385 0999 **e** info@worldfamousgroup.com **w** worldfamousgroup.com Chairman: Alon Shulman.

Worldmaster DJ Management PO Box 62, Lenham ME17 2WZ **t** 01622 858300 **f** 01622 858300 **e** info@eddielock.com **w** eddielock.co.uk Proprietor: Eddie Lock.

WS Management The Dog House, 32 Sullivan Crescent, Harefield, Uxbridge, Middlesex UB9 6NL **t** 01895 825757 **e** Bill@wsmgt.co.uk **w** wsmgt.co.uk Director: William L. Langdale-Smith.

Wyze Management 2-3 Fitzroy Mews, London W1T 6DJ **t** 020 7380 0999 **f** 020 7380 1555 **e** info@wyze.com **w** wyze.com MD: Kate Ross.

X FACTOR MANAGEMENT

PO Box 44198, London SW6 4XU **t** 0870 251 9540 **f** 0870 251 9560 **e** info@xfactorltd.com **w** xfactorltd.com MD: Natalie Swallow.

XL Talent Reverb House, Bennett Street, London W4 2AH **t** 020 8747 0660 **f** 020 8747 0880 **e** management@reverbxl.com **w** reverbxl.com Contact: Ian Wright, Maggi Hickman

Xosa Management 130A Uxbridge Road, London W12 8LR **t** 020 7854 1400 **f** 020 7854 1500 **e** info@xosagroup.com **w** xosagroup.com MD: Dean Zepherin.

Brian Yeates Associates Home Farm House, Canwell, Sutton Coldfield, West Midlands B75 5SH **t** 0121 323 2200 **f** 0121 323 2313 **e** ashley@brianyeates.co.uk **w** brianyeates.co.uk Partner: Ashley Yeates.

The Yukon Management 91 Saffron Hill, London EC1N 8PT **t** 020 7242 8408 **f** 020 7242 8408 **e** music@the-yukon.com **w** the-yukon.com MD: Andrew Maurice.

Z Management The Palm House, PO Box 19734, London SW15 2WU **t** 020 8874 3337 **f** 020 8874 3599 **e** office@zman.co.uk **w** zman.co.uk MD: Zita Wadwa-McQ.

Zeall Management Limited 5A Station Road, Twickenham, Middx TW1 4LL **t** 020 8607 9401 **e** info@zeall.com **w** zeall.com MD: David McGeachie. Director: Steve Crickmer.

Zen Management The Garden Office, 39A Ashburnham Road, London NW10 5SB **t** 020 8960 9171 or 07957 338 525 **e** sacha@zenmedia.net MD: Sacha Taylor-Cox.

Business Services

Artist Index

0898 DAVE: Mumbo Jumbo Mgmt
16 HORSEPOWER: Tender Prey Mgmt
2 TONE COLLECTIVE, The: Ro-lo Productions
21ST CENTURY SCHIZOID BAND: Paul Crockford Mgmt (PCM)
3Mi: SGO Music Mgmt
The 45s: First Column Mgmt
5 O'CLOCK HEROES: A.M.P./TBA
8.58: Fox Records (Mgmt)
A: Furtive Mass Transit Systems LLP
A:M LOVERS: Clown Mgmt
AADESH: Muirhead Mgmt
ABBA GOLD: The Psycho Mgmt Company
ABC/MARTIN FRY: Blueprint Mgmt
ABI: Jack 'N' Jill Artiste Mgmt
EVA ABRAHAM: Fruit
ABS: Safe Mgmt
ACOUSTIC ALCHEMY: The Art & Music Corporation
ACTOV LIFE: Future Mgmt
Actual Size: ARB Music Mgmt
ADAM'S FAMILY: Loose
BEN ADAMS: TForce
ADAMS, Justin: Spirit Music & Media
ADEM: Big Dipper Productions
ADVENTURES OF STEVIE V: RDPR Music Mgmt
The AFGHAN WHIGS: INS-YNC
AFRO CELT SOUND SYSTEM: Impro Mgmt
AFRO PUNKS: Congo Music
AFTER EDEN: Line-Up PMC
AFTER THE SILENCE: Jonny Paul Mgmt
The AFTERGLOW: JBM Mgmt
AGENT SUMO: Streetfeat Mgmt
AGUILLERA, Christina: azoffmusic mgmt
AIR ONE: Urban Control
AirHammer: Riot Club Mgmt
AKA THE FOX: Simon Lawlor Mgmt
ALAN 'MIDNIGHT' CONNOR: First Move Mgmt
ALBI: PopWorks
Aldergrove: Michael McDonagh Mgmt
HANNAH ALETHEA: JPS Mgmt
ROBERTA ALEXANDER: The Music Partnership
ALFIE: Steve Harrison Mgmt
ALFREDO: Worldmaster DJ Mgmt
ALLEN, Ross: David Dorrell Mgmt
ALPINESTARS: Riverman Mgmt
ALTERNATIVE 3: CEC Mgmt
AMBER MELODY: Pilot Mgmt
AMBERDOG: 4 Tunes
AMUSEMENT PARKS ON FIRE: Bermuda Mgmt
ANDAIN: Ornadel Mgmt
ANDERSON NOISE: Bulldozer Mgmt
BRETT ANDERSON: Altered States
ANDERSON, Paul Trouble: Prodmix DJ Mgmt & Production
ANDREAS, Lisa: Fox Records (Mgmt)
ANEMIC: Sugar Shack Mgmt
ANGEL CITY: Active Music Mgmt
ANGEL OAKS: Riviera Music Mgmt
ANIMAL CRUELTY: First Time Mgmt
ANNA ANN: Stan Green Mgmt
ANNIE CHRISTIAN: Schoolhouse Mgmt
ANONYMOUS: Urban Control
ANT AND DEC: James Grant Mgmt
APACHE INDIAN: Boom Mgmt
APOLLO 440: XL Talent
APPEAL, Neil: KlubDJ
APPLETON: Ruby Talent
APU FROM PERU: Line-Up PMC
ARCH ENEMY: Sanctuary Artist Mgmt
ARCHIVE: IE Music
ARENA: Billy Russell Mgmt
ARIEL: Zen Mgmt
CRAIG ARMSTRONG: IE Music
ARNOLD, Peter: First Time Mgmt
ASCENSION: Earth Music
ASH: Out There Mgmt
ASHCROFT, Richard: Terra Firma Mgmt
ASHLEY: Upside Mgmt
MARK ASTON: Liquid Mgmt
ASWAD: J Mgmt
ATLANTA: JBS Mgmt UK
ATLAS, Natacha: CEC Mgmt
ATTAR, Stella: Diamond Sounds Music Mgmt
AUBURN: Scarlet Mgmt
KATE AUMONIER: Sanctuary Artist Mgmt
The AUTEURS: INS-YNC
AUTOPIA: Starone
AVALANCHES: MBL
AZRAH: TK1 Mgmt.
AZURE: Urban Control
B MOVIE HEROES: FiveMilesHigh
mB, Emma: Wise Buddah Talent
BABYBIRD: DJT Mgmt
BACHELOR NUMBER ONE: JC Music
The BACHELORS (Con & Dec): The Party Palace
BAD NEWZ: Seven Music Promotions
BADLY DRAWN BOY: Big Life Mgmt
BAGHDADDIES: Line-Up PMC
BAKER, Cheryl: Razzamatazz Mgmt
BAKER, Duck: The Bechhofer Agency
BALBOA: Bizarre Mgmt
BARBARA BALDIERI: Asylum Artists
BAMBINO CASINO: Instinct Mgmt
A BAND CALLED FRANK: First Time Mgmt

BAND OF HOLY JOY: Charmenko
BANG OUT OF ORDER: Direct Heat Mgmt
BAPTISTE, Denys: The Dune Music Company
BARBER'S, Chris, JAZZ AND BLUES BAND: Cromwell Mgmt
BARBIERI, Richard: Medium Productions
BARCLAY JAMES HARVEST: Mad Mgmt
THE BARDO: 365 Artists
BARKER, Sophie: Emperor Mgmt
NEIL BARNES: LH Mgmt
BARRETT, Nick: Creative World Entertainment
BARRETT, Vicky: Jackie Davidson Mgmt
BARTON, Dean: NOW Music
TIM BASTMEYER: Future Mgmt
BBMAK: Daytime Entertainments
BC Sweet: Hal Carter Organisation
BEANGROWERS: Pure Delinquent
The BEARCATS: Swamp Music
BEAT FREAKS: Empire Artist Mgmt
THE BEATINGS: SuperVision Mgmt
THE BEAUTY ROOM: Consigliari
The BED BUGS: TSD Records
NATASHA BEDINGFIELD: Empire Artist Mgmt
BEDINGFIELD, Daniel: Empire Artist Mgmt
BEDOUIN: Doug Smith Associates
BEEDLE, Ashley: Whitenoise Mgmt
BELARUS: Boss Music
BELASCO: Mako Music
BELL & WADE: Metro Artist Mgmt
BELLE & SEBASTIAN: Banchory Mgmt
BELLE MONTENEGRO: Xosa Mgmt
BEN & JASON: Nettwerk Mgmt UK
MATTIE BENBROOK: CMO Mgmt International
BENNETT, Martyn: Braw Mgmt
BENNETT, Vernie: Shalit Global Entertainment & Mgmt
BRENDAN BENSON: Bermuda Mgmt
BENSON, Stephanie: Keep Hit Real Mgmt
BENSUSAN, Pierre: NEM Productions (UK)
JASON BERKMANN: Qaraj'
BERMEL, Derek: Music Company (London).
BERMUDA TRIANGLE: WonderWorld
BERTERO, Roberto: PVA Mgmt
BETH GIBBONS & RUSTIN MAN: Fruit
LAURA BETTINSON: Big Help Music
The BIG BOSSA: Streetfeat Mgmt
BIG CHIEF: Northstar Artist Mgmt
BIG SUR: Retaliate First Mgmt
BIGFELLA: Conception Artist Mgmt
The BIGGER THE GOD: OMC Mgmt
NED BIGHAM: Hope Mgmt
BIKINI ATOLL: Instinct Mgmt
BILK, Acker, AND HIS PARAMOUNT JAZZ BAND: Acker's International Jazz Agency
BIMBO JONES: Ambush Mgmt
BINI & MARTINI: Prodmix DJ Mgmt & Production
BIRD, Jez: Peter Haines Mgmt
BIS: TRC Mgmt
BITCH BITCH BITCH: Alan Whitehead Mgmt
BJORK: Quest Mgmt
BJORN AGAIN: BA Mgmt
BK: Ornadel Mgmt
BLACK BIKINI ALPHA: Arketek Mgmt
BLACK BOX RECORDER: INS-YNC
BLACK CANDY: SMI/Everyday Productions
The BLACK DOG: Feedback Communications
BLACK LACE: NOW Music
BLACK MOTH CONNECTION: RLM (Richard Law Mgmt)
BLACK SIFICHI: Feedback Communications
BLACK SMOKE: Feedback Communications
BLACK STAR LINER: W1 Music Mgmt
BLACK TOP PHOENIX: Simon King Mgmt (SKM)
BLACK VELVETS: Sanctuary Artist Mgmt
BLACK, Mary: Dara Mgmt
BLACK, Richard: Teleryngg UK
BLADES, Lynn: Keep Hit Real Mgmt
BLAKE, Paul: Little Piece of Jamaica (LPOJ)
BLAKE, Perry: NBM
BLAM, Geri: Direct Heat Mgmt
MELANIE BLATT: Redd Mgmt
BLAZIN SQUAD: Albert Samuel Mgmt
BLING DAWG: Jamdown
BLOCK 16 & 17: Solar Mgmt
BLOCK, Rory: NEM Productions (UK)
BLONDIE GOES TO HOLLYWOOD: Hal Carter Organisation
BLUE: Intelligent Music Mgmt
BLUE & RED: MWM Music Mgmt
BLUE BAMBOO: Asylum Artists
BLUE STAR: WonderWorld
SUSAN BLUECHILD: JW Mgmt
BLUR: CMO Mgmt International
BOB BROZMAN & WOODY MANN: NEM Productions (UK)
ALFRED BOE: FourFives Productions
BOG TOWN PLAYBOYS: MSM Music Consultants
BOHINTA: Ardent Music
BOLA: Kamara Artist Mgmt (UK)
BOLAN, Sha: Coda Mgmt UK
BOND: Mel Bush Organization
BOND, Scott: Serious Artist Mgmt
BONIFACE: Empire Artist Mgmt
BONZO DOG DOO DAH BAND: Right Mgmt
The BOOGIE BROTHERS: Denis Vaughan Mgmt
The BOOTLEG BEATLES: The Bootleg Beatles
BORDER CROSSING: Heavyweight Mgmt
BORISKIN, Michael: Music Company (London).
BOSTON: azoffmusic mgmt
BOUJAMAA BOUBOUL: Outerglobe (Global Fusion)
BOWIE, David: Outside Mgmt
BOY GEORGE: Sunhand
BOYCE, Max: International Artistes
THE BOYZ: The Flying Music Co
BOYZONE: Carol & Associates
BRAGG, Billy: Sincere Mgmt
The BRAND NEW HEAVIES: Wildlife Entertainment
BRANDED: Cultural Foundation
BRASSTOOTH: Boom Mgmt
BRAVE CAPTAIN: Rheoli Ankst Mgmt
BRAVEHEART: TForce
BREEZER, Jo: B&H Mgmt
BRENNAN, Maire: Gola Entertainment
POL BRENNAN: Muirhead Mgmt
The BRIDGE: Leap
JES BRIEDEN: Ornadel Mgmt
BROADCAST: Stereophonic Mgmt
BROKEN DOLLS: Safehouse Mgmt
BRONZE AGE FOX: Rheoli Ankst Mgmt
BROOK, Michael: Opium (Arts)
BROTHERHOOD OF MAN: Brotherhood Of Man Mgmt
BROTHERS: Shalit Global Entertainment & Mgmt
BROUDIE, Ian: JPR Mgmt
VANESSA BROWN: Empire Artist Mgmt
BROWN, Alex: Escape Music Mgmt
BROWN, Angie: DCM International
BROWN, Ian: Retaliate First Mgmt
BROWN, Joe: John Taylor Mgmt
BROWN, John Willy: Show Business Entertainment
BROWN, Lorna: Positive Mgmt
BROWN, Sam: One Fifteen
BROWN, Sarah: Eclipse-PJM
BRYDON, Mark: Graham Peacock Mgmt
BUCKLE: Quintessential Music
BUDAPEST: Easy Street Artist Mgmt
BUDDAHEAD: Sanctuary Artist Mgmt
BUDNUBAC: Bermuda Mgmt
THE BUFFSEEDS: Simon Lawlor Mgmt
BUMP & FLEX: Wyze Mgmt
BURKE, Joe, with Anne CONROY BURKE: The Bechhofer Agency
BURNING BUSH: Rose Rouge International
BUSH: azoffmusic mgmt
BUSTED: Prestige Mgmt
BUTTABALL: Menace Mgmt.

MARTIN BUTTRICH: Hope Mgmt
The BUZZCOCKS: Sentics
BYRNE: TARGO Ents Corp
C-JAGS: Formidable Mgmt
STUART CABLE: Marsupial Mgmt
CALCRAFT, Raymond: Music Company (London) .
CALDERONE, Victor: Sanctuary Artist Mgmt
CALE, John: Firebrand Mgmt
CALECHE: Caleche Studios
CALLA: PPM Artist Mgmt
CALLIER, Terry: Positive Mgmt
CAMPBELL, Ruu: Rough Trade Mgmt
Shanie CAMPBELL: O-Mix
CAMPI, Ray: Paul Barrett (Rock 'N' Roll Enterprises)
CAMPSIE, Colin: WG Stonebridge Artist Mgmt
The CANDYSKINS: Interzone Mgmt
LOUISE CANNON: The Music Partnership
CANTABILE: Seaview Music
CAPALDI, Jim: John Taylor Mgmt
CAPTAIN SOUL: 3rd Stone
Captain Wilberforce: Deluxxe Mgmt
THE CARDINALS: Jonny Paul Mgmt
CARLTON, Carl, & The Songdogs: What Mgmt
CARMELO: R2 Mgmt
The CARNIVAL BAND: Seaview Music
KENNY CARPENTER: Qaraj'
The CARPENTERS STORY: Hal Carter Organisation
CARRACK, Paul: Alan Wood Agency
CARRIE TREE: Z Mgmt
CARROL, Clive: NEM Productions (UK)
MARC CARROLL: Rough Trade Mgmt
CARTER, Derrick: Mumbo Jumbo Mgmt
CARTER, Jon: David Dorrell Mgmt
CARTHY, Eliza: Moneypenny Mgmt
CASABLANCA BOYS: McLeod Holden Enterprises
THE CASANOVAS: Emperor Mgmt
CASEY, Paddy: Principle Mgmt
CASSIDY, Eva: Tony Bramwell
Cast Iron Shores: Topaz Entertainment
CATACOUSTICS: Flick Productions
CATHEDRAL: One Fifteen
CAUTY, Jimmy: Feedback Communications
CAVAN, Crazy, & THE RHYTHM ROCKERS: Paul Barrett (Rock 'N' Roll Enterprises)
CAVE, Nick, & The BAD SEEDS: Tender Prey Mgmt
CEBEIRA, Asier: Onside Mgmt
CHAKRA: Earth Music
GUY CHAMBERS: Orgasmatron
The CHAMELEONS: Simon Lawlor Mgmt
CHAN: Wizard Mgmt
JAMES CHANT: White Tiger Mgmt
RICHARD A. CHAPMAN: Working Class Music Mgmt
CHARLAMAGNE, Diane: Streetfeat Mgmt
The CHARLATANS: Steve Harrison Mgmt
The CHEMICAL BROTHERS: MBL
CHERRY, Eagle-Eye: The Umbrella Group
CHERRY, Neneh: The Umbrella Group
CHIKINKI: Mumbo Jumbo Mgmt
The CHILDREN: Touched Productions
CHILI: MCM
CHILLAGE PEOPLE: Northstar Artist Mgmt
CHING: Little Piece of Jamaica (LPOJ)
STEVE CHRISANTHOU: Vex Mgmt
CHRISTIAN, Darren: Duty Free Artist Mgmt
CHRISTOPHER LAWRENCE: Represents Artist Mgmt
The CHUCKER BUTTY OCARINA QUARTET: Seaview Music
CHUMBAWAMBA: Doug Smith Associates
CHUNGKING: CEC Mgmt
CHARLOTTE CHURCH: Consigliari
CHURCH, Charlotte: azoffmusic mgmt
CICCONE: Zen Mgmt
The CIRCUS OF HORRORS: The Psycho Mgmt Company
CITIZEN K: Red Onion Productions
CJ Mackintosh: Safehouse Mgmt
CLARK, Michael: Modernwood Mgmt
CLARK, Petula: Denis Vaughan Mgmt
CLARKE, Steven: Wizard Mgmt
The CLASS OF '58: Paul Barrett (Rock 'N' Roll Enterprises)
The CLASSIC BUSKERS: Seaview Music
CLAUDIA: ECI Mgmt
CLAYDERMAN, Richard: Denis Vaughan Mgmt
CLEA: Upside Mgmt
CLEVE M: Yellow Balloon Productions
THE CLIENTS: Simon Lawlor Mgmt
ROBERT CLIVILLES: Safehouse Mgmt
CLOR: Big Dipper Productions
COAST: Zen Mgmt
COCCOLUTO, Claudio: Prodmix DJ Mgmt & Production
JARVIS COCKER: Rough Trade Mgmt
COCO VEGA Y LATINOS SALSA BAND: Line-Up PMC
COCO, Chris: 7pm Mgmt
CODY: Treasure Island Mgmt
RENATO COHEN: Bulldozer Mgmt
COLDPLAY: Coldplay Mgmt
COLE, BJ: Firebrand Mgmt
COLE, Paula: azoffmusic mgmt
COLLISTER, Christine: Robert Miller Mgmt
COLOUR OF FIRE: Riverman Mgmt
COMMONWEALTH: Keith Harris Music
CONDEMNED TO DANCE: Direct Heat Mgmt
CONVERSATION, The: MCM
COOK, Caroline: Yellow Balloon Productions
COOL BRITANNIA: McLeod Holden Enterprises
COOLIDGE, Rita: Numinous Mgmt
THE CORAL: Skeleton Key Mgmt
COSMIC JOKER: Future Mgmt
COSMIC ROUGH RIDERS: No Half Measures .
COUSINS, Tina: Cruisin' Music
COX, Carl: Safehouse Mgmt
COXON, Graham: CMO Mgmt International
CRACATILLA: FourFives Productions
CRADLE OF FILTH: In Phase Mgmt
CRASHLAND: CEC Mgmt
CRAVEN, Beverley: Blueprint Mgmt
CRAY, Aaron: Easy Street Artist Mgmt
CRAZY: Joe Bangay Enterprises
CRAZY PENIS: Bond Mgmt
CRESCENDO: A Crosse The World Mgmt
THE CRIMEA: Out There Mgmt
The CROCKETTS: Offside Mgmt
CROFT NO. FIVE: Martin Coull Mgmt
CROSBY, Gary: The Dune Music Company
CROSS, Christopher: azoffmusic mgmt
The Cubes: Topaz Entertainment
CUD: Wild Honey Mgmt
JAMIE CULLUM: Aire International (Air,)
THE CULT: Sanctuary Artist Mgmt
CULTURE CLUB: Sunhand
CUNNINGHAM, Carly: SGO Music Mgmt
CURLEY, Carlo: PVA Mgmt
CURTIS, Mac: Paul Barrett (Rock 'N' Roll Enterprises)
CUSHTY: FourFives Productions
CYRKA, Jan: Northern Music Company
D'VINE: Mel Tyler Mgmt
THE D4: Creation Mgmt
DA MUTTZ: Impro Mgmt
Da-Essence: Social Misfit Entertainment
DAINTIES, Penny: P3 Music Mgmt .
CAROLINE DALE: Spirit Music & Media
PAUL DALEY: LH Mgmt
DEE DALY: Mental Music Mgmt
Damien DEMPSEY: Spirit Music & Media
DANDYLIONS, The: Mighty Music Mgmt
DANKWORTH, Jacqueline: Cromwell Mgmt
DANNHOF, Regina: WonderWorld
DANNY S: Seven Music Promotions
DARIO G: Bond Mgmt
DARIUS: Brilliant 19
DARK BLUES, The: Dark Blues Mgmt

DARK FLOWER: SuperVision Mgmt
THE DARKNESS: Whitehouse Mgmt
DASHBOARD MADONNA: Clown Mgmt
THE DATSUNS: Thunderbird Mgmt
DAVID THOMAS: Charmenko
DAVID, Craig: Wildlife Entertainment
DAVIES, Dave: Sanctuary Artist Mgmt
DAVIES, Ray: Sanctuary Artist Mgmt
Spencer DAVIS Group: Richard Martin Mgmt
The DAWN: Ornadel Mgmt
DAY, Charlotte: Roger Boden Mgmt
DBA: Friars Mgmt
MICHEL DE HEY: Safehouse Mgmt
DEACON BLUE: CEC Mgmt
DEADLY AVENGER: Mumbo Jumbo Mgmt
DEAF SHEPHERD: Martin Coull Mgmt
DEAN, Hazell: DCM International
DEBOURG, Daniel: Xosa Mgmt
DECKER, Desmond: Ro-lo Productions
DEF INC: Ornadel Mgmt
DEL AMITRI: JPR Mgmt
DELMAR, Elaine: John Williams
DELMONACO: Karma Mgmt
DEMON: Spaced Out Music
DEMPSEY: Dellphonic Mgmt
THE DEPARTURE: Sanctuary Artist Mgmt
Derek Cox: Derek Boulton Mgmt
DES'REE: Outside Mgmt
PAUL DEVLIN: Got A Loser Job At The Diner Mgmt
ALEX DEW: Strongroom Mgmt
DEWI-SANDRA: Jack 'N' Jill Artiste Mgmt
Michael DEWIS: The Music Partnership
DEZIRE: DCM International
DICKINSON, Bruce: Sanctuary Artist Mgmt
DICKSON, Barbara: Theobald Dickson Productions
DIDO: Nettwerk Mgmt UK
DIE: Heavyweight Mgmt
DIFFERENT GEAR: Goldpush
DIFFORD, Chris: CBL
DIGITAL GNAWA: Outerglobe (Global Fusion)
DIGWEED, John: Safehouse Mgmt
DINNIGAN, Simon: P3 Music Mgmt.
DINO: Jackie Davidson Mgmt
DIRT CANDY: Leafman
DIRT DEVILS: Conception Artist Mgmt
DIRTY 3: Tender Prey Mgmt
DIRTY BLONDES: Massive Mgmt
DIRTY HARRY: Toni Medcalf Mgmt
DISCO INFERNO: The Psycho Mgmt Company
DISCO PARK: Graham Peacock Mgmt
DIVA FEVER: McLeod Holden Enterprises
DIVIDE & RULE: Conception Artist Mgmt
The DIVINE COMEDY: Divine Mgmt
DJ 279: KSO Records
DJ BADLY: Bastard Mgmt
DJ Daddy Cool: Mad As Toast
DJ DAZEE: Hope Mgmt
DJ EXCALIBUR: KSO Records
DJ MARKY: Bulldozer Mgmt
DJ MINISTER: ECI Mgmt
DJ PATIFE: Bulldozer Mgmt
DJ PLANKTON: Graham Peacock Mgmt
DJ TIESTO: Represents Artist Mgmt
DJ UNEEK: Urban Control
DNA DOLL: Wicked Wolf Mgmt
DO ME BAD THINGS: Bermuda Mgmt
DOBSTER: Public Symphony
DR HOOK featuring Ray SAWYER: Brian Gannon Mgmt
CRAIG DODDS: Daytime Entertainments
DODGY: TARGO Ents Corp
CARLOS ADOLFO DOMINGUEZ: Traxxevents
DON JUAN: Xosa Mgmt
SIOBHAN DONAGHY: CMO Mgmt International
Katarzyna DONDALSKA: The Music Partnership
DONE LYING DOWN: Black and White Indians
DONOVAN: Denis Vaughan Mgmt
DONOVAN, Jason: Me Me Me Mgmt
DOORS, Rufus: NVB Entertainments
Dopamine: Idle Eyes Mgmt
DOPE SMUGGLAZ: North
DORE, Charlie: Toni Medcalf Mgmt
DORRIAN: Madrigal Music
DOUGLAS, Craig: John Williams
DR HAZE: The Psycho Mgmt Company
DR OCTOPUS: Brian Yeates Associates
DR WATSON & SHERLOCK: Direct Heat Mgmt
DRACASS, Lindsay: Alan Wood Agency
DRAKE, Molly: Antar
DRAWBACKS: Strongroom Mgmt
DREAMCATCHER: Conception Artist Mgmt
THE DREEM TEEM: Dreem Teem
DAVE DRESDEN: Ornadel Mgmt
NICK DRESTI: Talent Call
THE DRIFTERS feat. RICK SHEPPARD: Malcolm Feld Agency
DRUMMOND, Bill: Antar
DUB PISTOLS: LH Mgmt
STEVE DUB: LH Mgmt
DUBDADDA: Bastard Mgmt
DUBPLATE DIVAS: Direct Heat Mgmt
UKDUEL: Adventures in Music Mgmt
DUFF, Patrick: Me Me Me Mgmt
DUFFY, Keith: Carol & Associates
DUGANI, Sherena: SuperVision Mgmt
THE DUKE SPIRIT: Heavenly Mgmt
GREG DULLI: INS-YNC
DUM DUMS: Modernwood Mgmt
ANDY DUNCAN: 7pm Mgmt
DUNKEL, Paul Lustig: Music Company (London).
DUNLOP, Marissa: Joe Bangay Enterprises
DUST: KAL Mgmt
DYNAMIC SYNCOPATION: KSO Records
DYNAMITE MC: Heavyweight Mgmt
DYNAMO DRESDEN: Lateral Artist Mgmt
DYNAMO PRODUCTIONS: Fruit
EAGLE PATROL: Urban Control
The EAGLES: azoffmusic mgmt
EAGLESHAM, Bobby: The Bechhofer Agency
EAR: 3rd Stone
EARTHTONE9: Northern Music Company
EASTERN LANE: JPR Mgmt
EAT STATIC: Elite Squad Mgmt
EATON, Chris: SGO Music Mgmt
ECHO: Ardent Music
ECHO AND THE BUNNYMEN: Porcupine Mgmt
EDEN: Hope Mgmt
EDEN, Michael: DJT Mgmt
EDWARDS, Mike: Gailforce Mgmt
RYAN EDWARDS: Subversive Music Mgmt
EDWARDS, Steve: Menace Mgmt.
EDWINA-O: ECI Mgmt
EGGSTONE: Formidable Mgmt
808 STATE: North
ELBOW: TRC Mgmt
ELECTRIC CIRCUS: Kickstart Mgmt
ELENA: Madrigal Music
ELESIS: Sphinx Mgmt
Louis ELIOT: Spirit Music & Media
ELLA & HARRIET: Mental Music Mgmt
ELLA GURU: War Zones and Associates
KATE ELSWORTH: TJM
The EMBEZZLERS: Bastard Mgmt
EMBRACE: Coalition Mgmt
EMERSON LAKE & PALMER: Part Rock Mgmt
EMMANUEL, Colin: Xosa Mgmt
EMMANUEL, Tommy: NEM Productions (UK)
ENO, Brian: Opal-Chant
ENRAP-TURE: Big Out
ENVY: Billy Russell Mgmt
ENZO: Represents Artist Mgmt
STEWART EPPS: Gerry Bron Mgmt
EQUATION: NEM Productions (UK)
ESCOFFERY, Shaun: Eclipse-PJM
ESP: KSO Records

ESSENCE: Earth Music
ESSEX, David: Mel Bush Organization
The Estate of Nick Drake: Antar
ESTELLE: Empire Artist Mgmt
ESTHER: GR Mgmt
EUROPAXL: Asylum Artists
EV.ON: KSO Records
EVA: Big Life Mgmt
EVALON: Pete Hawkins Mgmt
MARK EVANS: The Music Partnership
EVANS, Niki: Brian Yeates Associates
EVENSTAR: Sound Pets
F, Katie: Rose Rouge International
FABULOUS THUNDERBIRDS: azoffmusic mgmt
LUKE FAIR: Safehouse Mgmt
FAIRPORT CONVENTION: Denis Vaughan Mgmt
FAITHLESS: Faithless Live
FALLEN ANGEL: Massive Mgmt
FALLOUT 40: FiveMilesHigh
FANS OF KATE: Abbi Frutin Mgmt
FARIQ, Sona: Quest Mgmt
FARLEY, Andy: Media Records
FAT TUESDAY: Essential Entertainments
FAULTLINE: Ornadel Mgmt
FAY, Cecily: A Crosse The World Mgmt
Faze Action: Sublime Music
FBI: The Psycho Mgmt Company
FC ALLSTARS: Escape Music Mgmt
FC KAHUNA: Daddy Mgmt
FEEDER: Riot Mgmt
FEEL: Direct Heat Mgmt
The FEEL FOUNDATION: Direct Heat Mgmt
THE FEELING: XL Talent
FELON: Armstrong Academy Artist Mgmt
FERGUSON, Sheila D: Vashti
The FETCH: Loose
FIELD, RS "Bobby": Muirhead Mgmt
FIERCE: Jack 'N' Jill Artiste Mgmt
FIERCE BLACK: Instinct Mgmt
FIFTH AMENEDMENT F: Interceptor Enterprises
FIGHTCLUB: 7pm Mgmt
THE FIGHTIN' GATORS OF APALACHICOLA COUNTY: Got A Loser Job At The Diner Mgmt
FILTERHEADZ: Ornadel Mgmt
FILTRATE: North
FINLAYSON, Tucker, FUNCTION BAND, The: Acker's International Jazz Agency
FINLIN, Jeff: Tony Bramwell
FIRSTBORN: Midnight To Six Mgmt
FISH SWIM NAKED: Karma Mgmt
FLAM: Plus Artist Mgmt
FLAME TREES: WG Stonebridge Artist Mgmt
FLAMINGO FLEECE: Got A Loser Job At The Diner Mgmt
KEITH FLINT: Machine Mgmt
FLINT, Bernie: McLeod Holden Enterprises
FLIPPER: WonderWorld
FLIPRON: Up All Night Music
THE FLIPS: Z Mgmt
SERGIO FLORES: Active Music Mgmt
FLOYD, Keith: Stan Green Mgmt
FLUKE: Fools Paradise
FLYNT: Magic Kingdom Mgmt
FOGERTY, John: azoffmusic mgmt
FOLDS, Ben: CEC Mgmt
SEB FONTAINE: Represents Artist Mgmt
LENNY FONTANA: Qaraj'
FORCE MAJEURE: Earth Music
FORD, Frankie: Paul Barrett (Rock 'N' Roll Enterprises)
FOREIGNER: Part Rock Mgmt
The FORTUNES: Brian Yeates Associates
FORTUNES, The: Ro-lo Productions
The FOUR PENNIES: PVA
4 SENSATIONS: McLeod Holden Enterprises
FOUR STOREYS: Atomic Mgmt
FOX, Simon: Kickstart Mgmt
FOXX, John: Zeall Mgmt Limited
FRANC: Up All Night Music
FRANCIS, Louise: Xosa Mgmt
SKOTT FRANCIS: Lee & Co
FRANTI, Michael: Sincere Mgmt
FRANTIK: Flamecracker Mgmt
FRANZ FERDINAND: SuperVision Mgmt
FREAK NASTY: Unique Corp
FREAKS: Mumbo Jumbo Mgmt
FREDERIKA BABY DOLL: Qaraj'
FREEFALL: Madrigal Music
FREEFORM FIVE: Mumbo Jumbo Mgmt
FREEKSPERT: DJT Mgmt
FREEKSTAR: Craig Huxley Mgmt
THE FREESTYLERS: Heavyweight Mgmt
FRENCH, Nicki: DCM International
FREQ NASTY: LH Mgmt
FREUD: Numinous Mgmt
FREY, Glenn: azoffmusic mgmt
FRIEDMAN, Aron: Kudos Mgmt
FRIGID VINEGAR: Interzone Mgmt
JUSTINE FRISCHMANN: CMO Mgmt International
FRONTIER: TSD Records
FROU FROU: Modernwood Mgmt
FRUCTUOSO, Isabel: John Waller Mgmt & Marketing
RACHEL FULLER: Trinifold Mgmt
FUME: Madison Mgmt
FUNERAL FOR A FRIEND: Sanctuary Artist Mgmt
The FUTURE SOUND OF LONDON: Freedom Mgmt
THE FUTUREHEADS: Big Life Mgmt
FUTURESHOCK: Sanctuary Artist Mgmt
FYA: Jamdown
THE*GA*GA*S: Crisis Mgmt
GABO: Bulldozer Mgmt
GABRIEL & DRESDEN: Ornadel Mgmt
JOSH GABRIEL: Ornadel Mgmt
GABRIELLE: J Mgmt
GAGARIN: Charmenko
GARCIA, Francois: Bodo Music Co
MARK GARDENER: OMC Mgmt
GARRETT, Lesley: The Music Partnership
BEULAH GARSIDE: Blujay Mgmt
GARTNER, Steve: Cultural Foundation
GAYNOR, Rik: Show Business Entertainment
GAZZO, Jane: Goldpush
GEE BABY I LOVE YOU: PVA
CRAIG GEE (DJ): Traffik Productions
GEEZERS OF NAZARETH: North
GELDOF, Bob: Jukes Productions
GENASIDE 2: Jon Sexton Mgmt (JSM)
GENE: Automatic Mgmt
GENERAL MIDI: Hope Mgmt
GEORGE T (DJ): Traffik Productions
GEORGE,Ian: Subversive Music Mgmt
GHOSTLAND: Spirit Music & Media
GHOSTLY MAN: Simon King Mgmt (SKM)
GHOTTI: Redd Mgmt
GIANELLI, Tom: Wyze Mgmt
GIBBENS, John: Touched Productions
GIBBS, Helen: Monster Music Mgmt
GIN SAW: Cultural Foundation
GIPSY KINGS: Denis Vaughan Mgmt
A Girl Called Eddy: Deluxxe Mgmt
THE GLITTERATI: Mondo Mgmt
GO WEST: Blueprint Mgmt
GOLDFRAPP: Midnight To Six Mgmt
GOOBER PATROL: 3rd Stone
GOOD VIBES: NYJO - National Youth Jazz Orchestra
GOODACRE, Tony: Sylvantone Promotions
GORILLAZ: CMO Mgmt International
GORKYS ZYGOTIC MYNCI: Rheoli Ankst Mgmt
RACHEL GOSWELL: Menace Mgmt .
GOTHIC VOICES: Seaview Music
GOULDMAN, Graham: Harvey Lisberg Associates
GRABOWSKY, Paul: Muirhead Mgmt
KAREN GRACE: Alan Whitehead Mgmt
TOBY GRAFFTEY-SMITH: Muirhead Mgmt

GRAHAM, Max: Hope Mgmt
GRAHAM, Mikey: JC Music
GRAMME: David Dorrell Mgmt
GRAND DRIVE: Wild Honey Mgmt
GRAND ROSE BAND: Liquid Mgmt
GRAND TRANSMITTER: CMO Mgmt International
GRANT & FORESIGHT: Grant & Foresight
GRANT LEE BUFFALO: The Umbrella Group
GRANT, Kate: Hedgehog
GRANT, Noel: Little Piece of Jamaica (LPOJ)
RACHAEL GRAY: Easy Street Artist Mgmt
GRAY, David: Mondo Mgmt
GRAY, Elizabeth: Sublime Music
GREASED LIGHTNING: The Psycho Mgmt Company
JONNY GREEN & SATELLITE: TARGO Ents Corp
FARUK GREEN: Jon Sexton Mgmt (JSM)
GREEN, Jesse: Satellite Artists
GREEN, Leo: Lazarus Music & Media (LM2)
GROOVE ARMADA: Sanctuary Artist Mgmt
GROOVEZONE: Choir Connexion & London Community Gospel Choir
GUARD, Rick: MCM
GUAVA: The Dune Music Company
H: TForce
HACKETT, Steve: Kudos Mgmt
HADLEY, Tony: Blueprint Mgmt
HAINES, Luke: INS-YNC
HAKEEM: Jackie Davidson Mgmt
HAL: Independent Sound Mgmt (ISM)
HALL, Josie: Monster Music Mgmt
HALLELUJAH JOHNSON: Starone
HALSTEAD, Neil: Menace Mgmt .
HAMMILL, Peter: Gailforce Mgmt
PETE "MIXMASTER" HAMMOND: Active Music Mgmt
HAPPY DAYS: Les Hart (Southampton Entertainments)
The HAPPY VIBES CORPORATION: Direct Heat Mgmt
HARCOURT, Ed: Sanctuary Artist Mgmt
HARDKNOX: Deutsch-Englische Freundschaft
HARPER, Nick: Stress Mgmt
HARRISON, Sarah: Fruity Red Inc.
HARRY: Seaview Music
BRIAN HARVEY: B&H Mgmt
HARVEY, Polly: Principle Mgmt
HASAAN, Fahan: Modernwood Mgmt
HAVE MERCY: NoWHere Mgmt
HAWKESTRA: Money Talks Mgmt
HAWKWIND: MSM Music Consultants
HAYMAN, Andy: SMI/Everyday Productions
HAZE VS THE X FACTOR: Psycho Mgmt Company
HEADLINERS: Satellite Artists
HEADWAY: 7pm Mgmt
HEAP, Imogen: Modernwood Mgmt
HEARTFIELD: Blue Stack Music
JAMIE HEATH: Mental Music Mgmt
HEATHER NOVA: Bedlam Mgmt
HEAVEN 17: Subversive Music Mgmt
HECKLER: Madison Mgmt
WAYNE HECTOR: Jackie Davidson Mgmt
HEFNER: Machine Mgmt
HEKIMOVA, Yanka: PVA Mgmt
HELEN T: WonderWorld
HELENA: Grinning Rat Music Mgmt
DAVE HEMINGWAY: 7pm Mgmt
HENLEY, Don: azoffmusic mgmt
STEPHEN JOHN HENRY: Little Giant Music
ELIZABETH HENSHAW - "ZEPHYR": Muirhead Mgmt
HERINGMAN, Jacob: Music Company (London) .
HERON: Porcupine Mgmt
HEYOKA: Got A Loser Job At The Diner Mgmt
HEYWARD, Nick: Little Giant Music
HIGH STEPPERS: Z Mgmt
HIKINS, Rich: KlubDJ
HILLBILLY BOOGIEMEN: Sylvantone Promotions
HILLYER & JOHNSON: Asylum Artists
HINE, Rupert: Jukes Productions
NICOLA HITCHCOCK: Ardent Music
HOEY, Jade: Plus Artist Mgmt
HOLDEN, Darren: Crashed Music
ALEX HOLLAND: Black Magic Mgmt
HOLLAND, Chris: One Fifteen
HOLLAND, Jools, AND HIS RHYTHM & BLUES ORCHESTRA: One Fifteen
THE HONEYMOON: Sanctuary Artist Mgmt
HOODLUM PRIEST: DNA Artist Mgmt
HOOKS, Holli: Rose Rouge International
JON HOPKINS: Just Another Mgmt Co
HORACE & DUKE: Direct Heat Mgmt
HORN, Victoria: Divine Mgmt
HOT CHOCOLATE: Richard Martin Mgmt
HOUGH, Lisa: Split Music
TOM HOWE: Radius Music
DANNY HOWELLS: IMD
HOWIE B: Native Mgmt
HOY, Jayni: Diamond Sounds Music Mgmt
HUDSON, Mark: Little Piece of Jamaica (LPOJ)
HUE, Paul: Little Piece of Jamaica (LPOJ)
HUGGY (DJ): Traffik Productions
HUNDRED AND 3: Working Class Music Mgmt
HUNDRED REASONS: Furtive Mass Transit Systems LLP
HUNT, Miles: Spirit Music & Media
HUNTERZ: Wizard Mgmt
HUSK: Zeall Mgmt Limited
HUSSEY: Armstrong Academy Artist Mgmt
HUTTON, Chris: Safi Sounds Mgmt & Promotion
HYND, Richard: Goldpush
HYPERBOREA: Eurock
I MONSTER: Menace Mgmt .
I WANT YOUR SAX: Brian Yeates Associates
I'CHELMEE: Social Misfit Entertainment
THE IDJUT BOYS: Solar Mgmt
IGNITION TECHNICIAN: Archetype Mgmt
ILLEGAL EAGLES: Hal Carter Organisation
IMAGINATION featuring Leee JOHN: Johnboy Productions
IMMUNISE: Vex Mgmt
INCH BLUE: Pure Delinquent
INCOGNITO: Creation Mgmt
INDIAN ROPEMAN: CEC Mgmt
INDIGO: Wyze Mgmt
INJECTORS, The: Teleryngg UK
INME: Marsupial Mgmt
INNER CITY UNIT: Money Talks Mgmt
INNER MANTRA BAND: Liquid Mgmt
INSEMINATORS: Total Concept Mgmt (TCM)
THE INSPIRAL CARPETS: Key Music Mgmt
INTERCOOLER: Starone
INTIMATE STUDIOS: Gerry Bron Mgmt
THE IRISH TENORS: Pure Music Mgmt
IRON MAIDEN: Sanctuary Artist Mgmt
IRVINE, Andy: The Bechhofer Agency
JADE, Leah: Kamara Artist Mgmt (UK)
JAGWA: Jamdown
JAIMESON: Bermuda Mgmt
JAKE & ELWOOD: McLeod Holden Enterprises
The JAMES BROTHERS: Direct Heat Mgmt
NATALIE JAMES: Asylum Artists
NATE JAMES: >4 Mgmt
JANSEN, Steve: Medium Productions
JARRETT, Dennis: Wizard Mgmt
JAY, Norman: Serious Artist Mgmt
NINA JAYNE: B&H Mgmt
JAZZ JAMAICA ALL STARS: The Dune Music Company
JAZZUPSTARTS: Escape Music Mgmt
JEFFERSON: Brian Yeates Associates
JELAYJU: Maximum Music
JEM: Method Mgmt
JENGA HEADS: North
KATHERINE JENKINS: Bandana Mgmt
The JETS: Paul Barrett (Rock 'N' Roll Enterprises)

Business Services

Business Services

JG BROS: Qaraj'
JIMBO: Crashed Music
JO DAVIDSON: The Umbrella Group
JOBE: Retaliate First Mgmt
JODIE: FourFives Productions
JOHAN S: Seven Music Promotions
JOHNNY BOY: Emperor Mgmt
JOHNSON, Holly: Wolfgang Kuhle Artist Mgmt
JOHNSON, Wilko: Solid Senders
JOHNSTONE, Cressida: Andrew Miller Promotions Int.
JOI: Moksha Mgmt
JOKER: Les Hart (Southampton Entertainments)
JONES, Ben: Stress Mgmt
Dr BOB JONES: Positive Mgmt
JONES, Hannah: DCM International
JONES, Howard: Friars Mgmt
JONES, John Paul: Opium (Arts)
JONES, Salena: Vine Gate Music
JONES, Wayne: Kamara Artist Mgmt (UK)
JONNY L: Star-Write Mgmt
Jonny MALE: Spirit Music & Media
JONT: Nettwerk Mgmt UK
JONZ: Keith Harris Music
JOOLZ: Brian Yeates Associates
JORY, Sarah: Malcolm Feld Agency
JOSIAH: Big Brother Mgmt.
JOY ZIPPER: CMO Mgmt International
JOYCE, Jemma: John Waller Mgmt & Marketing
JUAN MARTIN'S FLAMENCO DANCE COMPANY: Flamencovision
JUDAS PRIEST: Trinifold Mgmt
JUDGE JULES: Serious Artist Mgmt
JUDGE, Chris: Billy Russell Mgmt
JUPITER ACE: Top Draw Music Mgmt
JX: Deutsch-Englische Freundschaft
K WARREN & LEE-O: SuperVision Mgmt
K+K: Mighty Music Mgmt
KALEIDOSCOPE: Bond Mgmt
KANE, Eden: Hal Carter Organisation
PAT KANE: Pat Kane
KAPITAHL: A: Kitchenware Mgmt
KARI KLEIV: 10 Mgmt
KARMENCHEETAH: Direct Heat Mgmt
KARN, Mick: Medium Productions
KATHRYN ROBERTS & SEAN LAKEMAN: NEM Productions (UK)
KAWALA: WG Stonebridge Artist Mgmt
KEATING, Ronan: Louis Walsh Mgmt
KEEP IT UP: Martin Coull Mgmt
KELLY, John: Serious Artist Mgmt
KEMI: Urban Control
KEVIN KENDLE: First Time Mgmt
KENNEDY, Bap: John Waller Mgmt & Marketing
David KENNEDY: Mad As Toast
KENYON, Carol: PEZ Mgmt
KERNIS, Aaron Jay: Music Company (London) .
KERR, Gordon: MCM
KERSHAW, Nik: Modernwood Mgmt
RICHIE KEYVAN: 7pm Mgmt
KHANER, Jeffrey: Music Company (London) .
KID CREOLE AND THE COCONUTS: Malcolm Feld Agency
KID GALLAHAD: Intuition Music
MICHAEL KILKIE (DJ): Traffik Productions
KILLING JOKE: Grand Union Mgmt
THE KILLS: Creation Mgmt
RACHEL MARI KIMBER: Marsupial Mgmt
KINESIS: Sanctuary Artist Mgmt
KING CRIMSON: DGM Mgmt
KING, Catherine: Music Company (London) .
KINGADORA: Fruition Mgmt
KINGS OF CONVENIENCE: INS-YNC
The KINKS: Sanctuary Artist Mgmt
KINOBE: CEC Mgmt
KIRSTEN: Sacred Mgmt
KITT, David: Interactive Music Mgmt
MYLEENE KLASS: Safe Mgmt
KNIGHT, Beverly: DWL (Dave Woolf), Outside Mgmt
KNOPFLER, Mark: Paul Crockford Mgmt (PCM)
KO-LA: Redd Mgmt
KOGLIN, Mike: Conception Artist Mgmt
KOOL & THE GANG: Unique Corp
KOOL KEITH: Jon Sexton Mgmt (JSM)
KOOP: Impro Mgmt
KOOT: Some Bizarre
KORNER, Damian: Gerry Bron Mgmt
DAVID KOSTNER: Ornadel Mgmt
KOWALSKI: Midnight To Six Mgmt
KRUST: Heavyweight Mgmt
KUBANO KICKASSO: Money Talks Mgmt
KUDA 8: Intuition Music
KUKANI PROJECT, The: Massive Mgmt
KUMO: O-Mix
BEN KWELLER: Nettwerk Mgmt UK
LACEY, Jon: Krack Music Mgmt
LACEY, Tiffany: Active Music Mgmt
LADY SOVEREIGN: Big Life Mgmt
LAFFERTY, Christopher: KAL Mgmt
Lagoon West: Firebrand Mgmt
LAHCEN LAHABIB: Outerglobe (Global Fusion)
LAHANNYA: Kabuki
LAIBACH: Charmenko
LAJ: Solar Mgmt
GREG LAKE: Trinifold Mgmt
LAMACQ, Steve: Wise Buddah Talent
LAMAI: Earth Music
LAMB: Blue Sky Entertainment
LANTAN: Little Piece of Jamaica (LPOJ)
LASHE: WonderWorld
LISA LASHES: Ornadel Mgmt
Last Man Standing: Sublime Music
LATE NIGHT MUSIC STORE: Lateral Artist Mgmt
AIDAN LAVELLE: Effective Mgmt
LAVELLE, Caroline: Ardent Music
JAMES LAVONZ: DNA Artist Mgmt
LAWSON, Jamie: Hedgehog
LE BLOND: Shalit Global Entertainment & Mgmt
LEE, Christopher: R2 Mgmt
LEE, Lorraine & Bennet HAMMOND: The Bechhofer Agency
LEE, Shawn: Impro Mgmt
LEE, Steve: Duty Free Artist Mgmt
LEEMING, Carol: O-Mix
LEMON JELLY: Terra Firma Mgmt
LENNOX, Annie: 19 Mgmt
LEON: First Move Mgmt
KYRAH LEONE: PPM Artist Mgmt
LETRIX: Parliament Mgmt
The LEVELLERS: First Column Mgmt
LEWIS, Linda Gale: Paul Barrett (Rock 'N' Roll Enterprises)
LEYTON, John: Hal Carter Organisation
THE LIBERTINES: Creation Mgmt
LICKETY SPLIT: Les Hart (Southampton Entertainments)
LIFEHOUSE: azoffmusic mgmt
LIFFORD: Mimi Music
LIGHTFOOT, Terry, & HIS BAND: Cromwell Mgmt
LIGHTFOOT, Terry, AND HIS BAND: John Williams
LIGHTHOUSE FAMILY: Independent Sound Mgmt (ISM), Kitchenware Mgmt
The LIGHTNING SEEDS: JPR Mgmt
LIMERICK, Alison: Blueprint Mgmt
LINCOLN BROWN: The ICE Group
LINOLEUM: Brown McLeod
LIPSTICK COLOURED MONKEYS: Kamara Artist Mgmt (UK)
LIQ, Ed: One Mgmt
LISTER, Mick: Modernwood Mgmt
DANNY LITCHFIELD: Armstrong Academy Artist Mgmt
LITTLE 10: Essential Entertainments
LIZARDSUN: Charles Salt Mgmt
LOAFER: Hope Mgmt
LOCK, Eddie: Worldmaster DJ Mgmt
The Lockdown Project: Deluxxe Mgmt
LOCORRIERE, Dennis: John Taylor Mgmt

LOGANSTONE: Bermuda Mgmt

LONDON COMMUNITY GOSPEL CHOIR, The: Choir Connexion & London Community Gospel Choir

The LONDON GIRLS: Peter Haines Mgmt

LONDON RAGTIME ORCHESTRA: Cromwell Mgmt

LONER: Vex Mgmt

LONGBONES: Coalition Mgmt

LONGRIGG, Francesca: One Fifteen

LOOP STORM: Onside Mgmt

JUDITH LORDE: Omoya Entertainment

LOST LOVE PROJECT: Direct Heat Mgmt

LOVE BITES: TK1 Mgmt .

LOVE TO INFINITY: JPS Mgmt

The LOVERS: TSD Records

LOWCRAFT: JC Music

LOWGOLD: Furtive Mass Transit Systems LLP

LUCA BRAZZI: Kickstart Mgmt

LUCAS, Adrian: PVA Mgmt

LUCAS, Huwey: Creative World Entertainment

LUCID: Black Magic Mgmt

LUCYS, The: PJ Music

LUIS PARIS: Represents Artist Mgmt

LULU: Louis Walsh Mgmt

LUNA, Eva: John Waller Mgmt & Marketing

LUNAR DRIVE: The Liaison and Promotion Company

LUNASA: SGO Music Mgmt

LUVDUP TWINS: Worldmaster DJ Mgmt

LYDIA: Little Giant Music

LYONESSE: Touched Productions

LYONS, Tim & Fintan VALLELY: The Bechhofer Agency

LYTTELTON, Humphrey, AND HIS BAND: John Williams

M DUBBS: Urban Control

M&S: F&G Mgmt

M&S PRODUCTIONS: Ambush Mgmt

M*A*S*H: JPS Mgmt

M-GEE: Wyze Mgmt

M.A.S.S.: TARGO Ents Corp

M.I.A.: CMO Mgmt International

MAAS, Timo: Hope Mgmt

STEVE MAC: IMD

MACKICHAN, Blair: Small World

MACLEAN, Dougie: NEM Productions (UK)

MACS: Jack 'N' Jill Artiste Mgmt

MACUMBA: Line-Up PMC

MAD DOG AND THE SOPHISTICATS: McLeod Holden Enterprises

MADDEN, Paul: Gerry Bron Mgmt

MAGNET: SuperVision Mgmt

MAGPIE: The Bechhofer Agency

MAHONEY, Gary: JBS Mgmt UK

JUDD MAHONEY: Sunhand

MAJOR: Fruit

VICTOR MALLOY: Machine Mgmt

MANCHILD: Midi Mgmt

MANDALAY: Interceptor Enterprises

MANEKI-NEKO: OPL Mgmt

RAY MANG: Solar Mgmt

MANHATTAN TRANSFER: Denis Vaughan Mgmt

MANIC STREET PREACHERS: Sanctuary Artist Mgmt

TANIA MANN: Top Draw Music Mgmt

MANNA PRODUCTIONS: Bermuda Mgmt

MANSTON, Andy: Duty Free Artist Mgmt

MANZANERA, Phil: Expression Mgmt

MARBLE FLOOR: Urban Control

THE MARIACHIS: The Yukon Mgmt

MARIE, Theresa: DCM International

MARR, Johnny: Ignition Mgmt

KYM MARSH: Safe Mgmt

MARSHALL, Bex: Numinous Mgmt

MARTIN STEPHENSON & THE DAINTEES: NEM Productions (UK)

MARTIN, Giles: CA Mgmt

MARTIN, Juan: Flamencovision

MARTIN, Linda: Denis Vaughan Mgmt

MARTIN, Sir George: CA Mgmt

MARYSIA: But! Mgmt

MASTERSON, Adam: Coalition Mgmt

PAUL MASTERSON: Top Draw Music Mgmt

MATCHBOX: Paul Barrett (Rock 'N' Roll Enterprises)

MATT BIANCO: Denis Vaughan Mgmt

CERYS MATTHEWS: Rough Trade Mgmt

JOHN MATTHIAS: LH Mgmt

THE MAU MAUS: Radius Music

MAUS: Vex Mgmt

MAX 'B': Davix Mgmt

MAY, Charlie: Ornadel Mgmt

CHARLIE MAY: Ornadel Mgmt

MAY, Joanne: Shalit Global Entertainment & Mgmt

MC BUZZ-BEE: Omoya Entertainment

MC CHICKABOO: Hope Mgmt

MC EMMANUEL: ECI Mgmt

MC HARDKAUR: Ambush Mgmt

MC J: ECI Mgmt

MCCABE, Mark: Ganz Mgmt

McCALL, Gordon: Lena Davis John Bishop Associates

McCANN, Susan: Dennis Heaney Promotions

KATHLEEN MCDERMOTT: Asylum Artists

DEREK MCDONALD: Asylum Artists

McEVOY, Jonny: Dara Mgmt

MCFLY: Prestige Mgmt

MCGOWAN, Alex: WonderWorld

STEPHANIE McKAY: Fruit

McLEOD, Rory: NEM Productions (UK)

MCLI: Little Piece of Jamaica (LPOJ)

MCRAFT: INS-YNC

MEDIAEVAL BAEBES: Strike Back Mgmt

MEKON: Fruit

MELLOTRAUMA: Social Misfit Entertainment

MELLOW: Fools Paradise

MELYS: Rheoli Ankst Mgmt

MERCURY REV: Ignition Mgmt

METCALFE, Bridget: Amber

METRO RIOTS: Zen Mgmt

MEW: Creation Mgmt

Michael English: Michael McDonagh Mgmt

MICKEY P: Jackie Davidson Mgmt

TOM MIDDLETON: Machine Mgmt

MIDGET: Sound Pets

MIKE MONDAY: Represents Artist Mgmt

MILEHIGH: 10 Mgmt

MILES, Robert: MuchMoreMusic Mgmt

The MILK & HONEY BAND: First Column Mgmt

MILLAR, Sam: Shalit Global Entertainment & Mgmt

MILLENNIA ENSEMBLE: Knifedge

MILLER, Ed: The Bechhofer Agency

MILLER, Larry, BAND: Flick Productions

MILLETT, Lisa: Menace Mgmt .

JEFF MILLS: IMD

MIM: Public Symphony

MINOGUE, Kylie: Terry Blamey Mgmt

MINT ROYALE: Nettwerk Mgmt UK

MINUTEMAN: A.M.P./TBA

MIRANDA, Nina: Evolution Mgmt

MISLED: Wyze Mgmt

The MISSION: Extreme Music Production

MISSISSIPPI FLY: Streetfeat Mgmt

MISTAKES: Yellow Balloon Productions

MISTY'S BIG ADVENTURE: TARGO Ents Corp

LIZ MITCHELL: P&P Music International

MITCHELL, Robert: The Dune Music Company

MOBY: Deutsch-Englische Freundschaft

MOJAVE 3: Menace Mgmt .

MOKE: Elite Squad Mgmt

SOPHIE MOLETA: Deluxe Mgmt

MOLOKO: Graham Peacock Mgmt

MOLSKY, Bruce: The Bechhofer Agency

MOLVAER, Nils Petter: Tim Prior - Artist & Rights Mgmt

MoMo (Music of Moroccan Origin): Outerglobe (Global Fusion)

MOMY: Leap

Business Services

MONACO: Evolution Mgmt
MONOMANIA: Future Mgmt
MONTGOMERY, Errington: Graham Peacock Mgmt
MONTGOMERY, Kevin: Tony Bramwell
MOOD INDIGO: Brian Yeates Associates
MOODY, James: BPR Productions
MOONFACE: But! Mgmt
MOONRAKER: The Umbrella Group
MOORE, Ceri: John Waller Mgmt & Marketing
MOORE, Gary: Part Rock Mgmt
MOORE, Tony: John Waller Mgmt & Marketing
MARTIN MORALES: Positive Mgmt
MORCHEEBA: CMO Mgmt International
MORE ROCKERS: MWM Music Mgmt
MORGAN, Jo: Streetfeat Mgmt
MORGAN, Tony: PJ Music
MORNING RUNNER: Coldplay Mgmt
MORPH: Intuition Music
JIM MORRAY: Sincere Mgmt
The MORRIGHAN: A Crosse The World Mgmt
MORRIS QUINLIN EXPERIENCE: Tony Bramwell
MORRIS, Andy: 7pm Mgmt
MORRISEY: Sanctuary Artist Mgmt
MOTORCYCLE: Ornadel Mgmt
MOTTA, Kai: Some Bizarre
THE MOUNTAINEERS: Key Music Mgmt
MOUSKOURI, Nana: Denis Vaughan Mgmt
MOUTH: Krack Music Mgmt
MOUTH MUSIC: Ardent Music
MOZEZ: Solar Mgmt
MR DAVID VINER: White Tiger Mgmt
Mr ROQUE: Just Another Mgmt Co
Mr Zippy: FiveMilesHigh
MRD: DNA Artist Mgmt
MS T REY: Little Piece of Jamaica (LPOJ)
MUGENKYO: Line-Up PMC
MULL HISTORICAL SOCIETY: Sanctuary Artist Mgmt
MUMBA, Samantha: Louis Walsh Mgmt
MUNGO JERRY: Satellite Artists
MURDOCH: White Tiger Mgmt
MURPHY, Roisin: Graham Peacock Mgmt
MURRAY: TFF Mgmt
MURRAY, Steve: Escape Music Mgmt
MUSAPHIA, Joey: Talent Call
THE MUSIC: Coalition Mgmt
MUSICA ALHAMBRA: Flamencovision
MUSIQUE: Conception Artist Mgmt
MUST: Toni Medcalf Mgmt
MUSTARD BANDITS: Broken Star Mgmt
MUZZI, Massimiliano: PVA Mgmt
MY VITRIOL: TRC Mgmt
MYNC PROJECT: Represents Artist Mgmt
MYONI: Peter Haines Mgmt
N 'N' G: Wyze Mgmt
NAILA BOSS: Impact Ventures
NARCOTIC THRUST: Z Mgmt
NASHER: Scarlet Mgmt
NEAT PEOPLE: Boss Music
NEBULA, The: Rose Rouge International
NEIL: JBS Mgmt UK
CHRIS NEIL: Sanctuary Artist Mgmt
TREVOR NELSON: In2music
NELSON, Bill: Opium (Arts)
NELSON, Grant: Wyze Mgmt
NELSON, Shelley: Fanatic Mgmt
NEVILLE, Luke: Serious Artist Mgmt
RITCHIE NEVILLE: Blueprint Mgmt
NEVILLE, Tom: Media Records
The NEW GODS OF AMERICA: Future Mgmt
NEW POLLUTION: Seven Music Promotions
The NEW SEEKERS: Hal Carter Organisation
NEW SOUND FOUNDATION: McLeod Holden Enterprises
NEW TELLERS: DJT Mgmt
The NEW VAUDEVILLE BAND: NVB Entertainments
NEX: Formidable Mgmt
The NEXTMEN: Leafman
GEOFF NICHOLLS: Brenda Brooker Enterprises
NICKELLE: Qaraj'
NIGHT GAMES: Malcolm Feld Agency
NIGHTMARES ON WAX: LH Mgmt
NIXON: Arketek Mgmt
NO CARS IN VENICE: TSD Records
NO HOPE IN NEW JERSEY: Jonny Paul Mgmt
NO PRISONERS: Sacred Mgmt
NO SLEEP NIGEL: KSO Records
NO-MAN: 3rd Stone
NOAKES, Rab: The Bechhofer Agency
NOBLE, Ian: Lena Davis John Bishop Associates
NOBLE, Karen: Yellow Balloon Productions
NODDING DOG: Marshall Arts Mgmt
NOFERINI, Stefano: Prodmix DJ Mgmt & Production
NORDENSTAM, Stina: Silentway Mgmt
NORMAN, Chris: Denis Vaughan Mgmt
CHRIS NORMAN: ACT Music
NOTCH, Mykie: Little Piece of Jamaica (LPOJ)
NU TROOP: The Dune Music Company
NYAH: Yellow Balloon Productions
NYJO: NYJO - National Youth Jazz Orchestra
NYJO 2: NYJO - National Youth Jazz Orchestra
NYLON PYLON: TRC Mgmt
NYUSTA: Sincere Mgmt
DAX O'CALLAGHAN: PPM Artist Mgmt
O'LEARY, Tony: Blue Stack Music
JAMIE O'NEAL: azoffmusic mgmt
O'SULLIVAN, Gilbert: Park Promotions
O, Jackie: DCM International
O.O.O.D.: Kabuki
OAKENFOLD, Paul: Terra Firma Mgmt
OAKENFULL, Ski: Impro Mgmt
OASIS: Ignition Mgmt
OATEN, Richard: Mal Spence Mgmt
SAM OBERNIK: Daytime Entertainments
OBI: Mako Music
OBSTOJ, Jeanette: Jukes Productions
0898 DUBPLATE: Direct Heat Mgmt
OI VA VOI: Positive Mgmt
OJEER, Thandi: Keep Hit Real Mgmt
OLDFIELD, Greg: Loose
OLIVER LIEB: Represents Artist Mgmt
OLIVER MACGREGOR: Represents Artist Mgmt
OLLIE 'D': Coda Mgmt UK
OLVEIRA, Elmar: Music Company (London) .
THE OMEGAS: JW Mgmt
ONE MINUTE SILENCE: Northern Music Company
THE OPERATION: Extreme Music Production
ORBITAL: Mondo Mgmt
ORCHESTRA, The: Knifedge
ORGANIC AUDIO: Autonomy Music
GUY ORNADEL: Represents Artist Mgmt
BETH ORTON: azoffmusic mgmt
OSIBISA: Denis Vaughan Mgmt
OTWAY, John: Interzone Mgmt
OUT 77: Loose
OUTRAGEOUS BLUES BROTHERS: McLeod Holden Enterprises
OVERSEAS EDITION: Social Misfit Entertainment
OVERSEER: Sanctuary Artist Mgmt
OWEN, Mark: 10 Mgmt
OWENS, Robert: Robert Owens/Musical Directions
OXIDE & NEUTRINO: Albert Samuel Mgmt
OXYGEN: Bond Mgmt
ERLEND OYE: INS-YNC
PABLO: W1 Music Mgmt
PACO OSUNA: Represents Artist Mgmt
The PADDIES: Right Mgmt
PAGANO, Lindsay: azoffmusic mgmt
PAL JOEY: Kickstart Mgmt
CARL PALMER: Trinifold Mgmt
PALOMINO: funky star
Johnny Panic: Prestige Mgmt
PARADISE LOST: Northern Music Company
SIOBHAN PARR: Emperor Mgmt

PARSONS, Gareth: Show Business Entertainment
PARTNERS IN RHYME: Wizard Mgmt
PASADENA ROOF ORCHESTRA: David Curtis Mgmt
PATERSON, Rod: The Bechhofer Agency
AMIT PAUL: Bandana Mgmt
POLLY PAULUSMA: Coldplay Mgmt
PAVE: Z Mgmt
PEARCE, Dave: Wise Buddah Talent
PEARSON, Ewan: Mumbo Jumbo Mgmt
PEELER SMALL QUARTET, The: Charles Salt Mgmt
PELLOW, Marti: Sanctuary Artist Mgmt
THE PENKILN BURN: Antar
PENTANGLE: Park Promotions
AMY PEPPERCORN: PPM Artist Mgmt
PERE UBU: Charmenko
PERFORMANCE: Big Life Mgmt
PERKINS, Polly: Lena Davis John Bishop Associates
THE PERSPIRATIONS: Direct Heat Mgmt
PESHAY: Evolution Mgmt
PETE SHELLEY: Sentics
PETERSON, Gilles: Impro Mgmt
PHANTASM: Music Company (London).
PHANTOM5000: Lamb Mgmt
PHAT MUSTARD: Ambush Mgmt
PHATS & SMALL: Deluxe Mgmt
PHELOUNG, Barrington: Barrington Pheloung Mgmt
PHELPS, Cynthia: Music Company (London).
PHIL LIFE CYPHER: KSO Records
PHILIPSZ, Kelia: Modernwood Mgmt
GRANT LEE PHILLIPS: The Umbrella Group
PHOR:U: TFF Mgmt
PICTURE HOUSE: Pete Hawkins Mgmt
PINA KOLLARS: Impro Mgmt
PINCH: Antar
PINE, Courtney: Collaboration
PING PONG BITCHES: Midi Mgmt
Pist.On: Total Concept Mgmt (TCM)
PLACEBO: Riverman Mgmt
PLANET FUNK: F&G Mgmt
PLANET OF WOMEN: Liquid Mgmt
PLANT, Robert: Trinifold Mgmt
PLASMA: Conception Artist Mgmt
PLASTIC SURGEONS: Z Mgmt
PLASTICA: Clown Mgmt
PLEASUREBEACH: Mental Music Mgmt
POB: WonderWorld
JULIETTE POCHIN: FourFives Productions
POCKET ANGEL: 7Hz Mgmt
POCOMAN: Parliament Mgmt
POINT BREAK: DCM International
POLOROID: 7pm Mgmt
THE POLYPHONIC SPREE: TRC Mgmt
POND DWELLERS: Loose
POOK, Jocelyn: Knifedge
POP!: TForce
The POPES: Scarlet Mgmt
PORCUPINE TREE: Big Brother Mgmt.
PORNSHOT: Evolution Mgmt
PORTISHEAD: Fruit
THE POUND BOYS: D2mm (Direct2 Music Mgmt)
ELROY 'SPOONFACE' POWELL: Keith Harris Music
HELEN POWNEY: Kev Bennison Mgmt
PQ: Social Misfit Entertainment
PRAHA: Conception Artist Mgmt
PREFAB SPROUT: Kitchenware Mgmt
PRENDO: Cultural Foundation
THE PRETENDERS: Gailforce Mgmt
PRICE, Alan: Cromwell Mgmt
The PRIEST: Worldmaster DJ Mgmt
PRIMAL SCREAM: GR Mgmt
PRIOR, Maddy: Park Promotions
The PROCLAIMERS: Braw Mgmt
PRODIGAL SUN: Top Banana Mgmt
PRODIGY: Midi Mgmt
PROJECT G: Roger Boden Mgmt
PSYCHE, Delia: Loose
PSYCHID: Bermuda Mgmt
PSYCHONAUTS: MBL
PUBLIC SYMPHONY: Public Symphony
PURPLE POLO: Direct Heat Mgmt
PUSSYCAT DOLLS: azoffmusic mgmt
SACHA PUTTNAM: 7pm Mgmt
QED: Massive Mgmt
QTEE: Pilot Mgmt
QUATRO, Suzi: Jive Entertainments
QUAYE, Finley: Jon Sexton Mgmt (JSM)
QUEMBY, Dee: Lena Davis John Bishop Associates
QUINN: GR Mgmt
R CAJUN AND THE ZYDECO BROTHERS: Swamp Music
RACHEL STAMP: Cruisin' Music
RADIOHEAD: Courtyard Mgmt
RADIOTONES: Buzz Artist Mgmt
RAFFLES: Les Hart (Southampton Entertainments)
RAGING SPEEDHORN: Grand Union Mgmt
THE RAILWAY CHILDREN: WonderWorld
The RAIN BAND: Steve Harrison Mgmt
RALF: Prodmix DJ Mgmt & Production
DANNY RAMPLING: IMD
RANX, Juki: Wizard Mgmt
NICK RAPACCIOLI: LH Mgmt
RAPID.LA: Fruity Red Inc.
RASCAL: Billy Russell Mgmt
RASCO: Jon Sexton Mgmt (JSM)
RAT PACK: Albert Samuel Mgmt
RAVENHALL, John: Right Mgmt
RAWAA: Urban Control
RE-MAIL: Maximum Music
RE4MATION: Right Mgmt
REACTOR: In Phase Mgmt
READER, Eddi: Sincere Mgmt
REAGAN: Me Me Me Mgmt
REAL, Ed: Media Records
THE REALM: Earth Music
REBEKAH RAIN: O-Mix
RED LAB: MCM
RED LIGHT: Braw Mgmt
REDBONE, Martha: JC Music
REEF: In Phase Mgmt
FIONN REGAN: CMO Mgmt International
REID, Don: Show Business Entertainment
REILLY & DURRANT: Top Draw Music Mgmt
RELAX: The Psycho Mgmt Company
RELISH: J Mgmt
RENBOURN, John: NEM Productions (UK)
REO SPEEDWAGON: azoffmusic mgmt
RESERVOIR CATS: Paul Barrett (Rock 'N' Roll Enterprises)
REVERB: Cultural Foundation
THE REVS: Treasure Island Mgmt
REYNOLDS, James: Gerry Bron Mgmt
RHINO'S REVENGE: Fanatic Mgmt
RHYTHM MASTERS: Seven Music Promotions
Ricci Benson: Derek Boulton Mgmt
DAMIEN RICE: Mondo Mgmt
RICHIE, Lionel: Marshall Arts Mgmt
RIG THE JIG: Crashed Music
The Rinse Out Brothers: PFB Mgmt
RISING SON CREW: Little Piece of Jamaica (LPOJ)
RITCHIE: Rose Rouge International
ROBERT FARNON: Derek Boulton Mgmt
ROBERTS, Juliet: The Dune Music Company
ROBERTS, Mark: WonderWorld
ROBSON, Bryan: Mumbo Jumbo Mgmt
ROCHELLE: DCM International
The ROCK OF TRAVOLTA: Interzone Mgmt
ROCKASTELLA: Broken Star Mgmt
Richard ROGERS: O-Mix
ROLLER: Key Music Mgmt
The ROLLING STONES: Rupert Loewenstein
ROMONE, Phil: 21st Artist
Roni Size and Reprazent: Heavyweight Mgmt

ROOTS MANUVA: LH Mgmt
The ROSENBERGS: DGM Mgmt
ANTHONY ROTHER: Archetype Mgmt
ROUND, Carina: White Tiger Mgmt
ROUSSOS, Demis: Denis Vaughan Mgmt
ROW Z: Atrium Music
ROWE, Jason: NBM
ROXANNE, Lisa: CBL
ROYKSOPP: Deutsch-Englische Freundschaft
ROZALLA: J Mgmt
RUBBLE, Pierre: Urban Control
RUBY CRUISER: Lateral Artist Mgmt
RUBY FUSION: X Factor Mgmt
Rudi: Coda Mgmt UK
RUE ST. DENIS: Conception Artist Mgmt
RUFF TOUCH: Upside Mgmt
RUMOURS OF FLEETWOOD MAC: Hal Carter Organisation
RUNRIG: Runrig Mgmt
ROBBIE RYAN: Indie Music Mgmt
S.O.R.: Armstrong Academy Artist Mgmt
SABBAMANGALANG: Bodo Music Co
SADLER, Sophie: Joe Bangay Enterprises
SAINT ETIENNE: Heavenly Mgmt
SALT TANK: Doug Smith Associates
CHRIS SALT: Effective Mgmt
SAMIA: Congo Music
SAMMY JAY: Xosa Mgmt
SANDS, Tommy: The Bechhofer Agency
SANTUCCI, Luca: Freedom Mgmt
Sarah-Ann Webb: Eclipse-PJM
SARJANT D: O-Mix
SAUNA: Friars Mgmt
KEVIN SAUNDERSON: Safehouse Mgmt
SAVERS: Represents Artist Mgmt
SAXON, Oliver Dawson: Total Concept Mgmt (TCM)
SAXSECTION: NYJO - National Youth Jazz Orchestra
SAXSECTION PLUS: NYJO - National Youth Jazz Orchestra
SAYER, Leo: Silverbird
PAULINE SCANLON: Spirit Music & Media
SCANNERS: Grand Union Mgmt
SCATTERGOOD, Caroline: Lena Davis John Bishop Associates
SCATTERGOOD, Cazz: Lena Davis John Bishop Associates
SCHMIDT, Jan: Les Hart (Southampton Entertainments)
ULRICH SCHNAUSS: Machine Mgmt
The SCORPIONS: Part Rock Mgmt
SCOTT & LEON: Boom Mgmt
SCOTT, Chris: Mumbo Jumbo Mgmt
SCOTT, Jack: Paul Barrett (Rock 'N' Roll Enterprises)
SCOTT, Shinri Tee: Shalit Global Entertainment & Mgmt
SCRATCHING POST: FiveMilesHigh
SCUBA Z: Braw Mgmt
SCUSI & HARD-DRIVE: Wizard Mgmt
SEAL: azoffmusic mgmt
DAVE SEAMAN: Ornadel Mgmt
SECRET KNOWLEDGE: Friars Mgmt
SELECTER, The: Ro-lo Productions
SEN, Richard: Sublime Music
SENSER: Ignite Marketing (UK)
SENTIENCE, Nick: Media Records
KATHY SEPTEMBER: Madrigal Music
SERENA: Magic Kingdom Mgmt
SERENITY SKY: TJM
SERNA: Caleche Studios
SERNA BAND: Caleche Studios
THE SERVANT: Firebrand Mgmt
SEVEN CHAIN OCTOPUS: Headstone Mgmt
SEX GANG CHILDREN:
SHAH: Unique Corp
SHAMEFACED: Anger Mgmt
SHAMEN: Moksha Mgmt
SHANE MACGOWAN: Michael McDonagh Mgmt
SHARNA SHANELLE: Quintessential Music
SHANIKA: Wizard Mgmt
SHANTI: Intuition Music
SHAPIRO, Helen, AND HER BAND: John Williams
SHARMAN, Dave: Flick Productions
THE SHARP BOYS: Ambush Mgmt
SHAW, Sandie: Shavian Enterprises
SHED SEVEN: Simon Lawlor Mgmt
SHEILA SOUTHERN: Derek Boulton Mgmt
Sheisty da Gypsy: Social Misfit Entertainment
SHELAN: O-Mix
SHINE: Martin Coull Mgmt
SHINE, Brendan: Denis Vaughan Mgmt
SHOP: Antar
SHOWADDYWADDY: Jive Entertainments
SIA: IE Music
SIGUR ROS: Big Dipper Productions
SILENT FRONT: Riot Club Mgmt
SILVA, Joy: Saphron Mgmt
SILVER, Jimmy: Plus Artist Mgmt
SILVERBACK: Conception Artist Mgmt
TIM SIMENON: Feedback Communications
SIMON, Emelie: NBM
SIMON, Vanessa: Congo Music
SIN E: Knifedge
Sir Prestige: Social Misfit Entertainment
SIRENS: Kitchenware Mgmt
SIRINU: Seaview Music
SISTER SLEDGE: Denis Vaughan Mgmt
SISTER SYSTEM: Sphinx Mgmt
SIX BY SEVEN: Emperor Mgmt
SIZER BARKER: Indie Music Mgmt
SKAHANA: Ambush Mgmt
Skandinavia: Deluxxe Mgmt
SKEET, Andrew: Knifedge
SKEEWIFF: Impro Mgmt
SKELLY: Mad As Toast
SKINDRED: Northern Music Company
SKITZ: Heavyweight Mgmt
SKY: Little Piece of Jamaica (LPOJ)
SKYE: CMO Mgmt International
SKYMOO: Graham Peacock Mgmt
SKYRATS: But! Mgmt
SLADE: Hal Carter Organisation
SLAMM: Creative World Entertainment
SLAUGHTER, John, BLUES BAND: Cromwell Mgmt
SLIDER: TSD Records
SLIGHTLY ALIEN: Big Blue Music
SLIP: Little Piece of Jamaica (LPOJ)
SLIPSTREAM: Pure Delinquent
SM TRAX: Unique Corp
HEATHER SMALL: Bandana Mgmt
SMITH & MIGHTY: MWM Music Mgmt
CRAIG SMITH (DJ): Traffik Productions
RICHARD SMITH: Atrium Music
SMITH, 'Legs' Larry: Right Mgmt
SMITH, Andy: Fruit
SMITH, Daryl: Yellow Balloon Productions
ROB SMITH: MWM Music Mgmt
SMOKE CITY: F&G Mgmt
SMOKIE: NOW Music
SMOOTHIE, Jean Jacques: Hope Mgmt
SNEAKER PIMPS: Splinter Mgmt
SNOW PATROL: Big Life Mgmt
SNOWDOGS: Pete Hawkins Mgmt
SNOWPONY: Ardent Music
SO SOLID CREW: Albert Samuel Mgmt
The Social Misfits: Social Misfit Entertainment
SODA CLUB: JPS Mgmt
SOMERVILLE, Jimmy: Solar Mgmt
SONIC BLOOM: Key Music Mgmt
SONIQUE: Deutsch-Englische Freundschaft
SONS & DAUGHTERS: Banchory Mgmt
SOSUEME: Feedback Communications
SOULSAVERS: Heavenly Mgmt
SOUNDS LIKE VIOLENCE: Motive Music Mgmt
THE SOUNDTRACK OF OUR LIVES: Sanctuary Artist Mgmt

SOWETO STRING QUARTET: Hutt Russell Organisation
SPACE: Indie Music Mgmt
The SPACE BROTHERS: Earth Music
SPACE COUNTY: Toni Medcalf Mgmt
SPACE RAIDERS: Sublime Music
SPACEFUNK: Mumbo Jumbo Mgmt
SPAN: SuperVision Mgmt
SPEAKING TONGUES: Positive Mgmt
SPEARHEAD: Sincere Mgmt
SPEARMINT: Charmenko
SPEARS, Billie Jo: Malcolm Feld Agency
SPECTRUM: 3rd Stone
SPEEDER: John Taylor Mgmt
SPEKTRUM: Big Life Mgmt
Jon SPENCER BLUES EXPLOSION: Sanctuary Artist Mgmt
PETE SPENCER: ACT Music
SPHYNX: Money Talks Mgmt
SPILLER: F&G Mgmt
SPIRITUAL BEGGARS: Sanctuary Artist Mgmt
SPRAGGA BENZ: Jamdown
SPRINGER, Marvin: Quintessential Music
SQUEEZE: Stress Mgmt
THE STANDS: Bermuda Mgmt
STARDUST, Alvin: Brian Yeates Associates
STARECASE: Hope Mgmt
STARSAILOR: Heavenly Mgmt
STARSEEDS: WonderWorld
STARSKEE: Ornadel Mgmt
STATELESS: Sanctuary Artist Mgmt
STATUS QUO: Duroc Media
STEEL PULSE: War Zones and Associates
STEELEYE SPAN: Park Promotions
STEEVI JAIMZ: Northstar Artist Mgmt
STEINSKI: CEC Mgmt
STEPHENS, Carla: Fox Records (Mgmt)
STEREO NATION: Wizard Mgmt
STEREOLAB: Stereophonic Mgmt
The STEREOPHONICS: Nettwerk Mgmt UK
Steve "Vann" Lange: WS Mgmt
RACHEL STEVENS: 19 Mgmt
STEWART, Allan: International Artistes
STEWART, Eric: Harvey Lisberg Associates
STIG: Loose
STIVELL, Alan: Denis Vaughan Mgmt
STOCKLEY, Miriam: Friars Mgmt
STOKES, Darren: Duty Free Artist Mgmt
STONE CIRCLE: Social Misfit Entertainment
STONEBRIDGE: Talent Call
STONECOLD ARTISTS: Little Piece of Jamaica (LPOJ)
The STRANGLERS: Cruisin' Music
STRATTON, Cindy: Charles Salt Mgmt
STREEBECK: NSMA
STREET, Andy: Yellow Balloon Productions
THE STREETS: Coalition Mgmt
STRETCH & VERN: Represents Artist Mgmt
STYLUS: Braw Mgmt
SUB-5: Headstone Mgmt
SUEDE: Interceptor Enterprises
SUGABABES: Metamorphosis Mgmt
KATE SULLIVAN: Armstrong Academy Artist Mgmt
SUN CYCLE CREW: Jamdown
The SUNDAYS: Raymond Coffer Mgmt
SUNGOVER: Deuce Mgmt
SUNNA: A.M.P./TBA
THE SUNS: Arketek Mgmt
SUNSHINE VARIETY CLUB: But! Mgmt
SUPER DELTA THREE: Dee O'Reilly Mgmt
SUPER FURRY ANIMALS: Rheoli Ankst Mgmt
SUPERGRASS: Courtyard Mgmt
SUZY WHO?: Kickstart Mgmt
SW1: B&H Mgmt
SWAN, Billy: Muirhead Mgmt
The SWANS: Metro Artist Mgmt
SWEET DREAMS: Direct Heat Mgmt
The SWEET WRAPPERS: Plus Artist Mgmt
SWERVEDRIVER: Offside Mgmt
SWINGING BLUE JEANS: Hal Carter Organisation
SYLVIAN, David: Opium (Arts)
SYNTAX: Fools Paradise
SYRINX: Music Company (London).
T-BABE: TFF Mgmt
TABOR, June: NEM Productions (UK)
TAF: OPL Mgmt
TAFFY: Active Music Mgmt
TAHITA 'TY' BULMER: Sublime Music
TALBOT, Joby: Manners McDade Artist Mgmt
TALI: Heavyweight Mgmt
TALL PAUL: Duty Free Artist Mgmt
TANGO SIEMPRE: Hal Carter Organisation
TASCHA TAH: Davix Mgmt
TATE, Darren: 7pm Mgmt
TAVENER, Sir John: Manners McDade Artist Mgmt
TAYLOR, Jay: Yellow Balloon Productions
TAYLOR, Martin: P3 Music Mgmt.
TAYLOR, Pauline: CMO Mgmt International
TC CURTIS: Right Mgmt
TD LIND: Sanctuary Artist Mgmt
TEALE: Top Banana Mgmt
TEEN SPIRIT: The Psycho Mgmt Company
TEENIDOL: Big Help Music
TENESEE KAIT: Buzz Artist Mgmt
TENOR FLY: Jamdown
TENTH PLANET: Conception Artist Mgmt
TERRA DIABLO: Big Life Mgmt
TESLA: Asylum Artists
COLIN TEVENDALE (DJ): Traffik Productions
TEXAS: GR Mgmt
The THE: Antar
THEESSINK, Hans: The Bechhofer Agency
THEO: First Move Mgmt
ROSIE THOMAS: Cool Badge Mgmt
DANNY THOMPSON: Paul Crockford Mgmt (PCM)
PHIL THOMPSON: Safehouse Mgmt
THOMPSON, Lindsey: Dee O'Reilly Mgmt
THOMSON: 4 Tunes
THORNALLEY, Phil: WG Stonebridge Artist Mgmt
JULIA THORNTON: Ardent Music
THUNDER: Toni Medcalf Mgmt
TIDEY, Dean: CA Mgmt
TILBROOK, Glenn: Stress Mgmt
TIM & ROB: Xosa Mgmt
TIME MACHINE: The Psycho Mgmt Company
TIPPING, Yvonne: No Half Measures.
TNT: Me Me Me Mgmt
TOADSTOOL: Flick Productions
TOMORROW'S FACE: NYJO - National Youth Jazz Orchestra
TONG, Pete: IMD
TONIC: azoffmusic mgmt
William TOPLEY: Paul Crockford Mgmt (PCM)
TOPLEY-BIRD, Martina: CEC Mgmt
TOSHACK HIGHWAY: Offside Mgmt
THE TRAMPS feat. Earl Young: Malcolm Feld Agency
TRAN, Catherine: Total Mgmt
TRASH PALACE: Firebrand Mgmt
TRASHCAN SINATRAS: Robin Morton Consultancy
TRAVIS: Wildlife Entertainment
TREANA: SMI/Everyday Productions
TRIBE: Satellite Artists
A TRIBUTE TO RIVERDANCE: Denis Vaughan Mgmt
TRIPLE 8: Safe Mgmt
The TROGGS: Stan Green Mgmt
TRUTH: Mal Spence Mgmt
TUESDAYS CHILD: Seven Music Promotions
TUNDE: Independent Sound Mgmt (ISM)
TURIN BRAKES: CMO Mgmt International
TURNER'S, Nik, FANTASTIC ALL STARS: Money Talks Mgmt
TURNER'S, Nik, SPACE RITUAL: Money Talks Mgmt

TURNER, Ruby: Saffa Music
TURTLE K: MCM
TUULI: Key Music Mgmt
THE TWIGHLIGHT SINGERS: INS-YNC
TWINS OF PLEASURE: Direct Heat Mgmt
TWIST: MSM Music Consultants
2 BANKS OF 4: Impro Mgmt
TWO DAY RULE: Sugar Shack Mgmt
TY: Sentinel Mgmt
TYLER, Bonnie: David Aspden Mgmt
TYMES 4: Kim Glover Mgmt
TZANT: PFB Mgmt
UBERNOISE: Mal Spence Mgmt
UB40: Part Rock Mgmt
CLARE UCHIMA: RLM (Richard Law Mgmt)
UFBI: Congo Music
UK SUBS: Subversive Music Mgmt
UN-CUT: Blue Sky Entertainment
UNA MAS: Z Mgmt
UNAMERICAN: Richman Mgmt
UNDERWORLD: Jukes Productions
CHRISTINA UNDJEM: Asylum Artists
UNITED FUTURE ORGANISATION: Impro Mgmt
UNYSON: Boom Mgmt
UP AND COMING: KlubDJ
UTAH SAINTS: North
UTOPIANS: Money Talks Mgmt
U2: Principle Mgmt
V: Prestige Mgmt
VALANCE, Ricky: Lena Davis John Bishop Associates
VALENTINO, Bobby: Line-Up PMC
VANELLI, Joe T: Prodmix DJ Mgmt & Production
CRISTIAN VARELA: Safehouse Mgmt
RUI VARGAS: Qaraj'
VEGA 4: Big Life Mgmt
VELOURIA: Sound Pets
THE VENUS EXPERIENCE: McLeod Holden Enterprises
VENUS RISING: RLM (Richard Law Mgmt)
VERBALICIOUS: Sunhand
THE VERNONS GIRLS: Hal Carter Organisation
VETO SILVER: Mobb Rule
VIBEBABY: Direct Heat Mgmt
VICIOUS CIRCLE: MSM Music Consultants
VIENNA: McLeod Holden Enterprises
VIKING SKULL: Grand Union Mgmt
VINCENT, Jean: Paul Barrett (Rock 'N' Roll Enterprises)
VIOLENT DELIGHT: Toni Medcalf Mgmt
VIRELAI: Music Company (London)
VIVIANNA: TK1 Mgmt
WADE, Colin: Future Mgmt
WAGON CHRIST: Consigliari
WALL STREET CRASH: Hal Carter Organisation
KATE WALSH: Kitchenware Mgmt
THE WANDERING STEP: Steve Harrison Mgmt
WANGFORD, Hank: Line-Up PMC
WankDen: Got A Loser Job At The Diner Mgmt
The WANNADIES: War Zones and Associates
WARD 21: Jamdown
THE WARLOCKS: Big Life Mgmt
WASHINGTON, Geno: KAL Mgmt
WATERFALL: W1 Music Mgmt
WATSON, Russell: Sanctuary Artist Mgmt
THE WAYWARD SHEIKS: Spirit Music & Media
WEAVER, Jane: TRC Mgmt
WEBB BROTHERS: SuperVision Mgmt
CHARLES WEBSTER: Deluxe Mgmt
FINDLAY WEBSTER: Numinous Mgmt
WEDLOCK, Fred: PVA
WEEKEND PLAYERS: Sanctuary Artist Mgmt
WELLINGTON BOOTLES: NVB Entertainments
HAYLEY WESTENRA: Bedlam Mgmt
WESTLIFE: Louis Walsh Mgmt
WHAM! DURAN: The Psycho Mgmt Company
WHEN TRAMS WERE KINGS: Dellphonic Mgmt
WHITE BUFFALO: Magic Kingdom Mgmt
WHITE TRASH: DJT Mgmt
Alison WHITE: Mad As Toast
WHITE, Rachel: Creative World Entertainment
The WHO: Trinifold Mgmt
WILDE, Kelly: DCM International
WILDE, Kim: Onside Mgmt
WILDE, Marty: Big M Productions
WILKIE, Ian: Hope Mgmt
LUCINDA WILLIAMS: azoffmusic mgmt
WILLIAMS, Hanif: Modernwood Mgmt
WILLIAMS, Robbie: IE Music
WILLOW: First Time Mgmt
WILSON, Gary: R2 Mgmt
WILT: Sanctuary Artist Mgmt
AMY WINEHOUSE: Brilliant 19
WINWOOD, Steve: Atomic Mgmt
WISEGUYS aka DJ TOUCHE: Fruit
WITHOUT GRACE: Indie Music Mgmt
WITHOUT PREJUDICE: Kickstart Mgmt
WITNESS: Coalition Mgmt
WOMACK, Bobby: David Morgan Mgmt
THE WONDERSTUFF: Furtive Mass Transit Systems LLP
WOOD, Roy: Ro-lo Productions
WOOLLEY: Wizard Mgmt
The WURZELS: Cruisin' Music
THE X FACTOR: TForce
X-PRESS 2: Whitenoise Mgmt
XCITE: Kamara Artist Mgmt (UK)
XRS: Bulldozer Mgmt
YARDE, James: Xosa Mgmt
YELLO:
YELLOWHAND: Kickstart Mgmt
YEN SUNG: Qaraj'
YORK, Nola: Chantelle Music
YOUNG HEART ATTACK: Grand Union Mgmt
YOUNG, Gareth: SMI/Everyday Productions
YOUNG, Paul: What Mgmt
YOUNGSTERS: Archetype Mgmt
YOURCODENAMEIS:MILO: Sanctuary Artist Mgmt
Z LIST: Positive Mgmt
ZEN BASEBALLBAT: Loose
Bryan ZENTZ: Archetype Mgmt
ZERO 7: Solar Mgmt
ZINGER, Earl: Impro Mgmt
ZOE: Big Help Music
ZOHAR: Goldpush
ZYDECOMOTION: Swamp Music

Recruitment Services

Barclays Executive Appointments Barclay House, 68 The Ridgeway, Stanmore, Middlesex HA7 4BD **t** 020 8954 4321 **f** 020 8954 5131 **e** barcexec@aol.com **w** barclaysexecutive.com MD: Lionel Rose.

CAREER MOVES

careermoves
Preferred suppliers to the Music Industry

Sutherland House, 5-6 Argyll Street, London W1F 7TE **t** 020 7292 2900 **e** music@cmoves.co.uk **w** cmoves.co.uk Music Consultants: Jessica Freeman, Kim Kidd. Rapidly becoming the leaders in music recruitment including search/selection and head hunting from Junior through to Senior Management positions.

Cat Entertainment Search Pinewood Studios, Pinewood Road, Iver Heath, Buckinghamshire SL0 0NH **t** 01753 630040 **f** 01753 630830 **e** cat@catentertainmentsearch.com **w** catentertainmentsearch.com GM: Catherine Pianta-McGill.

DNP Media 4th Floor, 2 Wedgwood Mews, 12 Greek Street, London W1D 4BB **t** 020 7439 3896 **f** 020 7734 7049 **e** john@dnpmedia.com Dir: John Dowson. MD: Mark Hilder.

Gottlieb Associates, Executive Search Consultants Garden Flat, 28 Oakley St, London SW3 5NT **t** 020 7351 0717 **f** 020 7351 0604 **e** stevegottlieb@stevegottlieb.com **w** stevegottlieb.com MD: Stephen Gottlieb.

Grosvenor Bureau Secretarial Recruitment 22 South Molton Street, London W1K 5RB **t** 020 7491 0884 **f** 020 7409 1524 **e** gb@grosvenorbureau.co.uk **w** grosvenorbureau.co.uk Contact: The Managing Director

HANDLE RECRUITMENT

THE MUSIC RECRUITMENT CONSULTANTS

4 Gees Court, London W1U 1JD **t** 020 7569 9999 **e** music@handle.co.uk w handle.co.uk Directors: Stella Walker and Peter Tafler. **THE No.1 Consultancy to the Music Industry. Permanent and Temporary recruitment solutions from Entry Level through to Executive Appointments. Secretarial/Support Staff • Finance/Accounts • Sales & Marketing • Press & PR • Production/Creative • A&R • Business Affairs • Licensing/Copyright • Human Resources • New Media • Supply Change Management**

Kingston Smith Executive Selection Quadrant House, (Air Street Entrance), 80-82 Regent Street, London W1R 5PA **t** 020 7306 5670 **f** 020 7306 5682 **e** jwest@kingstonsmith.co.uk **w** kingstonsmith.co.uk MD: John West.

MacMillan Davies Hodes 10 Regent's Wharf, All Saints Street, London N1 9RL **t** 020 7551 4732 **f** 020 7551 4682 **e** jbaker@mdh.co.uk **w** mdh.co.uk Head of Practice: John Baker.

Media Recruitment 1 Parkway, London NW1 7PG **t** 020 7267 0555 **f** 020 7482 3666 **e** tanya@mediarecruitment.co.uk **w** mediarecruitment.co.uk Senior Consultant: Tanya Ferris.

THE MUSIC MARKET

2nd Floor, 4 Paddington Street, London W1U 5QE **t** 020 7486 9102 **f** 020 7486 7512 **e** firstname@themusicmarket.co.uk **w** themusicmarket.co.uk MD: Helen Ward. Temporary Controller: Christine Knight. Recruitment Consultant: Jenny Dowler.

NJD Group (Executive Search Division) Pinewood Studios, Pinewood Road, Iver Heath, Buckinghamshire SL0 0NH **t** 01753 630040 **f** 01753 630830 **e** nicky@njdgroup.co.uk **w** njdgroup.co.uk Managing Consultant: Nicky Davis.

Positive Solutions Recruitment (Music & Media) Old Chambers, 93-94 West St, Farnham, Surrey GU9 7EB **t** 01252 720825 **f** 01252 720827 **e** music@positivejobs.com **w** positivejobs.com Dir: Craig Chuter.

Rose Inc 27 Phipp Street, London EC2A 4NP **t** 020 7613 5401 **f** 020 7739 7343 **e** nina@rose-inc.co.uk **w** rose-inc.co.uk MD: Rose Taylor.

Talentfile Red Bus Studios, 34 Salisbury Street, London NW8 8QE **t** 020 7734 2243 **f** 020 7724 2871 **e** info@crimson.globalnet.co.uk **w** talentfile.co.uk Joint MD: Joanne Cohen.

Conferences, Exhibitions & Events

Access Events International India House, 2nd Floor, 45 Curlew Street, London SE1 2ND **t** 020 7940 7070 **f** 020 7940 7071 **e** info@access-events.com **w** access-events.com Marketing Dir: Paul Gilbertson.

Airplay The Manse, 39 Northenden Road, Sale, Cheshire M33 2DH **t** 0161 962 2002 **f** 0161 962 2112 **e** mailbox@airplay.co.uk **w** airplay.co.uk MD: Peter Knott.

BALLISTIC EVENTS

2nd Floor, 13-19 Vine Hill, London EC1R 5DX **t** 020 7812 0097 or 020 7812 0096 **f** 020 7812 0099 **e** info@ballisticevents.com **w** ballisticevents.com Contacts: Louise Stevens, James Smith. **Independent events agency specialising in music: Music Week Awards, NME Awards, Digital Music Awards, Music Vision Awards, I See Music exhibition.**

Bandwagon Events 67 Kirkham, Biddick, Washington, Tyne & Wear NE38 7EY **t** 0191 4166419 or 07793 606195 **e** info@band-wagon.co.uk **w** bandwagon.co.uk Dirs: Paul Reay, Stephen Dodds.

Barracuda 3 Delta Way, Thorpe Industrial Park, Egham, Surrey TW20 8RX **t** 08451 284046 **f** 01784 435700 **e** info@barracudanet.co.uk **w** barracudanet.co.uk Sales/Marketing Dir: Ray Wallace.

Big Cat Group (Events) Vincent House, 92-93 Edward Street, Birmingham, West Midlands B1 2RA **t** 0121 248 4697 **e** info@bcguk.com **w** bcguk.com Dir: Nick Morgan.

Big Fish Events 115 Westbourne Studios, 242 Acklam Road, London W10 5JJ **t** 020 7524 7555 **f** 020 7524 7556 **e** bigfish@thefishpond.co.uk **w** thefishpond.co.uk MD: Robert Guterman.

Brickwerk 19, Wynell Road, London SE23 2LN **t** 020 7381 3524 **f** 020 8291 5053 **e** events@brickwerk.co.uk **w** brickwerk.co.uk Partners: Jo Brooks-Nevin / Maria Walker.

Camera0023 The Studio, 156-158 Grays Inn Road, London WC1X 8ED **t** 020 7358 4466 or 07901 808 606 **e** forlastingmemories@camera0023.com **w** camera0023.com Creative Dir: Alex Valdes.

Capitalize Specialist PR and Sponsorship 52 Thrale Street, London SE1 9HWor 020 7940 1700 or 020 7940 1739 **e** Info@capitalize.co.uk **w** capitalize.co.uk MD: Richard Moore.

Cup Promotions Suite 14-16, Marlborough BC, 96 George Lane, South Woodford, London E18 1AD **t** 020 8989 2204 **f** 020 8989 2219 **e** info@cup.uk.com **w** cup.uk.com Dir: Mark Abery.

The Day Job (Event Management) 14 Church Street, Twickenham, Middx TW1 3NJ **t** 020 8892 6446 **f** 020 8891 1895 **e** nina@thedayjob.com **w** thedayjob.com Contact: Nina Jackson

Event Management Systems (UK) 67 Plashet Road, London E13 0QA **t** 020 8472 9011 **f** 020 8472 9012 **e** info@emsltduk.com **w** emsltduk.com Marketing Manager: Imran Bashir.

Fabulous Events 130 Shaftesbury Ave, London W1D 5EU **t** 020 7031 0975 **e** ian@thesugargroup.com **w** thesugargroup.com Head of Business Dev't: Ian Milne.

Funevents Corporate Services PO Box 4040, Mayfair, London W1A 6NR **t** 0870 758 0619 **f** 0870 135 3338 **e** admin@funevents.com **w** funevents.com Dir: Harv Sethi.

Hawksmere plc 12-18 Grosvenor Gardens, London SW1W 0DH **t** 0845 120 9603 **f** 020 7730 4293 **e** business@hawksmere.co.uk **w** hawksmere.co.uk Event Co-ordinator: Jane Fullbrook.

IAAAM (Int Association Of African American Music) The Business Village, 3-9 Bromhill Road, London SW18 4JQ **t** 020 8870 8744 **f** 020 8874 1578 **e** info@hardzone.co.uk **w** hardzone.co.uk Co-Founder: Jackie Davidson.

Impact Ventures 38b Brixton Water Lane, London SW2 1QE **t** 020 7274 8509 **f** 020 7274 3543 **e** info@impactventures.co.uk **w** impactventures.co.uk MD: Rachael Bee.

In The City 8 Brewery Yard, Deva Centre, Trinity Way, Salford M3 7BB **t** 0161 839 3930 **f** 0161 839 3940 **e** info@inthecity.co.uk **w** inthecity.co.uk Director: Anthony Wilson.

International Live Music Conference (ILMC) 2-12 Pentonville Road, London N1 9PL **t** 020 7833 8998 **f** 020 7833 5992 **e** conference@ilmc.com **w** ilmc.com Producer: Alia Dann.

Jack Morton Worldwide 16-18 Acton Park Estate, Stanley Gardens, London W3 7QE **t** 020 8735 2000 **f** 020 8735 2020 **e** Asitha_Ameresekere@jackmorton.co.uk **w** jackmorton.com Sales/Mkt Dir: Chris Morris.

Lashed Worldwide Events Clearwater Yard, 35 Inverness Street, London NW1 7HB **t** 020 7424 7500 **f** 020 7424 7501 **e** roman@ornadel.com Contact: Roman Trystram

Mad As Toast Events 3 Broomlands Street, Paisley PA1 2LS **t** 0141 887 8888 **f** 0141 887 8888 **e** info@madastoast.com **w** madastoast.com Dirs: George Watson, John Richardson.

Midem (UK) Walmar House, 296 Regent Street, London W1B 3AB **t** 020 7528 0086 **f** 020 7895 0949 **e** emma.dallas@reedmidem.com **w** midem.com Sales Mgr: Emma Dallas.

MusicWorks 40a High St, Glasgow G1 1NL **t** 0141 552 6027 **f** 0141 552 6048 **e** musicworks@uzevents.com **w** musicworksUK.com Producer: Joanne Wain. Programme Co-ordinator: Peter Darnborough.

NUS Ents - Ents Convention 45 Underwood Street, London N1 7LG **t** 020 7490 0946 **f** 020 7490 1026 **e** steve@nus-ents.co.uk **w** nus-ents.co.uk NUS Ents Co-ordinator: Steve Hoyland.

onedotzero Unit 212c Curtain House, 136-146 Curtain Road, London EC2A 3AR **t** 020 7729 0072 **f** 020 7729 0057 **e** info@onedotzero.com **w** onedotzero.com Events Mgr: Anna Doyle.

Performance Exhibitions The Imperial Centre, Suite 102, Grange Road, Darlington, County Durham DL1 5NQ **t** 01325 467000 **f** 01325 351170 **e** brian.hum@ic24.net **w** performance-expo.com MD: Brian Launder.

The Radio Academy 5 Market Place, London W1W 8AE **t** 020 7255 2010 **f** 020 7255 2029 **e** info@radioacademy.org **w** radioacademy.org Dir: John Bradford.

Sensible Events 1st Floor, Regent Arcade House, 19-25 Argyll St, London W1F 7TS **t** 020 7009 3470 **e** Andrew@sensibleevents.com MD: Andrew Zweck.

SMi Group The Clove Building, Maguire Street, London SE1 2NQ **t** 020 7827 6000 **f** 020 7827 6001 **e** media@smi-online.co.uk **w** smi-online.co.uk

UZ Events 40a High Street, Glasgow G1 1NL **t** 0141 552 6027 **f** 0141 552 6048 **e** office@uzevents.com **w** uzevents.com Producer: Joanne Wain.

World Famous Group (Events) 467 Fulham Road, Fulham, London SW6 1HL **t** 020 7385 6838 **f** 020 7385 0999 **e** info@worldfamousgroup.com **w** worldfamousgroup.com Chairman: Alon Shulman.

Business Consultants & Misc

24 Carat (Music Sponsorship consultants) 21 Castle St, Castlefield, Manchester M3 4SW **t** 0161 827 8124 or 07770 633 458 **f** 0161 827 8129 **e** rose@twentyfourcarat.co.uk Contact: Rose Marley

>4 Marketing Consultant Morethan4 75c Perham Road, London W14 9SP **t** 020 7610 0963 **e** info@morethan4.com **w** morethan4.com MD: Anthony Hamer-Hodges.

Affinity Music 60 Kingly St, London W1B 5DS **t** 020 7453 4062 **f** 020 7453 4185 **e** info@affinitymusic.co.uk **w** affinitymusic.co.uk Co-MDs: Gordon Biggins, Simon Binns.

Air-Edel Music Supervision 18 Rodmarton Street, London W1U 8BJ **t** 020 7486 6466 **f** 020 7224 0344 **e** air-edel@air-edel.co.uk Contact: Maggie Rodford/Matt Biffa

AM-BA Enterprises 36 Ashville Road, London E11 4DT **t** 07970 198739 **e** anne-marie@amba-enterprises.co.uk **w** amba-enterprises.co.uk Dir: Anne-Marie Batson. Label management (urban), administration, artist management, UK and international licensing.

Elizabeth Andrews 15 Hawthorn Hill, Letchworth, Herts SG6 4HF **t** 01462 685333 **e** lizzie@music-consultancy.fsbusiness.co.uk Music Consultant: Elizabeth Andrews. International copyrights, compilations, premium product.

Aquarius Entertainments 132 Chase Way, London N14 5DH **t** 07958 592 526 or 020 8361 5002 **f** 020 8361 3757 **e** rdldisco@aol.com **w** webvert.co.uk/karaokediscos Mgr: C Jacques. Entertainment to corporate functions.

Art And Soul (Consultancy & Catalogue Compilers) 154 Gordon Road, Camberley, Surrey GU15 2JQ **t** 01276 505030 **f** 01276 508819 **e** davidsmith18@ntlworld.com MD: David Smith.

The Arts Clinic 14 Devonshire Place, London W1G 6HX **t** 020 7935 1242 **f** 020 7224 6256 **e** mail@artsclinic.co.uk **w** artsclinic.co.uk Director: Sandie Powell.

Edward Ashcroft Consultancy 101 High Street, Stetchworth, Newmarket, Suffolk CB8 9TH **t** 01638 508 582 or 07711 088 972 **e** ed@oneservice.co.uk MD: Edward Ashcroft.

Assential Arts Coxeter House, 21-27 Ock Street, Abingdon, Oxfordshire OX14 3ST **t** 01235 536008 **f** 01235 207070 **e** info@assentialarts.com **w** assentialarts.com MD: Mike Selway. Framers of BPI awards discs.

The Association Of Blind Piano Tuners 31 Wyre Crescent, Lynwood, Darwen, Lancs BB3 0JG **t** 01254 776148 **f** 01254 773158 **e** abpt@uk-piano.org **w** uk-piano.org Secretary: Barrie Heaton.

Autonomy Music Label Management & Consultancy Unit 212 Old Gramophone Works, 326 Kensal Road, London W10 5BZ **t** 020 8969 9111 **f** 020 8969 9955 **e** info@autonomy-music.co.uk **w** autonomy-music.co.uk MD: Grant Bishop.

Bonhams 65-69 Lots Road, Chelsea, London SW10 0RN **t** 020 7393 3952 **f** 020 7393 3906 **e** entertainment@bonhams.com **w** bonhams.com/ Entertainment Dept: Niki Roberts.

Bucks Music Group Onward House, 11 Uxbridge Street, London W8 7TQ **t** 020 7221 4275 **f** 020 7229 6893 **e** info@bucksmusicgroup.co.uk **w** bucksmusicgroup.com MD: Simon Platz. Music consultant.

Caligraving Brunel Way, Thetford, Norfolk IP24 1HP **t** 01842 752116 **f** 01842 755512 **e** info@caligraving.co.uk **w** caligraving.co.uk Sales Dir: Oliver Makings.

The Chain Music Services 30 Seby Rise, Uckfield TN22 5EE **t** 01825 769829 **e** mail@chainmusic.com MD: Giorgio Cuppini. General consultancy, Business Plan for Record Companies and Artists. Sales and Special Projects. Translations (texts, booklets, etc).

Chapman Freeborn Group 5 Hobart Place, London SW1W 0HU **t** 020 7393 1234 **f** 020 7393 1275 **e** lon@chapman-freeborn.com **w** chapman-freeborn.com MD: Carol Norman. Aircraft chartering and special travel arrangements.

Chart Moves-The Game 2 Move 2 PO Box 1099, London SE5 9HT **t** 020 7326 4824 **f** 020 7535 5901 **e** gamesmaster@chartmoves.com **w** chartmoves.com MD: David Klein. Multi-award-winning music business board game.

Christian Copyright Licensing (Europe) PO Box 1339, Eastbourne, East Sussex BN21 4YF **t** 01323 417711 **f** 01323 417722 **e** executive@ccli.co.uk **w** ccli.co.uk Sales Mgr: Chris Williams. Licensing hymn and worship song reproduction.

Christie's Pop Memorabilia Auctions 85 Old Brompton Road, London SW7 3LD **t** 020 7321 3281 or 020 7321 3280 **f** 020 7321 3321 **e** shodgson@christies.com **w** christies.com Head of Dept: Sarah Hodgson.

Churchill Howells Associates 24 Cornwall Road, Cheam, Surrey SM2 6DT **t** 020 8643 3353 **f** 020 8643 9423 **e** cha@c-h-a-ltd.demon.co.uk Chairman: Carole Howells. Dir: Graham Churchill.

Clancy Webster Partnership Penniwells, Edgwarebury Lane, Elstree, Hertfordshire WD6 3RG **t** 020 8953 8321 **f** 020 8953 2859 **e** jon@clancywebster.com Partner: Jon Webster. Music business (international) consultants.

cmac Music Consultancy 16 Sabine Road, London SW11 5LW **t** 020 7585 3876 **f** 020 7585 3876 **e** cmacmc@cfaz.demon.co.uk Music Consultant: Clive Farrell.

Collective Music The Collective, 2nd Floor, 80-82 Chiswick High Road, London W4 1SY **t** 020 8995 5544 **f** 020 8995 1133 **w** collective.mu MD: Phil Hardy. International Music Consutancy.

Consigliari 18 Hackford Walk, Hackford Road, London SW9 0QT **t** 020 7587 3799 **f** 020 7587 3818 Contact: Mark Melton & Sarah Blain Sample clearance specialist, music consultancy.

Cube Music The Factory, 2 Acre Road, Kingston upon Thames, Surrey KT2 6EF **t** 020 8547 1543 **f** 020 8547 1544 **e** info@cube-music.com **w** cube-music.com Music & Promotions Dir: Mick Hilton.

drive.information 60 Upper Walthamstow Road, Walthamstow, London E17 3QQ **t** 020 8281 8220 **f** 020 8281 8220 **e** info@driveinformation.com **w** driveinformation.com MD: Pete Dodge. Label management & consultancy.

Dynamik Music (Label Management) PO Box 32146, London N4 3AX **t** 020 7272 0090 **f** 020 7171 0101 **e** giles@dynamik-music.com **w** dynamik-music.com MD: Giles Goodman.

Eat Your Greens - Music Consultants 1 Crane Cottages, Dudset Lane, Cranford, Middx TW5 9UQ **t** 020 8759 2312 **e** info@eatyourgreens.ltd.uk **w** eatyourgreens.ltd.uk MD: Denzil Thomas.

EP Music Licensing Consultants 11 Richmond Way, East Grinstead, West Sussex RH19 4TG **t** 01342 313035 **f** 01342 313035 **e** clive@epmusic.f2s.com MD: Clive Wills. Music Licensing and Business Affairs Consultants.

Essential Business Services 131 Clermiston Road, Edinburgh, Midlothian EH12 6UR **t** 0131 334 3039 or 07774 161536 **f** 0131 334 3055 **e** jackie1ebs@aol.com **w** essentialbusiness.co.uk Owner: Jackie Grant, FIQPS. Word processing and business support services.

Feltwain 2000 1 Oakwood Parade, London N14 4HY **t** 020 8950 8732 **f** 020 8950 6648 **e** paul.lynton@btopenworld.com MD: Paul Lynton. Copyright clearance consultants.

Fleamusic PO Box 70, Witney, Oxon OX29 4GA **t** 01865 883671 or 07939 228435 **f** 01865 883671 **e** jerry@fleamusic.co.uk **w** fleamusic.co.uk Music Clearance Cons't: Jerry Butson.

Framous Unit 12/13 Impress House, Mansell Road, Acton, London W3 7QH **t** 020 8735 0047 **f** 020 8735 0048 **e** info@framous.ltd.uk **w** framous.ltd.uk Office Administrator: Lucy Walker. Coating/framing record and CD awards.

Liz Gallacher Music Supervision 23 Brickwood Road, Croydon, Surrey CR0 6UL **t** 020 8680 7784 **f** 020 8681 3000 **e** info@lizg.com Music Supervisor: Liz Gallacher.

Gas Music Tracking (GMT) Suite 1 Second Floor, 65 George Street, Oxford OX1 2BE **t** 01865 798791 **f** 01865 798792 **e** gmt@oxfordmusic.net Master Tracker: Dave Newton.

Genesis Trade Shows & Events Merlin House, 6 Boltro Road, Haywards Heath, West Sussex RH16 1BB **t** 01444 476 120 **f** 01444 476 121 **e** abigail@genesistravel.co.uk **w** genesistravel.co.uk Events Manager: Abigail Knight.

Green Consulting
30 Cranley Gardens, Muswell Hill, London N10 3AP **t** 020 8352 0973 **f** 020 8352 0973 **e** jonathangreen@blueyonder.co.uk MD: Jonathan Green.

Chris Griffin - Consultant/Management
69 Shakespeare Road, London W7 1LU **t** 07973 883 159 **f** 020 8357 9047 **e** chris@crgriffin.demon.co.uk

Hamilton House Mailings Earlstrees Court, Earlstrees Road, Corby, Northamptonshire NN17 4HH **t** 01536 399000 **f** 01536 399012 **e** sales@hamilton-house.com **w** hamilton-house.com MD: Stephen Mister.

Immediate Business Management 1st Floor, 1 Peterborough Road, Harrow, Middlesex HA1 2AZ **t** 020 8423 4307 **f** 020 8423 2082 **e** immbus@aol.com Partner: Derek Jones.

JN Promotions (Music Services) PO Box 6879, Wellingborough NN8 3YJ **t** 01933 228786 **e** jacqui@jnpromotions.biz **w** jnpromotions.biz MD: Jacqui Norton.

John Waller Management & Marketing
The Old Truman Brewery, 91 Brick Lane, London E1 6QL **t** 020 7247 1057 **f** 020 7377 0732 **e** john.waller@dial.pipex.com MD: John Waller.

The Licensing Team 23 Capel Road, Watford WD19 4QF **t** 01923 234021 **f** 01923 249251 **e** Info@TheLicensingTeam.com **w** thelicensingteam.com Dir: Lucy Winch. Director: Lucy Winch.

Keith RD Lowde F.C.A. Minoru, Pharaoh's Island, Shepperton, Middx TW17 9LN **t** 01932 222803 or 0771 444 9765 **f** 01932 222803 **e** k.lowde@btconnect.com Rights and royalties consultant.

Mandy Haynes-Music Business Consultant Covetous Corner, Hudnall Common, Little Gaddesden, Herts HP4 1QW **t** 01442 842039 **f** 01442 842082 **e** mandy@haynesco.fsnet.co.uk MD: Mandy Haynes.

Marken Time Critical Express Unit 2, Metro Centre, St Johns Road, Middlesex TW7 6NJ **t** 020 8388 8555 **f** 020 8388 8666 **e** marken.lon@exel.com **w** marken.com Bus Devel Mgr: Rob Paterson.

MBR Promotions 10 Hawthorn House, Forth Banks, Newcastle upon Tyne NE1 3SG **t** 0191 2211 666 **f** 0191 2211 777 **e** info@mbr-online.com **w** mbr-online.com Contact: Terry Hollingsworth

MECS (Music & Entertainment Consultancy Services)
14 Grasmere Ave, Kingston Vale, London SW15 3RB **t** 020 8974 5579 **f** 020 8974 5579 **e** tony@a-b-u.demon.co.uk MD: Tony Watts.

Mike Irving Music Consultancy 47 Longcroft Gardens, Welwyn Garden City, Herts AL8 6JR **t** 01707 376057 or 07071 881154 **f** 01707 393776 **e** MikeIrving@aol.com **w** mikeirvingpromotions.co.uk MD: Mike Irving.

MRD Consultancy 4, Wellington House, Messeter Place, London SE9 5DP **t** 020 8850 1060 **f** 020 8850 1060 **e** Mrdconsultancy@aol.com Proprietor: Sue Macauley.

MTD Group Stapleford Airfield, Nr Abridge, Romford, Essex RM4 1SJ **t** 01708 688652 **f** 01708 688697 **e** logistics@mtdgroup.co.uk **w** mtdgroup.co.uk Product Mgr: Patrick Malpass.

The Music & Media Partnership First Floor, 72-74 Notting Hill Gate, London W11 3HT **t** 020 7727 9111 **f** 020 7727 9911 **e** info@tmmp.co.uk MD: Rick Blaskey.

Music & Arts Security 13 Grove Mews, Hammersmith, London W6 7HS **t** 020 8563 9444 **f** 020 8563 9555 **e** sales@musicartssecurity.co.uk **w** music-and-arts-security.co.uk MD: Jerry Judge.

Music & Merit Consultancy 9 Griffin Avenue, Kidderminster, Worcs DY10 1NA **t** 07774 117678 **f** 01562 751330 **e** musicalmerit@blueyonder.co.uk Owner/consultant: Robin Vaughan.

The Music Broker **t** 0870 749 1117 **e** musicbroker@themusicbroker.org **w** TheMusicBroker.org Head of Licensing: Richard Jay.

Music Business Associates 1st Floor, 4 South Street, Epsom, Surrey KT18 7PF **t** 01372 840280 **f** 01372 840282 **e** info@musicbusinessassociates.com **w** musicbusinessassociates.com Contact: Lisa, David or Berry

Music Business Services (Accountancy & Publishing)
1 Freshfields Drive, Lancing, West Sussex BN15 9LN **t** 01903 530005 or 07950 274224 **f** 01903 530005 **e** ray@rowlesmusic.co.uk **w** rowlesmusic.co.uk MD: Ray Rowles.

Music Data Tracking (MDT) Unit 8 Acklam Workshops, 10 Acklam Road, London W10 5QZ **t** 020 8964 3300 **f** 020 8964 4400 **e** info@kickinmusic.com **w** kickinmusic.com Repertoire & Acquisitions: Andy Haeffele.

Musicalities Limited Snows Ride Farm, Snows Ride, Windlesham, Surrey GU20 6LA **t** 01276 474181 **f** 01276 452227 **e** enquiries@musicalities.co.uk **w** musicalities.co.uk MD: Ivan Chandler.

Musicare 16 Thorpewood Avenue, London SE26 4BX **t** 020 8699 1245 **f** 020 8291 5584 **e** peterfilleul@compuserve.com MDs: Peter Filleul & Sian Wynne.

MusikLine PO Box 1153, Bristol BS36 1DL **t** 0870 909 0500 **f** 0870 909 0600 **e** info@musikline.co.uk **w** musikline.com Operations Director: Peter Lockett. Audio telephone preview numbers, free, local, national or premium rate.

Network Chauffeur Drive Network House, Benacre Drive, Birmingham B5 5RF **t** 0870 242 2442 **f** 0870 242 2443 **e** info@networktransportgroup.com **w** neteurope.co.uk MD: Graham Adkins.

NiceMan Productions (Licensing & Repertoire Mgmt) 74 Pentland Close, London N9 0XN **t** 020 8245 5562 **f** 0870 922 3133 **e** scott@nicemanproductions.com **w** nicemanproductions.com Chairman: Scott Simons.

Pacific Entertainment PO Box 2154, Hove, East Sussex BN3 6RG **t** 01273 709228 **f** 01273 235043 **e** info@pacificentertainment.co.uk CEO: Howard Kruger.

Parallel Lines Marketing Unit 232, Canalot Studios, 222 Kensal Road, London W10 5BN **t** 020 8964 3489 **f** 020 8964 3489 **e** siona@parallellinesmusic.co.uk MD: Siona Ryan.

Peter Siggery - Information Consultant 28 Rosedene Gardens, Ilford, Essex IG2 6YE **t** 020 8551 6685 **f** 020 8551 6685 **e** Peter@Siggery.com Information Consultant: Peter Siggery.

Plan B Audio 15-17 Palace Street, London SW1E 5HS **t** 020 7821 8821 **f** 020 7821 8829 **e** info@planbaudio.com MD: Thomas Crowther.

The Product Exchange 45 Mount Ash Road, London SE26 6LY **t** 020 8699 5835 or 020 8291 1193 **f** 020 8699 5835 **e** music@productexchange.co.uk **w** productexchange.co.uk MD: Frank Rodgers.

Pure Delinquent (International Consultants) 134 Replingham Road, Southfields, London SW18 5LL **t** 07929 990 321 **f** 020 8870 0790 **e** julie@pure-delinquent.com **w** pure-delinquent.com Dir: Julie Pratt.

PVA 2 High Street, Westbury On Trym, Bristol BS9 3DU **t** 0117 950 4504 **f** 0117 959 1786 **e** enquiries@pva.ltd.uk **w** pva.ltd.uk Sales Director: John Hutchinson.

Quite Great Solutions 370 Old York Road, London SW18 1SP **t** 020 8877 3254 **f** 020 8877 3254 **e** solutions@quitegreat.co.uk **w** quitegreatsolutions.co.uk MD: Tony Lewis.

R&B Music Consultants 24 Beauval Road, Dulwich, London SE22 8UQ **t** 020 8693 6463 **f** 020 8299 0719 **e** stpierre.roger@ukf.net MD: Roger St Pierre.

RASHEED OGUNLARU LIFE COACH (FOR SINGERS AND PERFORMERS)

Rasheed Ogunlaru Coaching

The Coaching Studio, 223a Mayall Road, London SE24 0PS **t** 020 7207 1082 **e** rasaru_coaching@yahoo.com **w** rasaru.com Contact: Rasheed Ogunlaru - Founder. **Helping accomplished / aspiring artists fulfil their life and career: Confidence, direction, success, life-balance, motivation, creativity, performance. Serving artists / industry.**

Real Time Information The Unit, 2 Manor Gardens, London N7 6ER **t** 020 7561 6700 **f** 020 7561 6701 **e** hq@realtimeinfo.co.uk **w** realtimeinfo.co.uk Intl: Simon Edwards.

The Record Factory 38 Wharncliffe Gardens, London SE25 6DQ **t** 020 8239 8464 **f** 020 8239 8464 **e** davemcaleer@blueyonder.co.uk Owner: Dave McAleer.

Record-play Consultants Studio 203, 45-46 Charlotte Road, London EC2A 3PD **t** 07753 388275 **f** 020 7739 0939 **e** info@record-play.com **w** record-play.com Prop: Daniel Cross.

Ricall Limited Suites 1-4, 97 Mortimer Street, London W1W 7SU **t** 020 7927 8305 **f** 020 7927 8306 **e** mail@ricall.com **w** ricall.com MD: Richard Corbett.

Right Music Old Church Cottage, Wilby, Suffolk IP21 5LE **t** 01379 388365 **f** 01379 384731 **e** info@rightmusic.co.uk **w** rightmusic.co.uk MD: Kirsten Lane.

Rima Travel 10 Angel Gate, London EC1V 2PT **t** 020 7833 5071 **f** 020 7278 8676 **e** ernie.garcia@rima-travel.co.uk **w** rima-travel.co.uk MD: Ernie Garcia-Sheriff.

RPM Research Suite 4, 17 Pepper Street, London E14 9RP **t** 020 7537 3030 **f** 020 7537 0008 **e** info@rpmresearch.com Partners: Gary Trueman, David Lewis.

S4CDs Music Services 5 Rivett Close, Baldock, Herts SG7 6TW **t** 01462 892181 **e** inquiries@s4cds.co.uk **w** s4cds.co.uk MD: John Hall.

Screen And Music Travel 145 Station Road, West Drayton, Middx UB7 7ND **t** 01895 434057 **f** 01895 430279 **e** info@screenandmusictravel.co.uk **w** screeandmusictravel.co.uk Special Proj Mgr: Colin Doran.

SEARCH (a division of Jeff Wayne Music Group) 8-9 Ivor Place, London NW1 6BY **t** 020 7724 2471 **f** 020 7724 6245 **e** info@jeffwaynemusic.com Group Dir: Jane Jones.

Slice Marketing 2a Exmoor St, London W10 6BD **t** 020 8964 7605 **f** 020 8964 0101 **e** slice@slice.co.uk **w** slice.co.uk Director: Alec Samways.

Sound & Video Services (UK) Shentonfield Road, Sharston Industrial Estate, Manchester M22 4RW **t** 0161 491 6660 **f** 0161 491 6669 **e** sales@svsmedia.com **w** svsmedia.com MD: Mike Glasspole.

Sound Moves (UK) Unit 6, Planet Centre, Armadale Road, Feltham, Middx TW14 0LW **t** 020 8831 0500 or 07740 082 443 **f** 020 8831 0520 **e** john.corr@soundmoves.com **w** soundmoves.com MD: Martin Corr.

Spark Marketing Entertainment 3 Lansdowne Road, London N10 2AX **t** 0870 460 5439 **e** info@spark-me.com **w** spark-me.com Executive Director: Matthias Bauss.

T&S Immigration Services 27 Castle Street, Kircudbright DG6 4JD **t** 01557 339123 **f** 01557 330567 **e** steve@tandsimmigration.demon.co.uk Work Permit Specialists: Steve Richard.

Upside Productions (Music Consultancy) 14 Clarence Mews, Balham, London SW12 9SR **t** 020 8673 8549 **f** 020 8673 8498 **e** simon@upsideuk.com Co MDs: Simon Jones & Denise Beighton.

Westbury Music Consultants 72 Marylebone Lane, London W1U 2PL **t** 020 7487 5044 **f** 020 7935 2270 **e** rbradley@westburymusic.co.uk Consultant: Richard Bradley.

Ray Williams - Music Consultant South Lodge, Watlington Road, Shirburn, Oxon OX49 5DQ **t** 01491 613 555 **f** 01491 613 591 **e** crumbsmusic@btopenworld.com MD: Ray Williams.

Yewtree Media 20 Woodberry Avenue, Harrow, Middlesex HA2 6AU **t** 020 8427 9047 **f** 020 8861 1955 **e** yewtreemedia@aol.com **w** yewtreemedia.co.uk MD: Matthew Williams. Advice/Assistance incl. Licensing & Accounting.

Education

Academy of Contemporary Music (ACM) Rodboro Bld, Bridge Street, Guildford, Surrey GU1 4SB **t** 01483 500 800 **f** 01483 500 801 **e** enquiries@acm.ac.uk **w** acm.ac.uk

Access to Music 18 York Road, Leicester LE1 5TS **t** 0116 255 1936 **f** 0116 255 1938 **e** info@access-to-music.co.uk **w** access-to-music.co.uk Marketing Manager: Alan Ramsay.

Alchemea College of Audio Engineering The Windsor Centre, Windsor Street, London N1 8QG **t** 020 7359 4035 **e** info@alchemea.com **w** alchemea.com Contact: Mike Sinnott

Andy's Guitar Workshop 27 Denmark Street, London WC2H 8NJ **t** 020 7916 5080 **f** 020 7916 5714 **e** aguitar@btinternet.com MD: Andy Preston.

Armstrong Multimedia Arts Academy GMC Studio, Hollingbourne, Kent ME17 1UQ **t** 01622 880599 **f** 01622 880020 **e** records@triple-a.uk.com **w** triple-a.uk.com CEO: Terry Armstrong.

Associated Board of the Royal Schools of Music 24 Portland Place, London W1B 1LU **t** 020 7636 5400 **f** 020 7637 0234 **e** abrsm@abrsm.ac.uk **w** abrsm.ac.uk Fin Dir: Tim Leats.

Banana Row Drum School 47 Eyre Place, Edinburgh EH3 5EY **t** 0131 557 2088 **f** 0131 558 9848 **e** music@bananarow.com Drum Tutor: Craig Hunter.

Bear Storm South Bank Technopark, 90 London Road, London SE1 6LN **t** 020 7815 7744 **f** 020 7815 7793 **e** greg@bearstorm.com **w** bearstorm.com MD: Greg Tallent.

The Brighton Institute of Modern Music 7 Rock Place, Brighton, East Sussex BN2 1PF **t** 01273 626 666 **f** 01273 626 626 **e** info@bimm.co.uk **w** bimm.co.uk Dirs: Kevin Nixon, Sarah Clayman.

The Brit Performing Arts & Technology School 60 The Crescent, Croydon, Surrey CR0 2HN **t** 020 8665 5242 **f** 020 8665 8676 **e** admin@brit.croydon.sch.uk **w** brit.croydon.sch.uk Art Indust Liason Mgr: Arthur Boulton.

Buckinghamshire Chilterns University College Wellesbourne Campus, Kingshill Road, High Wycombe, Buckinghamshire HP13 5BB **t** 01494 522141 ex 4020 **f** 01494 465432 **e** fmacke01@bcuc.ac.uk **w** bcuc.ac.uk Head of Music: Frazer Mackenzie.

Canford Summer School of Music 5 Bushey Close, Old Barn Lane, Kenley, Surrey CR8 5AU **t** 020 8660 4766 **f** 020 8668 5273 **e** canfordsummersch@aol.com **w** canfordsummerschool.co.uk Director of Music: Malcolm Binney.

Centre For Voice The Tobacco Factory, Raleigh Road, Bristol BS3 1TF **t** 0117 902 6606 **f** 0117 902 6607 **e** info@centreforvoice.idps.co.uk **w** centrecords.com Principal: Andrew Hambly-Smith.

City University Music Department, Northampton Square, London EC1V 0HB **t** 020 7040 8284 **f** 020 7040 8576 **e** music@city.ac.uk **w** city.ac.uk/music Administrator: Andrew Pearce.

Collage Arts The Chocolate Factory, Unit 4, Building B, Clarendon Road, London N22 6XJ **t** 020 8365 7500 **f** 020 8365 8686 **e** info@collage-arts.org **w** collage-arts.org Training Mgr: Preti Dasgupta.

Community Music Wales Unit 8, 24 Norbury Road, Fairwater, Cardiff CF5 3AU **t** 029 2083 8060 **f** 029 2056 6573 **e** admin@communitymusicwales.org.uk **w** communitymusicwales.org.uk Music Dir: Simon Dancey.

Dartington College of Arts Totnes, Devon TQ9 6EJ **t** 01803 861650 **f** 01803 861685 **e** enterprise@dartington.ac.uk **w** dartington.ac.uk Cr've Enterprise Fellow: Adrian Bossey. Director of Music: Trevor Wiggins. Director of Arts & Cultural Management: Tracey Warr. Director, Centre for Creative Enterprise & Participation: Mary Schwarz.

Deep Recording Studios 187 Freston Road, London W10 6TH **t** 020 8964 8256 **f** 020 8969 1363 **e** deep.studios@virgin.net **w** deeprecordingstudios.com Studio Manager: Mark Rose. Education/Training Schools.

Drumtech 76 Stanley Gardens, London W3 7SZ **t** 020 8749 3131 **f** 020 8740 8422 **e** info@drum-tech.co.uk **w** drum-tech.co.uk GM: Andy Moorhouse.

Ebony and Ivory Vocal Tuition 11 Varley Parade, Edgware Road, Colindale, Londno NW9 6RR **t** 020 8200 5510 **f** 020 8205 1907 **e** svl@wsmgt.co.uk **w** wsmgt.co.uk Shop Mgr: Bill Smith.

Gateway Sound Education Trust The School of Music, Kingston Hill Centre, Kingston, Surrey KT2 7LB **t** 020 8549 0014 **f** 020 8547 7337 **e** info@gsr.org.uk **w** gsr.org.uk Course Administrator: Hilary Cohen.

Global Entertainment Group St Brides Institute, Bride Lane, Fleet Street, London EC4Y 8EQ **t** 020 7583 7900 **f** 020 7583 7900 **e** info@globalmusicbiz.co.uk **w** globalmusicbiz.co.uk Course Co-ordinator: Terry Hollingsworth.

Guildhall School of Music & Drama Silk Street, Barbican, London EC2Y 8DT **t** 020 7628 2571 **f** 020 7256 9438 **w** gsmd.ac.uk Contact: Principal

Guitar-X 76 Stanley Gardens, London W3 7SZ **t** 020 8749 3131 **f** 020 8740 8422 **e** info@guitar-x.co.uk **w** guitar-x.co.uk GM: Andy Moorhouse.

Hatchet Music Educational Resources 20 Intwood Road, Norwich, Norfolk NR4 6AA **t** 01603 458 488 **e** mark@hatchetmusic.co.uk MD: Mark Narayn. Training in Sound Engineering, Music Technology & Music Business.

Institute of Popular Music University of Liverpool, Roxby Building, Chatham Street, Liverpool L69 7ZT **t** 0151 794 3101 **f** 0151 794 2566 **e** ipm@liverpool.ac.uk **w** liv.ac.uk/ipm

iwanttoworkinmusic.com Music Dept., University of Westminster, Watford Road, Harrow, Middx. HA1 3TP **t** 020 7911 5000 **e** iwanttoworkinmusic@hotmail.com **w** iwanttoworkinmusic.com Contact: Rosie Hartnell

Jazzwise Direct 2B Gleneagle Mews, Ambleside Avenue, London SW16 6AE **t** 020 8769 7725 **f** 020 8677 7128 **e** admin@jazzwise.com **w** jazzwise.com Operations Mgr: Hugh Gledhill.

Jewel and Esk Valley College 24 Milton Road East, Edinburgh EH15 2PP **t** 0131 660 1010 **f** 0131 657 2276 **e** aduff@jevc.ac.uk **w** jevc.ac.uk Learning Manager: Althea Duff.

Jewish Music Institute School of Oriental & African, Studies, University of London, Thornhaugh Street, Russell Square, London WC1H 0XG **t** 020 8909 2445 **f** 020 8909 1030 **e** jewishmusic@jmi.org.uk **w** jmi.org.uk Director: Geraldine Auerbach MBE.

Leeds University School of Music, Leeds LS2 9JT **t** 0113 343 2583 **f** 0113 343 2586 **e** music@leeds.ac.uk **w** leeds.ac.uk/music/dept/courses/ug/pwm.htm Senior Teaching Fellow: Simon Warner.

The Liverpool Institute For Performing Arts Mount Street, Liverpool, Merseyside L1 9HF **t** 0151 330 3000 **f** 0151 330 3131 **e** admissions@lipa.ac.uk **w** lipa.ac.uk Admissions Manager: Rachel Bradbury.

The London College of Music & Media Thames Valley University, St Mary's Road, Ealing, London W5 5RF **t** 020 8231 2304 **f** 020 8231 2546 **e** clare.beckett@tvu.ac.uk **w** elgar.tvu.ac.uk Marketing Manager: Clare Beckett.

The London Music School 9-13 Osborn Street, London E1 6TD **t** 020 7265 0284 **f** 0709 202 0574 **e** music@londonmusicschool.com **w** londonmusicschool.com Admin Co-ordinator: Diana Mole.

Martin Belmont 101A Cricklewood Broadway, London NW2 3JG **t** 020 8450 2885 Guitar Teacher: Martin Belmont.

MBR Promotions 10 Hawthorn House, Forth Banks, Newcastle upon Tyne NE1 3SG **t** 0191 2211 666 **f** 0191 2211 777 **e** info@mbr-online.com **w** mbr-online.com Contact: Terry Hollingsworth

MMF Training 2nd Floor, Fourways House, 57 Hilton Street, Manchester M1 2EJ **t** 0161 228 3993 **f** 0161 228 3773 **e** admin@mmf-training.com **w** mmf-training.com Head of Training & Edu: Stuart Worthington.

Music For Youth 102 Point Pleasant, London SW18 1PP **t** 020 8870 9624 **f** 020 8870 9935 **e** mfy@mfy.org.uk **w** mfy.org.uk Executive Director: Larry Westland.

Music, Arts & Culture Hiltongrove Business Centre, 25 Hatherley Mews, London E17 4QP **t** 020 8520 3975 **f** 0208520 3975 **e** info@redonion-uk.com Manager: Dee Curtis.

Newark & Sherwood College Friary Road, Newark, Nottinghamshire NG24 1PB **t** 01636 680680 **f** 01636 680681 **e** enquiries@newark.ac.uk **w** newark.ac.uk Contact: Customer Services

Nordoff-Robbins Music Therapy 2 Lissenden Gardens, London NW5 1PP **t** 020 7267 4496 **f** 020 7267 4369 **e** admin@nordoff-robbins.org.uk **w** nordoff-robbins.org.uk Centre Director: Pauline Etkin.

North Glasgow College 110 Flemington Street, Glasgow, Lanarkshire G21 4BX **t** 0141 558 9001 **f** 0141 558 9905 **e** hbrankin@north-gla.ac.uk **w** north-gla.ac.uk Snr Lecturer Music: Hugh Brankin.

Panic Music 14 Trading Estate Road, Park Royal, London NW10 7LU **t** 020 8961 9540 **f** 020 8838 2194 **e** mroberts.drums@virgin.net Snr Tutor: Mark Roberts. Computer music and drum tuition.

Rasheed Ogunlaru Life Coaching (for Singers and Performers) The Coaching Studio, 223a Mayall Road, London SE24 0PS **t** 020 7207 1082 **e** rasaru_coaching@yahoo.com **w** rasaru.com Founder: Rasheed Ogunlaru.

The Recording Workshop Unit 10, Buspace Studios, Conlan Street, London W10 5AP **t** 020 8968 8222 **f** 020 7460 3164 **e** info@therecordingworkshop.co.uk **w** therecordingworkshop.co.uk Proprietor: Jose Gross.

The Royal Academy of Music University of London, Marylebone Road, London NW1 5HT **t** 020 7873 7373 **f** 020 7873 7374 **e** go@ram.ac.uk **w** ram.ac.uk

The Royal College Of Music Prince Consort Road, London SW7 2BS **t** 020 7589 3643 **f** 020 7589 7740 **e** info@rcm.ac.uk **w** rcm.ac.uk Secretary & Registrar: Kevin Porter.

Royal School of Church Music Cleveland Lodge, Westhumble, Dorking, Surrey RH5 6BW **t** 01306 872800 **f** 01306 887260 **e** enquiries@rscm.com **w** rscm.com Contact: RVN Administrator

Royal Welsh College of Music & Drama Castle Grounds, Cathays Park, Cardiff CF10 3ER **t** 029 2039 1361 **f** 029 2039 1305 **e** music.admissions@rwcmd.ac.uk **w** rwcmd.ac.uk Head of Music: Jeremy Ward.

SAE Technology College United House, North Road, London N7 9DP **t** 020 7609 2653 **f** 020 7609 6944 **e** saelondon@sae.edu **w** sae.edu Marketing Mgr: Angi Kuzma.

School of Music, University of Leeds Bretton Campus, West Bretton, West Yorkshire WF4 4LG **t** 0113 343 9024 **f** 0113 343 9181 **e** s.r.warner@leeds.ac.uk **w** leeds.ac.uk/music/dept/courses/ug/pwm.htm Popular Music BA Degree Co-ordinators: Vic Gammon/Simon Warner.

School Of Sound Recording 10 Tariff Street, Manchester M1 2FF **t** 0161 228 1830 **f** 0161 236 0078 **e** ian.hu@s-s-r.com **w** s-s-r.com Principal: Ian Hu.

Sense of Sound Training Parr Street Studios, 33-45 Parr St, Liverpool L1 4JN **t** 0151 707 1050 **f** 0151 709 8612 **e** info@senseofsound.demon.co.uk **w** senseofsound.net Artistic Director: Jennifer John.

Sonic Arts Network The Jerwood Space, 171 Union Street, London SE1 0LN **t** 020 7928 7337 **e** richard@sonicartsnetwork.org **w** sonicartsnetwork.org Edu Dir: Richard Whitelaw.

Training in Sound Recording The Studio, Tower Street, Hartlepool TS24 7HQ **t** 01429 424440 **f** 01429 424441 **e** studiohartlepool@btconnect.com **w** studiohartlepool.com Studio Manager: Liz Carter.

Tribal Tree 66C Chalk Farm Road, London NW1 8AN **t** 020 7482 6945 **f** 020 7485 9244 **e** enquiries@tribaltreemusic.co.uk **w** tribaltreemusic.co.uk Programme Mgr: Louise Nkosi. Charity funded music technology courses.

UCC (Warrington Campus) Resolution Records Crab Lane, Fearnhead, Warrington WA2 0DB **t** 01925 534308 **f** 01925 530001 **e** r.dyson@chester.ac.uk; j.mason@chester.ac.uk **w** chester.ac.uk/media Module Leaders: Russell Dyson, Jim Mason.

University of Surrey School of Performing Arts Dept of Music, Guildford, Surrey GU2 7XH **t** 01483 686500 **f** 01483 686501 **e** spa@surrey.ac.uk **w** surrey.ac.uk/music

University Of Westminster Watford Road, Harrow, Middlesex HA1 3TP **t** 020 7911 5903 **f** 020 7911 5943 **e** denise.stanley@virgin.net **w** wmin.ac.uk Head of Music: Denise Stanley.

Vocaltech Vocal School 76 Stanley Gardens, Acton, London W3 7BL **t** 020 8749 3131 **f** 020 8740 8422 **e** enquiries@vocal-tech.co.uk **w** vocal-tech.co.uk Operations Manager: Andy Moorhouse. Exceptional Contemporary Vocal Training.

Yes! You Can Sing! Vocal & Performance Tuition 32 Bunning Way, London N7 9UP **t** 020 7700 6379 **e** info@yesyoucansing.com **w** yesyoucansing.com MD: Gena Dry.

Zeall Music Business Training 5a Station Road, Twickenham, Middx TW1 4LL **t** 020 8607 9401 **e** info@zeall.com **w** zeall.com MD: David McGeachie.

Computer Services

Connolly Associates 6 Brookfields, Crickhowell, Powys NP8 1DJ **t** 01873 811633 **f** 01873 811992 **e** info@connolly-associates.co.uk **w** connolly-associates.co.uk MD: Steve Connolly.

Counterpoint Systems 74-80 Camden Street, London NW1 0EG **t** 020 7543 7500 **f** 020 7543 7600 **e** info@counterp.com **w** counterp.com CEO: Amos Biegun.

EP Music Services Pantiles Business Centre, 85 High Street, Tunbridge Wells, Kent TN1 1YG **t** 01892 506944 **f** 01892 506945 **e** info@epmusic.co.uk **w** epmusic.co.uk Dir: Edward Pardoe.

Essential Business Services 131 Clermiston Road, Edinburgh, Midlothian EH12 6UR **t** 0131 334 3039 or 07774 161536 **f** 0131 334 3055 **e** jackie1ebs@aol.com **w** essentialbusiness.co.uk Owner: Jackie Grant, FIQPS.

Music & Media Software Consultancy 24 Annandale Road, Greenwich, London SE10 0DA **t** 020 8858 6241 **e** info@backbeatsolutions.com **w** backbeatsolutions.com MD: Chris Chambers.

Musicalc Systems.(Royalty Accounting Software) 24 Grove Lane, Kingston-upon-Thames, Surrey KT1 2ST **t** 020 8541 5135 or 07785 234454 **f** 020 8541 1885 **e** info@musicalc.com **w** musicalc.com Marketing Manager: Asa Palmer.

Peter Siggery - Information Consultant 28 Rosedene Gardens, Ilford, Essex IG2 6YE **t** 020 8551 6685 **f** 020 8551 6685 **e** peter@siggery.com Information Consulant: Peter Siggery.

Portech Systems 501 The Green House, Gibb Street, Birmingham B9 4AA **t** 0121 624 2626 **f** 0121 624 0550 **e** s.naeem@portech.co.uk **w** portech.co.uk Sales Manager: S.Naeem.

Portman Music Services 38 Osnaburgh Street, London NW1 3ND **t** 01962 732033 or 07971 455920 **f** 01962 732032 **e** maria@portmanmusicservices.com Royalty & Copyright Mgr: Maria Comiskey.

Priam Software The Old Telephone Exchange, 32-42 Albert Street, Rugby CV21 2SA **t** 01788 558000 **f** 01788 558 001 **e** info@priamsoftware.com **w** priamsoftware.com Commercial Manager: Glyn Carvill.

Ranger Computers Ranger House, 2 Meeting Lane, Duston, Northamptonshire NN5 6JG **t** 01604 589200 **f** 01604 589505 **e** Postmaster@rangercom.com **w** ranger.demon.co.uk MD: David Viewing.

Spool Multi Media (UK) Unit 30, Deeside Industrial Park, Deeside, Flintshire CH5 2NU **t** 01244 280602 **f** 01244 288581 **e** rv@smmuk.co.uk **w** smmuk.co.uk MD: Roy Varley.

Summit Services Rosebery Avenue, High Wycombe, Buckinghamshire HP13 7YZ **t** 01494 447562 **f** 01494 441498 **e** summit@summit-services.co.uk **w** summit-services.co.uk MD: Bob Street.

Sypha 216A Gipsy Road, London SE27 9RB **t** 020 8761 1042 **e** sypha@syphaonline.com **w** DAWguide.com Partner: Yasmin Hashmi.

Totally Brilliant Software c/o Sphere Studios, 2 Shuttleworth Road, London SW11 3EU **t** 020 7326 9494 **f** 020 7326 9495 **e** support@totallybrilliant.com **w** totallybrilliant.com MD: Andy Hilton.

Willot Kingston Smith Quadrant House, (Air Street Entrance), 80-82 Regent Street, London W1B 5RP **t** 020 7304 4646 **f** 020 7304 4647 **e** eb@kingstonsmith.co.uk **w** kingstonsmith.co.uk Dir of IT Dep.: Ed Bayley.

Worldspan Communications Worldspan House, 80 Red Lion Road, Surbiton, Surrey KT6 7QW **t** 020 8288 8555 **f** 020 8288 8666 **e** sales@span.com **w** span.com

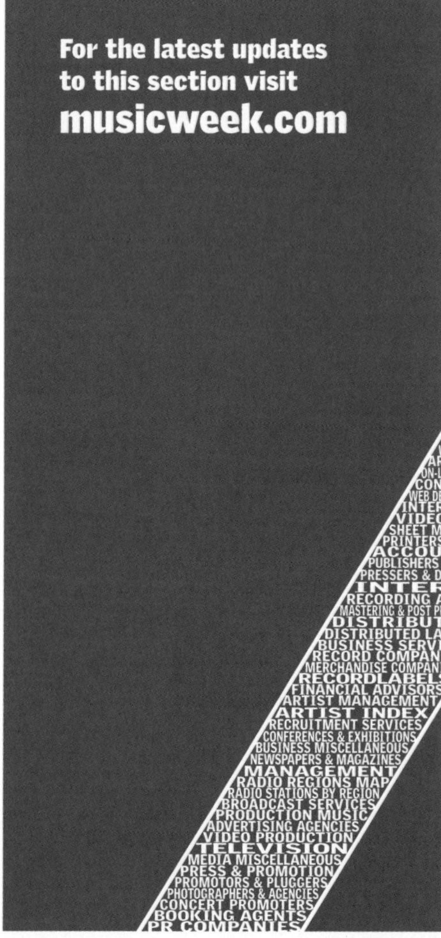

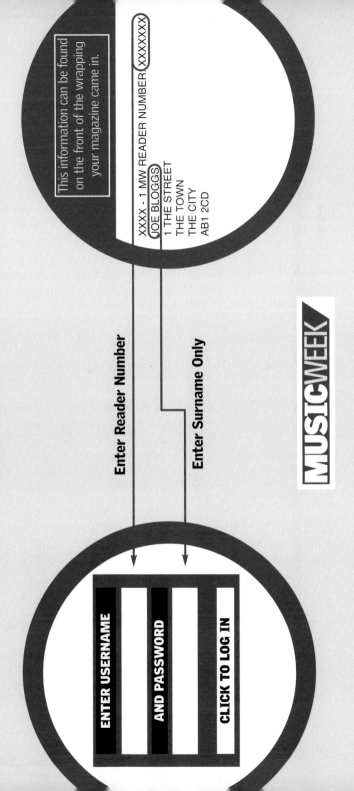

Media

Newspapers & Magazines

Access All Areas Inside Communications, One Canada Square, Canary Wharf, London E14 5AP **t** 020 7772 8300 **f** 024 7657 1002 **e** nic_howden@mrn.co.uk **w** access-aa.co.uk Editor: Nic Howden. Associate Pub: Nigel Waygood.

Artistes & Agents Richmond House Publishing Co, 70-76 Bell St, Marylebone, London NW1 6SP **t** 020 7224 9666 **f** 020 7224 9688 **e** sales@rhpco.co.uk **w** rhpco.co.uk Manager: Spencer Block.

Attitude Northern & Shell Tower, 4 Selsdon Way, City Harbour, London E14 9GL **t** 020 7308 5090 **f** 020 7308 5384 **e** attitude@attitudemag.co.uk **w** attitudemag.co.uk Ed: Adam Mattera.

Audience Miracle Publishing Ltd, 1 York St, London W1U 6PA **t** 020 7486 7007 **f** 020 7486 2002 **e** info@audience.uk.com **w** audience.uk.com Publisher/Managing Editor: Stephen Parker.

Audio Media Magazine 11 Station Rd, St Ives, Cambridgeshire PE27 5BH **t** 01480 461555 **f** 01480 461550 **e** mail@audiomedia.com **w** audiomedia.com Executive Editor: Paul Mac.

Bandit A&R Newsletter PO Box 22, Newport, Isle Of Wight PO30 1LZ **t** 01983 524110 **f** 0870 762 0132 **e** bandit@banditnewsletter.com **w** banditnewsletter.com MD: John Waterman.

BBC Music Magazine Origin Publishing, 14th Floor, Tower House, Fairfax St, Bristol BS1 3BN **t** 0117 927 9009 **f** 0117 934 9008 **e** music.magazine@bbc.co.uk **w** bbcmusicmagazine.co.uk Ed: Oliver Condy.

BBm Magazine Ireland PO Box 49, Lisburn, County Antrim, Northern Ireland BT28 5EF **t** 02892 667000 **f** 02892 668005 **e** judith@bbmag.com **w** bbmag.com Editor: Judith Farrell-Rowan.

The Beat 54 Canterbury Rd, Penn, Wolverhampton, West Midlands WV4 4EH **t** 01902 652759 or 07973 133416 **f** 01902 652759 **e** steve-morris@blueyonder.co.uk **w** http://surf.to/thebeat Ed: Steve Morris.

BETWEEN THE GROOVES

3 Tannsfeld Road, London SE26 5DQ **t** 020 8488 3677 **f** 020 8333 2572 **e** info@betweenthegrooves.com **w** betweenthegrooves.com Editor: Jonathan Sharif.

The Big Issue 1-5 Wandsworth Rd, London SW8 2LN **t** 020 7526 3201 **f** 020 7526 3301 **e** matt.ford@bigissue.com **w** bigissue.com Ed: Matt Ford.

Billboard Endeavour House, 5th floor, 189 Shaftesbury Avenue, London WC2H 8TJ **t** 020 7420 6003 **f** 020 7420 6014 **e** TFerguson@eu.billboard.com **w** billboard.com Int Ed: Tom Ferguson.

Blag Magazine PO Box 2423, London WC2E 9PG **t** 0870 138 9430 **f** 0870 138 9430 **e** blag@blagmagazine.com **w** blagmagazine.com Dirs: Sarah Edwards & Sally Edwards.

Blues & Soul 153 Praed St, London W2 1RL **t** 020 7402 6869 or 020 7402 7708 **f** 020 7224 8227 **e** editorial@bluesandsoul.demon.co.uk **w** bluesandsoul.com Ed: Bob Killbourn.

Blues Matters! PO Box 18, Bridgend CF33 6YW **t** 01656 743406 **e** blues.matters@ntlworld.com **w** bluesmatters.co.uk Editor: Alan Pearce.

Brass Band World Peak Press Building, Eccles Rd, Chapel-en-le-Frith, High Peak, Cheshire SK23 9RQ **t** 01298 812816 **f** 01298 812816 **e** advertising@brassbandworld.com **w** brassbandworld.com Ad Mgr: Liz Winter.

British & International Music Yearbook Rhinegold Publishing Ltd, 8 Mansell St, Stratford-upon-Avon, Warks CV37 6NR **t** 01789 209280 **f** 01789 264009 **e** sales@rhinegold.co.uk **w** rhinegold.co.uk Ed: Louise Head.

British Bandsman Harold Charles House, 64 London End, Beaconsfield, Buckinghamshire HP9 2JD **t** 01494 674411 **f** 01494 670932 **e** info@britishbandsman.com **w** britishbandsman.com MD: Nicola Bland.

British Hit Singles 338 Euston Rd, London NW1 3BD **t** 020 7891 4547 **f** 020 7891 4501 **e** david.roberts@guinnessworldrecords.com **w** britishhitsingles.com Editor: David Roberts.

Broadcast EMAP Media, 33-39 Bowling Green Lane, London EC1R 0DA **t** 020 7505 8014 or 020 7505 8040 **f** 020 7505 8050 **e** admin@broadcastnow.co.uk **w** broadcastnow.co.uk Ed: Katy Elliott.

Campaign 22 Bute Gardens, London W6 7HN **t** 020 8267 4683 **f** 020 8267 4915 **e** campaign@haynet.com Ed: Caroline Marshall.

Celebrity Service 4th Floor, Kingsland House, 122-124 Regent St, London W1B 5SA **t** 020 7439 9840 **f** 020 7494 3500 **e** celebritylondon@aol.com Contact: Diane Oliver

Chartwatch Magazine 34 Brybank Rd, Hanchett Village, Haverhill, Suffolk CB9 7WD **t** 01440 713859 **e** john@chartwatch.co.uk **w** chartwatch.co.uk Editors: Neil Rawlings/John Hancock.

City Life 164 Deansgate, Manchester M3 3RN **t** 0161 832 7200 **f** 0161 839 1488 **e**editor@citylife.co.uk **w** citylife.co.uk Editor: David Alan Lloyd. Deputy Ed & Listings Ed: Ra Page. Ad Mgr: Natalie May.

City Living Magazine 1st Floor, Weaman St, Birmingham B4 6AT **t** 0121 234 5202 **f** 0121 234 5757 **e** jamie_perry@mrn.co.uk **w** icbirmingham.co.uk/cityliving/ Product Mgr: Jamie Perry.

Clash Magazine 143C Nethergate, Dundee DD1 4DP **t** 01382 808808 **f** 01382 909909 **e** info@clashmagazine.com **w** clashmagazine.com MD: John O'Rourke.

Classic FM Magazine Haymarket Publishing, 38-42 Hampton Rd, Teddington, Middx TW11 0JE **t** 020 8267 5180 **f** 020 8267 5150 **e** classicfm@haynet.com **w** classicfm.com Editor in Chief: John Evans.

Classic Rock 99 Baker St, London W1U 6FP **t** 020 7317 2600 **f** 020 7317 2686 **e** firstname.lastname@futurenet.co.uk Ed: Sian Llewellyn.

Classic Rock (UK) Classic Rock Society 47 Brecks Lane, Rotherham, South Yorkshire S65 3JQ **t** 01709 702575 **e** martin@classicrocksociety.co.uk **w** classicrocksociety.com MD: Martin Hudson.

Classical Guitar Ashley Mark Publishing Co, 1 & 2 Vance Court, Trans Britannia Ent Park, Blaydon On Tyne NE21 5NH **t** 0191 414 9000 **f** 0191 414 9001 **e** classicalguitar@ashleymark.co.uk **w** ashleymark.co.uk Ed: Colin Cooper.

Classical Music Rhinegold Publishing, 241 Shaftesbury Avenue, London WC2H 8TF **t** 020 7333 1742 (Ed) or 020 7333 1733 (ads) **f** 020 7333 1769 (Ed) or 020 7333 1736 (ads) **e** classical.music@rhinegold.co.uk **w** rhinegold.co.uk Ed: Keith Clarke.

CMA Publications Strawberry Holt, Westfield Lane, Draycott, Somerset BS27 3TN **t** 01934 740270 **e** grp@cma-publications.co.uk **w** cma-publications.co.uk MD: Geraldine Russell-Price.

CMU Music Network UnLimited Media, Fl 3, Grampian House, Meridian Gate, London E14 9YT **t** 0870 744 2643 **f** 070 9231 4982 **e** cmu@unlimitedmedia.co.uk **w** cmuonline.co.uk Publishers: Chris Cooke, Caroline Moses.

Comes With A Smile 69 St Mary's Grove, Chiswick, London W4 3LW **t** 07941 010 250 **e** cwasmatt@yahoo.co.uk **w** comeswithasmile.com Editor: Matt Dornan.

Computer Music Future Publishing, 30 Monmouth St, Bath BA1 2BW **t** 01225 442244 **e** ronan.macdonald@futurenet.co.uk **w** computermusic.co.uk Ed: Ronan Macdonald.

Constantly Cliff 17 Podsmead Rd, Tuffley, Glos GLI 5PB **t** 01452 306104 **f** 01452 306104 **e** william@constantlycliff.freeserve.co.uk **w** cliffchartsite.co.uk Ed/Publisher: William Hooper.

Country Music People 1-3 Love Lane, London SE18 6QT **t** 020 8854 7217 **f** 020 8855 6370 **e** info@countrymusicpeople.com **w** countrymusicpeople.com Ed: Craig Baguley.

Country Music Round Up PO Box 111, Waltham, Grimsby, NE Lincs DN37 0YN **t** 01472 821808 **f** 01472 821808 **e** countrymusic_ru@hotmail.com **w** cmru.co.uk Publisher: John Emptage.

The Crack 1 Pink Lane, Newcastle upon Tyne NE1 5DW **t** 0191 230 3038 **f** 0191 230 4484 **e** rob@thecrackmagazine.com **w** thecrackmagazine.com Ed: Robert Meddes.

Cuesheet Music Report 23 Belsize Crescent, London NW3 5QY **t** 020 7794 2540 **f** 020 7794 7393 **e** cuesheet@songlink.com **w** cuesheet.net Editor/Publisher: David Stark.

Daily Mail Northcliffe House, 2 Derry St, London W8 5TT **t** 020 7938 6000 **f** 020 7937 3251 **e** editorial@dailymailonline.co.uk **w** dailymail.co.uk

Daily Record & Sunday Mail 1 Central Quay, GlasgowGlasgow G3 8DA **t** 0141 309 3000 **f** 0141 309 3340 **e** reporters@dailyrecord.co.uk **w** dailyrecord.co.uk

Daily Telegraph 1 Canada Square, Canary Wharf, London E14 5DT **t** 020 7538 5000 **f** 020 7538 7650 **w** telegraph.co.uk

The DAW Buyers Guide Gipsy Rd, London SE27 9RB **t** 020 8761 1042 **e** sypha@syphaonline.com **w** syphaonline.com Partner: Yasmin Hashmi.

Dazed & Confused 112 Old St, London EC1V 9BG **t** 020 7336 0766 or 020 7336 8272 **e** contact@confused.co.uk **w** confused.co.uk

Deuce Vision Publishing, 1 Trafalgar Mews, East Way, London E9 5JG **t** 020 8533 9320 **f** 020 8533 9320 **e** editor@deucemag.com **w** deucemag.com Ed: Colin Steven.

DJ Magazine Highgate Studios, 53-79 Highgate Rd, London NW5 1TW **t** 020 7331 1148 **f** 020 7331 1115 **e** info@djmag.com **w** DJmag.com Deputy Editor: Tom Kihl.

DMC Update DMC Publishing, 62 Lancaster Mews, London W2 3QG **t** 020 7262 6777 **f** 020 7706 9323 or 020 7706 9310 (ISDN) **e** info@dmcworld.com **w** dmcworld.com Ad & Sponsorship Mgr: John Saunderson.

Drowned in Sound 72 Palatine Rd, Stoke Newington, London N16 8ST **t** 020 8969 2498 **e** gareth@drownedinsound.com **w** drownedinsound.com Editor: Gareth Dobson.

Early Music Faculty of Music, University of Cambridge, 11 West Rd, Cambridge CB3 9DP **t** 01223 335 178 **f** 01223 335 178 **e** earlymusic@oupjournals.org **w** em.oupjournals.org Editor: Dr Tess Knighton.

Early Music Today Rhinegold Publishing, 241 Shaftesbury Avenue, London WC2H 8TF **t** 020 7333 1744 **f** 020 7333 1769 **e** emt@rhinegold.co.uk **w** rhinegold.co.uk Ed: Lucien Jenkins.

Echoes Unit LFB2, The Leathermarket, Weston St, London SE1 3HN **t** 020 7407 5858 **f** 020 7407 2929 **e** echoesmusic@aol.com Ed: Chris Wells.

Encyclopedia of Popular Music Suite 16, Arcade Chambers, 28 High St, Brentwood, Essex CM14 4AH **t** 01277 218088 **f** 01787 249161 **e** colinmuze@mac.com **w** muze.com Ed-in-Chief: Colin Larkin.

Essential Newcastle 5-11 Causey St, Newcastle-upon-Tyne NE3 4DJ **t** 0191 284 9994 **f** 0191 284 9995 **e** richard.holmes@accentmagazines.co.uk Editor: Richard Holmes.

Evening Standard Northcliffe House, 2 Derry St, London W8 5TT **t** 020 7938 6000 **f** 020 7937 7392 **e** editor@thisislondon.co.uk **w** thisislondon.co.uk

Financial Times 1 Southwark Bridge, London SE1 9HL **t** 020 7873 3000 **f** 020 7873 3062 **w** ft.com Ed: Richard Lambert.

The Fly 59-61 Farringdon Rd, London EC1M 3JB **t** 020 7691 4555 **f** 020 7691 4666 **e** info@channelfly.com **w** channelfly.com Ed: Will Kinsman.

Folk Music Journal 5 Hanborough Close, Eynsham, Witney OX29 4NR **t** 01865 880283 **e** michael.heaney@ouls.ox.ac.uk **w** efdss.org Ed: Mike Heaney.

Footloose Magazine 106-108 King St, London W6 0QP **t** 020 8563 8174 **f** 020 8563 8175 **e** info@footloosemagazine.com **w** footloosemagazine.com Editor: Matt Walker.

Foresight Bulletin/Planner Profile Group, Dragon Court, 27-29 Macklin St, London WC2B 5LX **t** 020 7190 7829 **f** 020 7190 7858 **e** info@profilegroup.co.uk **w** foresightonline.co.uk Editor: Vicki Ormiston.

Fresh Direction c/o Antonville Ltd, Ground Floor, 2 Ella Mews, Cressy Rd, London NW3 2NH **t** 020 7424 0400 **f** 020 7424 0100 **e** editor@freshdirection.co.uk **w** freshdirection.co.uk Editor: Paul Russell.

fRoots c/o Southern Rag Ltd, PO Box 337, London N4 1TW **t** 020 8340 9651 **f** 020 8348 5626 **e** froots@frootsmag.com **w** frootsmag.com Ed: Ian Anderson.

Fused Magazine Studio 315, The Greenhouse, Gibb St, Birmingham B9 4AA **t** 0121 246 1946 or 0121 246 1947 **e** enquiries@fusedmagazine.com **w** fusedmagazine.com Editor: David O'Coy.

Future Music Future Publishing, 30 Monmouth St, Bath, Somerset BA1 2BW **t** 01225 442244 **f** 01225 732353 **e** andy.jones@futurenet.co.uk **w** futuremusic.co.uk Snr Editor: Andy Jones.

Gargamel Campro Entertainment, PO Box 18542, London E17 5UY **t** 020 8527 2720 **f** 020 8531 6050 **e** mel@campro.freeserve.co.uk **w** mcsrecords.co.uk/gargamel.htm Editor/Publisher: Melissa Sinclair.

The Gen Generator North East, Black Swan Court, 69 Westgate Rd, Newcastle NE1 1SG **t** 0191 245 0099 or 07951 357 549 **f** 0191 245 0144 **e** mail@generator.org.uk **w** generator.org.uk Ed: David John Watton.

GQ Vogue House, Hanover Square, London W1R 0AD **t** 020 7499 9080 **f** 020 7495 1679 or 020 7629 2093 **e** gqletters@condenast.co.uk **w** gq-magazine.co.uk Ed: Dylan Jones.

Gramophone Haymarket Publications, 38-42 Hampton Rd, Teddington, Middlesex TW11 0JE **t** 020 8267 5050 **f** 020 8267 5844 **e** editor@gramophone.co.uk **w** gramophone.co.uk Deputy Editor: Michael Quinn.

Grove's Dictionaries Of Music The Macmillan Building, Crinan St, London N1 9XW **t** 020 7843 4612 **f** 020 7843 4601 **e** grove@macmillan.com **w** grovemusic.co.uk Marketing Manager: Richard Evans.

The Guardian 119 Farringdon Rd, London EC1R 3ER **t** 020 7278 2332 **f** 020 7713 4366 **e** arts.editor@guardianunlimited.co.uk **w** guardian.co.uk

The Guide The Guardian, 119 Farringdon Rd, London EC1R 3ER **t** 020 7713 4152 or 020 7239 9980 **f** 020 7713 4346

Guinness World Recs - British Hit Singles & Albums 338 Euston Rd, London NW1 3BD **t** 020 7891 4547 **f** 020 7891 4501 **e** editor@bibleofpop.com **w** bibleofpop.com Ed: David Roberts.

Guitar Magazine Link House, Dingwall Avenue, Croydon, Surrey CR9 2TA **t** 020 8774 0600 **f** 020 8774 0934 **e** guitar@ipcmedia.com Ed: Simon Weir.

Guitarist Future Publishing, 30 Monmouth St, Bath, Somerset BA1 2BW **t** 01225 442244 **f** 01225 732285 **e** neville.martin@futurenet.co.uk Ed: Neville Marten.

Heat Endeavor House, 189 Shaftesbury Avenue, London WC2H 8JG **t** 020 7295 5000 **f** 020 7859 8670 **e** heat@emap.com Ed: Mark Frith.

The Herald 200 Renfield St, Glasgow G2 3PR **t** 0141 302 7000 **f** 0141 302 7171 or 0141 302 6363 (Ad) **e** arts@theherald.co.uk **w** theherald.co.uk Ed: Mark Douglas-Home.

Hi-Fi Choice Future Publishing, 99 Baker St, London W1U 6FP **t** 020 7317 2600 **f** 020 7317 0275 **e** tim.bowern@futurenet.co.uk **w** hifichoice.co.uk Dep Ed: Tim Bowern.

Hi-Fi News Leon House, 233 High St, Croydon, Surrey CR9 1HZ **t** 020 8726 8310 **f** 020 8726 8397 **e** hi-finews@ipcmedia.com **w** hifinews.co.uk Ed: Steve Harris.

Hi-Fi World Audio Publishing, Unit G4, Imex House, Kilburn Park Rd, London W9 1EX **t** 020 7625 3134 **e** edit@hi-fiworld.co.uk **w** hi-fiworld.co.uk Ed: Simon Pulp.

Hip Hop Awards Magazine 46A Syon Lane, Isleworth, Middx TW7 5NQ **t** 020 8464 3071 **f** 020 8464 3071 **e** enquiries@hiphopawards.co.uk **w** hiphopawards.co.uk Editor: Jermaine Springer.

Hip Hop Connection Infamous Ink Ltd, PO Box 392, Cambridge CB1 3WH **t** 01223 210536 **f** 01223 210536 **e** hhc@hiphop.com **w** hiphop.co.uk Ed: Andy Cowan.

Hit Sheet 31 The Birches, London N21 1NJ **t** 020 8360 4088 **f** 020 8360 4088 **e** info@hitsheet.co.uk **w** hitsheet.co.uk Publisher: Paul Kramer.

Hokey Pokey Millham Lane, Dulverton, Somerset TA22 9HQ **t** 01398 324114 or 07831 103194 **f** 01398 324114 **e** hokey.pokey@bigfoot.com Ed: Andrew Quarrie.

The Hollywood Reporter Endeavour House, 189 Shaftesbury Ave, London WC2H 8TJ **t** 020 7420 6004 **f** 020 7420 6015 **e** rbennett@eu.hollywoodreporter.com **w** hollywoodreporter.com European Bureau Chief: Ray Bennett.

Honk Ty Cefn, Rectory Rd, Canton, Cardiff, South Glamorgan CF5 1QL **t** 029 2066 8127 **f** 029 2034 1622 **e** honk@welshmusicfoundation.com **w** welshmusicfoundation.com/honk Ed: James McLaren.

Hot Press Magazine 13 Trinity St, Dublin 2, Ireland **t** +353 1 241 1500 **f** +353 1 241 1538 **e** info@hotpress.ie **w** hotpress.com Ed: Niall Stokes.

i-D Magazine 124 Tabernacle St, London EC2A 4SA **t** 020 7490 9710 **f** 020 7251 2225 **e** editor@i-Dmagazine.co.uk **w** i-dmagazine.co.uk Ed: Avril Mair.

The Independent On Sunday Independent House, 191 Marsh Wall, London E14 9RS **t** 020 7345 2000 **f** 020 7293 2182 **e** arts@independent.co.uk **w** independent.co.uk

The Independent Independent House, 191 Marsh Wall, London E14 9RS **t** 020 7005 2000 **f** 020 7293 2182 **e** arts@independent.co.uk **w** independent.co.uk Ed: Simon Kelner.

International Broadcast Engineer BPL Business Media, Brooklyn House, 22 The Green, West Drayton, Middx UB7 7PQ **t** 01737 855102 **e** claresturzaker@dmgbm.com **w** ibeweb.com Publisher: Clare Sturzaker.

Into The Storm Studio 407, Bon Marche Centre, 241-251 Ferndale Rd, London SW9 8BJ **t** 020 7326 0345 **e** info@intothestorm.com **w** intothestorm.com Editorial Dir: Andy Crysell.

Irish Music Magazine 11 Clare St, Dublin 2, Ireland **t** +353 1 662 2266 **f** +353 1 662 4981 **e** info@selectmedialtd.com **w** irish-music.net Publisher: Robert Heuston.

Irish Music Scene Bunbeg, Letterkenny, Co Donegal, Ireland **t** +353 7495 31176 **e** donalkoboyle@eircom.net Ed/Publisher: Donal K O'Boyle.

Irish Times 10-16 D'Olier St, Dublin 2, Ireland **t** +353 1 679 2022 **e** (dept)@irish-times.ie **w** ireland.com

It's Hot! Woodlands, 80 Wood Lane, London W12 0TT **t** 020 8433 2447 **f** 020 8433 2763 **e** itshot@bbc.co.uk PA: Claire Blindell.

Jazz Journal International Jazz Journal Ltd, 3-3A Forest Rd, Loughton, Essex 1G10 1DR **t** 020 8532 0456 or 020 8532 0678 **f** 020 8532 0440 Publisher/Ed: Eddie Cook.

Jazz Newspapers 26 The Balcony, Castle Arcade, Cardiff CF10 1BY **t** 029 2066 5161 **f** 029 2066 5160 **e** jazzuk.cardiff@virgin.net **w** jazzservices.org.uk Administrator: Carolyn Williams.

The Jazz Rag PO Box 944, Birmingham, West Midlands B16 8UT **t** 0121 454 7020 **f** 0121 454 9996 **e** bigbearmusic@compuserve.com **w** bigbearmusic.com Ed: Jim Simpson.

Jazzwise Magazine 2B Gleneagle Mews, Ambleside Avenue, London SW16 6AE **t** 020 8664 7222 **f** 020 8677 7128 **e** jon@jazzwise.com **w** jazzwise.com Editor & Publisher: Jon Newey.

Jockey Slut 1b/c Zetland House, 5-25 Scrutton St, London EC2A 4HJ **t** 020 7729 3773 **f** 020 7729 8312 **e** letters@ockeyslut.com **w** jockeyslut.com Group Ed: Rob Wood.

Keep It Live! Glebe Cottage, Station Rd, Kildale, Whitby, North Yorkshire YO21 2RH **t** 01642 724470 **f** 01642 725143 **e** keepit.live@virgin.net **w** keepitlive.co.uk Editor: Colin McCosh.

Kerrang! EMAP Metro, Mappin House, 4 Winsley St, London W1R 7AR **t** 020 7436 1515 or 020 7312 8106 **f** 020 7312 8910 **e** kerrang@emap.com **w** kerrang.com

Keyboard Player 48 Mereway Rd, Twickenham, Middx TW2 6RG **t** 020 8245 5840 **e** stevemillerkp@blueyonder.co.uk **w** keyboardplayer.com Ed: Steve Miller.

Knowledge Magazine Vision Publishing, 1 Trafalger Mews, Eastway, London E9 5JG **t** 020 8533 9300 **e** editor@knowledgemag.co.uk **w** knowledgemag.co.uk Ed: Colin Steven.

The Knowledge CMP Information Ltd, Info Services, Riverbank House, Angel Lane, Tonbridge, Kent TN9 1SE **t** 01732 362666 **f** 01732 377440 **e** knowledge@cmpinformation.com **w** theknowledgeonline.com Grp Mktg Mgr: Katherine Jordan.

Leeds Guide 30-34 Aire St, Leeds, West Yorkshire LS1 4HT **t** 0113 244 1000 **f** 0113 244 1002 **e** editor@leedsguide.co.uk Ed: Dan Jeffrey.

The List 14 High St, Edinburgh EH1 1TE **t** 0131 558 1191 **f** 0131 557 8500 **e** editor@list.co.uk **w** thelist.co.uk Ed: Nick Barley.

Loaded IPC Magazines, Kings Reach Tower, Stamford St, London SE1 9LS **t** 020 7261 5562 **f** 020 7261 5640 **e** loadweb@ipc.co.uk **w** ipcloaded.com Ed: Scott Manson.

LOGO Mede House, Salisbury St, Southampton, Hampshire SO15 2TZ **t** 023 8034 6271 **f** 023 8034 8500 **e** info@logo-magazine.com **w** logo-magazine.com Editor: Alan Downes.

M2F First Floor, 62 Belgrave Gate, Leicester LE1 3GQ **t** 0116 251 2233 **f** 0116 299 0077 **e** enquiries@m2fonline.com **w** m2fonline.com Editor: Bina 'Bob' Mistry.

Mail On Sunday Northcliffe House, 2 Derry St, London W8 5TT **t** 020 7938 6000 **f** 020 7937 3829 **e** editorial@dailymailonline.co.uk **w** mailonsunday.co.uk

Marketing 174 Hammersmith Rd, London W6 7JP **t** 020 8267 4150 **e** Via website **w** marketing.haynet.com Ed: Craig Smith.

Marketing Week 12-26 Lexington St, 50 Poland St, London W1R 4 **t** 020 7970 4000 **f** 020 7970 6721 **e** stuart.smith@centaur.co.uk **w** marketing-week.co.uk Ed: Stuart Smith.

Media Research Publishing Lister House, 117 Milton Rd, Weston super Mare, Somerset BS23 2UX **t** 01934 644309 **f** 01934 644402 **e** cliffdane@tiscali.co.uk **w** mediaresearchpublishing.com Chairman: Cliff Dane.

M8 Magazine Trojan House, Phoenix Business Park, Paisley, Renfrewshire PA1 2BH **t** 0141 840 5980 **f** 0141 840 5995 **e** info@m8magazine.com **w** m8magazine.co.uk Ed: Kevin McFarlane.

Metal Hammer Future Publishing, 99 Baker St, London W1U 6FP **t** 020 7317 2688 **f** 020 7486 5678 **e** chris.ingham@futurenet.co.uk **w** metalhammer.co.uk Ed: Chris Ingham.

Metro Scotland 7th Floor, 144 St Vincent St, Glasgow G2 5LQ **t** 0141 225 3336 **f** 0141 225 3316 **e** scotlife@ukmetro.co.uk Arts Editor: Rory Weller.

MI Professional 35 High St, Marlow, Buckinghamshire SL7 1AU **t** 01628 487820 **e** news@mi-pro.com Dep Ed: Andy Barrett.

The Mirror 1 Canada Square, London E14 5AP **t** 020 7293 3000 **f** 020 7293 3405 **e** feedback@mirror.co.uk **w** mirror.co.uk

Mixmag EMAP Performance, Mappin House, 4 Winsley St, London W1W 8HF **t** 020 7436 1515 ed or 020 7437 9011 ads **f** 020 7312 8977 ed or 020 7323 0276 ads **e** mixmag@emap.com **w** mixmag.net Ed: Viv Craske.

Mizz IPC Magazines, Kings Reach Tower, Stamford St, London SE1 9LS **t** 020 7261 6319 **f** 020 7261 6032 **e** firstname_surname@ipcmedia.com

Mojo EMAP Performance, Mappin House, 4 Winsley St, London W1W 8HF **t** 020 7436 1515 **f** 020 7312 8296 **e** mojo@emap.com **w** mojo4music.com Ed: Pat Gilbert.

Music Business Journal 3 Winsdown House, Three Gates Lane, Haslemere, Surrey GU27 2LE **t** 01428 656 442 **e** info@musicjournal.org **w** musicjournal.org Managing Editors: JoJo Gould/Jonathan Little.

Music Education Yearbook (see British Music Yearbook)

Music Journal 10 Stratford Place, London W1C 1AA **t** 020 7629 4413 **f** 020 7408 1538 **e** membership@ism.org **w** ism.org Ed: Neil Hoyle.

Music Mart 1st Floor Edward House, Tindal Bridge, Edward St., Birmingham B1 2RA **t** 0121 233 8712 **f** 0121 233 8715 **e** jason.jones@trinitypub.co.uk **w** musicmart-mag.co.uk Ed: John Moore.

Music Master Retail Entertainment Data, Paulton House, 8 Shepherdess Walk, London N1 7LB **t** 020 7566 8216 **f** 020 7566 8259 **e** info@redmuze.com **w** redmuze.com

Music Teacher Rhinegold Publishing, 241 Shaftesbury Avenue, London WC2H 8EH **t** 020 7333 1747 **f** 020 7333 1769 **e** music.teacher@rhinegold.co.uk **w** rhinegold.co.uk Ed: Lucien Jenkins.

MUSIC WEEK

MUSICWEEK

CMP Information, Ludgate House, 245 Blackfriars Rd, London SE1 9UR **t** 020 7921 8348 **f** 020 7579 4011 **e** ascott@cmpinformation.com **w** musicweek.com Editor-in-chief: Ajax Scott.

Music Week Directory CMP Information, Ludgate House, 245 Blackfriars Rd, London SE1 9UR **t** 020 7921 8353 **f** 020 7579 4168 **e** mwdirectory@cmpinformation.com **w** musicweek.com Database manager: Nick Tesco.

Musical Opinion 2 Princes Rd, St Leonards-on-Sea, East Sussex TN37 6EL **t** 01424 715167 **f** 01424 712214 **e** musicalopinion2@aol.com **w** musicalopinion.com Publisher: Denby Richards.

The Musical Times PO Box 464, Berkhamsted, Herts HP4 2UR **t** 01442 879 097 **e** mustimes@aol.com **w** musicaltimes.co.uk Ed: Antony Bye.

Nerve Talbot Campus, Fern Barrow, Poole, Dorset BH12 5BB **t** 01202 595744 **f** 01202 535990 **e** suvpcomms@bournemouth.ac.uk **w** subu.org.uk Editor: Natalie Johnson.

A New Day - The Jethro Tull Magazine 75 Wren Way, Farnborough, Hampshire GU14 8TA **t** 01252 540270 or 07889 797482 **f** 01252 372001 **e** DAVIDREES1@compuserve.com **w** anewdayrecords.co.uk Editor: Dave Rees.

New Nation Newspaper Unit 2.1, Whitechapel Technology Centre, 65 Whitechapel Rd, London E1 IDU **t** 020 7650 2000 **f** 020 7650 2004 **e** thepulse@newnation.co.uk Music & Ent Ed: Justin Onyeka.

News Of The World News International, 1 Virginia St, London E1 9XR **t** 020 7782 7000 **f** 020 7583 9504 **e** Via website **w** newsoftheworld.co.uk

Night Magazine Mondiale Publishing Ltd, Waterloo Place, Watson Square, Stockport, Cheshire SK1 3AZ **t** 0161 429 7803 **f** 0161 476 0456 **e** night@mondiale.co.uk **w** mondiale.co.uk/night Ed: Ms Alex Eyre.

Nightshift PO Box 312, Kidlington, Oxford OX5 1ZU **t** 01865 372255 **e** nightshift@oxfordmusic.net **w** nightshift.oxfordmusic.net Editor: Ronan Munro.

NME IPC Music Magazines, Kings Reach Tower, Stamford St, London SE1 9LS **t** 020 7261 6472 **f** 020 7261 5185 **e** editor@nme.com **w** nme.com Ed: Conor McNicholas.

The Noise Buckinghamshire College SU, Queen Alexandra Rd, High Wycombe, Bucks HP11 2JZ **t** 01494 446330 **f** 01494 558195 **e** amanda.mcdowall@bcuc.ac.uk **w** bcsu.net Ed: Amanada McDowall.

Northdown Publishing PO Box 49, Bordon, Hants GU35 0AF **t** 01420 489474 **f** 01420 488797 **e** enquiries@northdown.demon.co.uk **w** northdown.demon.co.uk Dir: Michael Heatley.

The Observer 119 Farringdon Rd, London EC1R 3ER **t** 020 7278 2332 or 020 7713 4286 **f** 020 7713 4250 **e** firstname.lastname@observer.co.uk **w** observer.co.uk

ONE TO ONE

ONE TO ONE
The International Media Manufacturing Magazine

CMP Information, Ludgate House, 245 Blackfriars Rd, London SE1 9UR **t** 020 7921 8376 **f** 020 7921 8302 **e** tfrost@cmpinformation.com **w** oto-online.com Ed: Tim Frost.

onlinePOP PO Box 150, Chesterfield, Derbyshire S40 0YT **t** 0870 746 8478 **e** mail@onlinepopnews.com **w** onlinepopnews.com Editor: Tony Hedley.

Opera Now 241 Shaftesbury Avenue, London WC2H 8EH **t** 020 7333 1733 or 020 7333 1740 **f** 020 7333 1736 or 020 7333 1769 **e** opera.now@rhinegold.co.uk **w** rhiegold.co.uk Ed: Ashutosh Khandekar.

Organ Suite 212, The Old Gramophone Works, 326 Kensal Rd, London W10 5BZ **t** 020 8964 3066 **e** organ@organart.demon.co.uk **w** organart.com MD: Sean Worrall.

Original British Theatre Directory 70-76 Bell St, Marylebone, London NW1 6SP **t** 020 7224 9666 **f** 020 7224 9688 **e** sales@rhpco.co.uk **w** rhpco.co.uk Manager: Spencer Block.

Orpheus Publications 3 Waterhouse Square, 138-142 Holborn, London EC1N 2NY **t** 020 7882 1040 **f** 020 7882 1020 **w** thestrad.com Editor: Naomi Sadler.

The Piano Rhinegold Publishing, 241 Shaftesbury Avenue, London WC2H 8EH **t** 020 7333 1733 or 020 7333 1724 **f** 020 7333 1736 or 020 7333 1769 **e** piano@rhinegold.co.uk **w** rhinegold.co.uk Hd of Advertising: Joanna Sallnow.

Pipeline Instrumental Review 12 Thorkill Gardens, Thames Ditton, Surrey KT7 0UP **t** 020 8398 6684 **f** 020 8398 6684 **e** editor@pipelinemag.co.uk **w** pipelinemag.co.uk Ed: Alan Taylor.

Popular Music Cambridge University Press, The Edinburgh Building, Shaftesbury Rd, Cambridge CB2 2RU **t** 01223 325757 or 01223 325757 **f** 01223 315052 **w** journals.cambridge.org/public/door Eds: Lucy Green, David Laing.

Press Association, Rock Listings 4th Floor, 292 Vauxhall Bridge Rd, London SW1V 1AE **t** 020 7963 7749 **f** 020 7963 7800 **e** gigs@pa.press.net Rock & Pop Editor: Delia Barnard.

PRO SOUND NEWS EUROPE

Pro Sound News EUROPE

CMP Information Ltd., 8th Floor, Ludgate House, London SE1 9UY **t** 020 7921 8319 **f** 020 7921 8302 **e** david.robinson@cmpinformation.com **w** prosoundnewseurope.com Editor: David Robinson.

PROMO

CMP Information Ltd, Ludgate House, 245 Blackfriars Rd, London SE1 9UR **t** 020 7921 8318 **f** 020 7921 8327 **e** dknight@cmpinformation.com Ed: David Knight. Ad Sales: Scott Green.

Q EMAP Metro, Mappin House, 4 Winsley St, London W1N 7AR **t** 020 7312 8182 **f** 020 7312 8247 **e** q@ecm.emap.com **w** qonline.co.uk Editor: Paul Rees.

Q Sheet Markettiers 4DC, Northburgh House, 10a Northburgh St, London EC1V 0AT **t** 020 7253 8888 **f** 020 7253 8885 **e** editor@qsheet.com **w** qsheet.com Music Editor: Nik Harta.

The Radio Magazine Goldcrest Broadcasting, Crown House, 25 High St, Rothwell, Northants NN14 6AD **t** 01536 418558 **f** 01536 418539 **e** radiomagazine-goldcrestbroadcasting@btinternet.com **w** theradiomagazine.co.uk

Radio Times Woodlands, 80 Wood Lane, London W12 0TT **t** 020 8576 2000 **e** radio.times@bbc.co.uk **w** radiotimes.com

Record Collector Room 101, 140 Wales Farm Rd, London W3 6UG **t** 0870 732 8080 **f** 0870 732 6060 **e** firstname.lastname@metropolis.co.uk **w** recordcollectormag.com Ed: Alan Lewis.

Record Information Services Unit 8 (Hasmick), Forest Hill Ind Estate, London SE23 2LX **t** 020 8291 6777 **f** 020 8291 0081 **e** pp@brightguy.demon.co.uk Contact: Paul Pelletier

RECORD OF THE DAY

PO Box 49554, London E17 9WB **t** (PS) 020 8520 2130 or (DB) 020 8677 1847 **e** paul@recordoftheday.com **w** recordoftheday.com Eds: Paul Scaife, David Balfour.
Music industry news and a future hit – direct to your inbox. A sound read every morning. Free trial at website.

REDMuze Music Catalogues Paulton House, 8 Shepherdess Walk, London N1 7LB **t** 020 7566 8216 **f** 020 7566 8259 **e** sales@redmuze.com **w** redmuze.com Hd of Sales: Deborah Sass.

Revolutions 211 Western Rd, London SW19 2QD **t** 020 8646 7094 **f** 020 8646 7094 **e** john@revolutionsuk.com **w** revolutionsuk.com Editor: John Lonergan.

Rhythm Future Publishing, 30 Monmouth St, Bath, Somerset BA1 2BW **t** 01225 442244 **f** 01225 732353 **e** louise.king@futurenet.co.uk **w** futurenet.co.uk Editor: Louise King.

Rip&Burn Haymarket Publishing, 38-42 Hampton Rd, Teddington, Middlesex TW11 0JE **t** 020 8267 5120 **e** editor@ripandburn.it **w** ripandburn.it Editor: Tom Dunmore.

rock sound ixo Publishing UK Ltd, 50A Roseberry Avenue, London EC1R 4RP **t** 020 7278 5559 **f** 020 7278 4788 **e** rsvp.rocksound@ixopub.co.uk **w** rock-sound.net Publisher: Patrick Napier.

Roots And Branches 54 Canterbury Rd, Penn, Wolverhampton, West Midlands WV4 4EH **t** 01902 652759 or 07973 133416 **f** 01902 652759 **e** steve-morris@blueyonder.co.uk **w** roots-and-branches.com Ed: Steve Morris.

Rough Guides 62-70 Shorts Gardens, London WC2H 9AH **t** 020 7556 5000 **f** 020 7556 5050 **e** mail@roughguides.co.uk **w** roughguides.com Rights/Promo Ass.: Chloe Roberts.

RTE Guide TV Building, Donnybrook, Dublin 4, Ireland **t** +353 1 208 2919 **f** +353 1 208 3085 **e** Aoife.Byrne@rte.ie Ed: Aoife Byrne.

Sandman Magazine PO Box 3720, Sheffield S10 9AB **t** 0114 278 6727 **e** jan@sandmanmagazine.co.uk **w** sandmagazine.co.uk Ed: Jan Webster.

The Scotsman 108 Holyrood Rd, Edinburgh, Midlothian EH8 8AS **t** 0131 620 8620 **e** enquiries@scotsman.com **w** scotsman.com

Showcase Directory Harlequin House, 7 High St, Teddington, Middx TW11 8EL **t** 020 8943 3138 **f** 020 8943 5141 **e** gillie@hollis-pr.co.uk **w** showcase-music.com Ed: Gillie Mayer.

The Singer 241 Shaftesbury Avenue, London WC2H 8TF **t** 020 7333 1746 **f** 020 7333 1769 **e** the.singer@rhinegold.co.uk **w** rhinegold.co.uk Ed: Antonia Couling.

Sky TV Guide & Digital TV Guide The New Boathouse, 136-142 Bramley Rd, London W10 6SR **t** 020 7565 3000 **f** 020 7565 3056 **e** skymag@bcp.co.uk Ad Mgr: Amanda Pitt.

Sleazenation 1A Zetland House, 5-25 Scrutton St, London EC2A 4HJ **t** 020 7729 3773 or 020 7729 8311 **f** 020 7729 8312 **e** steve@sleazenation.com **w** sleazenation.com Publishing Dir: Rich Sutcliffe.

Smash Hits EMAP Metro, 4th Floor, Mappin House, 4 Winsley St, London W1N 7AR **t** 020 7436 1515 **f** 020 7636 5792 **e** smash_hits@emap.com; firstname.lastname@emap.com **w** smashhits.net Ed: Lisa Smosarski.

SongLink International 23 Belsize Crescent, London NW3 5QY **t** 020 7794 2540 or 07956 270 592 **f** 020 7794 7393 **e** david@songlink.com **w** songlink.com Ed/Publisher: David Stark.

Songsearch Monthly Mulberry House, 10 Hedgerows, Stanway, Colchester, Essex CO3 0GJ **t** 01206 364136 **f** 01206 364146 **e** songmag@aol.com **w** songwriters-guild.co.uk Ed: Colin Eade.

Songwriter International Songwriters' Ass, PO Box 46, Limerick City, Ireland **t** +353 61 228837 **f** +353 61 229464 **e** jliddane@songwriter.iol.ie **w** songwriter.co.uk MD: James D Liddane.

Songwriting and Composing Sovereign House, 12 Trewartha Rd, Praa Sands, Penzance, Cornwall TR20 9ST **t** 01736 762826 or 07721 449477 **f** 01736 763328 **e** panamus@aol.com **w** songwriters-guild.co.uk Ed: Roderick Jones.

Soul Trade PO Box 34539, London SE15 2XA **t** 020 7732 2287 **e** ash@soultrade.co.uk **w** soultrade.co.uk Manager: Ash Kamat.

Sound Nation Ty Cefn, Rectory Rd, Canton, Cardiff CF5 1QL **t** 029 2066 8127 **f** 029 2034 1622 **e** news@soundnation.net **w** soundnation.net Editor: James McLaren.

Sound On Sound Media House, Trafalgar Way, Bar Hill, Cambridgeshire CB3 8SQ **t** 01954 789888 **f** 01954 789895 **e** sos@sospubs.co.uk **w** sound-on-sound.com Publisher: Ian Gilby.

Southern Cross 14-15 Child's Place, London SW5 9RX **t** 020 7373 3377 or 020 7341 6642 **f** 020 7341 6630 **e** sxeditor@sxmagazine.com **w** tntmagazine.com Ed: Gordon Glyn-Jones.

The Stage Stage House, 47 Bermondsey St, London SE1 3XT **t** 020 7403 1818 **f** 020 7357 9287 **e** editor@thestage.co.uk **w** thestage.co.uk

Stage, Screen & Radio 373 -377 Clapham Rd, London SW9 9BT **t** 020 7346 0900 **f** 020 7346 0901 **e** info@bectu.org.uk **w** bectu.org.uk Ed: Janice Turner.

The Strad Newsquest Specialist Media, 30 Cannon St, London EC4M 6YJ **t** 020 7618 3456 **f** 020 7618 3483 **e** thestrad@orpheuspublications.com **w** thestrad.com Ed: Naomi Sadler. Ad Mgr: Emma Fielding.

Straight No Chaser 17D Ellingfort Rd, London E8 3PA **t** 020 8533 9999 **f** 020 8985 6447 or 020 8525 6647 **e** info@straightnochaser.co.uk **w** straightnochaser.co.uk Ed: Paul Bradshaw.

Sugar 64 North Row, London W1K 7LL **t** 020 7150 7972 **f** 020 7150 7572 **e** lysannecurrie@hf-uk.com **w** hf-uk.com Editorial Dir: Lysanne Currie. Ad Mgr: Caroline Connor.

The Sun News International, 1 Virginia St, London E1 9BD **t** 020 7782 4000 **f** 020 7782 4063 **e** talkback@he-sun.co.uk **w** thesun.co.uk

Sunday Mirror 1 Canada Square, London E14 5AD **t** 020 7510 3000 **f** 020 7293 3405 **e** Via website **w** sundaymirror.co.uk

Sunday People 1 Canada Square, London E14 5AP **t** 020 7293 3000 **f** 020 7293 3810 **e** feedback@mirror.co.uk **w** people.co.uk

Sunday Telegraph 1 Canada Square, London E14 5DT **t** 020 7538 5000 **e** firstname.lastname@telegraph.co.uk **w** telegraph.co.uk

Sunday Times News International, 1 Pennington St, London E1 9XW **t** 020 7782 5000 **f** 020 7782 5658 **e** artsed@thetimes.co.uk **w** timesonline.co.uk

Tele-Tunes Mike Preston Music, The Glengarry, Thornton Grove, Morecambe, Lancs LA4 5PU **t** 01524 421172 **f** 01524 421172 **e** mikepreston@beeb.net **w** teletunes.co.uk Research Ed: Mike Preston.

Tempo (A Quarterly Review of Modern Music) PO Box 171, Herne Bay CT6 6WD **t** 020 7291 7224 **e** tempo2@boosey.com **w** temporeview.com Ed: Calum MacDonald. Ad Mgr: Arthur Boyars.

Tense Magazine Top Floor, 24 Porden Rd, London SW2 5RT **t** 020 7642 2030 **f** 020 7274 3543 **e** editor@tensemagazine.com **w** tensemagazine.com Editor: Toussaint Davy.

Time Out Universal House, 251 Tottenham Court Rd, London W1T 7AB **t** 020 7813 3000 **f** 020 7813 6158 **e** music@timeout.com **w** timeout.com/london Music Ed: Chris Salmon.

The Times Metro News International, 1 Pennington St, London E98 1TE **t** 020 7782 5000 **f** 020 7782 5525 **e** metro@the-times.co.uk Ed: Rupert Mellor.

The Times 1 Pennington St, London E98 1XY **t** 020 7782 5000 **e** firstname.lastname@thetimes.co.uk **w** timesonline.co.uk

TNT Magazine 14-15 Childs Place, London SW5 9RX **t** 020 7341 6685 **f** 0870 752 2717 **e** arts@tntmag.co.uk **w** tntmagazine.com Entertainment Editor: Pierre de Villiers.

Top Of The Pops Magazine Room A1136, 80 Wood Lane, London W12 0TT **t** 020 8433 3910 **f** 020 8433 2763 **e** olivia.mclearon@bbc.co.uk **w** bbc.co.uk/totp PA to Editor: Olivia McLearon.

TV Hits 64 North Row, London W1K 7LL **t** 020 7150 7100 **f** 020 7150 7679 **e** tvhits@hf-uk.com **w** tvhits.co.uk Editorial Asst: Ami Neumann.

TV Times IPC Magazines, Kings Reach Tower, Stamford St, London SE1 9LS **t** 020 7261 7740 **e** firstname_lastname@ipcmedia.com **w** ipc.co.uk

---

TVB EUROPE

TVBEurope

CMP Information Ltd., Ludgate House, 245 Blackfriars Rd, London SE1 9UR **t** 020 7921 8307 **f** 020 7921 8302 **e** sgrice@cmpinformation.com **w** tvbeurope.com Grp Sales Mgr: Steve Grice.

Twenty4-Seven Magazine After Dark Media, Grosvenor House, Belgrave Lane, Mutley, Plymouth PL4 7DA **t** 01752 294130 **f** 01752 257320 **e** lucy@afterdarkmedia.net **w** 24-7magazine.co.uk Ed: Lucy Griffths.

Uncut IPC Music Magazines, Kings Reach Tower, Stamford St, London SE1 9LS **t** 020 7261 6992 **f** 020 7261 5573 **e** firstname_lastname@ipcmedia.com **w** uncut.net

Undercover Undercover Agents Ltd, Basement, 69 Kensington Gardens Sq, London W2 4DG **t** 020 7792 9392 **e** diagnostyx@hotmail.com Editor In Chief: Nat Illumine.

Venue Magazine 64-65 North Rd, St Andrews, Bristol BS6 5AQ **t** 0117 942 8491 **f** 0117 942 0369 **e** music@venue.co.uk **w** venue.co.uk Music Ed: Julian Owen.

The Voice 8/9th Fl's Bluestar House, 234-244 Stockwell Rd, London SW9 9UG **t** 020 7737 7377 **f** 020 7501 9465 **e** advertising@the-voice.co.uk **w** voice-online.co.uk GM: Simbo Nuga.

What Hi-Fi? Haymarket Magazines, 38-42 Hampton Rd, Teddington, Middlesex TW11 0JE **t** 020 8267 5000 **f** 020 8267 5019 **e** whathifi@haynet.com **w** whathifi.com Contact: Ed

What's On - Birmingham & Central England Weaman St, Birmingham B4 6AT **t** 0121 234 5202 **f** 0121 234 5757 **e** jamie_perry@mrn.co.uk Product Mgr: Jamie Perry.

What's On In London 180-182 Pentonville Rd, London N1 9LB **t** 020 7278 4393 **f** 020 7837 5838 **e** whatson.advertising@virgin.net Ed: Michael Darvell.

The White Book Inside Communications, Bank House, 23 Warwick Rd, Coventry, West Midlands CV1 2EW **t** 024 7657 1171 **f** 024 7657 1172 **e** inside_events@mrn.co.uk **w** whitebook.co.uk Business Manager: Clair Whitecross.

Media

The Wire 2nd Floor East, 88-94 Wentworth St, London E1 7SA **t** 020 7422 5010 **f** 020 7422 5011 **e** listings@thewire.co.uk **w** thewire.co.uk Ed-in-Chief/Publisher: Tony Herrington.

Consumer Websites

51 Degrees North Unit 9, The Old Truman Brewery, 91-95 Brick Lane, London E1 6QL. **t** 020 7770 6021 f 020 7770 6021 e sarah@clubinlondon.co.uk **w** ClubinLondon.co.uk; ClubinIbiza.co.uk Dir: Sarah Evans.

7 Digital Media Ltd 12-23 Hanson St, London W1W 6TW **t** 020 7631 5194 **f** 0871 733 4149 **e** ben.drury@7digitalmedia.com **w** 7digitalmedia.com Dir: Ben Drury.

Amazon.co.uk Patriot Court, The Grove, Slough SL1 1QP **t** 020 8636 9200 **f** 020 8636 9400 **e** info@amazon.co.uk **w** amazon.co.uk Contact: Judith Catton

Band Family Tree 2 Oakfield Terrace, Childer Thornton, Wirral CH66 7NY **t** 0870 011 6289 **e** admin@bandfamilytree.com **w** bandfamilytree.com MD: Rob Cowley.

Band Register PO Box 594, Richmond, Surrey TW10 6YT **t** 07973 297011 **e** peter@bandreg.com **w** bandreg.com MD: Peter Whitehead.

Bandname.com 21 Market Place, Blandford Forum, Devon DT11 7AF **e** information@bandname.com **w** bandname.com Manager: Crystal Beaubien.

C-Burn 33 Sekforde St, London EC1R 0HH **t** 020 7250 1133 **f** 020 7253 8553 **e** info@c-burn.com **w** c-burn.com Sales & Mkting: Neil Phillips.

Channelfly.com 59-61 Farringdon Rd, London EC1M 3JB **t** 020 7691 4555 **f** 020 7691 4666 **e** info@channelfly.com **w** channelfly.com Editor: Will Kinsman.

Classical.com Ltd 8 Bloomsbury Sq, London WC1A 2LP **t** 020 7916 2000 **f** 020 7916 2030 **e** info@classical.com **w** classical.com Dir: Tim Lloyd.

Clickmusic Ltd 58-60 Fitzroy St, London W1T 5BU **t** 020 7554 9743 **f** 0870 458 4183 **e** laurence@clickmusic.co.uk **w** clickmusic.co.uk Producer: Laurence Cooke.

Cliff Chart Site.co.uk 17, Podsmead Rd, Tuffley, Glos GL1 5PB **t** 01452 306104 **f** 01452 306104 **e** william@cliffchartsite.co.uk **w** cliffchartsite.co.uk Editor: William Hooper.

DanceMusic.com 41-44 Canalot Studios, 222 Kensal Rd, London W10 5BN **t** 020 8964 9020 **f** 020 8964 9090 **e** word@dancemusic.com **w** dancemusic.com CEO: Russel Coultart.

Drowned in Sound 72 Palatine Rd, Stoke Newington, London N16 8ST **t** 020 8969 2498 **e** gareth@drownedinsound.com **w** drownedinsound.com Editor: Gareth Dobson.

Drum & Bass Arena Unit 27, Sheffield Science Pk, Arundel St., Sheffield S1 2NS **t** 0114 281 4470 **f** 0114 281 4471 **e** info@breakbeat.co.uk/ ddias@breakbeat.co.uk **w** breakbeat.co.uk Commercial Dir: Del Dias.

FirstForMusic.com 23 New Mount St, Manchester M4 4DE **t** 0161 953 4081 **f** 0161 953 4091 **e** info@FirstForMusic.com **w** FirstForMusic.com Contact: Steven Oakes

Flash FM 9 Mansfield St, London W1M 9FH **t** 0701 071 2800 **f** 0701 071 2801 **e** info@flashfm.com **w** flashfm.com Dir: Steve Flint.

Freeflow UK International Media Centre, Adelphi House, The Crescent, Salford M3 6EN **t** 0161 295 7240 **f** 0161 834 0710 **e** info@freeflowuk.com **w** freeflowuk.com Project Manager: Ian Dobie.

Get Media Wilsons House, Wilsons Park, Newton Heath, Manchester M40 8WN **t** 0161 205 8885 **f** 0161 205 8887 **e** enquiries@getmediaplc.com **w** getmediaplc.com CEO: John Doyle.

Kent Gigs (One Kent) The Cedars, Elvington Lane, Hawkinge, Nr. Folkestone, Kent CT18 7AD **t** 01303 893472 **f** 01303 893833 **e** Chris@kentgigs.com **w** kentgigs.com MD: Chris Ashman.

Let's Talk Music The Dog House, 32 Sullivan Crescent, Harefield, Middlesex UB9 6NL **t** 01895 825 757 **e** Bill@letstalkmusic.com **w** letstalkmusic.com Contact: Bill Smith

livegigguide ltd The Windsor Centre, 15-29 Windsor St, London N1 8QG **t** 020 7359 2927 **f** 020 7359 7212 **e** info@livegigguide.com **w** livegigguide.com Dir of Operations: James Rodmell.

The Living Tradition PO Box 1026, Kilmarnock, Ayrshire, Scotland KA2 0LG **t** 01563 571220 **f** 01563 544855 **e** admin@livingtradition.co.uk **w** folkmusic.net Ed: Pete Heywood.

LoseControl Ltd 177 Wager St, London E3 4JR **t** 020 8980 1253 or 07887 912 678 **f** 020 7557 4771 **e** james@losecontrol.com **w** losecontrol.com Dir: James Hay.

Manchestermusic.co.uk Musicdash, PO Box 1977, Manchester M26 2YB **t** 0787 0727 075 **e** mancmusic@hotmail.com **w** manchestermusic.co.uk Editor: Jon Ashley.

Mania Entertainment Group Media House, 34 Salisbury St, London NW8 8QE **t** 020 7402 9111 **f** 020 7723 3064 **e** joanne@mania.net **w** mania.net Dir: Joanne Goldring-Cohen.

Mobiletones.com Unit 4, Handford Court, Garston Lane, Watford WD25 9EJ **t** 0870 444 7110 **f** 01923 675 299 **e** info@mobiletones.com **w** mobiletones.com Music Development Manager: Dominic Bignall.

New CD Weekly 56 Manston Rd, Exeter, Devon EX1 2QA **t** 01392 432 630 **f** 01392 432 630 **e** rod@newcdweekly.com **w** newcdweekly.com MD: Rod Walsom.

NME.COM IPC Music Magazines, Kingsreach Tower, Stamford St, London SE1 9LS **t** 020 7261 5000 **f** 020 7261 6022 **e** news@nme.com **w** nme.com Editor: Ben Perreau.

Noiseup.com Studio 407, Bon Marche Centre, 241-251 Ferndale Rd, London SW9 8BJ **t** 020 7326 0345 **e** info@rampindustry.co.uk **w** Noiseup.com Editorial Dir: Andy Crysell.

Odyssey.fm PO Box 18888, London SW7 4FQ **t** 020 7373 1614 **f** 020 7373 1614 **e** info@outer-media.co.uk **w** odyssey.fm Dir: Gregory Mihalcheon.

Online Classics Gnd & 1st Floors, 31 Eastcastle St, London W1W 8DL **t** 020 7636 1400 **f** 020 7637 1355 **e** team@onlineclassics.com **w** onlineclassics.com CEO: Christopher Hunt.

OnlineConcerts.com 2 Valentine Cottages, Petworth Rd, Witley, Godalming, Surrey GU8 5LS **t** 01428 684537 **e** jdoukas@onlineconcerts.com **w** onlineconcerts.com Founder: John Doukas.

Oxfordmusic.net Suite 1, 2nd Floor, 65 George St, Oxford OX1 2BE **t** 01865 798796 **f** 01865 798792 **e** info@oxfordmusic.net **w** oxfordmusic.net MD: Andy Clyde.

Playlouder 8-10 Rhoda St, London E2 7EF **t** 020 7729 4797 **f** 020 7739 8571 **e** site@playlouder.com **w** playlouder.com MDs: Paul Hitchman, Jim Gottlieb.

Popex.com 109x Regents Park Rd, London NW1 8UR **t** 020 7691 4555 **f** 020 7691 4666 **e** pauly@popex.com **w** popex.com Administrator: Paul Clarke.

Popworld Ltd. 21-23 Ransomes Dock, 35-37 Parkgate Rd, London SW11 4NP **t** 020 7350 5500 **f** 020 7350 5501 **e** promotions@popworld.com **w** popworld.com Gen Mgr: Emma Hill.

Primal Sounds.com PO Box 5, Alton, Hants GU34 2EN **t** 07967 155542 **e** mail@primalsounds.com **w** primalsounds.com Owner: Carl Saunders.

Raft, The Kensal House, 553-579 Harrow Rd, London W10 4RH **t** 020 8964 6000 **f** 020 8964 6003 **e** danny.van.emden@virginmusic.com **w** the-raft.com Multimedia Dir: Danny Van Emden.

Record Of The Day PO Box 49554, London E17 9WB **t** 020 8520 2130 or 020 8677 1847 **e** paul@recordoftheday.com **w** recordoftheday.com Eds: Paul Scaife, David Balfour.

Revolution 211 Western Rd, London SW19 2QD **t** 020 8646 7094 **f** 020 8646 7094 **e** info@revolutionsuk.com **w** revolutionsuk.com Ed: John Lonergan.

Shazam Entertainment Ltd. 4th Floor, block F, 375 Kensington High St, London W14 8QH **t** 020 7471 3440 **f** 020 7471 3477 **e** music@shazamteam.com **w** shazamentertainment.com Hd of Music: Will Mills.

Skrufff-E and Skrufff.com Available on request. **t** 020 7221 4794 **e** jonty@skrufff.com **w** skrufff.com Founder: Jonty Adderley.

sonic360 33 Riding House St, London W1W 7DZ **t** 020 7636 3939 **f** 020 7636 0033 **e** info@sonic360.com **w** sonic360.com Creative Dir: Hana Miya.

Spaced Unit 2, New North House, 202-208 New North Rd, London N1 7BJ **t** 020 7288 8150 **f** 020 7288 8151 **e** info@spaced.co.uk **w** spaced.co.uk Sales & marketing Dir: Vanessa Vigar.

Sypha's DAW Buyers Guide Gipsy Rd, London SE27 9RB **t** 020 8761 1042 **e** info@syphaonline.com **w** syphaonline.com Partner: Yasmin Hashmi.

thewhitelabel.com limited 1-3 Croft Lane, Henfield, W. Sussex BN5 9TT **t** 01273 491761 **f** 01273 491761 **e** contact@thewhitelabel.com **w** thewhitelabel.com GM: Nic Vine.

TOTP Online Room A400, Centre House, 56 Wood Lane, London W12 7SB **t** 020 8225 8917 **e** rob.cooper@bbc.co.uk **w** bbc.co.uk/totp Senior Producer: Rob Cooper.

TrustTheDJ.com Unit 13-14, Barley Shotts Bus.Park, 246 Acklam Rd, London W10 5YG **t** 020 8962 9944 **f** 020 8960 9660 **e** contact@trustthedj.com **w** trustthedj.com Editorial: Cameron McPhail.

Turnround Multi-Media 16 Berkeley Mews, 29 High St, Cheltenham, Gloucestershire GL50 1DY **t** 01242 224360 **f** 01242 226566 **e** studio@turnround.co.uk **w** turnround.co.uk MD: Ross Lammas.

UKMusic.com PO Box 50703, London NW6 6XG **t** 07949 828 910 **e** admin@ukmusic.com **w** ukmusic.com MD: Sarah Villegas.

Umusic.co.uk Universal UK, 22 St Peter's Square, London W6 9NW **t** 020 8910 3333 **f** 020 8748 0948 **e** info@umusic.co.uk **w** umusic.co.uk Hd of New Media: Rob Wells.

Virgin.net The Communications Bld, 48 Leicester Square, London WC2H 7LT **t** 020 7664 6069 **f** 020 7664 6006 **e** virgincontact@london.virgin.net **w** virgin.net Hd of Content: Caroline Hugh.

Virtual Festivals.com 4 Rowan Court, 56 High St, Wimbledon, London SW19 5EE **t** 020 8605 2691 **f** 020 8605 2255 **e** steve@virtualfestivals.com **w** virtualfestivals.com Managing Ed: Steve Jenner.

Vitaminic 20 Orange St, London WC2H 7NN **t** 020 7766 4000 **f** 020 7766 4001 **e** info@vitaminic.co.uk **w** vitaminic.co.uk UK MD: Chris Cass.

WEB SHERIFF

Argentum, 2 Queen Caroline Street, London W6 9DX **t** 020 8323 8013 **f** 020 8323 8080 **e** websheriff@websheriff.com **w** websheriff.com Contact: John Giacobbi. **Protecting Your Rights On The Internet.**

Yahoo! UK & Ireland 10 Ebury Bridge Rd, London SW1W 8PZ **t** 020 7808 4400 **f** 020 7808 4203 **e** mccraw@uk.yahoo-inc.com **w** yahoo.co.uk Ent/Media Prod (UK): Beth McCraw.

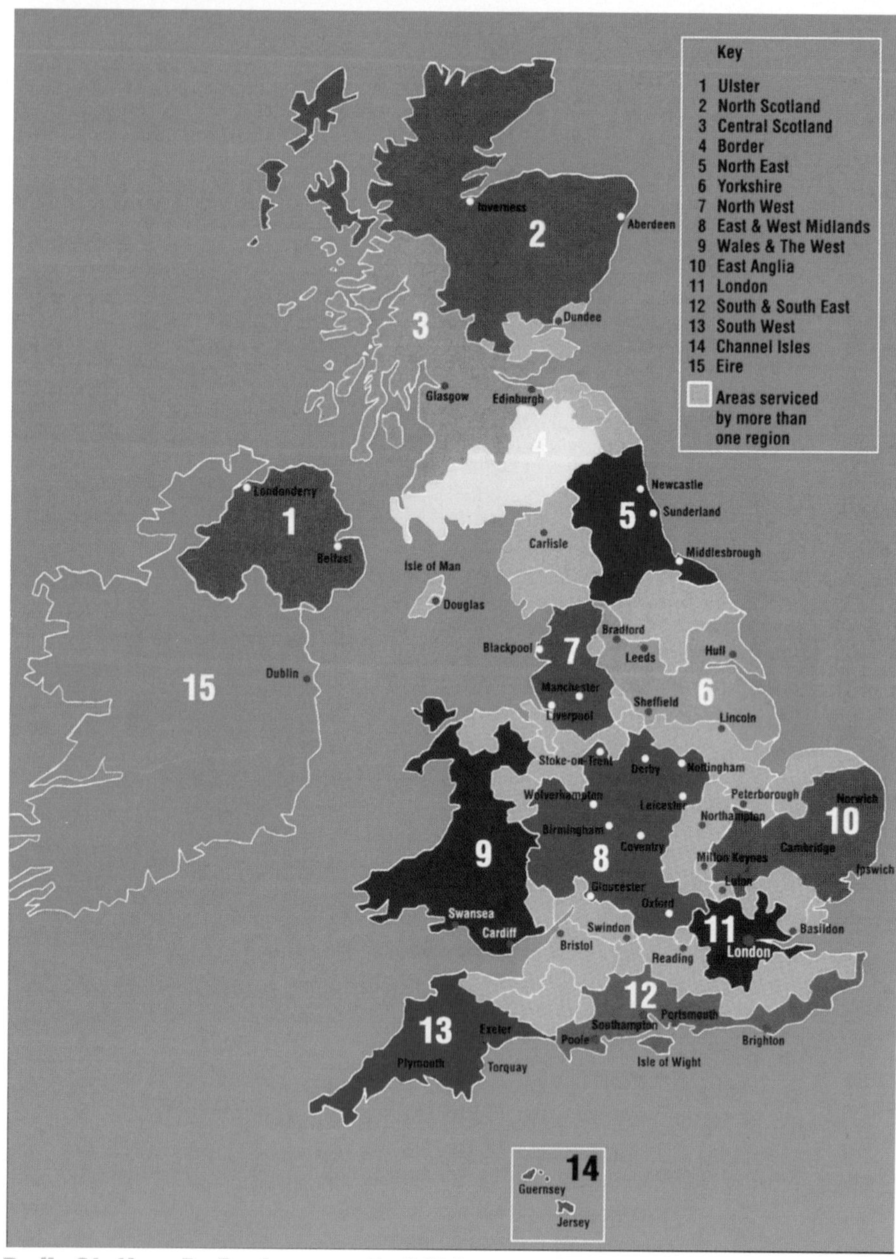

Radio Stations By Region

Region 1
Belfast City Beat
Cool FM
Downtown Radio/DTR
Manx Radio
Q101.2FM
Q102.9 FM
Q97.2FM
BBC Ulster

Region 2
Central FM
Isles FM 103
Lochbroom FM
Moray Firth Radio
NECR
BBC Nan Gaidheal
Nevis Radio
NorthSound One
NorthSound Two
Radio North Angus FM
SIBC
BBC Radio Shetland
Tay FM
Tay AM
Wave 102 FM
Waves Radio

Region 3
3C/Continuous Cool Country
Argyll FM
Beat 106
Clan FM
Classic VRN 1287
Clyde 1 FM
Clyde 2
Forth One
Forth 2
Heartland FM
Kingdom FM
Oban FM

Q96 FM
Real Radio FM
Saga 105.2
Score Digital Ltd
BBC Scotland
South West Sound
West FM
Westsound AM

Region 4
Radio Borders
CFM
BBC Radio Cumbria
Lakeland Radio

Region 5
103.4 Sun FM
Alpha 103.2
The Arrow
CFM
Century FM
BBC Radio Cleveland
BBC Radio Cumbria
Fresh Radio
Galaxy 105-106
Magic 1152
Magic 1170
Metro Radio
104.7 Minster FM
BBC Radio Newcastle
TFM
BBC Radio York
Yorkshire Coast Radio

Region 6
96.3 Radio Aire
BCB
Compass FM 96.4
Dearne FM
Fresh Radio
Galaxy 105
Hallam FM
Home 107.9
BBC Humber
BBC Leeds
BBC Radio Lincolnshire
Lincs FM 102.2
Magic 1161
Magic AM
Magic 828
104.7 Minster FM
Real Radio (Yorkshire)
BBC Radio Sheffield
97.2 Stray FM
Sunrise FM
radio2XS
96.9 Viking FM
107.2 Wire FM
BBC Radio York
Yorkshire Coast Radio

Region 7
The Arrow
Asian Sound Radio
The Bay
Buzz 97.1
Capital Gold - Manchester
105.4 Century FM
Radio City 96.7
Dee 106.3
Dune FM
BBC GMR (BBC Greater Manchester Radio)
Galaxy 102 FM
Imagine FM
Juice 107.6 FM
KCR 106.7
Key 103
Lakeland Radio
BBC Radio Lancashire
Magic 1548
Magic 999
Manx Radio
BBC Radio Merseyside
Real Radio
96.2 The Revolution
Ridings FM
97.4 Rock FM
BBC Shropshire
106.9 Silk FM
Smooth FM
Sunshine 855
2BR (Two Boroughs Radio)
107.4 Tower FM
Wave 96.5
102.4 Wish FM

Region 8
97.5 Scarlet FM
The Arrow
BCR FM
96.4 FM BRMB
Beacon FM
BBC Radio Berkshire
Capital Gold Birmingham
Carillon Radio
Centre FM
106 Century FM
Classic Gold 1260
Classic Gold 1359
Classic Gold 1557
Classic Gold 774
Classic Gold GEM
Classic Gold WABC
Classic Gold 1521
Classic Hits 954/1530AM
Herefordshire & Worcester
Connect FM
BBC Coventry & Warwickshire
BBC Radio Derby
FM 102 The Bear
Fosseway Radio
Fox FM
GWR FM
GWR FM
Galaxy 102.2
BBC Radio Gloucestershire
Heart FM 100.7
BBC Hereford & Worcester
Kerrang! Radio
Kix 96
BBC Leicester
Leicester Sound
BBC Radio Lincolnshire
Lincs FM 102.2
Mansfield 103.2
Mercia FM
BBC Radio Northampton
Northants 96
BBC Radio Nottingham
Oak 107
BBC Radio Oxford
Passion 107.9FM
Peak 107FM
Radio Pembrokeshire
RadioXL
102.8 Ram FM
107.1 Rugby FM
Rutland Radio
Sabras Radio
Saga 105.7FM
Saga 106.6fm
102.4 Severn Sound FM
BBC Shropshire
Signal 2
Signal 1
BBC Somerset Sound
Star 107
Star 107.5
BBC Stoke
Sunshine 855
107.4 Telford FM
Trax FM
Trax FM.
96 Trent FM
UCB Europe
BBC WM
BBC Radio Wiltshire
107.7 FM The Wolf
Wyvern FM

Region 9
97.5 Scarlet FM
The Arrow
107.9 Bath FM
106.3 Bridge FM
BBC Radio Bristol
Capital Gold - Red Dragon
Radio Ceredigion
Champion 103 FM
Classic Gold Marcher
Coast 96.3 FM
GTFM
GWR FM
MFM 103.4
Radio Maldwyn
Radio Carmarthenshire
Radio Pembrokeshire
Red Dragon FM
BBC Shropshire
Star 107.7
Sunshine 855
Swansea Sound 1170 MW
Valleys Radio
Vibe 101
BBC Wales/Cymru
96.4FM The Wave

Region 10
103.4 The Beach
Broadland 102
Cable Radio Milton Keynes (CRMK) 89.8FM
BBC Radio Cambridgeshire
96.9 Chiltern FM
97.6 Chiltern FM
Classic Gold 1332 AM
Classic Gold 1557
Classic Gold 792/828
Classic Gold Amber
Classic Gold Amber (Suffolk)
West Yorkshire's Classic Gold
Fen Radio 107.5
102.7 Hereward FM
HertBeat FM
FM 103 Horizon
KLFM
KM-fm (Thanet)
Lite FM
MIX 96
BBC Radio Norfolk
BBC Radio Northampton
Northants 96
The Pulse of West Yorkshire
Q103 FM
SGR Colchester
SGR-FM
Star 107.9
BBC Radio Suffolk
Ten-17
BBC Three Counties Radio
Vibe 105-108

Region 11
106.8 Time FM
107.3 Time FM
BBC Radio Berkshire
CMRPulse Radio
95.8 Capital FM
Capital Gold Kent
Capital Gold Network
96.9 Chiltern FM
97.6 Chiltern FM
Choice FM London
Classic Gold 1431/1485
Classic Gold Breeze
Classic Gold 1521
Club Asia Radio London
County Sound 1566 AM
Delta FM 97.1
Dream 100
96.4 The Eagle
Easy Radio London 1035
Essex FM
Heart 106.2
Invicta FM
102.2 Jazz FM
KM-fm (Canterbury)
KM-fm (Thanet)
KM-fm (West Kent)
BBC Radio Kent
107.6 Kestrel FM
Kick FM
Kiss 100 FM
Kool AM
LBC 97.3
BBC London
London Greek Radio
London Turkish Radio (LTR)
Magic 105.4
KM-fm (Medway)
Mercury 96.6
Mix 107
Premier Christian Radio
Radio Jackie
Reading 107fm
SGR Colchester
Soul City
BBC Southern Counties Radio
Spectrum Radio
Star 106.6 FM
Sunrise Radio
2-TEN FM
Ten-17
BBC Three Counties Radio
Virgin Radio
XFM 104.9
BBC Essex

Region 12
3TR FM
Arrow FM
BBC Radio Berkshire
Capital Gold Brighton
Capital Gold Hampshire
Capital Gold Kent
Classic Gold 1260
Classic Gold 828
Classic Gold 936/1161 AM
Dream 107.7FM
Fire 107.6
GWR FM
Invicta FM
Isle Of Wight Radio
Juice 107.2
KM-fm
BBC Radio Kent
107.6 Kestrel FM
Kick FM
102.7 Mercury FM
Ocean FM
103.2 Power FM
107.4 The Quay
Reading 107fm
The Saint
BBC Radio Solent
BBC Somerset Sound
Southern FM
107.5 Sovereign Radio
Spire FM
Spirit FM
2CR FM
Vale FM
Wave 105.2 FM
BBC Radio Wiltshire
Win 107.2 FM

Region 13
BCR FM
107.9 Bath FM
BBC Radio Bristol
Classic Gold Digital 666 & 954
Classic Gold Digital 1152
BBC Radio Cornwall
BBC Radio Devon
Gemini FM
Lantern FM
Orchard FM
Pirate FM102
97FM Plymouth Sound
Quaywest Radio
South Hams Radio
Star 107.7
Vibe 101
Wessex FM

Region 14
Channel 103 FM
BBC Radio Guernsey
Island FM
BBC Radio Jersey

Region 15
CKR FM (Carlow/Kildare)
Clare FM
Cork 96 FM
Dublin's 98 FM
Dublin's Country 106.8FM
East Coast FM
FM 104
Galway Bay FM
Highland Radio
Radio Kerry
LMFM Radio
Limerick's Live 95FM
Mid West Radio
Midlands 103
North West Radio
Q102
RLO 105 FM
RTE Radio 1
2FM
Red FM
Shannonside FM
South East Radio
Tipp FM
Tipperary Mid-West
100-102 Today FM
WLR FM
Wired FM
Raidio na Gaeltachta

Media

Radio

103.4 Sun FM, FM:103.4 PO Box 1034, Sunderland, Tyne and Wear SR5 2YL **t** 0191 548 1034 **f** 0191 548 7171 **e** progs@sun-fm.com **w** sun-fm.com Brand Mgr: Simon Grundy. Commercial Mgr: Helen Edmondson. AC/CHR[5]

106.8 Time FM, FM:106.8 2-6 Basildon Rd, London SE2 0EW **t** 020 8311 3112 **f** 020 8312 1930 **e** gary@timefm.com **w** time1068.com Grp Prog Cont: Gary Mulligan. Grp MD: Neil Romain. Grp Station Dir & Sales Dir: Mark Reason. Gold**[11]**

107.3 Time FM, FM:107.3 2-6 Basildon Rd, London SE2 0EW **t** 020 8311 3112 **f** 020 8312 1930 **e** gary@timefm.com **w** fusion1073.com Grp Prog Controller: Gary Mulligan. Group MD: Neil Romain. Grp Station Dir & Sales Dir: Mark Reason. Soul/RnB/Dance/Reggae**[11]**

3C/Continuous Cool Country, AM:DAB 3 South Avenue, Clydebank Business Park, Glasgow GB1 2RX **t** 0141 565 2307 **f** 0141 565 2340 **e** 3c@3cdigital.com **w** 3cdigital.com Station Manager: Pat Geary. Hd of Sales: Tracey McNellan. Country[3]

3TR FM, FM:107.5 Riverside Studios, Warminster, Wilts. BA12 9HQ **t** 01985 211111 **f** 01985 211110 **e** admin@3trfm.com **w** 3trfm.com Brand Mgr: Jonathan Fido. Commercial Mgr: Ceri Hurford-Jones. Sales Manager: Anne Holmes. AC[12]

97.5 Scarlet FM, FM:97.5 The Studios, Foothold Centre, Stebonheath Terrace, Llanelli SA15 1NE **t** 01834 869384 **f** 01834 861524 **e** keri@Scarletfm.com **w** Scarletfm.com MD/Prog Dir: Keri Jones. Hd of Sales: Aimee Bowen. AC[9, 8]

96.3 Radio Aire, FM:96.3 51 Burley Rd, Leeds, West Yorkshire LS3 1LR **t** 0113 283 5500 **f** 0113 283 5501 **e** firstname.lastname@radioaire.com **w** radioaire.co.uk Prog Dir: Stuart Baldwin. Commercial Dir: Tracy Eastwood. CHR[6]

Alpha 103.2, FM:103.2 11 Woodland Rd, Darlington, Co Durham DL3 7BJ **t** 01325 255552 **f** 01325 255551 **e** mail@alpha1032.com **w** alpha1032.com Prog Mgr/Hd of Music: Ricky Durkin. MD: Joe Radcliffe. Hd of Sales: Angela Bridgen. Gold[5]

Argyll FM, FM:106.5/107.1/107.7 27/29 Longrow, Campbeltown, Argyll PA28 6ER **t** 01586 551800 **f** 01586 551888 **e** argyllradio@hotmail.com **w** argyllfm.com Prog Dir: Kenny Johnson. Chairman/MD/HoM: Colin Middleton. Hd of Sales: John Armour. Full range[3]

Arrow FM, FM:107.8 Priory Meadow Centre, Hastings, East Sussex TN34 1PJ **t** 01424 461177 **f** 01424 422662 **e** info@arrowfm.co.uk **w** arrowfm.co.uk Station Mgr/Hd of Sales: Stuart Woodford. Brand Mgr: Mike Buxton. Hd of Music: Andy Knight. AC[12]

The Arrow, FM:DAB 1 The Square, 111 Broad St, Birmingham B15 1AS **t** 0121 695 0000 **f** 0121 695 0055 **e** feedback@thearrow.co.uk **w** thearrow.co.uk Prog Dir: Alan Carruthers. MD: Paul Fairburn. Hd of Music: Bev Hickman. Hd of Sales: Ian James. Rock **[7, 5, 8, 9]**

Asian Sound Radio, AM:1377/963 Globe House, Southall St, Manchester M3 1LG **t** 0161 288 1000 **f** 0161 288 9000 **e** info@asiansoundradio.co.uk **w** asiansoundradio.co.uk MD/Prog Cont: Shujat Ali. Sales Dir: Sufat Ali. Asian Film/Asian Dance[7]

107.9 Bath FM, FM:107.9 Station House, Ashley Avenue, Lower Weston, Bath BA1 3DS **t** 01225 471571 **f** 01225 471681 **e** studio@bath.fm **w** bath.fm Prog Controller: Steve Collins. MD: Jo Wood. Hd of Sales: Richard Thorogood. AC[13, 9]

The Bay, FM:96.9/102.3/103.2 PO Box 969, St Georges Quay, Lancaster LA1 3LD **t** 01524 848747 **f** 01524 844969 **e** info@thebay.fm **w** thebay.fm Prog Dir/Hd of Music: Tony Cookson. Station Dir: Bill Johnson. Grp Prog Dir: Mike Vitti. Hd of Sales: Cheri Ward. AC**[7]**

BBC 6 Music, FM:DAB Room 5661, Broadcasting House, London W1A 1AA **t** 020 7580 4468 **f** 020 7765 4571 **e** firstname.lastname@bbc.co.uk **w** bbc.co.uk/6music Hd of Music: Jon Myer. Network Controller: Lesley Douglas. Hd Of Programmes: Ric Blaxill. AC

BCB, FM:96.7 2 Forster Square, Bradford, West Yorkshire BD1 1DQ **t** 01274 771677 **f** 01274 771680 **e** info@bcb.yorks.com **w** bcb.yorks.com MD: Mary Dowson. Prog Dir/Hd of Sales: Jonathan Pinfield. Hd of Music: John Gill. World/Rock/Blues[6]

BCR FM, AM:1 FM:107.4 PO Box 1074, Bridgwater, Somerset TA6 4WE **t** 01278 727701 **f** 01278 727705 **e** info@bcrfm.co.uk **w** bcrfm.co.uk MD/Hd of Sales: Mark Painter. Programming Dir/Hd of Music: Dave Englefield. AC/MOR[8, 13]

103.4 The Beach, FM:103.4 PO Box 103.4, Lowestoft, Suffolk NR32 2TL **t** 0845 345 1035 **f** 0845 345 1036 **e** info@thebeach.co.uk **w** thebeach.co.uk Prog Contr: Tom Kaye. MD: David Blake. Hd of Music: Paul Carter. Hd of Sales: Sue Taylor. AC[10]

Beacon FM, FM:97.2/103.1 267 Tettenhall Rd, Wolverhampton, West Midlands WV6 0DE **t** 01902 461200 **f** 01902 461299 **e** firstname.lastname@creation.com **w** musicradio.com Station Mgr/Prog Cont: Chris Pegg. Hd of Music: Lisa Gibbons. Hd of Sales: Marie Wright. CHR[8]

Beat 106, FM:106.1/105.7 Four Winds Pavilion, Pacific Quay, Glasgow G51 1EB **t** 0141 566 6106 **f** 0141 566 6110 **e** info@beat106.com **w** beat106.com Prog Controller: Claire Pattenden. Hd of Music: Jim Gellatly. Hd of Sales: tbc. New Rock/Dance[3]

Belfast City Beat, FM:96.7 Lamont Buildings, 46, Stranmillis Embankment, Belfast, Co Antrim BT9 5FN **t** 028 9020 5967 **f** 028 9020 0023 **e** info@citybeat.co.uk **w** citybeat.co.uk Prog Dir: Owen Larkin. Hd of Music: Stuart Robinson. Sales Manager: Dorothy McDade. MOR[1]

BBC Radio Berkshire, FM:104.1/104.4/95.4/94.6 PO Box 104.4, Reading, Berkshire RG4 8FH **t** 0118 946 4200 **f** 0118 946 4555 **e** radio.berkshire@bbc.co.uk **w** bbc.co.uk/radioberkshire Managing Editor: Phil Ashworth. Programming Dir: Andrew Peach. News [8, 11, 12]

Radio Borders, FM:96.8/97.5/103.1/103.4 Tweedside Park, Galashiels, Selkirkshire TD1 3TD **t** 01896 759444 **f** 0845 345 7080 **e** firstname.lastname@radioborders.com **w** radioborders.com Station Mgr: Stuart McCulloch. Hd of Music: Keith Clarkson. Hd of Sales: Lynsey Law. AC[4]

106.3 Bridge FM, FM:106.3 PO Box 1063, Bridgend, Mid Glamorgan CF31 1ED **t** 01656 647777 **f** 01656 673618 **e** info@bridge.fm **w** bridge.fm M: Mark Franklin. Prog Cont/Hd of Music: Lee Thomas. Sales Manager: Nigel Hodgetts. AC[9]

Bright 106.4, FM:106.4 Market Place Shopping Centre, Burgess Hill, West Sussex RH15 9NP **t** 01444 248127 **f** 01444 248553 **e** reception@bright1064.com **w** bright1064.com Prog Dir/Hd of Music: Mark Chapple. MD: Allan Moulds. Hd of Sales: Mak Norman. AC [11, 12]

BBC Radio Bristol, AM:1548 FM:94.9/95.5 Broadcasting House, Whiteladies Rd, Bristol BS8 2LR **t** 0117 974 1111 **f** 0117 973 2549 **e** radio.bristol@bbc.co.uk **w** bbc.co.uk/radiobristol Station Manager: Ms Jenny Lacey. Hd of Music: Pat Wilson. MOR[13, 9]

British Forces Radio, Chalfont Grove, Narcot Lane, Chalfont St Peter, Gerrards Cross, Bucks SL9 8TN **t** 01494 874461 **f** 01494 870552 **e** admin.officer@bfbs.com **w** ssvc.com Prog Dir, BFBS Radio 1: Ian Noakes. Managing Editor: Alan Phillips. Hd of Music: Joanne Bell. Prog Planning Admin: Heidi Secker. CHR

96.4 FM BRMB, FM:96.4 9 Brindley Place, 4 Oozells Square, Birmingham, West Midlands B1 2DJ **t** 0121 245 5000 **f** 0121 245 5900 **e** info@brmb.co.uk **w** brmb.co.uk Prog Dir: Adam Bridge. Hd of Sales: Jane Davies. CHR[8]

Broadland 102, FM:102.4 St George's Plain, 47-49 Colegate, Norwich, Norfolk NR3 1DB **t** 01603 630621 **f** 01603 666252 **e** firstname.lastname@musicradio.com **w** musicradio.com Prog Cont: Steve Martin. Sales Centre Mgr: Sophie Crocker. AC[10]

Buzz 97.1, FM:97.1 The Studios, Mold Rd, Wrexham LL11 4AF **t 0151 650 1700 f** 0151 650 8109 **e** admin@mfm.musicradio.com **w** musicradio.com Grp ProgDir: Graham Ledger. MD: Sarah Smithard. Grp Hd of Music: Steve Simms. Hd of Music: Andy Parry. Hd of Sales: Clive Douthwaite. Chart/Gold[7]

Cable Radio Milton Keynes (CRMK) 89.8FM, FM:89.8 14 Vincent Avenue, Crownhill, Milton Keynes, Buckinghamshire MK8 0AB **t** 01908 265266 **f** 01908 564893 **e** Tony.White@crmk.co.uk **w** crmk.co.uk Programmer: Tony White. Station Mgr: Mike Barry/Andrew Hollinshead. Prog Dir/Hd of Music: Steve Wilson. Hd of Sales: Mike Barry. AC[10]

BBC Radio Cambridgeshire, AM:1026/1449 FM:96/95.7 PO Box 96, 104 Hills Rd, Cambridge CB2 1LD **t** 01223 259696 **f** 01223 460832 **e** Cambs@bbc.co.uk **w** bbc.co.uk/radiocambridgeshire Hd of Music/SBJ: Gerald Main. Managing Editor: David Martin. MOR[10]

95.8 Capital FM, FM:95.8 30 Leicester Square, London WC2H 7LA **t** 020 7766 6000 **f** 020 7766 6100 **e** firstname.lastname@capitalradio.com **w** capitalfm.com Hd of Music: Sheena Mason. Capital FM MD: Keith Pringle. Commercial Dir: Linda Smith. CHR[11]

Capital Gold - Red Dragon, AM:1305/1359 Radio House, Atlantic Wharf, Cardiff, South Glamorgan CF10 4DJ **t** 029 2066 2066 **f** 029 2066 2067 **e** info@capitalgold.com **w** capitalgold.co.uk Network Prog Dir: Andy Turner. MD: Lyn Long. Commercial Dir: Linda Smith. Gold[9]

Capital Gold - Manchester, AM:1458 4th Floor, Quay West, Trafford Wharf Rd, Trafford Park, Manchester M17 1FL **t** 0161 607 0420 **f** 0161 607 0443 **e** info@capitalgold.co.uk **w** capitalgold.com Network Prog Dir: Andy Turner. MD: Lyn Long. Commercial Dir: Linda Smith. Sales Mgr (Local): Allison Forshaw. Gold[7]

Capital Gold Birmingham, AM:1152 BRMB Radio Group, Nine Brindley Place, 4 Oozells Square, Birmingham B1 2DJ **t** 0121 245 5000 **f** 0121 245 5245 **e** info@capitalgold.co.uk **w** capitalgold.com Network Prog Dir: Andy Turner. MD: Lyn Long. Commercial Dir: Linda Smith. Gold[8]

Capital Gold Brighton, AM:945/1323 Radio House, PO Box 2000, Brighton, East Sussex BN41 2SS **t** 01273 430111 **f** 01273 430098 **e** info@capitalgold.co.uk **w** capitalgold.com Network Prog Controller: Andy Turner. MD: Lyn Long. Commercial Dir: Linda Smith. Gold[12]

Capital Gold Hampshire, AM:1170/1557 Radio House, Whittle Avenue, Segensworth West, Fareham, Hampshire PO15 5SH **t** 01489 589911 **f** 01489 587754 **e** info@capitalgold.com **w** capitalgold.com Group Prog Dir: Andy Turner. MD: Lyn Long. Commercial Dir: Linda Smith. Gold[12]

Capital Gold Kent, AM:1242/603 Radio House, John Wilson Business Park, Whitstable, Kent CT5 3QX **t** 01227 772004 **f** 01227 771560 **e** info@invictaradio.co.uk **w** capitalgold.com Network Prog Dir: Andy Turner. MD: Lyn Long. Commercial Dir: Linda Smith. Gold**[11, 12]**

Capital Gold Network, AM:1548 30 Leicester Square, London WC2H 7LA **t** 020 7766 6000 **f** 020 7766 6393 **e** andy.turner@capitalgold.com **w** capitalgold.com Prog Dir: Andy Turner. MD: Lyn Long. Hd of Sales: Linda Smith. Gold[11]

Carillon Radio, AM:1386 AM Loughborough General Hospital, Baxter Gate, Loughborough, Leics LE11 1TT **t** 01509 838 671 **f** 07973 987 554 **e** carillonradio@aol.com Station Sec/Engineer: John Sketchley. Station Manager: Colin Pytel.[8]

Central FM, FM:103.1 201-203 High St, Falkirk FK1 1DU **t 01324 611164 f** 01324 611168 **e** mail@centralfm.co.uk **w** centralfm.co.uk MD/Prog Dir: Tom Bell. Hd of Music: Gavin Orr. Hd of Sales: Anne Marie Miller. AC/GOLD[2]

Centre FM, FM:101.6/102.4 5-6 Aldergate, Tamworth, Staffordshire B79 7DJ **t** 01827 318000 **f** 01827 318002 **e** studio@centrefm.com **w** centrefm.com Prog Controller: Stuart Hickman. Station Dir/Hd of Sales: Phil Richardson. AC[8]

105.4 Century FM, FM:105.4 Laser House, Waterfront Quay, Salford Quays, Manchester M50 3XW **t** 0161 400 0105 **f** 0161 400 0173 or 0161 400 1105 **e** info@1054centuryfm.co.uk **w** 1054centuryfm.com Prog Dir: Ande Macpherson. MD: Nick Davidson. Hd of Music: Mike Walsh. Hd of Sales (Local): Allison Forshaw. AC[7]

106 Century FM, FM:106 City Link, Nottingham NG2 4NG **t** 0115 910 6100 or 08453 457 106 **f** 0115 910 6107 or 08453 454 106 **e** info106@centuryfm.co.uk **w** 106centuryfm.com Prog Controller: Anna Riggs. Hd of Music: Jim Davis. Commercial Controller: Marguerite Taylor. AC[8]

Century FM, FM:100 - 102 Century House, PO Box 100, Church St, Gateshead, Tyne and Wear NE8 2YY **t** 0191 477 6666 **f** 0191 477 5660 **e** info@centuryfm.co.uk **w** centuryfm.co.uk Prog Dir: Giles Squire. MD: Nick Davidson. Hd of Music: Paul Drogan. Hd of Sales: Debbie Bowman. MOR[5]

Radio Ceredigion, FM:103.3/96.6/97.4 Yr Hen Ysgol Gymraeg, Ffordd Alexandra, Aberystwyth, Ceredigion SY23 1LF **t** 01970 627999 **f** 01970 627206 **e** admin@ceredigionfm.f9.co.uk **w** ceredigionradio.co.uk Prog Cont: Myfanwy Jones. Station Manager: Dafydd Edwards. Hd of Music: Dylan Williams. Hd of Sales: June Forbes. CHR/Welsh/Country/Folk[9]

CFM, FM:96.4/102.2/102.5/103.4 PO Box 964, Carlisle, Cumbria CA1 3NG **t** 01228 818964 **f** 01228 819444 **e** studios@cfmradio.com **w** cfmradio.com Prog Controller/Hd of Mus: David Bain. MD: Cathy Kirk. Hd of Sales: Julie Currie. AC[5, 4]

Champion 103 FM, FM:103 Unit D1, Llys Y Dderwen, Parc Menai, Bangor, Gwynedd LL57 4BN **t** 01248 671888 **f** 01248 671971 **e** admin@mfm.musicradio.com **w** musicradio.com Prog Controller: Steve Simms. MD: Sarah Smithard. Prog Dir: Graham Ledger. Hd of Sales: Clive Douthwaite. MOR/Welsh[9]

Channel 103 FM, FM:103.7 6 Tunnell St, St Helier, Jersey, Channel Islands JE2 4LU **t** 01534 888103 **f** 01534 887799 **e** firstname@channel103.com **w** channel103.com Prog Controller: Matt Howells. MD: Linda Burnam. Sales Dir: Jenny Rhodes. AC[14]

96.9 Chiltern FM, FM:96.9 Broadcast Centre, 55 Goldington Rd, Bedford MK40 3LT **t** 01234 272400 **f** 01234 235009 **e** firstname.lastname@musicradio.com **w** musicradio.com Prog Cont: Stuart Davies. Hd of Music: Simon Marshall. Hd of Sales: Francis Flanagan. AC[11, 10]

97.6 Chiltern FM, FM:97.6 Chiltern Rd, Dunstable, Bedfordshire LU6 1HQ **t** 01582 676200 **f** 01582 676201 **e** firstname.surname@musicradio.com **w** musicradio.com Prog Controller: Stuart Davies. Hd of Music: Ben Dudley. Hd of Sales: Francis Flanagan. AC[11, 10]

Choice FM London, FM:96.9/107.1 291-299 Borough High St, London SE1 1JG **t** 020 7378 3969 **f** 020 7378 3911 **e** info@choicefm.com **w** choicefm.com Hd of Sales: Jeff Thomas. MD, Choice FM: Graham Bryce. Programming Controller: Ivor Etienne. Hd of Music: Kirk Anthony. Dance/Reggae/Soul/R&B[11]

Radio City 96.7, FM:96.7 St. John's Beacon, 1 Houghton St, Liverpool, Merseyside L1 1RL **t** 0151 472 6800 **f** 0151 472 6821 **e** firstname.lastname@radiocity.co.uk **w** radiocity.co.uk MD: Tom Hunter. Programming Dir: Richard Maddock. Sales Dir: Tracy King. CHR**[7]**

CKR FM (Carlow/Kildare), FM:97.3/97.6/107.4 Lismard House, Tullow St, Carlow, Ireland **t** +353 503 41044 **f** +353 503 41047 **e** info@ckrfm.ie **w** ckrfm.ie Station Manager: Terry Martin. Chief Exec/Prog Controller: Seamus Reddy. Hd of Sales: Dolores Gorman. AC**[15]**

Clan FM, FM:107.5/107.9 Radio House, Rowantree Ave, Newhouse Industrial Estate, Newhouse, Lanarkshire ML1 5RX **t** 01698 733107 **f** 01698 733318 **e** studio@clanfm.com **w** clanfm.com MD: Darren Stenhouse. Station Mgr: Janis Melville. AC**[3]**

Clare FM, FM:96.4/95.2/95.5/95.9 Abbeyfield Centre, Francis St, Ennis, Co. Clare, Ireland **t** +353 65 682 8888 **f** +353 65 682 9392 **e** info@clarefm.ie **w** clarefm.ie Prog Dir/Hd of Music: Pat Flynn. MD: Liam O'Shea. Hd of Sales: Susan Murphy. MOR[15]

Classic FM, FM:100.0/102.0 Classic FM House, 7 Swallow Place, Oxford Circus, London W1B 2AG **t** 020 7343 9000 **f** 020 7344 2703 **e** enquiries@classicfm.com **w** classicfm.com MD/Prog Dir: Darren Henley. Hd of Sales: Simon Daglish. Hd of Music: Joanna Wilson. Classical

Classic Gold 1260, AM:1260 PO Box 2020, One Passage St, Bristol BS99 7SN **t** 0117 984 3200 **f** 0117 984 3202 **e** admin@classicgolddigital.com **w** classicgolddigital.com Network Prog Controller: Don Douglas. MD: John Baish. Deputy Prog Controllers: Paul Baker and Tim Allen. AC[8, 12]

Classic Gold 1332 AM, AM:1332 PO Box 225, Queensgate Centre, Peterborough, Cambridgeshire PE1 1XJ **t** 01733 460460 **f** 01733 281445 **e** admin@classicgolddigital.com **w** classicgolddigital.com Prog Controller: Don Douglas. Sales Centre Mgr: Charlotte Durrant. Gold[10]

Classic Gold 1359, AM:1359 Hertford Place, Coventry, West Midlands CV1 3TT **t** 024 7686 8200 **f** 024 7686 8202 **e** admin@classicgolddigital.com **w** classicgolddigital.com Network Prog Controller: Don Douglas. Gold[8]

Classic Gold 1431/1485, AM:1431/1485 PO Box 2020, Reading, Berkshire RG31 7FG **t** 0118 945 4400 **f** 0118 928 8483 **e** admin@classicgolddigital.com **w** classicgolddigital.com Network Prog Controller: Don Douglas. Gold[11]

Classic Gold 1557, AM:1557 19-21 St Edmunds Rd, Northampton, Northants. NN1 5DY **t** 01604 795600 **f** 01604 795601 **e** admin@classicgolddigital.com **w** classicgolddigital.com Network Prog Controller: Don Douglas. Gold[8, 10]

Classic Gold Digital 666 & 954, AM:666/954 Hawthorn House, Exeter Business Park, Exeter, Devon EX1 3QS **t** 01392 444444 **f** 01392 354202 **e** admin@classicgolddigital.com **w** classicgolddigital.com Network Prog Controller: Don Douglas. Gold[13]

Classic Gold 774, AM:774 Bridge Studios, Eastgate Centre, Gloucester GL1 1SS **t** 01452 313200 **f** 01452 529446 **e** admin@classicgolddigital.com **w** classicgolddigital.com Network Prog Controller: Don Douglas. Gold[8]

Classic Gold 792/828, AM:792/828 Broadcast Centre, Chiltern Rd, Dunstable, Bedfordshire LU6 1HQ **t** 01582 676200 **f** 01582 676251 **e** admin@classicgolddigital.com **w** classicgolddigital.com Network Prog Controller: Don Douglas. Gold[10]

Classic Gold 828, AM:828 5-7 Southcote Rd, Bournemouth, Dorset BH1 3LR **t** 01202 259259 **f** 01202 255244 **e** admin@classicgolddigital.com **w** classicgolddigital.com Network Prog Controller: Don Douglas. Gold**[12]**

Classic Gold 936/1161 AM, AM:936/1161 PO Box 2000, Swindon, Wiltshire SN4 7EX **t** 01793 842600 **f** 01793 842602 **e** admin@classicgolddigital.com **w** classicgolddigital.com Network Prog Controller: Don Douglas. Gold/Chart[12]

Classic Gold Amber, AM:1152 St George's Plain, 47-49 Colegate, Norwich, Norfolk NR3 1DB **t** 01603 666000 **f** 01603 671167 **e** admin@classicgolddigital.com **w** classicgolddigital.com Network Prog Cont: Don Douglas. Gold[10]

Classic Gold Amber (Suffolk), AM:1170/1251 Alpha Business Park, 6-12 Whitehouse Rd, Ipswich, Suffolk IP1 5LT **t** 01473 744544 **f** 01473 741200 **e** admin@classicgolddigital.com **w** classicgolddigital.com Network Prog Controller: Don Douglas. Gold[10]

Classic Gold Breeze, AM:1359/1431 Radio House, Clifftown Rd, Southend-on-Sea, Essex SS1 1SX **t** 01702 333711 **f** 01702 333686 **e** admin@classicgolddigital.com **w** classicgolddigital.com Network Prog Cont: Don Douglas. Gold[11]

Classic Gold Digital 1152, AM:1152 Earls Acre, Alma Rd, Plymouth, Devon PL3 4HX **t** 01752 227272 **f** 01752 670730 **e** admin@classicgolddigital.com **w** classicgolddigital.com Network Prog Cont: Don Douglas. Gold[13]

Classic Gold 1521, AM:1521 The Stanley Centre, Kelvin Way, Crawley, West Sussex RH10 2SE **t** 01293 519161 **f** 01293 565663 **e** admin@classicgolddigital.com **w** classicgolddigital.com Network Prog Cont: Don Douglas. Gold[8, 11]

Classic Gold GEM, AM:945/999 29-31 Castle Gate, Nottingham NG1 7AP **t** 0115 952 7000 **f** 0115 912 9333 **e** admin@classicgolddigital.com **w** classicgolddigital.com Network Prog Cont: Don Douglas. Gold[8]

Classic Gold Marcher, AM:1260 The Studios, Mold Rd, Gwersyllt, Wrexham, Clwyd LL11 4AF **t** 01978 571818 **f** 01978 722209 **e** admin@classicgolddigital.com **w** classicgolddigital.com Network Prog Cont: Don Douglas. Gold[9]

Classic Gold WABC, AM:990/1017 267 Tettenhall Rd, Wolverhampton, West Midlands WV6 0DE **t** 01902 461300 **f** 01902 461299 **e** cgdl@classicgolddigital.com **w** classicgolddigital.com Network Prog Controller: Don Douglas. Gold[8]

West Yorkshire's Classic Gold, AM:1278/1530 Pennine House, Forster Square, Bradford, West Yorkshire BD1 5NE **t** 01274 203040 **f** 01274 203130 **e** westyorkshire@classicgolddigital.com **w** classicgolddigital.com/westyorkshire Prog Controller: Simon Walkington. MD: Esther Morton. Hd of Music: Tony Simon. Hd of Sales: Tony Wilkinson. Gold[10]

Classic Hits 954/1530AM Herefordshire & Worcester, AM:954/1530 Otherton Lane, Cotheridge, Worcester WR6 5ZE **t** 01905 740600 **f** 01905 740608 **e** studio@classichits.co.uk **w** classichits.co.uk Prog Cont/Hd of Music: Tim Boswell. MD & Hd of Sales: Chris Jeffries. Gold/Sport[8]

Classic VRN 1287, AM:1287 PO Box 1287, Kirkcaldy KY2 5SX **t** 01592 268530 **e** info@vrn1287.com **w** vrn1287.com Prog Dir: Sandy Izatt. MD: Hal London. MOR[3]

BBC Radio Cleveland, FM:95.0/95.8 PO Box 95FM, Broadcasting House, Newport Rd, Middlesborough, Cleveland TS1 5DG **t** 01642 225211 **f** 01642 211356 **e** bbcradiocleveland@bbc.co.uk **w** bbc.co.uk/tees Programmes Editor: Paul Smith. Managing Editor: Andrew Glover. Gold[5]

Club Asia Radio London, AM:963/972 Asia House, 227-247 Gascoigne Rd, Barking, Essex IG8 8LX **t** 020 8594 6662 **f** 020 8594 3523 **e** info@clubasiaonline.com **w** clubasiaonline.com Prog Dir: Sumerah Ahmad. Asian/Chart[11]

Clyde 1 FM, FM:102.5/97.0/103.3 Clydebank Business Park, Clydebank, Glasgow G81 2RX **t** 0141 565 2200 **f** 0141 565 2301 **e** Info@RadioClyde.com **w** RadioClyde.com Hd of Music: Paul Saunders. MD: Paul Cooney. Prog Cont-Clyde 1 & 2: Ross Macfadyen. Sales Dir: Tracey McNellan. CHR[3]

Clyde 2, AM:1152 Clydebank Business Park, Clydebank, Glasgow G81 2RX **t** 0141 565 2200 **f** 0141 565 2301 **e** Info@RadioClyde.com **w** RadioClyde.com Prog Cont-Clyde 1 & 2: Ross Macfadyen. MD: Paul Cooney. Sales Dir: Tracey McNellan. AOR/MOR[3]

CMRPulse Radio, FM:7.38/7.56 PO Box 7218, Hook, Hampshire RG27 8WG **t** 01252 842750 or 07956 888587 **f** 01252 842279 **e** cmr@cix.co.uk **w** cmrpulse.com MD: Lee Williams. Hd of Sales: Sarah Lawrenson. Country/Rock[11]

Coast 96.3 FM, FM:96.3 PO Box 963, Bangor LL57 4ZR **t** 01248 673272 **f** 01248 671971 **e** admin@mfm.musicradio.com **w** musicradio.com Prog Cont: Steve Simms. MD: Sarah Smithard. Grp Prog Dir: Graham Ledger. Hd of Sales: Clive Douthwaite. AC/CHR[9]

Compass FM 96.4, FM:96.4 26A Wellowgate, Grimsby, NE Lincs DN32 0RA **t** 01472 346666 **f** 01472 508811 **e** enquiries@compassfm.co.uk **w** compassfm.co.uk Prog Mgr/Hd of Music: Andy Marsh. Dir of Programming: Jane Hill. Hd of Sales: Chris Greig. Gold/MOR[6]

Connect FM, FM:97.2/107.4 Unit 1, Robinson Close, Telford Way, Kettering, Northants. NN16 8PU **t** 01536 412413 **f** 01536 517390 **e** info@connectfm.com **w** connectfm.com Prog Dir: Danny Gibson. Station Manager/Hd of Sales: Martyn Parr. AC[8]

Cool FM, FM:97.4 PO Box 974, Belfast, Co Antrim BT1 1RT **t** 028 9181 7181 **f** 028 9181 4974 **e** music@coolfm.co.uk **w** coolfm.co.uk Prog Dir/Hd of Music: John Paul Ballantine. MD: David Sloan. Hd of Sales: Richard Collett. CHR/AC[1]

Core, FM:(DAB Digital Radio) PO Box 2269, London W1A 5UQ **t** 020 7911 7300 **f** 020 7911 7302 **e** fresh@corefreshhits.com **w** corefreshhits.com Station Manager: Nick Piggott. Hd of Music: Bern Leckie. Hd of Sales: Steve Cray. Chart

Cork 96 FM, FM:96.4/103/103.7 Wellington Rd, Patrick's Place, Cork, Ireland **t** +353 21 4551596 **f** +353 21 4551500 **e** info@96fm.ie **w** 96fm.ie Prog Dir: Neil Prendeville. Station Manager: Ronan MacManamy. Hd of Music: Steve Hayes. Sales Dir: Sean Barry. Chart/Gold[15]

BBC Radio Cornwall, AM:657/630 FM:95.2/96/103.9 Phoenix Wharf, Truro, Cornwall TR1 1UA **t** 01872 275421 **f** 01872 275045 **e** radio.cornwall@bbc.co.uk **w** bbc.co.uk/radiocornwall Gram Librarian: Kath Peters. Managing Editor: Pauline Causey AC[13]

County Sound 1566 AM, AM:1566 Dolphin House, North St, Guildford, Surrey GU1 4AA **t** 01483 300964 **f** 01483 531612 **e** onair@countysound.co.uk **w** countysound.co.uk Prog Controller: Dave Johns. MD: Val Handley. Hd of Music: Mark Chivers/Stuart Clark. Hd of Sales: Sue Payne. AC/MOR[11]

BBC Coventry & Warwickshire, FM:94.8/103.7/104.0 Holt Court, 1 Greyfriars Rd, Coventry, West Midlands CV1 2WR **t** 024 7686 0086 **f** 024 7657 0100 **e** coventry@bbc.co.uk **w** bbc.co.uk/coventrywarwickshire Senior Broadcast Journ.: Sue Curtis. Station Manager: Keith Beech. Prog Dir: Tony Wadsworth. Hd of Music: Steve Woodhall. AC[8]

BBC Radio Cumbria, AM:756/837/1458 FM:95.6/96.1/95.2/104.2/104.1 Annetwell St, Carlisle, Cumbria CA3 8BB **t** 01228 592444 **f** 01228 511195 **e** radio.cumbria@bbc.co.uk **w** bbc.co.uk/radiocumbria SBJ/Programmes/Music: Paul Teague. Managing Editor: Nigel Dyson. MOR [5, 4]

Dearne FM, FM:97.1/102 Unit 7, Network Centre, Zenith Park, Whaley Rd, Barnsley S75 1HT **t** 01226 321733 **f** 01226 321755 **e** enquiries@dearnefm.co.uk **w** dearnefm.co.uk Prog Mgr: Paul Bromley. Hd of Sales: Sarah Hardy. CHR[6]

Dee 106.3, FM:106.3 2 Chantry Court, Chester CH1 4QN **t** 01244 391000 **f** 01244 391010 **e** studio@dee1063.com **w** dee1063.com Prog Dir/Hd of Music: Chris Buckley. Station Mgr & Hd of Sales: Sarah Vel. AC[7]

Delta FM 97.1, FM:97.1/101.6/102 65 Weyhill, Haslemere, Surrey GU27 1HN **t** 01428 651971 **f** 01428 658971 **e** news@deltaradio.co.uk **w** deltaradio.co.uk MD: David Wey. Prog Manager: Bill Sheldrake. Hd of Sales: Andy Wise. AC[11]

BBC Radio Derby, AM:1116 FM:104.5/95.3 PO Box 104.5, Derby DE1 3HL **t** 01332 361111 **f** 01332 290794 **e** radio.derby@bbc.co.uk **w** bbc.co.uk/derby Managing Editor: Simon Cornes. Hd of Programmes: David Harvey. Hd of Music: Bev Pickles. MOR/Pop[8]

BBC Radio Devon, AM:855/990/1458/801 FM:103.4/104.3/95.8/94.8/96.0 Broadcasting House, Seymour Rd, Plymouth, Devon PL3 5YQ **t** 01752 260323 **f** 01752 234564 **e** devon.online@bbc.co.uk **w** bbc.co.uk/radiodevon Managing Editor: John Lilley. Hd of Programmes: Ian Timms. Hd of Music: Matt Woodley. MOR[13]

Digital One, FM:Digital 20 Southampton St, London WC1E 7QH **t** 020 7288 4600 **f** 020 7288 4601 **e** info@digitalone.co.uk **w** ukdigitalradio.com Press Manager: Mandy Green. Chief Executive: Quentin Howard.

Downtown Radio/DTR, AM:1026 FM:96.4/96.6/97.1/102.3/102.4 Newtownards, Co Down BT23 4ES **t** 028 9181 5555 **f** 028 9181 5252 or 028 9181 8913 **e** programmes@downtown.co.uk **w** downtown.co.uk Hd of Music: Eddie West. MD/Prog Dir: David Sloan. Hd of Sales: Richard Collett. CHR/AC[1]

Dream 100, FM:100.2 Northgate House, St Peter's St, Colchester, Essex CO1 1HT **t** 01206 764466 **f** 01206 715102 **e** info@dream100.com **w** dream100.com Prog Cont/Hd of Music: Jonathan Hemmings. MD: Jamie Broadie. Hd of Sales: Mark Bird. AC[11]

Dream 107.7FM, FM:107.7 Cater House, High St, Chelmsford, Essex CM1 1AL **t 01245 259400 f** 01245 259558 **e** reception@dream107.com **w** dream107.com Station Mgr: Martyn Davies. Prog Mgr: Nick Hull. Hd of Music: John Leech. Hd of Sales: Annabelle Smail. AC[12]

Dublin's 98 FM, FM:98 The Malt House - South Block, Grand Canal Quay, Dublin 2, Ireland **t** +353 1 670 8970 **f** +353 1 670 8969 **e** online@98fm.ie **w** 98fm.ie Prog Dir: John Taylor. Station Manager: Dan Healy. Hd of Sales: Micheal Brady. AC[15]

Dublin's Country 106.8FM, FM:106.8 Radio Centre, Killarney Rd, Bray, Co. Wicklow, Ireland **t** +353 1 272 4770 **f** +353 1 272 4753 **e** mail@dublins1068.com **w** dublins1068.com Prog Dir: Robert Walshe. CEO: Sean Ashmore. Hd of Sales: Brian McGrath. MOR[15]

Dune FM, FM:107.9 The Power Station, Victoria Way, Southport, Merseyside PR8 1RR **t** 01704 502500 **f** 01704 502540 **e** info@dunefm.co.uk **w** dunefm.co.uk Station Mgr/Hd of Sales: Rob Halsall. Prog Mgr/Hd of Music: Jonathan Dean. AC[7]

96.4 The Eagle, FM:96.4 Dolphin House, North St, Guildford, Surrey GU1 4AA **t** 01483 300964 **f** 01483 531612 **e** onair@964eagle.co.uk **w** 964eagle.co.uk Prog Dir: Peter Gordon. MD: Val Handley. Hd of Music: Mark Chivers. Hd of Sales: Sue Payne. AC[11]

East Coast FM, FM:94.9/96.2/102.9/104.4 Radio Centre, Bray South Business Park, Bray, Co Wicklow, Ireland **t** +353 1 272 4700 **f** +353 1 272 4701 **e** mail@eastcoast.fm **w** eastcoast.fm Prog Dir/Hd of Music: Joe Harrington. Station Manager: Ciara O'Connor. Hd of Sales: Helen Clune. AC[15]

Easy Radio London 1035, AM:1035/DAB 43-51 Wembley Hill Rd, Wembley, London HA9 8AU **t** 020 8795 1035 **f** 020 8902 9657 **e** info@easy1035.com **w** easy1035.com Prog Controller: Natalie King. Station Manager/Sales Dir: Steve Wood. Country[11]

BBC Essex, AM:729/1530/765 FM:103.5/95.3 198 New London Rd, Chelmsford, Essex CM2 9XB **t** 01245 616000 **f** 01245 616025 **e** essex@bbc.co.uk **w** bbc.co.uk/essex Managing Editor: Margaret Hyde. Hd of Music: Steve Scruton. Programmes Editor: Tim Gillett. Assistant Editor: Lynne Wilson. Gold[11]

Essex FM, FM:96.3/102.6 Radio House, 19-20 Clifftown Rd, Southend-on-Sea, Essex SS1 1SX **t** 01702 333711 **f** 01702 345224 **e** firstname.lastname@musicradio.com **w** musicradio.com Programming Controller: Chris Cotton. Hd of Music: James Bassam. Hd of Sales: Brent Coulson. AC/Chart[11]

Fen Radio 107.5, FM:107.5 5 Church Mews, Wisbech, Cambridgeshire PE13 1HL **t 01945 467107 f** 01945 467464 **e** firstname.lastname@fenradio.co.uk **w** fenradio.co.uk Prog Mgr: Richard Grant. Group Prog Dir: Phil Angell. Hd of Music: Freddie Scherer. Sales Exec: Kathryn Vithray. Rock[10]

Fire 107.6, FM:107.6 PO Box 1234, Bournemouth, Dorset BH1 2AD **t** 01202 318100 **f** 01202 318110 **e** firstname@fire1076.com **w** fire1076.com Brand Manager: Max Hailey. Hd of Music: Paul Gerrard. Commercial Mgr: Jason Cawley. CHR/Rhythmic Contemporary[12]

BBC Radio 5 Live, AM:693/909 Room 2605, BBC TV Centre, London W12 7RJ **t** 020 8743 8000 **f** 020 8624 9588 **e** firstname.lastname@bbc.co.uk **w** bbc.co.uk/radio5live Controller: Bob Shennan. Hd of News: Cery Thomas. Hd of Network Management: Michael Hill. News/Sport

FM 102 The Bear, FM:102 The Guard House Studios, Banbury Rd, Stratford upon Avon, Warwickshire CV37 7HX **t** 01789 262636 **f** 01789 263102 **e** info@thebear.co.uk **w** thebear.co.uk Station Dir/Sales: Christine Arnold. Prog Mgr/Hd of Music: Steve Hyden. AC/MOR[8]

FM 104, FM:104.4 Hume House, Pembroke Rd, Balls Bridge, Dublin 4, Ireland **t** +353 1 500 6600 **f** +353 1 668 9401 **e** Firstname+initial@fm104.ie **w** fm104.ie Prog Dir: Dave Kelly. Hd of Music: Declan Pierce. Hd of Sales: Margaret Nelson. CHR[15]

Forth One, FM:97.3/97.6/102.2 Forth House, Forth St, Edinburgh, Lothian EH1 3LE **t** 0131 556 9255 **f** 0131 558 3277 **e** info@forthone.com **w** forthone.com Hd of Music: Sam Jackson. MD: Adam Findlay. Hd of Sales: Craig Lumsdaine. CHR[3]

Forth 2, AM:1548 Forth House, Forth St, Edinburgh, Lothian EH1 3LE **t** 0131 556 9255 **f** 0131 558 3277 **e** info@forth2.com **w** forth2.com Hd of Music: Sam Jackson. MD: Adam Findlay. Hd of Sales: Craig Lumsdaine. AC/Gold[3]

Fosseway Radio, FM:107.9 1 Castle St, Hinckley, Leicestershire LE10 1DA **t** 01455 614151 **f** 01455 616888 **e** enquiries@fossewayradio.co.uk **w** fossewayradio.co.uk Grp Prog Mgr: Jane Hill. Station Manager: Ian Ison. Group Hd of Music: Eddie Shaw. Sales Mgr: Sarah Washington. AC/Gold[8]

BBC Radio 4, FM:92.4/94.6 Broadcasting House, Portland Place, London W1A 1AA **t** 020 7580 4468 **f** 020 7765 3421 **e** firstname.lastname@bbc.co.uk **w** bbc.co.uk/radio4 Controller: Helen Boaden.

Fox FM, FM:97.4/102.6 Brush House, Pony Rd, Cowley, Oxfordshire OX4 2XR **t** 01865 871000 **f** 01865 871036 or 01865 871038 **e** reception@foxfm.co.uk **w** foxfm.co.uk Prog Controller: Sam Walker. Hd of Music: Adam Ball. Commercial Controller: Max Patey. AC[8]

Fresh Radio, AM:936/1413/1431 Firth Mill, Skipton, North Yorks BD23 2PT **t** 01756 799991 **f** 01756 799771 **e** info@freshradio.co.uk **w** freshradio.co.uk MD: Dave Parker. Prog Manager: Nick Bewes. Sales Mgr: Paul Mallett. AC[5, 6]

Galaxy 102 FM, FM:102.0 5th Floor, The Triangle, Hanging Ditch, Manchester M4 3TR **t** 0161 279 0300 **f** 0161 279 0303 **e** firstname.lastname@galaxy102.co.uk **w** galaxy102.co.uk Prog Dir: Vaughan Hobbs. MD: David Lloyd. Hd of Sales: Bev Holmes. Dance/Urban[7]

Galaxy 102.2, FM:102.2 1 The Square, 111 Broad St, Birmingham B15 1AS **t** 0121 695 0000 **f** 0121 696 1007 **e** firstname.lastname@galaxy1022.co.uk **w** galaxy1022.co.uk Prog Ctlr/Hd of Music: Neil Greenslade. MD: Paul Fairburn. Hd of Sales: Anita Wright. Urban[8]

Galaxy 105, FM:105.1/105.8 Joseph's Well, Hanover Walk, Leeds, West Yorkshire LS3 1AB **t** 0113 213 0105 **f** 0113 213 1054 **e** mail@galaxy105.co.uk **w** galaxy105.co.uk Prog Dir: Mike Cass. MD: David Lloyd. Hd of Sales: Bev Holmes. Dance/Urban**[6]**

Galaxy 105-106, FM:105.3/105.6/105.8/106.4 Kingfisher Way, Silverlink Business Park, Tyne & Wear NE28 9NX **t** 0191 206 8000 **f** 0191 206 8080 **e** reception@galaxy1056.co.uk **w** galaxy1056.co.uk Prog Dir: Matt McClure. MD: Martyn Healy. Hd of Music: Dan Archer. Hd of Sales: Ian Trotter. Dance[5]

Galway Bay FM, FM:95.8/96.0/96.8/97.4 Sandy Rd, Galway City, Galway, Ireland **t** +353 91 770000 **f** +353 91 752689 **e** info@galwaybayfm.ie **w** gbfm.galway.net CEO: Keith Finnegan. Hd of Music: John Richards. Hd of Sales: Paddy Madden. MOR/CHR[15]

Gemini FM, FM:97/96.4/103 Hawthorn House, Exeter Business Park, Exeter, Devon EX1 3QS **t** 01392 444444 **f** 01392 444433 **e** firstname.lastname@musicradio.com **w** musicradio.com Prog Cont/HoM: Gavin Marshall. Sales Centre Manager: Sara Burnell. Prog Mgr (Torquay): Al Dunn. CHR/Gold[13]

BBC Radio Gloucestershire, AM:1413 FM:104.7/95.8/95 London Rd, Gloucester GL1 1SW **t** 01452 308585 **f** 01452 306541 **e** radio.gloucestershire@bbc.co.uk **w** bbc.co.uk/radiogloucestershire Grams Librarian: Chris Fowler. Managing Editor: Mark Hurell. Hd of Programmes: David Aston. Hd of Music: Anna King. MOR[8]

BBC GMR (BBC Greater Manchester Radio), FM:95.1/104.6 PO Box 951, New Broadcasting House, Oxford Rd, Manchester M60 1SD **t** 0161 200 2020 **f** 0161 236 5804 **e** manchester.online@bbc.co.uk **w** bbc.co.uk/manchester Managing Editor: Steve Taylor. Prog Dir/Hd of Music: Lawrence Mann. AOR[7]

GTFM, FM:106.9 Pinewood Studios, Pinewood Avenue, Rhydyfelin, Pontypridd CF37 5EA **t** 01443 406111 **f** 01443 492744 **e** andrew@gtfm.co.uk **w** gtfm.co.uk Station Mgr/Prog Dir: Andrew Jones. CHR[9]

BBC Radio Guernsey, AM:116 FM:93.2 Commerce House, Les Banques, St Peter Port, Guernsey, Channel Islands GY1 2HS **t** 01481 728977 **f** 01481 713557 **e** radio.guernsey@bbc.co.uk **w** bbc.co.uk/radioguernsey Editor: Robert Wallace. Hd of Music: John Randall. Gold[14]

GWR FM, FM:96.3/103 PO Box 2000, 1 Passage St, Bristol BS99 7SN **t** 0117 984 3200 **f** 0117 984 3208 **e** firstname.lastname@musicradio.com **w** musicradio.com Prog Cont: Paul Andrew. Grp Hd of Music: Caroline Murphy. Hd of Sales: David Wenn. AC[8, 9]

GWR FM., FM:103/97.2/102.2 PO Box 2000, Wootton Bassett, Swindon, Wiltshire SN4 7EX **t** 01793 842600 **f** 01793 842602 **e** firstname.lastname@musicradio.com **w** musicradio.com Prog Controller: Sue Carter. Regional Sales Dir: Steve Jones. CHR[8, 12]

Hallam FM, FM:97.4/102.9/103.4 Radio House, 900 Herries Rd, Sheffield, South Yorkshire S6 1RH **t** 0114 209 1000 **f** 0114 285 3159 **e** programmes@hallamfm.co.uk **w** hallamfm.co.uk Temp Prog Dir: Paul Chantler. MD: Iain Clasper. Hd of Music: Chris Straw. Hd of Sales: Adrian Serle. CHR[6]

Heart 106.2, FM:106.2 The Chrysalis Building, Bramley Rd, London W10 6SP **t** 020 7468 1062 **f** 020 7465 6196 **e** onlineenquiries@heart1062.co.uk **w** heart1062.co.uk Prog Dir: Francis Currie. MD: Steve Parkinson. Hd of Sales: Gerrard Bridges. Hd of Music: Russ Evans. AC[11]

Heart FM 100.7, FM:100.7 1 The Square, 111 Broad St, Birmingham, West Midlands B15 1AS **t** 0121 695 0000 **f** 0121 696 1007 **e** heartfm@heartfm.co.uk **w** heartfm.co.uk Prog Dir: Alan Carruthers. MD: Paul Fairburn. Hd of Sales: Anita Wright. AC[8]

Heartland FM, FM:97.5 Lower Oakfield, Pitlochry, Perthshire PH16 5DS **t** 01796 474040 **f** 01796 474007 **e** mailbox@heartlandfm.co.uk **w** heartlandfm.co.uk Prog Dir/Hd of Music: Pete Ramsden. Hd of Sales: Georgina Lee. Soft AC/MOR/Speech[3]

Media

BBC Hereford & Worcester, AM:738 FM:94.7/104/104.6 Hylton Rd, Worcester WR2 5WW **t** 01905 748485 **f** 01905 337209 **e** worcester@bbc.co.uk **w** bbc.co.uk/herefordandworcester Managing Editor: James Coghill. News Editor: Mark Hellings. Programmes Editor: Glyn Johnson. Hereford Editor: Jane Gething-Lewis. AC[8]

102.7 Hereward FM, FM:102.7 PO Box 225, 98 Queensgate Centre, Peterborough, Cambridgeshire PE1 1XJ **t** 01733 460460 **f** 01733 281444 **e** firstname.lastname@musicradio.com **w** musicradio.com Prog Ctrl: Paul Green. Hd of Music: Matt Jarvis. Sales Centre Mgr: Phil Caborn. Chart/Gold[10]

HertBeat FM, FM:106.9/106.7 The Pump House, Knebworth Park, Hertford SG3 6HQ **t** 01438 810900 **f** 01438 815100 **e** info@hertbeat.com **w** hertbeat.com Prog Dir: Robbie Owen. Station Mgr/Hd of Sales: Darrell Thomas. Hd of Music: Tony James. AC[10]

Highland Radio, FM:95.2/103.3/94.7 Pine Hill, Letterkenny, Co Donegal, Ireland **t** +353 74 25000 **f** +353 74 25344 **e** enquiries@highlandradio.com **w** highlandradio.com Hd of Prog & Music: Linda McGroarty. MD/Hd of Sales: Charlie Collins. Hd of Promotions: Shaun Doherty. AC/Gold[15]

Home 107.9, FM:107.9 The Old Stableblock, Brewery Drive, Lockwood Park, Huddersfield HD1 3UR **t** 01484 321107 **f** 01484 311107 or 01484 311079 **e** info@home1079.co.uk **w** home1079.co.uk Brand Manager: Nick Hancock. MD: Phil Chadderton. Sales Manager: Ursula Johnson. Gold[6]

FM 103 Horizon, FM:103.3 14 Vincent Ave, Crownhill, Milton Keynes, Bucks MK8 0AB **t** 01908 269111 **f** 01908 591619 **e** firstname.lastname@musicradio.com **w** musicradio.com Prog Controller: Trevor Marshall. Hd of Music: Mark Sherry. Sales Manager: Iam Stuart. CHR[10]

BBC Humber, AM:1485 FM:95.9 9 Chapel St, Hull, East Yorkshire HU1 3NU **t** 01482 323232 **f** 01482 226409 **e** humber.online@bbc.co.uk **w** bbc.co.uk/radiohumberside Hd of Music: Sue Craft. Managing Editor: Helen Thomas. MOR[6]

Imagine FM, FM:104.9 Regent House, Heaton Lane, Stockport, Cheshire SK4 1BX **t** 0161 609 1400 **f** 0161 609 1401 **e** firstname.lastname@imaginefm.net **w** imaginefm.net Station Dir: Danny Holborn. Programming Controller: Ashley Byrne. Hd of Music: Paul Willett. Sales Mgr: Daniel Vincent. AC[7]

Independent Radio News Ltd, 200 Gray's Inn Rd, London WC1X 8XZ **t** 020 7430 4090 **f** 020 7430 4092 **e** news@irn.co.uk **w** irn.co.uk MD: John Perkins. Senior Editor: Jon Godel. News

Inflight Productions, 15 Stukeley St, London WC2B 5LT **t** 020 7400 0700 **f** 020 7400 0707 **e** firstname.lastname@inflightproductions.com **w** inflightproductions.com MD: Steve Harvey. Airline radio progs.

Invicta FM, FM:95.9/96.1/97/102.8/103.1 Radio House, John Wilson Business Park, Whitstable, Kent CT5 3QX **t** 01227 772004 **f** 01227 774450 **e** reception@invictaradio.co.uk **w** invictafm.com Prog Cont/Hd of Musi: Rebecca Trbojevich. Commercial Controller: Emma Liddiard. Marketing Cont: Mark Almond. AC[11, 12]

Island FM, FM:104.7/93.7 12 Westerbrook, St Sampson, Guernsey GY2 4QQ **t** 01481 242000 **f** 01481 249676 **e** news@islandfm.guernsey.net **w** islandfm.guernsey.net MD: Nick Creed. Prog Controller: Gary Burgess. Hd of Music: Carl Ward. Hd of Sales: Sue Campanella. CHR/AC[14]

Isle Of Wight Radio, FM:102/107 Dodnor Park, Newport, Isle Of Wight PO30 5XE **t** 01983 822557 **f** 01983 822109 **e** admin@iwradio.co.uk **w** iwradio.co.uk MD/Station Mgr: Andy Shier. Prog Controller: Tom Stroud. Hd of Sales: Sue Hudson. AC/Gold[12]

Isles FM 103, FM:103 PO Box 333, Stornoway, Isle Of Lewis, Western Isles HS1 2PU **t** 01851 703333 **f** 01851 703322 **e** studio@isles.fm **w** isles.fm Hd of Music: A.J. Kennedy. Station Mgrs: A.J. Kennedy & Kathleen Maciver. Progr Cont: David Morrison. Hd of Sales: Lionel Sewell. MOR/Scottish/Gaelic/News[2]

102.2 Jazz FM, FM:102.2 26-27 Castlereagh St, London W1H 5DL **t** 020 7706 4100 **f** 020 7723 9742 **e** music@jazzfm.com **w** jazzfm.com ProgCont/Hd of Music: Mark Walker. MD/Hd of Sales: Carter Tanner. Jazz/Soul/Blues/R'n'B[11]

BBC Radio Jersey, AM:1026 FM:88.8 18 Parade Rd, St Helier, Jersey, Channel Islands JE2 3PA **t** 01534 870000 **f** 01534 631208 **e** jersey@bbc.co.uk **w** bbc.co.uk/jersey Asst. Editor/Programmes: Matthew Price. Managing Editor: Denzil Dudley. Snr Broadcast Journalist/Hd of Music: Roger Bara. MOR/Specialist[14]

Juice 107.2, FM:107.2 170 North St, Brighton, East Sussex BN1 1EA **t** 01273 386107 **f** 01273 273107 **e** info@juicebrighton.com **w** juicebrighton.com MD/Prog Dir/Sales: Matthew Bashford. Hd of Music: Mark Brookes. Chart/Dance/Indie[12]

Juice 107.6 FM, FM:107.6 27 Fleet St, Liverpool L1 4AR **t** 0151 707 3107 **f** 0151 707 3109 **e** mail@juiceliverpool.com **w** juice.fm Prog Dir/Hd of Music: Grainne Landowski. MD: Donnach O'Driscoll. Hd of Sales: Jane Hunt. Dance/Indie**[7]**

KCR 106.7, FM:106.7 Cables Retail Park, Prescot, Merseyside L34 5SW **t** 0151 290 1501 **f** 0151 290 1505 **e** kcr106@btconnect.fm **w** kcr1067.com Prog Cont/Hd of Music: Brian Cullen. MD: Ray Ferguson. Gold[7]

BBC Radio Kent, AM:774 FM:96.7/104.2 The Great Hall, Mount Pleasant Rd, Royal Tunbridge Wells, Kent TN1 1QQ **t** 01892 670000 **f** 01892 549118 **e** radio.kent@bbc.co.uk **w** bbc.co.uk/kent Hd of Music/SBJ: Lynn Wallis-Eade. Managing Editor: Robert Wallace. Prog Dir: Andy Garland. MOR/Chart[11, 12]

Kerrang! Radio, AM:DAB FM:105.2 20 Lionel St, Kerrang! House, Birmingham B3 1AQ **t** 0845 053 1052 **e** kerrangradio@kerrangradio.co.uk **w** kerrangradio.co.uk Prog Dir: Andrew Jeffries. Station Mgr: Travis Baxter. Hd of Music: Adam Uytman. Hd of Sales: Linda Farren. Rock[8]

Radio Kerry, FM:96.2/96.6/97.6 Maine St, Tralee, Kerry, Ireland **t** +353 66 712 366**6** **f** +353 66 712 2282 **e** john@radiokerry.ie **w** radiokerry.ie Prog Dir: John Herlihy. MD: Paul Byrne. Hd of Music: Martin Howard. Hd of Sales: Melanie O'Sullivan. AC[15]

107.6 Kestrel FM, FM:107.6 2nd Floor, Paddington House, The Walks Shopping Centre, Basingstoke, Hampshire RG21 7LJ **t** 01256 694000 **f** 01256 694111 **e** studio@kestrelfm.com **w** kestrelfm.com Prog Manager: Mandy O'Neale. MD: Paul Allen. Hd of Sales: Susan Reynolds. AC[11, 12]

Key 103, FM:103 Castle Quay, Castlefield, Manchester M15 4PR **t** 0161 288 5000 **f** 0161 288 5071 **e** firstname.lastname@key103.co.uk **w** key103.co.uk Prog Dir/Hd of Music: Anthony Gay. MD: Gus MacKenzie. Hd of Sales: Alison Tootill. AC Chart[7]

Kick FM, FM:105.6/107.4 The Studios, 42 Bone Lane, Newbury, Berks RG14 5SD **t** 01635 841600 **f** 01635 841010 **e** mail@kickfm.com **w** kickfm.com Prog Dir: Andy Green. MD: Jeff Lee. Hd of Music: Mark Watson. Hd of Sales: Marie Hughes. Soft AC[11, 12]

Kingdom FM, FM:95.2/96.1/96.6/105.4/106.3 Haig House, Balgonie Rd, Markinch, Fife KY7 6AQ **t** 01592 753753 **f** 01592 757788 **e** kingdomfm@aol.com **w** kingdomfm.co.uk Prog Ctrl: Kevin Brady. Chief Exec: Ian Sewell. Hd of Sales: Linda McCrabbe. AC[3]

Kiss 100 FM, FM:100 Emap Performance, Mappin House, 4 Winsley St, London W1W 8HF **t** 020 7975 8100 **f** 020 7975 8150 **e** firstname.lastname@kiss100.com **w** kiss100.com Grp Prog Dir: Andy Roberts. Prog Dir: Simon Long. Hd of Music: Christian Smith. Prog Assistant: Claire Jago. Dance[11]

Kix 96, FM:96.2 Watch Close, Spon St, Coventry, West Midlands CV1 3LN **t** 024 7652 5656 **f** 024 7655 1744 **e** firstname@kix.fm **w** kix.fm Prog Dir/Hd of Music: Steffan Latouche. MD: Greg Parker. CHR**[8]**

KLFM, FM:96.7 18 Blackfriars St, Kings Lynn, Norfolk PE30 1NN **t** 01553 772777 **f** 01553 766453 **e** admin@klfm967.co.uk **w** klfm967.co.uk Station Mgr: Mark Pryke. Prog Controller: Steve Bradley. Hd of Music: Simon Rowe. Hd of Sales: Jason Smith. Gold[10]

KM-fm (Canterbury, Whitstable and Herne Bay), FM:106 9 St George's Place, Canterbury, Kent CT1 1UU **t** 01227 786106 **f** 01227 785106 **e** cfinn@kmfm.co.uk **w** kentonline.co.uk Prog Mgr: Chris Finn. Group Programming Cont: Mike Osbourne. Grp Hd of Music: Toby MacKenzie. Sales Mgr: Angela Smith. AC[11]

KM-fm (Folkestone, Dover, Sandwich and Deal), FM:96.4/106.8 93-95 Sandgate Rd, Folkestone, Kent CT20 2BQ **t** 01304 202505 **f** 01304 212717 **e** scork@kmradio.co.uk **w** kentonline.co.uk/kmfm Prog Mgr: Spencer Cork. Grp Prog Cont: Mike Osborne. Grp Hd of Music: Toby Mackenzie. Sales Mgr: Sarah Cooper. AC[12]

KM-fm (Thanet), FM:107.2 Imperial House, 2-14 High St, Margate, Kent CT9 1DH **t** 01843 220222 **f** 01843 299666 **e** ajohn@kmfm.co.uk **w** kentonline.co.uk/kmfm Prog Mgr: Adrian John. Grp Prog Cont: Mike Osborne. Grp Hd of Music: Toby Mackenzie. Sales Mgr: James Colton. AC[11, 10]

KM-fm (West Kent), FM:96.2/101.6 1 East St, Tonbridge, Kent TN9 1AR **t** 01732 369200 **f** 01732 369201 **e** bhaywood@kmfm.co.uk **w** kentonline.co.uk/kmfm Prog Mgr: Beccy Haywood. Grp Prog Cont: Mike Osborne. Grp Hd of Music: Toby Mackenzie. Sales Manager: Paul Harvey. AC[11]

Kool AM, PO Box 1072, Edmonton, London N9 0WQ **t** 020 8373 1073 **f** 020 8373 1074 **e** info@c4trt.co.uk **w** koolam.co.uk Group Station Mgr: Steve Saunders. Programming Dir: Joe Bone. Hd of Music: Peter Moore. Hd of Sales: James Fortune. AC[11]

Lakeland Radio, FM:100.1/100.8 Lakeland Food Park, Plumgarths, Crook Rd, Kendal, Cumbria LA8 8QJ **t** 01539 737380 **f** 01539 737390 **e** info@lakelandradio.co.uk **w** lakelandradio.co.uk Station Dir/Sales: Peter Fletcher. Hd of Music: Colin Yare. AC[7, 4]

BBC Radio Lancashire, AM:855/1557 FM:95.5/103.9/104.5 Darwen St, Blackburn, Lancashire BB2 2EA **t** 01254 262411 **f** 01254 680821 **e** radio.lancashire@bbc.co.uk **w** bbc.co.uk/lancashire Managing Editor: John Clayton. Hd of Music: Graham Liver. MOR[7]

Lantern FM, FM:96.2 Unit 2B, Lauder Lane, Barnstable, North Devon EX31 3TA **t** 01271 340340 **f** 01271 340345 **e** paul.hopper@creation.com **w** musicradio.com Prog Cont: Paul Hopper. Station Mgr/Hd of Sales: Jim Trevelyan. MOR[13]

LBC 97.3, AM:1152 FM:97.3 The Chrysalis Building, 13 Bramley Rd, London W10 6SP **t** 020 7314 7300 **f** 020 7314 7317 **e** website@lbc.co.uk **w** lbc.co.uk MD: Mark Flanagan. Editorial Dir: Steve Kyte. Hd of Sales: Gerrard Bridges. News/Current Affairs[11]

BBC Leeds, AM:774 FM:92.4/95.3/102.7/103.9 Broadcasting House, Woodhouse Lane, Leeds, West Yorkshire LS2 9PN **t** 0113 224 7300 **f** 0113 242 0652 **e** radio.leeds@bbc.co.uk **w** bbc.co.uk/leeds; bbc.co.uk/bradford Managing Ed: Ashley Peatfield. Programming Producer: Carmel Harrison. Hd of Music: David Crickmore. News/Talk[6]

BBC Leicester, FM:104.9 Epic House, Charles St, Leicester LE1 3SH **t** 0116 251 6688 **f** 0116 251 1463 **e** radio.leicester@bbc.co.uk **w** bbc.co.uk/radioleicester Hd of Music: Trish Dolman. Managing Editor: Liam McCarthy. AC[8]

Leicester Sound, FM:105.4 6 Dominus Way, Meridian Business Park, Leicester, Leicestershire LE19 1RP **t** 0116 256 1300 **f** 0116 256 1303 **e** firstname.lastname@musicradio.com **w** musicradio.com Prog Cont/Hd of Music: Craig Boddy. Sales Centre Mgr: Caroline Keeley. AC[8]

Limerick's Live 95FM, FM:95/95.3 Radio House, Richmond Court, Dock Rd, Limerick, Ireland **t** +353 61 400195 **f** +353 61 419595 **e** mail@live95fm.ie **w** live95fm.ie Prog Dir: Gary Connor. Hd of Music: Gary Connor. Hd of Sales: Gerry Long. CHR/AC[15]

BBC Radio Lincolnshire, AM:1368 FM:94.9/104.7 PO Box 219, Newport, Lincoln LN1 3XY **t** 01522 511411 **f** 01522 511058 **e** lincolnshire@bbc.co.uk **w** bbc.co.uk/lincolnshire Managing Editor: Charlie Partridge. Prog Editor: Les Sheehan. Hd of Music: Linda Rust. MOR/Gold[6, 8]

Lincs FM 102.2, FM:102.2 Witham Park, Waterside South, Lincoln LN5 7JN **t** 01522 549900 **f** 01522 549911 **e** enquiries@lincsfm.co.uk **w** lincsfm.co.uk Grp Dir of Prog: Jane Hill. Prog Mgr: John Marshall. Hd of Music: Eddie Shaw. Hd of Sales: Chris Grieg. Gold/AC[6, 8]

Lite FM, FM:106.8 2nd Floor, 5 Church St, Peterborough PE1 1XB **t** 01733 898106 **f** 01733 898107 **e** info@Lite1068.com **w** lite1068.com Prog Dir/Hd of Music: Kev Lawerence. MD: Dave Myatt. Hd of Sales: Dawn Trowsdale. AC[10]

LMFM Radio, FM:95.5/95.8/104.9 Broadcasting House, Rathmullen Rd, Drogheda, Co. Louth **t** +353 41 983 2000 **f** +353 41 983 2957 **e** info@lmfm.ie **w** lmfm.ie Prog Dir: Eamonn Doyle. MD: Michael Crawley. Hd of Music: Michael Gerrard. Hd of Sales: Eileen Duggan. Chart/MOR[15]

Lochbroom FM, FM:96.8/102.2 Radio House, Mill St, Ullapool, Ross-shire IV26 2UN **t** 01854 613131 **f** 01854 613132 **e** radio@lochbroomfm.co.uk **w** lochbroomfm.co.uk Station Mgr/Hd of Sales: Kevin Guy. Programming Dir/Hd of Music: Sheena Guy. AOR/Scottish[2]

BBC London, FM:94.9 PO Box 94.9, London W1A 6FL **t** 020 7224 2424 **f** 020 7208 9680 **e** yourlondon@bbc.co.uk **w** bbc.co.uk/london Managing Editor: David Robey. Assistant Editor (Prog Cont): Paul Leaper. Hd of Music: Jim Lahat. AC[11]

London Greek Radio, FM:103.3 LGR House, 437 High Rd, London N12 0AP **t 020 8349 6950 f** 020 8349 6960 **e** sales@lgr.co.uk **w** lgr.co.uk Prog Contr/Hd of Music: George Gregoriou. Station Manager: Kyriakos Tsioutras. Hd of Sales: Chris Harmantas. Greek[11]

London Turkish Radio (LTR), AM:1584 185B High Rd, London N22 6BA **t** 020 8881 0606 or 020 8881 2020 **f** 020 8881 5151 **e** ltr1584am@aol.com **w** londonturkishradio.com MD: Erkhan Pastirmacioglu. Programming Controller: Umit Dandul. Hd of Sales: Kelami Dedezade. Turkish**[11]**

Lyric FM, FM:96/99 Cornmarket Square, Limerick, Ireland **t** +353 61 207300 **f** +353 61 207390 **e** lyric@rte.ie **w** lyricfm.ie Station Mgr/Prog Dir: Aodan O Dubhghaill. Hd of Music: Sean McKenna. Light Classical/Jazz

Magic 1152, AM:1152 Radio House, Longrigg, Swalwell, Newcastle upon Tyne, Tyne and Wear NE99 1BB **t** 0191 420 0971 **f** 0191 488 9222 **e** enquiries@metroandmagic.com **w** metroradio.co.uk Prog Dir: Tony McKenzie. MD: Sally Aitchison. Hd of Music: Alex Roland. Hd of Sales: Kim Miljus. MOR[5]

Magic 1152 (Manchester), AM:1152 Castle Quay, Castlefield, Manchester M15 4PR **t** 0161 288 5000 **f** 0161 288 5151 **e** firstname.lastname@key103.co.uk **w** key103.co.uk Prog Dir: Anthony Gay. MD: Gus MacKenzie. Hd of Sales: Alison Tootill. Gold **[7]**

Magic 1161, AM:1161/258 The Boathouse, Commercial Rd, Hull, East Yorkshire HU1 2SG **t** 01482 325141 **f** 0845 4580 390 **e** firstname.lastname@vikingfm.co.uk **w** magic1161.co.uk Prog Dir: Darrell Woodman. MD: Mike Bawden. Hd of Sales: Mike Sarath. MOR**[6]**

Magic 1548, AM:1548 St.John's Beacon, 1 Houghton St, Liverpool, Merseyside L1 1RL **t** 0151 472 6800 **f** 0151 472 6821 **e** firstname.lastname@radiocity.co.uk **w** radiocity.co.uk MD: Tom Hunter. Prog Dir: Richard Maddock. Sales Dir: Tracy King. Gold[7]

Magic 999, AM:999 St Paul's Square, Preston, Lancashire PR1 1YE **t** 01772 477700 **f** 01772 477701 **e** firstname.lastname@magic999.com **w** magic999.com Prog Dir: Brian Paige. MD: Paul Jordan. Hd of Music: Dave Asher. Commercial Dir: Carrie Mosley. AC[7]

Magic AM, AM:990/1305/1548 Radio House, 900 Herries Rd, Sheffield, South Yorks S6 1RH **t** 0114 209 1000 **f** 0114 285 3159 **e** programmes@magicam.co.uk **w** magiccam.co.uk Hd of Music: Chris Straw. MD: Ian Clasper. Hd of Sales: Adrian Serle. Soft AC**[6]**

Magic 828, AM:828 PO Box 2000, 51 Burley Rd, Leeds, West Yorkshire LS3 1LR **t** 0113 283 5500 **f** 0113 283 5501 **e** firstname.lastname@radioaire.com **w** radioaire.co.uk Hd of Magic: Andy Siddell. Prog Dir: Stuart Baldwin. Commercial Dir: Tracy Eastwood. Soft AC[6]

Magic 105.4, FM:105.4 Emap Performance, Mappin House, 4 Winsley St, London W1W 8HF **t** 020 7975 8227 **f** 020 7975 8234 **e** studio@magicradio.com **w** magiclondon.co.uk Prog Dir/Hd of Music: Trevor White. Acting Sales Dir: Julieanne Toole. Soft AC[11]

Magic 1170, AM:1170 Radio House, Yales Crescent, Thornaby, Stockton-on-Tees TS17 6AA **t** 01642 888222 **f** 01642 868288 **e** tfm.reception@tfmradio.com Prog Dir: Colin Paterson. MD: Catherine Ellington. Hd of Music Magic: Peter Grant. Sales Dir: Colette Butler. MOR[5]

Radio Maldwyn, AM:756 The Magic 756, The Studios, The Park, Newtown, Powys SY16 2NZ **t** 01686 623555 or 01686 623777 (sales) **f** 01686 623666 **e** radio.maldwyn@ukonline.co.uk **w** magic756.net MD/Prog Controller: Austin Powell. Hd of Sales: Martin Adams. AC[9]

Mansfield 103.2, FM:103.2 The Media Suite, Brunts Business Centre, Samuel Brunts Way, Mansfield, Nottinghamshire NG18 2AH **t** 01623 646666 **f** 01623 660606 **e** info@mansfield103.co.uk **w** mansfield103.co.uk MD: Tony Delahunty. Prog Controller/Hd of Music: Katie Trinder. Hd of Sales: Gordon Pitman. Chart/Country/Gold[8]

Manx Radio, AM:1368 FM:89/97.2/103.7 PO Box 1368, Broadcasting House, Douglas, Isle Of Man IM99 1SW **t** 01624 682600 **f** 01624 682604 **e** postbox@manxradio.com **w** manxradio.com MD: Anthony Pugh. Prog Dir: Andy Wint. Business Dir: John Marsom. Dir of Technology: Darren Leeming. MOR[7, 1]

KM-fm (Medway), FM:100.4/107.9 Medway House, Ginsbury Close, Sir Thomas Longley Rd, Medway City Estate, Rochester, Kent ME2 4DU **t** 01634 841111 **f** 01634 841122 **e** rlowe@kmfm.co.uk **w** kentonline.co.uk/kmfm Prog Mgr: Russ Lowe. Grp Prog Cont: Mike Osborne. Grp Hd of Music: Toby MacKenzie. Sales Mgr: Julian Callis. AC/CHR**[11]**

Mercia FM, FM:97.0/102.9/Digital 1359 Hertford Place, Coventry, West Midlands CV1 3TT **t** 024 7686 8200 **f** 024 7686 8203 **e** mercia@musicradio.com **w** musicradio.com Prog Dir: Luis Clark. Hd of Music: Simon Clarke. Hd of Sales: Stella Kench. CHR[8]

Mercury 96.6, FM:96.6 Unit 5, The Metro Centre, Dwight Rd, Watford WD18 9SS **t** 01923 205470 **f** 01923 205471 **e** firstname.lastname@musicradio.com **w** musicradio.com Prog Controller: Rebecca Dundon. Hd of Sales: Francis Flanagan. AC[11]

102.7 Mercury FM, FM:102.7/97.5 9 The Stanley Centre, Kelvin Way, Crawley, West Sussex RH10 2SE **t** 01293 519161 **f** 01293 565663 **e** firstname.lastname@musicradio.com **w** musicradio.com Prog Cont: Chris Rick. Hd of Sales: Amanda Masters. CHR[12]

BBC Radio Merseyside, AM:1485 FM:95.8 55 Paradise St, Liverpool, Merseyside L1 3BP **t** 0151 708 5500 **f** 0151 794 0988 **e** radio.merseyside@bbc.co.uk **w** bbc.co.uk/liverpool Hd of Music: Nickie Mackay. Managing Editor: Mick Ord. MOR[7]

Metro Radio, FM:97.1/102.6/103/103.6 Radio House, Longrigg, Swalwell, Newcastle upon Tyne, Tyne and Wear NE99 1BB **t** 0191 420 0971 **f** 0191 488 9222 **e** enquiries@metroandmagic.com **w** metroradio.co.uk Prog Dir: Tony McKenzie. MD: Sally Aitchison. Hd of Music: Alex Roland. Hd of Sales: Kim Miljus. CHR[5]

MFM 103.4, FM:103.4 The Studios, Mold Rd, Gwersyllt, Wrexham, Clwyd LL11 4AF **t** 01978 752202 **f** 01978 722209 **e** admin@mfm.musicradio.com **w** musicradio.com Prog Mgr: Lisa Marrey. MD: Sarah Smithard. Grp Prog Controller: Graham Ledger. Hd of Music: Steve Simms. Hd of Sales: Clive Douthwaite. CHR[9]

Mid West Radio, FM:96.1/97.1 Abbey St, Ballyhaunis, Co. Mayo, Ireland **t** +353 94 963 0553 **f** +353 94 963 0285 **e** chris@mnwr.ie **w** mnwrfm.com Station Mgr/Hd of Music: Chris Carroll. Prog Dir: Paul Claffey. Hd of Sales: Tina Mitchell. MOR/Gold[15]

Midlands 103, FM:96.5/102.1/103.5 The Mall, William St, Tullamore, Co Offaly, Ireland **t** +353 506 51333 **f** +353 506 52546 **e** goodcompany@midlandsradio.fm **w** midlandsradio.fm GM Broadcasting: John McDonnell. Station Manager/Hd of Sales: Albert FitzGerald. MOR/Country/Chart[15]

104.7 Minster FM, FM:104.7/102.3 Chessingham House, Dunnington, York, North Yorkshire YO19 5SE **t** 01904 488888 **f** 01904 488811 **e** ed@minsterfm.com **w** ministerfm.com Brand Mgr/Hd of Music: Ed Bretten. Commercial Mgr: Sarah Barry. Hd of Sales: Peter Bilsborough. AC[5, 6]

Mix 107, FM:107.4/107.7 PO Box 1107, High Wycombe, Buckinghamshire HP13 6WQ **t** 01494 446611 **f** 01494 445400 **e** studio@mix107.co.uk **w** mix107.co.uk Prog Dir: Andy Muir. Station Mgr/Hd of Sales: Pranay Parmar. Hd of Music: Kate Beveridge. AC[11]

MIX 96, FM:96.2 Friars Square Studios, Bourbon St, Aylesbury, Bucks HP20 2PZ **t** 01296 399396 **f** 01296 398988 **e** mix@mix96.co.uk **w** mix96.co.uk Station Coordinator: Richard Carr. MD/Station Manager: Rachel Faulkner. Prog Dir/Hd of Music: Nathan Cooper. Hd of Sales: Lydia Flack. AC[10]

Moray Firth Radio, AM:1107 FM:97.4/96.6/96.7/102.5/102.8 PO Box 271, Inverness IV3 8UJ **t** 01463 224433 **f** 01463 243224 or 01463 227714 **e** mfr@mfr.co.uk **w** mfr.co.uk Prog Controller: Ray Atkinson. MD: Danny Gallagher. Hd of Music: Tich McCooey. Sales Dir: Hilary Cartwright. Chart/Gold/Scot/Country[2]

Music Choice (A member of Music Choice Europe), AM:Digital Provider Fleet House, 57-61 Clerkenwell Rd, London EC1M 5LA **t** 020 7014 8700 **f** 020 7253 8460 **e** contactus@musicchoice.co.uk **w** musicchoice.co.uk CEO: Margot Daly. Dir of Music & Marketing: Simon George.

Raidio na Gaeltachta, FM:92-94/102.7 Casla, Conamara, County na Gaillimhe, Ireland **t** +353 91 506677 **f** +353 91 506666 **e** rnag@rte.ie **w** rnag.ie Hd of Sales: Mairin Mhic Dhonnchada. Station Manager: Thomas Mac Con Iomaire. Programming Dir: Sean O Heanaigh. Hd of Music: Mairtin O Fatharta. Gaelic**[15]**

BBC Nan Gaidheal, FM:103.5-105 52 Church St, Stornoway, Isle of Lewis, Western Isles HS1 2LS **t** 01851 705000 **f** 01851 704633 **e** rapal@bbc.co.uk **w** bbc.co.uk/alba Music Prod: Mairead Maclennan. Prog Controller/Managing Editor: Marion MacKinnon. AC/Traditional[2]

NECR, FM:97.1/102.1/102.6/103.2 The Shed, School Rd, Kintore, Inverurie, Aberdeenshire AB51 0UX **t** 01467 632878 or 01467 632909 **f** 01467 632969 **e** necrradio102.1fm@supanet.com Prog Cont: John Dean. MD: Colin Strong. Hd of Sales: Maggie MacNaughton. Chart/Gold/Specialist[2]

Nevis Radio, FM:96.6/97/102.3/102.4 Ben Nevis Estate, Fort William, Inverness-shire PH33 6PR **t** 01397 700007 **f** 01397 701007 **e** firstname@nevisradio.co.uk **w** nevisradio.co.uk Station Manager: Willie Cameron. Programming Dir: Iain Ferguson. Hd of Music: Malcolm Brown. Hd of Sales: Gina Livingstone. Chart/AOR/Specialist[2]

BBC Radio Newcastle, AM:1458 FM:95.4/96/103.7/104.4 Broadcasting Centre, Barrack Rd, Newcastle upon Tyne, Tyne and Wear NE99 1RN **t** 0191 232 4141 **f** 0191 261 8907 **e** radio.newcastle@bbc.co.uk **w** bbc.co.uk/radionewcastle Senior Prod: Sarah Miller. Managing Editor: Sarah Drummond. Hd of Music: Paul Wappat. Pop**[5]**

BBC Radio Norfolk, FM:95.1/104.4 Norfolk Tower, Surrey St, Norwich, Norfolk NR1 3PA **t** 01603 617411 **f** 01603 633692 **e** norfolk@bbc.co.uk **w** bbc.co.uk/radionorfolk Editor: David Clayton. Managing Editor: David Clayton Gold/MOR[10]

North West Radio, FM:102.5/105 Market Yard, Sligo Town, Co Sligo, Ireland **t** +353 71 60108 **f** +353 71 60889 **e** maryd@mnwr.ie **w** mnwrfm.com Prog Dir: Paul Claffey. Station Manager: Mary Daly. Hd of Music: Chris Carroll. Hd of Sales: Tina Mitchell. MOR/Gold[15]

BBC Radio Northampton, FM:103.6/104.2 Broadcasting House, Abington St, Northampton NN1 2BH **t** 01604 239100 **f** 01604 230709 **e** northampton@bbc.co.uk **w** bbc.co.uk/radionorthampton Hd of Music: Anthony Isaacs. Managing Editor: David Clargo. Snr Broadcast Journalist: Nicci Holliday. Chart/AOR/Gold**[10, 8]**

Northants 96, FM:96.6 19-21 St Edmunds Rd, Northampton NN1 5DT **t** 01604 795600 **f** 01604 795601 **e** firstname.lastname@musicradio.com **w** musicradio.com Prog Cont: Richard Neale. Hd of Music: Tom Haynes. Sales Centre Mgr: Caroline Keeley. Chart[10, 8]

NorthSound One, FM:96.9/97.6/103 Abbotswell Rd, West Tullos, Aberdeen, Grampian AB12 3AG **t** 01224 337000 **f** 01224 400003 **e** firstname.lastname@northsound.co.uk **w** northsound1.co.uk Prog Cont: Luke McCullough. MD/Hd of Sales: Adam Findlay. Hd of Music: Chris Thomson. CHR[2]

NorthSound Two, AM:1035 Abbotswell Rd, West Tullos, Aberdeen AB12 3AJ **t** 01224 337000 **f** 01224 400222 **e** firstname.lastname@northsound.co.uk **w** northsound2.co.uk Prog Cont: Luke McCullough. MD/Hd of Sales: Adam Findlay. Hd of Music: Chris Thomson. AOR[2]

BBC Radio Nottingham, AM:1584 FM:95.5/103.8 London Rd, Nottingham NG2 4UU **t** 0115 955 0500 **f** 0115 902 1985 **e** radio.nottingham@bbc.co.uk **w** bbc.co.uk/nottingham Managing Editor: Mike Bettison. MOR[8]

Oak 107, FM:107 PO Box 107 Waldron Court, Prince William Rd, Loughborough, Leicestershire LE11 5GD **t** 01509 211711 **f** 01509 246107 **e** studio@oak107.co.uk **w** oak107.co.uk Station Dir: Bill Johnston. Prog Dir: Mike Vitti. Hd of Music: Dave James. Sales Manager: Annette Holgate. Chart/Gold[8]

Oban FM, FM:103.3 132 George St, Oban, Argyll PA34 5NT **t** 01631 570057 **f** 01631 570530 **e** obanfmradio@btconnect.com Station Manager: Ian MacKay. Programming Dir: Coll MacDougall. Hd of Music: Laura Johnston. Hd of Sales: Ian Simmonds. Various**[3]**

Ocean FM, FM:96.7/97.5 Radio House, Whittle Avenue, Segensworth West, Fareham, Hampshire PO15 5SH **t** 01489 589911 **f** 01489 587754 **e** info@oceanfm.com **w** oceanfm.com Prog Controller: Stuart Ellis. Century Group Hd of Music: Mike Walsh. Commercial Controller: Janet Jones. AC[12]

Olympic Radio (Webcasting Station), Plymouth PL4 8PL **t** 07050 664 071 **f** 0870 130 4868 **e** radio@olympicradio.co.uk **w** olympicradio.co.uk Hd of Music: Steve Elliott. Show Content Advisor: Den Barnes. Media: Paul Kingwell. AC

BBC Radio 1, FM:97-99 Yalding House, 152-156, Gt Portland St, London W1N 6AJ **t** 020 7580 4468 **f** 020 7765 1439 **e** firstname.lastname@bbc.co.uk **w** bbc.co.uk/radio1 Controller: Andy Parfitt. Editor of Music Policy: Alex Jones-Donelly. CHR

Orchard FM, FM:96.5/97.1/102.6 Haygrove House, Shoreditch Rd, Taunton, Somerset TA3 7BT **t** 01823 338448 **f** 01823 368319 **e** orchardfm@musicradio.com **w** musicradio.com Prog Cont/Hd of Music: Steve Bulley. Hd of Sales: Jim Trevelyan. AC/Gold[13]

BBC Radio Oxford, FM:95.2 269 Banbury Rd, Summertown, Oxford OX2 7DW **t** 08459 311444 **f** 08459 311555 **e** oxford.online@bbc.co.uk **w** bbc.co.uk/oxford Station Mgr: Phil Ashworth. Hd of Music: Mark Watson. Prog Dir: Colleen Joynt. MOR**[8]**

Passion 107.9FM, FM:107.9 270 Woodstock Rd, Oxford OX2 7NW **t** 01865 315980 **f** 01865 553355 **e** info@passion1079.com **w** passion1079.com Grp Prog Cont: Andy Green. MD: Nigel Taylor. Hd of Music: Adrian Brookbank. Hd of Sales: Lucinda Trotman. Chart/Dance/News[8]

Peak 107FM, FM:107.4/102.0 Radio House, Foxwood Rd, Chesterfield, Derbyshire S41 9RF **t** 01246 269107 **f** 01246 267108 **e** studio@peak107.com **w** peak107.com Prog Mgr/Hd of Music: Craig Pattison. Sales Dir: Chris Overend. AC[8]

Pirate FM102, FM:102.2/102.8 Carn Brea Studios, Wilson Way, Redruth, Cornwall TR15 3XX **t** 01209 314400 **f** 01209 315250 **e** onair@piratefm102.co.uk **w** piratefm102.co.uk Prog Dir: Bob McCreadie. Station Manager: Beverley Warne. Hd of Music: Neil Caddy. Hd of Sales: Colin Halfpenny. AC[13]

Planet Rock, FM:(DAB Digital Radio) PO Box 2269, London W1A 5UQ **t** 020 7911 7300 **f** 020 7911 7302 **e** joinus@planetrock.co.uk **w** planetrock.com MD/Prog Dir/Hd of Music: Nick Piggott. Hd of Sales: Steve Cray. Rock

97FM Plymouth Sound, FM:97 Earls Acre, Alma Rd, Plymouth, Devon PL3 4HX **t** 01752 227272 **f** 01752 670730 **e** firstname.lastname@musicradio.com **w** musicradio.com Prog Cont/Hd of Music: Dave England. Sales Centre Mgr: Alison Wyse. AC[13]

103.2 Power FM, FM:103.2 Radio House, Whittle Avenue, Segensworth West, Fareham, Hampshire PO15 5SH **t 01489 589911 f** 01489 589453 **e** info@powerfm.com **w** powerfm.com Prog Controller: Craig Morris. Hd of Music: John O'Hara. Commercial Controller: Janet Jones. CHR[12]

Premier Christian Radio, AM:1305/1332/1413 22 Chapter St, London SW1P 4NP **t** 020 7316 1300 **f** 020 7233 6706 **e** premier@premier.org.uk **w** premier.org.uk Prog Cont: Charmaine Noble-McLean. MD: Peter Kerridge. Hd of Sales: Claire Southall. Christian[11]

The Pulse of West Yorkshire, FM:97.5/102.5 Pennine House, Forster Square, Bradford, West Yorkshire BD1 5NE **t** 01274 203040 **f** 01274 203130 **e** general@pulse.co.uk **w** pulse.co.uk Prog Dir: Simon Walkington. MD: Esther Morton. Hd of Music: Jacqui Blay. Hd of Sales: Tony Wilkinson. AC[10]

Q101.2FM, FM:101.2 42A Market St, Omagh, Co. Tyrone BT78 1EH **t** 028 8224 5777 **f** 028 8225 9517 **e** manager@q101west.fm **w** q101west.fm AC[1]

Q102, FM:102.2 Glenageary Office Park, Glenageary, Co. Dublin **t** +353 1 662 1022 **f** +353 1 662 9974 **e** info@q102.ie **w** q102.ie Prog Manager: Ian Walker. MD: Scott Williams. Music Dir : Gerry O'Shea. Soft AC[15]

Q102.9 FM, FM:102.9 The Riverview Suite, 87 Rossdowney Rd, Waterside, Co Londonderry BT47 5SU **t** 028 7134 4449 **f** 028 7131 1177 **e** manager@q102.fm **w** q102.fm MD/Prog Dir: Frank McLaughlin. Station Manager: David Austin. Hd of Music: Steve Kirk. Hd of Sales: John O'Connor. CHR/AC[1]

Q96 FM, FM:96.3 65 Sussex St, Glasgow G41 1DX **t** 0141 429 9430 **f** 0141 429 9431 **e** firstname.lastname@q-fm.com **w** q-fm.com Prog Dir/Hd of Music: Mike Richardson. MD/Hd of Sales: Alan Shields. AC[3]

Q97.2FM, FM:97.2 24 Cloyfin Rd, Coleraine, Co Londonderry BT52 2NU **t** 028 7035 9100 **f** 028 7032 6666 **e** manager@q972.fm **w** q972.fm MD/Prog Dir: Frank McLaughlin. Station Manager: Damien Devenney. Hd of Music: Nick Davison. Hd of Sales: John O'Connor. AC/Gold[1]

Q103 FM, FM:103 The Vision Park, Histon, Cambridge CB4 9WW **t** 01223 235255 **f** 01223 235161 **e** firstname.lastname@musicradio.com **w** musicradio.com Prog Cont: Paul Green. Hd of Music: Danno Fox. Hd of Sales: Phil Caborn. AC[10]

107.4 The Quay, FM:107.4 PO Box 107.4, Portsmouth, Hampshire PO2 8PE **t** 023 9236 4141 **f** 023 9236 4151 **e** info@quayradio.com **w** quayradio.com Brand Mgr: Paul Owens. Station Manager/Hd of Sales: Paul Marcus. Hd of Music: Andy Shire. Gold/Chart/Dance[12]

Quaywest Radio, FM:102.4 Harbour Studios, The Esplande, Watchet, Somerset TA23 0AJ **t** 01984 634900 **f** 01984 634811 **e** studio@quaywest.fm **w** quaywest.fm MD/Prog Dir/Hd of Music: David Mortimer. Hd of Sales: Berny McLoughlin. AC[13]

Radio Carmarthenshire, FM:97.1/97.5 14 Old School Estate, Narberth SA67 7DU **t** 01834 869384 **f** 01834 861524 **e** keri@radiocarmarthenshire.com **w** radiocarmarthenshire.com MD/Prog Dir: Keri Jones. Hd of Sales: Aimee Bowen. AC[9]

Radio Jackie, FM:107.8 110 Tolworth Broadway, Surbiton, Surrey KT6 7JD **t** 020 8288 1300 **f** 020 8288 1312 **e** info@radiojackie.com **w** radiojackie.com Prog Dir: Dave Owen. General Manager: Peter Stremes. Soft AC**[11]**

Radio North Angus FM, FM:96.6/87.7 Arbroath Infirmary, Rosemount Rd, Arbroath, Angus DD11 2AT **t** 01241 879660 **f** 01241 439664 **e** info@radionorthangus.co.uk **w** radionorthangus.co.uk MD/Prog Dir: Malcolm J.B. Finlayson. News/Healthcare/MOR[2]

Radio Pembrokeshire, FM:102.5/107.5 14 Old School Estate, Narberth SA67 7DU **t** 01834 869384 **f** 01834 861524 **e** keri@radiopembrokeshire.com **w** radiopembrokeshire.com MD/Prog Dir: Keri Jones. Hd of Sales: Aimee Bowen. AC[8, 9]

RadioXL, AM:1296 KMS House, Bradford St, Birmingham, West Midlands B12 0JD **t** 0121 753 5353 **f** 0121 753 3111 **e** hardev@radioxl.net **w** radioxl.net Hd of Music/Sales: Sukhjinder Ghatoare. MD/Prog Dir: Arun Bajaj. Asian[8]

102.8 Ram FM, FM:102.8 35-36 Irongate, Derby DE1 3GA **t** 01332 205599 **f** 01332 851111 **e** firstname.lastname@musicradio.com **w** musicradio.com Prog Cont: James Daniels. Sales Centre Mgr: Margaret Dunn. AC[8]

Reading 107fm, Radio House, Madejski Stadium, Reading, Berkshire RG2 0FN **t** 0118 986 2555 **f** 0118 945 0809 **e** studio@reading107fm.com **w** reading107fm.com Prog Cont: Tim Grundy. Hd of Sales: Joanna Bishop.[11, 12]

Real Radio, FM:105.4/105.9/106 PO Box 6105, Ty-Nant Court, Cardiff CF15 8YF **t** 02920 315100 **f** 02920 315150 **e** firstname.lastname@realradiofm.com **w** realradiofm.com MD: Andy Carter. Prog Cont: Sarah Graham. Hd of Presentation: Chris Moore. Hd of Sales: Tony Downling. AC**[7]**

Real Radio (Yorkshire), FM:106/108 Sterling Court, Capitol Park, Leeds WF3 1EL **t** 0113 2381114 **f** 0113 3071450 **e** firstname.lastname@realradiofm.com **w** realradiofm.com Prog Dir/Grp Hd of Music: Terry Underhill. MD: Mike Pennington. Hd of Sales: Steve South. AC[6]

Real Radio FM, FM:100/101 PO Box 101, Glasgow Business Park, Glasgow G69 6GA **t** 0141 781 1011 **f** 0141 781 1112 **e** firstname.lastname@realradiofm.com **w** realradiofm.com MD: Shaun Bowron. Programming Dir: Jay Crawford. Hd of Sales: Billy Anderson. AC**[3]**

Red Dragon FM, FM:97.4/103.2 Atlantic Wharf, Cardiff Bay, South Glamorgan CF10 4DJ **t** 029 2066 2066 **f** 029 2066 2060 **e** info@reddragonfm.co.uk **w** reddragonfm.co.uk Prog Cont: David Rees. Commercial Cont: Jim Carpenter. Marketing Cont: Eirwen Parker. CHR/AC[9]

Red FM, FM:104-106 1, UTC, Bishopstown, Cork Ireland **t** +353 21 486 5500 **f** +353 21 486 5501 **e** info@redfm.ie **w** redfm.ie Prog Dir: Matt Dempsey. Chief Executive: Henry Condon. Hd of Sales: Niall Whelan. CHR[15]

96.2 The Revolution, FM:96.2 PO Box 962, Oldham, Lancashire OL1 3JF **t** 0161 621 6500 **f** 0161 621 6521 **e** studio@revolutiononline.co.uk **w** revolutiononline.co.uk Prog Manager: Chris Gregg. Station Manager: Dave Stankler. Hd of Music: Wayne Dutton. Hd of Sales: Jaqueline Sulkowski. AC[7]

Ridings FM, FM:106.8 PO Box 333, Wakefield, West Yorkshire WF2 7YQ **t** 01924 367177 **f** 01924 367133 **e** enquiries@ridingsfm.co.uk **w** ridingsfm.co.uk Prog Mgr: Phil Butler. Group Prog Dir: Jane Hill. Sales Mgr: Sarah Hardy. AC[7]

RLO 105 FM, FM:98.5-105 17 Patrick St, Limerick, Ireland **t** +353 61 319596 **f** +353 61 419890 **e** rlodj@hotmail.com **w** rlo105.com MD/Prog Cont: Gerrard Madden. Hd of Music: Fintan Maloney. Hd of Sales: Carmel Burke. Chart/Gold[15]

97.4 Rock FM, FM:97.4 St Paul's Square, Preston, Lancashire PR1 1YE **t** 01772 477700 **f** 01772 477701 **e** firstname.lastname@rockfm.co.uk **w** rockfm.co.uk Prog Dir: Brian Paige. MD: Paul Jordan. Hd of Music: Mark Kaye. Commercial Dir: Carrie Mosley. CHR[7]

RTE Radio 1, FM:88/89/90 Radio Centre, Donnybrook, Dublin 4, Ireland **t** +353 1 208 3111 **f** +353 1 208 4523 **e** radio1@rte.ie **w** rte.ie Production Manager: Gerry Kelly. Hd of Music: Peter Brown. Hd of Sales: Geraldine O'Leary. MOR/Country[15]

2FM, FM:90-92 RTE Radio Centre, Donnybrook, Dublin 4, Ireland **t** +353 1 208 3111 or 01850 715922 **f** +353 1 208 3092 **e** info@2fm.ie **w** 2fm.ie Station Mgr/Prog Dir: John Clarke. Hd of Music: Aidan Leonard. Group Hd of Sales: Geraldine O'Leary. CHR[15]

107.1 Rugby FM, FM:107.1 Suites 4-6, Dunsmore Business Centre, Spring St, Rugby CV21 3HH **t** 01788 541100 **f** 01788 541070 **e** mail@rugbyfm.co.uk **w** rugbyfm.co.uk MD/Hd of Sales: Martin Mumford. Hd of Music: Dave Barker. AC**[8]**

Rutland Radio, FM:107.2/97.4 40 Melton Rd, Oakham, Rutland LE15 6AY **t** 01572 757868 **f** 01572 757744 **e** enquiries@rutlandradio.co.uk **w** rutlandradio.co.uk Station Mgr: Julie Baker. Hd of Music: Rob Persani. Sales Manager: Sarah Washington. AC[8]

Sabras Radio, AM:1260 Radio House, 63 Melton Rd, Leicester LE3 6PN **t** 0116 261 0666 **f** 0116 266 7776 **e** don@sabrasradio.com **w** sabrasradio.com Station Mgr: Don Kotak. Grp Hd of Sales: Richard Scarle. Asian[8]

Saga 105.2, City Park, Alexandra Parade, Glasgow G31 3AU **t** 0141 551 1052 **f** 0141 551 1053 **e** firstname.lastname@saga1052.freeserve.co.uk w saga1052fm.co.uk MD: Norman Quirk. [3]

Saga 105.7FM, FM:105.7 Crown House, 123 Hagley Rd, Edgbaston, Birmingham B16 8LD **t** 0121 452 1057 **f** 0121 452 3222 **e** onair@saga1057fm.co.uk **w** saga1057fm.co.uk Prog Dir: Brian Savin. MD: Peter Tomlinson. Hd of Music: Mike Baker. Dir of Sales: Ian Smith. Gold/MOR**[8]**

Saga 106.6fm, FM:106.6 Saga Radio House, Alder Court, Riverside Business Park, Nottingham NG2 1RX **t** 0115 986 1066 **f** 0115 943 5065 **e** onair@saga1066fm.co.uk **w** saga1066fm.co.uk Prog Dir: Paul Robey. MD: Phil Dixon. Hd of Sales: Lisa MacDonald. MOR[8]

The Saint, FM:107.8 The Friends Provident, St Mary's Stadium, Brittania Rd, Southampton, Hampshire SO14 5fp **t** 023 8033 0300 **f** 023 8020 6400 **e** thesaint@saintsfc.co.uk **w** saintsfc.co.uk Prog Cont: Stewart Dennis. Station Dir: Tim Manns. AC[12]

Score Digital Ltd, AM:Digital Multiplex 3 South Avenues, Clydebank Business Park, Glasgow G81 2RX **t** 0141 565 2347 **f** 0141 565 2318 **e** scoredigital@srh.co.uk **w** scoredigital.co.uk Managing Dir: Grae Allan. Glasgow: Digital Channel 11C. Edinburgh: Digital Channel 12D. N.Ireland: Digital Channel 12C.[3]

BBC Scotland, FM:92 - 95 Queen Margaret Drive, Glasgow, Strathclyde G12 8DG **t** 0141 338 2000 **f** 0141 338 2346 **e** firstname.lastname@bbc.co.uk **w** bbc.co.uk/scotland Snr Prod Contemp. Music: Stewart Cruickshank. Hd of Radio: Maggie Cunningham. Indie/Dance/Celtic/Folk**[3]**

102.4 Severn Sound FM, FM:102.4 Bridge Studios, Eastgate Centre, Gloucester GL1 1SS **t** 01452 313200 **f** 01452 313213 **e** firstname.lastname@musicradio.com **w** musicradio.com Prog Dir: Russ Wilcox. Sales Centre Manager: Mark Wright. 80s/90s[8]

SGR Colchester, FM:96.1 Abbeygate Two, 9 Whitewell Rd, Colchester, Essex CO2 7DE **t** 01206 575859 **f** 01206 216149 **e** firstname.lastname@musicradio.com **w** musicradio.com Prog Dir: Paul Morris. Sales Manager: Sue Rudland. Gold/Chart[11, 10]

SGR-FM, FM:96.4/97.1 Radio House, Alpha Business Park, 6-12 White House Rd, Ipswich, Suffolk IP1 5LT **t** 01473 461000 **f** 01473 741200 **e** firstname.lastname@musicradio.com **w** musicradio.com Prog Dir: Tracy Cooper. Hd of Music: Nick Morrell. Sales Centre Mgr: Sophie Crocker. AC[10]

Shannonside FM, FM:94.8/95.7/104.1/103.1/104.8 Minard House, Sligo Rd, Longford, Ireland **t** +353 43 47777 **f** +353 43 48384 **e** info@shannonside.ie **w** shannonside.ie CEO: Richard Devlin. Programming Cont/Hd of Music: Joe Finnegan. Sales Manager: Kathy Casey. MOR/Country[15]

BBC Radio Sheffield, AM:1035 FM:88.6/94.7/104.1 54 Shoreham St, Sheffield, South Yorkshire S1 4RS **t** 0114 273 1177 **f** 0114 267 5454 **e** radio.sheffield@bbc.co.uk **w** bbc.co.uk/radiosheffield Hd of Music: Franca Marttella. Station Manager: Gary Keown. MOR/Specialist[6]

BBC Radio Shetland, FM:92.7 Pitt Lane, Lerwick, Shetland ZE1 0DW **t** 01595 694747 **f** 01595 694307 **e** radio.shetland@bbc.co.uk Senior Producer: Alisdair MacKinnon. Trad/Country/Some Indie[2]

BBC Shropshire, AM:1584 FM:95/96 2-4 Boscobel Drive, Shrewsbury, Shropshire SY1 3TT **t** 01743 248484 **f** 01743 271702 **e** shropshire@bbc.co.uk **w** bbc.co.uk/england/radioshropshire Hd of Music: Elaine Muir. Managing Editor: Tony Fish. Hd of Programmes: Rose Aston. MOR[9, 7, 8]

SIBC, FM:96.2/102.2 Market St, Lerwick, Shetland ZE1 0JN **t** 01595 695299 **f** 01595 695696 **e** info@sibc.co.uk **w** sibc.co.uk MD/Prog Cont: Inga Walterson. Hd of Sales: Ian Anderson. CHR[2]

Signal 2, AM:1170 Stoke Rd, Stoke-on-Trent, Staffordshire ST4 2SR **t** 01782 441300 **f** 01782 441301 **e** reception@signalradio.com **w** signal2.co.uk Prog Dir/Hd of Music: Kevin Howard. MD: Chris Hurst. Hd of Sales: Lee Williams. Gold[8]

Signal 1, FM:96.4/96.9/102.6 Stoke Rd, Stoke-on-Trent, Staffordshire ST4 2SR **t** 01782 441300 **f** 01782 441301 **e** reception@signalradio.com **w** signal1.com Prog Dir/Hd of Music: Kevin Howard. MD: Chris Hurst. Hd of Sales: Lisa Hughes. AC[8]

106.9 Silk FM, FM:106.9 Radio House, Bridge St, Macclesfield, Cheshire SK11 6DJ **t** 01625 268000 **f** 01625 269010 **e** mail@silkfm.com **w** silkfm.com Brand Mgr: Andy Bailey. Commercial Mgr: Rachel Barker. AC[7]

Smooth FM, FM:100.4 World Trade Centre, 8 Exchange Quay, Manchester M5 3EJ **t** 0845 050 1004 **f** 0845 054 1005 **e** info@smoothfm.com **w** smoothfm.com Prog Cont: Steve Collins. MD: Roy Bennett. Hd of Music: Derek Webster. Sales Dir: Joe Radcliffe. Jazz/Soul/Blues/R'n'B[7]

BBC Radio Solent, AM:999/1359 FM:96.1/103.8 Broadcasting House, Havelock Rd, Southampton, Hampshire SO14 7PW **t** 023 8063 2811 **f** 023 8033 9648 **e** radio.solent.news@bbc.co.uk **w** bbc.co.uk/england/radiosolent Managing Ed: Mia Costello. MOR[12]

BBC Somerset Sound, AM:1323 14-15 Paul St, Taunton, Somerset TA1 3PF **t** 01823 252437 **f** 01823 332539 **e** somerset.sound@bbc.co.uk **w** bbc.co.uk/england/radiobristol/somerset Managing Ed: Jenny Lacey. MOR/Specialist[8, 12]

Soul City, FM:107.5 Lambourne House, 7 Western Rd, Romford, Essex RM1 3LD **t** 01708 731 643 **f** 01708 730 383 **e** info@soulcity1075.com **w** soulcity1075.com Co-MD: Chris Slack. Co-MD: Roger Cutsforth. Hd of Music: Mick Jackson. Soul/RnB[11]

South East Radio, FM:95.6 - 96.4 Custom House Quay, Wexford, Ireland **t** +353 53 45200 **f** +353 53 45295 **e** info@southeastradio.ie **w** .southeastradio.ie Prog Dir/Hd of Music: Clive Roylance. MD: Eamonn Buttle. Hd of Sales: Marion Barry. AC[15]

South Hams Radio, FM:100.5-101.9 Unit 1G, South Hams Business Park, Churchstow, Devon TQ7 3QH **t** 01548 854595 **f** 01548 857345 **e** firstname.lastname@musicradio.com **w** musicradio.com Station Mgr/Hd of Music: David Fitzgerald. Sales Dir: Helen Barnett. AC/CHR/MOR[13]

South West Sound, FM:97/96.5/103 Unit 40, The Loreburne Centre, High St, Dunfries DG1 2BD **t** 01387 250999 **f** 01387 265629 **e** firstname.lastname@westsound.co.uk **w** southwestsound.co.uk Prog Dir/Hd of Music: Alan Toomey. Station Manager/Hd of Sales: Fiona Blackwood. MD: Sheena Borthwick. AC/Gold[3]

BBC Southern Counties Radio, FM:104-104.8/95-95.3 Broadcasting Centre, Guildford, Surrey GU6 7ER **t** 01483 306306 **f** 01483 304952 **e** southern.counties.radio@bbc.co.uk **w** bbc.co.uk/southerncounties Hd of Music: Neil Pringle. Hd of Programmes: Sam Hodgson. Managing Ed: Mike Hapgood. AC[11]

Southern FM, FM:102.4/103.5 Radio House, PO Box 2000, Brighton, East Sussex BN41 2SS **t** 01273 430111 **f** 01273 430098 **e** info@southernradio.co.uk **w** southernfm.com Prog Contr/Hd of Music: Tony Aldridge. Hd of Sales: Jason Kluver. CHR[12]

107.5 Sovereign Radio, FM:107.5 14 St Mary's Walk, Hailsham, East Sussex BN27 1AF **t** 01323 442700 **f** 01323 442866 **e** info@1075sovereignradio.co.uk **w** 1075sovereignradio.co.uk Brand Mgr: Nigel Ansell. Hd of Music: Andy Knight. Commercial Mgr: Karen Dyball. Soft AC[12]

Spectrum Radio, AM:558 4 Ingate Place, London SW8 3NS **t** 020 7627 4433 **f** 020 7627 3409 **e** enquiries@spectrumradio.net **w** spectrumradio.net Station Mgr: Paul Hogan. Multi Ethnic[11]

Spire FM, FM:102 City Hall Studios, Salisbury, Wiltshire SP2 7QQ **t** 01722 416644 **f** 01722 415102 **e** admin@spirefm.co.uk **w** spirefm.co.uk Station Mgr: Ceri Hurford-Jones. Prog Dir/Hd of Music: Darren Cee. Hd of Sales: Karen Bosley. Gold/Chart[12]

Spirit FM, FM:96.6/102.3 9-10 Dukes Court, Bognor Rd, Chichester, West Sussex PO19 8FX **t** 01243 773600 **f** 01243 786464 **e** info@spiritfm.net **w** spiritfm.net Prog Dir: Duncan Barkes. MD: Stephen Oates. Hd of Music: Ian Crouch. Hd of Sales: Marie Allen. AC[12]

Star 106.6 FM, FM:106.6 The Observatory, Slough, Berkshire SL1 1LH **t** 01753 551066 **f** 01753 512277 **e** onair@star1066.co.uk **w** star1066.co.uk Prog Dir: Anthony Ballard. Hd of Music: Mark Chivers. Hd of Sales: Gordon Drummond. AC[11]

Star 107, FM:107.2/107.9 Brunel Mall, London Rd, Stroud, Gloucestershire GL5 2BP **t** 01453 767369 **f** 01453 757107 **e** programming@star107.co.uk **w** star107.co.uk Prog Mgr: Marie Greenwood. MD: Dev Chakraborty. Hd of Sales: Rebecca Tansley. (Prog Dir & Hd of Music based at Star 107.3) AC[8]

Star 107.2 Bristol, FM:107.2 Bristol Evening Post Building, Temple Way, Bristol BS99 7HD **t** 0117 910 6600 **f** 0117 925 0941 **e** firstname.lastname@star1072.co.uk **w** star1072.co.uk Prog Cont: Ian Downs. MD: Dev Chakraborty. Hd of Music: Dave Coull. Hd of Sales: Paul Kurnyta. AC

Star 107.5, FM:107.5 1st Floor, West Suite, Cheltenham Film Studios, Hatherley Lane, Cheltenham, Gloucestershire GL51 6PN **t** 01242 699555 **f** 01242 699666 **e** studio@star1075.co.uk **w** star1075.co.uk Prog Mgr: Ian Timms. MD/Hd of Sales: Alan Knight. Hd of Music: Dave Coull. AOR[8]

Star 107.7, FM:107.7 11 Beaconsfield Rd, Weston-super-Mare, North Somerset BS23 1YE **t** 01934 624455 **f** 01934 629922 **e** firstname.lastname@star1077.co.uk **w** star1077.co.uk Acting Station Mgr: Mark Briggs. Prog Mgr: Scott Temple. Grp Sales Dir: Campbell Grant. AC**[13, 9]**

Star 107.9, FM:107.9 Radio House, Sturton St, Cambridge CB1 2QF **t** 01223 722300 **f** 01223 577686 **e** mail@star107.co.uk **w** star107.co.uk MD/Prog Cont: James Keen. Hd of Music: Freddie Scherer. Sales Dir: Darren Taylor. AC[10]

BBC Stoke, FM:94.6/104.1 Cheapside, Hanley, Stoke-on-Trent, Staffordshire ST1 1JJ **t** 01782 208080 **f** 01782 289115 **e** radio.stoke@bbc.co.uk **w** bbc.co.uk/radiostoke Managing Editor: Mark Hurrell. Hd of Programmes: Mary Fox. MOR[8]

The Storm, FM:(DAB Digital Radio) PO Box 2000, 1, Passage St, Bristol BS99 7SN **t** 0117 984 3200 **f** 0117 984 3202 **e** mail@stormradio.co.uk **w** stormradio.co.uk Digital Content Manager: Nick Piggott. Hd of Music: Bern Leckie.

97.2 Stray FM, FM:97.2 The Hamlet, Hornbeam Park Ave, Harrogate, North Yorkshire HG2 8RE **t** 01423 522972 **f** 01423 522922 **e** mail@strayfm.com **w** strayfm.com Hd of Music: Ed George. MD: Sarah Barry. Prog Dir: Ray Stroud. Hd of Sales: Rebecca Brooks. Hot AC[6]

BBC Radio Suffolk, FM:95.5/103.9/104.6 Broadcasting House, St Matthews St, Ipswich, Suffolk IP1 3EP **t** 01473 250000 **f** 01473 210887 **e** suffolk@bbc.co.uk **w** bbc.co.uk/radiosuffolk Senior Broadcast Journos: Pete Cook/Kate Hayward. Managing Editor: David Peel. Hd of Music: Stephen Foster. MOR[10]

Sunrise FM, FM:103.2 Sunrise House, 30 Chapel St, Little Germany, Bradford, West Yorkshire BD1 5DN **t** 01274 735043 **f** 01274 728534 **e** info@sunriseradio.fm **w** sunriseradio.fm MD/Prog Cont: Usha Parmar. Hd of Sales: Amir Shazad. Asian**[6]**

Sunrise Radio, AM:1458 Sunrise House, Merrick Rd, Southall, Middlesex UB2 4AU **t** 020 8574 6666 **f** 020 8813 9800 **e** tpatti@sunriseradio.com **w** sunriseradio.com Prog Dir/Hd of Music: Tony Patti. MD: Tony Lit. Hd of Sales: Kay McCarthy. Asian[11]

Sunshine 855, AM:855 Unit 11, Burway Trading Estate, Bromfield Rd, Ludlow, Shropshire SY8 1EN **t** 01584 873795 **f** 01584 875900 **e** firstname@sunshine855.com **w** sunshine855.com Operations Dir: Ginny Murfin. Hd of Music: Simon Doe. Hd of Sales: Iain Kerr. CHR/Gold**[9, 8, 7]**

Swansea Sound 1170 MW, AM:1170 Victoria Rd, Gowerton, Swansea SA4 3AB **t** 01792 511964 **f** 01792 511965 **e** info@swanseasound.co.uk **w** swanseasound.co.uk Station Dir: Esther Morton. Prog Mgr: Steve Barnes. Hd of Music: Andy Miles. Sales Dir: Christine Dunn. AC[9]

Talk Sport, AM:1053/1071/1089/1107 18 Hatfields, London SE1 8DJ **t** 020 7959 7800 **f** 020 7959 7808 **e** (via website 'Contact us') **w** talksport.net Station Mgr/Prog Dir: Mike Parry. Hd of Music: Peter Gee. Hd of Sales: Jason Trout. Sport/Talk/Phone-ins

Tay FM, FM:96.4/102.8 6 North Isla St, Dundee, Tayside DD3 7JQ **t** 01382 200800 **f** 01382 423252 **e** firstname.lastname@tayfm.co.uk **w** tayfm.co.uk Hd of Music: Graeme Waggott. MD/Prog Dir: Ally Ballingall. Hd of Sales: Lesley Mackenzie. Chart[2]

Tay AM, AM:1161/1584 6 North Isla St, Dundee DD3 7JQ **t** 01382 200800 **f** 01382 423231 **e** firstname.lastname@tayam.co.uk **w** Tayam.co.uk Hd of Music: Richard Allan. MD/Prog Dir: Arthur Ballingall. Hd of Sales: Lesley Mackenzie. Gold[2]

107.4 Telford FM, FM:107.4 Shropshire Star Building, Waterloo Rd, Ketley, Telford TF1 5UD **t** 01952 280011 **f** 01952 280010 **e** info@telfordfm.co.uk **w** telfordfm.co.uk MD/Prog Cont: Pete Wagstaff. Hd of Music: Paul Shuttleworth. Hd of Sales: Gaynor Morecroft. AC[8]

Ten-17, FM:101.7 Latton Bush Business Centre, Southern Way, Harlow, Essex CM18 7BU **t** 01279 431017 **f** 01279 445289 **e** firstname.lastname@musicradio.com Prog Dir/Hd of Music: James Lett. Hd of Sales: John Terry. AC[11, 10]

TFM, FM:96.6 Yale Crescent, Thornaby, Stockton on Tees, Cleveland TS17 6AA **t** 01642 888222 **f** 01642 868288 **e** tfm.reception@tfmradio.com **w** tfmradio.co.uk Prog Dir: Colin Paterson. MD: Catherine Ellington. Hd of Music-TFM: Rob Knight. Sales Dir: Colette Butler. AC[5]

BBC Radio 3, FM:90 - 93 Room 4119, Broadcasting House, London W1A 1AA **t** 020 7765 2512 **f** 020 7765 2511 **e** firstname.lastname@bbc.co.uk **w** bbc.co.uk/radio3 Cont: Roger Wright. Hd of Music Programming: Dr John Evans. Classical

BBC Three Counties Radio, FM:95.5/103.8/104.5 PO Box 3CR, Luton, Beds LU1 5XL **t** 01582 637400 **f** 01582 401467 **e** 3cr@bbc.co.uk **w** bbc.co.uk/threecounties Managing Editor: Marc Norman. MOR/Gold[11, 10]

Tipp FM, FM:95.3/97.1/103.9 Davis Rd, Clonmel, Co Tipperary, Ireland **t** +353 52 26222 **f** +353 52 25447 **e** onair@tippfm.com **w** tippfm.com CEO: Ethel Power. Hd of Sales: Eleanor Leharte. AC[15]

Tipperary Mid-West, FM:104.8 St Michael St, Tipperary, Ireland **t** +353 62 52555 **f** +353 62 52671 **e** tippmidwest@radio.fm **w** tipperarymidwestradio.com Station Mgr: Anne Power. CEO: Michael Maguire. Hd of Music & Sales: Breda Ryan. MOR[15]

100-102 Today FM, FM:100-102 124 Upper Abbey St, Dublin 1, Ireland **t** +353 1 804 9000 **f** +353 1 804 9099 **e** badams@todayfm.com **w** todayfm.com Hd of Music: Brian Adams. Chief Executive: Willie O'Reilly. Associate Prog Manager: Tom Hardy. Hd of Sales: Eamon Fitzpatrick. AC[15]

107.4 Tower FM, FM:107.4 The Mill, Brownlow Way, Bolton BL1 2RA **t** 01204 387000 **f** 01204 534065 **e** firstname+surname@towerfm.co.uk **w** towerfm.co.uk Prog Dir: Gary Stein. Hd of Sales: Matt Ramsbottom. AC[7]

Trax FM, FM:107.9 White Hart Yard, Bridge St, Worksop, Nottinghamshire S80 1HR **t** 01909 500611 **f** 01909 500445 **e** enquiries@traxfm.co.uk **w** traxfm.co.uk Admin Mgr: Paula Spencer. Hd of Sales: Peggy Watson. Prog Cont: Rob Wagstaff. Hd of Music: Mike Bargh. AC[8]

Trax FM., FM:107.1 5 Sidings Court, White Rose Way, Doncaster, South Yorkshire DN4 5SE **t** 01302 341166 **f** 01302 326104 **e** enquiries@traxfm.co.uk **w** traxfm.co.uk Admin Mgr: Paula Spencer. Hd of Sales: Peggy Watson. Prog Cont: Rob Wagstaff. Hd of Music: Mike Bargh. AC/CHR[8]

96 Trent FM, FM:96.2/96.5 29-31 Castle Gate, Nottingham NG1 7AP **t** 0115 952 7000 **f** 0115 952 7001 **e** firstname.lastname@musicradio.com **w** musicradio.com Prog Dir: Dick Stone. Sales Centre Manager: Margaret Dunn. AC[8]

BBC Radio 2, FM:88-91 Henry Wood House, 3 and 6 Langham Place, London W1A 1AA **t** 020 7580 4468 **f** 020 7725 2578 **e** firstname.lastname@bbc.co.uk **w** bbc.co.uk/radio2 Contact: Publicity Office Cont: Lesley Douglas. Exec Producer for Music: Colin Martin. AC/Gold/Specialist

2-TEN FM, FM:97/102.9/103.4 PO Box 2020, Reading, Berkshire RG31 7FG **t** 0118 945 4400 **f** 0118 945 4401 **e** 2progs@creation.com **w** musicradio.com Prog Cont: Tim Parker. Hd of Music: Ollie Hayes. Sales Centre Manager: Jane Suttie. AC[11]

2BR (Two Boroughs Radio), FM:99.8 IMEX Spaces, Nelson, Lancashire BB9 7DR **t** 01282 690000 **f** 01282 690001 **e** info@2br.co.uk **w** 2br.co.uk MD: Mark Matthews. Hd of Sales: Andrea Bury. AC[7]

2CR FM, FM:102.3 5-7 Southcote Rd, Bournemouth, Dorset BH1 3LR **t** 01202 259259 **f** 01202 255244 **e** firstname.lastname@musicradio.com **w** musicradio.com Prog Ctrl: Graham Mack. Hd of Music: Martyn Lee. Sales Mgr: Jane Suttie. AC[12]

radio2XS, FM:107.8 Manor Farm Studios, West Handley, Sheffield, South Yorkshire S21 5RZ **t** 0870 321 1242 **e** info@radio2xs.com **w** radio2XS.com MD/Prog Dir: Jeff Cooper. Hd of Sales: Paul Chadbourne. New/Alternative[6]

UCB Europe, FM:Sky Digital ch.941 Hanchurch Christian Centre, PO Box 255, Stoke On Trent, Staffordshire ST4 8YY **t** 01782 642000 **f** 01782 641121 **e** ucb@ucb.co.uk **w** ucb.co.uk Station Cont: Andrew Urquhart. Hd of Music: Fiona Day. Christian Contemporary/AC[8]

BBC Ulster, FM:92.4/95.4 Broadcasting House, Ormeau Avenue, Belfast, Co Antrim BT2 8HQ **t** 028 9033 8000 **f** 028 9033 8800 **e** firstname.lastname@bbc.co.uk **w** bbc.co.uk/northernireland/atl Senior Prod - Radio: Simon Taylor. Hd of Broadcast: Tim Cooke. All[1]

Vale FM, FM:96.6/97.4 Longmead Studios, Shaftesbury, Dorset SP7 8QQ **t** 01747 855711 **f** 01747 855722 **e** studio@valefm.co.uk **w** valefm.co.uk Prog Cont/Hd of Music: Stewart Smith. Hd of Sales: Will Brougham. AC[12]

Valleys Radio, AM:999/1116 PO Box 1116, Ebbw Vale NP23 8XW **t** 01495 301116 **f** 01495 300710 **e** sales@valleysradio.co.uk **w** valleysradio.co.uk Prog Ctrl/Hd of Music: Tony Peters. Station Mgr: Chris Hurst. Hd of Sales: Joanne Roberts. AC[9]

Vibe 101, FM:97.2/101 26 Baldwin St, Bristol BS1 1FE **t** 0117 901 0101 **f** 0117 930 9149 **e** info@vibe101.co.uk **w** vibe101.co.uk MD: Beverley Cleal Harding. Prog Cont: Trevor James. Hd of Music: Nathan Thomson. Hd of Sales: Louise Hayne. Prog Co-ordinator: Caroline Cook. Dance/RnB[13, 9]

Vibe 105-108, FM:105/108 Reflection House, Olding Rd, Bury St Edmunds, Suffolk IP33 3TA **t** 01284 715300 **f** 01284 715329 **e** firstname.lastname@vibefm.co.uk **w** vibefm.co.uk Prog Dir: Paul Saunders. MD: Beverley Cleall-Harding. Hd of Music: Glen White. Hd of Sales: Kelly Snook. Dance[10]

96.9 Viking FM, FM:96.9 The Boathouse, Commercial Rd, Hull, East Yorkshire HU1 2SG **t** 01482 325141 **f** 0845 4580 390 **e** programmes@vikingfm.co.uk **w** vikingfm.co.uk Prog Dir: Darrell Woodman. MD: Mike Bawden. Hd of Sales: Mike Sarath. AC/Chart[6]

Virgin Radio, AM:1215 FM:105.8 1 Golden Square, London W1F 9DJ **t** 020 7663 2000 **f** 020 7434 1197 **e** reception@virginradio.co.uk **w** virginradio.co.uk Hd of Music: James Curran. Prog Cont: Paul Jackson. MD: John Pearson. Hd of Sales: Lee Roberts. AC/Chart[11]

BBC Wales/Cymru, AM:882/1125/657 FM:92-105 Broadcasting House, Llantrisant Rd, Llandaff, Cardiff, South Glamorgan CF5 2YQ **t** 02920 322000 **f** 02920 323724 **e** radio.wales@bbc.co.uk **w** bbc.co.uk/wales Radio Wales Editor: Julie Barton. Classical/Welsh[9]

96.4FM The Wave, FM:96.4 Victoria Rd, Gowerton, Swansea SA4 3AB **t** 01792 511964 **f** 01792 511965 **e** info@thewave.co.uk **w** thewave.co.uk Regional MD: Esther Morton. Prog Mgr: Steve Barnes. Hd of Music: Andy Miles. Sales Dir: Christine Dunn. CHR[9]

Wave 96.5, FM:96.5 965 Mowbray Drive, Blackpool, Lancashire FY3 7JR **t** 01253 304965 **f** 01253 301965 **e** info@thewavefm.co.uk **w** wave965.com Prog Dir: Helen Bowden. MD: Mel Booth. Hd of Music: Roy Lynch. Hd of Sales: Paula Cliffe. AC[7]

Wave 102 FM, FM:102 8 South Tay St, Dundee DD1 1PA **t** 01382 901000 **f** 01382 900999 **e** studio@wave102.co.uk **w** wave102.co.uk Prog Mgr/Hd of Music: Peter Mac. Station Mgr: Esther Morton. Hd of Sales: Alan Shields. AC[2]

Wave 105.2 FM, FM:105.2/105.8 5 Manor Court, Barnes Wallis Rd, Segensworth East, Fareham, Hampshire PO15 5TH **t** 01489 481057 **f** 01489 481100 **e** studio@wave105.com **w** wave105.com MD: Martin Ball. Programming Cont: John Dash. Hd of Music: Steve Power. AC[12]

Waves Radio, FM:101.2 7 Blackhouse Circle, Peterhead, Aberdeenshire AB42 1BN **t** 01779 491012 **f** 01779 490802 **e** waves@radiophd.freeserve.co.uk **w** wavesfm.com MD: Norman Spence. Prog Dir/Hd of Music: Kenny King. Hd of Sales: David Milne. Chart/Gold**[2]**

Wessex FM, FM:97.2/96 Radio House, Trinity St, Dorchester, Dorset DT1 1DJ **t** 01305 250333 **f** 01305 266885 **e** admin@wessexfm.com **w** wessexfm.com Brand Mgr: Martin Lee. MD: John Baker. Hd of Music: Jason Herbert. Hd of Sales: Claire Evans. AC[13]

West FM, FM:96.7 Radio House, 54 Holmston Rd, Ayr KA7 3BE **t** 01292 283662 **f** 01292 283665 **e** info@westfm.co.uk **w** westfm.co.uk Prog Ctrl/Hd of Music: Alan Toomey. MD: Sheena Borthwick. Hd of Sales: Lynne Shirkie. CHR[3]

Westsound AM, AM:1035 Radio House, 54, Holmston Rd, Ayr KA7 3BE **t** 01292 283662 **f** 01292 283665 **e** info@westsound.co.uk **w** west-sound.co.uk Prog Cont/Hd of Music: Alan Toomey. MD: Sheena Borthwick. Hd of Sales: Lynne Shirkie. AC/Gold[3]

BBC Radio Wiltshire, AM:1368/1332 FM:103.6/104.3/103.5/104.9 Broadcasting House, Prospect Place, Swindon, Wiltshire SN1 3RW **t** 01793 513626 **f** 01793 513650 **e** radio.wiltshire@bbc.co.uk **w** bbc.co.uk/radiowiltshire (music contact): Graham Seaman. Gold/Chart/Classical[8, 12]

Win 107.2 FM, FM:107.2 PO Box 1072, The Brooks, Winchester, Hampshire SO23 8FT **t** 01962 841071 **f** 01962 841079 **e** admin@winfm.co.uk **w** winfm.co.uk Prog Dir/Hd of Music: Jane Danser. Hd of Sales: Jo Talbot. AC**[12]**

107.2 Wire FM, FM:107.2 , Warrington Business Park, Long Lane, Warrington, Cheshire WA2 8TX **t** 01925 445545 **f** 01925 657705 **e** info@wirefm.com **w** wirefm.com Prog Mgr: Paul Holmes. Station Dir: Matthew Allitt. Hd of Music: Pete Pinnington. Hd of Sales: Iain Fowler. AC[6]

Wired FM, FM:96.8/106.8 Mary Immaculate College, South Circular Rd, Limerick, Ireland **t** +353 61 315773 **f** +353 61 315776 **e** wiredfm@mic.ul.ie **w** listen.to/wiredfm Station Manager: Nessa McGann. Prog Dir: Aine Lynne. Hd of Music: Ciar†n Ryan. Indie/Local[15]

102.4 Wish FM, FM:102.4 Orrell Lodge, Orrell Rd, Orrell, Wigan WN5 8HJ **t** 01942 761024 **f** 01942 777694 **e** firstname.lastname@wish-fm.com **w** wishfm.net Prog Mgr: Jo Heuston. Station Dir/Hd of Sales: Matthew Allitt. Hd of Music: Andy Lawson. AC[, 7]

WLR FM, FM:95.1/97.5 The Broadcast Centre, Ardkeen, Co Waterford **t** +353 51 872248 **f** +353 51 877420 **e** studio@wlrfm.com **w** wlrfm.com Prog Cont: Billy McCarthy. MD: Des Whelan. Hd of Music: Ross Allen. Hd of Sales: Jonathan Earl. AC[15]

BBC WM, FM:95.6 PO Box 206, Birmingham, West Midlands B5 7SD **t** 08453 00 99 56 **f** 0121 472 3174 **e** bbcwm@bbc.co.uk **w** bbc.co.uk/radiowm Managing Editor: Keith Beech. AOR[8]

107.7 FM The Wolf, FM:107.7 10th Floor, Mander House, Wolverhampton, West Midlands WV1 3NB **t** 01902 571070 **f** 01902 571079 **e** studio@thewolf.co.uk **w** thewolf.co.uk Prog Dir: Kevin Howard. Station Dir & Hd of Sales: Lisa Hughes. Hd of Music: Tim Haycock. Gold[8]

World Radio Network (WRN), 10 Wyvil Court, Wyvil Rd, London SW8 2TG **t** 020 7896 9000 **f** 020 7896 9007 **e** info@wrn.org **w** wrn.org Marketing Manager: Tim Ayris. Broadcasting on - Sky Digital ch.937 & Telewest Active Digital ch.920Programming Dir: Edwina Jarvis. Hd of Sales: Tim Ayris. RnB/World

BBC World Service, Room 101, Henry Wood House, 3/6 Portland Place, London W1A 1AA **t** 020 7765 3938 **f** 020 7765 3945 **e** alan.rowett@bbc.co.uk **w** bbc.co.uk/worldservice Hd of Music: Alan Rowett. Dir, World Service: Mark Byford. Prog Dir: Phil Harding.

Wyvern FM, FM:96.7/97.6/102.8 5-6 Barbourne Terrace, Worcester WR1 3JZ **t** 01905 612212 **f** 01905 613549 **e** firstname.lastname@musicradio.com **w** musicradio.com Prog Cont: Simon Monk. Sales Centre Manager: Mark Wright. AC[8]

XFM 104.9, FM:104.9 30 Leicester Square, Lo WC2H 7LA **t** 020 7766 6600 **f** 020 7766 660 **e** firstname.lastname@xfm.co.uk **w** xfm.co.u Cont: Andy Ashton. MD: Graham Bryce. Hd Nigel Harding. Commercial Dir: Linda Smith. Alternative[11]

BBC Radio York, AM:666/1260 FM:95.5/103.7/104.3 20 Bootham Row, York, North Yorkshire YO30 7BR **t** 01904 641351 **f** 01904 610937 **e** northyorkshire.radio@bbc.co.uk **w** bbc.co.uk/radioyork Hd of Music/Librarian: Jan Moore. Managing Ed: Barrie Stephenson. Hd of Programmes: David Dunning. MOR/Specialist[6, 5]

Yorkshire Coast Radio, FM:96.2/103.1 PO Box 962, Scarborough, North Yorkshire YO11 3ZP **t** 01723 581700 **f** 01723 588990 **e** info@yorkshirecoastradio.com **w** yorkshirecoastradio.com Station Mgr/Prog Cont: Chris Sigsworth. Hd of Music: Ben Fry. Hd of Sales: Gaynor Preston-Routledge. AC[5, 6]

Television

Anglia Anglia House, Norwich, Norfolk NR1 3JG **t** 01603 615151 **f** 01603 631032 **e** angliatv@angliatv.co.uk **w** anglia.tv.co.uk

Big Eye Film & Television Lock Keepers Cottage, Century St, Whitworth St West, Manchester M3 4QL **t** 0161 832 6111 **f** 0161 834 8558 **e** eye@bigeye.u-net.com Contact: Steven Lock, Mary Richmond.

Blaze TV 43-45 Dorset St, London W1U 7NA **t** 020 7664 1600 **f** 020 7935 5907 **e** firstname.lastname@blaze.tv **w** zenith-enteretainment.com Dir of Programmes: Conor McAnally.

Bournemouth TV (see Southampton TV)

Brighter Pictures 10th Floor, Blue Star House, 234-244 Stockwell Rd, London SW9 9SP **t** 020 7733 7333 **f** 020 7733 6333 **e** info@brighter.co.uk **w** brighter.co.uk MD: Gavin Hay.

Carlton (Central) Carlton Studios, Television House, Nottingham NG7 2NA **t** 0115 986 3322 **f** 0115 964 5552 **w** carlton.com/central

Carlton UK 101 St Martin's Lane, London WC2N 4AZ **t** 020 7240 4000 **f** 020 7240 4171 **w** carlton.com

Carlton (Westcountry) Western Wood Way, Langage Science Park, Plymouth, Devon PL7 5BG **t** 01752 333333 **f** 01752 333444 **w** carlton.com/westcountry

CD:UK Contact: Blaze TV.

Media

Channel 4 124 Horseferry Rd, London SW1P 2TX **t** 020 7396 4444 **f** 020 7306 8630 **e** jwallace@channel4.co.uk **w** channel4.com Hd of Music: Jo Wallace. Commissioning Editor, Youth: Andi Peters.

Chart Show Channels 37 Harwood Rd, London SW6 4QP **t** 020 7371 5999 **f** 020 7384 2026 **e** info@chartshow.tv **w** chartshow.tv CEO: Gail Screene.

The Chart Show 37 Harwood Rd, London SW6 4QP **t** 020 7371 5999 **f** 020 7384 2026 **e** info@chartshow.tv **w** chartshow.tv

Chrysalis Television Ltd Mayward House, 46-52 Pentonville Rd, London N1 9HF **t** 020 7502 6000 **f** 020 7502 5622 **e** firstname+first letter of lastname@chrysalis.com MD: Neil Duncanson. Deputy MD/Dir of Business and Legal Affairs: John Wohlgemuth.

CYP Limited CYP Children's Audio, The Fairway, Bush Fair, Harlow, Essex CM18 6LY **t** 01279 444707 **f** 01279 445570 **e** enquiries@kidsmusic.co.uk **w** kidsmusic.co.uk Contact: John Bassett

DanceStar UK Ltd 1 Mission Grove, London E17 7DD **t** 020 8520 9316 or +1 305 371 2450 **f** +1 305 371 2460 **e** info@dancestar.com **w** dancestar.com Founder & CEO: Andy Ruffell.

BBC East St Catherine's Close, All Saints Green, Norwich, Norfolk NR1 3ND **t** 01603 619331 **f** 01603 284455 **e** look.east@bbc.co.uk **w** bbc.co.uk/england/lookeast

EMAP Performance TV Mappin House, 4 Winsley St, London W1W 8HF **t** 020 7436 1515 **f** 020 7376 1313 **e** tv@emap.com **w** emap.com Dir of Music: Simon Sadler. Channels: The Box, Kiss, Kerrang!, Smash Hits, Magic, Q & The Hits.

Endemol UK Productions Shepherds Building Central, Charecroft Way, London W14 0EE **t** 0870 333 1700 **f** 0870 333 1800 **e** info@endemoluk.com **w** endemoluk.com Music Supervisor: Amelia Hartley.

Somethin' Else Units 1-4, 1A Old Nichol St, London E2 7HR **t** 020 7613 3211 **f** 020 7739 9799 **e** jez@somethin-else.com **w** somethin-else.com Prog Dir: Jez Nelson. Hd of Commercial Radio: Steve Ackerman

Five 1 Stephen St, London W1T 1AL **t** 020 7691 6610 **f** 020 7691 6085 **e** firstname.lastname@five.tv **w** five.tv Mgr, Music Services: Martin Price.

GMTV London Television Centre, Upper Ground, London SE1 9TT **t** 020 7827 7000 **f** 020 7827 7001 **e** talk2us@gmtv.co.uk **w** gmtv.co.uk Contact: Press Office

Granada (Manchester) Granada Television, Quay St, Manchester M60 9EA **t** 0161 832 7211 **f** 0161 953 0298 **e** officers.duty@granadatv.co.uk **w** granadatv.co.uk Music & Fim Ent Dept: Louise Wilcockson.

Granada (News Centre) Albert Dock, Liverpool, Merseyside L3 4BA **t** 0151 709 9393 or 0161 832 7211 **f** 0151 709 3389 **w** granada.co.uk

Andy Holland - Independent TV Producer Firedup TV, 87 Lancaster Rd, London W11 1QQ **t** 020 7313 9156 or 07767 833 603 **e** andy.holland@firedup.tv **w** firedup.tv Exec Prod: Andy Holland.

Initial (an Endemol Company) Shepeherds Building Central, Charecroft Way, London W14 0EE **t** 0870 333 1700 **f** 0870 333 1800 **e** info@endemoluk.com **w** endemoluk.com Hd of Music: Phil Mount.

ITVWales Television Centre, Culverhouse Cross, Cardiff CF5 6XJ **t** 029 2059 0590 **f** 029 2059 7183 **e** info@itvwales.com **w** itvwales.com

Landscape Channel Europe Ltd Landscape Studios, Crowhurst, East Sussex TN33 9BX **t** 01424 830900 **f** 01424 830680 **e** info@landscapetv.com **w** landscapetv.com Chairman: Nick Austin.

Later With Jools Holland BBC TV Centre, Wood Lane, London W12 7RJ **t** 020 8743 8000 or 020 8576 0968 **f** 020 8749 4955 **w** bbc.co.uk/later

Mike Mansfield Television Ltd 5th Floor, 41-42 Berners St, London W1T 3NB **t** 020 7580 2581 **f** 020 7580 2582 **e** mikemantv@aol.com **w** cyberconcerts.com MD: Mike Mansfield. Producer: Hilary McLaren.

Mentorn Midlands 32 New Rd, Woodstock, Oxon OX20 1PB **t** 0199 381 0300 **f** 0199 381 0301 **e** midlands@mentorn.co.uk **w** mentorn.co.uk

Meridian Television Centre, Northam, Southampton, Hampshire SO14 0PZ **t** 023 8022 2555 **f** 023 8071 2012 **e** viewerliaison@meridiantv.com **w** meridiantv.co.uk

MTV Base 17-29 Hawley Crescent, London NW1 8TT **t** 020 7284 7777 **f** 020 7284 6466 **e** mtvbase@mtvne.com **w** mtv.co.uk/base MTV Base Channel Manager: Shurwin Beckford.

MTV Dance Hawley Crescent, London NW1 8TT **t** 020 7284 7777 **f** 020 7284 6466 **e** mtvdance@mtvne.com **w** mtv.co.uk/dance Channel Manager: Laurence Koe.

MTV Hits Hawley Crescent, London NW1 8TT **t** 020 7284 7777 **f** 020 7284 6466 **e** mtvhits@mtvne.com **w** mtv.co.uk/hits Channel Manager: Jon Lazarus.

MTV UK & Ireland Hawley Crescent, London NW1 0TT **t** 020 7284 7777 **f** 020 7284 6466 **e** parker.eleanor@mtvne.com **w** mtv.co.uk Hd of Production: Matthew Bowes. MD, MTV Networks UK & Ireland: Michiel Bakker. Hd of Talent: Jamie Caring.

MTV2 17-29 Hawley Crescent, London NW1 8TT **t** 020 7284 7777 **f** 020 7284 6466 **e** mtv2@mtvne.com **w** mtv2europe.com Channel Manager: Nick Hutchings.

Music Box 30 Sackville St, London W1X 1DB **t** 020 7478 7300 **f** 020 7478 7403 **w** music-bx.co.uk MD: John Leach.

Music Choice Ltd(A member of Music Choice Europe) Fleet House, 57-61 Clerkenwell Rd, London EC1M 5LA **t** 020 7014 8700 **f** 020 7253 8460 **e** sales@musicchoice.co.uk **w** musicchoice.co.uk CEO: Simon Bazalgette. Dir of Music & Marketing: Simon Bell. Media Sales Dir: Dominic Trigg. Hd of Trade Marketing: Stephen Peng.

BBC North BBC Broadcasting Centre, Woodhouse Lane, Leeds, West Yorkshire LS2 9PX **t** 0113 244 1188 **f** 0113 243 9387 **e** look.north@bbc.co.uk **w** bbc.co.uk/england/looknorthyorkslincs

BBC North East Broadcasting Centre, Barrack Rd, Newcastle upon Tyne, Tyne and Wear NE99 2NE **t** 0191 232 1313 **f** 0191 221 0112 **e** newcastlenews@bbc.co.uk **w** bbc.co.uk

BBC North West New Broadcasting House, Oxford Rd, Manchester M60 1SJ **t** 0161 200 2020 **f** 0161 236 1005 **e** nwt@bbc.co.uk **w** bbc.co.uk/england/northwesttonight

BBC Northern Ireland Ormeau Avenue, Belfast, Co Antrim BT2 8HQ **t** 028 9033 8000 **f** 028 9033 8800 **w** bbc.co.uk/northernireland

Oasis TV 6-7 Great Pulteney St, London W1R 3DF **t** 020 7434 4133 **f** 020 7494 2843 **e** sales@oasistv.co.uk **w** oasistv.co.uk Business Dev't Mgr: Matthew Lock.

Pearson Television Ltd 1 Stephen St, London W1P 1PJ **t** 020 7691 6000 **f** 020 7691 6100 **e** facilites.helpdesk@fremental.com **w** pearsontv.com

The Pop Factory / Avanti Television Welsh Hills Works, Jenkin St, Porth CF39 9PP **t** 01443 688500 **f** 01443 688501 **e** info@thepopfactory.com **w** thepopfactory.com Contact: Emyr Afan Davies

Remedy Productions Office 6, 9 Thorpe Close, London W10 5XL **t** 020 8964 4408 or 020 8964 4631 **f** 020 8964 4421 **e** toby@remedyproductions.tv MD: Toby Dormer.

RTE (Radio-Telefis Eireann) Donnybrook, Dublin 4, Ireland **t** +353 1 208 3111 **f** +353 1 208 3080 **e** webmaster@rte.ie **w** rte.ie

RTE Network 2 Donnybrook, Dublin 4, Ireland **t** +353 1 208 3111 **f** 00 353 1 208 2511 **e** television@rte.ie **w** rte.ie

RTE TG4 Donnybrook, Dublin 4, Ireland **t** +353 1 208 3111 **f** 00 353 1 208 2511 **w** tg4.ie/tg4.htm

BBC Scotland Queen Margaret Drive, Glasgow, Strathclyde G12 8DG **t** 0141 338 2000 **f** 0141 338 2773 **e** enquiries.scot@bbc.co.uk **w** bbc.co.uk/scotland

S4C (Sianel Pedwar Cymru) Parc Ty Glas, Llanishen, Cardiff, South Glamorgan CF4 5DU **t** 029 2074 7444 **f** 029 2074 1457 **e** hotline@s4c.co.uk **w** s4c.co.uk

SixTV The Oxford Channel 270 Woodstock Rd, Oxford OX2 7NW **t** 01865 557000 **f** 01865 553355 **e** ptv@oxfordchannel.com **w** sixtv.co.uk Producer: Tom Copeland.

Sky Box Office Skt Television, Unit 2, Grant Way, Isleworth, Middlesex TW7 5QD **t** 020 7805 8126 **f** 020 7805 8130 **e** marc.conneely@bskyb.com **w** sky.com Hd of Pay-Per-View Events: Marc Conneely.

Sky Music Channels Unit 4, Grant Way, Isleworth, Middlesex TW7 5QD **t** 020 7805 8526 **f** 020 7805 8522 **e** Ian.Greaves@bskyb.com Music Programming Manager: Ian Greaves.

BBC South Havelock Rd, Southampton, Hampshire SO1 0XQ **t** 023 8022 6201 **f** 023 8033 9931 **e** spotlight@bbc.co.uk **w** bbc.co.uk

BBC South West Broadcasting House, Seymour Rd, Plymouth, Devon PL3 5DB **t** 01752 229201**f** 01752 234595 **e** spotlight@bbc.co.uk **w** bbc.co.uk/england/spotlight Press Office: Marlene Crawley.

Southampton Television Sir James Mathews Building, 157-187 Above Bar St, Southampton SO14 7NN **t** 023 8023 2400 **f** 023 8038 6366 **e** James.Rostance@southamptontv.co.uk **w** southamptontv.co.uk Producer, Music & Ent.: James Rostance.

T4 At It Productions, Westbourne Studios, 242 Acklam Rd, London W10 5YG **t** 020 88964 2122 **f** 020 8964 2133 **e** lindsey.brill@atitproductions.com Entertainment Booker: Lindsey Brill.

BBC Television Centre Wood Lane, Shepherd's Bush, London W12 7RJ **t** 020 8743 8000 **f** 020 8749 7520 **e** info@bbc.co.uk **w** bbc.co.uk

Top Of The Pops Rm 385, Design Building, BBC Television Centre, Wood Lane, London W12 7RJ **t** 020 8743 8000 or 020 8624 8398 (Prod) **f** 020 8624 8395 (Prod) **e** firstname.lastname@bbc.co.uk **w** bbc.co.uk/totp Exec Prod: Andi Peters.

Upfront Television 39-41 New Oxford St, London WC1A 1BN **t** 020 7836 7702 **f** 020 7836 7701 **e** info@upfronttv.com **w** celebritiesworldwide.com Co-MDs: Claire Nye, Richard Brecker.

UTV (Ulster Television) Havelock House, Ormeau Rd, Belfast, Co Antrim BT7 1EB **t** 028 9032 8122 **f** 028 9024 6695 or 028 9026 2208 **w** utvlive.com

VH1/VH1 Classic Hawley Crescent, London NW1 8TT **t** 020 7284 7777 **f** 020 7284 6466 **e** vh1online@mtvne.com **w** vh1online.co.uk General Manager: Sally Habbershaw.

Videotech 131-151 Great Titchfield St., London W1W 5BB **t** 020 7665 8200 **f** 020 7665 8213 Producer: Diana Smith.

BBC Wales Broadcasting House, Meirion Rd, Bangor LL57 3BY **t** 01248 370880 **f** 01248 352784 **e** feedback.wales@bbc.co.uk **w** bbc.co.uk/wales

BBC West Midlands Pebble Mill Rd, Birmingham, West Midlands B5 7QQ **t** 0121 432 8888 **f** 0121 432 8634 **e** midlands.today@bbc.co.uk **w** bbc.co.uk

Yorkshire Television Ltd Television Centre, Leeds, West Yorkshire LS3 1JS **t** 0113 243 8283 **f** 0113 244 5107 **w** yorkshiretv.co.uk MD: David Croft.

Webcasting & Streaming

1000 Stream 61 Birkenhead St, London WC1H 8BB **t** 020 7843 4338 **e** info@1000stream.com **w** 1000stream.com

303 Ltd Suite 302-304, Golden House, 24 Great Pulteney St, London W1K 3DD **t** 020 7437 3030 **f** 020 7494 0956 **e** rufus@encoding.tv **w** encoding.tv MD: Rufus Collis.

Arawak Interactive Marketing Ltd 2-4 Rufus St, London N1 6PE **t** 020 7256 1111 **f** 020 7265 1122 **e** info@arawak.co.uk **w** arawak.co.uk Dir: Nick Corston.

Art Empire Industries Ltd 861 Ecclesall Rd, Sheffield S11 7AE **t** 0114 281 4470 **f** 0114 281 6001 **e** info@artempireindustries.com **w** artempireindustries.com Comm Dir: Del Dias.

Astream Limited 25 Denmark St, London WC2H 8NJ **t** 020 7628 9063 **f** 020 7638 2913 **e** info@astream.co.uk **w** astream.net Comm Dir: Mark Wilson.

BT Rich Media (a division of BT plc) PP4E, 4th Floor, 203 High Holborn, London WC1V 7BU **t** 020 7777 7444 **f** 020 7728 7474 **e** btrminfo@bt.com **w** btrichmedia.com Dir of Music: Marco Distefano.

Eunite :: The convergence company Bridgewater House, 58-60 Whitworth St, Manchester M1 6LT **t** 0161 237 4900 **f** 0161 237 4909 **e** info@eunite.co.uk **w** eunite.co.uk Ac Dir, music & streaming: Harry Leckstein.

Freeflow UK International Media Centre, Adelphi House, The Crescent, Salford M3 6EN **t** 0161 295 7240 **f** 0161 834 0710 **e** info@freeflowuk.com **w** freeflowuk.com Project Manager: Ian Dobie. Student music portal.

garageband.com Air Studios, Lyndhurst Rd, London NW3 5NG **t** 020 7794 0660 **f** 020 7916 2784 **e** artistmanager@garageband.com **w** garageband.com UK A&R: Adam Sharp.

Groovetech.com 10 Latimer Industrial Estate, Latimer Rd, London W10 6RQ **t** 020 8962 3350 **f** 020 8962 3355 **e** feedback@groovetech.com **w** groovetech.com Broadcast Content Manager: Ana Saskia Adang.

Media

Inner Ear Ltd/Radio Magnetic Argyle House, 16 Argyle Court, 1103 Argyle St, Glasgow G3 8ND **t** 0141 226 8808 **f** 0141 226 8818 **e** tom@radiomagnetic.com **w** inner.co.uk & radiomagnetic.com Sales & Marketing Dir: Tom Lousada.

INTEROUTE

Walbrook Building, 195 Marsh Wall, London E14 9SG **t** 020 7025 9000 **f** 020 7025 9854 **e** liza.autey@interoute.com **w** interoute.com Media Services Account Mgr Liza Autey . **Media Manager provides advanced media streaming solutions to securely upload, store, manage and syndicate online audio and video content.**

Matinée Sound & Vision Ltd 132-134 Oxford Rd, Reading, Berkshire RG1 7NL **t** 0118 958 4934 **f** 0118 959 4936 **e** info@matinee.co.uk **w** matinee.co.uk Marketing Co-ordinator: Miranda Harley.

MediaWave Group Ltd. Hudson House, Hudson Way, Pride Park, Derby DE24 8HS **t** 01332 866700 **f** 01322 208485 **e** kim.peatfield@mediawave.co.uk **w** mediawave.co.uk Mkt Mgr: Kim Peatfield.

Popex.com 109x Regents Park Rd, London NW1 8UR **t** 020 7691 4555 **f** 020 7691 4666 **e** Pauly@popex.com Contact: Paul Clarke

Purple Radio 6 Hanover St, Mayfair, London W1R 9HH **t** 020 7491 1001 **f** 020 7647 7678 **e** studio@purpleradio.com **w** purpleradio.net Hd of Programming: Peter Flynn.

Stream UK Ltd 1a Mornington Court, Arlington Rd, London NW1 7ER **t** 020 7387 6090 or 020 7387 6091 **f** 020 7383 9160 **e** joe@streamuk.com **w** streamuk.com Dir: Joe Bray.

thewhitelabel.com limited 1-3 Croft Lane, Henfield, W. Sussex BN5 9TT **t** 01273 491761 **f** 01273 491761 **e** contact@thewhitelabel.com **w** thewhitelabel.com GM: Nic Vine.

Tornado Virtue PLC Tornado House, Pound Lane, Marlow SL7 2AF **t** 01628 498600 **f** 01628 498610 **e** info@tornadovirtue.com **w** tornadovirtue.com Business Development Dir: Nick English.

Video-C 1 Bayham St, London NW1 OER **t** 020 7916 5483 **f** 020 7916 5482 **e** oisin@video-c.co.uk **w** video-c.co.uk Project Manager: Oisin Lunny.

VidZone 9 Tideway Yard, The Old Power Station, 125 Mortlake High St, London SW14 8SN **t** 020 8487 5880 **f** 020 8487 5883 **e** adrian@vidzone.tv **w** vidzone.tv CEO: Adrian Workman.

WAM TV (Worldart Media Television Ltd) 1 High St, Lasswade, Midlothian EH18 1NA **t** 0131 654 2372 **e** contact@wam.tv **w** wam.tv MD: Paul Blyth.

WembleyTV 1st Floor, 8-10 King St, Hammersmith, London W6 0QA **t** 020 8741 6113 **f** 020 8741 6113 **e** info@wembleytv.com **w** wembleytv.com Chief Executive: Ian Howard.

Broadcast Services

3DD Entertainment 190 Camden High St, London NW1 8QP **t** 020 7428 1800 **f** 020 7428 1818 **e** Sales@3dd-entertainment.co.uk **w** 3dd-entertainment.co.uk Publicity Co-ordinator: Sarah Andersen.

Alice Unit 34D, Hobbs Ind Estate, Newchapel, Lingfield, Surrey RH7 6HN **t** 01342 833500 **f** 01342 833350 **e** sales@alice.co.uk **w** alice.co.uk Sales Director: Garry Thompson. Radio studio equipment design, installation, servicing.

AMI Music Library 34 Salisbury Street, London NW8 8QE **t** 020 7402 9111 **f** 020 7723 3064 **e** eliot@amimedia.co.uk **w** amimedia.co.uk MD: Eliot Cohen.

Arcadia Production Music (UK) Greenlands, Payhembury, Devon EX14 3HY **t** 01404 841601 **f** 01404 841687 **e** admin@arcadiamusic.tv **w** arcadiamusic.tv Proprietor: John Brett.

Audio Processing Technology Edgewater Road, Belfast, Co Antrim BT3 9JQ **t** 028 9037 1110 **f** 028 9037 1137 **e** jmcclintock@aptx.com **w** aptx.com Sales Dept: Jon McClintock.

Audio Systems Components 1 Comet House, Calleva Park, Aldermaston, Berkshire RG7 8JB **t** 0118 981 1000 or 0118 981 9565 **f** 0118 981 9813 or 0118 981 9687 **e** sales@ascuk.com **w** ascuk.com Contact: Iain Elliott Radio studio equipment manufacture and supply.

Audionics Petre Drive, Sheffield S4 7PZ **t** 0114 242 2333 **f** 0114 243 3913 **e** online@audionics.co.uk **w** audionics.co.uk Production Director: Phil Myers. Radio studio equipment manufacture.

British Forces Broadcasting Services (BFBS) Chalfont Grove, Narcot Lane, Gerrard Cross, Buckinghamshire SL9 8TN **t** 01494 878354 **f** 01494 870552 **e** helen.marland@bfbs.com **w** bfbs.com Programme Dir: Ian Noakes. Radio for UK armed service worldwide.

Calrec Audio Nutclough Mill, Hebden Bridge, West Yorkshire HX7 8EZ **t** 01422 842159 **f** 01422 845244 **e** enquiries@calrec.com **w** calrec.com Sales & Mkting Dir: John Gluck. Manufacturers of audio equipment for broadcast.

Churches Media Council Box 6613, South Woodham Ferrers, Essex CM3 5DY **t** 01245 322158 **f** 01245 321957 **e** office@churchesmediacouncil.org.uk **w** churchesmediacouncil.org.uk Dir: Peter Blackman. Contacts, advice about churches and broadcasting.

Commercial Radio Companies Association 77 Shaftesbury Avenue, London W1V 7AD **t** 020 7306 2603 **f** 020 7470 0062 **e** info@crca.co.uk **w** crca.co.uk Contact: Paul Brown Trade association for UK commercial radio.

Community Media Asociation The Workstation, 15 Paternoster Row, Sheffield S1 2BX **t** 0114 279 5219 **f** 0114 279 8976 **e** cma@commedia.org.uk **w** commedia.org.uk Contact: Steve Buckley

Curious Yellow 33-37 Hatherley Mews, London E17 4QP **t** 020 8521 9595 **f** 020 8521 6363 **e** paul@curiousyellow.co.uk **w** curiousyellow.co.uk MD: Paul Penny.

delicious digital Suite GB, 39-40 Warple Way, Acton, London W3 0RG **t** 020 8749 7272 **f** 020 8749 7474 **e** info@deliciousdigital.com **w** deliciousdigital.com MD: Ollie Raphael.

DMX Music Forest Lodge, Westerham Road, Keston, Kent BR2 6HE **t** 01689 882200 **f** 01689 882288 **e** alex.martin@dmxmusic.co.uk **w** dmxmusic.co.uk Marketing Manager: Alex Martin.

Doctor Rock The Century, 2A Newlands Rd, Waterlooville, Hampshire PO7 5NF **t** 023 9225 4426 **e** DoctorRock@cwctv.net Producer: Bob Woodhead. Programme presenter/producer, pop expert/historian.

Done and Dusted 36 Howland St., London W1P 5FP **t** 07000 708 708 **f** 07000 708 709 **e** info@doneanddusted.com **w** www.doneanddusted.com Concert Prod/Events Dir.: Ian Stewart.

DT Productions Maygrove House, 67 Maygrove Rd, London NW6 2SP **t** 020 7644 8888 **f** 020 7644 8889 **e** info@dtproductions.co.uk **w** dtproductions.co.uk Music Programming: Lee Taylor.

DTP Radio Production Studios 35 Tower Way, Dunkeswell, Devon EX14 4XH **t** 01404 891598 MD: Don Todd MBE.

Eagle Media Productions Russell House, Ely Street, Stratford-upon-Avon, Warwickshire CV37 6LW **t** 01789 415 187 **f** 01789 415 210 **e** amy@eaglemp.co.uk **w** eagle-rock.com MD: Alan Ravenscroft. Executive Producer: Steve Gillham. Producer: Trevor Green. Producer: Audrey Healy. Technical Co-ordinator: David Rogers.

EAGLE ROCK ENTERTAINMENT LTD.

EAGLE ROCK
ENTERTAINMENT LIMITED

Eagle House, 22 Armoury Way, London SW18 1EZ **t** 020 8870 5670 **f** 020 8874 2333 **e** mail@eagle-rock.com **w** eagle-rock.com Executive Chairman: Terry Shand. Deputy Chairman: Julian Paul. Chief Operating Officer: Geoff Kempin. Group Finance Director: Jonathan Blanchard. Director of Business Affairs: Martin Dacre. General Manager: Chris Cole. Director of Marketing & Sales: Lindsay Brown.

EAGLE VISION

eagle vision

Eagle House, 22 Armoury Way, London SW18 1EZ **t** 020 8870 5670 **f** 020 8874 2333 **e** mail@eagle-rock.com **w** eagle-rock.com COO, Worldwide: Geoff Kempin. Dir of Intl. Acquisitions: John Gaydon. Dir of Intl. Sales & Marketing: Lindsay Brown. MD of Intl. Television: Peter Worsley. Dir. of Intl. TV Sales: Andrew Winter. Intl. Licensing Manager: Lesley Wilsdon. Intl. Product Manager: Nicola O'Donegan. Snr Production Manager: Claire Higgins. Business Affairs Manager: Melissa Roy.

Eleven Music Management 14 Church St, Twickenham, Middlesex TW1 3NJ **t** 020 8744 2777 or 0774 0643015 **f** 020 8891 1895 **e** nina@elevenmusic.co.uk Contact: Nina Jackson

Entertainment Media Research Studio One, Charter House, Crown Court, London WC2B 5EX **t** 020 7240 1222 **f** 020 7240 8877 **e** patrick.johnston@entertainmentmediaresearch.com **w** entertainmentmediaresearch.com Dir of Business Devt.: Patrick Johnston.

Fastrax Allan House, 10 John Prince's St, London W1G 0JW **t** 020 7468 6888 **f** 020 7468 6889 **e** info@fastrax.co.uk **w** fastrax.co.uk Ops Mgr: Ross Priestley. Digital distribution of music to radio.

Feltwain 2000 1 Oakwood Parade, London N14 4HY **t** 020 8950 8732 **f** 020 8950 6648 **e** paul.lynton@btopenworld.com MD: Paul Lynton.

Festival Productions PO Box 107, Brighton, East Sussex BN1 1QG **t** 01273 669595 **f** 01273 669596 **e** post@festivalradio.com **w** festivalradio.com MD: Steve Stark. Radio production and syndication.

Freeway Media Services 20 Windmill Road, Kirkcaldy, Fife KY1 3AQ **t** 01592 655309 or 07973 920488 **f** 01592 596177 **e** cronulla20@aol.com **w** voiceofscotland.co.uk Dir: John Murray. Training in radio presentation.

G One 50 Lisson St, London NW1 5DF **t** 020 7453 1655 or 020 7453 1619 **f** 020 7453 1665 **e** simon.poole@g-one.co.uk **w** g-one.co.uk Producer: Simon Poole.

Liz Gallacher Music Supervision 23 Brickwood Rd, Croydon, Surrey CR0 6UL **t** 020 8680 7784 **f** 020 8681 3000 **e** liz@lizg.com Music Supervisor: Liz Gallacher. Music consultancy to TV, film, advertising.

Generics R Us 3 Haversham Lodge, Melrose Avenue, London NW2 4JS **t** 020 8450 8882 **f** 020 8208 4219 **e** sharon@thepublicityconnection.com **w** thepublicityconnection.com Prop: Sharon Chevin.

The Hobo Partnership 18 Broadwick St, London W1F 8HS **t** 020 7434 2907 **f** 020 7437 9984 **e** info@hobopartnership.com **w** hobopartnership.com MD: Debbie Wheeler.

The Hospital Group 24 Endell Street, London WC2H 9HQ **t** 020 7170 9110 **f** 020 7170 9102 **e** studio@thehospital.co.uk **w** thehospital.co.uk Studio Sales Manager: Anne Marie Phelan.

Ig-nite 14 Panther House, 38 Mount Pleasant, London WC1X 0APEmail: info@ig-nite.com **w** ig-nite.com Director: Kary Stewart.

IMD Fastrax Allan House, 10 John Princes St, London W1G 0JW **t** 020 7468 6868 **f** 020 7468 6869 **e** info@fastrax.co.uk **w** fastrax.co.uk Operations Mgr: Ross Priestly.

Immedia Broadcasting 7-9 The Broadway, Newbury, Berks RG14 1AS **t** 01635 572 800 **f** 01635 572 801 **e** customerservices@immediabroadcasting.com **w** immediabroadcasting.com Office Mgr: Lesley Pye.

Independent Television News (ITN) 200 Grays Inn Road, London WC1X 8XZ **t** 020 7833 3000 **f** 020 7430 4016 **e** press.office@itn.co.uk **w** itn.co.uk Contact: Press Office

Inner Ear Argyle House, 16 Argyle Court, 1103 Argyle Street, Glasgow G3 8ND **t** 0141 226 8808 **f** 0141 226 8818 **e** info@innerear.co.uk **w** innerear.co.uk Sale & Marketing Dir: Tom Lousada.

Intelligent Media Kiln House, 210 New Kings Rd, London SW6 4NZ **t** 020 7731 2020 **f** 020 7731 1100 **e** jonm@intelligentmedia.com **w** intelligentmedia.com MD: Jon Mais.

ITC (Independent Television Commission) 33 Foley Street, London W1W 7TL **t** 0845 601 3608 **f** 020 7306 7800 **e** publicaffairs@itc.org.uk **w** itc.org.uk Contact: Viewer Relations Unit

ITV Network Centre 200 Gray's Inn Road, London WC1X 8HF **t** 020 7843 8000 **f** 020 7843 8158 **e** info@itv.co.uk **w** www.itv.co.uk

JW Media Music 4 Whitfield Street, London W1T 2RD **t** 020 7681 8900 **f** 020 7681 8911 **e** salesinfo@jwmediamusic.co.uk **w** jwmediamusic.com MD: George Barker.

MediaLane International The Old Garage, The Green, Great Milton, Oxon OX44 7NP **t** 01844 278534 **f** 01844 278538 **e** stratton@medialane-international.com **w** medialane-international.com Dir of Ops: Alan Stratton.

Mediatracks Music Library 93 Columbia Way, Blackburn, Lancashire BB2 7EA **t** 01254 691197 **f** 01254 723505 **e** info@mediatracks.co.uk **w** mediatracks.co.uk Proprieter: Steve Johnson.

Metrobroadcast 53 Great Suffolk Street, London SE1 0DB **t** 020 7202 2000 **f** 020 7202 2005 **e** info@metrobroadcast.com **w** metrobroadcast.com Director: Paul Braybrooke.

The Music Mall 1 Upper James St, London W1F 9DE **t** 020 7534 1444 **f** 020 7534 1440 **e** See website for contacts. **w** musicmall.co.uk

Musicalities Snows Ride Farm, Snows Ride, Windlesham, Surrey GU20 6LA **t** 01276 474181 **f** 01276 452227 **e** enquiries@musicalities.co.uk **w** musicalities.co.uk MD: Ivan Chandler.

NBC News 3 Shortlands, 4th Floor, Hammersmith, London W6 8HX **t** 020 8600 6600 **f** 020 8600 6601 **e** london.newsdesk@nbc.com

Neon Productions Studio One, 19 Marine Crescent, Kinning Park, Glasgow G51 1HD **t** 0141 429 6366 **f** 0141 429 6377 **e** mail@go2neon.com **w** go2neon.com Dir: Robert Noakes. Co-Dir: Stephanie Pordage.

Nielsen Music Control (Ireland) Top Floor, 6 Clare Street, Dublin 2, Ireland **t** +353 1 605 0686 **f** +353 1 678 5343 **e** f.byrne@music-control.com **w** music-control.com GM: Feidhlim Byrne.

Nielsen Music Control UK 5th Floor, Endeavour House, 189 Shaftesbury Avenue, London WC2H 8TJ **t** 020 7420 9292 **f** 020 7420 9295 **e** info@music-control.com Head of UK Ops: Ray Bonici.

OVC Media 88 Berkeley Court, Baker St, London NW1 5ND **t** 020 7402 9111 **f** 020 7723 3044 **e** Joanne.ovc@virgin.net **w** ovcmedia.com Dir: Joanne Cohen.

Q Sheet Markettiers 4DC, Northburgh House, 10a Northburgh St, London EC1V 0AT **t** 020 7253 8888 **f** 020 7253 8885 **e** editor@qsheet.com **w** qsheet.com Music Editor: Nik Harta.

Radica Broadcast Systems 18 Bolney Grange Industrial Pk, Hickstead, Haywards Heath, West Sussex RH17 5PB **t** 01444 258285 **f** 01444 258288 **e** sales@radica.com **w** radica.com/radio Sales Mgr: Graham Sloggett.

The Radio Academy 5 Market Place, London W1W 8AE **t** 020 7255 2010 **f** 020 7255 2029 **e** info@radioacademy.org **w** radioacademy.org Director: John Bradford.

The Radio Advertising Bureau 77 Shaftesbury Avenue, London W1V 5DU **t** 020 7306 2500 **f** 020 7306 2505 **e** aimee@rab.co.uk **w** rab.co.uk Operations Dir: Michael O'Brien.

RAJAR (Radio Joint Audience Research) Gainsborough House, 81 Oxford St, London W1D 2EU **t** 020 7903 5350 **f** 020 7903 5351 **e** info@rajar.co.uk **w** rajar.co.uk MD: Sally de la Bedoyere.

Rock Over London Inc 117 Grove Road, Sutton, Surrey SM1 2DB **t** 020 8661 2603 **f** 020 8661 2603 **e** psexton@blueyonder.co.uk MD: Paul Sexton.

Satellite Media Services Lawford Heath Teleport, Lawford Heath Lane, Rugby, Warwickshire CV23 9EU **t** 01788 523000 **f** 01788 523001 **e** sales@sms-internet.net **w** sms-internet.net MD: Tim Whittingham.

Sound Broadcast Services PO Box 100, Hastings, East Sussex TN34 3ZS **t** 01424 445588 **f** 01424 443388 **e** sales@sbsfm.com **w** sbsfm.com MD: Marcus Bekker.

searchtheyukon.com - Online Sync & Licensing 91 Saffron Hill, London EC1N 8PT **t** 020 7242 8408 **f** 020 7242 8408 **e** music@the-yukon.com **w** searchtheyukon.com MD: Andrew Maurice.

Somethin' Else Units 1-4, 1A Old Nichol Street, London E2 7HR **t** 020 7613 3211 **f** 020 7739 9799 **e** info@somethin-else.com **w** somethin-else.com Dir: Jez Nelson.

Straight TV 4th Floor, 121 Princess Street, Manchester M1 7AG **t** 0161 200 6000 **f** 0161 228 0228 **e** info@straight.tv **w** straight.tv Contact: Clare Winnick

Student Radio Association The Radio Academy, 5 Market Place, London W1W 8AE **t** 020 7255 2010 **f** 020 7255 2029 **e** chair@studentradio.org.uk **w** studentradio.org.uk Chair: Talia Kraines.

Talk Of The Devil 5 Ripley Rd, Worthing, West Sussex BN11 5NQ **t** 01903 526515 **f** 01903 539634 **e** steve.power@talk-of-the-devil.com **w** talk-of-the-devil.com MD: Steve Power.

Teletext Building 10, Chiswick Park, 566 Chiswick High Rd, London W4 5TS **t** 0870 731 3000 **e** listings@teletext.co.uk **w** teletext.co.uk

Totalrock 4 Fulham High Street, London SW6 3TZ **t** 020 7731 6696 **f** 020 7384 0319 **e** hq@totalrock.com **w** totalrock.com Head of Music/Dir of Prog: Tony Wilson.

Transorbital Productions 557 Street Lane, Leeds, West Yorkshire LS17 6JA **t** 0113 268 7886 or 07836 568 888 **f** 0113 266 0045 **e** carl@carlkingston.co.uk **w** carlkingston.co.uk MD: Carl Kingston.

Unique Facilities (Location Broadcasting Services & Radio Production Studios) 50 Lisson St, London NW1 5DF **t** 020 7723 0322 **f** 020 7453 1666 **e** info@uniquefacilities.com **w** uniquefacilities.com Facilities Mgr: Shane Wall.

Victoria Radio Network PO Box 1287, Kirkcaldy, Fife KY2 5ZX **t** 01592 268530 **e** info@vrn1287.com **w** vrn1287.com Programme Co-ordinator: Sandy Izatt. Presentation training and RSL management.

Waterfall Studios 2 Silver Rd, London W12 7SG **t** 020 8746 2000 **f** 020 8746 0180 **e** info@waterfall-studios.com **w** waterfall-studios.com Facilities Mgr: Samantha Leese.

Production Music

Abbeydale Music 6 Swinton Close, Kings Drive, Wembley Park, Middlesex HA9 9HW **t** 020 8904 9222 **f** 020 8904 9222 **e** jerry@abbeydale1.freeserve.co.uk Exec Producer: Jerry Freedman.

Adage Music 22 Gravesend Rd, London W12 OSZ **t** 07973 295113 **e** dobs@adagemusic.co.uk **w** adagemusic.co.uk MD: Dobs Vye.

Adelphoi Ltd 26 Litchfield Street, Covent Garden, London WC2H 9TZ **t** 020 7240 7250 **f** 020 7240 7260 **e** info@adelphoi.com **w** adelphoi.com Contact: Sophie Taylor

Admax Music 25 Heathmans RD, London SW6 4TJ **t** 020 7371 5756 **f** 020 7371 7731 **e** stirling@stakis.com **w** pureuk.com Contact: Ian Ferguson Brown

Air-Edel Associates 18 Rodmarton Street, London W1U 8BJ **t** 020 7486 6466 **f** 020 7224 0344 **e** mrodford@air-edel.co.uk **w** air-edel.co.uk MD: Maggie Rodford.

Arcadia Production Music (UK) Greenlands, Payhembury, Devon EX14 3HY **t** 01404 841601 **f** 01404 841687 **e** admin@arcadiamusic.tv **w** arcadiamusic.tv Proprietor: John Brett.

Arclite Productions Unit 303, Safe Store 5-10 Eastman Rd, London W3 7YG **t** O20 8743 4000 **e** info@arcliteproductions.com **w** arcliteproductions.com Prod: Alan Bleay.

David Arnold Music Unit 9, Dry Drayton Industries, Dry Drayton, Cambridge CB3 8AT **t** 01954 212020 **f** 01954 212222 **e** alex@davidarnoldmusic.com **w** davidarnoldmusic.com

Artemis Music Pinewood Studios, Pinewood Rd, Iver Heath, Bucks SL0 0NH **t** 01753 650766 **f** 01753 654774 **e** info@artemismusic.com **w** artemismusic.com MD: Mike Sheppard.

Atmosphere Music (see BMG Production Music)

Autograph Music & Media 19 Long Meadow Grove, St Lawrence Court, Manchester M34 2DA **t** 0161 336 9300 **f** 0161 221 3168 **e** autograph@ntlworld.com **w** autographmusicandmedia.com Owner: Derek Brandwood.

Barefoot Communications 24 Coronet Street, London N1 6HD **t** 020 7613 4697 **f** 020 7729 6613 **e** alex@barefootuk.co.uk **w** barefootuk.co.uk Dir: Alex Gover.

Bazza Productions 116 Ember Lane, Esher, Surrey KT10 8EL **t** 020 8398 1274 **f** 020 8398 1353 **e** bsguard@aol.com **w** barrieguard.com MD: Barrie Guard.

Beetroot Music 3/4 Portland Mews, D'Arblay St, London W1F 8JF **t** 020 7437 7889 **f** 020 7734 9230 **e** info@beetrootmusic.com **w** beetrootmusic.com Co MDs: Tish Lord & Danny Webster.

Big George and Sons PO Box 7094, Kiln Farm MK11 1LL **t** 01908 566453 **e** big.george@btinternet.com **w** biggeorge.co.uk Manager: Big George Webley.

BMG Zomba Production Music 10-11 St Martin's Court, London WC2N 4AJ **t** 020 7497 4808 **f** 020 7497 4801 **e** musicresearch@bmgzomba.com **w** bmgzomba.com Head of Mktg: Juliette Richards.

BOB 62 New Cavendish Street, London W1G 8TA **t** 020 7580 9373 **f** 020 7580 9375 **e** boblimited@aol.com Dir: Alex White.

Boom! Music 16 Blackwood Close, West Byfleet, Surrey KT14 6PP **t** 01932 336212 **e** Phil@music4media.tv **w** music4media.tv Composer: Phil Binding.

Boosey Media 295 Regent Street, London W1B 2JH **t** 020 7291 7222 **f** 020 7436 5675 **e** booseymedia@boosey.com **w** booseymedia.com Media Manager: Ann Dawson.

Brilliant Music Production Unit 2, The Quarry, Kewstoke Road, Worle, Weston-Super-Mare BS22 9LS **t** 01761 470023 or 01934 521555 **e** davidrees@brilliantmusicproductions.co.uk Partner: David Rees.

Burning Petals Production Music 5 Clover Ground, Shepton Mallet BA4 4AS **t** 0870 749 1117 **e** enquiries@burning-petals.com **w** burning-petals.com Contact: Richard Jay

Buzz-erk Music 17 Villiers Rd, Kingston Upon Thames, Surrey KT1 3AP **t** 020 8931 1044 **e** info@buzz-erk.com **w** Buzz-erk.com Dir: Niraj Chag.

Caleche Studios 175 Roundhay Road, Leeds LS8 5AN **t** 0113 219 4941 **f** 0113 249 4941 **e** caleche.studios@virgin.net MD: Leslie Coleman.

Candle 44 Southern Row, London W10 5AN **t** 020 8960 0111 or 07860 912 192 **f** 020 8968 7008 or (ISDN) 020 8960 4370 **e** email@candle.org.uk **w** candle.org.uk MD: Tony Satchell. Exec Producer: Charlie Spencer.

Capitol Studios 6 The White House, 42 The Terrace, Torquay, Devon TQ1 1DE **t** 01803 201918 **f** 01803 292323 **e** derek@radiojingles.com **w** radiojingles.com Commercial Prod: Julian Sharp.

Caritas Media Music (inc Caritas Music Library) 28 Dalrymple Crescent, Edinburgh EH9 2NX **t** 0131 667 3633 **f** 0131 667 3633 **e** media@caritas-music.co.uk **w** caritas-music.co.uk MD: James Douglas.

Chantelle Music 3A Ashheld Parade, London N14 5EH **t** 020 8886 6236 **e** info@chantellemusic.co.uk **w** chantellemusic.co.uk MD: Riss Chantelle.

Chicken Sounds PO Box 43829, London NW6 1WN **t** 020 7209 2586 **f** 020 7209 2586 **e** mail@whitehousemanagement.com Director: Sue Whitehouse.

Corporate Composition 7 Brunswick Close, Thames Ditton, Surrey KT7 0EU **t** 020 8398 1450 **f** 020 8398 1450 **e** smd.music@virgin.net Dir: Al Dickinson.

Crocodile Music 35 Gresse St, London W1T 1QY **t** 020 7580 0080 **f** 020 7637 0097 **e** music@crocodilemusic.com **w** crocodilemusic.com MD: Malcolm Ironton.

CYP The Fairway, Bush Fair, Harlow, Essex CM18 6LY **t** 01279 444707 **f** 01279 445570 **e** sales@cypmusic.co.uk **w** kidsmusic.co.uk Sales Manager: Gary Wilmot.

delicious digital Suite GB, 39-40 Warple Way, Acton, London W3 0RG **t** 020 8749 7272 **f** 020 8749 7474 **e** info@deliciousdigital.com **w** deliciousdigital.com Creative Director: Ed Moris.

Digital Vision India House, 45 Curlew St, London SE1 2ND **t** 020 7378 5555 **f** 020 7378 5735 **e** sales@digitalvisiononline.co.uk **w** digitalvisiononline.co.uk UK Sales: Joanne Rees.

Doodlehums 30 Cullesden Road, Kenley, Surrey CR8 5LR **t** 020 8668 4833 **f** 020 8668 4833 **e** oswinf@lineone.net Prop: Mr O Falquero.

Dreamscape Music 36 Eastcastle Street, London W1W 8DP **t** 020 7631 1799 **f** 020 7631 1720 **e** Bigsynths@aol.com Composer: Lester Barnes.

David Dundas Music 142 Battersea Park Road, London SW11 4NB **t** 020 7627 8017 **f** 020 7627 5412 **e** tai.dundas@virgin.net Producer: Tai Dundas.

veryday Productions 33 Mandarin Place, Grove, Oxfordshire OX12 0QH **t** 01235 767171 **e** smi_everyday_productions@yahoo.com VP Special Proj: David Wareham.

Geezers (Song Sourcing & Music Supervision) (see Beetroot Music)

G3 Music 13 Hales Prior, Calshot Street, London N1 9JW **t** 020 8361 2170 **f** 020 8361 2170 **e** g3music@g3music.com **w** g3music.com Creative Dir: Greg Heath.

Hear No Evil 6 Lillie Yard, London SW6 1UB **t** 020 7385 8244 **f** 020 7385 0700 **e** info@hearnoevil.net **w** hearnoevil.net MD: Sharon Rose-Parr.

Higher Ground Music Productions The Stables, Albury Lodge, Albury, Ware, Herts SG11 2LH **t** 01279 776 019 **e** info@highergrounduk.com **w** highergrounduk.com Creative & Commercial Dir: Greg Newman.

HotHouse Music Greenland Place, 115-123 Bayham St, London NW1 OAG **t** 020 7446 7446 **f** 020 7446 7448 **e** info@hot-house-music.com **w** hot-house-music.com Co-MDs: Becky Bentham, Karen Elliott.

Howarth & Johnston 61 Timber Bush, Leith, Edinburgh, Lothian EH6 6QH **t** 0131 555 2288 **f** 0131 555 0088 **e** doit@redfacilities.com **w** redfacilities.com Partner: Max Howarth.

HUM 31 Oval Road, London NW1 7EA **t** 020 7482 2345 **f** 020 7482 6242 **e** firstname@hum.co.uk **w** hum.co.uk Prod: Daniel Simmons.

Hydraphonic 127, Tottenham Road, London N1 4EA **t** 020 7923 7638 **e** info@hydraphonic.net Manager: Brian Betts.

In A City Unit 49, Carlisle Business Centre, 60 Carlisle Rd, Bradford BD8 8BD **t** 01904 438753 or 01274 223251 **f** 01274 223204 **e** cc@inacity.co.uk **w** inacity.co.uk MD: Carl Stipetic.

Inductive Music PO Box 20503, London NW8 0WY **t** 020 7586 5427 **f** 020 7483 2164 **e** inductrec@aol.com MD: Colin Peel.

Instant Music 14 Moorend Crescent, Cheltenham, Gloucestershire GL53 0EL **t** 01242 523304 or 07957 355630 **f** 01242 523304 **e** info@instantmusic.co.uk **w** instantmusic.co.uk MD: Martin Mitchell.

J Albert & Son (UK) Unit 29, Cygnus Business Centre, Dalmeyer Road, London NW10 2XA **t** 020 8830 0330 **f** 020 8830 0220 **e** anne@alberts.co.uk **w** alberts.co.uk TV & Screen Manager: Anne Miller.

Jingle Jangles The Strand, 156 Holywood Road, Belfast, Co Antrim BT4 1NY **t** 028 9065 6769 **f** 028 9067 3771 **e** steve@jinglejangles.tv **w** jinglejangles.tv MD: Steve Martin.

Joe & Co (Music) 59 Dean Street, London W1D 6AN **t** 020 7439 1272 **f** 020 7437 5504 **e** justine@joeandco.com **w** joeandco.com Office Mgr: Justine Campbell.

Killer Tracks (see BMG Zomba Production Music)

Carl Kingston 557 Street Lane, Leeds, West Yorkshire LS17 6JA **t** 0113 268 7886 or 07836 568888 **f** 0113 266 0045 **e** carl@carlkingston.co.uk **w** carlkingston.co.uk Contact: Carl Kingston

Knifedge 57b Riding House St, London W1W 7EF **t** 020 7436 5434 **f** 020 7436 5431 **e** info@knifedge.net **w** knifedge.net MD: Jonathan Brigden.

Koka Media (see BMG Zomba Production Music)

Dave Langer Creative Services 27 Cavendish Road, Salford, Manchester M7 4WP **t** 0161 740 7171 **f** 0161 792 9595 **e** info@jingle.org **w** jingle.org MD: Dave Langer.

LAS Music Productions PO Box 14303, London SE26 4ZH **t** 07000 472572 **f** 07000 472572 **e** info@latinartsgroup.com **w** latinartsgroup.com Director: Hector Rosquete.

LBS Manchester 11-13 Bamford Street, Stockport, Cheshire SK1 3NZ **t** 0161 477 2710 **f** 0161 480 9497 **e** info@lbs.co.uk **w** lbs.co.uk Prod: Adders.

LBS Music **t** 01865 725521 or 07071 225625 **e** richard@lbsmusic.demon.co.uk **w** lbsmusic.demon.co.uk MD: Richard Lewis.

Living Productions 39 Tadorne Road, Tadworth, Surrey KT20 5TF **t** 01737 812922 **f** 01737 812922 **e** Livingprods@ukgateway.net Dir/Co Sec: Norma Camby.

Loriana Music 30a Tudor Drive, Gidea Park, Romford RM2 5LH **t** 01708 750185 **f** 01708 750185 **e** info@lorianamusic.com **w** lorianamusic.com Owner: Jean-Louis Fargier.

Mad Hat Studios The Upper Hattons Media Centre, The Upper Hattons, Pendeford Hall Lane, Coven, Nr Wolverhampton WV9 5BD **t** 01902 840440 **f** 01902 840448 **e** studio@madhat.co.uk **w** madhat.co.uk Dir: Claire Swan.

Pete Martin Productions 305 Canalot Studios, 222 Kensal Rd, London W10 5BN **t** 020 8960 0700 **f** 020 8960 0762 **e** info@frontierrecordings.com **w** frontierrecordings.com Dir: Pete Martin.

Match Production Music (see BMG Production Music)

Mcasso Music Production 32-34 Great Marlborough St, London W1F 7JB **t** 020 7734 3664 **f** 020 7439 2375 **e** music@mcasso.com **w** mcasso.com Producer: Dan Hancock.

Meringue Productions 37 Church St, Twickenham, Middx TW1 3NR **t** 020 8744 2277 **f** 020 8744 9333 **e** enquiries@meringue.co.uk **w** meringue.co.uk Dir: Lynn Earnshaw.

Moments Music Library 7 Brunswick Close, Thames Ditton, Surrey KT7 0EU **t** 020 8398 1450 **f** 020 8398 1450 **e** smd.music@virgin.net Dir: Al Dickinson.

The Morrighan PO Box 23066, London W11 3FR **t** 07956 311810 **e** the@morrighan.com **w** morrighan.com Director: Jon Crosse.

Murfin Music International 1 Post Office Lane, Kempsey, Worcestershire WR5 3NS **t** 01905 820659 **f** 01905 820015 **e** muff.murfin@virgin.net **w** muffmurfin.com MD: Muff Murfin.

Music By Design 142 Wardour Street, London W1F 8ZU **t** 020 7434 3244 **f** 020 7434 1064 **e** enquiries@musicbydesign.co.uk **w** musicbydesign.co.uk Producer: Angela Allen.

North Star Music Publishing PO Box 868, Cambridge CB1 6SJ **t** 01787 278256 **f** 01787 279069 **e** info@northstarmusic.co.uk **w** northstarmusic.co.uk MD: Grahame Maclean.

Panama Productions Sovereign House, 12 Trewartha Road, Praa Sands, Penzance, Cornwall TR20 9ST **t** 01736 762826 or 07721 449477 **f** 01736 763328 **e** panamus@aol.com **w** panamamusic.co.uk MD: Roderick Jones.

Pluto Music Hulgrave Hall, Tiverton, Tarporley, Cheshire CW6 9UQ **t** 01829 732427 **f** 01829 733802 **e** info@plutomusic.com **w** plutomusic.com MD: Keith Hopwood.

Primrose Music Publishing 1 Leitrim House, 36 Worple Rd, London SW19 4EQ **t** 020 8946 7808 **f** 020 8946 3392 **e** jestersong@msn.com **w** primrosemusic.com Director: R B Rogers.

Quince Productions 62a Balcombe St, Marylebone, London NW1 6NE **t** 020 7723 4196 or 07810 752 765 **f** 020 7723 1010 **e** info@quincestudios.co.uk **w** quincestudios.co.uk Record Producer: Matt Walters.

RBM Composers Churchwood Studios, 1 Woodchurch Road, London NW6 3PL **t** 020 7372 2229 **f** 020 7372 3339 **e** rbm@easynet.co.uk MD: Ronnie Bond.

Resonant Matrix 10 Unity Wharf, London SE1 2BH **t** 020 7252 2661 **f** 0870 051 2594 **e** scott@movingshadow.com **w** movingshadow.com Business Manager: Scott Garrod.

Savin Productions 164 Streetsbrook Road, Solihull, Birmingham, West Midlands B90 3PH **t** 0121 240 1100 **f** 0121 240 4042 **e** info@savinproductions.com **w** savinproductions.com Prop: Brian Savin.

Select Music & Video Distribution 3 Wells Place, Redhill, Surrey RH1 3SL **t** 01737 645600 ext 306 or 01635 871338 **f** 01737 644065 **e** GBartholomew@selectmusic.co.uk **w** naxos.com Licensing Mgr: Graham Bartholomew.

Skyblue Recordings PO Box 44616, London N16 9WH **t** 0781 372 4854 **e** alyson@skybluerecordings.com **w** skybluerecordings.com Dir: Alyson Gilliland.

Somethin' Else Sound Direction Unit 1-4, 1A Old Nichol Street, London E2 7HR **t** 020 7613 3211 **f** 020 7739 9799 **e** info@somethin-else.com **w** somethin-else.com Dir: Steve Ackerman.

Sound Service Hill View, 93 Pointout Road, Bassett, Southampton, Hampshire SO16 7DL **t** 023 8070 1682 **f** 023 8079 0130 **e** colin@sound-service.co.uk **w** sound-service.co.uk Prop: Colin Willsher.

Soundbytes Promotions PO Box 1209, Stafford ST16 1XW **t** 01785 222382 **f** 0871 277 3060 **e** soundbytes@btinternet.com Creative Dir: Robert L Hicks.

Soundscape Music & Sounddesign 7 Goodge Place, London W1P 1FL **t** 020 7436 2211 or +31 35 622 9826 **f** +31 35 622 9826 **e** info@soundscape.nl **w** soundscape.nl Producer: Alex Nijmolen.

Soundtree Music Unit 124, Canalot Studios, 222 Kensal Road, London W10 5BN **t** 020 8968 1449 **f** 020 8968 1500 **e** post@soundtree.co.uk Business Mgr: Jo Feakes.

Space City Productions 77 Blythe Rd, London W14 0HP **t** 020 7371 4000 **f** 020 7371 4001 **e** info@spacecity.co.uk **w** spacecity.co.uk MD: Claire Rimmer.

Stevie "Vann" Lange (SVL) Productions Ebony and Ivory, 11 Varley Parade, Colindale, London NW9 **t** 020 8200 7090 **e** SVLProds@aol.com Contact: Stevie "Vann" Lange

Sumo Records 48 Cranbury Road, Reading, Berks. RG30 2XD **t** 0118 959 8282 **f** 0118 959 8282 **e** info@sumorecords.com MD: Jacqui Gresswell.

Tom Dick and Debbie Productions 43a Botley Rd, Oxford OX2 0BN **t** 01865 201564 **f** 01865 201935 **e** info@tomdickanddebbie.com **w** tomdickanddebbie.com Director: Richard Lewis.

Torchlight Music 34 Wycombe Gardens, London NW11 8AL **t** 020 8731 9858 **f** 020 8731 9858 **e** tony@torchlightmusic.com Dir: Tony Orchudesch.

Townend Music 44 Eastwick Crescent, Rickmansworth, Hertfordshire WD3 8YJ **t** 01923 720083 or 07974 048955 **f** 01923 710587 **e** townendmus@aol.com MD: Mike Townend.

Trimmer Music 13 Outram Road, London N22 7AB **t** 020 8881 7510 **e** trimmer@thejazzangels.fsnet.co.uk MD: Akane Abe.

Triple M Productions 31 Elmar Rd, Aigburth, Liverpool L17 0DA **t** 0151 727 7405 **f** 0151 727 7405 **e** mikemoran@breathemail.net **w** triplemproductions.mersinet.co.uk Producer/Composer: Mike Moarn.

Tsunami Sounds The Gables, Avenue Rd, Cranleigh, Surrey GU6 7LE **t** 01483 271200 **f** 01483 271200 **e** info@tsunami.co.uk **w** tsunami.co.uk Director: Ken Easter.

Ultimate Unit 6 Belfont Trading Estate, Mucklow Hill, Halesowen, West Midlands B62 8DR **t** 0121 585 8001 **f** 0121 585 8003 **e** info@ultimate1.co.uk **w** ultimate1.co.uk Manager: Andy Tain.

Visual Music West House, Forthaven, Shoreham by Sea, W Sussex BN43 5HY **t** 01273 453422 **f** 01273 452914 **e** richard@longman-records.com **w** richard-durrant.com Composer: Richard Durrant.

Wavsub Music Penvose Cottage, Summers Street, Lostwithiel, Cornwall PL22 0DH **t** 08700 702 265 **e** info@wavsub.com **w** wavsub.com Projects Manager: Lisa Baker.

Jeff Wayne Music Group 8-9 Ivor Place, London NW1 6BY **t** 020 7724 2471 **f** 020 7724 6245 **e** info@effwaynemusic.com **w** jeffwaynemusic.com Head of Production: Mandy Hughes.

Yellocello 49 Windmill Road, London W4 1RN **t** 020 8742 2001 **e** charlie@yellocello.com **w** yellocello.com MD: Charlie Carne.

Advertising Agencies

Abbott Mead Vickers BBDO 151 Marylebone Road, London NW1 5QE **t** 020 7616 3500 **f** 020 7616 3580 **e** linseyf@amvbbdo.com **w** amvbbdo.com Hd of TV Department: Francine Linsey.

adexchange The Old Garage, Gt Milton, Oxon OX44 7NP **t** 01844 278616 **f** 01844 278611 **e** enquiries@adexchange.co.uk **w** adexchange.co.uk Production Dir: Nick Herbert.

Gavin Anderson & Co 85 Strand, London WC2R 0DW **t** 020 7554 1400 **f** 020 7554 1499 **e** gavinfo@gavinanderson.co.uk **w** gavinanderson.co.uk

ARC Group Mortimer House, 37-41 Mortimer St, London W1T 3JH **t** 020 7017 5555 **f** 020 7017 5556 **e** info@arcgroup.com **w** argroup.com

ArtScience 172 Westminster Bridge Rd, London SE1 7RW **t** 020 7902 2780 **f** 020 7691 9755 **e** info@artscience.net **w** artscience.net Director: Douglas Coates, Liz Milward.

Bartle Bogle Hegarty 60 Kingly Street, London W1R 6DS **t** 020 7734 1677 **f** 020 7437 3666 **e** firstname.lastname@bbh.co.uk **w** bbh.co.uk

Bartlett Scott Edgar Bartlett House, 65-67 Wilson St, London EC2A 2LT **t** 020 7562 5700 **f** 020 7562 5706 **e** innovate@bartlett.co.uk **w** bartlett.co.uk

Bates UK 121-141 Westbourne Terrace, London W2 6JR **t** 020 7262 5077 **f** 020 7258 3757 **e** initialsurname@batesuk.com **w** batesuk.com

Bates Tavner Resources Int International House, World Trade Centre, 1 St Katharine's Way, London E1W 1UN **t** 020 7481 2000 **f** 020 7702 2271 **e** info@batestaverner.co.uk **w** batestaverner.co.uk

BBA Active 1 Hampstead West, 224 Iverson Road, London NW6 2HU **t** 020 7625 7575 **f** 020 7625 7007 **e** bba@bbagenius.com **w** bbagenius.com MD: Stephen Benjamin.

Big Blue Star Dunedin House, Harrow Yard, Akeman St, Tring, Herts HP23 6AA **t** 01442 826 240 **f** 01442 823 076 **e** paulgoodwin@bigbluestar.co.uk **w** bigbluestar.co.uk MD: Paul Goodwin.

BLM Group Eagle House, 50 Marshall St, London W1F 9BQ **t** 020 7437 1317 **f** 020 7437 1287 **e** info@blm.co.uk **w** blm.co.uk

BMP DDB 12 Bishops Bridge Road, London W2 6AA **t** 020 7258 3979 **f** 020 7402 4871 **e** firstname.lastnamename@bmpddb.com **w** bmp.co.uk

Leo Burnett Warwick Building, Kensington Village, Avonmore Rd, London W14 8HQ **t** 020 7591 9111 **f** 020 7591 9126 **e** firstname.lastname@leoburnett.co.uk **w** leoburnett.com

CDP-Travis Sully 9 Lower John Street, London W1F 9DZ **t** 020 7437 4224 **f** 020 7437 5445 **e** mail@cdp-travissully.com **w** cdp-travissully.com Office Manager: Melody Richards.

The Clinic 32-38 Saffron Hill, London EC1N 8FH **t** 020 7421 9333 **f** 020 7421 9334 **e** reception@clinic.co.uk **w** clinic.co.uk New Business: Mark Nicholls.

Cranham Advertising Suite 1, Essex House, Station Road, Upminster, Essex RM14 2SJ **t** 01708 641164 **f** 01708 220030 **e** cranham@globalnet.co.uk ISDN: 01708 225736.

Creative Marketing Services CMS House, 4 Spring Bank Place, Bradford BD8 7BX **t** 01274 820444 **f** 01274 822800 **e** mail@cmsadvertising.co.uk **w** cmsadvertising.co.uk Contact: Andrew Batty FCIM

Cunning Stunts Communications Top Floor, 24-28 Hatton Wall, London EC1N 8JH **t** 020 7691 0077 **f** 020 7691 0081 **e** info@cunningstunts.net **w** cunningstunts.net Account Manager: Nicky Keane.

Da Costa & Co 9 Gower Street, London WC1E 6HA **t** 020 7916 3791 **f** 020 7916 3799 **e** nickdc@dacosta.co.uk **w** dacosta.co.uk

Delaney Lund Knox Warren 25 Wellington Street, London WC2E 7DA **t** 020 7836 3474 **f** 020 7240 8739 **e** info@dlkw.co.uk **w** dlkw.co.uk

The Design & Advertising Business 10A Berners Place, London W1T 3AE **t** 020 7580 5566 **e** designbiz@easynet.co.uk **w** dabiz.co.uk Account Director: Richard Fearn.

Dewynters 48 Leicester Square, London WC2H 7QD **t** 020 7321 0488 **f** 020 7321 0104 **e** initial+lastname@dewynters.com **w** dewynters.com

Diabolical Liberties 1 Bayham St, London NW1 5OR **t** 020 7916 5483 **f** 020 7916 5482 **e** sales@diabolical.co.uk **w** diabolical.co.uk Head of Music: Karl Badger.

DKA 87 New Cavendish St, London171-177 Great Portland S W1W 6XD **t** 020 7467 7300 **f** 020 7467 7380 **e** enquiries@dka.uk.com **w** dka.uk.com

Euro RSCG London Cupola House, 15 Alfred Place, London WC1E 7EB **t** 020 7467 9200 **f** 020 7467 9210 **e** infouk@eurorscg.com **w** eurorscglondon.co.uk

Exposure (Nation-wide flyer distribution services) 3N Beehive Mill, Jersey St, Manchester M4 6JG **t** 0161 950 4241 **f** 0161 950 4240 **e** info@exposureuk.com **w** exposureuk.com MD: Keith Patterson.

Lee Golding Advertising & Communications Edinburgh House, 40 Great Portland Street, London W1W 7LZ **t** 020 7436 7910 or 020 7436 7978 **f** 020 7636 6091 **e** carol@leegolding.co.uk Contact: Carol Golding

Grey London 215-227 Great Portland St, London W1W 5PN **t** 020 7636 3399 **f** 020 7637 7473 **e** firstname.lastname@greyeu.com **w** grey.co.uk

Harry Monk Productions 24-28 Hatton Wall, London EC1N 8JH **t** 020 7691 0088 **f** 020 7691 0081 **e** production@harrymonk.net **w** harrymonk.net Dir: Sascha Darroch-Davies.

Hive Associates Bewlay House, 2 Swallow Place, London W1B 2AE **t** 020 7664 0480 **f** 020 7664 0481 **e** consult@hiveassociates.co.uk **w** hiveassociates.co.uk Account Director: Alex Moss.

JJ Stereo Units 13-14, Barley Shotts Business Park, 246 Acklam Road, London W10 5YG **t** 020 8969 5444 **f** 020 8969 5544 **e** info@jjstereo.com **w** jjstereo.com Dir: Ruth Paverly.

Lavery Rowe 69-71 Newington Causeway, London SE1 6BD **t** 020 7378 1780 **f** 020 7407 4612 **e** sales@laveryrowe.co.uk

Leagas Delaney 1 Alfred Place, London WC1E 7EB **t** 020 7758 1758 **f** 020 7758 1760 **e** infouk@leagasdelaney.com **w** leagasdelaney.com

The Leith Agency 37 The Shore, Leith, Edinburgh EH6 6QU **t** 0131 561 8600 **f** 0131 561 8601 **e** p.adams@leith.co.uk **w** leith.co.uk MD: Phil Adams.

The London Advertising Partnership 61-63 Portobello Road, london W11 3DB **t** 020 7229 9755 **f** 020 7229 6720 **e** london_ad@btinternet.com MD: Simon Dodds.

Lowe & Partners Bowater House, 3rd Floor, 68-114 Knightsbridge, London SW1X 7LT **t** 020 7584 5033 **f** 020 7581 9027 **e** info@loweworldwide.com **w** loweworldwide.com

M&C Saatchi 36 Golden Square, London W1F 9EE **t** 020 7543 4500 **f** 020 7543 4501 **e** firstnameinitialofsurname@mcsaatchi.com **w** mcsaatchi.com

M+H Communications (Inc Haymarket Advertising,, McCabes & Global Marketing) 36 Lexington Street, London W1F 0LJ **t** 020 7412 2000 **f** 020 7412 2020 **e** info@MandH.co.uk **w** MandH.co.uk Account Director: Mike McCraith. MD: Adrian Allen.

Matters Media 1st Floor, 146 Marylebone Rd, London NW1 5PH **t** 020 7224 6030 **f** 020 7224 6010 **e** mark@mattersmedia.co.uk Contact: Mark Riley

McCann-Erickson 7-11 Herbrand St, London WC1N 1EX **t** 020 7837 3737 **f** 020 7837 3773 **e** firstname.lastname@europe.mccann.com **w** mccann.com

McConnells McConnell House, Charlemont Place, Dublin, Ireland **t** +353 1 478 1544 **f** +353 1 478 0224 **e** firstname.lastname@mcconnells.ie **w** mcconnells.ie

Mearns & Gill Advertising 7 Carden Place, Aberdeen, Grampian AB10 1PP **t** 01224 646311 **f** 01224 631882 **e** alan@mearns-gill.com **w** mearns-gill.net

Media Campaign Services - MCS 20 Orange Street, London WC2H 7EW **t** 020 7389 0800 **f** 020 7839 6997 **e** dwoods@mediacampaign.co.uk **w** mediacampaign.co.uk Contact: David Woods

Media Junction 40a Old Compton St, London W1D 4TU **t** 020 7434 9919 **f** 020 7439 0794 **e** mailbox@mediajunction.co.uk **w** mediajunction.co.uk MD: Giles Cooper.

Mediacom EMG Entertainment Media Group 180 North Gower Street, London NW1 2NB **t** 020 7874 5500 **f** 020 7874 5999 **e** martin.cowie@mediacomuk.com **w** mediacomuk.com MD: Martin Cowie.

Ogilvy Primary Contact 5 Theobald's Rd, London WC1X 8SH **t** 020 7468 6900 **f** 020 7468 6950 **e** firstname.lastname@primary.co.uk **w** primary.co.uk MD: Gareth Richards.

Pawson Media 207 High Holborn, London WC1V 7BW **t** 020 7405 9080 **f** 020 7831 7391 **e** mail@pawson-media.co.uk Media Director: David Cecil.

PD Communications The Business Village, Broomhill Road, London SW18 4JQ **t** 020 8871 5033 **f** 020 8871 5034 **e** sales@pdcom.net **w** pdcom.net Creative Dir: Peter Saag.

Nick Pease Copywriting Services 290 Elgin Avenue, Maida Vale, London W9 1JS **t** 020 7286 8181 **f** 020 7286 8181 **e** nickpease@btconnect.com MD: Nick Pease.

Probe Media 2nd Floor, The Hogarth Centre, Hogarth Lane, London W4 2QN **t** 020 8742 3636 **f** 020 8995 1350 **e** john@probemedia.co.uk **w** probemedia.co.uk Account Dir: John Dicks.

Protege Design and Marketing East Dene, 5 Cromer Road, Southend on Sea, Essex SS1 2DU **t** 01702 300 176 **f** 01702 304 028 **e** info@protegedesign.co.uk **w** protegedesign.co.uk MD: Nic Cleeve.

Publicis 82 Baker Street, London W1M 2AE **t** 020 7935 4426 **f** 020 7487 5351 **e** re-fresh@publicis.co.uk **w** publicis.co.uk

QRBT Great Guildford Business Sq, 30 Great Guildford St, London SE1 0HS **t** 020 7921 9292 **f** 020 7921 9342 **e** qrbt@qrbt.com **w** qrbt.com

Rainey, Kelly, Camppbell, Rolfe/Y&R Greater London House, Hampstead Road, London NW1 7QP **t** 020 7387 9366 **f** 020 7611 6570 **e** firstname_lastname@uk.yr.com **w** rkcryr.com

Riley Advertising Riley House, 4 Red Lion Court, London EC4A 3EN **t** 020 7353 3223 **f** 020 7353 2338 **e** rileylondon@riley.co.uk **w** riley.co.uk MD: Rob Smith.

Robertson Saxby Associates Standard House, 107-115 Eastmoor Street, London SE7 8LX **t** 020 8858 3202 **f** 020 8853 2103 **e** dresource@aol.com Contact: Dick Saxby

RockBox (A Division of Clear Channel) 33 Golden Sq, London W1F 9JT **t** 020 7478 2200 **f** 020 7287 8129 **e** firstname.lastname@clearchannel.co.uk **w** clearchannel.co.uk Product Manager: Claire Cooch.

Rowleys:London One Port Hill, Hertford, Herts SG14 1PJ **t** 01992 587350 or 01992 551931 **f** 01992 586059 **e** info@rowleyslondon.co.uk **w** rowleyslondon.co.uk MD: Annie Rowley.

Saatchi & Saatchi plc 80 Charlotte St, London W1A 1AQ **t** 020 7636 5060 **f** 020 7637 8489 **e** fisrtname.surname@saatchi.co.uk **w** saatchi-saatchi.com

Small Japanese Soldier 4th Floor, 53-55 Beak St, London W1F 9SH **t** 020 7734 9956 **f** 020 7734 9957 **e** Jungle@smallJapanesesoldier.com **w** smalljapanesesoldier.com MD: Andy Hunns.

Sold Out The Windsor Centre, 16-29 Windsor Street, London N1 8QG **t** 020 7704 0409 **f** 020 7226 8249 **e** michelle@soldout.co.uk

Sonic Advertising The New Boathouse, 136-142 Bramley Road, London W10 6SR **t** 020 7727 7500 **f** 020 7727 7200 **e** lawrence@sonicadvertising.com **w** sonicadvertising.com Sales Mgr: Lawrence Cooke.

Sowerbykane 12 Burleigh St, Covent Garden, London WC2E 7PX **t** 020 7836 4561 **f** 020 7836 4073 **e** peter@sowerbykane.co.uk **w** sowerbykane.co.uk

Space Promotions Unit 12 Wellington Street, Unit Factory Development, 74 Eldon Street, Sheffield S1 4GT **t** 0114 2729211 **f** 0114 2756220 **e** post@spacegroup.co.uk **w** spacegroup.co.uk MD: Mark Platts.

Spark Marketing Entertainment 3 Lansdowne Rd, London N10 2AX **t** 0870 460 5439 **e** info@spark-me.com **w** spark-me.com Executive Director: Matthias Bauss.

St Luke's Communications 22 Dukes Rd, London WC1H 9PN **t** 020 7380 8888 **f** 020 7380 8899 **e** initial+lastname@stlukes.co.uk **w** stlukes.co.uk

Target NMI Middlesex House, 34-42 Cleveland Street, London W1T 4JE **t** 020 7462 5800 **f** 020 7462 5799 **e** mail@targetnmi.com **w** targetnmi.com MD: Robert Wilkerson.

TBWA London 76-80 Whitfield St, London W1T 4EZ **t** 020 7573 6666 **f** 020 7573 6728 **e** firstname.lastname@tbwa-london.com **w** tbwa.com MD: Jonathan Mildenhall.

TCS Media 35 Garway Rd, London W2 4QF **t** 020 7221 7292 **f** 020 7221 0460 **e** information@tcsmedia.co.uk **w** tcsmedia.com Dir: Mike Ashby.

J Walter Thompson Co 1 Knightsbridge Green, London SW1X 7NW **t** 020 7656 7000 **f** 020 7656 7010 **e** firstname.lastname@jwt.com **w** jwtworld.com

TMD Carat 43-49 Parker St, London WC2B 5PS **t** 020 7430 6000 **f** 020 7430 6299 **e** firstname_lastname@carat.co.uk **w** carat.com MD: Colin Mills.

TMP Worldwide Chancery House, 53-64 Chancery Lane, London WC2A 1QS **t** 020 7406 5000 **f** 020 7406 5001 **e** firstname.lastname@tmp.com **w** tmpw.co.uk

Two:Design Studio 20 The Arches, Hartland Rd, Camden, London NW1 8HR **t** 020 7267 1118 **f** 020 7482 0221 **e** studio@twodesign.net **w** twodesign.net Art Director: Graham Peake.

Martin Waxman Associates 56 St John St, London EC1M 4HG **t** 020 7253 5500 **f** 020 7490 2387 **e** info@waxman.co.uk **w** waxman.co.uk

Wood Brigdale Nisbet & Robinson Granville House, 132-135 Sloane Street, London SW1X 9AX **t** 020 7591 4800 **f** 020 7591 4801

Wunderman Greater London House, Hampstead Road, London NW1 7QP **t** 020 7611 6666 **f** 020 7611 6668 **e** firstname_lastname@uk.wunderman.com **w** wunderman.com

Young Euro RSCG 64 Lower Leeson Street, Dublin 2, Ireland **t** +353 1 661 5599 **f** +353 1 661 1992 **e** advertising@young-ad.ie **w** youngeurorscg.ie

Video Production

400 Company (Camera & Crew Hire) B3, The Workshops, 2A, Askew Crescent, London W12 9DP **t** 020 8746 1400 **f** 020 8746 0847 **e** info@the400.co.uk **w** the400.co.uk Sales & Mktg Mgr: Christian Riou.

422 Studios Battersea Rd, Heaton Mersey, Stockport SK4 3EA **t** 0161 432 9000 **f** 0161 443 1325 **e** rob@gym-tv.com MD: Robert Topliss.

46&2 Productions 19 Sommerville Road, St. Andrews, Bristol BS7 9AD **t** 07970 182168 **e** fortysixandtwo@blueyonder.co.uk Director: Stuart Brereton.

Abaco Video 212 Piccadilly, London W1J 9HG **t** 020 7917 2854 **f** 020 7439 0262 **e** info@abaco-music.com **w** abaco-music.com Production Manager: Vera Klefisch.

Abbey Road Studios 3 Abbey Road, London NW8 9AY **t** 020 7266 7366 **f** 020 7266 7367 **e** videoservices@abbeyroad.com **w** abbeyroad.com Video Services Mgr: Mark Fowler.

Aimimage Unit 5, 63 Pratt Street, London NW1 0BY **t** 020 7482 4340 **f** 020 7267 3972 **e** prods@aimimage.com **w** aimimage.com Prod Mgr: Rebecca Einhorn.

Autopsy Red Bus Studios, 34 Salisbury St, London NW8 8QE **t** 020 7724 2243 **f** 020 7724 2871 **e** info@crimson.globalnet.co.uk MD: Simon Crawley.

Banana Split Productions 11 Carlisle Road, London NW9 0HD **t** 020 8200 1234 **f** 020 8200 1121 **e** accounts@bananasplitprods.com **w** banana-split.com MD: Steve Kemsley.

Big Talk Productions 83 Great Titchfield Street, London W1W 6RH **t** 020 7255 1131 **f** 020 7436 9347 **e** talk@bigtalk.demon.co.uk MD: Nira Park.

Black Dog Films 42-44 Beak St, London W1F 9RH **t** 020 7434 0787 **f** 020 7734 4978 **e** initial+surname@rsafilms.co.uk **w** blackdogfilms.com Rep: Svana Gisla.

Blue Planet 96 York Street, London W1H 1DP **t** 020 7724 2267 **e** base@blueplanet.co.uk Contact: Bruce Robertson Specialise in classical music.

Blue Post Production 58 Old Compton Street, London W1D 4UF **t** 020 7437 2626 **f** 020 7439 2477 **e** info@bluepp.co.uk **w** bluepp.co.uk Facilities Manager: Ashley Ranson.

Blue Source The Fish Tank, The Saga Centre, 326 Kensal Road, London W10 5BZ **t** 020 7460 6020 **f** 020 7460 6021 **e** info@bluesource.com **w** bluesource.com MD: Seb Marling.

Box 5th floor, 121 Princess Street, Manchester M1 7AD **t** 0161 228 2399 **e** info@the-box.co.uk **w** the-box.co.uk Director: Mike Kirwin.

Cara Music The Studio, rear of 63 Station Rd, Winchmore Hill, London N21 3NB **t** 020 8364 3121 **f** 020 8364 3090 **e** caramusicltd@dial.pipex.com Dir: Michael McDonagh.

Channel 20-20 20-20 House, 26-28 Talbot Lane, Leicester LE1 4LR **t** 0116 233 2220 **f** 0116 222 1113 **e** info@channel2020.co.uk **w** channel2020.co.uk MD: Rob Potter.

Cinegenix at PBF Motion Pictures The Little Pickenhanger, Tuckey Grove, Ripley, Surrey GU23 6JG **t** 01483 225179 **f** 01483 224118 **e** image@pbf.co.uk **w** pbf.co.uk Creative Director: Peter Fairbrass.

Condor Post Production 54 Greek Street, London W1V 5LR **t** 020 7494 2552 **f** 020 7494 1166 **e** kirsty@condor-post.com **w** condor-post.com Bookings Manager: Kirsty Green.

Cowboy Films 11-29 Smiths Court, Great Windmill Street, London W1D 7DP **t** 020 7287 3808 **f** 020 7287 3785 **e** info@cowboyfilms.co.uk **w** cowboyfilms.co.uk Dir: Robert Bray.

Cube Music The Factory, 2 Acre Road, Kingston upon Thames, Surrey KT2 6EF **t** 020 8547 5143 **f** 020 8547 1544 **e** info@cube-music.com **w** cube-music.com Marketing Dir: Mick Hilton.

Curious Yellow 33-37 Hatherley Mews, London E17 4QP **t** 020 8521 9595 **f** 020 8521 6363 **e** paul@curiousyellow.co.uk **w** curiousyellow.co.uk MD: Paul Penny.

D-Fuse 13-14 Gt.Sutton St, London EC1V 0BX **t** 020 7253 3462 **e** info@dfuse.com **w** dfuse.com Dir: Michael Faulkner.

DMS Films 369 Burnt Oak Broadway, Edgware, Middlesex HA8 5XZ **t** 020 8951 6060 **f** 020 8951 6050 **e** danny@argonaut.com Producer: Daniel San.

Done and Dusted 87 Lancaster Rd, London W11 1QQ **t** 07000 708 708 **f** 07000 708 709 **e** info@doneanddusted.com **w** doneanddusted.com Director of Production: Simon Pizey.

Eagle Vision Eagle House, 22 Armoury Way, London SW18 1EZ **t** 020 8870 5670 **f** 020 8874 2333 **e** mail@eagle-rock.com **w** eagle-rock.com COO, Worldwide: Geoff Kempin. Dir of Intl. Acquisitions: John Gaydon.

11th Circle Films 79 Thorpe Bank Road, Shepherds Bush, London W12 0PG **t** 020 8740 6730 **f** 020 8740 6730 **e** 11th.circle@virgin.net Prod / Dir: Mark Turner.

Exceeda Films 110-116 Elmore Street, London N1 3AH **t** 020 7288 0433 **f** 020 7288 0735 **e** contact@exceeda.co.uk **w** exceeda.co.uk Producer: Sarah Davenport.

Fat Pictures 36C Aberdeen Road, London NW5 2UH **t** 020 7354 4109 **f** 020 7690 5129 **e** info@fatpictures.co.uk **w** fatpictures.co.uk Producer: Neil Thompson.

Fire House Productions 42 Glasshouse Street, London W1B 5DW **t** 020 7439 2220 **f** 020 7439 2210 **e** postie@hellofirehouse.com **w** hellofirehouse.com MD: Julie-Anne Edwards.

Flick Films 15 Golden Square, London W1F 9JG **t** 020 7734 7979 **f** 020 7287 9495 **e** info@flickmedia.co.uk **w** flickmedia.co.uk Dir: John Deery.

Flicks TV & Video Productions Classlane Studios, Bentley Lodge, Victoria Road, Beverley, East Yorkshire HU17 8PJ **t** 01482 873388 **f** 01482 873389 **e** dave_l@classlane.co.uk **w** classlane.co.uk Dir: David Lee.

Flynn Productions 64 Charlotte Road, London EC2A 3PE **t** 020 7729 7291 **f** 020 7729 7279 **e** mary@flynnproductions.com **w** flynnproductions.com Exec Producer: Mary Calderwood.

Four23 Films The Apex, 6 Southern St, Castlefield, Manchester M3 4NN **t** 0161 835 9466 **f** 0161 835 9468 **e** mailman@four23films.com **w** four23films.com Director: Warren Bramley.

Galaxi Television 11 Spruce Park, Crediton, Devon EX17 3HQ **t** 07968 163 866 **e** ross@galaxi.tv **w** galaxi.tv MD: Ross Hemsworth.

Glassworks 33-34 Great Poulteney Street, London W1F 9NP **t** 020 7434 1182 **f** 020 7434 1183 **e** tom@glassworks.co.uk **w** glassworks.co.uk Joint MD: Tom Jacomb.

Godman 76 Wardour Street, London W1F 0TG **t** 020 7287 6755 **f** 020 7287 6756 **e** jg@godman.co.uk Prod: Juliette Larthe.

Gorgeous Enterprises 23-24 Greek Street, London W1D 4DZ **t** 020 7287 4060 **f** 020 7287 4994 **e** gorgeous@gorgeous.co.uk **w** gorgeous.co.uk MD: Paul Rothwell.

Great Guns 43-45 Camden Road, London NW1 9LR **t** 020 7692 4444 **f** 020 7692 4422 **e** sheridan@greatguns.com **w** greatguns.com Prod Mgr: Sheridan Thomas.

Green Bandana Productions 7 Iron Bridge House, Bridge Approach, London NW1 8BD **t** 020 7722 1081 **f** 020 7483 0028 **e** james.hyman@virgin.net **w** jameshyman.com MD: James Hyman.

Groovy Badger PO Box 39002, London E2 9YP **t** 020 7613 5044 or 07956 272883 **f** 0870 124 5135 **e** info@groovybadger.com **w** groovybadger.com Dir: Sebastian Smith.

HLA 19-21 Great Portland Street, London W1W 8QB **t** 020 7299 1000 **f** 020 7299 1001 **e** postmaster@hla.net MD: Mike Wells.

The Hospital Group 24 Endell Street, London WC2H 9HQ **t** 020 7170 9110 **f** 020 7170 9102 **e** studio@thehospital.co.uk **w** thehospital.co.uk Studio Sales Manager: Anne Marie Phelan.

Illumina 8 Canham Mews, Canham Road, London W3 7SR **t** 020 8600 9300 **f** 020 8600 9333 **e** dannyn@illumina.co.uk **w** illumina.co.uk Exec Prod: Danny Nissim.

IMS Interactive Management Services Unit 19, Price St Business Centre, Birkenhead, Merseyside CH41 4JQ **t** 0151 651 0100 **f** 0151 652 0077 **e** daveims@compuserve.com **w** heritagevideo.co.uk MD: David McWilliam.

Independent Films 3rd Floor, 7A Langley Street, London WC2H 9JA **t** 020 7845 7474 **f** 020 7845 7475 **e** mail@independ.net Music Video Rep: Tess Wight.

Influential Films PO Box 306, Manchester M14 6GX **t** 07050 395 708 **e** info@influentialmedia.co.uk **w** influentialfilms.co.uk MD: Mike Swindells.

JJ Stereo Units 13-14, Barley Shotts Business Park, 246 Acklam Road, London W10 5YG **t** 020 8969 5444 **f** 020 8969 5544 **e** info@jjstereo.com **w** jjstereo.com Dir: Ruth Paverly.

Kick Screen 13 D'Arblay Street, London W1F 8DX **t** 020 7287 3757 **f** 020 7437 0125 **e** admin@kickproductions.co.uk MD: David Amphlett.

Kyng Films 50A Cross St, London N1 2BA **t** 020 7687 0380 **f** 020 7687 0380 **e** heather@kyngfilms.com MD: Heather Clarke.

Liquid Productions Reverb House, Bennett Street, London W4 2AH **t** 020 8995 6799 **f** 020 8995 6899 **e** liquidproductions@btinternet.com Director: Margot Quinn.

M Productions The Power House, 70 Chiswick High Rd, London W4 1SY **t** 020 8742 1111 **f** 020 8742 2626 **e** reception@metropolis-group.co.uk **w** metropolis-group.co.uk Producer: Anouk Fontaine.

Mad Cow Productions 75 Amberley Rd, London W9 2JL **t** 020 7289 0001 **f** 020 7289 0003 **e** info@madcowfilms.co.uk **w** madcowfilms.co.uk Head of Production: Anwen Rees-Myers.

Maguffin 10 Frith Street, London W1V 5TZ **t** 020 7437 2526 **f** 020 7437 1516 **e** maguffin.ltd@virgin.net MD: James Chads.

Masterpiece Media Unit 14 The Talina Centre, Bagleys Lane, London SW6 2BW **t** 020 7371 0700 **f** 020 7384 1750 **e** info@masterpiecelondon.com **w** masterpiecelondon.com Studio Manager: Johnnie Everton.

Melling White Productions West Hill Dairy, Avington, Winchester, Hants SO21 1DE **t** 01962 779002 **f** 01962 779002 **e** info@mellingwhite.co.uk Head Prod: Carol White.

The Mill 40-41 Great Marlborough Street, London W1F 7JQ **t** 020 7287 4041 **e** info@mill.co.uk **w** mill.co.uk Mktg Mgr: Emma Shield.

The Mob Film Company 10-11 Great Russell Street, London WC1B 3NH **t** 020 7580 8142 **f** 020 7255 1721 **e** mail@mobfilm.com Prod: John Brocklehurst.

Harry Monk 24-28 Hatton Wall, Farringdon, London EC1N 8JH **t** 020 7691 0088 **f** 020 7691 0081 **e** production@harrymonk.net **w** harrymonk.net MD: John Carver.

The Moving Picture Company 127 Wardour Street, London W1F 0NL **t** 020 7434 3100 **f** 020 7287 5187 **e** mailbox@moving-picture.co.uk **w** moving-picture.co.uk Snr Prod: Simon Gosling.

Mutiny Films 18 Soho Square, London W1V 3QL **t** 020 7025 8710 **f** 020 7025 8100 **e** info@mutinyfilms.co.uk **w** mutinyfilms.co.uk Company Directors: Adam Wimpenny, Sam Eastall.

Nexus Animation 113-114 Shoreditch High Street, London E1 6JN **t** 020 7749 7500 **f** 020 7749 7501 **e** chris@nexuslondon.com Prod: Chris O'Reilly.

Oasis TV 6-7 Great Poultney Street, London W1F 9NA **t** 020 7434 4133 **e** sales@oasistv.co.uk **w** oasistv.co.uk Business Dev't Mgr: Matthew Lock.

Oil Factory 5th Floor, 26 Little Portland Street, London W1W 8BX **t** 020 7255 6255 **f** 020 7255 6277 **e** musicvideo@oilfactory.net **w** oilfactory.com Head Of Music Video: Toby Hyde.

OVC Media 88 Berkely Court, Baker St, London NW1 5ND **t** 020 7402 9111 **f** 020 7723 3064 **e** joanne.ovc@virgin.net **w** ovcmedia.co.uk Dir: Joanne Cohen.

MUSIC WEEK DAILY
TOP STORIES
Chili Peppers debut at one on albums
Red Hot Chili Peppers Live From Hyde Park is
new entry in this week's album chart after
number one. [more]
Big Chill expands after
After an excellent sun-
Mylo, Bent, Lemon Jelly,
moves into a perma
success
weekend with acts such as
et and Magnet, Big Chill
e in London. [more]
share
leads pack with albums market
helped to rally EMI Music Publishing in
to its strongest performance in 12 months on the
market. [more]
releases set for quarter fo
studio albums for
radio licenses
September 1. [more]
The news as it happens
Register for your free
Music Week Daily update at
www.musicweek.com

Partizan 7 Westbourne Grove Mews, London W11 2RU **t** 020 7792 8483 **f** 020 7792 8870 **e** firstname.surname@partizan.com MD: Georges Bermann.

Passion Pictures 33-34 Rathbone Place, London W1T 1JN **t** 020 7323 9933 **f** 020 7323 9030 **e** info@passion-pictures.com Producer: Spencer Friend.

Picture Production Company 19-20 Poland St, London W1F 8QF **t** 020 7439 4944 **f** 020 7734 6635 **e** steve@theppc.com **w** theppc.co.uk Sales & Marketing Dir: Steve O`Pray.

Poisson Rouge Pictures 140 Battersea Park Road, London SW11 4NB **t** 020 7720 5666 **f** 020 7720 5757 **e** info@poissonrougepictures.com **w** poissonrougepictures.com Producer: Christopher Granier-Deferre.

POP @ Paul Weiland Film Co 14 Newburgh Street, London W1V 1LF **t** 020 7494 9600 **f** 020 7434 0146 **e** eatpop@aol.com Producer: Alex Johnson.

Punk Films Unit 2A Queens Studios, 121 Salusbury Road, London NW6 6RG **t** 020 7372 4474 **f** 020 7372 4484 or 020 7328 4447 **e** info@punk.uk.com **w** punk.uk.com Dir: Mark Logue.

QD Productions 93 Great Titchfield Street, London W1W 6RP **t** 020 7462 1700 **f** 020 7636 0653 **e** musicvideo@qotd.co.uk **w** qotd.co.uk Head of Music & Video: Andy Leahy.

The Rights Group Flat 2, 35 Lexham Gardens, London W8 **t** 07713 404 101 or 07976 924 902 **e** mwilkins@mbacorporatesolutions.com Dir: Grant Calton.

RnBTV.com PO Box 34539, London SE15 2XA **t** 020 7732 2287 **e** ash@soultrade.com **w** rnbtv.com Producer: Ash Kamat.

Rogue Films 70 Mortimer Street, London W1N 7DF **t** 020 7907 1000 **f** 020 7907 1001 **e** charlie@roguefilms.co.uk **w** roguefilms.com MD: Charlie Crompton.

David & Kathy Rose Productions 159 Earlsfield Road, London SW18 3DD **t** 020 8874 0744 **f** 020 8874 9136 **e** kathy@theroses.co.uk Partner: Kathy Rose.

Science Films 57 Great Portland Street, London W1W 7LH **t** 020 7636 7637 **f** 020 7636 7647 **e** films@sciencefilms.co.uk Exec Prod: Galia Ina.

Screen Edge St Annes House, 329 Clifton Drive South, Lytham St Annes, Lancashire FY8 1LP **t** 01253 712453 **f** 01253 712362 **e** andy@outlaw23.com **w** screenedge.com MD: John Bentham.

Serious Pictures Film 1A Rede Place, London W2 4TU **t** 020 7792 4477 **f** 020 7792 4488 **e** info@serious-pics.com **w** serious-pics.com Office Mgr: Ann-Marie Morris.

The Showreel Company 28 Cleveland Avenue, London W4 1SN **t** 020 8525 0058 **e** the.showreelcompany@virgin.net **w** theshowreelcompany.co.uk Director: John Gugolka.

Single Minded Production 11 Cambridge Court, 210 Shepherds Bush Rd, London W6 7NJ **t** 0870 011 3748 or 07860 391 902 **f** 0870 011 3749 **e** video@singleminded.com **w** singleminded.com MD: Tony Byrne.

Smoke & Mirrors 57-59 Beak Street, London W1R 3LF **t** 020 7468 1000 **f** 020 7468 1001 **w** smoke-mirrors.com Office Mgr: Matt Z.

Sounds Good 12 Chiltern Enterprise Centre, Station Rd, Theale, Berks RG7 4AA **t** 0118 930 1700 **f** 0118 930 1709 **e** sales-info@sounds-good.co.uk **w** sounds-good.co.uk Dir: Martin Maynard.

Spectre Vision 48 Beak Street, London W1F 9RL **t** 020 7851 2000 **e** spectre@spectrevision.com Contact: Janie Balcomb

Stink 87 Lancaster Road, London W11 1QQ **t** 020 7908 9400 **f** 020 7908 9400 **e** info@stink.tv **w** stink.tv Head of Promos: Alexa Hayward. MD: Daniel Bergmann.

Storm Film Productions 32 Great Marlborough Street, London W1F 7JB **t** 020 7439 1616 **f** 020 7439 4477 **e** sophie.storm@btclick.com Prod Mgr: Sophie Inman.

Stylorouge 57/60 Charlotte Rd, London EC2A 3QT **t** 020 7729 1005 **f** 020 7739 7124 **e** rob@stylorouge.co.uk **w** stylorouge.co.uk Dir: Rob O'Connor.

Sugar Vision 130 Shaftesbury Ave, London W1D 5EU **t** 020 7031 1140 **e** adamglen@thesugargroup.com **w** thesugargroup.com Head of Production: Adam Glen.

Swivel Films 23 Denmark Street, London WC2H 8NA **t** 020 7240 4485 **f** 020 7240 4486 **e** swivelfilms@btinternet.com Dir's Rep: Sarah Wills.

Syndicate Pictures Truman Brewery, 91-95 Brick Lane, London E1 6QL **t** 020 7247 7212 **f** 020 7247 7213 **e** syndicate@dial.pipex.com **w** synpics.com MD: Jonathan Hercock.

Tele-Cine 48 Charlotte Street, London W1T 2NS **t** 020 7208 2200 **f** 020 7208 2252 **e** telecine@telecine.co.uk **w** telecine.co.uk Music Bking Mgr: Claire Booth.

TheFireFactory.com 13 William Rd, Westbridgeford, Nottingham NG3 **t** 07870 553 717 **e** info@thefirefactory.com **w** thefirefactory.com Producer: Jake Shaw.

Tom Dick and Debbie 43A Botley Road, Oxford OX2 0BN **t** 01865 201564 **f** 01865 201935 **e** info@tomdickanddebbie.com **w** tomdickanddebbie.com Director: Richard Lewis.

Tomato Films 29-35 Lexington Street, London W1R 3HQ **t** 020 7434 0955 **f** 020 7434 0255 **e** films@tomato.co.uk **w** tomato.co.uk MD: Jeremy Barrett.

Tomboy Films 1st Floor, 74 Margaret Street, London W1W 8FU **t** 020 7436 3324 **f** 020 7436 3364 **e** info@tomboyfilms.co.uk **w** tomboyfilms.co.uk MD: Glynns Murray.

Treatment Unit 2, Queens Studio, 121 Salisbury Road, London NW6 6RG **t** 020 7372 4474 **f** 020 7372 4484 or 020 7372 4447 **e** sam@treatmentuk.com **w** treatmentuk.com Producer: Sam Pattinson.

TSI Video 10 Grape St, London WC2H 8TG **t** 020 7379 3435 **f** 020 7379 4589 **e** rwillcocks@tsi.co.uk Bkings Co-ord: Rebecca Willcocks.

The Valentine Music Group 7 Garrick Street, London WC2E 9AR **t** 020 7240 1628 **f** 020 7497 9242 **e** valentine@bandleader.co.uk **w** valentinemusic.co.uk MD: John Nice.

Jane Wallace The Corner House, Cidermill Lane, Chipping Campden, Gloucestershire GL55 6HL **t** 01386 841453 or 07885 749612 **f** 01386 841453 **e** successpr@hotmail.com Work with chart acts on pop videos.

Waterfall Studios 2 Silver Road, Wood Lane, London W12 7SG **t** 020 8746 2000 **f** 020 8746 0180 **e** info@waterfall-studios.com **w** waterfall-studios.com Facilities Mgr: Samantha Leese.

WembleyTV 1st Floor, 8-10 King Street, Hammersmith, London W6 0QA **t** 0208 741 6113 **f** 0208 741 6600 **e** info@wembleytv.com **w** wembleytv.com Commercial Director: Neil Osborne.

Yawning Dog Productions 70A Uxbridge Road, London W12 8LP **t** 020 8742 9067 **f** 020 8742 9118 **e** nina@yawningdog.fsnet.co.uk Prod: Nina Beck.

Yoyoandco Walnut Tree Cottage, Watercress Lane, Wingham Well, Canterbury, Kent CT3 1NR **t** 01227 728409 **f** 01227 728409 **e** info@yoyoand.co.uk MD: Blair Hart.

Media Miscellaneous

A United Production (U.P) 6 Shaftesbury Mews, Clapham, London SW4 9BP **t** 020 7720 9624 **f** 020 7720 9624 **e** info@united-productions.co.uk **w** united-productions.co.uk Choreographer: Lyndon Lloyd.

Abi Leland Music Supervision 1 Lonsdale Rd, London NW6 6RA **t** 020 7625 5757 or 07961 369 830 **f** 020 7625 0200 **e** abi.leland@virgin.net MD: Abi Leland.

Affinity Music 60 Kingly St, London W1B 5DS **t** 020 7453 4062 **f** 020 7453 4185 **e** info@affinitymusic.co.uk **w** affinitymusic.co.uk Co-MDs: Gordon Biggins, Simon Binns.

Elizabeth Andrews - Copyright clearances 15 Hawthorn Hill, Letchworth, Herts SG6 4HF **t** 01462 685333 **e** lizzie@music-consultancy.fsbusiness.co.uk Music Consultant: Elizabeth Andrews.

Box Music 2 Munro Terrace, 112 Cheyne Walk, London SW10 0DL **t** 020 7376 8736 **f** 020 7376 3376 **e** sam@boxmusicltd.com GM: Sam Hilsdon.

Broadchart Shelana House, 31-32 Eastcastle St, London W1W 8DW **t** 020 7341 0999 **f** 020 7341 0888 **e** info@broadchart.com **w** broadchart.com CEO: Andy Hill.

C-Burn 33 Sekforde St, London EC1R 0HH **t** 020 7250 1133 **f** 020 7253 8553 **e** info@c-burn.com **w** c-burn.com MD: Adam Smith. Ba

Celebrities Worldwide 39-41 New Oxford St, London WC1A 1BN **t** 020 7836 7702/3 **f** 020 7836 7701 **e** info@celebritiesworldwide.com **w** celebritiesworldwide.com Co-MDs: Claire Nye, Richard Brecker.

Constantly Cliff 17 Podsmead Rd, Tuffley, Glos GL1 5PB **t** 01452 306104 **f** 01452 306104 **e** william@constantlycliff.freeserve.co.uk **w** cliffchartsite.co.uk Ed: William Hooper.

Couchlife Devonshire House, 223 Upper Richmond Rd, London SW15 6SQ **t** 020 8780 0612 **f** 020 8789 8668 **e** info@couchlife.co.uk **w** couchlife.com Music Director: Rob Sawyer.

DT Productions Maygrove House, 67 Maygrove Rd, London NW6 2SP **t** 020 7644 8888 **f** 020 7644 8889 **e** info@dtproductions.co.uk **w** dtproductions.co.uk Sales Manager: Toby Hoyte.

Entertainment Press Cuttings Agency Unit 7, Lloyds Wharf, Mill Street, London SE1 2BD **t** 020 7237 1717 **f** 020 7237 3388 **e** epca@ukonline.co.uk Manager: Sally Miller.

Feltwain 2000 1 Oakwood Parade, London N14 4HY **t** 020 8950 8732 **f** 020 8950 6648 **e** paul.lynton@btopenworld.com MD: Paul Lynton.

Folktrax (Folktracks & Soundpost Publications) Heritage House, 16 Brunswick Square, Gloucester GL1 1UG **t** 01452 415110 **f** 01452 503643 **e** peter@folktrax.freeserve.co.uk **w** folktrax.org Dir: Peter Kennedy. International Library of Ethnic Traditions and World Archive of Recorded Traditions (Video and Audio).

Liz Gallacher Music Supervision 23 Brickwood Rd, Croydon, Surrey CR0 6UL **t** 020 8680 7784 **f** 020 8681 3000 **e** info@lizg.com Music Consultant: Liz Gallacher.

Giant Mobile 57 Kingsway, Woking, Surrey GU21 6NS **t** 01483 859 849 **e** mark.studio@ntlworld.com Contact: Mark Taylor

Green Island Promotions Unit 31, 56 Gloucester Road, London SW7 4UB **t** 0870 789 3377 **f** 0870 789 3414 **e** greenisland@btinternet.com **w** greenislandpromotions.com Dir: Steve Lucas.

Green Room Productions The Laurels, New Park Road, Harefield, Middlesex UB9 6EQ **t** 01895 822771 **f** 01895 824880 **e** tony@greenroom2.demon.co.uk **w** auracle.com/greenroom Partner: Tony Faulkner.

Carol Hayes Management (Hair, make up and fashion stylists) 1 Parkway, London NW1 7PG **t** 020 7482 1555 **f** 020 7482 3666 **e** info@carolhayesmanagement.co.uk **w** carolhayesmanagement.co.uk Head Booker: Julie Carter.

Jester Song 78 Gladstone Rd, London SW19 1QT **t** 020 8543 4056 **f** 020 8542 8225 **e** jestersong@msn.com MD: R B Rogers.

JN Associates 8 Broxash Rd, London SW11 6AB **t** 020 7223 5280 **f** 020 7223 9493 **e** jonnewey@btinternet.com Research & Archivist Dir: Jon Newey.

Klipjoint - Photo archive service 25 Plympton Ave, London NW6 7TL **t** 020 8357 3499 **f** 020 7372 2572 **e** mail@klipjoint.info **w** klipjoint.info MD: Duncan Brown.

The KRL Group Hartford House, Common Rd, Thorpe Salvin, Notts. S80 3JJ **t** 01909 774 111 **f** 01909 774 200 **e** enquiries@krlgroup.co.uk **w** kevroberts.com MD: Kev Roberts.

Lifeco UK PO Box 111, London W13 0ZH **t** 0870 741 5488 **f** 0870 131 5400 **e** john@lifecouk.co.uk **w** straighttalking.info Dir: John S Rushton.

MRIB Heckfield Place, 530 Fulham Road, London SW6 5NR **t** 020 7731 3555 **f** 020 7731 8545 **e** contactus@mrib.co.uk **w** mrib.co.uk MD: Paul Basford.

THE MUSIC ENGINE

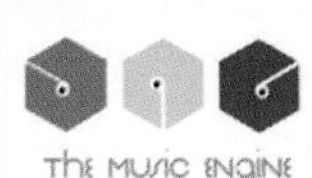

81 Rivington St, London EC2A 3AY **t** 020 7739 2611 **f** 020 7942 0573 **w** themusicengine.com **e** web@themusicengine.com. MD: Rob Atkin. Marketing Manager: Dan Brown. Sales: Ben Allen. Project Manager: Hamish Jackson. Admin: Ainhoa Acosta **Full service music e-commerce technology provider: MusicPay online/mobile payments; MP3 shops; ringtones; digital warehouse, delivery and distribution; fan-base management**

The Music & Media Partnership First Floor, 72-74 Notting Hill Gate, London W11 3HT **t** 020 7727 9111 **f** 020 7727 9911 **e** info@tmmp.co.uk MD: Rick Blaskey.

Music & Media Law Services Wychwood, Kencot, Oxon GL7 3QT **t** 01367 860256 **f** 01367 860116 **e** anicholas@btinternet.com MD: Alastair Nicholas.

Music Innovations 14 Ransomes Dock, 35 - 37 Parkgate Road, London SW11 4NP **t** 020 7350 5550 **f** 020 7350 5551 **e** firstname@musicinnovations.com MD: Robert Dodds.

Openplay Suite 106, Hiltongrove Business Centre, Hatherley Mews, London E17 4QP **t** 020 8520 6644 **f** 020 8520 7755 **e** info@openplay.co.uk **w** openplay.co.uk Director: David Hoskins.

Pro-Motion 33 Kendal Rd, Hove, East Sussex BN3 5HZ **t** 01273 327175 **e** info@martinjames.demon.co.uk Exec Producer: Martin James.

The Product Exchange 45 Mount Ash Rd, London SE26 6LY **t** 020 8699 5835 or 020 8291 1193 **f** 020 8699 5835 **e** music@productexchange.co.uk **w** productexchange.co.uk MD: Frank Rodgers.

Rasheed Ogunlaru Life Coaching (for Singers and Performers) The Coaching Studio, 223a Mayall Rd, London SE24 0PS **t** 020 7207 1082 **e** rasaru_coaching@yahoo.com **w** rasaru.com Contact: Rasheed Ogunlaru

REDMuze Paulton House, 8 Shepherdess Walk, London N1 7LB **t** 020 7566 8216 **f** 020 7566 8259 **e** sales@redmuze.com **w** redmuze.com Head of Sales: Deborah Sass.

Reflex Media Unit 5, Cirrus, Glebe Road, Huntingdon, Cambridgeshire PE29 7DL **t** 01480 412222 **f** 01480 411441 **e** sales@reflex-media.co.uk **w** reflex-media.co.uk MD: Roger Masterson.

Ricall Suites 1-4, 97 Mortimer St, London W1W 7SU **t** 020 7927 8305 **f** 020 7927 8306 **e** mail@ricall.com **w** ricall.com MD: Richard Corbett.

Shazam Entertainment 4th Floor, Block F, 375 Kensington High St, London W14 8QH **t** 020 7471 3440 **f** 020 7471 3477 **e** tim.porter@shazamteam.com **w** shazamentertainment.com Marketing Dir: Tim Porter.

Sound Moves (UK) Unit 6, Planet Centre, Armadale Road, Feltham, Middx TW14 0LW **t** 020 8831 0500 **f** 020 8831 0520 **e** London@soundmoves.com **w** soundmoves.com MD: Martin Corr.

Sound Stage Production Music Kerchesters, Waterhouse Lane, Kingswood, Surrey KT20 6HT **t** 01737 832837 **f** 01737 833812 **e** info@amphonic.co.uk **w** amphonic.com MD: Ian Dale.

Synchronicity 28 Howard House, 161 Cleveland St, London W1T 6QP **t** 020 7388 2099 or 07976 743081 **e** jp@synchronicity.uk.com **w** synchronicity.uk.com MD: Joanna Pearson.

Talk Of The Devil 5 Ripley Rd, Worthing, West Sussex BN11 5NQ **t** 01903 526515 **f** 01903 539634 **e** steve.power@talk-of-the-devil.com **w** talk-of-the-devil.com Dir: Steve Power.

UK Booking Agency Box 1, 404 Footscray Rd, London SE9 3TU **t** 020 8857 8775 or 07740 351 163 **f** 020 8857 8775 **e** spinners@dircon.co.uk **w** labelspinners.co.uk Owner: Steve Goddard. Events Organizer.

Upfront Promotions Unit 217 Buspace Studios, Conlan Street, London W10 5AP **t** 020 7565 0050 **f** 020 7565 0049 **e** terence@upfrontpromotions.com **w** upfrontpromotions.com Premiums Manager: Terence Scragg.

XK8 Organisation First Floor, 151 City Road, London EC1V 1JH **t** 020 7490 0666 **f** 020 7490 0660 **e** roger@xk8organisation.com **w** automaticpromotions.co.uk Dir: Roger Evans.

YR Media (YourRelease Ltd) Temple Gate Dojo, Herbert House, Lower Station Approach, Bristol BS1 6QS **t** 0870 909 0500 **e** info@YourRelease.com **w** yrmedia.com Marketing Manager: Seth Jackson.

Mobile Delivery & Aggregators

3 Star House, 20 Grenfell Rd, Maidenhead, Berks SL6 1EH **t** 01628 765 000 **f** 01628 767 031 **e** firstname.lastname@three.co.uk **w** three.co.uk Head of Music & Entertainment: Andrew Parker.

7 Digital Media 6th Floor, Palladium House, One Argyll Street, London W1F 7TA **t** 020 7494 6589 **f** 0871 733 4149 **e** info@7digitalmedia.com **w** 7digitalmedia.com Contact: Ben Drury

BT Rich Media (a division of BT plc) PP4E, 4th Floor, 203 High Holborn, London WC1V 7BU **t** 020 7777 7444 **f** 020 7728 7474 **e** btrminfo@bt.com **w** btrichmedia.com Dir of Music: Marco Distefano.

Direct Choice TV Communications 42 Edith Grove, London SW10 0NJ **t** 020 7352 6688 or 020 7352 6633 **f** 020 7352 6677 **e** jthomas@directchoicetv.com **w** directchoicetv.com Business Dev't Mgr: Johanna Thomas.

Kodime 39 The Woodlands, Esher, Surrey KT10 8DD **t** 0870 787 4652 **f** 020 8224 0033 **e** info@kodime.com **w** kodime.com MD: Nico Kopke.

Look Media Queen's Wharf, Queen Caroline St, London W6 9RJ **t** 020 8600 2615 **f** 020 8600 2501 **e** dedmonds@lookmediauk.com **w** lookmediauk.com Contact: Damien Edmonds

Melodi The Mill, Curborough Hall Farm, Lichfield, Staffordshire WS13 8ES **t** 0870 760 6495 **f** 0870 760 6495 **e** info@melodimedia.co.uk **w** melodimedia.co.uk MD: Iain Kerr.

Mobiq Tech House, Reddicap Trading Estate, Sutton Coldfield B75 7BU **t** 0121 311 9980 **f** 0121 311 9981 **e** info@mobiq.co.uk **w** mobiq.co.uk Commercial Dir: John Plant.

MusiWave UK 77 Oxford St, London W1D 2ES **t** 020 7659 2053 **f** 020 7659 2100 **e** janine@musicwave.com **w** musiwave.com Business Dev't Mgr: Janine Coughlan.

MyCokeMusic.com bd-ntwk, The Tea Building, 56 Shoreditch High Street, London E1 6PQ **t** 020 7749 5500 **f** 020 7749 5501 **e** enquiries@mycokemusic.com **w** mycokemusic.com Group Account Dir: Sam Needham.

Napster UK 57-61 Mortimer St, London W1W 8HS **t** 020 7101 7275 **f** 020 7101 7120 **e** firstname.lastname@napster.co.uk **w** napster.co.uk Programming Dir: Jeff Smith.

O2 Music O2UK, 260 Bath Rd, Slough SL14DX **t** 01132 722 000 **f** 01753 565010 **e** firstname.lastname@o2.com **w** o2.co.uk/music Hd, Mobile Data Mktg: Grahame Riddell. Hd, Content Dev't: John Ingham.

Oplayo UK 5th Floor, 5 Princes Gate, London SW7 1QJ **t** 0870 1999 989 **f** 0870 1991 816 **e** philip@oplayo.com **w** oplayo.com MD: Philip Bourchier O'Ferrall.

Phunky Phones 620 High Road, Leytonstone, London E11 3DA **t** 020 8556 0881 **f** 020 8556 0881 **e** laura@phunkyphones.net **w** phunkyphones.net Mgr: Laura Thrower.

ScreenFX Dudley House, 36-38 Southampton St, Covent Garden, London WC1E 7HE **t** 020 7240 0123 **f** 020 7240 0611 **e** info@screenfx.com **w** screenfx.com Sales Dir: Billy Howard.

SMS MusicMaker P.O. Box 44197, Fulham, London SW6 2XP **t** 07947 370 056 **e** info@smsmusicmaker.com **w** smsmusicmaker.com Dir: Barney Cordell.

T-Mobile International UK Waterfront, Hammersmith Embankment, Chancellors Rd, London W6 9RX **t** 020 8762 5000 **f** 020 8762 5222 **e** firstname.lastname@t-mobile.net **w** t-mobile.co.uk Snr Mgr, Content & Media: Keston Smith.

Vodafone Group Services 80 Strand, London WC2R 0RJ **t** 020 7212 0000 **f** 020 7212 0701 **e** firstname.lastname@vodafone.com **w** via.vodafone.com Head of Music: Edward Kershaw.

Xbox - Europe, Middle East & Africa Microsoft House, 10 Great Pulteney Street, London W1F 9NB **t** 020 7434 6172 **f** 020 7434 6495 **e** markcad@microsoft.com Hd, Strategic P'tnerships: Mark Cadogan.

QUITE GREAT

Promoters & Pluggers

3 Sound Promotions 10 Hilton St, Manchester M1 1JF **t** 0161 237 9413 **f** 0161 237 9413 **e** info@3soundpromotions.com **w** 3soundpromotions.com DJ Agent: Oliver Holland.

Absolute PR Hazlehurst Barn, Valley Road, Derbyshire SK22 2JP **t** 01663 747970 **f** 01663 747970 **e** neil@absolutepr.demon.co.uk **w** absolutepr.demon.co.uk Contact: Neil Cossar

ABSTRAKT 106B Saltram Crescent, London W9 3JX **t** 020 8968 1840 **f** 020 8968 1860 **e** abstrakt@btconnect.com MD: Anna Goodman.

Aire International 2a Ferry Rd, London SW13 9RX **t** 020 8834 7373 **f** 020 8834 7474 **e** info@airmtm.com **w** airmtm.com Director: Marc Connor.

Amanda Beel & Associates 27a Kings Gardens, West End Lane, London NW6 4PX **t** 020 7328 4836 or 07850 782 220 **e** amanda@allaboutpromo.co.uk Contact: Amanda Beel Lynn Blackwell (07850 216882). Bobbie Coppen (07833 365214). Trudie Myerscough-Harris (07801 459202).

Anglo Plugging Fulham Palace, Bishops Avenue, London SW6 6EA **t** 020 7384 7373 **f** 020 7371 9490 **e** firstname@angloplugging.co.uk **w** angloplugging.co.uk Promotions Co-ordinator: Alice Schofield.

Anonymous Groove PO Box 2, Leeds LS12 3WX **t** 0113 368 9912 or 0793 044 3048 **e** info@anonymous-groove.com **w** anonymous-groove.com MD: Chris Shipton.

Autograph Music & Media 19 Longmeadow Grove, St Lawrence Court, Manchester M34 2DA **t** 0161 336 9300 **f** 0161 221 3168 **e** autograph@ntlworld.com **w** autographmusicandmedia.com Owner: Derek Brandwood.

Avalon Public Relations 4A Exmoor Street, London W10 6BD **t** 020 7598 7222 **f** 020 7598 7223 **e** danielb@avalonuk.com Head of PR: Daniel Bee.

Backyard Promotion 106 Great Portland Street, London W1W 6PF **t** 020 7580 8881 **f** 020 7580 8882 **e** lil@back-yard.co.uk **w** back-yard.co.uk Booker: Mark Ngui.

Beatwax Communications 91 Berwick Street, London W1F 0NE **t** 020 7734 1965 **f** 020 7292 8333 **e** music@beatwax.com **w** beatwax.com Head of Music: Simon Bell.

Big Sister 78 Church Path, London W4 5BJ **t** 020 8747 2561 **f** 020 8747 2565 **e** karen@bigsisteruk.com Owner: Karen Williams.

Blurb 1-2 Anglers Lane, Kentish Town, London NW5 3DG **t** 020 7419 1221 **f** 020 7419 1222 **e** hello@blurbpr.com **w** blurbpr.com MD: Michael Plumley.

BR-Asian Media Consulting 45 Circus Rd, St Johns Wood, London NW8 9JH **t** 020 8550 9898 **f** 020 7289 9892 **e** moizvas@brasian.com **w** brasian.com MD: Moiz Vas.

Tony Bramwell 9 Brooking Barn, Ashprington, Totnes, Devon TQ9 7UL **t** 01803 732137 or 07762 583489 **f** 01803 732137 **e** bramwell@supanet.com MD: Tony Bramwell.

Breakout Promotions 36 Durnford St, Basford, Nottingham NG7 7EQ **t** 07961 014 303 **f** 0115 841 5994 **e** holmes_1978@hotmail.com MD: Rachel Holmes.

Brickwerk Unit 21, Rosaline Rd, London SW6 7QS **t** 020 7381 3524 **f** 020 7381 3524 **e** info@brickwerk.co.uk **w** brickwerk.co.uk Directors: Jo Brooks-Nevin.

CD POOL

Devonshire House, 223 Upper Richmond Road, London SW15 6SQ **t** 0845 458 8780 **f** 020 8789 8668 **e** admin@cdpool.co.uk **w** cdpool.com

Promoting Dance and Urban tunes across Europe on CD. House, Trance, Urban, Garage, Commercial Dance & Pop.

Chapple Davies 53 Great Portland Street, London W1W 7LG **t** 020 7299 7979 **f** 020 7299 7978 **e** gareth@chapdav.com; james@chapdav.com **w** chapdav.com Partner: Gareth Davies. Partner: James Chapple Gill.

Cool Badge Office 604, Oxford House, 49a Oxford Rd, London N4 3EY **t** 020 7272 8370 or 07766 233 368 **f** 020 7272 8371 **e** music@coolbadge.com **w** coolbadge.com MD: Russell Yates.

Crashed Music 162 Church Road, East Wall, Dublin 3, Ireland **t** +353 1 856 1011 **f** +353 1 856 1122 **e** shay@crashedmusic.com **w** crashedmusic.com MD: Shay Hennessy.

Crunk! Promotions Unit 11 Impress House, Mansell Road, London W3 7QH **t** 020 8932 3030 **f** 020 8932 3031 **e** duncan@crunk.co.uk **w** power.co.uk/crunk Promotions Mgr: Duncan Stump.

Cypher Press & Promotions Ltd Unit 2A Queens Studios, 121 Salusbury Road, London NW6 6RG **t** 020 7372 4464 or 020 7372 4474 **f** 020 7328 3808 or 020 7328 4447 **e** info@cypherpress.uk.com **w** cypherpress.uk.com Contact: Simon Ward/ Marion Sparks

Lisa Davies Promotions Caravela House, Waterhouse Lane, Kingswood, Surrey KT20 6DT **t** 01737 362444 **f** 01737 362555 **e** lisa@lisadaviespromotions.co.uk **w** lisadaviespromotions.co.uk MD: Lisa Davies.

Devolution 25 Pinehurst Court, Colville Gardens, London W11 2BH **t** 020 7229 5021 or 07776 196362 **f** 020 7229 5021 **e** geremy@devolution.freeserve.co.uk MD: Geremy O'Mahony.

djpromos.co.uk PO Box 34539, London sE15 2XA **t** 020 7732 2287 **e** ash@soultrade.com **w** djpromos.co.uk MD: Ash Kamat.

Earshot 5th Floor, 2-12 Pentonville Road, London N1 9PL **t** 020 7923 5560 **f** 020 7923 5564 **e** info@upshotcom.com **w** earshotmusic.net Contact: Tom Roberts, Stephen Barnes

Essential Entertainments Ltd 9 Church Street, Brighton, E. Sussex BN1 1US **t** 01273 888787 **f** 01273 888780 **e** info@essentialents.com **w** essentialfestival.com Events Organiser: Ish Ali.

Europropaganda Music House Media Services Ltd, PO BOX 5200, 103 Hammersmith Rd, London W14 0YP **t** 020 7348 5800 **f** 020 7348 5802 **e** scott@europropaganda.com **w** music-house.co.uk Contact: Scott Chester Pan-European promotion. UK & European holiday resort promotion.

EUROSOLUTION

Music House Group, Host Europe House, Kendal Avenue, London W3 0TT **t** 020 8896 8200 or 07973 670 545 **f** 020 8896 8201 **e** craig.eurosolution@music-house.co.uk **w** music-house.co.uk Promotions Mgr: Craig Jones. Full range of commercial, pop and urban club promotion services.

Richard Evans PR 15 Chesham St, Belgravia, London SW1X 8ND **t** 020 7235 3929 **e** r.evans@pipemedia.co.uk

Event One Music 5 Carlisle St, London W1D 3BL **t** 020 7437 4040 **f** 020 7437 1111 **e** hypemerchant@event-one.co.uk Director: Jeff Chegwin. Director: Nigel Wilton.

Exposure (Nation-wide flyer distribution services) 3N Beehive Mill, Jersey St, Manchester M4 6JG **t** 0161 950 4241 **f** 0161 950 4240 **e** info@exposureuk.com **w** exposureuk.com MD: Keith Patterson.

Fake Media PO Box 1020, High Wycombe, Buck HP10 0ZQ **t** 07966 233275 **e** Adam.fisher@fakemedia.com MD: Adam Fisher.

FLEMING CONNOLLY AND LANDER (FCL-PR)

Music House Group, Host Europe House, Kendal Avenue, London W3 0TT **t** 020 8896 8200 **f** 020 8896 8201 **e** nick@fclpr.com; judd@fclpr.com **w** music-house.co.uk Contact: Nick Fleming/Judd Lander **National radio & television promotion.**

Flying Sparks Promotion Garden House, Hayters Way, Alderholt, Hampshire SP6 3AX **t** 01425 658 000 **f** 01425 658 222 **e** flyingsparks@promotion100.fsnet.co.uk MD: Ian Brown.

Freeway Press 20 Windmill Road, Kirkcaldy, Fife KY1 3AQ **t** 01592 655309 **f** 01592 596177 **e** cronulla20@aol.com Dir: John Murray.

Frontier Promotions The Grange, Cockley Cley Rd, Hilborough, Thetford, Norfolk IP26 5BT **t** 01760 756394 **f** 01760 756398 **e** frontier@frontierUK.fsnet.co.uk MD: Sue Williams.

Future Studios International PO Box 10, London N1 3RJ **t** 020 7241 2183 **f** 020 7241 6233 **e** ladybelle888@blueyonder.co.uk **w** gigsonline.co.uk Director: Michelle L Goldberg.

GC Promotions 9 Preston Road, Leytonstone, London E11 1NL **t** 020 8989 5005 **f** 020 8989 5006 **e** jeffrey@gonecountry.net **w** gonecountry.net MD: Jeffrey Stothers.

Phil Gibbs Promotes... Faraday Cottage, Faraday Yard, Hampton Court Road, East Molesey, Surrey KT8 9BW **t** 020 8979 3505 or 07767 264154 **f** 020 8979 3505 **e** pgibbsprom@tiscali.co.uk Owner: Phil Gibbs. National and regional radio. 12 years' major label experience. A no-nonsense, professional service.

Groovefinder Productions Flat 1, 19 Craneswater Park, Southsea, Portsmouth PO4 0NU **t** 07831 450 241 **e** jeff@groovefinderproductions.com MD: Jeff Powell.

HardZone Full Service Marketing The Business Village, Gardiner House, 3-9 Broomhill Road, London SW18 4JQ **t** 020 8870 8744 **f** 020 8874 1578 **e** info@hardzone.co.uk **w** hardzone.co.uk Head of Marketing: Reggie Styles. MD: Jackie Davidson.

HART MEDIA LTD.

Primrose Hill Business Centre, 110 Gloucester Avenue, London NW1 8JA **t** 020 7209 3760 **f** 020 7209 3761 **e** info@hartmedia.co.uk **w** hartmedia.co.uk MD: Jo Hart. Head Of Promotions: Caroline Moore.

Taryn Hill Promotions Dolphin Court, 42 Carleton Road, London N7 0ER **t** 07971 575810 **e** hilltaryn@hotmail.com Contact: Taryn Hill

The Howlin' Plugging & Promotion Company 114 Lower Park Rd, Loughton, Essex IG10 4NE **t** 020 8508 4564 or 07831 430080 **e** djone@howardmarks.freeserve.co.uk Prop: Howard Marks.

HYPER ACTIVE

Music House Group, Host Europe House, Kendal Avenue, London W3 0TT **t** 020 8896 8200 **f** 020 8896 8201 **e** matt.hyperactive@music-house.co.uk **w** music-house.co.uk Contact: Matt Waterhouse **Full range of upfront house and mainstream club promotion services.**

Impact Ventures 38b Brixton Water Lane, London SW2 1QE **t** 020 7274 8509 **f** 020 7274 3543 **e** info@impactventures.co.uk **w** impactventures.co.uk MD: Rachel Bee.

Impel 1 Park Terrace, Glasgow G3 6BY **t** 0141 305 0011 **f** 0141 305 0015 **e** info@impelmusic.com **w** impelmusic.com MD: Alistair McGovern.

Indiscreet PR 10, Enfield Rd, Brentford, Middx TW8 9NX **t** 020 8847 0784 or 07813 290 474 **e** alan@indiscreetpr.co.uk **w** indiscreetpr.co.uk Dirs: Alan Robinson, Lesley Shone.

Infected 4th Floor, 40 Langham St, London W1W 7AS **t** 020 7580 7770 or 020 7580 6660 **f** 020 7580 6660 **e** mike.infected000@btclick.com MD: Mike Gourlay.

information communication ltd 6 Hornsey Lane Gardens, London N6 5PB **t** 020 8374 6040 **e** infocom@dial.pipex.com MD: Michael Thorne.

Instant Hit PO Box 34, Ventnor, Isle of Wight PO38 1YQ **t** 01983 857 079 **e** jkt@diamondisle.co.uk **w** diamondisle.co.uk MD: Jon Monks.

INTERMEDIA REGIONAL

Byron House, 112A Shirland Road, London W9 2EQ **t** 020 7266 0777 **f** 020 7266 7726 **e** info@intermediaregional.com MD: Steve Tandy. GM: Janice MacGregor. Regional Radio Promotions Managers: Gavin Hughes, Paul Akkermans. Reg TV Promotions: James Pegrum. Dance Promotions: Simon Hills. Alternative Promotions: Stacy Scurfield.

Iron Man Records PO Box 9121, Birmingham B13 8AU **t 0121 256 1303 f** 0121 256 1302 **e** info@ironmanrecords.co.uk Label Manager: Mark Badger.

ISH-MEDIA

2 Devonport Mews, Devonport Road, London W12 8NG **t** 020 8742 9191 **f** 020 8742 9102 **m** 07778 263533 **e** eden@ish-media.com **w** ish-media.com. Director: Eden Blackman

Mike Irving Promotions 47 Longcroft Gardens, Welwyn Garden City, Hertfordshire AL8 6JR **t** 01707 376057 or 07071 881154 **f** 01707 393776 **e** mikeirving@aol.com **w** mikeirvingpromotions.co.uk Director: Mike Irving.

Alan James PR Ground Floor, 60 Weston Street, London SE1 3QJ **t** 020 7403 9999 **f** 020 7403 0000 **e** promo@ajpr.co.uk **w** ajpr.co.uk MD: Alan James.

Jane Wallace Press & Promtion The Corner House, Cidermill Lane, Chipping Campden, Gloucestershire GL55 6HL **t** 01386 841453 **f** 01386 841453 **e** successpr@yahoo.co.uk Dir Press/Promo: Jane Wallace.

JBMusicMedia 2, The Bush, Newtown Road, Awbridge, Romsey, Hampshire SO51 0GG **t** 01794 342426 **f** 01794 432426 **e** jacqui@kwinstanley.free-online.co.uk GM: Jacqui Bateson.

Jeff Chegwin Promotions Suite 139, 2 Lansdowne Row, Berkerley Square, London W1J 6HL **t** 020 8579 7997 or 07957 939 072 **e** jeffchegwin@hotmail.com **w** jeffchegwin.com Dir: Jeff Chegwin.

Jelly Street Club Promotions 358 Chester Road, Manchester M16 9EZ **t** 0161 872 6006 **f** 0161 872 6468 **e** kevkinsella@aol.com MD: Kevin Kinsella.

Labels Enabled 34 Great James St, London WC1N 3HB **t** 020 7404 1050 **e** labelsenabled@get-it-signed.com **w** labelsenabled.co.uk Dir: Neil March.

LARGE PR LTD

39 Grafton Way, London W1T 5DE **t** 020 7388 6060 or 07885 332195 **f** 08700 518 459 **e** stuart@largepr.com Contact: Stuart Emery

Les Molloy 78 Church Path, Chiswick, London W4 5BJ **t** 020 8994 3791 **f** 020 8994 6845 **e** lmolloy@dircon.co.uk Contact: Les Molloy

LEYLINE PROMOTIONS

Studio 24, Westbourne Studios, 242 Acklam Road, London W10 5JJ **t** 020 7575 3285 **f** 020 7575 3286 **e** name@leylinepromotions.com **w** leylinepromotions.com. Director: Adrian Leigh. Head of Press & Marketing: Letitia Thomas. Technical Director: James Reid.
Dedicated & experienced team specialising in event management, festival production & programming, club promotions, press & marketing & new technology.

Phil Long PR 2/14 Park Terrace, The Park, Nottingham NG1 5DN **t** 0115 947 5440 **f** 0115 947 5440 **e** phil.long@pipemedia.co.uk MD: Phil Long.

Lucid PR Flat 9, 91 York St, London W1H 4QE **t** 020 7724 4472 **e** firstname.lastname@lucidpr.co.uk Dirs: Mick Garbutt, Charlie Lycett.

M P Promotions (MPP) 22 Hill Street, Romley, Stockport, Cheshire SK6 3AH **t** 0161 494 7934 **f** 0161 406 8500 **e** maria@mppromotions.co.uk Director: Maria Philippou.

Mad As Toast 3 Broomlands St, Paisley PA1 2LS **t** 0141 887 8888 **f** 0141 887 8888 **e** info@madastoast.com **w** madastoast.com Dirs: John Richardson, George Watson.

Mainstream Promotions The Music Village, 11B Osiers Road, London SW18 1NL **t** 07000 4 77666 or 020 8870 0011 **f** 020 8870 2101 **e** mainstream@rush-release.co.uk MD: Jo Underwood.

Making Waves Communications 45 Underwood St, London N1 7LG **t** 020 7490 0944 **f** 020 7490 1026 **e** info@makingwaves.co.uk **w** makingwaves.co.uk MD: Matt Williams.

Matthew Ryan Criel House, St. Leonards Road, London W13 8RG **t** 020 8566 3426 **f** 020 8567 3699 **e** mail@matthewryan.co.uk **w** matthewryan.co.uk Account Director: Matthew Ryan.

Mega Bullet Archway 74, Ranelagh Gardens, London SW6 3UR **t** 020 7384 3222 **f** 020 7384 3223 **e** info@megabullet.com **w** platin-m.com MD: Marilyn Rosen.

Mocking Bird Music PO Box 52, Marlow, Bucks SL7 2YB **t** 01491 579214 **f** 01491 579214 **e** mockingbirdmusic@aol.com Artiste Management: Leon B Fisk.

Mosquito Media PO Box 33790, 18 Chelsea Manor St, London SW3 6WF **t** 020 7286 0503 **f** 020 7286 0503 **e** mosquitomedia@aol.com **w** mosquito-media.co.uk Contact: Richard Abbott

Movement London PO Box 31835, London SE11 4WD **t** 020 7735 7255 **f** 020 7793 7225 **e** info@movement.co.uk **w** movement.co.uk Promoter: Nyeleti van Belle Freire.

MP Promotions Bexley Cottage, Haselor, Warwickshire B49 6LU **t** 01789 488988 **f** 01789 488998 **e** mppromotions@btinternet.com MD: Mike Perry.

Music House Group Host Europe House, Kendal Avenue, London W3 0TT **t** 020 8896 8200 **f** 020 8896 8201 **e** simon.walsh@music-house.co.uk **w** music-house.co.uk Dir: Simon Walsh. Directors: Simon Walsh, Judd Lander, Nick Fleming.

MVPD Queens House, 1 Leicester Place, Leicester Square, London WC2H 7BP **t** 020 7534 3340 **f** 020 7534 3341 **e** chris@mvpd.net **w** mvpd.net Dir: Chris Page.

NoBul Promotions 59 New River Crescent, Palmers Green, London N13 5RD **t** 020 8882 3677 **f** 020 8882 3688 **e** alex@nobul.prestel.co.uk MD: Alex Alexandrou.

NONSTOP PROMOTIONS

Studio 39, Aaron House Business Centre, 6 Bardolph Road, Richmond, Surrey TW9 2LS **t** 020 8334 9994 **f** 020 8334 9995 **e** info@nonstop1.co.uk Contact: Niki Sanderson, Stuart Kenning

Ny Sushi/Raw Fish 2 Fulmer Road, Sheffield, South Yorkshire S11 8UF **t** 0114 2671 869 **f** 0114 2671 783 **e** ny.sushi@virgin.net **w** nysushi.co.uk Dir: Christopher Bibby.

Out Promotion 4th Floor, 33 Newman Street, London W1T 1PY **t** 020 7637 3755 **f** 020 7637 3744 **e** caroline@out-london.co.uk Head Or Radio & TV: Caroline Poulton. Promotions manager: Caroline Poulton.

Outlet Promotions Holborn Gate,First Floor, 330 High Holborn, London WC1V 7QT **t** 020 7203 8366 **f** 020 7203 8409 **e** press@outlet-promotions.com **w** outlet-promotions.com Admin: Glenn Wilson.

THE OUTSIDE ORGANISATION LTD.

Butler House, 177-178 Tottenham Court Rd, London W1T 7NY **t** 020 7436 3633 **f** 020 7436 3632 **e** info@outside-org.co.uk **w** outside-org.co.uk

Overground Promotions PO Box 1NW, Newcastle upon Tyne NE99 1NW **t** 0191 232 6700 **f** 0191 232 6701 **e** lee@overground.co.uk MD: Lee Conlon.

Pacific Edge Promotions & Public Relations Charlestone House, 34 Poppleton Road, London E11 1LR **t** 020 8530 7748 **f** 020 8530 2571 **e** pacific.edge@btinternet.com MD: Jill Cramer.

Don Percival Artists' Promotion Shenandoah, Manor Park, Chislehurst, Kent BR7 5QD **t** 020 8295 0310 **f** 020 8295 0311 **e** don@dpap.demon.co.uk MD: Don Percival.

Phuture Trax Press & Events PR PO Box 48527, London NW4 4ZB **t** 020 8203 3968 **f** 020 8203 3968 **e** nix@phuturetrax.co.uk **w** phuturetrax.co.uk MD: Nicky Trax.

Pioneer Promotions 5 Emerson House, 14B Ballynahinch Rd, Belfast BT8 8DN **t** 028 9081 7111 **f** 028 9081 7444 **e** ppromo@musicni.co.uk MD: Johnny Davis.

Pivotal PR PO Box 47397, London NW3 1XY **t** 020 7692 7543 **f** 020 7813 4649 **e** bjorn@pivotalpr.co.uk **w** pivotalpr.co.uk Contact: Bjîrn Hall

Planetlovemusic 2 Gregg St, Lisburn, Co Antrim BT27 5AN **t** 02892 667 000 **f** 02892 668 000 **e** eddie@planetlovemusic.com **w** planetlovemusic.com Dir: Eddie Wray.

THE PLAY CENTRE

Unit 2 Devonport Mews, Shepherd's Bush, London W12 8NG **t** 020 8932 7705 **f** 020 8932 7723 **e** info@theplaycentre.com **w** theplaycentre.com Contact: MD & Head of Promotions: Shaun "STuCKee" Willoughby

PlugTwo 133 The Coal Exchange, Cardiff bay, Cardiff CF10 5ED **t** 02920 190151 **e** john@plugtwo.com **w** plugtwo.com Dir: John Rostron.

Poparazzi Unit 11, Impress House, Mansell Rd, London W3 7QH **t** 020 8932 3030 **f** 020 8932 3031 **e** Tracey@power.co.uk **w** power.co.uk Promotions Manager: Tracey Webb. Breaking commercial dance music through the clubs.

Power Promotions Unit 11, Impress House, Mansell Road, London W3 7QH **t** 020 8932 3030 **f** 020 8932 3031 **e** info@power.co.uk **w** power.co.uk MD: Terry Marks.

PRo Promotions Fulham Palace, Bishops Ave, London SW6 6EA **t** 020 7384 7373 **f** 020 7371 7940 **e** caroline@theprogroup.co.uk Director: Caroline Prothero.

Pro Urban Promotions Unit 11, Impress House, Mansell Rd, London W3 7QH **t** 020 8932 3030 **f** 020 8932 3031 **e** prourban@power.co.uk **w** power.co.uk Promotions Mgr: Tracey Webb.

Promobeats PO Box 6003, Birmingham B45 0AR **t 0121 477 9553 f** 0121 693 2954 **e** promobeats@gotham-records.com **w** gotham-records.com Manager: Tara Tomes.

RADIO PROMOTIONS

PO Box 20, Banbury, Oxon OX17 3YT
t 0129 581 4995 **e** music@radiopromotions.co.uk
w radiopromotions.co.uk
Contact: Steve Betts, Bill Whitney
Professional regional radio and TV promotion offering an individual service where every record is a priority.

Raised On Radio 23 Handley Court, Aigburth, Liverpool L19 3QS **t** 0151 427 9884 **f** 0151 427 9884 **e** steve.raisedonradio@tinyworld.co.uk Director of Promotion: Steve Dinwoodie.

Red Alert Promotions Sun House, 2-4 Little Peter Street, Manchester M15 4PS **t** 0161 834 7434 **f** 0161 834 8545 **e** liam@redalert.co.uk MD: Liam Walsh.

Red Shadow Wisteria House, 56 Cole Park Road, St Margarets, Twickenham, Middlx TW1 1HS **t** 020 8891 3333 **f** 020 8891 3222 **e** julian@redshadow.co.uk Director: Julian Spear. Promotion Manager: Justin Coombers.

RENEGADE

Music House Group, Host Europe House, Kendal Avenue, London W3 0TT **t** 020 8896 8200
f 020 8896 8201 **e** chris.renegade@music-house.co.uk
w music-house.co.uk Contact: Chris Smith
Indie/alternative/rock club & college promotion. Student/press & radio. Bars/cafes/retail promotion.

Richard Wootton Publicity The Manor House, 120 Kingston Rd, Wimbledon, London SW19 1LY **t** 020 8542 8101 **f** 020 8540 0691 **e** richard@rwpublicity.com MD: Richard Wootton.

Rocket The Brix at St Matthews Church, Brixton Hill, London SW2 1JF **t** 020 7326 1234 **e** Radio@Rocketpr.co.uk **w** rocketpr.co.uk
MD: Prudence Trapani.

Rocketscience Media Suite 36, 99-109 Lavender Hill, London SW11 5QL **t** 020 7738 9111 **f** 020 7738 9222
e office@rocketsciencemedia.com
w rocketsciencemedia.com Dir: Alex Black.

RPPR and Promotions The Collective, 2nd Floor, Chiswick High Rd, London W4 1SY **t** 020 8995 5544 **f** 020 8995 1133 **e** rppr1@ukonline.co.uk Head of Radio/TV: Richard Perry.

RUSH RELEASE

RUSH RELEASE LTD

Cranhurst Lodge, 37-39 Surbiton Hill Road, Surbiton, Surrey KT6 4TS **t** 020 8786 2121 **f** 020 8786 2123
e info@rush-release.co.uk **w** rushrelease.com
Established 1979, National Radio/TV & Regional Radio.
MD: Jo Underwood. **Club promotion, Urban Promotion & European Resort Promotion.** Contact: CarlyHodgson.
See our full page ad overleaf.

Scene Not Herd

Hillhead Cottage, Avonbridge, Falkirk FK1 2NL
t 01324 861744 or 24 Hour Operations Mobile 07866 265 666 **e** lesley@scenenotherd.co.uk
w scenenotherd.co.uk Sales & Marketing: Lesley Woodall. Operations: Jim Cumming.Deliveries: APC Depot 66, Unit 1, 239 Blairtummock Road, Glasgow G33 4ED. **Nationwide distribution of flyers and other promotional material, flyer printing, street teams, mailing service, data collection campaigns and event management.**

SCREAM PROMOTIONS

4th Floor, 57 Poland St, London W1F 7NW
t 020 7434 3446 **f** 020 7434 3449
e firstname@screampromotions.co.uk
w screampromotions.co.uk
Contact: Tony Cooke, Claire Jarvis, Phil Halliday

Scruffy Bird The Nest, 205 Victoria St, London SW1E 5NE **t** 020 7931 7990 **f** 020 7900 1557
e emily@scruffybird.com **w** scruffybird.com Head of Radio: Emily Cooper.

Seesaw PR Ltd 4th Floor, 22 Tower Street, London WC2H 9TW **t** 020 7539 8200/03 **e** firstname@seesawpr.net Contact: Sam Wright, Andrea Phipps

Sharp End Music Group Grafton House, 2-3 Golden Square, London W1F 9HR **t** 020 7439 8442 **f** 020 7434 3615 **e** sharpend2@aol.com Dir: Robert Lemon.

SINGLE MINDED PROMOTIONS

11 Cambridge Court, 210 Shepherds Bush Road, London W6 7NJ **t** 0870 011 3748 or 07860 391 902 **f** 0870 011 3749 **e** tony@singleminded.com **w** singleminded.com MD: Tony Byrne.

SIZE NINE

Music House Group, Host Europe House, Kendal Avenue, London W3 0TT **t** 020 8896 8200 **f** 020 8896 8201 **e** paul.sizenine@music-house.co.uk **w** music-house.co.uk Contact: Paul Kennedy (Radio), Simon Walsh, Mark Wilson (Radio) (mark@sizenine@music-house.co.uk).

Song And Media Promotions Mulberry House, 10 Hedgerows, Stanway, Colchester, Essex CO3 0GJ **t** 01206 364136 **f** 01206 364146 **e** songmag@aol.com **w** songwriters-guild.co.uk MD: Colin Eade.

Soul2Streets Unit 219, Canalot Production Studios, Kensal Rd, London W10 5BN **t** 020 8960 8950 **f** 020 8964 5968 **e** doug@soul2soul.co.uk **w** ukmusicworldwide.com Promotions Mgr: Doug Cooper.

Special D (SDDP) 29 St Barnabas Street, Belgravia, London SW1W 8QB **t** 020 7730 7697 or 0790 427 2668 **f** 020 7730 7697 **e** steve.stimpy@btinternet.com **w** special-d.com MD: Stimpy.

Steve Osborne Promotions PO Box 69, Daventry, Northamptonshire NN11 4SY **t** 01327 703968 or 01327 312545 **f** 0871 2772365 **e** steve@daventrynet.co.uk Proprietor: Steve Osborne.

Swell Music Marketing 147 Battersea Business Centre, 99-109 Lavender Hill, London SW11 5QF **t** 020 7223 2221 **f** 020 7223 7220 **e** info@swellmusic.co.uk Dir: Andrew Grainger.

TC Promotions 4 Gala Avenue, Dundee DD2 4EJ **t** 01382 644003 **f** 01382 646167 **e** tony@hotmix.co.uk Prop: Tony Cochrane.

Terrie Doherty Promotions 40 Princess St, Manchester M1 6DE **t** 0161 234 0044 **e** terriedoherty@zoo.co.uk Director: Terrie Doherty.

The Partnership 57-63 Old Church Street, London SW3 5BS **t** 020 7761 6005 **f** 020 7761 6035 **e** matthew@partnership2.com Partner: Matthew Austin. Partner: Billy MacLeod.

TIKKLE PR AND MUSIC PROMOTION

The Studio, 43 Bedford Street, Covent Garden, London WC2E 9HA **t** 020 7358 4466 or 07788 777 705 **e** getseen@tikkle.com **w** tikkle.com Creative Dir & Event Prod: Damien Chaos. Branding & Sponsorship Consultant: Mark Pearce. Youth Marketing & Under 18ns Events: Diane Worrell. Street Team Logistics & Event Photography: Chadissa Greenaway. Public Relations & Radio: Alex Valdes. **Managing the relationship between your promotional material and your target.**

TOMKINS PR

The Old Lampworks, Rodney Place, London SW19 2LQ **t** 020 8540 8166 **f** 020 8540 6056 **e** info@tomkinspr.com **w** tomkinspr.com MD: Susie Tomkins. Promotion Manager: Stroma Clark. **Regional Radio & TV Promotions.**

Traffic Marketing 2 Prowse Place, London NW1 9PH **t** 020 7485 7400 **f** 020 7485 6080 **e** info@trafficmarketing.co.uk **w** trafficmarketing.com MD: Lisa Paulon.

Upshot Communications Ltd 5th Floor, 2-12 Pentonville Rd, Angel, London N1 9PL **t** 020 7923 5560 **f** 020 7923 5564 **e** Info@Upshotcom.com **w** upshotcreek.com Contact: Tom Roberts, Stephen Barnes

Urban Marketeers PO Box 1345, Essex IG4 5FX **t** 07050 333 555 **f** 07020 923 292 **e** emmelleye@aol.com **w** urbanmarketeers.co.uk Joint MD: Trex Morton.

VISION

22 Upper Grosvenor St, London W1K 7PE **t** 020 7499 8024 **f** 020 7499 8032 **e** visionpromo@btconnect.com **w** visionmusic.co.uk MD: Rob Dallison.

WAXWORKS

WAXWORKS

Music House Group, Host Europe House, Kendal Avenue, London W3 0TT **t** 020 8896 8200 **f** 020 8896 8201 **e** aidan.waxworks@music-house.co.uk **w** music-house.co.uk Contact: Aidan Byrne **Breakbeat, leftfield house, hip hop, electronica, drum 'n' bass and alternative club promotion.**

Way To Blue 1st Floor, Suna House, 128-132 Curtain Road, London EC2A 3AR **t** 020 7749 8444 **f** 020 7749 8420 **e** lee@waytoblue.com **w** waytoblue.com Director: Lee Henshaw.

Whitenoise Promotions 8 Southam Street, London W10 5PH **t** 020 8964 0020 **f** 020 8964 0021 **e** info@whitenoisepromo.com **w** whitenoisepromo.com Promotions Mgr: Colin Hobbs. MD: Chris Butler.

XPOSURE

Music House Group, Host Europe House, Kendal Avenue, London W3 0TT **t** 020 8896 8200 **f** 020 8896 820 **e** kent@music-house.co.uk **w** music-house.co.uk Contact: Kent Da'Obry.
R&B/Hip Hop/Reggae/UK Grarage (Eski, Sub-low, Grime)/Club, Community/Specialist Radio promotion.

XK8 Organisation First Floor, 151 City Rd, London EC1V 1JH **t** 020 7490 0666 **f** 020 7490 0660 **e** roger@xk8organisation.com **w** automaticpromotions.co.uk Dir: Roger Evans.

ZZonked Unit 348, Stratford Workshops, Burford Road, London E15 2SP **t** 020 8503 1880 **f** 020 8534 0603 **e** info@zzonked.co.uk **w** zzonked.co.uk Contact: Harvey Jones

PR Companies

Absolute PR Hazlehurst Barn, Valley Road, Derbyshire SK22 2JP **t** 01663 747970 or 07768 652899 **f** 01663 747970 **e** neil@absolutepr.demon.co.uk **w** absolutepr.demon.co.uk MD: Neil Cossar.

Absolute Promotions & PR Ground Floor (Rear), 34 Maple Street, London W1T 6HD **t** 020 7323 2238 **f** 020 7323 2239 **e** info@absolutepromo.co.uk Partners: Stuart Emery.

ABSTRAKT

106B Saltram Crescent, London W9 3JX **t** 020 8968 1840 **f** 020 8968 1860 **e** abstrakt@btconnect.com MD: Anna Goodman. **Press/radio promotion for cutting-edge Hip-Hop, Dance, Jazz, World, Spoken Word & Alternative plus live shows/events. Labels are: Subliminal, Cyber, Ropeadope/Rykodisc, Sondos, Texture, Bambossa, Probe Plus, 7 Heads.**

AFC Publicity 24 Bray Gardens, Maidstone, Kent ME15 9TR **t** 01622 744481 **f** 01622 765014 **e** editor@maverick-country.com **w** maverick-country.com MD: Alan Cackett.

Aire International (Air,) 2a Ferry Rd, London SW13 9RX **t** 020 8834 7373 **f** 020 8834 7474 **e** info@airmtm.com **w** airmtm.com Director: Marc Connor.

Alchemy PR 212a The Bridge, 12-16 Clerkenwell Rd, London EC1M 5PQ **t** 020 7324 6260 **f** 020 7324 6001 **e** mail@alchemypr.com **w** alchemypr.com Dir: Matt Learmouth.

All About Promotions

ALL ABOUT PROMOTIONS

27a Kings Gardens, West End Lane, London NW6 4PX **t** 020 7328 4836 **f** 020 7372 3331 **e** info@allaboutpromo.com Contacts: Amanda Beel, Hayley Codd; Lynn Blackwell; Bobbie Coppen.

All Press 85 St Charles Square, London W10 6EB **t** 020 8969 3636 or 07931 557 970 **e** nienke.klop@all-press.co.uk MD: Nienke Klop.

Amanda Williams PR Top Floor Office, 95 Waldegrave Road, Teddington, Middlesex TW11 8LA **t** 020 8943 2804 **f** 020 8943 8874 **e** amanda@amandawilliamspr.co.uk **w** amandawilliamspr.co.uk Dir: Amanda Williams.

Stephen Anderson Publicity Cathedral Buildings, 64 Donegall Street, Belfast, Co Antrim BT1 2GT **t** 028 9031 0949 **f** 028 9031 5905 **e**stephen_anderson@btconnect.com **w** stephenandersonpublicty.co.uk MD: Stephen Anderson.

APB Studio 18, Westbourne Studios, 242 Acklam Road, London W10 5JJ **t** 020 8968 9000 **f** 020 8968 8500 **e** info@apb-pr.co.uk MD: Gordon Duncan.

Appetite PR 2 Coventry St, Brighton, E. Sussex BN1 5PQ **t** 01273 888099 or 07970 913494 **f** 01273 230189 **e** appetitepr@ntlworld.com MD: Judith Weaterton.

Ark PR The Basement, 11 Old Steine, Brighton, East Sussex BN1 1EJ **t** 01273 696 355 or 07759 528 006 **e** arkpr@tiscali.co.uk MD: Derek Day.

Arrested 49 Neal St, London WC2H 9PZ **t** 020 7240 6676 **f** 020 7240 1554 **e** Jody@arrestedpr.com MD: Jody Dunleavy.

ASAP Communications Ltd. Suite One, 2 Tunstall Rd, London SW9 8DA **t** 020 7978 9488 **f** 020 7978 9490 **e** info@asapcomms.co.uk **w** asapcomms.com MD: Yvonne Thompson.

The Associates UK 39-41 North Road, London N7 9DP **t** 020 7700 3388 **f** 020 7609 2249 **e** info@the-associates.co.uk **w** the-associates.co.uk PR Account Mgr: Rachael Marshall.

Autonomy PR Unit 212 The Gramophone Works, 326 Kensal Road, London W10 5BZ **t** 020 8969 9111 **f** 020 8969 9955 **e** jennie@autonomy-music.co.uk **w** autonomy-music.co.uk MD: Jennie Bishop.

Bad Girl PR 183 Anson Road, London NW2 4AU **t** 020 8452 2044 or 07909 691342 **f** 020 8452 2044 **e** joolz@badgirlpr.freeserve.co.uk MD: Joolz Bosson.

Bad Moon Publicity 19B All Saints Road, London W11 1HE **t** 020 7221 0499 **f** 020 7792 0405 **e** press@badmoon.co.uk MD: Anton Brookes.

Badger Promotions PO BOX9121, Birmingham B13 8AU **t** 0121 256 1303 **f** 0121 256 1302 **e** info@badgerpromotions.co.uk **w** badgerpromotions.co.uk Promoter: Mark Bager.

Barrington Harvey Troopers Yard, Bancroft, Hitchin, Hertfordshire SG5 1JW **t** 01462 456780 **f** 01462 456781 **e** simon@bhpr.co.uk **w** barringtonharvey.co.uk Dir: Simon Harvey.

Beatwax Communications 91 Berwick Street, London W1F 0NE **t** 020 7734 1965 **f** 020 7292 8333 **e** music@beatwax.com **w** beatwax.com Head of Music: Simon Bell.

Best PR 3rd Floor, 29-31 Cowper St, London EC2A 4AT **t** 020 7608 4590 **f** 020 7608 4599 **e** penny@bestest.co.uk Head Of Press: Penny Brignell. Press Officer: Simon Blackmore.

Big Cat Group Vincent House, 92-93 Edward St, Birmingham, West Midlands B1 2RA **t** 0121 248 4697 **e** info@bcguk.com **w** bcguk.com Dir: Nick Morgan.

Big Group Ltd 91 Princedale Road, Holland Park, London W11 4NS **t** 020 7229 8827 **f** 020 7243 1462 **e** info@biggroup.co.uk **w** biggroup.co.uk Account Director: Simon Broyd.

Blues Matters! PR PO Box 18, Bridgend CF33 6YW **t** 01656 743406 **f** 01656 743406 **e** blues.matters@ntlworld.com **w** bluesmatters.co.uk MD: Alan Pearce.

Blurb PR 7 Tower Mansions, 136 West End Lane, West Hampstead, London NW6 1SB **t** 020 7419 1221 **e** hello@blurbpr.com MD: Michael Plumley.

Borkowski PR 2nd Floor, 12 Oval Road, Camden, London NW1 7DH **t** 020 7482 4000 **f** 020 7482 5400 **e** larry@borkowski.co.uk **w** borkowski.co.uk New Bus Dev'**t** Mgr: Larry Franks.

BR-Asian Media Consulting 45 Circus Rd, St Johns Wood, London NW8 9JH **t** 020 8550 9898 **f** 020 7289 9892 **e** moizvas@brasian.com **w** brasian.com MD: Moiz Vas.

Brassneck Publicity 31A Almorah Road, London N1 3ER **t** 020 7226 3399 **f** 020 7226 7557 **e** brassneckpr@aol.com MD: Mick Houghton.

Buzz Publicity 14 Corsiehill Road, Perth PH2 7BZ **t** 01738 638140 **f** 01738 638140 **e** PR@thebuzzgroup.co.uk **w** thebuzzgroup.co.uk MD: Dave Arcari.

Cake Group Ltd 10 Stephen Mews, London W1T 1AG **t** 020 7307 3100 **f** 020 7307 3101 **e** info@cakemedia.com **w** cakegroup.com Director: Clare Craven.

Capitalize Ltd 52 Thrale Street, London SE1 9HW **t** 020 7940 1700 **f** 020 7940 1739 **e** Info@capitalize.co.uk **w** capitalize.co.uk MD: Richard Moore.

Casablanca PR 26 Porchester Sq, London W2 6AN **t** 020 7221 2287 or 07887 610 027 **f** 020 7221 2287 **e** fozia@casablancapr.co.uk MD: Fozia Shah.

Celebration PR Ltd 8 Ashington Court, Westwood Hill, Sydenham, London SE26 6BN **t** 020 8778 9918 **f** 020 8355 7708 **e** celebration@dial.pipex.com Dir: James Doheny.

Chapple Davies 53 Great Portland Street, London W1W 7LG **t** 020 7299 7979 **f** 020 7299 7978 **e** gareth@chapdav.com; james@chapdav.com **w** chapdav.com Partners: Gareth Davies, James C Gill.

Ian Cheek Press Suite 5, 51D New Briggate, Leeds, West Yorkshire LS2 8JD **t** 0113 246 9940 **f** 0113 246 9960 **e** iancheek@talk21.com Head of Press: Ian Cheek.

Sharon Chevin PR (see The Publicity Connection)

Circus PR Argo House, Kilburn Park Rd., Maida Vale, London NW6 5LF **t** 020 7644 0267 **f** 020 7644 0698 **e** bernard@circusrecords.net **w** circusrecords.net MD: Bernard MacMahon. Head Int'l: Paul Charles.

Max Clifford Associates 49-50 New Bond Street, London W1Y 9HA **t** 020 7408 2350 **f** 020 7409 2294 **e** max@mcapr.co.uk MD: Max Clifford.

CNC Associates 95 Tantallon Rd, London SW12 8DQ **t** 020 8673 0048 **f** 020 8673 0048 **e** office@cnclimited.co.uk **w** cnclimited.co.uk MD: Conor Nolan.

Coalition Group Devonshire House, 12 Barley Mow Passage, London W4 4PH **t** 020 8987 0123 **f** 020 8987 0345 **e** pr@coalitiongroup.co.uk MD, Music Division: Tony Linkin.

comm:union Criel House, St. Leonards Road, London W13 8RG **t** 020 8566 3426 **f** 020 8567 3699 **e** mail@comm-union.com **w** comm-union.com Account Dir: Matthew Ryan.

Complete PR PO Box 34126, London NW10 5BZ **t** 020 8830 3300 **f** 020 8830 0033 **e** alison@completepr.co.uk **w** completepr.co.uk MD: Alison McNichol.

Copperplate Consultants 68 Belleville Rd, London SW11 6PP **t** 020 7585 0357 **f** 020 7585 0357 **e** copperplate2000@yahoo.com **w** copperplateconsultants.com MD: Alan O'Leary.

Creative PR UK Unit 53, Simla House, Weston St, London SE1 3RN **t** 020 7378 1642 **f** 020 7378 1642 **e** general@creativepruk.com CEO: Dave Norton. Marketing & Promotions Manager: Ms Georgina Lewis.

Credibility PR 1st Floor, 34-35 Berwick Street, London W1F 8RP **t** 020 7851 2939 **f** 020 7851 2942 **e** jodie@credabilitypr.fsnet.co.uk Co MD: Jodie De Vere. Co MD: Stephanos Pantelas.

John Crosby & Mick Bovee Press & Promotions PO Box 230, Hastings, East Sussex TN34 3XZ **t** 0870 041 0576 **f** 0870 041 0577 **e** johncrosby@pressproms.demon.co.uk **w** pressproms.demon.co.uk Senior Partner: John Crosby.

Cunning Stunts Communications Top Floor, 24-28 Hatton Wall, London EC1N 8JH **t** 020 7691 0077 **f** 020 7691 0081 **e** info@cunningstunts.net **w** cunningstunts.net Account Manager: Nicky Keane.

Cutting Edge Littleton House, Littleton Rd, Ashford, Middx TW15 1UU **t** 01784 423214 **f** 01784 251245 **e** racheal@beechwoodmusic.co.uk **w** beechwoodmusic.co.uk PR Mgr: Racheal Edwards.

Cypher Press & Promotions Unit 2A Queens Studios, 121 Salusbury Road, London NW6 6RG **t** 020 7372 4464 or 020 7372 4474 **f** 020 7372 4484 or 020 7328 4447 **e** info@cypherpress.uk.com **w** cypherpress.uk.com Dir: Simon Ward.

DARLING DEPT

4th floor, 19 Denmark Street, London WC2H 8NA **t** 020 7379 8787 **f** 020 7379 5737 **e** info@darlinguk.com **w** darlingdepartment.com. Directors: Edward Cartwright/ Daniel Stevens.

David Hull Promotions 46 University St, Belfast BT7 1HB **t** 028 9024 0360 **f** 028 9024 7919 **e** info@dhpromotions.com **w** davidhullpromotions.com MD: David Hull.

Delta PR Consultancy PO Box 25285, London N12 7XG **t** 020 8446 3762 **f** 0870 051 6059 **e** mal@delta-music.co.uk **w** delta-music.co.uk Owner: Mal Smith.

Diffusion PR PO Box 2610, Mitcham, Surrey CR4 2YH **t** 020 7384 3200 **f** 0871 277 3055 **e** jodie@diffusionpr.co.uk **w** diffusionpr.co.uk MD: Jodie Stewart.

DNA Publicity Unit 4, Wellington Close, London W11 2AN **t** 020 7792 5100 or 020 7792 5200 **e** odaniaud@aol.com Director: Olly Daniaud.

Dorothy Howe Press & Publicity 1 Gunyah Court, 12 Spencer Rd, London W4 3SZ **t** 020 8995 3920 **f** 020 8994 9963 **e** dorothy.howe@virgin.net MD: Dorothy Howe.

DWL (Dave Woolf Ltd) 53 Goodge St, London W1T 1TG **t** 020 7436 5529 **f** 020 7637 8776 **e** kizzi@dwl.uk.net; dave@dwl.uk.net Account Manager: Kizzi Alleyne-Stewart. MD: Dave Woolf.

E22nd PR Fulham Palace, Bishops Ave, London SW6 6EA **t** 020 7384 7366 **f** 020 7384 7376 **e** tanya@e22nd.com MD: Tanya Gerber.

Electric PR 24A, Bartholomew Villas, London NW5 2LL **t** 020 7424 0405 **f** 020 7424 0305 **e** electric_pr@hotmail.com MD: Laurence Verfaillie.

EMMS PUBLICITY

100 Aberdeen House, 22-24 Highbury Grove, London N5 2EA **t** 020 7226 0990 **f** 020 7354 8600 **e** info@emmspublicity.com **w** emmspublicity.com MD: Stephen Emms.

ePM Unit 204, The Saga Centre, 326 Kensal Road, London W10 5BZ **t** 020 8964 4900 **f** 020 8962 9783 **e** jonas@electronicpm.co.uk **w** electronicpm.co.uk Partner: Jonas Stone.

Fake Media PO Box 1020, High Wycombe, Buck HP10 0ZQ **t** 07966 233275 **e** Adam.fisher@fakemedia.com MD: Adam Fisher.

Ferrara Pr 45 Empire Wharf, 235 Old Ford Rd, London E3 5NQ **t** 07946 523 007 **e** rosalia@ferrarapr.com **w** ferrarapr.com MD: Rosalia Ferrara.

Connie Filippello Publicity 49 Portland Road, London W11 4LJ **t** 020 7229 5400 **f** 020 7229 4804 **e** cfpublicity@aol.com MD: Connie Filippello.

FIFTH ELEMENT PUBLIC RELATIONS

258 Belsize Road, London NW6 4BT **t** 020 7372 2128 **f** 020 7624 3629 **e** info@fifthelement.biz **w** fifthelement.biz Directors: Chris Hewlett/Cat Hockley.
Covering National & Regional Press; a friendly, experienced team with clients including Smash Hits, Sneak magazine, Universal Music TV, Status Quo & Clear Channel.

Fleming Connolly Lander PR Music House Group, Host Europe House, Kendal Avenue, London W3 0TT **t** 020 8896 8200 **f** 020 8896 8201**e** nick@fclpr.com **w** music-house.co.uk Directors: Nick Fleming, Judd Lander.

Frontier Promotions The Grange, Cockley Cley Rd, Hilborough, Thetford, Norfolk IP26 5BT **t** 01760 756394 **f** 01760 756398 **e** frontier@frontierUK.fsnet.co.uk MD: Sue Williams.

Fullfill Studio 54, Canalot Studios, 222 Kensal Road, London W10 5BN **t** 020 8968 1231 **f** 020 8964 1181 **e** info@fullfill.co.uk **w** fullfill.co.uk Press Officer: Savanna Sparkes.

Future Studios International PO Box 10, London N1 3RJ **t** 020 7241 2183 **f** 020 7241 6233 **e** ladybelle888@blueyonder.co.uk **w** gigsonline.co.uk Contact: Michelle L Goldberg

Garrett Axford PR Harbour House, 27 High St, Shoreham by Sea, West Sussex BN43 5DD **t** 01273 441200 **f** 01273 441300 **e** mail@garrett-axford.co.uk Partners: Georgina Garrett/Simon Jones.

Gerry Lyseight PR 9 Hillworth Rd, London SW2 2DZ **t** 020 8674 1012 **f** 0870 120 6252 **e** gerry@mambo.eclipse.co.uk MD: Gerry Lyseight.

Get It On PR 13 Fairhazel Gardens, London NW6 3QE **t** 020 7328 4916 **e** kimshannon@madasafish.com MD: Kim Shannon.

Glass Ceiling PR 50 Stroud Green Rd, London N4 3ES **t** 020 7263 1240 **f** 020 7281 5671 **e** promo@glassceilingpr.com MD: Harriet Simms.

Global Guest List PR Suite 42, Pall Mall Deposits, 124-128 Barlby Road, London W10 6BL **t** 020 8962 0601 **f** 020 8962 0575 **e** info@globalguestlist.net **w** globalguestlist.net MD: Babs Epega. Marketing Director: Alistair Graham.

Gold Star Agency PO Box 130, Ross on Wye HR9 6WY **t** 01989 770 105 **f** 01989 770 039 **e** nitagoldstar@btinternet.com MD: Nita Patel.

Gone Country Promotions 9 Preston Road, Leytonstone, London E11 1NL **t** 020 8989 5005 **f** 020 8989 5006 **e** jeffrey@gonecountry.net **w** gonecountry.net MD: Jeffrey Stothers.

Greendesk Publicity 29a Waller Rd, London SE14 5LE **t** 020 7732 4624 or 07986 235 855 **f** 020 7732 4624 **e** helen@greendesk.demon.co.uk MD: Helen Maleed.

Greenroom Digital PR 87A Worship St, London EC2A 2BE **t** 020 7426 5700 or 07957 338 525 **e** sacha@greenroom-digital.com **w** greenroom-digital.com Communications Dir: Sacha Taylor-Cox.

Hackford Jones PR Third Floor, 16 Manette St, London W1D 4AR **t** 020 7287 9788 **f** 020 7287 9731 **e** info@hackfordjonespr.com **w** hackfordjonespr.com Co-MDs: Simon Jones, Jonathan Hackford.

Hall Or Nothing 11 Poplar Mews, Uxbridge Rd, London W12 7JS **t** 020 8740 6288 **f** 020 8749 5982 **e** press@hallornothing.com **w** hallornothing.com MD: Terri Hall. Senior PR: Gillian Porter.

Jennie Halsall Consultants PO Box 22467, London W6 0SG **t** 020 8741 0003 **f** 020 8846 9652 **e** jhc@dircon.co.uk MD: Jennie Halsall.

HardZone PR The Business Village, 3 Broomhill Rd, London SW18 4JQ **t** 020 8870 8744 **f** 020 8874 1578 **e** info@hardzone.co.uk **w** hardzone.co.uk Marketing Dir: Reggie Styles.

Henry's House PR 108 Gt. Russell Street, London WC1B 3NA **t** 020 7291 3000 **f** 020 7291 3001 **e** jane@henryshouse.com **w** henryshouse.com Dir: Jane Shaw. Commercial Director: Tim Bevan. Audio Sales Executive: Matt Shoults.

Hermana PR Unit 244, Bon Marche Centre, 241-251 Ferndale Rd, Brixton, London SW9 8BJ **t** 020 7733 8009 **f** 020 7733 0037 **e** ken@hermana.co.uk; pam@hermana.co.uk Directors: Ken Lower, Pam Ribbeck.

Hero PR 3 Tennyson Rd, Thatcham, Berks RG18 3FR **t** 01635 868 385 **f** 01635 868 385 **e** owen@heropr.com **w** heropr.com MD: Owen Packard.

Hill & Knowlton (UK) 35 Red Lion Square, London WC1R 4SG **t** 020 7413 3000 **f** 020 7413 3737 **e** jrivett@hillandknowlton.com **w** hillandknowlton.co.uk Business Dev Mgr: John Rivett.

hush-hush Suite 14-15, Old Truman Brewery, 91 Brick Lane, London E1 6QL **t** 020 8989 1726 or 020 7223 7456 **e** danielle@hush-hush.org.uk Press Officer: Danielle Richards. Partner: Sian Williams.

Hyperactive Publicity Ltd Unit 65, Pall Mall Deposit, 124-128 Barlby Rd, London W10 6BL **t** 020 8968 5480 **f** 020 8968 8480 **e** info@hyperactive-publicity.com Contact: Caroline Turner

ID Publicity 25 Britannia Row, London N1 8QH **t** 020 7359 4455 **f** 020 7704 1616 **e** info@idpublicity.com MD: Lisa Moskaluk.

Impel Music Group Ltd 1 Park Terrace, Glasgow G3 6BY **t** 0141 305 0011 **f** 0141 305 0015 **e** info@impelmusic.com **w** impelmusic.com Dir: Alistair McGovern.

IMPRESSIVE

9 Jeffrey's Place, Camden, London NW1 9PP **t** 020 7284 3444 **f** 020 7284 1840 **e** mel@impressivepr.com MD: Mel Brown. w impressivepr.com **National, regional, student, fanzine and internet press. Experienced, dedicated, enthusiastic, creative... the future is impressive.**

IN HOUSE PRESS

4th Floor, 20 Dale Street, Manchester M1 1EZ **t** 0161 228 2070 **f** 0161 228 3070 **e** info@inhousepress.com **w** inhousepress.com MD: David Cooper.

Indiscreet PR 10, Enfield Rd, Brentford, Middx TW8 9NX **t** 020 8847 0784 or 07813 290 474 **e** alan@indiscreetpr.co.uk **w** indiscreetpr.com Dirs: Alan Robinson, Lesley Shone.

INFECTED

INFECTED

18 Eddison Court, 253 Sussex Way, London N19 4DW **t** 020 7272 9620 or 07782 269 750/07762 130 510 **e** mike.infected000@btclick.com Contact: Mike Gourlay or Warren Higgins. **Regional and college press and college radio. Acts: Coldplay, Razorlight, Beastie Boys, The Black Velvets, The Others, Athlete, Idelwild, Kaiser Chiefs, Sum41, Ryan Adams etc.**

inform@tion communication ltd 6 Hornsey Lane Gardens, London N6 5PB **t** 020 8374 6040 **e** infocom@dial.pipex.com MD: Michael Thorne.

Intelligent Media Kiln House, 210 New Kings Road, London SW6 4NZ **t** 020 7731 2020 **f** 020 7731 1100 **e** jonm@intelligentmedia.com **w** intelligentmedia.com MD: Jon Mais.

The Italian Job Publicity 89 Borough High St, London SE1 1NL **t** 020 7403 2177 **f** 020 7357 9750 **e** aless.italianjob@lineone.net Dir: Alessandra Margarito.

Jackie Gill Promotions 2-3 Fitzroy Mews, London W1P 5DQ **t** 020 7383 5550 **f** 020 7383 3020 **e** jackie@jackiegill.co.uk MD: Jackie Gill.

Jane Wallace Press & Promotion The Corner House, Cidermill Lane, Chipping Campden, Gloucestershire GL55 6HL **t** 01386 841453 **f** 01386 841453 **e** successpr@yahoo.co.uk Contact: Jane Wallace

Karenstringer.pr 18 Landseer Rd, Hove, East Sussex BN3 7AF **t** 01273 240 246 or 07808 404 242

e karenstringer.pr@ntlworld.com MD: Karen Stringer.

Katherine Howard PR Eastwick Farm, Clay Lane, Braiseworth, Nr Eye, Suffolk IP23 7DZ **t** 01379 678811 **f** 08700 511 772 **e** info@katherinehoward.co.uk **w** katherinehoward.co.uk MD: Katherine Howard. London Office: 60a Oxford Gardens, W10 5UN.

Kelly Pike Publicity Suite 120, Park Royal Business Centre, 9-17 Park Royal Road, London NW10 7LQ **t** 020 8621 2345 **f** 020 8621 2344 **e** kpikepr@globalnet.co.uk MD: Kelly Pike.

KGA Press And Comunication 1st Floor, 20 Denmark Street, London WC2H 8NA **t** 020 7836 8088 **f** 020 7836 7980 **e** keith@kgapress.co.uk Contact: Keith Grant

LD Communications 58-59 Gt. Marlborough St, London W1F 7JY **t** 020 7439 7222 **f** 020 7734 2933 **e** info@ldpublicity.com **w** ldpublicity.com CEO: Bernard Doherty.

Leyline Promotions Studio 24, Westbourne Studios, 242 Acklam Road, London W10 5JJ **t** 020 7575 3285 **f** 020 7575 3286 **e** firstname@leylinepromotions.com **w** leylinepromotions.com Dir: Adrian Leigh. Head of Press & Marketing: Letitia Thomas. Technical Director: James Reid.

Lisa Agasee PR 10 Woodside Court, Northumberland Avenue, London E12 5HB **t** 020 8532 9145 or 07970 727801 **f** 020 8532 9145 **e** lisa@agasee.fsworld.co.uk Partners: Lisa Agasee.

Lucid PR Flat 9, 91 York St, London W1H 4QE **t** 020 7724 4472 **e** firstname.lastname@lucidpr.co.uk Dirs: Mick Garbutt, Charlie Lycett.

M P Promotions 22 Hill St, Stockport, Cheshire SK6 3AH **t** 0161 494 7934 **f** 0161 406 8500 **e** maria@mppromotions.co.uk Dir: Maria Philippou.

Magnum PR 41 Halcyon Wharf, 5 Wapping High St, London E1W 1LH **t** 020 7709 0914 or 07956 241542 **e** Tammy@magnumpr.co.uk MD: Tammy Arthur.

Making Waves Communications 45 Underwood Street, London N1 7LG **t** 020 7940 0944 **f** 020 7940 1026 **e** info@makingwaves.co.uk **w** makingwaves.co.uk PR Manager: Adam Buss.

MATERIAL

material

36 Washington Street, Glasgow, G3 8AZ
t 0141 204 7970 **f** 0141 248 5743
e info@materialmc.co.uk **w** materialmc.co.uk
Partners: Colin Spence and Sera Holland
Dynamic agency specialising in creation and delivery of brand experiences. Projects include T in the Park, T on the Fringe

Matthew Ryan Criel House, St. Leonards Road, London W13 8RG **t** 020 8566 3426 **f** 020 8567 3699 **e** mail@matthewryan.co.uk **w** matthewryan.co.uk MD: Matthew Ryan.

MBC PR Wellington Building, 28-32 Wellington Road, London NW8 9SP **t** 020 7483 9205 **f** 020 7483 9206 **e** barbara@mbcpr.com Co-MDs: Barbara Charone, Moira Bellas. Press Officer: Jane Reichardt.

Mercenary PR Suite 4, Canalot Studios, 222 Kensal Road, London W10 5BN **t** 020 8354 4111 or 07904 157720 **f** 020 8354 4112 **e** kas@mercenarypr.com **w** mercenarypr.com Dir: Kas Mercer.

Mi Live 55 St Albans Road, S.C.R., Dublin 8, Ireland **t** +353 1 416 9418 **f** +353 1 416 9418 **e** info@milive.net MD: Bernie McGrath.

Midas Public Relations 7-8 Kendrick Mews, London SW7 3HG **t** 020 7584 7474 **f** 020 7584 7123 **e** chris@midaspr.co.uk **w** midaspr.cdo.uk Dir: Chris Poole.

Midnight Communications 3 Lloyds Wharf, Mill St, London SE1 2BA **t** 020 7232 4517 **f** 020 7232 4540 **e** enquiries@midnight.co.uk **w** midnight.co.uk Director: Vicki Hughes.

Mingo PR Flat 3/1, 19 Duke St, Glasgow G4 0UL **t** 0141 552 3623 or 0780 372 8469 **e** mingo@easynet.co.uk **w** mingopr.co.uk MD: Jill Mingo.

Momentum PR 83 Great Titchfield St, London W1W 6RH **t** 0207 323 9789 or 07973 597 070 **e** general@momentumpr.co.uk MD: Maureen McCann.

Monopoly PR 34B Halliford Street, London N1 3EL **t** 020 7354 1057 **f** 020 7288 1571 **e** monopolyPR@aol.com Contact: Kate Comoshevski

Mosquito Media PO Box 33790, 18 Chelsea Manor St, London SW3 6WF **t** 020 7286 0503 **f** 020 7286 0503 **e** mosquitomedia@aol.com **w** mosquito-media.co.uk Contact: Richard Abbott

Music Company (London) Ltd. 103 Churston Drive, Morden SM4 4JE **t** 020 8540 7357 **f** 020 8542 4854 **e** musicco@musicco.f9.co.uk MD: Melanne Mueller.

Name Music Innovation Labs, Watford Rd, Harrow, Middx HA1 3TP **t** 020 8357 7305 **f** 020 8357 7326 **e** sam@name-uk.net MD: Sam Shemtob.

Nelson Bustock Compass House, 22 Redan Place, London W2 4SA **t** 020 7229 4400 **f** 020 7727 2025 **e** pr@nelsonbostock.com **w** nelsonbostock.com Snr Acc Exec: Kelly Finlay.

NOBLE PR

1

Mercers Mews, London N19 4PL **t** 020 7272 7772
f 020 7272 2227 **e** suzanne@noblepr.co.uk
w noblepr.co.uk Dirs: Suzanne & Peter Noble. **Check out our website for company brochure, client list and latest news.**

9PR 65-69 White Lion Street, 2nd Floor, London N1 9PR **t** 020 7833 9303 **f** 020 7833 9322 **e** julie@9pr.co.uk **w** 9pr.co.uk MD: Julie Bland.

No 9 Publicity Suite 216, Bon Marche Building, 241 Ferndale Road, London SW9 8BJ **t** 020 7733 1818 **e** no9@posteverything.com MD: Jim Johnstone. Press Officer: Lauren Zoric.

O PR PO Box 34002, London N21 3WX **t** 020 8886 3424 **f** 020 8482 9270 **e** info@o-pr.com **w** o-pr.com MD: Olga Hadjilambri.

Outerglobe 113 Cheeseman's Terrace, London W14 9XH **t** 020 7385 5447 **f** 020 7385 5447 **e** golden@outerglobe.freeserve.co.uk **w** outerglobe.com MD: Debbie Golt.

THE OUTSIDE ORGANISATION LTD.

Butler House, 177-178 Tottenham Court Road, London W1T 7NY **t** 020 7436 3633 **f** 020 7436 3632
e info@outside-org.co.uk **w** outside-org.co.uk

P&M (Public Relations & Marketing) 3rd Floor, Winchester House, 259-269 Old Marylebone Rd, London NW1 5RA **t** 020 7170 4189 or 020 7170 4188 **f** 020 7170 4001 **e** info@pmltd.co.uk Head of PR: Phyllisia Adjei.

Pacific Edge Promotions & Public Relations Charlstone House, 34 Poppleton Road, London E11 1LR **t** 020 8530 7748 **f** 020 8530 2571 **e** pacific.edge@btinternet.com MD: Jill Cramer.

Paddy Forwood PR The Studio, Manor Farmhouse, Stubhampton, Blandford, Dorset DT11 8JS **t** 01258 830014 or 07779 606533 **f** 01258 830014 **e** pad.forwood@virgin.net MD: Paddy Forwood.

Palmer Evans Associates 5 Landseer Rd, Hove, East Sussex BN3 7AF **t** 01273 775801 **e** jimevans@talk21.com MD: Jim Evans.

PB Communications Int 25 Fair Acres, Roehampton Lane, London SW15 5LX **t** 020 8876 9011 **f** 020 8876 9011 CEO: Peter Brown.

Phuture Trax Press & Events PR Ltd PO Box 48527, London NW4 4ZB **t** 020 8203 3968 **f** 020 8203 3968 **e** nix@phuturetrax.co.uk MD/Head of Press & PR: Nicky Trax.

Piranha PR Flat 7, 51 The Gardens, London SE22 9QQ **t** 020 8299 1928 or 07956 460 372 **e** rosie@piranha-pr.co.uk **w** piranha-pr.co.uk MD: Rosie Wilby.

Planet Earth Publicity 49 Rylstone Way, Saffron Walden, Essex CB11 3BL **t** 01799 501347 or 07966 557774 **f** 01799 501347 **e** info@planetearthpublicity.com **w** planetearthpublicity.com MD: Dave Clarke.

Planet Publicity 3rd Floor, 36 Langham St, London W1W 7AP **t** 020 7580 2400 **f** 020 7580 3500 **e** info@planetpublicity.com MD: Karen Johnson.

Platinum PR 42 Cheriton Close, Queens Walk, Ealing, London W5 1TR **t** 020 8997 8851 **f** 020 8997 8851 **e** carolyn@platinum.fsnet.co.uk MD: Carolyn Norman.

THE PLAY CENTRE

Unit 2 Devonport Mews, Shepherd's Bush, London W12 8NG **t** 020 8932 7705 **f** 020 8932 7723 **e** info@theplaycentre.com **w** theplaycentre.com Contact: Shaun 'STuCKee' Willoughby or Head of Press: Lisa Lindahl.

PMPR Business Communications Market House, Market Square, Winslow, Bucks MK18 3AF **t** 01296 715228 **f** 01296 715486 **e** musicpr@pmpr.co.uk **w** pmpr.co.uk Account Director: Peter Muir MIPR.

Pomona 36 Bridgegate, Hebden Bridge, West Yorks HX7 8EX **t** 01422 846900 **f** 01422 846880 **e** rob@pomonauk.co.uk **w** pomonauk.co.uk Office Manager: Rob Kerford.

POPLICITY

100 Aberdeen House, 22-24 Highbury Grove, London N5 2EA **t** 020 7226 0990 **f** 020 7354 8600 **e** info@poplicity.com **w** poplicity.com MD: Stephen Emms.

Porter Frith 26 Danbury Street, London N1 8JU **t** 020 7359 3734 **f** 020 7226 5897 **e** porterfrith@hotmail.com MD: Liz Frith.

Power Promotions Unit 11, Impress House, Mansell Road, London W3 7QH **t** 020 8932 3030 **f** 020 8932 3031 or i **e** info@power.co.uk **w** power.co.uk Promotions Mgr: Steve Stimpson (Stimpy).

PPR 623-625 Harrow Rd, London W10 4RA **t** 020 8960 1127 **f** 020 8964 9449 **e** info@pprpublicity.com **w** pprpublicity.com MD: Pete Flatt.

The PR Contact Garden Studio, 32 Newman St, London W1T 1PU **t** 020 7323 1200 **f** 020 7323 1070 **e** philsymes@theprcontact.com MD: Phil Symes.

Precious PR 3 Eliot Place, Blackheath, London SE3 0QL **t** 020 8318 0368 or 07958 495 199 **e** jack@preciouspr.plus.com MD: Jack McKillion.

PRESS COUNSEL PR

5-7 Vernon Yard, Off Portobello Rd, London W11 2DX **t** 020 7792 9400 **f** 020 7243 2262 **e** info@presscounsel.com **w** presscounsel.com MD: Charlie Caplowe. Consultant: Jayne Houghton.

PresStop Creatives 4E Oakdale Rd, London SW16 2HW **t** 020 8677 0193 **f** 0870 163 8615 **e** shazniz@aol.com MD: Shazia Nizam.

Psycho Media 111 Clarence Road, London SW19 8QB **t** 020 8540 8122 **f** 020 8715 2827 **e** info@psycho.co.uk **w** psycho.co.uk Dir: John Mabley.

Public Eye Communications Ltd Plaza Suite 318, 535 Kings Road, London SW10 0SZ **t** 020 7351 1555 **f** 020 7351 1010 **e** ciara@publiceye.co.uk MD: Ciara Parkes.

The Publicity Connection 3 Haversham Lodge, Melrose Avenue, London NW2 4JS **t** 020 8450 8882 **f** 020 8208 4219 **e** sharon@thepublicityconnection.com **w** thepublicityconnection.com MD: Sharon Chevin.

Purple PR (Entertainment) 28 Savile Row, London W1S 2EU **t** 020 7434 7092 **e** william@purplepr.com; carl@purplepr.com **w** purplepr.com Dirs: William Rice, Carl Fysh.

Quite Great Publicity 1C Langford Arch, London Rd Trading Estate, Cambridge CB2 4EG **t** 01223 830111 **e** news@quitegreat.co.uk **w** quitegreat.co.uk MD: Pete Bassett. Head of TV & Radio: Paul Clarkson.

Radical PR Suite 421, Southbank House, Black Prince Rd, London SE1 7SJ **t** 020 7463 0677 or 020 7463 0678 **f** 020 7463 0670 **e** info@radicalpr.com **w** radicalpr.com Dirs: Paul Ruiz & Mark Nicholls.

Random PR Studio 54, 222 Kensal Road, London W10 5BN **t** 020 8968 1545 **f** 020 8964 1181 **e** info@randompr.co.uk **w** randompr.co.uk Office Manager: Danni Chambers.

Razzle PR 66 Red Lion Street, Holborn, London WC1R 4NA **t** 020 7430 0444 **f** 020 7405 4391 **e** karen@razzlepr.com Head of Press: Karen Childs.

The Red Consultancy 77 Wimpole Street, London W1G 9RU **t** 020 7465 7700 **f** 020 7486 5260 **e** red@redconsultancy.com **w** redconsultancy.com MD: David Fuller.

Red Hot PR 62 Bell St, London NW1 6SP **t** 020 7723 9191 **f** 020 7723 6423 **e** info@redhotpr.co.uk **w** redhotpr.co.uk MD: Liz Bolton. Account Exec: Julia Gasiorowska.

Red Lorry Yellow Lorry 22 Warwick Street, London W1B 5NF **t** 020 7434 2950 **f** 020 7434 2951 **e** robe@rlyl.co.uk **w** rlyl.co.uk Director: Rob Ettridge.

Renegade Music House Group, Host Europe House, Kendal Avenue, London W3 0TT **t** 020 8896 8200 **f** 020 8896 8201 **e** renegade@music-house.co.uk **w** music-house.co.uk GM: Chris Smith.

Republic Media Ltd Studio 202, Westbourne Studios, 242 Acklam Rd, London W10 5JJ **t** 020 8960 7449 **f** 020 8960 7524 **e** info@republicmedia.net **w** republicmedia.net Director: Sue Harris.

RMP 9 Ivebury Court, 325 Latimer Rd, London W10 6RA **t** 020 8749 7999 **f** 020 8811 8162 **e** firstname@rmplondon.co.uk MD: Regine Moylett.

Rock Solid PR 11 Downton Avenue, Streatham Hill, London SW2 3TU **t** 020 8674 2224 or 07968 817 359 **f** 020 8674 2224 **e** rocksolidpr@aol.com MD: John Welsh.

Rocketscience Media Suite 36, 99-109 Lavender Hill, London SW11 5QL **t** 020 7738 9111 **f** 020 7738 9222 **e** office@rocketsciencemedia.com **w** rocketsciencemedia.com Dir: Alex Black.

RRR Management 96 Wentworth Rd, Birmingham B17 9SY **t** 0121 426 6820 **f** 0121 426 5700 **e** enquiries@rrrmanagement.com **w** rrrmanagement.com MD: Ruby Ryan.

Sainted PR Office 3, 9 Thorpe Close, London W10 5XL **t** 020 8962 5700 **f** 020 8962 5701 **e** heatherfinlay@saintedpr.com MD: Heather Finlay.

Sally Reeves PR 27 Burgess Rd, Waterbeach, Cambridge CB5 9ND **t** 01223 864710 **f** 01223 864727 **e** sallyreeves@btinternet.com MD: Sally Reeves.

Sarah J. Edwards PR PO Box 2423, London WC2E 9PG **t** 0870 138 9430 **f** 0870 138 9430 **e** blag@blagmagazine.com **w** blagmagazine.com Dir: Sarah J. Edwards.

Phill Savidge PR 8 Denton Rd, London N8 9NS **t** 020 8348 0373 **f** 020 8348 0373 **e** phill.savidge@btinternet.com **w** savagepr.com MD: Phill Savidge.

Scene Not Herd Hillhead Cottage, Avonbridge, Falkirk FK1 2NL **t** 01324 861744 or 07866 265 666 **e** lesley@scenenotherd.co.uk **w** scenenotherd.co.uk Sales & Marketing: Lesley Woodall. Operations: Jim Cumming.Deliveries: APC Depot 66, Unit 1, 239 Blairtummock Road, Glasgow G33 4ED.

SCRUFFY BIRD

The Nest, 205 Victoria St, London SW1E 5NE **t** 020 7931 7990 **f** 020 7900 1557 **e** info@scruffybird.com **w** scruffybird.com Press/Radio/Management/Mobile

SEASAW PR

seesaw pr

4th Floor, 22 Tower Street, London WC2H 9TW **t** 020 7539 8200/03 **e** firstname@seesawpr.net Contact Sam Wright, Andrea Phipps

Serious Press and PR 30 West Street, Stoke-sub-Hamdon, Somerset TA14 6PZ **t** 01935 823719 **f** 01935 823719 **e** janehamdon@yahoo.co.uk MD: Jane Osborne.

Sharp End Music Group Grafton House, 2-3 Golden Square, London W1F 9HR **t** 020 7439 8442 **f** 020 7434 3615 **e** sharpend2@aol.com Dir: Robert Lemon.

Silver PR 33 Belmont Court, 93 Highbury New Park, London N5 2HA **t** 020 7503 3920 **f** 020 7503 3920 **e** rachel.silver@silverpr.co.uk **w** silverpr.co.uk Dir: Rachel Silver.

Sketchpad 204 Ducie House, Ducie St, Manchester M1 2JW **t** 0845 458 8662 **f** 0845 458 8663 **e** info@sketchpadpr.com **w** sketchpadpr.com Snr Partner: Simon Morrison.

SLICE

2a Exmoor St, London W10 6BD**t** 020 8964 0064 **f** 020 8964 0101 **e** slice@slice.co.uk **w** slice.co.uk Contact: Damian Mould

Slidingdoors PR

PO Box 21469, Highgate, London N6 4ZG **t** 020 8340 3412 **f** 020 8340 3413 **e** roo@slidingdoorspr.com **w** slidingdoorspr.com. Senior Account Executive: Roo Farndon. MD: James Hamilton.

Smash Press 56 Ackroyd Road, London SE23 1DL **t** 020 8291 6466 or 07721 662 933 **e** smash.press@tiscali.co.uk MD: Nick White.

some friendly 2nd Floor, 334 Old Street, London EC1V 9DR **t** 020 7684 4830 **f** 020 7684 5432 **e** sophie@somefriendly.co.uk **w** somefriendly.com Director: Sophie Williams. Press Officer: Andy Fraser.

Soul Trade PO Box 34539, Peckham, London SE15 2XA **t** 020 7732 2287 **e** ash@soultrade.com **w** soultrade.com Manager: Ash Kamat.

Southern PR 6 Stucley Place, Camden, London NW1 8NT **t** 020 7267 3466 or 020 7267 3498 **e** lisa@southernpr.co.uk MD: Lisa Southern.

Spring PR and Marketing Studio 10, Rose Cottage, Aberdeen Centre, 22-24 Highbury Grove, London N5 2EA **t** 020 7704 0999 **f** 020 7704 6999 **e** rhiannon@spring-pr.com **w** spring-pr.com Dir: Rhiannon Sheehy.

St Pierre Publicity 24 Beauval Road, Dulwich, London SE22 8UQ **t** 020 8693 6463 **f** 020 8299 0719 **e** stpierre.roger@ukf.net MD: Roger St Pierre.

Starfish Communications 76 Oxford Street, London W1D 1BS **t** 020 7323 2121 **f** 020 7323 0234 **e** fearfield@star-fish.net **w** star-fish.net Managing Partner: Sally Fearfield.

Stone Immaculate Press Tunstall Studios, 34-44 Tunstall Rd, London SW9 8DA **t** 020 7737 6359 **f** 020 7274 8921 **e** stone@stoneimmaculate.co.uk **w** stoneimmaculate.co.uk MD: Chris Stone.

Street Life PO Box 23351, London SE16 4YQ **t** 020 7231 1393 **f** 020 7232 1373 **e** info@interactivem.co.uk **w** interactivem.co.uk MD: Jo Cerrone.

Street Press PR The Top Floor, The Outset Building, 2 Grange Rd, London E17 8AH **t** 020 8509 6073 **f** 020 8509 6021 **e** heather@streetpress.co.uk MD: Heather Moul.

StreetDrama PR Suite 7, Little Russell House, 22 Little Russell St, London WC1A 2HS **t** 020 7404 9898 or 07973 382341 **f** 020 7404 6868 **e** helen@streetdramapr.com MD: Helen Street.

Suzanne Parkes PR 2 Oseney Crescent, London NW5 2AU **t** 020 7485 5395 **f** 020 7485 3707 **e** suzanneparkespr@hotmail.com MD: Suzanne Parkes.

Talk Loud PR The Granary, Station Rd, Docking, Norfolk PE31 8LY **t** 01485 518910 **f** 01485 518920 **e** addie@talkloud.co.uk **w** talkloud.co.uk MD: Addie Churchill.

Tenacity Po Box 166, Hartlepool, Cleveland TS26 9JA **t** 01429 424603 **e** info@tenacitymusicpr.co.uk **w** tenacitymusicpr.co.uk Proprietor: Dave Hill.

Terrie Doherty Promotions 40, Princess St, Manchester M1 6DE **t** 0161 234 0044 **e** terriedoherty@zoo.co.uk Director, Regional Rad/TV: Terrie Doherty.

The Partnership 57-63 Old Church Street, London SW3 5BS **t** 020 7761 6005 **f** 020 7761 6035 **e** billy@partnership2.com Partner: Billy Macleod. Partner: Matthew Austin.

Peter Thompson Associates Flat 1, 12 Bourchier St., London W1D 4HZ **t** 020 7439 1210 **f** 020 7439 1202 **e** info@ptassociates.co.uk MD: Peter Thompson.

Tora! Company Clearwater Yard, 35 Inverness St, London NW1 7HB **t** 020 7424 7500 **f** 020 7424 7501 **e** gary@tora-co.demon.co.uk Dir: Gary Levermore.

scruffy bird
www.scruffybird.com
info@scruffybird.com
+44 (0) 207 931 7990
Press•Radio•TV•Promotions
Management•Events•Mobile

Judy Totton Publicity EBC House, Ranelagh Gardens, London SW6 3PA **t** 020 7371 8158 or 020 7371 8159 **f** 020 7371 7862 **e** judy@judytotton.com **w** judytotton.com MD: Judy Totton.

Traffic Marketing 6 Stucley Place, London NW1 8NS **t** 020 7485 7400 **f** 020 7485 5151 **e** info@trafficmarketing.co.uk **w** trafficmarketing.com MD: Lisa Paulon.

Trailer Suite 36, 99-109 Lavender Hill, London SW11 5QL **t** 020 7924 6443 **f** 020 7733 9966 **e** anton@trailermedia.com MD: Anton Hiscock.

Triad Publicity 164 New Cavendish Street, London W1W 6YT **t** 020 7436 7600 **f** 020 7436 7601 **e** info@triadpublicity.co.uk **w** triadpublicity.co.uk Director: Johnny Hopkins. Director: Vanessa Cotton. Director: Tones Sansom

UP-PR Studio 407, Bon Marche Centre, 241-251 Ferndale Rd, London SW9 8BJ **t** 020 7733 7493 **e** ian@up-pr.com **w** up-pr.com PR Manager: Ian Richardson.

Upshot Communications 5th Floor, 2-12 Pentonville Rd, London N1 9PL **t** 020 7923 5560 **f** 020 7923 5564 **e** info@upshotcom.com **w** upshotcreek.com Dirs: Stephen Barnes, Tom Roberts.

Velocity Communications Ground Floor, 4 Bourlet Close, London W1W 7BJ **t** 020 7323 1744 **f** 020 7436 4199 **e** andy@velocitypr.co.uk **w** velocitypr.co.uk MD: Andy Saunders.

Vision 22 Upper Grosvenor St, London W1K 7PE **t** 020 7499 8024 **f** 020 7499 8032 **e** visionpromotions@madasafish.com **w** visionmusic.co.uk MD/Head of Club and Radio Promotions: Rob Dallison.

Jane Wallace Press & Promotion The Corner House, Cider Mill Lane, Chipping Campden, Glocs GL55 6HL **t** 01386 841 453 **f** 01386 841 453 **e** successpr@yahoo.co.uk MD: Jane Wallace.

Wasted Youth 740 Alaska Buildings, 61 Grange Rd, London SE1 3BD **t** 020 7231 5123 **e** sarah@wastedyouth.uk.com MD: Sarah Pearson.

Way to Blue First Floor, Suna House, 65 Rivington St, London EC2A 3QQ **t** 020 7749 8444 **f** 020 7749 8420 **e** Lee@waytoblue.com **w** waytoblue.com Dir: Lee Henshaw.

Richard Wootton Publicity The Manor House, 120 Kingston Rd, Wimbledon, London SW19 1LY **t** 020 8542 8101 **f** 020 8540 0691 **e** richard@rwpublicity.com **w** rwpublicity.com MD: Richard Wootton.

Work Hard PR 35 Farm Avenue, London SW16 2UT **t** 020 8677 8466 or 020 8769 6713 **f** 020 8677 5374 **e** enquiries@workhardpr.com **w** workhardpr.com MD: Roland Hyams.

The Wright PR 44 Suffolk Rd, Ponders End, Middx EN3 4AZ **t** 020 8804 2993 or 07979 707 772 **e** TheWrightPR@aol.com MD: Doug Wright.

Yes Please PR 29 Harford House, 35 Tavistock Crescent, London W11 1AY **t** 020 7792 2843 **e** yespleasepr@btinternet.com MD: Ginny Luckhurst.

Chrissie Yiannou 16-24 Brewery Road, London N7 9NH **t** 020 7607 3608 **f** 020 7607 9608 **e** chrissie@positivenuisance.com MD: Chrissie Yiannou.

Zen Media Management The Garden Office, 39A Ashburnham Rd, London NW10 5SB **t** 020 8960 9171 or 07957 338 525 **e** sacha@zenmedia.net **w** zenmedia.net Dir:

ZZONKED Unit 348, Stratford Workshops, Burford Road, London E15 2SP **t** 020 8503 1880 **f** 020 8534 0603 **e** info@zzonked.co.uk **w** zzonked.co.uk Contact: David Silverman National music and press events press including the Big Chill, DMC/Technics, DL Finals, Roots Manuva, Coldcut, Lemon Jelly, Mr Scruff, Jazzanova.

Photographers & Agencies

aandr Photographic 16a Crane Grove, Islington, London N7 8LE **t** 020 7607 3030 **f** 020 7607 2190 **e** info@aandrphotographic.co.uk **w** aandrphotographic.co.uk Photographers Agents: Anita Grossman, Rosie Harrison.

All Action Digital 32 Great Sutton St, London EC1V 0NB **t** 020 7608 2988 **f** 020 7336 0491 **e** mo@allaction.co.uk **w** allactiondigital.com GM: Isabelle Vialle.

Mark Allan 30 Barry Road, London SE22 0HU **t** 020 8693 6625 or 07836 385352 **f** 020 8299 6566 **e** mark.allanphotos@btinternet.com

Ami Barwell - Music Photographer **t** 07787 188452 or +1 917 442 3588 **f** 01482 229921 **e** ami@musicphotographer.co.uk **w** musicphotographer.co.uk Contact: Ami Barwell

Aquarius Picture Library PO Box 5, Hastings, East Sussex TN34 1HR **t** 0116 229 0648 **e** sales@aquariuscollection.com **w** aquariuscollection.com Dir: David Corkill.

Peter Ashworth 107 South Hill Park, London NW3 2SP **t** 020 7435 4142 or 07714 952 292 **f** 020 7435 9988 **e** aaaashy@blueyonder.co.uk **w** ashworth-photos.com

Balcony Jump Management Unit 3, Round House Studios, 91 Saffron Hill, London EC1N 8PT **t** 020 7831 3355 **f** 020 7841 1356 **e** info@balconyjump.co.uk **w** balconyjump.co.uk MD: Tim Paton.

Joe Bangay Photography River House, Riverwoods, Marlow, Buckinghamshire SL7 1QY **t** 01628 486193 or 07860 812529 **f** 01628 890239 **e** william.b@btclick.com **w** JoeBangay.com MD: William Bangay.

Sheyi Antony Banks Photography 45 Indigo Mews, Carysfort Rd, London N16 9AA **t** 020 7254 5352 or 07956 312608 **f** 020 7254 5352 **e** info@sheyiantonybanks.com **w** sheyiantonybanks.com Contact: Sheyi Antony Banks

Colin Bell Contact: K2>music

Terri Berg Photographic PO Box 20072, London NW2 3ZU **t** 020 8450 6378 **f** 020 8450 7058 **e** tnb@dircon.co.uk **w** tbphoto.co.uk Contact: Terri N Berg

Big Photographic Ltd Unit D4, Metropolitan Wharf, Wapping Wall, London E1W 3SS **t** 020 7702 9365 **f** 020 7702 9366 **e** contact@bigactive.com **w** bigactive.com Directore: Richard Newton/Greg Burne.

Bijoux Graphics 10 L Peabody Bldgs, Clerkenwell Close, London EC1R 0AY **t** 020 7608 1316 **e** davies@bijouxgraphics.co.uk **w** bijouxgraphics.co.uk Director: David Davies.

Richard Birch Contact: M Agency

George Bodnar George Bodnar Productions, Churchill House, 137 Brent Street, London NW4 4DJ **t** 020 8457 2757 **f** 020 8457 2602 **e** george@gbimages.com **w** gbimages.com

Harry Borden Contact: K2>music

Sophie Broadbridge Contact: Coochie Mgmt

Jay Brooks Contact: M Agency

Ken Browar Contact: Serlin Associates

Ray Burmiston (see Shoot)

Cableimage **t** 01252 890222 or 07778 156925 **e** rob@cableimage.com **w** cableimage.com Director: Rob Cable.

Capital Pictures 49-51 Central St, London EC1V 8AB **t** 020 7253 1122 **f** 020 7253 1414 **e** sales@capitalpictures.com **w** capitalpictures.com Dir: Phil Loftus.

Carlos Cicchelli-Photographer 42B Medina Rd, London N7 7LA **t** 020 7686 2324 or 07960 726 957 **f** 020 7686 2324 **e** info@toshoot.com **w** toshoot.com Contact: Carlos Cicchelli

Davide Cernuschi Contact: M Agency

George Chin Photography **t** 020 8731 9300 or 07876 745943 **f** 020 8731 9290 **e** george@georgechin.com **w** georgechin.com MD: George Chin.

Claire Grogan Photography 12 Calverley Grove, Archway, London N19 3LG **t** 020 7272 1845 or 07932 635 381 **e** claire@clairegrogan.co.uk **w** clairegrogan.co.uk Contact: Claire Grogan

Coochie Management 26 Cosway Mansions, Shroton St, Marylebone, London NW1 6UE **t** 020 7724 9700 **f** 020 7724 2598 **e** amanda@coochie-management.com **w** coochie-management.com MD: Amanda G.

Pete Cronin 14 Lakes Rd, Keston, Kent BR2 6BN **t** 01689 858719 or 07860 391985 **e** pete@petecronin.com **w** petecronin.com

Daniel J.Scott **t** 020 7602 9382 or 07968 191 596 **e** mail@danieljscott.com **w** danieljscott.com Photographer: Daniel Scott.

Jack Daniels `The Photographer' Plot 2, The Plantation, Swanage, Dorset BH19 2TD **t** 07831 356719 or 01929 427429 **f** 01929 427471 **e** musicweek@jackdaniels.me.uk **w** jackdaniels.me.uk Contact: Jack Daniels

Dato Imaging 16A Pavilion Terrace, London W12 0HT **t** 07770 946058 **e** info@dato.co.uk **w** dato.co.uk MD: Chris Dato.

Dbox Contact: Eminent Mgmt

Dean Chalkley (see Shoot)

Digital Vision Ltd India House, 45 Curlew Street, London SE1 2ND **t** 020 7378 5555 **f** 020 7378 5533 **e** sales@digitalvision.com **w** digitalvisiononline.co.uk UK Sales: Joanne Rees.

Dirk Linder Contact: Skinny Dip

Mike Diver Contact: Eminent Mgmt

Paul Donohue Contact: Pearce Stoner

David Drebin Contact: Coochie Management

Liam Duke Contact: Pearce Stoner

Sandrine Dulermo & Michael Labica Contact: K2>music

Frederic Duval 6 Dorset Court, Hertford Road, London N1 4SD **t** 020 7503 6870 or 07876 481 279 **e** jenny_duval@hotmail.com

Andy Earl 29 Curlew Street, London SE1 2ND **t** 020 7403 1156 **f** 020 7403 1157 **e** mail@andyearl.com **w** andyearl.com

East Photographic 8 Iron Bridge House, 3 Bridge Approach, London NW1 8BD **t** 020 7722 3444 **f** 020 7722 3544 **e** hq@eastphotographic.com **w** eastphotographic.com Contact: Nick Selby

Eminent Management & Production Ltd The Old Truman Brewery, 91 Brick Lane, London E1 6QL **t** 020 7247 4750 **f** 020 7247 4712 **e** anita@eminentmanagement.co.uk **w** eminentmanagement.co.uk Dir: Anita Heryet.

Tim Evan-Cook Contact: Serlin Associates

Famous Pictures & Features Agency 13 Harwood Road, London SW6 4QP **t** 020 7731 9333 **f** 020 7731 9330 **e** info@famous.uk.com **w** famous.uk.com Library Manager: Dan Wigmore. ISDN: 0171 510 2515.

Jim Fiscus Contact: M Agency

Food 4 Foxes Concert, Event & Studio Photographers The Studio, 156-158 Grays Inn Road, London WC1X 8ED **t** 020 7713 1008 **e** onethousandwords@food4foxes.co.uk **w** food4foxes.co.uk MD: Damien Chaos.

Freelance Directory NUJ, Acorn House, 314-320 Gray's Inn Road, London WC1X 8DP **t** 020 7843 3703 **f** 020 7278 1812 **e** pamelam@nuj.org.uk **w** gn.apc.org/media/ Contact: Pamela Morton

Eric Frideen Contact: Serlin Associates

Future Earth Photography 59 Fitzwilliam St, Wath upon Dearne, Rotherham, South Yorks S63 7HG **t** 01709 872875 **e** david@future-earth.co.uk **w** future-earth.co.uk MD: David Moffitt.

Bob Glanville 77 Shelley House, Churchill Gardens, Pimlico, London SW1V 3JE **t** 07957 363 472 **e** info@bobglanville.com **w** bobglanville.com Photographer: Bob Glanville.

Mark Hadley Photography 25A Bridgnorth Avenue, Wombourne, Staffordshire WV5 0AD **t** 01902 896209 **f** 01902 896209 **e** thephotoagency@btinternet.com

Mischa Haller Contact: K2>music

Trevor Ray Hart Contact: PC.P

Jason Hetherington Contact: Pearce Stoner

Hugo Dixon Contact: Eminent Mgmt

John Beecher Photo Library Rock House, London Rd, St Mary's, Stroud, Gloucs GL6 8PU **t** 01453 886252 or 0845 456 9759 **f** 01453 885361 **e** photo@rollercoasterrecords.com **w** rollercoasterrecords.com Owner: John Beecher.

Judy Totton Photography EBC House, Ranelagh Gardens, London SW6 3PA **t** 020 7371 8159 or 07798 806079 **f** 020 7371 7862 **e** judy@judytotton.com **w** judytotton.com Photographer: Judy Totton.

Justine Contact: Serlin Associates

K2>music 109 Clifton St, London EC2A 4LD **t** 020 7749 6070 **f** 020 7749 6001 **e** nick@k2creatives.com **w** k2creatives.com Contact: Nick Bull

Karl Grant Contact: Eminent Mgmt

Kelly Pike Publicity Suite 120, Park Royal Business Centre, 9-17 Park Royal Road, London NW10 7LQ **t** 020 8621 2345 **f** 020 8621 2344 **e** kpikepr@globalnet.co.uk MD: Kelly Pike.

Jason Kelvin Contact: Skinny Dip

Luke Kirwan Contact: Pearce Stoner

Kochi Photography 33/37 Hatherley Mews, Walthamstow, London E17 4QP **t** 020 8521 9227 **f** 020 8520 5553 **e** xplosive@supanet.com Director: Terry McLeod.

Lacey Contact: Pearce Stoner

Robert Lakow Contact: M Agency

Jenny Lewis Contact: PC.P

Laurie Lewis 176 Camden Road, London NW1 9HG **t 020 7267 0315** Dir: Topsy Corian.

Link Picture Library 33 Greyhound Road, London W6 8NH **t** 020 7381 2261 or 020 7381 2433 **f** 020 7385 6244 **e** prints@linkpicturelibrary.com **w** linkpicturelibrary.com Proprietor: Orde Eliason.

London Features International Ltd 3 Boscobel St, London NW8 8PS **t** 020 7723 4204 **f** 020 7723 9201 **e** john@lfi.co.uk **w** lfi.co.uk Editorial Dir: John Halsall.

M Agency 7 Tyers Gate, London SE1 3HX **t** 020 7357 0622 **f** 020 7403 5424 **e** info@magency.co.uk **w** magency.co.uk Bookers: Emma Stanton, Grace Holbrook.

Mark McNulty 8E Sunnyside, Princes Park, Liverpool L8 3TD **t** 0151 727 2012 or 07885 847806 **e** mark@mcnulty.co.uk **w** mcnulty.co.uk

Michael Taylor Photography 412 Beersbridge Rd, Belfast BT5 5EB **t** 028 9065 4450 **f** 028 9047 1625 **e** michael@mtphoto.co.uk **w** mtphoto.co.uk Photographer: Michael Taylor.

One Photographic 4th Floor, 48 Poland St, London W1F 7ND **t** 020 7287 2311 **f** 020 7287 2313 **e** harriet@onephotographic.com **w** onephotographic.com Agents: Belinda Taylor, Harriet Essex.

Mike Parsons Contact: Coochie Management

PC.P 5-7 Vernon Yard, off Portobello Rd, London W11 2DX **t** 020 7313 9100 **f** 020 7313 9109 **e** penny@presscounsel.com **w** pcp-agency.com Dir: Penny Caplowe.

Pearce Stoner Associates 12b Links Yard, Spelman Street, London E1 5LX **t** 020 7247 7100 **f** 020 7247 7144 **e** info@pearcestoner.com **w** pearcestoner.com Directors: Eve Stoner, Victoria Pearce.

Rena Pearl 8A The Drive, London NW11 9SR **t** 020 8455 7661 or 07798 693756 **f** 020 8381 4050 **e** rena@renapearl.com **w** renapearl.com Contact: Rena Pearl

Photo-Stock Library International 14 Neville Avenue, Anchorsholme, Blackpool, Lancashire FY5 3BG **t** 01253 864598 **f** 01253 864598 **e** wayne@photo-stock.co.uk **w** photo-stock.co.uk Contact: Wayne Paulo

Pictorial Press Ltd Unit 1 Market Yard Mews, 194 Bermondsey Street, London SE1 3TQ **t** 020 7378 7211 **f** 020 7378 7194 **e** info@pictorialpress.co.uk **w** pictorialpress.com Director: Tony Gale.

Pilot Creative Agency Unit 208, Canalot Studios, 222 Kensal Road, London W10 5BN **t** 020 7565 2227 **f** 020 7565 2228 **e** Beverley@pilotcreativeagency.com **w** pilotcreativeagency.com MD: Beverley Kendall.

PR Pictures Ltd Cherry Trees, Loudwater Heights, Loudwater WD3 4AX **t** 01923 718555 **e** john@prpictures.co.uk **w** prpictures.co.uk Contact: John Willan

Rebecca Valentine Agency 37 Foley St, London W1W 7TN **t** 07968 190 411 **e** rebecca@rebeccavalentine.com **w** rebeccavalentine.com MD: Rebecca Valentine.

Red James , London EC2 **t** 020 7628 7853 **e** rj@redjam.com **w** redjam.com Dir: Red James.

Red represents 98 De Beauvoir Rd, London N1 4EN **t 020 7275 2725 f** 020 7572 2701 **e** rachel@redrepresents.com **w** redrepresents.com Contact: Rachel Thomas

Redferns Music Picture Library 7 Bramley Rd, London W10 6SZ **t** 020 7792 9914 **f** 020 7792 0921 **e** info@redferns.com **w** redferns.com Library Mgr: Jon Wilton.

Repfoto 74 Creffield Rd, London W3 9PS **t** 020 8992 2936 **f** 020 8992 9641 **e** repfoto@btinternet.com **w** repfoto.com Partner: Robert Ellis.

Retrograph Nostalgia Archive Ltd 10 Hanover Crescent, Brighton, E. Sussex BN2 9SB **t** 01273 687554 **e** retropix1@aol.com **w** Retrograph.com MD: Jilliana Ranicar-Breese.

Rex Features 18 Vine Hill, London EC1R 5DZ **t** 020 7278 7294 **f** 020 7837 4812 **e** rex@rexfeatures.com **w** rexfeatures.com Contact: John Melhuish

Ripley & Ripley Studio 31, 20 The Highway, Wapping, London E1W 2BE **t** 07739 745 495 **e** studio@ripleyandripley.com **w** ripleyandripley.com Contact: Colette Ripley or Rip

Jonathan Root 21 Ferdinand St, Chalk Farm, London NW1 8EU **t** 020 7485 5522 or 07768 292 666 **f** 020 7485 5532 **e** jonathan@jonathanroot.freeserve.co.uk **w** jonathanroot.freeserve.co.uk

Sarah-Photogirl Flat 4, 9 Belmont Rd, Scarborough, North Yorkshire YO11 2AA **t** 07803 108884 **e** sales@sarahphotogirl.com **w** sarahphotogirl.co.uk Photographer: Sarah Robinson.

Serlin Associates 258 Belsize Rd, Suite 402, London NW6 4BT **t** 020 7625 6060 **f** 020 7316 1891 **e** lisa@serlinassociates.com **w** serlinassociates.com Contact: Lisa Hughes

Shoot Production Ltd Unit 2.08, Tea Building, Shoreditch High St, London E1 6JJ **t** 020 7324 7500 **f** 020 7324 7514 **e** production@shootgroup.com **w** shootproduction.com MD: Adele Rider.

Skinny Dip Studio 301, Westbourne Studios, 242 Acklam Rd, London W10 5JJ **t** 020 7575 3222 **f** 020 8969 8696 **e** info@skinnydip.info **w** skinnydip.info Contact: Amy Foster, Pippa Hall

Paul Spencer Contact: Rebecca Valentine

Soren Solkaer Starbird Contact: PC.P

Steve Gullick Contact: Eminent Mgmt

Stewart Birch Photography 30 Kenilworth Rd, Bognor Regis, West Sussex PO21 5NF **t** 07789 648 646 **e** info@stewartbirch.co.uk **w** stewartbirch.co.uk Contact: Stewart Birch

The Street Studios 2 Dunston St, London E8 4EB **t** 020 7923 9430 **f** 020 7923 9429 **e** mail@streetstudios.co.uk **w** streetstudios.co.uk Studio Manager: Chris Purnell.

Susie Babchick Agency Top Floor, 6 Brewer St, London W1F 0SD **t** 020 7287 1497 **f** 020 7439 6030 **e** susan@babchick.freeserve.co.uk **w** susiebabchick.com Dir: Susie Babchick.

Syndicated International Network 89a North View Road, London N8 7LR **t 020 8348 8061 f** 020 8340 8517 **e** sales@sin-photo.co.uk **w** sin-photo.co.uk Contact: Marianne Lassen

Nick Tansley Pictures 1 Lopen Rd, London N18 1PN **t** 020 8807 6268 **f** 020 8351 1497 **e** popworks1@yahoo.com Contact: Nick Tansley

Tina McClelland Photography 34 Ashworth Place, Harlow, Essex CM17 9PU **t** 07855 715200 **e** tina.mcclelland@photo2000.co.uk **w** photo2000.co.uk Photographer: Tina McClelland.

TPhotographic.com 1 Heathgate Place, 75-83 Agincourt Rd, London NW3 2NU **t** 020 7428 6070 **f** 020 7428 6079 **e** liz@tphotographic.com **w** tphotographic.com Senior Producer: Liz Kaczmarski. MD: Peter Townsend.

Visualeyes Imaging Service 11 West Street, Covent Garden, London WC2H 9NE **t** 020 7836 3004 **f** 020 7240 0050 **e** imaging@visualeyes.ltd.uk **w** visualeyes.ltd.uk Sales Dir: Tony MacLean. Tech Dir: Leanda Newlyn. Pro Dir: Simon Perfect.

WildeHague Ltd Unit 9, The Coach Works, 80 Parsons Green Lane, London SW6 4HU **t** 020 7384 3444 **f** 020 7384 3449 **e** info@wildehague.com **w** wildehague.com Dirs: Janice Hague, Dilys Wilde.

XK8 Organisation First Floor, 151 City Rd, London EC1V 1JH **t** 020 7490 0666 **f** 020 7490 0660 **e** roger@xk8organisation.com **w** automaticpromotions.co.uk Dir: Jeff Davy.

FOR ALL YOUR LIVE MUSIC REQUIREMENTS

RECORD BREAKING EVENTS
MARKET LEADING VENUES
instantLIVE
AWARD-WINNING MARKETING
PARTNERSHIPS
OVER 7,000 LIVE EVENTS
AND 11 MILLION TICKETS SOLD*

*2003

Booking Agents

3 Sound Promotions 10 Hilton St, Manchester M1 1JF **t** 0161 237 9413 **f** 0161 237 9413 **e** info@3soundpromotions.com **w** 3soundpromotions.com Agency Mgr: Olly Holland.

ABA Booking 7 North Parade, Bath, Somerset BA2 4DD **t** 01225 428284 **f** 01225 400090 **e** aca_aba@freenet.co.uk MD: Harry Finegold.

ABS Agency 2 Elgin Avenue, London W9 3QP **t** 020 7289 1160 **f** 020 7289 1162 **e** nigel@absagency.u-net.com MD: Nigel Kerr.

Acker's International Jazz Agency 53 Cambridge Mansions, Cambridge Road, London SW11 4RX **t** 020 7978 5885 **e** pamela@ackersmusicagency.co.uk **w** ackersmusicagency.co.uk Prop: Pamela Francesa Sutton.

African Caribbean Asian Entertainment Agency Stars Building, 10 Silverhill Close, Nottingham NG8 6QL **t** 0115 951 9864 **f** 0115 951 9874 **e** acts@african-caribbean-ents.com **w** african-caribbean-ents.com Contact: Mr LI Sackey

The Agency Group Ltd 361-373 City Road, Islington, London EC1V 1PQ **t** 020 7278 3331 **f** 020 7837 4672 **e** agencylondon@theagencygroup.com **w** theagencygroup.com MD: Neil Warnock.

AIR (Artistes International Representation Ltd) AIR House, Spennymoor, Co Durham DL16 7SE **t** 01388 814632 **f** 01388 812445 **e** info@airagency.com **w** airagency.com Directors: Colin Pearson, John Wray.

Aire International (Air,) 2a Ferry Road, London SW13 9RX **t** 020 8287 4064 **f** 020 8834 7474 **e** tours@airmtm.com **w** airmtm.com Manager: Clive Johnson.

Steve Allen Entertainments 60 Broadway, Peterborough, Cambridgeshire PE1 1SU **t** 01733 569589 **f** 01733 561854 **e** steve@sallenent.co.uk **w** sallenent.co.uk MD: Steve Allen. Sales/Admin: Cherry Bradbury & Rebecca Ashworth.

Arcadia Music Agency 1 Felday Glade, Holmbury St Mary, Surrey RH5 6PG **t** 01306 730040 **f** 08700 526969 **e** enquiry@musi.co.uk **w** musi.co.uk MD: Max Rankin.

Asgard Promotions 125 Parkway, London NW1 7PS **t** 020 7387 5090 **f** 020 7387 8740 **e** info@asgard-uk.com Jnt MDs: Paul Fenn, Paul Charles.

Avenue Artistes 8 Winn Road, Southampton, Hampshire SO17 1EN **t** 02380 551000 **f** 02380 905703 **e** info@avenueartistes.com **w** avenueartistes.com Dir: Terence A Rolph.

Bandwagon 67 Kirkham, Biddick, Washington, Tyne & Wear NE38 7EY **t** 0191 4166419 or 07793 606195 **e** info@band-wagon.co.uk **w** bandwagon.co.uk Dirs: Paul Reay, Stephen Dodds.

Austin Baptiste Entertainments Agency 29 Courthouse Gardens, London N3 1PU **t** 020 8346 3984 **f** 020 8922 3770 **e** steelbands@aol.com **w** steelbands.uk.com MD: Austin Baptiste.

Barn Dance and Line Dance Agency 62 Beechwood Road, South Croydon, Surrey CR2 0AA **t** 020 8657 2813 **f** 020 8651 6080 **e** barndanceagency@btinternet.com **w** barn-dance.co.uk Dir: Derek Jones.

Paul Barrett (Rock'n'Roll Enterprises) 21 Grove Terrace, Penarth, South Glamorgan CF64 2NG **t** 029 2070 4279 **f** 029 2070 9989 **e** barrettrocknroll@amserve.com MD: Paul Barrett.

Barrucci Leisure Enterprises Ltd 45-47 Cheval Place, London SW7 1EW **t** 020 7225 2255 **f** 020 7581 2509 **e** barrucci@barrucci.com MD: Bryan Miller.

The Bechhofer Agency 51 Barnton Park View, Edinburgh EH4 6HH **t** 0131 339 4083 **f** 0131 339 9261 **e** agency@bechhofer.demon.co.uk **w** bechhoferagency.com Contact: Frank Bechhofer

John Bedford Enterprises 40 Stubbington Avenue, North End, Portsmouth, Hampshire PO2 0HY **t** 023 9266 1339 **f** 023 9264 3993 **e** agency@johnbedford.co.uk **w** johnbedford.co.uk Dir: John Bedford.

Tony Bennell Entertainment 10 Manor Way, Kidlington, Oxfordshire OX5 2BD **t** 0870 755 7645 **f** 0870 755 7646 **e** tonybennell@hotmail.com **w** tonybennell.btinternet.co.uk MD: Tony Bennell.

Best Kept Secret Queens Wharf, Queen Caroline St, London W6 9RJ **t** 020 8600 2664 **e** info@bestkeptsecret.uk.com **w** bestkeptsecret.uk.com GM: Nick Matthews.

Big Bear Music PO Box 944, Birmingham, West Midlands B16 8UT **t** 0121 454 7020 **f** 0121 454 9996 **e** bigbearmusic@compuserve.com **w** bigbearmusic.com MD: Jim Simpson.

John Boddy Agency 10 Southfield Gardens, Twickenham, Middx TW1 4SZ **t** 020 8892 0133 or 020 8891 3809 **f** 020 8892 4283 **e** jba@johnboddyagency.co.uk MD: John Boddy.

BPR Productions Ltd 36 Como Street, Romford, Essex RM7 7DR **t** 01708 725330 **f** 01708 725322 **e** bprmusic@compuserve.com **w** bprmusic.com MD: Brian Theobald.

Brian Gannon Management PO Box 106, Rochdale, Lancs OL15 0HY **t** 01706 374411 **f** 01706 377303 **e** brian@briangannon.co.uk **w** briangannon.co.uk Owner: Brian Gannon.

Garry Brown Associates (International) 27 Downs Side, Cheam, Surrey SM2 7EH **t** 020 8643 3991 or 020 8643 8375 **f** 020 8770 7241 **e** GBALTD@compuserve.com Chairman: Garry Brown. Director of Booking: John Cheney.

Hal Carter Organisation 101 Hazelwood Lane, Palmers Green, London N13 5HQ **t** 020 8886 2801 **f** 020 8882 7380 **e** artistes@halcarterorg.com **w** halcarterorg.com MD: Hal Carter.

Celtic Artists - Aisling Entertainments 95 Carshalton Park Road, Carshalton Beeches, Surrey SM5 3SJ **t** 020 8647 3084 **f** 020 8395 3560 **e** keirajennings@cwcom.net Dir: Keira Jennings.

Central Music Agency Hartfield House, 202 Wells Road, Malvern Wells, Worcestershire WR14 4HD **t** 01684 566102 **f** 01684 566100 **e** cmamalvern@aol.com **w** central-music.co.uk Agent/Promoter: Suzi Glantz.

Clear Channel Entertainment (CCE Europe) 1st Floor, Floor, Regent Arcade House, 19-25 Argyll St, London W1F 7TS **t** 020 7009 3333 **f** 0870 749 3191 **e** firstname.lastname@clearchannel.co.uk **w** getlive.co.uk Head of Music Promotions: Stuart Galbraith.

CODA Agency Ltd 81 Rivington St, London EC2A 3AY **t** 020 7012 1555 **f** 020 7012 1566 **e** agents@codaagency.com **w** codaagency.com MD: Phil Banfield.

Barry Collings Entertainments 21A Clifftown Road, Southend-On-Sea, Essex SS1 1AB **t** 01702 330005 **f** 01702 333309 **e** bcollent@aol.com **w** barrycollings.co.uk MD: Barry Collings.

Complete Entertainment Services PO Box 112, Seaford, East Sussex BN25 2DQ **t** 0870 755 7610 **f** 0870 755 7613 **e** info@completeentertainment.co.uk **w** completeentertainment.co.uk Events Mgr: Emalee Welsh.

Concorde International Artistes Concorde House, 101 Shepherds Bush Road, London W6 7LP **t** 020 7602 8822 **f** 020 7603 2352 **e** cia@cia.uk.com MD: Solomon Parker.

Continental Drifts Hilton Grove, Hatherley Mews, London E17 4QP **t** 020 8509 3353 **f** 020 8509 9531 **e** Chris@continentaldrifts.co.uk **w** continentaldrifts.uk.com Director: Chris Meikan.

Creeme Entertainments East Lynne, Harper Green Road, Doe Hey, Farnworth, Bolton, Lancashire BL4 7HT **t** 01204 793441 or 01204 793018 **f** 01204 792655 **e** info@creeme.co.uk **w** creeme.co.uk MD: Tom Ivers.

Crisp Productions PO Box 979, Sheffield, South Yorkshire S8 8YW **t** 0114 261 1649 **f** 0114 261 1649 **e** dc@cprod.win-uk.net MD: Darren Crisp.

Crown Entertainments 103 Bromley Common, Bromley, Kent BR2 9RN **t** 020 8464 0454 **f** 020 8290 4038 **e** info@crownentertainments.co.uk **w** crownentertainments.co.uk MD: David Nash.

Dark Blues Management Puddephats, Markyate, Herts AL3 8AZ **t** 01582 842226 **f** 01582 840010 **e** info@darkblues.co.uk **w** darkblues.co.uk Office Mgr: Fiona Hewetson.

David Hull Promotions 46 University St, Belfast BT7 1B **t** 028 9024 0360 **f** 028 9024 7919 **e** info@dhpromotions.com **w** davidhullpromotions.com MD: David Hull.

The Day Job 14 Church Street, Twickenham, Middx TW1 3NJ **t** 020 8892 6446 **f** 020 8891 1895 **e** nina@thedayjob.com **w** thedayjob.com Contact: Nina Jackson

DCM International Suite 3, 294-296 Nether Street, Finchley, London N3 1RJ **t** 020 8343 0848 **f** 020 8343 0747 **e** dancecm@aol.com **w** dancecrazy.co.uk MD: Kelly Isaacs.

Tony Denton Promotions Ltd 19 South Molton Lane, Mayfair, London W1Y 1AQ **t** 020 7629 4666 **f** 020 7629 4777 **e** mail@tdpromo.com **w** tdpromo.com MD: Tony Denton.

Derek Block Artistes Agency Ltd 70-76 Bell Street, Marylebone, London NW1 6SP **t** 020 7724 2101 **f** 020 7724 2102 **e** dbaa@derekblock.demon.co.uk MD: Derek Block.

Dexnfx Bookings Unit 13-14, Barley Shotts Business Park, 246 Acklam Road, London W10 5YG **t** 020 8964 9663 **f** 020 8960 9660 **e** jill@dexnfx.com **w** dexnfx.com Agents: Jill Thompson, Michelle Curry.

Dinosaur Promotions/Pulse (The Agency) 5 Heyburn Crescent, Westport Gardens, Stoke On Trent, Staffordshire ST6 4DL **t** 01782 824051 **f** 01782 761752 **e** alan@dinoprom.com **w** dinoprom.com MD: Alan Dutton.

The Dixon Agency 58 Hedley Street, Gosforth, Newcastle upon Tyne, Tyne and Wear NE3 1DL **t** 0191 213 1333 **f** 0191 213 1313 **e** bill@dixon-agency.com **w** dixon-agency.com Owner: Bill Dixon.

Steve Draper Entertainments 2 The Coppice, Beardwood Manor, Blackburn, Lancashire BB2 7BQ **t** 01254 679005 **f** 01254 679005 **e** steve@stevedraperents.fsbusiness.co.uk **w** stevedraper.co.uk Proprietor: Steve Draper. Agent: Tracey Kendall.

Duende Music Ltd PO Box 33436, London SW18 3WZ **t** 020 8879 1120 **e** info@duendemusic.co.uk **w** duendemusic.co.uk Creative Manager: Yvonne Mara.

Barry Dye Entertainments PO Box 888, Ipswich, Suffolk IP1 6BU **t** 01473 744287 **f** 01473 745442 **e** barrydye@aol.com Prop: Barry Dye.

Dyfel Management 19 Fontwell Drive, Bickley, Bromley, Kent BR2 8AB **t** 020 8467 9605 **f** 020 8249 1972 **e** jean@dyfel.co.uk **w** dyfel.co.uk Dir: J Dyne.

East Central One Agency Creeting House, All Saints Road, Creeting St Mary, Ipswich, Suffolk IP6 8PR **t** 01449 723244 **f** 01449 726067 **e** bob@eastcentralone.com **w** eastcentralone.com Co-Dir: Bob Paterson.

EC1 Music Agency Ltd 1 Cowcross Street, London EC1M 6DR **t** 020 7490 8990 **f** 020 7490 8987 **e** jack@ec1music.com MD: Alex Nightingale.

Elastic Artists Agency Flat 5, 3 Newhams Row, London SE1 3UZ **t** 020 7367 6224 **f** 020 7367 6206 **e** info@elasticartists.net **w** elasticartists.net MD: Jon Slade.

Elite Beats 23 Burleigh House, St.Charles Square, London W10 6HB **t** 020 89644313 **f** 07092 361057 **e** simon@elitebeats.com **w** elitebeats.com MD: Simon Sutcliffe.

Emkay Entertainments Nobel House, Regent Centre, Blackness Road, Linlithgow, Lothian EH49 7HU **t** 01506 845555 **f** 01506 845566 **e** emkay@cwcom.net Prop: Mike Kean.

ePM Unit 204, The Saga Centre, 326 Kensal Road, London W10 5BZ **t** 020 8964 4900 **f** 020 8962 9783 **e** oliver@electronicpm.co.uk **w** electronicpm.co.uk Partner: Oliver Way.

F&G Management & Booking Unit A105, 326 Kensal Road, London W10 5BZ **t** 020 8960 9562 **f** 020 8960 9971 **e** fgdjtrade@hotmail.com GM: Riccardo Carosi.

Faze 2 International DJ Agency, PO Box 263, Manchester M15 5WZ **t** 0161 953 4040 **f** 0161 953 4038 **e** iain@faze2agency.com **w** faze2agency.com Mgr: Iain Taylor.

First Contact Agency Ltd PO Box 35060, Camden, London NW1 7WD **t** 020 7691 1588 **f** 020 7691 1589 **e** ae@firstcontactagency.com **w** firstcontactagency.com Agents: Adam Elfin & Jon Vyner.

Fish Fry Agency Wellington House, Pollard Street East, Manchester M40 7FS **t** 0161 274 3700 **e** info@fishfryagency.com **w** fishfryagency.com Dirs: Will Brayne, Max Leader.

FiveMilesHigh 17 Maidavale Crescent, Styvechale, Coventry CV3 6FZ **t** 07811 469888 **e** tours@fivemileshigh.com MD: Dave Robinson.

Flick Productions PO Box 888, Penzance, Cornwall TR20 8ZP **t** 01736 788798 **f** 01736 787898 **e** Flickprouk@aol.com MD: Mark Shaw.

Fruit Pie Music Agency The Shop, 443 Streatham High Road, London SW16 3PH **t** 020 8679 9289 **f** 020 8679 9775 **e** info@fruitpiemusic.com **w** fruitpiemusic.com MD: Kumar Kamalagharan.

G Entertainment 16 Coney Green, Abbotts Barton, Winchester, Hants SO23 7JB **t** 0845 601 6285 **e** enquiries@g-entertaining.co.uk **w** g-entertaining.co.uk MD: Peter Nouwens.

GAA (Gold Artist Agency) 16 Princedale Road, London W11 4NJ **t** 020 7221 1864 **f** 020 7221 1606 **e** bob@goldartists.co.uk MD: Bob Gold.

Gentle Fire Music Ltd GFM House, Cox Lane, Chessington, Surrey KT9 1SD **t** 020 8397 3999 **f** 020 8397 1950 **e** info@gentlefiremusic.com **w** gentlefiremusic.com MD: Bill Shannon.

The Groove Company The Coach House, 29 Market Square, Bicester, Oxon OX26 6AG **t** 01869 250 647 **f** 01869 321 552 **e** tracey@groovecompany.co.uk Manager: Tracey Askem.

Hartbeat Entertainments Ltd PO Box 3, Plympton, Plymouth, Devon PL7 5YL **t** 01752 335000 **f** 01752 335060 **e** hartbeat@lineone.net **w** hartbeat.co.uk MD: Mr RJ Hart.

The Headline Agency 39 Churchfields, Milltown, Dublin 14, Ireland **t** +353 1 260 2560 **f** +353 1 261 1879 **e** info@musicheadline.com **w** musicheadline.com MD: Madeleine Seiler.

Helter Skelter The Plaza, 535 Kings Road, London SW10 0SZ **t** 020 7376 8501 **f** 020 7376 8336 or 020 7352 4759 **e** info@helterskelter.co.uk Snr Agent: Paul Franklin.

Hinc Inc Ltd PO Box 7, Ware, Hertfordshire SG12 9UD **t** 01920 467780 **f** 01920 466077 **e** hincdom@ntlworld.com Agent: Mike Hinc.

Hutt Russell Productions Ltd PO Box 64, Cirencester, Gloucestershire GL7 5YD **t** 01285 644622 **f** 01285 642291 e shows@huttrussell.co.uk w huttrussellorg.com Dir: Steven Hutt.

IMD Ltd PO Box 1200, London SW6 2GH **t** 020 7371 0995 **f** 020 7384 2999 **e** rachel@imd-info.com **w** imd-info.com MD: Rachel Birchwood-Gordon.

Imprint Bookings & Management Unit 13, Barley Shotts Business Park, 246 Acklam Road, London W10 5YG **t** 020 8964 1331 **f** 020 8960 9660 **e** gareth@imprintdjs.com **w** imprintdjs.com Contact: Gareth Rees

International Talent Booking (CCE Music) Ariel House, 74A Charlotte St, London W1T 4QH **t** 020 7637 6979 **f** 020 7637 6978 **e** mail@itb.co.uk **w** itb.co.uk MD: Barry Dickins. MD: Rod MacSween.

INSANITY ARTISTS AGENCY

8 Duncannon St, London WC2N 4JF **t** 08456 446625 **f** 08456 446627 **e** info@insanitygroup.com **w** insanitygroup.com MD: Andy Varley. Agents: James Marriott, Claire White.

Joe Borrow Agency 2 Conifer Drive, Stockton On Tees, Cleveland TS19 0LU **t** 01642 616710 **f** 01642 615737 **e** martintaylor2@netscapeonline.co.uk **w** joeborrowagency.co.uk Proprietor: Martin Taylor.

John Osborne Management PO Box 173, New Malden, Surrey KT3 3YR **t** 020 8949 7730 **f** 020 8949 7798 **e** john.osb1@btinternet.com Dir: John Osborne.

KlubDJ PO Box 5333, Daventry NN11 5FN **t** 07092 171780 **f** 07092 171790 **e** info@klubdj.co.uk **w** klubdj.co.uk Manager: John Barnet.

Label Spinners Box No 1, 404 Footscray Road, London SE9 3TU **t** 020 8857 8775 or 07740 351163 **f** 020 8857 8775 **e** spinners@dircon.co.uk **w** labelspinners.co.uk MD: Steve Goddard.

Limelight Entertainment 23 Westbury Avenue, Droitwich Spa, Worcestershire WR9 0RT **t** 01905 796816 **e** johnandlisanash@hotmail.com Owner: John Nash.

Main Stage Artists Clearwater Yard, 35 Inverness St, London NW1 7HB **t** 020 7424 7500 **f** 020 7424 7501 **e** simon@mainstageartists.com **w** mainstageartists.com MD: Simon Clarkson.

Malcolm Feld Agency Malina House, Sandforth Road, Liverpool L12 1JY **t** 0151 259 6565 **f** 0151 259 5006 **e** Malcolm@malcolmfeld.co.uk **w** malcolmfeld.co.uk Agent: Malcolm Feld.

Mike Malley Entertainments 10 Holly Park Gardens, Finchley, London N3 3NJ **t** 020 8346 4109 **f** 020 8346 1104 **e** mikemalley@ukstars.co.uk **w** ukstars.co.uk MD: Mike Malley. Agency Manager: Rebecca Fanner

Marshall Arts Ltd Leeder House, 6 Erskine Road, London NW3 3AJ **t** 020 7586 3831 **f** 020 7586 1422 **e** info@marshall-arts.co.uk **w** marshall-arts.co.uk MD: Barrie Marshall. Director: Jenny Marshall, Financial Director: Doris Dixon, Marketing & Production Manager: Mike Stewart, Financial Controller: John Chambers

McLeod Holden Enterprises Priory House, 1133 Hessle Road, Kingston-upon-Hull, East Yorkshire HU4 6SB **t** 01482 565444 **f** 01482 353635 **e** Peter.McLeod@mcleod-holden.com **w** mcleod-holden.com Dir: Peter McLeod.

MISSION CONTROL AGENCY

50 Business Centre, Lower Road, London SE16 2XB **t** 020 7252 3001 **f** 020 7252 2225 **e** gary@missioncontrol.net **w** www.missioncontrol.net MD: Gary Howard. Director: Richard Smith

Mi Live 55 St Albans Road, S.C.R., Dublin 8, Ireland **t** +353 1 416 9418 or +353 (0) 87 9817535 **f** +353 1 416 9418 **e** info@milive.net MD: Bernie McGrath.

Mike Stevens Music Canalot Studios, 222 Kensal Road, London W10 5BN **t** 020 8960 5069 **e** sue@msmusic.demon.co.uk Agent: Mike Stevens.

Miracle Artists 1 York Street, London W1U 6PA **t** 020 7935 9222 **f** 020 7935 6222 **e** info@miracle-artists.com Agency Dir: Steve Parker.

Money Talks Agency Cadillac Ranch, Pencraig Uchaf, Cwm Bach, Whitland, Carms. SA34 0DT **t** 01994 484466 **f** 01994 484294 **e** cadillacranch@telco4u.net Dir: Chick Augustino.

Moneypenny Agency The Stables, Westwood House, Main St, North Dalton, Driffield, East Yorks YO25 9XA **t** 01377 217815 or 07977 455882 **f** 01377 217754 **e** nigel@adastey.demon.co.uk **w** adastra-music.co.uk/moneypenny MD: Nigel Morton.

Music 4 Events 26 Carlisle Rd, London NW6 6TS **t** 020 8933 8844 or 07712 833876 **f** 020 7431 0621 **e** info@music4events.co.uk **w** muic4events.co.uk A&R: Toby Herschmann.

Nuphonic Management 93a Rivington Street, London EC2A 3AY **t** 020 7739 8757 or 020 7739 8755 **f** 020 7739 8761 **e** james@nuphonic.co.uk **w** nuphonic.co.uk Agents: James Hillard & Bille De Voil.

NVB Entertainments 80 Holywell Road, Studham, Dunstable, Bedfordshire LU6 2PD **t** 01582 873623 **f** 01582 873618 **e** NVBEnts@aol.com Bookers: H Harrison, Frances Harrison.

The Party Palace Balcony Floor, The Meridian Centre, Elm Lane, Havant, Hants PO9 1UN **t** 023 9247 7222 **f** 023 9247 7223 **e** info@thepartypalace.co.uk **w** thepartypalace.co.uk MD: Del Mitchell.

Peller Artistes Ltd. 47 Dean Street, London W1D 5BE **t** 020 7734 1502 or 0114 247 2365 **f** 020 7734 9996 or 0114 247 2156 **e** agent@pellerartistes.com **w** pellerartistes.com MD: Barry Peller.

Performance Artists Ltd Top Floor Suite, 197 Queens Crescent, London NW5 4DS **t** 020 7482 5080 **f** 020 7424 0631 **e** postmaster@performanceartists.biz **w** performance-artists.co.uk MD: Pete Whelan.

Gordon Poole Agency Ltd The Limes, Brockley, Bristol, Somerset BS48 3BB **t** 01275 463222 **f** 01275 462252 **e** agents@gordonpoole.com **w** gordonpoole.com MD: Gordon Poole.

Positive Nuisance Booking 16-24 Brewery Road, London N7 9NH **t** 020 7607 3608 **f** 020 7607 9608 **e** Chrissie@positivenuisance.com MD: Chrissie Yiannou.

Primary Talent International 2-12 Pentonville Road, London N1 9PL **t** 020 7833 8998 **f** 020 7833 5992 **e** mail@primary.uk.com **w** primary.uk.com/primary MD: Martin Hopewell.

Profile Artists Agency Unit 101, J Block, Tower Bridge Business Complex, 110 Clements Road, London SE16 4EG **t** 020 7394 0012 **f** 020 7394 0093 **e** enquiry@profileagency.co.uk **w** profileagency.co.uk Agent: Serena Parsons.

Psycho Management (Tribute & Retro Band Agency) 111 Clarence Road, London SW19 8QB **t** 020 8540 8122 or 01483 419429 **f** 020 8715 2827 **e** agents@psycho.co.uk **w** psycho.co.uk MD: JH Mabley.

Pure Energy Productions PO Box 4265, Poole, Dorset BH15 3YJ **t** 01202 777724 **f** 01202 777726 **e** sales@pepuk.com **w** pepuk.com Contact: Ian Walker

PVA Group Ltd 2 High Street, Westbury On Trym, Bristol BS9 3DU **t** 0117 950 4504 **f** 0117 959 1786 **e** enquiries@pva.ltd.uk **w** pva.ltd.uk MD: Pat Vincent. Sales Director: John Hutchinson. Marketing Director: Tim Cowlin.

Red Parrot DJ Management & Agency Unit B114, Faircharm Studios, 8-10 Creekside, London SE8 3DX **t** 020 8469 3541 **f** 020 8469 3542 **e** red.parrot@virgin.net **w** redparrot.co.uk Contact: Andria Law, Johnston Walker Partner: Andria Law. Agency: Johnston Walker.

Ro-Lo Productions 35 Dillotford Avenue, Styvechale, Coventry, West Midlands CV3 5DR **t** 024 7641 0388 or 07711 817475 **f** 024 7641 6615 **e** roger.lomas@virgin.net Proprietor: Roger Lomas.

RRR Management 96 Wentworth Road, Birmingham B17 9SY **t** 0121 426 6820 **f** 0121 426 5700 **e** enquiries@rrrmanagement.com **w** rrrmanagement.com MD: Ruby Ryan.

Sasa Music 309, Aberdeen House, 22-24 Highbury Grove, London N5 2EA **t** 020 7359 9232 **f** 020 7359 9233 **e** postroom@sasa.demon.co.uk **w** sasamusic.com MD: David Flower.

Dave Seamer Entertainments 46 Magdalen Road, Oxford OX4 1RB **t** 01865 240054 **f** 01865 240054 **e** dave@daveseamer.co.uk **w** daveseamer.co.uk MD: Dave Seamer.

Sensible Events 90-96 Brewery Road, London N7 9NT **t** 020 7700 9900 **f** 020 7700 7845 **e** zweckaz@aol.com MD: Andrew Zweck.

Serious Ltd Chapel House, 18 Hatton Place, London EC1N 8RU **t** 020 7405 9900 **f** 020 7405 9911 **e** david@serious.org.uk **w** serious.org.uk Dir: David Jones.

Solo (a division of CCE Europe) 2nd Floor, 53-55 Fulham High St, London SW6 3JJ **t** 020 7384 6644 **f** 0870 749 3174 **e** solo@solo.uk.com **w** solo.uk.com MD: John Giddings. Head of Promotions: Graham Pullen.

Sounds Fair Promotions 9 Park Place, Ashton Keynes, Nr Swindon, Wiltshire SN6 6NT **t** 01285 861486 **f** 01285 862302 **e** info@soundsfair.freeserve.co.uk **w** soundsfair.freeserve.co.uk Agent: Dave Beckley.

Stoneyport Agency 65a Dundas Street, Edinburgh EH3 6RS **t** 0131 539 8238 or 07968 131 737 **f** 0131 313 2083 **e** jb@stoneyport.demon.co.uk **w** stoneyport.demon.co.uk MD: John Barrow. Marketing Executive: David Francis. Creative Strategies Executive: Martin Coull. Corp Comm Exe: Bill Barclay.

Mike & Margaret Storey Entertainments Cliffe End Business Park, Dale Street, Longwood, Huddersfield, West Yorkshire HD3 4TG **t** 01484 657054 or 01484 657055 **f** 01484 657055 Owner: Mike Storey.

Swamp Music PO Box 94, Derby DE22 1XA **t** 01332 332336 or 07702 564804 **f** 01332 332336 **e** chrishall@swampmusic.co.uk **w** swampmusic.co.uk MD: Chris Hall.

Symphonic Music Units 13-14, Barley Shotts Business Park, 246 Acklam Road, London W10 5YG **t** 020 8962 5401 **f** 020 8962 5481 **e** abiblake@symphonic-music.com Agent: Abi Blake.

Talking Heads (Voice Agency) 88-90 Crawford Sreet, London W1H 2BS **t** 020 7258 6161 **f** 020 7258 6162 **e** voices@talkingheadsvoices.com **w** talkingheadsvoices.com Principal: John Sachs.

13 Artists 34 West Street, Brighton BN1 2RE **t** 01273 725 800 **f** 01273 733 247 **e** info@13artists.com MD: Charlie Myatt.

Top Talent Agency Yester Road, Chiselhurst, Kent BR7 5HN **t** 020 8467 0808 **f** 020 8467 0808 **e** top.talent.agency@virgin.net MD: John Day.

Total Concept Management (TCM) PO Box 128, Dewsbury, West Yorks WF12 9XS **t** 01924 438295 **f** 01924 525378 **e** tcm@totalconceptmanagement.com **w** totalconceptmanagement.com

TIMEWARP

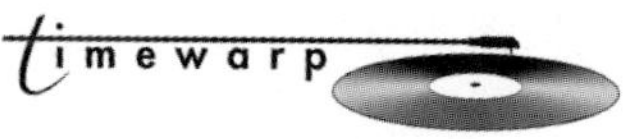

GFM House, Cox Lane, Chessington, Surrey KT9 1SD **t** 020 8397 4466 **f** 020 8397 1950 **e** info@timewarpdis.com **w** timewarpdis.com MD: Bill Shannon. [R]

Vagabond Artists Floor 2, Building B, Tower Bridge Business Complex, 100 Clements Road, London SE16 1ED **t** 020 7940 8587 **f** 020 7407 7081 **e** Info@vagabond.co.uk **w** vagabond.co.uk MD: Dexter Charles.

Value Added Talent 1 Purley Place, Islington, London N1 1QA **t** 020 7704 9720 **f** 020 7226 6135 **e** vat@vathq.co.uk **w** vathq.co.uk MD: Dan Silver. Booking Agent: Doug Smith PA/Office Manager: Heather Taylor.

Denis Vaughan PO Box 28286, London N21 3WT **t** 020 7486 5353 **f** 020 8224 0466 **e** dvaughanmusic@dial.pipex.com Dir: Denis Vaughan.

Vibe Promotions 91-95 Brick Lane, London E1 6QL **t** 020 7247 3479 **f** 020 7426 0491 **e** info@vibe-bar.co.uk **w** vibe-bar.co.uk Event & Bookings: Adelle Stripe.

Victor Hugo Salsa Show 19, Courtside Dartmouth Road, London SE26 4RE **t** 020 8291 9236 or 07956 446 342 **e** vhs@victorhugosalsa.com **w** victorhugosalsa.com MD: Victor Hugo.

Vision 22 Upper Grosvenor Street, London W1K 7PE **t** 020 7499 8024 **f** 020 7499 8032 **e** visionpromotions@madasafish.com MD: Rob Dallison.

Vital Edge Artist Agency PO Box 25965, London N18 1YT **t** 0870 350 1045 **f** 0870 350 1046 **e** info@vitaledgeagency.com **w** vitaledgeagency.com Prop: Nicky Jackson.

Wasted 15 Scott Street, Bognor Regis, West Sussex PO21 1UH **t** 01243 869115 or 07940 245724 **f** 01243 841252 **e** info@wastedonline.co.uk **w** wastedonline.co.uk Event co-ordinator: Tim Harris.

Jason West Agency Gables House, Saddle Bow, Kings Lynn, Norfolk PE34 3AR **t** 01553 617586 **f** 01553 617734 **e** info@jasonwest.com **w** jasonwest.com MD: Jason West.

XFactory 20 Boughton House, Bowling Green Place, London SE1 1YF **t** 020 7403 1980 **f** 020 7403 1830 **e** contact@xfactoryuk.com **w** xfactoryuk.com Dir: Nigel Proktor.

Concert Promoters

A.M.P. Level 2, 65 Newman Street, London W1T 3EG **t** 020 7224 1992 **f** 020 7224 0111 **e** mail@harveygoldsmith.com MD: Harvey Goldsmith CBE.

Active Carpenters Court, Lewes Road, Bromley, Kent BR1 2RN **t** 020 8466 8959 **f** 020 8466 8969 **e** info@active-group.co.uk **w** active-group.co.uk MD: Matthew Lewis.

Aiken Promotions 50-58 Vicar Street Theatre, Thomas Street, Dublin 8, Ireland **t** +353 1 454 6656 **f** +353 1 454 6787 **e** office@aikenpromotions.ie **w** aikenpromotions.com Office Mgrs: Mary Kelly / Sorcha.

Aiken Promotions Ltd Marlborough House, 348 Lisburn Road, Belfast BT9 6GH **t** 028 9038 1047 **f** 028 9068 2091 **e** office@aikenpromotions.ie **w** aikenpromotions.ie MD: Jim Aiken.

AIR (Artistes International Representation Ltd) AIR House, Spennymoor, Co Durham DL16 7SE **t** 01388 814632 **f** 01388 812445 **e** info@airagency.com **w** airagency.com Directors: Colin Pearson, John Wray.

Anonymous Groove 186 Town Street, Armley, Leeds LS12 3RF **t** 0113 225 1684 or 0793 044 3048 **f** 0113 225 1684 **e** info@anonymous-groove.com **w** anonymous-groove.com MD: Chris Shipton.

Artsun 18 Sparkle Street, Manchester M1 2NA **t** 0161 273 3435 **f** 0161 273 3695 **e** mailbox@pd-uk.com MD: Gary McClarnan.

Asgard Promotions 125 Parkway, London NW1 7PS **t** 020 7387 5090 **f** 020 7387 8740 **e** info@asgard-uk.com Jnt MDs: Paul Fenn, Paul Charles.

b-live 23 Newman Street, London W1T 1PL **t** 020 7291 5580 **f** 020 7291 5581 **e** info@b-live.co.uk **w** b-live.co.uk MD: Caroline Hollings.

Badger Promotions PO Box 9121, Birmingham B13 8AU **t** 0121 256 1303 **f** 0121 256 1302 **e** info@badgerpromotions.co.uk **w** badgerpromotions.co.uk Promoter: Mark Badger.

Barney Vernon Promotes PO Box 3418, Sheffield S11 7WJ **t** 0114 268 5441 **e** barney@frannyman.com **w** frannyman.com Promoter: Barney Vernon.

Paul Barrett (Rock 'n' Roll Enterprises) 21 Grove Terrace, Penarth, South Glamorgan CF64 2NG **t** 029 2070 4279 **f** 029 2070 9989 **e** barrettrocknroll@amserve.com MD: Paul Barrett.

BB Promotions 119 Beech Crescent, Netley View, Hythe, Southampton, Hampshire SO45 3QE **t** 023 8020 7877 Mgr: Doug Bailey.

BDA 32 Chiltern Road, Culcheth, Warrington, Cheshire WA3 4LL **t** 01925 766655 **f** 01925 765577 **e** brian.durkin@btinternet.com MD: Brian Durkin.

The Big Gig/Cent Events 500 Chiswick High Road, London W4 5RG **t** 020 8956 2391 or 020 8956 2393 **f** 020 8956 2394 **e** anne@centevents.com **w** thebiggig.biz Events Manager: Anne Jones. MD: Kevin Newton.

HMV Birmingham International Jazz Festival PO Box 944, Birmingham B16 8UT **t** 0121 454 7020 **f** 0121 454 9996 **e** bigbearmusic@compuserve.com **w** bigbearmusic.com Festival Dir: Jim Simpson.

BKO Productions Ltd The Old Truman Brewery, 91 Brick Lane, London E1 6QL **t** 020 7377 9373 **f** 020 7377 6523 **e** byron@bko-alarcon.co.uk Director: Byron Orme.

Derek Block Artistes Agency Ltd 70-76 Bell Street, Marylebone, London NW1 6SP **t** 020 7724 2101 **f** 020 7724 2102 **e** dbaa@derekblock.demon.co.uk MD: Derek Block.

Blow Up Unit 127, Stratford Workshops, Burford Road, London E15 2SP **t** 020 8534 7700 **f** 020 8534 7722 **e** webmaster@blowup.co.uk **w** blowup.co.uk MD: Paul Tunkin.

Broken Star Promotions 10 St Marys Close, Gt Plumstead, Norwich NR13 5EY **t** 01603 712495 **f** 01603 712495 **e** promotions@brokenstar.co.uk **w** brokenstar.co.uk Promoter: Jon Luton.

Bugbear Promotions 3A Highbury Crescent, London N5 1RN **t** 020 7700 0550 **f** 020 7700 0880 **e** bugbear@btconnect.com **w** bugbearbookings.com Contact: Jim Mattison, Tony Gleed

Mel Bush Organization Ltd Tanglewood, Arrowsmith Road, Wimbourne, Dorset BH21 3BG **t** 01202 691891 **f** 01202 691896 **e** mbobmth@aol.com MD: Mel Bush.

Cathouse Promotions Ltd 21 Sandyford Place, Glasgow G3 7NG **t** 0141 572 1120 **f** 0141 572 1121 **w** cplweb.com MD: Donald Macleod.

Channelfly Enterprises 59-61 Farringdon Road, London EC1M 3JB **t** 020 7691 4555 **f** 020 7691 4666 **e** info@channelfly.com **w** channelfly.com MD: Jason Bick.

Charabanc Promotions 18 Sparkle Street, Manchester M1 2NA **t** 0161 273 5554 **f** 0161 273 5554 **e** charabanc@btconnect.com **w** charabanc.net Promoter: Richard Lynch.

Classic Rock (UK) Ltd 47 Brecks Lane, Rotherham, South Yorkshire S65 3JQ **t** 01709 702575 **e** martin@classicrocksociety.co.uk **w** classicrocksociety.com MD: Martin Hudson.

Clear Channel Entertainment Music 1st Floor, Regent 1st Floor, Regent Arcade House, 19-25 Argyll St, London W1F 7TS **t** 020 7009 3333 **f** 0870 749 3191 **e** firstname.lastname@clearchannel.co.uk **w** getlive.co.uk Head of Music Promotions: Stuart Galbraith.

CMC PO Box 3, Newport NP20 3YB **t** 07973 715875 **f** 01633 677672 **e** alan.jones@amserve.com Principal: Alan Jones.

Concorde International Artistes Concorde House, 101 Shepherds Bush Road, London W6 7LP **t** 020 7602 8822 **f** 020 7603 2352 **e** cia@cia.uk.com MD: Paul Fitzgerald.

The Contemporary Music Centre 19 Fishamble Street, Temple Bar, Dublin 8, Ireland **t** +353 1 673 1922 **f** +353 1 648 9100 **e** info@cmc.ie **w** cmc.ie Director: Eve O'Kelly.

Cream Group Appleton House, 139 King Street, Hammersmith, London W6 9JG **t** 020 8735 6605 **f** 020 8735 6695 **e** gill@cream.co.uk **w** cream.co.uk Event & PR: Gill Nightingale/James Barton.

David Hull Promotions 46 University Street, Belfast BT7 1HB **t** 028 9024 0360 **f** 028 9024 7919 **e** info@dhpromotions.com **w** davidhullpromotions.com MD: David Hull.

Dead Or Alive PO Box 34204, London, NW5 1FS **t** 020 7482 3908 **e** gigs@deadoralive.org.uk **w** deadoralive.org.uk MD: Nicholas Barnett.

Tony Denton Promotions Ltd 19 South Molton Lane, Mayfair, London W1K 5LE **t** 020 7629 4666 **f** 020 7629 4777 **e** mail@tdpromo.com **w** tdpromo.com MD: Tony Denton.

DF Concerts 272 St Vincent Street, Glasgow G2 5RL **t** 0141 566 4999 **f** 0141 566 4998 **e** admin@dfconcerts.co.uk **w** gigsinscotland.com Promoter: Geoff Ellis.

Dig Promotions 115 Otley Road, Leeds LS6 3PX **t** 0113 230 2113 **f** 0113 278 9452 **e** eddie@digleeds.com **w** digleeds.com Partners: Eddie Roberts, Gip Dammone.

Domain Music Unit 9, TGEC, Town Hall Approach Road, London N15 4RX **t** 020 8375 3608 **f** 020 8375 3487 **e** info@domainmusic.co.uk **w** domainmusic.co.uk Dir: Michael Lowe.

Firestar Entertainments 10 Green Acres, Glyn Ave, Barnet, Herts EN4 9PJ **t** 01709 709633 or 07740 101347 **f** 020 8275 0502 **e** mailfirestar@aol.com **w** firestarentertainments.com Proprietor: Phivos Petrou.

Flick Productions PO Box 888, Penzance, Cornwall TR20 8ZP **t** 01736 788798 **f** 01736 787898 **e** Flickprouk@aol.com MD: Mark Shaw.

The Flying Music Company Ltd 110 Clarendon Road, London W11 2HR **t** 020 7221 7799 **f** 020 7221 5016 **e** info@flyingmusic.co.uk **w** flyingmusic.com Joint MD: Paul Walden.

Folk in the Fall (see Mrs Casey Music)

Geronimo! 29 Gillian Avenue, Aldershot, Hampshire GU12 4HS **t** 07960 187529 **f** 01252 408041 **e** barneyjeavons@supanet.com **w** geronimo-music.net Promoter: Barney Jeavons.

Get Real Promotions 141 Malmesbury Park Road, Charminster, Bournemouth BH8 8PU **t** 08707 40 65 58 **f** 08707 40 65 59 **e** info@getreal2000.co.uk **w** getreal2000.co.uk Promotions Manager: Andy Freeman.

Hallogen Ltd The Bridgewater Hall, Manchester M2 3WS **t** 0161 950 0000 **f** 0161 950 0001 **e** admin@bridgewater-hall.co.uk **w** bridgewater-hall.co.uk Programming Manager: Sara Unwin.

Jef Hanlon Promotions Ltd 1 York Street, London W1U 6PA **t** 020 7487 2558 **f** 020 7487 2584 **e** jhanlon@agents-uk.com MD: Jef Hanlon.

Head Music Ltd 2 Munro Terrace, London SW10 0DL **t** 020 7376 4456 **f** 020 7351 5569 **e** straight@freeuk.com Contact: John Curd

The Headline Agency 30 Churchfields, Milltown, Dublin 14 **t** +353 1 261 1879 **f** +353 1 261 1879 **e** info@musicheadline.com **w** musicheadline.com MD: Madeleine Seiler.

Homeless Productions 1 Tranent Grove, Dundee, Tayside DD4 0XP **t** 0790 535 3301 **e** headz@onaireast.com **w** onaireast.com Admins: Rika Wanatabee.

Chester Hopkins Int Ltd PO Box 536, Headington, Oxford OX3 7LR **t** 01865 766 766 or 020 8441 1555 **f** 01865 769 736 **e** office@chesterhopkins.co.uk **w** chesterhopkins.co.uk MDs: Adrian Hopkins, Jo Chester.

Hutt Russell Organisation PO Box 64, Cirencester, Gloucestershire GL7 5YD **t** 01285 644622 **f** 01285 642291 **e** shows@huttrussellorg.com **w** huttrussellorg.com Dir: Steve Hutt.

Infinite Events Ltd 2 Dickson Road, Blackpool, Lancashire FY1 2AA **t** 01253 299 606 **f** 01253 299 454 **e** infinite@mct-online.com Contact: Julian Murray

Insanity Artists Agency 8 Duncannon Street, London WC2N 4JF **t** 08456 446625 **f** 08456 446627 **e** info@insanitygroup.com **w** insanitygroup.com MD: Andy Varley. Agents: James Marriott, Claire White.

Jay Taylor Flat 114, India House, 75 Whitworth Street, Manchester M1 6HB **t** 0161 278 6087 or 07931 797 982 **e** jaytaylor@cwcom.net **w** bone-box.com Promoter: Jay Taylor.

Kennedy Street Enterprises Ltd Kennedy House, 31 Stamford St, Altrincham, Cheshire WA14 1ES **t** 0161 941 5151 **f** 0161 928 9491 **e** kse@kennedystreet.com Dir: Danny Betesh.

King Tut's Wah Wah Hut/DF Concerts 272A St Vincent Street, Glasgow G2 5RL **t** 0141 248 5158 **f** 0141 248 5202 **e** kingtuts@dfconcerts.co.uk **w** kingtuts.co.uk Promoter/Venue Manager: Dave McGeachan.

Line-Up PMC 9A Tankerville Place, Newcastle upon Tyne, Tyne and Wear NE2 3AT **t** 0191 281 6449 **f** 0191 212 0913 **e** c.a.murtagh@btinternet.com **w** on-line-records.co.uk Prop: Chris Murtagh.

Scott Mackenzie Associates 6 Gardner Way, Kenilworth, Warwickshire CV8 1QW **t** 01926 859102 or 01962 859103 **f** 01926 858966 **e** scottmackenzie4u@hotmail.com **w** scottmackenzie.co.uk MD: Scott Mackenzie.

Marshall Arts Leeder House, 6 Erskine Road, London NW3 3AJ **t** 020 7586 3831 **f** 020 7586 1422 **e** info@marshall-arts.co.uk **w** marshall-arts.co.uk MD: Barrie Marshall.

Matpro Ltd Cary Point, Babbacombe Downs, Torquay, Devon TQ1 3LU **t** 01803 322233 **f** 01803 322244 **e** matpro@btinternet.com **w** babbacombe-theatre.com MD: Colin Matthews.

Maxrock Masefield House, 271 Four Ashes Road, Dorridge, Solihull, West Midlands B93 8NR **t** 07801 562801 **f** 01564 77 1078 **e** robert@maxrock.co.uk **w** maxrock.co.uk MD: Robert Smith.

Phil McIntyre Promotions 2nd Floor, 35 Soho Square, London W1D 3QX **t** 020 7439 2270 **f** 020 7439 2280 **e** reception@mcintyre-ents.com Promoter: Paul Roberts.

McLeod Holden Presentations Ltd Priory House, 1133 Hessle Road, Kingston-upon-Hull, East Yorkshire HU4 6SB **t** 01482 565444 **f** 01482 353635 **e** Peter.McLeod@mcleod-holden.com **w** mcleod-holden.com Dir: Peter McLeod.

Mean Fiddler Concerts 16 High Street, Harlesden, London NW10 4LX **t** 020 8961 5490 **f** 020 8961 9238 **w** meanfiddler.com CEO: Vince Power. Director: Rob Hallett.

Metropolis Music 69 Caversham Road, London NW5 2DR **t** 020 7424 6800 **f** 020 7424 6849 **e** mail@metropolismusic.com **w** gigsandtours.com MD: Bob Angus.

Andrew Miller Promotions Int. Ltd 35 Ashcombe Street, Fulham, London SW6 3AW **t** 020 7471 4775 **f** 020 7371 5545 **e** AMPILtd@aol.co.uk **w** ampi.co.uk Dir: Faye Miller.

Montana Concerts 174 Camden High St, London NW1 0NE **t** 020 7267 3939 **f** 020 7482 1955 **e** jon@theunderworldcamden.co.uk Promoter: Jon Vyner.

Mrs Casey Music PO Box 296, Matlock, Derbyshire DE4 3XU **t** 01629 760345 **f** 01629 760777 **e** office@mrscasey.co.uk **w** mrscasey.co.uk MD: Steve Heap.

Musicdash Musicdash, PO Box 1977, Manchester M26 2YB **t** 0787 0727 075 **e** jon@musicdash.co.uk **w** manchestermusic.co.uk Director: Jon Ashley.

New Vision Arts Management Empire House, Penthouse Suite, 175 Piccadilly, London W1V 9DB **t** 0870 444 2506 **f** 07000 785 845 **e** info@newvisionarts.com **w** newvisionarts.com Head of Promotions: Mark Foker.

NSMA Concerts The Old Laundry, 100 Irving Road, Bournemouth BH6 5BL **t** 0870 040 6767 **e** info@nsma.com **w** nsma.com MD: Dan Harris.

Partners In Crime 18 Chenies Street, London WC1E 7PA **t** 020 8521 7764 or 07973 415 167 **e** saphron@msn.com Promoter: Annette Bennett.

Perfect Words & Music 2 The Teak House, 37 The Avenue, Branksome Park, Poole, Dorset BH13 6LJ **t** 01202 763208 or 07810 437179 **e** philmurray.pac@talk21.com Booker: Allison Longstaff.

Performing Arts Management Canal 7, Clarence Mill, Bollington, Macclesfield, Cheshire SK10 5JZ **t** 01625 575681 **f** 01625 572839 **e** info@performingarts.co.uk **w** performingarts.co.uk Marketing Manager: Fifi Butler. General Manager/Orchestra Manager: Clare Scott.

Planet Of Sound - Live (Scotland) 236 High Street, Ayr, South Ayrshire KA7 1RN **t** 01292 265913 **f** 01292 265493 **e** planet-of-sound@btconnect.com Dir: Ian Hollins.

Plum Promotions 56b Farringdon Road, London EC1R 3BL **t** 020 7336 7326 **f** 020 7336 7326 **e** info@plummusic.com **w** plummusic.com Dirs: Allan North, Sarah Thirtle.

Pollytone Weekenders PO Box 124, Ruislip, Middx HA4 9BB **t** 01895 638584 **f** 01895 624793 **e** val@pollyton.demon.co.uk **w** pollytone.com Owner: Val Bird.

Gordon Poole Agency The Limes, Brockley, Bristol, Somerset BS48 3BB **t** 01275 463222 **f** 01275 462252 **e** agents@gordonpoole.com **w** gordonpoole.com Consultant: James Poole.

Psychic Pig Promotions 46-47 Church Street, Trowbridge, Wilts BA14 8PB **t** 07973 314237 **e** alloutmgmt@hotmail.com Promotions: George Hodgson.

PVC 51 Bath Road, Southsea, Portsmouth, Hampshire PO4 0HX **t** 023 9275 2782 **f** 023 9275 2782 **e** ianbpvc@hotmail.com Contact: Ian Binnington

Real Promotions 140 Cross Lane, Crookes, Sheffield S10 1WP **t** 07989 347 645 **e** mark@realpromo.co.uk **w** realpromo.co.uk Promoter: Mark Roberts.

Regular Music 100B Constitution Street, Leith, Edinburgh EH6 6AW **t** 0131 554 7444 **f** 0131 554 7222 **e** barry@regularmusic.co.uk **w** regularmusic.co.uk MD: Barry Wright.

Rideout Lillie House, 1a Conduit Street, Leicester LE2 0JN **t** 0116 2230318 **e** rideout@stayfree.co.uk **w** themusicianpub.co.uk Booker: Darren Nockles.

Riverman Concerts Top Floor, George House, Brecon Road, London W6 8PY **t** 020 7381 4000 **f** 020 7381 9666 **e** info@riverman.co.uk **w** riverman.co.uk Dir: David McLean.

RK Promo 78 Church Road, Northenden, Manchester M22 4WD **t** 0161 998 8903 **f** 0161 998 8903 **e** JasonSingh78@aol.com **w** RockKitchen.com Promoter: Jason Singh.

RLM Promotions 2A Old Mill Complex, Brown Street, Dundee DD1 5EG **t** 01382 224405 **f** 01382 224406 **e** mail@rlm-promotions.com **w** rlm-promotions.com Owner: John Macdonald.

Rock Garden 6-7 The Piazza, Covent Garden, London WC2E 8HA **t** 020 7836 4052 or 07768 8904262 **f** 020 7379 4793 **e** sean@rockgarden.co.uk **w** rockgarden.co.uk Entertainment Dir: Sean McDonnell.

Sensible Events 90-96 Brewery Road, London N7 9NT **t** 020 7700 9900 **f** 020 7700 7845 **e** zweckaz@aol.com Agent: Andrew Zweck.

Serious Chapel House, 18 Hatton Place, London EC1N 8RU **t** 020 7405 9900 **f** 020 7405 9911 **e** info@serious.org.uk **w** serious.org.uk Director: David Jones.

Serious Club Promotions PO Box 13143, London N6 5BG **t** 020 8731 7300 **f** 020 8458 0045 **e** sam@seriousworld.com **w** seriousworld.com Contact: Sam O'Riordan

Shark Promotions 23 Rolls Court Avenue, Herne Hill, London SE24 0EA **t** 020 7737 4580 **f** 020 7737 4580 **e** mellor@organix.fsbusiness.co.uk MD: MH Mellor.

Sidmouth International Festival (see Mrs Casey Music)

SJM Concerts St Matthews, Liverpool Road, Manchester M3 4NQ **t** 0161 907 3443 **f** 0161 907 3446 **e** vicky@sjmconcerts.com **w** gigsandtours.com Office Manager: Vicky Potts.

Solo Agency & Promotions 1st Floor, Regent Arcade House, 252-260 Regent Street, London W1B 3BX **t** 020 7009 3361 **f** 0870 749 3174 **e** solo@solo.uk.com **w** solo.uk.com MD: John Giddings.

Sonic Arts Network The Jerwood Space, 171 Union Street, London SE1 0LN **t** 020 7928 7337 **e** phil@sonicartsnetwork.org **w** sonicartsnetwork.org Chief Exec: Phil Hallett.

Sound Advice 30 Artesian Road, London W2 5DD **t** 020 7229 2219 **f** 020 7229 9870 **e** info@soundadvice.uk.com **w** soundadvice.uk.com MD: Hugh Phillimore.

Straight Music 2 Munro Terrace, London SW10 0DL **t** 020 7376 4456 **f** 020 7351 5569 **e** shelley@straightmusic.com MD: John Curd.

Sub Zero Music The Leisure Factory, Oldfields, Cradley Heath, West Midlands B64 6BS **t** 01384 637776 **f** 01384 637227 **e** Music@therobin.co.uk MD: Mike Hamblett.

The Talent Scout 2nd Floor, Swiss Center, 10 Wardour Street, London W1D 6QF **t** 020 7864 1300 **f** 020 7437 1029 **e** info@thetalentscout.co.uk **w** thetalentscout.co.uk Dir: Karen Smyth, Helen Douglas.

TKO Music Group Ltd PO Box 130, Hove, E. Sussex BN3 6QU **t** 01273 550088 **f** 01273 540969 **e** management@tkogroup.com **w** tkogroup.com Contact: Warren Heal

Towersey Village Festival (see Mrs Casey Music)

Traxxevents 3/2, 1 Kennoway Drive, Glasgow G11 7UA **t** 0141 341 0691 **f** 0141 341 0691 **e** info@traxxevents.com **w** traxxevents.com Dir: Mark MacKechnie.

Truck 15 Percy Street, Oxford OX4 3AA **t** 01865 722333 **e** paul@truckrecords.com **w** truckrecords.com MD: Paul Bonham.

Up All Night Music 20 Denmark Street, London WC2H 8NA **t** 020 7419 4696 **e** info@upallnightmusic.com **w** upallnightmusic.com MD: Phil Taylor.

Urban Music Entertainment Network (U-Men) Group PO Box 7874, London SW20 9XD **t** 07050 605219 **f** 07050 605239 **e** sam@pan-africa.org CEO: Oscar Sam Carrol Jnr.

Denis Vaughan Promotions PO Box 28286, London N21 3WT **t** 020 7486 5353 **f** 020 8224 0466 **e** dvaughanmusic@dial.pipex.com MD: Denis Vaughan.

Weekender Promotions PO Box 571, Taunton, Somerset TA1 3ZW **t** 01823 321605 **e** weekenderlive@btopenworld.com **w** weekenderlive.co.uk Dir: Paul Dimond.

World Famous Group Ltd. Stamford Gate House, Chelsea Village, Fulham Road, London SW6 1HS **t** 020 7385 6838 **f** 020 7385 0999 **e** info@worldfamousgroup.com **w** worldfamousgroup.com Chairman: Alan Shulman.

The World Music Foundation (WMF) Please, visit website for detailse events@musicaid.org **w** musicaid.org

World Unlimited 34, Rothesay Croft, Kitwell, Birmingham, West Midlands B32 4JG **t** 01803 324089 **f** 01803 324089 **e** graham@rootitooti.freeserve.co.uk **w** worldunlimited.freeuk.com Music Programmer: Graham Radley.

Zoot Promotions PO Box 3932, Birmingham B30 2EQ **t** 0121 458 3811 or 07958 340162 **f** 0870 055 7785 **e** jackie@zootmusic.net **w** zootmusic.net Promoter: Jackie Wade.

Concert Hire

▲ Concert Hire Lighting
● Concert Hire PA
*** Concert Hire Both**

A.C. Lighting Ltd (Equipment Supply) Centauri House, Hillbottom Road, High Wycombe, Bucks HP12 4HQ **t** 01494 446000 **f** 01494 461024 **e** info@aclighting.co.uk **w** aclighting.co.uk Marketing Director: Glyn O'Donoghue. ▲

A-C Technology Ltd 30 Grove Road, Pinner, Middlesex HA5 5HW **t** 020 8429 3111 **f** 020 8429 4240 **e** actech@btclick.com MD: George Ashley-Cound. *

Adlib Audio Ltd Adlib House, Fleming Road, Speke, Liverpool L24 9LS **t** 0151 486 2216 **f** 0151 448 1454 **e** hire@adlibaudio.co.uk **w** adlibaudio.co.uk MDs: Andy Dockerty, Dave Kay. ●

Alliance Music Hire 92A Parchmor Road, Thornton Heath, Surrey CR7 8LX **t** 020 8239 8815 **f** 020 8239 8816 **e** john@jofish-muzik.com MD: John Fisher. *

Apollo Sound 32 Ellerdale Road, London NW3 6BB **t** 020 7435 5255 **f** 020 7431 0621 **e** info@apollosound.com **w** apollosound.com MD: Toby Herschmann. ●

Aquarius Acoustics Unit 1, Stanley Street, Colne, Lancashire BB9 8HT **t** 01282 693575 or 01282 859797 **f** 01282 863250 **e** dave@aquac.demon.co.uk **w** aquariusacoustics.com MD: Dave Pickering. ●

Astra Audio Fairview Farm, Fiddling Lane, Monks Horton, Ashford, Kent TN25 6AP **t** 01303 812715 **f** 01303 812715 **e** astraaudio@aol.com **w** astraaudio.co.uk Studio Mgr: Gwen Woolgar. ●

Atlantic Hire 4 The Limes, North End Way, London NW3 7HG **t** 020 8209 0025 **e** atlantichire@aol.com Contact: Jez Strode *

Audile Unit 110, Cariocca Business Park, Ardwick, Manchester M12 4AH **t** 0161 272 7883 or 07968 156 499 **f** 0161 272 7883 **e** mail@audile.co.uk **w** audile.co.uk Partner: Rob Ashworth. *

Audio & Acoustics United House, North Road, London N7 9DP **t** 020 7700 2900 **f** 020 7700 6900 **e** aaaco@aol.com Dir: Nick Kantoch. ●

Audioforum Ltd Unit 20, Dixon Business Centre, Dixon Road, Brislington, Bristol BS4 5QW **t** 0870 240 6444 **f** 0117 972 3926 **e** sales@audioforum.co.uk **w** audioforum.co.uk MD: Mike Reeves. *

Autograph Sales Ltd. 102 Grafton Road, London NW5 4BA **t** 020 7485 3749 **f** 020 7485 0681 **e** sales@autograph.co.uk **w** autograph.co.uk Dir: Graham Paddon. ●

Avolites Ltd 184 Park Avenue, Park Royal, London NW10 7XL **t** 020 8965 8522 **f** 020 8965 0290 **e** avosales@avolites.com **w** avolites.com Sales Manager: May Lee. ▲

B&H Sound Services Ltd The Old School, Crowland Road, Eye, Peterborough, Cambrigeshire PE6 7TN **t** 01733 223535 **f** 01733 223545 **e** sound@bhsound.co.uk **w** bhsound.co.uk PA Mgr: Julian Stanford. ✻

Banana Row Backline Hire 47 Eyre Place, Edinburgh EH3 5EY **t** 0131 557 2088 **f** 0131 558 9848 **e** music@bananarow.com MD: Craig Hunter. ✻

Bandit Lites Ltd Unit 4C, Portland Industrial Estate, Hitchin Road, Arlesey, Bedfordshire SG15 6SG **t** 01462 731739 **f** 01462 731570 **e** banditUK@banditlites.com **w** banditlites.com GM: Jason Tang. ▲

Batmink Beckery Road, Glastonbury, Somerset BA6 9NX **t** 01458 833186 **f** 01458 835320 **e** batmink@aol.com **w** batmink.co.uk Dir: D Churches. ✻

Bennett Audio 41 Sherriff Road, London NW6 2AS **t** 020 7372 1077 or 07748 705 067 **e** bennettaudio@f2s.com **w** bennettaudio.co.uk Dir. and Audio Engineer: Clem Bennett. ●

John Boddy Agency 10 Southfield Gardens, Twickenham, Middlesex TW1 4SZ **t** 020 8892 0133 or 020 8891 3809 **f** 020 8892 4283 **e** jba@johnboddyagency.co.uk MD: John Boddy. ✻

Bonza Sound Services Ltd Alfriston House, Guildford Road, Normandy, Surrey GU3 2AR **t** 01483 235313 **f** 01483 236015 **e** ray@bonza.co.uk **w** bonza.co.uk MD: Ray Bradman. ●

Canegreen Unit 2, 12-48 Northumberland Park, London N17 0TX **t** 020 8801 8133 **f** 020 8801 8139 **e** yan@canegreen.com **w** canegreen.co.uk MD: Yan Stile. ●

Capital Sound Hire Unit K, Bridges Wharf, off York Road, London SW11 3QS **t** 020 7978 5825 **f** 020 7978 5826 **e** info@capital-sound.co.uk **w** capital-sound.co.uk Owner: Keith Davis. ●

CAV Unit F2, Bath Road Trading Estate, Stroud, Gloucestershire GL5 3QF **t** 01453 751865 **f** 01453 751866 **e** sales@cav.co.uk **w** cav.co.uk Prop: Hans Beier. ✻

Celco Midas House, Willow Way, London SE26 4QP **t** 020 8699 6788 **f** 020 8699 5056 **e** sales@celco.co.uk **w** celco.co.uk Sales: Mark Buss. ✻

Chameleon Pro Audio & Lighting Unit 10, Orton Industrial Estate, London Road, Coalville, Leicestershire LE67 3JA **t** 01530 831337 **f** 01530 838319 **e** stewart@chameleon-pa.co.uk **w** chameleon-pa.co.uk Partner: Stewart Duckworth. ✻

Chaps Production Co 4 Fairdene Road, Coulsdon, Surrey CR5 1RA **t** 01737 551144 **f** 01737 552244 **e** hires@chapsproduction.com Dir: Steve Ludlam. ✻

Cheltenham Stage Services ltd Unit 31, Ullenwood Court, Ullenwood, Cheltenham, Gloucestershire GL53 9QS **t** 01242 244978 **f** 01242 250618 **e** enquiries@ullenwood.co.uk **w** ullenwood.co.uk/css Business Manager: Chris Davey. ✻

The Cloud One Group of Companies 24 Proctor Street, Birmingham B7 4EE **t** 0121 333 7711 **f** 0121 333 7799 **e** admin@cloudone.net **w** cloudone.net MD: Paul Stratford. ▲

Coast To Coast 3 Lane Top Cottages, Whalley Lane, Denholme, Bradford, West Yorkshire BD13 4LE **t** 01274 835558 **f** 01274 835558 **e** gerardrolfe@orange.net Dir: Gerard Rolfe. ●

Complete Entertainment Services PO Box 112, Seaford, East Sussex BN25 2DQ **t** 0870 755 7610 **f** 0870 755 7613 **e** info@completeentertainment.co.uk **w** completeentertainment.co.uk CEO: Chris Bray. ✻

Concert Lights (UK) Ltd Undershore Works, Brookside Road, Bolton, Lancs BL2 2SE **t** 01204 391343 **f** 01204 363238 **e** clightuk@aol.com **w** concertlights.com Hire Manager: Chris Sinnott. ▲

Concert Sound Unit C, Park Avenue Ind Estate, Sundon Park Road, Luton, Bedfordshire LU3 3BP **t** 01582 565855 or 07768 418413 **f** 01582 565856 **e** davec@concert-sound.co.uk **w** concert-sound.co.uk GM: David Catlin. ●

Concert Systems Unit 4D, Stag Industrial Est, Atlantic Street, Altrincham, Cheshire WA14 5DW **t** 0161 927 7700 **f** 0161 927 7722 **e** hire@concert-systems.com **w** concert-systems.com Prop: Paul Tandy. ●

Corporate Events UK Ltd Gratitude, Foxley Lane, Binfield, Berkshire RG42 4EE **t** 01344 649549 **f** 01344 649549 **e** info@corporateeventsuk.co.uk **w** corporateeventsuk.co.uk Dir: Paul Donnelly. ✻

CPL 18 St Albans Road, Dartford, Kent DA1 1TF **t** 01322 229923 or 07860 419728 **f** 01322 284145 **e** cshroff@aol.com Contact: Cyrus Shroff ▲

Creative Lighting And Sound Unit 6, Spires Business Units, Mugiemoss Road, Bucksburn, Aberdeen AB21 9NY **t** 01224 683111 **f** 01224 686611 **e** clsabdn@aol.com Owner: Mr Flett. ✻

DHA Lighting 284-302 Waterloo Road, London SE1 8RQ **t** 020 7771 2900 **f** 020 7771 2901 **e** sales@dhalighting.co.uk **w** dhalighting.co.uk MD: Diane Grant. ▲

Dimension Audio Unit 3, 307-309 Merton Road, London SW18 5JS **t** 020 8877 3414 **f** 020 8877 3410 **e** mail@dimension.co.uk **w** dimension.co.uk MD: Colin Duncan. ●

Disaster Area PA 44 Arfryn, Llanrhos, Llandudno, Gwynedd LL30 1PB **t** 01492 584065 or 07778 138463 **f** 01492 584065 **e** berenice.hardman@virgin.net **w** touringproductionservices.co.uk Contact: Berenice Hardman ●

DM Audio 22 Duddingston Road, Edinburgh EH15 1NE **t** 0131 620 0456 **f** 0131 620 1423 **e** info@dmaudio.co.uk **w** dmaudio.co.uk Partner: Deano Martino. ●

DPL Production Lighting Units 2 & 3 Dodds Farm, Hatfield Broad Oak, Bishop's Stortford, Herts CM22 7JX **t** 0870 1610 141 **f** 0870 1610 151 **e** darren@dplighting.com **w** dplighting.com Contact: Darren Parker ▲

Empire Mobile Services 15 Hildens Drive, Tilehurst, Berkshire RG31 5HW **t** 0118 942 7062 **f** 0118 942 7062 **e** geoffwemp@aol.com Prop: Geoff West. ✻

EMS Audio Ltd 12 Balloo Avenue, Bangor, Co. Down BT19 7QT **t** 028 9127 4411 **f** 028 9127 4412 **e** ems@musicshop.to **w** musicshop.to Director: William Thompson. ●

Enlightened Lighting Ltd 2B - 2C, Bath Riverside Business Park, Riverside Road, Bath, Somerset BA2 3DW **t** 01225 311964 **f** 01225 445454 **e** enq@enlightenedlighting.co.uk **w** enlightenedlighting.co.uk Dir: Simon Marcus. ▲

Entec Sound And Light 517 Yeading Lane, Northolt, Middlesex UB5 6LN **t** 020 8842 4004 **f** 020 8842 3310 **e** dick@entec-soundandlight.com **w** entec-soundandlight.com Sound Dept Mgr: Dick Hayes. ✻

The Entertainment Company 13 Appledore, Bracknell, Berkshire RG12 8QY **t** 01344 867089 **f** 01344 305294 **e** info@entertainmentcompany.co.uk **w** entertainmentcompany.co.uk Dir: Paul James. ✻

ESE Audio Great Job's Cross Farm, Hastings Road, Rolvenden, Kent TN17 4PL **t** 01580 243330 **f** 01580 243216 **e** janewinterese@hotmail.com Partner: Jane Winter. ●

ESS Unit 14, Bleak Hill Way, Hermitage Lane Ind Estate, Mansfield, Nottinghamshire NG18 5EZ **t** 01623 647291 **f** 01623 622500 **e** richardjohn@orange.net Partner: Richard John. ●

Eurosound (UK) Unit 12, Station Court, Clayton West, Huddersfield, West Yorkshire HD8 9XJ **t** 01484 866066 **f** 01484 866299 **e** sales@eurosound.co.uk **w** eurosound.co.uk Prod Mgr: Tony Bottomley. ✻

Fineline The Old Quarry, Clevedon Road, Failand, Bristol BS8 3TU **t** 01275 395000 **f** 01275 395001 **e** darren@fineline.uk.com **w** fineline.uk.com MD: Darren Wring. ▲

Futurist Projects 136 Thornes Lane, Wakefield, West Yorkshire WF2 7RE **t** 01924 298900 **f** 01924 298700 **e** info@futurist.co.uk **w** futurist.co.uk MD: Michael Lister. ▲

FX Music Unit 1B, Atlas Business Centre, Oxgate Lane, London NW2 7HJ **t** 020 8208 1771 **f** 020 8208 1883 **e** sales@fx-music.co.uk **w** fx-music.co.uk Hire Mgr: Dave Beck. ●

FX Rentals 38-40 Telford Way, London W3 7XS **t** 020 8746 2121 **f** 020 8746 4100 **e** info@fxrentals.co.uk **w** fxgroup.net Op's Dir: Peter Brooks. ●

GB Audio Unit D, 51 Brunswick Road, Edinburgh EH7 5PD **t** 0131 661 0022 **f** 0131 661 0022 **e** info@gbaudio.co.uk **w** gbaudio.co.uk Contact: G Bodenham ●

HSL Productions Ltd Unit 11, Appleby Business Centre, Appleby Street, Blackburn BB1 3BL **t** 01254 698808 or 01254 697800 **f** 01254 698835 **e** simon@hslproductions.com **w** hslproductions.com MD: Simon Stuart. ✻

IllumiNation 75 Leicester Road, Quorn, Leicestershire LE12 8BA **t** 01509 415374 **f** 01509 620976 **e** andy@quorndon.com Lighting Designer: Andy Liddle. ▲

Intasound PA (NO THIRD PARTY USE) Unit 15, Highgrove Farm Ind Estate, Pinvin, Pershore, Worcestershire WR10 2LF **t** 01905 841591 **f** 01905 841590 **e** sales@intasoundpa.co.uk **w** intasoundpa.co.uk Lighting Manager: Chris Dale. ✻

Intrak 6 Delaney Drive, Freckleton, Preston, Lancashire PR4 1SJ **t** 01772 633697 **f** 01772 634875 **e** mail@intrak.co.uk **w** intraksoundandlight.co.uk Prop: JA Foley. ✻

Jive Entertainment Services PO Box 5865, Corby, Northamptonshire NN17 5ZT **t** 01536 406406 or 07831 835635 **f** 01536 400082 **e** hojive@aol.com MD: Dave Bartram. ▲

John Henry's 16-24 Brewery Road, London N7 9NH **t** 020 7609 9181 **f** 020 7700 7040 **e** johnh@johnhenrys.com **w** johnhenrys.com MD: John Henry. ●

Juice Lighting & Sound 9-10 Gresley Close, Drayton Fields, Daventry, Northants NN11 5RZ **t** 01327 876883 **f** 01327 310094 **e** sales@juicesound.co.uk **w** juicesound.co.uk Prop: John Silk. ✻

Lancelyn Theatre Supplies Poulton Road, Bebington, Wirral, Cheshire CH63 9LN **t** 0151 334 8991 or 0151 334 3000 **f** 0151 334 4047 or 0151 334 0831 **e** sales@lancelyn.co.uk **w** lancelyn.co.uk Mgr: Bob Baxter. ▲

Light & Sound Design 201 Coventry Road, Birmingham B10 0RA **t** 0121 766 6400 **f** 0121 766 6150 **e** uksales@lsdicon.com **w** fourthphase.com Ops Mgr: Kevin Forbes. ▲

Lighting Design Services Ltd Crede Barn, Crede Lane, Old Bosham, Chichester, West Sussex PO18 8NX **t** 01243 575373 **f** 01243 572076 **e** jon@light-design.co.uk MD: Jon Pope. ▲

Lighting Technology Projects Industry Road, Heaton, Newcastle-upon-Tyne, Tyne and Wear NE6 5XB **t** 0191 265 2500 **f** 0191 265 8595 **e** craig.greiveson@lighting-tech.com **w** lighting-tech.com Hire Mgr: Craig Greiveson. ✻

Lite Alternative Unit 4, Shadsworth Business Park, Duttons Way, Blackburn, Lancashire BB1 2QR **t** 01254 279654 **f** 01254 278539 **e** anyone@lite-alternative.com **w** lite-alternative.com Hire Mgr: Jon Greaves. ▲

LXCO Ltd 32A St Stephens Gardens, London W2 5QX **t** 020 7467 0810 **f** 020 7467 0811 **e** info@lxco.co.uk **w** lxco.co.uk Dir: James Cobb. ▲

Martin Bradley Sound & Light 69A Broad Lane, Hampton, Middlesex TW12 3AX **t** 020 8979 0672 **f** 020 8979 0672 **e** mslbradley@aol.com **w** polytone.co.uk Contact: Martin Bradley ✻

MCL 18 Lord Byron Square, Stowell Technical Park, Salford Quays, Manchester M50 2XH **t** 0161 745 9933 **f** 0161 745 9975 **e** jleah@mcl-manchester.com **w** mclwebsite.com Marketing Manager: John Leah. ✻

Media Control (UK) Ltd 69 Dartmouth Middleway, Birmingham, West Midlands B7 4UA **t** 0121 333 3333 **f** 0121 333 3347 **e** hire@mcl-birmingham.com **w** mcl-europe.com MD: Tony Cant. ●

Midnight Electronics Off Quay Building, Foundry Lane, Newcastle upon Tyne, Tyne and Wear NE6 1LH **t** 0191 224 0088 **f** 0191 224 0080 **e** dx@compuserve.com **w** midnightelectronics.co.uk Manager: Dave Cross. ●

Mikam Sound (Ireland) Ltd 38 Parkwest Enterprise Centre, Park West, Dublin 12, Ireland **t** 00 353 1 623 7277 **f** 00 353 1 623 7350 **e** mikam@iol.ie Contact: Paul Aungier ●

Moonlite Productions Unit 4, Bridgewater Business Park, Gatehouse Way, Aylesbury, Buckinghamshire HP19 8XN **t** 01296 331000 **f** 01296 437220 **e** moonliteprod@btinternet.com **w** moonlite.co.uk Dir: James Iyengar. ✻

Multiplex Productions 239 Clarendon Park Road, Leicester LE2 3AN **t** 0116 270 4007 **f** 0116 270 4007 **e** dave.davies1@virgin.net Mgr: Teri Wyncoll. ●

Mushroom Hire & Event Services Ltd 3 Encon Court, Owl Close, Moulton Park Industrial Estate, Northampton NN3 6HZ **t** 01604 790900 **f** 01604 491118 **e** info@mushroomevents.co.uk **w** mushroomevents.co.uk Hire Mgr: Andy Slevin. Events Mgr: Paul Butler. ▲

Music Bank (Hire) Ltd Buildings C & D, Tower Bridge Business Complex, 100 Clement's Road, London SE16 4DG **t** 020 7252 0001 **f** 020 7231 3002 **e** nunu@musicbank.org **w** musicbank.org Dir: Nunu Whiting. ●

Music Room The Old Library, 116-118 New Cross Road, London SE14 5BA **t** 020 7252 8271 **f** 020 7252 8252 **e** sales@musicroom.web.com **w** musicroom.web.com MD: Gordon Gapper. ✻

Nightair Productions Unit 1, Eastfield Side, Sutton In Ashfield, Nottinghamshire NG17 4JW **t** 01623 557040 or 01623 455051 **f** 01623 555586 **e** nightair@inmansfield.freeserve.co.uk **w** nightair.co.uk Prop: Andrew Monk. ✻

Nitelites Unit 3E, Howdon Green Ind Est, Norman Terrace, Wallsend, Tyne and Wear NE28 6SX **t** 0191 295 0009 **f** 0191 295 0009 **e** nitelites@onyxnet.co.uk Partner: Gordon Reay. ✻

Northern Light 35-41 Assembly Street, Leith, Edinburgh, Lothian EH6 7RG **t** 0131 553 2383 or 0131 440 1771 **f** 0131 553 3296 **e** enquiries@northernlight.co.uk **w** northernlight.co.uk Hire Mgr: Gordon Blackburn. ✻

OPTI 38 Cromwell Road, Luton, Bedfordshire LU3 1DN **t** 01582 411413 **f** 01582 400613 **e** optiuk@optikinetics.com **w** optikinetics.com Sales Dir: Neil Rice. ▲

Otto Lighting & Production Co Unit 20, Earlsdon Business Centre, Earlsdon Street, Coventry, West Midlands CV5 6EJ **t** 024 7645 1231 or 07721 012003 **f** 024 7645 1231 or 024 7667 0111 **e** peter@olpc.freeserve.co.uk **w** scoot.co.uk/otto_lighting/ Prop: Pete Hopkins. ✻

The PA Company Unit 7, Ashway Centre, Elm Crescent, Kingston-Upon-Thames, Surrey KT2 6HH **t** 020 8546 6640 or 07836 600 081 **f** 020 8547 1469 **e** thepacompany@aol.com MD: Doug Beveridge. ●

PA Music 172 High Road, East Finchley, London N2 9AS **t** 020 8883 4350 **f** 020 8883 5117 **e** mail@pamusic.net **w** pamusic.net Prop: Mr MW Lowe. ✻

Pandora Productions Unit 38 Hallmark Trading Ctr, Fourth Way, Wembley, Middlesex HA9 0LB **t** 020 8795 2432 **f** 020 8795 2431 **e** pandoraprods@btconnect.com Prop: John Montier. ✻

Pearce Hire Unit 27, Second Drove, Industrial Estate, Fengate, Peterborough, Cambridgeshire PE1 5XA **t** 01733 554950 or 07850 363543 **f** 01733 892807 **e** sales@pearcehire.co.uk **w** pearcehire.co.uk Prop: Shaun Pearce. ✻

Pegasus Sound & Light 23-25 Canongate, The Royal Mile, Edinburgh, Lothian EH8 8BX **t** 0131 556 1300 **f** 0131 557 6466 **e** pegasussl@aol.com **w** pegasussl.co.uk Sales Mgr: David Hunter. ✻

PG Stage Electrical Studio House, Northstage, Broadway, Salford M50 2UW **t** 0161 877 4933 **f** 0161 877 4944 **e** sales@pgstage.co.uk **w** pgstage.co.uk MD: Paul Holt. ▲

Phase 5 Enterprise (Europe) Ltd **t** 0151 353 8163 **f** 0151 353 1892 **e** info@phase5.uk.com **w** phase5.uk.com Dir: Haydn Gregson. ▲

Playtime (Agency) Ltd The Leisure Factory, Oldfields, Cradley Heath, West Midlands B64 6BS **t** 01384 637776 **f** 01384 637227 **e** playtime@agents-uk.com **w** playtimeagency.co.uk Director: Keith Evans.

Prism Lighting Unit 5A, Hampton Industrial Estate, Malpas, Cheshire SY14 8JQ **t** 01948 820201 **f** 01948 820480 **e** sales@prismlighting.co.uk **w** prismlighting.co.uk Partner: John Mellen. ▲

Presentation Services Ltd The Heights, Cranborne Industrial Estate, Potters Bar, Herts EN6 3JN **t** 01707 648120 **f** 01707 648121 **e** info@presservgroup.com **w** presservgroup.com Manager, Concert & Touring: Pod Bluman.

Pure Energy Productions PO Box 4265, Poole, Dorset BH15 3YJ **t** 01202 777724 **f** 01202 777726 **e** sales@pepuk.com **w** pepuk.com Dir: Ian Walker. ✻

RG Jones Sound Engineering 16 Endeavour Way, London SW19 8UH **t** 020 8971 3100 **f** 020 8971 3101 **e** info@rgjones.co.uk **w** rgjones.co.uk Hire Dept Mgr: John Carroll. ●

Rhythm Audio Rhythm House, King Street, Carlisle, Cumbria CA1 1SJ **t** 01228 515141 **f** 01228 515161 **e** hire@rhythmaudio.co.uk **w** rhythmaudio.co.uk Head of Prod: Ian Howe. ✻

Runway UK 163 Victoria Road, Horley, Gatwick, Surrey RH6 7BF **t** 01293 820758 **f** 01293 408885 **e** info@runwayuk.com **w** runwayuk.com Prop: Andy Wildy. ✻

SAV Ltd Party House, Mowbray Drive, Blackpool FY3 7JR **t** 01253 302602 **f** 01253 301000 **e** sales@stardream.co.uk Technical Director: Steve Salisbury. ✻

Sensible Music (Ireland) Unit 53, Parkwest Enterprise Centre, Ningor Road, Dublin 12 Ireland **t** +353 1 620 8321 **f** +353 1 620 8322 **e** info@sensiblemusic.ie **w** sensiblemusic.ie Dir: John Munnis. ✻

Show Presentations 6 Commerce Road, Brentford, Middx TW8 8LE **t** 020 8569 9292 **f** 020 8569 9293 **e** sps@showpres.co.uk **w** showpres.com MD: Robin Coles. ✻

The Small PA Company 49 Liddington Road, London E15 3PL **t** 020 8536 0649 or 07785 584 273 **f** 07092 022 897 **e** ian@soundengineer.co.uk **w** soundengineer.co.uk MD: Ian Hasell. ●

Matt Snowball Music Unit 2, 3-9 Brewery Road, London N7 9QJ **t** 020 7700 6555 **f** 020 7700 6990 **e** enquiries@mattsnowball.com **w** mattsnowball.com Hire/Sales: Kent Jolly. ●

Sound And Light Productions PO Box 32295, London W5 1WD **t** 0870 066 0272 **f** 0870 066 0273 **e** info@soundandlightproductions.co.uk **w** soundandlightproductions.co.uk Partner: John Denby. ✻

Sound Hire Unit 7, Kimpton Trade Business Centre, Minden Road, Sutton, Surrey SM3 9PF **t** 020 8644 1248 **f** 020 8644 6642 **e** richard@sound-hire.com **w** sound-hire.com MD: Richard Lienard. ●

Sound of Music 14 Runswick Drive, Wollaton, Nottingham NG8 1JD **t** 0115 875 6359 or 07946 739 384 **e** info@pahire.com **w** pahire.com Mgr: Sash Pochibko. ●

SouthWestern Management 13 Portland Road, Street, Somerset BA16 9PX **t** 01458 445186 or 07831 437062 **f** 01458 841186 **e** info@sw-management.co.uk **w** sw-management.co.uk Dir: Chris Hannam. ✻

SRS (Norwich) 59 Darrell Place, Norwich, Norfolk NR5 8QN **t** 01603 250486 or 07850 235161 **f** 01603 250486 **e** srs@deafgeoff.co.uk Owner: Geoff Lowther. ●

SSE Hire Ltd Burnt Meadow House, Burnt Meadow Rd, North Moons Moat, Redditch, Worcs B98 9PA **t** 0152 172 8822 **f** 0152 172 8840 **e** postmaster@sse-hire.com **w** sse-hire.com Dir: Chris Beale. ●

Stage Audio Services Unit 2, Bridge Street, Wordsley, Stourbridge DY8 5YU **t** 01384 263629 **f** 01384 263620 **e** kevinmobers@aol.com Dir: Kevin Mobberley. ●

Stage Light Design Unit 11, College Fields Business Ctr, Prince George's Road, London SW19 2PT **t** 020 8640 4100 **f** 020 8640 3400 **e** mw@stagelightdesign.com **w** stagelightdesign.com MD: John Rinaldi. ▲

Stage Two Hire Services Unit J, Penfold Trading Estate, Imperial Way, Watford, Hertfordshire WD24 4YY **t** 01923 230789 or 01923 244822 **f** 01923 255048 **e** richard.ford@stage-two.co.uk **w** stagetwo.co.uk Hire Mgr: Richard Ford. ✻

Star Events Group Milton Road, Thurleigh, Bedfordshire MK44 2DG **t** 01234 772233 **f** 01234 772272 **e** firstname.lastname@stareventsgroup.com **w** StarEventsGroup.com Dir: Jane Russen. ✻

Stratford Acoustics 24 Procter Street, Birmingham B7 4EE **t** 0121 333 7711 **f** 0121 333 7799 **e** admin@cloudone.net **w** cloudone.net MD: Paul Stratford. ●

STS Touring Productions Ltd Unit 103-104, Cariocca Business Park, Hellidon Close, Ardwick, Manchester M12 4AH **t** 0161 273 5984 **f** 0161 272 7772 **e** ststouring@aol.com **w** ststouring.co.uk Director: Peter Dutton. ✻

Sub Zero Music The Leisure Factory, Oldfields, Cradley Heath, West Midlands B64 6BS **t** 01384 637776 **f** 01384 637227 **e** music@therobin.co.uk **w** subzeromusic.com Dir: Mike Hamblett. ✻

System Sound (UK) Ltd 1 Liddall Way, Horton Road, West Drayton, Middlesex UB7 8PG **t** 01895 432995 **f** 01895 432976 **e** design@systemsound.com **w** systemsound.com Dir: Simon Biddulph. ●

Terminal Studios 4-10 Lamb Walk, London Bridge, London SE1 3TT **t** 020 7403 3050 **f** 020 7407 6123 **e** info@terminal.co.uk **w** terminal.co.uk Prop: Charlie Barrett. ●

Tiger Hire Unit 3, Grove Farms, Milton Hill, Abingdon, Oxfordshire OX14 4DP **t** 01235 834000 **f** 01235 820022 **e** jimtigerhire@cs.com **w** ourworld.compuserve.com/homepages/tiger_hire Owner: Jim Parsons. ●

TMC Hillam Road, off Canal Road, Bradford, West Yorkshire BD2 1QN **t** 01274 370966 **f** 01274 308706 **e** enquiries@tmc.ltd.uk **w** tmc.ltd.uk Sales Mgr: Nick Bolton. ●

TMS Show Services Chichester Road, Sidlesham Common, Sidlesham, Chichester PO20 7PY **t** 01243 641166 **f** 01243 641888 **e** info@tms1.co.uk Partner: Dick Edney. ✻

Tourtech 3 Quarry Park Close, Moulton Park Industrial Estate, Northampton NN3 6QB **t** 01604 494846 **f** 01604 642454 **e** tourtecuk@aol.com **w** tourtech.co.uk MD: Dick Rabel. ●

Travelling Light (Birmingham) Ltd Unit 34, Boulton Industrial Centre, Icknield Street, Birmingham, West Midlands B18 5AU **t** 0121 523 3297 **f** 0121 551 2360 Dir: Chris Osborn. ✻

Roy Truman Sound Services Unit 23, Atlas Business Centre, Oxgate Lane, London NW2 7HJ **t** 020 8208 2468 **f** 020 8208 3320 **e** rtss@london.com Mgr: Elisabeth Wirrer. ●

TSProfessional Audio Ltd 7 Hove Park Villas, Hove, East Sussex BN3 6HP **t** 01273 822485 **f** 01273 772664 **e** sales@tsproaudio.co.uk **w** tsproaudio.co.uk MD: Keith Upton. ✻

Up All Night Music 20 Denmark Street, London WC2H 8NA **t** 020 7419 4696 **e** info@upallnightmusic.com **w** upallnightmusic.com MD: Phil Taylor. ✻

Utopium Lighting Unit B The Old Workhouse, Hudds Vale Road, St George, Bristol BS5 7HY **t** 0117 955 8848 **f** 0117 939 3927 **e** colin@utopium.co.uk **w** utopium.co.uk Prod Mgr: Colin Bodenham. ▲

Vari-Lite Europe Ltd 20-22 Fairway Drive, Greenford, Middlesex UB6 8PW **t** 020 8575 6666 **f** 020 8575 0424 **e** info@vari-lite.eu.com **w** vari-lite.com GM: Edward Pagett. ▲

Villa Audio Ltd Baileys Yard, Chatham Green, Little Waltham, Essex CM3 3LE **t** 01245 361694 **f** 01245 362281 **e** sales@villa-audio.com **w** villa-audio.com MD: Gareth Jones. ●

VLPS Lighting Services 20-22 Fairway Drive, Greenford, Middlesex UB6 8PW **t** 020 8575 6666 **f** 020 8575 0424 **e** info@vlps.co.uk **w** vlps.co.uk GM: Edward Pagett. ✻

Volume Audio 6 All Saints Crescent, Garston, Watford, Hertfordshire WD25 0LU **t** 01923 673027 **f** 01923 893733 **e** david@finn.com Dir: David Finn. ●

Whitelight Electrics Ltd 20 Merton Park Ind Est, Jubilee Way, London SW19 3WL **t** 020 8254 4820 **f** 020 8254 4821 **e** info@whitelight.ltd.uk **w** whitelight.ltd.uk Gen Mgr: Bryan Raven. ▲

Wigwam Unit 6, Junction 19 Ind Est, Green Lane, Haywood, Lancashire OL10 1NB **t** 01706 363400 or 01706 363800 **f** 01706 363410 or 01706 363810 **e** events@wigwam.co.uk **w** wigwam.co.uk MD: Mike Spratt. ●

World Unlimited 34 Rothesay Croft, Birmingham B32 4JG **t** 01803 324089 **f** 01803 324089 **e** graham@tooti.freeserve.co.uk **w** worldunlimited.freeuk.com Programmer: Graham Radley. ✻

Zig Zag Lighting (South) 68 Morton Gardens, Wallington, Surrey SM6 8EX **t** 020 8647 1968 **f** 020 8401 2216 **e** kev@zigzag-lighting.com Prop: Kevin Ludlam. ▲

Zique Audio Highfield Works, John Street, Hinkley, Leicestershire LE10 1UY **t** 01455 610364 or 07831 342355 **f** 01455 610164 Prop: Gary Hargraves. ✻

Zisys AVMN Ltd. 1 Alexander Place, Irvine, Ayrshire KA12 0UR **t** 01294 204213 **e** danny@zisysavmn.co.uk **w** zisysavmn.co.uk Director: Danny Anderson. ✻

Venues

42nd Street Nightclub 2 Bootle Street, off Deansgate, Manchester M2 5GU **t** 0161 831 7108 **f** 0161 831 7108 **e** info@42ndstreetnightclub.com **w** 42ndstreetnightclub.com Manager: Simon Jackson.

Albert Halls Dumbarton Road, Stirling FK8 2QL **t** 01786 473544 or 01786 443109 **f** 01786 448933 or 01786 442538 **e** mccarthya@stirling.gov.uk Venues Mgr: Anne Marie-McCarthy. Seated Capacity: 893 Standing Capacity: 1200

Aberdeen Exhibition and Conference Centre Bridge of Don, Aberdeen AB23 8BL **t** 01224 824824 **f** 01224 825276 **e** aecc@aecc.co.uk Contact: Jim Francis Seated Capacity: 4700 Standing Capacity: 8000

Aberdeen Music Hall Union Street, Aberdeen AB10 1QS **t** 01224 632080 **f** 01224 632400 **e** musichall@arts-rec.aberdeen.net.uk **w** musichallaberdeen.com Ops Mgr: Julie Sinclair. Seated Capacity: 1282 Standing Capacity: 1500

Aberdeen University Union Gallowgate, Aberdeen AB10 1SZ **t** 01224 647751 **f** 01224 633326 **e** entertainments@ausaunion.com **w** abdn.ac.uk\union Ents Mgr/Clubs Mgr: Mike Wharton/Mike MacKenzie. Seated Capacity: 500 Standing Capacity: 600

Aberystwyth Arts Centre Penglais, Aberystwyth, Ceredigion SY23 3DE **t** 01970 622882 **f** 01970 622883 **e** lla@aber.ac.uk **w** aber.ac.uk/~arcwww/index.htm Dir: Alan Hewson. Seated Capacity: 1000

Aberystwyth University Guild Of Students, Panglais Campus, Penglais, Aberystwyth, Dyfed SY23 3DX **t** 01970 621700 **f** 01970 621701 Standing Capacity: 850

The Academy Cleveland Road, Uxbridge, Middlesex UB8 3PH **t** 01895 462200 **f** 01895 462301 or 01895 462300 Contact: Dan Harris Seated Capacity: 450 Standing Capacity: 600

Accrington Town Hall Blackburn Road, Accrington, Lancashire BB5 1LA **t** 01254 380297 **f** 01254 380291 **e** leisure@hyndburnbc.gov.uk **w** leisureinhyndburn.co.uk Marketing & Events Officer: Nigel Green. Seated Capacity: 400 Standing Capacity: 360

AK Bell Library York Place, Perth PH2 8EP **t** 01738 444949 or 01738 477017 **f** 01738 477010 **e** kmcwilliam@pkc.gov.uk **w** pkc.gov.uk Theatre Mgr: Kenny McWilliam. Seated Capacity: 125

The Alban Arena Civic Centre, St Albans, Hertfordshire AL1 3LD **t** 01727 861078 **f** 01727 865755 **e** info@alban-arena.co.uk **w** alban-arena.co.uk Mgr: Roger Cramer. Seated Capacity: 856 Standing Capacity: 1132

The Albany Douglas Way, London SE8 4AG **t** 020 8692 0231 or 020 8692 4446 **f** 020 8469 2253 Programmer: Geraldine Marsh. Seated Capacity: 250 Standing Capacity: 425

Alexandra Palace Alexandra Palace Way, Wood Green, London N22 7AY **t** 020 8365 4313 **f** 020 8365 2662 **e** alexandrapalace@dial.pipex.com **w** alexandrapalace.com Head of Sales & Marketing: Chris Gothard. Seated Capacity: 7250 Standing Capacity: 7250

Alexandra Theatre Station Street, Birmingham, West Midlands B5 4DS **t** 0121 643 5536 **f** 0121 632 6841 Gen Mgr: Charlie Ingham. Seated Capacity: 1365

The Alfred McAlpine Stadium Stadium Way, West Yorkshire HD1 6PG **t** 01484 450000 **f** 01484 450144 **w** the_stadium.co.uk Contact: Kevin Collinge Seated Capacity: 20000 Standing Capacity: 40000

Alloa Town Hall Mars Hill, Alloa, Clackmannan FK10 1AB **t** 01259 213131 **f** 01259 721313 Contact: Bookings Supervisor Seated Capacity: 500

Angel Centre Angel Lane, Tonbridge, Kent TN9 1SF **t** 01732 359588 **f** 01732 363677 Seated Capacity: 1100 Standing Capacity: 1500

Anglia Polytechnic University Students Union, East Road, Cambridge CB1 1PT **t** 01223 460008 **f** 01223 417718 **e** d.low@asu.anglia.ac.uk **w** anglia.ac.uk Ents Mgr: Daz Low. Seated Capacity: 230 Standing Capacity: 300

The Anvil Churchill Way, Basingstoke, Hampshire RG21 7QR **t** 01256 819797 **f** 01256 331733 **e** Ann.Dickson@theanvil.org.uk **w** theanvil.org.uk Prog Mgr: Ann Dickson. Seated Capacity: 1400

Apollo Theatre Shaftesbury Avenue, London W1V 7HD **t** 020 7494 5200 **f** 020 7434 1217 **e** info@rutheatres.com **w** rutheatres.com Concerts & Hirings Mgr: Mike Townsend. Seated Capacity: 775

Apollo Theatre George Street, Oxford OX1 2AG **t** 01865 243041 **f** 01865 791976 Gen Mgr: Louise Clifford. Seated Capacity: 1826

Apollo Victoria 17 Wilton Road, London SW1V 1LG **t** 020 7834 6318 **f** 020 7630 7716 Contact: Jamie Baskeyfield Seated Capacity: 1564

Aqua Cafe Bar Albion Wharf, Albion Street, Manchester M1 5LN **t** 0161 228 1800 Contact: John Houghton

The Arches 253 Argyle Street, Glasgow, Lanarkshire G1 4PR **t** 0141 565 1009 **f** 0141 565 1001 **e** tamsin@thearches.co.uk **w** thearches.co.uk Music Programmer: Tamsin Austin. Seated Capacity: 550 Standing Capacity: 800

Area Gade House, 46 The Parade, High Street, Watford, Herts WD17 1AY **t** 01923 281100 or 01923 281500 **f** 01923 281101 **e** chris@areaclub.com **w** areaclub.com Events & PR Manager: Lisa Worton. Seated Capacity: 1500 Standing Capacity: 1500

The Arena 208 Newport Road, Middlesborough TS1 5PS **t** 01642 804444 **f** 01642 804455 Bookings Manager: Nik Cook. Standing Capacity: 600

Artslink Theatre Knoll Road, Camberley, Surrey GU15 3SY **t** 01276 707612 **f** 01276 707644 Contact: Pat Pembridge Seated Capacity: 400 Standing Capacity: 600

Ashcroft Theatre Park Lane, Croydon, Surrey CR9 1DG **t** 020 8681 0821 **f** 020 8760 0835 **e** dbarr@fairfield.co.uk Contact: Nick Leigh

Assembly Hall Stoke Abbott Road, Worthing, West Sussex BN11 1HQ **t** 01903 239999 or 01903 206206 **f** 01903 821124 Theatre Mgr: Peter Bailey. Seated Capacity: 840 Standing Capacity: 1100

Assembly Hall Theatre Crescent Road, Royal Tunbridge Wells, Kent TN1 2LU **t** 01892 510971 or 01892 554103 **f** 01892 525203 or 01892 539078 **e** info@tunbridgewells.gov.uk **w** tunbridgewells.gov.uk/ah Contact: Pat Casey Seated Capacity: 930 Standing Capacity: 1000

Assembly Rooms Market Place, Derby DE1 3AH **t** 01332 255443 **f** 01332 255788 Gen Mgr: Chris Ward-Brown. Seated Capacity: 1500 Standing Capacity: 2000

Assembly Rooms 54 George Street, Edinburgh, Midlothian EH2 2LR **t** 0131 220 4348 **f** 0131 220 6812 **e** assemblyrooms@dial.pipex.com Mgr: Simon Robson. Seated Capacity: 700 Standing Capacity: 750

Aston University Students Guild The Triangle, Birmingham B4 7ES **t** 0121 359 6531 **f** 0121 333 4218 Contact: The Ents Mgr Seated Capacity: 400 Standing Capacity: 942

Aylesbury Civic Centre Market Square, Aylesbury, Buckinghamshire HP20 1UF **t** 01296 585527 **f** 01296 392091 **e** aabbott@aylesburyvaledc.gov.uk **w** aylesburyciviccentre.co.uk Dept Mgr: Sam McCaffrey. Seated Capacity: 640 Standing Capacity: 1000

Ayr Pavilion Esplanade, Ayr KA7 1DT **t** 01292 265489 **f** 01292 611614 Contact: F Macintyre Seated Capacity: 1000

Babbacombe Theatre Babbacombe Downs, Torquay, Devon TQ1 3LU **t** 01803 322233 **f** 01803 322244 **e** matpro@btinternet.com **w** babbacombe-theatre.co.uk Resident Dir: Colin Matthews. Seated Capacity: 600

BAC Lavender Hill, London SW11 5TN **t** 020 7223 6557 or 020 7223 2223 (box) **f** 020 7978 5207 **e** mailbox@bac.org.uk **w** bac.org.uk Asst Administrator: Joana Crowley. Seated Capacity: 170

Band On The Wall 25 Swan Street, Manchester M4 5JQ **t** 0161 832 6625 or 0161 834 1786 **f** 0161 834 2559 **w** bandonthewall.com Contact: The promotor Seated Capacity: 240 Standing Capacity: 240

Bar Cuba Ltd Pickford Street, Macclesfield, Cheshire SK11 6HB **t** 01625 66 99 44 **f** 01625 66 99 77 **w** barcuba.tv Operations Director: Daniel Phillips. Standing Capacity: 400

Barbican Centre Silk Street, Barbican, London EC2Y 8DS **t** 020 7638 4141 or 020 7382 7242 **f** 020 7382 7037 Head of Music: Robert Van Leer. Seated Capacity: 1989

Barfly - Liverpool 90 Seel Street, Liverpool L1 4BH **t** 0151 707 6171 **e** liverpool.info@barflyclub.com **w** barflyclub.com/liverpool

Barfly Camden The Monarch, 49 Chalk Farm Road, London NW1 8AN **t** 020 7691 4244 or 020 7691 4246 **f** 020 7691 4245 **e** info@barflyclub.com **w** barflyclub.com MD: Be Rozzo. Standing Capacity: 200

Barfly Cardiff Ty Cefn, Rectory Road, Cardiff CF5 1QL **t** 02920 667 658 **f** 02920 341 622 **e** cardiff.info@barflyclub.com **w** barflyclub.com Booker: Jon Wing. Standing Capacity: 200

Barfly Glasgow Riverside House, 260 Clyde Street, Glasgow, Lanarkshire G1 4JH **t** 0141 221 0414 **f** 0141 204 5711 **e** glasgow.info@barflyclub.com **w** barflyclub.com Manager: David Dempster. Standing Capacity: 400

Barnsley College Student Union, 6B Eastgate, Barnsley, South Yorkshire S7D 2EP **t** 01226 249886 **f** 01226 249886 Contact: Jennifer Hulme Seated Capacity: 350 Standing Capacity: 400

Barrowlands Ballroom 244 Gallowgate, Glasgow, Lanarkshire G4 0TT **t** 0141 552 4601 **f** 0141 552 4997 Contact: Stan Riddet Standing Capacity: 1900

Bartok 78-79 Chalk Farm Road, London NW1 8AR **t** 020 7916 0595 **w** meanfiddler.com

Bath Pavilion North Parade Road, Bath BA2 4ET **t** 01225 462565 **f** 01225 481306 Seated Capacity: 1000 Standing Capacity: 800

Bath Spa University College Students Union, Newton Park, Bath BA2 9BN **t** 01225 875588 **f** 01225 874765 **e** bathspasu@bathspa.ac.uk **w** bathspasu.co.uk Events Mgr: Diane Starling. Standing Capacity: 250

Bath Theatre Royal St John's Place, Sawclose, Bath BA1 1ET **t** 01225 448815 **f** 01225 444080 Seated Capacity: 978

Beach Ballroom Beach Leisure Centre, Beach Promenade, Aberdeen AB2 1NR **t** 01224 647647 **f** 01224 648693 Seated Capacity: 1200

Beau Sejour Centre Amherst, St Peter Port, Guernsey, Channel Islands GY1 2DL **t** 01481 727211 **f** 01481 714102 Events Manager: Penny Weaver. Seated Capacity: 1500 Standing Capacity: 2000

Beck Theatre, Hayes Grange Road, Hayes, Middlesex UB3 2UE **t** 020 8561 7506 **f** 020 8569 1072 **w** tickest-direct.co.uk Contact: Graham Bradbury Seated Capacity: 600

Bedford Corn Exchange - CSD Events St Paul's Square, Bedford MK40 1SL **t** 01234 344813 **f** 01234 325358 **e** cornexch@bedford.btinternet.com **w** bedfordcornexchange.co.uk Manager: Carl Amos. Seated Capacity: 830 Standing Capacity: 1000

Belgrade Theatre Belgrade Square, Coventry CV1 1GS **t** 024 7625 6431 **f** 024 7655 0680 **e** admin@belgrade.co.uk **w** belgrade.co.uk GM: David Beidas. Seated Capacity: 865

The Betsey Trotwood 56 Farringdon Road, London EC1R 3BL **t** 020 7336 7326 **e** info@plummusic.com **w** plummusic.com Promoter: Sarah Thirtle.

Birbeck College Student Union, Malet Street, London WC1E 7HX **t** 020 7631 6335 **f** 020 7631 6270 **e** president@bcsu.bbk.ac.uk **w** bbk.ac.uk/su Contact: Lucy Reed Seated Capacity: 100

Bivouac @ The Duke of Wellington 37 Broadgate, Lincoln, Lincolnshire LN2 5AE **t** 01522 539883 **f** 01522 528964 **e** steve.hawkins@easynet.co.uk Booker: Steve Hawkins. Standing Capacity: 200

Blackburn Arena Blackburn Waterside, Lower Audley, Blackburn, Lancashire BB1 1BB **t** 01254 263063 **f** 01254 691516

Blackheath Halls 23 Lee Road, London SE3 9RQ **t** 020 8318 9758 **f** 020 8852 5154 **e** mail@blackheathhalls.com **w** blackheathhalls.com Operation Mgr: Jenni Darwin. Seated Capacity: 700 Standing Capacity: 1000

Blackpool Grand Theatre 33 Church Street, Blackpool, Lancashire FY1 1HT **t** 01253 290111 **f** 01253 751767 **e** geninfo@blackpoolgrand.co.uk **w** blackpoolgrand.co.uk GM: Stephanie Sirr. Seated Capacity: 1192

Blackpool Pleasure Beach Arena Ocean Boulevard, Blackpool, Lancashire FY4 1EZ **t** 01253 341033 **f** 01253 401098 or 01253 405467 **e** michelle.barratt@bpbltd.com **w** bpbltd.com Contact: Michelle Barratt Seated Capacity: 1800

Blackpool Winter Gardens Church Street, Blackpool, Lancashire FY1 1HW **t** 01253 292029 **f** 01253 751204 Contact: Martin Witts Seated Capacity: 3250 Standing Capacity: 4000

Bletchley Leisure Centre Princes Way, Bletchley, Milton Keynes, Buckinghamshire MK2 2HQ **t** 01908 377251 **f** 01908 374094 Contact: Dean Woods Seated Capacity: 1300 Standing Capacity: 1500

Bloomsbury Theatre 15 Gordon Street, London WC1H 0AH **t** 020 7679 2777 or 020 7388 8822 **f** 020 7383 4080 **e** blooms.theatre@ucl.ac.uk **w** thebloomsbury.com Administrator: Mark Feakins. Seated Capacity: 550 Standing Capacity: 550

Bluecoat Arts Centre Bluecoat Chambers, School Lane, Liverpool, Merseyside L1 3BX **t** 0151 709 5297 **f** 0151 709 0048 **e** bluecoat@dircon.co.uk

The Borderline Orange Yard, Off Manette Street, Charing Cross Road, London W1V 5LB **t** 020 7424 9592 or 020 7734 5547 **f** 020 7434 2698 **e** beveritt@meanfiddler.co.uk **w** borderline.co.uk Promoter: Barry Everitt. Standing Capacity: 275

Borough Hall Middlegate, Headland, Hartlepool TS24 8AY **t** 01429 266522 **f** 01429 523005

Bournemouth International Centre (Tregonwell Hall) Exeter Road, Bournemouth, Dorset BH2 5BH **t** 01202 456513 **f** 01202 456432 **e** chris.jenkins.bic@bournemouth.gov.uk **w** bic.co.uk Entertainment & Events: Chris Jenkins. Standing Capacity: 1202

Bournemouth International Centre (Windsor Hall) Exeter Road, Bournemouth, Dorset BH2 5BH **t** 01202 456513 **f** 01202 456432 **e** chris.jenkins.bic@bournemouth.gov.uk **w** bic.co.uk Entertainment & Events: Chris Jenkins. Seated Capacity: 3500 Standing Capacity: 4100

Bournemouth Pavilion Ballroom Westover Road, Bournemouth, Dorset **t** 01202 456436 **f** 01202 456432 **e** sara.orford.bic@bournemouth.gov.uk **w** bic.co.uk Head of Entertainments: Rob Zuradzki. Seated Capacity: 752 Standing Capacity: 900

Bournemouth Pavilion Theatre Westover Road, Bournemouth, Dorset BH1 2BU **t** 01202 456436 **f** 01202 456432 **e** sara.orford.bic@bournemouth.gov.uk **w** bic.co.uk Entertainment Manager: Rob Zuradzki. Seated Capacity: 1512

Bournemouth University The Old Fire Station, 36 Holdenhurst Road, Bournemouth, Dorset BH8 8AD **t** 01202 503888 **f** 01202 503913 **e** info@oldfirestation.co.uk **w** oldfirestation.co.uk Events & Marketing Mgr: Angus Carter. Seated Capacity: 300 Standing Capacity: 600

Bradford University Commmunal Building Students Union, Richmond Road, Bradford, West Yorkshire BD7 1DP **t** 01274 233245 **f** 01274 235530 **e** ubu-ents@bradford.ac.uk **w** ubuonline.co.uk Standing Capacity: 1300

Braehead Arena Glasgow Braehead, Kings Inch Road, Glasgow G51 4BN **t** 0141 886 8300 **f** 0141 885 4620 **e** fiona-curran@capshop.co.uk **w** braehead.co.uk Business Liaison Mgr: Fiona Curran. Seated Capacity: 5100

Braintree Towerlands Arena Panfield Road, Braintree, Essex CM7 5BJ **t** 01376 326802 **f** 01376 552487 Marketing Mgr: Michael Smillie. Seated Capacity: 3600 Standing Capacity: 4000

Brangwyn Hall The Guildhall, Swansea SA1 4PE **t** 01792 635489 **f** 01792 635488 **e** brangwyn.hall@swansea.gov.uk **w** swansea.gov.uk/brangwynhall Manager: Tracy Ellicott. Seated Capacity: 1070 Standing Capacity: 1286

Brentford Fountain Leisure Centre 658 Chiswick High Road, Brentford, Middlesex TW8 0HJ **t** 020 8994 9596 **f** 020 8994 4956 Contact: Alan Boulden Seated Capacity: 1200 Standing Capacity: 1500

Brentwood Centre Doddinghurst Road, Brentwood, Essex CM15 9NN **t** 01277 261111 x 381 **f** 01277 200152 Concerts & Promotions Mgr: Steve Allen. Seated Capacity: 1900 Standing Capacity: 1900

Brewery Arts Centre Highgate, Kendal, Cumbria LA9 4HE **t** 01539 725133 **f** 01539 730257 **e** admin@breweryarts.co.uk **w** breweryarts.co.uk Music Officer: Gavin Sharp. Seated Capacity: 300 Standing Capacity: 450

Bridge Lane Theatre Bridge Lane, London SW11 3AD **t** 020 7228 5185 or 020 7228 8828 **f** 020 7262 0090 Artistic Dir: Terry Adams. Seated Capacity: 200

The Bridgewater Hall Lower Mosley Street, Manchester M2 3WS **t** 0161 950 0000 **f** 0161 950 0001 **e** admin@bridgewater-hall.co.uk **w** bridgewater-hall.co.uk Chief Executive: Howard Raynor.

Bridgwater Arts Centre 11-13 Castle Street, Bridgwater, Somerset TA6 3DD **t** 01278 422700 or 01278 422701 **f** 01278 447402 Contact: Charlie Dearden Seated Capacity: 196 Standing Capacity: 186

Bridlington Spa Theatre And Royal Hall South Marine Drive, Bridlington, East Yorkshire YO15 3JH **t** 01262 678255 **f** 01262 604625 Contact: Rob Clutterham Seated Capacity: 1800 Standing Capacity: 3200

Brighton Centre Kings Road, Brighton, Sussex BN1 2GR **t** 01273 290131 or 0870 9009100 **f** 01273 779980 **e** b-centre@pavilion.co.uk **w** brightoncentre.co.uk Gen Mgr: Steve Piper. Seated Capacity: 4273 Standing Capacity: 5127

Brighton Dome 29 New Road, Brighton, East Sussex BN1 1UG **t** 01273 261530 **f** 01273 261543 **e** events.admin@brighton-dome.org.uk **w** brighton-dome.org.uk GM: Steve Bagnall. Seated Capacity: 1800 Standing Capacity: 1800

Bristol Hippodrome St Augustine's Parade, Bristol BS1 4UZ **t** 0117 926 5524 **f** 0117 925 1661 Gen Mgr: John Wood. Seated Capacity: 1981

Bristol University, Anson Rooms University of Bristol Union, Queens Road, Clifton, Bristol BS8 1LN **t** 0117 954 5810 **f** 0117 954 5817 **e** ents-ubu@bristol.ac.uk **w** ansonrooms.co.uk Ents Mgr: Kay Lowrie. Seated Capacity: 600 Standing Capacity: 900

Broadstairs Pavilion Harbour Street, Broadstairs, Kent CT9 1EY **t** 01843 865726 Seated Capacity: 260 Standing Capacity: 340

The Bruce Hotel Cornwall Street, East Kilbride, Lanarkshire G74 1AF **t** 013552 29771 **f** 013552 42216

Brunel University Student Union, Runnymede Campus, Coopers Hill Lane, Egham, Surrey TW20 0JZ **t** 01784 435508 Standing Capacity: 320

Brunton Theatre Ladywell Way, Musselburgh, Edinburgh EH21 6AA **t** 0131 665 9900 **f** 0131 665 7495 Contact: Lesley Smith Seated Capacity: 302

Buckinghamshire College Newland Park Campus, Gorelands Lane, Chalfont St Giles, Buckinghamshire HP8 4AD **t** 01494 871225 **f** 01494 871954

Bull & Gate Promotions 389 Kentish Town Road, London NW5 2TJ **t** 020 7093 4820 or 020 7485 5358 **f** 020 7093 4821 **e** info@bullandgate.co.uk **w** bullandgate.co.uk Bookers: Andy Clarke & Phil Avey. Standing Capacity: 150

The Bullingdon Arms 162 Cowley Road, Oxford OX4 1UE **t** 01865 244516 **f** 01865 202457 **e** info@thebullingdon.com **w** thebullingdon.co.uk Manager: Mike Laudat. Seated Capacity: 200 Standing Capacity: 280

Burnley Mechanics Manchester Road, Burnley, Lancashire BB11 1HH **t** 01282 664411

Caird Hall Complex City Square, Dundee, Tayside DD1 3BB **t** 01382 434451 **f** 01382 434451 Contact: Susan Pasfield Seated Capacity: 2400 Standing Capacity: 2300

Cambridge Arts Theatre 6 St Edward's Passage, Cambridge CB2 3PJ **t** 01223 578933 **f** 01223 578997 **e** smarsh@cambridgeartstheatre.com **w** cambridgeartstheatre.com Contact: Ian Ross Seated Capacity: 660

Cambridge Corn Exchange 3 Parsons Court, Wheeler St, Cambridge CB2 3QE **t** 01223 457555 admin or 01223 357851 **f** 01223 457559 admin **e** admin.cornex@cambridge.gov.uk **w** cornex.co.uk Asst Head - Arts & Ents: Graham Saxby. Seated Capacity: 1200 Standing Capacity: 1837

Cambridge Guildhall Cambridge City Council, Market Square, Cambridge CB2 3QJ **t** 01223 457000 **f** 01223 463364 Seated Capacity: 699 Standing Capacity: 400

Cambridge University Student Union, 11-12 Trumpington Street, Cambridge CB2 1QA **t 01223 356454** f 01223 323244

Canterbury Christ Church University College Student Union, North Holmes Road, Canterbury, Kent CT1 1QU **t** 01227 782080 **f** 01227 458287 **e** ents@cant.ac.uk **w** c4online.net Ents & Marketing Mgr: Matt Wynter. Standing Capacity: 450

Cardiff International Arena Mary Ann Street, Cardiff CF10 2EQ **t** 029 2023 4500 or 029 2023 4600 **f** 029 2023 4501 **w** sfx-europe.com/cia GM: Graham Walters. Seated Capacity: 4994 Standing Capacity: 6700

Cardiff University Students Union, Park Place, Cardiff CF10 3QN **t** 029 2078 1400 or 029 2078 1456 **f** 029 2078 1407 **e** westawayj@cardiff.ac.uk **w** cardiffstudents.com Ents Mgr: Josh Westaway. Seated Capacity: 100 Standing Capacity: 300

Cargo Kingsland Viaduct, 83 Rivington St, Shoreditch, London EC2A 3AY **t** 020 7739 3440 **f** 020 7739 3441 **e** info@cargo-london.com **w** cargo-london.com Events & Bookings Mgr: Ben Robertson. Seated Capacity: 500

Carling Academy Birmingham/Bar Academy 52-54 Dale End, Birmingham, West Midlands B4 7LS **t** 0121 262 3000 **f** 0121 236 2241 **e** mail@birmingham-academy.co.uk **w** birmingham-academy.co.uk GM: Richard Maides. Standing Capacity: 2700

Carling Academy Bristol Frogmore St, Bristol BS1 5NA **t** 0117 927 9227 **f** 0117 927 9295 **e** mail@bristol-academy.co.uk **w** bristol-academy.co.uk GM: Helen Spillane. Standing Capacity: 1900

Carling Academy Brixton 211 Stockwell Road, Brixton, London SW9 9SL **t** 020 7771 3000 admin **f** 020 7738 4427 **e** mail@brixton-academy.co.uk **w** brixton-academy.co.uk Gen Mgr: Nigel Downs. Standing Capacity: 4921

Carling Academy Glasgow 121 Eglinton Street, Glasgow G5 9NT **t** 0141 418 3000 **f** 0141 418 3001 **e** mail@glasgow-academy.co.uk **w** glasgow-academy.co.uk GM: David Laing. Standing Capacity: 2500

Carling Academy Islington / Bar Academy N1 Centre, 16 Parkfield Street, London N1 0PS **t** 020 7288 4400 or 020 7288 4403 **f** 020 7288 4401 **e** mail@islington-academy.co.uk **w** islington-academy.co.uk GM: Lucinda Brown. Standing Capacity: 800

Carling Academy Liverpool 11-13 Hotham Street, Liverpool L3 5UF **t** 0151 707 3200 **f** 0151 707 3201 **e** mail@liverpool-academy.co.uk **w** liverpool-academy.co.uk GM: Steve Hoyland. Admin: 11-13 Hotham Street, Liverpool L3 5UF. Standing Capacity: 1200

Carling Apollo Manchester Stockport Road, Ardwick Green, Manchester M12 6AP **t** 0161 273 6921 **f** 0870 749 0779 **e** manchester.apollo@clearchannel.co.uk **w** ccLive.co.uk GM: Rob O'Shea. Seated Capacity: 2693 Standing Capacity: 3500

Carlisle Sands Centre The Sands, Carlisle, Cumbria CA1 1JQ **t** 01228 625208 **f** 01228 625666 **e** sueb@carlisle-city.gov.uk **w** 4leisure.org.uk Ents Prog Mgr: Sue Baty. Seated Capacity: 1414 Standing Capacity: 1750

Carnegie Hall East Port, Dunfermline, Fife KY12 7JA **t** 01383 314110 or 01383 314127 **f** 01383 314131 Arts Co-ordinator: Evan Henderson. Seated Capacity: 590

Carnegie Theatre Finkle Street, Workington, Cumbria CA14 2BD **t** 01900 602122 **f** 01900 67143 **e** carnegie@allerdale.gov.uk Mgr: Paul Sherwin. Seated Capacity: 354

Cathouse 15 Union Street, Glasgow, Lanarkshire G1 3RB **t** 0141 248 6606 **f** 0141 248 6741

The Cathouse 15 Union Street, Glasgow G1 3RB **t** 0141 248 6606 **f** 0141 248 6741 **w** cplweb.com MD: Donald Macleod. Standing Capacity: 400

The Cavern Club 83-84 Queen Street, Exeter, Devon EX4 3RP **t** 01392 495370 or 01392 258070 **f** 01392 271625 **e** exetercavern@hotmail.com **w** cavernclub.co.uk Dir: Patrick Cunningham. Standing Capacity: 250

The Cavern Club. 8 Mathew Street, Liverpool, Merseyside L2 6RE **t** 0151 236 1964

Cecil Sharp House 2 Regents Park Road, London NW1 7AY **t** 020 7485 2206 **f** 020 7284 0534 **e** info@efdss.org **w** efdss.org Events Mgr: Nicola Elwell. Seated Capacity: 400 Standing Capacity: 450

University of Central England Student Union, Franchise Street, Perry Barr, Birmingham B42 2SU **t** 0121 331 6801 **f** 0121 331 6802 **w** uce.ac.uk Standing Capacity: 350

Central Hall, Westminster Storey's Gate, Westminster, London SW1H 9NH **t** 020 7222 8010 **f** 020 7222 6883 **e** info@c-h-w.co.uk **w** c-h-w.co.uk GM: Michael Sharp. Seated Capacity: 2350

Central Lancashire University Student Union, Fylde Road, Preston, Lancashire PR1 2TQ **t** 01772 513200 **f** 01772 894975 **e** suents@uclan.ac.uk **w** yourunion.co.uk Ents Mgr: David Evans. Standing Capacity: 1460

Central Pier Theatre Promenade, Blackpool, Lancashire FY1 5BB **t** 01253 623422 **f** 01253 752427 Seated Capacity: 550

The Central Theatre 170 High Street, Chatham, Kent ME4 4AS **t** 01634 848584 **f** 01634 827711 Contact: Tony Hill Seated Capacity: 945

The Charlotte 8 Oxford Street, Leicester LE1 5XZ **t** 0116 255 3956 **e** charlotte@stayfree.co.uk **w** thecharlotte.co.uk Manager/Owner: Andy Wright. Standing Capacity: 390

Charter Hall Colchester Leisure World, Cowdray Avenue, Colchester, Essex CO1 1YH **t** 01206 282946 or 01206 282020 **f** 01206 282916 or 01206 282024 **e** claire.jackson@colchester.gov.uk Event Co-ordinator: Claire Jackson. Seated Capacity: 1216 Standing Capacity: 1216

Cheese & Grain Market Yard, Frome, Somerset BA11 1BE **t** 01373 455768 **f** 01373 455765 **e** office@cheeseandgrain.co.uk **w** cheeseandgrain.co.uk Event Mgr: Nial Joyce. Standing Capacity: 800

Chelsea School Of Art Student Union, 388-396 Oxford Street, London W1N 9HE **t** 020 7514 6270 **f** 020 7514 7838

Cheltenham Town Hall Imperial Square, Cheltenham, Gloucestershire GL50 1QA **t** 01242 521621 or 01242 227979 **f** 01242 573902 **e** TimHu@cheltenham.gov.uk **w** cheltenham.gov.uk/events Ents & Mktg Mgr: Tim Hulse. Seated Capacity: 1008 Standing Capacity: 1008

Chequer Mead Theatre & Arts Centre De La Warr Road, East Grinstead, West Sussex RH19 3BS **t** 01342 325577 **f** 01342 325587 **e** info@chequermead.org.uk **w** chequermead.org.uk Head of Programming: Annie Carpenter. Seated Capacity: 320

Chester College - Warrington Campus Student Union, Padgate Campus, Fearnhead, Warrington, Cheshire WA2 0DB **t** 01925 821336 **f** 01925 838085 **e** studentsunion@warr.ac.uk Entertainments Officer: Vasilis Stylianos. Seated Capacity: 400 Standing Capacity: 500

Chesterfield Arts Centre Chesterfield College, Sheffield Road, Chesterfield, Derbyshire S41 7LL **t** 01246 500578 **f** 01246 500578 Co-ordinator: Bernie Hayter. Seated Capacity: 250

Chingford Assembly Hall Station Road, Chingford, London E4 8NU **t** 020 8529 0555 Contact: Halls Mgr

The Citadel Arts Centre Waterloo Street, St Helens, Merseyside WA10 1PX **t** 01744 735436

City Varieties Music Hall Swan Street, Leeds LS1 6LW **t** 0113 242 5045 **f** 0113 234 1800 Contact: Mr P Sandeman Seated Capacity: 531

Clair Hall Perrymount Road, Haywards Heath, West Sussex RH19 3DN **t** 01444 455440 **f** 01444 440041

Clickimin Leisure Complex Lochside, Lerwick, Mainland, Shetland Islands ZE1 0PJ **t** 01595 741000 **f** 01595 741001 Contact: Mrs Shona Nisbet Seated Capacity: 1200 Standing Capacity: 1500

Cliffs Pavilion Station Road, Southend-on-Sea, Essex SS0 7RA **t** 01702 331852 or 01702 390657 **f** 01702 433015 or 01702 391573 **e** chasm@cliffspavilion.demon.co.uk Gen Mgr: Charles Mumford. Seated Capacity: 1630 Standing Capacity: 2000

Colchester Arts Centre Church Street, Colchester, Essex CO1 1NF **t** 01206 500900 **f** 01206 500187 **e** colchester.artscentre@virgin.net **w** colchesterartscentre.com Dir: Anthony Roberts. Seated Capacity: 300 Standing Capacity: 400

Colne Municipal Hall Bank House, 61 Albert Road, Colne, Lancashire BB8 0PB **t** 01282 661220 **f** 01282 661221 **e** ghood@pendleleisuretrust.co.uk Devel / Mkt Mgr: Gary Hood. Seated Capacity: 600 Standing Capacity: 700

Colston Hall Colston Street, Bristol BS1 5AR **t** 0117 922 3693 **f** 0117 922 3681 **e** ken_lovell@bristol-city.gov.uk **w** bristol-city.gov.uk/colstonhall General Manager: Ken Lovell. Seated Capacity: 1840 Standing Capacity: 1940

Commonwealth Conference & Events Centre Commonwealth Institute, Kensington High Street, London W8 6NQ **t** 020 7603 3412 **f** 020 7603 9634 **e** coference@commonwealth.org.uk Seated Capacity: 460 Standing Capacity: 800

The Complex 1-5 Parkfield Street, London N1 6NU **t** 020 8961 5490 or 020 7288 1986 **f** 020 8961 9238 or 020 7288 1997 Contact: David Green Standing Capacity: 800

Concordia Leisure Centre Forum Way, Cramlington, Northumberland NE23 6YB **t** 01670 717421 **f** 01670 590648 Seated Capacity: 920

The Congress Theatre Carlisle Road, Eastbourne, East Sussex BN21 4BP **t** 01323 415500 **f** 01323 727369 **e** theatres@eastbourne.gov.uk **w** eastbourne.org Gen Mgr: Chris Jordan. Seated Capacity: 1689

Conway Hall South Place Ethical Society, 25 Red Lion Square, London WC1R 4RL **t** 020 7242 8032 **f** 020 7242 8036 **e** info@conwayhall.org.uk **w** conwayhall.org.uk Hall Manager: Peter Vlachos. Seated Capacity: 300 Standing Capacity: 500

Corby Festival Hall and Theatre Complex George Street, Corby, Northamptonshire NN17 1QB **t** 01536 402551 or 01536 402233 **f** 01536 403748 or 01536 400200 Contact: Gen Mgr Seated Capacity: 970

The Corn Exchange Market Place, Newbury, Berkshire RG14 5BD **t** 01635 582666 **f** 01635 582223 **e** admin@cornexchangenew.co.uk **w** cornexchangenew.com Dir: Michael Bewick. Seated Capacity: 400

Cornwall Coliseum Cornwall Leisure World, Carlyon Bay, St Austell, Cornwall PL25 3RG **t** 01726 814004 or 01726 814261 **f** 01726 817231 Gen Mgr: Sallie Polmounter. Seated Capacity: 2306 Standing Capacity: 3326

Corporation Milton Street, Sheffield, South Yorkshire S1 4JU **t** 0114 276 0262 **f** 0114 252 7606 **e** enquiries@corporation.org.uk **w** corporation.org.uk Contact: Mr M Hobson Seated Capacity: 700 Standing Capacity: 700

Coventry University - The Planet Nightclub Students Union, Priory Street, Coventry, West Midlands CV1 5FJ **t** 01203 571231 or 01203 571228 Gen Mgr: William Blake. Seated Capacity: 1000

Crawley Leisure Centre Haslett Avenue, Crawley, West Sussex RH10 1TS **t** 01293 552941 **f** 01293 533362 **e** dave.watmore@crawley.gov.uk **w** hawth.co.uk Promotions & Ents Mgr: David Watmore. Seated Capacity: 1550 Standing Capacity: 2400

The Crypt 53 Robertson Street, Hastings, East Sussex TN34 1HY **t** 01424 444675 or 01424 424458 **f** 01424 722847 **e** pete@the-crypt.co.uk **w** the-crypt.co.uk Seated Capacity: 350

Cumbernauld Theatre Kildrum, Cumbernauld, Glasgow, Lanarkshire G67 2BN **t** 01236 737235 **f** 01236 738408 or 01236 738408 Artistic Dir: Simon Sharkey. Seated Capacity: 258 Standing Capacity: 300

Dancehouse Theatre 10 Oxford Road, Manchester M1 5QA **t** 0161 237 1413 **f** 0161 237 1408 Mgr: Chrispin Radcliffe. Seated Capacity: 433

Darlaston Town Hall Victoria Road, Wednesbury, West Midlands WS10 8AA **t** 01922 653171 **f** 01922 720885

Darlington Arts Centre Vane Terrace, Darlington, Co Durham DL3 7AX **t** 01325 483271 **f** 01325 365794 Music Programmer: Lynda Winstanley. Seated Capacity: 320

Darlington Civic Theatre Parkgate, Darlington, Co Durham DL1 1RR **t** 01325 468006 **f** 01325 368278 **e** marketing@darlington-arts.co.uk **w** darlington-arts.co.uk Head of Theatre & Arts: Peter Cutchie. Seated Capacity: 909

De La Warr Pavilion Marina, Bexhill-on-Sea, Sussex TN40 1DP **t** 01424 787900 **f** 01424 787940 **e** dlwp@rother.gov.uk Contact: Mike Jolly Seated Capacity: 1004 Standing Capacity: 800

De Montfort Hall Granville Road, Leicester LE1 7RU **t** 0116 233 3111 or 0116 233 3113 **f** 0116 233 3182 **w** demontforthall.co.uk Mgr: Richard Haswell. Seated Capacity: 1973 Standing Capacity: 2300

De Montfort Student Union First Floor, Campus Centre Building, Mill Lane, Leicester LE2 7DR **t** 0116 255 5576 **f** 0116 257 6309 **e** initial+surname@dmu.ac.uk **w** mydsu.com Standing Capacity: 1200

De Montfort University, Bedford Students Union, Pole Hill Avenue, Bedford MK41 9EA **t** 01234 793155 **f** 01234 217738 **e** rhurll@dmu.ac.uk **w** mydsu.com Bar & Events Mgr: Robert Hurll. Standing Capacity: 200

Debates Chamber, Glasgow University Glasgow University, 32 University Avenue, Glasgow G12 8LX **t** 0141 339 8697 **f** 0141 339 8931 **e** libraries@guu.co.uk **w** guu.co.uk Contact: The Porter's Box Standing Capacity: 900

Deeside Leisure Centre Chester Road West, Queensferry, Deeside, Clwyd CH5 1SA **t** 01244 812311 **f** 01244 836287 Seated Capacity: 3500

University of Derby UDSU, Kedleston Road, Derby DE22 1GB **t** 01332 622238 **f** 01332 348846 **e** m.j.shepherd@derby.ac.uk **w** derby.ac.uk/udsu Ents Mgr: Matt Shepherd. Seated Capacity: 700

Derngate 19-21 Guildhall Road, Northampton NN1 1DP **t** 01604 626222 or 01604 624811 **f** 01604 250901 or 01604 233095 **e** postbox@derngate.demon.co.uk **w** derngate.org Contact: Rosemary Jones Seated Capacity: 1500 Standing Capacity: 1550

Dominion Theatre Tottenham Court Road, London W1A 0AQ **t** 01865 782900 **f** 01865 782910 Contact: Nicky Monk Seated Capacity: 2205

Doncaster Dome Doncaster Leisure Park, Bawtry Road, Doncaster, South Yorkshire DN4 7PD **t** 01302 370777 or 01302 370999 **f** 01302 379135 Contact: Michael Hart Seated Capacity: 1850 Standing Capacity: 3264

Doncaster Odeon Hallgate, Doncaster, South Yorkshire DN1 3NL **t** 01302 344626 **f** 01302 340492 Seated Capacity: 1003

Dover Town Hall Biggin Street, Dover, Kent CT16 1DL **t** 01304 201200 **f** 01304 201200 **e** townhall@dover.gov.uk Trevor S Jones: Gen Mgr. Seated Capacity: 500 Standing Capacity: 600

Dublin Castle 94 Parkway, London NW1 7NN **t** 020 8806 2668 or 07956 313239 **f** 020 8806 6444 **e** info@bugbear18.freeserve.co.uk **w** bugbearbookings.com Promoters: Jim & Tony. Standing Capacity: 134

Duchess Of York 71 Vicar Lane, Leeds, West Yorkshire LS1 6QA **t** 0113 268 2184 or 0113 242 2110 **e** duchess@btinternet.com **w** fibbers.co.uk Contact: John Keenan Seated Capacity: 250 Standing Capacity: 250

Dudley Town Hall St James's Road, Dudley, West Midlands DY1 1HF **t** 01384 815544 or 01384 815577 **f** 01384 815534 or 01384 815599 Hall Mgr: Andrew Grimshaw. Seated Capacity: 1060 Standing Capacity: 1000

Dundee University Student Association, Airlie Place, Dundee, Tayside DD1 4HP **t** 01382 221841 **f** 01382 227124 **w** dusa.dundee.ac.uk Ents & Publicity Mgr: Trevor San. Seated Capacity: 600 Standing Capacity: 600

Durham University Student Union, Dunelm House, New Elvet, Co Durham DH1 3AN **t** 0191 374 3331 **f** 0191 374 3328 **e** dsu.ents@dur.ac.uk Contact: Jez Light Seated Capacity: 550 Standing Capacity: 800

Ealing Town Hall Halls & Events, Ground Floor, Perceval House, London W5 2HL **t** 020 8758 5624 or 020 8758 8079 **f** 020 8566 5088 **e** HandM@Ealing.Gov.uk **w** Ealing.Gov.uk/HE&M Head of Halls & Events: M Hand. Seated Capacity: 500 Standing Capacity: 500

Earls Court/Olympia Group Ltd Earls Court Exhibition Centre, Warwick Road, London SW5 9TA **t** 020 7370 8009 **f** 020 7370 8223 **e** marketing@eco.co.uk **w** eco.co.uk Commercial Director: Nigel Nathan. Seated Capacity: 18000 Standing Capacity: 22000

East Kilbride Civic Centre Andrew Street, East Kilbride, Lanarkshire G74 1AB **t** 01355 806000

East London University Romford Road, London E15 4LZ **t** 020 8223 3000 **f** 020 8223 3000

University of East London Union Building, Longbridge Road, Dagenham, Essex RM8 2AS **t** 020 8590 6017 **f** 020 8597 6987

Eastbourne Theatres - Winter Garden Compton Street, Eastbourne, East Sussex BN21 4BP **t** 01323 415500 **f** 01323 727369 **e** theatres@eastbourne.gov.uk **w** eastbourne.org Gen Mgr: Chris Jordan. Seated Capacity: 1100 Standing Capacity: 1200

Eden Court Theatre Bishops Road, Inverness IV3 5SA **t** 01463 239841 or 01463 234234 **f** 01463 713810 **e** ecmail@cali.co.uk **w** edencourt.uk.com Contact: Colin Marr Seated Capacity: 810

Edinburgh International Conference Centre The Exchange, Morrison Street, Edinburgh EH3 8EE **t** 0131 300 3000 **f** 0131 300 3030 **e** sales@eicc.co.uk **w** eicc.co.uk Snr Sales Team Leader: Lesley Stephen. Seated Capacity: 1200 Standing Capacity: 1200

Edinburgh Playhouse 18-22 Greenside Place, Edinburgh EH1 3AA **t** 0131 557 2692 **f** 0131 557 6520 **w** edinburgh-playhouse.co.uk Gen Mgr: Andrew Lyst. Seated Capacity: 3056

Edinburgh University Students Association, Mandela Centre, 5/2 Bristo Square, Edinburgh EH8 9AL **t** 0131 650 2656 or 0131 650 2649 **f** 0131 668 4177 **e** ian.evans@eusa.ed.ac.uk **w** eusa.ed.ac.uk Entertainments Manager: Ian Evans. Standing Capacity: 1200

Electric Ballroom 184 Camden High Street, London NW1 8QP **t** 020 7485 9006 or 020 7485 9007 **f** 020 7284 0745 **e** info@electricballroom.co.uk Standing Capacity: 1100

Elgin Town Hall 5 Trinity Place, Elgin IV30 1VL **t** 01343 543451 **f** 01343 563410 Contact: Eric McGilvery Seated Capacity: 723

Ellesmere Port Civic Hall Civic Way, Ellesmere Port, South Wirral, Cheshire CH65 0BE **t** 0151 356 6780 or 0151 356 6890 **f** 0151 355 0508 Contact: Miles Veitch Seated Capacity: 636

Embassy Centre Grand Parade, Skegness, Lincolnshire PE25 2UN **t** 01754 768444 or 01507 329411 **f** 01754 761737 or 01507 327149 Head of Leisure & Tourism: Bob Suich. Seated Capacity: 1158 Standing Capacity: 1158

Empire Theatre High Street West, Sunderland, Tyne and Wear SR1 3EX **t** 0191 510 0545 or 0191 514 2517 **f** 0191 553 7427 **e** ticketmaster.com **w** empiretheatre.co.uk Contact: Stuart Anderson Seated Capacity: 1875 Standing Capacity: 1875

The Empire Milton Keynes Leisure Plaza, 1 South Row, Charles Way, Milton Keynes, Buckinghamshire MK9 1BL **t** 01908 394 074 **f** 01908 696 768 **e** info@empire-mk.co.uk **w** empire-mk.co.uk Promotions Manager: Nicky Harris. Standing Capacity: 2000

The English Folk Dance and Song Society Cecil Sharp House, 2 Regent's Park Road, London NW1 7AY **t** 020 7485 2206 **f** 020 7284 0534 **e** info@efdss.org **w** efdss.org Publications Manager: Felicity Greenland. Events Co-ordinator: Nicola Elwell. Seated Capacity: 400 Standing Capacity: 540

English National Opera The London Coliseum, St Martin's Lane, London WC2N 4ES **t** 020 7836 0111 Gen Mgr: Nicholas Payne. Seated Capacity: 2358

Esquires 60A Bromham Road, Bedford MK40 2QG **t** 01234 340120 **f** 01234 356630

The Event II Kingswest, West Street, Brighton, East Sussex **t** 01273 732627 **f** 01273 208996 Info Mgr: Dan Boorman. Standing Capacity: 1920

Everyman Theatre 5-9 Hope Street, Liverpool, Merseyside **t** 0151 708 0338 **f** 0151 709 0398 **e** info@everymanplayhouse.com **w** everyman.merseyworld.com/ Contact: The General Mgr Seated Capacity: 450

Evesham Arts Centre Victoria Avenue, Evesham, Worcestershire WR11 4QH **t** 01386 48883 Contact: LA Griffith-Jones Seated Capacity: 300

Exeter Phoenix Bradninch Place, Gandy Street, Exeter, Devon EX4 3LS **t** 01392 667056 **f** 01392 667599 The Arts Mgr: Andy Morley. Seated Capacity: 216 Standing Capacity: 500

Fairfield Halls Park Lane, Croydon, Surrey CR9 1DG **t** 020 8681 0821 **e** dbarr@fairfield.co.uk **w** croydon.qou.uk/fairfield/ Head of Artistic Planning: Nick Leigh. Seated Capacity: 1550

Falmouth Arts Centre Church Street, Falmouth, Cornwall TR11 3EG **t** 01326 212719 **e** jon@falmouthharts.org **w** falmouthharts.org GM: Shaun Kavanagh. Seated Capacity: 200

Farnborough Recreation Centre 1 Westmead, Farnborough, Hampshire GU14 7LD **t** 01252 370411 **f** 01252 372280 Standing Capacity: 2100

Fat Sam's 31 South Ward Road, Dundee, Angus DD1 1PU **t** 01382 228181 **f** 01382 228181 **e** sam@fatsams.co.uk **w** fatsams.co.uk Mgr: Derek Anderson. Seated Capacity: 480 Standing Capacity: 480

Ferneham Hall, Fareham Osborn Road, Fareham, Hampshire PO16 0TL **t** 01329 824864 **f** 01329 281486 **e** rdavies@fareham.gov.uk **w** fareham.gov.uk Head of Arts & Ents: Russell Davies. Seated Capacity: 752 Standing Capacity: 800

Festival City Theatres Trust 13/29 Nicolson Street, Edinburgh EH8 9FT **t** 0131 662 1112 **f** 0131 667 0744 **e** empire@eft.co.uk **w** eft.co.uk Acting GM: David W S Todd. Seated Capacity: 1900

The Fibbers Group Units 8-12, Stonebow House, Stonebow, York, North Yorkshire YO1 7NP **t** 01904 466148 **f** 01904 675315 **e** fibbers@fibbers.co.uk **w** fibbers.co.uk MD: Tim Hornsby. Seated Capacity: 200 Standing Capacity: 250

Fibbers Stonebow House, The Stonebow, York YO1 7NP **t** 01904 651250 **f** 01904 651250 **e** fibbers@fibbers.co.uk **w** fibbers.co.uk

Fleece & Firkin 12 St Thomas Street, Bristol BS1 6JJ **t** 0117 927 7150

Fort Regent Leisure Centre St Helier, Jersey, Channel Islands JE2 4UX **t** 01534 500009 **f** 01534 500225 **e** c.stanier@gov.je **w** esc.gov.je Events Mgr: Colin Stanier. Seated Capacity: 1974 Standing Capacity: 2500

Forum 28 28 Duke Street, Barrow-in-Furness, Cumbria LA14 1HH **t** 01229 820000 **f** 01229 894942 **e** nward@barrowbc.gov.uk **w** barrowbc.gov.uk Bookings Mgr: Neil Ward. Seated Capacity: 485 Standing Capacity: 720

The Forum 9-17 Highgate Road, London NW5 1JY **t** 020 7284 1001 **f** 020 7284 1102 **w** meanfiddler.com Seated Capacity: 1400 Standing Capacity: 2110

The Foundry Beak Street, Birmingham, West Midlands B1 1LS **t** 0121 622 1894 **w** dr-p.demon.co.uk/foundry.html

The Fridge 1 Town Hall Parade, Brixton Hill, London SW2 1RJ **t** 020 7326 5100 **f** 020 7274 2879 **e** info@fridge.co.uk **w** fridge.co.uk Mgr: Gary Baker. Seated Capacity: 1100 Standing Capacity: 1100

Futurist Theatre Foreshore Road, Scarborough, North Yorkshire YO11 1NT **t** 01723 370742 **f** 01723 365456 Standing Capacity: 2155

G-MEX Centre Windmill Street, City Centre, Manchester M2 3GX **t** 0161 834 2700 **f** 0161 833 3168 **e** email@g-mex.co.uk **w** g-mex.co.uk Contact: Paul Ashton Standing Capacity: 10500

Gaiety Theatre , Douglas, Isle of Man **t** 01624 620046

Garage 20-22 Highbury Corner, London N5 1RD **t** 020 8961 5490 or 020 7607 1818 **f** 020 8961 9238 or 020 7609 0846 **e** joady@meanfiddler.co.uk Bking Mgr: Joady Thornton. Standing Capacity: 500

The Garage 490 Sauchiehall Street, Glasgow G2 3LW **t** 0141 332 1120 **f** 0141 332 1130 **w** cplweb.com MD: Donald Macleod. Standing Capacity: 700

The Gardner Arts Centre University Of Sussex, Falmer, Brighton, East Sussex BN1 9RA **t** 01273 685447 **f** 01273 678551 **e** gardner-arts@pavilion.co.uk **w** gardnerarts.co.uk Dir: Sue Webster. Seated Capacity: 476 Standing Capacity: 476

Garrick Theatre Barrington Road, Altrincham, Cheshire WA14 1HZ **t** 0161 929 8779 (mktg) or 0161 928 1677 (box) Seated Capacity: 472

Gateshead International Stadium Neilson Road, Gateshead, Tyne & Wear NE10 0EF **t** 0191 478 1687 **f** 0191 477 1315 Seated Capacity: 11000 Standing Capacity: 38000

Glamorgan University Student Union, Forest Grove, Treforest, Pontypridd, Mid Glamorgan CF37 1UF **t** 01443 408227 **f** 01443 491589 Contact: Jason Crimmins Seated Capacity: 200 Standing Capacity: 500

Glasgow Caledonian University Students Union, 70 Cowcaddens Road, Glasgow, Lanarkshire G4 0BA **t** 0141 332 0681 **f** 0141 353 0029 **e** d.boner@gcal.ac.uk **w** sa.gcal.ac.uk Contact: Denis Boner Standing Capacity: 595

Glasgow City Halls 32 Albion Street, Glasgow, Lanarkshire G1 1QU **t** 0141 287 5005 **f** 0141 287 5533 Susan Deighan: Head of Programming. Seated Capacity: 1121 Standing Capacity: 800

Glasgow Garage 490 Sauchiehall Street, Glasgow, Lanarkshire G2 3LW **t** 0141 332 1120 **f** 0141 332 1120 Contact: Donald Macleod Standing Capacity: 600

Glasgow King's Theatre Glasgow City Council, Cultural and Leisure Services, 229 George Street, Glasgow G1 1QU **t** 0141 287 3922 **f** 0141 287 5533 Contact: Pauline Murphy Seated Capacity: 1785

Glasgow Pavilion Theatre 121 Renfield Street, Glasgow, Lanarkshire G2 3AX **t** 0141 332 7579 or 0141 332 1846 **f** 0141 331 2745 Theatre Mgr: Iain Gordon. Seated Capacity: 1449

Glasgow Royal Concert Hall 2 Sauchiehall Street, Glasgow, Lanarkshire G2 3NY **t** 0141 332 6633 **f** 0141 333 9123 **e** grch@grch.scotnet.co.uk **w** grch.com Seated Capacity: 2417

Glastonbury Festival Worthy Farm, Pilton, Shepton Mallet, Somerset BA4 4BY **t** 01749 890470 **f** 01749 890285 **e** worthy@glastonbury-festivals.co.uk **w** glastonburyfestivals.co.uk Standing Capacity: 100000

Glee Club The Arcadian Centre, Hurst Street, Birmingham, West Midlands B5 4TD **t** 0870 241 5093 or 07973 121 95 **e** markus_sargeant@yahoo.com **w** glee.co.uk Promoter: Markus Sargeant. Seated Capacity: 400 Standing Capacity: 400

The Globe Blackpool Pleasure Beach, Ocean Boulevard, Blackpool, Lancashire FY4 1EZ **t** 01253 341033 **f** 01253 401098 Contact: Michelle Barratt Seated Capacity: 940

Gloucester Leisure Centre Bruton Way, Gloucester GL1 1DT **t** 01452 385310 or 01452 306498 Seated Capacity: 2100 Standing Capacity: 2500

Goldiggers Timber Street, Chippenham, Wiltshire SN15 3BP **t** 01249 656444 **f** 01249 443835 **e** goldinfo@aol.com Standing Capacity: 1540

Goldsmiths College Student Union Dixon Road, New Cross, London SE14 6NW **t** 020 8692 1406 **f** 020 8694 6789 **e** info@gold.ac.uk **w** gold.ac.uk Entertainment Manager: Nat Perkins. Seated Capacity: 350 Standing Capacity: 600

Gordon Craig Theatre Stevenage Arts & Leisure Ctr, Lytton Way, Stevenage, Hertfordshire SG1 1LZ **t** 01438 242642 **f** 01438 242342 **e** gordoncraig@stevenage-leisure.co.uk **w** stevenage.gov.uk/GordonCraig Bookings Mgr: Bob Bustance. Standing Capacity: 500

Robert Gordon University Student Union, 60 Schoolhill, Aberdeen, Grampian AB10 1JQ **t** 01224 262262 **f** 01224 262268 **e** rgusa@rgu.ac.uk **w** rgu.ac.uk Seated Capacity: 150 Standing Capacity: 200

The Grafton West Derby Road, Liverpool L6 9BY **t** 0151 263 2303 **f** 0151 263 4985 Seated Capacity: 1425

Grand Opera House Great Victoria Street, Belfast, Co Antrim BT2 7HR **t** 028 9024 0411 **f** 028 9023 6842 **w** goh.co.uk Contact: Derek Nicholls Seated Capacity: 1001

Grand Theatre Church Street, Blackpool, Lancashire FY1 1HT **t** 01253 290111 **f** 01253 751767 **e** gm@blackpoolgrand.co.uk **w** blackpoolgrand.co.uk Contact: Stephanie Sir Seated Capacity: 1200

Grand Theatre Wolverhampton, West Midlands **t** 01902 429212

Great Grimsby Town Hall Town Hall Square, Great Grimsby, North East Lincolnshire DN31 1HX **t** 01472 324109 **f** 01472 324108 Contact: John Callison Seated Capacity: 350 Standing Capacity: 400

Grimsby Auditorium Cromwell Road, Grimsby, South Humberside DN31 2BH **t** 01472 323100 **f** 01472 323102 Contact: Mr Morris

Group Theatre Bedford Street, Belfast, Co Antrim BT2 7FF **t** 028 9032 3900 **f** 028 9024 7199 Contact: Pat Falls Seated Capacity: 221

Guildford Civic London Road, Guildford, Surrey GU1 2AA **t** 01483 444720 **f** 01483 301982 **e** info@guildford-civic.co.uk **w** guildford-civic.co.uk Dep Mgr, Sales & Dev't: Heather Richardson. Seated Capacity: 1150 Standing Capacity: 1500

Guildhall 23 Eastgate Street, Gloucester GL1 1QR **t** 01452 505089

Guildhall Lancaster Road, Preston, Lancashire PR1 1HT **t** 01772 203456

Hackney Empire Ltd. 291 Mare Street, London E8 1EJ **t** 020 8510 4500 **f** 020 8510 4530 **e** info@hackneyempire.co.uk **w** hackneyempire.co.uk Programmer: Claire Muldoon. Seated Capacity: 1300 Standing Capacity: 1500

Halfmoon, Putney 93 Lower Richmond Road, London SW15 1EU **t** 020 8780 9383 **f** 020 8789 7863 **e** office@halfmoon.co.uk **w** halfmoon.co.uk Bookings/Promotions Mgr: Carrie Davies. Seated Capacity: 150 Standing Capacity: 230

Hare And Hounds High Street, King's Heath, Birmingham B14 7JZ **t** 0121 444 2081 or 0121 444 3578 Contact: The Manager Seated Capacity: 140

Harlow Bandstand Harlow Council Leisure Service, Latton Bush Centre, Southern Way, Harlow, Essex CM18 7BL **t** 01279 446404 **f** 01279 446431 Contact: Recreation Services Officer Standing Capacity: 5000

Harlow Showground Harlow Council Leisure Service, Latton Bush Centre, Southern Way, Harlow, Essex CM18 7BL **t** 01279 446404 **f** 01279 446431 Contact: Recreation Services Officer Standing Capacity: 15000

Harrogate International Centre Kings Road, Harrogate, North Yorkshire HG1 5LA **t** 01423 500500 **f** 01423 537270 **e** sales@harrogateinternationalcentre.co.uk **w** harrogateinternationalcentre.co.uk Dir: Paul Lewis. Seated Capacity: 2009 Standing Capacity: 1431

The Hawth, Crawley Hawth Avenue, Crawley, West Sussex RH10 6YZ **t** 01293 552941 **f** 01293 533362 **e** info@hawth.co.uk **w** hawth.co.uk Head Of Arts: Kevin Eason. Seated Capacity: 850 Standing Capacity: 950

Haymarket Theatre 1 Belgrave Gate, Garrick Walk, Leicester LE1 3YQ **t** 0116 253 0021 **f** 0116 251 3310 Seated Capacity: 732

Hazlitt Theatre Earl Street, Maidstone, Kent ME14 1PL **t** 01622 602178 **f** 01622 602194 **e** mandyhare@hazlitt.maidstone.gov.uk **w** hazlitt.org.uk Mgr: Mandy Hare. Seated Capacity: 381 Standing Capacity: 400

Heriot-Watt University Students Asso. Students Association, The Union, Riccarton Campus, Edinburgh EH14 4AS **t** 0131 451 5333 **f** 0131 451 5344 **e** K.Easton@hw.ac.uk **w** hwusa.org Entertainment Mgr: Keith Easton. Seated Capacity: 250 Standing Capacity: 450

University of Hertfordshire Student Union, College Lane, Hatfield, Hertfordshire AL10 9AB **t** 01707 285008 or 01707 285000 **f** 01707 286151 **e** uhsu@herts.ac.uk **w** uhsu.herts.ac.uk/ Contact: Venue Mgr Seated Capacity: 450 Standing Capacity: 1300

Hexagon Queen's Walk, Reading, Berkshire RG1 7UA **t** 0118 939 0123 **f** 0118 939 0028 or 0118 939 0004 **e** boxoffice@readingarts.com **w** readingarts.com Prog Co-ordinator: Charity Gordon. Seated Capacity: 1484 Standing Capacity: 1686

Hippodrome Leicester Square, London WC2 7JH **t** 020 7437 4311 **f** 020 7434 4225 **w** londonhippodrome.com Contact: Annette Morris Seated Capacity: 700 Standing Capacity: 1945

His Majesty's Theatre Rosemount Viaduct, Aberdeen AB25 1GL **t** 01224 637788 **f** 01224 632519 **e** venues@arts-rec.aberdeen.net.uk **w** aberdeencity.gov.uk/venues GM: Duncan Hendry. Seated Capacity: 1446

The Hive, Glasgow University Glasgow University, 32 University Avenue, Glasgow G12 8LX **t** 0141 339 8697 **f** 0141 339 8931 **e** libraries@guu.co.uk **w** guu.co.uk Contact: The Porter's Box Standing Capacity: 1000

The Hope & Anchor 207 Upper Street, London N1 1BZ **t** 020 8806 2668 or 07956 313239 **f** 020 8806 6444 **e** info@bugbear18.freeserve.co.uk **w** bugbearbookings.com Promoters: Jim & Tony. Standing Capacity: 80

Horseshoe Bar Blackpool Pleasure Beach, Ocean Boulevard, Blackpool, Lancashire FY4 1EZ **t** 01253 341033 **f** 01253 401098 **e** michelle.barratt@bpbltd.com **w** bpbltd.com Contact: Michelle Barratt Seated Capacity: 400

Horsham Arts Centre North Street, Horsham, West Sussex RH12 1RL **t** 01403 259708 or 01403 268689 **f** 01403 211502 Mgr: Michael Gattrell. Seated Capacity: 438

Hove Centre @ Hove Town Hall Norton Road, Hove, East Sussex BN3 4AH **t** 01273 292902 **f** 01273 292936 **e** venuehire@brighton-hove.gov.uk Admins Officer: Amanda-Jane Stone. Seated Capacity: 1000 Standing Capacity: 1000

Huddersfield Town Hall (also Batley, Dewsbury) Cultural Services HQ, Red Doles Lane, Huddersfield, West Yorkshire HD2 1YF **t** 01484 226300 **f** 01484 221541 **e** julia.robinson@kirkleesmc.gov.uk Town Halls Manager: Julia Robinson. Seated Capacity: 1200 Standing Capacity: 700

Huddersfield University Student Union, Queensgate, Huddersfield HD1 3DH **t** 01484 538156 **f** 01484 432333 **e**su-comms@hud.ac.uk Venue Mgr: Jerome Curran. Ents Co-ordinator: Kerry Stead. Seated Capacity: 250 Standing Capacity: 300

Hull Arena Kingston Street, Hull, East Yorkshire HU1 2DZ **t** 01482 325252 **f** 01482 216066 **w** hullarena.co.uk Contact: Linda Parker Seated Capacity: 3250 Standing Capacity: 3750

Hull City Hall Victoria Square, Hull, East Yorkshire HU1 3NA **t** 01482 613880 **f** 01482 613961 Programming Mgr: Mike Lister. Seated Capacity: 1400 Standing Capacity: 1800

Hull New Theatre Kingston Square, Kingston Upon Hull, East Yorkshire HU1 3HF **t** 01482 613880 **f** 01482 613961 Programming Mgr: Michael Lister. Seated Capacity: 1189

Hull University University House, Cottingham Road, Hull, East Yorkshire HU2 9BT **t** 01482 466253 **f** 01482 466280 **e** j.a.brooks@hull.ac.uk **w** hull.ac.uk Ents Co-ordinator: James Brooks. Standing Capacity: 1500

ICA Theatre The Mall, London SW1Y 5AH **t** 020 7930 0493 **f** 020 7306 0122 **e** jamiee@ica.org.uk **w** ica.org.uk Dir of Live Arts: Andrew Missingham. Seated Capacity: 167 Standing Capacity: 350

Imperial College Union, Beit Quad, Prince Consort Road, London SW7 2BB **t** 020 7594 8068 **f** 020 7594 8065 **e** ents@ic.ac.uk **w** union.ic.ac.uk Ents Manager: Ham Al-Rubaie. Seated Capacity: 300 Standing Capacity: 450

Imperial Gardens 299 Camberwell New Road, London SE5 0TF **t** 020 7252 6000 **f** 020 7252 7180 **e** info@imperialgardens.co.uk **w** imperialgardens.co.uk

Inverurie Town Hall Market Place, Inverurie, Aberdeenshire **t** 01467 621610 Seated Capacity: 400

ION 161-165 Ladbroke Grove, London W10 6HJ **t** 020 8960 1702 **w** meanfiddler.com

Ipswich Corn Exchange King Street, Ipswich, Suffolk IP1 1DH **t** 01473 433133 **f** 01473 433450 **e** firstname.lastname@ipswich.gov.uk **w** ipswichcornexchange.com Operations & Events Mgr: Craig Oldfield. East Anglia's largest multi-purpose hiring venue. Seated Capacity: 900 Standing Capacity: 1000

Ipswich Regent Theatre 3 St Helens Street, Ipswich, Suffolk IP4 1HE **t** 01473 433555 **f** 01473 433727 **e** firstname.lastname@ipswich.gov.uk **w** ipswichregent.com Manager: Hazel Clover. Seated Capacity: 1781 Standing Capacity: 1781

Irish Centre York Road, Leeds, West Yorkshire LS9 9NT **t** 0113 248 0613

Jackson's Nightclub 4-8 Fisher Street, Carlisle, Cumbria CA3 8RN **t** 01228 596868 **f** 01228 534168 **e** Jnightclub@aol.com **w** Jnightclub.co.uk Promoter/Owner: David Jackson. Standing Capacity: 600

The Jaffa Cake 28 Kings Stables Road, Edinburgh, Lothian EH1 2JY **t** 0131 229 9438

JAGZ At the Station, Station Hill, Ascot, Berks SL5 9EG **t** 01344 878 100 **f** 01344 878 102 **e** roland@jagz.co.uk **w** jagz.co.uk Promotions Manager: Roland Monger. Seated Capacity: 100 Standing Capacity: 150

Jazz Cafe 5 Parkway, Camden Town, London NW1 7PG **t** 020 7916 6060 **f** 020 7267 9219 **e** info@jazzcafe.co.uk **w** jazzcafe.co.uk Promoter: Adrian Gibson. Seated Capacity: 250 Standing Capacity: 400

Jersey Opera House Gloucester Street, St Hellier, Jersey, Channel Islands JE2 3QL **t** 01534 617521 **f** 01534 610624 Contact: Ian Stephens Seated Capacity: 680

Joiner's Arms 141 St Mary Street, Southampton, Hampshire SO14 1NS **t** 023 8022 5612 **f** 01962 878812 **e** vic@liveattherailway.co.uk **w** joinerslive.com Promoter: Vic Toms. Standing Capacity: 250

Jug Of Ale 43 Alcester Road, Moseley, Birmingham, West Midlands B13 8AA **t** 0121 449 1082

The Junction Clifton Road, Cambridge CB1 7GX **t** 01223 578000 **f** 01223 565600 **e** spiral@junction.co.uk **w** junction.co.uk Commercial Prog Mgr: Rob Tinkler. Seated Capacity: 278 Standing Capacity: 850

Kartouche Princes Street, Ipswich, Suffolk IP2 9TD **t** 01473 230666 **f** 01473 232579 **e** info@kartouche.net **w** kartouche.net Manager: Georgie Smith. Standing Capacity: 1450

Keele University Student Union, Keele, Newcastle-under-Lyme, Staffordshire ST5 5BJ **t** 01782 583700 **f** 01782 712671 **e** l.fitzmaurice@keele.ac.uk **w** kusu.net Ents Mgr: Luke Fitzmaurice. Seated Capacity: 400 Standing Capacity: 1100

Kendal Town Hall Highgate, Kendal, Cumbria LA9 4DL **t** 01539 725758 **f** 01539 734457 Bookings: Debbie Mckee. Seated Capacity: 400 Standing Capacity: 400

Kensington Town Hall Royal Borough Kensington & Chelsea, Horton Street, London W8 7NX **t** 020 7361 2220 **f** 020 7361 3442 **e** hall-let@rbkc.gov.uk **w** rbkc.gov.uk Conference/Events Office: Maxine Howitt. Seated Capacity: 860 Standing Capacity: 900

Kettering Arena Thurston Drive, Kettering, Northamptonshire NN15 6PB **t** 01536 414141 **f** 01536 414334 Contact: Tony Remington Seated Capacity: 2000 Standing Capacity: 3000

Kidderminster Town Hall Vicar Street, Kidderminster, Worcestershire DY10 2BL **t** 01562 732158 **f** 01562 750708 Contact: The Mgr Seated Capacity: 450

Kilmarnock Palace Theatre 9 Green Street, Kilmarnock KA1 3BN **t** 01563 537710 or 01563 523590 **f** 01563 573047 Asst Theatre & Ents Mgr: Laura Brown. Standing Capacity: 1100

King Georges Hall Northgate, Blackburn, Lancashire BB2 1AA **t** 01254 582579 **f** 01254 667277 **e** geoff.peake@blackburn.gov.uk **w** kinggeorgeshall.com Events/Promo Mgr: Geoff Peake. Seated Capacity: 1853 Standing Capacity: 2000

King Tut's Wah Wah Hut 272A St Vincent Street, Glasgow G2 5RL **t** 0141 248 5158 **f** 0141 248 5202 **e** kingtuts@dfconcerts.co.uk **w** kingtuts.co.uk Promoter/Venue Mgr: Dave McGeachan. Standing Capacity: 300

King's Hall Exhibition & Conference Centre Balmoral, Belfast, Co Antrim BT9 6GW **t** 028 9066 5225 **f** 028 9066 1264 **e** info@kingshall.co.uk **w** kingshall.co.uk Comm Dir: Philip M Rees. Seated Capacity: 5000 Standing Capacity: 8000

The King's Head 4 Fulham High Street, London SW6 3LQ **t** 020 7751 1044 or 07958 967666 **f** 020 7348 3911 **e** livegigs@mail.com **w** orangepromotions.com Booker & Promoter: Phil Brydon. Seated Capacity: 180

King's Lynn Arts Centre 27-29 King Street, King's Lynn, Norfolk PE30 1HA **t** 01553 765565 **f** 01553 762141 **e** howard.barnes@dial.pipex.com **w** west-norfolk.gov.uk Gen Mgr: Mr Howard Barnes. Seated Capacity: 349

King's Theatre Edinburgh 2 Leven Street, Edinburgh EH3 9LQ **t** 0131 662 1112 **f** 0131 667 0744 **e** empire@eft.co.uk **w** eft.co.uk Gen Mgr & Chief Exec: Stephen Barry. Seated Capacity: 1300

King's WC2 King's College London, Students Union, Macadam Bldg, Surrey Street, London WC2R 2NS **t** 020 7836 7132 **f** 020 7379 9833 **e** Rob.Massy@kclsu.org **w** kclsu.org/events Events Mgr: Rob Massy. Seated Capacity: 400 Standing Capacity: 620

Kingston University Guild Of Students Penrhyn Road, Kingston upon Thames, Surrey KT1 2EE **t** 020 8547 2000 **f** 020 8255 0032 **w** kingston.ac.uk Standing Capacity: 700

Koko (formerly known as Camden Palace) 1A Camden High Street, London NW1 7JE **t** 0870 432 5527 **f** 020 7388 4388 **e** info@koko.uk.com **w** koko.uk.com Manager: Eddie Hill. Standing Capacity: 1500

Komedia 44-47 Gardner Street, Brighton, East Sussex BN1 1KN **t** 01273 647100 or 01273 647101 **f** 01273 647102 **e** admin@komedia.co.uk **w** komedia.co.uk Venue Mgr: Jackie Alexander. Seated Capacity: 210

University of Wales - Lampeter Student Union, Ty Ceredig, Lampeter, Ceredigion SA48 7ED **t** 01570 422619 **f** 01570 422480 **e** ents@lamp.ac.uk **w** lamp.ac.uk Ents Officer: Ian Larsen.

Lancaster University (The Sugar House) Student Union, Slaidburn House, Lancaster LA1 4YT **t** 01524 593765 **f** 01524 846732 **e** c.burston@lancaster.ac.uk **w** lancs.ac.uk/lusu

The Landmark Seafront, Wilder Road, Ilfracombe, Devon EX34 9BZ **t** 01271 865655 **f** 01271 867707 **e** info@northdevontheatres.org.uk **w** northdevontheatres.org.uk Programming Dir: Karen Turner. Seated Capacity: 483

Larkfield Leisure Centre New Hythe Lane, Larkfield, Aylesford, Kent ME20 6RH **t** 01622 719345 **f** 01622 710822 Contact: Operations Mgr Seated Capacity: 600

LA2 165 Charing Cross Road, London WC2H 0EN **t** 020 7434 9592 or 020 7734 6963 **f** 020 7437 1781 **e** chrisalexander@alexanderc.freeserve.co.uk Contact: Chris Alexander Standing Capacity: 1000

The Lava Club 9 Belmont St, Aberdeen AB10 1JR **t** 01224 645328 or 01224 648000 **f** 01224 644737 **e** angela@lavaclub.co.uk **w** lavaclub.co.uk Manager: Angela Stirling. Seated Capacity: 120 Standing Capacity: 150

The Leadmill 6 Leadmill Road, Sheffield, South Yorkshire S1 4SE **t** 0114 221 2828 **f** 0114 221 2848 **e** promotions@leadmill.co.uk **w** leadmill.co.uk Live Promoter: Rupert Dell. Seated Capacity: 500 Standing Capacity: 900

Leas Cliff Hall The Leas, Folkestone, Kent CT20 2DZ **t** 01303 228600 **f** 01303 221175 **e** mail@leascliffhall.co.uk **w** leascliffhall.co.uk GM: Stephen Levine. Seated Capacity: 1000 Standing Capacity: 1500

Leeds Civic Theatre Cookridge Street, Leeds, West Yorkshire LS2 8BH **t** 0113 245 6343 **f** 0113 246 5906 **w** leeds.gov.uk/tourinfo/theatre Seated Capacity: 521

Leeds Grand Theatre & Opera House 46 New Briggate, Leeds, West Yorkshire LS1 6NZ **t** 0113 245 6014 **f** 0113 246 5906 **w** leeds.gov.uk/GrandTheatre General Mgr: Warren Smith. Seated Capacity: 1550

Leeds Metropolitan University Student Union, Calverley Street, Leeds, West Yorkshire LS1 3HE **t** 0113 209 8416 **f** 0113 234 2973 **e** events@lmusu.org.uk **w** lmusu.org.uk Seated Capacity: 500 Standing Capacity: 1050

Leeds Town & Country 55 Cookridge Street, Leeds, West Yorkshire LS2 3AW **t** 0113 280 0100 **f** 0113 283 3383 Contact: Steve Phelan Standing Capacity: 1800

Leeds University PO Box 157, Leeds, West Yorkshire LS1 1UH **t** 0113 380 1334 **f** 0113 380 1336 **e** ents@luu.leeds.ac.uk **w** luuonline.com Ents Mgr: Steve Keeble. Standing Capacity: 1750

Leicester University Student Union, University Road, Leicester LE1 7RH **t** 0116 223 1169 or 0116 223 1122 **f** 0116 223 1207 **e** jk69@le.ac.uk **w** le.ac.uk/su Bars & Ents Manager: Jo Kenning. Seated Capacity: 500 Standing Capacity: 1300

The Lemon Tree 5 West North Street, Aberdeen AB24 5AT **t** 01224 647999 **f** 01224 630888 **e** info@lemontree.org **w** lemontree.org Music Programmer: Andy Shearer. Seated Capacity: 300 Standing Capacity: 500

Lewisham Theatre (Studio) Rushey Green, Catford, London SE6 4RU **t** 020 8690 2317 or 020 8690 1000 **f** 020 8314 3144 **e** info@lewishamtheatre.co.uk **w** lewishamtheatre.co.uk Contact: Chris Hare Seated Capacity: 855 Standing Capacity: 1000

Lighthouse Pooles' Centre for the Arts, Kingland Road, Poole, Dorset BH15 1UG **t** 01202 665 334 **f** 01202 670 016 **e** jamesg@lighthousepoole.co.uk **w** lighthousepoole.co.uk Programmer: James Greenwood. Seated Capacity: 1463 Standing Capacity: 2459

Limelight 17 Ormeau Aveue, Belfast, Co Antrim BT2 8HD **t** 028 9066 5771 **f** 028 9066 8811 Contact: Eamonn McCann Standing Capacity: 500

Limelight Theatre Queens Park Centre, Queens Park, Aylesbury, Buckinghamshire HP21 7RT **t** 01296 431272 or 01296 424332 **f** 01296 337363 Artistic Dir: Amanda Eels. Seated Capacity: 120 Standing Capacity: 120

Link Centre Whitehill Way, Westlea, Swindon, Wiltshire SN5 7DL **t** 01793 465148 **f** 01793 445569 Recreation Mgr: G Byrne. Seated Capacity: 1580 Standing Capacity: 1900

The Little Civic North Street, Wolverhampton, West Midlands WV1 1RQ **t** 01902 552122 **f** 01902 713665

Liverpool Empire Theatre Lime Street, Liverpool, Merseyside L1 1JE **t** 0151 708 3200 **f** 0151 709 6757 Gen Mgr: Rachel Miller. Seated Capacity: 2370

Liverpool Hope University College Students Union Derwent House, Hope Park, Liverpool L16 9JD **t** 0151 291 3663 **f** 0151 291 3535 **e** union@livhope.ac.uk Contact: Chas Jenkins Seated Capacity: 500 Standing Capacity: 500

Liverpool Students Union 160 Mount Pleasant, Liverpool L69 7BR **t** 0151 794 4116 or 0151 794 4143 **f** 0151 794 4174 **e** guild@liv.ac.uk **w** liverpoolguild.org.uk Ents Mgr: Carl Bathgate. Standing Capacity: 500

Liverpool University Mountford Hall Guild of Students, PO Box 187, 160 Mount Pleasant, Liverpool, Merseyside L69 7BR **t** 0151 709 9108 or 0151 794 4143 **f** 0151 794 4174 **e** bathgate@liv.ac.uk **w** liverpoolguild.org.uk/ Ents Mgr: Carl Bathgate. Seated Capacity: 700 Standing Capacity: 1530

Lock 17 (formerly Dingwalls) Middle Yard, Camden Lock, Camden High St., London NW1 8AB **t** 020 7428 5929 **e** lock17.camden@regent-inns.plc.uk GM: Matt Ward. Standing Capacity: 487

Logan Hall Institute of Education, 20 Bedford Way, London WC1H 0AL **t** 020 7612 6401 **f** 020 7612 6402 **e** s.nazim@ioe.ac.uk **w** ioe.ac.uk Conference Office Mgr: Sittika Nazim. Seated Capacity: 933

London Apollo Complex Queen Caroline Street, London W6 9QH **t** 020 8748 8660 **f** 020 8846 9320 Seated Capacity: 3485

London Arena Limeharbour, London E14 9TH **t** 020 7538 8880 **f** 020 7538 5572 **e** sales@londonarena.co.uk **w** londonarena.co.uk Dir of European Events: Eve Hewitt. Seated Capacity: 11500 Standing Capacity: 12500

London Astoria 157 Charing Cross Road, London WC2H 0EN **t** 020 7434 9592 **f** 020 7437 1781 **e** chrisalexander@alexanderc.freeserve.co.uk Bookings Mgr: Chris Alexander. Seated Capacity: 520 Standing Capacity: 2000

London Palladium Argyll Street, London W1A 3AB **t** 020 7494 5020 or 020 7734 6846 **f** 020 7437 4010 Contact: Gareth Parnell Seated Capacity: 2291

Lordswood Leisure Centre North Dane Way, Lordswood, Chatham, Kent ME5 8YE **t** 01634 682862 **f** 01634 201897 **e** llcentre@freenetname.co.uk **w** lordswood-leisure-centre.co.uk Contact: Gen Mgr Seated Capacity: 500 Standing Capacity: 750

Loreburn Hall Newall Terrace, Dumfries DG1 1LN **t** 01387 260243 **f** 01387 2672255 Area Mgr East: John MacMillan. Seated Capacity: 800 Standing Capacity: 1400

Loughborough Student Union, Ashby Road, Loughborough, Leicestershire LE11 3TT **t** 01509 632020 **f** 01509 235593 **e** davehowes@lborosu.org.uk **w** lborosu.org.uk Ents Mgr: Dave Howes. Seated Capacity: 400 Standing Capacity: 2500

The Lowry Pier 8, Salford Quays, Manchester M50 3AZ **t** 0161 876 2020 **f** 0161 876 2021 **e** info@thelowry.com **w** thelowry.com

LSE SU Entertainments LSE SU East Building, East Building, Houghton Street, London WC2A 2AE **t** 020 7955 7136 **f** 020 7955 6789 **e** su.ents@lse.ac.uk **w** lse.ac.uk/union Ents Officer: George Ioannou. Seated Capacity: 440 Standing Capacity: 550

LSO St Luke's 161 Old St, London EC1V 9NG **t** 020 7490 3939 **f** 020 7566 2881 **e** lsostlukes@lso.co.uk **w** lso.co.uk/lsostlukes Centre Director: Simon Wales. Seated Capacity: 370

University of Luton Student Union Europa House, Vicarage Street, Bedfordshire LU1 3JU **t** 01582 489366 or 01582 743268 **f** 01582 457187 **e** michael.lawrence@luton.ac.uk Ents Co-ordinator: Michael Lawrence. Seated Capacity: 1000 Standing Capacity: 1000

Lyric Theatre, Hammersmith King Street, London W6 0QL **t** 020 8741 0824 **f** 020 8741 7694 **e** foh@lyric.co.uk **w** lyric.co.uk Theatre Mgr: Howard Meaden. Seated Capacity: 560

Magnum Theatre Magnum Leisure Centre, Harbourside, Irvine KA12 8PP **t** 01294 316463 **f** 01294 311228 Ents Officer: Willie Freckleton. Seated Capacity: 1164 Standing Capacity: 1700

Malvern Theatres Grange Road, Malvern, Worcestershire WR14 3HB **t** 01684 569256 or 01684 892277 **f** 01684 893300 **e** post@malvern-theatres.co.uk **w** malvern-theaters.co.uk Chief Exec: Nicolas Lloyd. Seated Capacity: 850

Manchester Academy & University Student Union, Oxford Road, Manchester M13 9PR **t** 0161 275 2930 **f** 0161 275 2936 **e** maximum@umu.man.ac.uk **w** umu.man.ac.uk Events Manager: Sean Morgan. Standing Capacity: 1800

Manchester Boardwalk Little Peter Street, Manchester M15 4PS **t** 0161 228 3555 **f** 0161 237 1037 **e** colindsinclair@msn.com **w** boardwalk.co.uk Contact: Lee Donnelly Standing Capacity: 500

Manchester Evening News Arena Victoria Station, Manchester M3 1AR **t** 0161 950 5333 or 0161 950 5667 **f** 0161 950 6000 **e** john.knight@men-arena.com Dir Sales/Mkting: John Knight. Seated Capacity: 19500

Manchester Met Students' Union 99 Oxford Road, Manchester M1 7EL **t** 0161 247 6468 **f** 0161 247 6314 **e** s.u.ents@mmu.ac.uk **w** mmsu.com Ents Mgr: Ben Casasola. Seated Capacity: 950 Standing Capacity: 1100

Manchester Opera House Quay Street, Manchester M3 3HP **t** 0161 834 1787 **f** 0161 834 5243 **w** manchestertheatres.co.uk Seated Capacity: 1909

Manchester Palace Theatre Oxford Street, Manchester M1 6FT **t** 0161 228 6255 **f** 0161 237 5746 **w** manchestertheatres.co.uk Contact: Rachel Miller Seated Capacity: 1996

Mansfield Leisure Centre Chesterfield Road South, Mansfield, Nottinghamshire NG19 7BQ **t** 01623 463800 **f** 01623 463912 Mgr: M Darnell. Seated Capacity: 1100 Standing Capacity: 1500

Marcus Garvey Centre Lenton Boulevard, Nottingham NG7 2BY **t** 0115 942 0297 **f** 0115 942 0297 Contact: Mr T Brown

Margate Winter Gardens Fort Crescent, Margate, Kent CT9 1HX **t** 01843 296111 **f** 01843 295180 Ops Mgr: Mr S Davis. Seated Capacity: 1400 Standing Capacity: 1900

Marina Theatre The Marina, Lowestoft, Suffolk NR32 1HH **t** 01502 533200 (Box) or 01502 533203 **f** 01502 538179 **e** info@marinatheatre.co.uk Contact: David Shepheard Seated Capacity: 751

Marlowe Theatre The Friars, Canterbury, Kent CT1 2AS **t** 01227 763262 **f** 01227 781802 **e** markeverett@canterbury.gov.uk **w** marlowetheatre.com Theatre Dir: Mark Everett. Seated Capacity: 993

The Marquee Club 1 Leicester Square, London WC2H 7NA **t** 020 7336 7326 or 020 7495 6770 **e** info@plummusic.com **w** plummusic.com Contact: Allan North

Mayfield Leisure Centre 10 Mayfield Place, Mayfield, Dalkeith, Midlothian EH22 5JG **t** 0131 663 2219 **f** 0131 660 9539 Contact: Area Leisure Mgr Seated Capacity: 400 Standing Capacity: 600

The Mayflower Commercial Road, Southampton, Hampshire S015 1GE **t** 023 8071 1800 **f** 023 8071 1801 **e** Dennis.hall@mayflower.org.uk **w** the-mayflower.com Chief Executive: Dennis Hall. Seated Capacity: 2406

Medina Theatre Mountbatten Centre, Fairlee Road, Newport, Isle of Wight PO30 2DX **t** 01983 527020 **f** 01983 822821 Contact: Paul Broome Seated Capacity: 425

Mercury Theatre Balkerne Gate, Colchester, Essex CO1 1PT **t** 01206 577006 **f** 01206 769607 **e** info@mercurytheatre.co.uk Marketing Director: Philip Bray. Seated Capacity: 496

The Met Arts Centre Market Street, Bury, Lancashire BL9 0BW **t** 0161 761 7107 or 0161 761 2216 **f** 0161 763 5056 **e** metarts.demon.co.uk Dir: Alan Oatey. Seated Capacity: 230 Standing Capacity: 300

Metro Club 19-23 Oxford St, London **t** 020 7437 0964 **f** 020 7494 4795 **e** bookings@blowupmetro.com **w** blowupmetro.com Dir: Paul Tunkin. Standing Capacity: 175

The Metropole Galleries The Metropole Galleries, The Leas, Folkestone, Kent CT20 2LS **t** 01303 255070 **f** 01303 851353 **e** info@metropole.org.uk **w** mertopole.org.uk Dir: Nick Ewbank. Seated Capacity: 140 Standing Capacity: 200

Middlesbrough Town Hall PO Box 69, Albert Road, Middlesbrough, Cleveland TS1 1EL **t** 01642 263848 or 01642 263850 **f** 01642 221866 Bookings Mgr: Jean Hewitt. Seated Capacity: 1190 Standing Capacity: 1352

Middlesex University Student Union, Bramley Road, London N14 4YZ **t** 020 8362 6450 **f** 020 8440 5944 **e** d.medawar@mdx.ac.uk **w** musu.mdx.ac.uk VP Ents: David Medawar. Seated Capacity: 400 Standing Capacity: 850

Milton Keynes College Chaffron Way, Leadenhall, Milton Keynes MK6 5LP **t** 01908 230797 **f** 01908 684399

Ministry of Sound 103 Gaunt Street, London SE1 6DP **t** 020 7378 6528 **f** 020 7403 5348 **e** arnie@ministryofsound.com **w** ministryofsound.com General Manager: Gary Smart. Standing Capacity: 1500

Mitchell Theatre Exchange House, 229 George Street, Glasgow, Lanarkshire G1 1QU **t** 0141 287 4855 **f** 0141 221 0695 Seated Capacity: 418

Moles Club 14 George Street, Bath BA1 2EN **t** 01225 404445 **f** 01225 404447 **e** moles@moles.co.uk **w** moles.co.uk Bookings Mgr: Louise Evans. Standing Capacity: 200

Michael Monroes Bar Carnegie Theatre, Finkle Street, Workington, Cumbria CA14 2BD **t** 01900 602122 **f** 01900 67143 Mgr: Paul Sherwin. Standing Capacity: 200

Morfa Stadium Upper Bank, Pentrechwyth, Swansea SA1 7DF **t** 01792 476578 **f** 01792 467995

Mote Hall Maidstone Leisure Centre, Mote Park, Maidstone, Kent ME15 7RN **t** 01622 220234 **f** 01622 672462 Events Mgr: Barry Reynolds. Seated Capacity: 1200 Standing Capacity: 1080

Motherwell Concert Hall & Theatre PO Box 14, Civic Centre, Motherwell, Lanarkshire ML1 1TW **t** 01698 267515 **f** 01698 268806 Contact: Theatre Mgr Seated Capacity: 883 Standing Capacity: 1800

Motherwell Theatre, Civic Centre PO Box 14, Motherwell, North Lanarkshire ML1 1TW **t** 01698 267515 **f** 01698 268806 Theatre Mgr: Lynn McDougal. Seated Capacity: 395

The Musician Clyde Street, Leicester LE1 2DE **t** 0116 251 0080 **f** 0116 251 0474 **e** rideout@stayfree.co.uk **w** themusicianpub.co.uk Booker/Mgr: Darren Nockles. Seated Capacity: 120 Standing Capacity: 150

Napier Student Association 12 Merchiston Place, Edinburgh EH10 4NR **t** 0131 229 8791 **f** 0131 228 3462 **e** e.reynolds@napier.ac.uk **w** napierstudents.com Contact: Ents Officer Standing Capacity: 100

The National Bowl at Milton Keynes c/o BS Group plc, Abbey Stadium, Lady Lane, Swindon, Wiltshire SW2 4DW **t** 0117 952 0600 **f** 0117 952 5500 Contact: Gordon Cockhill Standing Capacity: 65000

National Club 234 Kilburn High Road, London NW6 4JR **t** 020 7625 4444 or 020 7328 3141 Contact: PJ Carey Standing Capacity: 1200

The National Indoor Arena King Edward's Road, Birmingham, West Midlands B1 2AA **t** 0121 767 2754 **f** 0121 644 7181 **e** tc-7002@mail.necgroup.co.uk **w** necgroup.co.uk Contact: Linda Barrow Seated Capacity: 8000 Standing Capacity: 12000

NEC Arena The NEC, Birmingham, West Midlands B40 1NT **t** 0121 767 3981 **f** 0121 767 3858 **e** nec-arena@necgroup.co.uk **w** necgroup.co.uk Dir of Arenas: Linda Barrow.

New Theatre Royal Guildhall Walk, Portsmouth, Hampshire PO1 2DD **t** 01705 646477 or 01705 649000 **f** 01705 646488 Contact: Fiona Cole Seated Capacity: 320 Standing Capacity: 450

New Theatre, Cardiff Park Place, Cardiff CF10 3LN **t** 029 2087 8787 or 029 2087 8889 **f** 029 2087 8788 or 029 2087 8880 Contact: Giles Ballisat Seated Capacity: 1156

New Victoria Theatre Woking, Surrey **t** 01483 761144

Newcastle City Hall Northumberland Road, Newcastle upon Tyne, Tyne and Wear NE1 8SF **t** 0191 222 1778 or 0191 261 2606 **f** 0191 261 8102 Mgr: Peter Brennan. Seated Capacity: 2133

Newcastle University Union Student Union, Kings Walk, Newcastle upon Tyne, Tyne & Wear NE1 8QB **t** 0191 239 3926 **f** 0191 222 1876 **e** union-entertainments@ncl.ac.uk **w** union.ncl.ac.uk/entertainments Entertainments Manager: Polly Woodbridge. Standing Capacity: 1200

Newham Leisure Centre 281 Prince Regent Lane, London E13 8SD **t** 020 7511 4477 **f** 020 7511 6463

Newman College Of Education Student Union, Jenners Lane, Bartley Green, Birmingham B32 3NT **t** 0121 475 6714 **f** 0121 475 6714 **e** ncsu@newman.ac.uk Contact: Louise Beasley Seated Capacity: 160 Standing Capacity: 300

Newport Centre Kingsway, Newport, Gwent NP20 1UH **t** 01633 662663 **f** 01633 662675 Events Mgr: Roger Broome. Seated Capacity: 2000 Standing Capacity: 1600

Nice 'n' Sleazy 421 Sauchiehall Street, Glasgow, Lanarkshire G2 3LG **t** 0141 333 9637 or 0141 333 0900 **f** 0141 333 0900 **e** sleazys@hotmail.com **w** nicensleazy.com Promoter: Mig. Standing Capacity: 200

North Wales Theatre And Conference Centre The Promenade, Llandudno, Conwy LL30 1BB **t** 01492 872000 **f** 01492 879771 **e** info@nwtheatre.co.uk **w** nwtheatre.co.uk GM: Nick Reed. Seated Capacity: 1500 Standing Capacity: 1100

North Worcestershire College Student Union, Burcot Lane, Bromsgrove, Worcestershire B60 1PQ **t** 01527 570020 **f** 01527 572900

Northgate Arena Victoria Road, Chester CH2 2AU **t** 01244 377086 **f** 01244 381693 **e** cadsart@compuserve.com **w** northgatearena.com Business Development Mgr: Jon Kelly. Seated Capacity: 800 Standing Capacity: 1800

Northumbria University Union Building, 2 Sandyford Road, Newcastle upon Tyne NE1 8SB **t** 0191 227 3791 **f** 0191 227 3776 **e** s.collier@unn.ac.uk Ents Mgr: Sue Collier. Standing Capacity: 1680

Norwich Arts Centre Reeves Yard, St Benedicts, Norfolk NR2 4PG **t** 01603 660387 **f** 01603 660352 Centre Mgr: Pam Reekie. Seated Capacity: 120 Standing Capacity: 250

Norwich City Hall St Peters Street, Norwich, Norfolk NR2 1NH **t** 01603 622233 **f** 01603 213000

Notting Hill Arts Club 21 Notting Hill Gate, London W11 3JQ **t** 020 7460 4459

Nottingham Albert Hall North Circus Street, Off Derby Road, Nottinghamshire NG1 5AA **t** 0115 950 0411 **f** 0115 947 6512 Events Mgr: Sarah Robinson. Seated Capacity: 900

Nottingham Trent University Student Union, Byron House, Shakespeare Street, Nottingham NG1 4GH **t** 0115 848 6200 **f** 0115 848 6201 **e** keri.stephenson@su.ntu.ac.uk Ents Manager: Keri Stephenson. Standing Capacity: 640

University of Nottingham Student Union, Portland Building, University Park, Nottingham NG7 2RD **t** 0115 935 1100 Social Sec: Tanya Nathan. Seated Capacity: 200

Number10 10 Golborne Road, London W10 5PE **t** 020 8969 8922 **f** 020 8969 8933 **e** tris@number10london.com **w** number10london.com Events Co-ordinator: Tris Dickin.

Oakengates Theatre Lines Walk, Oakengates, Telford, Shropshire TF2 6EP **t** 01952 619020 **f** 01552 610164 **e** oakthea@telford.gov.uk **w** oakengates.ws Theatre Mgr: Psyche Hudson. Seated Capacity: 650 Standing Capacity: 780

Oasis Leisure Centre North Star Avenue, Swindon, Wiltshire SN2 1EP **t** 01793 445401 or 01793 465173 **f** 01793 445569 **e** mljones@swindon.gov.uk **w** swindon.gov.uk/oasis Bookings Mgr: Michelle Jones. Seated Capacity: 1580 Standing Capacity: 2400

Ocean 270 Mare Street, Hackney, London E8 1HE **t** 020 8533 0111 **f** 020 8533 1991 **e** mail@ocean.org.uk **w** ocean.org.uk Venue Manager: Alan Henehan. Promoters: Jane Cotter (jane.cotter@ocean.org.uk) Emma Bownes (emma@ocean.org.uk). Stage Manager: Brian Concannon. 3 rooms - Ocean 1: 3000 Cap. Ocean 2: 450 Cap. Ocean 3: 170 Cap. Seated Capacity: 2100 Standing Capacity: 900

Octagon Theatre Howell Croft South, Bolton, Lancashire BL1 1SB **t** 01204 529407 or 01204 520661 **f** 01204 380110 Contact: The Administrator Seated Capacity: 420

Odyssey Arena 2 Queen's Quay, Belfast BT3 9QQ **t** 028 9076 6000 **f** 028 9076 6111 **e** info@smg-sheridan.com **w** odysseyarena.com Executive Director: Nicky Dunn. Seated Capacity: 9500 Standing Capacity: 7000

The Old Institute 9 The Strand, Derby DE1 1BJ **t** 01332 381770 **f** 01332 381745 **e** paul.needham7@btopenworld.com GM/Promoter: Paul Needham. Standing Capacity: 500

The Old Market Upper Market Street, Hove, E. Sussex BN3 1AS **t** 01273 736 222 **f** 01273 329 636 **e** carolinebrown@theoldmarket.co.uk **w** theoldmarket.co.uk Artistic Dir: Caroline Brown. Seated Capacity: 300 Standing Capacity: 500

Old Town Hall High Street, Hemel Hempstead, Hertfordshire HP1 3AE **t** 01442 228097 **f** 01442 234072 **e** othadmin@dacorum.gov.uk **w** oldtownhall.co.uk Marketing & Publicity: Ranjit Atwal. Seated Capacity: 120

The Old Vic The Cut, Waterloo, London SE1 8NB **t** 020 7231 1393 f 020 7232 1373 **e** jo@interactivem.co.uk Promoter: Jo Cerrone. Seated Capacity: 1100

Olympia (see Earls Court)

100 Club 100 Oxford Street, London W1D 1LL **t** 020 7636 0933 **f** 020 7436 1958 **e** info@the100club.co.uk **w** the100club.co.uk Prop: Jeff Horton. Seated Capacity: 290 Standing Capacity: 290

The Orange 3 North End Crescent, North End Road, West Kensington, London W14 8TG **t** 020 7751 1044 **f** 020 7348 3911 **e** livegigs@mail.com **w** orangepromotions.com Booker/Promoter: Phil Brydon. Seated Capacity: 300 Standing Capacity: 300

The Orchard Home Gardens, Dartford, Kent DA1 1ED **t** 01322 220099 **f** 01322 227122 Contact: Theatre Mgr Seated Capacity: 950

Ormond Multi Media Centre 14 Lower Ormond Quay, Dublin 1, Ireland **t** 00 353 1 872 3500 **f** 00 353 1 872 3348

The Overdraft 300-310 High Road, Ilford, Essex IG1 1QW **t** 020 8514 4400

Oxford University Student Union New Barnet House, Little Clarendon Street, Oxford 0X1 2HU **t** 01865 270777 or 01865 270769 **f** 01865 270776 **e** president@ousu.org **w** ousu.org President: Ruth Hunt.

Paisley Arts Centre New Street, Paisley, Renfrewshire PA1 1EZ **t** 0141 887 1010 **f** 0141 887 6300 **e** artsinfo@renfrewshire.gov.uk Principle Arts Officer: John Harding. Seated Capacity: 158

University of Paisley - Ayr Campus Student Association, Beech Grove, Ayr KA8 0SR **t** 01292 886330 office or 01292 886362 union **f** 01292 886271 or 01292 886000 **e** dpa@upsa.org.uk Deputy President: Kim Macintyre. contact **e** dpa@upsa.org.uk Seated Capacity: 100 Standing Capacity: 200

Paradise Bar 460 New Cross Road, London SE14 6TJ **t** 020 8692 1530 **f** 020 8691 0445 **w** paradisebar.co.uk Contact: David Roberts Standing Capacity: 300

The Paradise Room Blackpool Pleasure Peach, Ocean Boulevard, Blackpool, Lancashire FY4 1EZ **t** 01253 341033 **f** 01253 407609 **e** debbie.hawksey@bpbltd.com **w** bpbltd.com Contact: Debbie Hawksey Seated Capacity: 600 Standing Capacity: 750

Parr Hall Palmyra Square South, Warrington, Cheshire WA1 1BL **t** 01925 442345 **f** 01925 443228 **e** parrhall@warrington.gov.uk **w** parrhall.co.uk Arts & Project Mgr: John Perry. Seated Capacity: 1000 Standing Capacity: 1100

Peacock Arts And Entertainment Centre Victoria Way, Woking, Surrey GU21 1GQ **t** 01483 747422 **f** 01483 770477 Standing Capacity: 500

The Penny 30-31 Northgate, Canterbury, Kent CT1 1BL **t** 01227 450333 or 01227 470512 **f** 01227 450333 Contact: Ian Mills Seated Capacity: 100 Standing Capacity: 200

Perth City Hall King Edward Street, Perth PH1 5UT **t** 01738 624055 **f** 01738 630566 Gen Mgr: Drew Scott. Seated Capacity: 1350 Standing Capacity: 1627

Philharmonic Hall Hope Street, Liverpool, Merseyside L1 9BP **t** 0151 210 1945 **f** 0151 210 2902 **e** publicity@rlps.co.uk **w** liverpoolphil.com Hall Dir: Pat Peter. Seated Capacity: 1682

The Platform Old Station Buildings, Central Promenade, Morecambe, Lancashire LA4 4DB **t** 01524 582801 **f** 01524 831704 **e** lancasterarts@tinyonline.co.uk **w** artsandevents.co.uk Head of Arts and Events: Jon Harris. Seated Capacity: 350 Standing Capacity: 1000

The Playhouse Harlow Playhouse Square, Harlow, Essex CM20 1LS **t** 01279 446760 **f** 01279 424391 **e** playhouse@harlow.gov.uk **w** playhouseharlow.com Theatre Mgr: Phillip Dale. Seated Capacity: 419

Playhouse Theatre High Street, Weston-Super-Mare, North Somerset BS23 1HP **t** 01934 417117 **f** 01934 612182 **e** playhouse@n-somerset.gov.uk Gen Mgr: Vivienne Thomson. Seated Capacity: 664

Plymouth College Of Art & Design Student Union, Tavistock Place, Plymouth, Devon PL4 8AT **t** 01752 203434 **f** 01752 203444

Plymouth Pavilions Millbay Road, Plymouth, Devon PL1 3LF **t** 01752 222200 **f** 01752 262226 **e** enquires@plymouthpavilions.com **w** plymouthpavilions.com Mktg Mgr: Shona Dipino. Seated Capacity: 2400 Standing Capacity: 4000

Plymouth University Student Union, Drake Circus, Plymouth, Devon PL4 8AA **t** 01752 663337 **f** 01752 251669 Contact: Mark Witherall Standing Capacity: 600

Po Na Na Hammersmith 242 Shepherd's Bush Road, London W6 7NL **t** 020 8600 2300 **f** 020 86002332 **w** ponana.co.uk

The Point Arena and Theatre East Link Bridge, Dublin 1, Ireland **t** 00 353 1 836 6777 **f** 00 353 1 836 6422 Gen Mgr: Cormal Rennick. Seated Capacity: 6500 Standing Capacity: 8500

The Point The Plain, Oxford OX4 1EA **t** 01865 798794 **f** 01865 798794 **e** mac@thepoint.oxfordmusic.net **w** thepoint.oxfordmusic.net Promoter: Mac. Seated Capacity: 220 Standing Capacity: 220

The Pop Factory Welsh Hills Works, Jenkin St, Porth CF39 9PP **t** 01443 688500 or 01443 688504 **f** 01443 688501 **e** info@thepopfactory.com **w** thepopfactory.com Contact: Mair Afan Davies Standing Capacity: 300

Portobello Town Hall 147 Portobello High Street, Edinburgh, Lothian EH15 1AF **t** 0131 669 5800 **f** 0131 669 5800 Hall Keeper: Andrew Crazy. Seated Capacity: 771

Portsmouth Guildhall Guildhall Square, Portsmouth, Hampshire PO1 2AB **t** 01705 834146 **f** 01705 834177 Gen Mgr: Martin Dodd. Seated Capacity: 2017 Standing Capacity: 2228

Portsmouth University Student Union, Alexandra House, Museum Road, Portsmouth, Hampshire PO1 2QH **t** 02392 843679 **f** 02392 843667 **e** janet.hillier@port.ac.uk **w** upsu.net Trad Op's Exec: Janet Hillier. Standing Capacity: 450

Prince of Wales Theatre Coventry Street, London W1V 8AS **t** 020 7930 9901 **f** 020 7976 1336 Contact: George Biggs Seated Capacity: 1100 Standing Capacity: 100

Princes Hall Princes Way, Aldershot, Hampshire GU11 1NX **t** 01252 327671 **f** 01252 320269 **w** rushmoor.gov.uk/princes/index.htm Gen Mgr: Steven Pugh. Seated Capacity: 700 Standing Capacity: 700

Princes Theatre Station Road, Clacton-on-Sea, Essex CO15 1SE **t** 01255 253208 **f** 01255 253200 **e** rfoster@tendringdc.gov.uk **w** tendringdc.gov.uk Ents Officer: Bob Foster. Seated Capacity: 820 Standing Capacity: 800

Princess Pavilion Theatre & Gyllyndune Gardens 41 Melvill Road, Falmouth, Cornwall TR11 4AR **t** 01326 311277 or 01326 211222 **f** 01326 315382 Contact: Mr RHD Phipps Seated Capacity: 400 Standing Capacity: 400

Princess Theatre Torbay Road, Torquay, Devon TQ2 5EZ **t** 01803 290288 or 01803 290290 (BO) **f** 01803 290170 Gen Mgr: Wendy Bennett. Seated Capacity: 1487

Purcell Room Royal Festival Hall, Belvedere Road, London SE1 8XX **t** 020 7921 0952 **f** 020 7928 2049 **e** calexander@rfh.org.uk **w** rfh.org.uk Prog Planning Mgr: Catherine Alexander. Seated Capacity: 367

Purple Turtle 9 Gunn Street, Reading, Berkshire RG1 2JR **t** 0118 959 7196 Standing Capacity: 470

Quay Arts Centre Sea Street, Newport, Isle Of Wight PO30 5BD **t** 01983 822490 **f** 01938 526606 **e** info@quayarts.demon.co.uk **w** quayarts.org Centre Director: Virgil Philpott. Seated Capacity: 130

Queen Elizabeth Hall Belvedere Road, London SE1 8XX **t** 020 7921 0815 **f** 020 7928 2049 **e** pchowhan@rfh.org.uk **w** rfh.org.uk Prog Planning Mgr: Pam Chowhan. Seated Capacity: 902

Queen Elizabeth Hall West Street, Oldham, Lancashire OL1 1UT **t** 0161 911 4071 **f** 0161 911 3094 Admin Mgr: Shelagh Malley. Seated Capacity: 1300 Standing Capacity: 2000

Queen Margaret University College Student's Union, 36 Clerwood Terrace, Edinburgh EH12 8TS **t** 0131 317 3403 **f** 0131 317 3402 **e** stanpern@hotmail.com Ents Mgr: Stan Pern. Seated Capacity: 300 Standing Capacity: 400

Queen's Hall Arts Centre Beaumont Street, Hexham, Northumberland NE46 3LS **t** 01434 606787 or 01434 607272 **f** 01434 606043 Arts Mgr: Geoff Keys. Seated Capacity: 399

Queen's Hall Victoria Road, Widnes, Cheshire WA8 7RF **t** 0151 424 2339 **f** 0151 420 5762 Contact: Brian Pridmore Seated Capacity: 640 Standing Capacity: 810

Queen's Theatre Boutport Street, Barnstaple, Devon EX31 1SY **t** 01271 327357 or 01271 865655 **f** 01271 326412 or 01271 867707 **e** info@northdevontheatres.org.uk **w** northdevontheatres.org.uk Karen Turner: Programming Dir. Seated Capacity: 688

Queens Hall Victoria Road, Widnes, Cheshire WA8 7RF **t** 0151 424 2339 **f** 0151 420 5762 **e** queenshall@halton-borough.gov.uk **w** queenshall-widnes.com Entertainments Manager: Brian Pridmore. Asst Manager: Pat Kershaw. Tech Manager: Duncan Armstrong. Marketing Officer: Peter Bentham ext 4067. Seated Capacity: 640 Standing Capacity: 810

The Queens Hall Edinburgh Clerk Street, Edinburgh, Lothian EH8 9JG **t** 0131 668 3456 **f** 0131 668 2656 Hall Mgr: Iain McQueen. Seated Capacity: 868 Standing Capacity: 900

Queens University Students Union, 79-81 University Road, Belfast, Co Antrim BT7 1PE **t** 028 9032 4803 **f** 028 9023 6900 **e** info@qubsu-ents.com **w** qubsu-ents.com Standing Capacity: 800

Queensway Hall Vernon Place, Dunstable, Bedfordshire LU5 4EU **t** 01582 603326 **f** 01582 471190 Gen Mgr: Yvonne Mullens. Seated Capacity: 900 Standing Capacity: 1200

RADA Bar Malet St, London WC1E 7PA **t** 020 7636 7076 **f** 020 7908 4895 **e** finance@rada.ac.uk **w** rada.ac.uk Manager: Annette Bennett. Standing Capacity: 100

Radius Goslett Yard, off Charing Cross Road, London WC2H 0EA **t** 020 7437 8595 **f** 020 7437 0479 **e** radiuscc@sfigroup.co.uk **w** radiusbar.com GM: Victor Zuriaga. Seated Capacity: 250 Standing Capacity: 275

Reading Town Hall 3 B's Bar and Cafe, Blagrave Street, Reading, Berkshire RG1 1QH **t** 0118 939 9803 or 0118 939 9815 **f** 0118 956 6719 Bookings Mgr: Stefano Buratta. Seated Capacity: 95 Standing Capacity: 150

Reading University PO Box 230, Whiteknights, Reading, Berkshire RG6 2AZ **t** 0118 986 0222 **f** 0118 975 5283 Standing Capacity: 1400

The Red Brick Theatre Aqueduct Road, Blackburn, Lancashire BB2 4HT **t** 01254 698859 or 01254 265566 **f** 01254 265640 Contact: Miss C Kay Seated Capacity: 380

Redditch Palace Theatre Alcester Street, Redditch, Worcestershire B98 8AE **t** 01527 61544 or 01527 65203 **f** 01527 60243 Bookings Mgr: Michael Dyer. Seated Capacity: 399

The Rex 361 Stratford High Street, London E15 4QZ **t** 020 8215 6003 **f** 020 8215 6004 **w** meanfiddler.com

The Rhythm Station Station House, Station Court, Newhallhey Road, Rawtenstall, Rossendale, Lancashire BB4 6AJ **t** 01706 214039

Richmond Theatre The Green, Richmond, Surrey TW9 IQJ **t** 020 8940 0220 **f** 020 8948 3601 Theatre Dir: Karin Gartzke. Seated Capacity: 830

The Richmond 10 Fisher Street, Carlisle, Cumbria CA3 8R **t** 01228 512220 **f** 01228 534168 **e** Rvenue@aol.com **w** jnightclub.co.uk Promoter/Owner: David Jackson. Standing Capacity: 325

The Ritz Ballroom Whitworth Street West, Manchester M1 5NQ **t** 0161 236 4355 **f** 0161 236 7515 **e** eddieritz@hotmail.com GM: Eddie Challiner. Standing Capacity: 1500

Rivermead Leisure Complex Richfield Avenue, Reading, Berkshire RG1 8EQ **t** 0118 901 5014 **f** 0118 901 5006 Seated Capacity: 2400 Standing Capacity: 3000

Riverside Studios Crisp Road, Hammersmith, London W6 9RL **t** 020 8237 1000 **f** 020 8237 1011 **e** jonfawcett@riversidestudios.co.uk **w** riversidestudios.co.uk Hires Mgr: Jon Fawcett. Seated Capacity: 500 Standing Capacity: 500

The Roadhouse 8 Newton St, Piccadilly, Manchester M1 2AN **t** 0161 237 9789 or 0161 228 1789 **f** 0161 236 9289 **e** kris@theroadhouselive.co.uk **w** theroadhouselive.co.uk Promoter: Kris Reid. Standing Capacity: 350

The Roadmender 1 Ladys Lane, Northampton NN1 3AH **t** 01604 604 603 **f** 01604 603 166 **w** roadmender.uk Contact: Jon Dunn Seated Capacity: 300 Standing Capacity: 900

The Robin 1 The Robin Hood, Merry Hill, Brierley Hill, West Midlands DY5 1TD **t** 01384 637747 or 01384 77756(venue) **f** 01384 637227 **e** music@therobin.co.uk **w** therobin.co.uk Prop: Mike Hamblett. Standing Capacity: 350

The Robin 2 28 Mount Pleasent, Bilston, Wolverhampton, West Midlands WV14 7LJ **t** 01384 637747 or 01902 497860 (venue) **f** 01384 637227 **e** music@therobin.co.uk **w** therobin.co.uk Director: Mike Hamblett. Standing Capacity: 400

Rock City 8 Talbot Street, Nottingham NG1 5GG **t** 0115 941 2544 **f** 0115 941 8438 **e** jen@rock-city.co.uk **w** rock-city.co.uk Director: George Akins. Standing Capacity: 1900

The Rock Garden/Gardening Club Bedford Chambers, The Piazza, Covent Garden, London WC2E 8HA **t** 07779 582 927 **f** 020 7379 4793 **e** platform_music@yahoo.co.uk **w** rockgarden.co.uk Platform Promoter: Lisa Cowan. Standing Capacity: 250

The Rocket Complex 166-220 Holloway Rd, London N7 8DB **t** 020 7133 2238 **e** info.rocket@londonmet.ac.uk **w** rocket-complex.net Events Mgr: Geoff Barnett.

Ronnie Scott's 47 Frith Street, London W1D 4HT **t** 020 7439 0747 **f** 020 7437 5081 **e** ronniescotts@ronniescotts.co.uk **w** ronniescotts.co.uk Owner/Club Director: Pete King. Seated Capacity: 300 Standing Capacity: 100

Rothes Halls The Kingdom Centre, Glenrothes, Fife KY7 5NX **t** 01592 612121 or 01592 611101 (box) **f** 01592 612220 **e** admin@rotheshalls.org.uk **w** rotheshalls.org.uk Halls Mgr: Frank Chinn. Seated Capacity: 706 Standing Capacity: 1500

Royal Albert Hall Kensington Gore, London SW7 2AP **t** 020 7589 3203 **f** 020 7823 7725 **e** sales@royalalberthall.com **w** royalalberthall.com Head of Sales & Mkting: Tracy Cooper. Seated Capacity: 5266

Royal Centre Theatre Square, Nottingham NG1 5ND **t** 0115 989 5500 **f** 0115 947 4218 **e** enquiry@royalcentre-nottingham.co.uk **w** royalcentre-nottingham.co.uk Acting Director: James Ashworth. Seated Capacity: 2499

Royal Concert Hall Theatre Square, Nottingham NG1 5ND **t** 0115 989 5500 **f** 0115 947 4218 **e** mgrayson@royalcentre.co.uk **w** royalcentre-nottingham.co.uk MD: J Michael Grayson. Seated Capacity: 2499 Standing Capacity: 10000

Royal Court Theatre 1 Roe Street, Liverpool, Merseyside L1 1HL **t** 0151 709 1808 or 0151 709 4321 **f** 0151 709 7611 or 0151 709 2678 **e** Richard.Maides@iclway.co.uk **w** royalcourttheatre.net Theatre Manager: Richard Maides. Seated Capacity: 1525 Standing Capacity: 1796

Royal Court Theatre Sloane Square, London SW1W 8AS **t** 020 7565 5050 **f** 020 7565 5001 **e** info@royalcourttheatre.com **w** royalcourttheatre.com Exec Dir: Vikki Heywood. Seated Capacity: 396

Royal Exchange Theatre St Ann's Square, Manchester M2 7DH **t** 0161 833 9333 **f** 0161 832 0881 **e** Philp.Lord@royalexchange.co.uk **w** royalexchange.co.uk Contact: Philip Lord Seated Capacity: 700

Royal Festival Hall Belvedere Road, London SE1 8XX **t** 020 7921 0843 **f** 020 7928 2049 **e** emcbain@rfh.org.uk **w** rfh.org.uk Head of Hall Prog Planner: Elspeth McBain. Seated Capacity: 2900

Royal Hall Ripon Road, Harrogate, North Yorkshire HG1 2RD **t** 01423 500500 **f** 01423 537210 **e** sales@harrogateinternationalcentre.co.uk **w** harrogateinternationalcentre.co.uk Dir: Paul Lewis. Seated Capacity: 1260 Standing Capacity: 723

Royal Lyceum Theatre Grindlay Street, Edinburgh EH3 9AX **t** 0131 248 4800 or 0131 248 4848 **f** 0131 228 3955 **e** administration@lyceum.org.uk **w** lyceum.org.uk Admin Mgr: Ruth Butterworth. Seated Capacity: 658

Royal Spa Centre Newbold Terrace, Leamington Spa, Warwickshire CV32 4HN **t** 01926 334418 **f** 01926 832054 Gen Mgr: Peter Nicholson. Seated Capacity: 800 Standing Capacity: 800

Royal Victoria Hall London Road, Southborough, Tunbridge Wells, Kent TN4 0ND **t** 01892 529176 **f** 01892 541402 Seated Capacity: 322

The Royal Pall Mall, Hanley, Stoke On Trent, Staffordshire ST1 1EE **t** 01782 206000 or 01782 207777 box off **f** 01782 204955 **w** webfactory.co.uk/theroyal/ Dir: Mike Lloyd. Seated Capacity: 1451 Standing Capacity: 1900

St David's Hall The Hayes, Cardiff CF10 1SH **t** 029 2087 8500 **f** 029 2087 8599 Head Arts & Cultural Serv: Judi Richards. Seated Capacity: 1956

St George's Concert Hall Bridge Street, Bradford, West Yorkshire BD1 1JS **t** 01274 752186 **f** 01274 720736 **e** christine.raby@bradford.gov.uk **w** bradford-theatres.co.uk Programme Booking Admin.: Christine Raby. Seated Capacity: 1574 Standing Capacity: 1872

St George's Hall Market Street, Exeter, Devon EX1 1BU **t** 01392 265866 or 01392 422137 **f** 01392 422137 **e** markets.halls@exeter.gov.uk Mgr: David Lewis. Seated Capacity: 500 Standing Capacity: 500

St John's Tavern 91 Junction Road, London N19 5QU **t** 020 7272 1587 **f** 020 7371 8797 Contact: Nick Sharpe

St Mary's College Student Union, Waldergrave Road, Strawberry Hill, Twickenham, Middlesex TW1 4SX **t** 020 8240 4314 **f** 020 8744 1700 Contact: Kieran Renihan Seated Capacity: 300 Standing Capacity: 600

Salford University Student Union, University House, The Crescent, Salford, Greater Manchester M5 4WT **t** 0161 736 7811 **f** 0161 737 1633 **e** entsorg-ussu@salford.ac.uk **w** salfordstudents.com

Salisbury Arts Centre Bedwin Street, Salisbury, Wiltshire SP1 3UT **t** 01722 430700 **f** 01722 331742 **e** info@salisburyarts.co.uk **w** salisburyarts.co.uk Centre Mgr: Catherine Sandbook. Seated Capacity: 300 Standing Capacity: 400

Salisbury City Hall Malthouse Lane, Salisbury, Wiltshire SP2 7TU **t** 01722 334432 **f** 01722 337059 **e** gpettifer@salisbury.gov.uk Sales & Marketing Mgr: Gail Pettifer. Seated Capacity: 953 Standing Capacity: 1116

Scarborough Univerity College Student Union, Filey Road, Scarborough, North Yorkshire YO11 3AZ **t** 01723 362392 **f** 01723 370815 Contact: Nick Evans Standing Capacity: 250

Scottish Exhibition & Conference Centre Glasgow, Lanarkshire G3 8YW **t** 0141 248 3000 **f** 0141 226 3423 Acct Mgr, Concerts: Susan Verlaque. Seated Capacity: 9300 Standing Capacity: 10000

Sheffield Arena Broughton Lane, Sheffield, South Yorkshire S9 2DF **t** 0114 256 2002 **f** 0114 256 5520 **e** info@clearchannel.co.uk **w** sheffield-arena.co.uk GM: David Vickers. Seated Capacity: 12500

Sheffield City Hall Barkers Pool, Sheffield, South Yorkshire S1 2JA **t** 0114 223 3740 **f** 0114 276 9866 **e** info@sheffieldcityhall.co.uk **w** sheffieldcityhall.com GM: Jo Barnes. Seated Capacity: 2346

Sheffield Hallam University Student's Union, Nelson Mandela Building, Pond Street, Sheffield, South Yorksire S1 2BW **t** 0114 225 4122 **f** 0114 225 4140 **e** a.sewell@shu.ac.uk **w** shu.ac.uk/su Ents Co-ordinator: Alice Sewell. Seated Capacity: 250 Standing Capacity: 900

Sheffield University Students Union, Western Bank, Sheffield, South Yorkshire S10 2TG **t** 0114 222 8556 **f** 0114 222 8574 **e** j.hann@sheffield.ac.uk **w** sheffieldunion.com Ents Manager: James Hann. Seated Capacity: 1000 Standing Capacity: 1500

Shepherd's Bush Empire Shepherd's Bush Green, London W12 8TT **t** 020 8354 3300 or 0905 020 3999 **f** 020 8743 3218 **e** mail@shepherds-bush-empire.co.uk **w** shepherds-bush-empire.co.uk GM: Bill Marshall. Seated Capacity: 1278 Standing Capacity: 2000

Shrewsbury Music Hall The Square, Shrewsbury, Shropshire SY1 1LH **t** 01743 281281 **f** 01743 281283 **e** mail@musichall.co.uk **w** musichall.co.uk Marketing Officer: Adam Burgan. Seated Capacity: 384 Standing Capacity: 500

606 Club 90 Lots Road, London SW10 0QD **t** 020 7352 5953 **f** 020 7349 0655 **e** jazz@606club.co.uk **w** 606club.co.uk Owner: Steve Rubie. Seated Capacity: 130 Standing Capacity: 165

Snape Maltings Concert Hall High Street, Aldeburgh, Suffolk IP15 5AX **t** 01728 687100 **f** 01728 687120 **e** enquiries@aldeburghfestivals.org **w** aldeburgh.co.uk Concert Mgr: Sharon Godard. Seated Capacity: 820

Sound Swiss Centre, 10 Wardour Street, London W1V 3HG **t** 020 7287 1010 **f** 020 7437 1029 **e** info@soundlondon.com **w** soundlondon.com Head of Corporate: Phil Bridges. Seated Capacity: 300 Standing Capacity: 1335

South Bank University Student Union, Keyworth Street, London SE1 6NG **t** 020 7815 6060 **f** 020 7815 6061 Ents Mgr: Tom Dinnis. Seated Capacity: 400 Standing Capacity: 800

South Hill Park Arts Centre Ringmead, Birch Hill, Bracknell, Berkshire RG12 7PA **t** 01344 484858 **f** 01344 411427 **e** music@southhillpark.org.uk **w** southhillpark.org.uk Music Officer: Simon Chatterton. Seated Capacity: 330 Standing Capacity: 600

South Holland Centre 23 Market Place, Spalding, Lincolnshire PE11 1SS **t** 01775 725031

Southampton Guildhall Civic Centre, Southampton, Hampshire SO14 7LP **t** 023 8083 2453 **f** 023 8023 3359 or 023 8033 7802 **e** h.richardson@southampton.gov.uk **w** southampton.gov.uk Events/Ents Services Mgr: Sue Cheriton. Seated Capacity: 1350 Standing Capacity: 1700

Southampton University Student Union, Highfield Campus, University Road, Southampton SO17 1BJ **t** 023 8059 5213 or 023 8059 5221 **f** 023 8059 5245 **e** em@susu.org **w** susu.org Entertainments Manager: Melissa Taylor. Standing Capacity: 800

Southport Arts Centre Lord Street, Southport, Merseyside PR8 1DB **t** 0151 934 2134 **f** 0151 934 2126 **e** jake.roney@leisure.sefton.gov.uk **w** seftonarts.co.uk Programme Mgr: Jake Roney. Seated Capacity: 472

Southport Theatre & Floral Hall Promenade, Southport, Merseyside PR9 0DZ **t** 01704 540454 **f** 01704 536841 Contact: Lisa Chu Seated Capacity: 1631

Spa Pavilion Theatre Seafront, Felixstowe, Suffolk IP11 8AQ **t** 01394 282126 **f** 01394 278978

The Spitz 109 Commercial Street, Old Spitalfields Market, London E1 6BG **t** 020 7392 9032 **f** 020 7377 8915 **e** mail@spitz.co.uk **w** spitz.co.uk Music Promoter: Tris Dickin. Seated Capacity: 180 Standing Capacity: 230

The Square Fourth Avenue, Harlow, Essex CM20 1DW **t** 01279 305000 **f** 01279 866151 **e** promotion@harlowsquare.com **w** harlowsquare.com Music Promoter: Tom Hawkins. Standing Capacity: 325

St Andrews Music Centre North Street, St Andrews, Fife KY16 9AJ **t** 01334 462226 **e** music@st-andrews.ac.uk **w** st-andrews.ac.uk/services/music Office Manager: Alison Malcolm. Seated Capacity: 450 Standing Capacity: 1000

St George's Bristol Great George Street, (off Park Street), Bristol BS1 5RR **t** 0117 929 4929 **f** 0117 927 6537 **e** administration@stgeorgesbristol.co.uk **w** stgeorgesbristol.co.uk Dir: Jonathan Stracey. Seated Capacity: 562

The St Helens Citadel Waterloo Street, St Helens, Merseyside WA10 1PX **t** 01744 735436 **f** 01744 20836 Contact: Jake Roney Seated Capacity: 172 Standing Capacity: 300

Stables Theatre Stockwell Lane, Wavendon, Milton Keynes, Buckinghamshire MK17 8LU **t** 01908 280814 **f** 01908 280827 **e** stables@stables.org **w** stables.org Programmer: Penny Griffiths. Seated Capacity: 396

Stafford Gatehouse Eastgate Street, Stafford ST16 2LT **t** 01785 253595 **f** 01785 225622 Mgr: Daniel Shaw. Seated Capacity: 564

Staffordshire University, Legends Nightclub Student Union, Beaconside, Stafford, Staffordshire ST18 0AD **t** 01785 353311 **f** 01785 353599 **e** l.gilbert@staffs.ac.uk **w** staffs.ac.uk Ents Manager: Luke Gilbert. Standing Capacity: 500

Staffordshire University, Stoke On Trent Student Union, College Road, Stoke On Trent, Staffordshire ST4 2DE **t** 01782 294629 **f** 01782 295736 **e** d.trigg@staffs.ac.uk **w** staffs.ac.uk Ents manager: Don Trigg.

The Standard Music Venue 1 Blackhorse Lane, London E17 6DS **t** 020 8503 2523 or 020 8527 1966 **f** 020 8527 1944 **e** thestandard@btinternet.com **w** standardmusicvenue.co.uk Contact: Nigel Henson Standing Capacity: 400

Stantonbury Leisure Centre Purbeck, Stantonbury, Milton Keynes, Buckinghamshire MK14 6BN **t** 01908 314466 **f** 01908 318754 Mgr: Matthew Partridge. Seated Capacity: 1000 Standing Capacity: 1000

Stirling University Students Association Student Union, The Robbins Centre, Stirling University, Stirling FK9 4LA **t** 01786 467189 **f** 01786 467190 **e** nicola.mcdonough@stir.ac.uk **w** susaonline.org Events Manager: Nicola McDonough. Seated Capacity: 1100

Stour Centre Tannery Lane, Ashford, Kent TN23 1PL **t** 01233 625801 f 01233 645654 Seated Capacity: 1500 Standing Capacity: 1800

Stourbridge Town Hall Crown Centre, Stourbridge, West Midlands DY8 1YE **t** 01384 812948 or 01384 812960 **f** 01384 812963 Contact: Laurence Hanna Seated Capacity: 300 Standing Capacity: 650

University of Strathcylde Students Association, 90 John Street, Glasgow, Lanarkshire G1 1JH **t** 0141 567 5023 **f** 0141 567 5033 **e** a.j.mawn@strath.ac.uk Seated Capacity: 300 Standing Capacity: 700

The Studio Tower Street, Hartlepool TS24 7HQ **t** 01429 424440 **f** 01429 424441 **e** studiohartlepool@btconnect.com **w** studiohartlepool.com Studio Manager: Liz Carter. Standing Capacity: 200

The Sub Club 2 Goulston St, Aldgate, London E1 7TP **t** 020 7133 2238 **e** info.rocket@londonmet.ac.uk Events Mgr: Geoff Barnett.

Subterania 12 Acklam Road, London W10 5QZ **t** 020 8960 4590 **f** 020 8961 9238 Promoter: Poorang Shahabi. Standing Capacity: 600

Sunderland University Student Union, Manor Quay, Charles Street, Sunderland SR6 0AN **t** 0191 515 3583 **f** 0191 515 2499 **e** andy.fitzpatrick@sunderland.ac.uk **w** mq@sunderland.co.uk Contact: A Fitzpatrick Seated Capacity: 1200 Standing Capacity: 1200

The Superdome Ocean Boulevard, Blackpool, Lancashire FY4 1EZ **t** 01253 341033 **f** 01253 401098 Seated Capacity: 1000

University of Surrey Union Club Union House, University of Surrey, Guildford, Surrey GU2 7XH **t** 01483 689983 **e** ents@ussu.co.uk **w** ussu.co.uk Events Mgr: Alan Roy. Standing Capacity: 1600

Sussex University Student Union, Falmer House, Falmer, Brighton BN1 9QF **t** 01273 678555 **f** 01273 678875 Contact: Entertainments Dept

The Swan 215 Clapham Road, London SW9 91E **t** 020 7978 9778 or 020 7738 3065 **f** 020 7738 6722 **w** swanstockwell.com Contact: John McCormack Seated Capacity: 300 Standing Capacity: 500

The Swan Abbey Barn Road, High Wycombe, Buckinghamshire HP11 1RS **t** 01494 539482

University of Wales - Swansea Student Union, Fulton House, Singleton Park, Swansea SA2 8PP **t** 01792 295485 **f** 01792 513006 **e** suents@swansea.ac.uk **w** swansea-union.co.uk/ents Seated Capacity: 800 Standing Capacity: 800

Symphony Hall International Convention Centre, Broad Street, Birmingham B1 2EA **t** 0121 200 2000 **f** 0121 212 1982 **e** symphony-hall@necgroup.co.uk **w** necgroup.co.uk MD: Andrew Jowett. Seated Capacity: 2260

Tameside Hippodrome Oldham Road, Ashton-under-Lyne, Tameside OL6 7SE **t** 0161 330 2095 **f** 0161 343 5839 **e** beth.loughran@clearchannel.co.uk Theatre Manager: Beth Loughran. Seated Capacity: 1262

Tamworth Arts Centre Church Street, Tamworth, Staffordshire B79 7BX **t** 01827 53092 **f** 01827 53092 Contact: The Arts Venue Mgr Seated Capacity: 360 Standing Capacity: 200

Teesside University University of Teesside Union, Southfield Road, Middlesbrough, Cleveland TS1 3BA **t** 01642 342234 **f** 01642 342241 **e** L.Stretton@utsu.org.uk **w** utsu.org.uk Ent & Promotions Mgr: Luke Stretton. Seated Capacity: 450 Standing Capacity: 1000

Telewest Arena Arena Way, Newcastle upon Tyne NE4 7NA **t** 0191 260 6002 **f** 0191 260 2200 **w** telewestarena.co.uk Exec Dir: Colin Revel. Seated Capacity: 9700 Standing Capacity: 11321

Telford Ice Rink Telford Town Centre, Telford, Shropshire TF3 4JQ **t** 01952 291511 **f** 01952 291543 Mgr: Robert Fountain. Seated Capacity: 3300 Standing Capacity: 4000

Thames Valley University Students Union, St Mary's Road, London W5 5RF **t** 020 8231 2531 **f** 020 8231 2589

Theatre Royal 282 Hope Street, Glasgow G2 3QA **t** 0141 332 3321 admin or 0141 332 9000 box **f** 0141 332 4477 **w** theatreroyalglasgow.com Theatre Mgr: Martin Ritchie. Seated Capacity: 1555

Theatre Royal Grey Street, Newcastle upon Tyne, Tyne and Wear NE1 6BR **t** 0191 232 0997 **f** 0191 261 1906 Contact: Peter Sarah Seated Capacity: 1294

Theatre Royal Theatre Street, Norwich, Norfolk NR2 1RL **t** 01603 598500 **f** 01603 598501 Contact: Peter Wilson Seated Capacity: 1314

Theatre Royal Theatre Square, Nottingham NG1 5ND **t** 0115 989 5500 **f** 0115 947 4218 **e** enquiry@royalcentre.co.uk **w** royalcentre-nottingham.co.uk MD: JM Grayson. Seated Capacity: 1135

Theatre Royal Royal Parade, Plymouth, Devon PL1 2TR **t** 01752 668282 or 01752 267222 **f** 01752 671179 or 01752 252546 **e** info@theatreroyal.com **w** theatreroyal.com Chief Exec: Adrian Vinken. Seated Capacity: 1296

Theatre Royal Corporation Street, St Helens, Merseyside WA10 1LQ **t** 01744 756333 admin or 01744 756000 bo **f** 01744 756777 Gen Mgr: Basil Soper. Seated Capacity: 698

Time Bangor Student Union, Deiniol Road, Bangor, Gwynedd LL57 2TH **t** 01248 388033 **f** 01248 388033 **e** ents@underbangor.ac.uk Ents Dir: Shaun Casey. Standing Capacity: 700

Tiverton New Hall Barrington Street, Tiverton, Devon, Exeter EX16 6QP **t** 01884 253404 **f** 01884 243677 Town Clerk: B Lough. Seated Capacity: 222 Standing Capacity: 300

TJ's Disco 16-18 Clarence Place, Newport, South Wales NP19 0AE **t** 01633 216608 **e** sam@tjs-newport.demon.co.uk **w** tjs-newport.demon.co.uk Manager: John Sicolo. Seated Capacity: 500

The Top of Reilly's 10 Thurland Street, Nottingham NG1 3DR **t** 0115 941 7709 **f** 0115 941 5604 Standing Capacity: 450

Torbay Leisure Centre Clennon Valley, Penwill Way, Paignton, Devon TQ4 5JR **t** 01803 522240 **w** torbay.gov.uk Seated Capacity: 2000 Standing Capacity: 3400

Torquay Town Hall Lymington Road, Torquay, Devon TQ1 3DR **t** 01803 201201 **f** 01803 208856 **e** pete.carpenter@torbay.gov.uk Contact: Mr P Carpenter Seated Capacity: 1000 Standing Capacity: 1000

The Tower Ballroom Reservoir Road, Edgbaston, Birmingham, West Midlands B16 9EE **t** 0121 454 0107 **f** 0121 455 9313 **e** tower@zanzibar.co.uk **w** zanzibar.co.uk MD: Susan Prince. Seated Capacity: 1000 Standing Capacity: 1200

The Tower Ballroom Blackpool Tower, Promenade, Blackpool, Lancashire FY1 4BJ **t** 01253 622242 **f** 01253 625194 **e** Blackpool.Tower@FLC.co.uk Contact: Gen Mgr Seated Capacity: 1650 Standing Capacity: 1700

Town Hall High Street, Hawick TD9 9EF **t** 01450 364743 Contact: Alister Murdie Seated Capacity: 600 Standing Capacity: 900

Tramway 25 Albert Drive, Pollockshields, Glasgow, Lanarkshire G41 2PE **t** 0141 422 2023 **f** 0141 422 2021 Seated Capacity: 1000 Standing Capacity: 1500

Trentham Gardens Stone Road, Trentham, toke On Trent, Staffordshire ST4 8AX **t** 01782 657341 Sales Dir: Karen Nixon. Seated Capacity: 1500 Standing Capacity: 2000

Trinity & All Saints College The Base, Brownberrie Lane, Horsforth, Leeds, West Yorkshire LS18 5HD **t** 0113 258 5793 **f** 0113 258 6831 Standing Capacity: 600

Truro Hall for Cornwall Back Quay, Truro, Cornwall TR1 2LL **t** 01872 262468 **f** 01872 260246 **e** hallforcornwall@enterprise.net **w** hallforcornwall.co.uk Contact: Chief Exec Seated Capacity: 1000 Standing Capacity: 1700

Turnmills 63b Clerkenwell Rd, London EC1M 5NP **t** 020 7250 3409 **f** 020 7250 1046 **e** info@turnmills.co.uk **w** turnmills.co.uk Corporate Events Mgr: Linda Ransome.

21 South Street 21 South Street, Reading, Berkshire RG1 4QU **t** 0118 901 5234 **f** 0118 901 5235 **w** readingarts.com Venue Mgr: Matthew Linley. Seated Capacity: 120 Standing Capacity: 200

University of Ulster Cromore Road, Coleraine, Co Antrim BT52 1SA **t** 028 9036 5121 **f** 028 9036 6817

Ulster Hall Bedford Street, Belfast, Co Antrim BT2 7FF **t** 028 9032 3900 **f** 028 9024 7199 Contact: Pat Falls Seated Capacity: 1600 Standing Capacity: 1800

Ulster University Students' Association, York Street, Belfast, Co Antrim BT15 1ED **t** 028 9032 8515 **f** 028 9026 7351 Club Sec: Joseph Mathews. Standing Capacity: 450

ULU (University of London Union) Malet St, London WC1E 7HY **t** 020 7664 2022 or 020 7664 2092 **f** 020 7436 4604 **e** entsinfo@ulu.lon.ac.uk **w** ulucube.com Venue Manager: Laurie Pegg. Seated Capacity: 320 Standing Capacity: 828

UMIST Union PO Box 88, Sackville Street, Manchester M60 1QD **t** 0161 200 3286 or 0161 200 3276 **f** 0161 200 3268 or 0161 200 3296 **e** paul.parkes@su.umist.ac.uk Contact: Paul Parkes Seated Capacity: 350 Standing Capacity: 600

The Underworld 174 Camden High Street, London NW1 0NE **t** 020 7267 3939 or 020 7482 1932 **f** 020 7482 1955 **e** contact@theunderworldcamden.co.uk **w** theunderworldcamden.co.uk Bookings Mgr: Jon Vyner Seated Capacity: 500 Standing Capacity: 500

Union Chapel Project Compton Avenue, London N1 2XD **t** 020 7226 1686 **f** 020 7354 8343 Contact: Julia Farrington Seated Capacity: 1000

University College London Student Union, 25 Gordon Street, London WC1H 0AH **t** 020 7387 3611 **f** 020 7383 3937 **e** A.davis@ucl.ac.uk Contact: Andy Davis Standing Capacity: 600

University College Of St Martin Student Union, Rydal Road, Ambleside, Cumbria LA22 9BB **t** 01539 430216 **f** 01539 430309

University of East Anglia Students Union, University Plain, Norwich, Norfolk NR4 7TJ **t** 01603 505401 or 01603 593460 **f** 01603 593465 or 01603 250144 **e** ents@uea.ac.uk **w** ueaticketbookings.co.uk Ents Mgr: Nick Rayns. Seated Capacity: 780 Standing Capacity: 1470

University of Essex Students' Union Students' Union, Uni of Essex, Colchester, Essex CO4 3SQ **t** 01206 863211 **f** 01206 870915 **e** ents@essex.ac.uk **w** essexentsonline.com Ents & Venues Mgr: Lee Pugh. Seated Capacity: 400 Standing Capacity: 1000

University of Gloucestershire Students' Union Student Union, PO Box 220, The Park, Cheltenham GL52 2EH **t** 01242 532848 **f** 01242 361381 **e** union@uqsu.org; space@glos.ac.uk **w** ugsu.org VP Communications: Mathew Loach. Seated Capacity: 600 Standing Capacity: 1200

University of Greenwich Student Union, Bathway, Woolwich, London SE18 6QX **t** 020 8331 8268 **f** 020 8331 8591

Upstairs @ Garage 20/22 Highbury Corner, London N5 1RD **t** 020 7607 1818 or 020 8961 5490 **f** 020 7609 0846 or 020 8961 9238 **e** joady@meanfiddler.co.uk Bking Mgr: Joady Thornton. Standing Capacity: 150

Usher Hall Lothian Road, Edinburgh EH1 2EA **t** 0131 228 8616 **f** 0131 228 8848 Mgr: Moira McKenzie. Seated Capacity: 2200 Standing Capacity: 2737

The Venue at Kent University Kent Student Union, Mandela Building, Canterbury, Kent CT2 7NW **t** 01227 824235 **f** 01227 824207 **e** d.stepto@ukc.ac.uk Entertainments Manager: Danny Stepto. Seated Capacity: 1500 Standing Capacity: 1500

Venue 1 Theatre Student Union, St Mary's Place, St Andrews KY16 9UZ **t** 01334 462700 **f** 01334 462740 **e** nhll@st-and.ac.uk **w** st-and.ac.uk/union Bldg Supervisor: Bruce Turner. Seated Capacity: 450 Standing Capacity: 1000

The Venue Bath University, Students Union, Claverton Down, Bath BA2 7AY **t** 01225 826613 **f** 01225 444061 **e** ents@union.bath.ac.uk **w** bath.ac.uk/~su4su/ent/ Ents Co-ordinator: Steve Backman. Seated Capacity: 250 Standing Capacity: 500

Verdis 38A Maiden Street, Weymouth, Dorset DT4 8AZ **t** 01305 779842 **f** 01305 776869 **e** schultzy@verdis.co.uk **w** verdis.co.uk Prop: Michael Shalts. Standing Capacity: 450

Vibe Bar 91-95 Brick Lane, London E1 6QL **t** 020 7247 3479 **f** 020 7426 0641 **e** info@vibe-bar.co.uk **w** vibe-bar.co.uk Events Manager: Adelle Stripe.

Victoria Community Centre Oakley Building, West Street, Crewe, Cheshire CW1 2PZ **t** 01270 211422 **f** 01270 537960 Centre Mgr: Mrs E McFahn. Seated Capacity: 550 Standing Capacity: 1000

The Victoria Hall Bagnall Street, Hanley, Stoke-on-Trent, Staffordshire ST1 3AD **t** 0117 932 1952 **f** 0117 932 1953 **e** Paul.Mazy@ukonline.co.uk Seated Capacity: 1700 Standing Capacity: 637

Victoria Theatre Wards End, Halifax, West Yorkshire HX1 1BU **t** 01422 351156 or 01422 351158 **f** 01422 320552 **e** admin@victoria-theatre.yorks.co.uk Contact: George Candler Seated Capacity: 1585 Standing Capacity: 1585

Vivid & Elite Atlanta Boulevard, Romford, Essex RM1 1TB **t** 01708 742289 **f** 01708 733905 **e** vividelite.romford@firstleisure.com **w** applebelly.com General Manager: John Mercer. Seated Capacity: 1625 Standing Capacity: 1300

Wakefield Theatre Royal & Opera House Drury Lane, Wakefield, West Yorks WF1 2TE **t** 01924 215531 **f** 01924 215525 **e** mail@wakefieldtheatres.co.uk **w** wakefieldtheatres.co.uk Gen Mgr: Murray Edwards. Seated Capacity: 509 Standing Capacity: 509

Warwick Arts Centre University Of Warwick, Coventry, West Midlands CV4 7AL **t** 024 7652 4524 **f** 024 4652 4777 **e** box.office@warwick.ac.uk **w** warwickartscentre.co.uk Dir: Alan Rivett. Seated Capacity: 1462 Standing Capacity: 1462

Warwick University Student Union, Gibbet Hill Road, Coventry, West Midlands CV4 7AL **t** 024 7657 3056 **f** 024 7657 3070 **e** dwalter@sunion.warwick.ac.uk **w** sunion.warwick.ac.uk/ents Entertainments Manager: Darren Walter. Standing Capacity: 2700

The Water Rats 328 Grays Inn Road, Kings Cross, London WC1X 8BZ **t** 020 7336 7326 **e** info@plummusic.com **w** plummusic.com Contact: Allan North, Sarah Thirtle Standing Capacity: 100

The Waterfront 139 King Street, Norwich, Norfolk NR1 1QH **t** 01603 632717 **f** 01603 615463 **e** p.ingleby@uea.ac.uk **w** ueaticketbookings.co.uk Programmer: Paul Ingleby. Standing Capacity: 700

Watermans Arts Centre 40 High Street, Brentford, Middlesex TW8 0DS **t** 020 8847 5651 **f** 020 8569 8592 Contact: Lorna O'Leary Standing Capacity: 500

Watford Colosseum Rickmansworth Road, Watford, Hertfordshire WD1 7JN **t** 01923 445300 **f** 01923 445225 Contact: John Wallace Seated Capacity: 1440 Standing Capacity: 1800

The Wedgewood Rooms 147B Albert Road, Southsea, Portsmouth, Hampshire P04 0JW **t** 023 9286 3911 **f** 023 9285 1326 **e** tickets@wedgewood-rooms.co.uk **w** wedgewood-rooms.co.uk GM: Geoff Priestley. Seated Capacity: 300 Standing Capacity: 400

The Welly Club 105-107 Beverley Road, Hull HU3 1TS **t** 01482 221113 **f** 01482 221113 **e** thewelly@hull24.com **w** yo-yo-indie.com Promotions Mgr: Andrew Coe.

Wembley Arena Empire Way, Wembley, London HA9 0DW **t** 020 8902 8833 **f** 020 8585 3879 **e** newbusiness@wembley.co.uk **w** whatsonwembley.com Mgr: Caroline McNamara. Seated Capacity: 11000 Standing Capacity: 12000

Wembley Arena Pavillion Empire Way, Wembley, Middx HA9 0DW **t** 020 8902 8833 **f** 020 8585 3879 **e** newbusiness@wembley.co.uk **w** whatsonwembley.com Snr Sales Mgr: Caroline McNamara. Seated Capacity: 10000

Wembley Conference and Exhibition Centre Wembley Conference, and Exhibition Centre, Elvin House, Stadium Way, Wembley, Middlesex HA9 0DW **t** 020 8795 8073 **f** 020 8585 3879 **e** newbusiness@wembley.co.uk **w** wembley.co.uk Sales & Mktg Dir: Peter Tudor. Seated Capacity: 11000 Standing Capacity: 12000

West End Centre Queens Road, Aldershot, Hampshire GU11 3JD **t** 01252 408040 **f** 01252 408041 **e** westendcentre@hants.gov.uk **w** westendcentre.co.uk Programme Co-ordinator: Barney Jeavons. Seated Capacity: 150 Standing Capacity: 200

University of West England Student Union, Coldharbour Lane, Frenchay, Bristol B16 1QY **t** 0117 965 6261 x 2580 **f** 0117 976 3909 **e** union@uwe.ac.uk **w** gate.uwe.ac.uk:8000/union/ents/index.html Contact: Programming Asst Seated Capacity: 400 Standing Capacity: 1500

Westex Royal Bath & West Showground, Shepton Mallet, Somerset BA4 6QN **t** 01749 822219 **f** 01749 823137 **e** bwwestex@ukonline.co.uk **w** westex.uk.com Gen Mgr: Jo Perry. Seated Capacity: 4000 Standing Capacity: 5250

University of Westminster Student Union, 32 Wells Street, London W1T 3UW **t** 020 7911 5000 x 2306 **f** 020 7911 5848 **e** edfrith@hotmail.com Events Mgr: Ed Frith. Seated Capacity: 150 Standing Capacity: 450

Westpoint Arena Clyst St Mary, Exeter, Devon EX5 1DJ **t** 01392 446000 **f** 01392 445843 **e** info@westpoint-devonshow.co.uk **w** westpoint-devonshow.co.uk Events Mgr: Sarah Symons. Seated Capacity: 6000 Standing Capacity: 7500

Weymouth Pavilion The Esplanade, Weymouth, Dorset DT4 8ED **t** 01305 765218 or 01305 765214 **f** 01305 789922 Arts & Entertainments Mgr: Stephen Young. Seated Capacity: 1000

White Rock Theatre White Rock, Hastings, East Sussex TN34 1JX **t** 01424 781010 or 01424 781000 **f** 01424 781170 Contact: Andy Mould Seated Capacity: 1165 Standing Capacity: 1500

Whitley Bay Ice Rink Hillheads Road, Whitley Bay, Tyne and Wear NE25 8HP **t** 0191 291 1000 **f** 0191 291 1001 Contact: Francis Smith Seated Capacity: 6000 Standing Capacity: 6000

Wigmore Hall 36 Wigmore Street, London W1H 0BP **t** 020 7258 8200 **f** 020 7258 8201 **e** info@wigmore-hall.org.uk **w** wigmore-hall.org.uk Contact: Management Office Seated Capacity: 540

Wimbledon Theatre 93 The Broadway, London SW19 1QG **t** 020 8543 4549 **f** 020 8543 6637 **e** live@wimbledontheatre.co.uk **w** uktw.co.uk/info/wimbledon.htm Gen Mgr: Ian Alexander. Seated Capacity: 1665

Winchester Guildhall The Broadway, Winchester, Hampshire SO23 9LJ **t** 01962 840820 **e** gbuchanan@winchester.gov.uk **w** winchester.gov.uk/guildhall Sales & Mktg Officer: Geraldine Buchanan. Seated Capacity: 600 Standing Capacity: 800

Winchester School Of Art Student Union, Park Avenue, Winchester, Hampshire SO23 8DL **t** 01962 840772 **f** 01962 840772 **e** cvasudev@hotmail.com **w** soton.ac.uk/~wsasu President: Chetan. Seated Capacity: 250 Standing Capacity: 250

Windmill Brixton 22 Blenheim Gardens, (off Brixton Hill), London SW2 5BZ **t** 020 8671 0700 or 07931 351 971 **e** windmillbrixton@yahoo.co.uk **w** windmillbrixton.co.uk Booker: Tim Perry. Standing Capacity: 120

Windsor Arts Centre St Leonard's Road, Windsor, Berkshire SL4 3BL **t** 01753 859421 or 01753 859336 **f** 01753 621527 Contact: Debbie Stubbs Seated Capacity: 179 Standing Capacity: 100

Wolverhampton Civic North Street, Wolverhampton, West Midlands WV1 1RQ **t** 01902 552122 **f** 01902 552123 **e** markb@wolvescivic.co.uk **w** wolvescivic.co.uk Gen Mgr: Mark Blackstock. Seated Capacity: 2200 Standing Capacity: 3000

Wolverhampton University Students Union, Wulfruna Street, Wolverhampton, West Midlands WV1 1LY **t** 01902 322021 **f** 01902 322020 **w** wlv.ac.uk Seated Capacity: 200 Standing Capacity: 600

WOMAD Festival (see Rivermead Leisure Complex)

Woodville Halls Theatre Woodville Place, Gravesend, Kent DA12 1DD **t** 01474 337456 or 01474 337611 **f** 01474 337458 **e** woodville.halls@gravesham.gov.uk **w** gravesham.gov.uk/woodvillehalls.htm Contact: Rob Allen Seated Capacity: 814 Standing Capacity: 1000

Worthing Assembly Hall Stoke Abbott Road, Worthing, Sussex BN11 1HQ **t** 01903 239999 **f** 01903 821124 Theatre Mgr: Peter Bailey. Seated Capacity: 930

Worthing Pavilion Theatre Marine Parade, Worthing, Sussex BN11 3PX **t** 01903 239999 **f** 01903 821124 Theatre Mgr: Peter Bailey. Seated Capacity: 850

Wyvern Theatre Theatre Square, Swindon, Wiltshire SN1 1QN **t** 01865 782900 **f** 01865 782910 Contact: Nicky Monk Seated Capacity: 617

Yeovil Octagon Theatre Hendford, Yeovil, Somerset BA20 1UX **t** 01935 422836 or 01935 422720 **f** 01935 475281 Gen Mgr: John G White. Seated Capacity: 625

York Barbican Centre Barbican Road, York, North Yorkshire YO10 4NT **t** 01904 628991 or 01904 621477 **f** 01904 628227 or 01904 621477 **e** craig.smart@york.gov.uk **w** fibbers.co.uk/barbican Contact: Craig Smart Seated Capacity: 1500 Standing Capacity: 1860

York University Students Union, Goodricke College, Heslington, York, North Yorkshire YO1 5DD **t** 01904 433724 **f** 01904 434664 **e** ents@york.ac.uk **w** york.ac.uk/student/su/index.shtml Andrew Windsor: Entertainments Officer. Seated Capacity: 300 Standing Capacity: 540

Younger Graduation Hall North Street, St Andrews KY16 9AJ **t** 01334 462226 **f** 01334 462570 **e** music@st-and.ac.uk **w** st-and.ac.uk/services/music Contact: The Secretary Seated Capacity: 900

Zanzibar 43 Seel Street, Liverpool, Merseyside L1 4AZ **t** 0151 707 0633 **f** 0151 707 0633 Sleeper coaches.

Tour Miscellaneous

23 Management **t** 07785 228000 or +61 415 498 955 **f** 0870 130 5365 **e** ifan@23management.com **w** 23management.com Tour Manager: Ifan Thomas. Artist, tour and production management.

5 Star Cases Broad End Industrial Estate, Broad End Road, Walsoken, Wisbech, Cambs PE14 7BQ **t** 01945 427000 **f** 01945 427015 **e** info@5star-cases.com **w** 5star-cases.com MD: Keith Sykes.

Air Brokers International Charity Farm, Fulborough Road, Parham, Sussex RH20 4HP **t** 01903 740200 **f** 01903 740102 **e** bugle@instoneair.com Contact: Mike Bugle

AIR CHARTER SERVICE

Brentham House, 45C High Street, Hampton Wick, Kingston upon Thames, Surrey KT1 4DG **t** 020 8614 6299 **f** 020 8943 1062 **e** london@aircharter.co.uk **w** aircharter.co.uk Passenger Sales Manager: Gavin Copus.

Anglo Pacific International Units 1 & 2, Bush Industrial Estate, Standard Road, London NW10 6DF **t** 020 8965 1234 **f** 020 8965 4954 **e** info@anglopacific.co.uk **w** anglopacific.co.uk MD: Steve Perry.

Anonymous Groove 186 Town Street, Armley, Leeds LS12 3RF **t** 0113 225 1684 or 0793 044 3048 **f** 0113 225 1684 **e** chris@anonymous-groove.com **w** anonymous-groove.com MD: Chris Shipton.

Any Time Any Place Unit 1A, Riverside Road, London SW17 0BA **t** 020 8944 1022 or 07831 420002 **f** 020 8944 9434

Audile Unit 110, Cariocca Business Park, Ardwick, Manchester M12 4AH **t** 0161 272 7883 or 07968 156 499 **f** 0161 272 7883 **e** mail@audile.co.uk **w** audile.co.uk Partner: Rob Ashworth.

BCS Multi Media (Computer Visuals) Grantham House, Macclesfield, Cheshire SK10 3NP **t** 01625 615379 **f** 01625 429667 **e** dpl@bcsmm.fsnet.co.uk **w** bcsmm.fsnet.co.uk Director: Duncan Latham.

Beat The Street UK (Tour Coaches) Unit 103, Cariocca Business Park, Hellidon Close, Ardwick, Manchester M12 4AH **t** 0161 273 5984 **f** 0161 272 7772 **e** beatthestreetuk@aol.com **w** beatthestreet.net Manager: Paul Collis.

BENNETT AUDIO

41 Sherriff Road, London NW6 2AS, t 020 7372 1077 or 07748 705 067 e bennettaudio@f2s.com w bennettaudio.co.uk Dir and Audio Engineer: Clem Bennett

Capes UK Security Services Ltd Unit 1, West Street Business Park, Stamford, Lincolnshire PE9 2PR **t** 01780 480712 **f** 01780 480824 Security.

Lee Charteris Associates 10 Marco Road, London W6 0PN **t** 020 8741 2500 or 07801 663700 **f** 020 8741 2577 **e** LCharteris@compuserve.com Production Mgr: Lee Charteris.

The Chevalier Catering Company Studio 4-5, Garnet Close, Watford, Herts WD24 7GN **t** 020 8950 8998 or 01923 211703 **f** 01923 211704 **e** bonnie@chevalier.co.uk **w** chevalier.co.uk Ops Manager: Sarah 'Bonnie' May.

The Concert Travel Company Taw Vale, Barnstaple, Devon EX32 8NJ **t** 01271 323355 **f** 01271 375902 **e** sales@ticketzone.co.uk Contact: Robert Cotton

Crawfords Luxury Cars And Coaches 8 Concord Business Centre, Concord Road, London W3 0TJ **t** 020 8896 3030 **f** 020 8896 3300 **e** crawfords@btconnect.com **w** crawfordscars.co.uk Divisional Manager: Ivor Davies.

Crisp Productions Tour Mgmt & Support Services, 21 Stupton Road, Sheffield S9 1BQ **t** 0114 261 1649 **f** 0114 261 1649 **e** dc@cprod.win-uk.net MD: Darren Crisp.

Curious Yellow Ltd 33-37 Hatherley Mews, London E17 4QP **t** 020 8521 9595 **f** 020 8521 6363 **e** info@curiousyellow.co.uk **w** curiousyellow.co.uk Creative Dir: Paul Penny.

The Departure Lounge 29 Kingdon Road, London NW6 1PJ **t** 020 7431 2070 **f** 020 7431 2070 Contact: Susan Ransom

Displaybox Hatches Barn, Bradden Lane, Gaddesden Row, Hemel Hempstead, Hertfordshire HP2 6JB **t** 01442 843737 **f** 01442 843727 **e** dbox@displaybox.co.uk MD: Joe Redmond.

Dunn-Line Travel The Coach Station, Dunn-Line Corporation House, Park Lane, Basford, Nottinghamshire NG6 0RD **t** 0115 916 9000 **f** 0115 942 0578 **w** dunn-line.co.uk

Eat To The Beat Studio 4-5, Garnet Close, Greycaine Road, Watford, Hertfordshire WD2 4JN **t** 01923 211702 **f** 01923 211704 **e** catering@eattothebeat.com **w** eattothebeat.com Ops Manager: Mary Shelley-Smith.

Eat Your Hearts Out Basement Flat, 108A Elgin Avenue, London W9 2HD **t** 020 7289 9446 **f** 020 7266 3160 **e** eyho@dial.pipex.com MD: Kim Davenport.

EST Ltd Marshgate Sidings, Marshgate Lane, London E15 2PB **t** 020 8522 1000 **f** 020 8522 1002 **e** delr@est-uk.com **w** yourock-weroll.co.uk Dir: Del Roll. Transport & logistics.

ET Travel 35 Britannia Row, Islington, London N1 8QH **t** 020 7359 7161 **f** 020 7354 3270 **e** info@ettravel.demon.co.uk **w** et-travel-ltd.co.uk Dir: Melanie Weston.

Event Experts 3 Walpole Court, Ealing Green, London W5 5ED **t** 020 8326 3290 **f** 020 8326 3299 **e** info@event-experts.co.uk **w** event-experts.co.uk Production Manager: John Denby.

Extreme Music Production - Tour Management 4-7 Forewoods Common, Holt, Wilts BA14 6PJ **t** 01225 782984 or 07909 995011 **e** george@xtrememusic.co.uk **w** xtrememusic.co.uk MD: George Allen.

Fexx Live Sound 159A High Road, Romford, Essex RM6 6NL **t** 07931 752641 **e** adamfexx@yahoo.co.uk **w** fexx.co.uk Sound Engineer: Adam Taylor.

Fineminster - Air Charter Ltd. Worth Corner, Pound Hill, Crawley, West Sussex RH10 7SL **t** 01293 885888 **f** 01293 883238 **e** charter@fineminster.com **w** fineminster.com MD: Graham Plunkett.

FM Productions Great Bossinghamn Farmhouse, Bossingham, Kent CT4 6EB **t** 01227 709790 **f** 01227 709730 **e** kenfmprod@aol.com Prod Designer/Mgr: Ken Watts.

Front Of House Productions 81 Harriet Street, Trecynon, Aberdare, Rhondda Cynon Taff CF44 8PL **t** 01685 881006 **f** 01685 881006 **e** fohproductions@yahoo.co.uk Production Mgr: Jules Jones.

Fruit Pie Music Productions Ltd The Shop, 443 Streatham High Road, London SW16 3PH **t** 020 8679 9289 **f** 020 8679 9775 **e** info@fruitpiemusic.com **w** fruitpiemusic.com Dir: Matthew Bradbury.

Fruition Chestnut Farm, Frodsham, Cheshire **t** 01928 734422 or 020 7430 0700 **f** 01928 734433 or 020 7430 2122 **e** musicevents@fruition.co.uk **w** fruition.co.uk Contact: Mark Tasker

Funevents Corporate Services PO Box 4040, Mayfair, London W1A 6NR **t** 0870 758 0619 **f** 0870 135 3338 **e** admin@funevents.com **w** funevents.com Director: Harv Sethi.

Future Management & Tour Logistics PO Box 183, Chelmsford, Essex CM2 9XN **t** 01245 601910 **f** 01245 601048 **e** Futuremgt@aol.com **w** futuremanagement.co.uk MD: Joe Ferrari.

Future Studios International PO Box 10, London N1 3RJ **t** 020 7241 2183 **f** 020 7241 6233 **e** ladybelle888@blueyonder.co.uk **w** gigsonline.co.uk Contact: Michelle L Goldberg

Gatecrasher PO Box 6571, Birmingham B31 3TB **t** 0121 445 6699 **f** 0121 445 6633 **e** name@gatecrasher.co.uk

Grand Tours 93b Scrubs Lane, London NW10 6QU **t** 020 8968 7798 **f** 020 8968 3377 **e** johndawkins@granduniongroup.com **w** grand-tours.net Manager: John Dawkins.

GWH Backline Rental GWH, Hillcroft Business Park, Whisby Road, Lincoln LN6 3QT **t** 01522 501815 **f** 01522 501816 **e** gary@gwhmusic.com **w** gwhmusic.com Director: Gary Weight.

Health & Safety Advice PO Box 32295, London W5 1WD **t** 0870 066 0272 **f** 0870 066 0273 **e** info@health-safetyadvice.co.uk **w** health-safetyadvice.co.uk Dir: Jan Goodwin.

Hooligan Flightcases GWH, Hillcroft Business Park, Whisby Road, Lincoln LN6 3QT **t** 01522 501815 **f** 01522 501816 **e** dean@gwhmusic.com Sales manager: Dean Anderton. Flightcase design and manufacture.

Jam DVD Unit 6 Buspace studios, Colan St. London, London W10 5AP **t** 07976 820774 **f** 07092 003937 **e** jamdvd@mancunlimited.net Recording Engineer/Mixer: Julie Gardner. Live sound and recording.

John Henry's 16-24 Brewery Road, London N7 9NH **t** 020 7609 9181 **f** 020 7700 7040 **e** info@johnhenrys.com **w** johnhenrys.com MD: John Henry.

Judgeday Ltd The Manor House, Box, Corsham, Wiltshire SN13 8NF **t** 01225 744226 **f** 01225 742155 **e** judgedaybeck@dial.pipex.com Contact: Dave T

K West Hotel & Spa Richmond Way, London W14 0AX **t** 020 7674 1000 or 020 7674 1059 **f** 020 7674 1050 **e** ej@k-west.co.uk **w** k-west.co.uk Entertainment Sales Mgr: Emma Jenkins.

Key Cargo International 6 Millbrook Business Centre, Floats Road, Roundthorn, Manchester M23 9YJ **t** 0161 283 2471 **f** 0161 283 2472 **e** touring@keycargo.net Operations Director: Steve Plant.

Knights Guitar Electronics and Flight Cases 28 Hill Grove, Romford, Essex RM1 4JP **t** 07788 740793 **f** 07092 231176 **e** kge@freeuk.com **w** http://welcome.to/kge MD: Ron Knights.

Mad As Toast (Tour Management) 3 Broomlands Street, Paisley PA1 2LS **t** 0141 887 8888 **f** 0141 887 8888 **e** info@madastoast.com **w** madastoast.com Dirs: John Richardson, George Watson.

MDMA 1A, 1 Adelaide Mansions, Hove, Sussex BN3 2FD **t** 01273 321602 **f** 0870 1213472 **e** tourmanric@aol.com Manager: Rick French.

MEDIA TRAVEL LTD

mediatravel★

travel management for the entertainment industry

Studio 1, Cloisters House, 8 Battersea Park Road, London SW8 4BG **t** 020 7627 2200 **f** 020 7627 2221 **e** info@mediatravel.com **w** mediatravel.com MD: Guy Lindsay-Watson.

Midland Custom Cases 24 Proctor Street, Birmingham B7 4EE **t** 0121 333 7711 **f** 0121 333 7799 **e** admin@cloudone.net **w** cloudone.net MD: Paul Stratford.

Midnight Costume Design & Wardrobe **t** 07941 313 223 **e** Midnight_wardrobe@hotmail.com Designer/Wardrobe: Midnight.

Millennium Concert Travel 2 Dickson Road, Blackpool, Lancashire FY1 2AA **t** 01253 299 266 **f** 01253 299 454 **e** sales@mct-online.com Contact: Julian Murray

Millsea Production Services 2A Rotherwood Mansion, 78 Madeira Road, Streatham, London SW16 2DE **t** 020 8677 2370 or 07770 428 096 **f** 020 8677 8690 **e** millsea@aol.com Tour Manager: Caron Malcolm.

Movin' Music Ltd (London) Suite 1, 52 Highfield Road, Purley, Surrey CRB 2JG **t** 020 8763 0767 **f** 020 8668 2214 **e** info@movinmusic.net **w** movinmusic.net Dir: Brenda Lillywhite. Travel agent, tour management & splitter bus hire.

Movin' Music Ltd (Manchester) Studio 2, 33 Albany Road, Chorlton, Manchester M21 0BH **t** 0161 881 9227 **f** 0161 881 9089 **e** info@movinmusic.net **w** movinmusic.net Dir: Nick Robinson.

Moving Space Rentals 93b Scrubs Lane, London NW10 6QU **t** 020 8968 7798 **f** 020 8968 3377 **e** nickyeatman@granduniongroup.com **w** movingspaceuk.co.uk Manager: Nick Yeatman, John Dawkins.

MTFX Velt House, Velt House Lane, Elmore, Gloucester GL2 3NY **t** 01452 729903 **f** 01452 729904 **e** info@mtfx.com **w** mtfx.com MD: Mark Turner.

Music & Arts Security Ltd 13 Grove Mews, Hammersmith, London W6 7HS **t** 020 8563 9444 **f** 020 8563 9555 **e** sales@musicartssecurity.co.uk **w** music-and-arts-security.co.uk MD: Jerry Judge.

Music By Appointment (MBA) - Travel Agents The Linen House, 253 Kilburn Lane, London W10 4BQ **t** 020 8962 6795 **f** 020 8962 1255 **e** byron.carr@appointmentgroup.com **w** appointmentgroup.com GM: Byron Carr.

The Music Room 35 Bradford Road, Cleckheaton, West Yorkshire BD19 3JN **t** 01274 879768 **f** 01274 852280 **e** info@the-music-room.com **w** the-music-room.com Shop Mgr: Terry Evans.

Nova Travel 20 Old Lydd Road, Camber, East Sussex TN31 7RH **t** 01797 225528 or East Sussex **f** 01797 225577 **e** nova@sleepercoaches.co.uk **w** sleepercoaches.co.uk Contact: Peter Davie

Pa-Boom Phenomenal Fireworks Ltd 49 Carters Close, Sherington, Buckinghamshire MK16 9NW **t** 01908 612 593 or 0860 439 380 **f** 01908 216 400 **e** pa@boom.demon.co.uk **w** pa-boom.com Contact: Neil Canham

Packhorse Case Co 9 Stapledon Road, Orton Southgate, Peterborough, Cambs PE2 6TB **t** 01733 232440 **f** 01733 232556 Contact: Sam Robinson

Pod Bluman 65 Coppetts Road, London N10 1JH **t** 020 8374 8400 **f** 020 8374 2982 **e** pod.projects@blueyonder.co.uk

Poiesis 14 Fairlawn Court, London W4 5EE **t** 020 8995 2494 or 07785 770424 **e** connect@poiesis.org **w** poiesis.org Dir: Indra Adnan.

Polar Arts The Old Court House, Market Place, Castle Combe, Wilts SN14 7HT **t** 01249 783850 **f** 020 7681 1900 **e** info@PolarArts.com **w** polararts.com Directors: Juliette Devine/Jane Kelly. Tour Production & Management.

Premier Aviation Units 1&2, Newhouse Business Centre, Old Crawley Road, Faygate, W. Sussex RH12 4RU **t** 01293 852688 **f** 01293 852699 **e** operations@premieraviation.com **w** premieraviation.com MD: Adrian Whitmarsh.

Pyramid Productions & Promotions Cadillac Ranch, Pencraig Uchaf, Cwm Bach, Whitland, Carms. SA34 0DT **t** 01994 484466 **f** 01994 484294 **e** cadillacranch@telco4u.net Dir: Nik Turner.

Rhythm Of Life Ltd Rhythm House, King Street, Carlisle, Cumbria CA1 1SJ **t** 01228 515141 **f** 01228 515161 **e** events@rhythm.co.uk **w** rhythm.co.uk MD: Andrew Lennie.

Rima Travel 10 Angel Gate, London EC1V 2PT **t** 020 7833 5071 **f** 020 7278 4700 **e** ernie.garcia@rima-travel.co.uk **w** rima-travel.co.uk MD: Ernie Garcia.

Rooti-Tooti Music 69 Windsor Road, Torquay TQ1 1SY **t** 01803 324089 **f** 01803 324089 **e** graham@rootitooti.freeserve.co.uk Venue Programmer: Graham Radley.

Sanctuary Set Construction 8 Olaf Street, London W11 4BE **t** 020 7221 9041 **f** 020 7221 9399 **e** iain.hill@sanctuarygroup.com **w** sanctuarystudios.co.uk Construction Manager: Iain Hill.

Saucery Catering Watchcott, Nordan, Leominster, Herefordshire HR6 0AJ **t** 01568 614221 **f** 01568 610256 **e** saucery@aol.com MD: Alison Taylor.

Screen And Music Travel Ltd 145 Station Road, West Drayton, Middx UB7 7ND **t** 01895 434057 **f** 01895 430279 **e** info@screenandmusictravel.co.uk **w** screenandmusictravel.co.uk Special Projects Mgr: Colin Doran.

Sensible Events 90-96 Brewery Road, London N7 9NT **t** 020 7700 9900 **f** 020 7700 7845 **e** zweckaz@aol.com MD: Andrew Zweck.

Shell Shock Firework Ltd Furze Hill Farm, Knossington, Oakham, Leics LE15 8LX **t** 01664 454 994 **f** 01664 454 995 **e** zoe@shell-shock.co.uk **w** shell-shock.co.uk Dir: Zoe Gibson.

So Touring Services PO Box 20750, London E3 2YU **t** 020 8573 6652 **f** 020 8573 6784 **e** sotouring@aol.com Contact: Sean O'Neill

Sonic Movement Flat 2, 110 Chepstow Road, London W2 5QS **t** 020 7229 0196 **f** 020 7691 7276 **e** JOwens666@btinternet.com Tour Manager: Jamie Owens.

Sound & Light Productions PO Box 32295, London W5 1WD **t** 0870 066 0272 **f** 0870 066 0273 **e** info@soundandlightproductions.co.uk **w** soundandlightproductions.co.uk Contact: John Denby

Sound Moves (UK) Ltd Unit 6, Planet Centre, Armadale Road, Feltham, Middlesex TW14 0LW **t** 020 8831 0500 or 07740 082 443 **f** 020 8831 0520 **e** john.corr@soundmoves.com **w** soundmoves.com MD: Martin Corr.

SouthWestern Management 13 Portland Road, Street, Somerset BA16 9PX **t** 01458 445186 or 07831 437062 **f** 01458 841186 **e** info@sw-management.co.uk **w** sw-management.co.uk Dir: Chris Hannam.

SPA Catering Services 44 Oak Hill Road, London SW15 2QR **t** 020 7563 2550 or 07788 785 493 **f** 020 8871 4579 **e** spacatering@hotmail.com MD: Simon Peter.

SR Management Ltd 4 Monkton House, 130A Haverstock Hill, London NW3 2AY **t** 020 7722 4373 **e** srmgmt@aol.com MD/Pilates Trainer: Sarah Rosenfield. Tour management & Pilates training.

Stardes Ashes Buildings, Old Lane, Holbrook Industrial Estate, Halfway, Sheffield S20 3GZ **t** 0114 251 0051 **f** 0114 251 0555 **e** dhs@totalise.co.uk **w** stardes.co.uk Contact: David Harvey-Steinberg

Stevie "Vann" Lange (SVL) Vocal Productions Ebony and Ivory, 11 Varley Parade, Colindale, London NW9 6RR **t** 020 8200 7090 **e** SVLProds@aol.com Contact: Stevie "Vann" Lange

T&S Immigration Services 27 Castle Street, Kirkcudbright DG6 4JD **t** 01557 339123 **f** 01557 330567 **e** tina@tandsimmigration.demon.co.uk Work Permit Specialists: Tina Richard.

Taurus Self Drive Ltd 55 Wyverne Road, Chorlton, Manchester M21 0ZW **t** 0161 434 9823 or 020 7434 9823 **f** 0161 434 9823 or 020 7434 9823 Contact: Sean Shannon

TCP International Ltd 101 Shepherds Bush Road, London W6 7LP **t** 020 7602 8822 **f** 020 7603 2352 **e** hello@tcpinternational.com Live Manager/Event Prod: John Fairs.

Teri Wyncoll Tour Management 239 Clarendon Park Road, Leicester LE2 3AN **t** 0116 270 4007 **f** 0116 270 4007 **e** dave.davies1@virgin.net MD: Teri Wyncoll.

Terminal Studios 4-10 Lamb Walk, London Bridge, London SE1 3TT **t** 020 7403 3050 **f** 020 7407 6123 **e** info@terminal.co.uk **w** terminal.co.uk Prop: Charlie Barrett.

That's EnTEEtainment 59 Prince Street, Bristol BS1 4QH **t** 0117 904 4116 **f** 0117 904 4117 **e** dick@dicktee.com **w** dicktee.com MD: Dick Tee.

Ticket Zone Taw Vale, Barnstaple, Devon EX32 8NJ **t** 01271 323355 **f** 01271 375902 **e** sales@ticketzone.co.uk **w** ticketzone.co.uk Contact: Domingo Tjornelund

Ticketmaster UK 48 Leicester Square, London WC2H 7LR **t** 020 7344 4000 **f** 020 7915 0411 **e** sales@ticketmaster.co.uk **w** ticketmaster.co.uk National Sales Mgr: Tim Chambers.

Ticketweb (UK) Ltd 48 Leicester Square, London WC2H 7LR **t** 020 7316 3550 **f** 020 7344 0331 **e** info@ticketweb.co.uk; clients@ticketweb.co.uk **w** ticketweb.co.uk

TM International 4 Badby Road, Newnham, Northamptonshire NN11 3HE **t** 01327 705032 or 07785 267751 **f** 01327 300037 **e** hitme@cwcom.net MD: Harry Isles.

The Tough Enough Touring Company Tour Mngmt & Splitter Van Hire, 88 Calvert Road, Greenwich, London SE10 0DF **t** 020 8333 9447 or 07985 142 193 **e** sam.towers@ganzmanagement.com Contact: Sam Towers

Trathens Travel Services Ltd Burrington Way, Plymouth, Devon PL5 3LS **t** 01752 772000 **f** 01752 769629 Contact: The Manager

24/7 Productions 62 Canalot Studios, 222 Kensal Road, London W10 5BN **t** 020 8964 4888 **f** 020 8964 4777

Violation Tour Production 26 Mill Street, Gamlingay, Sandy, Bedfordshire SG19 3JW **t** 01767 651552 or 07768 667076 **f** 01767 651228 **e** dicky_boy@msn.com Manager: Dick Meredith.

Len Wright Band Services 9 Elton Way, Watford, Hertfordshire WD2 8HH **t** 01923 238611 or 07831 811201 **f** 01923 230134 **e** lwbs1@aol.com Contact: Les Collins Transport suppliers, sleeper coaches.

Pro Sound News
Innovative control surface console from Australian ergonomics champion
Smart ARC de triomphe
Installation
AUDIO, VIDEO AND LIGHTING IN THE BUILT ENVIRONMENT
EUROPE
Playing the field
Behind the scenes of an Italian stadium re-fit
Primal screen
Why cinema projects face an uncertain future
Seas of change
State-of-the-art systems onboard Queen Mary 2
Ears first, eyes later?
Audio puts lighting in the shade at PLASA
Systems in concert
Designing for live venues
The European Systems Yearbook
2005
Pro Sound News VOLUME 5

Recording studios

▲ Indicates **APRS STUDIO MEMBERS**

10th Planet 40 Newman St, London W1T 1QJ **t** 020 7637 9500 **f** 020 7637 9599 **e** studio@10thplanet.net **w** 10thplanet.net Dirs: Ben Woolley & Jon Voda.

2KHz Studios 97a Scrubs Lane, London NW10 6QU **t** 020 8960 1331 **f** 020 8968 3377 **e** info@2khzstudios.co.uk **w** 2khzstudios.co.uk Studio Manager: Mike Nelson. **EMI TG Desk 28 Channel1964 Design, Boxer 3 Way Monitors, Yamaha Ns10, B&W Dm1200, 1A80 MKI , Protools 24 Mix Plus 24bit, Protools 5, 24tk Studer.**

▲ABBEY ROAD STUDIOS

3 Abbey Road, London NW8 9AY Tel: 020 7266 7000 **f** 020 7266 7250 **e** bookings@abbeyroad.com **w** abbeyroad.com Studio Mgr: Colette Barber. Post Production Manager: Lucy Launder. **Studio 1: 72 channel Neve 88RS with full surround capabilities and stem section Studio 2: Neve VRP 60 Channel. Studio 3: SSL9000J series 96 channel. Penthouse: Neve Capricorn Digital.**

ADS Studios 16A Westhaven, Clonsilla, Dublin 15, Ireland **t** +353 1 822 2268 or +353 87 2372787 **f** +353 1 822 4657 **e** sales@duplication.ie **w** duplication.ie Sales Manager: Tom Byrne. Studio Mgr: Colin Turner. **STUDIO 1: Hard Disk 24 trk digital.**

AGM Studios 1927 Building, 2 Michael Rd, London SW6 2AD **t** 020 7371 0234 **e** contacts@agmstudios.com **w** agmstudios.com MD: Alex Golding.

▲Air Studios (Lyndhurst) Lyndhurst Hall, Lyndhurst Road, London NW3 5NG **t** 020 7794 0660 **f** 020 7794 8518 **e** info@airstudios.com **w** airstudios.com Bookings Mgr: Alison Burton. Gen Mgr: Jacqui Howell. **LYNDHURST HALL: Neve 88R 96ch. STUDIO 1: Custom Neve 72ch. STUDIO 2: SSL 8000G Plus 72ch with full 5.1 monitoring. STUDIO 3: AMS Logic 2 with AudoFile S24. DUBBING: AMS Logics 2 & 3 with AudioFile S24. All studios with full 5.1 monitoring.**

▲Air-Edel Recording Studios 18 Rodmarton Street, London W1U 8BJ **t** 020 7486 6466 **f** 020 7224 0344 **e** trevorbest@air-edel.co.uk **w** air-edel.co.uk Studio Mgr: Trevor Best. **Cadac 72 input.**

Airtight Productions Unit 16, Albany Rd Trading Estate, Albany Rd, Chorlton M21 OAZ **t** 0161 881 5157 **e** info@airtightproductions.co.uk **w** airtightproductions.co.uk Director: Anthony Davey.

Alaska @ Waterloo Bridge Studios 127-129 Alaska Street, London SE1 8XE **t** 020 7928 7440 **f** 020 7928 8070 **e** blodge_uk@yahoo.com **w** soundrecordingstudio.net Studio Mgr: Beverley Lodge. **MCI 36 input JH 600 series (automated).**

Albert Studios Unit 29, Cygnus Business Centre, Dalmeyer Road, London NW10 2XA **t** 020 8830 0330 **f** 020 8830 0220 **e** info@alberts.co.uk **w** albertmusic.co.uk Studio Manager: Paul Hoare. **Neve VR60 channel state of the art recording/mixing room. Two fully equipped programming rooms.**

Angel Recording Studios Ltd 311 Upper Street, London N1 2TU **t** 020 7354 2525 **f** 020 7226 9624 **e** angel@angelstudios.co.uk **w** angelstudios.co.uk Studio Mgr: Lucy Jones. **STUDIO 1: Neve VR 60. STUDIO 2: Soundtracks Jade 48. STUDIO 3: Neve VXS.**

Angel Studios The Brainyard, 156-158 Gray's Inn Road, London WC1X 8ED **t** 020 7209 0536 **e** info@arriba-records.com Dir: S-J Henry.

Mark Angelo Studios Unit 13, Impress House, Mansell Road, London W3 7QH **t** 020 8735 0040 **f** 020 8735 0041 **e** mimi@markangelo.co.uk **w** markangelo.co.uk Studio Manager: Mimi Kerns.

AngelSword Productions Ltd Little Barn, Plaistow Road, Loxwood, West Sussex RH14 0SX **t** 01403 751 862 **f** 01403 753 564 **e** jonn@jonnsavannah.co.uk **w** jonnsavannah.co.uk Dir: Jonn Savannah.

APE Recording 19 Market Street, Castle Donington, Derby DE74 2JB **t** 01332 810933 **f** 01332 850123 **e** info@APE.co.uk **w** APE.co.uk Studio Mgr: Nira Amba. **Studiomaster Series 2.**

Apollo Studio (see Temple Lane Recording)

Arclite Studios Unit 303 Safestore, 5-10 Eastman Rd, London W3 7YG **t** 020 8743 4000 **e** Info@arcliteproductions.com **w** arcliteproductions.com Studio Mgrs: Alan Bleay/Laurie Jenkins.

Are We Mad? Studios 34 Whitehorse Lane, London SE25 6RE **t** 020 8653 7744 or 020 8771 1470 **f** 020 8771 1911 **e** info@ariwa.com **w** ariwa.com Studio Mgr: Kamal Fraser.

Ariwa Sounds 34 Whitehorse Lane, London SE25 6RE **t** 020 8653 7744 or 020 8771 1470 **f** 020 8771 1911 **e** info@ariwa.com **w** ariwa.com Studio Mgr: Joseph Fraser. **Soundcraft 52 channel.**

Arriba Studios 256-258 Gray's Inn Road, London WC1X 8ED **t** 020 7713 0998 **e** info@arriba-records.com **w** arriba-records.com Contact: SJ/Baby Doc

The Audio Workshop 217 Askew Road, London W12 9AZ **t** 020 8742 9242 **f** 020 8743 4231 MD: Martin Cook. **Studios 1, 2, 3 & 4: DDA.**

AudioEdit 15 Popes Grove, Strawberry Hill, Twickenham, Middlesex TW2 5TA **t** 020 8755 2349 **e** timhandley@freenet.co.uk Studio Mgr: Tim Handley.

Audiolab West Street 3 West St, Buckingham, Bucks MK18 1HL **t** 01280 822814 **f** 01280 822814 **e** office@alab.co.uk **w** alab.co.uk Studio Manager: Jamie Masters.

Axis Recording Studios 3 Brown Street, Sheffield, South Yorkshire S1 2BS **t** 0114 275 0283 **f** 0114 275 4915 **e** axis@syol.com **w** axisrecordingstudios.co.uk Studio Mgr: Paul R Bower. **Neve 51.**

B&H Sound Services Ltd The Old School Studio, Crowland Road, Eye, Peterborough PE6 7TN **t** 01733 223535 **f** 01733 223545 **e** sound@bhsound.co.uk **w** bhsound.co.uk Recording Co-ordinator: Nicola Tonge.

Band On The Wall Studio 25 Swan Street, Northern Quarter, Manchester M4 5JZ **t** 0161 834 1786 **f** 0161 834 2559 **w** bandonthewall.org Promotions: Gavin Sharp.

Bandwagon Studios Westfield Folkhouse, Westfield Lane, Mansfield, Notts NG18 1TL **t** 01623 422962 **f** 01623 633449 **e** info@bandwagonstudios.co.uk **w** bandwagonstudios.co.uk Studio Mgr: Andy Dawson. Bookings Mgr: Mark Allsop. **Soundtracs Megas 40-24-2.**

Bark Studio 1A Blenheim Road, London E17 6HS **t** 020 8523 0110 **f** 020 8523 0110 **e** Brian@barkstudio.co.uk **w** barkstudio.co.uk Studio Manager: Brian O'Shaughnessy. **MCI Series 600.**

BBC Resources (London) Maida Vale Music Studios, Delaware Road, London W9 2LH **t** 020 7765 3374 **f** 020 7765 3203 **e** adam.askew@bbc.co.uk Ops Mgr: Adam Askew. Studio Mgr: Mark Diamond. **SSL 4000G.**

Be-Bop Recording Studio Unit 4 Indian Queens Workshops, Moorland Rd, Indian Queens, Cornwall TR9 6JP **t** 01726 861068 **e** sales@be-bop.co.uk **w** be-bop.co.uk Prop: Steve White.

Beaumont Street Studios Ltd St Peters Chambers, St Peters Street, Huddersfield, West Yorkshire HD1 1RA **t** 01484 452013 **f** 01484 435861 **e** info@beaumontstreet.co.uk Studio Mgr: Sam Roberts. **Amek Rembrandt desk.**

Beechpark Studios Newtown, Rathcoole, Co Dublin, Ireland **t** +353 1 458 8500 **f** +353 1 458 8577 **e** info@beechpark.com **w** beechpark.com Studio Manager: Dara Winston. DDA.

Beige Phunk Productions 54 Great Marlborough St, London W1F 7JU **t** 020 7434 9199 **f** 020 7434 3994 **e** info@beigephunk.com **w** beigephunk.com Director: Khaled Bin Ali. Studio Manager: Lysha Davis. **Makie 32 Channel Mixer, Dynaudio acoustics BM6A, ProTools 64track Hard Disk recording.**

Berlin Recording Studios Caxton House, Caxton Avenue, Blackpool, Lancashire FY2 9AP **t** 01253 591169 **f** 01253 508670 **e** berlin.studios@virgin.net **w** berlinstudios.co.uk MD: Ron Sharples. **Soundtracs Quartz 48 channel.**

Biffco 20 Ringsend Road, Dublin 4, Ireland **t** +353 1 668 5567 **f** +353 1 667 0114 **e** biffco1@indigo.ie **w** biffco.net Studio Mgr: Dave Morgan.

Big Noise Recordings 12 Gregory Street, Northampton NN1 1TA **t 01604 634455** Studio Mgr: Ben Gordelier.

Blah Street Studios The Hop Kiln, Hillside, Odiham, Hants RG29 1HX **t** 01256 701112 **f** 01256 701106 **e** studio@blahstreet.co.uk **w** blahstreet.co.uk Producer: Nick Hannan.

Blakamix International Garvey House, 42 Margetts Road, Bedford MK42 8DS **t** 01234 302115 **f** 01234 854344 **e** blakamix@aol.com **w** blakamix.co.uk MD: Dennis Bedeau.

Blank Tape Studios 16 Sidney Street, Sheffield, South Yorkshire S1 4RH **t** 0114 275 7757 **w** blanktape.fsnet.co.uk Studio Mgr: Tom Chester.

Blueprint Studios Elizabeth House, 39 Queen Street, Salford, Manchester M3 4DQ **t** 08700 11 27 60 **f** 08700 11 27 80 **e** info@blueprint-studios.com **w** blueprint-studios.com Studio Manager: Tim Thomas.

BonaFideStudio Burbage House, 83-85 Curtain Road, London EC2A 3BS **t** 020 7684 5350 or 020 7684 5351 **f** 020 7613 1185 **e** info@bonafidestudio.co.uk **w** bonafidestudio.co.uk Studio Director: Deanna Gardner.

Boomtown (ProTools) Studio Valetta Road, London W3 7TG **t** 020 8723 9548 or 07961 405 140 **e** info@boomtownstudio.co.uk **w** boomtownstudio.co.uk Contact: Simon Wilkinson

Born To Dance Studios Unit 34, DRCA Business Centre, Charlotte Despard Ave, Battersea, London SW11 5JH **t** 01273 301555 **f** 01273 305266 **e** studio@borntodance.com **w** borntodance.com Studio Mgr: Gavin McCall. **Mackie D8B - 72 channel.**

The Bridge Facilities Ltd 55-57 Great Marlborough St, London W1F 7JX **t** 020 7434 9861 **f** 020 7494 4658 **e** bookings@thebridge.co.uk **w** thebridge.co.uk Facilities Mgr: Tom McConville. Bookings Mgr: Angela Parkinson. **SSL 6032 x 2 Lexicon Opus.**

Broadley Studios Broadley House, 48 Broadley Terrace, London NW1 6LG **t** 020 7258 0324 f 020 7724 2361 e manny@broadleystudios.com w broadleystudios.com GM: Manny Elias. Studio Mgr: Peter Griffiths. Yamaha 02R with Pro-Tools.

BRITANNIA ROW STUDIOS

3 Bridge Studios, 318-326 Wandsworth Bridge Road, London SW6 2TZ **t** 020 7371 5872 **f** 020 7371 8641 **e** info@britanniarowstudios.co.uk **w** britanniarowstudios.co.uk Studio Manager: Kate Koumi. STUDIO 1: Vintage Neve 60ch. with moving faders + Protools HD3 Accel. STUDIO 2: Mackie D8B + Protools Mix 3. STUDIO 3: Yamaha 02R + Protools Mix+.

Bryn Derwen Studio Coed-y-Parc, Bethesda, Gwynedd LL57 4YW **t** 01248 600234 f 01248 601933 e Laurie@brynderwen.co.uk w brynderwen.co.uk Manager: Laurie Gane. DDA AMR 36 analogue and digital 48 track.

The Building 37 Rowley Street, Stafford, Staffs ST16 2RH **t** 01785 245649 or 07866 718010 **e** info@thebuilding.co.uk **w** thebuilding.co.uk Studio Mgr: Tim Simmons. **Soundtracs Solitaire 32, G5 Mac with MOTU 192 kHz AD/DAs, Genelec 1037 and Blue Sky 5.1**

The Bunker Recording Studio Borras Road, Borras, Wrexham LL13 9TW **t** 01978 263295 **f** 01978 263295 **e** kklass@btconnect.com **w** k-klass.com Contact: Andrew Willimas

Ca Va Sound Workshops 30 Bentinck Street, Kelvingrove, Glasgow, Strathclyde G3 7TU **t** 0141 334 5099 **f** 0141 339 0271 **e** helen@cavastudios.co.uk **w** cavastudios.co.uk Bookings Mgr: Helen Clark. Studio Mgr: Brian Young.

Cabin Studios 82 London Rd, Coventry, Warwickshire CV1 2JT **t** 024 7622 0749 **e** office@sonar-records.demon.co.uk **w** cabinstudio.co.uk MD: Jon Lord. **Soundcraft 2400, 24 track digital and analogue.**

CAP Recording Studios Crask Of Aigas, By Beauly, Inverness-Shire IV4 7AD **t** 01463 782364 f 01463 782525 **e** capdonna@cali.co.uk Studio/Bkings Mgr: Donna Cunningham. **Yamaha 02R.**

Castlesound Studios The Old School, Park View, Pencaitland, East Lothian EH34 5DW **t** 0131 666 1024 **f** 0131 666 1024 **e** info@castlesound.co.uk **w** castlesound.co.uk Studio & Bookings Mgr: Freeland Barbour. **Neve Series 51 Classic 72 ch 40 trk digital and 24 trk analogue + 24 trk Radar II.**

The Cave Studio 155 Acton Lane, Park Royal, London NW10 7NJ **t** 020 8961 5818 **f** 020 8965 7008 **e** cavestudio@jet-star.co.uk Contact: Danny Ray Amek **Einstein Console, Soundcraft DC2000.**

Cent Music Melbourne House, Chamberlain St, Wells BA5 2PJ **t** 01749 689074 **f** 01749 670315 **e** kevin@centrecords.com **w** centrecords.com MD: Kevin Newton.

Chamber Recording Studio 120A West Granton Road, Edinburgh, Midlothian EH5 1PF **t** 0131 551 6632 **f** 0131 551 6632 **e** mail@humancondition.co.uk **w** chamberstudio.co.uk Studio Mgr: Jamie Watson. **AMEK 24 track.**

Chapel Studios Bryants Corner, South Thorseby, Lincolnshire LN13 0AS **t** 01507 480305 or 01507 480761 **f** 01507 480752 Studio Mgr: Andy Dransfield. **STUDIO 1: AMEK 2500. STUDIO 2: Neotek Elite.**

Chem19 Recording Studios Unit 5C, Peacock Cross Trading Estate, Burnbank Road, Hamilton ML3 9AQ **t** 01698 286882 **e** mail@chem19studios.co.uk **w** chem19studios.co.uk Manager: Peter Black.

▲Classic Sound Ltd 5 Falcon Park, Neasden Lane, London NW10 1RZ **t** 020 8208 8100 **f** 020 8208 8111 **e** info@classicsound.net **w** classicsound.net Director: Neil Hutchinson.

Coad Mountain Studios Coad, Caherdaniel, Co Kerry, Ireland **t +353 66 947 5171 f** +353 66 947 5264 **e** coadmountain@eircom.net Bookings Mgr: Simon Taylor. **Studio 1: Soundcraft Spirit Auto 24:8:2. Studio 2: PC Cubase UST.**

Compression Studios 56 Frazer Road, Perivale, Middlesex UB6 7AL **t** 020 8723 6158 **e** suli.hirani@btinternet.com Studio Manager: Suli.

Contour Studios Unit 4 Hallam Mill, Hallam St, Stockport, Cheshire **t** 07974 236 275 **e** danfunk@breathe.com **w** contourstudios.co.uk Producer: Daniel Broad.

Conversion Studios Woolfields, Milton On Stour, Gillingham, Dorset **t** 01747 824729 **e** info@conversionstudios.co.uk **w** conversionstudios.co.uk Studio Manager: Owen Thomas.

Cordella Music 35 Britannia Gdns, Hedge End, Hants SO30 2RN **t** 08450 616616 or 01489 780909 **e** barry@cordellamusic.co.uk **w** cordellamusic.co.uk MD: Barry Upton. **Allen & Heath Sabre.**

Core Studios Kings Court, 7 Osborne St, Glasgow G1 5QN **t** 0141 552 6677 **f** 0141 552 1354 **e** mail@corestudios.co.uk w corestudios.co.uk Co-Dir: Alan Walsh. **STUDIO ONE: Tascam, ProTools HD. STUDIO TWO: Soundcraft Ghost, ProTools LE.**

Cottage Recording Studios 2 Gawsworth Road, Macclesfield, Cheshire SK11 8UE **t** 01625 420163 **f** 01625 420168 **e** info@cottagegroup.co.uk **w** cottagegroup.co.uk MD: Roger Boden. Bookings Mgr: Wesley Boden. Studio Mgr: Glenn Lockley.

Courtyard Recording Studios Gorsey Mount Street, Waterloo Road, Stockport, Cheshire SK1 3BU **t** 0161 477 6531 **e** tim@courtyardrecordingstudios.co.uk **w** courtyardrecordingstudios.co.uk Studio Mgr: Tim Woodward.

Courtyard Studio 21 The Nursery, Sutton Courtenay, Abingdon, Oxon OX14 4UA **t** 01235 845800 **f** 01235 847692 **e** kate@cyard.com Studio Mgr: Kate Cotter. Bookings Mgr: Kate Cotter. **MTA 980.**

Cuan Studios Spiddal, Conamara, Co Galway, Ireland **t** +353 91 553838 **f** +353 91 553837 **e** info@cuan.com **w** cuan.com Studio Director: Eilis Lennon. Bookings Mgr: Fionnuala Mannion. **STUDIO 1: ProControl 128 track. STUDIO 2: Yamaha 02R.**

The Cutting Rooms Abraham Moss Centre, Crescent Road, Manchester M8 5UF **t** 0161 740 9438 **f** 0161 740 9438 **e** cuttingrooms@hotmail.com **w** citycol.com/cuttingrooms Studio Mgr: Andrew Harris. Studio Mgr: Andrew Harris. **Studio 1: Raindirk Symphony 56 inputs with Flying Faders. Studio 2: Berringer MX8000. Studio 3: Yamaha 02R Total Recall.**

Dada Studios 157A Hubert Grove, Stockwell, London SW9 9NZ **t** 020 7501 9545 or 07956 945 417 **f** 020 7501 9216 **e** dadastudios@mac.com Studio Manager: George Holt. **Amek 2500, 2" 24 Track and Logic Audio on Digidesign Protools, KRK 9000B/Yamaha NS10's.**

▲The Dairy 43-45 Tunstall Rd, London SW9 8BZ **t** 020 7738 7777 **f** 020 7738 7007 **e** info@thedairy.co.uk **w** thedairy.co.uk Contact: Emily Taylor **Studio 1: Neve VR Legend 60ch. Studio 2: DDA AMR 24.**

DB Entertainments Ltd PO Box 147, Peterborough, Cambridgeshire PE1 4XU **t** 01733 311755 **f** 01733 709449 **e** info@dbentertainments.com **w** dbentertainments.com Director/Producer: Russell Dawson-Butterworth.

De-Mix Productions 7 Croxley Rd, London W9 3HH **t** 020 8960 1115 **e** martin.lascelles@virgin.net MD: Martin Lascelles. **STUDIO 1: Soundcraft TS12.**

deBrett Studios 42 Wood Vale, Muswell Hill, London N10 3DP **t** 020 8372 6179 **e** jwest@debrett41.freeserve.co.uk Proprietor: Jon West.

Deep Recording Studios 187 Freston Road, London W10 6TH **t** 020 8964 8256 **f** 020 8969 1363 **e** deep.studios@virgin.net w deeprecordingstudios.com Studio Manager: Mark Rose. Bookings Mgr: Mark Rose. Studio Mgr: Mark Rose. **48trk Radars, 96 channel asp 8024 Audient Desk, Quested Monitors.**

Delta Recording Studios Deanery Farm, Bolts Hill, Chatham, Kent CT4 7LD **t** 01227 732140 **f** 01227 732140 **e** delta.studios@virgin.net **w** deltastudios.co.uk Contact: Julian Whitfield

The Den Studio Archers Close, Archers Fields, Basildon, Essex SS13 1DH **t** 0956 887 162 or 07932 521 516 **e** leo294@dircon.co.uk **w** biglionproductions.com Manager: Michelle Alexander.

DEP International Studios 1 Andover Street, Birmingham, West Midlands B5 5RG **t** 0121 633 4742 **f** 0121 643 4904 **e** enquiries@ub40.co.uk **w** ub40.co.uk Bkngs/Studio Mgr: Dan Sprigg. **STUDIO 1: SSLE 4056e Total Recall. STUDIO 2: DDA AMR 24.**

Digital Hit Factory 613 Anlaby Road, Hull **t** 01482 573759 **e** marsh@digihitfactory.demon.co.uk **w** digitalhitfactory.co.uk Contact: Dean Marshall

The Dog House Studio Little Purbeck, Bolney Rd, Lower Shiplake, Henley-On-Thames, Oxon RG9 3NS **t** 0118 940 3516 **f** 0118 940 3516 **e** barrie.barlow@virgin.net **w** doghousestudios.com Studio Manager: Barrie Barlow. **Amek, Amek Angela, MCI, UREI. AMS, Neuman etc.**

Dreamhouse Studio (Rive Droite Music) Home Park House, Hampton Court Road, Kingston Upon Thames, Surrey KT1 4AE **t** 020 8977 0666 **f** 020 8977 0660 **e** sirharry@rivedroitemusic.com **w** rivedroitemusic.com MD: Sir Harry.

Earth Productions 163 Gerrard Street, Birmingham, West Midlands B19 2AP **t** 0121 554 7424 **f** 0121 554 9250 **e** earth.p@virgin.net Studio Mgr: Natasha Godfrey. **Studio 1: Soundtrac IL 48/32. Studio 2: Mackie Digital D8B r-drive HDR 24 track digital.**

Earthworks Music Studios 62 The Rear, Barnet High Street, Herts EN5 5SL **t** 020 8449 2258 or 07989 549 730 **e** ljdarlow@aol.com **w** earthworksstudio.co.uk Head Engineer: Leigh Darlow. **24 track digital recording and digital editing, Soundcraft DC2000 (32:32)**

Eastcote Studios Ltd 249 Kensal Road, London W10 5DB **t** 020 8969 3739 **f** 020 8960 1836 **e** peggy@eastcotestudios.co.uk **w** eastcotestudios.co.uk Studio Mgr: Peggy Fussell. Studio Owner: Philip Bagenal. **STUDIO 1:48 track with MCI JH542C automated. STUDIO 2: 24 track with Mackie 56/8/2.**

Ebony & Ivory Productions 11 Varley Parade, Edgware Road, Colindale, London NW9 6RR **t** 020 8200 7090 **e** SVLProds@aol.com Studio Manager: Alan Bradshaw.

▲Eden Studios Ltd 20-24 Beaumont Road, Chiswick, London W4 5AP **t** 020 8995 5432 **f** 020 8747 1931 **e** eden@edenstudios.com **w** edenstudios.com Studio Mgr: Natalie Horton. **Studio 1: SSL 6056G (48 trk). Studio 2: 6060E. Out Of Eden Programming Suite: Fame2 + ProTools.**

Elektra Studio (see Temple Lane Recording)

EMS Audio Ltd 12 Balloo Avenue, Bangor, Co Down BT19 7QT **t** 028 9127 4411 **f** 028 9127 4412 **e** ems@musicshop.to **w** musicshop.to Director: William Thompson. Studio Mgr: Leslie Hume. Bookings Mgr: William Thompson. **STUDIO 1: Mackie 48 Channel.**

English West Coast Music The Old Bakehouse, 150 High Street, Honiton, Devon EX14 1JX **t** 01404 42234 **f** 07767 869029 **e** studio@ewcm.co.uk **w** ewcm.co.uk Snr Prod: Ian Dent. Studio Mgr: Paul Bateman. Bookings Mgr: Sean Brown. **STUDIO 1: Helios/Soundtracs.**

The Factory Sound (Woldingham) Toftrees, Church Rd, Woldingham, Surrey CR3 7JX **t** 01883 652386 **f** 01883 652457 **e** mackay@dircon.co.uk Producer/Engineer: David Mackay. Studio Mgr: Ron Challis. **Harrison 32-24.**

Fairview Music Cavewood Grange Farm, Common Lane, North Cave, Brough, East Yorks HU15 2PE **t** 01430 425546 **f** 01430 425547 **e** sales@fairviewstudios.co.uk **w** fairviewstudios.co.uk Studio Manager: Andy Newlove.

Farm Studios Windyhill Farm, Houston, Renfrewshire, Scotland PA6 7AA **t** 01505 325111 **f** 01505 382841 Studio Mgr: Andy Kinning. **Studio 1: Otari Status/Pro Tools Mix Plus System. Studio 2: O2R Pro Tools/Programming Suite. Studio 3: O2R Pro Tools/Programming Suite.**

Fat Fox Studios 24a Radley Mews, Kensington, London W8 6JP **t** 020 7376 9666 **f** 020 7937 6246 **e** info@fatfox.co.uk **w** fatfoxstudios.co.uk Studio Manager: Richie Kayvan. **Focusrite, Mackie, Genelec, Protools HD.**

Firebird Studios Kyrle House Studios, Edde Cross Street, Ross-on-Wye, Herefordshire HR9 7BZ **t** 01989 762269 **f** 01989 566337 **e** info@firebird.com **w** firebird.com CEO: Peter Martin.

Fisher Lane Farm Fisher Lane, Chiddingfold, Surrey GU8 4TB **t** 01428 684475 **f** 01428 684947 Contact: Dale Newman SSL 4056.

Foel Studio Llanfair, Caereinion, Powys SY21 0DS **t** 01938 810758 **f** 01938 810758 **e** foel.studio@dial.pipex.com **w** foelstudio.co.uk MD: Dave Anderson. Studio Mgr: Dave Anderson. Bookings Mgr: Dave Anderson. **48 track Trident 80 B with Optifile automation**

FourFives Music 21d Heathman's Rd, London SW6 4TJ **t** 020 7731 6555 **f** 020 7371 5005 **e** mp@fourfives-music.com **w** fourfives-music.com Bookings Mgr: Mia Pillay.

Frog Studios Unit 2B, Banquay Trading Estate, Slutchers Lane, Warrington, Cheshire WA1 1PJ **t** 01925 445742 **f** 01925 445742 **e** info@frogstudios.co.uk **w** frogstudios.co.uk Studio Mgr: Steve Millington. Bookings Mgr: Steve Oates. **STUDIO 1: Soundtracks Quartz 48. STUDIO 2: Soundtracks Solitaire full automation.**

▲Gateway Studio Kingston Hill Centre, Kingston, Surrey KT2 7LB **t** 020 8547 8167 or 020 8549 0014 ex 202 **f** 020 8547 8167 **e** studio@gsr.org.uk **w** gsr.org.uk Studio Mgr: Gurjit Dhinsa. Bookings Mgr: Andy Smith. Studio Mgr: Jason Edge. **Soundcraft DC 2020 40 channel.**

Jeffrey Ginn 11 Haycroft, Wootton, Bedford MK43 9PB **t** 01234 765602 **f** 01234 765602 **e** jeffginn@onetel.net

Golden Acrid 78 Albion Road, Edinburgh, Lothian EH7 5QZ **t** 0131 659 6673 **e** info@goldenacrid.com **w** goldenacrid.com Studio Mgr: James Locke.

Gorse Road Studios 2 Longlane, Staines, Middlesex TW19 7AA **t** 01784 255629 **f** 01784 420672 **e** cliffrandall@compuserve.com Studio Mgr: Cliff Randall.

The Granary Studio Bewlbridge Farm, Lamberhurst, Kent TN3 8JJ **t** 01892 891128 **e** guydenning@tgas.co.uk **w** tgas.co.uk Studio Mgr: Guy Denning. **TAC Matchless.**

Grand Central Studios 25-32 Marshall Street, London W1F 7ES **t** 020 7306 5600 **f** 020 7306 5616 **e** info@grand-central-studios.com **w** grand-central-studios.com MD: Carole Humphrey. Studio Mgr: Oscar Kugblenu. Bookings Mgr: Louise Allen. **Four studio complex with AMS Neve Logic 2. 24 track Spectra Audiofile, SFX Fileserver, E4s, 2 x Dolby 5.1 cinema rooms.**

Great Linford Manor Great Linford Manor, Great Linford, Milton Keynes, Buckinghamshire MK14 5AX **t** 01908 667432 **f** 01908 668164 **e** bookings@greatlinfordmanor.com **w** greatlinfordmanor.com Studio Manager: Sue Dawson. **Neve VR60 Legend, 2 x Studer A820 analogue, 4-way Quested monitoring.**

Greystoke Studios 39 Greystoke Park Terrace, Ealing, London W5 1JL **t** 020 8998 5529 or 07850 735591 **e** andy@greystokeproductions.co.uk **w** greystokeproductions.co.uk Owner/Director: Andy Whitmore. Bookings Mgr: Tom Garrad-Cole. **Mackie 56 channel desk with automation, protools 64trk. Logic Audio Platinum V$. STUDIO B: Preproduction programing suite.**

Ground Zero Studios 43-45 Coombe Terrace, Lewes Rd, Brighton BN2 4AD **t** 01273 819 617 **f** 01273 272 830 **e** james@g-zero.co.uk **w** g-zero.co.uk Studio Mgr: James Stringfellow. **Sony DMX-R100, Otari MTR90 MK II, Dynaudio BM15-A.**

The Hanger Recording Studio Unit H, 4 Doman Rd, Yorktown Ind Est., Camberley, Surrey GU15 3DF **t** 01276 685808 **f** 01276 683060 **e** info@thehanger.co.uk **w** thehanger.co.uk Owner: Tom Gibbs. **Tascam DM24, Yamaha MSP5s, Hard Drive Recording.**

Harewood Farm Studios Little Harewood Farm, Clamgoose Lane, Staffs ST10 2EG **t** 07782 306251 **f** 01538 755735 **e** gilroy@fenetre.co.uk **w** harewoodfarmstudios.com Studio Mgr: Kristian Gilroy.

Hatch Farm Studios Chertsey Rd, Addlestone, Surrey KT15 2EH **t** 01932 828715 **f** 01932 828717 **e** brian.adams@dial.pipex.com MD: Brian Adams. Studio Mgr: Felix Reisch.

Hear No Evil 6 Lillie Yard, London SW6 1UB **t** 020 7385 8244 **f** 020 7385 0700 **e** info@hearnoevil.net **w** hearnoevil.net MD: Sharon Rose. **Euphonix CS2000.**

Heartbeat Recording Studio Guildie House Farm, North Middleton, Gorbridge, Mid Lothian EH23 4QP **t** 01875 821102 **f** 01875 821102 **e** eddie@logane.freeserve.co.uk Engineer/Prod: David L Valentine. **Hard disk/analogue recording.**

Helicon Mountain The Station, Station Terrace Mews, London SE3 7LP **t** 020 8858 0984 **f** 020 8293 4555 Studio Mgr: Richard Holland. **Soundtracs Quartz 48 channel in line.**

Hi Street 25 Churchfield Road, London W3 6BD **t** 020 8896 1925 Studio Manager: Gareth Redfarn.

High Barn Studio The Bardfield Centre, Great Bardfield, Braintree, Essex CM7 4SL **t** 01371 811291 **f** 01371 811404 **e** info@high-barn.com **w** high-barn.com Studio Manager: Simon Allen.

The Hospital Group 24 Endell Street, London WC2H 9HQ **t** 020 7170 9110 **f** 020 7170 9102 **e** studio@thehospital.co.uk **w** thehospital.co.uk Studio Sales Manager: Anne Marie Phelan. **96 Channel SSL MT+ fully automated digital consoleProTools HD3 with Logic & Digital PerformerStuder A827Ampex ATR100Sony PCM-7040Tascam DA-98HRPMC Surround Sound**

H20 Enterprises Sphere Studios, 2 Shuttleworth Road, Battersea, London SW11 3EA **t** 020 7737 9700 **f** 020 7326 9499 **e** simonb@h2o.co.uk **w** h2o.co.uk Bkngs/Studio Mgr: Patti Nilder.

▲ICC Studios 4 Regency Mews, Silverdale Road, Eastbourne, East Sussex BN20 7AB **t** 01323 643341 **f** 01323 649240 **e** info@iccstudios.co.uk **w** iccstudios.co.uk Studio Mgr: Helmut Kaufmann. Bookings Mgr: Gayle Price. Studio Mgr: Helmut Kaufmann. Bookings Mgr: Gayle Price. **Soundtracs Jade desk, Otan Radar II, Protools, 2" analogue with Dolby SR, Vintage mics & outboard gear, self-catering apartment.**

The ICE Group 3 St Andrews Street, Lincoln, Lincolnshire LN5 7NE **t** 01522 539883 **f** 01522 528964 **e** steve.hawkins@easynet.co.uk **w** icegroup.co.uk MD: Steve Hawkins.

▲Iguana Studios Unit 1, 88a Acre Lane, London SW2 5QN **t** 020 7924 0496 **e** info@iguanastudio.co.uk **w** iguanastudio.co.uk MD: Andrea Terrano. **Studio 1 & 2: Mackie D8B, HHB Circle 5, Logic Audio Pro 6, 24 Tracks Pro-Tools, 24 Tracks Soundscape.**

Impulse Studio 71 High Street East, Wallsend, Tyne and Wear NE28 7RJ **t** 0191 262 4999 **f** 0191 263 7082 MD: David Wood. **Soundtracs 32-16-24.**

In A City Studio & Services Unit 49, Business Centre, 60 Carlisle Road, Bradford BD8 8BD **t** 01904 438753 or 01274 223251 **f** 01274 223204 **e** cc@inacity.co.uk **w** inacity.co.uk MD: Carl Stipetic. **24-Track Analogue & Digital. Cubase vst.**

INFX Recording Studios Wellesbourne Campus, Kingshill Rd, High Wycombe, Bucks HP13 5BB **t** 01494 522141 ex 4020 **f** 01494 465432 **e** fmacke01@bcuc.ac.uk Studio Manager: Frazer Mackenzie. **Focusrite & Mackie, Genelec (5.1 surround) & Tannoy, Protools Promix 24, ADAT & Mackie.**

Instant Music 14 Moorend Crescent, Cheltenham, Gloucestershire GL53 0EL **t** 07957 355630 **f** 01242 523304 **e** info@instantmusic.co.uk **w** instantmusic.co.uk MD: Martin Mitchell.

Intimate Recording Studios The Smokehouse, 120 Pennington St, London E1 9BB **t** 020 7702 0789 **f** 020 7813 2766 **e** p.madden1@ntlworld.com **w** intimatestudios.com MDs: Paul Madden/Gerry Bron. Bookings Mgr: Gerry Bron. **Studio Mgr: Paul Madden. Harrison MR2.**

▲Jacob's Studios Ltd Ridgway House, Dippenhall, Farnham, Surrey GU10 5EE **t** 01252 715546 **f** 01252 712846 **e** andy@jacobs-studios.co.uk **w** jacobs-studios.co.uk Studio Mgr: Andy Fernbach. **STUDIO 1: Neve VR Flying Faders, tracking and mixing. STUDIO 2: SSL 4064 EG, computer and mixing.**

Jam Central Studio Unit 8, College Road Business Park, College Road North, Aston Clinton, Bucks HP22 5EY **t** 01296 633311 or 07765 258225 **f** 01296 633311 **e** admin@jamcentralrecords.co.uk **w** jamcentralrecords.co.uk MD: Stuart Robb.

Jingle Jangles The Strand, 156 Holywood Rd, Belfast, Co Antrim BT4 1NY **t** 028 9065 6769 **f** 028 9067 3771 **e** steve@jinglejangles.tv **w** jinglejangles.tv MD: Steve Martin.

Jumbo Music Complex 387-389 Chapter Road, London NW2 5NG **t** 020 8459 7256 **f** 020 8459 7256 Contact: The Facilities Mgr

KD's Studio 78 Church Path, London W4 5BJ **t** 020 8994 3142 **f** 020 8755 1124 **e** sue@kdees.co.uk **w** kdees.co.uk Studio Mgr: Kenny Denton. Bookings Mgr: Sue Denton.

▲Keynote Studios Green Lane, Burghfield Bridge, Reading RG30 3XN **t** 01189 599 944 **f** 01189 596442 **e** lizzie@keynotestudios.com **w** keynotestudios.com Studio Mgr: Lizzie Mills.

▲Konk Studios 84-86 Tottenham Lane, London N8 7EE **t** 020 8340 4757 or 020 8340 7873 **f** 020 8348 3952 **e** linda@konkstudio.com Studio Mgr: Sarah Lockwood. Bookings Mgr: Linda McBride. **STUDIO 1: Neve with GML Automation. STUDIO 2: SSL G series.**

La Rocka Studios Post Mark House, Cross Lane, Hornsey, London N8 7SA **t** 020 8348 2822 **e** info@larockastudios.co.uk **w** larockastudios.co.uk Director: Pete Chapman.

Lab 24 346 Kingsland Road, Ground Floor, London E8 4DA **t** 07970 309470 Studio Mgr: Hamish Dzewu. Studio Master 24:16:8:2 ; Yamaha NS 10's ; 24 track 2 inch reel to reel.

Bob Lamb's Recording Studio 122A Highbury Road, Kings Heath, Birmingham, West Midlands B14 7QP **t** 0121 443 2186 **e** boblamb@recklessltd.freeserve.co.uk Studio Mgr/Prop: Bob Lamb. **Tascam.**

▲Lansdowne Recording Studios Lansdowne House, Lansdowne Road, London W11 3LP **t** 020 7727 0041 **f** 020 7792 8904 **e** info@cts-lansdowne.co.uk **w** cts-lansdowne.co.uk Studio Mgr: Chris Dibble. Bookings Mgr: Vicki Pyrkos. **Neve VXS 72 channel with Flying Faders and Recall.**

The Leisure Factory Ltd The Leisure Factory, Oldfields, Cradley Heath, West Midlands B64 6BS **t** 01384 637776 **f** 01384 637227 **e** music@therobin.co.uk Director: Mike Hamblett.

Liberty City Studios 1 Tabley Close, Victoria Mansions, Macclesfield, Cheshire SK10 3SL **t** 07812 201 133 **e** darren@libertycity.biz **w** LibertyCity.Biz Contact: Darren Eager

The Library 2 Sybil Mews, London N4 1EP **t** 07956 412 209 **e** jules@librarystudio.com **w** librarystudio.com Owner: Julian Standen.

Lime Street Sound 3 Lime Court, Lime Street, Dublin 2, Ireland **t** +353 1 671 7271 **f** +353 1 670 7639 **e** limesound@eircom.net **w** limesound.com Dir: Steve McGrath.

LimeTree Studios Welgate, Mattishall, Dereham, Norfolk NR20 3PJ **t 01362 858015 f** 01362 858016 **e** info@limetreestudios.com **w** limetreestudios.com Proprietor: Stephen Pitkethly. **STUDIO 1: D&R Triton.**

Linden Studio Laurel Bank, Motherby, Penrith, Cumbria CA11 0RL **t** 01768 483181 **f** 01768 483181 **e** guy@lindenstudio.co.uk **w** lindenstudio.co.uk Producer/Engineer: Guy Forrester. Studio Mgr: Maire Morgan. **Soundcraft 2400.**

Livingston Recording Studios Brook Road, off Mayes Road, London N22 6TR **t** 020 8889 6558 **f** 020 8888 2698 **e** mail@livingstonstudios.co.uk **w** livingstonstudios.co.uk Bkings/Studio Mgr: Alina Syed. **STUDIO 1: SSL 4056E. STUDIO 2: Amek Rembrandt.**

Loco Studios Plas Llecha, Llanhennock, Newport, Monmouthshire NP18 1LU **t** 01633 450 603 **f** 01633 450 670 **e** asia@globalnet.co.uk **w** locostudios.com Studio Manager: Alison Durran-Beasley.

The Lodge 23 Abington Square, Northampton NN1 4AE **t** 01604 475399 **f** 01604 516999 **e** studio@lodgstud.demon.co.uk **w** demon.co.uk/lodgstud Snr Engineer/Owner: Max Read. Studio Mgr: Max Read. **Cadac.**

Lomax Entertainments Ltd 57-63 Great Crosshall Street, Liverpool L3 2AS **t** 0151 236 4443 **f** 0151 236 8616 **e** lomax.studios@amserve.net **w** lomaxentertainment.com Studio Director: Tommy Longmate.

Loose 11, Stanley Villas, Greenway Road, Runcorn, Cheshire WA7 4NW **t** 01928 566261 **e** jaki.florek@virgin.net Studio manager: Bill Leach. Engineer: Bill Leach.

Lost Boys Studio Hillgreen Farm, Bourne End, Cranfield, Bedfordshire MK43 0AX **t** 01234 750730 **f** 01234 751277 **e** info@lostboysstudio.com **w** lostboysstudio.com Studio Mgr:` Rupert Cook. **48 track digital production facility with Total Recall.**

MA Music Studios PO Box 106, Potton, Bedfordshire SG19 2ZS **t** 01767 262040 **e** info@mamusicstudios.co.uk **w** mamusicstudios.co.uk Studio MGR: Noel Rafferty. **Mackie 72Ch DB8; 24Trk Mackie HDR/Pro Tools LE/Adats; Mackie/NS10/Genelec.**

Mad Hat Studios The Upper Hattons Media Centre, The Upper Hattons, Pendeford Hall Lane, Coven, Nr Wolverhampton WV9 5BD **t** 01902 840440 **f** 01902 840448 **e** studio@madhat.co.uk **w** madhat.co.uk Dir: Claire Swan. **Amek Einstein Super 40 Ch.**

Manic One Studio PO Box 2251, London SE1 2FH **t** 020 7252 2661 **f** 0870 0512594 **e** manicone@movingshadow.com **w** movingshadow.com Studio Mgr: Gavin Johnson. Studio Mgr: Gavin Johnson. **Mackie Digital 8 bus.**

Map Music Ltd 46 Grafton Road, London NW5 3DU **t** 020 7916 0544 or 020 7916 0545 **f** 020 7284 4232 **e** info@mapmusic.net **w** mapmusic.net MD: Chris Townsend.

Matrix Recording Studios 91 Peterborough Road, London SW6 3BU **t** 020 7384 6400 **f** 020 7384 6401 **e** flip@matrix-studios.co.uk Office Mgr: Flip Dewar. Sales Mgr: Jason Wallbank. **SSL, Neve.**

Mayfair Recording Studios 11A Sharpleshall Street, London NW1 8YN **t** 020 7586 7746 **f** 020 7586 9721 **e** bookings@mayfair-studios.co.uk **w** mayfair-studios.co.uk Bkings/Studio Mgr: Daniel Mills. **Studio 1: SSL 6048 G series. Studio 2: Neve VR60. Studio 3: Amek Big computerised. Studio 4: Programming.**

MCS Studio 7 Northington Street, London WC1N 2JF **t** 020 7404 2647 **f** 020 7404 2647 **e** kevin.delascasas@lineone.net Prod/Engineer: Kevin de Las Casas. IZ Radar 24 trk digital & DDA Profile 56 channels.

Meridian Studios Holmdene Court, Southlands Grove, Bickley, Kent BR1 2DA **t** 020 8289 0466 **e** rricktb@aol.com Contact: Ricky Turner Brown

▲Metropolis Studios The Power House, 70 Chiswick High Road, London W4 1SY **t** 020 8742 1111 **f** 020 8742 2626 **e** reception@metropolis-group.co.uk **w** metropolis-group.co.uk Studio Bookings: Sophie Downs. Bookings: Julie Bateman, Sophie Downs. **STUDIO A: Focusrite 72 channel. STUDIO B: SSL 4000 G series. STUDIO C: Neve VR 72 channel. STUDIO D: E Series SSL 48 channel. STUDIO E: SSL 9000 J Series.**

Metway Studios 55 Canning Street, Brighton, East Sussex BN2 2EF **t** 01273 698171 **f** 01273 624884 **e** lois@levellers.co.uk **w** metwaystudios.co.uk Studio Manager: Lois Teague. **Soundtracks Jade 48 Tr, Otari MX-80 2", Dynaudio M4.**

Mex One Recordings The Basement, 3 Eaton Place, Brighton, East Sussex BN2 1EH **t** 01273 572090 **f** 01273 572090 **e** mexone@mexone.co.uk **w** mexonerecordings.co.uk MD: Paul Mex.

Mighty Atom Studios Dylan Thomas House, 32 Alexandra Rd, Swansea SA1 5DT **t** 01792 476567 **f** 01792 476564 **e** info@mightyatom.co.uk **w** mightyatom.co.uk Producer/Engineer: Joe Gibb. Producer: Joe Gibb. **Soundtracs Jade, Otari MTR90 and Soundscape Red 24, ATC 100's, Yamaha NS10's, Dynaudio BM 15's.**

Mill Hill Recording Company Ltd Unit 7, Bunns Lane Works, Bunns Lane, Mill Hill, London NW7 2AJ **t** 020 8906 5038 **f** 020 8906 9991 **e** enquiries@millhillmusic.co.uk **w** millhillmusic.co.uk MD: Roger Tichborne.

Miloco 36 Leroy St, London SE1 4SP **t** 020 7232 0008 **f** 020 7237 6109 **e** info@milomusic.co.uk **w** miloco.co.uk Bookings Mgr: Jess Gerry. Bookings Mgr: Mark Cox. **Studio 1: Neve VR 60 with Flying Faders. Studio 2: DDA QMR 48 channels (96 inputs) including protools. Studio 3: Amek G2520 with automation.Studio 4: Neve V3 48 channels with Flying Faders.**

Moles Studio 14 George Street, Bath BA1 2EN **t** 01225 404446 **f** 01225 404447 **e** studio@moles.co.uk **w** moles.co.uk Studio Mgr: Jan Brown. **SSL 4056E, TR, G+computer, (48 trk), Protools 24 mix, pre-production/programming.**

Monnow Valley Studio Old Mill House, Rockfield Road, Monmouth NP25 5QE **t** 01600 712761 or 07770 988503 **f** 01600 715039 **e** enquiries@monnowvalleystudio.com **w** monnowvalleystudio.com Bookings Mgr: Jo Hunt. **SSL4064 G+, Pro Tools HD, ATC 200, Tannoy PBM 6.5, Yamaha NS10.**

Monroe Production Co 103-105 Holloway Road, London N7 8LT **t** 020 7700 1411 **e** monroehq@netscapeonline.co.uk Studio Mgr: Halina Ciechanowska. **STUDIO 1: Neve 48 with SSL compression to 2 inch analogue multitrack. STUDIO 2: 48 track digital to audio - PC & Applemac hard disk recording.**

Moon Recording Studio 41 Leslie Park Rd, Croydon CR0 6TP **t** 020 8654 1197 **e** enquiries@beanos.co.uk **w** beanos.co.uk Studio Mgr: Quentin Fletcher.

Mother Digital Studio 30 Redchurch St, Shoreditch, London E2 7DP **t** 020 7739 8887 **e** studio@motherdigitalstudio.com **w** motherdigitalstudio.com Owner: Justin Morey. **Yamaha 02R. Logic Audio Platinum.**

Motor Museum Studios 1 Hesketh Street, Liverpool, Merseyside L17 8XJ **t** 0151 726 9808 **f** 0151 222 2760 **e** office@whitenoiseuk.com Contact: Bookings Mgr Bookings Mgr: Patrice Haines. Studio Mgr: Martin O'Shea. **Pro Tools TDM Mix3, expanded to 5 Farms. Otari MTR90 MKII. Urei, Neve, Avalon.**

MuchMoreMusic Studios Unit 29, Cygnus Business Centre, Dalmeyer Road, London NW10 2XA **t** 020 8830 0330 **f** 020 8830 0220 **e** info@muchmoremusic.net **w** robert-miles.com MD: Sandra Ceschia. **2 commercial studios, both with Pro Tools 24 bit system.**

The Music Barn PO Box 92, Gloucester GL4 8HW **t** 01452 814321 **f** 01452 812106 **e** vic_coppersmith@hotmail.com MD: Vic Coppersmith-Heaven.

Music City Ltd 122 New Cross Road, London SE14 5BA **t** 020 7277 9057 **f** 0870 7572004 **e** info@musiccity.co.uk **w** musiccity.co.uk Studio Mgr: Miles Bradley. Studio & Bookings Mgr: Myles Bradley. **STUDIO A: Allen & Heath Sabre 36. STUDIO B: Mackie SR32.**

The Music Factory Hawthorne House, Fitzwilliam Street, Parkgate, Rotherham, South Yorkshire S62 6EP **t** 01709 710022 **f** 01709 523141 **e** info@musicfactory.co.uk **w** mfeg.com CEO: Andy Pickles. MD: John Pickles. **Amek Mozart.**

Musowire PO Box 100, Gainsborough DN21 3XH **t** 01427 628826 **e** info@musoswire.com **w** musoswire.com Proprietor: Dan Nash.

MVD Studios Unit 4, Rampart Business Pk, Greenbank Ind, Estate, Newry, Co Down BT34 2QU **t** 028 3026 2926 **f** 028 3026 2671 **e** mail@wren.ie **w** soundsirish.com Studio Manager: Jim McGirr. **Soundcraft 2400.**

MWA Studios 20 Middle Row, Ladbroke Grove, London W10 5AT **t** 020 8964 4555 **f** 020 8964 4666 **e** studios@musicwithattitude.com **w** musicwithattitude.com Studio Engineer: Matt Foster.

Natural Grooves Studio 3 Tannsfeld, London SE26 5DQ **t** 020 8488 3677 **f** 020 8333 2572 **e** jon@naturalgrooves.co.uk **w** naturalgrooves.co.uk Studio Manager: Jonathan Sharif.

Network Studios (Nophonex) Network House, 22A Forest Road West, Nottingham NG7 4EQ **t** 0115 978 4714 **f** 0115 942 4183 Studio Mgr: Mick Vaughan. Bookings Mgr: Linda Davey. **Amek Angela 36 input with C mix.**

Nimbus Performing Arts Centre Wyastone Leys, Monmouth, Monmouthshire NP25 3SR **t** 01600 891090 **f** 01600 891052 **e** adrian@wyastone.co.uk **w** wyastone.co.uk Director: Adrian Farmer.

Nomis Studios (see Sanctuary Studios)**SSL 64 channel 4000 G Series.**

Nucool Studios 34 Beaumont Rd, London W4 5AP **t** 020 8248 2157 **e** r.niles@richardniles.com **w** richardniles.com Director: Richard Niles.

Odessa Wharf Studios 38 Upper Clapton Road, London E5 8BQ **t** 020 8806 5508 **f** 020 8806 5508 **e** odessa@mathias.idps.co.uk **w** surf.to/odessa MD: Gwyn Mathias. **Studio 1: 24T 2" Analogue and hard disk recording. Amek console, Urei 815.Studio 2: Yamaha 02R digiytal console, hard disk recording.**

Old Smithy Recording Studio 1 Post Office Lane, Kempsey, Worcestershire WR5 3NS **t** 01905 820659 **f** 01905 820015 **e** muff.murfin@virgin.net Bookings Mgr: Janet Allsopp. **Tweed Audio.**

Online Studios Unit 18-19 Croydon House, 1 Peall Road, Croydon, Surrey CR0 3EX **t** 020 8287 8585 **f** 020 8287 0220 **e** info@onlinestudios.co.uk **w** onlinestudios.co.uk MD: Rob Pearson.

Open Ear Productions Ltd. Main Street, Oughterard, Co Galway, Ireland **t** +353 91 552816 **f** +353 91 557967 **e** info@openear.ie **w** openear.ie MD: Bruno Staehelin.

Opus23 Sound Studio 23 New Mount St, Manchester M4 4DE **t** 0161 953 4077 **f** 0161 953 4001 **e** info@opus23.co.uk **w** opus23.co.uk Owner: Sean Flynn.

Ovni Audio 33-37 Hatherley Mews, London E17 4QP **t** 020 8521 9595 or 07967 615647 or 020 8521 6363 **e** flavio.uk@ukonline.co.uk **w** curiousyellow.co.uk Owner: Flavio Curras.

OxRecs Digital 37 Inkerman Close, Abingdon, Oxon OX14 1NH **t** 01235 550589 **e** info@oxrecs.com **w** oxrecs.com Dir: Bernard Martin.

Panther Recording Studios 5 Doods Rd, Reigate, Surrey RH2 0NT **t** 01737 210848 **f** 01737 210848 **e** studios@dial.pipex.com **w** ds.dial.pipex.com/sema/panther.htm Studio Manager: Richard Coppen.

Park Lane 974 Pollokshaws Road, Glasgow, Strathclyde G41 2HA **t** 0141 636 1218 **f** 0141 649 0042 **e** graccounts@btconnect.com **w** pls.uk.com Studio Mgr: Alan Connell. Bookings Mgr: Alan Connell. **DDA 232 56 channel.**

Parkgate Studios Catsfield, Battle, East Sussex TN33 9DT **t** 01424 774088 **f** 01424 774810 **e** parkgatestudio@hotmail.com **w** parkgatestudio.co.uk Contact: Dan Priest **Neve VR 60 Ch + Flying Faders, Sony DMX-R100 Digital, PMC/Bryston, 5:1 Surround Sound Mixing, Genelac 1035A's, ProTools, Studer A800.**

Parkland Studios The Old Garage, 37a Grosvenor St, Hull HU3 1RU **t** 01482 211 529 **e** suzanne@thedeebees.com Studio Manager: Suzanne Pinder.

▲Parr Street Studios 33-45 Parr Street, Liverpool L1 4JN **t** 0151 707 1050 **f** 0151 707 1813 **e** info@parrstreet.co.uk **w** parrstreet.co.uk Bookings Managers: Paul Lewis & Anne Lewis. **STUDIO 1: SSL 4064. STUDIO 2: Neve Legend. STUDIO 3: AHB Saber. STUDIO 4: Pro Tools.**

The Pierce Rooms Pierce House, London Apollo Complex, Queen Caroline Street, London W6 9QH **t** 020 8563 1234 **f** 020 8563 1337 **e** meredith@pierce-entertainment.com **w** pierce-entertainment.com Studio Mgr: Meredith Leung. **Studio 1: NEVE VR-60/72, Dynaudio M4 SurroundStudio 2: Mackie 56, Studer 827 (x2)48 track, Protools D24 System, Protools Mix Plus System.**

Pisces Studios 20 Middle Row, Ladbroke Grove, London W10 5AT **t** 020 8964 4555 **f** 020 8964 4666 **e** matt@musicwithattitude.com **w** musicwithattitude.com Head Engineer: Matt Foster. **Studio 1: Soundtracs IL34/32 eith Tracmix II Automation. Studio 2: Yamaha 02R + 03D.**

Planet Audio Studios Travel House, Spring Villa Road, Edgware, London HA8 7EB **t** 020 8952 4355 **f** 020 8952 4548 **e** helen@planetaudiostudios.com **w** planetaudiostudios.com GM: Helen Gammons. Studio Mgr: Nick Downing. Bookings Mgr: Helen Gammons. **A Neve VR Legend Mix room including Huge Pro Tools system.**

Pluto Studios Hulgrave Hall, Tiverton, Tarporley, Cheshire CW6 9UQ **t** 01829 732427 **f** 01829 733802 **e** info@plutomusic.com **w** plutomusic.com Studio Mgr: Keith Hopwood. **Reims 32/24.**

Point Blank 23-28 Penn St, London N1 5DL **t** 020 7729 4884 **f** 020 7729 8789 **e** studio@pointblanklondon.com **w** pointblanklondon.com CEO: Rob Cowan.

Pollen Studios 97 Main Street, Bishop Wilton, York, North Yorkshire YO42 1SQ **t** 01759 368223 **e** sales@pollenstudio.co.uk **w** pollenstudio.co.uk Prop: Dick Sefton. **ACES 24:16:2, Otari MX70.**

OLYMPIC STUDIOS

117 Church Road, Barnes, London SW13 9HL **t** 020 8286 8600 **f** 020 8286 8625 **e** siobhan@olympicstudios.co.uk **w** olympicstudios.co.uk Studio Mgr: Siobhan Paine. **Studio 1: SL 9072J. Studio 2: SSL G Series 56:32:4. Studio 3: SSL G+ series 80:32:4. Mix suite: SSL series 64:32:4. Studio 4: Amek 9098i 48 input.**

The Pop Factory Welsh Hills Works, Jenkin St, Porth CF39 9PP **t** 01443 688500 **f** 01443 688501 **e** info@thepopfactory.com **w** thepopfactory.com Contact: Emyr Afan Davies

Power Recording Studios Unit 11, Impress House, Mansell Rd, London W3 7QH **t** 020 8932 3033 **f** 0870 139 3608 **e** Keith@power.co.uk **w** power.co.uk Studio Mgr: Keith Neill.

The Premises Studios Ltd 201-205 Hackney Road, Shoreditch, London E2 8JL **t** 020 7729 7593 **f** 020 7739 5600 **e** info@premises.demon.co.uk **w** premises.demon.co.uk CEO: Viv Broughton. **Amek Einstein Super E.**

Presshouse PO Box 6, Colyton, Devon EX24 6YS **t** 01297 553508 **f** 01297 553709 **e** presshouse@zetnet.co.uk Studio Mgr: Mark Tucker. **56 input Amex Hendrix.**

Priderock Recording Studios Deppers Bridge Farm, Southam, Warwicks CV47 2SZ **t** 01926 614640 or 07782 172 101 **e** studio@bighelpmusic.com **w** bighelpmusic.com MD: Dutch Van Spall. **Allen & Heath GS3000 valve, ProTools 64-track, Genelec, Tannoy, NS10.**

Priory Recording Studios 3 The Priory, London Rd, Canwell, Sutton Coldfield, West Midlands B75 5SH **t** 0121 323 3332 **f** 0121 308 8815 **e** greg@prioryrecordingstudios.co.uk **w** prioryrecordingstudios.co.uk Studio Mgr: Greg Chandler.

The Pro Tools Room Sanctuary House, 45-53 Sinclair Road, London W14 0NS **t** 020 8932 3200 **f** 020 8932 3207 **e** protools@sanctuarystudios.co.uk **w** sanctuarystudios.co.uk Studio Manager: Nikki Affleck.

The Propagation House Studios East Lodge, Ogbeare, North Tamerton, Holsworthy, Devon EX22 6SE **t** 01409 271111 **f** 01409 271111 **e** office@propagationhouse.com **w** propagationhouse.com Studio Mgr: Mark Ellis.

Pulse Recording Studios 67 Pleasants Place, Dublin 8, Ireland **t** +353 1 478 4045 **f** +353 1 475 8730 **e** engineroom@pulserecording.com **w** pulserecording.com Studio Mgr: Tony Perrey. Bookings Mgr: Naomi Moore. **Studio 1: 80 Input AMEK 'Rembrandt' w/Superture Automation & Virtual Dynamics. Otari MTR 90 MKII w/Dolby SR & Tascam DA88 (24-tk) w/SY-88 sync. Motionworker total synchronisation system + 42" Plasma Screen. Studio 2: Protools AV Mix +24 V.5.**

Quince Recording Studio 62a Balcombe St, Marylebone, London NW1 6NE **t** 020 7723 4196 or 07810 752 765 **f** 020 7723 1010 **e** info@quincestudios.co.uk **w** quincestudios.co.uk Studio Manager: Matt Walters.

Quo Vadis Recording Studio Unit 1 Morrison Yard, 551A High Rd, London N17 6SB **t** 020 8365 1999 **e** quovadis_2002@yahoo.co.uk **w** quovadisstudios.com Studio Mgr: Don MacKenzie.

Raezor Studio 25 Frogmore, London SW18 1JA **t** 020 8870 4036 **f** 020 8874 4133 Studio Mgr: Ian Wilkinson. Bookings Mgr: Anni Wilkinson. **SSL 4048E.**

Rainmaker Music Music Bank, Building D, Tower Bridge Business Complex, 100 Clements Rd, London SE16 4DG **t** 020 7252 0001 or 07980 607 808 **f** 020 7231 3002 **e** rainmakermusic@aol.com **w** rainmakermusic.com MD: Chris Tsangarides. **Desk: TL Audio VTC Valve ConsoleRecorder: Otari Radar (HD/Exabyte)Monitors: Genelec 1031A's & Yamaha NS-10M's**

▲RAK Recording Studios 42-48 Charlbert Street, London NW8 7BU **t** 020 7586 2012 **f** 020 7722 5823 e trisha@rakstudios.co.uk **w** rakstudios.co.uk Bookings Mgr: Trisha Wegg. **STUDIO 1: AP1. STUDIO 2: AP1. STUDIO 3: SSL 4056G.**

Ray Hayden Productions & Studios 293 Mare Street, London E8 1EJ **t** 020 8986 8066 **f** 020 8533 7978 **e** rayopaz@aol.com **w** rayhayden.com Studio Mgr: Shanin Noronha. **Neve 72 channels.**

Raya Recording Studios Unit 6, The Saga Centre, 326 Kensal Rd, London W10 5BZ **t** 020 7240 8055 **f** 020 7379 3653 **e** RRS@plasticfantastic.co.uk **w** rayarecordingstudios.co.uk Studio Manager: Luis Paris.

React Studios 3 Fleece Yard, Market Hill, Buckingham MK18 1JX **t** 01280 821840 or 01280 823546 **f** 01280 821840 **e** info@reactstudios.co.uk **w** reactstudios.co.uk Studio Mgr: Tom Thackwray.

The Real Stereo Recording Company 14 Moorend Crescent, Cheltenham, Gloucestershire GL53 0EL **t** 01242 523304 **f** 01242 523304 **e** martin@instantmusic.co.uk **w** instantmusic.co.uk Prod Mgr: Martin Mitchell.

▲Real World Studios Box Mill, Mill Lane, Box, Corsham, Wiltshire SN13 8PL **t** 01225 743188 **f** 01225 743787 **e** studios@realworld.on.net **w** realworld.on.net/studios Studio Mgr: Owen Leech. **STUDIO 1: SSL 4080G 72 ch G Series w/tr. STUDIO 2: SSL 4052E 48 ch w/c G Series computer. STUDIO 3: Sony OXF-R3.**

Red Bus Recording Studios 34 Salisbury Street, London NW8 8QE **t** 020 7402 9111 **f** 020 7723 3064 **e** eliot@amimedia.co.uk **w** amimedia.co.uk MD: Eliot Cohen. Studio Mgr: Elliott S Cohen. **STUDIO 1: MCI JH500. STUDIO 2: SSL SL605E.**

Red Fort The Sight And Sound Centre, Priory Way, Southall, Middlesex UB2 5EB **t** 020 8843 1546 **f** 020 8574 4243 **e** kuljit@compuserve.com **w** keda.co.uk MD: Kuljit Bhamra. Bookings Mgr: Anita Masih. **Soundtracs IL 4832 Automation.**

Redwood Studios Ltd 20 Great Chapel St, London W1F 8FW **t** 020 7287 3799 **f** 020 7287 3751 **e** andrestudios@yahoo.co.uk **w** sound-design.net MD/Producer: Andre Jacquemin. **Mackie D8b-Protools24 Mix Plus VER5, HD System.**

Revolution Studios 11 Church Road, Cheadle Hulme, Cheadle, Cheshire SK8 6LS **t** 0161 485 8942 or 0161 486 6903 **f** 0161 485 8942 **e** revolution@wahtup.com Prop: Andrew MacPherson. Bookings Mgr: Karen Hemsley. **STUDIO 1: AMEK 2500. STUDIO 2: AMEK 2500. 32 digital/24 analogue.**

Ridge Farm Studio Rusper Road, Capel, Dorking, Surrey RH5 5HG **t** 01306 711202 **e** info@ridgefarmstudio.com w ridgefarmstudio.com Bookings & Admin. Mgr: Ann Needham.

Riff Raff Studios Penvale Cottage, Siliverwell, Truro, Cornwall TR4 8JE **t** 01872 561 331 **e** info@Riffraffmusic.co.uk **w** riffraffmusic.net Studio Manager: Baz Cox.

River Recordings 3 Grange Yard, London SE1 3AG **t** 020 7231 4805 **f** 020 7237 0633 **e** sales@riverproaudio.co.uk **w** riverstudios.co.uk MD: Joel Monger. **Studio 1: Soundtracs CP6800.**

River Studio's 3 Grange Yard, London SE1 3AG **t** 020 7231 4805 **f** 020 7237 0633 **e** sales@riverproaudio.co.uk **w** riverstudios.co.uk Contact: Joel Monger

RMS Studios 43-45 Clifton Rd, London SE25 6PX **t** 020 8653 4965 **f** 020 8653 4965 **e** studiosrms@aol.com w rms-studios.co.uk Bookings Mgr: Alan Jones.

RNT Studios Pinetree Farm, Cranborne, Dorset BH21 5RR **t** 01725 517204 **f** 01725 517801 **e** info@rntstudios.com **w** rntstudios.com Studio Manager: Rick Parkhouse. Pro Tools Mix Plus System / Digidesign Control 24.

▲Rockfield Studios Amberley Court, Rockfield Road, Monmouth, Monmouthshire NP25 5ST **t** 01600 712449 **f** 01600 714421 **e** rockfieldstudios@compuserve.com **w** rockfieldstudios.com Bookings Mgr: Lisa Ward. **COACH HOUSE: Neve VR 60 input. QUADRANGLE STUDIO: Neve VR 60 mono input, 8 stereo input.**

Rogue Studios RA 4 Bermondsey Trading Estate, Rotherhithe New Road, London SE16 3LL **t** 020 7231 3257 **f** 020 7231 7358 **e** info@RogueStudios.co.uk **w** roguestudios.co.uk Contact: Jon Paul Harper/Jim Down

Rollover Studios 29 Beethoven Street, London W10 4LJ **t** 020 8969 0299 **f** 020 8968 1047 **e** bookings@rollover.co.uk Studio Mgr: Phillip Jacobs. **Studio 1: Soundtracs Jade 48. Studio 2: Soundtracs Jade 48. Studio 3: Mackie 32. Studio 4: Yamaha 02R.**

Room With A View 167, Ringwood Rd, St. Leonards, Ringwood, Hants BH24 2NP **t** 01425 473432 **f** 01425 473432 **e** info@rwav.co.uk **w** rwav.co.uk Studio Manager: Bonnie Smith. **24-Track Otari Radar / Soundtracs Solitaire.**

Rooster 117 Sinclair Road, London W14 0NP **t** 020 7602 2881 **e** roosteraud@aol.com **w** roosterstudios.com Proprietor: Nick Sykes. **Otari Status S18-R 48.**

Rotator Studios Ltd Interzone House, 74-77 Magdalen Road, Oxford OX4 1RE **t** 01865 205600 **f** 01865 205700 **e** studios@rotator.co.uk **w** rotator.co.uk MD: Richard Cotton. Senior Manager: Phill Honey.

▲Roundhouse Recording Studios 91 Saffron Hill, Clerkenwell, London EC1N 8PT **t** 020 7404 3333 **f** 020 7404 2947 **e** roundhouse@stardiamond.com **w** stardiamond.com/roundhouse Studio Managers: Lisa Gunther & Maddy Clarke. Studio Mgr: Lisa Shimidzu. **Studio 1: SSL 4056G+SE. Studio 2: Yamaha DM2000, Protools HD 2, 5.1 Surround Sound. Studio 3: SSL 6048. Genelec monitoring, Floating Protools Mix plus, SADiE Digital Editing,**

▲Sain Canolfan Sain, Llandwrog, Caernarfon, Gwynedd LL54 5TG **t** 01286 831111 **f** 01286 831497 **e** studio@sain.wales.com **w** sain.wales.com Studio Mgr: Eryl Davies. **STUDIO 1: Harrison MR 3. STUDIO 2: DDA M series.**

Sam's 7 St Nicholas Churchyard, Newcastle-Upon-Tyne, Tyne and Wear NE1 1PF **t** 0191 233 0289 Studio Mgr: Nick Booth.

▲Sanctuary Town House 150 Goldhawk Road, London W12 8HH **t** 020 8932 3200 **f** 020 8932 3207 **e** recording@sanctuarystudios.co.uk **w** sanctuarystudios.co.uk Studio Mgr: Nikki Affleck. **Studio 1: SSL 4000G+. Studio 2: SSL 8072 G (5.1 surround monitoring). Studio 4: SSL 4000E (with G series computer). Pro Tools Suite.**

SARM HOOK END

Hook End Manor, Checkendon, Nr Reading, Berks RG8 0UE t 020 7229 1229 **f** 020 7221 9247 **e** jo@spz.com **w** sarmstudios.com Studio Mgr: Jo Buckley. MD: Jill Sinclair. **An Elizabethan country manor house occupying a 22-acre estate. 1 hour from London. Separate studio with 1000sq ft control room, plus SSL 9080 J series.**

Sarm West 8-10 Basing Street, London W11 1ET t 020 7229 1229 f 020 7221 9247 e jo@spz.com w sarmstudios.com Studio Mgr: Jo Buckley. MD: Jill Sinclair. **Studio 1: SSL 9080J Series. Natural daylight. Studio 2: SSL 4048 E/G Series. Studio 3: SSL 9072 J Series. Studio 4: Pro Tools.**

▲Sawmills Studio Golant, Fowey, Cornwall PL23 1LW **t** 01726 833338 or 01726 833752 **f** 01726 832015 **e** ruth@sawmills.co.uk **w** sawmills.co.uk Studio Mgr: Ruth Taylor. MD: Dennis Smith. **Trident 80B 54:24:24.**

Schoool of Sound Recording 10 Tariff Street, Manchester M1 2FF **t** 0161 228 1830 **f** 0161 236 0078 **e** info@s-s-r.com w s-s-r.com Principal: Ian Hu. Studio Mgr: Chris Mayo. **Studio 1: Amek BIG. Studio 2: Amek Einstein. Studio 3: Soudcraft Spirit. Studio 4: Soundcraft Spirit. Studio 5: Allen & Heath S8. Studio 6: Roland VM7200**

Sensible Studios 90-96 Brewery Road, London N7 9NT **t** 020 7700 9900 **f** 020 7609 9478 **e** studio@sensible-music.co.uk **w** sensiblemusic.com MD: Jeff Allen. Studio Mgr: Jeff Allen. **Euphonix CS2000 CS11 with 96 faders (28 moving).**

Silk Sound Ltd 13 Berwick Street, London W1F 0PW **t** 020 7434 3461 **f** 020 7494 1748 **e** bookings@silk.co.uk **w** silk.co.uk Studio Mgr: Paula Ryman. Bookings Mgr: Paula Ryman. **4 x Lexicon Opus digital systems.**

Silk Studios 23 New Mount St, Manchester M4 4DE **t** 0161 953 4045 or 07887 564 485 **f** 0161 953 4001 **e** leestanley@silkstudios.co.uk Dir: Lee Stanley.

▲Soho Recording Studios The Heals Building, 22-24 Torrington Place, London WC2E 7AJ **t** 020 7419 2444 or 020 7419 2555 **f** 020 7419 2333 **e** dominic@sohostudios.co.uk **w** sohostudios.co.uk Bkngs/Studio Mgr: Dominic Sanders. **Studio 1: SSL 4056G+.**

Soleil Studios Unit 10, Buspace Studios, Conlan Street, London W10 5AP **t** 020 7460 2117 **f** 020 7460 3164 **e** soleil@trwuk.com Proprietor: Jose Gross.

Solitaire Recording Studio C/O North Kerry Arts, Main St, Ballybunion, Co Kerry, Ireland **t** +353 68 28003 **f** +353 68 28006 **e** info@solitairestudio.com **w** solitairestudio.com MD: Alan Whelan.

Songwriting & Musical Productions Sovereign House, 12 Trewartha Road, Praa Sands, Penzance, Cornwall TR20 9ST **t** 01736 762826 or 07721 449477 **f** 01736 763328 **e** panamus@aol.com **w** songwriters-guild.co.uk MD: Colin Eade. Bookings Mgr: Ann Eade. **Soundcraft, Pro tools, digital & anologue systems.**

Sonic Music Production 8 Berkley Grove, Primrose Hill, London NW1 8XY **t** 020 7722 9494 **f** 020 7722 7179 **e** reception@sonic.uk.com **w** sonic.uk.com MD: Adrienne Aiken.

Soul II Soul Studios 36-38 Rochester Place, London NW1 9JX **t** 020 7284 0393 **f** 020 7284 2290 **e** sales@soul2soul.co.uk **w** soul2soul.co.uk Contact: Louise Howells/Ed Colman **3 studios (all with Genelec monitoring), 2 mixdown studios, 48 track digital, 24/48 track analogue formats, Otari RADAR, Tascam DA88, Alesis ADAT (optional).**

The Sound Joint 10 Parade Mews, London SE27 9AX **t** 020 8678 1404 **f** 020 8671 0380 **e** info@soundjoint.fsnet.co.uk **w** soundjoint.fsnet.co.uk Director: Barnaby Smith. Director: Chris Bachmann.

▲Sound Recording Technology Audio House, Edison Road, St Ives, Cambridge PE27 3LF **t** 01480 461880 **f** 01480 496100 **e** srt@btinternet.com **w** soundrecordingtechnology.co.uk Dirs: Sarah Pownall, Karen Kenney. Bookings Mgr: Emma Dooley. **Six studios, CD mastering. PQ encoding, Sonic Solutions 20 bit digital recording and editing. HDCD, enhanced CD. Dolby Surround.**

Sound Studios 25 Castlereagh Street, London W1H 5YR **t** 020 7724 1331 **f** 020 7724 4900 **w** soundstudios.co.uk Studio Mgr: Henry Anthony.

The Sound Suite 92 Camden Mews, London NW1 9AG **t** 020 7485 4881 **f** 020 7482 2210 **e** peterrackham@soundsuite.freeserve.co.uk Studio Mgr: Peter Rackham. Bookings Mgr: Kate Fox. **Amek Hendrix Supertrue.**

Soundbyte Promotions PO Box 1209, Stafford ST16 1XW **t** 01785 222382 f 0871 277 3060 **e** soundbytes@btinternet.com Prop: Robert Hicks.

Soundtree Music Unit 124, Canalot Studios, 222 Kensal Road, London W10 5BN **t** 020 8968 1449 **f** 020 8968 1500 **e** post@soundtree.co.uk Business Mgr: Jo Feakes.

Southern Studios 10 Myddleton Rd, London N22 8NS **t** 020 8888 8036 **f** 020 8889 6166 **e** studio@southern.com **w** southern.com/studio Studio Manager/Engineer: Harvey Birrell. Studio Mgr: Harvey Birrell. Bookings Mgr: Harvey Birrell. **Desk - Raindirk series III, Studer A827 24tk, Protools 5.**

Space Facilities 16 Dufours Place, London W1F 7SP **t** 020 7494 1020 **f** 020 7494 2861 **e** bookings@space.co.uk **w** space.co.uk Facility Manager: Tom McConville. Studio Mgr: Tom McConville. Bookings Mgr: Marie McWilliam.

Spatial Audio Pinewood Studios, Pinewood Rd, Iver, Bucks SLO 0NH **t** 07802 657 258 **f** 020 8932 3465 **e** gerry@spatial-audio.co.uk **w** spatial-audio.co.uk Chief Engineer: Gerry O'Riordan. **Studio 1: DDA AMR 24, 36 input, automated. Studio 2: DDA AMR 24, 28 input.**

▲Sphere Studios 2 Shuttleworth Road, London SW11 3EA **t** 020 7326 9450 **f** 020 7326 9499 **e** info@spherestudios.com **w** spherestudios.com Studio Manager: Graham Carpenter.

SPM Studios 9 Lichfield Way, South Croydon, Surrey CR2 8SD **t** 020 8657 8363 or 07970 646 166 f 020 8657 8380 e steve@spmstudios.co.uk **w** spmstudios.co.uk Prop: Steve Parkes.

Sprint Music Ltd High Jarmany Farm, Jarmany Hill, Barton St David, Somerton,Somerset TA11 6DA **t** 01458 851010 **f** 01458 851029 **e** info@sprintmusic.co.uk **w** sprintmusic.co.uk Consultant: John Ratcliff.

The Square Fourth Avenue, Harlow, Essex CM20 1DW **t** 01279 305000 **f** 01279 866151 **e** des@square1.demon.co.uk **w** square1.demon.co.uk Studio Manager: Des Wiltshire. Studio Mgr: John Sellings.

St George's Bristol Great George Street, off Park Street, Bristol BS1 5RR **t** 0117 929 4929 **f** 0117 927 6537 **e** administration@stgeorgesbristol.co.uk **w** stgeorgesbristol.co.uk Director: Jonathan Stracey. **Soundcraft Spirit Digital Mixing Desk RW5548, 2 x Dat Recorders Tascam DA-45HR, CDR HHB850 Recorder, Monitors ATC SCM 50A Pro.**

Stanley House Stanley House, 39 Stanley Gardens, London W3 7SY **t** 020 8735 0280 **f** 020 8743 6365 **e** sh@stanley-house.co.uk Studio & Bookings Mgr: Jess Gentle. **SSL J Series.**

Steelworks Studio Unit D, 3 Brown St, Sheffield S1 2BS **t** 0114 272 0300 **f** 0114 272 0303 **e** steelworksmu@aol.com **w** steelworks-studios.com Studio Mgr: Dan Panton. **Neve Capricorn Desk, Cubase, Genelec 1039A & 1031A, Dynaudio BM15A, Sony SMS1P.**

Stickysongs Ltd Sticky Studios, Kennel Lane, Windlesham, Surrey GU20 6AA **t** 01276 479255 **f** 01276 479255 **e** stickysong@aol.com MD: Pete Gosling.

▲Strongroom Ltd 120-124 Curtain Road, London EC2A 3SQ **t** 020 7426 5100 **f** 020 7426 5102 **e** mix@strongroom.com **w** strongroom.com Studio Manager: Nina Mistry. Studio Mgr: Jane Holloway. Bookings Mgr: Nina Mistry. **Studio 1: Neve VR60 Legend with Encore Automation. Studio 2: Euphonix CS3000 5.1 Mix room. Studio 3: SSL 4000 G Plus with Ultimation. Studio 4: Pro Tools tracking room. Studio 5: Pro Control/Pro Tools mix room. Studio 6: DVD encoding room - Pro Tools 24 Mix plus systems 48 I/O with Apogee convertors.**

Studio 17 17 David's Road, London SE23 3EP **t** 020 8291 6253 **f** 020 8291 1097 **e** chris@dubvendor.co.uk Dir: Chris Lane. **Soundcraft Sapphyre 28/24 with Optifile Automation.**

Studio 24 60 Benedict Close, Romsey, Hampshire SO51 8PN **t** 01794 501774 or 07754 969326 **f** 01794 501774 **e** info@studiotwentyfour.co.uk **w** studiotwentyfour.co.uk Studio Manager: Alan Cotty.

Studio 125 125 Junction Road, Burgess Hill, West Sussex RH15 0JL **t** 01444 871818 **e** i.herron@btinternet.com Studio Mgr: Ian Herron. **Soundcraft TS 24.**

The Studio Tower Street, Tower Street, Hartlepool TS24 7HQ **t** 01429 424440 **f** 01429 424441 **e** studiohartlepool@btconnect.com **w** studiohartlepool.com Studio Manager: Liz Carter. **Studio 1: Amek Big Langley, Tascam 24 HD, Quested & Mackie. Studio 2: Amek Mozart, Otari Mtr 90/Pto Tools 24, Quested & Mackie HR824. Studio 3: Mackie, Alesis 24 ADAT, Tannoy & Fostex. Subsidised rates for unwaged.**

Sun Studios - 1 & 2 8 Crow Street, Dublin 2, Ireland **t** +353 1 677 7255 **f** +353 1 679 1968 **e** info@sunrecording.com Studio Mgr: Denis Lovett. **Amek Einstein Super 80 channels, 48 track digital / analog Saturn 824 2".**

Sweet Georgia Browns Unit 12, 407 Hornsey Road, London N19 4DX **t** 020 7263 1219 **f** 020 7263 3270 **e** info@sweetgeorgiabrowns.co.uk **w** sweetgeorgiabrowns.co.uk Studio Mgr: Dani.

Swing City Studios 59 Riding House Street, London W1T 6DJ **t** 020 7380 0999 **f** 020 7380 1555 **e** info@wyze.com **w** wyze.com Contact: Kate Ross Studio Mgr: Grant Nelson. Bookings Mgr: Kate Ross.

Sync City Media Ltd 16-18 Millmead Business Centre, Millmead Road, Tottenham Hale, London N17 9QU **t 020 8808 0472** **e** sales@synccity.co.uk **w** synccity.co.uk Studio Manager: Ron Niblett.

Tall Order Studios The Basement, 346 North End Road, London SW6 1NB **t** 020 7385 1816 **f** 020 7385 1816 **e** paul@tallorder.org.uk **w** tallorder.org.uk Studio Mgr: Paul Southby. **Soundcraft 1600.**

Temple Lane Recording Studios 8 Crow Street, Temple Bar, Dublin 2, Ireland **t** +353 1 677 7255 **f** +353 1 679 1968 **e** info@templelanestudios.com Studio Mgr: Denis Lovett. **Studio 1: Soundcraft 3200. Studio 2: Amek Einstein. Studio 3: Yamaha 02R (Digi 8). Studio 4: Soundcraft 6000.**

Temple Music Studios 48 The Ridgway, Sutton, Surrey SM2 5JU **t** 020 8642 3210 or 07802 822 006 f 020 8642 8692 **e** jh@temple-music.com **w** temple-music.com Chief Bottlewasher: Jon Hiseman.

Temple Records Shillinghill, Temple, Midlothian EH23 4SH **t f** 01875 830392 **e** info@templerecords.co.uk **w** templerecords.co.uk Studio Mgr: Robin Morton. **Tascam M-600.**

Temptation Studio Unit 3B, Ballybane Industrial Est, Tuam Road, Galway, Ireland **t** +353 91 756266 **f** +353 91 789001 **e** tron@indigo.ie; secret@indigo.ie **w** indigo.ie/~tron Partners: Pat Neary/John O'Shaughnessy.

Ten21 Little Milgate, Otham Lane, Bearsted, Maidstone, Kent ME15 8SJ **t** 0622 735 200 **f** 0622 735 200 **e** info@ten21.biz **w** ten21.biz Contact: Sean Kenny and Juliet Ward

Touchwood Audio Productions 6 Hyde Park Terrace, Leeds, West Yorkshire LS6 1BJ **t** 0113 278 7180 f 0113 278 7180 **e** bruce.w@appleonline.net **w** touchwood/20m.com Studio Mgr: Bruce Wood. Tascam M3500 - 32.

Tribal Sound + Vision 66C Chalk Farm Road, London NW1 8AN **t** 020 7482 6945 **f** 020 7485 9244 **e** tribal.sound@virgin.net **w** tribaltreemusic.co.uk Studio Manager: Kate Greenslade.

Tweeters Unit C1, Business Park 7, Brookway, Kingston Rd, Leatherhead, Surrey KT22 7NA **t** 01372 386592 **e** info@tweeters2studios.co.uk **w** tweeters2studios.co.uk Studio Eng: Nigel Wade. **24 track Tascam, Tascam M3700.**

Twin Peaks Studio Ty Neuadd, Torpantau, Brecon Beacons, Mid Glamorgan CF48 2UT **t** 01685 359932 **f** 01685 376500 **e** TwinPeaksStudio@aol.com **w** TwinPeaksStudio.com Director: Adele Nozedar. **2 x Yamaha 02R 80 trk digital.**

▲Unit 21 Recording 21 London Lane, London Fields, London E8 3PR **t** 020 8525 1101 **f** 0870 161 7619 **e** info@unit21recording.com **w** unit21recording.com Studio Mgr: Beth Shuttleworth. **Studio 1: Euphonix CS3000 72 fader, Euphonix 48T & ProTools HD3 w Accel, PMC. Studio 2: ProTools & ProControl 5.1 Surround.**

Unit Q Studio Unit Q The Maltings, Station Rd, Sawbridgeworth, Herts CM21 9JX **t** 01279 600078 **e** darren@orgyrecords.com **w** unitq.com Contact: Darren Bazzoni **Digital Studio, Mac G4. Logic 6, Yamaha 02R, Genelec.**

Vertical Rooms Road Farm, Ermine Way, Arrington, Herts SG8 3YY **t** 01223 207007 **f** 01223 207007 **e** info@verticalrooms.com **w** verticalrooms.com Studio Manager: Phil Culbertson. Bookings Mgr: Steve Bunting. **Studio 1: 56 channel mackie 8-buss, NS 10's, OHM monitors, Tascam Hi 8's (24trck). Studio 2 Soundtracks Topaz 32CH 8-buss, Tascam Hi 8's (24trck), Soundcraft 2inch 24trck, monitors-Tannoys/Keff/OHM.**

Vital Spark Studios 1 Waterloo, Isle Of Skye IV42 8QE **t** 01471 822484 **f** 01471 822952 **e** chris@vitalsparkmusic.demon.co.uk Manager: Chris Harley.

Warehouse 60 Sandford Lane, Kennington, Oxford OX1 5RW **t** 01865 736411 **e** info@warehousestudios.com **w** warehousestudios.com Studio Mgr: Steve Watkins.

Waterfront Studios Riverside House, 260 Clyde St, Glasgow G1 4JH **t** 0141 248 9100 **f** 0141 248 5020 **e** waterfront@picardy.co.uk **w** picardy.co.uk

WaterRat Music Studios Unit 2 Monument Way East, Woking, Surrey GU21 5LY **t** 01483 764444 **e** jayne@waterrat.co.uk **w** waterrat.co.uk Proprietor: Jayne Wallis.

Welsh Media Music Gorwelion, LLanfynydd, Carmarthen, Dyfed SA32 7TG **t** 01558 668525 or 0774 100430 **f** 01558 668750 **e** dpierce@welshmediamusic.f9.co.uk Studio & Bkings Mgr: Dave Pierce. **Soundcraft 6000 48 channel, Yamaha Promix.**

West Orange Unit 1, 16B Pechell Street, Ashton, Preston, Lancashire PR2 2RN **t** 01772 722626 **f** 01772 722626 **e** westorange@btclick.com Studio Mgr: Alan Gregson. **D&R Dayner.**

Westland Studios Ltd 5-6 Lombard Street East, Dublin 2, Ireland **t** +353 1 677 9762 **f** +353 1 671 0421 **e** westland@indigo.ie **w** westlandstudios.ie Studio Mgr: Deirdre Costello. **SSL 4048 G, 48 track recording studio.**

Westpoint Studio Unit GA, Westpoint, 39-40 Warple Way, London W3 0RG **t** 020 8740 1616 **f** 020 8740 4488 **e** respect@mailbox.co.uk Studio Manager: Ian Sherwin. **Euphonix CS3000, ATC SCM200, ProTools 24 Mix-plus, Otari MTR90, Sony 3348.**

Westside Studios Olaf Centre, 10 Olaf Street, London W11 4BE **t** 020 7221 9494 **f** 020 7727 0008 **e** westsidestudios@btconnect.com GM: Olly Henshell. **Studio 1: Neve VR 72, 60 Channels, EMI TG Mk2. Studio 2: 64 channel SSL Console.**

Westsound 95 Carshalton Park Road, Carshalton Beeches, Surrey SM5 3SJ **t** 020 8647 3084 **f** 020 8395 3560 **e** tomjennings@cwcom.net Studio Mgr: Tom Jennings. **Soundtracs.**

▲White's Farm Studios Whites Farm, Wilton Lane, Kenyon Culcheth WA3 4BA **t** 0161 790 4830 **f** 0161 703 8521 **e** whitesfarmstudio@aol.com **w** whitesfarmstudios.com Dir: Gary Hastings. **Amek, Dynaudio, Genelec, Yamaha, Lexicon, AMS, VST, Logic, Pro-tools, 48/24 track, Analogue, Digital, Neve, SSL.**

▲Whitfield Street Studios 31-37 Whitfield Street, London W1T 2SF **t** 020 7636 3434 **f** 020 7580 2219 **e** info@whitfield-street.com **w** whitfield-street.com Studio Bookings Mgr: Rebecca Duncan. **STUDIO 1: 72 channel Neve VRP, Recall & Flying Faders. STUDIO 2: 72 channel Neve VRP, Recall & Flying Faders. STUDIO 3: SSL 9072J.**

Windmill Lane Studios 20 Ringsend Road, Dublin 4, Ireland **t** +353 1 668 5567 **f** +353 1 668 5352 **e** catherine@windmill.ie **w** windmill.ie Studio Mgr: Catherine Rutter. **Studio 1: Neve VRP Legend. Studio 2: SSL E Series with G Up-Dates.**

Wired Studios Ltd 26-28 Silver Street, Reading, Berkshire RG1 2ST **t** 0118 986 0973 **e** office@wiredstudios.demon.co.uk **w** wiredstudios.demon.co.uk Manager: Chris Britton. **25 track facility.**

Wise Buddah Creative 74 Great Titchfield St, London W1W 7QP **t** 020 7307 1600 **f** 020 7307 1601 **e** paul.plant@wisebuddah.com **w** wisebuddah.com Manager: Paul Plant. Bookings Mgr: Emma Pyne. Studio Mgr: Paul Plant.

Wolf Studios 83 Brixton Water Lane, London SW2 1PH **t** 020 7733 8088 **f** 020 7326 4016 **e** bret@wolfen.netkonect.co.uk **w** wolfstudios.co.uk Director: Dominique Brethes. **Studio 1: Amek Angela. Studio 2: Yamaha 02R.**

Woodbine Street Recording Studio 1 St Mary's Crescent, Leamington Spa, Warwickshire CV31 1JL **t** 01926 338971 e jony2r@ntlworld.com w woodbinestreet.com MD/Studio Mgr: John A Rivers. **ASP 8024, Pro Tools HD3, Mission & Genelec.**

Woodlands Recording Perseverance Works, Morrison St, Castleford, West Yorkshire WF10 4BE **t** 01977 556868 **f** 01977 603180 **e** sales@jarberry-music.co.uk **w** woodlandsrecording.co.uk Studio Mgr: Simon Humphrey. **IZ Radar, DDA AMR 24.**

Woodside Studio Woodside, Eason's Green, Framfield, Nr. Uckfield, East Sussex TN22 5RE **t** 01825 841484 **f** 01825 880019 **e** studio@woodside1.idps.co.uk **w** surf.to/woodside Studio Manager: Terri Myles. **Automated Soundtracs console, 24 Tr ADAT, Dynaudio Monitoring, Logic Audio Platinum.**

Xplosive Studios 33/37 Hatherley Mews, Walthamstow, London E17 4QP **t** 020 8521 9227 **f** 020 8520 5553 **e** xplosive@supanet.com **w** xplosiverecords.co.uk Directors: Terry McLeod/Tapps Bandawe.

Zoo Studios 145 Wardour Street, London W1F 8WB **t** 020 7734 2000 **f** 020 7734 2200 **e** mail@zoostudios.co.uk Bking Mgr: Danielle Jones. Studio Mgr: Graham Ebbs. **Amek Einstein.**

Mobile studios

Abbey Road Mobiles 3 Abbey Road, London NW8 9AY **t** 020 7266 7000 **f** 020 7266 7250 **e** bookings@abbeyroad.com **w** abbeyroad.com Studio Mgr: Colette Barber.

As The Crow Flies The Retreat, Pidney, Hazlebury Bryan, Dorset DT10 2EB **t** 01258 817214 or 07971 686961 **f** 01258 817207 **e** PeteFreshney@compuserve.com **w** petefreshney.co.uk Contact: Pete Freshney

BBC Radio Outside Broadcasts (London) Brock House, 19 Langham St, London W1A 1AA **t** 020 7765 4888 **f** 020 7765 5504 **e** will.garnett@bbc.co.uk Operations Mgr: Will Garnett.

Black Mountain Recordings 1 Squire Court, The Marina, Swansea SA1 3XB **t** 01792 301500 **f** 01792 301500 **e** info@blackmountainmobile.co.uk **w** blackmountainmobile.co.uk MD: Michael Evans.

▲Circle Sound Services Circle House, 14 Waveney Close, Bicester, Oxfordshire OX26 2GP **t** 01869 240051 **f** 0870 7059679 **e** sound@circlesound.net **w** circlesound.net Owner: John Willett.

Classic Sound 5 Falcon Park, Neasden Lane, London NW10 1RZ **t** 020 8208 8100 **f** 020 8208 8111 **e** info@classicsound.net **w** classicsound.net Dir: Neil Hutchinson.

The Classical Recording Co.Ltd 16-17 Wolsey Mews, Kentish Town, London NW5 2DX **t** 020 7482 2303 **f** 020 7482 2302 **e** info@classicalrecording.com **w** classicalrecording.com Snr Producer: Simon Weir.

Doyen Recordings Ltd The Doyen Centre, Vulcan Street, Oldham, Lancashire OL1 4EP **t** 0161 628 3799 **f** 0161 628 0177 **e** sales@doyen-recordings.co.uk **w** doyen-recordings.co.uk MD: Nicholas J Childs.

Emglow Records Norton Cottage, Colchester Road, Wivenhoe, Essex CO7 9HT **t** 01206 826342 **e** Marcelg@aspects.net Contact: Marcel Glover

The Eureka Factor 12 Laxford House, Cundy Street, London SW1W 9JU **t** 020 7259 9903 **f** 020 7259 9903 **e** Recordings@theeurekafactor.com Recording Engineer: Mike Jeremiah.

▲Fleetwood (see Sanctuary Mobiles) **t** 08700 771071 **f** 08700 771068 **e** mobiles@sanctuarystudios.co.uk **w** sanctuarystudios.co.uk Bookings Mgr: Ian Dyckhoff.

Floating Earth Unit 14, 21 Wadsworth Road, Perivale, Middx UB6 7JD **t** 020 8997 4000 **f** 020 8998 5767 **e** record@floatingearth.com **w** floatingearth.com Director: Steve Long.

Green Room Productions The Laurels, New Park Road, Harefield, Middlesex UB9 6EQ **t** 01895 822771 **f** 01895 824880 **e** tony@greenroom2.demon.co.uk Rec Engineer: Tony Faulkner.

Hazard Chase 25 City Rd, Cambridge CB1 1DP **t** 01223 312400 **f** 01223 460827 **e** info@hazardchase.co.uk **w** hazardchase.co.uk MD: James Brown.

Innocent Ear 14 Andrews Way, Marlow Bottom, Buckinghamshire SL7 3QJ **t** 01628 473918 **f** 01628 473918 **e** Innocent.Ear@which.net **w** innocentear.com Contact: Chris Burmajster

K&A Productions 5 Wyllyotts Place, Potters Bar, Hertfordshire EN6 2HN **t** 01707 661200 **f** 01707 661400 **e** info@kaproductions.co.uk **w** kaproductions.co.uk MD: Andrew Walton.

Leapfrog Audiovisual 1 Currievale Farm Cottages, Currie, Midlothian EH14 4AA **t** 0131 449 5808 or 07941 346813 **e** claudeharper@supanet.com Prop: Claude Harper.

MACH2 412 Beersbridge Rd, Belfast BT5 5EB **t** 08707 300 030 or 07850 663 089 **f** 08707 300 040 **e** michael@machtwo.co.uk **w** machtwo.co.uk Director: Michael Taylor.

Manor Mobiles (see Sanctuary Mobiles) **t** 08700 771071 **f** 08700 771068 **e** mobiles@sanctuarystudios.co.uk **w** sanctuarystudios.co.uk

Ninth Wave Audio 46 Elizabeth Road, Moseley, Birmingham, West Midlands B13 8QJ **t** 0121 442 2276 or 07770 364 464 **f** 0121 689 1902 **e** ninthwave@blueyonder.co.uk Studio Mgr: Tony Wass.

Regent Records PO Box 528, Wolverhampton, West Midlands WV3 9YW **t** 01902 424377 **f** 01902 717661 **e** regent.records@btinternet.com **w** regentrecords.com Contact: Gary Cole

Sanctuary Mobiles Bray Film Studios, Windsor Road, Windsor, Berks SL4 5UG **t** 08700 771071 **f** 08700 771068 **e** mobiles@sanctuarygroup.com **w** sanctuarystudios.co.uk Studio Mgr: Ian Dyckhoff.

Sound Moves The Oaks, Cross Lane, Smallfield, Surrey RH6 9SA **t** 01342 844 190 **f** 01342 844 290 **e** steve@sound-moves.com **w** sound-moves.com Owner: Steve Williams.

Zipper Mobile Studio 272 Cricklewood Lane, London NW2 2PU **t** 020 8450 4130 **f** 020 8450 4130 **e** jay@zippermobile.co.uk **w** zippermobile.co.uk Bookings Mgr: Jeffrey Jay.

Producers & Producer Management

0510 Management 7 Smeaton Road, London SW18 5JJ **t** 020 8870 0510 **e** mgmt0510@btinternet.com Contact: Maureen Moore

0898 Dave Contact: Mumbo Jumbo Management

140dB Management 133 Kilburn Lane, London W10 4AN **t** 020 8354 2900 **f** 020 8354 2091 **e** ros@140db.co.uk: katrina@140db.co.uk **w** 140db.co.uk Managers: Ros Earls, Katrina Berry.

24 Management Westfield Cottage, Scragged Oak Rd, Maidstone, Kent ME143HA **t** 01622 632 634 **f** 01622 632 634 **e** info@24twentyfour.com MD: Andy Rutherford.

365 Artists 91 Peterborough Rd, London SW6 3BU **t** 020 7384 6500 **f** 020 7384 6504 **e** info@365artists.com **w** 365artists.com Dirs: Adam Clough.

3kHz 54 Pentney Rd, London SW12 0NY **t** 020 8772 0108 **f** 020 8675 1636 **e** threekhz@hotmail.com Manager: Jessica Norbury.

4 Tunes Management PO Box 36534, London W4 3XE **t** 020 8994 2739 **f** 020 8742 0399 **e** andy@4-tunes.com **w** 4-tunes.com MD: Andy Murray.

7Hz Management 57b Riding House St, London W1W 7EF **t** 020 7436 5434 **f** 020 7436 5431 **e** barry@7hz.co.uk Director: Barry Campbell.

a Side Productions (David Kreuger & Per Magnusson) Contact: XL Talent

Jim Abbiss Contact: This Much Talent

Absolute Contact: Native Management

AC Burrell Contact: Dig-It-All

John Acock Contact: Bright Tracks Productions

Active Music Management (AMM Suite 401, 29 Margaret St, London W1N 7LB **t** 0870 120 7668 **f** 0870 120 9880 **e** ActiveMM@lineone.net MD: Mark Winters.

Adage Music 22 Gravesend Rd, London W12 OSZ **t** 07973 295113 **e** Dobs@adagemusic.co.uk **w** adagemusic.co.uk Manager: Dobs Vye.

John Adams Contact: Alan Bown Management

Justin Adams Contact: David Jaymes Associates Ltd

Afrikan Cowboy Unit 1 Greenwich Quay, Clarence Rd, London SE8 3EY **t** 07957 391418 or 020 8305 2448 **e** afrikancowboyltd@aol.com Director: Dean Hart.

AGM Studios 1927 Building, 2 Michael Road, London SW6 2AD **t** 020 7371 0234 **e** contacts@agmstudios.com Producer: Alex Golding.

Matt Aitken Contact: Menace Management

Alan Branch Contact: 7hz Productions

Alchemy Remix Management 2a-6a Southam St, London W10 5PH **t** 020 8960 3253 or 078555 07170 **f** 020 8968 5111 **e** info@alchemy-remix.com **w** alchemy-remix.com Partner: Howie Martinez.

Alex Golding Contact: AGM Studios

Ash Alexander Contact: Rive Droite Music Productions

Ali Staton Contact: Sanctuary Producer Management

The All Seeing I Contact: Menace Mgmt

Almighty Productions PO Box 12173, London N19 4SQ **t** 020 7281 3212 **f** 020 7281 8002 **e** info@almightyrecords.com **w** almightyrecords.com Manager: Andy Wetson.

John Altman Contact: SMA Talent

Amazonia Contact: Seedpod

Ambush Management 32 Ransome's Dock, 35-37 Parkgate Road, London SW11 4NP **t** 020 7801 1919 **f** 020 7738 1819 **e** alambush.native@19.co.uk **w** ambushgroup.co.uk MD: Alister Jamieson.

Amco Music Productions 2 Gawsworth Road, Macclesfield, Cheshire SK11 8UE **t** 01625 420163 **f** 01625 420168 **e** amco@cottagegroup.co.uk **w** cottagegroup.co.uk Contact: Roger Boden

Paul Anderson Contact: Prodmix Artist Mgmt

Andy Perring Contact: Sublime Mgmt.

Andy Richards Contact: Out Of Eden

Andy Whitmore Productions 39 Greystoke Park Terrace, London W5 1JL **t** 020 8998 5529 or 07850 735591 **e** andy@greystokeproductions.co.uk **w** greystokeproductions.co.uk Prod: Andy Whitmore.

AngelSword Productions Little Barn, Plaistow Rd, Loxwood, West Sussex RH14 0SX **t** 01403 751862 **f** 01403 753564 **e** jonn@jonnsavannah.co.uk **w** jonnsavannah.co.uk Director: Jonn Savannah.

Apollo 440 Contact: XL Talent Partnership

Appawsa Contact: Bronco Records

Arclite Productions Unit 303, Safe Store 5-10 Eastman Rd, London W3 7YG **t** 020 8743 4000 **e** info@arcliteproductions.com **w** arcliteproductions.com Prod: Alan Bleay/Laurie Jenkins.

Craig Armstrong Contact: Silent Mgmt

Peter Arnold Contact: Panama Productions

Arpeggio Music Bell Farm House, Eton Wick, Windsor, Berkshire SL4 6LH **t** 01753 864910 or 01753 884810 MD: Beverley Campion.

Artfield 5 Grosvenor Square, London W1K 4AF **t** 020 7499 9941 **f** 020 7499 5519 **e** bb@artfieldmusic.com **w** artfieldmusic.com MD: B B Cooper.

Artist, Music & Talent International PO Box 43, Manchester M8 0BB **t** 0161 795 7717 or 07905 001 687 **f** 0161 795 7717 **e** amti@btconnect.com MD: Peter Lewyckyj.

Peter Asher Contact: Sanctuary Producer Management

Ron Aslan Contact: Z management

Jon Astley Contact: Positive

Asylum Artists PO Box 121, Hove, East Sussex BN3 4YY **t** 01273 774468 **f** 08709 223099 **e** info@AsylumGroup.com **w** AsylumGroup.com Contact: Bob James, Steve Gilmour, Scott Chester.

Atkinson, David Contact: TD Prods

Atlantis Management PO Box 1419, Croydon CR9 7XG **t** 07974 755217 **e** richardbelcher1@btopenworld.com **w** atlantismanagement.co.uk Dir: Richard Belcher.

Atlas Realisations Music Trendalls Cottage, Beacons Bottom, Bucks HP14 3XF **t** 01494 483121 **f** 01494 484303 **e** info@craigleon.com **w** craigleon.com Producer: Craig Leon.

Audio Authority Management 77 Addiscombe Rd, Croydon, Surrey CR0 6SE **t** 07980 607 808 **e** tim.hole@audioauthority.co.uk **w** audioauthority.co.uk Contact: Tim Hole

Dan Austin Contact: 140db Management

Avril Eventhal 26 Dovedale Avenue, Prestwich, Manchester M25 0BU **t** 0161 795 8545 Producer: Avril Eventhal.

Baby T Contact: Seedpod

Chris Bachmann Contact: The Sound Joint

Arthur Baker Contact: Stephen Budd Mgmt

Luke Baldry The Kilns, Snails Lynch, Farnham, Surrey GU9 8AP **t** 01252 710244

Bamn Management Ltd 25 Heathmans Road, London SW6 4TY **t** 020 7371 7223 **f** 020 7731 8566 Contact: Will Stoppard

Barnaby Smith Contact: The Sound Joint

Rick Barraclough Contact: Stephen Budd Mgt

Dave Bascombe Contact: Sanctuary Producer Management

Basecamp Contact: Atlantis Management

Bastone & Burnz Contact: Stephen Budd Mgmt

Cathy Battistessa Contact: Stephen Budd Mgmt

Beat Factory Productions PO Box 189, Hastings TN34 2WE **t** 01424 435693 **f** 01424 461058 **e** jimsrbmusic@aol.com Producer: Jim Beadle.

Beatguru The Townhouse, 150 Goldhawk Rd, London W12 8HH **t** 020 8743 1111 or 07951 406 938 **e** andrian@beatguru.com **w** beatguru.com Dirs: Magnus Fiennes, Andrian Adams.

Andy Bell Contact: Ricochet

Ben E & Pyro Man Contact: Loriana Music

Haydn Bendall Contact: Schtum Limited

Myles Benedict Contact: Freshwater Mgmt

Vito Benito Contact: NUFF Productions

Richard Bennett Contact: Muirhead Management

Gary Benson Contact: Menace Management

Neelu Berry Contact: TMR Prods

Biffco 20 Ringsend Road, Dublin 4, Ireland **t** 00353 1 668 5567 **f** 00353 1 667 0114 **e** biffco1@indigo.ie **w** biffco.net Studio Manager: Dave Morgan.

Big Chief 152 Trinity Road, London SW17 **t** 020 8767 3199 **f** 020 8682 3346 Contact: Edwina Berthold

Big George & Sons Hit House, Vicarage Walk, Stony Stratford, Buckinghamshire MK11 1BS **t** 01908 566453 or 01908 263050 **e** biggeorge@btinternet.com **w** lostboysstudio.com/georgewebley

Big Life Management 67-69 Chalton Street, London NW1 1HY **t** 020 7554 2100 **f** 020 7554 2154 **e** biglife@biglife.co.uk **w** biglife.co.uk Contact: Zak Biddu

Big Lion Productions 30 Holgate, Pitsea, Basildon, Essex SS13 1JD **t** 01268 728 274 or 0956 887 162 **f** 01268 728 274 **e** leo294@dircon.co.uk **w** biglionproductions.com Director: Phillip Leo.

Big M Productions Thatched Rest, Queen Hoo Lane, Tewin, Herts AL6 0LT **t** 01438 798395 **f** 01438 798395 **e** joyce@bigmgroup.freeserve.co.uk **w** martywilde.com MD: Joyce Wilde.

Big Noise PO Box 632, Cardiff CF10 4WJ **t** 02920 233144 **e** greg.haver@bignoise.co.uk **w** bignoise.co.uk Contact: Greg Haver

Big Out 27 Smithwood Close, Wimbledon, London SW19 6JL **t** 020 8780 0085 or 07703 165146 **f** 020 8785 4004 **e** BigOutLtd@aol.com **w** mis-teeq.com MD: Louise Porter.

The BigPockets Contact: CBL

David Billing Contact: Bold Management

Henry Binns Contact: Solar Management

Bird & Bush Contact: Paul Brown Management

Dan Bizaro Contact: Seedpod

BJ Contact: Zomba Mgmt

Blah Street Productions The Hop Kiln, Hillside, Odiham, Hants RG29 1HX **t** 01256 701112 **f** 01256 701106 **e** studio@blahstreet.co.uk **w** blahstreet.co.uk Contact: John Stimpson/Patch Hannan

Paul Blake Contact: Bamn Mgmt

Tchad Blake Contact: Paul Brown Management

David Blaylock Productions 39 Leyton Road, Harpenden, Hertfordshire AL5 2JB **t** 01582 715098 **f** 01582 715098 MD: David Blaylock.

Blindside Contact: Sublime

Blinkered Vision 4-10 Lamb Walk, London SE1 3TT **t** 020 7921 8353 **f** 020 7407 7081 **e** Info@blinkvis.co.uk **w** blinkvis.co.uk Creative Director: Fabian Enculez.

Nikolaj Bloch Contact: Solar Management

Blueprint Management PO Box 593, Woking, Surrey GU23 7YF **t** 01483 7153363 **f** 01483 7574904 **e** blueprint@lineone.net Contact: John Glover

Bluff Contact: GR Management

Bluntfunkers Contact: NUFF Productions

Bob Noxious Contact: Extreme Music

Bobby B Contact: Split Music

Bobfalola Music Production 628 Old Kent Road, London SE15 1JB **t** 07989 471263 **e** bobfalola@aol.com Dir: Bob Falola.

Roger Boden Contact: Amco Music Productions

Phil Bodger Contact: Pachuco Management

Bodyrockers Contact: 24 Management

Bold Management Ground Floor, 39 Mowbray Rd, London NW6 7QS **t** 020 8830 2655 **e** jayne@boldmanagement.com MD: Jayne Griffiths.

Boomfactory 22 Stephenson Way, London NW1 2HD **t** 020 7419 1800 **f** 020 7419 1600 **e** andy.ruffell@boomfactory.com **w** boomfactory.com CEO: Andy Ruffell.

Daniel Boone Contact: Value Added Talent

David Bottril Contact: Paul Brown Mgmt

Alan Bown Management 71 Shaggy Calf Lane, Slough, Berkshire SL2 5HN **t** 01344 890001 or 01753 524227 **f** 01344 885323 Contact: Alan Bown

Julian Bown Contact: Alan Bown Mgmt

Brad Carter Contact: Pure Stirling

Andy Bradfield Contact: 365 Artists

Derek Bramble Contact: Freshwater Mgmt

David Brant Contact: XL Talent Partnership

Martin Brass Contact: SGM Mgmt

Michael Brauer Contact: SJP/Dodgy Productions

Brenda Brooker Enterprises 9 Cork St, Mayfair, London W1S 3LL **t** 020 7544 2893 **e** BrookerB@aol.com MD: Brenda Brooker.

Brian Rawling Productions 78 Portland Road, London W11 4LQ **t** 01483 225226 **f** 01483 479606 **e** info@metrophonic.com **w** metrophonic.com MD: Brian Rawling.

Bright Tracks Productions PO Box 27, Stroud, Gloucestershire GL6 0YQ **t** 01453 836877 **f** 01453 836877 **e** info@johnnycoppin.co.uk **w** johnnycoppin.co.uk MD: Johnny Coppin.

Pete Briquette Contact: Pachuco Management

Neil Brockbank Contact: Pete Hawkins Management

Gerry Bron Management 17 Priory Road, London NW6 4NN **t** 020 7209 2766 **f** 020 7813 2766 **e** gerrybron@easynet.co.uk **w** gerrybron.com Contact: Gerry Bron

Michael Brook Contact: Opium (Arts

Brothers Grimm Music Productions The Sound Factory, PO Box 681, Birmingham, West Midlands B17 9AU **t** 0121 681 8881 **f** 0121 681 8881 Contact: Mark Thorley

Ian Broudie Contact: JPR Management

John Brough Contact: Stephen Budd Mgmt

Chris Brown Contact: Z Management

Paul Brown Management 103 Devonshire Rd, London W4 2HU **t** 020 8994 8887 **f** 020 8994 2221 **e** paulb@pbmanagement.co.uk **w** pbmanagement.co.uk MD: Paul Brown.

Phil Brown Contact: 0510 Management

Wayne Brown Contact: LJE

Jim Brumby Contact: Engine Ears Management

Stephen Budd Management 109x Regents Park Road, London NW1 8UR **t** 020 7916 3303 **f** 020 7916 3302 **e** info@record-producers.com **w** record-producers.com MD: Stephen Budd. GM: Louise Smith.

Bukowski Productions PO Box 33849, London N8 9XJ **t** 07092 047 780 **e** bukowskiproductions@btinternet.com Contact: Michael Bukowski

Jonny Bull Contact: Spirit Music & Media

Richard Burton Contact: TNR Music

Lukas Burton Contact: XL Talent Partnership

Adrian Bushby Contact: This Much Talent

David Butcher Contact: First Step Mgmt

Ian John Button Contact: The Day Job

Buzz-erk Music 17 Villers Rd, Kingston Upon Thames, Surrey KT1 3AP **t** 020 8931 1044 **e** info@buzz-erk.com **w** buzz-erk.com Dir: Niraj Chag.

John Cale Contact: Firebrand Management

Cameron Craig Contact: The Day Job

Ian Cameron 29 North End Road, London NW11 7RJ **t** 020 8455 4707

Matt 'Qualified' Campbell Contact: The Yukon Mgmt

Colin Campsie W.G.Stonebridge Artist Mgmnt, The Chapel, 57 St Dionis Road, London SW6 4BU **t** 020 7731 2100 **f** 020 7371 7722

Gil Cang Contact: Twenty Four Seven Music Mgmt

Ian Caple Contact: SJP/Dodgy Productions

Cargogold Productions 39 Clitterhouse Crescent, Cricklewood, London NW2 1DB **t** 020 8458 1020 **f** 020 8458 1020 **e** mike@mikecarr.co.uk **w** mikecarr.co.uk MD: Mike Carr.

Carl Stipetic Contact: In A City Mgmnt

Carpe Diem Contact: Worldmaster Dj Mgmt

Nick Carpenter PO Box 22626, London N15 3WW **t** 020 8211 0272 **f** 020 8211 0272

Derrick Carter Contact: Mumbo Jumbo Management

CBL 1 Glenthorne Mews, 115A Glenthorne Road, London W6 0LJ **t** 020 8748 5036 **f** 020 8748 3356 **e** mail@clivebanks.com Management Assistant: Sharon Wheeler.

Guy Chambers Contact: Orgasmatron

Ben Chapman Contact: 140dB Management

Ed Cherney Contact: Sanctuary Producer Management

Chris Harley Contact: Vital Spark

Chunk Management 97a Scrubs Lane, London NW10 6QU **t** 020 8960 1331 **f** 020 8968 3377 **e** info@chunkmanagement.com **w** chunkmanagement.com MD: Mike Nelson.

City Hi-Fi Contact: Jamdown Mgmt.

Jason Clift Contact: Silent Mgmt

Simon Climie Contact: Signia Productions

Claudio Coccoluto Contact: Prodmix Artisdt Management

Coda Recordings 9, Springfield House, Marsden Green, Welwyn Garden City, Herts AL8 6UZ **t** 01707 322793 or 07957 861656 **f** 01707 322793 **e** coda@coda-uk.co.uk **w** coda-uk.co.uk MD: Colin Frechter.

BJ Cole Contact: Firebrand Management

Jude Cole Contact: Sanctuary Producer Management

Jon Collyer Contact: Strongroom

Con Fitzpatrick Productions Unit 3, Gravity Shack, Rear of 328 Balham High Rd, London SW17 7AA **t** 020 8672 4772 **e** con.fitzpatrick@virgin.net Contact: Con Fitzpatrick

Connect 2 Music Ltd 20 Woodlands Rd, Bushey, Hertfordshire WD2 2LR **t** 01923 244673 **f** 01923 244693 **e** info@connectmusic.com **w** connectmusic.com MD: Barry Blue.

Steve Constantine Contact: SCO Prods

Paul Cooke Contact: PCM

Copy Katz Productions 6 Liberty Hall Road, Addlestone, Surrey KT15 1SS **t** 01932 840 616 or 07702 272100 **f** 01932 840 616 **e** meltyler@talk21.com MD: Mel Tyler.

Cordella Music 35 Britannia Gardens, Hedge End, Hants SO30 2RN **t** 08450 616616 or 01489 780909 **e** barry@cordellamusic.co.uk **w** cordellamusic.co.uk Producer: Barry Upton.

John Cornfield Contact: SJP/Dodgy Productions

Simon Cotsworth Contact: Ricochet

Simon Cottsworth Contact: Ricochet

Courtyard Productions 22 The Nursery, Sutton Courtenay, Oxfordshire OX14 4UA **t** 01235 845800 **f** 01235 847692 **e** brian@cyard.com Dir: Brian Message.

Carl Cox Contact: International Mgmt Div

DJ CP Contact: Global Mgmt

Craig Leon Contact: Atlas Realisations Music

Pete Craigie Contact: Z Mgmt

Creation Management 2 Berkley Grove, Primrose Hill, London NW1 8XY **t** 020 7483 2541 **f** 020 7722 8412 **e** Creation.management@dial.pipex.com Office Manager: Peter Jackson.

Creative Dialogue Air Studios, Lyndhurst Road, London NW3 5NG **t** 020 7794 0660 **e** creativedialogueltd@btinternet.com **w** creativedialogue.co.uk Director: Ian Dean.

Stuart Crichton Contact: Z Management

Crisis Media The Old Granary, Ammerham, Somerset TA20 4LB **t** 01460 30846 **e** ronnie@crisis-management.org Dirs: Ronnie Gleeson, Meredith Cork.

Crocodile Music 35 Gresse St, London W1T 1QY **t** 020 7580 0080 **f** 020 7637 0097 **e** music@crocodilemusic.com **w** crocodilemusic.com Production Mgr: Ray Tattle.

David Cunningham 30 Fournier Street, London E1 6QE **t** 020 7247 1346 **f** 020 7247 1346 **w** stalk.net/piano/dcbio.htm Contact: David Cunningham

Cutfather & Joe Contact: XL Talent Partnership

The Cutting Room Abraham Moss Centre, Crescent Centre, Manchester M8 5UF **t** 0161 740 9438 **f** 0161 740 0583

Tommy D Contact: This Much Talent

Graham D'Ancey Contact: Panama Productions

Caroline Dale Contact: Spirit Music & Media

Danny D Contact: 19 Mgmt

Darah Music 21C Heathmans Road, London SW6 4TJ **t** 020 7731 9313 **f** 020 7731 9314 **e** admin@darah.co.uk MD: David Howells.

Dave The Drummer Contact: Tortured Artists

David Jaymes Associates PO Box 30884, London W12 9AZ **t** 020 8746 7461 **f** 020 8749 7441 **e** info@spiritmm.com **w** spiritmm.com Directors: David Jaymes, Tom Haxell.

Neil Davidge Contact: 7Hz Productions

Pete Davis Contact: Native Management

Charlotte Day Contact: Amco Music Productions

The Day Job 14 Church St, Twickenham, Middx TW1 3NJ **t** 020 8892 6446 **f** 020 8891 1895 **e** nina@thedayjob.com **w** thedayjob.com Contact: Nina Jackson

dB Entertainments PO Box 147, Peterborough, Cambs. PE1 4XU **t** 01733 311755 **f** 01733 709449 **e** info@dbentertainments.com **w** dbentertainments.com Director/Producer: Russell Dawson-Butterworth.

Edward de Bono Contact: Wingfoot Prods

John de Bono Contact: Wingfoot Prods

Ted de Bono 41A Cavendish Road, London NW6 7XR **t** 020 8459 2833 **e** ted.de_bono@virgin.net Contact: Ted de Bono

Merv de Peyer Contact: Stephen Budd Mgmt

Marius De Vries Contact: Native Management

De-Mix Productions 7 Croxley Rd, London W9 3HH **t** 020 8960 1115 **e** martin.lascelles@virgin.net MD: Martin Lascelles.

Deadly Avenger Contact: Mumbo Jumbo Management

Ian Dean Contact: Creative Dialogue

Death and Hotdog Contact: Pure Stirling

DeeKay Contact: Asylum Artists

Deekay Music Contact: Asylum Artists

Deep Production Contact: Deep Recording Studios

Fred De Faye Contact: Match Mgmt

Delta Rhythm Contact: The Day Job

Deluxe Management PO Box 5753, Nottingham NG2 7WN **t** 0115 914 1429 **f** 0115 914 1429 **e** management@deluxeaudio.com Contact: Nick Gordon Brown

Deluxxe Management PO Box 373, Teddington TW11 8ZQ **t** 020 8755 3630 or 07771 861 054 **f** 020 8404 7771 **e** info@deluxxe.co.uk **w** deluxxe.co.uk MD: Diane Wagg.

Gez Dewar Contact: XL Talent Partnership

Ron Dickson Contact: Value For Money

Dirty Beatniks Contact: Me One Mgmt

Disclab Contact: Zomba Mgmt

DJ Dan Contact: International Mgmt Div

DND Productions Contact: XL Talent Partnership

Ben Dobie Contact: Strongroom

Dobs Vye Contact: Adage Music

Mark Dodson Contact: Rive Droite Music Productions

Sean Doherty Contact: Roundhouse Mgmnt

Mick Dolan Contact: Bright Tracks Productions

Johnny Dollar Contact: Bamn Mgmt

Domain Music Unit 9, TGEC, Town Hall Approach Road, London N15 4RX **t** 020 8375 3608 **f** 020 8375 3487 **e** info@domainmusic.co.uk **w** domainmusic.co.uk Dir: Michael Lowe.

Don Wise Contact: SJP/Dodgy Productions

Tim Dorney Contact: David Jaymes Associates Ltd

Double Jointed Productions (address witheld by request **t** 020 7836 7553 **e** djp@musicard.co.uk Production Mgr: David Newell.

Johnny Douglas Contact: Twenty Four Seven Music Mgmt

Tim Downey Contact: Spirit Music & Media

George Drakoulias Contact: Sanctuary Producer Management

Markus Dravs Contact: Sanctuary Producer Management

Drawbacks Contact: Strongroom

Dreamscape Music 36 Eastcastle Street, London W1W 8DP **t** 020 7631 1799 **f** 020 7631 1720 **e** Bigsynths@aol.com Producer: Lester Barnes. Composer/Producer: Lester Barnes.

Dave Dresden Contact: Ornadel Management

Richard Drummie Contact: Blueprint Mgmt

Dub Organiser Contact: Fashion Productions

Matt Dunkley Contact: SMA Talent

Duran Duran Productions 55 Loudoun Rd, London NW8 0DL **t** 020 7625 3555 **e** evon@ddproductions.easynet.co.uk **w** duranduran.com Programmer/Engineer: Mark Tinley.

Joe Dwomiak Contact: This Much Talent

Floyd Dyce Onward House, 11 Uxbridge St, London W8 7TQ **t** 020 7221 4275 **f** 020 7229 6893 **e** info@bucksmusicgroup.co.uk **w** bucksmusicgroup.co.uk Publisher: Simon Platz.

E-Poppi Contact: The Yukon Mgmt

Colin Eade Contact: Panama Productions

EasyUK Contact: Seedpod

Eclectic Method Contact: The Day Job

Eden Contact: Stephen Budd Mgmt

Steve Edwards Contact: Menace Management

Bruce Elliott-Smith Contact: Active Music Mgmt

Colin Emmanuel (C Swing Contact: Stephen Budd Mgmt

Engine Contact: XL Talent Partnership

Engine Ears Management 2 Shuttleworth Rd, London SW11 3EA **t** 020 7326 9450 or 07966 195 890 **f** 020 7326 9499 **e** engine-ears@spherestudios.com Manager: Amanda Todd.

Dave Eringa Contact: Solar Management

EuropaXL Contact: Asylum Artists

Evolver Contact: Music Factory

Extreme Music Productions 4-7 Forewoods Common, Holt, Wilts BA14 6PJ **t** 01225 782984 **f** 01255 782281 **e** george@xtrememusic.co.uk **w** xtrememusic.co.uk MD: George D Allen.

Bob Ezrin Contact: Sanctuary Producer Management

Face Music 13 Elvendon Road, London N13 4SJ **t** 020 8889 1959 **f** 020 8889 1959 **e** sue@facemusic.freeserve.co.uk Managers: Sue Carling.

Michael Fallon Contact: Atlantis Management

Jean-Louis Fargier Contact: Loriana Music

Sasha Farhadian Contact: The Day Job

Fashion Productions 17 David's Road, London SE23 3EP **t** 020 8291 6253 **f** 020 8291 1097 Studio Manager: Chris Lane.

Faze Action Contact: Sublime Mgmnt

Richie Fermie Contact: This Much Talent

The Fern Organisation Fern Studios, 5 Low Road, Conisbrough, Doncaster, South Yorkshire DN12 3AB **t** 01709 868511 **f** 01709 867274 Contact: Howard Johnson

Fexx 159A High Road, Chadwell Heath, Romford, Essex RM6 6NL **t** 07931 752641 **e** adamfexx@yahoo.co.uk **w** fexx.co.uk Prod/Engineer: Adam Taylor.

RS "Bobby" Field Contact: Muirhead Management

Magnus Fiennes Contact: Beatguru

Daniel Figgis Contact: The Day Job

Filo Contact: Sublime Mgmt

Filterheadz Contact: Ornadel Management

Firebrand Management 12 Rickett Street, London SW6 1RJ **t** 020 7381 2375 or 07885 282 165 **e** vernfire@aol.com Contact: Mark Vernon

Steve Fitzmaurice Contact: Native Management

Richard Flack Contact: Engine Ears Management

Andrew Flintham Productions Titlow Rd, Harleston, Norfolk IP20 9DH **t** 01379 853982 **e** andrew.flintham@talk21.com Freelance Producer: Andrew Flintham.

Flood Contact: 140dB Management

John Fortis Contact: XL Talent Partnership

FourFives Productions 21d Heathman's Rd, London SW6 4TJ **t** 020 7731 6555 **f** 020 7371 5005 **e** mp@fourfives-music.com **w** fourfives-music.com Dir: Andrew Greasley.

Henry Frampton 11 Devonshire Gardens, London W4 3TN **t** 020 8580 2667

Lenny Franchi Contact: Sanctuary Producer Management

Charlie Francis Contact: Paul Brown Management

Simon Franglen Contact: Native Management

Freaks Contact: Mumbo Jumbo Management

Freedom Management 218 Canalot Studios, 222 Kensal Rd, London W10 5BN **t** 020 8960 4443 **f** 020 8960 9889 **e** freedom@frdm.co.uk MD: Martyn Barter.

Freeform Five Contact: Mumbo Jumbo Management

Mark Freegard Contact: 140dB Management

Michael Freeman Contact: Tracy-Carter Mgmt

Freshwater Management PO Box 54, Northaw, Hertfordshire EN6 4PY **t** 01707 661431 **f** 01707 664141 **e** fresh@btconnect.com Contact: Brian Freshwater

Aron Friedman Contact: Kudos Management

Mark Frith Contact: Positive

Full Phatt Produtions Contact: 365 Artists

Fume Productions 30 Kilburn Lane, Kensal Green, London W10 4AH **t** 020 8969 2909 **f** 020 8969 3825 **e** info@fume.co.uk **w** fume.co.uk MD: Seamus Morley.

Fundamental Music 64 Manor Road, Wheathampstead, Hertfordshire AL4 8JD **t** 01582 622757 **f** 01582 621718 **e** chickers@ntlworld.com Manager: Karen Ciccone.

Josh Gabriel Contact: Ornadel Management

Pascal Gabriel Contact: This Much Talent

Toby Gafftey-Smith Contact: Muirhead Management

Pete Gage Production 47 Prout Grove, London NW10 1PU **t** 020 8450 5789 **f** 020 8450 0150 MD: Pete Gage.

Gailforce Management 55 Fulham High Street, London SW6 3JJ **t** 020 7384 8989 **f** 020 7384 8988 **e** gail@gailforcemanagement.co.uk MD: Gail Colson.

Galaxy P Contact: Jamdown Mgmt.

Julian Gallagher Contact: Native Management

Rod Gammons Contact: Match Mgmt

Vince Garcia Contact: Match Management

Davey Garnish Contact: Roundhouse Mgmt

Ger McDonnell Contact: 3kHz

Jeremy Gill see Roundhouse Mgmnt

Richard Gillinson Contact: Lionheart

Kristian Gilroy Harewood Farm Studios, Little Harewood Farm, Clamgoose Lane, StaffS ST10 2EG **t** 07782 306251 **f** 01538 755735 **e** gilroy@fenetre.co.uk **w** harewoodfarmstudios.com

Pete Glenister Contact: Maximum Music

Glenn A Payne Contact: Matiz Music/Mystic Prod

Mick Glossop Contact: Stephen Budd Mgmt

Go Crazy Music The Studio, Penybryn, Tydcombe Rd, Warlingham, Surrey CR6 9LU **t** 01883 626859 **e** gocrazymusic@aol.com GM: Sara Watts.

Goatboy Contact: Stephen Budd Mgmt

Jem Godfrey Contact: Wise Buddah Music

Goetz B Contact: 365 Artists

Goldman Associates 16 Red Hill Lane, Great Shelford, Cambridge CB2 5JR **t** 01223 840436 **f** 01223 840436 **e** dox@goldman.co.uk **w** goldman.co.uk Contact: Martin Goldman

Tim Goldsworthy Contact: This Much Talent

Gone to Lunch Productions PO Box 28013, London SE27 0PG **t** 020 8761 6890 **e** michael.music@virgin.net Contact: Michael Natkanski

Dave Goodman Contact: Line-Up PMC

Nigel Godrich Contact: Solar Management

Peter Gordeno Contact: XL Talent Partnership

GR Management 974 Pollokshaws Road, Shawlands, Glasgow, Strathclyde G41 2HA **t** 0141 632 1111 **f** 0141 649 0042 **e** g.r@dial.pipex.com Dirs: Rab Andrew/Gerry McElhone.

Paul Grabowsky Contact: Muirhead Management

Graeme Stewart Contact: Solar Management

Noel Grant Contact: Little Piece of Jamaica

Michael Graves Contact: JC Music

Andy Gray Contact: 140dB Management

Howard Gray Contact: XL Talent Partnership

Ian Green Contact: Bamn Management

Leo Green Contact: LJE

Nigel Green Contact: Sanctuary Producer Management

Glen Gregory Contact: Stephen Budd Mgmt

John Gregory Contact: Arpeggio Music

Nick Griffiths Contact: SJP/Dodgy Productions

Ian Grimble Contact: Stephen Budd Mgmt

Groove Collision/Manhattan Clique Contact: 365 Artists

Raj Gupta Contact: Solar Management

Robin Guthrie Contact: The Day Job

Guy Massey Contact: 140db Management

DJ H (Queasyrider Contact: The Day Job

Steve Hackett Contact: Kudos Management

Stephen Hague Contact: Solar Management

James Hallawell Contact: Stephen Budd Mgmt

Jason Halliday PO Box 1257, London E5 0UD **t** 07956 398 152 **f** 020 8986 7451

Pete Hammond Contact: Futurescope Ltd

Steve Hammond Contact: Active Music Mgmt

Handbaggers Contact: Music Factory

John Hanlon Contact: SJP/Dodgy Productions

Hannah Management 102 Dean St, London W1D 3TQ **t** 020 7758 1494 **e** hgadsdon@barberamusic.co.uk MD: Hugh Gadsdon.

Phil Harding Contact: P.J. Music

Iain Harive Contact: JPR Management

Martin Harrington Contact: Native Management

Hu Harris Contact: Ricochet

Shannon Harris Contact: The Oxford Music Co

Simon Harris Unit 9b, Wingbury Business Village, Upper Wingbury Farm, Wingrave, Bucks HP11 4LW **t** 07770 364 268 **e** chris@musicoflife.com **w** musicoflife.com Contact: Chris France

Danny Harrison Contact: Bold Management

Greg Haver Contact: Stephen Budd Mgmt

Pete Hawkins Management 3 Vincent Close, Bromley, Kent BR2 9ED **t** 020 8402 9199 or 07836 266 328 **e** pvhawkins@ntlworld.com MD: Pete Hawkins.

Matt Hay Contact: Engine Ears Management

Head Contact: Paul Brown Mgmt

Mike Hedges Contact: 3kHz Mgmt

Zeus B Held Contact: LJE

Sally Herbert Contact: Solar Management

Dennis Herring Contact: Sanctuary Producer Management

Max Heyes Contact: Z Management

High Barn The Bardfield Centre, Great Bardfield, Braintree, Essex CM7 4SL **t** 01371 811291 **f** 01371 811404 **e** info@high-barn.com **w** high-barn.com MD: Chris Bullen. Manager: Iain Court.

Mark Hill Contact: Zomba Mgmt

Ben Hillier Contact: 140dB Management

Hillyer & Johnson Contact: Asylum Artists

Paul Hillyer Contact: Asylum Artists

Stephen Hilton Contact: Silent Mgmt

Rupert Hine Contact: Jukes Prods

Hip-Hop Cow Management 27 Church Drive, North Harrow, Middx HA2 7NR **t** 020 8866 2454 **f** 020 8429 4383 **e** hiphopcow@aol.com **w** hiphopcow.com MD: Andrew East.

Jimmy Hogarth Contact: Native Management

Ross Hogarth Contact: Sanctuary Producer Management

Holdings Ecosse 9/1 Tweeddale Court, 14 High Street, Edinburgh, Lothian EH1 1TE **t** 0131 557 2678 **f** 0131 557 4954 **e** contact@holdingsAV.com Contact: Bob Last

Recording Studios & Services

John Holliday Contact: WC Stonebridge

Holyrood Recording & Film Productions 86 Causewayside, Edinburgh EH9 1PY **t** 0131 668 3366 **f** 0131 662 4463 **e** neil@holyroodproductions.com MD: Neil Ross.

Dean Honer Contact: Menace Management

Claude Hopper Productions Ltd 21 Napier Place, London W14 8LG **t** 020 7603 9261 **f** 020 8878 7849 Dir: Tony Prior.

Trevor Horn Contact: Sarm Management

Thor House Contact: Gerry Bron Management

Howard Hughes 8 Mentmore Terrace, London E8 3PN **t** 020 8525 4179 or 07714 202 435 **e** exbetts@aol.com **w** howardhughes.co.uk Contact: Producer

Howarth & Johnston **t** 0131 555 2288 or 07976 209105 **e** h+j@daveandmax.co.uk **w** daveandmax.co.uk Contact: Max Howarth, David Johnston

Ash Howes Contact: Native Management

Howie B Contact: Native Management

Hoxton Whores Contact: 24 Management

Mark Hudson Contact: Little Piece of Jamaica

Paul Hue Contact: Little Piece of Jamaica

Chris Hughes Contact: Isisglow

Miles Hunt Contact: David Jaymes Associates

Hush Productions 14 Raynham Road, London W6 0HY **t** 020 8846 9912 **f** 020 8748 6683 Contact: Judy Lipson

Hyperlogic Contact: Music Factory

I Monster Contact: Menace Mgmnt

Ian Catt Contact: Jester Music

Ils & Richie Contact: Bamn Mgmt

The Insects Contact: Paul Brown Management

Instant Music 14 Moorend Crescent, Cheltenham, Gloucestershire GL53 0EL **t** 07957 355360 **f** 01242 523304 **e** info@instantmusic.co.uk **w** instantmusic.co.uk Producer: Martin Mitchell.

Jack Clark Contact: Out Of Eden

Andre Jacquemin Contact: Redwood Studios

Jadell Contact: Mumbo Jumbo Management

Jam DVD 1st floor, 17 Mortimer Crescent, London NW6 5NP **t** 07976 820774 **e** julieg@dircon.co.uk Recording Engineer/Mixer: Julie Gardner.

Jamdown Stanley House, 39 Stanley Gardens, London W3 7SY **t** 020 8735 0280 **f** 020 8930 1073 **e** othman@jamdown-music.com **w** jamdown-music.com MD: Othman Mukhlis.

David James (Audio Drive Contact: Stephen Budd Mgmt

James Reynolds Contact: Match Management

Stewart & Bradley James 28 Horton Road, London E8 1DP **t** 020 7254 9257 **f** 020 7254 4928

Eli Janney Contact: Paul Brown Management

Jeff Jarratt Hotrock Music, Forestdene, Barnet, Hertfordshire EN5 4PP **t** 020 8449 0830 **f** 020 8447 1210 **e** jeff@abbeyroadcafe.com MD: Jeff Jarratt.

JAY Productions 107 Kentish Town Rd, London NW1 8PD **t** 020 7485 9593 **f** 020 7485 2282 **e** john@jayrecords.com **w** jayrecords.com Producer: John Yap.

Jay Taylor Flat 114, India House, 75 Whitworth St, Manchester M1 6HB **t** 0161 278 6087 or 07931 797 982 **e** jaytaylor@cwcom.net **w** bone-box.com Producer: Jay Taylor.

Jazzwad Contact: Jamdown Mgmt.

JC Music 111 Power Road, London W4 5PY **t** 020 8995 0989 **f** 020 8995 0878 **e** jcmusic@dial.pipex.com MD: John Campbell.

Jeff Knowler Contact: Out Of Eden

Jester Music PO Box 903, Sutton, Surrey SM2 6BY **t** 020 8642 1679 **f** 020 8642 5203 **e** info@jestermusic.co.uk **w** jestermusic.co.uk MD: Andy Cook.

Jewels & Stone Contact: Freedom Management

Jimmy Thomas PO Box 38805, London W12 7XL **t** 020 8740 8898 **e** jimmythomas@osceolarecords.com **w** osceolarecords.com

Joe Brown Productions PO Box 272, London N20 0BY **t** 020 8368 0340 **f** 020 8361 3370 **e** john@jt-management.demon.co.uk MD: John Taylor.

Tore Johansson Contact: Stephen Budd Mgmt

John Boy Productions PO Box 5303-03180, Alicante, SPAINor 020 7624 6167 **f** 0870 284 7322 or 0870 063 6118 **e** johnboyproductions@hotmail.com **w** leeejohn.com Contact: Gina Smith

Leee John Contact: John Boy Prods

Ethan Johns Contact: Sanctuary Producer Management

Glyn Johns Contact: Sanctuary Producer Management

Gary Johnson Contact: Asylum Artists

Rich Johnstone Contact: Pachuco Management

Cliff Jones Contact: Audio Authority Management

David Jones Contact: Panama Productions

Hugh Jones Contact: Sanctuary Producer Management

John Paul Jones Contact: Opium (Arts

Roderick Jones Contact: Panama Productions

Jordan Contact: Richard Law Mgmt

Jos Jorgensen Contact: XL Talent Partnership

Jay Joyce Contact: Sanctuary Producer Management

JPR Management Suite 25, 9-12 Middle St, Brighton, East Sussex BN1 1AL **t** 01273 236969 **f** 01273 386291 **e** info@jprmanagement.co.uk **w** jprmanagement.co.uk Contact: John Reid

Julian Sandell Contact: Tortured Artist

Jeff Juliano Contact: Sanctuary Producer Management

June Productions Toftrees, Church Road, Woldingham, Surrey CR3 7JX **t** 01883 652386 **f** 01883 652457 **e** mackay@dircon.co.uk Producer: David Mackay. Harrison 48-32.

Junior Dubbs Contact: Fashion Prods

K-Gee Contact: RPM Management

K-Klass The Bunker Recording Studio, Borras Road, Borras, Wrexham LL13 9TW **t** 01978 263295 **f** 01978 263295 **e** kklass@btconnect.com **w** k-klass.com Contact: Andrew Willimas/Carl Thomas

K-Warren Contact: Stephen Budd Mgmt

DJ Kane Contact: Congo Music

Karon Productions 20 Radstone Court, Hillview Rd, Woking, Surrey GU22 7NB **t** 01483 755153 **e** ron.roker@btinternet.com MD: Ron Roker.

Keep Calm Music The Music Village, 11B Osiers Road, London SW18 1NL **t** 020 8870 0011 **f** 020 8870 2101 **e** info@keepcalm.co.uk **w** keepcalm.co.uk Contact: Colin Peter/Carl Ward

Jon Kelly Contact: Stephen Budd Mgmt

Kevin Kendle Contact: Panama Prods

Eliot Kennedy Contact: Freedom Mgmt

Kick Production 13 D'Arblay Street, London W1V 3FP **t** 020 7287 3757 **f** 020 7437 0125 Contact: Terry J Neale

Lucy King Contact: PCM

King Unique Contact: 24 Management

Rob Kirwan Contact: 140dB Management

Kite Music Binny Estate, Ecclesmachan, West Lothian, Edinburgh EH52 6NL **t** 01506 858885 **f** 01506 858155 **e** kitemusic@aol.com **w** kitemusic.com MD: Billy Russell.

KK Kerrigan Contact: Stephen Budd Mgmt

Mike Koglin Contact: Red Parrot Mgmt

Jagz Kooner Contact: Big Life Mgmt

Damian Korner Contact: Gerry Bron Management

Kostas Contact: PCM

David Kostner Contact: Ornadel Management

Andy Kowalski Contact: Bamn Mgmt

Bob Kraushaar 24 Arlington Gardens, London W4 4EY **t** 020 8995 0676 **f** 020 8987 9656 **e** mail@bobkraushaar.com **w** bobkraushaar.com

Carsten Kroeyer Contact: Stephen Budd Mgmt

Kudos Management Crown Studios, 16-18 Crown Road, Twickenham, Middlesex TW1 3EE **t** 020 8891 4233 **f** 020 8891 2339 **e** kudos@camino.co.uk MD: Billy Budis.

Jan 'Stan' Kybert Contact: Lee Management

Kynance Cove 58-60 Berners Street, London W1P 4JS **t** 020 7747 4296 **f** 020 7747 4470 **e** max.hole@umusic.com Contact: Rhona Levene

Bob Lamb 122A Highbury Road, Kings Heath, Birmingham B14 7QP **t** 0121 443 2186

Gary Langan Contact: Positive

Mutt Lange Contact: Zomba Mgmt

Stevie "Vann" Lange Contact: W S Management

Clive Langer Contact: Hannah or Muirhead Mgmt.

Quiz Larossi Contact: XL Talent Partnership

Phil Larsen Contact: Active Music Mgmt

Nathan Larson Contact: Sanctuary Producer Management

LAS Music Production PO Box 14303, London SE26 4ZH **t** 07000 472 572 **f** 07000 472 572 **e** info@latinartsgroup.com **w** latinartsgroup.com Director: Hector Rosquete.

Martin Lascelles Contact: De-Mix Prods

Simon Law & Lee Hamblin Contact: Z Management

Peter Lawlor c/o Water Music Productions, 1st Floor, Block 2, 6 Erskine Road, London NW3 3AJ **t** 020 7722 3478 **f** 020 7722 6605 Contact: Tessa Sturridge

Matt Lawrence Contact: Audio Authority Management

Tim Laws Contact: Bamn Mgmt

Mike Lawson Contact: Value Added Talent

Graham Le Fevre 59 Park View Road, London NW10 1AJ **t** 020 8450 5154 **f** 020 8452 0187 **w** rubiconrecords.co.uk

Leafman Reverb House, Bennett St, London W4 2AH **t** 020 8747 0660 **f** 020 8747 0880 **e** liam@leafsongs.com **w** leafsongs.com MD: Liam Teeling.

John Leckie Contact: SJP/Dodgy Productions

Lectrolux Contact: Tortured Artist

Garret Lee Contact: Big Life Mgmt

Lee Management 19 Denmark Mews, Hove, East Sussex BN3 3TX **t** 01273 746449 or 07808 489553 **e** jazzlb@leemanagement.co.uk MD: Jasmin Lee.

Xavier Lee Contact: Value For Money

Damian Le Gassick Contact: XL Talent Partnership

Damian Legassick Contact: ACM

Leon Sylvers 3rd & 4th Contact: The Yukon Mgmt

Pat Leonard Contact: Sanctuary Producer Management

Paul Leonard-Morgan Contact: SMA Talent

Bernard Lermit & Bob Templar Contact: Loriana Music

Lester Barnes Contact: Dreamscape Music

Deni Lew Contact: Maximum Music

Steve & Pete Lewinson Contact: Sanctuary Producer Management

Mark Lewis Contact: International Mgmt Div

Richard Lewis Contact: The Oxford Music Co

The Liaison & Promotion Company 124 Great Portland St, London W1W 6PP **t** 020 7636 2345 **f** 020 7580 0045 **e** garydavison@fmware.com Dir: Gary Davison.

Chris Liberator Contact: Tortured Artists

Stephen Lipson Contact: Native Management

Steve Lironi Contact: Stephen Budd Mgmt

Robert Lissalde Contact: Loriana Music

Alan Little 2 Kingswood Way, Wallington, Surrey SM6 8PB **t** 07802 723 124 or 020 8395 2289 **e** cyberfletch@blueyonder.co.uk

Little Piece of Jamaica 55 Finsbury Park Road, London N4 2JY **t** 020 7359 0788 **f** 020 7226 2168 **e** paulhuelpoj@yahoo.co.uk Contact: Paul Hue

Living Productions 39 Tadorne Rd, Tadworth, Surrey KT20 5TF **t** 01737 812922 **f** 01737 812922 **e** livingprods@ukgateway.net Director: Norma Camby.

LJE 32 Willesden Lane, London NW6 7ST **t** 020 7625 0231 **f** 020 7372 5439 **e** lauriejay@btconnect.com Contact: Laurie Jay

Eddie Lock Contact: Worldmaster Dj Mgmt

Pete Lockett Contact: Silent Mgmt

Roger Lomas Ro-Lo Productions, 35 Dillotford Avenue, Styvechale, Coventry, West Midlands CV3 5DR **t** 024 7641 0388 or 07711 817475 **f** 024 7641 6615 **e** roger.lomas@virgin.net

Loriana Music 30A Tudor Drive, Gidea Park, Romford, Essex RM2 5LH **t** 01708 750185 **f** 01708 750185 **e** info@lorianamusic.com **w** lorianamusic.com MD: Jean-Louis Fargier.

James Lott Contact: Muirhead Management

James Loughrey Contact: Strongroom

Andy Love Contact: XL Talent Partnership

Love To Infinity Contact: JPS Prods

Steve Lovell Contact: Popcorp

Larry Lush Contact: SeedPod

Ged Lynch Contact: SGM Mgmt

Steve Lyon Contact: Stephen Budd Mgmt

M&S Productions Contact: 19 Mgmt

Steve Mac Contact: Darah Music

David Mackay Contact: June Prods

Paul Madden Contact: Gerry Bron Management

Made Backwards Contact: Asylum Artists

Majic Production PO Box 66, Manchester M12 4XJ **t** 0161 225 9991 **f** 0161 225 9991 **e** info@majicmusic.co.uk **w** sirenstorm.com Dir: Mike Coppock.

Major Seven 47 Combemartin Road, London SW18 5PP **t** 020 8788 9147 **f** 020 8785 7291 **e** major.seven@virgin.net Dir: Jane Wingfield. Producer: Pete Wingfield.

Mak Togashi Contact: see 1 2 One Mgmt

Jonny Male Contact: David Jaymes Associates Ltd

Keith Mansfield Contact: Alan Bown Mgmt

Tony Mansfield Contact: SJP/Dodgy Productions

Richard Manwaring 25 Waldeck Road, London W13 8LY **t** 020 8991 0495

Manygate Production Trees, Ockham Road South, East Horsley, Surrey KT24 6QE **t** 01483 281300 **f** 01483 281811 **e** manygate@easynet.co.uk Administrator: Edward Price.

MAP Productions 27 Abercorn Place, London NW8 9DX **t** 07905 116 455 **f** 020 7624 7219 **e** hkhan@greycoat.co.uk Contact: Helen Khan

Mark Hill Productions Regus House, George Curl Way, Southampton, Hants SO18 2RZ **t** 0870 240 4232 **f** 0870 240 4233 **e** Tanya.dominey@otwp.co.uk Contact: Tanya Dominey, Howard Lucas

Mark Picchiotti (aka Basstoy Contact: Stephen Budd Mgmt

Martin 101 Contact: Martin101.com

Clive Martin Contact: Paul Brown Mgmt

Marty Wilde Productions (sse Big M Productions

Dare Mason Contact: Young Producers Stable

Poj Masta Contact: The Yukon Mgmt

Jim Masters Contact: International Mgmt Div

Match Management 91 Saffron Hill, Farringdon, London EC1N 8PT **t** 020 7242 9677 **f** 020 7242 4336 **e** Info@matchmgt.fsnet.co.uk Dirs: Catrina Barnes & Matt Steggles.

Matinee Sound and Vision 132-134 Oxford Road, Reading, Berkshire RG1 7NL **t** 0118 958 4934 **f** 0118 959 4936 Dir: Timm Baldwin.

Danny de Matos Contact: Simon King Mgmt

Matpro Cary Point, Babbacombe Downs, Torquay, Devon TQ1 3LU **t** 01803 322233 **f** 01803 322244 **e** matpro@btinternet.com MD: Colin Matthews.

Matt Black Music 21c Heathmans Rd, Parsons Green, London SW6 4TJ **t** 020 7731 9313 **e** mattblack@darah.co.uk Producer: Matt Black.

Jean Paul Maunick Contact: Ricochet

Maximum Music 9 Heathmans Road, Parsons Green, London SW6 4TJ **t** 020 7731 1112 **f** 020 7731 1113 **e** info@maximummusic.co.uk MD: Nicky Graham, Deni Lew. MD: Deni Lew.

Guy McAffer Contact: Tortured Artists

Mcasso Music Production 32-34 Great Marlborough St, London W1F 7JB **t** 020 7734 3664 **f** 020 7439 2375 **e** music@mcasso.com **w** mcasso.com MD: Mike Connaris.

Andy McCluskey Contact: XL Talent Partnership

Dave McCracken Contact: 140dB Management

Rafe McKenna Contact: Stephen Budd Mgmt

Reg McLean RMO Music, 37 Philip Close, carshalton, Surrey SM5 2FE **t** 020 8646 3378 **f** 020 8646 3376

Neil McLellan Contact: This Much Talent

Dave Meegan Contact: Z Management

Menace Management 2 Park Road, Radlett, Hertfordshire WD7 8EQ **t** 01923 853789 **f** 01923 853318 **e** menacemusicmanagement@btopenworld.com MD: Dennis Collopy.

Messy Productions Studio 2, Soho Recording Studios, 22-24 Torrington Place, London WC1E 7HJ **t** 020 7813 7202 **f** 020 7419 2333 **e** info@messypro.com **w** messypro.com MD: Zak Vracelli.

Metro Contact: MumboJumbo Mgmnt

Micky Modelle/Electro Headz Contact: Tortured Artist

Teo Miller Contact: Stephen Budd Mgmt

Gordon Mills Contact: 4 Tunes Management

Jorden Milnes Contact: Asylum Artists

Miloco Management 36 Leroy Street, London SE1 4SP **t** 020 7232 0008 **f** 020 7237 6109 **e** info@milomusic.co.uk **w** miloco.co.uk Bookings Mgr: Mark Cox.

Misfits Contact: Maximum Music

Grant Mitchell Contact: Sarm Management

Martin Mitchell Commercial Music Productions 14 Moorend Crescent, Cheltenham, Gloucestershire GL53 0EL **t** 01242 523304 **f** 01242 523304 **e** mmitchell@hrpl.u-net.com MD: Martin Mitchell.

Ben Mitchell Contact: Stephen Budd Mgmt

MJS Productions 86 Birmingham Road, Lichfield, Staffordshire WS13 6PJ **t** 01543 253576 or 07585 341745 **f** 01543 253576 **e**106454.2270@compuserve.com

Mobb Rule Productions PO Box 26335, London N8 9ZA **t** 020 8340 8050 **e** info@mobbrule.com **w** mobbrule.com MD: Stewart Pettey, Wayne Clements.

Moneypenny The Stables, Westwood House, Main Street, North Dalton, Driffield, East Yorkshire YO25 9XA **t** 01377 217815 **f** 01377 217754 **e** nigel@adastey.demon.co.uk MD: Nigel Morton.

Mike Moran Contact: SMA Talent

Pat Moran Contact: SJP/Dodgy Productions

The Morrighan PO Box 23066, London W11 3FR **t** 07956 311810 **e** the@morrighan.com **w** morrighan.com Director: Jon X.

Owen Morris Contact: Redemption Music Management

Simon Morris Contact: Roundhouse Mgmnt

Ian Morrow Contact: Sarm Management

David Motion Contact: Holdings Ecosse

Motive Music Management 13 Bexhill Rd, London SW14 7NF **t** 07779 257 577 or 07808 939 919 **e** info@motivemusic.co.uk Contact: Paul Flanagan, Nathan Leeks

Alan Moulder Contact: Fundamental Management

Mozez Contact: Solar Management

MPG (The Music Producers Guild Ltd. PO Box 29912, London SW6 4FR **t** 020 7371 8888 **f** 020 7371 8887 **e** office@mpg.org.uk **w** mpg.org.uk Office Manager: Susie Sparrow.

Muirhead Management Anchor House, 2nd Floor, 15-19 Britten St, London SW3 3TY **t** 020 7351 5167 or 07785 226 542 **f** 0870 136 3878 **e** info@muirheadmanagement.co.uk **w** muirheadmanagement.co.uk CEO: Dennis Muirhead.

Multiplay Music 19 Eagle Way, Harrold, Bedford MK43 7EW **t** 01234 720785 or 07971 885375 **f** 01234 720664 **e** kevin@multiplaymusic.com **w** multiplaymusic.com MD: Kevin White.

MumboJumbo Management 2a-6a Southam St, London W10 5PH **t** 020 8960 3253 **f** 020 8968 5111 **e** caroline@mumbojumbo.co.uk **w** mumbojumbo.co.uk Contact: Caroline Hayes

Jon Musgrave Contact: Roundhouse Mgmt

MUSIC 4

music⁴

90 Long Acre, London WC2E 9RZ **t** 020 7240 7444 **e** office@music4.com **w** music4.com. Managing/A&R Director: Sandy Beech. Music Director: Roger Dexter. Commercial Director: Alan Bell. Operations Director: Christine Chapman. Business Development: Phil Bird. **Custom music for all media projects / World class library music / New songs for the music industry.**

The Music Barn Contact: Vision Discs

Music Company Recording Services (London Ltd. 103 Churston Drive, Morden, Surrey SM4 4JE **t** 020 8540 7357 **f** 020 8540 7357 **e** simon@musicco.force9.co.uk Executive Director: Simon Foster.

Music Factory Entertainment Group Hawthorne House, Fitzwilliam Street, Parkgate, Rotherham, South Yorkshire S62 6EP **t** 01709 710022 **f** 01709 523141 **e** information@musicfactory.co.uk **w** musicfactory.co.uk Contact: Andy Pickles

Music Masters Orchard End, Upper Oddington, Moreton-in-Marsh, Gloucestershire GL56 0XH **t** 01451 812288 **f** 01451 870702 **e** info@music-masters.co.uk **w** music-masters.co.uk MD: Nick John.

The Music Sculptors 32-34 Rathbone Place, London W1P 1AD **t** 020 7636 1001 **f** 020 7636 1506

Paul Mysiak Contact: Match Management

Nick Nasmyth Contact: Solar Management

Native Management Unit 32, Ransomes Dock, 35-37 Parkgate Road, London SW11 4NP **t** 020 7801 1919 **f** 020 7738 1819 **e** marie.native@19.co.uk **w** nativemanagement.com Contact: Peter Evans

Michael Natkanski Contact: Gone To Lunch Productions

Ned Bigham Contact: Ocean Bloem Productions

Negus-Fancey Company 78 Portland Road, London W11 4LQ **t** 020 7727 2063 **f** 020 7229 4188 **e** negfan@aol.com Contact: Charles Negus-Fancey

Chris Neil Contact: Sanctuary Producer Management

Nel E Contact: MDMA Mgmt

Bill Nelson Contact: Opium (Arts

Ken Nelson Contact: Oxygen Music Management

Yoad Nevo Contact: 365 Artists

Howard New Contact: JC Music

The Next Room Contact: Split Music

The Nextmen Contact: Leafman

Ted Niceley Contact: Paul Brown Management

Tom Nichols Contact: Freedom Management

Nick Franglen Contact: Town House Managment

Hugo Nicolson Contact: Big Life Mgmt

Mike Nielsen Contact: Strongroom

Niles Productions 34 Beaumont Rd, London W4 5AP **t** 020 8248 2157 **e** r.niles@richardniles.com **w** richardniles.com Dir: Richard Niles.

19 Management Unit 32 Ransome Dock, 35-37 Parkgate Road, London SW11 4NP **t** 020 7801 1919 **f** 020 7801 1920 **e** info@19.co.uk **w** 19.co.uk Contact: Simon Fuller

Rab Noakes Studio 1, 19 Marine Crescent, Kinning Park, Glasgow G51 1HD **t** 0141 423 9811 **f** 0141 423 9811 **e** stephy@go2neon.com **w** rabnoakes.com Production Organiser: Stephanie Pordage.

Paul Noble Contact: The Day Job

Noiz Studios 1 Sutherland House, 2 Greencroft Gardens, London NW6 3LR **t** 0870 240 7596 **f** 0787 686 7836 **e** info@noizstudios.co.uk **w** noizstudios.co.uk Producer: Noel da Costa.

Chuck Norman Contact: Solar Management

Richard Norris Contact: Solar Management

North Star Music PO Box 868, Cambridge CB1 6SJ **t** 01787 278256 **f** 01787 279069 **e** info@northstarmusic.co.uk **w** northstarmusic.co.uk MD: Grahame Maclean.

Northern Light Music Noyna Lodge, Manor Road, Colne, Lancashire BB8 7AS **t** 01282 611547 or 0797 072 8210 **f** 01282 718901 **e** ajjh@freenetname.co.uk Contact: Andrew Hall

Gil Norton Contact: JPR Management

Tristin Norwell Contact: TLS

Rick Nowels Contact: Stephen Budd Mgt

NUFF Productions 139c Whitfield Street, London W1T 5EN **t** 020 7380 1000 **f** 020 7380 1000 **e** Neil@Nuff.co.uk MD: Neil Stainton.

Nursery Cottage Productions PO Box 370, Newquay, Cornwall TR8 5YZ **t** 01637 831011 **f** 01637 831037 **e** nurseryco@aol.com Manager: Rod Buckle.

Paul Staveley O'Duffy Contact: WG Stonebridge Artist Mgmn

O2 Contact: Silent Mgmt

Richard Oaten Contact: Mal Spence Mgmt

Ocean Bloem Productions Unit 127, Canalot Production Studios, 222 Kensal Road, London W10 5BN **t** 020 8960 3888 **e** ned@oceanbloem.com **w** oceanbloem.com Producer: Ned Bigham.

Octave One Contact: Match Music

OD Hunte Contact: Treasure Hunte

Dave Odlum Contact: Motive Music Management

Gabriel Olegavich Contact: Big Life Mgmt

Tim Oliver Contact: Positive

Matthew Ollivier Contact: 365 Artists

Roger Olsson Contact: Stephen Budd Mgt

One Horse Man Contact: Global Mgmt

Opium (Arts 49 Portland Road, London W11 4LJ **t** 020 7229 5080 **f** 020 7229 4841 **e** opium@aol.com MD: Richard Chadwick.

Orgasmatron 4 Bourlet Close, (off Riding House St, London W1W 7BJ **t** 020 7580 4170 **f** 020 7900 6244 **e** info@orgasmatron.co.uk **w** guychambers.com Contact: Dylan Chambers, Louise Jeremy

Ornadel Management Clearwater Yard, 35 Inverness St, London NW1 7HB **t** 020 7424 7500 **f** 020 7424 7501 **e** guy@ornadel.com **w** ornadel.com MD: Guy Ornadel.

Steve Osborne Contact: 140dB Management

Out Of Eden 20-24 Beaumont Road, Chiswick, London W4 5AP **t** 020 8995 5432 **f** 020 8747 1931 **e** eden@edenstudios.com **w** edenstudios.com Studio Manager: Natalie Horton.

Oven Ready Productions PO Box 30446, London NW6 6FW **t** 07050 803 933 **f** 07050 693 471 **e** info@ovenready.net **w** ovenready.net MD: Moussa Clarke.

Ovni Audio 33-37 Hatherley Mews, London E17 4QP **t** 020 8521 9595 or 07967 615647 **f** 020 8521 6363 **e** flavio.uk@ukonline.co.uk **w** curiousyellow.co.uk Owner: Flavio Curras.

Gorwel Owen Ein Hoff Le, Llanfaelog, Ty Croes, Ynys Mon LL63 5TN **t** 01407 810742 or 07987 672824 **f** 01407 810742 **e** besyn.digwydd@virgin.net

Oxbridge Records (Classical, Choral & Organ only 1 Abbey Street, Eynsham, Oxford OX8 1HR **t** 01865 880240 **f** 01865 880240 MD: HF Mudd.

The Oxford Music Company Music House, 43A Botley Road, Oxford OX2 0BN **t** 01865 725533 **e** omc@lbsmusic.demon.co.uk **w** lbsmusic.demon.co.uk MD: Richard Lewis.

Oxygen Music Management 33-45 Parr St, Liverpool, Merseyside L1 4JN **t** 0151 707 1050 **f** 0151 709 4090 **e** oxygenmusic@btinternet.com MD: Pete Byrne.

P.J. Music Willow Barn, Wrenshall Farm, Walsham-Le-Willows, Bury St Edmunds, Suffolk IP31 3AS **t** 01359 258686 **f** 01359 258686 **e** phil.harding@virgin.net MD: Phil Harding.

Pachuco Management Priestlands, Letchmore Heath, Herts WD2 8EW **t** 01923 854334 **f** 01923 857884 **e** graham@spz.com MD: Graham Carpenter.

Bill Padley Contact: Wise Buddah Music

Palladium Contact: XL Talent Partnership

Panama Productions Sovereign House, 12 Trewartha Road, Praa Sands, Penzance, Cornwall TR20 9ST **t** 01736 762826 or 07721 449477 **f** 01736 763328 **e** panamus@aol.com **w** panamamusic.co.uk MD: Roderick Jones.

P+E Music Contact: P.J. Music

Paradigm Productions 143 West Vale, Neston, South Wirral, Cheshire CM64 0TJ **t** 0151 336 6657 or 07974 900740 **f** 0151 336 6657 **e** paraprod@cwcom.net **w** mp3.com/subsymphonic MD: Andy Williams.

Parks & Wilson Contact: Red Parrot Mgmt

Paul Ballance Music PO Box 72, Beckenham, Kent BR3 5UR **t** 020 8650 2976 **f** 0870 922 3582 **e** info@megabop.plus.com **w** megabop.com MD: Paul Ballance.

Paul Hicks Contact: Abbey Road or 3kHz

Oskar Paul Contact: Stephen Budd Mgt

PCM 6 Cheyne Walk, Hornsea, East Yorkshire HU18 1BX **t** 01964 533982 **f** 01964 536193 **e** paulcooke@88interactive.com **w** 88interactive.com MD: Paul Cooke.

Ewan Pearson Contact: Mumbo Jumbo Management

Harry Peat Contact: 365 Artists

Mike Peden Contact: Native Management

Mike Pelanconi Contact: Motive Music Management

Dave Pemberton Contact: Strongroom

Pete Cobbin Contact: Abbey Road or 3kHz

Kevin Petrie Contact: Young Producers Stable

Tim Pettit Contact: Solar Management

PHAB High Notes, Sheerwater Avenue, Woodham, Surrey KT15 3DS **t** 019323 48174 **f** 019323 40921 MD: Philip HA Bailey.

Phats & Small Contact: Deluxe Management

Philly B Contact: MJM

Photek Contact: Stephen Budd Mgmt

Pierce c/o Pierce Ent., Pierce House, Hammersmith Apollo, Queen Caroline Street, London W6 9QH **t** 020 8563 1234 **f** 020 8563 1337 Contact: Deborah Cable

Giulio Pierucci Contact: 365 Artists

Tony Platt Contact: Schtum Limited

Rob Playford Contact: Stephen Budd mgmt

Point4 Productions Unit 16 Talina Centre, Bagleys Lane, Fulham, London SW6 2BW **t** 07788 420 315 **e** info@point4music.com **w** point4music.com Dirs: Paul Newton, Peter Day.

Iestyn Polson Contact: Big Life Mgmt

Pop Muzik Haslemere, 40 Broomfield Road, Henfield, W. Sussex BN5 9UA **t** 01273 491416 **f** 01273 491417 **e** info@popmuzik.co.uk **w** popmuzik.co.uk Dir: Robin Scott.

Chris Porter Contact: Shalit Mgmt

Positive Management 16, Abbey Churchyard, Bath BA1 1LY **t** 01225 311661 **f** 01225 482013 **e** carole@helium.co.uk **w** positivebiz.com Mgr: Carole Davies.

Chris Potter Contact: Z Mgmt

Steve Power Contact: Zomba Mgmt

Guy Pratt Contact: SMA Talent

Matt Prime Contact: Native Management

Principle Management 30-32 Sir John Rogersons Quay, Dublin 2, Ireland **t** 00353 1 677 7330 **f** 00353 1 677 7276 **e** jenn@numb.ie Contact: Sally-Anne McKeown MD: Paul McGuinness.

Prodmix Artist Management & Production Railway Arch 61, Cambridge Grove, London W6 0LD **t** 020 8742 6600 or 07768 877426 **f** 020 8742 6677 **e** info@prodmix.com **w** prodmix.com Dir: Karen Goldie Sauve.

Project G Contact: Amco Music Productions

Mos Props Contact: De-Mix Prods

Craig Pruess Contact: SMA Talent

Nick Pyall Contact: SGM Mgmt

Q Productions The Red Cottage, East Tytherley Road, East Tytherley, Hampshire SO51 0LW **t** 01794 341181 **f** 01794 511810 Contact: Ian Baddon

QD Music 72A Lilyville Rd, London SW6 5DW **t** 07779 653930 **f** 0870 0511 879 **e** info@qdmusic.demon.co.uk **w** kooldesac.com MD: Drew Todd.

QFM PO Box 77, Leeds LS13 2WZ **t** 08709 905 078 **f** 0113 256 1315 **e** info@qfm.com MD: Katherine Canoville.

Tom Quick Contact: Submlime Mgmt

Quince Productions 62a Balcombe St, Marylebone, London NW1 6NE **t** 020 7723 4196 or 07810 752 765 **f** 020 7723 1010 **e** info@quincestudios.co.uk **w** quincestudios.co.uk Record Producer: Matt Walters.

Quintessential Music PO Box 546, Bromley, Kent BR2 0RS **t** 020 8402 1984 **f** 020 8325 0708 Contact: Quincey

Quivver Contact: Red PArrot Mgmt

Q-Zone 21C Heathmans Road, Parsons Green, London SW6 4TJ **t** 020 7731 9313 **f** 020 7731 9314 **e** mail@darah.co.uk Contact: Nicki L'Amy

Rachel Auburn Contact: Tortured Artist

Rae & Christian Contact: Paul Brown Management

Peter Raeburn Contact: Soundtree Music

Chris Rainbow Contact: Vital Spark Management

Marc Ramaer Contact: SGM Mgmt

RandM Productions 72 Marylebone Lane, London W1U 2PL **t** 020 7486 7458 **f** 020 8467 6997 **e** mike@randm.co.uk **w** randm.co.uk MDs: Mike Andrews, Roy Eldridge.

Ray Hayden Productions 293 Mare Street, London E8 1EJ **t** 020 8986 8066 **f** 020 8533 7978 **e** rayopaz@aol.com **w** rayhayden.com Prod: Ray Hayden.

Simon Raymonde Contact: The Day Job

Louis Read Contact: Sanctuary Producer Management

Really Wicked Productions 8 Martin Dene, Bexleyheath, Kent DA6 8NA **t** 020 8301 2828 **f** 020 8301 2424 **e** htdrecords@aol.com Contact: Barry Riddington

Realsound Nottingham NG5 1JU **t** 0115 978 7745 or 07973 279 652 **f** 0115 978 7745 **e** john@realsound.fsnet.co.uk **w** realsound-uk.com Engineer: John Moon.

Red Fort Studios The Sight And Sound Centre, Priory Way, Southall, Middlesex UB2 5EB **t** 020 8843 1546 **f** 020 8574 4243 Contact: Kuljit Bhamra Soundtracs IL 48/32.

Red Hand Gang Contact: Music Factory

Red Parrrot Management B114 Faircharm Studios, 8-10 Creekside, London SE8 3DX **t** 020 8469 3541 **f** 020 8469 3542 **e** red.parrot@virgin.net **w** redparrot.co.uk Contact: John Cecchini

Red Rhythm Productions Red Rhythm Towers, 2 Longlane, Stains, Middlesex TW19 7AA **t** 01784 255629 **f** 01784 420672 **e** cliffrandall@compuserve.com Ace Production Team: Cliff Randall.

Red Sky Records PO Box 27, Stroud, Gloucestershire GL6 0YQ **t** 0845 644 1447 **f** 01453 836877 **e** info@redskyrecords.co.uk **w** redskyrecords.co.uk MD: Johnny Coppin.

Redemption Music Management 13 Bexhill Rd, London SW14 7NF **t** 07779 257 577 **e** info@redemptionmusicmanagement.co.uk Mgr: Paul Flanagan.

Redwood Studios 20 Great Chapel St, London W1V 3AQ **t** 020 7287 3799 **f** 020 7287 3751 **e** andrestudios@yahoo.co.uk **w** sound-design.net Producer: Andre Jacquemin.

Paul Reeve Contact: SJP/Dodgy Productions

David Renwick Contact: Livid

Respect Productions Unit GA, 39-40 Westpoint, Warple Way, London W3 0RG **t** 020 8740 1616 **f** 020 8740 4488 **e** respect@mailbox.co.uk Studio Manager: Ian Sherwin.

Mark Revell Contact: The Oxford Music Co

Jay Reynolds Contact: 247 Artists

John Reynolds Contact: David Jaymes Associates

Rhythm of Life Lazonby, Penrith CA10 1BG **t** 01768 898888 **f** 01768 898809 **e** events@rhythm.co.uk **w** rhythm.co.uk MD: Andrew Lennie.

Rishi Rich Contact: TwoPointNine Productions

Richard Lightman Productions 353 St. Margaret's Road, Twickenham, Middx TW1 1PW **t** 020 8891 3293 **f** 020 8744 0811 **e** richard@lightman.demon.co.uk Producer: Richard Lightman.

Richard Rainey Contact: Sanctuary Producer Management

Richard Robson Contact: DAT Productions

James Richards Contact: Big M Prods

Richie Boy Contact: Split Music

Neil Richmond 12 Fairwall House, Peckham Road, London SE5 8QW **t** 020 7703 4668 or 0799 0932850 **f** 020 7703 4668

Riff Raff Music Stanley House, 39 Stanley Gardens, Acton, London W3 7SY **t** 020 8735 0280 **e** roy@riffraffmanagement.com **w** riffraffmusic.net Director/Producer: Roy Jackson/ Gareth Young.

Mike Rigley Contact: PCM

Rise Management First Floor, 8 Wendell Road, London W12 9RT **t** 020 8740 8444 **f** 020 8749 1877 **e** info@risemanagement.co.uk **w** risemanagement.co.uk Contact: Tom Haxell

Rising Son Contact: Little Piece of Jamaica

RIve Droite Music Productions Home Park House, Hampton Court Rd, Kingston upon Thames, Surrey KT1 4AE **t** 020 8977 0666 **f** 020 8977 0660 **e** sirharry@rivedroitemusic.com **w** rivedroitemusic.com MD: Sir Harry.

John A Rivers c/o Woodbine Street Recording, 1 St Mary's Crescent, Leamington Spa, Warwickshire CV31 1JL **t** 01926 338971 **f** withheld

Riviera Music Productions 83 Dolphin Crescent, Paignton, Devon TQ3 1JZ **t** 07071 226078 **f** 01803 665728 **e** Info@rivieramusic.net **w** rivieramusic.net MD: Kevin Jarvis.

Tom Rixton Contact: The Day Job

RNT Music Pinetree Farm, Cranborne, Dorset BH21 5RR **t** 01725 517204 **f** 01725 517801 **e** info@rntmusic.com **w** rntmusic.com Producers: Rick & Tim Parkhouse.

Ben 'Jammin' Robbins Contact: Rive Droite Music Productions

Robert Miles Contact: MuchMoreMusic Artist Mgmt

Iain Roberton Contact: Sarm Management

Ian Robertson Contact: Bronco Records

Robin Millar Contact: SJP/Dodgy Productions

Joe Robinson Contact: Paul Brown Management

Bryan Robson Contact: Mumbo Jumbo Management

Jony Rockstar Contact: Z Management

Roland Herrington Contact: see Pachuco Mgmt.

David Rolfe Contact: Sanctuary Producer Management

Roll Over Productions 29 Beethoven Street, london W10 4LJ **t** 020 8968 0299 **f** 020 8968 1047 **w** rollover.co.uk Contact: Phil Jacobs

Rose & Foster Contact: Native Management

Rose Rouge International Aws House, Trinity Square, St. Peter Port, Guernsey, Channel Islands GY1 1LX **t** 01481 728 283 **f** 01481 714 118 **e** awsgroup@cwgsy.net Director: Steve Free.

Matt Rowe Contact: Native Management

RPM Management Pierce House, London Apollo Complex, Queen Caroline Street, London W6 9QU **t** 020 8741 5557 **f** 020 8741 5888 **e** marlene-rpm@pierce-entertainment.com **w** pierce-entertainment.com MD: Marlene Gaynor.

RuffNTumble 23 Corbyn St, London N4 3BY **t** 020 7281 1313 **e** info@ruffntumble.co.uk **w** ruffntumble.co.uk Dirs: Dave Longmore, Andreas Monoyos.

Rugged Expression Productions 138A Chiswick High Road, London W4 1PU **t** 020 8994 4443 **f** 020 8995 1051 **e** harry@ruggedexpression.com **w** ruggedexpression.com MD: Harry Bozadjian.

Ralph P Ruppert 23 Gatton Rd, Bristol BS2 9TF **t** 0117 983 8050 **f** 0117 983 8063 **e** ralphruppert@onetel.net.uk

Jamie Ryan Contact: Bronco Records

Marco Sabiu Contact: Paul Brown Management

Barry Sage Contact: Schtum Limited

Ron Saint Germain Contact: SJP/Dodgy Productions

Jean Saint-Girons & Robert De Coulaoun Contact: Loriana Music

Sanctuary Producer Management UK Sanctuary Townhouse Studios, 150 Goldhawk Rd, London W12 8HH **t** 020 8932 3200 **f** 020 8740 6100 **e** alan.cowderoy@sanctuarygroup.com **w** sanctuarygroup.com MD: Alan Cowderoy.

Johnny Sandlin Contact: Zane Prods

Solvieg Sandnes Contact: Stephen Budd Mgmt

Sarm Management The Blue Building, 8-10 Basing St, London W11 1ET **t** 020 7229 1229 **f** 020 7221 9247 **e** jill@spz.com **w** sarm.com MD: Jill Sinclair.

Mike Satori Management Email for address, London **t** 07963 011 302 or +43 650 407 1527 **e** mike.satori@deep9music.com **w** martin101.com Manager: Mike Satori.

DJ Savage Contact: Global Mgmt

Andy Scarth Contact: Engine Ears Management

Scatta Contact: Jamdown Mgmt.

Brian Scheuble Contact: Sanctuary Producer Management

Schmusicmusic 156a High Street, London Colney, Hertfordshire AL2 1QF **t** 01727 827017 or 07860 902361 **f** 01727 827017 **e** pjmusic@ukonline.co.uk **w** shmusicmusic.com Dir: Paul J Bowrey.

Schtum 11 Osram Road, East Lane Business Park, Wembley, Middx. HA9 7NG **t** 020 8904 4422 **f** 020 8904 3777 **e** info@schtum.co.uk **w** schtum.co.uk

SCO Productions 29 Oakroyd Ave, Potters Bar, Herts EN6 2EL **t** 01707 651439 **f** 01707 651439 **e** constantine@steveconstantine.freeserve.co.uk MD: Steve Constantine.

Chris Scott Contact: Mumbo Jumbo Management

Dave Seaman Contact: Ornadel Management

Seedpod 11 Lindal Rd, Crofton Park, London SE4 1EJ **t** 020 8691 1564 **f** 020 8691 1564 **e** music@seedpod.biz **w** seedpod.biz Production Manager: Natalie Cummings.

Sentinel Management 60 Sellons Avenue, London NW10 4HH **t** 020 8961 6992 or 07932 737 547 **e** sentinel7@hotmail.com Dirs: RJ, Sandra Scott.

Session Connection 110-112 Disraeli Road, London SW15 2DX **t** 020 8871 1212 or 020 8672 7055 **f** 020 8682 1772 **e** sessionconnection@mac.com **w** thesessionconnection.com MD: Tina Hamilton.

Charlie Sexton Contact: Sanctuary Producer Management

Shalit Global Entertainment & Management 7 Moor St, Soho, London W1D 5NB **t** 020 7851 9155 **f** 020 7851 9156 **e** info@shalitglobal.com MD: Jonathan Shalit.

Chris Sheldon Contact: Sanctuary Producer Management

Adrian Sherwood Contact: 140dB Management

Signia Productions 20 Stamford Brook Avenue, London W6 0YD **t** 020 8846 9469 **f** 020 8741 5152 **e** info@signia.com **w** signiamusic.com MD: Dee Harrington.

Valgeir Sigurdsson Contact: Stephen Budd Mgmt

Silent Management 225A Camden Road, London NW1 9AA **t** 020 7916 0366 **f** 020 7916 0367 **e** sarah.dolan@virgin.net Contact: Sarah Dolan

Silver Lion Productions 10 Oakwood Road, London NW11 6QX **t** 07937 345368 Contact: Tony Wilson

Silver Road Studios 2 Silver Road, Wood Lane, London W12 7SG **t** 020 8746 2000 **f** 020 8746 0180 **e** enquiries@silver-road-studios.co.uk **w** silver-road-studios.co.uk Contact: Samantha Leese Amek Angela.

Tim Simenon Contact: Wildlife Entertainment

Simon Sheridan Contact: DAT Productions

Sir Harry Contact: Rive Droite Music Productions

SJP/Dodgy Productions 263 Putney Bridge Road, London SW15 2PU **t** 020 8780 3311 **f** 020 8785 9894 **e** mike@tastemedia.com **w** sjpdodgy.co.uk Creative Manager: Mike Audley.

Skylark Contact: 24 Management

Slave Productions (UK PO Box 200, South Shore, Blackpool, Lancs FY1 6GR **t** 07714 910257 **e** sploj3@yahoo.co.uk Contact: Rob Powell

Sly & Robbie Contact: Z Managment

Small World 18A Farm Lane Trading Centre, 101 Farm Lane, London SW6 1QJ **t** 020 7385 3233 **f** 020 7386 0473 **e** tina@smallworldmanagement.com MD: Tina Matthews.

SMA Talent The Cottage, Church St, Fressingfield, Suffolk IP21 5PA **t** 01379 586734 **f** 01379 586131 **e** carolynne@smatalent.com MD: Carolynne Wyper.

Alexis Smith Contact: 365 Artists

Arthur Smith Contact: Bold Management

Christian Smith Contact: International Mgmt Div

Sniffy Dog 26 Cosway Mansions, Shroton St, London NW1 6UE **t** 020 7724 9700 **f** 020 7724 2598 **e** amanda@coochie-management.com **w** sniffy-dog.com Contact: Michael Blainey

Soda Club Contact: JPS Prods

Sodi Contact: SJP/Dodgy Productions

Solar Management 13 Rosemont Rd, London NW3 6NG **t** 020 7794 3388 **f** 020 7794 5588 **e** info@solarmanagement.co.uk **w** solarmanagement.co.uk Manager: Carol Crabtree.

Sonic Music Production 8 Berkley Grove, Primrose Hill, London NW1 8XY **t** 020 7722 9494 **f** 020 7722 7179 **e** reception@sonic.uk.com **w** sonic.uk.com MD: Adrienne Aiken.

Soulpower Contact: Stephen Budd Mgmt

Sound Alibi Productions 92 Hartley Avenue, Leeds, West Yorkshire LS6 2HZ **t** 0113 243 0177 **f** 0113 243 0177 **e** andy@soundalibi.co.uk **w** soundalibi.co.uk Partner: Andy Wood.

Sound Image Productions c/o Frog Recording Services, Unit 2B Bankquay Trading Est, Warrington, Cheshire WA1 1PJ **t** 01925 445742 **f** 01925 445742 **e** info@frogstudios.co.uk **w** soundimageproductions.co.uk MD: Steve Millington.

The Sound Joint 10 Parade Mews, London SE27 9AX **t** 020 8678 1404 **f** 020 8671 0380 **e** info@soundjoint.fsnet.co.uk **w** soundjoint.fsnet.co.uk Director: Chris Bachmann.

Soundcakes 14A Hornsey Rise, London N19 3SB **t** 020 7281 0018 **f** 020 7272 9609 Gen Mgr: Kris Hoffmann.

Soundtree Music Unit 124, Canalot Studios, 222 Kensal Road, London W10 5BN **t** 020 8968 1449 **f** 020 8968 1500 **e** post@soundtree.co.uk Business Mgr: Jo Feakes.

Soundz Of Muzik The Courtyard, 42 Colwith Road, London W6 9EY **t** 020 8741 1419 **f** 020 8741 3289 **e** firstname@evolverecords.co.uk Director: Trevor Porter.

The Source Contact: Tortured Artist

Spacefunk Contact: Mumbo Jumbo Management

Sam Spacey Contact: Tortured Artist

Spatts Contact: Match Management

John Spence - Freelance Engineer/Producer 20 Churchside, Appleby, North Lincs DN15 OAJ **t** 01724 732062 or 07718 061 297 **e** john@spence252.wanadoo.co.uk

Mal Spence Management Cherry Tree Lodge, Copmanthorpe, York, North Yorkshire YO23 3SH **t** 01904 703764 **f** 01904 702312 **e** malspence@aol.com **w** sugarstar.com Contact: Mal Spence

Jim Spencer Contact: Paul Brown Management

Spirit Music & Media Contact: David Jaymes Associates Ltd

Roy Spong Contact: Pachuco Mgmt

John Springate 61 Lansdowne Lane, London SE7 8TN **t** 020 8853 0728 **f** 020 8853 0728 **e** handbagmusic@cwcom.net **w** starguitar.mcmail.com/johnspring.html

SRB Music PO Box 189, Hastings TN34 2WE **t** 01424 435693 **f** 01424 461058 **e** jimsrbmusic@aol.com Dir: Jim Beadle.

Jeremy Stacey Contact: Sarm Management

Neil Stainton Contact: NUFF Productions

Ian Stanley Contact: Sanctuary Producer Management

Tom Stanley Contact: 247 Artists

Richard 'Biff' Stannard Contact: Native Management

Marshall Star Contact: Global Mgmt

Steel & Holliday Contact: WG Stonebridge

Steelworks Productions Contact: Freedom Management

Billy Steinberg Contact: Stephen Budd Mgt

Mark 'Spike' Stent Contact: TLS Mgmt

STEPHEN BUDD MANAGEMENT

SBM Stephen Budd Management
www.record-producers.com
Home of the best producers, mixers and songwriters

Zeppelin Building, 59-61 Farringdon Road, London EC1M 3JB **t** 020 7916 3303 **f** 020 7916 3302 **e** info@record-producers.com **w** record-producers.com Contacts: Stephen Budd, Simon Dix, Louise Smith, Jo Beckett. **Representing producers including: Rick Nowels, Tore Johansson, Arthur Baker, Jon Kelly, MJ Cole, Greg Haver, Steve Lironi, Peter Biker & Delgardo (Soul Power), Mark Wallis, Colin Emmanuel (C Swing), Rick Barraclough, Ian Grimble, Photek, Steve Lyon, Mark Picchiotti, Martijn ten Velden, Valgeir Sigurdsson, K-Warren, Colin Richardson, Steve Hilton, Mick Glossop and Billy Steinberg.**

Steve Smith 167, Ringwood Rd, St. Leonards, Ringwood, Hants BH24 2NP **t** 01425 473432 **f** 01425 473432 **e** info@rwav.co.uk **w** rwav.co.uk

Steven Chrisanthou Contact: Vex Management

Stonebridge Contact: X-Management

WG Stonebridge Artist Management PO Box 49155, London SW20 0YL **t** 020 8946 7242 Dir: Bill Stonebridge.

Stephen Street Contact: Gailforce Mgmt

Streetfeat Management 26 Bradmore Park Road, London W6 0DT **t** 020 8846 9984 MDs: Colin Schaverien, Simon Napier-Bell.

Strongroom Management 120-124 Curtain Rd, London EC2A 3SQ **t** 020 7426 5130 **f** 020 7426 5102 **e** coral@strongroom.com **w** strongroom.com/management Dir: Coral Worman.

Studio 24 Production 60 Benedict Close, Romsey, Hants SO51 8PN **t** 01794 501774 or 07754 969326 **f** 01794 501774 **e** info@studiotwentyfour.co.uk **w** studiotwentyfour.co.uk Producer: Alan Cotty.

Subsymphonic 143 West Vale, Neston, South Wirral, Cheshire CH64 0TJ **t** 0151 336 6657 **e** andy@subsymphonic.com **w** subsymphonic.com Producer: Andy Williams.

Suburban Soul Productions Contact: Quintessential Music

Suck My Deck Contact: Asylum Artists

Sugarcane Music The Shed, Cooper House, 2 Michael Road, London SW6 2AD **t** 020 8847 2695 **f** 020 8847 2695 Contact: Richard Bailey

Suli n' Stef Productions 56 Fraser Road, Perivale, Middlesex UB6 7AL **t** 020 8723 6158 **f** 020 7738 1764 **e** suli.hirani@btinternet.com Producer: Suli.

Sunship Contact: Jamdown Mgmt

Danton Supple Contact: 140dB Management

Billy Swan Contact: Muirhead Management

Swiss American Federation Contact: The Yukon Mgmt

Switch Contact: Global Mgmt

Synesthesia Contact: The Yukon Mgmt

Fraser T Smith Contact: Match Management

T-W-A-D Productions 72A Lilyville Rd, Fulham, London SW6 5DW **t** 07779 653930 **f** 0870 0511879 **e** twad@qdmusic.demon.co.uk **w** twad.co.uk Dir: Drew Todd.

Brio Taliaferro Contact: 365 Artists

Shel Talmy Productions 14 Raynham Road, London W6 0HY **t** 020 8846 9912 **f** 020 8748 6683 Contact: Judy Lipson

TAT Productions Contact: 2B3 Prooduction

Simon Tauber Contact: ARC Mgmt

Mark Taylor Contact: PCM

Temple Studios 97A Kenilworth Road, Edgware, Middlesex HA8 8XB **t** 020 8958 4332 or 07956 510620 **f** 020 8958 4332 **e** contact@templestudios.co.uk **w** templestudios.co.uk Producer: Howard Temple.

J Templeman Contact: Respect Prods

Terpsichord PO Box 794, High Wycombe, Buckinghamshire HP10 9FD **t** 01628 667515 **f** 01628 667515 **e** paul@terpsichord.com **w** terpsichord.com Producer: Paul Dakeyne.

Tesla Contact: Asylum Artists

Bob Thiele Contact: XL Talent Partnership

This Much Talent The Fan Club, 133 Kilburn Lane, London W10 4AN **t** 020 8354 2900 **f** 020 8354 2095 **e** contact@ThisMuchTalent.co.uk **w** ThisMuchTalent.co.uk MD: Sandy Dworniak.

Ken Thomas Contact: Strongroom

Peter Thompson Contact: Zane Prods

Rod Thompson Music 73 Bromfelde Road, London SW4 6PP **t** 020 7720 0866 **f** 020 7720 0866

Ali Thomson Contact: Sarm Management

Paul Thomson Contact: Match Management

Phil Thornalley Contact: WG Stonebridge

Three Saints Productions 241 Union Street, Middlesborough, Cleveland TS1 4EF **t** 01642 211741 Contact: Paul Mooney

TidyTrax Contact: Music Factory

Dimitri Tikovoi Contact: 140db Management

Emmitt Till Contact: Value For Money

Tilt Contact: Red Parrot Mgmt

Mark Tinley Unit 462, 405 Kings Rd, London SW10 0BB **t** 0709 212 6916 **f** 0709 212 6916 **e** marktinley@hotmail.com **w** tinley.net/mark Producer: Mark Tinley.

Paul Tipler Contact: 140dB Management

TLS Management Unit 32, Ransome's Dock, 35-37 Parkgate Road, London SW11 4NP **t** 020 7801 1919 or 020 7801 1956 **f** 020 7738 1819 **e** tls@19.co.uk MD: Tracy Slater.

TMC Records PO Box 150, Chesterfield, Derbyshire S40 0YT **t** 01246 236667 or 07711 774369 **f** 01246 236667

TNT Explosive Contact: Copy Katz Productions

Pete Tong Contact: International Mgmt Div

Tony Price Contact: Sublime Mgmt.

Tortured Artists 19F Tower Workshops, Riley Rd, London SE1 3DG **t** 020 7252 2900 **f** 020 7252 2890 **e** torture@truelove.co.uk **w** truelove.co.uk MD: John Truelove.

Townend Music 44 Eastwick Crescent, Rickmansworth, Hertfordshire WD3 8YJ **t** 01923 720083 or 07974 048955 **f** 01923 710587 **e** townendmus@aol.com MD: Mike Townend.

Cenzo Townshend Contact: Sanctuary Producer Management

Toy Productions Contact: Principle Management

Trackboyz Contact: The Yukon Mgmt

Traxx Music Production 6 Lillie Yard, London SW6 1UB **t** 020 7385 9000 **f** 020 7385 0700 **e** sharonrose@traxx.co.uk **w** traxx.co.uk Contact: Sharon Rose

Treasure Hunte Productions Global House, 92 De Beauvoir Rd, London N1 4EN **t** 07774 265 211 **f** 020 7254 6580 **e** od@thp-online.com **w** odhunte.com Producer: OD Hunte.

Tribal Sound & Vision 66C Chalk Farm Road, London NW1 8AN **t** 020 7482 6944 **e** tribal.sound@virgin.net **w** tribaltreemusic.co.uk Contact: Tony Jay

Triple M Productions 31 Elmar Rd, Aigburth, Liverpool L17 0DA **t** 0151 727 7405 **f** 0151 727 7405 **e** mikemoran@breathemail.net **w** triplemproductions.mersinet.co.uk Producer/Composer: Mike Moran.

Triple X + Bassman Contact: Simon Harris

Tropical Fish Music 351 Long Lane, London N2 8JW **t** 0870 444 5468 or 07973 386 279 **f** 0870 132 3318 **e** info@tropicalfishmusic.com **w** tropicalfishmusic.com MD: Grishma Jashapara.

Terry Trower Contact: Panama Productions

True North Productions Contact: Freedom Management

John Truelove Contact: Tortured Artist

Chris Tsangerides Contact: Audio Authority Management

Twenty Four Seven Music Management PO Box 2470, The Studio, Chobham, Surrey GU24 8ZD **t** 01276 855247 **f** 01276 856897 **e** info@24-7musicmanagement.com MD: Craig Logan.

21st Century Fix 78 Crown Lodge, Elystan Street, London SW3 3PR **t** 020 7581 3044 **f** 020 7589 5162 **e** grant.calton@btinternet.com **w** loramunro.com Director: Grant Calton.

2B3 Production Suite B, 2 Tunstall Road, London SW9 8DA **t** 020 7733 5400 or 020 7274 0782 **f** 020 7733 4449 Contact: Neville Thomas

TwoPointNine Productions 7-9 Wadsworth Rd, Perivale, Middx UB6 7JD **t** 020 8566 8633 **e** info@2point9.com **w** 2point9.com Dirs: Billy Grant, Rob Stuart.

Ty Contact: Sentinel Management

U-Freqs 20 Athol Court, 13 Pine Grove, London N4 3GU **t** 07831 770 394 **f** 0870 131 0432 **e** info@u-freqs.com **w** u-freqs.com Partner: Stevino.

UK Gold Contact: Music Factory

The Umbrella Group Call for address. **t** 07802 535 696 **f** 020 7603 9930 **e** Tommy@Umbrella-Group.com **w** Umbrella-Group.com Dir: Tommy Manzi.

UMU Productions 144 Princes Avenue, London W3 8LT **t** 020 8992 7351 **f** 020 8400 4931 **e** promo@ciscoeurope.co.uk MD: Mimi Kobayashi.

Untidy DJs Contact: Music Factory

Barry Upton Contact: Cordella Music

Utopia Records/Video Utopia Village, 7 Chalcot Road, London NW1 8LH **t** 020 7586 3434 **f** 020 7586 3438 **e** utopiarec@aol.com MD: Phil Wainman.

Peter Vale Contact: Freshwater Mgmt

Value Added Talent 1, Purley Place, London N1 1QA **t** 020 7704 9720 **f** 020 7226 6135 **e** vat@vathq.co.uk **w** vathq.co.uk MD: Dan Silver.

Value For Money (VFM Productions White House Farm, Shropshire TF9 4HA **t** 01630 647374 **f** 01630 647612 A&R Dept: Xavier Lee.

Martijn Ten Velden (Audio Drive Contact: Stephen Budd Mgmt

Vernandaz Productions 15 St Johns Church Road, Folkestone, Kent CT19 5BQ **t** 01303 257714 or 01303 257285 **e** vernon@songlife.co.uk MD: Vernon Woodward.

Vex Management 21c Tressillian Rd, London SE4 1YG **t** 020 8469 0800 **f** 020 8469 0800 **e** paul@vexmgmt.demon.co.uk **w** vexmanagement.com MD: Paul Ablett.

Dan Vickers Contact: Sarm Management

Phil Vinall Contact: Deluxxe Management

Tony Visconte Productions Inc, PO Box 314, Pomona, NY, USA 10970 **t** 001 845 362 8876 **f** 001 845 362 9190 **w** tonyvisconti.com Contact: May Pang

Vision Discs PO Box 92, Gloucester GL4 8HW **t** 01452 814321 **f** 01452 812106 **e** vic_coppersmith@hotmail.com **w** visiondiscs.com MD: Vic Coppersmith-Heaven.

Klas B. Wahl Contact: Stephen Budd Mgt

Bob Wainright Contact: TNR Music

Simon Wall Contact: 0510 Management

Mark Wallis Contact: Stephen Budd Mgmt

Greg Walsh Contact: The Liaison Promotion Company

Peter Walsh Contact: The Liaison Promotion Company

Rik Walton Giffords Oasthouse, Battle Rd, Dallington, East Sussex TN21 9LH **t** 01424 838148 or 07808 453321 **f** 01424 838148 **e** rik.walton@virgin.net Producer/Engineer: Rik Walton.

Ward 21 Contact: Jamdown mgmt.

Martyn Ware Contact: Stephen Budd Mgmt

Jim Warren Contact: SJP/Dodgy Productions

Ron Warshow Contact: 247 Artists

Marc Waterman Contact: Strongroom

The WBs Contact: Vernandez Prods

Weatherman c/o Mansfield & Co, 55 Kentish Town Rd, London NW1 8NX **t** 020 8800 1011 **f** 020 7681 3135 **e** Weatherman@ryanedwards.com MD: Nick Ashton-Hart.

Charles Webster Contact: Deluxe Management

Greg Wells Contact: Sanctuary Producer Management

West HQ Contact: Sublime Mgmt

Jeremy Wheatley Contact: 365 Artists

David White Contact: The Liaison Promotion Company

Wife Beaters PO Box 697, Wembley HA9 8WQ **t** 07956 583 221 **f** +44(0207 681 1007 **e** harry@hiphop.com CEO: Harold Anthony.

Ricki Wilde Contact: Big M Prod

Wilf Frost Contact: SeedPod

Mark Williams Contact: 140db Management

Pip Williams Contact: Pachuco

Sam Williams Contact: Sanctuary Producer Management

Tim Wills Contact: Z Management

James Wiltshire Contact: Respect Prods

Pete Wingfield Contact: Major Seven

Wingfoot Productions 15 Flower Lane, London NW7 2JA **t** 020 8959 5913 **f** 020 8959 5913 **e** info@wingfoot.co.uk **w** wingfoot.co.uk MD: John de Bono.

Alan Winstanley Contact: Hannah or Muirhead Mgmt.

Wise Buddah Music 74 Great Titchfield St, London W1W 7QP **t** 020 7307 1600 **f** 020 7307 1601 **e** mark.goodier@wisebuddah.com Contact: Mark Goodier

Wonky Contact: Ripe Productions

Denis Woods Contact: Muirhead Management

Darrell Woodward Contact: Vernandez Prods

Woolven Productions 55a Ditton Road, Surbiton, Surrey KT6 6RF **t** 020 8390 4583 **f** 020 8390 4583 **e** kitw@cygnet.co.uk Producer/engineer: Kit Woolven.

World Unlimited 88 Melton Road, Kings Heath, Birmingham B14 7ES **t** 0121 443 5765 **f** 0121 443 5765 **e** worldunlimited@hotmail.com **w** worldunlimited.freeuk.com Co-ordinator: Graham Radley.

Worldmaster Dj Management The Coachhouse, Mansion Farm, Liverton Hill, Sandway, Maidstone, Kent ME17 2NJ **t** 01622 858 300 **f** 01622 858 300 **e** info@eddielock.com **w** eddielock.co.uk Prop: Eddie Lock.

DJ Wright Contact: Global Mgmt

Paul Wright Contact: 365 Artists

Wyze Management 2-3 Fitzroy Mews, London W1T 6DJ **t** 020 7380 0999 **f** 020 7380 1555 **e** info@wyze.com **w** wyze.com MD: Kate Ross.

X-Management London House, 100 New Kings Road, London SW6 4LX **t** 0207 348 6150 **f** 0207 348 6056 **e** stone@stoneyboy.com **w** stoneyboy.com

XL Talent Reverb House, Bennett Street, London W4 2AH **t** 020 8747 0660 **f** 020 8747 0880 **e** management@reverbxl.com **w** reverbxl.com Contact: Ian Wright, Liam Teeling

Gota Yashiki Contact: Respect Prods

Yazuka Productions 30 West Block, Rosebery Square, London EC1A 4PT **t** 020 7916 9205 Contact: Brett Hunter

Yekuana Contact: Music Factory

Youth Contact: Big Life Mgmt

YoYo Contact: Solar Management

The Yukon Management 91 Saffron Hill, London EC1N 8PT **t** 020 7242 8408 **f** 020 7242 8408 **e** music@the-yukon.com **w** the-yukon.com MD: Andrew Maurice.

Z Management The Palm House, PO Box 19734, London SW15 2WU **t** 020 8874 3337 **f** 020 8874 3599 **e** office@zman.co.uk **w** zman.co.uk MD: Zita McHugh.

Zah Media Group 11 West Highland Rd, Ash Brake, Swindon SN5 4EX **t** 07831 205562 **e** howard@zahmedia.com **w** zahmedia.com MD: Howard Ritchie.

Zane Productions 162 Castle Hill, Reading, Berkshire RG1 7RP **t** 0118 957 4567 **f** 0118 956 1261 **e** Pete@zaneproductions.demon.co.uk **w** zanerecords.com Producer: Peter Thompson.

Zarjaz PO Box 16671, London W8 6ZYEmail: incoming@freakapuss.co.uk **w** freakapuss.co.uk PR Manager: Harlean Carpenter.

Zomba Management Zomba House, 165-167 High Rd, Willesden, London NW10 2SG **t** 020 8459 8899 **f** 020 8830 2801 **e** tim.smith@zomba.co.uk Creative Mgr: Tim Smith.

Rehearsal studios

chieve Fitness New Islington Mill, Regent Trading Estate, Oldfield Road, Manchester M5 7DE **t** 0161 832 9310 **f** 0161 832 9310 Prop: Glenn Ashton.

Alaska @ Waterloo Bridge Studios 127-129 Alaska Street, London SE1 8XE **t** 020 7928 7440 **f** 020 7928 8070 **e** blodge_uk@yahoo.com **w** soundrecordingstudio.net Studio Mgr: Beverley Lodge. MCI JH 636 Automated.

Ariwa Rehearsal Studios 34 Whitehorse Lane, London SE25 6RE **t** 020 8653 7744 or 020 8771 1470 **f** 020 8771 1911 **e** info@ariwa.com **w** ariwa.com Studio Manager: Joseph Fraser.

Backstreet Rehearsal Studios 313 Holloway Road, London N7 9SU **t** 020 7609 1313 **f** 020 7609 5229 **e** backstreet.studios@virgin.net **w** backstreet.co.uk Prop: John Dalligan.

Banana Row 47 Eyre Place, Edinburgh, Midlothian EH3 5EY **t** 0131 557 2088 **f** 0131 558 9848 **e** music@bananarow.com Studio Mgr: Craig Hunter.

Berkeley 2 54 Washington Street, Glasgow G3 8AZ **t** 0141 248 7290 **f** 0141 204 1138 Prop: Steve Cheyne.

Big City Studios (Dance only) 159-161 Balls Pond Road, London N1 4BG **t** 020 7241 6655 **f** 020 7241 3006 **e** pineapple.agency@btinternet.com **w** pineapple-agency.com Prop: Rebecca Paton.

Big Noise 12 Gregory Street, Northampton NN1 1TA **t** 01604 634455 Studio Mgr: Kim Gordelier.

Blueprint Studios Elizabeth House, 39 Queen Street, Salford, Manchester M3 4DQ **t** 08700 11 27 60 **f** 08700 11 27 80 **e** info@blueprint-studios.com **w** blueprint-studios.com Studio Manager: Tim Thomas.

BonaFideStudio Burbage House, 83-85 Curtain Road, London EC2A 3BS **t** 020 7684 5350 or 020 7684 5351 **f** 020 7613 1185 **e** info@bonafidestudio.co.uk **w** www.bonafidestudio.co.uk Studio Director: Deanna Gardner.

Charlton Farm Rehearsal Solutions (Residential) Charlton Farm, Hemington, Bath BA3 5XS **t** 01373 834161 **f** 01373 834167 **e** al@cruisin.co.uk **w** cruisin.co.uk GM: Al Hale.

Chem19 Rehearsal Studios Unit 5C, Peacock Cross Trading Estate, Burnbank Road, Hamilton ML3 9AQ **t** 01698 286882 **e** mail@chem19studios.co.uk **w** www.chem19studios.co.uk Manager: Peter Black.

Colorsound Audio 68 Fountainbridge, Edinburgh, Midlothian EH3 9PY **t** 0131 229 3588 **f** 0131 221 1454 **e** r.heatlie@virgin.net **w** colorsound.mu MD: Bob Heatlie.

Core Studios Kings Court, 7 Osborne St, Glasgow G1 5QN **t** 0141 552 6677 **f** 0141 552 1354 **e** mail@corestudios.co.uk **w** corestudios.co.uk Co-Dir: Alan Walsh.

Crash Rehearsal Studios Imperial Warehouse, 11 Davies Street, Liverpool, Merseyside L1 6HB **t** 0151 236 0989 **f** 0151 236 0989 Directors: John White, Mark Davies.

Cruisin' Music Charlton Farm, Hemington, Bath BA3 5XS **t** 01373 834161 **f** 01373 834164 **e** sil@cruisin.co.uk **w** cruisin.co.uk MD: Sil Wilcox.

Falling Anvil Studios Unit 114 Stratford Workshops, Burford Road, London E15 2SP **t** 020 8503 0415

e necker@falling-anvil.freeserve.co.uk **w** fallinganvil.co.uk Studio Mgr: Necker.

Golden Acrid 78 Albion Road, Edinburgh, Lothian EH7 5QZ **t** 0131 659 6673 **e** info@goldenacrid.com **w** goldenacrid.com Studio Mgr: James Locke.

Gracelands East Acton Lane, London W3 7HD **t** 020 8740 8922 **f** 020 8740 8922 Prop: Paul Burrows.

Ground Zero Studios 43-45 Coombe Terrace, Lewes Rd, Brighton BN2 4AD **t** 01273 819 617 **f** 01273 272 830 **e** james@g-zero.co.uk **w** g-zero.co.uk Studio Mgr: James Stringfellow.

The Hanger Rehearsal Rooms Unit H, 4 Doman Rd, Yorktown Ind Est., Camberley, Surrey GU15 3DF **t** 01276 685808 **f** 01276 683060 **e** info@thehanger.co.uk **w** thehanger.co.uk Studio Manager: Tom Gibbs.

House of Mook Studios Unit 1, Authorpe Works, Authorpe Road, Leeds LS6 4JB **t** 0113 230 4008 **e** mail@mookhouse.ndo.co.uk **w** mookhouse.ndo.co.uk Studio Mgr: Phil Mayne.

Islington Arts Factory 2 Parkhurst Road, Holloway, London N7 0SF **t** 020 7607 0561 **f** 020 7700 7229 **e** IAF@islingtonartsfactory.fsnet.co.uk **w** islingtonartsfactory.org.uk Bookings: Mathew Coates.

JJM Studios 20 Pool St, Walsall, West Midlands WS1 2EN **t** 01922 629 700 **e** jjmstudios@hotmail.com **w** jjmstudios.com Contact: Jay Mitchell

John Henry's 16-24 Brewery Rd, London N7 9NH **t** 020 7609 9181 **f** 020 7700 7040 **e** johnh@johnhenrys.com **w** johnhenrys.com MD: John Henry.

La Rocka Studios Post Mark House, Cross Lane, Hornsey, London N8 7SA **t** 020 8348 2822 **e** info@larockastudios.co.uk **w** larockastudios.co.uk Director: Pete Chapman.

Lab 24 346 Kingsland Road, Ground Floor, London E8 4DA **t** 07970 309470 Studio Mgr: Hamish Dzewu.

Music City 122 New Cross Road, London SE14 5BA **t** 020 7277 9657 **f** 0870 7572004 **e** info@musiccity.co.uk **w** musiccity.co.uk Rehearsal Mgr: Chris Raw.

Music Room The Old Library, 116-118 New Cross Road, London SE14 5BA **t** 020 7252 8271 **f** 020 7252 8252 **e** sales@musicroom.web.com **w** musicroom.web.com MD: Gordon Gapper.

Opus23 Sound Studio 23 New Mount Street, Manchester M4 4DE **t** 0161 953 4077 **f** 0161 953 4001 **e** info@opus23.co.uk **w** opus23.co.uk Owner: Sean Flynn.

Panic Rehearsal Studios 14 Trading Estate Rd, Park Royal, London NW10 7LU **t** 020 8961 9540 **f** 020 8838 2194 **e** mroberts.drums@virgin.net Studio Mgr: Mark Roberts.

The Premises Studios 201-205 Hackney Road, Shoreditch, London E2 8JL **t** 020 7729 7593 **f** 020 7739 5600 **e** info@premises.demon.co.uk **w** premises.demon.co.uk CEO: Viv Broughton.

React Studios 3 Fleece Yard, Market Hill, Buckingham MK18 1JX **t** 01280 821840 or 01280 823546 **f** 01280 821840 **e** info@reactstudios.co.uk **w** reactstudios.co.uk Studio Mgr: Tom Thackwray.

Red Onion Rehearsal Studio 25 Hatherley Mews, Hilton Grove Business Centre, Walthamstow, London E17 4QP **t** 020 8520 3975 **f** 020 8521 6646 **e** info@redonion.uk.com **w** redonion.uk.com Administrator: Lucy Hickin.

Rich Bitch 505 Bristol Road, Selly Oak, Birmingham, West Midlands B29 6AU **t** 0121 471 1339 **f** 0121 471 2070 **e** richbitchstudios@aol.com **w** rich-bitch.co.uk Owner: Rob Bruce.

Riot Club Unit 4, 27A Spring Grove Rd, Hounslow, Middx TW3 4BE **t** 020 8572 8809 **f** 020 8572 9590 **e** riot@riotclub.co.uk **w** riotclub.co.uk Studio Manager: Ben Smith.

Ritz Studios 110-112 Disraeli Road, Putney, London SW15 2DX **t** 020 8870 1335 **f** 020 8877 1036 **e** lee.webber@virgin.net Dir: Lee Webber.

River Studio's 3 Grange Yard, London SE1 3AG **t** 020 7231 4805 **f** 020 7237 0633 **e** sales@riverproaudio.co.uk **w** riverstudios.co.uk Contact: Joel Monger

Rogue Studios RA 4, Bermondsey Trading Estate, Rotherhithe New Road, London SE16 3LL **t** 020 7231 3257 **f** 020 7231 7358 **e** info@roguestudios.co.uk **w** roguestudios.co.uk Contact: Jon-Paul Harper/Jim Down

The Rooms Rehearsal Studios Lynchford Lane, North Camp, Farnborough, Hants GU14 6JD **t** 01252 371177 **e** minister.g@ntlworld.com **w** theroomsstudios.com Directors: Gerry Bryant/Shaun Streams.

Rooz Studios 2A Corsham Street, London N1 6DP **t** 020 7490 1919 Studio Mgr: Graham Clarke.

Rotator Rehearsal Studios 74-77 Magdalen Road, Oxford OX4 1RE **t** 01865 205600 **f** 01865 205700 **e** rehearse@rotator.co.uk **w** rotator.co.uk Senior Manager: Phill Honey. MD: Richard Cotton.

Soundbite Studios Unit 32, 17 Cumberland Business Park, Cumberland Avenue, London NW10 7RG **t** 020 8961 8509 **f** 020 8961 8994 Owner: Ranj Kumar.

The Studio Tower Street, Hartlepool TS24 7HQ **t** 01429 424440 **f** 01429 424441 **e** studiohartlepool@btconnect.com **w** studiohartlepool.com Studio Manager: Liz Carter.

Survival Studios Unit B18, Acton Business Centre, School Road, London NW10 6TD **t** 020 8961 1977 Mgr: Simon Elson.

Sync City Media 16-18 Millmead Business Centre, Millmead Road, Tottenham Hale, London N17 9QU **t** 020 8808 0472 **e** sales@synccity.co.uk **w** synccity.co.uk Studio Manager: Ron Niblett.

Terminal Studios 4-10 Lamb Walk, London SE1 3TT **t** 020 7403 3050 **f** 020 7407 6123 **e** info@terminal.co.uk **w** www.terminal.co.uk Prop: Charlie Barrett. Quality restaurant, secure parking and storage, extensive equipment hire on site.

Tweeters Unit C1, Business Park 7, Brookway, Kingston Road, Leatherhead, Surrey KT22 7NA **t** 01372 386592 **f** 020 8241 9427 **e** info@tweeters2studios.co.uk **w** tweeters2studios.co.uk Studio Eng: Mr Wade.

Unit 25 - Mill Hill Music Complex Bunns Lane Works, Bunns Lane, London NW7 2AJ **t** 020 8906 9991 **f** 020 8906 9991 **e** enquiries@millhillmusic.co.uk **w** millhillmusic.co.uk Dir: Roger Tichbourne.

Warehouse 60 Sandford Lane, Kennington, Oxford OX1 5RW **t** 01865 736411 **e** info@warehousestudios.com **w** warehousestudios.com Studio Mgr: Steve Watkins.

Warwick Hall of Sound Banastre Avenue, Heath, Cardiff CF14 3NR **t** 029 2069 4455 **f** 029 2069 4450 **e** booking@ffvinyl.co.uk **w** warwickhall.co.uk MD: Martin Bowen.

Waterloo Sunset Tower Bridge Business Complex, 100 Clements Road, London SE16 4DG **t** 020 7252 0001 **f** 020 7231 3002 **e** nunu@musicbank.org **w** musicbank.org/waterloo.html Studio Mgr: Dave Whiting.

WaterRat Rehearsal Unit 2 Monument Way East, Woking, Surrey GU21 5LY **t** 01483 764444 **e** jayne@waterrat.co.uk **w** waterrat.co.uk Prop: Jayne Wallis.

WESTBOURNE REHEARSAL STUDIOS

The Rear Basement, 92-98 Bourne Terrace, Little Venice, London W2 5TH **t** 020 7289 8142 **f** 020 7289 8142 Studio Mgr: Chris Thomas. Large, air-conditioned, mirrored studios. Acoustically conditioned rooms with superb PA. Backline. Free parking. Refreshments. Storage. Shop. Mention Music Week for extra discount.

WhiteRooms Rehearsal Studios Roden House, Alfred St South, Nottingham NG3 1JH **t** 01726 861068 **e** admin@whiterooms.co.uk **w** whiterooms.co.uk Prop: Steve White.

Session Fixers

B&H Management/B&H Musicians PO Box 475, Amersham, Bucks HP8 4ZN **t** 01494 737414 **f** 01494 737415 **e** simon@bandhmanagement.demon.co.uk MD: Simon Harrison.

Choir Connexion Brookdale House, 75 Brookdale Rd, Walthamstow, London E17 6QH **t** 020 8509 7288 **f** 020 8509 7299 **e** choirconnexion@btconnect.com **w** lcgc.org.uk Principal: Bazil Meade.

Cool Music 62A Warwick Gardens, London W14 8PP **t** 020 7565 2665 **f** 020 7603 8431 **e** enquiries@coolmusicltd.com **w** coolmusicltd.com Musicians Contractor: Richard Nelson.

CyberStrings (Powerbase) 1 Norlington Road, London E11 4BE **t** 020 8279 8286 **f** 020 8928 0613 **e** rjwardroden@argonet.co.uk MD: Richard Ward-Roden.

Eclipse-PJM (Vocalists) PO Box 3059, South Croydon, Surrey CR2 8TL **t** 020 8657 2627 or 07798 651691 **f** 020 8657 2627 **e** Eclipsepjm@btinternet.com Mgr & PA: Paul Johnson & Iris Sutherland.

First Move Management 137 Shooters Hill Rd, Blackheath, London SE3 8UQ **t** 020 8305 2077 or 07717 473 433 **f** 020 8305 2077 **e** firstmoves@aol.com **w** firstmove.biz Creative Dir: Janis MacIlwaine.

Isobel Griffiths **t** 020 7351 7383 **f** 020 7376 3034 **e** isobel@isobelgriffiths.co.uk Contact: MD

Hornography 180 Lyndhurst Rd, London N22 5AU **t** 020 8365 8862 or 07956 510 112 **e** mat@hornography.freeserve.co.uk Contact: Mat Colman

In A City Management Unit 49, Carlisle Business Centre, 60 Carlisle Road, Bradford BD8 8BD **t** 01904 438753 or 01274 223251 **f** 01274 223204 **e** cc@inacity.co.uk **w** inacity.co.uk MD: Carl Stipetic.

Kick Horns 158 Upland Road, London SE22 0DQ **t** 020 8693 5991 or 07931 776155 **f** 020 8693 5991 **e** info@kickhorns.com **w** kickhorns.com Director: Simon C Clarke.

Knifedge 57b Riding House St, London W1W 7EF **t** 020 7436 5434 **f** 020 7436 5431 **e** info@knifedge.net **w** knifedge.net Contact: Jonathan Brigden

Lager Productions 10 Barley Rise, Baldock, Herts SG7 6RT **t** 01462 636799 **f** 01462 636799 **e** dan@Lockupmusic.co.uk Dir: Steve Knight.

London Musicians Cedar House, Vine Lane, Hillingdon, Middlesex UB10 0BX **t** 01895 252555 **f** 01895 252556 **e** mail@lonmus.demon.co.uk MD: David White.

London Symphony Orchestra Barbican Centre, London EC2Y 8DS **t** 020 7588 1116 **f** 020 7374 0127 **e** smallet@lso.co.uk **w** lso.co.uk Administrator: Sue Mallet.

Millennia Ensemble Contact: Knifedge

More Music PO Box 306, Harrow, Middlesex HA2 0XL **t** 020 8423 1078 or 07721 623171 **f** 020 8423 1078 **e** dwmoremusic@yahoo.com Contact: Debra Williams

PEZ Management (for singers) 15 Sutherland House, 137-139 Queenstown Road, London SW8 3RJ **t** 020 7978 1503 **f** 020 7978 1502 **e** perryfmorgan@hotmail.com Management: Perry Morgan.

Red Onion Productions Suite 100, Hilton Grove Business Centre, 25 Hatherley Mews, London E17 4QP **t** 020 8520 3975 **f** 020 8521 6646 **e** info@redonion.uk.com **w** redonion.uk.com MD: Dee Curtis.

Rhythm & Bookings **t** 020 8892 4810 **f** 020 8744 0413 **e** gpm@pennies.demon.co.uk **w** rhythmandbookings.com Booker/Contractor: Graeme Perkins.

Royal Philharmonic Orchestra 16 Clerkenwell Green, London EC1R 0QT **t** 020 7608 8800 **f** 020 7608 8801 **e** info@rpo.co.uk **w** rpo.co.uk MD: Ian Maclay.

SD Creative 113b Leander Road, London SW2 2NB **t** 020 7652 9676 **e** office@sdcreative.co.uk Session Coordinator: Suzann Douglas.

Sense of Sound Training Parr Street Studios, 33-45 Parr St, Liverpool L1 4JN **t** 0151 707 1050 **f** 0151 709 8612 **e** info@senseofsound.demon.co.uk **w** senseofsound.net Artistic Director: Jennifer John.

SESSION CONNECTION

SESSION CONNECTION

110-112 Disraeli Rd, London SW15 2DX **t** 020 8871 1212 or 020 8672 7055 **f** 020 8682 1772 **e** sessionconnection@mac.com **w** thesessionconnection.com MD: Tina Hamilton.

Sugarcane Music 32 Blackmore Avenue, Southall, Middlesex UB1 3ES **t** 020 8574 2130 **f** 020 8574 2130 MD: Astrid Pringsheim.

Tropical Fish Music 351 Long Lane, London N2 8JW **t** 0870 444 5468 or 07973 386 279 **f** 0870 132 3318 **e** info@tropicalfishmusic.com **w** tropicalfishmusic.com MD: Grishma Jashapara.

Tuff The Session Agency United House, North Rd, London N7 9DP **t** 020 7700 6262 **f** 020 7700 6179 **e** info@tuffsessions.com **w** tuffsessions.com Business Manager: Joanne Costello.

Wired Strings 92 Uplands Road, London N8 9NJ **t** 07976 157 277 **f** 020 8347 8455 **e** rosie@wiredstrings.com **w** wiredstrings.com Director: Rosie Wetters.

The Wrecking Crew 15 Westmeads Rd, Whitstable, Kent CT5 1LP **t** 01227 264 966 or 07957 686 152 **f** 01227 264 966 **e** sophie@thewreckingcrew.co.uk **w** thewreckingcrew.co.uk Bookings: Sophie Sirota.

XFactory 20 Boughton House, Bowling Green Place, London SE1 1YF **t** 020 7403 1980 **f** 020 7403 1830 **e** contact@xfactory.co.uk **w** xfactory.co.uk Director: Nigel Proktor.

Studio Equipment Hire

20th Century Vintage and Rare Guitars 6 Denmark St, London WC2 8LX **t** 020 7240 7500 **f** 020 7240 8900 **e** enquiries@vintageandrareguitars.com Website: vintageandrareguitars.com Mgr: Adam Newman. Also: 7-8 Saville Row, Bath, BA1 2QP. **t** 01225 330 888 **f** 01225 335 999. Mgr: Andy Lewis.

Advanced Sounds Admin address on request. **t** 01305 757088 **f** 01305 268947 **e** advancedsoundsltd@btinternet.com Website: advancedsounds.co.uk Hire, Sales & Repairs: Mike Moreton.

Audile Unit 110, Cariocca Business Park, Ardwick, Manchester M12 4AH **t** 0161 272 7883 or 07968 156 499 **f** 0161 272 7883 **e** mail@audile.co.uk Website: audile.co.uk Partner: Rob Ashworth.

Audio Technica Technica House, Royal London Ind Est, Old Lane, Leeds LS11 8AG **t** 0113 277 1441 **f** 0113 270 4836 **e** sales@audio-technica.co.uk Website: audio-technica.co.uk Sales Manager UK & Export: Tony Cooper.

Audiohire The Old Dairy, 133-137 Kilburn Lane, London W10 4AN **t** 020 8960 4466 **f** 020 8964 0343 **e** admin@audiohire.co.uk Website: audiohire.co.uk Manager: Richard Zamet.

Circle Sound Services Circle House, 14 Waveney Close, Bicester, Oxon OX26 2GP **t** 01869 240051 **f** 0870 705 9679 **e** sound@circlesound.net Website: circlesound.net Owner: John Willett.

Delta Concert Systems Unit 4, Springside, Trinity, Jersey, Channel Islands JE3 5DG **t** 01534 865885 **f** 01534 863759 **e** hire@delta-av.com Website: delta-av.com Director: Cristin Bouchet.

FX Rentals 38-40 Telford Way, London W3 7XS **t** 020 8746 2121 **f** 020 8746 4100 **e** info@fxrentals.co.uk Website: fxgroup.net Operations Director: Peter Brooks. Marketing Dir: Tony Andrews. (TonyAndrews@fxgroup.net)

GearBox (Sound and Vision) Unit 15 Alliance Court, Alliance Road, London W3 ORB **t** 020 8992 4499 **f** 020 8992 4466 **e** mail@gearbox.com Website: gearbox.com Contact: Danny Simmonds

GearBox Express (Soho) 36-44 Brewer St, Entrance 1 Lexington St, London W1F 9LX **t** 020 7437 4832 **f** 020 7437 5402 **e** express@gearbox.com Website: gearbox.com Contact: Danny Simmonds

GWH Backline Rental GWH, Hillcroft Business Park, Whisby Road, Lincoln LN6 3QT **t** 01522 501815 **f** 01522 501816 **e** gary@gwhmusic.com Website: gwhmusic.com Director: Gary Weight.

Harris Hire 49 Hayes Way, Park Langley, Beckenham, Kent BR3 6RR **t** 020 8663 1807 **f** 020 8658 2803 **e** info@harris-hire.co.uk Website: harris-hire.co.uk MD: Mr P Harris.

John Henry's 16-24 Brewery Road, London N7 9NH **t** 020 7609 9181 **f** 020 7700 7040 **e** johnh@johnhenrys.com Website: johnhenrys.com MD: John Henry.

Midnight Electronics Off Quay Building, Foundry Lane, Newcastle upon Tyne, Tyne and Wear NE6 1LH **t** 0191 224 0088 **f** 0191 224 0080 **e** dx@compuserve.com Website: midnightelectronics.co.uk MD: Dave Cross.

Music City 122 New Cross Road, London SE14 5BA **t** 020 7277 9657 **f** 0870 7572004 **e** info@musiccity.co.uk Website: musiccity.co.uk Hire Mgr: Jim Woodward.

Music Room Hire The Old Library, 116-118 New Cross Road, London SE14 5BA **t** 020 7252 8271 **f** 020 7252 8252 **e** sales@musicroom.web.com Website: musicroom.web.com MD: Gordon Gapper.

Ovni Audio 33-37 Hatherley Mews, London E17 4QP **t** 020 8521 9595 or 07967 615647 **f** 020 8521 6363 **e** flavio.uk@ukonline.co.uk Website: curiousyellow.co.uk Owner: Flavio Curras.

Sensible Music Rebond House, 98-124 Brewery Road, London N7 9PG **t** 020 7700 6655 **f** 020 7609 9478 sales **e** rental@sensible-music.co.uk Website: sensiblemusic.com Hire Mgr: Matt Russell.

Matt Snowball Music Unit 2, 3-9 Brewery Road, London N7 9QJ **t** 020 7700 6555 **f** 020 7700 6990 Website: mattsnowball.com Hire/Sales: Kent Jolly.

Strong Hire 120-124 Curtain Road, London EC2A 3SQ **t** 020 7426 5150 **f** 020 7426 5102 **e** hire@stronghire.com Website: stronghire.com Bookings Manager: Nina Mistry.

Studiocare Professional Audio 51-53 Highfield St, Liverpool L3 6AA **t** 0845 345 8910 **f** 0845 345 8911 **e** hire@studiocare.com Website: studiocare.com Hire Mgr: Drew Culshaw.

Studiohire 8 Daleham Mews, London NW3 5DB **t** 020 7431 0212 **f** 020 7431 1134 **e** mail@studiohire.net Website: studiohire.net General Manager: Sam Thomas.

Terminal Studios Hire 4-10 Lamb Walk, London SE1 3TT **t** 020 7403 3050 **f** 020 7407 6123 **e** info@terminal.co.uk Website: terminal.co.uk MD: Charlie Barrett.

Tickle Music Hire The Old Dairy, 133-137 Kilburn Lane, London W10 4AN **t** 020 8964 3399 **f** 020 8964 0343 **e** hire@ticklemusichire.com Director: Tad Barker.

TL Commerce Unit 2 Iceni Court, Icknield Way, Letchworth SG6 1TN **t** 01462 492095 **f** 01462 492097 **e** info@tlcommerce.co.uk Website: tlcommerce.co.uk MD: Tony Larking.

Peter Webber Hire 110-112 Disraeli Road, Putney, London SW15 2DX **t** 020 8870 1335 **f** 020 8877 1036 **e** lee.webber@virgin.net Dir: Lee Webber.

Studio Equipment Manufacture & Distribution

AES Pro Audio North Lodge, Stonehill Road, Ottershaw, Surrey KT16 0AQ **t** 01932 872672 **f** 01932 874364 **e** aesaudio@intonet.co.uk **w** aesproaudio.com Dir: Mike Stockdale.

Allen & Heath Kernick Industrial Estate, Penryn, Cornwall TR10 9LU **t** 0870 755 6250 **f** 0870 755 6251 **e** marketing@allen-heath.com **w** allen-heath.com Sales and Mktg Dir: Bob Goleniowski.

Amek Ltd Harman Inter'l Industries, Cranbourne House, Cranbourne Rd, Potters Bar, Herts EN6 3JN **t** 01707 660667 **f** 01707 660755 **e** amek@amek.com **w** amek.com Marketing Manager: David Neal.

AMG Electronics 2 High Street, Haslemere, Surrey GU27 2LR **t** 01428 658775 **f** 01428 658438 **e** amg@c-ducer.com **w** c-ducer.com Proprietor: AW French.

AMS Neve plc Billington Road, Burnley, Lancashire BB11 5UB **t** 01282 457011 **f** 01282 417282 **e** enquiry@ams-neve.com **w** ams-neve.com Dir of Commercial Oper.: Greg Cluskey.

Arbiter Group Wilberforce Road, London NW9 6AX **t** 020 8202 1199 **f** 020 8202 7076 **e** mtsales@arbitergroup.com **w** arbitergroup.com Mktg Mgr: Nick Sharples.

Audio Agency PO Box 4601, Kiln Farm, Milton Keynes, Bucks MK19 7ZN **t** 01908 510123 **f** 01908 511123 **w** audioagency.co.uk Sales Mgr: Paul Eastwood.

Audio & Design (Recording) Ltd Unit 20d, Horseshoe Park, Pangbourne, Reading, Berkshire RG8 7JW **t** 0118 984 4545 **f** 0118 984 2604 **e** sales@proaudio.uk.com **w** proaudio.uk.com Dir: Ian Harley.

Audio Developments Ltd Hall Lane, Walsall Wood, Walsall, West Midlands WS9 9AU **t** 01543 375351 **f** 01543 361051 **e** sales@audio.co.uk **w** audio.co.uk Sales Director: Antony Levesley.

Audio Digital Technology Ltd Manor Road, Teddington, Middx TW11 8BG **t** 020 8977 4546 **f** 020 8977 4576 **e** info@audiodigitaltech.com **w** audiodigitaltech.com Director: Jim Dowler.

Audio Processing Technology Edgewater Road, Belfast, Co Antrim BT3 9JQ **t** 028 9037 1110 **f** 028 9037 1137 **e** jmcclintock@aptx.com **w** aptx.com Commercial Dir: Jon McClintock.

Audio-Technica Technica House, Royal London Industrial Estate, Old Lane, Leeds, West Yorkshire LS11 8AG **t** 0113 277 1441 **f** 0113 270 4836 **e** sales@audio-technica.co.uk **w** audio-technica.co.uk UK Marketing Manager: Tony Cooper.

Audionics Petre Drive, Sheffield, South Yorkshire S4 7PZ **t** 0114 242 2333 **f** 0114 243 3913 **e** info@audionics.co.uk **w** audionics.co.uk Prod Dir: Phil Myers.

BBM Electronics Group Ltd Cherry Garth, Station Road, Holme, Cumbria LA6 1QY **t** 07971 083038 **f** 01524 782988 **e** tim@trantec.co.uk **w** trantec.co.uk Mkting Mgr: Tim Riley.

Beyerdynamic GB Ltd 17 Albert Drive, Burgess Hill, West Sussex RH15 9TN **t** 01444 258258 **f** 01444 258444 **e** sales@beyerdynamic.co.uk **w** beyerdynamic.co.uk MD: John Midgley.

BSS Audio Cranbourne House, Cranbourne Road, Potters Bar, Hertfordshire EN6 3JN **t** 01707 660667 **f** 01707 660755 **e** info@bss.co.uk **w** bss.co.uk Marketing Manager: David Neal.

Canford Audio plc Crowther Industrial Estate, Crowther Road, Washington, Tyne and Wear NE38 0BW **t** 0191 418 1000 **f** 0191 418 1001 **e** info@canford.co.uk **w** canford.co.uk Sales & Mktg Director: Barry Revels.

Chevin Research Ltd 4A Ilkley Road, Otley, West Yorkshire LS21 3JP **t** 01943 466060 **f** 01943 466020 **e** sales@chevin-research.com **w** chevin-research.com MD: Martin Clinch.

Chiswick Reach Ltd TBA **t** 07977 427535 **e** chiswick.reach@virgin.net **w** chiswickreach.co.uk MD: Nigel Woodward.

ComSec Int. 26 Penwinnick Road, St Austell, Cornwall PL25 5DS **t** 01726 874180 or 01235 550791 (Sales) **f** 01726 874185 or 01235 550874 (Sales) **e** steve@comsecint.com **w** comsecint.com Sales Manager: Steve Smith.

Connectronics PO Box 22618, London N4 1LZ **t** 07000 422253 **f** 07000 283461 **e** sales@connectronics.co.uk **w** connectronics.co.uk Sales Manager: Gary Ash.

Cunnings Recording Associates Brodrick Hall, Brodrick Road, London SW17 7DY **t** 0870 90 66 44 0 **f** 020 8767 8525 **e** info@cunnings.co.uk **w** cunnings.co.uk Proprietor: Malcolm J Cunnings.

D&M Professional Chiltern Hill, Chalfont St Peter, Buckinghamshire SL9 9UG **t** 01753 888447 **f** 01753 880109 **e** info@d-mpro.eu.com **w** d-mpro.eu.com Sales & Marketing Mgr: Simon Curtis.

dBm Ltd. The Barn, Mill Lane, Little Hallingbury, Bishop's Stortford, Hertfordshire CM22 7QT **t** 01279 721434 **f** 01279 721391 **e** info@dbmltd.com **w** dbmltd.com Sales & Marketing Dirs.: Janice Glen, Richard Watts.

dCS Ltd Mull House, Great Chesterford Court, Great Chesterford, Saffron Walden, Essex CB10 1PF **t** 01799 531999 **f** 01799 531681 **e** sales@dcsltd.co.uk **w** dcsltd.co.uk Mktg Mgr: Robert Kelly.

J Decor Interiors 159-161 High Street, Epsom, Surrey KT19 8EW **t** 01372 721773 **f** 01372 742765 **e** jdecor@btconnect.com Dir: Judith Newbit.

Deltron Emcon Ltd Deltron Emcon House, Hargreaves Way,, Scunthorpe, N. Lincs DN15 8RF **t** 01724 273200 **f** 01724 270230 **e** media@deltron-emcon.com **w** deltron-emcon.com Mktng Co-ord: Diane Kilminster.

Digital Audio Research Harman Int'l Industries, Cranbourne House, Cranbiurne Rd, Potters Bar, Herts EN6 3JN **t** 01707 665000 **f** 01707 660482 **e** mail@dar.uk.com **w** dar.uk.com Product Specialist: Inder Biant.

Direct Distribution Unit 6 Belfont Trading Estate, Mucklow Hill, Halesowen, West Midlands B62 8DR **t** 0121 550 2777 **f** 0121 585 8003 **e** info@directdistribution.uk.com **w** directdistribution.uk.com UK Manager: Andrew Scott.

Dolby Laboratories, Inc. Interface, Wootton Bassett, Wiltshire SN4 8QJ **t** 01793 842100 **f** 01793 842101 **e** info@dolby.co.uk **w** dolby.com Sound Consultant: Andrea Borgato.

Drawmer Distribution Ltd Charlotte St Business Centre, Charlotte Street, Wakefield, West Yorkshire WF1 1UH **t** 01924 378669 **f** 01924 290460 **e** sales@drawmer.com **w** drawmer.com MD: Ken Giles.

eJay Empire Interactive Europe Ltd., The Spires, 677 High Rd, North Finchley, London N12 0DA **t** 020 8492 1049 **f** 020 8343 7447 **e** eJayinfo@empire.co.uk **w** eJay.com Brand Manager: Cate Swift.

Euphonix Europe Ltd Linton House, 39-51 Highgate Rd, London NW5 1RS **t** 020 7267 1226 **f** 020 7267 1227 **e** rusty@euphonix.com **w** euphonix.com VP Int'l Sales: Rusty Waite.

Focusrite Audio Engineering 19 Lincoln Road, Cressex Business Park, High Wycombe, Bucks HP12 3FX **t** 01494 462246 **f** 01494 459920 **e** sales@focusrite.com **w** focusrite.com Marketing Manager: Giles Orford.

Graff Electronic Machines Ltd Wood Hill Road, Collingham, Newark, Nottinghamshire NG23 7NR **t** 01636 893036 **f** 01636 893317 **e** sales@graffelectronics.co.uk **w** graffelectronics.co.uk Sales Mgr: Roger Platts.

Groove Tubes Europe - Guitar XS 12a Waterside, Upper Brents, Faversham, Kent ME13 7AU **t** 01795 538877 **f** 01795 538877 **e** sales@guitarXS.com **w** guitarXS.com Contact: Doug Chandler, Tina Sharpe.

Harbeth Audio Ltd Unit 3, Enterprise Park, Lindfield, West Sussex RH16 2LH **t** 01444 484371 **f** 01444 487629 **e** sound@harbeth.com **w** harbeth.com MD: Alan Shaw.

HHB Communications 73-75 Scrubs Lane, London NW10 6QU **t** 020 8962 5000 **f** 020 8962 5050 **e** sales@hhb.co.uk **w** hhb.co.uk Sales & Marketing Dir.: Steve Angel.

HIQ Sound Units 2 & 3, Cedars Farm, South Carlton, Lincolnshire LN1 2RH **t** 01522 730810 **f** 01522 731055 **e** sales@hiqsound.co.uk **w** hiqsound.co.uk Contact: Tony Hopkinson

Jarberry Pro Audio Perseverance Works, Morrison St, Castleford WF10 4BE **t** 01977 556868 **f** 01977 603180 **e** sales@jarberry-music.co.uk **w** jarberry-music.co.uk Director: Ryan Davis.

Junger Audio Invicta Works, Elliott Road, Bromley, Kent BR2 9NT **t** 020 8460 7299 **f** 020 8460 0499 **e** sales@michael-stevens.com **w** michael-stevens.com UL Sales Manager: Simon Adamson.

Kelsey Acoustics 9 Lyon Road, Walton on Thames, Surrey KT12 3PU **t** 01932 886060 **f** 01932 885565 **e** kelsey@yahoo.com Op's Mgr: Michael Whiteside.

Klark Teknik Group Klark Teknik Building, Walter Nash Road, Kidderminster, Worcestershire DY11 7HJ **t** 01562 741515 **f** 01562 745371 **e** webbmeister@compuserve.com **w** klarkteknik.com Marketing Manager: James Godbehear.

Logic System Pro Audio Unit 46, Corringham Road Industrial Est, Gainsborough, Lincolnshire DN21 1QB **t** 01427 611791 **f** 01427 677008 **e** sales@logic-system.co.uk **w** logic-system.co.uk MD: Chris Scott.

Marquee Audio Shepperton Film Studios, Studio Road, Shepperton, Middlesex TW17 0QD **t** 01932 566 777 **f** 01932 565 861 **e** info@marqueeaudio.co.uk **w** marqueeaudio.co.uk Office Mgr: Tim Cowling.

A&F McKay Audio/Oktava The Studios, Hoe Farm, Hascombe, Surrey GU8 4JQ **t** 01483 208511 **f** 01483 208538 **e** fergus@mckay.org **w** oktava.net Contact: Fergus McKay

MC2 Audio Units 6 & 7 Kingsgate, Heathpark Industrial Estate, Honiton, Devon EX14 1YG **t** 01404 44633 **f** 01404 44660 **e** mc2@mc2-audio.co.uk **w** mc2-audio.co.uk MD: Ian McCarthy.

Mitsubishi Electric UK Travellers Lane, Hatfield, Hertfordshire AL10 8XB **t** 01707 276100 **f** 01707 278690 **e** yoshinori.miyata@meuk.mee.com **w** meuk.mee.com President: Yoshinori Miyata.

MJQ (Studio Consultants) Swillett House, 52 Heronsgate Road, Chorleywood, Hertfordshire WD3 5BB **t** 01923 285266 **f** 01923 285168 **e** sales@mjq.co.uk **w** mjq.co.uk MD: Malcolm Jackson.

MTR Ltd Ford House, 58 Cross Road, Bushey, Hertfordshire WD19 4DQ **t** 01923 234050 **f** 01923 255746 **e** mtrltd@aol.com **w** mtraudio.com MD: Tony Reeves.

Munro Acoustics Unit 21, Riverside Studios, 28 Park Street, London SE1 9EQ **t** 020 7403 3808 **f** 020 7403 0957 **e** info@munro.co.uk **w** munro.co.uk Prop: Andy Munro.

The Music Corporation 679 Christchurch Road, Boscombe, Bournemouth, Dorset BH7 6AE **t** 01202 395135 **f** 01202 397622 **e** ask@themcorporation.com **w** themcorporation.com GM: Alan Barclay.

Musisca (Music Stands & Accessories) Piccaddilly Mill, Lower St, Stroud, Glos. GL5 2HT **t** 01453 751911 **f** 01453 751911 **e** info@musisca.co.uk **w** musisca.co.uk Director: Marc Oboussier.

Mutronics Unit 12 Impress House, Mansell Road, London W3 7QH **t** 020 8735 0042 **f** 020 8735 0041 **e** mutronics@mutronics.co.uk **w** mutronics.co.uk Technical Dir: James Dunbar.

Nemesis Professional Audio Products Ltd (see SHEP Associates)

Ohm (UK) Ltd Wellington Close, Parkgate, Knutsford, Cheshire WA16 8XL **t** 01565 654641 **f** 01565 755641 **e** info@ohm.co.uk **w** ohm.co.uk Dir: Paul Adamson.

Orange Amplifiers Ltd T/A Omec Ltd, 4th Floor, 28 Denmark Street, London WC2H 8NJ **t** 020 7240 8292 **f** 020 7240 8112 **e** info@orange-amps.com **w** orangeamps.com Marketing/Press: Michelle Printer.

Peavey Electronics Great Folds Rd, Oakley Hay, Corby, Northants NN18 9ET **t** 01536 461234 **f** 01536 747222 **e** sales@peavey-eu.com **w** peavey-eu.com Contact: Ken Achard

Penny & Giles Controls Ltd Nine Mile Point Ind Estate, Cwmfelinfach, Gwent NP1 7HZ **t** 01495 202000 **f** 01495 202006 **e** sales@pennyandgiles.com **w** pennyandgiles.com Product Manager: Andrew Clarke.

PRECO (Broadcast Systems) Ltd 3 Four Seasons Crescent, Kimpton Road, Sutton, Surrey SM3 9QR **t** 020 8644 4447 **f** 020 8644 0474 **e** sales@preco.co.uk **w** preco.co.uk MD: Tony Costello.

Quantegy Europa Ltd Unit 3, Commerce Park, Brunel Road, Theale, Reading, Berkshire RG7 4AB **t** 0118 930 2240 **f** 0118 930 2235 **e** sales.uk/eire@quantegy-eu.com **w** quantegy.com Sales Co-ordinator: Rose McCormack.

Quested Monitoring Systems Ltd Units 6&7 Kingsgate, Heathpark Industrial Estate, Honiton, Devon EX14 1YG **t** 01404 41500 **f** 01404 44660 **e** sales@quested.com **w** quested.com MD: Ian McCarthy.

Ridge Farm Industries Rusper Road, Capel, Surrey RH5 5HG **t** 01306 711202 **e** info@ridgefarmindustries.com **w** ridgefarmindustries.com MD: Frank Andrews.

River Pro Audio 3 Grange Yard, London SE1 3AG **t** 020 7231 4805 **f** 020 7237 0633 **e** sales@riverproaudio.co.uk **w** http://riverproaudio.com Contact: Joel Monger

RMPA & Rauch Amplification 42 Lower Ferry Lane, Callow End, Worcester WR2 4UN **t** 01905 831877 or 07836 617158 **f** 01905 830906 **e** rmpaworcester@aol.com **w** rmpa.co.uk Owner: Richard Bailey.

Roland (UK) Atlantic Close, Swansea Enterprise Park, Swansea, West Glamorgan SA7 9FJ **t** 01792 515 020 **f** 01792 600 527 **e** customers@roland.co.uk **w** roland.co.uk

SADiE UK The Old School, Stretham, Ely, Cambs CB6 3LD **t** 01353 648 888 **f** 01353 648 867 **e** sales@sadie.com **w** sadie.com Sales & Mkt Mgr: Geoff Calver.

SCV London 40 Chigwell Lane, Oakwood Hill Ind. Estate, Loughton, Essex IG10 3NY **t** 020 8418 0778 **f** 020 8418 0624 **e** orders@scvlondon.co.uk **w** scvlondon.co.uk Marketing Manager: Steve McDonald.

Sennheiser UK 3 Century Point, Halifax Road, High Wycombe, Buckinghamshire HP12 3SL **t** 01494 551 551 **f** 01494 551 550 **e** info@sennheiser.co.uk **w** sennheiser.co.uk Director of Marketing: John Steven.

Shep Associates Long Barn, North End, Meldrith, Royston, Hertfordshire SG8 6NT **t** 01763 261 686 **f** 01763 262 154 **e** info@shep.co.uk **w** shep.co.uk MD: Derek Stoddart.

Shure Distribution UK 167-171 Willoughby Lane, London N17 0SB **t 020 8808 2222 f** 020 8808 5599 **e** info@shuredistribution.co.uk **w** shuredistribution.co.uk Sales Manager: Mike Gibson.

Shuttlesound 4 The Willows Centre, Willow Lane, Mitcham, Surrey CR4 4NX **t** 020 8646 7114 **f** 020 8254 5666 **e** info@shuttlesound.com **w** shuttlesound.com MD: Paul Barretta.

Silver Productions 29 Castle Street, Salisbury, Wiltshire SP1 1TT **t 01722 336221 f** 01722 336227 **e** info@silver.co.uk **w** silver.co.uk IT & Systems Director: Riza Pacalioglu.

Solid State Logic Spring Hill Road, Oxford OX5 1RU **t** 01865 842300 **f** 01865 842118 **e** info@solid-state-logic.com **w** solid-state-logic.com Sales Dir: Niall Feldman.

The Solutions Company (TSC) 1 Amalgamated Drive, West Cross Centre, Great West Road, London TW8 9EZ **t** 020 8400 4333 **f** 020 8400 9444 **e** andy.campbell@gotsc.com **w** gotsc.com Sales Director: Andrew Campbell.

Sound and Video Services UK Shentonfield Road, Sharston Industrial Estate, Manchester M22 4RW **t** 0161 491 6660 **f** 0161 491 6669 **e** sales@svsmedia.com **w** svsmedia.com Dir: Mike Glasspole.

Sound Control 61 Jamaica Street, Glasgow G1 4NN **t** 0141 204 2774 or 0141 204 0322 **f** 0141 204 0614 **e** sales@soundcontrol.co.uk **w** soundcontrol.co.uk GM: Kenny Graham.

Sound Technology plc 17 Letchworth Point, Letchworth, Hertfordshire SG6 1ND **t** 01462 480000 **f** 01462 480800 **e** info@soundtech.co.uk **w** soundtech.co.uk Sales Office Manager: Colin Haines.

Soundcraft, Harman International Industries Cranborne House, Cranborne Road, Potters Bar, Hertfordshire EN6 3JN **t** 01707 665000 **f** 01707 660482 **e** info@soundcraft.com **w** soundcraft.com Intl Sales Dir: Adrian Curtis.

Soundtracs DiGiCo Unit 10, Silverglade Buisness Park, Leatherhead Rd, Chessington, Surrey KT18 7LX **t** 01372 845 600 **f** 01372 845 656 **e** info@digiconsoles.com **w** soundtracs.co.uk Sales Dir: James Gordon.

EA Sowter Ltd The Boatyard, Cullingham Road, Suffolk IP1 2EL **t** 01473 252794 **f** 01473 236188 **e** sales@sowter.co.uk **w** sowter.co.uk MD: Brian W Last.

Speed Music PLC 1 West Street, Baneswell, South Wales NP20 4DD **t** 01633 215577 **f** 01633 213214 **e** info@speedmusic.co.uk **w** speedmusic.co.uk Director: Nick Fowler.

Michael Stevens & Partners Ltd Invicta Works, Elliott Road, Bromley, Kent BR2 9NT **t** 020 8460 7299 **f** 020 8460 0499 **e** sales@michael-stevens.com **w** michael-stevens.com UL Sales Mgr: Simon Adamson.

Stirling Syco Systems 5 The Chase Centre, Chase Rd, London NW10 6QD **t** 020 8963 4790 **f** 020 8963 4799 **e** info@stirlingsyco.com **w** stirlingsyco.com MD: Andrew Stirling.

Straight Edge Manufacturing Ltd Bladewater Marina, The Esplanade, Mayland, Chelmsford, Essex CM3 6FD **t 01621 742000 f** 01621 742222 **e** info@straight-edge.co.uk **w** straight-edge.co.uk MD: Ian Wilson.

Studer UK Cranbourne House, Cranborne Rd, Potters Bar, Herts EN6 3JN **t** 01635 254 719 **e** andrew@studer.co.uk **w** studer.ch Sales: Andrew Hills.

Studio Spares 61-63 Rochester Place, London NW1 9JU **t** 020 7482 1692 **f** 020 7485 4168 **e** sales@studiospares.com **w** studiospares.com Mgrs: Richard Venables/Mike Dowsett.

The Studio Wizard Organisation Station Masters House, County School, Dereham, Norfolk NR20 5LE **t** 07092 123666 or 01362 668900 **f** 07092 123666 **e** info@studiowizard.com **w** studiowizard.com MD: Howard Turner.

Tannoy Professional Rosehall Industrial Estate, Coatbridge, Strathclyde ML5 4TF **t** 01236 420199 **f** 01236 428230 **e** prosales@tannoy.com **w** tannoy.com Sales Mgr: Sean Martin.

Tapematic UK Unit 13 Hurricane Close, Hurricane Way, Wickford, Essex SS11 8YR **t** 01268 561999 **f** 01268 561709 **e** uk@tapematic.com **w** tapematic.com MD: David Hill.

TDK UK Ltd TDK House, 5-7 Queensway, Redhill, Surrey RH1 1YB **t** 01737 773773 **f** 01737 773809 or 01737 773805 **w** tdk-europe.com Brand Dev Mgr: Donna de Souza.

TEAC UK Limited (TASCAM) Marlin House, The Croxley Centre, Watford, Hertfordshire WD18 8TE **t** 01923 438880 **f** 01923 236290 **e** info@teac.co.uk **w** teac.co.uk Sales Mgr: Neil Wells.

Thurlby Thandar Instruments Ltd Glebe Road, Huntingdon, Cambridgeshire PE29 7DR **t** 01480 412451 **f** 01480 450409 **e** sales@tti-test.com **w** tti-test.com Dir: John Cornwell.

TL Audio Sonic Touch, ICENI Court, Icknield Way, Letchworth, Herts SG6 1TN **t** 01462 492 090 **f** 01462 492 097 **e** info@tlaudio.co.uk **w** tlaudio.co.uk MD: Tony Larkin.

Turbosound Star Road, Partridge Green, West Sussex RH13 8RY **t** 01403 711 447 **f** 01403 710 155 **e** sales@turbosound.com **w** turbosound.com Sales Dir: Rik Kirby.

Denis Tyler Ltd 59 High Street, Great Missenden, Buckinghamshire HP16 0AL **t** 01494 866262 **f** 01494 864959 **e** denistylerlimited@btinternet.com **w** denistyler.com MD: Elizabeth Tyler.

Vestax (Europe) Ltd Unit 5, Riverwey Industrial Park, Alton, Hampshire GU34 2QL **t** 01420 83000 **f** 01420 80040 **e** sales@vestax.co.uk **w** vestax.co.uk MD: Andy Williams.

Volt Loudspeakers Ltd Enterprise House, Blyth Road, Hayes, Middlesex UB3 1DD **t** 020 8573 4260 **f** 020 8813 7551 **e** info@voltloudspeakers.co.uk **w** voltloudspeakers.co.uk MD: David Lyth.

Wharfedale Professional Ltd IAG House, Sovereign Court, Ermine Business Park, Huntingdon, Cambridgeshire PE29 6XU **t** 01480 447709 **f** 01480 431767 **e** marketing@wharfedale.co.uk **w** wharfedalepro.com Int'l Marketing Manager: Lisa Fletcher.

Yamaha-Kemble Music (UK) Sherbourne Drive, Tilbrook, Milton Keynes, Buckinghamshire MK7 8BL **t** 01908 366700 **f** 01908 368872 **w** yamaha-music.co.uk MD: Andrew Kemble.

Studio Design & Construction

Acoustics Design Group 30 Pewley Hill, Guildford, Surrey GU1 3SN **t** 01483 503681 **f** 01483 303217 **e** acousticsdesign@aol.com Prop: John Flynn.

Asadul Ltd Hophouse, Colchester Road, West Bergholt, Colchester, Essex CO6 3TJ **t** 01206 241600 **f** 01206 241988 **e** 2cv@Beeb.net Dir: Stuart Bailey.

The Audionet Unit 13 Impress House, Mansell Rd, London W3 7QH **t** 020 8735 0040 **f** 020 8735 0041 **e** james@theaudionet.ltd.uk MD: Mark Lusardi.

Autograph Sales Ltd. 102 Grafton Rd, London NW5 4BA **t** 020 7267 6677 **f** 020 7485 0681 **e** sales@autograph.co.uk **w** autograph.co.uk Directors: Rob Piddington & Graham Paddon.

AVD (FM) Ltd PO Box 15, Swaffham, Norfolk PE37 8JE **t** 01362 822444 **f** 01362 822488 **e** info@avdco.com **w** avdco.com Dir: Alan Stewart.

Black Box Ltd (UK) 1 Greenwich Quay, London SE10 9HZ **t** 020 8858 6883 **f** 020 8692 6957 **e** ra@aaa-design.com **w** aaa-design.com Director: Hugh Flynn.

Cablesystems 8 Woodend, London SE19 3NU **t** 020 8653 5451 or 07771 755 339 **e** cablesystems@yahoo.com Owner: Alan Maskall.

J Decor Interiors 159-161 High Street, Epsom, Kent KT19 8EW **t** 01372 721773 **f** 01372 742765 **e** jdecor@btconnect.com Dir: Judith Newbit.

Eastlake Audio (UK) PO Box 6016, London W2 1WH **t** 020 7262 3198 **f** 020 7706 1918 **e** info@eastlake-audio.co.uk **w** eastlake-audio.co.uk Director: David Hawkins.

H2O Enterprises Sphere Studios, 2 Shuttleworth Road, London SW11 3EA **t** 020 7326 9460 **f** 020 7326 9499 **e** simonb@h2o.co.uk **w** h2o.co.uk Contact: Simon Bohannon

Hi-Fi Services - Studio Electronics White House Farm, Shropshire TF9 4HA **t** 01630 647374 **f** 01630 647612 Service Mgr: Don Stewart.

IAC IAC House, Moorside Road, Winchester, Hampshire SO23 7US **t** 01962 873000 **f** 01962 873111 **e** info@iacl.co.uk **w** iacl.co.uk Sales Manager: Ian Rich.

Clive Kavan 9B Ashbourne Parade, Hanger Lane, London W5 3QS **t** 020 8998 8127 **f** 020 8997 0608

Kelsey Acoustics (Cables & Interconnections) 9 Lyon Road, Walton On Thames, Surrey KT12 3PU **t** 01932 886060 **f** 01932 885565 **e** kelsey@fuzion.co.uk **w** kelseyweb.co.uk Op's Mgr: Michael Whiteside.

R&W Sound Engineering Unit 7u, Long Spring, Porters Wood, St Albans AL3 6EN **t** 01727 756999 **f** 01737 765777 **e** enquiries@rwsound.co.uk **w** rwsound.co.uk Technical Director: Jon Raper.

Recording Architecture Ltd (UK) 1 Greenwich Quay, Greenwich, London SE8 3EY **t** 020 8692 6992 **f** 020 8692 6957 **e** ra@aaa-design.com **w** aaa-design.com MD: Roger D'Arcy.

Sacred Space Design 28 Hollerith Rise, Bracknell, Berks RG12 7TJ **t** 0845 345 2750 or 07734 513 345 **e** info@sacredspacedesign.ltd.uk **w** sacredspacedesign.ltd.uk Senior Designer: Daphne Rotenberg.

Sound Workshop (Sound System Design/Installation) 19-21 Queens Road, Halifax, West Yorkshire HX1 3NS **t** 01422 345021 **f** 01422 363440 **e** enquiries@thesoundworkshop.co.uk **w** thesoundworkshop.co.uk MD: David Mitchell.

The Studio Wizard Organisation Station Master's House, County School, Dereham, Norfolk NR20 5LE **t** 07092 123666 or 01362 668900 **f** 07092 123666 **e** info@studiowizard.com **w** studiowizard.com MD: Howard Turner.

Veale Associates 16 North Rd, Stevenage, Hertfordshire SG1 4AL **t** 01438 747666 **f** 01438 742500 **e** info@vealea.com **w** vealea.com MD: Edward Veale.

Studio Miscellaneous

0510 Management 7 Smeaton Road, London SW18 5JJ **t** 020 8870 0510 **e** mgmt0510@btinternet.com Contact: Maureen Moore.

5 Star Cases Broad End Industrial Estate, Broad End Road, Walsoken, Wisbech, Cambs PE14 7BQ **t** 01945 427000 **f** 01945 427015 **e** info@5star-cases.com **w** 5star-cases.com MD: Keith Sykes.

Audio Motion Ltd Osney Mead House, Osney Mead, Oxford, Oxon OX2 0ES **t** 08701 600 504 **f** 01865 728 319 **e** info@audiomotion.com **w** audiomotion.com Audio Mgr: Des Tong.

Audio Transfers @ Inflight Studios 15 Stukeley St, Covent Garden, London WC2B 5LT **t** 020 7400 8569 or 020 7400 0725 **e** keith.knowles@inflightstudios.com **w** ifsaudiotransfers.com Facility Mgr: Keith Knowles.

Casmara 16 West Park, Mottingham, London SE9 4RQ **t** 020 8857 3213 **f** 020 8857 0731 **e** mail@meridian-records.co.uk **w** casmara.supanet.com Owner: Richard Hughes.

GTek 10 Barley Mow Passage, London W4 4PH **t** 020 8994 6477 **e** gtek@jgtek.demon.co.uk Prop: Jon Griffin.

Hear No Evil 6 Lillie Yard, London SW6 1UB **t** 020 7385 8244 **f** 020 7385 0700 **e** info@hearnoevil.net **w** hearnoevil.net MD: Sharon Rose-Parr.

John Henry's 16-24 Brewery Road, London N7 9NH **t** 020 7609 9181 **f** 020 7700 7040 **e** johnh@johnhenrys.com **w** johnhenrys.com MD: John Henry.

The M Corporation Audio The Market Place, Ringwood, Hampshire BH24 1AP **t** 01425 479090 **f** 01425 480569 **e** ask@theMcorporation.com **w** www.theMcorporation.com Sales Manager: Douglas Sinclair.

Melissa Miguel Vocal Training 33/37 Hatherley Mews, Walthamstow, London E17 4QP **t** 020 8521 9227 **f** 020 8520 5553 **e** xplosive@supanet.com

Meltones Media 3 King Edward Drive, Chessington, Surrey KT9 1DW **t** 020 8391 9406 **f** 020 8391 8924 **e** tony@meltones.com **w** meltones-media.co.uk Sale/Mkt Dir: Tony Fernandez.

The Music Room 35 Bradford Rd, Cleckheaton, West Yorkshire BD19 3JN **t** 01274 879768 **f** 01274 852280 **e** info@the-music-room.com **w** the-music-room.com Shop Mgr: Terry Evans.

Studio Electronics- Hi Fi Services White House Farm, Shropshire TF9 4HA **t** 01630 647374 **f** 01630 647612 Service Mgr: Don Stewart.

ADVERTISERS INDEX